40 Years of Research on Rent Seeking 2

Roger D. Congleton • Arye L. Hillman
Kai A. Konrad (Eds.)

40 Years of Research on Rent Seeking 2

Applications: Rent Seeking in Practice

 Springer

Prof. Roger D. Congleton
George Mason University
Center for the Study
of Public Choice
MSN 1D3
Fairfax, Virginia 22030
USA
congleto@gmu.edu

Prof. Arye L. Hillman
Bar-Ilan University
Department of Economics
52900 Ramat-Gan
Israel
hillman@mail.biu.ac.il

Prof. Kai A. Konrad
Wissenschaftszentrum Berlin
für Sozialforschung
Reichpietschufer 50
10785 Berlin
Germany
kkonrad@wzb.eu

ISBN: 978-3-540-79185-0

Library of Congress Control Number: 2008926320

Cover design: WMX Design GmbH, Heidelberg

Printed on acid-free paper

9 8 7 6 5 4 3 2 1

springer.com

Preface

The last survey of the rent-seeking literature took place more than a decade ago. Since that time a great deal of new research has been published in a wide variety of journals, covering a wide variety of topics. The scope of that research is such that very few researchers will be familiar with more than a small part of contemporary research, and very few libraries will be able to provide access to the full breadth of that research. This two-volume collection provides an extensive overview of 40 years of rent-seeking research.

The volumes include the foundational papers, many of which have not been in print for two decades. They include recent game-theoretic analyses of rent-seeking contests and also applications of the rent-seeking concepts and methodology to economic regulation, international trade policy, economic history, political competition, and other social phenomena. The new collection is more than twice as large as any previous collection and both updates and extends the earlier surveys. Volume I contains previously published research on the theory of rent-seeking contests, which is an important strand of contemporary game theory. Volume II contains previously published research that uses the theory of rent-seeking to analyze a broad range of public policy and social science topics.

The editors spent more than a year assembling possible papers and, although the selections fill two large volumes, many more papers could have been included. Our aim has been to include the most important contributions in the literature and give a broad overview of secondary contributions. The end result is a fine collection that shows the flexibility and power of the rent-seeking methodology, and the light shed on a broad range of political, social, and institutional research issues. Each volume begins with an extensive survey of the literature written by the editors and an overview of the contributions included in the two volumes.

Although responsibility for the papers included and organization of the volumes rests entirely with the editors, a number of debts must be acknowledged. The Center for Study of Public Choice provided a grant that made the publication of these volumes possible. Professor Congleton's contribution to the project was supported by the Center for Study of Public Choice at George Mason University and the Department of Political Science at the University of Southern Denmark. Professor Hillman's contribution was supported by the Department of Economics at Bar Ilan University. Professor Konrad's contribution was supported by the Social Science Research Center (WZB) and the Department of Economics at the Free University of Berlin. Thanks are due to Nina Bonge for her administrative assistance and to Martina Bihn of Springer for her encouragement and oversight of the production of the two volumes. Numerous colleagues provided suggestions for the contents and commented on our selection.

Roger D. Congleton
Arye L. Hillman
Kai A. Konrad

Contents Volume II

Contents

Contents

Contents Volume I

Contents

Part 5   Experiments

Forty Years of Research on Rent Seeking: An Overview

Roger D. Congleton, Arye L. Hillman and Kai A. Konrad

The quest for rents has always been part of human behavior. People have long fought and contended over possessions, rather than directing abilities and resources to productive activity. The great empires and conquests were the consequences of successful rent seeking. Resources were also expended in defending the rents that the empires provided. The unproductive use of resources to contest, rather than create wealth, also occurred within societies in attempts to replace incumbent rulers and in seeking the favor of rulers who dispensed rewards and indeed often determined life and death. Sacrifices made by early peoples to their deities were instances of rent seeking; valuable possessions were given up with the intent of seeking to influence assignment of other rewards. In contemporary times, rent seeking takes place within democratic institutions and also under conditions of autocracy that are akin to the circumstances of the earlier rent-dispensing despots. Incentives for rent seeking are present whenever decisions of others influence personal outcomes or more broadly when resources can be used to affect distributional outcomes.

The search for rents, defined as rewards and prizes not earned or not consistent with competitive market returns, is, thus, clearly ancient. Efforts to understand how wealth, status, and other rewards can be acquired, and how contests for such prizes can be designed to reduce losses associated with unproductive conflict and encourage productive forms of competition, are also likely to have begun at the dawn of social life. The academic rent-seeking literature, however, is relatively new and emerged from papers by Gordon Tullock, Anne Krueger, and Richard Posner published during the course of some 10 years in the 1960s and 1970s (reprinted in these volumes). The early rent-seeking analyses sought accurate measures of social losses from public policies and monopoly. Tullock, Krueger, and Posner argued that the resources used to establish, maintain, or eliminate trade restrictions and monopolies are part of the social cost of those policies, but had previously been neglected.

The idea that resources are unproductively used in rent-seeking contests has much broader application than the initial rent-seeking papers suggested. The rent-seeking logic has been applied to issues in history, sociology, anthropology, biology, and philosophy. The core idea has also been formalized and analyzed more rigorously, using the tools of modern game theory. The modern rent-seeking literature describes the rational decision to invest in contesting pre-existing wealth or income, rather than undertaking productive activity.

The starting point of this literature is often considered to be Gordon Tullock's paper on the "Welfare Costs of Tariffs, Monopolies, and Theft" in 1967. Tullock focused on the efficiency consequences of income transfers and observed that "Transfers themselves cost society nothing, but for the people engaging in them they are just like any other activity, and this means large resources may be invested in attempting to make or prevent transfers. These largely offsetting commitments of resources are totally wasted from the standpoint of society as a whole." Tullock's observations implied that there was more to inefficiency than deadweight losses. Beneficiaries of inefficient policies have personal incentives to influence creation and assignment of income and wealth created by political decisions. Tullock reasoned that the resources used in activities of persuasion should be counted as a cost to society.

The quests for income and wealth redistribution through public policy are comparable to the activities of thieves, who also use personal resources and initiative in unproductive endeavors to redistribute, rather than create wealth. The act of theft results in an income transfer that does not change total national income, but social losses do arise before a theft takes place, because the aspiring thieves' contest who in the end will be successful in the act of theft, and prospective victims' invest in various means for resisting the thieves' efforts. These resources could have been used to produce goods and services with a positive value, rather than devoted to distributional conflict. The social loss from rent seeking similarly occurs ex ante, through unproductively used resources and initiative before policy decisions are made. Public policies often directly or indirectly transfer income or wealth among people. Of course, there is no suggestion that all public policies are akin to theft. The theory of rent seeking, however, is based on the possibility of influencing public policies for personal gain. The quest for personal advantage may be masked with the rhetoric of social advantage. A focal question of the rent-seeking literature is the computation of social loss through the value of the resources unproductively used because of the presence of the rents or prizes that are assigned by the personal discretion of others, as when political decision makers determine public policies.

After four decades of research following the publication of Tullock's paper, the literature expanding on the rent-seeking idea is substantial. The *JStor* data base of academic journals reports that 74 papers include the term "rent seeking" in their titles. The *Scopus* on-line search reports 170 papers. The more representative *EconLit* data base of academic journals and books reports 401. The broader *Google Scholar* search engine reports that the titles of more than 1,500 papers on the Web include the term "rent seeking." Moreover, not every paper on rent seeking includes those words in its title. *EconLit*'s data base reports that more than 8,000 published papers and books use the terms "rent seeking" or "rent seeker" somewhere within their pages.

The quite different backgrounds of the editors of these two volumes provide a balance in perspectives on rent seeking and indeed on public choice. Roger Congleton was present from the beginning in the Center for the Study of Public Choice as a member of the Virginia School when the rent-seeking concept developed, and was an editor of a previous collection and contributed to the influential first compendium on rent seeking published in 1980. Arye Hillman, a former president of the European Public Choice Society, has pursued political economy research, but not as a member of the Virginia School. Kai Konrad provides a perspective that includes rent seeking in the more general study of contests.

It was, of course, a difficult task to choose papers for inclusion in these volumes. The decision rule for inclusion of papers was consensus among the editors. The prediction of the theoretical literature (Buchanan and Tullock 1962) that decision costs increase with a consensus rule for collective decision making was borne out in the natural experiment of selecting papers for these volumes, which continued for more than a year. Other scholars were also consulted and recommendations heeded. The two volumes include classics and major extensions of the rent-seeking literature. Papers were valued that expressed informative novel ideas and that directed attention to applications that expanded the scope of the rent-seeking concept. Many were initially published in journals and books to which few readers have easy access. Books that contain seminal contributions are out of print, including the now classic 1980 edited volume. Many papers that have proven to be significant were not published in "leading" journals. Our choice of papers confirms the more general finding of Andrew Oswald (2007) that the most significant papers are not always published in the most prominent economic journals.

The papers are organized to provide a sense of the development of the rent-seeking literature by topic rather than by date of publication. The papers in volume I are analytical developments on the rent-seeking theme. The papers in volume II are applications of the rent-seeking concept. Our introduction provides an overview of the literature and summarizes the contributions of the papers in the two volumes.

Origins of the Literature

In the second half of the twentieth century, there were a variety of efforts to place the normative analysis of public policy on firmer analytical ground. The first efforts, like the positive theories of that time, attempted to rank order allocations of real resources without considering how or why particular allocations might have arisen (Bergson 1938, Samuelson 1947, Harsanyi 1955). Governments and therefore political decision makers were described as seeking social optimality. Yet individuals and firms in the private sector were at the same time viewed as having self-interested objectives. The argument was that, if governments were making decisions, the decisions were in the best interest of society, because government is socially benevolent. The public choice view proposed consistency in application of the principle of rationality and self-interest. If utility- and profit-maximizing models explain a good deal of private sector behavior, they are also likely to explain a good deal of the behavior of political and bureaucratic decision makers. In applied research, the public choice view could provide an answer as to why governments often adopt economically inefficient policies. In contrast, the mainstream literature used the classic analysis of monopoly by Arnold Harberger (1954) to measure "deadweight" losses of such public policies, ignoring how they might have come to be adopted. The evaluations of deadweight losses were influential and soon found their way into textbooks as the core of modern welfare economics. The perceived benevolence of government made policies in these studies exogenous, rather than endogenous, consequences of choices made under specific legal and political institutions.

Public policies that result in deadweight losses do not come into existence spontaneously. Yet the welfare implications of interest group activities and politically endogenous policies were either not fully appreciated in the mainstream literature or else were simply neglected to avoid confronting the question as to why political and bureaucratic decision makers created and assigned rents – and extracted political rents for themselves. A prime case was the literature on international economics: here the deadweight efficiency losses from protectionist policies were studied, but the mainstream literature of the time did not address the question as to why Pareto-inefficient departures from free trade took place. Yet, the protectionist policies clearly reduced national income while benefiting some people at the expense of others.

In his 1967 paper inaugurating the modern literature on rent seeking, Tullock made the fundamental observation that, if inefficient public policies, such as trade policies, were politically endogenous, part of the social cost of those policies was the use of scarce personal abilities and resources in efforts to influence policy decisions. Tullock thus pointed to a source of social loss beyond Harberger triangles.

The next important step in Tullock's analysis – and for the rent-seeking literature that later emerged – was to investigate the extent to which resources are attracted to rent-seeking activities. Tullock reasoned that, if government could be induced to redistribute wealth, the rate of return from political wealth-enhancing activities would equal the return from other investments in long-run competitive equilibrium. This implies that social losses from contesting rents are equal to the values of observed contested rents. Although profits and other rents could often be measured, the value of the resources used in rent seeking is usually not observable. Tullock's logic suggests that the value of rents generated by public policies can be used as a proxy for the resources used in rent seeking. That is, rent dissipation could be viewed as complete. Given this, the mainstream accounts of losses from monopoly, tariffs, and other public policies that had been carefully worked out in the previous two decades substantially understated the true extent of the losses that a society incurred from inefficient public policies.

Tullock's insight was slow to find its way into print (see Brady and Tollison 1994) and slow to be integrated into new research. The rent-seeking idea was not totally neglected after publication in 1967; however, wider recognition of the worth of Tullock's idea required re-publication and re-expression in a more prominent place and the accompaniment of an appropriate pithy phrase. Anne Krueger (1974: reprinted in volume II) provided the descriptive term "rent seeking" and thereafter the literature could refer to "rent seekers." Krueger set out a general equilibrium model of social loss from contesting quota rents and presented estimates of losses in Turkey and India. She based her measures on the complete dissipation presumption that rents would attract resources of equal value. Richard Posner (1975: reprinted in volume II) used the complete-dissipation presumption to estimate losses from monopoly in U.S. industries. Keith Cowling and Dennis Mueller (1978: reprinted in volume II) followed with estimates of the cost of monopoly for the U.S. and U.K. economies. These and other empirical studies, for example, David Laband and John Sophocleus (1992) and Martin Paldam (1997), suggest social losses considerably greater than the rather small losses that had been reported from measurement of Harberger triangles.

With its new appellation and evidence of its importance, and also the expression of the idea outside of the public choice school, the literature on rent seeking began to expand, although not very rapidly at first. In the beginning, the rent-seeking concept was, in a sense, proprietary to the Virginia School that Tullock had been instrumental in founding. Much of the early research was by faculty and students associated with the Center for Study of Public Choice, where the new research on rent seeking stimulated several papers that were presented in an evening seminar series in 1978. It was in that seminar series that Tullock noted that the complete rent dissipation presumption that Krueger, Posner, and others had also adopted was not necessarily appropriate. Tullock (1980: reprinted in volume I) set out a rent-seeking game and, with assistance from his colleagues Nicolas Tideman and Joseph Greenberg and his graduate student assistant, characterized the Nash equilibrium for a contest success function that probabilistically designated the winner of a contest according to how much individual contenders spend. The mathematical and simulation results confirmed that complete dissipation was a special case. Actual rent dissipation depended on the number of players and on a returns-to-scale parameter in the contest success function. The seminar inspired many of the papers that appeared in the first rent-seeking volume edited by Buchanan, Tollison, and Tullock (1980), in which Tullock's paper with the probabilistic contest success function first appeared.

The explanatory power of the rent-seeking idea arises from its linkage of neoclassical economics to modern game theory and rational choice politics. Tullock's lottery-based characterization of the contest success function of a rent-seeking game was an important advance in demonstrating that the "rules of the game" matter. The institutions and technologies that determine the parameters of rent-seeking contests affect society's losses from rent seeking. Tullock's 1980 paper was also important for the development of the literature, because his characterization of rent-seeking contests as lotteries was relatively easy to generalize and extend. Intuition and a preference for a simple and elegant mapping that transforms competing players' efforts into probabilities of success guided Tullock in his choice of a contest success function. Later axiomatic work by Skaperdas (1996: reprinted in volume I), Kooreman and Schoonbeek (1997), and Clark and Riis (1998: reprinted in volume I) confirmed that only the functional form that Tullock chose is compatible with a number of desirable and plausible properties of a contest success function.

The first collection of rent-seeking papers that appeared in the 1980 volume launched the broader literature that emerged during the next 25 years. The 1980 collection included 22 papers, only 10 of which had been previously published. The 12 new papers covered a broad range of topics. The papers in that first collection were for the most part by colleagues and students of Tullock, including James Buchanan and an editor (Congleton) of the present collection. The inclusion of Tullock's *efficient rent seeking* paper, which had now been provided with a natural publication outlet, allowed the research on rent dissipation to begin in earnest.

The 1980 volume influenced scholars in societies outside of the United States. Far away from Virginia, in Israel, where economic liberalization was yet a decade away, another editor of the present collection (Hillman) observed the substantial presence of non-market allocation and non-market-determined personal rewards in the self-managed worker sector of the economy. As in Virginia, the Bar-Ilan School set out to investigate efficiency consequences of the presence of politically assigned rents. The scholarly divisions were amazingly similar to those in the United States where rent seeking was not a topic favored outside of the Virginia School. In Israel, only scholars at Bar-Ilan University or graduates of Bar-Ilan undertook research on rent seeking. The first contribution of the Bar-Ilan School to the study of rent-seeking contests, by Hillman and Katz (1984: reprinted in volume I), investigated rent dissipation in winner-take-all contests, such as those for monopoly. They demonstrated that complete rent dissipation emerges if rent seekers are risk neutral and rent-seeking contests can be freely entered, but not if rent seekers are risk averse or there are barriers to entry into contests. Hillman and Samet (1987: reprinted in volume I) solved the rent-seeking game for the case of an all-pay auction in which the highest spending individual or group wins the prize. Their results provide another justification for the complete-dissipation presumption. Subsequently Shmuel Nitzan and others at Bar-Ilan made contributions to the rent-seeking literature.

The analysis of rent seeking also attracted the attention of scholars in Korea, including in particular Kyung Hwan Baik. In Korea substantial rent-creating non-market allocation occurred through the interaction between government and vertically integrated conglomerates. Scholars from the Philippines and sub-Saharan Africa where corruption and non-benevolent governments created and assigned significant rents also contributed to the rent-seeking literature. However, in many autocratic societies where rent seeking has been endemic, there appear to have been impediments to analyses and discussion of rent seeking by local scholars.

The post-1980 literature was often theoretical and positive, rather than empirical or normative as the first papers had been. The extent of rent dissipation was studied, often in abstract terms without description of the types of policies that gave rise to the rents and to rent seeking. Other contest success functions were considered and changes were made to incorporate more general assumptions. The analysis gained in precision and increased in complexity. The literature has explored how contest structures affect resource use in rent-seeking activities and has investigated the efficiency properties of alternative methods of allocating "prizes." Collective goods, free-riding incentives in contests, hold-up problems from repeated rent seeking, issues of endogenous timing, budget constraints, nested contests, and the role of incomplete information have been analyzed in this context. The papers in volume I are largely from this theoretical strand of the rent-seeking literature.[1]

The idea of rent seeking has been acknowledged as important for understanding a broad range of long-standing applied economic topics encompassing regulation, international trade policy, economic development, the transition from socialism, and communal property. An approach based on political economy of protection, which gradually became part of the mainstream economics literature, clearly pointed out the link between trade policies and rents for protected groups (Hillman 1989). The rent-seeking concept has also been applied to deepen our understanding of topics in economic history, law, sociology, and biology. If rent-seeking contests can be created and conditions of contests revised, many aspects of institutional design and evolution are also part of the applied rent-seeking research program. A broad selection of applications of the rent-seeking concept is included in volume II.

Criteria for inclusion

A general principle for inclusion of papers in these volumes is consistency with the political-economy and institutional origins of the rent-seeking concept. Rent seeking is a political economy concept. The intent of Gordon Tullock, the Virginia-based Public Choice School, and the Bar-Ilan School was to show that societies incur efficiency losses beyond the traditional economic deadweight losses when personal benefits and costs are politically assigned rather than market determined. Their research generally implies that reducing rent-seeking losses requires institutional reform.

Not all contests involve rent-seeking activities, although most involve decisions about how much to invest in a given contest. A decision was therefore confronted whether to include literature in which contests similar in structure to rent seeking are studied outside of the domain of political economy. One such literature involves the theory of the firm. This literature is extensive and revolves around internal principal-agent problems. Another question was whether to include literature that was in principle about rent creation and rent seeking but did not use or acknowledge the rent-seeking concept. Prominent among such cases is again the firm-related literature in which private-sector internal-firm tournaments or

---

[1] A strand of more technically oriented research analyzed a large set of formal structures that can be applied to analyze rent-seeking contests. Konrad (2007) surveys the literature focusing on strategic aspects of contests.

contests for promotion have structures similar to rent seeking.[2] In a literature on research and development (R&D) contests, winners provide productive outputs rather than contests being purely distributional. In sports contests also, effort is a source of benefit for spectators. We have excluded the literature on R&D contests and the literature explicitly on sports contests.[3] We have, however, included representative papers on the rents created and contested within the firm.

Contests are also described in a large body of literature known as conflict theory. We have excluded most of this literature. Conflict theory emerged from the recognition that, without the rule of law and without possibilities for contractual enforcement, property rights are established endogenously by efforts to defend own wealth or efforts to acquire the wealth of others. In the 1990s conflict theory developed for the most part parallel and apart from the theory of rent-seeking literature. Models of rent seeking and models of conflict share the common element of contestability of wealth or income, although conflict models do not in general focus on the core rent-seeking issue of dissipation. There is also a difference in institutional setting: most rent-seeking models are motivated by the *presence of government* that can be influenced to create and assign rents, whereas most models of conflict are motivated by the *absence of government* and thereby absence of the rule of law.[4]

Questions were faced about how to categorize papers in which authors did not relate their analyses and conclusions to the prior insights of the rent-seeking literature, even though their papers described circumstances in which politically created and assigned rents are contested. A general rule was to exclude papers if they are not described by authors as being about rents or rent seeking. However, exceptions were made in the applications volume when the behavior being described clearly constitutes rent creation by government and rent seeking by interest groups. The principal sources of papers in the present collection are the *American Economic Review*, *Public Choice*, the *Economic Journal*, and the *European Journal of Political Economy*, which in the mid-1990s adopted a political economy focus that attracted authors of papers on rent seeking.

Attitudes to the concept and terminology of rent seeking are of interest for understanding academic economics. As we have observed, in the beginning, rent seeking as a descriptive and explanatory concept was not accepted into the "main-

---

[2] The literature on tournaments began with seminal contributions of Lazear and Rosen (1981) and Rosen (1986).

[3] Early influential contributions to the R&D contest literature were Loury (1979), Dasgupta and Stiglitz (1980), and Nalebuff and Stiglitz (1983). Fullerton and McAfee (1999) and Baye and Hoppe (2003) provide microfoundations of Tullock's contest success function in applications to R&D contests. On sports contests, see Szymanski (2003).

[4] For elaboration on the distinction between rent seeking due to the response of government and conflict theory based on anarchy and the absence of government, see Hillman (2003, chapter 6). See also Tullock (1974) on conflict in anarchy. Skaperdas (2003) and Garfinkel and Skaperdas (2007) survey the conflict literature. See Fearon (1995) on military conflict and Hillman (2004) on conflict between strong and weak under Nietzschean conditions in anarchy.

stream" of academic economics. Tullock's 1967 paper appeared in a relatively new regional journal and his 1980 paper had to await the edited volume for publication. In the 1990s rational political behavior and political economy concepts came to be more broadly recognized as descriptive of realities of government decision making. However, there seemed to be a reluctance to acknowledge the antecedents of the public-choice school. For example, a "new" political economy literature emerged in the 1990s that often failed to acknowledge that their research addressed questions that had previously been addressed by public choice scholars. When asked (by one of the present editors) in 1990s why the contributions of public choice scholars were not being acknowledged, a prominent contributor to the "new" political economy literature replied that "we cannot cite everyone since Adam Smith". The answer was not "what is public choice?" Or "what is rent seeking?" The answer suggests that the concept of rent seeking has had wider influence than indicated by the rent-seeking literature per se.

We proceed now to describe the structure of the two volumes and to link and summarize the papers.

Volume I – Theory of Rent Seeking

The focus of volume I is on conceptual and theoretical developments.

Theory Part 1 – Rents

1.1 The social cost of rent seeking

The early papers followed Tullock's original exposition in further considering the social cost of contestable rents.

> Gordon Tullock, 1967. The welfare costs of tariffs, monopolies, and theft. *Western Economic Journal* 5, 224–32.

> James M. Buchanan, 1980. Rent seeking and profit seeking. In James M. Buchanan, Robert D. Tollison, and Gordon Tullock (eds.), *Toward a Theory of the Rent-Seeking Society*. Texas A&M University Press, College Station, pp. 3–15.

> Roger D. Congleton, 1980. Competitive process, competitive waste, and institutions. In James M. Buchanan, Robert D. Tollison, and Gordon Tullock (eds.), *Toward a Theory of the Rent-Seeking Society*. Texas A&M University Press, College Station, pp. 153–79.

> Arye L. Hillman and Eliakim Katz, 1984. Risk-averse rent seekers and the social cost of monopoly power. *Economic Journal* 94, 104–10.

Tullock (1967) is the seminal paper that points out the social losses from unproductive use of resources in quests to influence political decisions about income distribution. Buchanan (1980) distinguishes socially productive and unproductive competition. Congleton (1980) explicitly analyzes the role of institutions, or "the rules of the game," using deterministic models that would later be called all-pay auctions. His analysis suggests that rent dissipation can be reduced by majority-rule allocation of prizes and by rules that distribute the "prize" in proportion to effort, rather than through winner-take-all contests. Hillman and Katz (1984) use a general contest success function in which the probability of winning increases with own rent-seeking effort and decreases with opponents' effort to show that the complete dissipation presumption (that the value of a contested rent is equal to the value of the resources used in contesting the rent) is valid in contests with large numbers of risk neutral players; however, rent dissipation is incomplete when rent seekers are risk averse.

The early literature thus established that contestable rents create social losses, that we should distinguish between socially productive and unproductive forms of competition, that institutions matter, and that complete dissipation in competitive contests is the predicted outcome when rent seekers are risk neutral and when the rent-seeking game is fully competitive but not otherwise.

1.2 Tullock contests

Tullock (1980) introduced the probabilistic contest success function for which personal expenditures on rent seeking are like buying lottery tickets. Other studies subsequently amended and extended the Tullock contest success function. A primary issue was whether over-dissipation of a rent could ever occur.

> Gordon Tullock 1980. Efficient rent seeking. In James M. Buchanan, Robert D. Tollison, and Gordon Tullock (eds.), *Towards a Theory of the Rent-Seeking Society*. Texas A&M University Press, College Station, pp. 97–112.

> Richard S. Higgins, William F. Shughart II, and Robert D. Tollison, 1985. Free entry and efficient rent seeking. *Public Choice* 46, 247–58.

> J. David Pérez-Castrillo and Thierry Verdier, 1992. A general analysis of rent-seeking games. *Public Choice* 73, 335–50.

> Kofi O. Nti, 1999. Rent seeking with asymmetric valuations. *Public Choice* 98, 415–30.

A scale parameter was included in Tullock's lottery model of rent seeking, which (partly) determines the return from purchasing lottery tickets and implicitly represents institutional aspects of rent-seeking contests. Tullock showed that with constant returns from rent-seeking expenditures two contenders dissipate half of the rent in the unique Nash equilibrium. Rent-seeking losses increase as the number of contenders increase and with increases in the scale parameter. Tullock's results suggest that over-dissipation occurs if there are large economies of scale in rent-seeking. Higgins, Shughart, and Tollison (1985) point out that the value of the scale parameter determines whether the Tullock contest success function is consistent with existence of Nash equilibria. In a generalization that that does not rely on the Tullock contest success function, Higgins et al consider a case in which effort of risk-neutral rent seekers is observed subject to error and rent seekers choose a probability with which to participate in a contest. In a symmetric zero-profit mixed-strategy equilibrium, rents are on average completely dissipated, although ex post, under-, or over-dissipation may be observed (depending on the realizations of the mixed strategies). Over-dissipation is inconsistent with Nash equilibrium when participation in rent-seeking contests is voluntary. Pérez-Castrillo and Verdier (1992) reformulate the Tullock contest using reaction curves and consider consequences of free entry and Stackelberg equilibrium. Nti (1999) extends Tullock's contest to asymmetric valuations of a prize. Equilibria depend on the different valuations of rent seekers as well as on the scale parameter of the contest success function. The asymmetric valuations determine a favorite and an "underdog." A player with a higher valuation expends more effort to win. The "underdog" values the prize less and in consequence chooses to spend less to obtain the prize. Asymmetry in practice requires either a discriminatory contest design or disagreements about the estimated value of the prize, such as might arise in contests for a mate, for ego rents from political office, or for a non-pecuniary honor bestowed on a winner.

1.3 Contests as all-pay auctions

In the Tullock contest, random elements through the lottery nature of the contest success function determine the identity of the winner. An alternative contest success function designates the participant exerting the highest effort as the winner with certainty.

> Arye L. Hillman and Dov Samet, 1987. Dissipation of contestable rents by small numbers of contenders. *Public Choice* 54, 63–82.
>
> Arye L. Hillman and John G. Riley, 1989. Politically contestable rents and transfers. *Economics and Politics* 1, 17–39.
>
> Michael R. Baye, Dan Kovenock, and Casper G. de Vries, 1996. The all-pay auction with complete information. *Economic Theory* 8, 291–305.
>
> Simon P. Anderson, Jacob K. Goeree, and Charles A. Holt, 1998. Rent seeking with bounded rationality: An analysis of the all-pay auction. *Journal of Political Economy* 106, 828–53.

The possibility of a contest success function in which the highest effort wins was noted in Congleton (1980) above. Hillman and Riley (1989) introduce the terminology of a discriminating contest to describe such a contest success function. The Tullock lottery implies an inability to discern with precision the efforts of different contestants and accounts for sources of noise. The discriminating rent-seeking contest is an all-pay auction: contenders bid for the rent, the highest bid wins, and all contenders lose the value of their bids whether they win or not. Hillman and Samet (1987) derive the mixed strategy solution for such success functions. A Nash equilibrium in pure strategies does not exist in such contests, as noted in Congleton (1980).[5] They show that in a mixed-strategy equilibrium, with risk neutrality and equal valuations of the rent, complete dissipation on average holds, in that the expected value of resources used in rent seeking by all contenders is equal to the value of the rent. They conclude that the rent is on average fully dissipated for any number of contestants larger than one. A justification other than competitive rent seeking by risk-neutral rent seekers is thereby provided for the descriptions of social losses from rent seeking by Tullock, Krueger, and Posner, and others, in which it is taken for granted that rent dissipation is complete.

Hillman and Riley (1989) also extend the all-pay auction to cases in which contestants have different valuations of the prize. Only the two highest valuation

---

[5] If everybody makes the same bid (less than the value of the prize), there is an incentive to bid a little more. If someone bids the value of the prize, others bid zero, in which case the contender who bid the value of the prize can reduce his or her bid to a little above zero, but then others will not bid zero – and so on.

contenders contest the prize. Others are deterred by the high valuations of competitors for the rent. In this case, the outcome can be less than complete rent dissipation, and an inefficient allocation of the prize (through the low-value contender winning) can occur. Hillman and Riley distinguish between contests for pre-existing rents and contests for transfers (in which one person's gain is another person's loss). Baye, Kovenock, and de Vries (1996) provide a complete characterization of the various types of equilibria that can emerge in an all-pay auction in the case of many players with different valuations of the prize, and when the equilibrium is unique.

The all-pay contest is used as a building block in more complex contests and in many applications. Anderson, Goeree, and Holt (1998) study all-pay auctions when there is bounded rationality. Rational behavior is inconsistent with systematic over-dissipation of rents, yet over-dissipation is observed in experiments. Bounded rationality, in which decisions with higher expected payoffs are more likely to be made, but not with probability one, is proposed as an explanation for the over-dissipation observed in some laboratory experiments. A generalization of Nash equilibrium obtained by incorporating bounded rationality into the determination of equilibrium yields a prediction of over-dissipation similar to that of Tullock's (1980) analysis. The extent of rent dissipation increases with the number of players

1.4 Contest success functions reconsidered

The contest success function was reconsidered in different contexts.

> Jack Hirshleifer, 1989. Conflict and rent-seeking success functions: Ratio vs. difference models of relative success. *Public Choice* 63, 101–12.

> Stergios Skaperdas, 1996. Contest success functions. *Economic Theory* 7, 283–90.

> Ferenc Szidarovszky and Koji Okuguchi, 1997. On the existence and uniqueness of pure Nash equilibrium in rent-seeking games. *Games and Economic Behavior* 18, 135–40.

Hirshleifer (1989) compared the Tullock ratio (lottery) contest success function with a specification based on differences in effort. In the Tullock case, non-conflict cannot be an equilibrium, and there is never an equilibrium in which one side just gives up. Hirshleifer's difference-based specification for the contest success function is consistent with equilibrium outcomes of mutual non-conflict and submission, the latter occurring when there are sufficiently large differences in the valuation of the prize. Skaperdas (1996) shows that the Tullock lottery is the only contest success function that is consistent with seven reasonable axioms about the relationship between efforts and win probabilities. The most important axiom needed is an independence of irrelevant alternatives property. Szidarovszky and Okuguchi (1997) use a clever transformation to provide sufficient conditions for the existence and uniqueness of equilibrium for contests with contest success functions that are considerably more general than the Tullock contest success function.

Theory Part 2 – Collective Dimensions

2.1 Collective decisions, collective effort, and shared rents

Rent seeking often involves collective choices of various kinds. Collective decisions are often made about who receives rents. There might also be collective effort. Indeed, rent-seeking contests often involve groups, rather than single individuals, and collective action issues can arise, as noted by Mancur Olson (1965). In such cases, the prize might be shared by members of successful rent-seeking teams. Outcomes depend on whether the prize is allocated by casting votes, is a group-specific public good that can be enjoyed in a non-rival manner by all members of the winning group, or is a private good that needs to be allocated among the members of the winning group.

> Roger D. Congleton, 1984. Committees and rent-seeking effort. *Journal of Public Economics* 25, 197–209.
>
> Ngo Van Long and Neil Vousden, 1987. Risk-averse rent seeking with shared rents. *Economic Journal* 97, 971–85.
>
> Shmuel Nitzan, 1991. Collective rent dissipation. *Economic Journal* 101, 1522–34.
>
> Joan Esteban and Debraj Ray, 2001. Collective action and the group size paradox. *American Political Science Review* 95, 663–72.
>
> Kyung Hwan Baik, Bouwe R. Dijkstra, Sanghack Lee, and Shi Young Lee, 2006. The equivalence of rent-seeking outcomes for competitive-share and strategic groups. *European Journal of Political Economy* 22, 337–42.

Congleton (1984) extends his 1980 analysis of the effects of institutions on rent dissipation in deterministic contests between two groups. In two-party contests, he shows that investments in deterministic rent-seeking contests tend to be lower when decisions are made by committees through majority rule rather than by a single person, because investing resources to form majority coalitions tends to deescalate, rather than escalate. This conclusion provides an explanation for the widespread use of committees to make decisions within both democratic and non-democratic organizations. Investments in such contests also tend to be smaller under deterministic proportional sharing rules than under winner-take-all rules.

Long and Vousden (1987) analyze the case in which rents are shared and shares are not deterministic and demonstrate that dissipation falls with the extent of risk aversion of rent seekers and with uncertainty about the shares received by individual participants. They also explore the case in which the prize distributed is increased by the total effort of rent seekers. In such cases, individual efforts produce both positive (larger prize) and negative (reduced probability of winning) externalities for fellow players. As a consequence, individual investments increase, because investments provide a higher rate of return by increasing the value of the rent to be distributed to winners. Total resources invested in rent-seeking games thus increase, although overall dissipation rates do not necessarily increase. Nitzan (1991) considered shared rents and showed that rules specifying the division of collectively sought rents within a winning group determine the magnitude of the free-riding problem among group members and determine thereby a group's effectiveness in an inter-group contest. Assignment rules that make a group member's share in the prize an appropriately chosen function of personal and other group members' efforts countervail free-riding incentives and increase equilibrium rent-seeking effort and also overall rent dissipation. A critical role is demonstrated for the rule by which the prize is shared among the members of the winning group, as a function of their number, type, or contest effort. Baik, Dijkstra, Lee, and Lee (2006) synthesize previous portrayals of contests by showing equivalence between contests in which groups compete for shared rents that are assigned to members of the group through distribution rules and contests in which members of a group compete individually for a rent and a winner is obliged to share with group members.

2.2 Rent seeking for public goods

The above papers are about sharing of benefits when the benefits are private. For example, money might simply be shared. In other cases, however, the rent that is contested provides a public-good benefit to a group. Public expenditure may, for example, provide local public goods that benefit regional populations. The following papers describe rent seeking for public goods.

Heinrich W. Ursprung, 1990. Public goods, rent dissipation, and candidate competition. *Economics and Politics* 2, 115–32.

Kyung Hwan Baik, 1993. Effort levels in contests: The public-good prize case. *Economics Letters* 41, 363–67.

Mark Gradstein, 1993. Rent seeking and the provision of public goods. *Economic Journal* 103, 1236–43.

Khalid Riaz, Jason F. Shogren, and Stanley R. Johnson, 1995. A general model of rent seeking for public goods. *Public Choice* 82, 243–59.

Joan Esteban and Debraj Ray, 2001. Collective action and the group size paradox. *American Political Science Review* 95, 663–72.

Ursprung (1990) embeds rent seeking for a public good in a model of political competition. Individual utility is additively separable so there are only substitution effects when the size of a group supporting a political candidate increases. Free-riding incentives through substitution effects between own-spending and spending by others reduce a group's total rent-seeking effort. In the Nash equilibrium, the total effort of a group is independent of the size of the group, and there is substantial under-dissipation of the public-good rent that the groups contest.[6] Riaz, Shogren, and Johnson (1995) point out that an income effect would increase total group effort when group size increases. Convex contribution costs have a similar effect of making total contributions to group rent-seeking effort increase in the group size: Esteban and Ray (2001) show this in a model that allows also for a mix between private and public components of the prize. Gradstein (1993) draws attention to the choice between inefficient private, uncoordinated provision of a public good, and governmental provision. Rent seeking uses resources unproductively, but the private supply of public goods is also generally inefficient because of free-riding incentives. Although the government can overcome the free-rider problem by compelling payment, the government may also be lobbied, which is costly in using resources and also does not ensure first-best provision. Baik (1993) describes groups composed of people with different valuations of a public good. The groups compete for the public good. Free riding tends to be complete within each group, with one high valuation contender active on behalf of the group. In effect, the contest becomes one of high-value individuals representing their group. Rent dissipation is clearly low.

Theory Part 3 – Extensions

3.1 Opposition

The losers from public policies, such as assigning monopoly rights, protectionist international trade policies, and privileged budgetary allocations, and other cases in which income is transferred, have incentives to resist the transfer. Hillman and Riley (1989) call such cases transfer contests to distinguish them from contests in which a pre-existing prize or rent exists and the providers of the rent are not identified or do not resist. There is a social cost associated with rent seeking, even if the rent seekers are not successful in persuading political decision makers to create rents. Those who have been successful in blocking such policies have nonetheless used resources in their opposition to the rent seekers. These losses highlight the point that the source of the social cost of rent seeking is the ex ante contest, rather than the ex post policy outcome.

Elie Appelbaum and Eliakim Katz, 1986. Transfer seeking and avoidance: On the full social costs of rent seeking. *Public Choice* 48, 175–81.

Tore Ellingsen, 1991. Strategic buyers and the social cost of monopoly. *American Economic Review* 81, 648–57.

---

[6] Katz, Nitzan, and Rosenberg (1990, reprinted in Lockard and Tullock 2001) likewise study rent seeking for a public good when there are no income effects, and demonstrate precisely the same result.

Kai A. Konrad, 2000. Sabotage in rent-seeking contests. *Journal of Law, Economics, and Organization* 16, 155–65.

Gil S. Epstein and Shmuel Nitzan, 2004. Strategic restraint in contests. *European Economic Review* 48, 201–10.

Appelbaum and Katz (1986) point out that the size of the stakes and the group of rent seekers need to be considered, as well as whether people can abstain from the contest. Ellingsen (1991) considers the consequences of active transfer-avoidance behavior by consumers opposing the creation of monopoly rents. He shows that pre-existing rent seekers will change their behavior if new players enter and that this will generally prevent the players from over-dissipating the rent. Konrad (2000) explores contests in which there are two types of rent-seeking effort. He distinguishes between efforts that improve one's own competitive position with respect to all other contestants, and efforts that disadvantage a subset of the other competitors. The latter, sabotaging a subset of the other contenders, has the characteristics of a public good, because it benefits all but the contestants who are sabotaged. For this reason, sabotage as a form of opposition is a phenomenon that is more likely to occur in games with a small number of players. Epstein and Nitzan (2004) show that competition over policy alternatives induces strategic restraint in policy proposals (the prizes sought), which reduces resources used in rent seeking.[7]

3.2 Choice of timing

Nash equilibrium is often based on simultaneity in choice of strategies, but one player may move first and commit to a strategy, which introduces issues of timing.

Avinash K. Dixit, 1987. Strategic behavior in contests. *American Economic Review* 77, 891–98.

Kyung Hwan Baik and Jason F. Shogren, 1992. Strategic behavior in contests: Comment. *American Economic Review* 82, 359–62.

Dixit (1987) investigated the incentives of players to commit to choose a level of effort other than their Nash equilibrium effort if a player can act as a Stackelberg leader, and asked how the choice of commitment depends on the valuations of the prize. Baik and Shogren (1992) showed that Stackelberg-leader-follower behavior emerges endogenously in a non-discriminating probabilistic contest, with the weaker player or "underdog" moving first. The weaker player has a lower valuation of the prize than the stronger player, or has a probability of winning the contest of

---

[7] See also Leidy (1994) on reduced rent dissipation when monopoly is threatened by regulatory policy.

less than 50 percent in the simultaneous-move Nash equilibrium. Rent dissipation is less than in the simultaneous-move Nash equilibrium.[8]

3.3 Time

Rent seeking can take place sequentially, in the course of time, and in repeated contests. Two important time-related aspects of rent-seeking contests concern asymmetries in living on to compete again and the properties of evolutionary equilibria.

> Joerg Stephan and Heinrich W. Ursprung, 1998. The social cost of rent seeking when victories are potentially transient and losses final. In Karl-Josef Koch and Klaus Jaeger (eds.), *Trade, Growth, and Economic Policy in Open Economies: Essays in Honour of Hans-Jürgen Vosgerau*. Springer, Berlin, pp. 369–80.

> Nava Kahana and Shmuel Nitzan, 1999. Uncertain preassigned non-contestable and contestable rents. *European Economic Review* 43, 1705–21.

> Burkhard Hehenkamp, Wolfgang Leininger, and Alex Possajennikov, 2004. Evolutionary equilibrium in Tullock contests: Spite and overdissipation. *European Journal of Political Economy* 20, 1045–57.

Stephan and Ursprung (1998) describe rent seeking in sequential contests over time, with the important asymmetry that one side can lose in a contest and nonetheless return to contest the rent in a future contest, whereas for the other side any loss is permanent. For example, an incumbent once ousted may not be able to return to office or a new policy, once adopted, may not be easily reversed. The possibility that one side wins once and forever does not necessarily reduce the social cost of rent seeking. Kahana and Nitzan (1999) describe a government bureaucracy that procrastinates and does not deliver assigned payments or rents in a timely way, or may never deliver. The uncertainty about timing of payment affects the value of the rent. They examine circumstances in which the rent if delivered has been pre-assigned and the purpose of rent seeking is to elicit the payment from the bureaucracy, and also in which the rent is contestable. They evaluate rent dissipation in each case. When there is no uncertainty regarding timing of delivery of a contestable rent, the model reduces to the standard Tullock contest.

Hehenkamp, Leininger, and Possajennikov (2004) provide a dynamic analysis of the Tullock contest using the concept of evolutionary stable strategies (ESS).[9] An evolutionary contest is a contest for survival and has a natural rent-seeking connotation. Hehenkamp et al derive the equilibrium in ESS for Tullock contests and show that more resources are used in rent seeking than in the unique Nash

---

[8] An equivalent result is derived by Leininger (1993, reprinted in Lockard and Tullock 2001). For observations on the two formulations, see Nitzan (1994, reprinted in Lockard and Tullock 2001).

[9] An ESS has the property that, if generally adopted by the group, there is no alternative strategy that can give a higher payoff to a member of the group. For finite populations, an ESS can differ from Nash equilibrium.

equilibrium. Total use of resources in rent seeking does not depend on the number of players and is solely determined by the contest success function and the value of the rent. Whether there is over-dissipation depends on the scale parameter of the contest function. Over-dissipation is interpreted as the consequence of "spite". Given the nature of ESS, it pays to reduce one's own prospects of success by increasing rent-seeking outlays, if this reduces the other strategy's success even more, which is what a person using ESS will do. An equilibrium in ESS is consistent with over-dissipation. Vindication is therefore provided for Tullock's observations on over-dissipation, although not in the usual context of Nash equilibrium.

3.4 Information

Information is expected to affect the outcome of rent-seeking contests. Most of the literature on contests assumes that players are completely informed, or at least symmetrically informed. As in many other games, the information of players may not always be symmetric. Information asymmetries can exist with respect to a number of aspects of a contest.

> Karl Wärneryd, 2003. Information in conflicts. *Journal of Economic Theory* 110, 121–36.

> David A. Malueg and Andrew J. Yates, 2004. Rent seeking with private values. *Public Choice* 119, 161–78.

Wärneryd (2003) considers a contest for a prize, the value of which is the same for both players, but known only by one of the players. He finds that the less informed player may win with a higher probability. Malueg and Yates (2004) consider the case in which each player's valuation of the prize is private information and drawn from the same binary probability distribution.

Theory Part 4 – Structure of Contests

4.1 Hierarchies and nested contests

Contests can take place in hierarchies, or similarly can be nested in that the results of one contest give rise to another contest.

> Arye L. Hillman and Eliakim Katz, 1987. Hierarchical structure and the social costs of bribes and transfers. *Journal of Public Economics* 34, 129–42.

> Eliakim Katz and Julia Tokatlidu, 1996. Group competition for rents. *European Journal of Political Economy* 12, 599–607.

> Kai A. Konrad, 2004. Bidding in hierarchies. *European Economic Review* 48, 1301–08.

Hillman and Katz (1987) described rent seeking in bureaucratic hierarchies in which bribes are transferred up the hierarchy (for example, from the corrupt police officer to the senior officer to the minister of police, to the president). Bribes are transfers and do not in themselves indicate social losses through rent seeking. Contests to occupy the positions to which bribes accrue at each level of the hierarchy, however, attract resources into rent seeking. Katz and Tokatlidu (1996) describe a nested contest in which initially members of a group compete for a rent, and in a second stage the members of the group that has won the rent compete for the rent among themselves. In the absence of risk aversion, whether or not the rent is divisible is of no significance. The rent is a collective benefit in the stage at which groups compete and is a private benefit when members of the winning group compete among themselves. Rent dissipation depends on the relative sizes of the groups. The model describes cases in which, first, a coalition is formed to contest or create a rent and, second, if the rent is won or made available, the personal division of the rent becomes the issue of contention. Konrad (2004) shows that group composition effects become important in nested contests if the group members are asymmetric. For some group compositions, players who value the prize very little may win the prize with high probability and with very little effort.

4.2 Contest design

The structures of contests affect the effort that contenders exert. The consequences are similar to different distributional rules for contenders. The literature demonstrates that fine-grained rules and the structure of contests have a wide variety of subtle effects on the investments in effort made by participants. Under slightly different rules for entry, sequencing, or dividing the prize, the social losses associated with rent-seeking contests can differ substantially. These are important conclusions because structures of rent-seeking contests are not entirely historical accidents. Rather, contests are often contrived with various ends in mind. The rules of the game are often affected by the gains of those who contrive the contests. Although effort used in rent seeking is a cost for rent seekers, and so potentially a source of social loss, those efforts can be a source of benefit for government officials.[10] In principle, the rules of the game can be revised to reduce or to increase social losses by inducing changes in both the extent and kind of competitive effort (Congleton 1980).

Elie Appelbaum and Eliakim Katz, 1987. Seeking rents by setting rents: The political economy of rent seeking. *Economic Journal* 97, 685–99.

Mark Gradstein and Kai A. Konrad, 1999. Orchestrating rent seeking contests. *Economic Journal* 109, 536–45.

---

[10] See Congleton (1988) for a discussion of the extent to which rent-seeking efforts may be regarded as completely wasteful.

Kofi O. Nti, 2004. Maximum efforts in contests with asymmetric valuations. *European Journal of Political Economy* 20, 1059–66.

Appelbaum and Katz (1987) point out the active role that the "rent setter" may have in devising rent-seeking contests. Gradstein and Konrad (1999) show that organizing a contest in a structure with multiple rounds, in which there are period contests among subgroups of players and only the winners advance to the next round, may induce higher total rent-seeking effort, in particular, if the discriminatory power of the contest at each round is low. Nti (2004) considers the choice of the contest success function that maximizes effort when contestants have asymmetric valuations of the prize. Although the Tullock function with constant returns is optimal in circumstances in which valuations are symmetric and contest success functions are restricted, in the unconstrained case the optimal contest success function is equivalent to an all-pay auction with a reserve price. The optimal design internalizes the incentives to exert effort that derive from different valuations of the prize and discounts the incentive of a high-valuation contestant to evoke more effort.

4.3 The structure of prizes

The early studies proposed a single prize for the winner of a contest. The structure of prizes is, however, an important determinant of effort in contests. There can be more than one prize, and the prizes can have different values.

Amihai Glazer and Refael Hassin, 1988. Optimal contests. *Economic Inquiry* 26, 133–43.

Derek J. Clark and Christian Riis, 1998. Competition over more than one prize. *American Economic Review* 88, 276–89.

Benny Moldovanu and Aner Sela, 2001. The optimal allocation of prizes in contests. *American Economic Review* 91, 542–58.

Stefan Szymanski and Tommaso M. Valletti, 2005. Incentive effects of second prizes. *European Journal of Political Economy* 21, 467–81.

Glazer and Hassin (1988) examined the structure of prizes as incentive mechanisms. With prizes allocated in accord with individuals' output or effort rankings, they derived properties of a structure of prizes that maximizes the output (or effort) of contestants and found different optimal structures of prizes in different circumstances. Clark and Riis (1998) and Moldovanu and Sela (2001) investigate the structure of prizes in optimal design of contests under conditions of both complete and incomplete information. They find that splitting the prize into several smaller prizes is typically not a good strategy for inducing higher overall effort. Convex cost of effort is one of the cases for which multiple prizes may, however, generate higher overall effort. Szymanski and Valletti (2005) investigate the effect of introducing a second place prize in contests in which contestants have asymmetric abilities. In a three-person contest, a second prize increases total effort if one contestant is favored to win the first prize. The model directly applies to sports contests in which the efforts of contestants provide utility for spectators; however, other applications are proposed in which there is asymmetry in the abilities of contenders. The second prize is an alternative to an exclusion rule that would deny participation to a contestant whose likelihood of winning is so high as to make the outcome of a contest almost a foregone conclusion.

Theory Part 5 – Experiments

Many of the predictions of the theory have been tested in experiments.

> Jason F. Shogren and Kyung Hwan Baik, 1991. Reexamining efficient rent seeking in laboratory markets. *Public Choice* 69, 69–79.

> Jan Potters, Casper G. de Vries, and Frans van Winden, 1998. An experimental examination of rational rent seeking. *European Journal of Political Economy* 14, 783–800.

> Carsten Vogt, Joachim Weimann, and Chun-Lei Yang, 2002. Efficient rent seeking in experiment. *Public Choice* 110, 67–78.

Shogren and Baik (1991) report on experimental behavior in Tullock's efficient rent-seeking game and find outcomes consistent with predicted behavior and rent dissipation. Potters, de Vries, and van Winden (1998) report on experiments using both the Tullock probabilistic and highest-bid (discriminating or all-pay auction) contest success functions. In the Tullock contests, rent dissipation was initially greater than the predicted 50 percent for two contenders but declined toward the predicted outcome as further games were played. In the contests in which the highest bidder won, ex post rent dissipation fluctuated around the Hillman-Samet predicted on-average complete dissipation. Some participants showed learning from experience and changed their behavior, while others in both types of contests did not approach the consistent rational behavior predicted by the models. Vogt, Weimann, and Yang (2002) report rational behavior in variants of the Tullock contest.

Volume II – Applications: Rent Seeking in Practice

Volume II focuses on applications of the rent-seeking approach. The earliest applied papers demonstrate that the rent-seeking approach can be used to shed light on the behavior of politically active individuals and interest groups, and to provide a rational choice – based explanation for the wide range of unproductive economic regulations observed in the present and past. The rent-seeking approach has also been used to investigate a variety of other contest-like settings in which the resources invested by participants may be socially unproductive. For example, rent-seeking models have been used to analyze electoral contests, court proceedings, status seeking, terrorism, war, and revolution. Again, the literature is large and selection was required. Our decision was to focus on classics, significant contributions, and to sample the breadth of the applied work. Many more papers could have been included.

In the second volume we have sorted papers into areas of application by institutional setting and sector of the economy: regulation of industry, protectionist rent seeking, soft budgets and moral hazard, rent seeking in the context of economic development, the relationship between rent seeking and economic growth, rent seeking inside the firm, rent seeking between insiders and outsiders, office seeking and rent creation in democratic politics, litigation, history, and the civil society.

Applications Part 1 – Regulation and Protection

1.1 Monopoly and regulation of industry

Tullock's (1967) observations of the social cost of rent seeking included monopoly. Subsequent studies focused on measuring the social costs of monopoly due to rent seeking.

> Richard A. Posner, 1975. The social costs of monopoly and regulation. *Journal of Political Economy* 83, 807–27.
>
> Keith Cowling and Dennis C. Mueller, 1978. The social costs of monopoly power. *Economic Journal* 88, 727–48.
>
> Stephen C. Littlechild, 1981. Misleading calculations of the social costs of monopoly power. *Economic Journal* 91, 348–63.

Posner (1975) set out assumptions consistent with complete dissipation of monopoly rents and computed a formula for the relation between deadweight losses and social costs of full-dissipation rent seeking. The elasticity of demand is critical for evaluating social costs. Estimates of elasticities and social loss were computed for a number of U.S. industries. Posner's calculations suggested that between 1.7 and 3.5 percent of GNP may have been lost through monopolization. He also noted that, in price-regulated industries, rent dissipation occurs through non-price competition.[11] Posner extended his observations to tax policy, the effects of monopoly power on the distribution of income, and the internal practices of labor unions. For example, he argued that taxes that increase government revenue also provide greater incentives for taxpayers to seek means of avoiding the tax payments, and so, when rent avoidance costs are taken into account, broader tax bases can be socially costly. Cowling and Mueller (1978) took the full-dissipation assumption to its logical conclusion and assigned social loss to all profits and all expenditures on advertising. They estimate social losses for relatively large firms and for the economies as a whole in the U.S. and the U.K. Estimated welfare losses ranged from 3.0 to 7.2 percent of GNP. Littlechild (1981) re-evaluated the Cowling-Mueller study and suggested that their estimates overstate the true social cost of monopoly.

1.2 Protectionist international trade policies

Tullock (1967) also referred to tariffs. Beyond monopoly and regulation, policies that restrict international trade have been a significant source of rents. The following papers view protectionist policies as means of rent creation. Rent seeking is introduced through the issue of who is to be protected.

> Arye L. Hillman, 1982. Declining industries and political-support protectionist motives. *American Economic Review* 72, 1180–87.
>
> Arye L. Hillman and Heinrich W. Ursprung, 1988. Domestic politics, foreign interests, and international trade policy. *American Economic Review* 78, 729–45.
>
> Gene M. Grossman and Elhanan Helpman, 1994. Protection for sale. *American Economic Review* 84, 833–50.

In normative international trade models, protectionism was shown to be socially optimal under various second-best circumstances; in particular, subsidizing domestic firms was proposed as socially optimal when international markets are imperfectly competitive. Hillman (1982) pointed out that protection to industries in decline because of changing comparative advantage could be explained by political-support motives. Protection increased industry-specific rents and benefited an identifiable group. When industries are in decline, new entry does not occur and the beneficiaries of protection can readily identify themselves and express political gratitude, whereas costs of protection of any industry are widely dispersed over the population. The view of protection as politically motivated rent creation and protection contrasted with the prior views of protection as reflecting social welfare objectives in second-best situations.

Hillman and Ursprung (1988) describe trade policy as the outcome of a contest between competing political candidates who have committed to implement the

---

[11] Posner's (1975) description of non-price competition as a form of rent seeking was preceded by studies of structurally similar processes in markets with promotional competition in the form of marketing and advertising effort (e.g., Friedman 1958).

preferred policies of domestic import-competing and foreign exporting producers. When tariffs are the means of protection, the candidates announce polarized policies that benefit their respective political supporters. Tariff revenue is assumed to be without political value. Voluntary export restraints that replace tariffs transform the tariff revenue to quota rents that are transferred to foreign exporters. Domestic producers gain from protection and foreign producers gain from the quota rents. The rents to foreign producers are compensation – and indeed overcompensation – for the protectionist policies. When voluntary export restraints restrict international trade, political candidates choose identical Hotelling-type policies, so ending the political tensions when tariffs are the means of protection. Grossman and Helpman (1994) describe a policy maker who stands ready to accept offers for "sale of protection" to industry interests. The industry producer groups are perfectly organized and consumers are not organized at all, which is the source of the industry's political advantage. The model solves a common agency problem in which the politician selling protection secures all rents (at the margin). Market characteristics determine the structure of protection chosen to maximize political rents. Each of these papers describes rent creation and rent assignment through political discretion over international trade policy.

Applications Part 2 – Economic Development and Growth

2.1 Economic development

> Anne O. Krueger, 1974. The political economy of the rent-seeking society. *American Economic Review* 64, 291–303.

> Jakob Svensson, 2000. Foreign aid and rent seeking. *Journal of International Economics* 51, 437–61.

> Philip Verwimp, 2003. The political economy of coffee, dictatorship, and genocide. *European Journal of Political Economy* 19, 161–81.

Krueger (1974) observed that rents from import quotas attracted resources to rent seeking and computed estimates of the social cost of rent seeking for quota rents in India and Turkey. She set out a general equilibrium model using the complete-dissipation assumption. The rent dissipation arose in the course of the government assigning import quotas based on firms' productive capacities. The method for assigning quotas provided incentives for excessive productive capacity. Resources were also used in seeking to influence government officials' decisions regarding quota assignments. She estimated that rent dissipation accounted for 7.3 percent of national income for India and 15 percent for Turkey. Svensson (2000) points to the evidence that foreign aid has been ineffective in increasing incomes in poor countries and notes that foreign aid made up more than half of the government budgets of the 50 most aid-dependent countries in the 1975-1995 period. He describes a repeated game among competing domestic groups in which aid is provided, and considers an aid policy that takes account of losses from rent seeking. In an empirical section, ethnic diversity is used as a proxy for the number of competing groups and an index of corruption is a proxy for rent seeking. Foreign aid is positively associated with rent seeking (proxied by corruption). Verwimp (2003) describes how the antecedents to the Rwanda genocide centered on government responses to the value of rents that were tied to the price of coffee.

2.2 Property rights and corruption

Conditions are favorable for rent seeking when the rule of law is not present to protect property rights and where there is corruption.

> Kevin M. Murphy, Andrei Shleifer, and Robert W. Vishny, 1993. Why is rent seeking so costly to growth? *American Economic Review* 83, 409–14.

> Arye L. Hillman and Heinrich W. Ursprung, 2000. Political culture and economic decline. *European Journal of Political Economy* 16, 189–213.

> Halvor Mehlum, Karl Moene, and Ragnar Torvik, 2006. Institutions and the resource curse. *Economic Journal* 116, 1–20.

Murphy, Shleifer, and Vishney (1993) observe that effectiveness of protection of property rights determines returns from rent seeking and propose that rent seeking inhibits economic growth for two principal reasons: because of increasing returns to rent seeking relative to productive activity and because bureaucratic rent seeking deters innovation more so than ongoing productive activity. In their model with increasing returns, a "bad" equilibrium exists that is stable and is not affected by minor improvement in property rights protection. Countries can also slide into this equilibrium as the consequence of civil turmoil. With respect to innovation, they note that rent seeking by government officials impedes growth because of the need for licenses, etc. to start new business activities. Also, whereas large pre-existing firms have political influence and can protect themselves from a rent-seeking bureaucracy, innovators are least protected from the rent seeking by government officials and can least afford bribes. Innovative projects are also long-term risky investments that are most vulnerable to rent extraction by government officials. Hillman and Ursprung (2000) use the background of the transition from socialism to address the question as to why rent seeking appears to increase with political liberalization. The transition from socialism offered substantial rents through the processes of privatization. The privatization occurred with initial property rights not defined, and after rounds of privatization property rights could at times remain not well protected. The processes of privatization often involved corruption by political insiders who had the authority and means to designate owners of property and natural resources. Hillman and Ursprung use a nested model to describe the privileged insiders competing for rents, while at the same time outsiders compete to become insiders. Political liberalization gives outsiders direct access to contests for rents and thereby increases social costs of rent seeking, as long as a political culture of rent seeking persists.[12] Mehlum, Moene, and Torvik (2006) confirm that institutions conducive to rent seeking underlie failures of societies to realize benefits from natural resource wealth. Natural-resource wealth is a "curse," rather than a source of social benefit when property rights are not defined or respected and the wealth becomes a rent-seeking prize.[13]

2.3 Migration

Rents and rent-seeking losses are associated with migration and migration policies. When people emigrate, they may be escaping a rent-seeking society or they may be attracted by rents available in new locations.

> Gil S. Epstein, Arye L. Hillman, and Heinrich W. Ursprung, 1999. The king never emigrates. *Review of Development Economics* 3, 107–21.

> Peter Nannestad, 2004. Immigration as a challenge to the Danish welfare state? *European Journal of Political Economy* 20, 755–67.

Epstein, Hillman, and Ursprung (1999) describe a king or ruler who creates and assigns rents by taxing part of the population for both own personal benefit and for the benefit of other privileged parts of the population. Whether people in the population gain or lose depends on the outcome of a contest that determines proximity to the king. People differ in personal comparative advantage in productive and rent-seeking activities. The contest success function determines whether the most productive people or the superior rent seekers are closest to the king. Those furthest from the king have the greatest incentives to emigrate. Rents provided by welfare systems make immigration a form of rent seeking. Nannestad (2004) describes the creation of rents for immigrants through the welfare budget of Denmark.

Applications Part 3 – Political and Legal Institutions

3.1 Electoral politics

Rent-seeking contests within political systems take place at several levels, as noted in volume I. Analysis of the efforts of would-be monopolists, transfer recipients, and beneficiaries of entry barriers to change the policies of standing governments and regulatory agencies is the focus of most of the research described in volume II. In other cases, however, the government and the rent at issue are determined simultaneously. Contests to become the government – through electoral competition in democracies – exhibit some of the properties of rent-seeking games. Moreover, incumbent politicians and political parties may create or threaten to create

---

[12] Gelb, Hillman, and Ursprung (1998) describe the institutional background of rent seeking in the transition from socialism.

[13] Ollson (2007) considers the case of diamonds.

rent-seeking contests to attract campaign "contributions," insofar as campaign resources increase their prospects for electoral success.

Roger D. Congleton, 1986. Rent-seeking aspects of political advertising. *Public Choice* 49, 249–63.

Fred S. McChesney, 1987. Rent extraction and rent creation in the economic theory of regulation. *Journal of Legal Studies* 16, 101–18.

Michael R. Baye, Dan Kovenock, and Casper G. de Vries, 1993. Rigging the lobbying process: An application of the all-pay auction. *American Economic Review* 83, 289–94.

Yeon-Koo Che and Ian L. Gale, 1998. Caps on political lobbying. *American Economic Review* 88, 643–51.

Kai A. Konrad, 2004. Inverse campaigning. *Economic Journal* 114, 69–82.

Congleton (1986) notes that competition among candidates (and parties) for the votes of their electorates often resembles a rent-seeking contest. Advertising is often used to affect voter expectations about the relative merits of the policies and candidates. To the extent that political advertising is effective, but provides biased information, the quality of voter information may be eroded by persuasive campaigns, at least at the margin. This may occur even in cases in which the efforts of proponents and opponents of a given policy exactly offset each other, because such persuasive campaigns tend to increase the variance of voter estimates of policy consequences. When the informational value of political advertising to voters is less than the expenditures of opposing candidates, at least some political advertising is wasteful in the sense of a rent-seeking contest.

McChesney (1987) suggests that the demand for campaign contributions can induce competing candidates and political parties to create new rent-seeking games. Incumbent politicians, may for example, threaten to eliminate existing rents, or threaten firms with new taxation, to obtain additional political support. Such contests increase rent-seeking losses by creating new contests for political influence with costs greater than benefits. They may also create conventional deadweight losses by affecting the allocation of investment resources and the flow of indirect payments to politicians. Baye, Kovenock, and de Vries (1993) demonstrate how a rent-maximizing official can benefit by creating a two-stage lobbying game when participants disagree about the value of the prize to be awarded. Lobbyists in the second stage actively compete for favor by providing services or campaign contributions, and the closer the lobbyists in the second round are in valuing the prize, the higher the total lobbying expenditure tends to be. Consequently, it is clear that conditions exist in which officials will exclude the highest bidder from the final group of participants. Similarly, Che and Gale (1998) demonstrate that caps on the amounts that may be given to political candidates can increase total expenditures in cases in which substantial valuation disagreements exist.

Konrad (2004) explores a setting in which campaign expenditures are informative, but nonetheless give rise to a deadweight cost through the electoral process. Uninformed voters have sufficient information in the absence of campaign expenditures to make the correct (welfare-enhancing) choice. Voters initially know that a majority benefits from the program of one of the two parties, but not who actually benefits. In a process termed "inverse campaigning", parties each diminish political support for political opponents by informing uninformed voters about the beneficiaries of the opponent's programs. The expected benefits of the uninformed voters from the opponent's program are reduced (the voters realize that they are less likely to be members of the favored subset of voters). In equilibrium, voters become informed, but are no better off because they knew enough in the first place to make the correct decision in the election. Campaign expenditures have been wasted in the political contest.

3.2 The courts, the judiciary, and litigation

A good deal of mainstream economics rests on the assumption that property rights are both secure and clearly understood by one and all. This allows trade to take place and contracts to be negotiated with participating parties all expecting to benefit from exchange. Although this is a useful first approximation of legal systems, disagreements can exist about the nature of a contract and about property rights. The result is then litigation that aims at clarifying or establishing property rights. The outcome of a civil suit redistributes wealth between defendants and plaintiffs. Civil law proceedings are thus rent-seeking contests in which the "prize" is dissipated through conflict.

Gordon Tullock, 1975. On the efficient organization of trials. *Kyklos* 28, 745–62.

Amy Farmer and Paul Pecorino, 1999. Legal expenditure as a rent-seeking game. *Public Choice* 100, 271–88.

Francesco Parisi, 2002. Rent-seeking through litigation: Adversarial and inquisitorial systems compared. *International Review of Law and Economics* 22, 193–216.

Michael R. Baye, Dan Kovenock, and Casper G. de Vries, 2005. Comparative analysis of litigation systems: An auction-theoretic approach. *Economic Journal* 115, 583–601.

Tullock (1975) developed an early version of his contest success function to describe a legal contest between two sides of a civil law suit. In related research, Tullock used the resources committed to litigation as an index of the cost-effectiveness of legal systems. By that measure, he argues that the judge-run continental system is superior to the adversarial proceedings of the Anglo-Saxon system. The technique of using rent dissipation as an index of court performance was developed further by Farmer and Peccorino (1999), Parisi (2002), and Baye, Kovenock, and de Vries (2005), who highlight different aspects of court procedures and outcomes. Farmer and Peccorino and Baye, Kovenock and de Vries show how the design of the legal system, in particular fee shifting rules, that is, the allocation of litigation fees as a function of the court decision, influences the efficiency of the litigation system. Parisi notes the existence of a continuum of court procedures, rather than the dichotomous Anglo-Continental Europe choice.

Applications Part 4 – Institutions and History

4.1 Institutions

The rules of a rent-seeking contest determine both the feasible range of rent-seeking methods and the net returns from private investments in rent-seeking contests. The "rules of the game" are simply another name for the array of formal and informal institutions under which the rent-seeking contest takes place. To the extent that existing formal and informal rules can be modified or new formal rules introduced, rent-seeking expenditures can be reduced (or increased) through institutional design (Congleton, 1980, 1984: reprinted in volume I). Since institutions can both induce and curtail rent-seeking activities, normative research on institutional design attempts to identify rules that reduce or increase unproductive conflict and to suggest reforms that can improve on existing rules. For example, the research on court systems and alternative ownership structures for firms noted above falls into this general category of research. The rent-seeking approach can also be applied to understand the law itself and other civil institutions.

James M. Buchanan, 1983. Rent seeking, noncompensated transfers, and laws of succession. *Journal of Law and Economics* 26, 71–85.

Kevin Sylwester, 2001. A model of institutional formation within a rent-seeking environment. *Journal of Economic Behavior and Organization* 44, 169–76.

J. Atsu Amegashie, 2006. The 2002 winter Olympics scandal: Rent seeking and committees. *Social Choice and Welfare* 26, 183–89.

Buchanan (1983) explores an area of civil law that is one of the oldest and most important, namely inheritance law. Many models assume that agents live forever, although this is not a reasonable assumption for long-term analysis. Even if intra-generational law is efficient in the sense that it minimizes rent-seeking losses by channeling conflict into productive activities, resources may still be dissipated in intergenerational conflict. Such large-scale conflict is most evident in great dynastic conflicts for power and wealth, but may also occur in any household that has wealth that may be passed on to the next generation, or even within governments or bureaucracies insofar as an office may be said to be created and passed on to the next office holder. Buchanan notes that some legal institutions clearly tend to reduce conflict levels, as with primogeniture and requirements for equal division, while others clearly increase conflict over what he terms uncompensated transfers.

The logic of rent seeking can also be used to explain the emergence of the law and state enforcement of the law itself as a means of avoiding losses from wasteful conflict. This approach to political theory was first clearly stated by Thomas Hobbes in 1651, and rational choice–based analysis of the state as a device for reducing conflict in a setting of anarchy has existed since the early 1970s (see for example Tullock 1974).[14] Sylwester (2001) analyzes an intermediate setting in which a group of producers confronts rent seeking by a large group of pragmatists who can choose either to be productive or to rent seek (steal) from the producers. Additional protection through the rule of law can be provided collectively by the producers to reduce losses from rent seeking, although this is not always consistent with individual producers' incentives, because additional security is a public good for the producers. Sylwester suggests that the larger the initial productive group is relative to the group of rent seekers, and the more productive are the producers, the more likely it is that additional law enforcement will be provided. In a relatively simple model, he demonstrates a clear interdependence between production technology (income), rent-seeking, and effective legal institutions. Societies with effective legal institutions are more prosperous because of reduced rent-seeking activity, although more costly legal institutions can be adopted only by societies that are relatively prosperous. In effect, the results suggest that some societies "boot strap" themselves out of poverty by adopting successively more effective legal institutions that curtail rent seeking and enhance productivity.

Determining the outcome of rent-seeking contests requires the choice of judges. When measures of performance are not entirely objective, but involve subjective aesthetics, the choice of winners can be influenced by extraneous considerations or corruption. Amegashie (2006) uses the case of the skating judgment scandal at the 2002 winter Olympic Games as background to investigate the consequence of change in the rules of committee decisions.[15] Because of the scandal, not all judges' evaluations were included in determination of winners. Rather, there was random selection of which judges' evaluations were used. Although the identity of which judges' opinions will count is then not known, Amegashie finds no systematic effects that reduce the incentives for rent seeking through influence on judges. If the intent was to diminish rent seeking, this was a case of institutional design that failed.

---

[14] As noted, we have elected to exclude the theoretical literature on anarchy from the present volume for space considerations and in order to focus on settings in which a political and legal system of some sort already exists.

[15] This was a case of corruption. If the decisions of an international committee and international organizations reflect the values or behavioral norms of individual national members, we expect corruption to emerge, and rent-seeking contests to replace objective decisions.

4.2 Mercantilism

Mercantilism has been studied as an example of a rent-seeking society.[16]

> Barry Baysinger, Robert B. Ekelund Jr., and Robert D. Tollison, 1980. Mercantilism as a rent-seeking society. In James M. Buchanan, Robert D. Tollison, and Gordon Tullock (eds.), *Towards a Theory of the Rent-Seeking Society*. Texas A&M University Press, College Station, pp. 235–68.

> S. R. H. Jones and Simon P. Ville, 1996. Efficient transactors or rent-seeking monopolists? The rationale for early chartered trading companies. *Journal of Economic History* 56, 898–915.

> Oliver Volckart, 2000. The open constitution and its enemies: Competition, rent seeking, and the rise of the modern state. *Journal of Economic Behavior and Organization* 42, 1–17.

Baysinger, Ekelund, and Tollison (1980) quote Adam Smith that "mercantilism is nothing but a tissue of protectionist fallacies foisted upon a venal parliament by our merchants and manufacturers" based on the idea that "wealth consists in money." They describe mercantilism using a model of the state as a source of private rents, with applications to the different political and legal institutions of England and France. Mercantilism in France persisted into the nineteenth century, whereas mercantilism in England was compromised by a competitive judiciary that created uncertainty about whether monopoly rights could be sustained, and also by the intellectual arguments of economists and philosophers.[17] Volckart (2000) analyzes the emergence of the early mercantilist state in the late Middle Ages as an exercise in rent extraction by lords and vassals providing military protection for peasants in exchange for other services. The rent-extracting ability arose because of reductions in information and transaction costs, along with increasing population, which together shifted bargaining power and military authority to regional lords. In the early Middle Ages, labor had been scarce and competition between large landowners and fortified towns for labor resulted in contracts that were relatively favorable to peasants. As population increased, regional political authorities were able to create and enforce new laws that generated new rents for those controlling large blocks of land and supplying military services. Rents were created for towns, for example, by requiring farmers to sell their grain to the nearest grain dealer, reducing competition among resellers for grain, who in turn would obtain this profitable privilege by accepting the regional lord's provision of military services. Jones and Ville (1996) propose that joint stock companies that emerged in the seventeenth and eighteenth centuries held exclusive trading rights in particular goods and/or regions of the world, not because they reduced transactions costs associated with

---

[16] Prior to mercantilism, Ekelund et al (1996) describe the medieval church as an economic firm.

[17] For an extended study, see Ekelund and Tollison (1997).

long-distance trade, but because they maximized monopoly rents. This, in turn, maximized the fees that the crown could charge for issuing such charters. For example, in 1687, private traders to West Africa paid a premium of 40 percent of the value of their cargoes for the right to trade. Very few of these companies survived in the more competitive environment that emerged in the late eighteenth century.

4.3 Authoritarian regimes

Rent seeking has historically been prevalent under authoritarian regimes. The following papers describe communism and the Roman Empire.

> Arye L. Hillman and Adi Schnytzer, 1986. Illegal economic activities and purges in a Soviet-type economy: A rent-seeking perspective. *International Review of Law and Economics* 6, 87–99.

> Charles D. DeLorme Jr., Stacey Isom, and David R. Kamershen, 2005. Rent seeking and taxation in the Ancient Roman Empire. *Applied Economics* 37, 705–11.

Hillman and Schnytzer (1986) describe the role of rents and rent seeking under communism, under which rewards were non-market determined and market transactions constituted economic crimes. Purges were means of protecting the incumbent ruler from rent seekers. Data from the prosecution of economic crimes reveals the large magnitudes of rents from personal transactions within the planned system. A puzzle is that large rents were contested and secured when there were limited opportunities for spending wealth because of the limited presence of markets. Data is also presented on the value of payments made to obtain positions in the official hierarchy. The payments are indicative of the rents that could be extracted. DeLorme, Isom, and Kamershen (2005) describe the role of rent seeking in the demise of the Roman Empire. The change in political institutions from republic to rule by an emperor changed the behavior of the ruling classes. Rent seeking resulted in use of tax revenue for privileged benefits. Military control by the emperor prevented popular expression of discontent with the privileged assignment of tax revenue.

Applications Part 5 – The Firm

5.1 Soft budgets and moral hazard

The interface between firms and benefits through public policy introduces the idea of the soft budget, which is closely related to rent seeking. "Soft" budgets are budgets that are not binding and that can thereby be manipulated to create rents. Government subsidies that cover producers' costs provide soft budgets for the subsidy recipients. Soft budgets are associated with moral hazard.

Jànos Kornai, 1980. 'Hard' and 'soft' budget constraint. *Acta Oeconomica* 25, 231–46.

Arye L. Hillman, Eliakim Katz, and Jacob Rosenberg, 1987. Workers as insurance: Anticipated government intervention and factor demand. *Oxford Economic Papers* 39, 813–20.

Steven T. Buccola and James E. McCandish, 1999. Rent seeking and rent dissipation in state enterprises. *Review of Agricultural Economics* 21, 358–73.

Kornai (1980) described soft budgets in a context in which state-owned firms function in markets but cannot become bankrupt, because of the political unacceptability of unemployment or the closure of a state-owned firm. A state guarantee to cover all losses allows rent creation and rent extraction by managers and workers in the state-owned firms. Kornai's soft budgets also apply in market economies to government departments and bureaucracies, which similarly are protected from bankruptcy. Hillman, Katz, and Rosenberg (1987) describe a firm whose owners are aware that the political disutility of unemployment and the likelihood of protectionist policies increase with the number of workers who would lose their jobs if the firm were to confront low-cost import competition. Rents in the form of returns to industry-specific capital are protected by employing more than the profit-maximizing number of workers. Firms producing output under conditions of market risk have incentives to produce in peripheral locations where the political disutility of unemployment is greater. Beyond moral hazard, there is therefore adverse selection. Buccola and McCandish (1999) provide a case study from Africa in which a private firm competes against a privatized former state enterprise that retains its ties to government officials and thereby its privileges. The case study is the background for a description of how state-owned firms seek to maximize costs subject to the aid that is provided by international donors. In this case, the source of the soft budget is development assistance.

5.2 Rent seeking within the firm

When rent seeking occurs within the firm, government need not be involved and so political economy issues need not arise. The firm is an institution of economic organization based on the incentives of markets and private property. In principle, the competitive firm is devoid of rents. The logic of the rent-seeking approach suggests, however, that a firm's labor force, management, and owners have incentives to invest resources in socially (and organizationally) fruitless disputes over their firm's profits.

Aaron S. Edlin and Joseph E. Stiglitz, 1995. Discouraging rivals: Managerial rent seeking and economic inefficiencies. *American Economic Review* 85, 1301–12.

David S. Scharfstein and Jeremy C. Stein, 2000. The dark side of internal capital markets: Divisional rent-seeking and inefficient investment. *The Journal of Finance* 55, 2527–64.

Amihai Glazer, 2002. Allies as rivals: Internal and external rent seeking. *Journal of Economic Behavior and Organization* 48, 155–62.

Edlin and Stiglitz (1995) present a model in which managers entrench themselves in their positions by making investment decisions that discourage rivals from applying for or contesting their positions. The rents of entrenchment are achieved by creating asymmetric information and by making acquisitions that require the personal information of the incumbent managers for the realization of potential synergies. Incumbent managers, thus, increase uncertainty about the firm's prospects to reduce competition for their positions, given the reservation rewards of other prospective applicants. Edlin and Stiglitz thereby suggest that acquisitions and mergers reflect rent seeking by incumbent managers.

Scharfstein and Stein (2000) note the empirical evidence that diversified firms or conglomerates trade on the stock market at a discount compared with firms that are more specialized in their activities. A CEO personally gains from empire building or from increasing total investment beyond levels that maximize the value of the firm. Nonetheless the CEO has an incentive to allocate capital efficiently within the firm. Scharfstein and Stein (2000) suggest, however, that the internal allocation of capital within the firm is inefficient because rent seeking by divisional managers results in value-reducing cross-subsidization among the divisions of conglomerates. Rent seeking increases the bargaining power of the weaker divisional managers. Weaker divisions of the firm are subsidized by stronger divisions, because the opportunity cost of allocating time to rent seeking, rather than productive activities, is lower for the managers of the weaker divisions. With accountability constraining the CEO from increasing managerial incomes directly, managerial incomes are increased by increasing investment and thereby managerial responsibility, which can be used to justify increases in manager incomes. Glazer (2002) notes that employees have the option of using their rent-seeking abilities on behalf of the firm in confronting external competitors, or in rent seeking for personal benefit within the firm, which reduces the firm's profits. The ability or means to use rent seeking in either way reduces the incentives of the firm to hire proficient rent seekers.

5.3 Firm ownership, outsiders, and rents

Rent seeking within the firm provides an explanation for the existence of outside ownership and for unemployment.

Assar Lindbeck and Dennis J. Snower, 1987. Efficiency wages versus insiders and outsiders. *European Economic Review* 31, 407–16.

Roger D. Congleton, 1989. Monitoring rent-seeking managers: Advantages of diffuse ownership. *Canadian Journal of Economics* 22, 662–72.

Holger M. Müller and Karl Wärneryd, 2001. Inside versus outside ownership: A political theory of the firm. *Rand Journal of Economics* 32, 527–41.

Intra-firm rent-seeking opportunities arise because the institutional structure of the firm is unable to align perfectly the interests of the parties participating in joint production. This may be a consequence of informational asymmetries within the firm, contract and institutional imperfections, and/or a firm's market power. It is clear that intra-firm conflict over profits tends to reduce a firm's efficiency and thereby its prospects for survival in competitive markets. And, it is equally clear that firms with an organizational structure that reduces such losses will be relatively more efficient and more likely to survive. Thus, the rent-seeking approach predicts the emergence of organizational structures that reduce intra-firm rent-seeking activities. Congleton (1989) and Müller and Wärneryd (2001) suggest that a firm's ownership structure is such a device. Congleton (1989) notes that owner efforts to monitor shirking employees create a rent seeking-like contest in which owners may over-monitor their employees. Owners may sacrifice total firm profits, as long as their own share of the profits can be increases sufficiently through monitoring. In some cases, diffuse ownership can increase a firm's profits by reducing monitoring by owners, because productivity increases as employee profit shares increase. The more profit seeking are employees, the more diffuse ownership should be, if a firm's profits are to be maximized. Müller and Wärneryd explore distinctions between partnerships (inside ownership) and outside owners. They demonstrate that adding outside owners has the effect of creating a hierarchical game in which investments in rent seeking tend to fall relative to the single-level game among partners (insiders). In effect, insiders free ride in the contest, with outside owners leaving less on the insider's table to contest. They explore incentives for insider sell-outs to outsiders and suggest that the common evolution of firm organizational structures from partnerships to corporations reflects diminishing returns to investments in firm-specific human capital and increasing intra-firm distributional conflict.

Lindbeck and Snower (1987) use the firm insider-outsider relation to propose an explanation for unemployment. The "efficiency wage" hypothesis suggests that unemployment is the outcome of a Nash equilibrium in which higher than market-clearing wages are paid to employees to provide incentives for workers not to shirk. Efficiency wages therefore create rents, at the same time that they increase the opportunity cost of shirking. Such rents produce unemployment. Snower and Lindbeck describe rents as created by insiders within the firm, who decide on the number of workers who are hired.

Applications Part 6 – Societal Relations

Societal relations involve forms of rent seeking, as expounded by Thorstein Veblen (1899) in his classic book, *The Theory of the Leisure Class*. Veblen described the quest for social status as a rent-seeking contest that involved conspicuously refraining from engaging in productive activity, or if more expedient, conspicuously engaging in consumption or having unwarranted servants for the purpose of conspicuous display. Resources were wastefully used in the display of status. More recent literature extends Veblen's observations.

6.1 Status

A great many social settings resemble rent-seeking contests, in that a prize of one kind or another is to be awarded in a manner that depends on the relative efforts of the persons seeking the prize. In some cases the prize is distributed among all those seeking it, as might be said of status in a status game. In other cases, the prize tends to be of the winner-take-all variety, as might be said of the quest for sainthood. Whether the resources used in attempting to secure the prize are socially wasted depends upon the nature of the activities that influence the distribution of the prize or probability of obtaining the prize. If status is conferred by good works or public goods, the game may consume resources but external benefits may exceed the cost of seeking the status, in which case the game may be efficiency enhancing. On the other hand, if the resources used produce no positive externalities outside the game, the game is wasteful in the usual sense of a rent-seeking contest. All contestants would benefit from a proportionate reduction in their expenditures, because this would not diminish their relative position (which determines their share of honor or probability of winning), but would free resources for other purposes. The following papers consider the quest for status.

Roger D. Congleton, 1989. Efficient status seeking: Externalities and the evolution of status games. *Journal of Economic Behavior and Organization* 11, 175–90.

Amihai Glazer and Kai A. Konrad, 1996. A signaling explanation for charity. *American Economic Review* 86, 1019–28.

Mario Ferrero, 2002. Competing for sainthood and the millennial church. *Kyklos* 55, 335–60.

Bruno S. Frey, 2003. Publishing as prostitution? Choosing between one's own ideas and academic success. *Public Choice* 116, 205–23.

Congleton (1989) suggests that there is a tendency for status games to evolve toward more productive contests in which games with negative externalities (private duals and criminal competition) are replaced by games producing no or positive externalities for non-participants, as in gift-giving contests. Good deeds and knowledge accumulate as a consequence of the latter contests. Yet this process of social evolution is slow and imperfect. Glazer and Konrad (1996) describe charitable giving as a contest for status.

Ferrero (2002) describes contests for the status of sainthood, in which proponents of candidates use resources in post-mortem contests to attract attention to the case for status. Frey (2003) considers status conferred by academic publishing. Rent seeking occurs insofar as personal honor and higher personal income are sought through socially unproductive uses of time and ability. Frey observes that authors seeking publications exhibit a willingness to make any and all changes that an editor or reviewers demand in order to ensure publication of their papers. Frey points out that there is no honor in such quests for honor. Frey also proposes changes in responsibilities of editors to make the quest for publication less like prostitution.

6.2 Civil society and rent seeking

Two final papers consider the role of rent seeking in the context of civil society.

> Roger D. Congleton, 1991. Ideological conviction and persuasion in the rent-seeking society. *Journal of Public Economics* 44, 65–86.

> Arye L. Hillman, 1998. Political economy and political correctness. *Public Choice* 96, 219–39.

Rent-seeking activity in democracies involves persuasion: directly of voters, and indirectly of political decision makers who exercise some policy discretion, because of specialization and the rational ignorance of uniformed voters. Inefficient policies that create rents can be adopted at little cost to responsible politicians or bureaucrats, if few voters know about the specific policies at issues. To understand why voters often support policies favoring more wealthy interest groups, however, requires a more finely grained representation of voter interests than provided by models that focus exclusively on economic wealth. Relatively well-informed voters often favor such programs, and it bears noting that the public arguments of economic interest groups rarely directly mention their own economic stakes or those of voters. Rather, political campaigns tend to use arguments based on the interests that voters have in a more attractive society, which usually reflects implications of broadly shared norms and ideology. Congleton (1991) explores how economic and ideological groups conduct advertising and lobbying campaigns to persuade voters and bureaucrats of the merits of particular policies. He demonstrates that persuasive contests among ideological groups are more likely to escalate than are contests among economic interest groups, and so rent-seeking losses tend to be higher for ideological than economic persuasive campaigns. Persuasive campaigns of rent seekers are more likely to be successful during times of ideological confusion or uncertainty, because at such times, voters are more open to persuasion.

Hillman (1998) considers the slow acceptance of the rent-seeking concept in its first two decades. He argues that contemporary ideology requires that democratic government be perceived as acting in the public interest. Consequently, the idea that rent seekers might be able to persuade others that their personal interests are actually the public's interest was simply rejected by the "mainstream orthodoxy," as impossible or at least politically incorrect. The policies that create and assign rents are then left unexplained, as simply part of the error term of democratic theory. It might be argued that the intent of a democratic theory that did not countenance rent seeking was pedagogical. Perhaps, education in the ways of normatively desirable behavior required not exposing students to the possibility of undeserved rewards obtained through unproductive activities. Yet assuming rent seeking out of existence, or assuming that all assignments of income and wealth affected by democratic governance are meritorious, also teaches students that all politically assigned rewards reflect intrinsic merit. Students are thereby not taught to be wary of political assignments of personal rewards.

Eventually, as these volumes demonstrate, the social costs associated with rent creation, rent assignment, and rent extraction by political decision makers have come to be widely acknowledged among social scientists and in the public domain, where the term "rent seeking" has emerged in an increasingly wide range of academic publications and in newspaper editorial pages around the world. The literature on corruption (for example, Tanzi 1998, Aidt 2003) and the willingness of international organizations, such as the World Bank and the International Monetary Fund, to ascribe ineffectiveness of aid to rent seeking and other political problems has also increased the awareness and application of the rent-seeking approach (for example, Easterly 2001, Abed and Gupta 2002).

The fear of those who acknowledge that rent seeking takes place, but oppose the academic research program, is that democratic institutions will be undermined by that research. In contrast, the hope of those who engage in that research is that, by raising awareness of the problems of political decision making, voters will exercise better oversight of their elected representatives. Democratic governments, although imperfect, sustain more attractive societies than other systems that we are aware of, and their policies are likely to be improved by more informed monitoring of the activities of rent seekers. And, moreover, as suggested in Congleton (1980: reprinted in volume I, 2000, 2003a, 2003b), the research may lead to improvements in our institutions for developing and implementing public policies. Without acknowledging the problems, improvements are unlikely to be forthcoming.

Forty Years of Rent-Seeking Research: A Progress Report

The importance of a theory can be judged in different ways. Within academia itself, the importance of a new idea can be gauged by its ability to capture the attention and imagination of other academics. The breadth and depth of the academic research on rent seeking undertaken in the past 40 years clearly suggests that this test has been passed. The analytical literature on rent-seeking contests represented in volume I demonstrates that the properties of rent-seeking contests are widely regarded to be interesting, subtle, and important. The applied literature represented in volume II demonstrates that the rent-seeking model provides a powerful and versatile tool for understanding a wide variety of social, economic, and political phenomena. The phenomenon identified by Gordon Tullock in 1967 has clearly proven to be both subtle and general.

The collection of papers in these two volumes provides an overview of important contributions of the literature. The result is an especially interesting and broad subset of the literature as a whole that should be of interest to economists, political scientists, and policy makers, whether for their own research or to better understand the world.

References (papers referred to in the introduction, but not included in the volumes)

Abed, George T. and Sanyeev Gupta (eds.), 2002. *Governance, Corruption, and Economic Performance*. International Monetary Fund, Washington DC.

Aidt, Toke S., 2003. Economic analysis of corruption: A survey. *Economic Journal* 113, 632–52.

Baye, Michael R. and Heidrun C. Hoppe, 2003. The strategic equivalence of rent-seeking, innovation, and patent-race games. *Games and Economic Behavior* 44, 217–26.

Bergson, Abram, 1938. A reformulation of certain aspects of welfare economics. *Quarterly Journal of Economics* 52, 310–34.

Brady, Gordon and Robert D. Tollison, 1994. *On The Trail of Homo Economicus: Essays by Gordon Tullock*. George Mason University Press, Fairfax.

Buchanan, James M. and Gordon Tullock, 1962. *The Calculus of Consent: Logical Foundations of Constitutional Democracy*. University of Michigan Press, Ann Arbor.

Buchanan, James M., Robert D. Tollison, and Gordon Tullock (eds.), 1980. *Toward a Theory of the Rent-Seeking Society*. Texas A&M University Press, College Station.

Congleton, Roger D., 1988. Evaluating rent-seeking losses. *Public Choice* 56, 181–84.

Congleton, Roger D., 2000. A political-efficiency case for federalism in multinational states: Controlling ethnic rent seeking. In Gianluigi Galeotti, Pierre Salmon, and Ronald Wintrobe (eds.), *Competition and Structure: The Political Economy of Collective Decisions: Essays in Honor of Albert Breton*. Cambridge University Press, New York, pp. 284–308.

Congleton, Roger D., 2003a. Rent seeking and political institutions. In Charles K. Rowley and Friedrich Schneider (eds.), *The Encyclopedia of Public Choice*. Kluwer Academic Publishers, Dordrecht, pp. 499–501.

Congleton, Roger D., 2003b. *Improving Democracy through Constitutional Reform: Some Swedish Lessons*. Kluwer Academic Publishers, Dordrecht.

Dasgupta, Partha and Joseph E. Stiglitz, 1980. Uncertainty, industrial structure, and the speed of R&D. *Bell Journal of Economics* 11, 1–28.

Easterly, William, 2001. *The Elusive Quest for Growth: Economists' Adventures and Misadventures in the Tropics*. MIT Press, Cambridge MA.

Ekelund, Robert B. Jr. and Robert D. Tollison, 1997. *Politicized Economies: Monarchy, Monopoly, and Mercantilism*. Texas A&M University Press, College Station.

Ekelund, Robert B. Jr., Robert D. Tollison, Gary M. Anderson, Robert F. Hébert, and Audrey B. Davidson, 1996. *Sacred Trust: The Medieval Church as an Economic Firm*. Oxford University Press, Oxford.

Fearon, James D., 1995. Rationalist explanations for war. *International Organization* 49, 379–414.

Friedman, Lawrence, 1958. Game-theory models in the allocation of advertising expenditures. *Operations Research* 6, 699–709.

Fullerton, Richard L. and R. Preston McAfee, 1999. Auctioning entry into tournaments. *Journal of Political Economy* 107, 573–605.

Garfinkel, Michelle R. and Stergios Skaperdas, 2007. Economics of conflict: An overview. In Todd Sandler and Keith Hartley (eds.), *Handbook of Defense Economics*, Vol. 2. Elsevier, Amsterdam, pp. 649–709.

Gelb, Alan, Arye L. Hillman, and Heinrich W. Ursprung, 1998. Rents as distractions: Why the exit from transition is prolonged. In Nicolas C. Baltas, George Demopoulos, and Joseph Hassid (eds.), *Economic Interdependence and Cooperation in Europe*. Springer, Berlin, 1998, pp. 21–38.

Harberger, Arnold C., 1954. Monopoly and resource allocation. *American Economic Review* 44, 77–87.

Harsanyi, John C., 1955. Cardinal welfare, individualistic ethics, and interpersonal comparisons of utility. *Journal of Political Economy* 63, 309–21.

Hillman, Arye L., 1989. *The Political Economy of Protection*. Harwood Academic Publishers, Chur. Reprinted 2001 by Routledge, London.

Hillman, Arye L., 2003. *Public Finance and Public Policy: Responsibilities and Limitations of Government*. Cambridge University Press, New York.

Hillman, Arye L., 2004. Nietzschean development failures. *Public Choice* 119, 263–80.

Katz, Eliakim, Shmuel Nitzan, and Jacob Rosenberg, 1990. Rent seeking for pure public goods. *Public Choice* 65, 49–60. Reprinted in: Alan Lockard and Gordon Tullock (eds.), *Efficient Rent Seeking: Chronicle of an Intellectual Quagmire*. Kluwer Academic Publishers, Dordrecht, 2001, pp. 137–48.

Konrad, Kai A., 2007. Strategy in contests: An introduction. Wissenschaftszentrum Berlin, Discussion Paper SP II 2007–01.

Kooreman, Peter and Lambert Schoonbeek, 1997. The specification of the probability functions in Tullock's rent-seeking contest. *Economics Letters* 56, 59–61.

Laband, David N. and John P. Sophocleus, 1992. An estimate of resource expenditure on transfer activity in the United States. *Quarterly Journal of Economics* 107, 959–83.

Lazear, Edward P., and Sherwin Rosen, 1981. Rank-order tournaments as optimum labor contracts. *Journal of Political Economy* 89, 841–64.

Leidy, Michael P., 1994. Rent dissipation through self-regulation: The social cost of monopoly under threat of reform. *Public Choice* 80, 105–28.

Leininger, Wolfgang, 1993. More efficient rent-seeking – A Münchhausen solution. *Public Choice* 75, 43–62. Reprinted in Alan Lockard and Gordon Tullock (eds.), *Efficient Rent Seeking: Chronicle of an Intellectual Quagmire*. Kluwer Academic Publishers, Dordrecht, 2001, pp. 187–206.

Lockard, Alan, and Gordon Tullock, 2001. *Efficient Rent-seeking: Chronicle of an Intellectual Quagmire*. Kluwer Academic Publishers, Dordrecht.

Loury, Greg C., 1979. Market structure and innovation. *Quarterly Journal of Economics* 93, 395–410.

Nalebuff, Barry J. and Joseph E. Stiglitz, 1983. Prizes and incentives: Towards a general theory of compensation and competition. *Bell Journal of Economics* 14, 21–43.

Nitzan, Shmuel, 1994. More on more efficient rent seeking and strategic behavior in contests: Comment. *Public Choice* 79, 355–56. Reprinted in Alan Lockard and Gordon Tullock (eds.), *Efficient Rent Seeking: Chronicle of an Intellectual Quagmire*. Kluwer Academic Publishers, Dordrecht, 2001, pp. 239–40.

Olson, Mancur, 1965. *The Logic of Collective Action, Public Goods and the Theory of Groups*. Harvard University Press, Cambridge MA.

Olsson, Ola, 2007. Conflict diamonds. *Journal of Development Economics* 82, 267–86.

Oswald, Andrew J., 2007. An examination of the reliability of prestigious scholarly journals: Evidence and implications for decision-makers. *Economica* 74, 21–31.

Paldam, Martin, 1997. Dutch disease and rent seeking: The Greenland model. *European Journal of Political Economy* 13, 591–614.

Rosen, Sherwin, 1986. Prizes and incentives in elimination tournaments. *American Economic Review* 76, 701–15.

Samuelson, Paul A., 1947. *Foundations of Economic Analysis*. Harvard University Press, Cambridge MA.

Skaperdas, Stergios, 2003. Restraining the genuine homo economicus: Why the economy cannot be divorced from its governance. *Economics and Politics* 15, 135–62.

Szymanski, Stefan, 2003. The economic design of sporting contests. *Journal of Economic Literature* 41, 1137–87.

Tanzi, Vito, 1998. Corruption around the world: Causes, consequences, scope, and cures. *IMF Staff Papers* 45, 559–94.

Tullock, Gordon, 1974. *The Social Dilemma: The Economics of War and Revolution*. University Publications, Blacksburg.

Veblen, Thorstein, 1934 (1899). *The Theory of the Leisure Class*. Modern Library, New York.

★　★　★

A Prince had some Monkeys trained to dance. Being naturally great mimics of men's actions, they showed themselves most apt pupils, and when arrayed in their rich clothes and masks, they danced as well as any of the courtiers. The spectacle was often repeated with great applause, till on one occasion a courtier, bent on mischief, took from his pocket a handful of nuts and threw them upon the stage. The Monkeys at the sight of the nuts forgot their dancing and became (as indeed they were) monkeys instead of actors. Pulling off their masks and tearing their robes, they fought with one another for the nuts. The dancing spectacle thus came to an end amidst the laughter and ridicule of the audience.

(Aesop, circa 600 BCE, "Fable of the Dancing Monkeys")

Part 1

Regulation and Protection

The Social Costs of Monopoly and Regulation

Richard A. Posner

University of Chicago Law School and National Bureau of Economic Research

This paper presents a model and some highly tentative empirical estimates of the social costs of monopoly and monopoly-inducing regulation in the United States. Unlike the previous studies, it assumes that competition to obtain a monopoly results in the transformation of expected monopoly profits into social costs. A major conclusion is that public regulation is probably a larger source of social costs than private monopoly. The implications of the analysis for several public policy issues, such as appropriate policy toward mergers and price discrimination, are also discussed.

When market price rises above the competitive level, consumers who continue to purchase the sellers' product at the new, higher price suffer a loss (L in fig. 1) exactly offset by the additional revenue that the sellers obtain at the higher price. Those who stop buying the product suffer a loss (D) not offset by any gain to the sellers. This is the "deadweight loss" from supracompetitive pricing and in traditional analysis its only social cost, L being regarded merely as a transfer from consumers to producers. Loss D, however, underestimates the social costs of monopoly. The existence of an opportunity to obtain monopoly profits will attract resources into efforts to obtain monopolies, and the opportunity costs of those resources are social costs of monopoly too (Tullock 1967). Theft provides an instructive analogy. The transfer of wealth from victim to

Research on this paper was supported by a grant from the National Science Foundation to the National Bureau of Economic Research for research in law and economics. The paper is not an official National Bureau publication, since it has not yet undergone the full critical review accorded Bureau publications, including approval by the Bureau's Board of Directors. I am grateful to William F. Baxter, Gary S. Becker, Harold Demsetz, Victor R. Fuchs, William M. Landes, Sam Peltzman, and George J. Stigler for helpful comments on previous drafts of the paper.

[*Journal of Political Economy*, 1975, vol. 83, no. 4]

Richard A. Posner

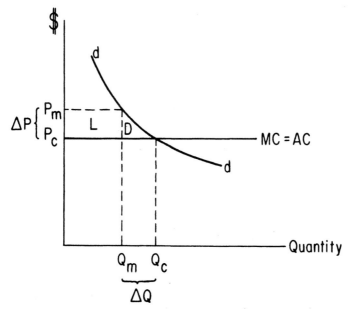

FIG. 1.—Social costs of supracompetitive pricing

thief involves no artificial limitation of output,[1] but it does not follow that the social cost of theft is zero. The opportunity for such transfers draws resources into thieving and in turn into protection against theft, and the opportunity costs of the resources consumed are social costs of theft (Tullock 1967; Becker 1968, p. 171, n. 3).

This sort of analysis has long been familiar in a few special contexts. Plant's criticism of the patent system, made more than a generation ago, was based on the effect of the patent monopoly in drawing greater resources into invention than into activities that yield only competitive returns (Plant 1934). Telser's theory of resale price maintenance is in the same vein (Telser 1960), as is the literature on nonprice competition among members of a cartel (Stigler 1968, pp. 23–28; Douglas and Miller 1974). But, while the tendency of monopoly rents to be transformed into costs is no longer a novel insight, its implications both for the measurement of the aggregate social costs of monopoly and for a variety of other important issues relating to monopoly and public regulation (including tax policy) continue for the most part to be ignored. The present paper is an effort to rectify this neglect.[2]

[1] If a thief took three radios from a home and on the way out dropped one, which broke, the resulting loss would correspond to the deadweight loss of monopoly.

[2] See Krueger (1974) for a parallel approach to the measurement of the social costs of import licenses in India and Turkey.

Part I presents a simple model of the social costs of monopoly, conceived as the sum of the deadweight loss and the additional loss resulting from the competition to become a monopolist. Part II uses the model to estimate the social costs of monopoly in the United States and the social benefits of antitrust enforcement. The estimates are crude; their primary value may simply be to induce skepticism about the existing empirical literature on the social costs of monopoly. Part III considers the implications of the analysis for several qualitative issues relating to monopoly and public regulation.

I. A Model of the Social Costs of Monopoly

A. Assumptions

The critical assumptions underlying the model are the following:

1. Obtaining a monopoly is itself a competitive activity, so that, at the margin, the cost of obtaining a monopoly is exactly equal to the expected profit of being a monopolist. An important corollary of this assumption is that there are no intramarginal monopolies—no cases, that is, where the expected profits of monopoly exceed the total supply price of the inputs used to obtain the monopoly. If there were such an excess, competition in the activity of obtaining the monopoly would induce the competing firms (or new entrants) to hire additional inputs in an effort to engross the additional monopoly profits.

2. The long-run supply of all inputs used in obtaining monopolies is perfectly elastic. Hence, the total supply price of these inputs includes no rents.

3. The costs incurred in obtaining a monopoly have no socially valuable by-products.

The first two assumptions assure that all expected monopoly rents are transformed into social costs, and the third that these costs do not generate any social benefits.[3] But how reasonable are such assumptions?

1. The first is a standard assumption of economics and, pending better evidence than we have, seems a reasonable one in the present context. Anyone can try to obtain a patent, a certificate of public convenience and necessity, a television license, a tariff, an import quota, or a minimum-wage law; and anyone can try to form a cartel with his competitors or, if he is a member of a cartelized industry, try to engross a greater share of the monopoly profits of the industry.[4] Nonprice competition in the airline

---

[3] Another assumption, but one that does not affect the analysis, is that the monopoly is enjoyed for one period only; otherwise the optimum expenditures on obtaining a monopoly could not be compared directly with L in fig. 1.

[4] Other than by reducing price, a method of obtaining a larger share of the cartel's profits that would not involve a socially wasteful use of resources.

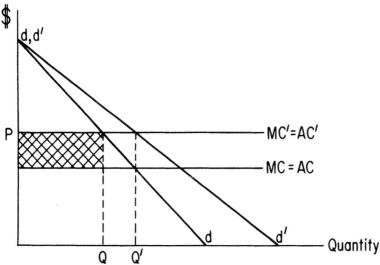

Fig. 2.—Nonprice competition when market price exceeds competitive level

industry illustrates the last point. If the Civil Aeronautics Board places a floor under airline prices that exceeds the marginal cost of providing air transportation under competitive conditions, the situation initially is as depicted in figure 2 and is unstable. Since nonprice competition is not constrained, the airlines will expend resources on such competition (better service, etc.) until the marginal costs of air transportation rise to the level (P in fig. 2) where the industry is earning only a normal return (see Douglas and Miller 1974). The result will be the transformation of the monopoly profits initially generated by the regulatory price floor—the shaded rectangle—into higher costs for the industry. The demand curve shifts to the right because the increased expenditures on service improve the product from the standpoint of the consumer. But the additional consumer surplus is not great enough to offset the higher costs—otherwise the higher level of service would have been provided without the spur of monopoly pricing.

If nonprice competition were forbidden (say, at zero cost) or were somehow not feasible, it would not follow that our assumption that monopolizing is a competitive activity would be overthrown. It would mean simply that the expected profits of the airline business would be greater than if the airlines could expect those profits to be dissipated in nonprice competition. Hence, more resources would be devoted to obtaining a license from the CAB in the first place. The expected profits from monopoly pricing of air transportation would still be zero.

2. Although the assumption that obtaining monopolies involves constant costs seems plausible as a first approximation—there seems little

reason to think that it involves using resources whose long-run supply is inelastic—a more important point is that the assumption may not be a crucial one. Assume that suppliers of inputs into monopolizing do obtain rents. In the long run, the availability of such rents will attract additional resources into the production of those inputs, and these resources will be wasted from a social standpoint. Some possible exceptions are considered in part III(7). Clearly, however, the production function of monopolies requires greater attention than I give it in this paper. The assumption of a perfectly elastic long-run supply may fail for an input as foreign to conventional economic analysis as political power.

3. In the airline example, the expenditures on monopolizing had a socially valuable by-product (improved service), although the value was less than its cost. However, the possibility that expenditures on monopolizing will yield such by-products will be ignored in the development of the model, and its principal relevance, therefore, is to methods of monopolizing that have little or no social value. The formation of a cartel, the procuring of a tariff or other protective legislation, and the merging of competing firms in a market to produce a monopoly (where the merger does not enable economies of scale or other efficiencies to be realized) are examples of such methods. (Even in these cases, there will be some socially valuable by-products [e.g., information] if, for example, the cartel agreement fails to limit nonprice competition.) At the opposite extreme, obtaining a monopoly by cutting costs or prices or by innovation will normally yield social benefits greater than the expenditures on monopolizing.

Several more preliminary points should be noted briefly.

1. Legal and illegal monopolies must be distinguished. The threat of punishment can be used to increase the expected costs of monopolizing and thereby reduce the amount of resources invested in the activity. To the extent that enforcers' resources are merely substituted for monopolizers', there will be no social savings (see Becker 1971, p. 101); but the literature on punishment (e.g., Becker 1968) suggests that activities such as monopolizing can be deterred at low social cost by combining heavy monetary penalties (i.e., transfer payments) with modest resources devoted to apprehending and convicting offenders.[5] Hence, under an optimum system of penalties, the social costs of *illegal* monopolies might be quite low.

2. As an extension of the last point, note that the observed monopoly profits in an industry may actually underestimate the social costs of monopoly in that industry. Considerable resources may have been

---

[5] This could, to be sure, merely shift the problem to a new level: the opportunity to obtain substantial rents from apprehending and convicting monopolists will induce enforcers to pour resources into enforcement activities. This problem is analyzed in Landes and Posner (1975).

expended by consumers or enforcers to reduce those profits. Monopoly profits in an industry could be zero, yet the social costs of monopoly in that industry very high, if enforcement of antimonopoly measures were both expensive and effective.

3. Given uncertainty, the expected monopoly profits of any firm seeking a monopoly may be much smaller than the actual monopoly profits, and so will its expenditures. If 10 firms are vying for a monopoly having a present value of $1 million, and each of them has an equal chance of obtaining it and is risk neutral, each will spend $100,000 (assuming constant costs) on trying to obtain the monopoly. Only one will succeed, and *his* costs will be much smaller than the monopoly profits, but the total costs of obtaining the monopoly—counting losers' expenditures as well as winners'—will be the same as under certainty. If the market for monopoly is in fact characterized by a high degree of uncertainty, this would explain why the costs of obtaining monopoly have largely eluded detection. Most of the costs are incurred in unsuccessful efforts to obtain a monopoly—the lobbying campaign that fails, the unsuccessful attempt to obtain a bank charter or form a cartel.

4. It might seem that where monopoly is obtained by bribery of government officials, the additional loss of monopoly with which this paper is concerned would be eliminated, since a bribe is a pure transfer. In fact, however, bribery merely shifts the monopoly profits from the monopolist to the officials receiving the bribe and draws real resources into the activity of becoming an official who is in a position to receive these bribes (Krueger 1974, pp. 292–93).

B. The Model

Given the assumptions explained above, the total social costs of monopoly prices in figure 1 are simply $D + L$, and since $D \simeq \frac{1}{2}\Delta P \Delta Q$ and $L = \Delta P(Q_c - \Delta Q)$, the relative sizes of D and L are given by

$$\frac{D}{L} \simeq \frac{\Delta Q}{2(Q_c - \Delta Q)}. \tag{1}$$

This ratio can also be expressed in terms of the elasticity of demand for the product in question at the competitive price and the percentage increase in price brought about by monopolization (p):

$$\frac{D}{L} \simeq \frac{p}{2(1/\varepsilon - p)}. \tag{2}$$

The partial derivatives are

$$\frac{\partial(D/L)}{\partial \varepsilon} \simeq \frac{2p}{(2 - 2p\varepsilon)^2} > 0;$$

$$\frac{\partial(D/L)}{\partial p} \simeq \frac{2\varepsilon}{(2 - 2p\varepsilon)^2} > 0. \tag{3}$$

In words, the ratio of D to L is smaller, the less elastic the demand for the industry's product at the competitive price and the smaller the percentage price increase over the competitive level. At moderate elasticities and percentage price increases, D is only a small fraction of L (and hence of the total costs of monopoly). For example, at an elasticity of one[6] and a price increase over the competitive level of 10 percent, D is only 5.6 percent of L.

Observe that the model does *not* assume that the actual supracompetitive price being charged (P_m in fig. 1) is the optimum monopoly price for the industry (otherwise the supracompetitive price increase would not be determined independently of the elasticity of demand, as in [2]). The rationale of this procedure is that perfect monopoly is presumably rare; it will, however, be considered as a special case later.

Using R_c to denote total sales revenues at the competitive price, C, the total social costs of monopoly, is approximated by

$$D + L = pR_c - \tfrac{1}{2}\Delta P \Delta Q \tag{4a}$$

$$= R_c(p - \tfrac{1}{2}\varepsilon p^2). \tag{4b}$$

The partial derivatives of C are (approximately)

$$\frac{\partial C}{\partial R_c} = p - \tfrac{1}{2}\varepsilon p^2 > 0 \text{ iff } \varepsilon p < 2;$$

$$\frac{\partial C}{\partial p} = R_c(1 - \varepsilon p) > 0 \text{ iff } \varepsilon p < 1; \tag{5}$$

$$\frac{\partial C}{\partial \varepsilon} = -\tfrac{1}{2}p^2 R_c < 0.$$

In words, the social costs of monopoly will usually—not always—be higher, the larger the industry's sales revenues at the competitive price and output and the greater the percentage price increase over the competitive level. And they will always be higher, the less elastic the demand for the product at the competitive price—the costs of monopoly being greatest when demand is totally inelastic at the competitive price.

Formulas (2) and (4b) are accurate only for small changes in the price level. Yet monopolization might result in large price increases. Hence (1) and (4a) remain useful. For purposes of empirical estimation, it is helpful to derive two additional formulas: one for the case where data on the deadweight loss, the elasticity of demand, and the monopoly price increase are available and the elasticity of demand is assumed to be constant, and the other for the case where data on the monopoly price increase, the monopoly output, and the elasticity of demand at the

---

[6] Throughout this paper, ΔQ is treated as a positive number. Therefore, $\varepsilon \, [= (\Delta Q/\Delta P)/(Q/P)]$ is also positive.

monopoly price are available and the demand curve is assumed to be linear.

1. For the case of constant elasticity, let $k \equiv P_c/P_m$ and $R_m \equiv$ total sales revenue at the monopoly price and output. Then, since $Q_c = \alpha P_c^{-\varepsilon}$ and $Q_m = \alpha P_m^{-\varepsilon}$, and therefore $\Delta Q = \alpha(P_c^{-\varepsilon} - P_m^{-\varepsilon})$, D/L and C are approximately

$$\frac{D}{L} = \frac{(kP_m)^{-\varepsilon} - P_m^{-\varepsilon}}{2P_m^{-\varepsilon}} = \frac{k^{-\varepsilon} - 1}{2}; \tag{6}$$

$$C = D + L = D\left(1 + \frac{2}{k^{-\varepsilon} - 1}\right) = R_m(1 - k)\left(\frac{k^{-\varepsilon} + 1}{2}\right). \tag{7}$$

The partial derivatives of D/L are (approximately)

$$\frac{\partial(D/L)}{\partial k} = \frac{-\varepsilon}{2k^{\varepsilon+1}} < 0;$$

$$\frac{\partial(D/L)}{\partial \varepsilon} = \frac{-k^{-\varepsilon} \ln k}{2} > 0. \tag{8}$$

[7] For the special case where the firm is able to charge the optimum monopoly price for the industry, so that $P_c = MC = P_m(1 - 1/\varepsilon)$, equation (6) becomes

$$\frac{D}{L} = \frac{(1 - 1/\varepsilon)^{-\varepsilon} - 1}{2} \tag{6'}$$

and equation (7) becomes

$$C = \frac{R_m[(1 - 1/\varepsilon)^{-\varepsilon} + 1]}{2\varepsilon}. \tag{7'}$$

Since a demand curve of constant elasticity is nonlinear, the question arises whether the linear approximation of the deadweight loss used in equations (6) and (7) (and [6'] and [7']) introduces a source of serious inaccuracy. It appears not to, at least in the simple case where $\varepsilon = 1$ and therefore

$$\frac{D}{L} = \frac{\int_{Q_m}^{Q_c} P \, dQ - P_c \, \Delta Q}{(P_m - P_c)Q_m} = \frac{\ln (1/k) - 1 + k}{1 - k}. \tag{6''}$$

Table 1, which compares D/L as calculated from equation (6) (with $\varepsilon = 1$) and from equation (6''), shows that the linear approximation overestimates the deadweight loss, but not seriously.

TABLE 1

P* (%)	D/L† Eq. (6)	Eq. (6'')
5	.025	.025
10	.050	.049
15	.075	.072
20	.100	.094
50	.250	.216

* Monopoly price increase.
† Ratio of deadweight to additional loss.

In words, the ratio of the deadweight loss of monopoly to the additional loss is smaller, the smaller the monopoly price increase (k, the ratio of the competitive to the monopoly price, is larger, the smaller the relative price increase) and greater, the more elastic the demand.

2. For the case where the elasticity of demand at the monopoly price (as well as the monopoly price increase and the quantity sold at the monopoly price) is known or can be computed, and the demand curve can be approximated by a straight line, we begin by determining the slope of the demand curve at the monopoly price:

$$\frac{\Delta Q}{\Delta P} = \frac{\varepsilon Q_m}{P_m}.$$ (9)

Since the slope of a linear demand curve is constant, this equation can be used to find ΔQ and hence C and D/L:

$$C = R_m(1 - k)[1 + \tfrac{1}{2}\varepsilon(1 - k)];$$ (10)

$$\frac{D}{L} = \frac{\varepsilon(1 - k)}{2} . \text{[8]}$$ (11)

The estimates produced by our two formulas for the ratio of the deadweight to the additional loss from monopoly—equations (6) and (11)—turn out not to be very different for price increases of less than 25 percent, and even for much larger price increases if the elasticity of demand is no greater than one (see fig. 3).

II. Empirical Estimates

The formulas developed in the preceding part can be used to derive, from the estimates of the deadweight loss of monopoly made by Arnold Harberger and others, an estimate of the total social cost of monopoly. Harberger (1954), estimating an average monopoly price increase of about 6 percent and assuming that the elasticity of demand was constant and equal to unity, found the deadweight loss from monopoly in the manufacturing sector to be equal to (at most) 0.1 percent of GNP. Harberger's (implicit) k is 0.9434, and from equation (6) the ratio of D to L in Harberger's analysis is, therefore, 0.03. Hence, if D is 0.1

---

[8] In the special case where the firm is able to charge the optimum monopoly price,

$$C = \frac{R_m}{2\varepsilon};$$ (10′)

$$\frac{D}{L} = \frac{1}{2}.$$ (11′)

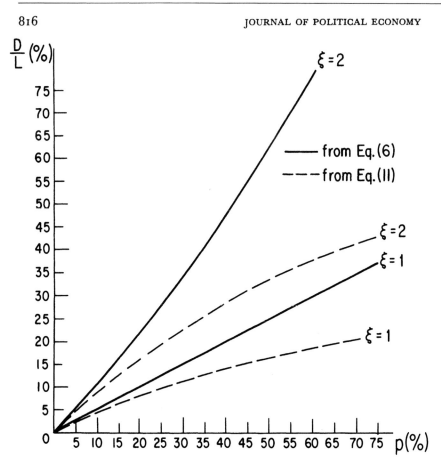

FIG. 3.—Ratio of deadweight to additional loss of monopoly, for different price increases and demand elasticities.

percent of GNP, L is about 3.3 percent and C about 3.4 percent of GNP. Schwartzman (1960) used similar methods and found D equal to about 0.1 percent of GNP too. But he assumed a price increase of 8.3 percent and an elasticity of demand of 1.5. Plugging these values into equation (6) yields $D/L = 0.06$. Hence, if $D = 0.1$ percent of GNP, $L = 1.7$ percent and $C = 1.8$ percent.

Neither estimate can be given much credence, however, because of the method that both Harberger and Schwartzman employed to determine the monopoly price increase. Persistently above average rates of return were used both (1) to identify the monopolized industries and (2) to calculate the monopoly price increase. If the approach of this paper is correct, such a procedure is improper, especially the second step. Because of uncertainty, many monopolists may enjoy supernormal rates of return ex post, but those rates will understate the percentage of the monopolist's revenues that is attributable to monopoly pricing, unless no cost whatever was incurred in obtaining (or maintaining) the monopoly.[9]

A better method of calculating the social costs of monopoly (deadweight plus additional loss) is to obtain from industry studies estimates of the monopoly price increase and of the elasticity of demand at the relevant points along the demand curve. An independent estimate of the elasticity of demand would be unnecessary if we could assume that, after the price increase, the price charged was the optimum monopoly price; and where an independent estimate of ε is available, it can serve as a check on that assumption. To illustrate, there have been a number of estimates of the percentage by which CAB regulation has increased the price of airline travel. The simple average of these estimates is .66 (computed from Caves 1962, p. 372; Jordan 1970, pp. 110–11, 124–25; and Yale Law Journal 1965, pp. 1435–36). If a 66 percent price increase over competitive levels is assumed to raise the price of air travel to the optimum monopoly level, then the elasticity of demand at the monopoly price can be calculated, from the formula which equates marginal cost to marginal revenue,[10] to be 2.5 at the monopoly price. An independent estimate of the long-run elasticity of demand for air travel made by Houthakker and Taylor (1966, p. 124) is 2.36,[11] which is virtually identical to my calculation.

If we assume a constant elasticity of 2.5 and solve for D/L using equation (6'), $D = 1.29L$, and (from equation [7']) it is readily calculable that the total social cost of the airline monopoly is equal to 92 percent of the total revenue of the industry at the monopoly price. However, the assumption of a linear demand curve seems more plausible than the assumption of constant elasticity, especially for large relative price increases, which one expects to find associated with a rising elasticity of demand as substitutes become increasingly attractive. If, therefore, equations (10') and (11') are used instead of (6') and (7'), $D = 0.5L$ and $C = 0.2R_m$—still a very large social loss from the regulation-induced airline monopoly. (These estimates ignore, however, the partially offsetting benefits of excessive nonprice competition in the airline industry.)

[9] This point is distinct from the (also valid) objections to Harberger's procedure raised by Stigler (1956)—that monopoly profits are often capitalized into the valuation of a firm's assets and that some of the profits may be received as rents by suppliers of the firm's inputs.

[10] This was essentially the procedure used by Kamerschen (1966) to estimate the deadweight loss from monopoly in manufacturing. He has been criticized, rightly, for assuming that firms in concentrated industries subject to the Sherman Act's prohibition of collusive pricing are typically able to charge the profit-maximizing monopoly price. The assumption is more plausible with regard to a regulated industry in which entry and price competition are limited by the regulatory agency and the Sherman Act is inapplicable.

[11] This is presumably the elasticity of demand at the regulated price, since only a small part of the airline industry is exempt from CAB regulation.

Richard A. Posner

TABLE 2

SOCIAL COSTS OF REGULATION

INDUSTRY	REGULATORY PRICE INCREASE (%)	ELASTICITY		COSTS (AS % OF INDUSTRY'S SALES)	
		ε_1	ε_2	C_1*	C_2*
Physicians' services	.40†	3.500	0.575‡	.14	.31
Eyeglasses........	.34§	0.394	0.450‖	.13	.24
Milk	.11#	10.000	0.339**	.05	.10
Motor carriers ...	.62††	2.630	1.140‡‡	.19	.30
Oil	.65§§	2.500	0.900§§	.20	.32
Airlines	.66	2.500	2.360	.20	.19

* C_1 based on ε_1; C_2 based on ε_2.
† Kessel 1972, p. 119.
‡ Houthakker and Taylor 1966, p. 99 (short run).
§ Benham 1973, p. 19.
‖ Benham 1973, p. 30 (simple average).
Kessel 1967, p. 73.
** Houthakker 1965, p. 286. This estimate is for all food; an estimate limited to dairy products in the Netherlands was not significantly different (Ayaynian 1969).
†† Average estimates in Department of Agriculture studies cited in Moore (1972) and Farmer (1964).
‡‡ Simple averages of various estimates for transportation in Scandinavia (see Frisch 1959 and Parks 1969, p. 649).
§§ Cabinet Task Force on Oil Import Control 1970.

All of the previous studies of the cost of monopoly to the economy have been based on supposed monopoly pricing in manufacturing alone. Yet the ability of firms to maintain supracompetitive prices must be greater in industries in which a regulatory agency limits entry and price competition than in the manufacturing sector, where express collusion is forbidden by the Sherman Act. Table 2 collects estimates of the regulation-induced price increase and the elasticity of demand at the current price for several industries for which these data are available. Two estimates of elasticity are given: one (ε_1) is derived from the price-increase data, on the assumption that the industry is charging the optimum monopoly price; the other (ε_2) is an independent estimate of elasticity. The estimates of the total social costs of the regulation in question (C_1, where ε_1 is the estimate of elasticity used, and C_2, where ε_2 is used) are based on the assumption that the industry's demand curve is linear in the relevant region and are expressed as a percentage of the total revenues of the industry.

These estimates are, of course, very crude, but they do suggest that the total costs of regulation may be extremely high, given that about 17 percent of GNP originates in industries—such as agriculture, transportation, communications, power, banking, insurance, and medical services—that contain the sorts of controls over competition that might be expected to lead to supracompetitive prices.[12] Indeed, the costs of

[12] Of course, not all of the markets in the regulated industries are in fact subject to the relevant regulatory controls (almost half of the trucking industry, for example, is exempt from regulation by the Interstate Commerce Commission). On the other hand, tariffs and similar restrictions (e.g., the oil import quota) are excluded from the estimate of the percentage of GNP affected by regulation.

regulation probably exceed the costs of private monopoly. To be sure, a higher percentage of GNP—30 percent—originates in manufacturing and mining, a highly concentrated sector of the economy, and the conventional wisdom associates high concentration with supracompetitive pricing. But only about one-fifth of the output of this sector comes from industries in which four firms account for 60 percent or more of sales, and there is little theoretical basis for believing that the sellers in less concentrated industries could collude effectively without engaging in behavior prohibited by the Sherman Act.[13] Not all violations of the Sherman Act are detected and punished, but the secret conspiracies that escape detection are probably not very effective—even the great electrical conspiracy, an elaborate and relatively durable conspiracy among a very small group of firms, apparently succeeded in raising prices by less than 10 percent on average (see U.S. Congress 1965, p. 39). It would be surprising if the price level of the manufacturing and mining sector as a whole were more than about 2 percent above the competitive level.[14] Assume that it is 2 percent, and that the average elasticity of demand for the products of this sector, at current prices, is 1.1607.[15] Then the total social costs of monopoly in this sector are 1.9 percent of the total revenues generated in the sector (from equation [10]). This amounts to a total dollar loss substantially smaller than that generated in the regulated sector.[16] And this is true even if we assume that prices in the manufacturing and mining sector are, on average, 4 percent above the competitive level, rather than 2 percent.[17]

This comparison excludes, of course, both the relative costs of regulation

[13] Thus, Kessel's study of underwriting costs (1971, p. 723) shows that an increase beyond eight in the number of bids does not reduce those costs substantially—and an industry where the four largest firms have less than 60 percent of the market is apt to contain at least eight significant competitors.

[14] If we assume that only in industries where the four-firm concentration ratio exceeds 60 percent is effective, undetected collusion likely, and that collusion allows these industries to maintain prices, on average, 5 percent above the competitive level while in the rest of the manufacturing and mining sector the average price level is only 1 percent above the competitive level, then average prices for the entire sector would be only 1.83 percent above the competitive price level. (Statistics on the distribution of output among industries in different four-firm concentration ratio groups are from the 1963 Census of Manufactures.)

[15] This figure is a simple average of the long-run price elasticities for nine product groups within the manufacturing and mining sector estimated in Houthakker and Taylor (1966, pp. 72, 74, 83, 112–14, 116, 128–31).

[16] The simple average of the social-cost estimates presented in table 2 is 19.8 percent of the total revenues of the regulated industry. Assuming that 50 percent of the output of that sector is produced in markets that are regulated in a manner similar to the industries in table 2 and that the average social cost of regulation in each such market is 19.8 percent of total revenue, the social costs of regulation would be equal to 1.7 percent of GNP, while the social costs of monopoly in manufacturing and mining would be equal to 0.6 percent of GNP.

[17] In which event the social costs of monopoly in that sector would be about 1.2 percent of GNP.

TABLE 3

SOCIAL COSTS OF CARTELIZATION

INDUSTRY	CARTEL PRICE INCREASE (%)	ELASTICITY		COSTS (AS % OF INDUSTRY'S SALES)	
		ε_1	ε_2	C_1	C_2
Nitrogen	0.75*	2.3256	1.4493†	.21	.30
Sugar	0.30‡	4.3276	0.3390§	.12	.22
Aluminum	1.00‖	2.0000	...	.25	...
Aluminum	0.38#	3.6311	...	.14	...
Rubber	1.00**	2.0000	...	.25	...
Electric bulbs	0.37††	3.7023	...	.14	...
Copper	0.31‡‡	4.2499	...	.12	...
Cast-iron pipe	0.39§§	3.5641	...	.14	...

* Stocking and Watkins 1946, p. 163.
† Stocking and Watkins 1946, p. 166.
‡ Stocking and Watkins 1946, p. 46.
§ Houthakker 1965, p. 286; obviously a much too low estimate for one food product sold at a cartel price!
‖ Stocking and Watkins 1946, p. 228.
Stocking and Watkins 1946, p. 251.
** Stocking and Watkins 1946, p. 64–65.
†† Stocking and Watkins 1946, p. 343.
‡‡ Stocking and Watkins 1948, p. 127.
§§ United States v. Addyston Pipe & Steel Co., 85 F. 271 (6th Cir. 1898).

and of antitrust enforcement and the relative benefits of monopoly in the two sectors.[18] Were these additional factors included, however, it is doubtful that the comparison would become more favorable to the regulated sector. In particular, while there are theoretical reasons for believing that concentration in unregulated markets is associated with economies of scale and other efficiencies (Demsetz 1973), there is no accepted theory or body of evidence that ascribes social benefits to regulation limiting entry and price competition.

The analysis developed here can also be used to estimate the social benefits of the antitrust laws. Table 3, which is constructed on the same basis as table 2, presents estimates of the social costs of several well-organized (mainly international) private cartels.[19]

Presumably, collusive price increases of this magnitude and the attendant very substantial social costs are deterred by current enforcement of the American antitrust laws. A complete cost-benefit analysis of the antitrust laws would, however, also require estimation of (1) the costs of administering those laws[20] and (2) the large social costs imposed by the

[18] To recur to an earlier point, the assumed monopoly price increase in the manufacturing and mining sector may underestimate the social costs of monopoly in that sector. Those costs may be reflected in expenditures by consumers and enforcers in preventing monopoly pricing.

[19] As distinct from the sorts of covert conspiracies that might escape detection under present enforcement of the Sherman Act (see Stigler 1968, pp. 268–70).

[20] A point to be kept in mind is that, while these costs are incurred annually, private—unlike governmentally protected—cartels eventually collapse (although they often re-form later). Hence, table 3 gives an exaggerated picture of the *average* annual costs of cartelization as it would exist in the absence of the Sherman Act.

many perverse applications of antitrust laws that are, perhaps, an inevitable by-product of having such laws.

A very large disclaimer concerning the accuracy of the estimates presented in this part of the paper needs to be entered at this point. Quite apart from any reservations about the realism of the assumptions on which the model used to generate these estimates is based, the crudeness of the data on price increases and elasticities of demand precludes treating the estimates of the costs of the monopoly and regulation as anything more than suggestive. The suggestions are, however, interesting ones: (1) previous studies of the costs of monopoly may have grossly underestimated those costs; and (2) the costs of monopoly are quite probably much greater in the regulated than in the unregulated sector of the economy, despite the greater size of the latter sector.

III. Other Applications

1. In a recent paper Comanor and Smiley (in press) attempt to show that a large part of the inequality in the distribution of wealth in contemporary America is attributable to monopoly. They use studies such as Harberger's (1954) to determine the aggregate wealth transfer from consumers to the owners of monopoly firms and, by a series of additional assumptions concerning the incomes of consumers and shareholders, family size, the savings rate, etc., derive an estimate of the distributive impact of monopoly. Many of the assumptions are questionable, but even if their correctness were conceded the conclusion would be highly doubtful. There is no reason to think that monopoly has a significant distributive effect. Consumers' wealth is not transferred to the shareholders of monopoly firms; it is dissipated in the purchase of inputs into the activity of becoming a monopolist.

2. Oliver Williamson (1968) has argued that the refusal of the courts to recognize a defense of economies of scale in merger cases under the Clayton Act is questionable because, under plausible assumptions concerning the elasticity of demand, only a small reduction in the merging firms' costs is necessary to offset any deadweight loss created by the price increase that the merger enables the firms to make (see fig. 4).

This analysis is incomplete, however. The expected profits of the merger ($ABEF$) will generate an equivalent amount of costs as the firms vie to make such mergers or, after they are made, to engross the profits generated by the higher postmerger price through service competition or whatever. As a first approximation, the total social cost of the merger is $ABEF + BCD$ and exceeds the cost savings ($GDEF$) made possible by it. The curves could, of course, be drawn in such a way that the merger would generate net cost savings; the point is only that there is no presumption that anticompetitive mergers generate net savings. This consideration, together with the high cost of litigating issues of cost

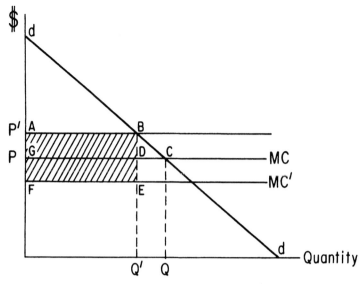

FIG. 4.—The costs of mergers

savings, may provide a justification for refusing to recognize a defense of efficiencies in merger cases where the merger is likely to produce a substantial increase in monopoly power.

3. It has been argued (e.g., Bowman 1973) that the antitrust laws should not concern themselves with practices that are merely methods of price discrimination, since there is no basis for thinking that discrimination increases the deadweight loss of monopoly, and it may reduce it (it will reduce it to zero if discrimination is perfect). The conclusion may be justifiable by reference to the costs of administering antidiscrimination rules, but the basis on which it has been defended by its proponents is incorrect. Even when price discrimination is perfect, so that the deadweight loss of monopoly is zero, the total social costs of a discriminating monopoly are greater than those of a single-price monopoly.[21] Under perfect price discrimination, C is the entire area between the demand curve and the marginal (= average) cost curve, and it is greater than $D + L$ at any single price (see fig. 1).

4. It is occasionally suggested that the case for antitrust enforcement has been gravely weakened by the theory of the second best. Since the elimination of one monopoly in an economy containing other monopolies (or other sources of divergence between price and marginal cost, such as

[21] I abstract from the costs of administering the price-discrimination scheme; these increase the costs of discriminating monopoly relative to those of nondiscriminating monopoly.

taxation) may reduce the efficiency of resource allocation, antitrust enforcement may increase, rather than reduce, D. The true economic basis for antitrust enforcement, however, is not D but $D + L$, and we have seen that, under plausible assumptions as to the elasticity of demand, D is only a small fraction of $D + L$, at least for moderate increases in price above the competitive level. The social costs measured by L, like the social costs of theft (i.e., the opportunity costs of thieves' and police-men's time and of the labor and capital inputs into locks, burglar tools, etc.), are unaffected by the existence of second-best problems (cf. Markovits 1972).

5. The analysis in this paper suggests a possible explanation for the positive correlation that has been found between concentration and advertising.[22] It may be easier to collude on price than on the amount of advertising. Although there is no great trick to establishing an agreed-upon level of advertising and detecting departures from it, the incentives to violate any such agreement are strong, because the gains from a successful advertising campaign may be difficult to offset immediately and hence offer promise of a more durable advantage than a price cut would. In that event the situation is similar to nonprice competition in the airline industry. If price is fixed by the cartel but the level of advertising is not, or at least not effectively, the monopoly profits generated by the cartel price will be transformed into additional expenditures on advertising. Cartelization is presumably more common in concentrated industries.

This analysis suggests, incidentally, a possible difficulty in distinguishing empirically between Telser's theory of resale price maintenance (1960) and an alternative explanation which stresses cartelization by dealers. In Telser's theory, manufacturers impose resale price maintenance in order to induce dealers to provide services in connection with the resale of the manufacturer's brand. If Telser's theory is correct, we would expect to find resale price maintenance imposed where the efficient merchandising of a product involved the provision of extensive point-of-sale services. However, a dealer's cartel might also result in the dealers' competing away the cartel profits through service competition.

6. Discussions of the "social responsibility" of large corporations generally assume that a firm (or group of firms) having some monopoly power could, without courting bankruptcy, decide to incur somewhat higher costs in order to discharge its social responsibilities. Thus, in figure 1, even if MC rose to P_m the firm would still be covering its costs. However, if the analysis in this paper is correct and the expected profits of monopolizing are zero, it follows that the entire area L in figure 1 will represent fixed costs to the firm unless the monopoly was obtained under conditions

---

[22] The finding has been questioned, however (e.g., Ekelund and Gramm 1970).

of uncertainty. In the latter case the fixed costs will be somewhat lower, but in the former *any* increase in *MC* will jeopardize the firm's solvency.

7. Assuming that the decision to create or tolerate a monopoly has been made, it may still be possible to prevent the expected monopoly profits from being completely transformed into social costs. The basic technique is to reduce the elasticity of supply of the inputs into monopolizing. (Thus, the present discussion modifies my original assumption of perfect supply elasticity.) Consider, for example, a market that is a natural monopoly. If the monopolist is permitted to charge a monopoly price—and suppose that he is—he may set a price that exceeds the average costs of new entrants, albeit those costs are higher than his; and new entry will presumably occur. The resulting increase in the average costs of serving the market is an example of the social costs of monopoly (independent of the welfare triangle). These costs can be reduced, however, by a rule limiting entry. Such a rule will reduce the responsiveness of a key input into monopolizing—capacity to produce the monopolized product—to increases in the expected value of the monopoly. But the rule is not very satisfactory. Prospective entrants will have an incentive to expend resources on persuading the agency to change or waive the rule—and the monopolist to expend them on dissuasion. Moreover, the more efficient the rule is at keeping out new entrants at low cost to the monopolist, the greater will be the expected value of having a natural monopoly—and, hence, the greater will be the resources that firms expend on trying to become the first to occupy a natural-monopoly market.[23]

As another example, consider the recurrent proposal to replace the present method of assigning television licenses (now awarded to the applicant who convinces the Federal Communications Commission in a formal hearing of his superior ability to serve the public interest) by an auction system. This proposal is frequently supported on distributive grounds—why should the licensee, rather than the public, receive the rents generated by the limited allocation of electromagnetic spectrum for broadcasting? But there is also an efficiency justification for the proposal. The auction would substitute a transfer payment for a real cost, the expenditures on the hearing process by competing applicants. To be sure, these expenditures might simply be redirected into rigging the bidding. But this could be discouraged, possibly at low cost, by appropriate legal penalties. The objective would be to increase the expected costs of obtaining the license (other than by an honest bid), which include any expected punishment costs, to the point where the applicants are induced to make the costless transfer rather than to expend real resources on trying to obtain the license outside the auction

---

[23] This is the obverse of the situation discussed in Demsetz (1968), where competition to become a monopolist results in a competitive price level.

process. As mentioned earlier, in an optimum system of penalties the resources expended on enforcement would be slight.

The patent laws embody a somewhat similar economizing technique. In their absence inventors would expend substantial resources on preserving the secrecy of their inventions. Their efforts in this direction would generate indirect as well as direct social costs, by retarding the spread of knowledge. By providing a legal remedy against "stealing" inventions, the patent laws reduce the level of such expenditures in much the same way as the existence of legal penalties for theft reduces the level of resources that people devote to protecting their property from thieves.

An interesting method of reducing the social costs of monopoly is used by labor unions. The existence of a monopoly wage might be expected to induce the expenditure of more and more resources by workers seeking entry into the union, until the expected benefits of union membership were reduced to zero. However, unions traditionally have rationed membership in a way that greatly reduces the marginal benefits of expenditures on obtaining membership, and hence the resources expended in that pursuit, by conditioning membership on a status that is difficult or impossible for the job seeker to buy at any price—such as being white or the son of a union member.[24] In the limit, this method of rationing would reduce the elasticity of the supply of inputs into obtaining union membership, and hence the social costs of labor monopolies (excluding the welfare triangle), to zero, disregarding the costs resulting from the exclusion of possibly better qualified workers who do not meet the membership criterion. Yet even this method may not be ultimately effective in preventing the transformation of monopoly rents into social costs. The more profitable union membership is, the greater are the resources that workers will be willing to invest (e.g., in forgone earnings due to being on strike) in union-organizing activities.

8. One reason why most students of tax policy prefer income to excise taxes is that the misallocative effect of an income tax is believed to be less than that of an excise tax: the cross-elasticity of demand between work and leisure is assumed to be lower than that between a commodity and its substitutes. Even if correct, this does not mean that the total social costs of collecting a given amount of revenue by means of an income tax are lower than those of an excise tax. The amount of the tax transfer represents potential gain to the taxpayer, and he will expend real resources on trying to avoid the tax until, at the margin, cost and gain are equated. A critical question in comparing the costs of income and excise taxation is therefore the shape and location of the supply curves for avoiding income tax liability and excise tax liability, respectively. In the case of a highly progressive income tax system in which

[24] The use of these methods by unions is being increasingly limited by government regulations designed to eliminate racial discrimination.

expenses for the production of income are deductible, the comparison is likely to be unfavorable to income taxation. Were the marginal income tax rate in the highest bracket 90 percent (as it once was in this country), the taxpayer would continue expending resources on tax avoidance until the expected value of a dollar so expended fell below 10 cents. Thus, he might spend as much as 10 times his marginal tax liability in order to reduce that liability to zero. (How much he would actually spend would depend on the location and shape of the supply curve for avoidance and on his resources and attitude toward risk.) This analysis is not conclusive against the income tax. It might be possible to increase the private marginal costs of avoidance by punishment or by disallowing the deduction of expenses on avoidance. The main problem would be to distinguish legitimate from illegitimate avoidance efforts.[25] Still, no general presumption that excise taxation is less costly than income taxation can be derived from an analysis limited to the allocative costs of taxation, corresponding to the deadweight loss of monopoly.

References

Ayaynian, Robert. "A Comparison of Barten's Estimated Demand Elasticities with Those Obtained Using Frisch's Method." *Econometrica* 37 (January 1969): 79–94.

Becker, Gary S. "Crime and Punishment: An Economic Approach." *J.P.E.* 76, no. 2 (March/April 1968): 169–217.

———. *Economic Theory*. New York: Knopf, 1971.

Benham, Lee. "Price Structure and Professional Control of Information." Mimeographed. Univ. Chicago Graduate School Bus. (March 1973).

Bowman, Ward S., Jr. *Patent and Antitrust Law: A Legal and Economic Appraisal*. Chicago: Univ. Chicago Press, 1973.

Cabinet Task Force on Oil Import Control. *The Oil Import Question*. Washington: Government Printing Office, 1970.

Caves, Richard E. *Air Transport and Its Regulators*. Cambridge, Mass.: Harvard Univ. Press, 1962.

Comanor, William S., and Smiley, Robert H. "Monopoly and the Distribution of Wealth." *Q.J.E.* (in press).

Demsetz, Harold. "Why Regulate Utilities?" *J. Law and Econ.* 11 (April 1968): 55–65.

———. "Industry Structure, Market Rivalry, and Public Policy." *J. Law and Econ.* 16 (April 1973): 1–9.

Douglas, George W., and Miller, James C., III. "The CAB's Domestic Passenger Fare Investigation." *Bell J. Econ. and Management Sci.* 5 (Spring 1974): 204–22.

Ekelund, Robert B., Jr., and Gramm, William P. "Advertising and Concentration: Some New Evidence." *Antitrust Bull.* 15 (Summer 1970): 243–49.

Farmer, Richard N. "The Case for Unregulated Truck Transportation." *J. Farm Econ.* 46 (May 1964): 398–409.

---

[25] It would make no sense to punish everyone who believed that some provision of the Internal Revenue Code was not intended to apply to his activity.

Frisch, Ragnar. "A Complete Scheme for Computing All Direct Costs and Cross Demand Elasticities in a Market with Many Sectors." *Econometrica* 27 (April 1959): 177–96.

Harberger, Arnold C. "Monopoly and Resource Allocation." *A.E.R.* 44 (May 1954): 77–87.

Houthakker, H. S. "New Evidence on Demand Elasticities." *Econometrica* 33 (April 1965): 277–88.

Houthakker, H. S., and Taylor, Lester D. *Consumer Demand in the United States, 1929–1970.* Cambridge, Mass.: Harvard Univ. Press, 1966.

Jordan, William A. *Airline Regulation in America.* Baltimore: Johns Hopkins Univ. Press, 1970.

Kamerschen, David. "Estimation of the Welfare Losses from Monopoly in the American Economy." *Western Econ. J.* 4 (Summer 1966): 221–36.

Kessel, Reuben A. "Economic Effects of Federal Regulation of Milk Markets." *J. Law and Econ.* 10 (October 1967): 51–78.

————. "A Study of the Effects of Competition in the Tax-exempt Bond Market." *J.P.E.* 79, no. 4 (July/August 1971): 706–38.

————. "Higher Education and the Nation's Health: A Review of the Carnegie Commission Report on Medical Education." *J. Law and Econ.* 15 (April 1972): 115–27.

Krueger, Anne O. "The Political Economy of the Rent-seeking Society." *A.E.R.* 64 (June 1974): 291–303.

Landes, William M., and Posner, Richard A. "The Private Enforcement of Law." *J. Legal Studies* 5 (January 1975): 1–46.

Markovits, Richard S. "Fixed Input (Investment) Competition and the Variability of Fixed Inputs (Investment): Their Nature, Determinants, and Significance." *Stanford Law Rev.* 24 (February 1972): 507–30.

Moore, Thomas Gale. *Freight Transportation Regulation.* Washington: American Enterprise Inst., 1972.

Parks, Richard W. "Systems of Demand Equations: An Empirical Comparison of Alternative Functional Forms." *Econometrica* 37 (October 1969): 629–50.

Plant, Arnold. "The Economic Theory Concerning Patents." *Economica* 1 (n.s.) (February 1934): 30–51.

Schwartzman, David. "The Burden of Monopoly." *J.P.E.* 68, no. 6 (November/December 1960): 627–30.

Stigler, George J. "The Statistics of Monopoly and Mergers." *J.P.E.* 64, no. 1 (January/February 1956): 33–40.

————. *The Organization of Industry.* Homewood, Ill.: Irwin, 1968.

Stocking, George W., and Watkins, Myron W. *Cartels in Action.* New York: Twentieth Century Fund, 1946.

————. *Cartels or Competition?* New York: Twentieth Century Fund, 1948.

Telser, Lester. "Why Should Manufacturers Want Fair Trade?" *J. Law and Econ.* 3 (October 1960): 86–105.

Tullock, Gordon. "The Welfare Costs of Tariffs, Monopolies, and Theft." *Western Econ. J.* 5 (June 1967): 224–32.

U.S. Congress, Joint Committee on Internal Revenue Taxation. *Staff Study of Income Tax Treatment of Treble Damage Payments under the Antitrust Laws.* Washington: Government Printing Office, 1965.

Williamson, Oliver E. "Economics as an Antitrust Defense: The Welfare Tradeoffs." *A.E.R.* 58 (March 1968): 18–36.

Yale Law Journal. "Is Regulation Necessary? California Air Transportation and National Regulatory Policy." *Yale Law J.* 74 (July 1965): 1416–47.

The Economic Journal, **88** (*December* 1978), 727–748
Printed in Great Britain

THE SOCIAL COSTS OF MONOPOLY POWER*

In 1954, Arnold Harberger estimated the welfare losses from monopoly for the United States at 0·1 of 1 % of GNP. Several studies have appeared since, re-confirming Harberger's early low estimates using different assumptions (e.g. Schwartzman, 1960; Scherer, 1970; Worcester, 1973). These papers have firmly established as part of the conventional wisdom the idea that welfare losses from monopoly are insignificant.

The Harberger position has been, almost from the start, subject to attack, however (e.g. Stigler, 1956); Kamerschen (1966) followed essentially the Harberger methodology, but assumed an elasticity of demand consistent with monopoly pricing behaviour at the industry level and obtained welfare loss estimates as high as 6 %. Posner (1975) made some rough estimates of the social costs of acquiring monopoly power, but, using Harberger's calculations, con-cluded that the real problem was the social cost imposed by regulation rather than of private market power.

The most sophisticated critique of Harberger's approach has been offered by Abram Bergson (1973). Bergson criticises the partial equilibrium framework employed by Harberger and all previous studies, and puts forward a general equilibrium model as an alternative. He then produces a series of hypothetical estimates of the welfare losses from monopoly, some of them quite large, for various combinations of the two key parameters in this model, the elasticity of substitution in consumption and the difference between monopoly and com-petitive price. Not surprisingly Bergson's estimates, suggesting as they do that monopoly can be a matter of some consequence, have induced a sharp reaction (see Carson, 1975; Worcester, 1975).[1]

The present paper levels several objections against the Harberger-type approach. It then calculates estimates of the welfare loss from monopoly using procedures derived to meet these objections, and obtains estimates significantly greater than those of previous studies. Although several of the objections we make have been made by other writers, none has systematically adjusted the basic Harberger technique to take them into account. Thus all previous esti-mates of monopoly welfare losses suffer in varying degrees from the same biases incorporated in Harberger's original estimates.

We do, however, employ a partial equilibrium framework as followed by Harberger and all subsequent empirical studies. Although a general equilibrium framework would be preferable, such an approach requires simplifying assump-

* This paper was started during the summer of 1975 when Keith Cowling visited the International Institute of Management and completed during the summer of 1976 when Dennis Mueller participated in the University of Warwick's Summer Workshop. Thanks are extended to both of these institutions for their support. In addition, special thanks are due to Gerald Nelson, who made the welfare loss calculations for the United States and Clive Hicks for making the estimates for the United Kingdom.

[1] In addition to the points Bergson (1975) raises in his own defence, we have serious objections to the arguments made by Carson (1975) and Worcester (1975). Some of these are presented below in our critique of previous studies.

tions which to our mind are just as restrictive as those needed to justify the partial equilibrium approach. For example, Bergson must assume that social welfare can be captured via a social indifference curve, and further that this indifference curve is the CES variety. The assumption that the elasticity of substitution (σ) is constant further implies, for a disaggregated analysis, that the elasticity of demand for each product (η_i) is the same, since $\eta_i \rightarrow \sigma$ as the share of the ith product in total output approaches zero. But the assumption that η_i is the same for all i is the same assumption made by Harberger and most other previous studies. It introduces a basic inconsistency between the observed variations in price cost margins and the assumed constant elasticities in demand, which the present study seeks to avoid. Given such problems, we have adopted the partial equilibrium framework, with all the necessary assumptions it requires (see Bergson, 1973). We present estimates for both the United States and the United Kingdom based on data gathered at the firm level.

I. THEORETICAL ANALYSIS

We have four substantive criticisms of the Harberger approach:

(1) In the partial equilibrium formula for welfare loss $\frac{1}{2}dp\,dq$, where dp is the change in price from competition to monopoly and dq is the change in quantity, dp and dq were considered to be independent of each other. Generally low values of dp were *observed* and low values of dq were *assumed*. In Harberger's case he assumed that price elasticities of demand in all industries were unitary. This must inevitably lead to small estimates of welfare loss.

(2) The competitive profit rate was identified with the mean profit rate and thus automatically incorporated an element of monopoly. In fact the underlying approach was a "constant degree of monopoly" – one in which distortions in output were associated with deviations of profit rate from the mean, rather than from the competitive return on capital.

(3) The use of industry profit rates introduces an immediate aggregation bias into the calculation by allowing the high monopoly profits of those firms with the most market power to be offset by the losses of other firms in the same industry. Given assumption (1), a further aggregation bias is introduced, which can easily be shown to result in additional downward bias in the estimates.

(4) The entire social loss due to monopoly was assumed to arise from the deviation of monopoly output from competitive levels. To this should be added the social cost of attempts to acquire monopoly positions, existing or potential.

We now seek to justify each of these four criticisms.

(A) *Interdependence of dp_i and dq_i*

Assuming profit maximising behaviour we can define the implied price elasticity of demand for a specific firm by observing the mark-up of price on marginal cost:

$$\hat{\eta}_i = p_i/(p_i - mc_i). \tag{1}$$

For a pure monopolist or perfectly colluding oligopolist $\hat{\eta}_i$ is the industry elasticity of demand. In other cases $\hat{\eta}_i$ reflects both the industry demand elasticity and the degree of rivals' response to a change in price the ith firm perceives (Cubbin, 1975). Using (1) we shall obtain welfare loss estimates by individual firms from their price/cost margins. These estimates indicate the amount of welfare loss associated with a single firm's decision to set price above marginal cost, given the change in its output implied by $\hat{\eta}_i$.[1] To the extent other firms also charge higher prices, because firm i sets its price above marginal cost, the total welfare loss associated with firm i's market power exceeds the welfare loss we estimate. To the extent that a simultaneous reduction to zero of all price cost margins is contemplated, however, $\hat{\eta}_i$ overestimates the net effect of the reduction in p_i on the ith firm's output. What the latter effect on output and welfare would be is a matter for general equilibrium analysis and is not the focus here. Rather, we attempt an estimate of the relative importance of the distortions in individual firm outputs, on a firm by firm basis, on the assumption that each does possess some monopoly power, as implied by the price cost margin it chooses, and uses it.

This approach emphasising the interdependence of observed price distortions and changes in output contrasts with the methodology of Harberger (1954), Schwartzman (1960), Worcester (1973) and Bergson (1973), who observe (or, in Bergson's case, assume) $(p_i - mc_i)/p_i$ and then *assume* a value of η_i.[2] Harberger observed generally low values of dp_i and yet chose to assume that $\eta_i = 1$, and therefore that dq_i was also very small. But, it is inconsistent to observe low values of dp_i and infer low elasticities unless one has assumed that the firm or industry cannot price as a monopolist, i.e. unless one has already assumed the monopoly problem away.[3] Assuming interdependence we obtain the following definition of welfare loss:

$$dW_i = \frac{1}{2} \frac{dp_i}{p_i} \frac{dq_i}{q_i} p_i q_i, \tag{2}$$

where

$$\frac{dp_i}{p_i} = \frac{1}{\hat{\eta}_i} \quad \text{and} \quad \frac{dq_i}{q_i} = \hat{\eta}_i \frac{dp_i}{p_i} = 1,[4]$$

therefore

$$dW_i = \frac{dp_i}{p_i} \frac{p_i q_i}{2}. \tag{3}$$

Assuming constant costs we can rewrite (3) in terms of profits:

$$dW_i = \frac{\Pi_i}{p_i q_i} \frac{p_i q_i}{2} = \frac{\Pi_i}{2}. \tag{4}$$

[1] We need here an assumption of perfect competition everywhere else, of course. We shall ignore problems of the second best, along with the general equilibrium issue more generally, throughout the paper.

[2] The Harberger and Schwartzman estimates are at the industry level.

[3] This position is questioned by Wenders (1967) and others who attempt to show how implausible the implied η_i's are. However, their calculations are erroneous because they fail to recognise (a) that the degree of collusion is a variable – we need not assume perfect joint profit maximisation and (b) that entry is conditional on the same variables (plus others) that determine $(p_i - mc_i)/p_i$, for example η, the degree of concentration and, for differentiated products, advertising also.

[4] This is true so long as the firm is in equilibrium, i.e. that the firms' expectations about the behaviour of rivals are actually borne out. If this were not the case then the elasticity on which the pricing decision was made would not correspond to the elasticity implied by the change in output. We assume firm equilibrium in our calculations.

This formulation obviously contrasts sharply with Harberger's:

$$dW_i = \tfrac{1}{2} p_i q_i \eta_i t_i^2, \tag{5}$$

where

$$t_i = dp_i/p_i, \quad \eta_i = 1.$$

It is obvious that if t_i is small the welfare loss is going to be insignificant. If t_i were a price increase due to tariff or tax then it might be assumed to be independent of η_i,[1] and equation (5) would give a reasonable estimate of welfare loss. But where t_i is a firm decision variable, η_i and t_i must be interdependent, and formulae for calculating welfare losses should take this interdependence into account. Interesting here is the Worcester (1975) critique of Bergson for doing essentially this with his hypothetical general equilibrium calculations when Worcester himself followed the Harberger line without demure (Worcester, 1973).[2] In contrast to Harberger and Worcester, Bergson (1973) allowed himself to pick some combinations of t_i and η_i, which implied high values of welfare loss.

Harberger defended his choice of a demand elasticity of 1·0 across all products on the grounds that what was "envisage[d was] not the substitution of one industry's product against all other products, but rather the substitution of one great aggregate of products (those yielding high rates of return) for another aggregate (those yielding low rates of return)" (p. 79). Thus, the use of $\eta = 1$·0 was an attempt at compensating for the disadvantages of employing a partial equilibrium measure of welfare loss to examine a general equilibrium structural change. But certainly this is a very awkward way of handling the problem which neither answers the criticisms raised by Bergson (1973) against the partial equilibrium approach, nor those we have just presented. For this reason we have chosen to define the partial equilibrium methodology properly and obtain the best estimates we can with this approach, recognising that it leaves unanswered the issues raised by general equilibrium analysis and the theory of second best regarding the net effect of a simultaneous elimination of all monopoly power. We return to this point below in Subsection E.

(B) The Measurement of Monopoly Profits

The obvious measure of monopoly profit is the excess of actual profits over long-run competitive returns. For an economy in equilibrium, the competitive profit rate is the minimum profit rate compatible with long-run survival, after making appropriate allowances for risk. Monopoly profit is thus the difference between actual profits and profits consistent with this minimum rate.

Harberger (1954) and all subsequent studies have based their monopoly profit estimates on the size of the deviation between actual profit rates and the mean rate. To the extent that observed profits contain elements of monopoly

---

[1] But not necessarily so. Taxes and tariffs may be applied according to elasticity expectations.

[2] Worcester (1975) also offers some empirical support. His collection of industry price elasticities is either irrelevant (including many agricultural products and few manufacturing ones) or suspect (no allowance having been made in the studies quoted for quality change over time), and is certainly not comprehensive.

rent, the mean profit rate exceeds the minimum rate consistent with long-run survival. The deviations between profit rates above the mean and the mean rate underestimate the level of monopoly returns, and the estimate of monopoly welfare is biased downwards.[1] Indeed, if all firms and industries were in long-run equilibrium, all would earn profits equal to or greater than the minimum and the use of deviations from the mean would minimize the size of the measured monopoly profits.

It is unreasonable to assume that the time periods investigated in Harberger's study, the others which followed, or our own, are long enough or stable enough so that all firms and industries are in equilibrium. The presence of firms earning profits less than the competitive norm creates a methodological problem for a study of monopoly welfare losses. All studies to date have implicitly assumed that a monopolist's costs are the same as those of a firm in competitive equilibrium, and that all welfare loss is from the loss of consumers' surplus from a monopoly price above marginal cost. But, what is the appropriate assumption to make for a firm experiencing losses? It seems unrealistic to assume that its costs are at competitive levels and its prices below them. More reasonable seems the assumption that these firms are in disequilibrium, probably with costs currently above competitive levels. When calculating monopoly welfare losses, therefore, we simply drop all firms (or industries where relevant) with profits below the competitive return on capital, in effect assuming that they will eventually return to a position where they are earning normal profits or disappear. In either case, they represent no long-run loss to society. (It is possible that some of these losses represent expenditures by firms hoping to secure monopoly positions from other firms in the industry, as discussed below. These losses are then part of the social costs of monopoly. We attempt to account for them in one of our welfare loss formulae.)

Previous studies, to the extent we can ascertain, have followed Harberger and treated deviations in profits below and above the mean symmetrically. That is, an industry whose profit rate was 5 % below the mean profit rate was considered to have created as large a welfare loss as an industry whose profits are 5 % above the mean.[2] Thus, these studies have not actually estimated welfare loss under monopoly using perfect competition as the standard of comparison, but have effectively compared welfare loss under the present regime with that which would exist were the degree of monopoly equalised across all firms and industries. Under their procedures, a constant degree of monopoly power, however high, would result in no welfare loss. While such an approach has some theoretical support, it raises practical difficulties. How is this elusive concept of a constant degree of monopoly defined and measured? How is such a world created without an omniscient planner or regulator? In addition,

---

[1] Worcester (1973) makes some allowance for this bias by using 90 % of the median profit rate, but this adjustment is obviously rather *ad hoc*.

[2] One might believe that the losses by firms earning profits below the norm represent a form of *factor surplus loss* which must be added to the consumer surplus loss to obtain the full losses from monopoly. But, as Worcester (1973) has shown, these factor-surplus losses, if properly measured, are *an alternative way* of estimating the consumer surplus losses and should be used *instead of* the consumer surplus measure, rather than in addition to it, if used at all.

monopoly in product markets could be expected to induce distortions in factor markets. Finally, as developed below, the existence of monopoly power in product markets attracts resources to its acquisition and protection, which are part of the social cost of monopoly apart from the distortions in output accompanying it. For these reasons, and because it appears to be most directly in the spirit of the analysis, we have compared monopoly profits to competitive returns, and considered only deviations above the competitive rate when estimating welfare losses.

Following Harberger and other previous studies we have attempted to minimise the transitory component in our estimates by using averages of firm profits over several years.[1] Nevertheless, some of the companies earning profits above competitive levels in our samples are in temporary disequilibrium, and the welfare losses associated with these firms can be expected to disappear over time. Thus, our estimates of monopoly profits are a combination of both long-run monopoly profits and short-run disequilibrium profits. To the extent the time periods we have chosen are representative of the U.K. and U.S. economies under "normal" conditions, our calculations are accurate estimates of the annual losses from monopoly, both permanent and transitory, that can be expected in these countries. A further effort to eliminate the transitory monopoly components from the data would require a specification of what is meant by "permanent" and "transitory" monopolies. Many economists would take it for granted that in the "long run" all monopolies are dead and thus monopoly like unemployment is a "short run" phenomenon. As with unemployment, the question is how serious is the problem when it exists, and how long does it last. Our paper addresses the first of these questions. A full answer to the second question is clearly beyond the scope of our essentially cross-section analysis.

(C) *The Aggregation Biases from Using Industry Data*

Previous studies of monopoly welfare losses with the exception of Worcester (1973) used industry data at a fairly high level of aggregation. At any point in time some firms in an industry are likely to be earning profits below the competitive level. We have already discussed the methodological issues raised in a study of monopoly welfare losses by firms earning negative economic profits. If our interpretation of these firms as being in short-run disequilibrium is correct, then they should be dropped from an industry before calculating the industry's profit rate. Previous studies which have based their calculations solely on industry data have effectively combined the negative profits of some firms with the positive profits of others in estimating the welfare losses from monopoly. Thus they have implicitly assumed that the monopoly profits earned by the most profitable firms in the industry are somehow offset or mitigated by

---

[1] Harberger chose 5 years of "normal" business activity in the 1920s for his original study of the United States. Following his lead we have chosen 4 years in the 1960s for the U.S. estimates falling between a recession and the Vietnam War boom. The results reported below for the United Kingdom are for only two years, 1968/9. The U.K. results for 1970/4 indicate that averaging profits over five years does not change the nature of the outcome.

those experiencing transitory losses. But if there is a monopoly problem in an industry, it is represented by the positive rents earned by those firms with profits above the norm, and the losses of firms that are temporarily unable to compete successfully in no way alleviates the social costs arising from the monopoly positions of the other firms. The present study therefore measures monopoly welfare losses using firm level monopoly profit estimates.

A second aggregation bias is introduced into the estimates of all previous studies other than Kamerschen's (1966) through the assumption of a constant elasticity of demand across all industries. This results in the profit margin's appearance as a squared term in the welfare loss formula. The use of average firm profit margins (including firms with negative profits) implicit in the use of industry data, further biases the welfare loss estimates downwards. The extent of this bias is measured below.

(D) Welfare Loss in the Acquisition of Monopoly Power

Tullock (1967) and Posner (1975) have argued that previous studies under-state the social costs of monopoly by failing to recognise the costs involved in attempts to gain and retain monopoly power. These costs could take the form of investment in excess production capacity, excessive accumulation of adver-tising goodwill stocks, and excessive product differentiation through R and D.[1] Efforts to obtain tariff protection, patent protection and other types of pre-ferential government treatment through campaign contributions, lobbying or bribery are parts of the social costs of the existence of monopoly as defined by Tullock and Posner. To the extent that these expenditures enter reported costs in the form of higher payments to factor owners and legitimate business ex-penses, firm costs in the presence of monopoly exceed costs under perfect com-petition. Estimates of welfare loss based on those profits remaining *net* of these expenditures *under*estimate the social cost of monopoly in two ways: first, by understating monopoly rents they understate the distortions in output mono-poly produces; secondly, by failing to include these additional expenditures as part of the costs of monopoly.

Three adjustments to the usual welfare triangle measure of monopoly welfare loss are made to account for the additional expenditures to redistribute mono-poly rents, monopoly power induces. First, advertising is added to monopoly profit in calculating the welfare triangle loss to allow for the understatement of monopoly profit expenditures of this type produce. Second, all of advertising is added to the welfare loss. This takes the extreme view of advertising as merely an instrument for securing market power. To the extent advertising provides useful information to consumers, this measure overstates the cost of mono-poly.[2] Thirdly, all of measured, after-tax profits above the competitive cost of

---

[1] See Spence (1974). It is interesting to note that this type of activity generally dominates the entry-limiting pricing response. Entry-limiting pricing can be thought of as having extra capacity because of potential entry and actually using it to produce output. Thus the profits associated with restricting output are lost. From this viewpoint we cannot accept Posner's position that the elimination of entry regulation would eliminate waste. As the probability of entry increases so would the optimal degree of excess capacity. Monopoly pricing would be maintained but social waste would still occur.

[2] There will always be an inherent bias in the information provided given the interests of the agent

capital are used as the estimate of the expenditures incurred by others to obtain control of these monopoly rents. Obviously this estimate is but a first approximation. It is an underestimate, if the firm has incurred expenditures in the acquisition and maintenance of its monopoly position, which are included in current costs. It is an overstatement if actual and potential competitors can successfully collude to avoid these wasteful outlays. This type of argument can always be rebutted, however, by carrying the Tullock/Posner analysis one stage back and positing expenditures of resources to enter the potential competitor's position, and so on. The arguments that after-tax profits underestimate the additional costs associated with monopoly seem at least as reasonable as those suggesting overestimation.

(E) *An Objection and Alternative Estimating Technique*

The assumption that demand elasticity equals the reciprocal of the price–cost margin, equation (1), can give rise, when price–cost margins are small, to firm level elasticity estimates much greater than existing industry level estimates, and imply large increases in output from the elimination of monopoly. This has led several observers to criticise the use of the Lerner formula, and the underlying assumption that firms set price as if they possess and utilise market power. Worcester (1969) has made the argument most forcefully.

> Serious error...arise[s] if the "monopolist" is only an oligopolist who fears entry, unfavourable publicity, government regulation or a weaker position at the bargaining table should profits be too high, and for such reasons prices at P_0 (Fig. 1) and sells output Q_E in spite of the fact that the marginal revenue is far below zero at that point. [1969, p. 237, note that our Fig. 1 and Worcester's are drawn to scale.]

The elasticity of demand is lower at P_0 than at P_M, and the expansion in output following a reduction in price to competitive price P_c is obviously much smaller if we assume the "monopolist" sets price equal to P_0. Thus Worcester's depiction of the problem does meet the objections many have raised against the use of the Lerner formula to estimate demand elasticities. We observe only that if one assumes from the start that "monopolists" are so constrained in their behaviour that they must set price so low that marginal revenue is negative, it can be no surprise that calculations incorporating this assumption indicate insignificant welfare losses. But any estimates of welfare losses within a partial equilibrium framework, which impose demand elasticities significantly below those implied via the Lerner formula, must implicitly be assuming that firms set price in such an environment, if the data on price/cost margins are accepted at face value.

The latter assumption may not be valid, however, and its abandonment allows a reconciliation of existing profit-margin data with lower demand

---

doing the advertising so the argument for advertising as a provider of information should not be taken too seriously. Even if we base our welfare measures on post-advertising preferences it is still possible to demonstrate that monopolies (and *a fortiori* oligopolies) invest in too much advertising (see Dixit and Norman, 1975).

elasticity figures without also introducing the assumption that monopolists are either irrational or impotent. The preceding section discusses several business outlays that are made to maintain or preserve monopoly positions. Conceptually these are best treated as *investments* out of current profits made to secure future monopoly rents than as current production costs as is done for accounting purposes, and is carried through into the economist's calculations based on accounting data. A rational monopolist will not take these into account in making his short-run pricing decision. We can thus reconcile the monopoly pricing assumption with small demand elasticity estimates by assuming that average costs contain much investment-type expenditure and that marginal production costs are below these.

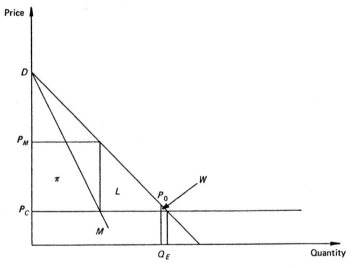

Fig. 1. π, Monopoly profit rectangle. L, Deadweight loss assuming firm exercises monopoly power. W, Worcester's proposed deadweight loss.

In Fig. 2 let C_0 be observed costs, including investment-type outlays, and P_0 observed price. For such price and cost figures to be consistent with monopoly pricing behaviour the firm's demand schedule would have to be D_0. Price P_0 would be consistent with a much more inelastic demand schedule, D_a say, if actual production costs were at C_a. Note that both profits (π), and the welfare triangle losses (L) are much larger under the more inelastic demand schedule assumption.

Thus, an alternative procedure for calculating the welfare losses from monopoly to the one described above would be to estimate price/cost margins from data on demand elasticities, where now we estimate demand elasticities from data on price/cost margins. We do not pursue these calculations here. First, because we do not have demand elasticity data applicable to firms, and the imposition of any constant η across all firms is obviously *ad hoc*. Secondly, the choice of any η in line with existing industry estimates would lead to welfare loss estimates far greater than those calculated here. The highest of the elasticities used in previous studies has been $\eta = 2 \cdot 0$. This implies a profit margin of 50 % and a welfare triangle loss equal to one-quarter of sales. These estimates exceed those reported here, whenever the firm's profits are *less* than one-half of sales. Since this is true for all our firms, our welfare loss estimates are all smaller than under the alternative procedure.

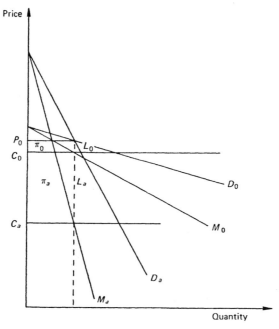

Fig. 2

We believe that reported costs do contain large amounts of investment-type expenditures beyond the advertising we allow for, that production costs are lower therefore, and that individual firm demand elasticities are typically lower than we implicitly estimate. We emphasise, however, that any attempt to take these costs into account, and adjust demand elasticities accordingly, while maintaining the assumption that companies do possess and exercise market power, will lead to larger estimates of welfare loss underlining again the conservative nature of our calculations.

II. EMPIRICAL ESTIMATES

Empirical estimates of the social cost of monopoly power were obtained for both the United States and United Kingdom. We provide two sets of estimates, one based on our assumptions (ΔW_{CM}^k), the other based on Harberger-type assumptions (ΔW_H^k), both measured at the firm-level. For each approach we give a range of four estimates defined in Table 1.

Thus for $k = 1$ we define two alternative estimates of the welfare triangle, the one (ΔW^k_{CM}) based on interdependence of dp_i and dq_i, the other (ΔW^1_H) based on the Harberger methodology. This latter estimate is included for comparison with previous results especially from the viewpoint of bias due to aggregation. For $k = 2$, the same calculations are performed but in calculating dp_i, advertising expenditure (A_i) is deducted from cost. For $k = 3$ we add in advertising expenditure as a social cost, and for $k = 4$ we also add in monopoly profits *after tax* as a further element of social cost. It should be noted at this point that in calculating dp_i the appropriate profit measure is *before tax*

Table 1

Alternative Definitions of Social Cost

k	ΔW^k_{CM}	ΔW^k_H
1	$\Pi/2$	$(R/2)\,(\Pi/R)^2$
2	$(\Pi+A)/2$	$(R/2)\,[(\Pi+A)/R]^2$
3	$A+(\Pi+A)/2$	$(R/2)\,[(\Pi+A)/R]^2+A$
4	$\Pi'+A+(\Pi+A)/2$	$(R/2)\,[(\Pi+A)/R]^2+A+\Pi'$

Π, before tax profit; Π', after tax profit; A, advertising; R, total revenue.

profit since the price and quantity choice of a monopolist should not be affected by a tax on profits. Thus, in contrast to most previous studies, we use before-tax profits to measure the distortion between price and costs under monopoly (the ΔW's for $k = 1, 2, 3$). However, it is *after-tax* monopoly profits which provide an inducement to additional expenditures to gain monopoly, and it is these that are added in to obtain our fourth measure of welfare loss.

To estimate monopoly profits an estimate of the return on capital of a firm in a competitive industry is needed. Any estimates based on actual returns earned in existing industries run the danger of including monopoly rents. The stock market might be regarded as coming fairly close to satisfying the free-entry and -exit requirement of a competitive industry, however. The returns on corporate stock will include monopoly rents to the extent that they become capitalised over the period for which the rate is estimated. The use of these returns for the United States is therefore equivalent to assuming that (1) all existing monopoly rents are fully capitalised at the beginning of the period, and (2) changes in monopoly rents over the period are accurately anticipated.

For the United States we use as our estimate of the competitive return on capital the Fisher–Lorie index of returns on a fully diversified portfolio of listed stocks for the same period for which our monopoly profit estimates are made (1963–6). This estimate was 12% which might be compared with the average return on capital earned by the firms in our sample of 14%.

For the United Kingdom we use the pre-tax real cost of capital as calculated by Flemming *et al.* (1976). These estimates avoid the newly capitalised monopoly rent problem mentioned above entirely. For the 1968/9 period they yield an estimate of the cost of capital of 8·15 %.[1]

[1] It may be argued that because of inflation we are undervaluing land or capital. This should not be a serious problem for the United States since our data follow a period of quite modest price increases.

The firms in our samples include companies operating in both intermediate and final goods markets. To justify the addition of triangular type measures of welfare loss for final and intermediate products, we must assume that the demand schedule for an intermediate product represents a derived demand schedule as in traditional Marshallian analysis. Under this assumption, triangular measures of welfare loss calculated from intermediate product demand schedules fully capture the loss in consumer welfare monopoly distortions in the intermediate markets cause, as Wisecarver (1974) has recently demonstrated. Assuming advertising and other efforts to obtain monopoly power are as wasteful when undertaken in intermediate markets as in final goods markets, the formulae presented in Table 1 can be applied for both intermediate and final good producers.

(A) U.S. Estimates

The range of welfare loss estimates for the United States are presented in Table 2. They refer to the 1963–6 period and the sample comprises the 734 firms on the COMPUSTAT tape with useable information.[1] The firms are ranked according to the size of welfare loss as measured by ΔW^4_{CM}. General Motors leads the list with an annual welfare loss of over \$1¾ billion, which alone is over ¼ of 1 % of average GNP during the period, and exceeds Harberger's original welfare loss estimate for the entire economy. Most of the other members of the top 20 are names one also might have expected. One possible exception is AT & T. AT & T's gross profit rate was, in fact, less than our estimate of the cost of capital ($\approx$ 0·12). Its advertising entry on the COMPUSTAT tape (and in this case we did have a COMPUSTAT figure, see appendix) was \$¾ billion, and it is AT & T's advertising which leads to the high ΔW_{CM} estimate we have for it. Advertising also weighs heavily in the ΔW^4_{CM} estimates for Unilever, Proctor and Gamble, Sears Roebuck, Genesco, Colgate–Palmolive, Pan Am and Pacific Tel. At first sight this might seem surprising, particularly with respect to regulated firms like AT & T and Pacific Tel. But, as Posner (1975) has argued, this is precisely what one expects to find in industries with high market power, and, as Posner himself stresses, firms under regulatory constraint can be expected to engage, if anything, in more wasteful dissipation of their

Given that inflation in the United Kingdom in 1968/9 was substantial, although very much less than in the seventies, we have corrected our data at the company level. Using data from Walker (1974), we multiplied the profit figure derived from the company accounts by the ratio of the average rate of return at replacement cost to the average rate of return at historical cost and subtracted from this the estimated book value of assets times the cost of capital. The ratio of rates of return used was 9·4 : 13·4 in 1968 and 8·2 : 12·4 in 1969. We should in fact be using the ratio of the rate of return at replacement cost to the rate of return at book value but the latter rate was not available on a comparable basis (see Walker, 1974, table 3). This means that our measure of excess profits and therefore of welfare loss will tend to be biased down, given that (a) asset revaluations generally take place at merger, when acquired assets are given a current market valuation, and (b) revaluations, of land and buildings especially, do take place periodically, their frequency being related to the rate of inflation. The cost of capital measure used was the forward-looking, pre-tax measure which was estimated at 8·15 % for the period 1968/9 (Flemming et al. 1976).

[1] The COMPUSTAT tape contains data on a sample of large firms, mostly in manufacturing, listed on U.S. stock exchanges. The data definitions used in making the estimates are discussed in the appendix.

monopoly rents than non-regulated firms through expenditures like advertising. It is interesting to note in this regard that 6 of the 40 largest welfare losses are accounted for by regulated firms (3 telephone companies and 3 airlines) in which advertising made up all or most of the losses.

At the bottom of Table 2 the losses are summed over the firms with positive profit margins as defined for the ΔW^1 and ΔW^2 measures (see table notes), and then expressed as a proportion of our estimate of the Gross Corporate Product originating in the 734 firms in the sample. It should be stressed here, again, that the totals do not represent the estimated gains from the simultaneous elimination of all monopoly power. The answer to this question could be obtained only via a general equilibrium analysis. What we estimate via our partial equilibrium analysis is the relative cost of monopoly for each firm, and the column totals present average estimates of these costs for our sample of firms. Note, however, that the *additions* to our cost estimates that occur in moving from the W^2_{CM} to the W^3_{CM} and W^4_{CM} columns do sum across all firms, since these are estimates of the wasted expenditures made in pursuit of monopoly. If we see product market power as a ubiquitous characteristic of the economy, then it might be reasonable to assume that this estimate of monopoly welfare loss could be generalised to the entire economy. To the extent one believes monopoly power is more (e.g. see again Posner, 1975) or less pervasive in other sectors our estimates must be raised or lowered. Assuming the social costs of monopoly are the same across all sectors, we obtain estimates for our preferred model (ΔW^k_{CM}) ranging between 4 and 13 % of GCP. Thus, all losses are significant, but the range is considerable depending upon what components of social cost one includes. For the Harberger approach, the range is between 0·4 and 7 %. The lowest of these follows the Harberger assumptions most closely, but nevertheless we estimate a welfare loss four times as big as he did. This difference in large part is explained by the aggregation bias incorporated into the industry level estimates.

The extent of this bias can be seen by considering Table 3. Its entries are made by assigning each firm to an industry at the appropriate level of aggregation, and aggregating over the firms in each industry. Just as negative profit firms were excluded in calculating welfare losses at the firm level, negative profit industries are excluded in calculating welfare losses across industries. For the ΔW^k_{CM} measures aggregation bias is due simply to the inclusion of losses by some firms in the calculation of each industry's profits. Table 3 shows how this bias varies with the level of aggregation and with the choice of measure. Industry estimates are between ˙78 and 98 % of the firm level estimates in aggregate. For the ΔW^k_H estimates, a further cause of bias is introduced by the squared term, $(\Pi/R)^2$, in the formula. It can be seen from Table 3 that for the ΔW^1_H measures, the 2-digit industry estimates aggregate to only 40% of the firm level estimates.[1] Note, however, that the biases are much smaller for the ΔW^3 and ΔW^4 measures and in the case of the ΔW^3_H measure at the

[1] Worcester (1973) plays down the extent of the bias by focusing on the *absolute* differences between the measures. Given that the absolute values of losses are small using ΔW^1_H, even very large relative biases result in small absolute distortions, as one would expect. For additional evidence on the importance of aggregation bias in previous studies, see Siegfried and Tiemann (1974).

Table 2

Monopoly Welfare Losses by Firm (yearly averages in $ millions) : U.S. 1963/6

Company	$\Delta W^1_{\hat{O}M}$	$\Delta W^2_{\hat{O}M}$	$\Delta W^3_{\hat{O}M}$	$\Delta W^4_{\hat{O}M}$	ΔW^1_H	ΔW^2_H	ΔW^3_H	ΔW^4_H
1. General Motors	1,060·5	1,156·3	1,347·8	1,780·3	123·4	146·2	337·8	770·2
2. AT & T	0·0	257·3	1,025·0	1,025·0	0·0	13·4	781·1	781·1
3. Unilever	0·0	160·0	490·5	490·5	0·0	19·5	350·0	350·0
4. Procter & Gamble	56·7	180·1	427·0	427·0	3·3	33·0	279·9	279·2
5. Dupont	225·1	241·9	275·4	375·3	36·3	41·7	75·2	175·2
6. Ford Motor	160·4	217·5	331·7	331·7	5·2	9·3	123·5	123·5
7. IBM	251·7	264·0	288·7	319·8	36·8	40·5	65·2	96·3
8. Reynolds, R. J.	73·1	138·5	269·3	278·8	10·8	38·5	169·3	178·8
9. Sears Roebuck	36·2	115·0	272·5	272·5	0·5	4·4	162·0	162·0
10. Eastman Kodak	136·3	157·9	201·1	258·5	27·7	36·8	80·0	137·4
11. American Cyanamid Co.	27·6	98·7	240·8	240·8	1·9	23·6	165·8	165·8
12. Genesco, Inc.	0·0	67·5	202·6	292·6	0·0	14·9	150·0	150·0
13. Exxon Corp.	115·6	143·0	197·8	197·8	2·4	3·7	58·5	58·5
14. Colgate–Palmolive Co.	3·9	56·7	160·3	160·3	0·0	7·6	111·8	111·8
15. Chrysler Corp.	39·8	78·4	155·5	155·5	1·1	3·0	80·1	80·1
16. General Electric Co.	83·4	105·2	148·8	148·8	2·6	4·0	47·6	47·6
17. Pan Am Airways	1·1	49·8	147·2	147·2	0·1	7·5	104·9	104·9
18. Pacific Tel. & Tel.	0·0	18·4	138·1	138·1	0·0	0·8	128·5	128·5
19. Gillette Co.	27·8	56·0	112·3	129·2	4·7	18·9	75·3	92·2
20. Minnesota Mining & Mfg.	62·5	77·7	107·1	129·1	8·2	12·6	42·3	64·3
Totals all firms*	4,527·1	7,454·9	14,005·4	14,997·6†	448·2	897·8	7,448·3	8,440·1†
Total/GCP‡	0·0396	0·0652	0·1227	0·13137	0·0040	0·0079	0·0652	0·0739

* The ΔW's for all firms having monopoly profits (Π) less than zero were set equal to zero. The ΔW^2, ΔW^3, and ΔW^4's for all firms with $(\Pi + A) < 0$ were set equal to zero. The latter was based on the assumption that these firms would not survive in the long run and hence represent no *long run* welfare loss to society. There are 421 firms with Π > 0 and 525 firms with $(\Pi + A) > 0$ in the sample of 734 firms.

† When profits, after deducting taxes and the cost of capital (Π'), are less than zero, $\Delta W^4 = \Delta W^3$.

‡ The total welfare loss for all firms by each ΔW measure is first divided by the total sales of the 734 firms in the sample, and then multiplied by the ratio of corporate sales to gross corporate product over all industries (2·873) as given in Laffer (1969).

Table 3

Comparison of Firm and Industry Welfare Loss Estimates: U.S. 1963/6

	ΔW^1_{OM}	ΔW^2_{OM}	ΔW^3_{OM}	ΔW^4_{OM}	ΔW^1_{H}	ΔW^2_{H}	ΔW^3_{H}	ΔW^4_{H}
(1) Summation over firms	4,527·1	7,454·9	14,005·4	14,997·6	448·2	897·8	7,448·3	8,440·1
(2) Summation over 4 digit industries	3,767·8	6,902·5	13,752·6	14,052·8	276·9	628·8	7,478·9	7,790·2
(3) Summation over 3 digit industries	3,619·0	6,680·5	13,355·4	13,512·8	237·4	577·7	7,252·5	7,410·4
(4) Summation over 2 digit industries	3,515·2	6,634·5	13,262·7	13,287·9	178·9	485·3	7,113·5	7,148·8
(5) (2)/(1)	0·832	0·926	0·982	0·937	0·618	0·700	1·004	0·923
(6) (3)/(1)	0·799	0·896	0·954	0·901	0·530	0·643	0·974	0·878
(7) (4)/(1)	0·776	0·890	0·947	0·886	0·399	0·541	0·955	0·847

4-digit level the bias goes slightly the other way. This comes about because of the inclusion in the industry estimates of advertising for firms earning less

Table 4

Monopoly Welfare Losses by Firm (£ million): U.K. 1968/9

Company	ΔW^1_{CM}	ΔW^2_{CM}	ΔW^3_{CM}	ΔW^4_{CM}	ΔW^1_{H}	ΔW^2_{H}	ΔW^3_{H}	ΔW^4_{H}
1. British Petroleum	74·1	74·4	75·1	82·7	5·1	5·1	5·8	13·4
2. Shell Transport & Trading	49·4	50·8	53·6	53·6	2·2	2·3	5·1	5·1
3. British American Tobacco	26 8	27·0	27·5	49·1	1·0	1·1	1·6	23·1
4. Unilever	2·8	11·3	28·2	29·0	0·0	0·2	17·2	18·0
5. I.C.I.	17·6	18·8	21·1	27·9	0·5	0·5	2·9	9·6
6. Rank Xerox	13·9	14·0	14·2	27·5	3·4	3·4	3·5	16·9
7. I.B.M. (U.K.)	11·1	11·2	11·3	21·9	2·2	2·2	2·4	12·9
8. Great Universal Stores	9·6	10·0	11·0	21·6	0·5	0·5	1·5	12·1
9. Beecham	6·2	8·9	14·3	20·4	0·6	1·3	6·7	12·8
10. Imperial Group	2·8	8·6	20·1	20·1	0·0	0·1	11·7	11·7
11. Marks & Spencer	9·8	9·8	9·8	18·6	0·6	0·6	0·6	9·5
12. Ford	7·2	7·8	8·8	16·6	0·2	0·2	1·3	9·1
13. F. W. Woolworth	7·3	7·4	7·8	15·9	0·3	0·4	0·7	8·9
14. J. Lyon	0·0	0·7	2·8	14·2	0·0	0·0	2·1	13·4
15. Burmah	5·3	5·5	5·9	13·9	0·2	0·3	0·7	8·7
16. Distillers	5·6	6·1	7·1	13·4	0·2	0·2	1·2	7·5
17. Rank Organisation	11·5	11·7	12·1	12·5	1·2	1·2	1·7	2·1
18. Thorn	5·6	6·1	7·1	12·5	0·3	0·3	1·4	6·7
19. Cadbury Schweppes	1·8	5·0	11·4	12·3	0·0	0·3	6·7	7·6
20. Reckitt & Coleman	2·9	4·7	8·3	10·4	0·1	0·3	3·9	6·0
Total all firms (102)	385·8	435·0	537·4	719·3	21·4	24·2	118·8	304·4
Total ÷ GCP	0·0386	0·0436	0·0539	0·0720	0·0021	0·0024	0·0119	0·0305

No. of firms with $\Pi > 0 = 82$.
No. of firms with $\Pi + A > 0 = 86$.

than normal profits. Thus in future work along these lines, when data are limited to industry level observations, the ΔW^3 and ΔW^4 measures have an additional advantage over the other two measures.

(B) *U.K. Estimates*

These have been calculated on the same basis as the U.S. estimates, but since no convenient computer tape was available we contented ourselves with an analysis of the top 103 firms in the United Kingdom for the periods 1968/9 and 1970/4.[1] Over the periods in question these firms were responsible for roughly one-third of the GNP and were therefore proportionally more important than the 734 firms sample from the COMPUSTAT tape for the United States. The time-periods used have been dictated by the availability of data. The basic source has been EXTEL cards but advertising expenditure was estimated by aggregating up from the brand level, using estimates of press and TV

[1] The top 100 varies somewhat over time.

advertising contained in MEAL. We can therefore expect that our advertising expenditure figures will be biased down by the amount of non-media advertising, as is true also for the United States. Table 4 gives the results for 1968/9, with firms again being ranked by ΔW_{CM}^4. The two major oil companies, BP and Shell, dominate the table. The social cost associated with BP alone is roughly a quarter of 1 % of GNP. The other members of the Top Ten are industry leaders plus British–American Tobacco. Two interesting features of the Top Twenty are the high ranking of Rank Xerox despite its size (explained presumably by its U.K. patent rights) and, in contrast to the United States, the low ranking of motor-car manufacturers (absent from the Top Twenty in 1970/4). We have computed estimates of welfare loss for the 1970/4 period, but we have not reported these results here. It is well known that the early seventies was a period of very rapid inflation in the United Kingdom and this undoubtedly raises problems such as how to account for stock appreciation and the revaluation of capital adequately. Despite these problems, it is somewhat reassuring to note that the 1970–4 results look very much like the 1968/9 results except that the oil companies become even more dominant.[1]

The aggregate estimates of welfare loss for ΔW_{CM}^k range between 3·9 and 7·2 % of GCP for the 1968/9 period. The estimate for ΔW_{CM}^1 is almost identical with that for the United States but in each of the other cases the value for the United Kingdom is well below that for the United States. The obvious and important difference between the two sets of results is the apparent greater expenditure on advertising in the United States. Taking direct account of advertising quadruples the welfare loss estimate for the United States but in the case of the United Kingdom welfare loss goes up by only about 40 % (compare ΔW_{CM}^1 with ΔW_{CM}^3).[2] Using the Harberger approach estimates of welfare loss vary between 0·2 and 3 % of GCP for the United Kingdom in the same 1968/9 period.

Again, we must conclude that our evidence suggests significant welfare loss due to monopoly power. One other point is also brought out particularly by the U.K. results (e.g. in the case of the oil companies) and that is the international distribution of these social costs. Monopoly power held by U.K. companies in foreign markets may be advantageous to the U.K. economy whilst being disadvantageous in the global sense. Thus the issue is a distributional one and adds an international dimension to the distributional issues already implicit in our analysis. In any national evaluation of the social costs imposed by the actions of a particular company, the international distribution of these costs would presumably gain some prominence.

---

[1] Indeed, comparing the results for the two periods indicates the large extent to which oil companies have benefited from the recent "oil crisis". However, this inference has to be qualified by the problems raised for the measurement of profit by stock appreciation during a period of rapid inflation of oil prices.

[2] This does not of course mean that advertising implies no additional social costs, since profit-margins and the level of excess profits may both be partly determined by advertising in so far as elasticities of demand and entry barriers are influenced by the level of advertising in monopolistic industries. We should also note that in some cases our direct adjustment for advertising is very significant (e.g. Unilever, Imperial Group and Beecham Group).

III. IMPLICATIONS AND CONCLUSIONS

Previous studies of the social costs of monopoly have generally (and often unconsciously) assumed that "monopolies" set prices as if they did not possess market power, that the only important distortions in output are brought about through the deviations in one firm's market power from the average level of market power, that the losses of some firms (perhaps incurred in unsuccessful attempts to obtain monopoly power) legitimately offset the monopoly rents of others, and that all of the expenditures made in the creation and preservation of monopoly positions are part of the normal costs which would exist in a world without monopolies. With the problem so defined, it is not surprising that most of these studies have found the welfare losses from monopoly to be small.

Since we know from general equilibrium analysis that monopoly allocation distortions may be offsetting, the conclusion that partial equilibrium analysis yields small welfare loss estimates has seemed all the more impressive. Yet each of the studies that has come up with low estimates has done so in large part because it has made assumptions (e.g. demand elasticities equal to $1\cdot0$, monopoly profits are deviations from mean profits) that can be rationalised only as *ad hoc* attempts to answer the general equilibrium question. In contrast, the present study defines a procedure for estimating the costs of monopoly that is consistent with a partial equilibrium analysis that assumes market power does (or may) exist. Our results reveal that the costs of monopoly power, calculated on an individual firm basis, are on average large. The conclusion that "even" a partial equilibrium analysis of monopoly indicates that its costs are insignificant no longer seems warranted.

This conclusion has potentially important policy implications. Antitrust policy consists typically not of a frontal attack on all existing market power, but of selective assaults on the most flagrant offenders. Our partial equilibrium estimates of monopoly welfare losses indicate the most significant contributors to these losses. The tops of our lists of the largest welfare losses by firm are logical starting points for intensified enforcement of antitrust policy. Our figures and supporting analysis further demonstrate that "the monopoly problem" is broader than traditionally suggested. A large part of this problem lies not in the height of monopoly prices and profits *per se*, but in the resources wasted in their creation and protection. These costs of monopoly should be considered when selecting targets for antitrust enforcement.

One might argue that the high profits of some firms reflect economies of scale advantages, and, therefore, these firms should not be the victims of antitrust policy. This argument points to some form of regulatory or public enterprise solution to the monopoly problem. With respect to this type of policy, our estimates of the losses from monopoly represent a still further understatement of their potential magnitude. If a policy were adopted forcing the most efficient size or organisational structure upon the entire industry, the welfare loss under the existing structure would have to be calculated using the profit margin of the most efficient *firm and the output of the entire industry*, rather than the profit margins of the individual firms and their outputs.

These considerations suggest the difficulty in estimating the social gains from the elimination of all monopoly power, since one almost has to know what form of policy is to be used (antitrust, regulation), and what the underlying cause of monopoly power is, before answering this question. Nevertheless, this has been the question that has traditionally been asked in studies of monopoly welfare losses, and the reader who has persisted to this point can justifiably ask what light our figures cast on this question. By their very nature partial equilibrium calculations cannot give very *precise* estimates of these gains, but they may establish orders of magnitude. As stressed above, we regard the Harberger-type calculations based on uniform demand elasticities of 1·0 as essentially efforts to solve the general equilibrium problem inherent in this question. As such, we regard them as the most conservative estimates of what the elimination of all monopoly would produce. Thus, we would expect the elimination of all monopoly to yield gains at least as large as the 7 and 3 % of gross corporate product we estimate for the United States and United Kingdom, respectively, using ΔW_H^4. To the extent that firms sell differentiated products, and operate in separate markets, i.e. to the extent that they have and utilise market power, these gains are pushed in the direction of our ΔW_{CM}^4 estimates of 13 and 7 %. Further upward pressure on these estimates is created by considering some of the other factors ignored in our calculations. We have already emphasised that reported profits understate true profits to the extent that firms compete for monopoly power by investing in excess plant capacity, advertising, patent lawyers, and so on. But much of the competition for *control* over monopoly rents may take place within the firm itself among the factor owners. Such competition will lead to an understatement of actual monopoly rents both through the inflation of costs that wasteful competition among factors owners brings about, and through the inclusion of part of the winning factor owners' shares of monopoly rents as reported costs. A large literature now exists on the variety of objectives managers have and the ways in which these objectives are satisfied through their discretionary control over company revenues. To the extent that managerial control over firm revenues is the reward for competing against other factor groups and potential managers successfully, reported profits understate the true profitability. By ignoring these possibilities we have erred in being conservative when estimating the social cost of monopoly. It is our reasoned guess that these additional costs would at least equal the "washing out" effect of the simultaneous elimination of all monopoly power on our partial equilibrium estimates and, therefore, that these latter figures are, if anything, underestimates of the true social costs of monopoly.

In this respect, it is useful to note an alternative, aggregative approach to the question. Phillips, in an appendix to Baran and Sweezy (1966), isolated several categories of expenditure dependent on the existence of "Monopoly Capitalism" (e.g. advertising, corporate profits, lawyers' fees). Their sum came to over 50 % of U.S. GNP. Although the assumptions upon which these calculations were made are rather extreme, they do suggest both an alternative method of analysis and the potential magnitude of the problem. Here too it should be noted that our approach has been essentially micro-orientated and neoclassical in that we have taken the returns on corporate stocks as our cost of capital. From a more aggregative view it could be argued that profits are not required at all to generate the savings required to sustain a given rate of growth, since alternative macro policies are available. From this perspective, all profits are excess profits and our estimates of social cost are too conservative. Still further weight would be added against the position that monopoly power is unimportant if the link with the distribution of political power were considered.

Of course, any public policy has its own sets of costs and inefficiencies. For Tullock–Posner reasons a concerted effort to apply or strengthen the anti-trust laws induces large, defensive expenditures on the part of business. Price and profit regulation leads to efforts to change, influence, or circumvent the application of the rules. The public enterprise solution raises the same sort of problems, with members of the bureaucracy participating in the competition for monopoly rents. Thus it might be that any alternative for dealing with existing monopoly power would involve higher costs than the monopolies themselves create. The present study does not answer this question. What it does do is dispel the notion that it need not even be asked, since the costs of monopoly within the present environment are necessarily small. The question of what the costs and benefits from alternative antimonopoly policies are still seems worth asking.

Warwick University   KEITH COWLING
University of Maryland   DENNIS C. MUELLER

Date of receipt of final typescript: April 1978

REFERENCES

Baran, P. and Sweezy, P. (1966). *Monopoly Capital*. New York: Monthly Review Press.
Bergson, A. (1973). "On Monopoly Welfare Losses." *American Economic Review*, vol. 63 (December), pp. 853–70.
Carson, R. (1975). "On Monopoly Welfare Losses: Comment." *American Economic Review*, vol. 65 (December), pp. 1008–14.
Cubbin, J. (1975). "Apparent Collusion, Price–Cost Margins and Advertising in Oligopoly." Mimeo, University of Warwick.
Dixit, A. and Norman, V. (1978). "Advertising and Welfare." *Bell Journal of Economics* (June).
Flemming, J. S., Price, L. D. D. and Byers, S. A. (1976). "The Cost of Capital, Finance and Investment." *Bank of England Quarterly Bulletin*, vol. 16 (June), pp. 193–205.
Harberger, A. C. (1954). "Monopoly and Resource Allocation." *American Economic Review*, vol. 45 (May), pp. 77–87.
Kamerschen, D. R. (1966). "An Estimation of the Welfare Losses from Monopoly in the American Economy." *Western Economic Journal*, vol. 4 (Summer), pp. 221–36.
Laffer, A. B. (1965). "Vertical Integration by Corporations, 1929–65." *Review of Economics and Statistics*, vol. 51 (February), pp. 91–3.
Posner, R. A. (1975). "The Social Costs of Monopoly and Regulation." *Journal of Political Economy*, vol. 83 (August), pp. 807–27.
Scherer, F. M. (1970). *Industrial Market Structure and Market Performance*. Chicago: Rand McNally.
Schwartzman, D. (1960). "The Burden of Monopoly." *Journal of Political Economy*, vol. 68 (December), pp. 627–30.
Siegfried, J. J. and Tiemann, T. K. (1974). "The Welfare Cost of Monopoly: An Inter-Industry Analysis." *Economic Inquiry*, vol. 12 (June), pp. 190–202.

Spence, M. (1974). "Entry, Capacity, Investment and Oligopolistic Pricing." Technical Report 131, Institute for Mathematical Studies in the Social Sciences, Stanford University.

Stigler, G. J. (1956). "The Statistics of Monopoly and Merger." *Journal of Political Economy*, vol. 64 (February), pp. 33–40.

Tullock, G. (1967). "The Welfare Costs of Tariffs, Monopolies and Theft." *Western Economic Journal*, vol. 5 (June), pp. 224–32.

Walker, J. L. (1974). "Estimating Companies' Rate of Return on Capital Employed." *Economic Trends*, November, pp. xx–xxix.

Wenders, J. L. (1967). "Entry and Monopoly Pricing." *Journal of Political Economy*, vol. 75, pp. 755–60.

Wisecarver, D. (1974). "The Social Costs of Input-Market Distortions." *American Economic Review*, vol. 64 (June), pp. 359–72.

Worcester Jr., D. A. (1969). "Innovations in the calculations of welfare loss to monopoly." *Western, Economic Journal*, vol. 7 (September), pp. 234–43.

—— (1973). "New Estimates of the Welfare Loss to Monopoly: U.S. 1956–69." *Southern Economic Journal*, vol. 40 (October), pp. 234–46.

—— (1975). "On Monopoly Welfare Losses: Comment." *American Economic Review*, vol. 65 (December), pp. 1015–23.

APPENDIX

Data: Definitions and Sources

United States

All data on individual firms with one exception were taken from the COMPUSTAT tape of 1969, and all definitions conform therefore to those given in the COMPUSTAT manual. The numbers in brackets { } refer to the variable numbers assigned on the COMPUSTAT annual industrial file.

The competitive return on capital used in calculating monopoly profits was 0·1197, the geometric mean of the monthly Fisher–Lorie index of returns on the market portfolio between January 1963 to December 1967. The firm's capital was measured as Total Assets/Liabilities and Net Worth less Intangibles (goodwill, patents, etc.). The latter were deducted on the grounds that they largely represent capitalised monopoly rents (see Stigler, 1956; Kamerschen, 1966). Thus, the firm's opportunity cost of capital was estimated as:

$$CC = 0·1197\ (DATA\{6\} - DATA\{33\}).$$

Two estimates of monopoly profits were formed to compute the triangle-type measures. The first is gross profit flow (net income + interest expense + income taxes) less the cost of capital (*CC*).

$$\Pi = DATA\{18\} + DATA\{15\} + DATA\{16\} - CC.$$

The second is the first plus advertising ($A = DATA\{45\}$). For roughly 85 % of the sample firms the COMPUSTAT entry for advertising was missing, however. The product of the firm's Sales ($DATA\{12\}$) and the industry advertising to sales ratio for the firm's industry as given in *Advertising Age* (7 June 1965, pp. 101–3) was substituted for this entry in these cases.

To calculate the ΔW^4 measures, income taxes ($DATA\{16\}$) were subtracted from Π to obtain Π'.

United Kingdom

All the data on individual firms with the exception of advertising has its origin in the data tabulations of the Exchange Telegraph Statistics Service (EXTEL). Most of the relevant data in a summarised form was available in various issues of *The Times Review of Industry and Technology*. In the case of advertising the firm data had to be estimated via a process of aggregating estimates of press and TV advertising of the various products produced by each firm. These data were extracted from various issues of *MEAL* (*Advertisers' Annual Analysis of Media Expenditure*) and, in the case of 1968, from the *Statistical Review of Press and T.V. Advertising* (Legion Publishing Company). *Who Owns Whom* was used in the process of aggregation.

Each firm's capital was measured as total tangible assets less current liabilities (excluding bank loans, overdrafts and future tax). Profit was measured before interest and tax and then adjusted for the estimated cost of capital (taken from Flemming *et al.* 1976).

The Economic Journal, **91** (*June* 1981), 348–363
Printed in Great Britain

MISLEADING CALCULATIONS OF THE SOCIAL COSTS OF MONOPOLY POWER*

It has long been thought that monopoly is 'bad', but only comparatively recently have economists attempted to measure 'how bad'. The first and most influential of such studies (Harberger, 1954) found that the welfare losses attributable to monopoly were surprisingly small – of the order of one tenth of one percent of national income in the United States during the 1920s.

Harberger's work inspired a number of further studies, the latest of which is by Cowling and Mueller (1978)[1]. According to their calculations, 734 large firms in the United States generated welfare losses totalling $15 billion annually over the period 1963–6. This figure represents 13 % of Gross Corporate Product (GCP).[2] General Motors and A T & T lead the list with annual welfare losses of over $1·7 and $1 billion respectively, which together represent over $1\frac{1}{2}$ % of GCP during that period. In the United Kingdom, the top 103 firms generated welfare losses of £719m in the year 1968–9; this represents over 7 % of GCP. More than a quarter of these losses are accounted for by three firms: BP (£83m), Shell (£54m) and BAT (£49m).

In the light of these results, Cowling and Mueller conclude that previous beliefs that the costs of monopoly are insignificant are no longer warranted. Indeed, they suggest that 'the tops of our lists of the largest welfare losses by firm are the logical starting points for intensified enforcement of anti-trust policy'. Elsewhere, Cowling (1978) advocates standing parliamentary committees to provide continuous surveillance of these 'major private centres of economic power'.

How reliable are these various calculations of the cost of monopoly? Previous studies have not lacked critics,[3] hence it is appropriate to begin by examining those modifications adopted by Cowling and Mueller which have not previously been discussed. However, the main purpose of this note is to examine the adequacy of the conceptual framework within which *all* the calculations have been made, and which has tacitly been accepted by all the critics. I shall argue (*a*) that even within the framework of their own model, Cowling and Mueller have overestimated the costs of monopoly in four major respects; (*b*) that the very framework of long-run equilibrium, used by all writers from Harberger onwards, precludes the recognition of profits due to uncertainty and innovation,

* I should like to acknowledge helpful comments from A. Charnes, M. E. Beesley, D. Friedman, I. M. Kirzner, D. S. Lees, A. J. McGuinness, J. McKie, W. D. Reekie, J. Wiseman, B. S. Yamey, two referees and numerous seminar participants.

[1] A reply by Cowling and Mueller to the present paper will be published in the September 1981 issue of the *Economic Journal*.

[2] Gross Corporate Product is a concept reportedly used by the US Department of Commerce in unpublished calculations. It is presumably less than national income, but it is not clear how Cowling and Mueller's results compare to those of previous authors. The calculated welfare losses for the firms they actually examine are of the order of 1 % of national income.

[3] See papers by Bergson, Kamerschen, Schwartzman, Siegfield and Tiemann, Stigler, Wenders, Wisecarver and Worcester, as referred by Cowling and Mueller.

[348]

and wrongly interprets them as due to monopoly; (c) that in consequence all these studies are completely misleading as to the location, extent, duration and costs of monopoly power; and (d) that such studies are therefore quite inappropriate as a basis for public policy.

The ideas presented here are by no means original, and no fresh calculations of the costs of monopoly power are made. Nevertheless, the fact that academic and government economists appear to take the previous studies seriously suggests that the present brief critique may not be out of place, and the alternative approach which is suggested here may help to stimulate more reliable empirical studies.

I. THE STUDY BY HARBERGER

According to textbook economic theory, the main effects of monopoly are to misallocate resources, to reduce aggregate welfare and to redistribute income in favour of monopolists. Assuming that long run average costs are approximately constant, for both firm and industry, Harberger represents the situation as in Fig. 1. If price were set equal to unit cost C (which includes the cost of capital), then output equal to the competitive level Q^* would be demanded and produced. If, instead, a monopolist is able to raise price to P and restrict output to Q, he enjoys a monopoly profit π, given by the rectangle $ABCP$. However, this profit is merely a transfer of wealth from consumers to the monopolist producer. Assuming that we are interested only in the aggregate net value of output, regardless of who obtains it, the net loss to society as a whole is given by the 'welfare triangle' ABE, denoted Δ. This represents the net value (to consumers) of the lost output QQ^* over and above the value of the resources (BEQ^*Q) used to produce it.

To calculate the cost of monopoly in the economy as a whole it is necessary to estimate empirically the size of the welfare triangles Δ for each industry. This involves making assumptions about the magnitudes of profit rates PC (equal to AB) and output restrictions BE. These two magnitudes are related by the elasticity of demand. Harberger calculated average profit rates for 2,046 corporations in 73 industries in 1924–8, which accounted for some 45% of total manufacturing output in the United States, and assumed a unit elastic demand curve for each industry. Grossing up the resulting figures yielded an estimated annual welfare loss of $59m for the manufacturing sector of the United States economy. This represented less than one tenth of one percent of national income, or less than $1·50 for every man, woman and child in the United States at 1953 prices.

Harberger concluded that, although monopoly might be a serious problem in certain industries, the United States economy as a whole was emphatically not an example of 'monopoly capitalism', and for many purposes the entire manufacturing sector of the economy could be treated as competitive.

II. THE STUDY BY COWLING AND MUELLER

Cowling and Mueller (henceforth CM) retain Harberger's partial equilibrium approach, and also his welfare criterion of aggregate net benefits to whomever

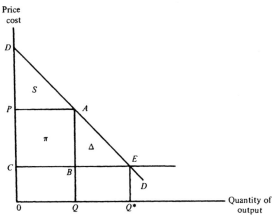

Fig. 1. The conventional welfare loss due to monopoly. *DD*, Demand function; *P*, monopoly price; *C*, unit cost (including cost of capital); π, profit (above normal return on capital); *S*, consumer surplus; Δ, welfare triangle.

they accrue. However, they make four criticisms and modifications of his procedure.

(i) *Pricing and elasticity of demand*

Prices and elasticities of demand are not independent, as Harberger assumed, since a monopolist will take elasticity into account in setting his price. In fact, the area of the welfare triangle will be approximately equal to half the (pre-tax) level of profit, so there is no need to make independent calculations of elasticities.[1]

(ii) *Cost of capital*

Harberger identified the normal competitive profit rate with the average profit rate earned, but the latter already includes an element of monopoly profit. CM therefore use an independent (and lower) estimate of the cost of capital as a yardstick by which to calculate monopoly profit rates. Furthermore, intangible assets such as goodwill and patents are subtracted from capital on the grounds that they largely represent capitalised monopoly rents.

(iii) *Aggregation*

The use of industry profit rates introduces an immediate aggregation bias into the calculation by allowing the high monopoly profits of those firms with the most market power to be offset by the losses of other firms in the industry. Calculations are therefore performed for individual firms rather than for industries.

[1] Briefly, the welfare triangle may be approximated by

$$\Delta \simeq \tfrac{1}{2}(P-C)^2 dQ/dP = (\pi/2)\ \eta(P-C)/P,$$

where η denotes absolute elasticity of demand. A profit-maxising monopolist will set price such that $\eta = P/(P-C)$, hence $\Delta \simeq \pi/2$.

Stephen C. Littlechild

(iv) Cost of gaining and retaining monopoly power

Tullock (1967) and Posner (1975) have pointed out that firms will find it worthwhile to expend resources in order to receive or preserve an inflow of monopoly rents. If necessary, firms in competition for the monopoly will pay up to the whole amount of the prospective monopoly rent. Such expenses are considered social costs because they affect only the distribution of wealth, and not its magnitude. Moreover, to the extent that these expenses enter reported costs, estimates of welfare losses based on remaining profits will underestimate the monopolistic distortions in output.

CM assume that advertising expenditure is 'merely an instrument for securing market power', and make three adjustments to the calculation of welfare loss: advertising expenditure is added (back) to monopoly profit when calculating the welfare triangle, all of advertising expenditure is added to the welfare loss; all of after-tax profits above the competitive cost of capital are used as the estimate of the expenditures incurred by other (unsuccessful) firms to obtain control of monopoly rents.

As a result of these modifications, the social cost due to monopoly is defined for each firm by the computation

$$\frac{\pi}{2} + \frac{A}{2} + A + \pi - T \quad \text{or} \quad \tfrac{3}{2}(\pi + A) - T,$$

where A denotes advertising expenditure, T denotes the tax paid, and π denotes pre-tax book profit adjusted (upwards) by substituting a calculated competitive cost of capital (competitive rate of return times net assets less intangibles) for the firm's interest expenses. *The net effect is that the welfare loss imposed on society by any firm is defined as one and a half times its pre-tax profit (adjusted upwards) plus one and a half times its advertising expenditure less its tax payment.*

These assumptions provide the basis for the estimates reported in the introduction to this paper. Calculations are also provided for the separate components of welfare loss. These may be presented as illustrated in Table 1 to show the proportions of total welfare loss contributed by restrictions in output, advertising expenditure and expenses of rivals in rent-seeking activities. According to these calculations, advertising accounts for nearly two thirds of total welfare loss in the United States, and restrictions in output account for most of the remainder. In the United Kingdom restrictions in output account for over half of total welfare loss, while the other two components account about equally for the other half.[1]

III. THE NATURE OF PROFIT IN LONG RUN EQUILIBRIUM

All authors from Harberger to CM take as their reference point an economy in long-run equilibrium. If this economy were perfectly competitive, no profits or losses would be observed, i.e. rates of return would be precisely equal to the

---

[1] If our interpretation is correct, after-tax profits in the United States amount to only $992/(4,527 \times 2) = 11\%$ of pre-tax profits; the corresponding figure for the United Kingdom is $23 \cdot 5\%$. These figures seem to imply average tax rates which are implausibly high (89% and $76 \cdot 5\%$ respectively).

Table 1

Calculations of Monopoly Welfare Losses

	Restrictions in output $\frac{1}{2}\pi$	Advertising $A + \frac{1}{2}A$	Expenses of rivals $\pi - T$	Total welfare loss
U.S.A. ($m p.a.) 1963/6				
General Motors	1,061	287	433	1,780
AT & T	0	1,025	0	1,025
...	...	...	...	...
Total 734 firms	4,527	9,478	992	14,998
% of total welfare loss	30%	63%	7%	100%
U.K. (£m) 1968/9				
British Petroleum	74	1	8	83
Shell	49	4	0	54
British American Tobacco	27	1	22	49
...	...	...	...	...
Total 102 firms	386	152	182	719
% of total welfare loss	54%	21%	25%	100%

Source. Cowling and Mueller (1978), Table 4, cols. 1, 3–1, 4–3, 4 respectively.

cost of capital. If the economy were not perfectly competitive, positive profits would be observed which would be due to monopoly; strictly speaking, they would be monopoly rents.

In long-run equilibrium, there are essentially only two distinct sources of monopoly:

(1) a grant by the government protecting the recipient(s) from competition by others, e.g. via statutory monopoly, licensed entry, import duties, quotas, patents, etc.

(2) a permanent advantage enjoyed by the incumbent firm(s) over potential entrants, e.g. sole ownership of some necessary input, access to superior techniques of production, an ineradicable belief by customers in the superiority of established products (brand loyalty) etc. (Indivisibilities in capacity and economies of scale, which render new entry uneconomic given a competitive response, may be considered variants of this advantage to incumbents.)

Two other considerations are often mentioned in connection with monopoly profit. (i) The necessity of entering an industry on a large scale, with heavy investments in research and development or advertising, will limit the type of firm which can enter, and reduce the rate at which the entrant can put together the necessary resources. This consideration undoubtedly affects the rate at which (temporary) profits are computed away but the situation is not an equilibrium. (ii) As long as potential entrants expect incumbents to maintain or increase output in the face of entry, and to be better able to withstand the resulting price war, an incumbent firm (or firms) may enjoy positive profits by the use of 'limit pricing'. This situation is an equilibrium, but insofar as it relies on unjustified beliefs it is not a *long-run* equilibrium.

IV. AN EVALUATION OF THE CALCULATIONS BY COWLING AND MUELLER

Our first task is to evaluate CM's calculations within the framework of their model, i.e. assuming that the economy is in long-run equilibrium and that all profits are due to monopoly.

(1) *The welfare triangle*

CM assume that each firm maximises profit, leading to a welfare triangle approximately equal to half the level of profit. In practice, however, firms make extensive use of price discrimination, either directly or via multipart tariffs, tie-in sales, full-line forcing, retrospective discounts, etc. Price discrimination may well lead to increased output, a reduced welfare loss and a welfare triangle which is *less* than half of pre-tax profit.[1] Furthermore, firms may operate in competitive industries but obtain rents on superior assets or resources which they own. Even though reported profits are positive, there is no restriction of output, and consequently no welfare triangle.[2] Finally, for those companies with large export and/or overseas operations (such as BP, Shell and BAT), a restriction of output does not necessarily generate a welfare loss *in the United Kingdom*, and if higher prices generate more foreign exchange this is surely a welfare *gain* to the United Kingdom.

(2) *Advertising*

It is not entirely clear what role advertising plays in long-run equilibrium, but there appear to be two strands of thought in CM's model.

(i) Excess advertising, together with excess capacity and excess product differentiation, is assumed to be a means of dissuading potential entrants via limit pricing (Spence, 1977). We have already indicated that limit-pricing is incompatible with long-run equilibrium.

(ii) Firms are assumed to agree on prices, but advertising is one of the dimensions of non-price competition through which profits are dissipated (Baran and Sweezy, 1966). In this case, the monopoly must be conferred by the government, otherwise new rivals would enter the industry and compete on price alone. However, CM do not restrict their calculations to such monopolies.

CM admit that taking all of advertising expenditure to be a social loss 'takes the extreme view of advertising as merely an instrument for securing market power. To the extent that advertising provides useful information to consumers, this measure overstates the cost of monopoly'. If advertising affects market share, then it must provide information which consumers find relevant. To assume that most advertising is pure waste arguably implies a rather condescending view of ordinary consumers.[3]

---

[1] It is also possible to construct cases in which price discrimination reduces output and welfare (Yamey, 1974).

[2] It has also been argued that, in long-run equilibrium, sole owners of durable assets will not even be able to restrict output and command a monopoly rent (Coase, 1972).

[3] Dixit and Norman (1978) point out that a monopolist may reduce social welfare by advertising to exploit his monopoly power, but the advertising itself is neither the source of the monopoly nor a

(3) *Expenses of monopoly rent-seeking*

CM rightly take into account the notion that firms will spend resources to acquire monopoly rents. Not only the exercise of monopoly, but also the acquisition of it, may involve a welfare loss. But is it reasonable to assume that expenditures incurred by unsuccessful firms will *equal* the monopoly rents earned by successful firms? Posner (1975) argued that this would be so, provided that obtaining a monopoly is itself a perfectly competitive activity, and that the long-run supply of all inputs used to obtain monopolies is perfectly elastic. If the expected monopoly profit were positive, then the competing firms (or new entrants) would hire additional inputs in an effort to secure this profit. Even if the monopoly were obtained by bribery or any other transfer of income, which in itself would not generate a welfare loss, in the long-run resources would be drawn into the activity of becoming the official or supplier who receives such payments, and the use of these resources would constitute a social waste.

Posner does point out, however, that 'the production function of monopolies requires greater attention than I give it in this paper. The assumption of a perfectly elastic long-run supply may fail for an input as foreign to conventional economic analysis as political power' (p. 811). In the conventional neo-classical model, the extent and distribution of resources are assumed given, together with a set of property rights. Initial resource-owners will ultimately receive at least part of monopoly rents, and to this extent achieved post-tax profits are an overstatement of socially wasteful expenditures on acquiring monopoly.

(4) *Accounting conventions*

In calculating economic profit rates, both Harberger and CM adjust the reported profit rates *upwards* on the grounds that book-keeping assets such as patents and goodwill represent a capitalisation of monopoly profits, so that the accounting profit rate is an understatement of the actual profit rate on 'real capital'.

A quite opposite argument has been made. Advertising and research and development expenditures are generally 'expensed', i.e. written off as current expenses in the year in which they are incurred. However, to the extent that they generate income in future years, they should be treated as 'intangible assets', i.e. capitalised then depreciated against subsequent income. This approach will generally show different time-streams of asset values, net income and return on capital.

Several authors have shown that corrected rates of return on capital are significantly different from reported rates in those industries which engage in substantial advertising and R & D (Comanor and Wilson, 1967; Bloch, 1974; Ayanian, 1975; Clarkson, 1977). The balance of the empirical evidence suggests

---

measure of the welfare loss. Advertising may have other socially-useful by-products – e.g. in facilitating the supply of public goods such as newspapers and television programmes, which would otherwise be curtailed or require financial subsidy – but it could also lead to the over-supply of such products.

that corrected rates of return are in fact *lower* (Brozen, 1977a; Reekie and Bhoyrub, 1980). For example, the average corrected return in US pharmaceuticals over 1959–73 is 5·4 percentage points lower than the accounting return, leading Brozen to conclude that 'the higher profitability of the pharmaceutical industry turns out to be, in large part, an accounting illusion'.

To summarise this section, we have assumed with CM that the economy is in long-run equilibrium, and that all profits are due to monopoly. Nevertheless, we have argued that (1) the welfare triangle is probably less than half pre-tax profit; (2) advertising neither dissipates profit where monopoly is not conferred by government nor prevents long-run entry, and on the contrary provides relevant information to consumers; (3) the expenses of monopoly rent-seeking need to be taken into account, but are less than post-tax profits; (4) reported profit rates need to be corrected (downwards) to reflect the intangible assets generated by advertising and R & D. *In sum, even within the context of their own model, CM have overestimated the social cost of monopoly in four major respects.*

V. INADEQUACY OF THE EQUILIBRIUM FRAMEWORK

We now turn from the details of the calculations to the framework within which these calculations are made. The central notion is that of long-run equilibrium. Bergson (1973) has argued that a partial equilibrium approach is misleading, and shown that a general equilibrium approach can generate much higher estimates of the cost of monopoly.[1] In similar vein, a referee of the present paper argues that the welfare triangle cannot possibly be an appropriate measure of the cost of monopoly. For suppose each industry is a profit-maximising monopoly, and all industries face identical demand elasticities, then all industries will have the same markup of price over marginal cost. But this is precisely the competitive equilibrium which maximises welfare: there is no distortion and hence no social cost.[2]

But is an equilibrium approach, whether partial or general, justified at all? Following Harberger, all authors consciously choose data from a period 'reasonably close to a long-run equilibrium period' and then take an average of profits over these periods in order further to minimise transitory components. Yet embarrassing evidence of disequilibrium still remains. In Harberger's study, firms weaving woollens earned an average of only 2·6 % on capital over the five years 1924–8 (compared to an overall sample mean of 10·4 %). CM report that 421 of the 734 firms in their US sample enjoyed positive average pre-tax profits over the period 1963–6 (their Table 2), so that presumably 313 out of 734 – about 40 % of their sample – made losses.

Now as CM remark, 'the presence of firms earning profits less than the competitive norm creates a methodological problem' (p. 731). Presumably these firms did not intend to make losses. They found themselves with costs

---

[1] See, however, the argument by Pearce (1975) that the equilibrium model with monopoly is logically impossible, in that 'no point of general equilibrium with all firms maximising profits can exist'.

[2] It is not clear that this criticism applies to Harberger's calculation, which is based on divergences from mean profit rates.

above competitive levels through bad luck and/or inadequate foresight. By the same token, there were presumably other firms which found themselves with costs below competitive levels through good luck and/or superior foresight. That is, *some firms enjoyed profits above the competitive norm, because of luck and/or fore-sight, and not because of any monopoly power.*

The presence of loss-making firms compelled CM to the following frank admission.

> It is unreasonable to assume that the time periods investigated in Har-berger's study, the others which followed, or our own, are long enough or stable enough so that all firms and industries are in equilibrium ... Some of the companies earning profits above competitive levels in our samples are in temporary disequilibrium, and the welfare losses associated with these firms can be expected to disappear over time. Thus, *our estimates of monopoly profits are a combination of both long-run monopoly profits and short-run disequilibrium profits* [p. 732, italics added].

Similarly, Harberger admits that

> We have actually included in the measurement *not only monopoly mis-allocations but also misallocations coming out of the dynamics of economic growth and development* and all other elements which would cause divergent profit rates to persist for some time even in an effectively competitive economy [p. 84, italics added].

In other words, the empirical calculations made by all these authors are un-able to distinguish the *source and nature* of observed profit rates, nor are they able to estimate their *duration*. As for the long-run equilibrium model which is used as a framework, it can scarcely shed light on these questions because it does not even acknowledge the problem! Within this model, as remarked in section III, all profits are necessarily permanent monopoly profits: there is no such thing as a 'temporary profit'.

Furthermore, in the long-run equilibrium model, *all profits necessarily imply a welfare loss.* There is no scope for profits which might be harmless, let alone any scope for profits to play a socially beneficial role in the operation of the economy. Thus *the very choice of a long-run equilibrium framework within which to analyse monopoly misinterprets the nature of profits, overestimates the extent of monopoly power, and thereby overestimates the social cost of monopoly.* As a result of this inappropriate framework, retailers such as Great Universal Stores, Marks & Spencers and F. W. Wool-worth, who have proved successful in one of the most actively competitive industries in the United Kingdom, are implausibly held responsible for welfare losses totalling £56m in 1968/9.

VI. THE INTRODUCTION OF UNCERTAINTY AND INNOVATION

In order adequately to analyse the nature and extent of monopoly power, it is necessary to employ a model of the economy which allows above-average rates of return to be derived from sources other than monopoly. These alternative sources are twofold:

(1) the occurrence of unexpected events, whether generated by 'nature' or the unanticipated actions of other market participants, which may augment intended profits or convert them into losses;

(2) differences between firms in the ability to create or notice profitable opportunities that are, in principle, available to anyone.

Thus, the rate of return obtained by any company actually comprises three elements: monopoly rent, 'windfall' gains and losses, and 'entrepreneurial' profit.[1]

In a risky environment, not all firms will succeed. Even if investment in an industry is carried forward to the point where the return expected ex ante is equal to the cost of capital (i.e. to the competitive level), the results achieved ex post will show that some firms obtained an above-average return and others a below-average return. But here, an above-average return does not imply any welfare loss. To select only the successful firms, and to assume that their above-average returns represent monopoly profit, with a corresponding welfare loss, would be a blatant error. Yet this is precisely what CM have done, by carrying out their calculations in terms of firms rather than industries (as Harberger did), and ignoring the losses made by unsuccessful firms.[2]

Furthermore, if certain industries are riskier than others, the companies operating therein will need to pay a 'risk premium' to attract capital. This premium is presumably reflected to some extent in the interest expenses reported in the company's books, but the company will also need to earn higher rates of return in order to pay higher dividends. Not only do CM not adjust rates of return for the risk premium, they in fact substitute a common cost of capital for a company's actual interest payments, and thereby misinterpret the costs of risk as monopoly profit.

VII. COMPETITION AS AN ENTREPRENEURIAL PROCESS

The notion of perfect competition as a static equilibrium state is a relatively recent development in economics. For Adam Smith and the classical writers, competition was a process of rivalry taking place over time (McNulty 1967). This latter view of competition was maintained and developed by members of the 'Austrian School'.[3] A similar approach has also been used by other authors in recent empirical work.[4]

As is well known, Schumpeter saw competition as 'a perennial gale of creative destruction'. Entrepreneurial profits can be earned by creativity and superior foresight, by being 'first in the field'. However, a profitable firm is always at the mercy of rivals attempting to develop new and better products. In the absence of artificial restrictions, there is always a tendency for entrepreneurial profits to be competed away.

[1] It might be argued that entrepreneurial profits could be attributed to monopoly if entrepreneurial ability were regarded as a factor of production in limited supply; for an argument against this, see Kirzner (1979, chapters 9, 10; 1980, pp. 10–2).

[2] For more extensive discussion and numerical examples, see Mancke (1974) and Brozen (1977b).

[3] Cf. Schumpeter (1950), von Mises (1949), Hayek (1948), Kirzner (1973, 1979).

[4] Cf. Alchian and Allen (1974), Brozen (1970), Demsetz (1973). For an exposition and integration of Austrian and other models of the competitive process see Littlechild (1978) or Reekie (1979).

With this idea of a competitive process in mind, we can reinterpret Fig. 1 to analyse the behaviour of an entrepreneur who discovers a new product before the rest of the market realises its potential. Assume he charges a monopoly price P, since for the moment he is the sole seller. It is true that he is restricting output compared to what he could produce, or compared to what would be produced if all his rivals shared his own insight. But they do *not* share his insight; this is not the relevant alternative. For the time being *the relevant alternative to his action is no product at all*. It would therefore be inappropriate to characterise his action as generating a social loss given by the welfare triangle Δ. On the contrary, *his action generates a social gain given by his own entrepreneurial profit π plus the consumer surplus S.*[1]

This social gain is enjoyed from the time at which the entrepreneur discovers and exploits the new product until the time at which the market would other-wise have done so. However, it is likely that the action of the first entrepreneur will stimulate the market to an earlier awareness of the situation, i.e. rivals will step in and compete the price down to cost. Insofar as entrepreneurial profit π is converted to consumer surplus, this is merely a transfer of income. However, there is a *further* social gain, namely, the *earlier* enjoyment of consumer surplus on output QQ^*, which of course is equal in value to the area of the welfare triangle Δ.

It may be argued, along Tullock–Posner lines, that the lure of entrepreneurial profits will stimulate other firms to spend resources in order to achieve such insights (e.g. via market research), and that such use of resources constitutes a social waste which will fully offset any social gains. There are at least four reasons (in addition to the property rights consideration of section IV. 3) why this argument is untenable here. (i) Firms typically differ in ability (there is not perfect competition) so the more efficient firms will not need to expend re-sources equal to prospective profits in order to match the efforts of rivals. (ii) If resources have to be spent in order to clarify the nature of profit opportunities, this merely pushes back the entrepreneurial element to an earlier stage (e.g. to the location of profitable opportunities for engaging in market research) (Kirzner, 1973, pp. 65–9). Differences in entrepreneurial ability at this earlier stage provide a further reason why successful firms can gain their prize without the expenditure of resources equal to the value of prospective profit – indeed, in the extreme case, an entrepreneur may achieve his innovation before his potential rivals realise that market research in that area would have been worth-while. (iii) Just as copying an existing innovation generates social benefits from the earlier enjoyment of lower prices, so too the very process of competing to make the innovation may bring forward the time of discovery and initial pro-duction, with corresponding welfare gains. (iv) Even if resources are expended to the value of private profit, the social benefits of innovation include, in addition, the consumer surplus which initially accompanies this profit and subsequently replaces it.

---

[1] For simplicity of exposition, we ignore the effects of introducing the new product on the demand for other products.

VIII. MONOPOLY AND THE COMPETITIVE PROCESS

Monopoly can still exist in the competitive process, deriving either from government protection or from ownership of superior resources. In the former case, rivals are legally prevented from providing specified products, while in the latter case they do not have access to equally effective techniques of production. As in the equilibrium model, the effect is to confer a monopoly rent. Two points of difference should be emphasised, however.

In the static equilibrium model, monopoly is permanent. There are no forces acting within the model to reduce the loss which it induces. In the dynamic process model, by contrast, there is both opportunity and incentive to discover new products or techniques which might *bypass* the monopoly, thereby reducing over time the extent of welfare loss. The market process thus continues *around* the monopoly, rather than being eliminated by it. (And of course the monopolist himself will simultaneously be searching for better ways to apply or extend his monopoly.) The loss imposed by a monopoly will thus depend crucially upon its scope, and will be reflected not merely by the restriction in current output, but by the restriction in access by others to potential but as yet undiscovered products and techniques. For this reason, a statutory monopoly which prohibits all potential rivals in some field is likely to be more onerous than a monopoly based on sole ownership of some input, since alternative techniques of production may render than input no longer crucial.[1]

Second, firms may use resources in order to acquire or retain a monopoly rent. But, just as with entrepreneurial profit, it does not follow that the total value of these expended resources is equal to monopoly rent, since potential monopolists differ in ability and alertness. Similarly, competition to acquire a monopoly may bring forward the date of producing the monopoly product; it may therefore be socially beneficial to *create* certain monopolies. (Indeed, this is the usual defence for patents.)

Finally, it is worth remarking that concepts such as limit pricing, predatory pricing and related phenomena, which are awkward to analyse in terms of long-run equilibrium, fit naturally into a framework of competitive process. If potential entrants are unsure about future demand and cost conditions, or apprehensive about the likely reactions of incumbents, they may delay entry (or use a safer alternative route such as merger). Incumbents may (in principle) be able to influence these decisions of entrants, at least temporarily. By the same token, however, the prospect of being able to delay subsequent entrants is an added incentive to be first in the field.

IX. EVIDENCE FOR THE COMPETITIVE PROCESS

If high rates of return can result from monopoly rent, windfall gains or entrepreneurial profit, how far, in practice, is it possible to ascertain the precise proportions of these three ingredients?

[1] An excellent example is the potential development of radio beams from satellites direct to homes and offices, which would make telephone exchanges obsolete, thereby removing the local monopoly currently enjoyed by the telephone company.

Detailed case-studies of particular firms could perhaps provide some insights e.g. by identifying areas where the firm enjoys some government protection from competition, by contrasting plans and achieved results, by comparing its costs of production with those of rivals, etc. (Thus, AT & T probably earned substantial monopoly rents from its position protected by the Federal Communications Commission, BP and Shell probably received larger windfall gains than companies in less risky industries, etc.)

Taking a broader view of the unregulated sector of the economy as a whole, there is accumulating evidence that monopoly rents are considerably less important than windfall gains and entrepreneurial profits.

It was once widely believed by economists that highly concentrated industries allowed explicit or implicit collusion, which in turn led to higher profit rates. The original evidence by Bain (1951), who himself was rather cautious, is now known to be in error (Brozen, 1971). Recent empirical work has shown that the effect of concentration on profits has at best been overstated, and may be negligible (Brozen, 1970, 1977*b*; Demsetz, 1973, 1974; Peltzman, 1977; Carter, 1978; and for the United Kingdom, Hart and Clarke, 1980). The evidence shows that industries with relatively high rates of return in one year tend to descend towards a middle rank in later years, whereas those with low returns tend to ascend (Brozen, 1970, 1977*b*). Additional resources are systematically attracted into high-return industries, causing capacity and supply to rise and prices and profits to fall. This would not be the case if high rates of return were based on monopoly power.

Secondly, the fact that, even within industries, firms exhibit 'higgledy-piggledy growth' (Little and Rayner, 1978; Prais, 1976) shows that success in the past, whether due to luck or foresight, does not guarantee success in the future. Mere size does not convey monopoly power.[1]

Finally, the empirical evidence suggests that advertising facilitates entry and leads to reductions in price i.e. it is primarily a means of competing rather than a means of preventing competition (Benham, 1972; Brozen, 1974).[2]

X. THE ANALYSIS OF POLICY

In the equilibrium framework the current situation is evaluated against the ideal benchmark of perfect competition. Profit is assumed due to monopoly, and as such is not only wasteful in itself but also the cause of waste in other firms. The task of public policy is therefore to eliminate profit (e.g. by controlling mergers or prices) – although, as CM rather belatedly acknowledged, 'any public policy has its own sets of costs and inefficiencies ... Thus it might be that any alternative for dealing with existing monopoly power would involve higher costs than the monopolies themselves create' (p. 746).

In the competitive process framework, there is no such ideal benchmark. One

---

[1] Larger firms tend to earn higher profit rates, but it is more plausible to interpret size as the *consequence*, rather than the *cause*, of profits. (Demsetz 1973).

[2] For contrary views on concentration and advertising, see papers by Weiss and Mann in Goldschmid (1974).

process is superior to another if, ceteris paribus, new products and techniques are discovered, exploited and diffused sooner. But in a world in which the number of potential discoveries is infinite, there is no 'soonest' time at which they can be made. The 'ideal benchmark' approach must therefore be abandoned in favour of a 'comparative institutions' approach (Demsetz, 1969), i.e. a comparison of the likely path of the market process as a result of alternative available government policies.

This point may be briefly illustrated. With respect to monopoly stemming from government-imposed barriers to entry (e.g. the statutory monopolies enjoyed by many nationalised industries, patent laws, import duties and quotas, 'self-regulation' based on government charters, etc.), the practical question is whether the benefits so obtained (e.g. as a result of diverted investment and output, reduced uncertainty, higher quality, income redistribution, etc.) are sufficient to offset the costs of intervention (e.g. higher prices, less initiative, slower response to change, expenses of intervention, etc.). With respect to monopoly stemming from sole ownership of necessary inputs, and 'barriers to entry' stemming from the conduct of firms (e.g. limit pricing, predatory pricing, 'tying' arrangements, restrictive practices, etc.), the relevant question is whether government action to remove such 'barriers' will in fact stimulate entry by previously thwarted firms, without at the same time reducing the ability of existing firms to cope with their uncertain and ever-changing environments, and without reducing the incentives to create, notice and exploit opportunities arising in future (Schumpeter, 1950; Richardson, 1960).[1]

XI. CONCLUSIONS

The recent work by Professors Cowling and Mueller is the latest in a series of papers designed to extend or reappraise the pioneering attempt by Harberger to measure the welfare loss due to monopoly. The principle innovation introduced by CM is a measurement of the waste of resources employed in trying to gain or retain a monopoly position. In principle, this element ought to be included. However, we have argued that, even within the context of the model employed by CM, there are serious deficiencies in the calculation of this and other components of welfare loss, so that the resulting figures are quite unreliable as an estimate of the social cost of monopoly (but surely a serious overestimate).

More importantly, we have further argued that the choice by all these authors of a long-run equilibrium framework in which to analyse monopoly is itself a source of bias and the cause of major difficulties. Within this framework, *all* profit is due to monopoly, and necessarily implies a serious welfare loss. The equilibrium model precludes any neutral or socially beneficial interpretation of profit.

An alternative model of competition as a continuing process of rivalry and

---

[1] Thus, the Petrol Report of the Monopolies and Mergers Commission (1979) found that selective price support did restrict and distort competition but that any attempts to control the practice would have even more adverse effects (due to administrative costs and delays and the facilitation of collusion).

adjustment in an uncertain environment was then sketched out. Within this framework, windfall gains and losses result from unanticipated shifts in demand and cost conditions, while creativity and alertness generate entrepreneurial profits which reflect innovation and increased co-ordination rather than monopoly. Empirical evidence concerning 'higgledy-piggledy growth' and the tendency of extreme profit rates to return over time to the mean suggests that these two sources of profit are more important than monopoly power. Finally, this model of competition as a process suggests that the attention of policy makers be directed away from the size of firms and concentration of industries to the conditions of entry into those industries. If one is concerned to promote competition, the obvious starting point is the wide variety of government restrictions which serve to protect vested interest groups. A policy of systematically attempting to eliminate profit, regardless of its source, is less likely to stimulate the competitive process than to destroy it.

University of Birmingham   S. C. LITTLECHILD

Date of receipt of final typescript: December 1980

REFERENCES

Alchian, A. A. and Allen, W. R. (1974). *University Economics*, 3rd ed. London: Prentice-Hall.
Ayanian, R. (1975). 'Advertising and rate of return.' *Journal of Law and Economics*, vol. 18, no. 2 (October), pp. 479–506.
Bain, J. S. (1951). 'Relation of profit rate to industry concentration: American manufacturing 1936–40.' *Quarterly Journal of Economics*, vol. 65, p. 293.
Baran, P. and Sweezy, P. (1966). *Monopoly Capital*. New York: Monthly Review Press.
Benham, L. (1972). 'The effect of advertising on the price of eyeglasses.' *Journal of Law and Economics*, vol. 15, no. 2 (October), pp. 337–52.
Bergson, A. (1973). 'On monopoly welfare losses.' *American Economic Review*, vol. 63 (December), pp. 853–70.
Bloch, H. (1974). 'Advertising and profitability: a reappraisal.' *Journal of Political Economy*, vol. 82, no. 2, part 1.
Brozen, Y. (1970). 'The antitrust-task force deconcentration recommendation', *Journal of Law and Economics*, vol. 13, no. 2 (October).
—— (1971). 'Bain's concentration and rates of return.' *Journal of Law and Economics*, vol. 14, no. 2 (October), pp. 351–70.
—— (1974). 'Entry barriers: advertising and product differentiation.' In Goldschmid (1974), pp. 115–37.
—— (1977a). *Foreword* to Clarkson (1977).
—— (1977b). 'The concentration–collusion doctrine.' *Antitrust Law Journal*, vol. 4, no. 3 (summer), pp. 826–62.
Carter, J. R. (1978). 'Collusion, efficiency, and antitrust.' *The Journal of Law and Economics*, vol. 21 (2) (October), pp. 435–44.
Clarkson, K. W. (1977). *Intangible Capital and Rates of Return*, American Enterprise Institute, Washington.
Comanor, W. S. and Wilson, T. S. (1967). 'Advertising, market structure and performance.' *Review of Economics and Statistics*, vol. 49, pp. 423–40.
Coase, R. H. (1972). 'Durability and monopoly'. *Journal of Law and Economics*, vol. 15, no. 1, (April), pp. 143–50.
Cowling, K. (1978). 'Monopolies and mergers policy: a view on the Green Paper.' University of Warwick (August).
—— and Mueller, D. C. (1978). 'The social costs of monopoly power,' ECONOMIC JOURNAL, vol. 88, (December), pp. 727–48.
Demsetz, H. (1969). 'Information and efficiency: another viewpoint'. *Journal of Law and Economics*, vol. 12, no. 1 (April), pp. 1–22.
—— (1973). 'Industry structure, market rivalry and public policy.' *Journal of Law and Economics*, vol. 16, no. 1 (April), pp. 1–10.
—— (1974). 'Two systems of belief about monopoly.' In Goldschmid (1974), pp. 164–84.

Dixit, A. and Norman, V. (1978). 'Advertising and welfare.' *Bell Journal of Economics*, vol. 9, no. 1 (spring), pp. 1–17.

Goldschmid, H. J. *et al.* (eds) (1974). *Industrial Concentration: The New Learning* Boston: Little, Brown.

Harberger, A. C. (1954). 'Monopoly and resource allocation.' *American Economic Review, Proceedings*, vol. 44 (May), pp. 73–87.

Hart, P. E. and Clarke, R. (1980). *Concentration in British Industry 1935–75*. Cambridge University Press (National Institute of Economic and Social Research, Occasional Papers, 32.)

Hayek, F. A. (1948) 'The meaning of competition.' In *Individualism and Economic Order*. Chicago: University of Chicago Press.

Kirzner, I. M. (1973). *Competition and Entrepreneurship*. Chicago: University of Chicago Press.

—— (1975). 'The social costs of monopoly: a comment.' Mimeo, New York University.

—— (1979) *Perception, Opportunity and Profit*. Chicago: University of Chicago Press.

—— (1980). 'The primacy of entrepreneurial discovery.' In *The Prime Mover of Progress* (ed. A. Seldon), pp. 3–28. London: Institute of Economic Affairs.

Little, I. M. D. and Rayner, A. C. (1978). *Higgledy Piggledy Growth Again: Investigation of the Predictability of Company Earnings in the U.K. 1951–1961*. Kelly.

Littlechild, S. C. (1978). *The Fallacy of the Mixed Economy*. Hobart Paper no. 80 (June). London: Institute of Economic Affairs.

Mancke, R. B. (1974). 'Interfirm profitability differences.' *The Quarterly Journal of Economics*. vol. 88, no. 2 (May), pp. 181–94.

McNulty, P. J. (1967). 'A note on the history of perfect competition.' *Journal of Political Economy*, vol. 75 (August).

Mises, L. von (1949). *Human Action*, 1st ed. Chicago: Henry Regnery. (3rd rev. ed. 1963).

Monopolies and Mergers Commission (1979). *Petrol* Cmnd. 7433. London: HMSO (January).

Pearce, I. F. (1975). 'Monopolistic competition and general equilibrium.' In *Current Economic Problems*. (ed. M. Parkin and A. R. Nobay) Cambridge University Press.

Peltzman, S. (1977). 'The gains and losses from industrial concentration.' *Journal of Law and Economics*, vol. 20, no. 2, (October), pp. 229–64.

Posner, R. A. (1975). 'The social costs of monopoly and regulation.' *Journal of Political Economy*, vol. 83 (August), pp. 807–27.

Prais, S. (1976). *The Evolution of Giant Firms in Britain: A Study of the Growth of Concentration in Manufacturing Industry in Britain, 1909–1970*. Cambridge University Press.

Reekie, W. Duncan (1979). *Industry, Prices and Markets*. Oxford: Philip Allan.

—— and Bhoyrub, P. (1980). 'Profitability and intangible assets – Another look at advertising and entry barriers.' Discussion Paper.

Richardson, G. B. (1960). *Information and Investment*. Oxford University Press.

Schumpeter, J. A. (1950). *Capitalism, Socialism and Democracy*, 3rd ed. New York: Harper & Row.

Spence, A. M. (1977). 'Entry, capacity, investment and oligopolistic pricing.' *Bell Journal of Economics*, vol. 8, no. 2 (Autumn), pp. 534–44.

Tullock, G. (1967). 'The welfare costs of tariffs, monopolies and theft.' *Western Economic Journal*, vol. 5 (June), pp. 224–32.

Yamey, B. (1974). 'Monopolistic price discrimination and economic welfare.' *Journal of Law and Economics*. vol. 17, no. 2 (1974), pp. 377–80.

Declining Industries and Political-Support Protectionist Motives

By Arye L. Hillman*

Protection provided to declining industries is generally explained as founded in the judgement that specific factors, which do not have the opportunities for adjustment available to mobile factors,[1] ought be cushioned against income losses due to falls in the world price of their industry's output. The argument is that moral hazard causes private insurance markets for income maintenance to fail, so obligating governments to provide social insurance against income losses; or, alternatively, some form of altruistic notion of fairness is viewed as underlying protection of individuals' incomes in face of exogenous change. Whether the social insurance or altruism view is taken, the authorities are seen as responding to *social justice* considerations in providing industries adversely affected by changes in world prices with compensating protection, at least temporarily to ease difficulties in adjustment—although the industry itself may influence the level and timing of protection by lobbying to make its plight known.[2]

This paper presents an alternative to social justice perspectives on declining industry protection. Protective responses for declining industries are considered when the authorities, rather than seeking social welfare objectives, pursue their own self-interest motives to maximize political support.[3]

An adaptation of the Stigler-Peltzman regulatory model is used herein to describe a political support equilibrium for a protected industry. Section I reviews their model for background purposes, and reinterprets the gainers and losers from government intervention in a Ricardo-Viner setting. Section II introduces a distinction in the evocation of political-support response between changes in the gainers' and losers' welfare that derive from administrative decisions and changes that are the consequence of exogenous market forces. The authorities' self-interest response to declines in the world price of an industry's output is then established. Section III presents a brief concluding summary and contrasts social justice perspectives on declining industry protection with the outcome when political self-interest motives underly intervention.

I. Introduction

A. *Background: The Stigler-Peltzman Regulatory Model*

Let us begin with a background review of the Stigler-Peltzman model of regulation.

*Department of economics, Bar Ilan University, Israel, and Centre of Policy Studies, Monash University, Australia. I am grateful to Peter Hartley and Chris Trengove for observations which prompted a revision of a previous draft of this paper.

[1] The specific mobile-factor distinction is emphasized by the Ricardo-Viner model of international trade: see Ronald Jones (1971, 1975); Wolfgang Mayer; Michael Mussa; Roy Ruffin and Jones; Peter Neary; David Burgess.

[2] See Peter Gray (1973, 1975) for an example of a social justice plea for protection for declining industries, and also the discussion of Gray's plea by Geoffrey Wood, and myself. Max Corden (1974, pp. 109–10) suggests that a social objective of maintaining individuals' incomes gives rise to a conservative social welfare function which explains provision of protection to "senescent" (i.e., declining) industries. On social insurance aspects, see Corden (1974, p. 321) and myself (1977, p. 159). Parallels with adjustment assistance are considered by James Cassing (1980). An overview of various social choice considerations affecting protection decisions is provided by Robert Baldwin. This view places the protection decision in the general framework of social choice theory, as reviewed by Dennis Mueller.

[3] There is now a considerable literature, both theoretical and empirical, examining political support motives for protection: see, for example, Jonathan Pincus (1975, 1977), Richard Caves, G. K. Helleiner, William Brock and Steven Magee, Ronald Saunders, Kym Anderson, and Baldwin. Relatedly, on governments' protectionist responses to rent and revenue-seeking overtures of private agents, see Anne Krueger, and Jagdish Bhagwati and T. N. Srinivasan. More generally, various aspects of rent-seeking—and rent-avoiding—behavior are considered in James Buchanan, Robert Tollison, and Gordon Tullock.

Arye L. Hillman

This model is concerned with establishing the effects of political-support motives on the determination of regulated prices. The price of a particular industry's output derives from maximization by the authorities of a political support function for that industry,[4]

$$(1) \qquad \tilde{M}(P) = M[\Pi(P), P],$$

where P is price and $\Pi(P)$ is the industry's profit function. Higher industry profits elicit greater political support from industry-specific interests, which is reflected in $M_\Pi > 0$, but consumers are antagonized by higher prices, so $M_P < 0$.

The function $M[\Pi, P]$ is a strictly quasiconcave preference function exhibiting diminishing marginal industry support as profits are increased by increases in the regulated price and increasing marginal consumer antagonism as consumers' welfare is decreased, so $M_{\Pi\Pi} < 0$ and $M_{PP} < 0$. If consumers' antagonism towards the authorities increases the more the industry has already benefited from higher prices, there is an envy effect reflected in $M_{\Pi P} < 0$.[5]

The authorities use their regulatory powers to maximize political support by choosing the industry's price to satisfy

$$(2) \qquad \tilde{M}_P = M_\Pi \Pi_P + M_P = 0,$$

so balancing at the margin support from industry-specific interests who favor price rises against political disfavor due to consumer opposition.

The regulatory price which solves (2) to yield a maximum for $\tilde{M}(P)$ lies between the profit-maximizing and competitive prices. That the regulated price is less than the monopolistic price is indicated by rearrangement of terms in (2) to establish $\Pi_P = -M_P/M_\Pi > 0$;[6] and, although the authorities are ultimately accountable to the electorate, consumers fail to enforce a competitive price, because voting takes place on

packages of issues, and because of the different transactions costs incurred by industry-specific interests and consumers-at-large in organizing to influence a particular industry's price.[7]

B. *The Gains to Industry-Specific Interests*

The Stigler-Peltzman model protrays the regulatory gains to industry-specific interests in terms of noncompetitively sustained supernormal profits earned by firms in the industry. However, industry rewards and political support coalitions can also be viewed in the Ricardo-Viner general equilibrium setting of international trade theory.[8] In that setting, output is produced by competitive firms employing mobile and industry-specific factors. Mobile factors receive a competitive return, whereas industry-specific factors receive residual rents. Individuals whose incomes derive from ownership of industry-specific factors unambiguously benefit from protection of their industry. Mobile factors may or may not support protection for a particular industry, although either way with many commodities the stake of mobile factors in the outcome of a change in protection in any one industry will generally tend to be small. Factors specific to industries other than those receiving an increase in protection lose, and hence oppose protection of any industry but their own.[9]

---

[4]All functions in this paper are continuous and differentiable.

[5]Peltzman assumes $M_{\Pi P} = 0$. More generally, we can assume $M_{\Pi P} \leq 0$.

[6]That is, in the neighborhood of the political-support equilibrium, profits would be increased by further increases in price.

[7]Such a compromise between the outcomes sought by industry-specific interests and consumers supposes, of course, that neither the industry nor consumers have sufficient political leverage to enable either to dominate entirely the authorities' regulatory response. Free-rider problems limit different industries' abilities to organize a cohesive industry front (see Stigler, 1974), but impose a much more constraining influence in attempts to secure the participation of individual consumers in lobbying activities directed against any particular industry.

[8]Of course, the Heckscher-Ohlin model wherein all factors are mobile also implies anti- and pro-trade coalitions; see, for example, Cassing (1981). But this model fails to encompass the specific factors which are central to any discussion of declining industry protection. See Magee for empirical confirmation of the pertinence of the Ricardo-Viner model, in contrast to the longer-run view of the Heckscher-Ohlin model, in explaining individuals' stances on protection and free trade.

[9]See in particular Jones (1975), and Anderson (appendix). Ruffin and Jones propose that there is a presumption that protection will tend to harm mobile fac-

1182   *THE AMERICAN ECONOMIC REVIEW*   *DECEMBER 1982*

Whether beneficiaries of protection are viewed as firms earning supernormal profits, or as individuals deriving income from the rents secured by industry-specific factors, entry barriers are of some importance.

Taking the Stigler-Peltzman view of firms as the beneficiaries of the authorities' intervention, and supernormal profits as the measure of gain to industry-specific interests, either entry barriers existing in the absence of regulation persist to sustain supernormal profits in the regulatory equilibrium or, alternatively, the industry may have been initially competitive, in which case entry barriers must have been erected in conjunction with regulation to prevent the dissipation of profits by new entrants. Analogous considerations apply to the dissipation of rents of industry-specific factors: although, at a point in time, industry-specific factors are inelastically supplied, over time, the availability of such factors may be augmented, so reducing factor rents. And, of course, if rents are dissipated, so is political support.[10]

A *declining* industry has, however, the particular characteristic that entry is unattractive. Hence the problem of ensuring that incumbent industry-specific interests continue to benefit from protection is mitigated. But, of course, unattractiveness of entry persists only if protection does not reverse the industry's decline.[11]

II. Political-Support Protectionist Responses

A. *Displacement of Equilibrium by a Fall in the World Price*

Figure 1 depicts an import-competing industry protected in an initial equilibrium at world price P_1^* by a nonprohibitive tariff. Adopting a Ricardo-Viner setting, assume

---

tors. The informational requirements for identifying gainers and losers become more stringent and possible outcomes more varied when allowance is made for the presence of intermediate goods: see Burgess.

[10]See Dwight Lee and Daniel Orr.

[11]Baldwin suggests unattractiveness of entry as a reason why declining industries are more amenable to benefit from politically motivated tariff protection, and hence more inclined to be granted protection than industries which are expanding.

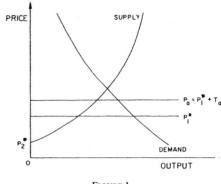

FIGURE 1

competition and individuals earning income from ownership of industry-specific factors as beneficiaries of protection. The industry's (general equilibrium) supply function exhibits increasing marginal cost because of diminishing marginal factor productivity. Suppose the tariff to have been determined in accord with the authorities' political-support motives. With domestic price as the sum of the exogenous world price of industry output and the (specific) tariff T, so that

$$(3) \qquad P = P^* + T,$$

the particular political-support maximizing domestic price P_a when the world price is P_1^* is sustained by a tariff T_a.

Now let the world price of the industry's output decline below P_1^*—and suppose that the world price continues to decline.

B. *Domestic Price as the Indicator of Political-Support Response*

Suppose that it were so as assumed in the Stigler-Peltzman regulatory model that political support depended upon gainers' and losers' welfare levels as determined by the level of domestic industry price in itself. Then the predicted political self-interest response of the authorities to a decrease in the world price of the industry's output would be an exactly offsetting increase in the tariff to maintain the previously prevailing domestic

Arye L. Hillman

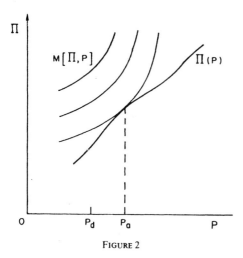

FIGURE 2

price. In terms of Figure 2,[12] a fall in the world price that, for a given tariff, reduces the domestic price to P_d would simply lead the authorities to increase the tariff so as to return the domestic price to the previous political-support maximizing price P_a; for with the given political-support and industry profit functions $\tilde{M}(P)$ and $\Pi(P)$, this is the domestic price which continues to yield maximal political support.[13] That P_a is constant in these circumstances is readily confirmed by totally differentiating the political support equilibrium condition (2) to obtain

(4)　　　$dT/dP^* = -\tilde{M}_{PP^*}/\tilde{M}_{PP}.$

---

[12] In the Stigler-Peltzman regulatory model, industry profits are assumed strictly concave in price and to attain a unique maximum. In the setting of the Ricardo-Viner model, industry-specific factors' real rentals are, on the other hand, strictly increasing in the price of their industry's output, as depicted in Figure 2. While an analogous course to assuming profits concave in output price is to assume factors' real rentals similarly concave, it suffices to assume as in Figure 2 that $\tilde{M}(P)$ attains a unique global maximum on $\Pi(P)$.

[13] Given competition, the tariff can of course sustain no more than the autarkic price, but if as in the Stigler-Peltzman regulatory model there may be noncompetitive firms earning monopoly profits, then the tariff remains an effective instrument beyond the autarkic price. See Gideon Fishelson and myself on the limits to protection which a tariff can provide when there is domestic monopoly.

Via equation (3), $\tilde{M}_{PP^*}$ and $\tilde{M}_{PP}$ are identical, which means (4) implies the equal offset tariff-adjustment rule

(5)　　　　　$dT = -dP^*.$

C. Asymmetric Administrative and Market Effects on Political Support

The tariff-adjustment rule (5) maintains a static domestic price invariant to changes in the world price. However, the assumption underlying this rule that political support is independent of the constituent components of domestic price fails to encompass an important asymmetry in agents' perceptions of politically imposed change.

Consider industry-specific interests. They gain as a consequence of increases in the domestic price of their industry's output. But should their welfare have increased because exogenous influences in the world market have led to an increase in the world price of their industry's output, there is no reason to expect these interests to be behoving to the domestic tariff-setting authority for the ensuing gain. Nor could the tariff-setting authority be blamed for losses suffered by industry-specific interests because of exogenous falls in the world price. On the other hand, industry-specific interests *will* be appreciative of increases in their incomes that are due to increased protection, and be disparaging of reductions in domestic price that have occurred because of administrative decisions to reduce previous levels of protection.

The same considerations apply as well to consumers. While they may with justification blame the authorities for welfare losses due to domestic price rises that have been the consequence of tariff increases, they could not harbor ill will against the authorities for losses incurred because the domestic price of an industry's output has risen due to an increase in the world price—an event for which the local tariff-setting authorities can be assigned no responsibility.

Suppose, therefore, that the political support function reflects the constituent components of industry price, with agents responsive in their political support only to gains and losses that are due to the authorities' acting to cause the domestic price to deviate from the world price via tariff intervention. Let $\Pi(P, P^*)$ denote the *increase* in industry-specific returns due to the domestic price being maintained at P when the world price is P^*. Clearly, $\Pi_P > 0$ and $\Pi_{P^*} < 0$. And let $V(P, P^*)$ measure the utility derived by agents harmed by the tariff when the domestic price is P, relative to the welfare level that would obtain were there no tariff and were the domestic price given by the world price P^*, where then $V_P < 0$ and $V_{P^*} > 0$. With these functions forming the basis of agents' political response, the political support function is, in contrast to the Stigler-Peltzman function (1),

$$(6) \quad \tilde{M}(P, P^*) = M[\Pi(P, P^*), V(P, P^*)].$$

The condition describing the authorities' political-support maximizing choice of domestic price is

$$(7) \qquad \tilde{M}_P = M_\Pi \Pi_P + M_V V_P = 0.$$

This has the same interpretation of balance of political support at the margin as (2).

With the authorities choosing the tariff that sustains the domestic price given by (7), now consider a change in the world price. The response of domestic price is given by

$$(8) \qquad dP/dP^* = -\tilde{M}_{PP^*}/\tilde{M}_{PP}.$$

Expansion of (7) yields

$$(9) \quad \tilde{M}_{PP} = \Pi_{PP}M_\Pi + \Pi_P^2 M_{\Pi\Pi}$$
$$+ V_{PP}M_V + V_P^2 M_{VV} + 2\Pi_P V_P M_{V\Pi};$$

$$(10) \quad \tilde{M}_{PP^*} = \Pi_P \Pi_{P^*} M_{\Pi\Pi}$$
$$+ V_P V_{P^*} M_{VV} + 2\Pi_{P^*} V_{P^*} M_{\Pi V}.$$

Applying the same characterizations of positive diminishing political support from the beneficiaries of intervention, and increasing antagonism by those harmed by intervention and maintaining the same envy assumption in (6) as specified for (1), it follows that (9) is negative[14] (as we would require it to be to

satisfy the second-order condition for maximization of political support) whereas (10) is positive.[15] Thus (8) indicates that

$$(8') \qquad dP/dP^* > 0.$$

This reveals that the authorities adjust the domestic price in the same direction as the movement in world price. Consequently, when the world price declines, so does the domestic price sustained by the authorities' tariff intervention. In terms of Figure 1, when P_1^* falls, the authorities permit the domestic price to fall, maintaining a lower value of P_a via the choice of the tariff level for the industry. Since falls in the world price lead to falls in the domestic price, the industry's decline is not arrested by the authorities. Under free trade, domestic production would cease at a world price of P_2^*. Eventually, if the world price continues falling, protection will be insufficient to sustain a domestic price inclusive of the tariff above P_2^*, so even though protected the industry will cease to produce. Political-support motivated protection to a declining industry is accordingly transient, and terminal.

D. Changes in the Tariff: Retardation and Acceleration of Decline

In the course of the industry's decline, the level of the tariff set by the authorities is changing. Since, from (3), the tariff is adjusted in response to changes in the world price via

$$(11) \qquad dT/dP^* = dP/dP^* - 1,$$

it follows that

$$(12) \quad dT/dP^* \underset{<}{\overset{>}{=}} 0 \quad \text{as} \quad dP/dP^* \underset{<}{\overset{>}{=}} 1.$$

Examination of (9) and (10) reveals that, in principle, dP/dP^* as determined by (8) may

---

[14] In (9) the assumptions are that $M_\Pi > 0$, $M_{\Pi\Pi} < 0$, $\Pi_P > 0$, $\Pi_{PP} < 0$, $M_V > 0$, $M_{VV} < 0$, $M_{V\Pi} \geq 0$, $V_P < 0$ and $V_{PP} < 0$.

[15] In (10) the assumptions are that $M_{\Pi\Pi} < 0$, $M_{VV} < 0$, $M_{\Pi V} \geq 0$, $\Pi_P > 0$, $\Pi_{P^*} < 0$, and $V_{P^*} > 0$. It is assumed that $\Pi_{PP^*} = V_{PP^*} = 0$; i.e., that $\Pi(P, P^*) = \Pi(P) - \Pi(P^*)$ and that a similar linear decomposition can be made in ascertaining the loss of individuals harmed by protection.

exceed or may be less than unity. Hence in the course of the industry's decline, the authorities may be either increasing or decreasing the tariff.

If the tariff is increased, it is, however, never increased to the extent that complete or overcompensation is provided for the fall in the world price. For (8') obtains as a general result—the domestic price falls when the world price falls, a tariff increase never being sufficient to reverse an industry's decline. The most that industry-specific interests can expect is that the authorities may act to retard their industry's decline. And it is quite possible that the authorities' response to a decrease in the world price of the industry's output will be to accelerate the industry's decline.

III. Concluding Remarks

As noted in the introduction, previous literature in confronting the phenomenon of declining industry protection has focused on the *social merit* in ameliorating reductions in industry-specific earnings which occur due to reduced world prices. In contrast, in this paper, the phenomenon of declining industry protection has been considered beginning from the premise that authorities will choose protective levels on the basis of political support motives. So not perceptions of social justice, but rather the authorities' perceptions of their own political self-interest determine the assistance which factors specific to a declining industry can expect to receive. To portray politically motivated interventionist behavior, I have adapted the Stigler-Peltzman regulatory model to view the beneficiaries of gainers and losers from intervention in a Ricardo-Viner setting. I have also proposed that responses of gratitude or antagonism towards the authorities will be evoked only as a consequence of administratively decided change in agents' welfare.

The basic conclusion that emerges from the analysis of politically motivated protection of declining industries is that, over time, an industry that changing comparative advantage in international trade indicates ought decline, still declines when political-support motives tie the industry's domestic price endogenously to the world price. This outcome is in accord with the general political cross-subsidization theorem. When the world price falls, those who would benefit if the level of protection were not linked to the world price still benefit via a lower domestic price in the politically determined equilibrium.

That changes in protection do not reverse industry decline is important if one is to adopt a political-influence view of the behavior of the authorities, for this means that entry into the industry is not encouraged and investment in augmentation of industry-specific factors remains unattractive. Incumbent industry-specific interests therefore reap the benefits of the tariff protecting their industry, and the political support offset against those opposed to the persistence of the industry's tariff is assured.

Although a declining industry continues to decline when political influence motives determine protective levels, the analysis indicates that the authorities may respond either way with respect to the *rate* of the industry's decline. An industry's political weight may be sufficiently great for the authorities to find it in their own self-interest to retard its decline, in which event a compensatory tariff increase cushions the losses of those individuals whose incomes fall when the world price declines. But since the tariff *under*compensates these individuals for the decline in the world price, individuals opposed to protection still derive some benefit from the lower world price, their gain, however, then being less than it would be, were the industry's tariff not linked via political-support motives to the world price.

An industry's political weight may, on the other hand, be such that the outcome is acceleration rather than retardation of its demise. So a political-influence perspective on declining industry protection is consistent with instances where the authorities raise the tariff to ameliorate the plight of industry-specific interests, and where the authorities' response is to aggravate the position of industry-specific interests by reducing the tariff in response to a fall in the world price.

Consider now the relationship to social justice pleas for declining industry protection. In one interpretation, such pleas would have individuals' incomes be sustained in the face of exogenous change. This is, for example, what follows from Corden's notion of a conservative social welfare function. In that case, the link between incomes of industry-specific factors and output prices suggests that intervention ought be directed at arresting industry decline. But we have seen that political self-interest motives do not affect the direction of change—industry expansion or contraction—evoked by world market forces. Even if its decline is retarded by compensating tariff increases, a declining industry for which protection derives from considerations of political self-interest continues its decline, and eventually ceases to produce if falls in the world price of its output persist. A downward slide of incomes of industry-specific factors is not impeded, and industry extinction is not prevented. So a plea on social justice grounds for sustaining individuals' incomes by arresting industry decline will not be acted upon by authorities choosing protective levels in accord with their own political self-interest motives.

In yet another interpretation, social justice pleas for declining industry protection would have the authorities intervene to *slow down* the market-determined decline of an industry. Such a plea may, however, not evoke a sympathetic response from the authorities, who may find it politically expedient to accelerate an industry's decline. So then not only do incomes of industry-specific factors fall, but they fall at a faster rate than market outcomes expressed in world prices would dictate. On the other hand, a social justice plea for retarding an industry's decline *may* appear to be heeded. But then retardation of decline may be the very consequence of authorities' deciding on protective responses in accord with their own political self-interest motives and need not at all be explained as a social expression of altruism towards the disadvantaged. Although, in responding by retarding an industry's decline, the authorities provide individuals with longer periods during which to write off the value of their industry-specific capital to zero, and thereby provide derivatively, via their own political self-interest motives, the very increased time for adjustment which underlies such a social justice exposition of the declining industry case for protection.

REFERENCES

Anderson, Kym, "The Political Market for Government Assistance to Australian Manufacturing Industries," *Economic Record*, June 1980, *56*, 132–44.

Baldwin, Robert E., "The Political Economy of Protection," in J. N. Bhagwati and T. N. Srinivasan, eds., *Import Competition and Response*, Chicago: University of Chicago Press, forthcoming.

Bhagwati, Jagdish N., "Lobbying and Welfare," *Journal of Public Economics*, December 1980, *14*, 355–63.

_____ **and Srinivasan, T. N.,** "Revenue Seeking: A Generalization of the Theory of Tariffs," *Journal of Political Economy*, December 1980, *88*, 1069–87.

Brock, William A. and Magee, Steven P., "The Economics of Special Interest Politics: The Case of the Tariff," *American Economic Review Proceedings*, May 1978, *68*, 246–50.

Buchanan, James M., Tollison, Robert D. and Tullock, Gordon, *Toward a Theory of the Rent-Seeking Society*, College Station: Texas A&M University Press, 1980.

Burgess, David F., "Protection, Real Wages and the Neo-Classical Ambiguity with Interindustry Flows," *Journal of Political Economy*, August 1980, *88*, 783–802.

Cassing, James H., "Alternatives to Protectionism," in I. Levenson and J. Wheeler, eds., *Western Economies in Transition: Structural Change and Adjustment Policies in Industrial Countries*, Westview: Croom Helm, 1980, 391–424.

_____ , "On the Relationship Between Commodity Price Changes and Factor Owners' Real Positions," *Journal of Political Economy*, June 1981, *89*, 593–95.

Caves, Richard E., "Economic Models of Political Choice: Canada's Tariff Structure," *Canadian Journal of Economics*, May 1976, *9*, 278–300.

Corden, W. M., *Trade Policy and Economic Welfare*, Oxford: Clarendon Press, 1974.

Fishelson, Gideon and Hillman, Arye L., "Domestic Monopoly and Redundant Tariff Protection," *Journal of International Economics*, February 1979, *9*, 47–55.

Gray, H. Peter, "Senile Industry Protection: A Proposal," *Southern Economic Journal*, April 1973, *40*, 569–74.

111

_____, "Senile Industry Protection: Reply," *Southern Economic Journal*, January 1975, *41*, 538–41.

Helleiner, G. K., "The Political Economy of Canada's Tariff Structure: An Alternative Model," *Canadian Journal of Economics*, May 1977, *10*, 318–26.

Hillman, Arye L., "The Case for Terminal Protection for Declining Industries," *Southern Economic Journal*, July 1977, *44*, 155–60.

Jones, Ronald W., "A Three Factor Model in Theory, Trade and History," in J. N. Bhagwati et al., eds., *Trade, Growth and the Balance of Payments: Essays in Honor of C. B. Kindleberger*, Amsterdam: North-Holland, 1971, 3–21.

_____, "Income Distribution and Effective Protection in a Multicommodity Trade Model," *Journal of Economic Theory*, August 1975, *11*, 1–15.

Krueger, Anne, O., "The Political Economy of the Rent-Seeking Society," *American Economic Review*, June 1974, *64*, 291–303; reprinted in J. M. Buchanan et al., eds., *Toward a Theory of the Rent-Seeking Society*, College Station: Texas A&M University Press, 1980, 51–70.

Lee, Dwight R. and Orr, Daniel, "Two Laws of Survival for Ascriptive Government Policies," in J. M. Buchanan et al., eds., *Toward a Theory of the Rent-Seeking Society*, College Station: Texas A&M University Press, 1980, 113–24.

Magee, Steven P., "Three Simple Tests of the Stolper-Samuelson Theorem," in P. Oppenheimer, ed., *Issues in International Economics*, London: Oriel Press, 1980, 138–53.

Mayer, Wolfgang, "Short-Run and Long-Run Equilibrium for a Small Open Economy," *Journal of Political Economy*, October 1974, *82*, 955–67.

Mueller, Dennis C., *Public Choice*, Cambridge: Cambridge University Press, 1979.

Mussa Michael, "Tariffs and the Distribution of Income: The Importance of Factor Specificity, Substitutability and Intensity in the Short and Long Run," *Journal of Political Economy*, December 1974, *82*, 1191–203.

Neary, J. Peter, "Short-Run Capital Specificity and the Pure Theory of International Trade," *Economic Journal*, September 1978, *88*, 488–510.

Peltzman, Sam, "Towards a More General Theory of Regulation," *Journal of Law and Economics*, August 1976, *19*, 211–40.

Pincus, Jonathon J., "Pressure Groups and the Pattern of Tariffs," *Journal of Political Economy*, August 1975, *83*, 757–78.

_____, *Pressure Groups and Politics in Antebellum Tariffs*, New York: Columbia University Press, 1977.

Ruffin, Roy and Jones, Ronald W., "Real Wages and Protection: The Neoclassical Ambiguity," *Journal of Economic Theory*, April 1977, *14*, 337–48.

Saunders, Ronald S., "The Political Economy of Effective Protection in Canada's Manufacturing Sector," *Canadian Journal of Economics*, May 1980, *13*, 340–48.

Stigler, George, J., "The Theory of Economic Regulation," *Bell Journal of Economics*, Spring 1971, *2*, 3–21.

_____, "Free Riders and Collective Action," *Bell Journal of Economics*, Autumn 1974, *2*, 359–65.

Wood, Geoffrey, E., "Senile Industry Protection: Comment," *Southern Economic Journal*, January 1975, *41*, 535–37.

Domestic Politics, Foreign Interests, and International Trade Policy

By Arye L. Hillman and Heinrich W. Ursprung*

This paper incorporates the foreign interest in the determination of a country's international trade policy into a model of political competition between candidates contesting elective office. We envisage foreign and domestic producer interests as expressing political support for a candidate via campaign contributions, and candidates as making trade policy pronouncements to maximize political support from producer interests. Tariffs are divisive, but VERs are consistent with conciliatory policy positions yielding mutual gain to foreign and domestic interests. No candidate has an interest in formulating a trade policy position using a tariff if a VER is a policy option.

Protection in the developed countries has in recent years often taken the form of bilaterally negotiated voluntary export restraints (VERs) rather than the more traditional unilaterally imposed import restrictions.[1] The use of voluntary export restraints has been paralleled by interest in the theoretical literature. The effects of VERs have been compared with tariffs and quotas, and VERs have been examined in a political-economy framework with a view to identifying the gainers and losers from this form of restriction of international trade.[2] Foreign interests figure prominently in these analyses. VERs are, like import quotas which have been assigned to domestic interests, quantitative restrictions, but it is foreigners who secure the rents created by the restraint on trade. If a VER is a substitute for a tariff, revenue which would have accrued to the home government is transferred to foreigners.

The rent or revenue transfer to foreigners has given rise to two interrelated perspectives on VERs. By negotiating VERs, home governments have been seen as providing compensation in seeking foreign acquiescence with domestic protectionist policies which violate prior negotiated GATT commitments; and by consenting to VERs, foreign governments have on their part been seen as preempting other more costly protectionist measures in export markets.[3]

*Bar-Ilan University, Ramat Gan, 52100 Israel and University of Konstanz, Konstanz, D7750 F.R.G., respectively. Ursprung acknowledges the support of the Swiss National Science Foundation. We thank Peter Bernholz, Harold Demsetz, Sebastian Edwards, Wolfgang Mayer, Michael Waldman, and two anonymous referees for comments on a previous draft. We have also benefited from seminars at Bar-Ilan University, the University of California-Los Angeles, the University of Konstanz, the University of Pennsylvania, the University of Pittsburgh, and Princeton University.

[1] The various instances include the restraints on U.S. imports of Japanese automobiles, initially implemented in 1981 and renewed in subsequent years to date. Japanese automobile exports to the U.K., France, and Italy are also subject to voluntary restraints, as are European exports of steel to the United States, various developing countries' exports of clothing to the United States, and the EEC, and exports of consumer electronics goods from the newly industrializing countries of Asia to some developed countries. VERs as a component of U.S. trade policy date back at least to 1957 when the United States announced that Japan would "voluntarily" restrict exports of cotton textiles and apparel for the subsequent five years.

[2] See Kent Jones (1984), who also reviews prior theoretical literature.

[3] Other proposed explanations for VERs include the suggestion by Jagdish Bhagwati (1985) that export restraints may be linked to incentives for domestic investment by the foreign industry whose exports are subject to restriction. Since it is Japanese exports which have been prominently involved, it has also been suggested that VERs may reflect a traditional Japanese preference for undertaking unavoidable, unpleasant acts oneself rather than leaving the execution of such acts to others.

American Economic Review **78**, 729–745

VERs as protectionist options thus introduce a focus on the foreign interest in the domestic determination of international trade policy, and more particularly in the *form* which protectionist policies take. This paper presents a model of the political formulation of protectionist policies which takes explicit account of this foreign interest. In a setting of representative democracy, rival candidates for political office are viewed as making trade policy pronouncements so as to maximize political support, which may derive from foreign or domestic producer interests.[4]

Foreigners, lacking the necessary franchise, cannot influence the determination of trade policy directly by voting in domestic political contests. However, under representative democracy, foreign participation in domestic politics can take the form of campaign contributions, or other transfers directed at influencing the trade-policy position taken by a political candidate. Evidence confirming the foreign interest in participation in domestic politics is provided by the comprehensive account of foreign lobbying expenditures documented by Steven Husted (1986).

We shall portray the foreign interests seeking to influence the domestic formulation of international trade policy as residual claimants in a foreign export industry. The foreign industry is composed of identical Cournot firms acting noncooperatively, unless directed to comply with negotiated VERs by collectively restraining exports and preallocating market shares. A Cournot portrayal of firms is likewise adopted in the domestic

import-competing industry. Firms in the domestic industry remain however at all times in compliance with domestic antitrust laws and do not behave collusively.[5]

Firms choose campaign contributions to a favored candidate to maximize expected profits, which depend upon the rival candidates' prospects for election and upon the trade policy to which a candidate commits himself if elected. The campaign contributions made by firms have a public-good character. Any one firm's outlays benefit other firms which stand to gain or lose in the same way from a candidate's policy commitment. Firms' political outlays thus constitute an instance of private provision of public goods, here the collective benefit derived from influence over policy.[6]

In this endogenous policy setting, we investigate the characteristics of protectionist proposals when the alternative forms of trade intervention are tariffs and quantitative restrictions in the form of VERs.[7] The outcome of political competition depends upon the instrument used by the rival candidates to make trade-policy pronouncements. The tariff equilibrium is politically divisive in

---

[4] Economic policy is thus politically determined (see, for example, Peter Bernholz, 1974, 1977). The international economics literature has in recent years emphasized the inherently political nature of protectionist decisions. See, for example, Robert Baldwin, 1982, 1984, 1985; Arye Hillman, 1982; Wolfgang Mayer, 1984; Leslie Young and Stephen Magee, 1986; and James Cassing and Hillman, 1985, 1986. Our model of political competition under representative democracy is in particular of the genre of models of political contestability as formulated by Young and Magee. The literature on the political economy of trade policy is reviewed in Hillman, 1988.

[5] Firms are viewed as identical, so that the number of firms can be used as a simple measure of industry competitiveness. More generally, of course, because of efficiency differences (see Harold Demsetz, 1973), firms will have different market shares. However, we abstract from such differences among firms to focus on the quest to influence trade policy via the political process.

[6] See Richard Cornes and Todd Sandler (1986) for an exposition of the theory of noncooperative voluntary provision of public goods.

[7] We do not compare auctioned import quotas with VERs because under our assumptions (which we shall subsequently make explicit) concerning property rights to revenue assignment, political candidates prefer VERs to auctioned quotas as protectionist instruments. The literature offers other perspectives on political choice of the means of protection. The choice between tariffs and quotas by a government trading off political support from domestic gainers and losers from protection is considered by Cassing and Hillman, 1985. On terms of trade uncertainty, domestic interests, and the political choice between tariffs and quotas, see Rodney Falvey and Peter Lloyd, 1986. Again in settings concerned only with the domestic interests influenced by trade policy, Dani Rodrik, 1986, and Mayer and Raymond Riezman, 1987, consider aspects of the choice between tax/subsidy instruments and tariffs.

that a protectionist candidate announces a prohibitive tariff and a liberal trade-policy candidate announces free trade as his policy platform. Associated with the political divisiveness in the candidates' policy pronouncements is divisiveness in the attribution of economic gains and losses associated with candidates' pronounced policies. The policy platform chosen by the protectionist candidate maximizes domestic profits and minimizes foreign profits, while the opposite is true of the equilibrium policy platform chosen by the liberal trade-policy candidate.

However, when candidates' policy proposals are formulated in terms of export restraints, trade-policy platforms converge to a Hotelling-type equilibrium. There is thus political conciliation. At the same time, the prospect emerges of compromise between the conflicting economic interests of domestic and foreign producers. An interior equilibrium (which cannot arise under a tariff) is characterized by a level of export restraint which is more restrictive than foreigners would wish in order to maximize collusively joint profits, but less restrictive than the prohibitive level of restraint of imports sought by domestic import-competing firms.[8]

Beyond compromise, the political equilibrium associated with VERs is consistent with mutual economic gain to foreign and domestic producer interests.[9] Our conception of voluntariness of export restraints is based on the prospect of such mutual gain. We shall term an export restraint as voluntary if foreign and domestic industry rents both increase as the consequence of foreigners' coordinated restriction of export sales. This conception of voluntariness differs from the more traditional perspective that export restraints are imposed restrictions which are only voluntary in the sense that foreigners find negotiation and compli-

ance preferable to a threatened alternative trade restriction.[10]

Whether an export restraint facilitates increases in producer rents at home and abroad will be shown to be determined by a relationship linking foreign and domestic market structures and the substitutability of foreign and domestic goods in domestic consumption. In particular, a change in substitutability as for example effected by upgrading of exports can make an initially involuntary constraint voluntary.[11]

We also investigate the political choice between VERs and tariffs. Export restraints are shown to dominate tariffs, in that political equilibria are inconsistent with any candidate's making a protectionist policy pronouncement in terms of a tariff when the option of using export restraints is available.

Two aspects of our model of the political contestability of trade policy merit preliminary comment. We assume that rival candidates place no value on revenue derived from a tariff. Such revenue accrues to the general fund of government receipts to which the candidates have no claim.[12] However, while the candidates have no means of appropriating or benefiting from the revenue from a tariff which they might propose, there

---

[8] For consistent evidence, see Schlesinger, *Wall Street Journal*, Jan. 28, 1987, "Japan's Extension of Auto-Export Curb Fails to Mollify Strongest U.S. Critics."
[9] For recognition of collusive aspects of VERs, see Richard Harris, 1985; Jurgen Eichenberger and Ian Harper, 1987, and Kala Krishna (forthcoming 1988).

[10] There is a related view in the literature (see Bhagwati and T. N. Srinivasan, 1976) that foreigners may themselves initiate voluntary restraints on exports to preempt protectionist measures in export markets. Consistent with this view, the *Economist* (May 30, 1987) reported: "Taiwan and South Korea may be about to introduce voluntary export restraints on some goods, including shoes. Legislation in the United States Congress is trying to limit shoe imports to their 1986 levels."
[11] Thus the United States indicated its readiness in 1985 to dispense with the voluntary export restraints on Japanese automobiles which had been introduced in 1981. However, the voluntary export restraints were nonetheless renewed by the Japanese government. At the same time there is evidence of quality upgrading of Japanese automobile exports to the United States (see Robert Feenstra, 1984, 1985; and Charles Collyns and Steven Dunaway, 1987).
[12] See Baldwin (1984) for observations on limitations to the assignment of property rights to tariff revenues. For an analysis encompassing voluntary export restrictions which does on the other hand assume that individuals can secure claims to revenue from tariffs, see Richard Brecher and Bhagwati (1987).

is a prospective benefit from the creation of rents which can be transferred to private economic interests via export restraints. The latter rents can be transformed via the political process into campaign contributions, thereby bearing upon the candidates' ultimate concern, their probabilities of attaining political office.

Second, our formulation of political competition does not assign an active role to consumer interests. The focus is on those interests with the principal economic stakes in influencing the political formulation of trade policy, domestic and foreign residual claimants who benefit or lose according to the trade policy adopted. Consumers are viewed as passively influenced in their voting behavior by campaign expenditures, hence the importance assigned to campaign contributions by the candidates. The vote which consumers cast is, moreover, preconditioned on the policy positions taken by the candidates on a range of issues and is not dominated by any one single issue. Out of "rational ignorance," consumer–voters have no reason to have acquired detailed information on the consequences of policies proposed regarding the extent and form of protection for a particular industry. This is, however, not to deny that consumer interests can influence the trade policies proposed by candidates for political office. To the extent that consumer interests matter, the protectionist outcomes which we shall portray will be moderated.

I. The Model

We consider an import-competing industry producing a homogeneous good which is imperfectly substitutable in domestic consumption for imports. The domestic demand functions for the domestic good and imports are

$$(1) \qquad P = a - bx + \gamma P^*$$

$$(2) \qquad P^* = a - bx^* + \gamma P,$$

where x and x^* denote quantities of domestically produced and foreign goods, and P and P^* are the respective domestic

prices of the two goods; γ is a constant with values $0 \le \gamma < 1$ which measures substitutability in consumption between domestic and foreign goods.[13]

The domestic industry consists of n identical profit-maximizing Cournot firms. Each firm makes a campaign contribution L_i to influence the outcome of an electoral contest between two candidates, one of whom is predisposed to a protectionist and the other to a liberal trade policy.[14] Firms' per unit production costs are a constant c. A domestic firm chooses output and a campaign contribution to the protectionist candidate to maximize profits given by

$$(3) \qquad \max_{x_i, L_e} \pi_i = (P - c)x_i - L_i,$$

$$i = 1, \dots, n.$$

The foreign industry consists of m Cournot firms also seeking to influence domestic trade policy. Foreign firms have the same per unit cost of production as domestic firms. When a tariff is the means of domestic protection, the profit-maximization problem confronting a foreign firm is

$$(4) \qquad \max_{x_i^*, L_i^*} \pi_i^* = (P^* - c - t)x_i^* - L_i^*,$$

$$i = 1, \dots, m,$$

where t is a specific tariff. Alternatively, with an export restraint V, foreign firms maximize

---

[13] If $\gamma = 0$, demand for each good depends only upon its own price, reflecting zero substitutability. With $\gamma > 0$, if $P = P^*$, then $x = x^*$; but $P > P^*$ is consistent with $x > 0$, so not all domestic firms' sales are lost to competitive imports when the price of the domestic good exceeds that of imports. For the specification of consumption preferences underlying the above demand functions and another application to an analysis of export restraints, see Harris (1985). Using Bertrand price adjustment (as distinct from our formulation of Cournot quantity-adjustment), Harris shows that an export restraint set at the free-trade quantity of imports can be voluntary, in the sense of facilitating an increase in foreign firms' profits. See also Eichenberger and Harper, 1987, and Krishna, forthcoming 1988.

[14] Ideology has no role here. We assume a policy predisposition to distinguish the candidates.

profits subject to the coordinated market-sharing condition

$$(5) \qquad x_i^* \leq V/m.$$

Each candidate seeks to maximize his probability of election, which is determined by campaign contributions received relative to total contributions. The protectionist candidate, who is the beneficiary of domestic firms' contributions, thus seeks to maximize

$$(6) \qquad W = \frac{L}{L + L^*},$$

where

$$L = \sum_{i=1}^{n} L_i \quad \text{and} \quad L^* = \sum_{i=1}^{m} L_i^*.$$

On the other hand, the candidate predisposed to a liberal trade policy seeks to minimize W. It will be assumed that if the two candidates propose identical policies, then each has equal probability of election.

II. Political Competition with a Tariff

A. Tariffs and Profits

Let candidates' policy pronouncements be made in terms of tariffs. For given tariff policies, each firm maximizes profits, assuming that other firms do not respond to its output choice. The symmetric Nash equilibrium that results is given by the respective outputs for domestic and foreign firms,

$$(7) \quad x_i = \frac{[m(1-\gamma)+1]B}{bA}$$
$$+ \frac{[\gamma(1-\gamma^2)m]t}{bA}, \quad i=1,\ldots,n$$

and

$$(8) \quad x_i^* = \frac{[n(1-\gamma)+1]B}{bA}$$
$$- \frac{(1-\gamma^2)(n+1)t}{bA}, \quad i=1,\ldots,m$$

where $A \equiv (m+1)(n+1) - mn\gamma^2 > 0$ and $B \equiv (1+\gamma)(a - c(1-\gamma)) > 0$.

Denote by $\bar{t}$ the prohibitive tariff in a symmetric Nash equilibrium, established by solving (8) for $x_i^* = 0$. For $x_i, x_i^* \geq 0$, $\gamma > 0$ and $0 \leq t \leq \bar{t}$, (7) and (8) indicate that equilibrium domestic sales are linear functions of the tariff, increasing for domestic firms and decreasing for foreign firms. As the tariff is increased, domestic consumers substitute domestic output for imports, the extent of substitution depending on the value of γ. If $\gamma = 0$, the output x_i of domestic firms is independent of the tariff, but the domestic sales x_i^* of foreign firms still decline as the tariff is increased.

Post-election profits depend upon the tariff via[15]

$$(9) \quad \pi_i(t) = \frac{1}{b(1-\gamma^2)A^2}$$
$$\times \left\{ [m(1-\gamma)+1]B \right.$$
$$\left. + (1-\gamma^2)\gamma mt \right\}^2$$

$$(10) \quad \pi_i^*(t) = \frac{1}{b(1-\gamma^2)A^2}$$
$$\times \left\{ [n(1-\gamma)+1]B \right.$$
$$\left. - (n+1)(1-\gamma^2)t \right\}^2.$$

It follows that as depicted in Figure 1, for nonprohibitive tariffs, profits of domestic and foreign firms are respectively strictly increasing and decreasing, but both strictly convex, functions of the tariff.

B. Choice of Campaign Contributions

Perceiving the ex post (or post election) dependence of profits on the tariff, firms make campaign contributions ex ante to influence political candidates' trade policy pro-

---

[15] To derive the profit functions (9) and (10), substitute the equilibrium quantities (7) and (8) into (3) and (4), respectively.

Arye L. Hillman and Heinrich W. Ursprung

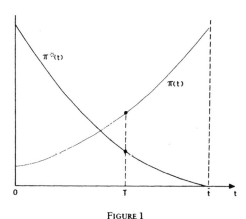

FIGURE 1

nouncements. Firms choose their individual contributions as Nash equilibria. The outlays made reflect the public-good nature of the benefits to other firms in the industry. The value of campaign contributions is a deduction from *ex post* profits given by (9) and (10).[16]

When deciding on campaign contributions, firms confront the uncertainty of not knowing which candidate will be elected. Firms are risk-neutral and choose campaign contributions to maximize expected profits. For a domestic firm, expected profits are

$$(11) \quad E\pi_i = \theta \left[\pi_i(t_0) - L_i \right]$$
$$+ (1-\theta)\left[\pi_i(t_1) - L_i \right]$$
$$= \theta\pi_i(t_0) + (1-\theta)\pi_i(t_1) - L_i,$$

where θ and $(1-\theta)$ are the respective probabilities of election of the liberal trade-policy and protectionist candidates, and t_0 and t_1 ($t_0 \le t_1$) are the candidates' respective tariff pronouncements. The expected profits of a

foreign firm, $E\pi_i^*$, likewise encompass the two states of the world described by the policy pronouncements of the rival candidates, and take the same form as (11).

Campaign contributions determine the candidates' probabilities of electoral success, via

$$(12) \quad \theta = L^*/(L+L^*) = W(L,L^*)$$
$$1 - \theta = L/(L+L^*) = 1 - W(L,L^*),$$

where L and L^* are as defined in (6) total contributions by domestic and foreign firms.

On substituting (12) into (11), it follows that domestic firms choose campaign contributions which satisfy

$$(13) \quad \frac{\partial E\pi_i}{\partial L_i} = \frac{L^*}{(L+L^*)^2}$$
$$\times \left[\pi_i(t_1) - \pi_i(t_0) \right] - 1 = 0,$$
$$i = 1,\dots,n.$$

The condition (13) can be expressed as

$$(14) \quad \frac{L^*}{(L+L^*)^2}\Delta\pi_i = 1, \quad i = 1,\dots,n$$

where $\Delta\pi_i = \left[\pi_i(t_1) - \pi_i(t_0)\right]$ is the difference in domestic firms' profits for the states associated with the rival candidates' tariff pronouncements.

For foreign firms, the expected profit-maximizing choice of campaign contributions satisfies a similar condition

$$(15) \quad \frac{L}{(L+L^*)^2}\Delta\pi_i^* = 1, \quad i = 1,\dots,m.$$

Combining (14) and (15) yields the relationship between equilibrium campaign contributions

$$(16) \quad \frac{L}{L^*} = \frac{\Delta\pi_i}{\Delta\pi_i^*} = \frac{\pi_i(t_1) - \pi_i(t_0)}{\pi_i^*(t_0) - \pi_i^*(t_1)}$$
$$\equiv R(t_0,t_1).$$

---

[16]Observe the relation here to the portrayals of contestability of rents in the literature (for example, Hillman and Eliakim Katz, 1984; and Hillman and John Riley, 1987). The outlays L_i made in seeking to influence the outcome of the political contest (and thereby the political allocation of producer rents) are irretrievably lost.

VOL. 78 NO. 4   HILLMAN AND URSPRUNG: DOMESTIC POLITICS   735

C. Candidates' Policy Pronouncements

The rival candidates choose policy positions to maximize their respective probabilities of electoral success, as expressed by (12).[17] The protectionist candidate accordingly seeks to maximize $L/(L + L^*)$. This is however equivalent to maximizing L/L^*, and thus entails adopting a policy position which maximizes $R(t_0, t_1)$ as defined in (16). Hence, maximization of the protectionist candidate's probability of electoral success implies choice of a tariff which maximizes $\Delta\pi_i/\Delta\pi_i^*$, the state-contingent difference in domestic relative to foreign profits.

The relation (16) therefore links candidates' political motives and firms' profit-maximizing objectives. Each candidate has a political interest in maximizing the gains which his constituency secures from his announced policy relative to the gains which his political opponent's constituency secures from the opponent's policy.[18]

D. Equilibrium Tariff Pronouncements

A candidate's choice of tariff pronouncement evidently affects the profits which domestic and foreign firms would secure on his election. An increase in the tariff proposed by the protectionist candidate may increase $\Delta\pi_i$, but at the same time may also increase $\Delta\pi_i^*$. One cannot therefore presume that the protectionist candidate will necessarily announce a prohibitive tariff or that his rival will announce a policy of free trade.

---

[17] The candidates for political office are thus Stackelberg leaders with respect to the domestic and foreign interests making campaign contributions.

[18] Satya Das (1988) derives a condition similar to (16). Das presents an alternative scenario which recognizes the motives of foreigners in seeking to influence domestic policy decisions. The model presented by Das has elements in common with our formulation. However, rather than rival candidates engaged in political competition making political-support maximizing trade-policy pronouncements, Das views domestic and foreign firms as seeking to influence a single policymaker's decision, and whereas we compare tariffs and voluntary export restraints as alternative instruments of trade restriction, Das focuses on the policymaker's response in choosing to implement an import quota.

This is however the equilibrium outcome. The result of political competition via tariff pronouncements is described by

PROPOSITION 1: *The equilibrium platform combination when political-support maximizing candidates for political office make policy pronouncements in terms of tariffs is characterized by the protectionist candidate's announcing a prohibitive tariff and the liberal trade-policy candidate's announcing a policy of free trade.*

PROOF:

Let the candidates' policy pronouncements differ. Evaluating $\Delta\pi_i$ and $\Delta\pi_i^*$ when $t_0 < t_1$ and substituting into (16) yields

$$(17) \quad R(t_0, t_1)\big|_{t_0 < t_1}$$

$$= \frac{2[m(1-\gamma)+1]m\gamma B + m^2\gamma^2(1-\gamma^2)(t_0+t_1)}{2[n(1-\gamma)+1](n+1)B - (n+1)^2(1-\gamma^2)(t_0+t_1)}.$$

The expression (17) is strictly increasing in both t_0 and t_1. Hence the protectionist candidate increases his probability of election by announcing increasingly greater tariffs, up to $\bar{t}$. Conversely, the liberal trade-policy candidate increases his probability of election by announcing ever smaller tariffs, until free trade.

Now suppose that the candidates were to announce the same positive nonprohibitive tariff T, where as in Figure 1 $0 < T < \bar{t}$. (17) (which is derived subject to $t_0 < t_1$) then no longer defines election probabilities. Since identical tariff pronouncements imply equal state-contingent profits ($\Delta\pi_i = \Delta\pi_i^* = 0$), R in (16) is also not defined. However, since identical policy pronouncements imply equal probabilities of election,

$$(18) \quad W = \frac{L}{L + L^*} = \frac{R}{1+R} = \frac{1}{2},$$

and $R(T, T) = 1$. The liberal trade-policy candidate improves his prospects of electoral success by deviating from T to announce free trade if $R(0, T) < R(T, T) = 1$, which

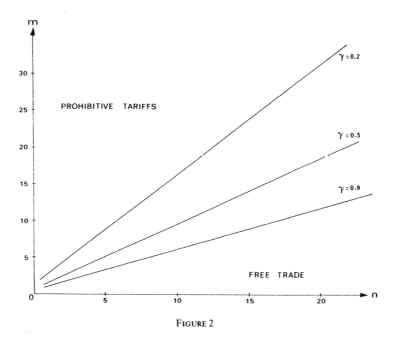

FIGURE 2

from (18) requires that

$$(19) \quad T < \frac{2B[(n+1)(n(1-\gamma)+1) - \gamma m(m(1-\gamma)+1]}{(1-\gamma^2)(m^2\gamma^2 + (n+1)^2)}$$

$$\equiv \bar{t}.$$

The protectionist candidate increases his probability of election by deviating from the common pronouncement T to announce a prohibitive tariff if $R(T, \bar{t}) > R(T, T) = 1$, which from (17) and (19) implies $T > \bar{t} - \bar{t} \equiv \hat{t}$. If $\bar{t} \leq \bar{t}$, then $\hat{t} \leq 0$ and this latter condition is satisfied for all $T \in (0, \bar{t})$. If however $\bar{t} > \bar{t}$, then (19) is satisfied for all $T \in (0, \bar{t})$. Hence at least one of the candidates can improve his election prospects by deviating from the common pronouncement T, which therefore cannot be an equilibrium. We have thus eliminated a common interior Hotelling-type policy platform as an equilibrium; and we have demonstrated that when tariff pronouncements differ, the equilibrium platform consists of free-trade and prohibitive tariff pronouncements.

The tariff equilibrium is accordingly politically divisive, and is also maximally conflicting in terms of the state-contingent outcomes for foreign and domestic producer interests. A candidate's policy proposal either maximizes domestic profits by altogether excluding imports from the domestic market, or serves foreign interest by permitting free trade.[19]

E. *Comparative Statics of the Tariff Equilibrium*

Which of the two candidates will enjoy the greater likelihood of electoral success, and therefore which policy will have the greater

[19]In equilibrium, one candidate will in general have a higher probability of success than the other. The candidate with the lower probability of success could duplicate the policy of his opponent. Then one equilibrium policy emerges as supported by both candidates. The characteristic of no-compromise in the tariff equilibrium is retained.

likelihood of implementation, is determined by the exogenous characteristics of market structure and substitutability in domestic consumption between imports and domestic goods.

Figure 2 depicts three contours (which are necessarily increasing and nonintersecting) along which $R(0, \bar{t}) = 1$ and hence along which free trade and protectionist outcomes are equally likely.[20] As the value of the substitution parameter γ increases, the zone wherein the protectionist candidate has the greater probability of election expands. The greater is γ, the more substitutable are domestically produced goods for imports, and hence the greater the gain to domestic interests from protection relative to free trade. Domestic interests accordingly have a greater incentive to make campaign contributions to the protectionist candidate. At the same time, foreign interests have less to lose from a denial of access to the domestic market, and make smaller campaign contributions to their candidate.

Increased competition, whether in terms of more competitors in a firm's own industry or abroad, decreases firms' profits, but *ceteris paribus* profits are decreased more by increased competitiveness in a firm's own industry, since domestic goods and imports are only imperfectly substitutable. As competition increases, profits fall, and the voluntary public-good outlays for campaign contributions fall. An increase in the number of domestic firms therefore reduces the benefits to domestic firms from a protectionist outcome by more than the reduction in benefit to foreign firms from a free-trade outcome. Hence, in Figure 2, for given γ, an increase in n holding m constant increases the probability of election of the free-trade candidate.

III. Export Restraints

Now let the candidates for political office formulate their policy pronouncements in

[20] $R(0, \bar{t}) = [2\gamma m(m(1 - \gamma) + 1)]/[(n + 1)(n(1 - \gamma) + 1] + (\gamma^2 m^2)/(n + 1)^2$ which follows from (17) after appropriate substitution.

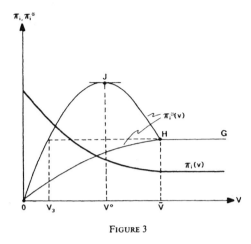

FIGURE 3

terms of export restraints. We begin by establishing the relation between export restraints and firms' profits.

A. *Domestic Profits*

When foreign firms confront the binding export constraint V, the equilibrium output of domestic firms is

$$(20) \qquad x_i = \frac{B}{b(n + 1)} - \frac{\gamma V}{n + 1}$$

and profits are

$$(21) \qquad \pi_i(V) = \frac{[B - b\gamma V]^2}{b(n + 1)^2(1 - \gamma^2)}.$$

Let $\bar{V}$ denote the free-trade quantity of imports. For export restraints less than $\bar{V}$, $\pi_i(V)$ is a strictly decreasing convex function. Hence, as depicted in Figure 3, max $\pi_i(V) = \pi_i(0)$, confirming that domestic profits are maximized by an export restraint which excludes competitive imports from the domestic market.

The profits of a domestic firm in (21) depend upon domestic market structure (via n) but are independent of foreign market structure (i.e., m). Export restraints thus eliminate the dependence, present under a tariff, of domestic profits on foreign market structure.

B. *Foreign Profits*

A binding export constraint leads foreign firms to decrease their domestic sales from the level of free trade to the constrained quantity $x_i^* = V/m$. Profits subject to the export restraint are

$$(22) \quad \pi_i^*(V) = \frac{V\left[\left(n(1-\gamma)+1\right)B - b\left(n(1-\gamma^2)+V\right)\right]}{m(n+1)(1-\gamma^2)},$$

where

$$(23) \quad \frac{\partial \pi_i^*}{\partial V} = \frac{\left\{ B\left(n(1-\gamma)+1-2b\left[n(1-\gamma^2)+1\right]\right)\right\}}{m(n+1)(1-\gamma^2)} \gtreqless 0.$$

Hence, while domestic profits necessarily fall, foreign profits may increase or decrease as an export restraint is marginally relaxed.

The export restraint which maximizes foreign profits and which foreign interests would therefore seek to have imposed is derived from (23) as

$$(24) \quad V^0 = \min\left\{ \frac{B[n(1-\gamma)+1]}{2b[n(1-\gamma^2)+1]}, \bar{V}\right\}.$$

There are two possibilities encompassed in (24). If foreigners can only lose from a restriction of exports, V^0 is given by free-trade domestic sales. In that case, the foreign profit function in Figure 3 is of the form OHG. Alternatively, joint profit maximization by foreign firms may require restricting exports below the free-trade quantity. V^0 is then given by the first expression in braces in (24) and the profit function is of the form OJH.

C. *Voluntariness*

We shall term an export restraint as "voluntary" if a foreigners' reduction in domestic sales increases foreign profits. From (23) voluntariness requires

$$(25) \quad m > \frac{n+1}{n(1-\gamma^2)+1}.$$

Should this condition hold, foreign and domestic firms have a common interest in restricting trade.

The right-hand side of (25) exceeds unity as long as there is substitutability in domestic consumption between domestic and foreign goods ($\gamma > 0$). (25) therefore confirms that if the foreign industry were to consist of a single firm or were collusively organized as a joint profit-maximizing cartel ($m = 1$), an export restraint could only be involuntary.

Increased competitiveness in the foreign industry can make an initially involuntary export restraint voluntary. The voluntary restraint affects the domestic market in the manner of a collusive restriction of sales: a more competitive foreign industry secures greater benefit from the implicit collusion.

The right-hand side of (25) is increasing in the substitution parameter γ. Hence, if, for example, as a consequence of upgrading imports become closer substitutes for domestic output, a voluntary restraint can become involuntary.

D. *Candidates' Export-Restraint Pronouncements*

Consider now the behavior of the rival candidates for political office. We shall demonstrate

PROPOSITION 2: *When the candidates choose levels of export restraint to maximize their respective probabilities of election, the political equilibrium is characterized by the announcement of a common policy.*

PROOF:

The proof proceeds along the same general line as that demonstrating the nature of the political equilibrium with tariffs. Let V_1 be the level of restraint announced by the protectionist candidate, and let the liberal trade-policy candidate announce V_0 (where $V_0 \geq V_1$). The candidates' political objectives and firms' profits are interconnected via

$$(26) \quad \frac{L}{L^*} = \frac{\Delta\pi_i}{\Delta\pi_i^*} \equiv R(V_0, V_1),$$

where $\Delta\pi_i$ and $\Delta\pi_i^*$ are established via (21) and (22). Let the candidates' policy pronouncements differ (with $V_0 > V_1$). Then substituting from (21) and (22) into (26) establishes that

$$(27) \quad R(V_0, V_1)|_{V_0 > V_1} =$$

$$\frac{m\gamma[b\gamma(V_0 + V_1) - 2B]}{(n+1)[b(n(1-\gamma^2)+1)(V_0 + V_1) - (n(1-\gamma)+1)B]},$$

which is increasing in V_0 and V_1. The liberal trade-policy candidate therefore improves his election prospects by decreasing V_0 and the protectionist candidate improves his prospects by increasing V_1. Thus when policy pronouncements differ, V_0 and V_1 converge.

Let the policies converge to V^*. (27) is defined for $V_0 > V_1$. In particular $R(V^*, V^*)$ can therefore not be evaluated using (27). However, since, when the same policy is announced, candidates have the same probability of election, $R(V^*, V^*) = 1$.

The common pronouncement V^* is an interior equilibrium if and only if, for $\varepsilon > 0$ arbitrarily small,

$$(28) \quad R(V^* + \varepsilon, V^*) \geq R(V^*, V^*) = 1,$$

$$(29) \quad R(V^*, V^* - \varepsilon) \leq R(V^*, V^*) = 1.$$

If V^* prohibits imports (i.e., $V^* = 0$) (28) alone needs to be satisfied; if V^* entails no restriction of trade (i.e., $V^* = \tilde{V}$), then (29) alone needs to be satisfied.

Let $\quad g(V) \equiv \lim_{\varepsilon \to 0} R(V + \varepsilon, V)$

$$= \lim_{\varepsilon \to 0} R(V, V - \varepsilon).$$

Then (28) and (29) imply

$$(30) \quad g(V^*)$$

$$= \frac{2m\gamma[B - b\gamma V^*]}{(n+1)[n(1-\gamma)+1)B - 2b(n(1-\gamma^2)+1)V^*]}$$

$$= 1 \qquad \text{for } 0 < V^* < \tilde{V}$$

$$g(V^*) \geq 1 \qquad \text{for } V^* = 0$$

$$g(V^*) \leq 1 \qquad \text{for } V^* = \tilde{V}.$$

The function $g(V)$ is depicted in Figure 4.[21]

[21] $g(V)$ converges to infinity at the regular maximum of $\pi_i^*(V)$ if $V^0 < \tilde{V}$. $g(0) = 2m\gamma/(n+1)[n(1-\gamma)+1] > 0$; if $g(0) < 1$, then V^* is necessarily nonprohibitive.

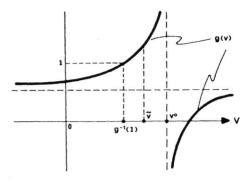

FIGURE 4

If, as depicted in Figure 4, $g(0) < 1$ and $g^{-1}(1) < \tilde{V}$, there exists a unique interior solution to (30) given by

$$(31) \quad V^* = g^{-1}(1)$$

$$= \frac{B[(n+1)(n(1-\gamma)+1) - 2m\gamma]}{2b[(n+1)(n(1-\gamma^2)+1) - m\gamma^2]}.$$

Alternatively, if $g(0) < 1$ but $g^{-1}(1) \geq \tilde{V}$, the solution to (31) is $V^* = \tilde{V}$ and the unique equilibrium is free trade. If $g(0) \geq 1$, the unique solution is prohibition of imports, or $V^* = 0$.

E. Political Compromise and Economic Gain

When policy pronouncements are made in terms of export restraints, candidates thus announce a common policy. But to whose advantage? Clearly, if political competition results in a policy pronouncement prohibiting imports, the outcome is to the exclusive advantage of domestic import-competing interests. Or, if the political equilibrium entails free trade, and if at the same time foreigners can only lose from a curtailment of their domestic sales, the outcome is to the exclusive advantage of foreign interests. In these latter instances, the economic division of gains and losses from pronounced export-restraint policies is no different from that under tariffs. The export-restraint equilibrium is politically conciliatory in that both candidates announce the same policy, but still as with the tariff the equilibrium is divi-

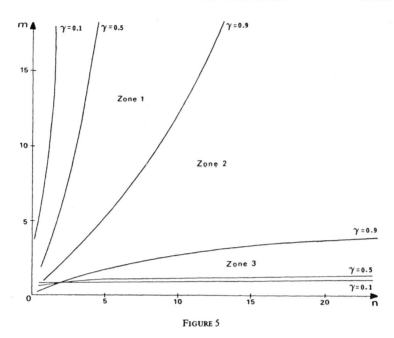

FIGURE 5

sive in offering no compromise between foreign and domestic economic interests.

The distinguishing characteristic of export-restraint equilibria is however that political competition is consistent with interior solutions. Such solutions may or may not benefit foreign interests. Whether foreign interests can gain is determined by whether condition (25) holds.

Suppose that (25) is satisfied. So export restraints can benefit foreigners. For any level of restraint announced by the protectionist candidate, let the liberal trade-policy candidate announce as his policy the foreign collusive profit-maximizing level of restraint V^0. However,

$$(\partial \pi_i^*/\partial V)|_{V^0} = 0 \quad \text{and} \quad (\partial \pi_i/\partial V)|_{V^0} < 0.$$

Hence this latter candidate, in seeking to minimize $R = \Delta \pi_i/\Delta \pi_i^*$, can gain by marginally decreasing his pronouncement below V^0. The liberal trade-policy candidate has thus an incentive to deviate from the foreign joint profit-maximizing level of export restraint to propose a more restrictive trade

policy than sought by foreign interests. The protectionist candidate similarly has an incentive to deviate from a policy pronouncement of prohibition of imports, to announce a policy allowing some imports, which is then inconsistent with maximizing domestic firms' profits. The candidates' policy pronouncements converge in the manner we have described. The political equilibrium is a compromise between the outcomes sought by foreign and domestic interests, but also provides mutual gain to both sets of producer interests.

The compromise character of an export-restraint equilibrium is likewise reflected in an interior equilibrium where mutual gain is absent. Although foreigners lose, they lose less than they would were the equilibrium policy exclusively to accommodate domestic interests.

F. Comparative Statics

Comparative static properties of export-restraint equilibria are described in Figure 5. In region 1 $g(0) = 2m\gamma/(n+1)(n(1-\gamma)+1)$

≥ 1 and the political equilibrium yields an export restraint which is prohibitive. In regions 2 and 3, $g(0) < 1$ and the equilibrium policy allows imports. For a given number of domestic firms, the outcome is free trade (region 3) if the foreign industry is sufficiently concentrated. In region 2 characterizing interior equilibria, the equilibrium export restraint is more stringent the more competitive is the foreign export industry, since from (31) $\partial V^*/\partial m < 0$. Also, since $\partial V^*/\partial n > 0$, the equilibrium export restraint is conversely less stringent, the more competitive is the domestic industry.

The boundaries in Figure 5 are determined by substitutability between domestic goods and imports in domestic consumption. As γ decreases, regions 1 and 3 diminish and region 2 which is consistent with interior solutions correspondingly expands. Region 1 diminishes because with decreased substitutability between imports and domestic goods a restriction on imports is of less value to domestic firms. In the limit as $\gamma \to 0$, domestic firms have no interest in restraining imports, and hence region 1 disappears. The foreign interest in influencing trade policy however remains. Indeed, as γ falls, the foreign gain from domestic market access increases. Foreigners seek the imposition of the collusive foreign profit-maximizing export restraint, which whatever the values of n and m does not entail free trade. Hence, in the limit as $\gamma \to 0$, region 3 also disappears.

IV. Political Choice of Instrument

The choice between an export restraint and a tariff as the means of protection is also a choice between assigning rents to foreigners and revenue to government. Our specification of political optimization supposes that individual candidates for political office do not themselves value the revenue derived from any tariff which they might propose. The Treasury has rights to tariff revenue. Candidates for political office can only benefit from tariff revenue via discretion in budgetary allocation—contingent on election—and then such discretion via budgetary allocations is exercised only over some small share of the revenue from any particular tariff. However, while the candidates have very limited scope for allocation of tariff revenue, their announced export-restraint policies directly influence the transfer of foreigners and the allocation of rents between domestic and foreign interests. The rent creation and rent allocation is reflected in campaign contributions received.

Because of the rent transfer, a candidate seeking support from foreign interests evidently has reason to prefer an export restraint to a tariff as the instrument for formulating his policy proposal. However, need the same be true for the protectionist candidate seeking support from domestic import-competing interests? Since it is the difference between rents secured by domestic and foreign interests in different policy regimes which determines campaign contributions and hence probabilities of election, one might propose that the protectionist candidate also prefers, given the option, to formulate his policy proposal in terms of an export restraint rather than a tariff. This is confirmed by

PROPOSITION 3: *When candidates have the choice of making policy pronouncements in terms of export restraints or tariffs, both candidates choose export restraints. The political equilibrium in the presence of a tariff option is that obtained when only export restraints are feasible.*

PROOF:
Combinations of tariffs and export restraints among which domestic firms are indifferent follow from equating profits $\pi_i(t)$ and $\pi_i(V)$ as given by (9) and (21) to obtain

$$(32) \quad V = \frac{B}{b\gamma} - \frac{n+1}{b\gamma A}$$
$$\times \left\{ [m(1-\gamma)+1]B + (1-\gamma^2)\gamma mt \right\}.$$

The linear function (32) is depicted as GH in Figure 6. The point G represents free trade, with either $V = \tilde{V}$ or $t = 0$; at H, there are no competitive imports and either $V = 0$ or $t = \bar{t}$. In zone 1, $\pi_i(t) > \pi_i(V)$ and domestic firms thus support a candidate announcing a tariff;

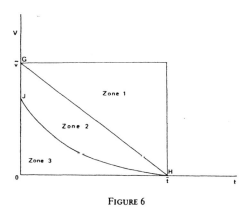

FIGURE 6

in zones 2 and 3 $\pi_i(t) < \pi_i(V)$, so domestic firms support a candidate announcing an export restraint.

JH is the corresponding policy indifference locus for foreign firms, when export restraints can increase foreign profits. (If foreign profits cannot be increased by an export restraint, J coincides with G; otherwise J lies below G, since some restraint below $\bar{V}$ (at G) is beneficial for foreign firms.) To establish JH, use (10) and (22) to equate $\pi_i^*(t)$ and $\pi_i^*(V)$, which yields the convex relation depicted. In zones 1 and 2, $\pi_i^*(t) < \pi_i^*(V)$ and hence foreign firms support the candidate announcing an export restraint. In zone 3 $\pi_i^*(t) > \pi_i^*(V)$, so foreign firms support the candidate announcing a tariff.

In zone 2 the candidate announcing a tariff thus is supported by neither foreign nor domestic interests. In zone 1 foreign interests support the candidate proposing an export restraint and domestic interests the candidates proposing a tariff. However, the export-restraint candidate can secure the support of domestic interests by announcing a policy which moves him into zone 2. In zone 3 foreign interests support the tariff candidate and domestic interests the export-restraint candidate, but similarly the latter candidate can amend his policy so as to move into zone 2, thereby also securing support from foreign interests.

Policy combinations in zones 1 and 3 therefore are inconsistent with political equi-

librium, and in zone 2 only the candidate announcing an export restraint has political support. Hence there exists no equilibrium characterized by a candidate's announcing a policy in terms of a tariff $t \in (0, \bar{t})$ when export restraints are available policy instruments.

Moreover, since $t = 0$ corresponds to $V = \bar{V}$ and $t = \bar{t}$ to $V = 0$, tariffs are completely dominated by export restraints as policy instruments. In particular, this means that tariff equilibria which are not of the form $(t_0 = 0, t_1 = \bar{t})$ are not sustainable in the presence of the opportunity to use an export restraint.

It remains to demonstrate that an export-restraint equilibrium is unaffected by the option to use a tariff. To show this, begin with an equilibrium (V^*, V^*) and let one candidate deviate by announcing a tariff t' which attracts the support of domestic interests: so $\pi_i(t') > \pi_i(V^*)$. Proceed by introducing an export restraint V' such that domestic firms are indifferent between V' and t', that is, $\pi_i(V') = \pi_i(t')$. It can then be shown that $R(V^*, t') < R(V^*, V')$. However, since (V^*, V^*) is an equilibrium, $R(V^*, V') < R(V^*, V^*)$. Hence $R(V^*, t') < R(V^*, V^*)$, which proves that the deviating candidate cannot benefit. A candidate who deviates from (V^*, V^*) by announcing a tariff that attracts the support of foreign interests cannot benefit for similar reasons.

An important determinant of the result that export restraints drive out tariffs in the domestic political contest is the nonappropriability of tariff revenue by the political candidates. The candidates also cannot directly secure the rents associated with the restriction of trade via export restraints. However, these latter rents are a prize for foreigners and accordingly bear upon the value of campaign contributions received by the candidates. Thus, indirectly, the rents from restriction of trade under export restraints become part of campaign contributions and hence are of significance in the political contest. Tariff revenue has no corresponding political significance.

Campaign contributions made in the divergent tariff equilibrium will be greater than in the compromise export-restraint equilibrium. Indeed, since the export-restraint pronouncements converge in a Hotelling manner, there is nothing in equilibrium to distinguish the candidates. Strictly positive political outlays would however be made if the candidates kept part of the contributions for themselves, since then candidates can have an incentive not to converge completely in their policy pronouncements. A candidate's objective function would in that case encompass more than the probability of election. Introducing such a qualified objective function for political candidates does not change the comparative forms taken by the tariff and export-restraint equilibria. Tariff pronouncements still diverge and export-restraint pronouncements converge, but the latter convergence is less than complete.

V. Concluding Remarks

In prior analyses of the relation between political-influence motives and protection, a cohesive industry coalition has been set against a diffuse coalition of domestic losers from protection. Recognition of the domestic political-influence role of foreigners introduces another cohesive coalition to counter the domestic industry-specific interests seeking protection, and the tariff then becomes too divisive an instrument to be politically appealing. Our model of protectionist proposals as the equilibrium outcome of political competition has shown how tariffs are inconsistent with but export restraints facilitate the types of distributive compromises and opportunities for mutual collusive gain favored in political outcomes. Two questions remain.

First, if, as our model proposes, voluntary export restraints are the equilibrium outcome of political contestability of trade policy when tariffs can be used, why have export restraints become prominent only in recent years? We suggest that a political analogue to international integration of goods and financial markets has facilitated increased participation by foreign interests in domestic politics. Also, while there are certain legal complexities attendant on foreigners making domestic political outlays, campaign contributions are facilitated by the domestic legal entities which are subsidiaries of or have interests coincident with foreign corporations. Beyond these considerations, our model also suggests a role for changes in market structure. A more competitive foreign export industry has *ceteris paribus* more to gain from securing regulation of sales in its foreign markets. And a less competitive domestic import-competing industry has more to gain from supporting the restraint on domestic sales of its principal foreign competitors.

The second question is, given the prospect of collusive gain, why should foreign interests participate in the domestic political process rather than use their own home political process to secure a regulated restriction of exports? We would propose that such a collusive restriction of trade invites retaliation in export markets. The foreign cartel would be exposed as engaging in an unfair trade practice, in defiance of national trade laws and the General Agreement on Tariffs and Trade. However, this can clearly not be so when the export restraint is the outcome of the political process in the importing country which itself requests foreign exporters to cooperate in coordinating the restraint of trade.

REFERENCES

Baldwin, Robert, "The Political Economy of Protectionism," in *Import Competition and Response*, J. N. Bhagwati, ed., Chicago: University of Chicago Press, 1982, 263–86.
_____, "Rent Seeking and Trade Policy: An Industry Approach," *Weltwirtschaftliches Archiv*, Heft 4, 1984, *120*, 662–77.
_____, *The Political Economy of U.S. Import Policy*, Cambridge, MA: MIT Press, 1985.
Bernholz, Peter, "On the Reasons for the Influence of Interest Groups on Political Decision Making," *Zeitschrift für Wirtschafts und Socialwissenschaft*, 1974, *94*, 45–63.
_____, "Dominant Interest Groups and Powerless Parties," *Kyklos*, 1977, *30*, 411–20.
Bhagwati, Jagdish N., "Protectionism: Old Wine in New Bottles," *Journal of Policy Modeling*, Spring 1985, *7*, 23–33.

_____ and Srinivasan, T. N., "Optimal Trade Policy and Compensation Under Endogenous Uncertainty: The Phenomenon of Market Disruption," *Journal of International Economics*, November 1976, *6*, 317–36.

Brecher, Richard A. and Bhagwati, Jagdish N., "Voluntary Export Restrictions Versus Import Restrictions: A Welfare-Theoretic Comparison," in H. Kierzkowski, ed., *Protection and Competition in International Trade: Essays in Honor of Max Corden*, Oxford: Basil Blackwell, 1987.

Cassing, James H. and Hillman, Arye L., "Political Influence Motives and the Choice Between Tariffs and Quotas," *Journal of International Economics*, November 1985, *19*, 279–90.

_____ and _____, "Shifting Comparative Advantage and Senescent Industry Collapse," *American Economic Review*, June 1986, *76*, 516–23.

Collyns, Charles and Dunaway, Steven, "The Cost of Trade Restraints: The Case of Japanese Automobile Exports to the United States," *IMF Staff Papers*, March 1987, *34*, 150–75.

Cornes, Richard and Sandler, Todd, *The Theory of Externalities, Public Goods and Club Goods*, Cambridge: Cambridge University Press, 1986.

Das, Satya P., "Foreign Lobbying and the Political Economy of Protection," Indiana University, 1988.

Demsetz, Harold, "Industry Structure, Market Rivalry, and Public Policy," *Journal of Law and Economics*, April 1973, *16*, 1–10.

Eichenberger, Jurgen and Harper, Ian, "Price and Quantity Controls as Facilitating Devices," *Economics Letters*, 1987, *23*, 223–28.

Falvey, Rodney and Lloyd, Peter J., "The Choice of the Instrument of Industry Protection," in Richard N. Snape, ed., *Issues in World Trade Policy: GATT at the Crossroads*, New York: Macmillan, 1986, 152–70.

Feenstra, Robert C., "Voluntary Export Restraint in U.S. Autos 1980–1981: Quality, Employment and Welfare Effects," in Robert E. Baldwin and Anne O. Krueger, eds., *The Structure and Evolution of Recent U.S. Trade Policy*, Chicago: The University of Chicago Press for NBER, 1984, 298–325.

_____, "Automobile Prices and Protection: The U.S.-Japan Trade Restraint," *Journal of Policy Modeling*, Spring 1985, *7*, 49–68.

Harris, Richard, "Why Voluntary Export Restraints Are Voluntary," *Canadian Journal of Economics*, November 1985, *18*, 799–809.

Hillman, Arye L., "Declining Industries and Political Support Protectionist Motives," *American Economic Review*, December 1982, *72*, 1180–87.

_____, *The Political Economy of Protection*, in the series Fundamentals of Pure and Applied Economics, Chur, New York, London, Paris: Harwood Academic Publishers, 1988.

_____ and Katz, Eliakim "Risk-averse Rent Seekers and the Social Cost of Monopoly Power," *Economic Journal*, March 1984, *94*, 104–10, reprinted in C. Rowley, R. Tollison, and G. Tullock, eds., *The Political Economy of Rent Seeking*, Boston: Kluwer Academic Publishers, 1988, 81–90.

_____ and Riley, John, "Politically Contestable Rents and Transfers," presented at the conference on *Political Economy: Theory and Policy Implications*, World Bank, Washington D.C., June 1987, forthcoming in *Economics and Politics*, inaugural issue.

Husted, Steven, "Foreign Lobbying and the Formation of Domestic Trade Policy," presented at the Meetings of the Western Economic Association, San Francisco, July 1986.

Jones, Kent, "The Political Economy of Voluntary Export Restraints," *Kyklos*, 1984, *37*, 82–101.

Krishna, Kala, "Trade Restrictions as Facilitating Practices," *Journal of International Economics*, forthcoming 1988.

Mayer, Wolfgang, "Endogenous Tariff Formation," *American Economic Review*, December 1984, *74*, 970–85.

_____ and Riezman, Raymond, "Endogenous Choice of Trade Policy Instruments," *Journal of International Economics*, November 1987, *23*, 377–81.

_____ and _____, "Tariff Formation in

Political-Economy Models," presented at the conference on *Political Economy: Theory and Policy Implications*, World Bank, Washington D.C., June 1987.

Rodrik, Dani, "Tariffs, Subsidies and Welfare with Endogenous Policy," *Journal of International Economics*, November 1986, *21*, 285–99.

Young, Leslie and Magee, Stephen P., "Endogenous Protection, Factor Returns, and Resource Allocation," *Review of Economic Studies*, July 1986, *53*, 407–19.

Protection for Sale

By GENE M. GROSSMAN AND ELHANAN HELPMAN*

We develop a model in which special-interest groups make political contributions in order to influence an incumbent government's choice of trade policy. The interest groups bid for protection with their campaign support. Politicians maximize their own welfare, which depends on total contributions collected and on the welfare of voters. We study the structure of protection that emerges in the political equilibrium and the contributions by different lobbies that support the policy outcome. We also discuss why the lobbies may in some cases prefer to have the government use trade policy to transfer income, rather than more efficient means. (JEL F13, D72)

When asked why free trade is so often preached and so rarely practiced, most international economists blame "politics." In representative democracies, governments shape trade policy in response not only to the concerns of the general electorate, but also to the pressures applied by special interests. Interest groups participate in the political process in order to influence policy outcomes. Politicians respond to the incentives they face, trading off the financial and other support that comes from heeding the interest groups' demands against the alienation of voters that may result from the implementation of socially costly policies.

Research on the political economy of trade policy seeks to explain the equilibrium outcome of this political process. Two different approaches are prominent in the literature (which is nicely surveyed by Arye Hillman [1989]). One approach stresses *political competition* between opposing candidates. In the work of Stephen Magee et al.

(1989) and Hillman and Heinrich Ursprung (1988), competing parties announce trade policies that they are committed to implement, if elected. Organized lobby groups evaluate their members' prospects under the alternative policy proposals and contribute resources to the party that promises them the highest level of welfare. The parties use the resources to sway voters, who are presumed to be imperfectly informed about candidates' positions. In making their giving decisions, the lobbies weigh the benefit of an increased probability of their favorite party being elected against the direct cost of the donation. Clearly, the motivation for political contributions in this setting is to influence the election outcome.

The second approach, pioneered by George Stigler (1971) and first used to study endogenous protection by Hillman (1982), sees economic policies as being set by an incumbent government seeking to maximize its *political support*. The "political-support function" has as arguments the welfare that designated interest groups derive from the chosen policies and the deadweight loss that the policies impose on society at large. In this formulation, campaign contributions do not enter directly into the analysis (although they may be implicit in the notion of "support" by special interests), and the political competition of the next election is kept in the background. While the incumbent government maximizes support with the apparent goal of being reelected, the election

*Grossman: Woodrow Wilson School, Princeton University, Princeton, NJ 08544; Helpman: Department of Economics, Tel Aviv University, Tel Aviv 69978, Israel, and the Canadian Institute for Advanced Research. We are grateful to Robert Baldwin, Avinash Dixit, Joanne Gowa, Arye Hillman, Paul Krugman, Tom Romer, Henry Ursprung, and two anonymous referees for helpful suggestions and the National Science Foundation and the U.S.–Israel Binational Science Foundation for financial support.

833

American Economic Review **84**, 833–850

131

itself is not explicitly considered, nor are the positions of potential rivals.

Both of these approaches contribute to our understanding of the political optimization underlying the endogenous determination of trade policy. Political competition seems most important for explaining the broader contours of trade policy: Will it be liberal or interventionist? Benefit capital or labor? Benefit the rich or the poor? At this level of generality, competing parties can articulate opposing positions and can inform (at least some) voters of the differences among them. For the finer details of policy—such as the extent to which different industries will be favored, or the designation of what sorts of instruments will be used—the political-support approach seems more appropriate. Often incumbent governments find themselves in a position to make the detailed policy choices unencumbered by immediate competition from political rivals. Of course, if the choices made by the government turn out to be ill-advised, the incumbent officeholders may be held accountable in subsequent elections.

This paper seeks to explain the equilibrium *structure of trade protection*. We are interested in understanding which special interest groups will be especially successful in capturing private benefits from the political process. We are also interested in understanding why lobbies may hold preferences over the types of policies that are used to redistribute income and why they may support institutional constraints on the set of instruments available to the government. For these purposes we adopt the perspective of the political-support approach; we model incumbent politicians who make policy choices while being aware that their decisions may affect their chances for reelection.

In developing our model of political support we take what we feel are significant steps beyond the existing literature. Previous authors have specified a reduced form for the politicians' objective function, assuming that the government places different fixed weights on the welfare levels of different groups in society. Here we derive the government's objective from more primitive

preferences defined over campaign contributions and voter well-being. While it might be argued that these preferences too have more fundamental determinants in the details of the political process, our formulation does offer a distinct advantage over more reduced-form approaches for some types of questions. One can easily imagine changes in the international rules of the game that would affect government's willingness and ability to protect particular sectoral interests but would not affect politicians' weighting of campaign contributions relative to general voter dissatisfaction. We believe that our approach could be used (in future research) to investigate how such institutional changes would affect equilibrium policies *by endogenously changing the shape of the political-support function*.

Not only do we derive the weights that the government places on different groups endogenously, but we also make explicit the process by which the government comes to pay special attention to the concerns of particular interests. Organized interest groups are able to offer political contributions, which politicians value for their potential use in the coming election (and perhaps otherwise). It is this ability to contribute (as well as the ability to deliver blocks of votes, a channel of influence that we neglect in the current paper) that gives special interests their favored position in the eyes of the government.

In our model, lobbies represent industry interests. The lobbies make (implicit) offers that relate prospective contributions to the trade policies chosen by the incumbent government. The government then sets policy —a vector of import and export taxes and subsidies—to maximize a weighted sum of aggregate social welfare and total contributions. In this process the various interest groups vie for the government's favor. The lobbies' equilibrium bids are each optimal, given the contributions promised by the others. Here, in contrast to the literature on political competition, an individual interest group does not see a link between its own (relatively small) contribution and the election outcome; rather, the groups are motivated to make contributions by the prospect of *influencing policy*. In other words, politicians' penchant for campaign gifts makes "protection for sale."[1]

We proceed to show that equilibrium trade policies obey a modified Ramsey rule: all else equal, industries with higher import demand or export supply elasticities will have smaller deviations from free trade; but the rates of protection also reflect the relative political strengths of the various interest groups and parameters describing the nation's political economy. The paper goes on to discuss the determinants of the relative sizes of the political contributions that the various interest groups must make to support the equilibrium policy choices. Finally, we examine the reasons why lobbies may prefer in some circumstances to constrain the set of policy instruments that governments can use to redistribute income.

I. Overview

We begin with an overview of our analytical approach, postponing the formal development of our model until the next section. We consider a small, competitive economy that faces exogenously given world prices. Free trade is efficient for such an economy, so any policy interventions can be ascribed to the political process. The economy produces a numeraire good, with labor alone, and each of n additional products using labor and an input that is specific to the particular sector. We assume that there is a high degree of concentration in the ownership of many of the n specific inputs and that the various owners of some of these inputs have banded together to form lobby groups. We do not at this point have a theory of lobby formation; rather we take it as given that some factor owners overcome the free-rider problem to conduct joint lobbying activities, while others do not.

The lobby groups may offer political contributions to the incumbent officeholders, who are in a position to set the current trade policy. The lobbies do not contribute to any challenger candidates, nor do they take into account any effect of their contribution on the likelihood that the incumbents will be reelected. Although we recognize the absence of explicit political competition as a potential shortcoming of our approach, we believe that the available evidence for the United States supports our assumptions as a reasonable first approximation. In particular, political action committees (PAC's) gave more than three-quarters of their total contributions in the 1988 Congressional campaigns to incumbent candidates. If elections for open seats are excluded, incumbents received 6.3 times as much in contributions from PAC's as did their challengers (David Magelby and Candice Nelson, 1990 p. 86). Moreover, 62 percent of the campaign contributions by PAC's in the 1987–1988 campaign occurred in the first 18 months of the election cycle, often before a challenger to the incumbent had even been identified (Magelby and Nelson, 1990 p. 67). Many of these incumbents would not be involved in close races when the elections came. Also, few single contributions were large relative to total spending by any candidate. In short, PAC contributions can best be seen as attempts to curry favor.[2]

While the lobby groups ignore the effects of their individual contributions on the election probabilities, the incumbent politicians may see a relationship between *total* collections (which can be used to finance campaign spending) and their

---

[1] We recognize, of course, that influence-peddling is illegal in most political systems. The policy-contingent contribution offers that we have in mind need not be explicit. Special-interest groups can readily make it known, as indeed most do, that they intend to support more generously those politicians who take positions that benefit their cause.

[2] Magelby and Nelson (1990 p. 55) report that, of the 255 incumbent Congress members who received the greatest portion of their funding from PAC's, only 19 took part in races where the challenger received 45 percent or more of the vote. They conclude from their review of the evidence that "PAC money is interested money" with "more than an electoral objective in mind."

reelection prospects.[3] At the same time, they may believe that their odds of survival depend on the utility level achieved by the average voter. With these considerations in mind, we suppose that the incumbent politicians' objective is to maximize a weighted sum of total political contributions and aggregate social welfare. Such an objective function seems plausible for a government that is concerned about the next election, but broader interpretations also are possible. For example, aggregate welfare might enter the government's objective if some representatives are civil-minded. In addition, politicians may value contributions not only for financing future campaigns, but also for retiring debts from previous elections (which many times are owed to the politician's personal estate), for deterring competition from quality challengers,[4] and for showing the candidates' abilities as fundraisers and thereby establishing their credibility as potential candidates for higher political or party office. In any event, politicians have, over the years, revealed their considerable taste for amassing such contributions.

We model the lobbying process as follows. Each organized interest group representing one of the sector-specific factors confronts the government with a *contribution schedule*. The schedule maps every policy vector that the government might choose (where policies are import and export taxes and subsidies on the n nonnumeraire goods) into a campaign contribution level. Of course, some policies may evoke a contribution of zero from some lobbies. The government then sets a policy vector and collects from each lobby the contribution associated with its policy choice. An equilibrium is a set of contribution schedules such that each lobby's schedule maximizes the aggregate utility of the lobby's members, taking as given the schedules of the other lobby groups. In calculating their optimal schedules, the lobbies recognize that the politicians ultimately will set policy to maximize their own welfare. The Nash-equilibrium contribution schedules implement an equilibrium trade-policy choice.

Our model has the structure of a *common agency problem*, that is, a situation that arises when several principals attempt to induce a single agent to take an action that may be costly for the agent to perform. The government here serves as an agent for the various (and conflicting) special interest groups, while bearing a cost for implementing an inefficient policy that stems from its accountability to the general electorate. B. Douglas Bernheim and Michael D. Whinston (1986) have coined the term *menu auction* to describe a situation of complete information where bidders announce a "menu" of offers for various possible actions open to an "auctioneer" and then pay the bids associated with the action selected. They have analyzed a class of such auctions and derived several results that will prove useful below for characterizing the political equilibrium in our economy.

II. Formal Framework

A small economy is populated by individuals with identical preferences but different factor endowments. Each individual maximizes utility given by

$$(1) \qquad u = x_0 + \sum_{i=1}^{n} u_i(x_i)$$

where x_0 is consumption of good 0 and x_i is consumption of good i, $i = 1, 2, \ldots, n$. The sub-utility functions $u_i(\cdot)$ are differentiable,

---

[3] Gary C. Jacobson (1978, 1987) has argued that an incumbent's campaign spending level has little quantifiable effect on his or her chance of winning reelection. However, Donald Philip Green and Jonathan S. Krasno (1988) challenge this view, pointing out that Jacobson has either failed to control for the correlation between spending and the quality of the opponent or has used inappropriate instruments. They find a much larger influence of incumbent spending on election outcomes once challenger quality is taken into account.

[4] In their study of campaign spending in the 1978 Congressional election, Edie N. Goldenberg et al. (1986) suggest that incumbents stockpiled contributions and made early campaign expenditures in order to dissuade strong challengers from entering the race. However, Krasno and Green (1988) find little evidence of such strategic spending in their regression analysis of challenger quality.

increasing, and strictly concave. Good 0 serves as numeraire, with a world and domestic price equal to 1. We denote by p_i^* the exogenous world price of good i, while p_i represents its domestic price. With these preferences, an individual spending an amount E consumes $x_i = d_i(p_i)$ of good i, $i = 1, 2, \ldots, n$ [where the demand function $d_i(\cdot)$ is the inverse of $u_i'(x_i)$] and $x_0 = E - \Sigma_i p_i d_i(p_i)$ of the numeraire good. Indirect utility takes the form

$$(2) \qquad V(\mathbf{p}, E) = E + s(\mathbf{p})$$

where $\mathbf{p} = (p_1, p_2, \ldots, p_n)$ is the vector of domestic prices of the nonnumeraire goods and $s(\mathbf{p}) \equiv \Sigma_i u_i[d_i(p_i)] - \Sigma_i p_i d_i(p_i)$ is the consumer surplus derived from these goods.

Good 0 is manufactured from labor alone with constant returns to scale and an input–output coefficient equal to 1. We assume that the aggregate supply of labor is large enough to ensure a positive supply of this good. Then the wage rate equals 1 in a competitive equilibrium. Production of each nonnumeraire good requires labor and a sector-specific input. The technologies for these goods exhibit constant returns to scale, and the various specific inputs are available in inelastic supply. With the wage rate fixed at 1, the aggregate reward to the specific factor used in producing good i depends only on the domestic price of that good. We denote this reward by $\pi_i(p_i)$.

In this paper, we restrict the set of policy instruments available to politicians. For now, we allow the government to implement only trade taxes and subsidies. These policies drive a wedge between domestic and world prices. A domestic price in excess of the world price implies an import tariff for a good that is imported and an export subsidy for one that is exported. Domestic prices below world prices correspond to import subsidies and export taxes. The net revenue from all taxes and subsidies, expressed on a per capita basis, is given by

$$(3) \quad r(\mathbf{p})$$

$$= \sum_i (p_i - p_i^*) \left[d_i(p_i) - \frac{1}{N} y_i(p_i) \right]$$

where N measures the total (voting) population and $y_i(p_i) = \pi_i'(p_i)$ is domestic output of good i. We assume that the government redistributes revenue uniformly to all of the country's voters. Then $r(\mathbf{p})$ gives the net government transfer to each individual.

A typical individual derives income from wages and government transfers, and possibly from the ownership of some sector-specific input. We assume that claims to the specific inputs are indivisible and nontradable (e.g., claims to sector-specific human capital) and that individuals own at most one type. Clearly, those who own some of the specific input used in producing good i will see their income tied to the domestic price of that good. These individuals will have a direct stake in the tax or subsidy applicable to trade in good i that goes beyond their general interest as consumers in trade policies that affect any domestic prices.

The various owners of the specific factor used in industry i, with their common interest in protection (or export subsidies) for their sector, may choose to join forces for political activity. Mancur Olson (1965) has discussed "the logic of collective action," but also the difficulties associated with overcoming free-rider problems. We have nothing to add to his discussion here, so we simply assume that in some exogenous set of sectors, denoted L, the specific-factor owners have been able to organize themselves into lobby groups. The lobbies serve to coordinate campaign giving decisions and to communicate the political "offers" to the government. In the remaining sectors (if any), the individual owners of the specific factors remain unorganized. Any individual perceives himself or herself as too small to communicate political demands effectively or to influence policy. Therefore, the unorganized factor owners, as well as all individuals who own no claims to a specific input, refrain from making political contributions.

The lobby representing an organized sector i makes its political contribution contingent on the trade-policy vector implemented by the government. Since the country is small, it can equivalently relate the gift to the realized vector of domestic prices. We denote by $C_i(\mathbf{p})$ the contribution schedule tendered by lobby i. The lobby tailors this schedule to maximize the total welfare (income plus consumer surplus less contributions) of its members. It then collects the necessary donations from its members in such a way as to allow all to share in the gains from political coordination.

It will prove convenient in what follows to express the joint welfare of the members of lobby group i as $V_i = W_i - C_i$, where W_i is their gross-of-contributions joint welfare. We note that

$$(4) \quad W_i(\mathbf{p}) \equiv \ell_i + \pi_i(p_i)$$
$$+ \alpha_i N[r(\mathbf{p}) + s(\mathbf{p})]$$

where ℓ_i is the total labor supply (and also the labor income) of owners of the specific input used in industry i and α_i is the fraction of the voting population that owns some of this factor.

The incumbent government cares about the total level of political contributions and about aggregate well-being. The government values contributions, because they can be used to finance campaign spending, and as noted above, they may provide other direct benefits to the officeholders. Social welfare will be of concern to the incumbent government if voters are more likely to re-elect a government that has delivered a high standard of living. We choose a linear form for the government's objective function, namely,

$$(5) \quad G = \sum_{i \in L} C_i(\mathbf{p}) + aW(\mathbf{p}) \qquad a \geq 0$$

where W represents aggregate, gross-of-contributions welfare.[5] Aggregate gross welfare equals aggregate income plus trade tax revenues plus total consumer surplus; that is,

$$(6) \quad W(\mathbf{p}) = \ell + \sum_{i=1}^{n} \pi_i(p_i)$$
$$+ N[r(\mathbf{p}) + s(\mathbf{p})].$$

We are interested in the political equilibrium of a two-stage noncooperative game in which the lobbies simultaneously choose their political contribution schedules in the first stage and the government sets policy in the second. An equilibrium is a set of contribution functions $\{C_i^o(\mathbf{p})\}$, one for each organized lobby group, such that each one maximizes the joint welfare of the group's members given the schedules set by the other groups and the anticipated political optimization by the government; and a domestic price vector $\mathbf{p}^o$ that maximizes the government's objective taking the contribution schedules as given. We characterize the equilibrium structure of protection in the next section and the political contributions that underlie the government's policy choice in the section that follows.

III. The Structure of Protection

As we noted near the end of Section II, the interaction between the various lobbies and the government in this economy has the structure of a menu-auction problem. Bernheim and Whinston (1986) have characterized the equilibrium for a class of such problems. Although they limited their analysis to situations where players bid for a finite set of objects, it is clear that their main results apply also when, as here, the auctioneer can choose from a continuum of possible actions. Accordingly, we allow the government's choice set (of domestic price vectors) to be continuous.

Let $\mathcal{P}$ denote the set of domestic price vectors from which the government may choose. We bound $\mathcal{P}$ so that each domestic price p_i must lie between some minimum $\underline{p}_i$ and some maximum $\bar{p}_i$. For the most part, we restrict attention to equilibria that lie in

---

[5] We could equally well write the government's welfare function as $\hat{G} = a_1 \Sigma_{i \in L} C_i + a_2(W_i - \Sigma_{i \in L} C_i)$, where a_1 is the weight the government attaches to campaign contributions and a_2 is the weight it attaches to *net* aggregate welfare. Maximizing $\hat{G}$ is equivalent to maximizing G in (5) with $a = a_2/(a_1 - a_2)$, provided that $a_1 > a_2$. We assume that this is so (i.e., that politicians value a dollar in their campaign coffers more highly than a dollar in the hands of the public). This assumption implies no restriction on the size of the parameter a.

the interior of $\mathcal{P}$. Lemma 2 of Bernheim and Whinston (1986) implies that an equilibrium to the trade-policy game can be characterized as follows:

PROPOSITION 1 (B-W): $(\{C_i^\circ\}_{i \in L}, \mathbf{p}^\circ)$ *is a subgame-perfect Nash equilibrium of the trade-policy game if and only if:*

(a) C_i° *is feasible for all $i \in L$;*
(b) $\mathbf{p}^\circ$ *maximizes $\sum_{i \in L} C_i^\circ(\mathbf{p}) + aW(\mathbf{p})$ on $\mathcal{P}$;*
(c) $\mathbf{p}^\circ$ *maximizes*

$$W_j(\mathbf{p}) - C_j^\circ(\mathbf{p}) + \sum_{i \in L} C_i^\circ(\mathbf{p}) + aW(\mathbf{p})$$

on $\mathcal{P}$ for every $j \in L$;
(d) *for every $j \in L$ there exists a $\mathbf{p}^j \in \mathcal{P}$ that maximizes $\sum_{i \in L} C_i^\circ(\mathbf{p}) + aW(\mathbf{p})$ on $\mathcal{P}$ such that $C_j^\circ(\mathbf{p}^j) = 0$.*

Condition (a) restricts each lobby's contribution schedule to be among those that are feasible (i.e., contributions must be nonnegative and no greater than the aggregate income available to the lobby's members). Condition (b) states that, given the contribution schedules offered by the lobbies, the government sets trade policy to maximize its own welfare. The last two conditions allow us to characterize the equilibrium structure of protection and the equilibrium pattern of political contributions, respectively. We derive and apply condition (c) here, while postponing discussion of condition (d) until the next section.

Condition (c) stipulates that, for every lobby j, the equilibrium price vector must maximize the joint welfare of that lobby and the government, given the contribution schedules offered by the other lobbies. If this were not the case, then lobby j could reformulate its policy bids to induce the government to choose the jointly optimal price vector and could appropriate some (in fact, nearly all) of the surplus from the switch in policy. Suppose, for example, that the government contemplated choosing the price vector $\bar{\mathbf{p}}$, whereas $\hat{\mathbf{p}}$ is jointly optimal for lobby j and the government. All lobby j need do is design a new contribution schedule that pays the government for any price

vector $\mathbf{p}$ the difference between its welfare at $\bar{\mathbf{p}}$ and its welfare at $\mathbf{p}$, plus a little bit more for choosing $\mathbf{p}$. The "little bit more" would vary with $\mathbf{p}$ and would be maximal for $\mathbf{p} = \hat{\mathbf{p}}$. Then the government would gain by choosing $\hat{\mathbf{p}}$ in place of $\bar{\mathbf{p}}$, and would prefer $\hat{\mathbf{p}}$ to any other policy choice. The government's gain would be small, however, and the lobby would capture nearly all of the surplus.[6] In equilibrium, no such unexploited profit opportunities can exist for any lobby.

Let us assume now that the lobbies set political-contribution functions that are differentiable, at least around the equilibrium point $\mathbf{p}^\circ$. In a moment we will argue that there are some compelling reasons for focusing on contribution schedules that have this property. With contribution functions that are differentiable, the fact that $\mathbf{p}^\circ$ maximizes $V_j + G$ implies that a first-order condition is satisfied at $\mathbf{p}^\circ$, namely,

$$(7) \quad \nabla W_j^\circ(\mathbf{p}^\circ) - \nabla C_j^\circ(\mathbf{p}^\circ) + \sum_{i \in L} \nabla C_i^\circ(\mathbf{p}^\circ)$$

$$+ a\nabla W(\mathbf{p}^\circ) = 0 \quad \text{for all } j \in L.$$

However, the government's maximization of G requires the first-order condition

$$(8) \quad \sum_{i \in L} \nabla C_i^\circ(\mathbf{p}^\circ) + a\nabla W(\mathbf{p}^\circ) = 0.$$

Taken together, (7) and (8) imply

$$(9) \quad \nabla C_i^\circ(\mathbf{p}^\circ) = \nabla W_i(\mathbf{p}^\circ) \quad \text{for all } i \in L.$$

Equation (9) establishes that the contribution schedules all are *locally truthful* around $\mathbf{p}^\circ$; that is, each lobby sets its contri-

---

[6] More formally, let $\tilde{C}_i(\mathbf{p})$ be the contemplated bid schedules for the lobbies $i \in L$. Suppose they induce the government to choose $\bar{\mathbf{p}}$, but $\hat{\mathbf{p}} \neq \bar{\mathbf{p}}$ maximizes $V_j + G$, given $\{\tilde{C}_i(\mathbf{p})\}$ for $i \neq j$. Now let lobby j reformulate its contribution schedule as $\hat{C}_j(\mathbf{p}) \equiv \sum_{i \in L} \tilde{C}_i(\bar{\mathbf{p}}) + aW(\bar{\mathbf{p}}) - \sum_{i \in L, i \neq j} \tilde{C}_i(\mathbf{p}) - aW(\mathbf{p}) + \varepsilon h(\mathbf{p})$, where $h(\cdot)$ is any nonnegative function that reaches a unique maximum at $\mathbf{p} = \hat{\mathbf{p}}$. Faced with this new schedule in place of $\tilde{C}_j(\mathbf{p})$, the government maximizes G by choosing the policy vector $\hat{\mathbf{p}}$ as long as $\varepsilon > 0$. Lobby j's welfare becomes $W_j(\hat{\mathbf{p}}) - \hat{C}_j(\hat{\mathbf{p}}) = W_j(\bar{\mathbf{p}}) - \tilde{C}_j(\bar{\mathbf{p}}) + \Delta - \varepsilon h(\hat{\mathbf{p}})$, where $\Delta > 0$ represents the gain in joint welfare $V_j + G$ that results from replacing $\bar{\mathbf{p}}$ with $\hat{\mathbf{p}}$. For ε small enough, we have $\Delta > \varepsilon h(\hat{\mathbf{p}})$, which implies $W_j(\hat{\mathbf{p}}) - \hat{C}_j(\hat{\mathbf{p}}) > W_j(\bar{\mathbf{p}}) - \tilde{C}_j(\bar{\mathbf{p}})$ (i.e., the lobby gains from this change in its contribution schedule).

Gene M. Grossman and Elhanan Helpman

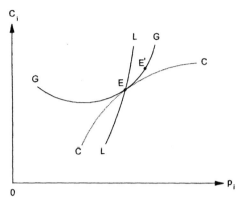

FIGURE 1. LOCAL TRUTHFULNESS

bution schedule so that the marginal change in the contribution for a small change in policy matches the effect of the policy change on the lobby's gross welfare. In other words, the shapes of the schedules reveal the lobbies' true preferences in the neighborhood of the equilibrium. The intuition for this result can be seen in Figure 1, where we plot the contribution C_i made by lobby i along the vertical axis and the domestic price p_i along the horizontal axis. The curve labeled GG is an indifference curve for the government. It shows the contributions from lobby i that would compensate the government for altering the price of good i, in view of the change in aggregate welfare *and* the change in contributions from all other lobbies that would result from the price change. The curve labeled LL depicts an indifference curve for lobby i. These curves must be upward-sloping in the neighborhood of the equilibrium, although this fact is not needed for the present argument. Now suppose that the lobby offers the contribution schedule CC, inducing the government to maximize its welfare at point E. Since CC is not tangent to LL at E, there exists a point E' along GG that yields greater welfare to lobby i than point E. The lobby could induce the government to choose E' instead of E by offering a contribution schedule that coincides with CC until a point somewhere below point E, falls below CC at that point and then rises to be tangent with

GG at E'. It will always be possible for the lobby to reconfigure its contribution schedule like this so as to raise its net welfare, unless CC and LL are tangent to one another (and to GG) at the equilibrium point.

We can extend this notion of "truthfulness" to define (as Bernheim and Whinston [1986] do) a *truthful contribution schedule*. This is a contribution schedule that *everywhere* reflects the true preferences of the lobby. It pays to the government for any policy **p** the excess (if any) of lobby j's gross welfare at **p** relative to some base level of welfare. Formally, a truthful contribution function takes the form

$$(10) \quad C_j^T(\mathbf{p}, B_j) = \max[0, W_j(\mathbf{p}) - B_j]$$

for some B_j. Notice that truthful schedules are differentiable, except possibly where the contribution becomes nil, because the gross benefit functions are differentiable. Bernheim and Whinston (1986) have shown that players bear essentially no cost from playing truthful strategies, because the set of best responses to *any* strategies played by one's opponents includes a strategy that is truthful. They have also shown that all equilibria supported by truthful strategies, and only these equilibria, are stable to nonbinding communication among the players (i.e., they are "coalition-proof"). For these reasons they argue that *truthful Nash equilibria* (those equilibria supported by truthful bid functions) may be focal among the set of Nash equilibria.

Truthful Nash equilibria (TNE) have an interesting property. The equilibrium price vector of any TNE satisfies[7]

$$(11) \quad \mathbf{p}^\circ = \underset{\mathbf{p} \in \mathcal{P}}{\arg\max}\left[\sum_{j \in L} W_j(\mathbf{p}) + aW(\mathbf{p})\right].$$

---

[7]To see this, note that condition (b) of Proposition 1 implies that $\sum_{j \in L} C_j^\circ(\mathbf{p}^\circ) + aW(\mathbf{p}^\circ) \geq \sum_{j \in L} C_j^\circ(\mathbf{p}) + aW(\mathbf{p})$ for all $\mathbf{p} \in \mathcal{P}$. If the contribution functions are truthful, then from the definition (10), $C_j^\circ(\mathbf{p}^\circ) = W_j(\mathbf{p}^\circ) - B_j^\circ$ (where B_j° is the equilibrium net benefit to lobby j) and $C_j^\circ(\mathbf{p}) \geq W_j(\mathbf{p}) - B_j^\circ$ for all $j \in L$ and all $\mathbf{p} \in \mathcal{P}$. Therefore $\sum_{j \in L} W_j(\mathbf{p}^\circ) + aW(\mathbf{p}^\circ) \geq \sum_{j \in L} W_j(\mathbf{p}) + aW(\mathbf{p})$ for all $\mathbf{p} \in \mathcal{P}$.

Equation (11) says that, in equilibrium, truthful contribution schedules induce the government to behave as if it were maximizing a social-welfare function that weights different members of society differently, with individuals represented by a lobby group receiving a weight of $1 + a$ and those not so represented receiving the smaller weight of a. Our model thus provides microanalytic foundations for the reduced-form political-support function used by, for example, Ngo Van Long and Neil Vousden (1991).

We return now to the characterization of equilibrium trade policies that can be supported by differentiable—although not necessarily globally truthful—contribution schedules.[8] We sum (9) over i and substitute the result into (8) to derive

$$(12) \quad \sum_{i \in L} \nabla W_i(\mathbf{p}^o) + a \nabla W(\mathbf{p}^o) = 0.$$

This equation characterizes the equilibrium domestic prices supported by differentiable contribution functions. Notice that this is just the first-order condition that is necessary for the maximization in (11), although we see that it must hold more generally (i.e., for all differentiable contribution schedules, not just those that are everywhere truthful).

Our next step is to calculate how marginal policy changes affect the welfare of the various groups in society. Looking first at the members of some lobby i we find from (3) and (4) that

$$(13) \quad \frac{\partial W_i}{\partial p_j} = (\delta_{ij} - \alpha_i) y_j(p_j)$$
$$+ \alpha_i (p_j - p_j^*) m_j'(p_j)$$

where $m_j(p_j) \equiv N d_j(p_j) - y_j(p_j)$ denotes the

net import demand function and δ_{ij} is an indicator variable that equals 1 if $i = j$ and 0 otherwise. Equation (13) states that lobby i gains from an increase in the domestic price of good i above its free-trade level and gains from a decrease in the price of any other good (because $m_j' < 0$). The specific-factor owners benefit more from an increase in the price of their industry's output the larger is the free-trade supply of the good. The benefit to lobby i that results from a decline in the price of another good j falls as the share of the members of lobby i in the total population shrinks, and it vanishes completely in the limit when $\alpha_i = 0$. When the members of lobby i are a negligible fraction of the total population, they receive only a negligible share of the transfers generated by taxes on good j, and they enjoy only a negligible share of the surplus that derives from consumption of good j. In this case, they are unaffected by changes in the domestic price of that good.

Since all organized interest groups submit locally truthful contribution schedules, we need to know how a policy change impinges on the gross welfare of the entire group of individuals who are actively trying to influence policy. Accordingly, we sum the expressions in (13) for all $i \in L$ to derive

$$(14) \quad \sum_{i \in L} \frac{\partial W_i}{\partial p_j} = (I_j - \alpha_L) y_j(p_j)$$
$$+ \alpha_L (p_j - p_j^*) m_j'(p_j)$$

where $I_j \equiv \sum_{i \in L} \delta_{ij}$ is an indicator variable that equals 1 if industry j is organized and 0 otherwise, while $\alpha_L \equiv \sum_{i \in L} \alpha_i$ denotes the fraction of the total population of voters who are represented by a lobby. Equation (14) reveals that, starting from free-trade prices, lobby members as a whole benefit from a small increase in the domestic price of any good that is produced by an organized industry and (provided $\alpha_L > 0$) from a small decline in the price of any good that is produced by an unorganized industry.

Finally, we compute the effect of a marginal price change on aggregate welfare.

---

[8] Even if one does not accept the Bernheim-Whinston argument for TNE, one might want to require that contribution schedules be differentiable, because these schedules will be robust to small mistakes in calculation on the part of the lobbies, whereas a lobby might suffer a large penalty for a small miscalculation if it used a nondifferentiable payment schedule.

Gene M. Grossman and Elhanan Helpman

Using the definition of W in (6), we find

$$(15) \qquad \frac{\partial W}{\partial p_j} = (p_j - p_j^*)m_j'(p_j)$$

which reveals, of course, that marginal deadweight loss grows as the economy deviates further and further from free trade. Substituting (14) and (15) into (12) allows us to solve for the domestic prices in political equilibrium, assuming that these prices lie in the interior of $\mathcal{P}$.[9] We express the result in terms of the equilibrium ad valorem trade taxes and subsidies, which are defined by $t_i^o \equiv (p_i^o - p_i^*)/p_i^*$.

PROPOSITION 2 (Equilibrium Policies): *If the lobbies use contribution schedules that are differentiable around the equilibrium point, and if the equilibrium lies in the interior of $\mathcal{P}$, then the government chooses trade taxes and subsidies that satisfy*

$$\frac{t_i^o}{1 + t_i^o} = \frac{I_i - \alpha_L}{a + \alpha_L}\left(\frac{z_i^o}{e_i^o}\right) \qquad \text{for } i = 1, 2, \ldots, n$$

where $z_i^o = y_i(p_i^o)/m_i(p_i^o)$ is the equilibrium ratio of domestic output to imports (negative for exports) and $e_i^o = -m_i'(p_i^o)p_i^o/m_i(p_i^o)$ is the elasticity of import demand or of export supply (the former defined to be positive, the latter negative).

Proposition 2 describes a modified Ramsey rule. All else equal, industries that have

<hr>

[9]The domestic price of good i may be driven to the boundary of $\mathcal{P}$ if one of several constraints becomes binding. First, the owners of the specific factor used in industry i may not have sufficient resources to "protect themselves" from other lobbies (i.e., the political contributions needed to keep p_i above $\underline{p}_i$ may exceed their aggregate income). Second, some lobby group j may bid for such a large export subsidy that the income of some individuals will not be sufficient to cover the per capita levy needed to finance the subsidy. Then p_j will be driven to $\bar{p}_j$. These extreme outcomes, which are made possible by the linearity in our specification, are not an especially interesting feature of the model. Thus, we do not pursue the equilibria with corner solutions any further.

high import demand or export supply elasticities (in absolute value) will have smaller ad valorem deviations from free trade. This is true for two reasons. First, the government may bear a political cost from creating deadweight loss (if $a > 0$). To the extent that this is so, all else equal, it will prefer to raise contributions from sectors where the cost is small. Second, even if $a = 0$, if $\alpha_L > 0$ the members of lobbies as a group will share in any deadweight loss that results from trade policy. The owners of specific inputs in industries other than i will bid more to avoid protection in sector i the greater is the social cost of that protection.

Considerations of deadweight loss are modified by political variables in the determination of the equilibrium structure of protection. First, note that *all* sectors that are represented by lobbies are protected by import tariffs or export subsidies in the political equilibrium.[10] In contrast, import subsidies and export taxes are applied to all sectors that have no organized representation. In other words, the organized interest groups collectively manage to raise the domestic prices of goods from which they derive profit income and to lower the prices of goods that they only consume. The political power of a particular organized sector is reflected by the ratio of domestic output to imports. In sectors with a large domestic output, the specific-factor owners have much to gain from an increase in the domestic price, while (for a given import demand elasticity) the economy has relatively little to lose from protection when the volume of imports is low.[11]

<hr>

[10]The formula for the equilibrium trade tax can be expressed as

$$t_i^o = \frac{I_i - \alpha_L}{a + \alpha_L}\left(\frac{y_i(p_i^o)}{[-p_i^* m_i'(p_i^o)]}\right).$$

If this equation has a solution for a case where $I_i = 1$, then it must involve $t_i^o > 0$. If the equation has no solution, then $p_i^o = \bar{p}_i$, and again $t_i^o > 0$.

[11]Our formula suggests that only two variables (the elasticity of import demand and the ratio of domestic output to imports) should explain the cross-industry

The smaller is the weight that the government places on a dollar of aggregate welfare compared with a dollar of campaign financing, the larger in absolute value are all trade taxes and subsidies. An interior solution remains possible, however, even if the government cares only about contributions ($a = 0$). This is because the interest groups themselves do not want the distortions to grow too large. As the share of voters who are members of one interest group or another increases, equilibrium rates of protection for the organized industries decline. At the extreme, when all voters belong to an interest group ($\alpha_L = 1$) and all sectors are represented ($I_i = 1$ for all i), then free trade prevails in all markets. In this case, the various interest groups neutralize one another, so that an industry's demand for protection is matched in equilibrium by the opposing interest groups' bids for a low domestic price. On the other hand, if interest-group members comprise a negligible fraction of the voting population ($\alpha_L = 0$), then no trade taxes or subsidies will be applied to goods not represented by a lobby (for which $I_i = 0$). When the potential political contributors are few in number, they stand little to gain from trade interventions in sectors other than their own.

IV. Political Contributions

We have characterized the structure of protection that emerges from the political process whenever the interest groups use contribution schedules that are locally differentiable. This restriction on the contribution functions leaves latitude for schedules with many different shapes (away from equi-

librium), and in fact the set of contribution schedules that supports the equilibrium policy vector is not unique. Different sets of equilibrium contribution schedules give rise to different equilibrium donations by the various lobby groups and thus to different net payoffs for the groups' members. If we are to say something more about which lobbies contribute the most to influence policy, we must introduce additional assumptions that allow us to select among the set of Nash equilibria.

We focus henceforth on truthful Nash equilibria; recall that these are equilibria that arise when lobbies announce truthful contribution schedules. With this restriction on the nature of the policy bids the competition between the lobbies involves only a choice of the scalars $\{B_i\}$. Given these "anchors" for the contribution functions, the truthfulness requirement dictates the shapes of the schedules [see the definition in (10)].

What incentive does a lobby i face with regard to its choice of B_i? From the definition of a truthful contribution schedule, we see that the net welfare to lobby i will be B_i whenever the lobby makes a positive contribution to the government in equilibrium. The lobby therefore wishes to make B_i as large as possible (and the contribution as small as possible), but without going so far as to induce the government to deviate from $\mathbf{p}^o$ to some alternative policy that might be damaging to its interests.

This point can be made clear with an example. Suppose for the moment that there are exactly two lobbies and that the government cares only about campaign financing ($a = 0$). Let the lobbies contemplate setting the anchors $\hat{B}_1$ and $\hat{B}_2$ for their truthful contribution schedules. With these anchors the lobbies' contributions will be $C_1^T(\mathbf{p}, \hat{B}_1)$ and $C_2^T(\mathbf{p}, \hat{B}_2)$, which depend of course on the policy action taken by the government. In Figure 2, the shaded area represents the set of contribution pairs (C_1, C_2) that the government might collect for all of the various policy choices open to it. Given this shaded opportunity set, a government that cares only about maximizing total contribu-

---

variation in protection levels. Empirical studies of the structure of protection are reviewed by Robert E. Baldwin (1984) and Kym Anderson and Baldwin (1987). However, the existing studies fail to control for import demand elasticities, while including many variables that are not indicated by our model (but which may be correlated with the omitted variable), thus rendering the regression results impossible to interpret in the light of our theory.

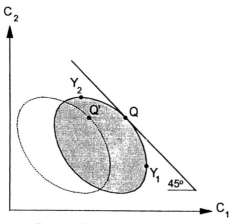

FIGURE 2. EXCESSIVE CONTRIBUTIONS

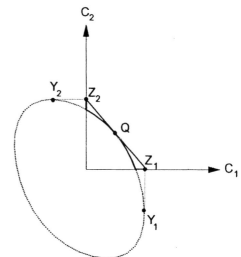

FIGURE 3. EQUILIBRIUM CONTRIBUTIONS

tions will opt for point Q, where the outer frontier is tangent to a line with a slope of -1. Underlying this point is some policy vector. If the figure is to represent an equilibrium situation, it must be the policy identified in Proposition 2.

Now we examine whether lobby 1 might wish to raise B_1 slightly above $\hat{B}_1$. By doing so, it would reduce all of its contributions *by the same amount*. The shaded area would shift uniformly to the left, to the location indicated by the dotted lines. The government would then be faced with a new set of possibilities and would choose the point Q', a leftward displacement of point Q. But the policy underlying point Q' must be the same as that for point Q, since the relative desirability of different policies has not changed from the government's (political) perspective. Evidently, lobby 1 must benefit from this increase in B_1. Of course, the situation illustrated in the figure affords lobby 2 the same opportunity to improve its net welfare; so Figure 2 cannot represent an equilibrium situation.

The lobbies will continue to see an incentive to raise their B_i's at least as long as the contributions associated with the entire set of feasible policies remain positive. But eventually, when B_i gets sufficiently large, some policies will elicit a contribution of zero from lobby i [again see (10)]. Subsequent increases in B_i no longer affect the government's choices uniformly; the positive reward associated with a policy that is favorable to lobby i is reduced by an increase in B_i, but the nil contribution corresponding to a policy that is unfavorable to lobby i does not change. Lobby i must be careful not to raise B_i so far that the government decides to adopt one of these disadvantageous policies.

Figure 3 depicts an equilibrium configuration. Here both lobbies have increased their B_i's (relative to the situation depicted in Fig. 2), so that some policy choices available to the government generate a contribution of zero from one or the other of the lobbies. Consider, for example, the point Y_1, which corresponds to the similarly labeled point in Figure 2. This point is not feasible now, because lobby 2 cannot offer a negative contribution as implied. Rather, if the government were to choose the policy underlying this point (which, incidentally, is the policy most preferred by lobby 1) it would receive the pair of contributions at Z_1: a large donation from a thankful lobby 1 and a nil contribution from lobby 2. In

Figure 3, the government collects the same total donations for choosing any one of Q, Z_1, and Z_2. No other point offers contributions as great as these, so the policies that underlie these three points comprise the set of welfare-maximizing choices for the government. The government willingly chooses point Q; and neither lobby wishes to raise its B_i any further, for fear that the government then would select the policy most preferred by its rival.

Notice that our equilibrium conforms to condition (d) of Proposition 1. That condition requires that for every i there must exist a policy that elicits a contribution of zero from lobby i which the government finds equally attractive as the equilibrium policy $\mathbf{p}^\circ$. In the figure, these policies are, for lobbies 1 and 2, the ones that underlie points Z_2 and Z_1, respectively.

In our 1992a working paper we present a formal procedure for calculating the equilibrium contributions and net welfare levels when an arbitrary number of lobbies set truthful contribution schedules and the government has the more general objective function described in (5). Here we will present the procedure informally, relying on the intuition developed for the special case just discussed. Then we will calculate the contributions for several examples, showing in the process how the political environment determines the division of surplus between the interest groups and the politicians.

Our special case suggests that each lobby must worry about what policy would be chosen if it were to raise its B_i to a level where the government would opt to neglect its interests entirely. We define $\mathbf{p}^{-i}$ as the policy that would emerge from political maximization by the government, if the contribution offered by lobby i were zero; that is,

$$(16) \quad \mathbf{p}^{-i} = \arg\max_{\mathbf{p} \in \mathcal{P}} \sum_{\substack{j \in L \\ j \neq i}} C_j^T(\mathbf{p}, B_j^\circ) + aW(\mathbf{p})$$

$$\text{for } i \in L.$$

We have seen in the example that lobby i

will raise its B_i to the point where the government is just indifferent between choosing the policy $\mathbf{p}^{-i}$ and choosing the equilibrium policy $\mathbf{p}^\circ$. The following equation expresses this indifference:

$$(17) \quad \sum_{\substack{j \in L \\ j \neq i}} C_j^T\left(\mathbf{p}^{-i}, B_j^\circ\right) + aW(\mathbf{p}^{-i})$$

$$= \sum_{j \in L} C_j^T(\mathbf{p}^\circ, B_j^\circ) + aW(\mathbf{p}^\circ)$$

$$\text{for all } i \in L.$$

These two sets of equations allow us to solve for the net welfare levels of the various lobbies in a truthful Nash equilibrium (TNE) with positive contributions by all lobbies. As a consistency check, we must make sure that at B_i°, lobby i would make no contribution were the policy $\mathbf{p}^{-i}$ to be chosen by the government. This requires $W_i(\mathbf{p}^{-i}) \leq B_i^\circ$ for all $i \in L$. If this inequality fails for some i, then that lobby benefits from raising its B_i (reducing its equilibrium contributions) until the constraint that payments must be nonnegative becomes binding. Such a lobby would contribute nothing in the political equilibrium, and the equilibrium policy would be the same as if the factor owners represented by this lobby were politically unorganized.

We now examine three special cases, to see how the equilibrium contributions are determined in different situations.

Example 1: A Single Organized Lobby. —Suppose that there is only one politically active lobby group, which represents the interests of the specific-factor owners in some industry i. The equilibrium policy vector in this case provides protection for sector i ($p_i^\circ > p_i^*$), and so long as $\alpha_i > 0$, it calls for import subsidies and export taxes on all other goods ($p_j^\circ < p_j^*$ for $j \neq i$). We know that the government would opt for free trade in the absence of any contributions from the one and only special-interest group; thus (16) gives $\mathbf{p}^{-i} = \mathbf{p}^*$. Using (17),

Gene M. Grossman and Elhanan Helpman

we find the equilibrium campaign contribution of lobby i, $C_i^T(\mathbf{p}^\circ, B_i^\circ) = aW(\mathbf{p}^*) - aW(\mathbf{p}^\circ)$. We see that the lobby contributes an amount that is proportional to the excess burden that the equilibrium trade policies impose on society. The factor of proportionality is the weight that the government attaches to aggregate gross welfare (relative to campaign contributions) in its own objective function. In this political equilibrium, the politicians derive exactly the same utility as they would have achieved by allowing free trade in a world without influence payments. In other words, *a lobby that faces no opposition from competing interests captures all of the surplus from its political relationship with the government.*

Example 2: All Voters Represented as Special Interests. —The next example is one in which all of the voters are represented in the political process by one lobby group or another. We have seen that the political competition in this case results in free trade ($\mathbf{p}^\circ = \mathbf{p}^*$). Nonetheless, each lobby must make a positive campaign contribution in order to induce the government to choose this outcome rather than one that would be still worse from its perspective. Take for example the case where there are only two nonnumeraire goods and two lobbies. Using (17), we have

$$(18) \quad C_i^T(\mathbf{p}^\circ, B_i^\circ) = \left[C_j^T(\mathbf{p}^{-i}, B_j^\circ) + aW(\mathbf{p}^{-i}) \right]$$
$$- \left[C_j^T(\mathbf{p}^\circ, B_j^\circ) + aW(\mathbf{p}^\circ) \right]$$
$$\text{for } i = 1, 2; j \neq i.$$

By the definition of $\mathbf{p}^{-i}$ and the fact that $\mathbf{p}^{-i} \neq \mathbf{p}^* = \mathbf{p}^\circ$, we know that the right-hand side of (18) is positive for $i = 1, 2$. Thus, both lobbies must actively contribute to the incumbent government in order to support the free-trade outcome. *When all voters are active in the process of buying influence, the rivalry among competing interests is most intense, and the government captures all of the surplus from the political relationships.*

Which of the two lobbies makes the larger contribution? To answer this question, we

rewrite equation (18) as[12]

$$(19) \quad C_i^T(\mathbf{p}^\circ, B_i^\circ) = \left[W_j(\mathbf{p}^{-i}) + aW(\mathbf{p}^{-i}) \right]$$
$$- \left[W_j(\mathbf{p}^*) + aW(\mathbf{p}^*) \right]$$
$$\text{for } i = 1, 2; j \neq i.$$

This equation says that each lobby i must contribute to the politicians an amount equal to the difference between what its rival and the government could jointly achieve were lobby i not itself active in the political process and what the two actually attain in the full political equilibrium. Thus, *each lobby pays according to the political strength of its rival.* Take for example the case in which the industries are symmetric except that they have different, perfectly inelastic supply functions $y_i(\mathbf{p}) = \bar{y}_i$. Then the interest group representing factor owners with the smaller endowment makes *larger* political contribution.

Example 3: Represented Special Interests Are Highly Concentrated. —The final example is one where the ownership of the specific factors is so highly concentrated that interest-group members account for a negligible fraction of the total voting population. The political equilibrium in this case has positive protection for all organized sectors. But since $\alpha_i = 0$ for all i, the members of each interest group receive only a negligible share of government transfer payments and derive only a negligible share of the surplus from consuming nonnumeraire products. Thus, no lobby is willing to contribute toward trade intervention in any sector other than its own. The policy $\mathbf{p}^{-i}$ that the government would choose if lobby i failed to contribute allows free trade in good i (since

[12]In order to do so, we need $C_j^T(\mathbf{p}^{-i}, B_j^\circ) - C_j^T(\mathbf{p}^*, B_j^\circ) = W_j(\mathbf{p}^{-i}) - W_j(\mathbf{p}^*)$. Given that the contribution schedules are truthful, this will be the case if both $C_j^T(\mathbf{p}^{-i}, B_j^\circ)$ and $C_j^T(\mathbf{p}^*, B_j^\circ)$ are positive. We have already seen that the latter is true. Since the right-hand side of (18) is positive and $W(\mathbf{p}^{-i}) < W(\mathbf{p}^*)$, we have $C_j^T(\mathbf{p}^{-i}, B_j^\circ) > C_j^T(\mathbf{p}^*, B_j^\circ)$. Thus, the former must be true as well.

this policy is socially efficient and no other lobby bids for any intervention) but has the same protection on all other goods as in the full equilibrium (since the presence or absence of lobby i has no bearing on the political interaction between the government and those with interests in these other sectors). The common agency problem here is the same as for a set of separate principal–agent arrangements between each industry lobby and the government. As in Example 1, each lobby i must compensate the government for the political cost of providing protection (it pays a times the deadweight loss imposed by the industry policy p_i^o). *But with no political rivalry between the special interests, each industry group captures all of the surplus from its own political relationship with the government.*[13]

V. Why Lobbies May Prefer Trade Policies

In deriving the political-economic equilibrium, we have limited the government's choice of policy instruments to trade taxes and subsidies. It may seem that the interest groups would prefer to have the government use more efficient means to transfer income. Our model implies that this is not necessarily the case. In fact, the lobby groups may support institutions that constrain the government to transfer income as inefficiently as possible. Accordingly, a regime that allows only voluntary export restraints (with quota rents transferred to foreigners) may be even more desirable to the lobbies than one that allows for import tariffs. We will discuss now why this is so.[14]

Suppose that the government could use output subsidies instead of (or in addition

to) trade policies to transfer income to groups that bid for special treatment. It is well known that such subsidies generate less deadweight loss than tariffs and export subsidies, for an equivalent amount of income transfer. But would the interest groups share in these efficiency gains?

Consider first the case where factor ownership is highly concentrated, so that the members of the lobby groups account for a negligible fraction of the total population. In this case the interests of the industry lobbies are not directly opposed. As we have seen, no lobby would bid against policies that favored other interest groups under these circumstances. The equilibrium output subsidies would be the ones that maximized the joint welfare of each lobby and the government. Of course, joint welfare is higher in a regime that allows output subsidies than in one that does not, because the output subsidies generate less deadweight loss than the trade policies. Moreover, each lobby compensates the government only for the political cost associated with its special treatment (an amount a times the deadweight loss). Therefore, the lobbies capture *all* of the surplus from the use of the more efficient policy instrument.

However, consider now the case where all voters are represented by an organized lobby group. In this situation, as we have seen, the political competition among the groups is quite intense. We know that the equilibrium policy in any TNE maximizes a weighted sum of the utilities of represented and unrepresented voters, and that when all voters are represented in the bidding process the equilibrium policy maximizes aggregate welfare. So the equilibrium entails laissez-faire, just as free trade emerged as the political equilibrium when the government could invoke only trade policies. However, the lobbies must make larger political contributions to induce the laissez-faire outcome in the equilibrium with output subsidies than they must make to support a free-trade outcome in the regime that allows only trade interventions. This is because each lobby must contribute in equilibrium the difference between what rival lobbies and the government could jointly achieve in the ab-

---

[13]The interested reader can refer to our 1992a working paper for further details.

[14]Our point is related to, but not the same as, one made by Dani Rodrik (1986) and John D. Wilson (1990). These two have argued that a policy regime with tariffs only may be socially preferred to one with output subsidies, because the distortions that endogeneously emerge in the former regime may be smaller than those in the latter. Our arguments concern the institutional preferences of special-interest groups, not those of an external observer.

sence of its own participation in the political process and what they in fact achieve in the political equilibrium. The equilibrium entails the same joint welfare under either regime; but the rival lobbies and the government can jointly attain greater welfare in a policy regime that allows output subsidies (or other, more efficient policies) than in one that does not. It follows that the lobbies' contributions will be higher and net welfare lower if the political regime allows output subsidies.

These examples suggest that the extent of competition between rival interest groups determines their preferences among alternative policy regimes. When competition between interest groups is intense (because their interests are in direct opposition), the availability of an efficient income-transfer tool makes credible an implicit government threat to join forces with the opposing lobbies. Individual interest groups have little political power under these conditions, and they prefer to tie the hands of the government. However, when the interests of the lobbies are orthogonal to one another, the groups do not compete for favors, but instead seek to extract gains at the expense of the underrepresented masses. Then each lobby prefers to grant politicians access to the most efficient means possible for transferring income.

VI. Summary and Extensions

We have developed a new approach to analyzing the formation of trade policy in a representative democracy. Like many previous authors we view politicians as maximizing agents who pursue their own selfish interests rather than as benevolent agents seeking to maximize aggregate welfare. Our modeling focuses on the political interactions between a government that is concerned both with campaign contributions and with the welfare of the average voter and a set of organized special-interest groups that care only about the welfare of their members. What is distinctive in our approach is the role that we ascribe to political contributions: we see the gifts made by interest groups not so much as investments in the outcomes of elections, but more as a

means to influence government policy. In our view, the manner of campaign and party finance in many democratic nations creates powerful incentives for politicians to peddle their policy influence. Then the structure of trade protection is bound to reflect the outcome of a competition for political favors; this is the central theme in our story.

In our model, lobbies make implicit offers of political contributions as functions of the vector of trade policies (import and export taxes and subsidies) adopted by the government. Taking account of these offers, the government sets policy to further its own objectives, which include (perhaps among other things) a concern for reelection. In the political equilibrium neither the government nor any lobby has an incentive to alter its behavior; no lobby can revise its contribution schedule so as to induce the government to choose a policy that would yield its members higher net welfare, nor can the government realize political gains by changing policy given the contribution offers it faces.

We have derived an explicit formula for the structure of protection that emerges in such a setting. Our formula relates an industry's equilibrium protection to the state of its political organization, the ratio of domestic output in the industry to net trade, and the elasticity of import demand or export supply. Also, the protection provided to all politically organized industries increases with the relative weight the government attaches to campaign contributions vis-à-vis voter welfare and falls with the fraction of voters that belong to an organized lobby group. We have discussed in some detail the determinants of the size of the equilibrium contributions made by different interest groups, the relative political power of these groups, and the division of political surplus between the government and the lobbies.

The questions we have addressed in this paper are of considerable independent interest. Beyond this, the tools that we have developed for studying the relationship between special interest groups and policymakers may be applicable to many additional problems. For example, our approach could be used to study the endogenous de-

VOL. 84 NO. 4   GROSSMAN AND HELPMAN: PROTECTION FOR SALE   849

sign of social transfer schemes, environmental regulations, or government spending programs. We conclude the paper with a brief discussion of two possible extensions, still within the area of trade policy, that show the flexibility and potential usefulness of our approach.

The first extension allows for more political competition among the special-interest groups. In our model such competition is highly circumscribed, because the various industry groups oppose one another only to the extent that owners of specific factors also protect their interests as ordinary *consumers*. In reality, the most serious political opposition to protection arises when higher prices stand to harm other *producer* interests downstream. The users of intermediate inputs often are as politically active against import barriers as are the domestic manufacturers who favor such protection.

The model can readily be extended to allow for imported intermediate inputs. Suppose, for example, that there is one such good, producible at home with labor and a sector-specific input. Suppose further that the intermediate good is used in some or all of the sectors producing nonnumeraire goods, but not in the sector that produces good 0. Then the aggregate reward to the owners of the specific factor used in the production of final good i becomes $\pi_i(p_i, q)$, where q is the domestic price of the intermediate good. The reward to the owners of the specific factor used in domestic production of the intermediate good depends only on q. We can proceed as before to derive the equilibrium trade policies and campaign contributions.

Two notable results emerge from such an exercise. First, imports of the intermediate good may be subsidized in the political equilibrium, even if the interests of the owners of the specific factor used in producing that good are represented in the political process. This contrasts with the situation for politically organized final-good producers, all of whom succeed in securing at least some (effective) trade protection. Producers of intermediates are more vulnerable politically, because the representatives of the final-goods producers bid vigorously against tariffs on intermediates, whereas opposition

to protection on consumer goods is much less intense. Second, the formula for the equilibrium import tariff or export subsidy applicable to trade in any final good can be decomposed into two terms, one with the same form as in Proposition 2, the other being an increasing function of the equilibrium tariff applicable to intermediate inputs. Both of these results suggest that the political process tends to favor the interests of final-good producers relative to those of intermediate-good producers.

The second extension incorporates policy interdependence among large trading economies. The literature on tariff wars, starting with the classic paper by Harry Johnson (1953), examines noncooperative policy games between governments that single-mindedly serve the public interest. Similarly, studies of negotiated tariff agreements (see e.g., Wolfgang Mayer, 1981) generally begin with the assumption that the state enters international negotiations with the aim of maximizing aggregate welfare. Greater insight could be gained into international economic relations, we believe, by considering governments that are guided in their external dealings by domestic political pressures. Our 1992b working paper takes a first step in this direction, applying our approach to domestic politics in an analysis of international trade wars and trade talks. A next step might be to assess the relative desirability of alternative international "rules of the game." Such rules limit the policy choices open to national governments and change the nature of the strategic interactions between elected officials and their constituents. Our framework could be used to generate predictions about what domestic policies will emerge from the political process in different institutional settings, and therefore to evaluate which rules give rise to preferred policy outcomes.

REFERENCES

Anderson, Kym and Baldwin, Robert E. "The Political Market for Protection in Industrial Countries," in A. M. El-Agraa, ed., *Protection, cooperation, integration and development: Essays in honour of Profes-*

sor Hiroshi Kitamura. London: Macmillan, 1987, pp. 20–36.

Baldwin, Robert E. "Trade Policies in Developed Countries," in R. W. Jones and P. B. Kenen, eds., *Handbook of international economics*, Vol. 1. Amsterdam: North-Holland, 1984, pp. 571–611.

Bernheim, B. Douglas and Whinston, Michael D. "Menu Auctions, Resource Allocation, and Economic Influence." *Quarterly Journal of Economics*, February 1986, *101*(1), pp. 1–31.

Goldenberg, Edie N.; Traugott, Michael W. and Baumgartner, Frank R. "Preemptive and Reactive Spending in U.S. House Races." *Political Behavior*, 1986, *8*(1), pp. 3–20.

Green, Donald Philip and Krasno, Johnathan S. "Salvation for the Spendthrift Incumbent: Reestimating the Effects of Campaign Spending in House Elections." *American Journal of Political Science*, November 1988, *32*(4), pp. 884–907.

Grossman, Gene M. and Helpman, Elhanan. "Protection for Sale." National Bureau of Economic Research (Cambridge, MA) Working Paper No. 4149, 1992a.

_____. "Trade Wars and Trade Talks." Discussion Paper in Economics No. 163, Woodrow Wilson School of Public and International Affairs, Princeton University, 1992b.

Hillman, Arye L. "Declining Industries and Political-Support Protectionist Motives." *American Economic Review*, December 1982, *72*(5), pp. 1180–87.

_____. *The political economy of protection.* Chur: Harwood, 1989.

Hillman, Arye and Ursprung, Heinrich W. "Domestic Politics, Foreign Interests, and International Trade Policy." *American Economic Review*, September 1988, *78*(4), pp. 729–45.

Jacobson, Gary C. "The Effects of Campaign Spending in Congressional Elections."

American Political Science Review, June 1978, *72*(2), pp. 769–83.

_____. *The politics of Congressional elections*, 2nd Ed. Boston: Little, Brown, 1987.

Johnson, Harry G. "Optimal Tariffs and Retaliation." *Review of Economic Studies*, 1953, *21*(2), pp. 142–53.

Krasno, Jonathan S. and Green, Donald Philip. "Preempting Quality Challengers in House Elections." *Journal of Politics*, November 1988, *50*(4), pp. 920–36.

Long, Ngo Van and Vousden, Neil. "Protectionist Responses and Declining Industries." *Journal of International Economics*, February 1991, *30*(1-2), pp. 87–103.

Magee, Stephen P.; Brock, William A. and Young, Leslie. *Black hole tariffs and endogenous policy theory: Political economy in general equilibrium.* Cambridge: Cambridge University Press, 1989.

Magelby, David B. and Nelson, Candice J. *The money chase: Congressional campaign finance reform.* Washington, DC: Brookings Institution, 1990.

Mayer, Wolfgang. "Theoretical Considerations on Negotiated Tariff Adjustments." *Oxford Economic Papers*, March 1981, *33*(1), pp. 135–53.

Olsen, Mancur. *The logic of collective action.* Cambridge, MA: Harvard University Press, 1965.

Rodrik, Dani. "Tariffs, Subsidies, and Welfare with Endogenous Policy." *Journal of International Economics*, November 1986, *21*(3/4), pp. 285–96.

Stigler, George J. "The Theory of Economic Regulation." *Bell Journal of Economics*, Spring 1971, *2*(1), pp. 359–65.

Wilson, John D. "Are Efficiency Improvements in Government Transfer Policies Self-Defeating in Political Equilibrium?" *Economics and Politics*, November 1990, *2*(3), pp. 241–58.

Part 2

Economic Development and Growth

The Political Economy of the Rent-Seeking Society

By Anne O. Krueger*

In many market-oriented economies, government restrictions upon economic activity are pervasive facts of life. These restrictions give rise to rents of a variety of forms, and people often compete for the rents. Sometimes, such competition is perfectly legal. In other instances, rent seeking takes other forms, such as bribery, corruption, smuggling, and black markets.

It is the purpose of this paper to show some of the ways in which rent seeking is competitive, and to develop a simple model of competitive rent seeking for the important case when rents originate from quantitative restrictions upon international trade. In such a case 1) competitive rent seeking leads to the operation of the economy inside its transformation curve; 2) the welfare loss associated with quantitative restrictions is unequivocally greater than the loss from the tariff equivalent of those quantitative restrictions; and 3) competitive rent seeking results in a divergence between the private and social costs of certain activities. Although the analysis is general, the model has particular applicability for developing countries, where government interventions are frequently all-embracing.

A preliminary section of the paper is concerned with the competitive nature of rent seeking and the quantitative importance of rents for two countries, India and Turkey. In the second section, a formal model of rent seeking under quantitative

restrictions on trade is developed and the propositions indicated above are established. A final section outlines some other forms of rent seeking and suggests some implications of the analysis.

I. Competitive Rent Seeking

A. *Means of Competition*

When quantitative restrictions are imposed upon and effectively constrain imports, an import license is a valuable commodity. It is well known that under some circumstances, one can estimate the tariff equivalents of a set of quantitative restrictions and analyze the effects of those restrictions in the same manner as one would the tariff equivalents. In other circumstances, the resource-allocational effects of import licensing will vary, depending upon who receives the license.[1]

It has always been recognized that there are *some* costs associated with licensing: paperwork, the time spent by entrepreneurs in obtaining their licenses, the cost of the administrative apparatus necessary to issue licenses, and so on. Here, the argument is carried one step further: in many circumstances resources are devoted to competing for those licenses.

The consequences of that rent seeking are examined below. First, however, it will be argued that rent-seeking activities are often competitive and resources are devoted to competing for rents. It is difficult, if not impossible, to find empirically observable measures of the degree to which rent seeking is competitive. Instead, some

* Professor of economics, University of Minnesota. I am indebted to James M. Henderson for invaluable advice and discussion on successive drafts. Jagdish Bhagwati and John C. Hause made helpful comments on earlier drafts of this paper.

[1] This phenomenon is explored in detail in Bhagwati and Krueger.

mechanisms under which rent seeking is almost certain to be competitive are examined. Then other cases are considered in which it is less obvious, but perhaps equally plausible, that competition results.

Consider first the results of an import-licensing mechanism when licenses for imports of intermediate goods are allocated in proportion to firms' capacities. That system is frequently used, and has been analyzed for the Indian case by Jagdish Bhagwati and Padma Desai. When licenses are allocated in proportion to firms' capacities, investment in additional physical plant confers upon the investor a higher expected receipt of import licenses. Even with initial excess capacity (due to quantitative restrictions upon imports of intermediate goods), a rational entrepreneur may still expand his plant if the expected gains from the additional import licenses he will receive, divided by the cost of the investment, equal the returns on investment in other activities.[2] This behavior could be perfectly rational even if, for all entrepreneurs, the total number of import licenses will remain fixed. In fact, if imports are held constant as domestic income grows, one would expect the domestic value of a constant quantity of imports to increase over time, and hence installed capacity would increase while output remained constant. By investing in additional capacity, entrepreneurs devote resources to compete for import licenses.

A second sort of licensing mechanism frequently found in developing countries is used for imports of consumer goods. There, licenses are allocated *pro rata* in proportion to the applications for those licenses from importers-wholesalers. Entry

is generally free into importing-wholesaling, and firms usually have U-shaped cost curves. The result is a larger-than-optimal number of firms, operating on the downward sloping portion of their cost curves, yet earning a "normal" rate of return. Each importer-wholesaler receives fewer imports than he would buy at existing prices in the absence of licensing, but realizes a sufficient return on those licenses he does receive to make it profitable to stay in business. In this case, competition for rents occurs through entry into the industry with smaller-than-optimally sized firms, and resources are used in that the same volume of imports could be efficiently distributed with fewer inputs if firms were of optimal size.

A third sort of licensing mechanism is less systematic in that government officials decide on license allocations. Competition occurs to some extent through both mechanisms already mentioned as businessmen base their decisions on expected values. But, in addition, competition can also occur through allocating resources to influencing the probability, or expected size, of license allocations. Some means of influencing the expected allocation—trips to the capital city, locating the firm in the capital, and so on—are straightforward. Others, including bribery, hiring relatives of officials or employing the officials themselves upon retirement, are less so. In the former case, competition occurs through choice of location, expenditure of resources upon travel, and so on. In the latter case, government officials themselves receive part of the rents.

Bribery has often been treated as a transfer payment. However, there is competition for government jobs and it is reasonable to believe that expected total remuneration is the relevant decision variable for persons deciding upon careers. Generally, entry into government service requires above-average educational at-

[2] Note that: 1) one would expect to find greater excess capacity in those industries where rents are higher; and 2) within an industry, more efficient firms will have greater excess capacity than less efficient firms, since the return on a given amount of investment will be higher with greater efficiency.

VOL. 64 NO. 3   *KRUEGER: RENT-SEEKING SOCIETY*   293

tainments. The human capital literature provides evidence that choices as to how much to invest in human capital are strongly influenced by rates of return upon the investment. For a given level of educational attainment, one would expect the rate of return to be approximately equated among various lines of endeavor. Thus, if there appear to be high official-plus-unofficial incomes accruing to government officials and higher education is a prerequisite for seeking a government job, more individuals will invest in higher education. It is not necessary that government officials earn the same total income as other college graduates. All that is necessary is that there is an excess supply of persons seeking government employment, or that highly educated persons make sustained efforts to enter government services. Competition takes place through attaining the appropriate credentials for entry into government service and through accepting unemployment while making efforts to obtain appointments. Efforts to influence those in charge of making appointments, of course, just carry the argument one step further back.

To argue that competition for entry into government service is, in part, a competition for rents does not imply that all government servants accept bribes nor that they would leave government service in their absence. Successful competitors for government jobs might experience large windfall gains even at their official salaries. However, if the possibility of those gains induces others to expend time, energy, and resources in seeking entry into government services, the activity is competitive for present purposes.

In all these license-allocation cases, there are means, legal and illegal, for competing for rents. If individuals choose their activities on the basis of expected returns, rates of return on alternative activities will be equated and, in that sense, markets will be competitive.[3] In most cases, people do not perceive themselves to be rent seekers and, generally speaking, individuals and firms do not specialize in rent seeking. Rather, rent seeking is one part of an economic activity, such as distribution or production, and part of the firm's resources are devoted to the activity (including, of course, the hiring of expediters). The fact that rent seeking and other economic activities are not generally conducted by separate economic entities provides the motivation for the form of the model developed below.

B. *Are Rents Quantitatively Important?*

Granted that rent seeking may be highly competitive, the question remains whether rents are important. Data from two countries, India and Turkey, suggest that they are. Gunnar Myrdal believes India may "... on the balance, be judged to have somewhat less corruption than any other country in South Asia" (p. 943). Nonetheless, it is generally believed that "corruption" has been increasing, and that much of the blame lies with the proliferation of economic controls following independence.[4]

Table 1 presents crude estimates, based on fairly conservative assumptions of the value of rents of all sorts in 1964. One important source of rents—investment licensing—is not included for lack of any valid basis on which to estimate its value. Many smaller controls are also excluded. Nonetheless, it is apparent from Table 1 that

---

[3] It may be objected that illegal means of competition may be sufficiently distasteful that perfect competition will not result. Three comments are called for. First, it requires only that enough people at the margin do not incur disutility from engaging in these activities. Second, most lines of economic activity in many countries cannot be entered without some rent-seeking activity. Third, risks of detection (especially when bribery is expected) and the value judgments associated with illegal activities differ from society to society. See Ronald Wraith and Edgar Simpkins.

[4] Santhanam Committee, pp. 7-8.

TABLE 1—ESTIMATES OF VALUE OF RENTS: INDIA, 1964

Source of Rent	Amount of Rent (Rs. million)
Public investment	365
Imports	10,271
Controlled commodities	3,000
Credit rationing	407
Railways	602
Total	14,645

Sources:

1) Public investment: The Santhanam Committee, pp. 11–12, placed the loss in public investment at *at least* 5 percent of investment. That figure was multiplied by the average annual public investment in the *Third Five Year Plan.*

2) Imports: The Santhanam Committee, p. 18, stated that import licenses were worth 100 to 500 percent of their face value. Seventy-five percent of the value of 1964 imports was used here as a conservative estimate.

3) Controlled commodities: These commodities include steel, cement, coal, passenger cars, scooters, food, and other price—and/or distribution-controlled commodities, as well as foreign exchange used for illegal imports and other unrecorded transactions. The figure is the lower bound estimate given by John Monteiro, p. 60. Monteiro puts the upper bound estimate at Rs. 30,000 billion, although he rejects the figure on the (dubious) ground that notes in circulation are less than that sum.

4) Credit rationing: The bank rate in 1964 was 6 percent; Rs. 20.3 billion of loans were outstanding. It is assumed that *at least* an 8 percent interest rate would have been required to clear the market, and that 3 percent of bank loans outstanding would be equivalent to the present value of new loans at 5 percent. Data source: Reserve Bank of India, Tables 534 and 554.

5) Railways: Monteiro, p. 45, cites commissions of 20 percent on railway purchases, and extra-official fees of Rs. 0.15 per wagon and Rs. 1.4 per 100 maunds loaded. These figures were multiplied by the 1964 traffic volume; 203 million tons of revenue-paying traffic originated in that year. Third plan expenditure on railroads was Rs. 13,260 million. There were 350,000 railroad goods wagons in 1964–65. If a wagon was loaded once a week, there were 17,500,000 wagons of freight. At Rs. 0.15 per load, this would be Rs. 2.6 million; 100 maunds equal 8,228 pounds so at 1.4 Rs. per 100 maunds, Rs. 69 million changed hands; if one-fifth of railroad expenditures were made in 1964–65, Rs. 2652 million was spent in 1964; at 20 percent, this would be Rs. 530 million, for a total of Rs. 602 million.

import licenses provided the largest source of rents. The total value of rents of Rs. 14.6 billion contrasts with Indian national income of Rs. 201 billion in 1964. At 7.3 percent of national income, rents must be judged large relative to India's problems in attempting to raise her savings rate.

For Turkey, excellent detailed estimates of the value of import licenses in 1968 are available.[5] Data on the c.i.f. prices of individual imports, their landed cost (c.i.f. price plus all duties, taxes, and landing charges), and wholesale prices were collected for a sizeable sample of commodities representing about 10 percent of total imports in 1968. The c.i.f. value of imports in the sample was TL 547 million and the landed cost of the imports was TL 1,443 million. The value at the wholesale level of these same imports was TL 3,568 million. Of course, wholesalers incur some handling, storage, and transport costs. The question, therefore, is the amount that can be attributed to normal wholesaling costs. If one assumes that a 50 percent markup would be adequate, then the value of import licenses was TL 1,404 million, or almost three times the c.i.f. value of imports. Imports in 1968 were recorded (c.i.f.) as 6 percent of national income. On the basis of Aker's data, this would imply that rents from import licenses in Turkey in 1968 were about 15 percent of *GNP.*

Both the Indian and the Turkish estimates are necessarily somewhat rough. But they clearly indicate that the value of import licenses to the recipients was sizeable. Since means were available of competing for the licenses, it would be surprising if competition did not occur for prizes that large. We turn, therefore, to an examination of the consequences of competitive rent seeking.

---

[5] I am indebted to Ahmet Aker of Robert College who kindly made his data available to me. Details and a description of the data can be found in my forthcoming book.

II. The Effects of Competitive Rent Seeking

The major proposition of this paper is that competitive rent seeking for import licenses entails a welfare cost in addition to the welfare cost that would be incurred if the same level of imports were achieved through tariffs. The effects of tariffs upon production, trade, and welfare are well known, and attention is focussed here upon the additional cost of competitive rent seeking. A simple model is used to develop the argument. Initially, free trade is assumed. Then, a tariff or equivalent import restriction is introduced. Finally, an equal import restriction with competitive rent seeking is examined.

A. *The Basic Model*

Two commodities are consumed by the country under investigation: food and consumption goods. Food is produced domestically and exported. Consumption goods are imported. Distribution is a productive activity whereby food is purchased from the agricultural sector, exported, and the proceeds are used to import consumption goods which are sold in the domestic market. Labor is assumed to be the only domestic factor of production.[6] It is assumed that the country under consideration is small and cannot affect its international terms of trade. Physical units are selected so that the fixed international prices of both goods are unity.

The agricultural production function is

$$(1) \quad A = A(L_A) \quad A' > 0, \ A'' < 0$$

where A is the output of food and L_A is the quantity of labor employed in agriculture. The sign of the second derivative reflects a diminishing marginal physical product of labor in agriculture, due, presumably, to fixity in the supply of land.

The level of distribution output, D, is defined to equal the level of consumption-goods imports, M:

$$(2) \quad D = M$$

One unit of distributive services entails exchanging one unit of imports for food with the agricultural sector at the domestic terms of trade, and exporting the food in exchange for imports at the international terms of trade. Constant returns to scale are assumed for the distribution activity; one unit of distribution requires k units of labor. Total labor employed in distribution, L_D, is

$$(3) \quad L_D = kD$$

A distribution charge of p_D per unit is added to the international price of imports:

$$(4) \quad p_M = 1 + p_D$$

where p_M is the domestic price of imports. The domestic price of food is assumed to equal its unit international price.[7]

Society's demand for imports depends upon the domestic price of imports and total income generated in agriculture:[8]

$$(5) \quad M = M(p_M, A)$$

where $\partial M/\partial p_M < 0$ and $\partial M/\partial A > 0$. Demand decreases with increases in the price of imports, and increases with increases in agricultural output (income). Equation (5) is derived from micro utility maximization with the assumption that farmers, distributors, and rent seekers all have the same consumption behavior. Domestic

---

[6] Labor could be regarded as a composite domestic factor of production. Extensions to two or more factors would complicate the analysis, but would not alter its basic results.

[7] These assumptions establish a domestic numeraire. The real analysis would be unaffected by proportional changes in the domestic prices.

[8] Food and imports are consumed. But, by choice of food as the numeraire (see equation (6)) and the assumed constancy of international prices, agricultural output serves as a measure of income.

food consumption, F, is simply the quantity not exported:

(6) $F = A - M$

Since the fixed international terms of trade equal unity, food exports equal consumption goods imports.

Finally, it is assumed that the economy under consideration has a fixed labor supply, $\overline{L}$:

(7) $\overline{L} = L_A + L_D + L_R$

where L_R is the quantity of labor engaged in rent seeking.

B. Free Trade

Under free trade, there is free entry into both agriculture and distribution and competition equates the wage in the two activities:

(8) $A' = p_D/k$

Equations (1) to (8) constitute the free-trade system. These eight equations contain the eight variables A, M, D, F, L_A, L_D, p_M, and p_D. Since there is no rent seeking under free trade, $L_R \equiv 0$.

It is easily established that free trade is optimal in the sense that the domestic price ratio under free trade equals the marginal rate of transformation between food consumption and imports. The consumption possibility locus is obtained by substituting into (6) from (1) and (7)

$$F = A(\overline{L} - kM) - M$$

The locus has a marginal rate of transformation greater than one:

(9) $\dfrac{-dF}{dM} = kA' + 1 > 1$

which reflects the positive distribution cost of substituting imports for food consumption. The locus is concave:

$$\dfrac{d^2F}{dM^2} = k^2 A'' < 0$$

since $A'' < 0$, which follows from diminishing returns in food production. Substituting from (8) into (9),

$$\dfrac{-dF}{dM} = 1 + p_D$$

which establishes the aforementioned equality.

A free-trade solution is depicted in Figure 1. Domestic food consumption and import consumption are measured along OF and OM, respectively. The consumption possibility locus is $\hat{F}\hat{M}$. At the point $\hat{F}$ no imports are consumed and hence there is no distribution. If distribution were costless, society could choose its consumption point from the line $\hat{F}A$. However, to consume one unit of import requires exchanging one unit of food *and* withdrawing k workers from agriculture to provide the requisite distributive services. With diminishing marginal product of labor in agriculture, the cost of additional imports in terms of foregone food production rises. Thus, the price of distribution, and hence the domestic price of imports, increases in moving northwest from $\hat{F}$. The consump-

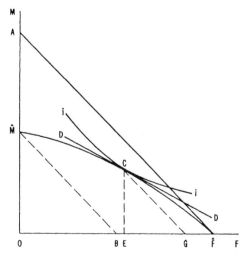

FIGURE 1. FREE TRADE

VOL. 64 NO. 3   *KRUEGER: RENT-SEEKING SOCIETY*   297

tion point $\hat{M}$ has OB food exchanged for $O\hat{M}$ of imports. The distance $\hat{F}B$ is the agricultural output foregone to distribute $O\hat{M}$ imports.

If society's preferences are given by the indifference curve ii, point C is optimal. The price of distribution is reflected in the difference between the slope of $\hat{F}A$ and the slope of DD at C. At the point C, OG food would be produced, with EG $(=EC)$ exported, and the rest domestically consumed.

C. A Tariff or an Import Restriction Without Rent Seeking

Consider now a case in which there is a restriction upon the quantity of imports

$$(10) \qquad M = \overline{M}$$

where $\overline{M}$ is less than the import quantity that would be realized under free trade. Since entry into distribution is now limited, the competitive wage equality (8) will no longer hold. The relevant system contains (1) to (7) and (10). The variables are the same as in the free-trade case and again $L_R = 0$. The system may be solved sequentially: given (10), D follows from (2), L_D from (3), L_A from (7), A from (1), F from (6), p_M from (5), and p_D from (4). Since equations (1), (6), and (7) remain intact, the solution for this case is also on the consumption possibility locus.

It is useful to establish the directions of change for the variables following a switch from free trade to import restriction. The reduced import level will reduce the labor employed in distribution and increase the labor force in agriculture. Diminishing returns will reduce the agricultural wage. The domestic price of imports, the distributive margin, and the wage of distributors will increase. Distributors will earn a rent in the sense that their wage will exceed the wage of those engaged in agriculture.

In the absence of rent seeking, a tariff

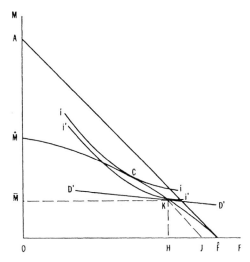

FIGURE 2. IMPORT RESTRICTION WITHOUT RENT SEEKING

and a quantitative restriction are equivalent[9] aside from the resultant income distribution. Under a quantitative restriction the distributive wage is higher than the agricultural. If instead there were an equivalent tariff with redistribution of the proceeds, the marginal product of labor in agriculture would be unchanged, but agricultural workers would benefit by the amount of tariff proceeds redistributed to them whereas traders' income would be lower. Since the allocation of labor under a tariff and quantitative restriction without rent seeking is the same and domestic prices are the same, the only difference between the two situations lies in income distribution.

The solution under a quantitative restriction is illustrated in Figure 2, where $\hat{F}\hat{M}$ is again the consumption possibility locus and C the free-trade solution. With a quantitative restriction on imports in the amount $O\overline{M}$, the domestic prices of

[9] The change in the price of the import from the free-trade solution is the tariff equivalent of the quantitative restriction described here.

imports, and hence of distribution, rise from free trade to import restriction. Food output (OJ) and domestic consumption of food increase, and exports decline to HJ ($=OM$). The indifference curve $i'i'$ lies below ii (and the point C), and the welfare loss may be described by the consumption and production cost measure given by Harry Johnson.

The wage rate in distribution unequivocally rises for a movement from free trade to a quantitative restriction. The total income of distributors will increase, decrease, or remain unchanged depending upon whether the proportionate increase in p_D is greater than, less than, or equal to the absolute value of the proportionate decrease of imports. For the moment, let p_D, p_M, and M represent free-trade solution values, and let p_D^*, p_M^*, and $\overline{M}$ represent import-restriction solution values. The total arc elasticity of demand for imports for the interval under consideration, η, is

$$(11) \qquad \eta = \frac{-(\overline{M} - M)}{\overline{M} + M} \cdot \frac{p_M^* + p_M}{p_M^* - p_M}$$

Total expenditures on imports will increase, decrease, or remain unchanged as η is less than one, greater than one, or equal to one. The total income of distributors will increase if

$$p_D^*\overline{M} > p_D M$$

Multiplying both sides of this inequality by $(p_M^* + p_M)/(p_M^* - p_M)$, substituting from (11), and using (4),

$$(12) \qquad 1 + 2/(p_D^* + p_D) > \eta$$

Hence, distributors' total income can increase even if the demand for imports is price elastic.[10] The smaller is the free-trade

distributive markup, the more likely it is that the distributors' total income will increase with a curtailment of imports. The reason is that an increase in the domestic price of imports results in a proportionately greater increase in the price of distribution.

D. *An Import Restriction with Competitive Rent Seeking*

In the import-restriction model just presented, the wage in distribution p_D/k exceeds the wage in agriculture A'. Under this circumstance, it would be surprising if people did not endeavor to enter distribution in response to its higher return. Resources can be devoted to rent seeking in all the ways indicated in Section IA. This rent-seeking activity can be specified in a number of different ways. A simple and intuitively plausible specification is that people will seek distributive rents until the average wage in distribution and rent seeking equals the agricultural wage:[11]

$$(13) \qquad A' = \frac{p_D \overline{M}}{L_D + L_R}$$

One can regard all distributors and rent seekers as being partially engaged in each activity or one can think of rent seekers as entering in the expectation of receiving import licenses. In the latter case, the final solution classifies the successful seekers in L_D and the unsuccessful ones in L_R. Equation (13) implies risk neutrality in this circumstance.

The model for import restriction with rent seeking contains the same equations,

---

[10] Proof of (12) uses the step that $p_D^*\overline{M} > p_D M$ implies $(p_D^* - p_D)/(p_D^* + p_D) > -(\overline{M} - M)/(\overline{M} + M)$. Note that in the continuous case, (12) reduces to $1 + 1/p_D > \eta$.

[11] As an alternative, the distributive production function (3) can be altered to treat all persons competing for import licenses as distributors so that L_D also encompasses L_R and $A' = p_D \overline{M}/L_D$. Another alternative is to introduce a rent-seeking activity distinct from distribution with a wage determined from total rents $(p_D - A'k)\overline{M}/L_R$, and require that this wage equal the wages in distribution and agriculture. These specifications give results equivalent to those that follow from (13).

VOL. 64 NO. 3   *KRUEGER: RENT-SEEKING SOCIETY*   299

(1) to (7) and (10), and the same variables as the model for import restrictions without rent seeking. In addition, the new model contains (13) and the introduction of L_R as a variable. The essential factor of rent seeking is that L_R becomes positive.

Let us start with a solution for an import restriction without rent seeking and ask what happens to the values of the variables when rent seeking is introduced. By assumption $M = \overline{M}$ is unchanged, so that L_D is unchanged. Therefore, $dL_A = -dL_R$, because the labor that enters rent seeking can only come from agriculture. Substituting into the total differential of (1) and using (6),

$$(14) \qquad dF = dA = -A'dL_R < 0$$

Agricultural production and food consumption are reduced by the introduction of rent seeking. Since the import level remains unchanged, rent seeking entails a welfare loss beyond that for an import restriction without rent seeking. The concavity of the agricultural production function results in a food loss that is less than proportional to decrements in L_A. Differentiating (5) totally,

$$(15) \qquad 0 = M_1 dp_M + M_2 dA$$

where M_1 and M_2 are the partial derivatives of (5) with respect to p_M and A, respectively. Solving (15) for dp_M, and substituting from (4) and (14),

$$(16) \qquad dp_D = dp_M = \frac{M_2}{M_1} A'dL_R < 0$$

since $M_1 < 0$ and $M_2 > 0$. The domestic cost of imports will be lower under rent-seeking competition. This follows from the decrease in the consumption of food relative to imports.

The results of (14) and (16) are not dependent upon the particular form of the equilibrium of the labor market. They hold for any specification of competitive rent seeking. Equation (13) serves to determine particular values for L_R and other variables of the system. The mere existence of competitive rent seeking is enough to determine the directions of change of the variables.

The above results are sufficient to indicate that, for any given level of import restrictions, competition among rent seekers is clearly inferior to the tariff equivalent of the restrictions, in that there could be more food consumed with no fewer imports under the latter case than the former. To the extent that rent seeking is competitive, the welfare cost of import restrictions is equal to the welfare cost of the tariff equivalent *plus the additional cost of rent-seeking activities.* Measurement of that excess cost is considered below.

The tariff-equivalent and rent-seeking equilibria are contrasted in Figure 3. Equilibrium under rent seeking will be at some point such as L, with the same consumption of imports, but smaller production and consumption of food than occurs under a tariff. The points K and C are the tariff-equivalent and free-trade equilibria, respectively. The line $D'D'$ cor-

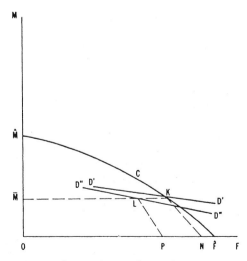

FIGURE 3. RENT-SEEKING IMPORT RESTRICTION

responds to the domestic price of imports in Figure 2, and the steeper line $D''D''$ corresponds to the lower domestic price of imports under competitive rent seeking.

So far, it has been shown that for any given level of import restriction, a tariff is Pareto-superior to competitive rent seeking, and the properties of rent-seeking equilibrium have been contrasted with those of the tariff-equivalent case in the absence of competition for the rents. A natural question is whether anything can be said about the properties of rent-seeking equilibrium in contrast to those of a free-trade equilibrium, which is, after all, the optimal solution. It has been seen that the number of persons engaged in distribution declines from free trade to import restriction without rent seeking, and increases as one goes from that situation to competition for import licenses. Likewise, agricultural output increases between free trade and the tariff-equivalent case, and declines between that and rent seeking. The question is whether any unambiguous signs can be placed on the direction of these changes between free trade and rent seeking and, in particular, is it possible that society might produce and consume less of both goods under rent seeking than under free trade?

The answer is that if inequality (12) is satisfied, the absolute number of persons (L_D+L_R) in distribution will increase going from a free-trade to a rent-seeking equilibrium. If import demand is more elastic, the number of persons in distribution will decline. Contrasted with a free-trade equilibrium, there would be less agricultural output *and* fewer imports when inequality (12) holds. If, with import restriction, the income from distribution $p_D^*\overline{M}$ is greater than distributors' income at free trade, more persons will be employed in distribution-cum-rent seeking with import restriction than are employed under free trade.

E. Measuring the Welfare Loss from Rent Seeking

A tariff has both production and consumption costs, and it has already been shown that rent seeking entails costs in addition to those of a tariff. Many forms of competition for rents, however, are by their nature difficult to observe and quantify and one might therefore question the empirical content of the result so far obtained.

Fortunately, there is a way to estimate the production cost of rent seeking. That cost, in fact, is equal to the value of the rents. This can be shown as follows. The rent per import license, r, is:

$$(17) \qquad r = p_D - kA'$$

This follows because the labor required to distribute one unit of imports is k, which could be used in agriculture with a return A'. Note that at free trade r equals zero. A distributor could efficiently distribute an import and earn his opportunity cost in agriculture with zero rent. The total value of rents, R, with competitive rent seeking is thus the rent per unit of imports times the amount imported.

$$(18) \qquad R = r\overline{M} = (p_D - kA')\overline{M}$$

Using (3) and (13),

$$(19) \qquad R = \left(p_D - \frac{kp_D\overline{M}}{L_D + L_R}\right)\overline{M}$$

$$= p_D\left(1 - \frac{L_D}{L_D + L_R}\right)\overline{M}$$

$$= \frac{p_D\overline{M}L_R}{L_D + L_R}$$

Thus the total value of rents reflects the agricultural wage (A') times the number of rent seekers.

The value of rents reflects the value (at current prices) of the domestic factors of production which could be extracted from the economy with no change in the final

VOL. 64 NO. 3   *KREUGER: RENT-SEEKING SOCIETY*   *301*

goods and services available for society's utilization. Thus, if the value of rents is known, it indicates the volume of resources that could be transferred out of distribution and into other activities, with no loss of distributive services from an initial position of rent-seeking activity. The estimates of rents in India and Turkey, therefore, may be interpreted as the deadweight loss from quantitative restrictions in addition to the welfare cost of their associated tariff equivalents if one believes that there is competition for the rents.

The value of the rents overstates the increase in food output and consumption that could be attained with a tariff to the extent that the marginal product of labor in agriculture is diminishing, since the equilibrium wage will rise between the tariff and the competitive rent-seeking situation. In the case of a constant marginal product of labor in alternative uses, the value of rents will exactly measure foregone output.

F. *The Implications of Rent Seeking for Trade Theory*

Recognition of the fact of rent seeking alters a variety of conclusions normally obtained in the trade literature and examination of such cases is well beyond the scope of this paper. A few immediately derivable results are worth brief mention, however.

First, an import prohibition might be preferable to a nonprohibitive quota if there is competition for licenses under the quota. This follows immediately from the fact that a prohibition would release resources from rent seeking and the excess cost of domestic production might be less than the value of the rents. Second, one could not, in general, rank the tariff-equivalents of two (or more) quotas, since the value of rents is a function of both the amount of rent per unit (the tariff equiva-

lent) and the volume of imports of each item.[12] Third, it has generally been accepted that the more inelastic domestic demand the less is likely to be the welfare cost of a given tariff. For the quota-cum-rents case, the opposite is true: the more price inelastic is demand, the greater will be the value of rents and the greater, therefore, the deadweight loss associated with rent seeking. Fourth, it is usually believed that competition among importers will result in a better allocation of resources than will a monopoly. If rent seeking is a possibility, however, creating a monopoly position for one importer will generally result in a higher real income if not in a preferable income distribution for society. Finally, devaluation under quantitative restrictions may have important allocation effects because it diminishes the value of import licenses, and hence the amount of rent-seeking activity, in addition to its effects upon exports.

III. Conclusions and Implications

In this paper, focus has been on the effects of competition for import licenses under a quantitative restriction of imports. Empirical evidence suggests that the value of rents associated with import licenses can be relatively large, and it has been shown that the welfare cost of quantitative restrictions equals that of their tariff equivalents plus the value of the rents.

While import licenses constitute a large and visible rent resulting from government intervention, the phenomenon of rent seeking is far more general. Fair trade laws result in firms of less-than-optimal size. Minimum wage legislation generates equilibrium levels of unemployment above the optimum with associated deadweight losses, as shown by John Harris and

---

[12] I am indebted to Bhagwati for pointing out this implication.

Michael Todaro, and Todaro. Ceilings on interest rates and consequent credit rationing lead to competition for loans and deposits and/or high-cost banking operations. Regulating taxi fares affects the average waiting time for a taxi and the percent of time taxis are idle, but probably not their owners' incomes, unless taxis are also licensed. Capital gains tax treatment results in overbuilding of apartments and uneconomic oil exploration. And so on.

Each of these and other interventions lead people to compete for the rents although the competitors often do not perceive themselves as such. In each case there is a deadweight loss associated with that competition over and above the traditional triangle. In general, prevention of that loss can be achieved only by restricting entry into the activity for which a rent has been created.

That, in turn, has political implications. First, even if they *can* limit competition for the rents, governments which consider they must impose restrictions are caught on the horns of a dilemma: if they do restrict entry, they are clearly "showing favoritism" to one group in society and are choosing an unequal distribution of income. If, instead, competition for the rents is allowed (or cannot be prevented), income distribution may be less unequal and certainly there will be less appearance of favoring special groups, although the economic costs associated with quantitative restrictions will be higher.

Second, the existence of rent seeking surely affects people's perception of the economic system. If income distribution is viewed as the outcome of a lottery where wealthy individuals are successful (or lucky) rent seekers, whereas the poor are those precluded from or unsuccessful in rent seeking, the market mechanism is bound to be suspect. In the United States, rightly or wrongly, societal consensus has

been that high incomes reflect—at least to some degree—high social product. As such, the high American per capita income is seen as a result of a relatively free market mechanism and an unequal distribution is tolerated as a by-product. If, instead, it is believed that few businesses would survive without exerting "influence," even if only to bribe government officials to do what they ought in any event to do, it is difficult to associate pecuniary rewards with social product. The perception of the price system as a mechanism rewarding the rich and well-connected may also be important in influencing political decisions about economic policy. If the market mechanism is suspect, the inevitable temptation is to resort to greater and greater intervention, thereby increasing the amount of economic activity devoted to rent seeking. As such, a political "vicious circle" may develop. People perceive that the market mechanism does not function in a way compatible with socially approved goals because of competitive rent seeking. A political consensus therefore emerges to intervene further in the market, rent seeking increases, and further intervention results. While it is beyond the competence of an economist to evaluate the political impact of rent seeking, the suspicion of the market mechanism so frequently voiced in some developing countries may result from it.

Finally, all market economies have some rent-generating restrictions. One can conceive of a continuum between a system of no restrictions and a perfectly restricted system. With no restrictions, entrepreneurs would seek to achieve windfall gains by adopting new technology, anticipating market shifts correctly, and so on. With perfect restrictions, regulations would be so all-pervasive that rent seeking would be the only route to gain. In such a system, entrepreneurs would devote all their time and resources to capturing windfall rents.

While neither of these extreme types could ever exist, one can perhaps ask whether there might be some point along the continuum beyond which the market fails to perform its allocative function to any satisfactory degree. It will remain for further work to formalize these conjectures and to test their significance. It is hoped, however, that enough has been said to stimulate interest and research on the subject.

REFERENCES

J. Bhagwati, "On the Equivalence of Tariffs and Quotas," in his *Trade, Tariffs and Growth*, London 1969.

——— and P. Desai, *Planning for Industrialization: A Study of India's Trade and Industrial Policies Since 1950*, Cambridge 1970.

——— and A. Krueger, *Foreign Trade Regimes and Economic Development: Experience and Analysis*, New York forthcoming.

J. R. Harris and M. P. Todaro, "Migration, Unemployment, and Development: A Two-Sector Analysis," *Amer. Econ. Rev.*, Mar. 1970, *60*, 126–42.

H. G. Johnson, "The Cost of Protection and the Scientific Tariff," *J. Polit. Econ.*, Aug. 1960, *68*, 327–45.

A. Krueger, *Foreign Trade Regimes and Economic Development: Turkey*, New York 1974.

J. B. Monteiro, *Corruption*, Bombay 1966.

G. Myrdal, *Asian Drama*, Vol. III, New York 1968.

M. P. Todaro, "A Model of Labor Migration and Urban Employment in Less Developed Countries," *Amer. Econ. Rev.*, Mar. 1969, *59*, 138–48.

R. Wraith and E. Simpkins, *Corruption in Developing Countries*, London 1963.

Government of India, Planning Commission, *Third Five Year Plan*, New Delhi, Aug. 1961.

Reserve Bank of India, *Report on Currency and Finance*, 1967–68.

Santhanam Committee, *Report on the Committee on Prevention of Corruption*, Government of India, Ministry of Home Affairs, New Delhi 1964.

N·H

ELSEVIER

Journal of International Economics 51 (2000) 437–461

Journal of INTERNATIONAL ECONOMICS

www.elsevier.nl/locate/econbase

Foreign aid and rent-seeking

Jakob Svensson[*]

Development Research Group, World Bank, 1818 H Street NW, Washington, DC 20433, USA

Received 13 November 1997; received in revised form 29 June 1998; accepted 1 February 1999

Abstract

Why has the macroeconomic impact of foreign aid seemingly been so poor? Is there a relationship between the widespread level of corruption and other types of rent-seeking activities and concessional assistance? To answer these questions we provide a simple game-theoretic rent-seeking model. The model has a number of implications. First, under certain circumstances, an increase in government revenue lowers the provision of public goods. Second, the mere expectation of aid may suffice to increase rent dissipation and reduce productive public spending. This result may be reversed, however, if the donor community can enter into a binding policy commitment. We also provide some preliminary empirical evidence in support of the hypothesis that foreign aid and windfalls are on average associated with higher corruption in countries more likely to suffer from competing social groups. We find no evidence that the donors systematically allocate aid to countries with less corruption. © 2000 Elsevier Science B.V. All rights reserved.

Keywords: Corruption; Foreign aid; Rent-seeking

JEL classification: D72; F35

1. Introduction

Empirical evidence indicates that rent-seeking is a serious problem in developing countries. This type of discretionary redistribution also tends to be particularly severe in "good" times. A country-specific example illustrates the point. "Public

Tel.: +1-202-477-1234; fax: +1-202-522-3518.

E-mail address: jsvensson@worldbank.org (J. Svensson)

438   *J. Svensson / Journal of International Economics 51 (2000) 437–461*

spending in Nigeria during the oil boom in the early 1990s increased by more than 50 percent, yet over the same period school enrollment shrunk due to tight education funding. The Nigerian Nobel Prize winner and dissident writer Wole Soyinka (1996) notes that a government-appointed commission of inquiry was unable to account for what happened to much of the 1990s government oil windfall" (Easterly and Levine, 1997).

Causal empiricism suggests that the dramatic increase in foreign aid over the past three decades has had a similar effect in many countries. The World Bank, for instance, reports that the rapid increase in foreign exchange resources, mainly due to large concessional flows, has greatly expanded the opportunities of malfeasance (World Bank, 1989, pp. 27, 61), and Klitgaard (1990) gives a vivid description of aid-related corruption in Africa. In many developing countries foreign assistance is an important source of revenue. For the 50 most aid-dependent countries the mean value of aid as share of central government expenditures for the period 1975–95 was 53.8 percent (World Bank, 1998). Despite this vast resource transfer, a number of empirical studies have shown that the macroeconomic effects of aid are, at best, ambiguous (Boone, 1996).

To explain this puzzle we develop a game-theoretic rent-seeking model in which (social) groups compete over common-pool resources. The common resources can either be invested in public goods, or be appropriated for private consumption. The latter either by means of direct appropriation (e.g., seizure of power) or manipulations of bureaucrats and politicians to implement favorable transfers, regulations or other redistributive policies. In a static setting it is not hard to see how this setup can lead to a Pareto-inefficient Nash equilibrium: each group will be strictly better off if all reduced their costly appropriation efforts, but a unilateral decrease is not rational for the individual social group. However, since the social groups interact repeatedly, this may provide a mechanism that can reduce the conflict of interest.[1] At the same time, these forces may not suffice to deliver the first-best outcome since full cooperation maximizes the reward of behaving opportunistically. Hence, it is possible to envision an economy where the degree of cooperation among social groups is, at the margin, balancing the benefit of cooperative behavior with the cost of sustaining the equilibrium.[2]

Within this setup, we show that an increase in government revenues may lower the provision of public goods. This provides an explanation for why large disbursements of aid, or windfalls, do not necessarily lead to increased welfare. Second, we show that mere expectation of aid according to the recipients' future needs may increase rent dissipation and reduce the expected number of periods in which efficient policies can be sustained. This may be an important observation

---

[1] See Benhabib and Rustichini (1996) for a dynamic model with this ingredient.
[2] The general idea was initially proposed by Rotemberg and Saloner (1986) to explain how tacit coordination among producers varies throughout the business cycle.

J. Svensson / Journal of International Economics 51 (2000) 437–461   439

because a positive correlation between recipients' needs and aid flows has been noted in the literature.

These results have three novel implications. First, since concessional assistance may influence policy in the recipient country even without any resources actually being disbursed, evaluations of project and sector assistance may overestimate the total impact of foreign aid. Second, the effects of development aid critically depend on the political equilibrium in the recipient country. An empirical investigation of the impact of aid that does not explicitly take this into account may be biased. Finally, if the donor community can enter into a binding policy commitment, aid may mitigate the incentives for social groups to engage in rent-seeking activities.

The empirical prediction of the model is that discretionary aid, and windfalls, in countries suffering from competing social groups will on average be associated with increased rent-seeking. Motivated by the theory we specify a simultaneous equation system to test this implication. To this end, we try to identify characteristics of the political and socio-political structure of a country which are plausibly correlated with the existence of influential social groups. As dependent variable we employ an index of corruption. The model's prediction hold up when confronted with cross-country data and is robust to a number of prospective statistical problems.

There is only limited work on foreign aid and endogenous macroeconomic policy. Casella and Eichengreen (1994) show, in line with our results, using the Alesina and Drazen (1991) model, that the prospect of aid can actually exacerbate the delay in stabilization, by inducing the social groups to postpone making sacrifices until aid actually materializes. In our model, the adverse impact of aid holds irrespective of specific timing assumptions. Further, Ranis and Mahmood (1992) argue that the availability of external resources tends to promote irresponsible policies. Boycko et al. (1996) discuss the impact of foreign assistance in countries characterized by a divided government, arguing that aid may be counterproductive if based on the wrong premise of government. This is an argument which accords well with our model's prediction. The papers closest in spirit to ours are Lane and Tornell (1995, 1996). They show that in a growth model with several powerful interest groups, a change in productivity (or terms of trade) may lead to a reduction in the growth rate. Our analysis, by studying a repeated rather than a dynamic game, should be regarded as complementing their work. However, our model differs from that of Lane and Tornell in a number of ways. First, the shocks are stochastic, rather than a one-time change in a perfect-foresight model as in Lane and Tornell. More important, in Lane and Tornell, the voracity effect whereby an increase in the raw return to aggregate capital leads to a more than proportional increase in redistributive transfers, is due to a coordination failure across interest groups. Our results, on the contrary, arise from Pareto constrained responses by the social groups to changing incentives to deviate. The main difference though is that we focus on foreign aid. Foreign aid

Jakob Svensson

differs from other sources of windfalls in that the outcome depends on the donors' actions. When explicitly taking this into account, we find that foreign aid also affects the equilibrium through a less tangible mechanism – the mechanism that enforces the control of rent dissipation in the economy.

Recently a number of studies have empirically investigated the macroeconomic impact of foreign aid. Boone (1996) concludes that aid primarily goes to consumption and that there is no relationship between aid and growth, nor does it benefit the poor as measured by improvements in human development indicators. Burnside and Dollar (1997) find that aid has a positive impact on growth in countries with "good" fiscal, monetary and trade policies, while Svensson (1998a) shows that the long-run growth impact of aid is conditional on the degree of political rights. The empirical section of the paper provides additional evidence on the aggregate impact of foreign aid, but rather than studying the relationship between aid and growth, we study the relationship between aid and corruption.

This paper is organized as follows. In Section 2 the model is presented. In Section 3, the noncooperative and the fully cooperative equilibria in the stage game are derived. The second-best equilibrium is studied in Section 4. In Section 5 the model is extended by explicitly modeling the donor's behavior. Section 6 provides some empirical results. Section 7 discusses the interpretation of these findings, while Section 8 concludes.

2. A political model of public spending and rent dissipation

2.1. The model

Consider an economy consisting of n powerful social groups. All groups have "common access" to the government's budget constraint. Specifically, at the beginning of each time period the government receives income (revenue) y_t. Income can be used either on local public goods, or appropriated by each individual social group. Appropriation of common resources is costly. Rent-seeking outlays by group i, denoted by z_i, result in total appropriation equal to $d_i = y(z_{it}/\sum_{j=1}^{n} z_{jt})$ for $z_{it} > 0$, and $d_i = 0$ for $z_{it} = 0$. Thus, private consumption is

$$
c_{it} =
\begin{cases}
y_i, & \text{for } z_{it} = 0, \\
y(\theta_t)\dfrac{z_{it}}{\sum_{j=1}^{n} z_{jt}} - z_{it} + y_i, & \text{for } z_{it} > 0,
\end{cases}
\tag{1}
$$

where $y(\theta_t)$ is government revenue, c_{it} denotes private consumption of the ith group, and z_{it} is rent-seeking outlays by social group i, all expressed in time period t.[3] The last term in (1), y_i, denotes the exogenously given income received by

[3]This setup builds on Tullock (1980).

J. Svensson / Journal of International Economics 51 (2000) 437–461   441

group i at the beginning of each time period. We think of this as income derived from the informal sector or from capital held abroad. It is assumed that y_i is secure from appropriation from others. Eq. (1) warrants two remarks. First, income for private consumption is derived from two sources: appropriation of government revenue, the first two terms in (1), and from the secure stock of capital (y_i). Second, the appropriation technology is exogenously given. This should be interpreted as a reduced form of a more structural model in which organized social groups can capture a large share of government income either by means of direct appropriation, or by manipulating the political system to implement favorable transfers, regulations, and other redistributive policies. Thus z_{it} is a composite variable of both direct costs of redistribution (e.g., bribes), and indirect costs of political competition (e.g., protection costs, resources employed to seize, or attempt to seize, power and restrict opponents' political activities).

Government income, $y(\theta_t)$, is stochastic, where θ_t is the realization at t of the observable shock to revenues with $y'(\theta_t) > 0$. We assume that the shocks are independently and identically distributed over time. θ_t has domain $[\underline{\theta}, \overline{\theta}]$, and a distribution function $F(\theta_t)$.

Each social group has a population of size 1. There is no heterogeneity within groups. Citizens derive utility from private consumption and public projects. Group i's per period utility is $u_{it} = b_{it} + c_{it}$, where $b_i = [y(\theta_t) - \sum_{j=1}^n d_j]/n$ is the amount of local public goods benefiting group i.

The social groups interact strategically, each maximizing expected utility

$$E \sum_{t=0}^{\infty} \delta^t u_{it} \tag{2}$$

subject to the per period budget constraint $z_{it} \leq y_i$.

This model defines a repeated game among the n social groups. At the beginning of each period, θ_t becomes common knowledge. The social groups then simultaneously choose rent seeking outlays $z_i \in [0, y_c]$. Resources not appropriated by the social groups are thereafter spent on local public goods in a symmetric fashion. A strategy for the individual social group is a policy function $z_i(\theta_t)$ that specifies the amount of rent-seeking outlays for each realization of θ_t.

3. The stage game

To solve the problem we start by calculating the symmetric Nash (NE) and cooperative (CE) equilibria in the stage game.

3.1. Nash equilibrium

Each social group determines the optimal level of rent-seeking outlays, z_{it}, taking z_{jt} for $j \neq i$ as given. The first-order condition for this problem can be written as

Jakob Svensson

$$\frac{y(\theta_t)}{\sum_{j=1}^{n} z_{jt}} \left[1 - \frac{z_{it}}{\sum_{j=1}^{n} z_{jt}} \right] - 1 = 0. \tag{3}$$

Hence, in equilibrium the marginal gain of rent-seeking, taking the form of a higher share of total net income, should be equal to the marginal cost, unity. Solving for z_{it} and summing over i gives us the aggregate level of rent dissipation

$$Z^n(\theta_t) = \frac{(n-1)}{n} y(\theta_t), \tag{4}$$

where superscript n denotes the symmetric NE. Clearly, rent dissipation is an increasing function of the number of social groups and income.

In the NE, all common resources will be appropriated from the budget. Hence, $b_i^n(\theta) = 0$ and $\sum_i^n d_i^n(\theta_t) = y(\theta_t)$. However, as appropriation is costly, only a fraction of the appropriated resources will actually benefit the social groups through higher private consumption.

3.2. Cooperation among the social groups

Now consider instead the fully cooperative equilibrium (CE). The symmetric CE is a vector of feasible policy functions $[z_i(\theta_t), \ldots z_n(\theta_t)]$ such that all social groups exert the same level of rent-seeking activities and $z_i(\theta_t) = \arg\max E\sum_{i=1}^{n} u_{it}$.

Clearly, since rent-seeking is a zero-sum game in influence, but a negative-sum game in total resources, $z_i^c(\theta_t) = 0 \; \forall i$, where superscript c denotes the CE. Hence, in the CE all resources will be spent on public projects, $b_i^c(\theta) = y(\theta_t)/n$, and utility will be strictly higher.

4. The repeated game

4.1. Second-best equilibrium (SBE)

The game described in Section 2 is a repeated game. Hence, one equilibrium is the NE in the stage game repeated infinitely. However, infinitely played games of the type described above are usually able to sustain an equilibrium that strictly dominates the outcome in the corresponding static NE played repeatedly, even if the groups cannot sign binding contracts. The extreme case would be if the social groups could sustain the CE in all states. In reality the actual outcome may lie between the extreme regimes of either full cooperation or noncooperative behavior. This is so because, on the one hand, repeated interaction provides a mechanism which can sustain a subgame perfect equilibrium with higher payoffs for all groups with trigger strategies. On the other hand, these forces may not

J. Svensson / Journal of International Economics 51 (2000) 437–461   443

suffice to deliver the fully cooperative outcome in all states, since full cooperation maximizes the reward of behaving opportunistically. Hence, it is possible to envision an economy where the degree of cooperation among the social groups is, at the margin, balancing the benefit of cooperative behavior with the cost of sustaining the equilibrium.

To deter groups from deviating, the equilibrium must involve a mechanism that punishes deviations. One such mechanism would be the use of punishment against defecting groups in periods following the defection (Friedman, 1971). A simple, but not the only, way to ensure sequential rationality is for the punishment to involve playing of the static NE for the reminder of the game after the first defection is detected. We restrict attention to these strategies.[4]

Definition 4.1. The second-best equilibrium (SBE) is a sequence of feasible policy functions $[z_i(\theta_t), \ldots, z_n(\theta_t)]$ such that: (i) all social groups exert the same level of rent-seeking activities; (ii) the rent-seeking configuration is sustainable in equilibrium; (iii) the expected present discounted utility of each group along the equilibrium path is not Pareto dominated by other equilibrium payoffs.

The equilibrium is solved in two steps. First, the highest sustainable level of income is determined for a given punishment. Second, the optimal punishment as a function of the highest sustainable level of income is derived. This defines a mapping from the set of possible punishments into itself. The fixed point of this mapping, then, defines a threshold value for θ_t.

We start by exploring the social groups' options for each value of θ_t. Let $v^c(\theta_t) = y(\theta_t)/n$ be the equilibrium level of "net" utility (i.e. net of own income y_i) for each social group under full cooperation. Since $y(\theta_t)$ is increasing in θ_t, "net-utility" is increasing in θ_t.

Along the cooperative equilibrium path, an increase in z_i with an arbitrary small amount raises net-utility for the group that deviates to almost $y(\theta_t)$. Thus, group i would deviate from the joint utility-maximizing strategy if

$$y(\theta_t) > \frac{n}{n-1}P, \tag{5}$$

where P is the punishment inflicted on group i in the future if it deviates at time t. Note that the higher θ_t, the higher is $y(\theta_t)$, and the greater are the incentives to deviate for a given P. Since $y'(\theta_t) > 0$, there exist some $\hat{\theta}_t$, for which $y(\hat{\theta}_t) = (n/(n-1))P$. Thus, if $v(\hat{\theta}_t, \theta_t)$ denotes the highest level of net-utility each group can sustain in the SBE

---

[4]As discussed in the working paper version of this paper, switching forever to the stage-game Nash equilibrium is the strongest credible punishment (i.e. optimal punishment) provided that the number of social groups are sufficiently high (Svensson, 1998b).

Jakob Svensson

$$v(\hat{\theta}_t,\theta_t) = \begin{cases} v^c(\theta_t), & \text{for } \theta_t \le \hat{\theta}_t, \\ v^c(\hat{\theta}_t) = \dfrac{1}{n-1}P, & \text{for } \theta_t > \hat{\theta}_t. \end{cases} \tag{6}$$

Clearly, the higher the punishment, P, the higher the equilibrium level of net-utility. The future loss from deviation at some date, discounted at the same date, can be stated as

$$P(\hat{\theta}_t,\theta_t) = \frac{\delta}{(1-\delta)} \int_{\underline{\theta}}^{\bar{\theta}} [v(\hat{\theta}_t,\theta_t) - v''(\theta_t)] dF(\theta_t). \tag{7}$$

That is, P is the difference between the expected discounted value of net utility from time $t+1$ to ∞ between the SBE and the repeated NE.

Eq. (7) gives a mapping from the set of possible punishments into itself: a given P implies a cutoff value $\hat{\theta}_t$ from (6), which in turn defines a punishment level from (7). The equilibrium of the model is the fixed point of this mapping with the highest value of P; i.e. the highest level of utility for the social groups.

In Appendix B we show that sufficient conditions for the existence of a fixed point are

$$(i) \ y(\underline{\theta})\Gamma < -(\beta/n^2)E[y(\theta_t)], \quad (ii) \ y(\bar{\theta})/E[y(\theta_t)] > \frac{\delta}{(1-\delta)n^2},$$

where $\beta \equiv \delta/(1-\delta)$, $\Gamma \equiv (1 - \beta/(n-1))$ and E is the expectation operator.

Condition (i) states that the discount factor must be sufficiently high. Otherwise the social groups discount the future too much, implying that the punishment become less important and it will no longer be possible to sustain the fully cooperative equilibrium. Condition (ii) ensures that full cooperation is not the only solution in every state. This condition is satisfied provided that there is sufficient dispersion in the distribution of revenues.

Lemma 4.2. *If conditions (i) and (ii) are satisfied, there exists a fixed point $\hat{\theta}_t$ such that (6) holds with P defined in Eq. (7).*

Proposition 4.3. *An increase in revenue above the threshold value, $\hat{\theta}$, lowers the provision of public projects, leaving total utility unchanged. The equilibrium configuration for the endogenous variables are*

$$b_i(\theta_t) = y(\theta_t)/n, \ c_i(\theta_t) = y_i, z_i(\theta_t) = 0, \qquad \text{for } \theta_t \le \hat{\theta}_t,$$

$$b_i(\theta_t) = 0, \ c_i(\theta_t) = y(\hat{\theta}_t)/n + y_i, z_i(\theta_t) = [y(\theta_t) - y(\hat{\theta}_t)]/n, \quad \text{for } \theta_t > \hat{\theta}_t.$$

Proof. Follows from Lemma 4.2 and the first-order condition (3). ■

The higher the income the higher the incentive to deviate from the cooperative conduct. To counter-balance this, the social groups must increase their appropria-tion rate so as to reduce the aggregate net level of resources for redistribution. In equilibrium, all incomes above $y(\hat{\theta}_t)$ are dissipated, leaving welfare unchanged. Note that in the SBE aggregate appropriation must increase by more than the rise in income, implying that the provision of public projects actually falls with an increase in income above $y(\hat{\theta}_t)$.

This finding has one important implication. If the political game described in the paper is relevant, and provided that θ_t is near $\hat{\theta}_t$, we should observe surprisingly small or in fact even contractible effects on welfare and public project provision following increased inflows of foreign aid, or windfall gains in revenue.[5]

5. Aid and rent dissipation: the indirect linkage

The main point highlighted in this section is that foreign aid may affect the equilibrium outcome not only through the direct effect explored in the previous section, but also through a less tangible mechanism – the mechanism enforcing the control of rent dissipation in the economy.

5.1. A modified model

Consider the following extension of the model. Besides the n social groups there is also a donor. The donor's problem is to maximize its expected utility

$$E\sum_{t=1}^{\infty} \delta^t[\varphi f_t + w(s_t)] \tag{8}$$

subject to the budget constraint $f_t + a_t \leq r$. In (8), f_t denotes the domestic activity of the donor at time t, $s_t \equiv \Sigma_i^n u_{it}$, a_t is the level of aid disbursed at time t, r is the income received at the beginning of each period and $w(\cdot)$ is a concave, increasing function. Alternatively, f_t captures the welfare of giving aid to other recipient countries or to activities not valued by the recipient. Assuming that the donor's utility is linear in its domestic activity simplifies the analysis. However, the qualitative results do not hinge on this specification (see Svensson, 1998b). The parameter φ is the constant marginal utility of the domestic activity.

We believe that (8) is a realistic and rather general characterization of the donor's preferences. The empirical literature on the determinants of foreign aid have found that aid is driven both by the donor's own interests (captured by f) and by recipients' needs (captured by s) (see, e.g., Burnside and Dollar, 1997).

---

[5]The comparative statics with respect to n and δ are analyzed in Svensson (1998b). Contrary to the results in Lane and Tornell (1995) and the standard result in the rent-seeking literature, the effect of n on $\hat{\theta}$ is non-monotonic. An increase in δ raises $\hat{\theta}$.

446   *J. Svensson / Journal of International Economics 51 (2000) 437–461*

We assume initially that aid is given in the form of public projects. Assuming that aid is disbursed as untied program support does not alter the qualitative result. In fact, we consider the alternative in Section 5.1.2.

5.1.1. Foreign aid with discretion

Consider first a discretionary aid regime where it is impossible to commit policy in advance. Thus, the sequencing of events are as described in Section 2.1 with the exception that the donor now determines the level of aid disbursed simultaneously with the choices of the n social groups, taking $[z_i(\theta), \ldots, z_n(\theta)]$ as given.

The equilibrium in the stage game is characterized by two conditions. The first condition defines the amount of rent-seeking outlays and is described in Section 3. The second concerns the disbursement of foreign aid, and is given by the first-order condition of the donor's maximization program

$$w'\left(\sum_{i=1}^{n}[c_i(\theta_t|a_t) + b_i(\theta_t|a_t)]\right) - \varphi \leq 0, \tag{9}$$

where r is assumed to be sufficiently large to guarantee an interior solution. $c_i(\theta_t|a_t)$ is defined in (1) and

$$b_i(\theta_t|a_t) = \frac{1}{n}[y(\theta_t) + a_t] - \frac{1}{n}\sum_{i=1}^{n}\left[y(\theta_t)\frac{z_i(\theta_t)}{\sum_{j=1}^{n}z_j(\theta_t)}\right] \tag{10}$$

when the groups act noncooperatively, and $c_i = y_c$ and $b_i = (1/n)[y(\theta_t) + a_t]$ when they act cooperatively. Thus, the donor will provide assistance up to the point where the marginal utility of aid is equal to the opportunity cost, φ. As evident from Eq. (9), the inclusion of a donor sets a lower bound on the welfare of the agents.[6] Since the payoff in the NE is strictly smaller than the payoff in the CE for all θ, foreign aid will affect the two scenarios asymmetrically. Specifically, more aid will be given in the NE. Thus, the presence of a donor increases expected welfare in the NE relative the CE. As the punishment is the expected discounted difference in utility between the second-best and Nash equilibrium, foreign aid will undermine the enforcement mechanism available for the social groups.

Proposition 5.1. *A discretionary aid policy will make cooperative behavior more difficult to sustain thereby lowering the threshold value $\hat{\theta}_t$.*

Proof. See Appendix C. ■

A discretionary aid policy of higher aid disbursements when income is low will undermine the enforcement mechanism available for the social groups. Since harsh

---

[6]We assume that $w_c^{-1}(\varphi) < \sum_{i=1}^{n} u_i^c(\bar{\theta})$ so that consumption is not constant in the fully cooperative equilibrium.

J. Svensson / Journal of International Economics 51 (2000) 437–461   447

punishment facilitates cooperation, foreign aid makes cooperation more difficult to sustain. As a result, the social groups must content themselves with fewer periods in which the fully cooperative outcome can be sustained. Consequently, the expected level of rent dissipation increases.

This result warrants four remarks. First, it is not the actual increased disbursement of aid in bad states that drives the result, but the expectation that this will happen. Hence, the fact that the donor acts according to recipients' needs may by itself increase rent dissipation in the recipient country, and reduce the number of periods in which efficient policies can be sustained.[7]

Second, aid is effective at the micro-level while having adverse macroeconomic consequences. Hence, the model provides a possible explanation for the "macro–micro paradox" that has been discussed in the aid literature (see, e.g., Mosley, 1987).[8] Moreover, even though aid is given as project support, project evaluations would yield biased estimates of the overall impact of the aid program.

Third, even though the aid relationship causes corruption, the social groups are better off (in expected terms) with aid than without.

Finally, taking the model literally, rent-seeking and aid cannot coexist in the SBE. The reason for this is that as long as the country receives aid, i.e. $y(\theta) < y(\theta_1)$ where $y(\theta_1)$ denote the cutoff value of $y(\theta)$ for which (9) no longer binds in the fully cooperative equilibrium, welfare is constant along the equilibrium path. Thus, if it is profitable to deviate at some $y(\theta) < y(\theta_1)$, it must be profitable to deviate for all $y(\theta)$. In this case, of course, there exists no equilibrium. Hence, $\hat{\theta} > \theta_1$. It is straightforward to generalize the model so that rent-seeking and aid can co-exist in the SBE. As shown in Svensson (1998b), a sufficient condition is that the donor's utility function over the domestic activity is concave rather than linear.

5.1.2. Foreign aid with commitments

Now consider instead an environment in which the donor can enter into a binding policy commitment before the social groups choose rent-seeking outlays. That is, suppose the timing is such that the donor first chooses aid as a function of θ and $z_i \ldots z_n$. Then, observing $a(\theta_t, \mathbf{z}(\theta_t))$, the social groups choose $z_i(\theta), \ldots, z_n(\theta)$. To simplify the exposition we now assume that aid is given as untied program support. Consequently, aggregate government income in each period is $y(\theta_t) + a(\theta_t, \mathbf{z}(\theta_t))$, where $\mathbf{z}(\theta_t)$ is the vector of rent-seeking outlays.

The equilibrium can be computed by backward induction. We need to consider

---

[7]Note that this result differs from the Samaritan's dilemma problem explored in the literature on altruism and transfers (see, e.g., Svensson, 1997), in which the recipient strategically tries to free-ride on the donor's concern. Here, on the contrary, the linkage is more subtle: expectation of aid undermines the mechanism enforcing the control of rent dissipation.

[8]The paradox is that whilst micro-level evaluations have been, by and large, positive, those of the macro evidence have, at best, been ambiguous.

Jakob Svensson

aid disbursement under two different institutional settings: when the social groups
cooperate and when they interact noncooperatively. In both cases, the last stage of
the game is identical to that described in Section 3, with $y(\theta_t)$ replaced by
$y(\theta_t) + a(\theta_t, \mathbf{z}(\theta_t))$. These conditions act as incentive constraints on the donor's
maximization program in the first stage of the game. The first-order condition of
the donor's problem is

$$
w'\left(a(\theta_t, \mathbf{z}(\theta_t)) + \sum_{i=1}^{n} u_i^c(\theta_t) \right) - \varphi \le 0 \tag{11}
$$

when the social groups cooperate and

$$
w'\left(\frac{1}{n} a(\theta_t, \mathbf{z}(\theta_t)) + \sum_{i=1}^{n} u_i^n(\theta_t) \right) \frac{1}{n} - \varphi \le 0 \tag{12}
$$

when they interact noncooperatively. As evident, the donor now internalizes the
cost of rent dissipation. The political competition over the common resources
creates a wedge, $1/n$, between the marginal utility of the recipients' consumption
and the opportunity cost of foreign aid. In other words, the rent-seeking contest
results in a "tax" on foreign aid. If the tax effect dominates, more aid will be
given in the cooperative setting for each θ, implying that the mechanism enforcing
cooperation is strengthened.

Proposition 5.2. *A donor with access to a binding policy commitment generally
strengthens the mechanism that enforces cooperation, thereby increasing the
threshold value $\hat{\theta}_t$.*

Proof. See Appendix D. ∎

6. Some preliminary evidence

6.1. Empirical prediction

   In this section we take a first step to empirically test the prediction of the model.
The test, however, is bound to be only suggestive. First, time series observations
for sufficiently long periods are only available for a small subset of the relevant
variables, implying that we are constrained to analyze the medium-term implications of the model. Second, since manipulations of the political system are seldom
done in the open and are almost never recorded, we cannot directly measure the
degree of competition among powerful social groups. As an alternative, we try to
identify characteristics of the political and socio-political structure of a country
which are plausibly correlated with the existence of influential social groups.
Finally, since we cannot a priori determine the cutoff value $\hat{\theta}$ and as actual

J. Svensson / Journal of International Economics 51 (2000) 437–461   449

disbursements of aid are likely to be (highly) correlated with expectations of future assistance, we are not able to distinguish between the two mechanisms summarized in Propositions 4.3 and 5.1.

With these limitations in mind, the model's main prediction can be stated as: *discretionary aid (or expectations thereof) and windfalls, in countries suffering from competing social groups, will on average increase the level of rent-seeking activities.*

To test this implication, we specify the following equation

$$z_{it} = \beta^z \mathbf{x}_{it} + \gamma^z d_{it} + \zeta^z \mathbf{w}_{it} + \theta^z (\mathbf{w}_{it} d_{it}) + \varepsilon_{it}^r, \tag{13}$$

where z_{it} is a measure of the average level of rent-seeking activities in period t for country i, d_{it} is a proxy of the existence of powerful social groups, $\mathbf{w}_{it}$ is a vector of windfalls proxies including the level of aid disbursed to country i, denoted by a_{it}, and $\mathbf{x}_{it}$ is a vector of other variables that affect the level of rent dissipation. The model suggests that a should be treated as an endogenous variable. For this reason we also specify an aid-determinants equation

$$a_{it} = \beta^a \mathbf{v}_{it} + \phi^a z_{it} + \varepsilon_{it}^a, \tag{14}$$

where $\mathbf{v}_{it}$ is a vector of other variables influencing the amount of aid disbursed to country i. Once we properly instrument for aid, we can test our null hypothesis that the marginal impact of aid and windfalls on z depends on the political equilibrium.

6.2. Data and base specification

Following Easterly and Levine (1997), we choose a measure of ethnic diversity (*ethnic*) as proxy for the likelihood of competing social groups in a country. A vast political science literature links ethnic groups with redistributive policies in developing countries, particularly in Africa. *ethnic* measures the probability that two randomly selected individuals in a country will belong to different ethnolinguistic groups. The raw data for *ethnic* refers to 1960. *ethnic* increases with the number of groups and the more equal is the size of the groups. Since coalitions with power to extract transfers from the rest of society may be formed along many other lines, ethnic fractionalization is obviously not a necessary, and much less a sufficient, condition for the existence of competing social groups. Consequently, we do not claim that *ethnic* is a valid measure for all countries.

To proxy for the dependent variable rent-seeking, we employ an index of corruption drawn from ICRG (see Knack and Keefer, 1995). The index is on a scale from 0 to 6. We reverse the scale so that 0 indicates least corrupt and 6 most corrupt and denote the re-scaled variable by *cor*. Obviously, rent-seeking can take many other forms than corruption, e.g. protection costs, resources employed to seize, or attempt to seize, power and restrict opponents' political activities.

450   *J. Svensson / Journal of International Economics 51 (2000) 437–461*

However, this type of data is not readily available. Moreover, it is hard to see why increased pressure for redistribution would manifest itself only through certain channels (e.g., costs of political competition) and not through all different types available for the social groups (e.g., corruption). Presumably the social groups are equalizing the marginal costs and benefits of the different forms of rent-seeking.

We use aid data from a new World Bank data base on foreign aid. The data combines the grant component of each concessional loan with outright grants to provide a more accurate measure of foreign assistance. The data, denoted by *aid*, is converted into constant dollars and scaled by real GDP.

We also employ two additional proxies of windfalls: term of trade shocks (*tt*), and the share of exports of primary products in GDP (*sxp*). The latter measure captures discoveries of natural (mineral) resources that are important sources of windfall gains in many developing countries.

The level of rent-seeking is also a function of the discount factor δ. A lower δ leads to a higher expected *z*. To proxy for δ we employ regional-specific dummy variables for Sub-Saharan Africa (*africa*), and Central America (*centam*), and the log of initial per capita GDP (*lgdp*).

Motivated by the theory we assume that aid is driven both by donors' interests and recipients' needs. In the base specification we include the log of population (*lpop*) to proxy for donors' interests, and (*lgdp*) to control for recipients' needs motives. We also include *tt*. According to the model, a negative income shock will result in increased aid flows.

We are able to collect data for 66 aid recipient countries starting from 1980. To increase the size of the sample, but also to explore the time dimension in the data, we divide the cross-country data into three 5-year periods. Thus, each country has three observations, data permitting. The system of equations is estimated by 2SLS, with standard errors adjusted for country-specific random effects.[9] Data sources and summary statistics are reported in Appendix A.

6.3. Results

As a benchmark, the simple regression of corruption on *ethnic* is highly significant, with a *t*-statistic of 3.71. If we add the vector of windfall proxies and *aid* to this regression we obtain the equation system reported in Table 1, columns (1a) and (1b). If we do not control for the political equilibrium, there is no significant correlation between *cor* and the regressors *aid*, *sxp* and *tt*. In the aid regression, both initial income and the log of population are highly significant. *cor* and *tt* enter with negative signs in (1b), but are insignificant. If the donor could credibly commit to a policy rule we would expect the coefficient on *cor* to be different from zero. However, in the model of aid with discretion, *a* is constant for

---

[9]Because we use 2SLS we must also specify an equation for the interaction term *a*d*. See the discussion in the text below.

Table 1
IV-regressions on corruption and aid[a,b]

Equation Dep. var.	(1a)[c] cor	(1b)[d] aid	(1c)[c] cor	(1d)[e] aid	(1e)[c] cor	(1f)[c] cor	(1g)[c] cor
ethnic	0.734 (2.56)		−1.20 (−1.83)		−0.679 (−1.56)	−1.67 (−2.31)	−1.01 (−2.19)
aid	0.018 (0.24)		(−0.406) (−2.47)			−0.433 (−2.27)	
sxp	0.4E−3 (0.05)		−0.024 (−1.65)		−0.026 (−2.14)	−0.035 (−1.59)	−0.043 (−2.46)
tt	−0.61 (−1.25)	−0.133 (−0.98)	−0.194 (−2.47)	−0.066 (−0.61)		−0.171 (−1.95)	
lgdp	−0.081 (−0.38)	−2.36 (−10.7)	−5.10 (−2.16)	−2.17 (15.4)	−0.552 (−3.74)	−0.582 (−2.49)	−0.551 (−3.30)
aid*ethnic			0.833 (3.66)			0.785 (3.05)	
sxp*ethnic			0.057 (2.52)		0.065 (3.14)	0.075 (2.40)	0.088 (3.23)
tt*ethnic			0.233 (1.34)			0.215 (1.22)	
(aid + tt)*ethnic					0.520 (4.36)		0.466 (3.69)
aid + tt					−0.278 (−4.04)		−0.255 (−3.21)
africa			−1.24 (−5.49)		−1.09 (−5.33)	−1.20 (−5.38)	−1.12 (−5.35)
centam			−0.064 (−0.24)		−0.200 (−0.80)	−0.131 (−0.51)	−0.236 (−1.00)
cor		−0.815 (−1.33)		−0.096 (−0.38)			
lpop		−0.828 (−8.87)		−0.829 (−9.23)			
time[f]	5%	No	No	1%	5%	No	No
Observations	182	182	182	182	182	162	162

[a] 2SLS estimation on pooled data (1980–84, 85–89, 90–94), with *t*-statistics adjusted for country-specific random effects in parentheses.

[b] Each regression includes a constant and two time dummies not reported here.

[c] The instruments for *aid* are given in (1b).

[d] The instruments for *cor* in (1b) are given in (1a).

[e] The instruments for *cor* in (1d) are given in (1c).

[f] *time* indicates if the time dummies are jointly significant at the 5 (1)% level.

all z if $\theta > \hat{\theta}$. Hence, the data suggests that the donor community acts with discretion and does not systematically allocate aid to countries with less corruption. Overall, our instruments for aid are rather powerful. The R^2 in the first-stage regression of *aid* increases from 0.10 to 0.60 when *lgdp* and *lpop* are included.

Adding the regional dummies and the interaction terms yield the base specification reported in columns (1c) and (1d). We instrument for *aid*ethnic* by

452   *J. Svensson / Journal of International Economics 51 (2000) 437–461*

including *ethnic* interacted with several of the regressors in Eq. (14).[10] In column (1c), *aid*ethnic* and *sxp*ethnic* are positive and highly significant, while *tt*ethnic* enters insignificantly, although with the predicted sign. The joint hypothesis that the coefficients on all interaction terms are zero is rejected by a wide margin (F-statistic 4.40). In accordance with the prediction of the model, the partial derivatives of corruption with respect to *aid* and *sxp* are positive for high levels of *ethnic*. The marginal impact of *aid* (*sxp*) on *cor* is positive for *ethnic* > 0.49 (*ethnic* > 0.42) implying that for 31 (33) out of 66 countries in the sample, increased aid (discovery of exploitable resources) is associated with higher corruption. The magnitude of the correlation between aid and corruption is considerable. For the most fractionalized country (*ethnic* $= 0.93$), a one standard deviation increase in predicted aid (2.0 percentage points) is associated with a 0.8 standard deviation increase in the corruption index (0.8 points).

As reported above, there is no significant relationship between the level of aid and *tt*. However, a closer look at the data reveals that changes in aid during sub-periods, Δaid, is responsive to terms of trade shocks, particularly in fractionalized countries. The simple correlation between *tt* and Δaid for the most fractionalized countries (top 20%) is -0.27.[11] If terms of trade shocks are (partly) counterbalanced by aid flows, it is not surprising that *tt*ethnic* is insignificantly different from zero. In column (1e) we try to circumvent the multicollinearity problem by including the sum of *aid* and *tt* as a regressor. Note that both variables are measured as a share of GDP. *aid* $+$ *tt* then provides a measure of the flow of "windfalls" into the country. As shown in (1e), the result improves with this specification. Using *aid* $+$ *tt* as regressor, the cutoff point for the derivative of *cor* with respect to *aid* $+$ *tt* is 0.54, implying that for 53 percent of the countries in the sample, an increase in "adjusted" aid is associated with higher corruption. Note also that the marginal effect of aid on corruption in countries less likely to suffer from competing social groups is significantly negative.

It is reasonable to assume that the mechanism described in the model is more relevant for countries with a sufficiently high level of aid. Therefore, we estimated the effect of aid on corruption for countries with a share of aid to GDP above 0.1 percent.[12] The results of this exercise are shown in (1f) and (1g). As evident, the results are very similar to those reported above.

Summarizing the preliminary findings, when properly instrumenting for aid, the

---

[10]In the base specification *ethnic* is interacted with the time and regional dummies. These interaction terms are highly correlated with *ethnic*aid* (the F-statistic on the joint hypothesis that the coefficients on the interaction variables are zero in the first-stage regression is 5.28), but uncorrelated with *aid* (F-statistic in the first-stage regression is 1.20), which make them good candidates for instruments. *ethnic* interacted with the additional regressors in Eq. (14), *lpop, lgdp,* are less suitable as instruments since they are highly correlated with *aid* (F-statistic in the first-stage regression is 12.18).

[11]If Nigeria is excluded the correlation jumps to -0.36.

[12]There are 12 countries with a share of aid to GDP below 0.1 percent in at least one of the three sub-periods.

J. Svensson / Journal of International Economics 51 (2000) 437–461   453

interaction term neatly separates the effects of aid on corruption. On average, foreign aid is positively associated with corruption in countries more likely to suffer from competing social groups. This partitioning fits the prediction of the model and underlies the general idea that the effects of aid critically depend on the political equilibrium in the recipient country. Additional proxies of windfalls show a similar pattern. We find a weakly robust negative relationship between aid and corruption in countries less likely to suffer from competing social groups, while there is no evidence that the donors systematically allocate aid to countries with less corruption.

6.4. Sensitivity analyses

We conducted several robustness checks. We have already shown that the results are robust to the sample of countries. Another important question is whether the findings are robust to alternative specifications. To check this we included additional controls in both the aid regression (infant mortality rate at the start of the period, arms imports as a share of total imports lagged one period), and the corruption regression [regional dummies for South America and East Asia, share of trade to GDP, and a composite measure of openness from Sachs and Warner (1995)]. The original rent-seeking literature emphasized trade restrictions as the primary source of (government-induced) rents (Krueger, 1974). More generally, protection from international competition generates rents that business may be willing to pay for. Overall, once we control for *ethnic* in the corruption regression, the additional controls have only a minor effect on *cor*. Sachs and Warner's openness measure enters significantly in some specifications, but the result is not robust. The share of trade to GDP and the additional regional dummies enter insignificantly. The results of the other regressors, in particular *aid*ethnic*, remain qualitatively unaffected. We find no evidence that the level of aid is significantly correlated with arms imports or infant mortality rate, even though arms imports enters with the predicted sign and a *P*-value of around 0.10 in most specifications.

We also experimented with other proxies of wasteful rent-seeking activities. In Table 2, column (2a), we report the base specification with black-market premium (*bmp*) as dependent variable. *bmp* is a measure of (trade) distortions/regulations in the economy. With the presumption that (trade) regulations are mechanisms for redistribution to special interests, *bmp* should be positively correlated with *z*. An additional proxy of regulations is the "Freedom from Government Regulation" (*fgr*) rating from the Fraser Institute (1997), reported in column (2b). We also combined the two variables to create a composite measure of regulations, denoted by *regulation*, column (2c). As evident from Table 2, the interaction term, (*aid* + *tt*)*ethnic, enters significantly [at the 10% level in (2b)] and with right sign in all three specifications and the partial derivatives of rent-seeking with respect to *aid* + *tt* are positive for high levels of *ethnic*. Thus, the result reported above is

Table 2
IV-regressions on corruption[a,b]

Equation Dep. var.	(2a)[c] bmp	(2b)[c] fgr	(2c)[c] regulation	(2d)[c] cor	(2e)[c] cor
ethnic	−0.151	−4.70	−2.01	−0.430	0.630
	(−0.68)	(−2.76)	(−2.68)	(−1.04)	(1.12)
aid + tt	−0.080	−0.859	−0.401	−0.241	−0.111
	(−2.31)	(−2.75)	(−3.08)	(−3.25)	(−0.82)
sxp	0.020	0.072	0.026	−0.022	0.008
	(3.26)	(1.36)	(1.17)	(−1.85)	(1.12)
lgdp	−0.142	−1.81	−0.671	−0.398	−0.358
	(−2.09)	(−4.05)	(−3.64)	(−2.40)	(−1.29)
(aid + tt)*ethnic	0.103	−0.859	0.424	0.485	
	(2.06)	(1.76)	(2.14)	(4.23)	
sxp*ethnic	0.019	−0.042	−0.003	0.056	
	(1.97)	(−0.48)	(−0.07)	(2.69)	
africa	0.014	1.08	0.474	−1.20	−0.940
	(0.11)	(1.28)	(1.16)	(−5.73)	(−3.76)
centam	0.478	−1.53	0.376	−0.160	−0.306
	(2.36)	(0.81)	(0.75)	(−0.70)	(−1.21)
dem				−0.114	−0.174
				(−2.26)	(−2.86)
(aid + tt)*ethnic*dem					0.080
					(2.38)
sxp*ethnic*dem					0.4E−3
					(0.05)
time[d]	No	No	No	No	No
Observations	188	167	160	182	182

[a] 2SLS estimation on pooled data (1980–84, 85–89, 90–94), with t-statistics adjusted for country-specific random effects in parentheses.

[b] Each regression includes a constant and two time dummies not reported here.

[c] The instruments for aid are given in (1b).

[d] time indicates if the time dummies are jointly significant at the 5 (1)% level.

robust to other proxies of rent-seeking activities. The main difference from Table 1 is that sxp*ethnic is no longer significantly different from zero.

Another feature which might influence the link between aid and rent-seeking is the nature of the political system. To control for this we include an index of democracy (dem) from Freedom House (1997). dem enters with a negative sign in (2d), and is significantly different from zero. Thus, more democratic countries tend to experience lower corruption. Note that dem is not simply proxying for income levels, since lgdp remains significant, and that the interaction term (aid + tt)*ethnic as well as the partial derivative remain qualitatively unaffected. Interacting dem with the two interactions terms in (1e) yields the specification reported in (2e). The partial derivative of cor with respect to dem is significantly negative, even for a country with ethnic = 1 (evaluated at the mean level of aid).

J. Svensson / Journal of International Economics 51 (2000) 437–461 455

Thus, the mechanism explored in the paper seems to be of less importance in democratic countries.[13]

Finally, we did a Hausman test of the over-identifying restrictions on the base specification reported in columns (1c) and (1d). We cannot reject the over-identifying restrictions, i.e. we find no evidence that the instruments for *aid* (*cor*) belong in the corruption (*aid*) regression.[14]

7. Discussion

We have shown that foreign aid and windfalls are associated with higher corruption in countries more likely to suffer from powerful competing social groups. We believe this result is supportive of the theory. The model we have laid out is built around a standard rent-seeking specification. Admittedly, this is a black box approach to policy formation. It should be viewed as a reduced form of a more structural model in which organized social groups can capture a large share of government income, either by means of direct appropriation, or by manipulating the political system to implement favorable transfers, regulations and other redistributive policies.

In the empirical section we use corruption as a proxy of rent-seeking. We believe that corruption is likely to be highly correlated with other forms of discretionary redistribution, and therefore able to capture more than the empirical relationship between aid, corruption and the political equilibrium. This assertion also finds support in the data – the empirical results are robust to other proxies of wasteful rent-seeking.

The key insights we want to capture in the model are that "economically irrational" responses to windfalls that has been noted in the literature may be "politically rational", and that foreign aid may affect the outcome (and the political equilibrium) through a less tangible mechanism.

These results rely on four general assumptions. First, economic policy is determined jointly by a number of powerful social groups. In the long run, the groups are better off if they cooperate than if the act noncooperatively. There is a large literature both in economics (see, e.g., Easterly and Levine, 1997; Rodrik, 1998) and in political science that links interest/social groups with redistributive policies in developing countries. Problems of coordination and cooperation are at the heart of this literature. Thus, we believe that our reduced form model captures an important aspect of reality.

---

[13] The specification in column (2e) is restricted, in that the various two-way interactions are excluded. When adding all two-way interactions to (2e), they enter insignificantly. To minimize the loss of degrees of freedom, we choose to drop them from the specification.

[14] The test statistics are 5.37 and 10.17, respectively. The 5 (1) percent critical values from the χ^2 distribution are 7.82 (11.34) for regression (1c), and 16.92 (21.67) for regression (1d).

456   *J. Svensson / Journal of International Economics 51 (2000) 437–461*

Second, we assume that the deviating group can capture the entire government budget. An objection to this is that a slight increase in rent-seeking by one group when all others refrain yields a very large payoff. While technically correct, this critique takes the model's structure too much at face value. Rent-seeking is a composite variable of both direct cost of redistribution (e.g., bribes), and indirect costs of political competition (e.g., resources employed to seize or attempt to seize power). In these dimensions, deviating from a cooperative code of conduct is likely to yield high short-run payoffs.

Third, the larger the government budget, the larger the incentives to deviate. An objection to this assumption is that it implies that the richer the economy, the more rent-seeking, and the type of discretionary redistribution analyzed in the model is not associated with policies in many rich developed countries. In response, it is important to make clear that the focus in the paper is on the relationship between rent-seeking, windfalls and foreign aid, and we have purposely assumed away other incentives to engage in rent-seeking.[15] An intuitive way to think about the setup is that government income takes two forms, a constant flow and a stochastic flow. $y(\theta_t)$ is the stochastic part, and there are pre-existing institutional arrangements determining the distribution of the constant flow. The constant part could vary between countries, implying that rich countries are not necessarily more prone to rent-seeking. The focus of this paper is the conflict arising when a country receives income above the level that its pre-existing institutional arrangements can handle, i.e. windfalls, and how expectations of foreign aid influence this response.

Finally, we assume that the donor (partly) cares about the recipient's welfare. There is plenty of empirical support for this assertion.

8. Concluding remarks

The present model has abstracted from a number of issues influencing public policy in developing countries. The analysis may therefore be biased and it would be inappropriate to draw any definite conclusions. Nevertheless, some important insights emerge from the analysis. First, we have shown that the provision of public goods does not need to increase with government income, thus providing a political-economy rationale for why large windfall gains in revenue, or large inflows of foreign aid, do not necessarily result in general welfare gains. Second, we have shown that expectations of aid in the future may suffice to increase rent dissipation and reduce the expected level of public goods provision.

From a policy perspective, there are four main implications of these findings. First, the model points to the importance of studying the interaction between the political process shaping public policy and foreign aid. Second, concessional

---

[15] One can imagine other situations in which rent-seeking is intensified when the cake starts to shrink (see, e.g., Rodrik, 1998).

J. Svensson / Journal of International Economics 51 (2000) 437–461   457

assistance may influence policy in the recipient country even without any resources actually being disbursed, implying that evaluations of project and sector assistance may overestimate the total impact of foreign aid. Third, the analysis stresses the important issue of commitment in foreign aid policy. If the donor community can enter into a binding policy commitment, aid may mitigate the incentives for social groups to engage in rent-seeking activities. However, such a regime shift would involve an aid policy that in the short run provides more assistance to countries in less need, and less assistance to those in most need. Enforcing such a regime shift may be difficult (Svensson, 1997). Finally, the fact that democracies seem to be less subjective to the perverse effect of aid on corruption suggests that political liberalization should have an important priority in the donors' policy agenda.

We provide some empirical evidence supporting the mechanism we propose. Foreign aid and windfalls are associated with increased corruption in countries more likely to suffer from competing social groups. We find a weakly robust negative relationship between aid and corruption in countries where these conditions are less likely, while there is no evidence that the donors systematically allocate aid to countries with less corruption. These results are robust to a number of statistical problems.

Acknowledgements

The views expressed here do not represent official opinions of the World Bank. The author is grateful for comments by Allan Drazen, William Easterly, Aart Kraay, Peter Norman, Lars Persson, Torsten Persson, Peter Svedberg, Aaron Tornell, several seminar participants as well as three anonymous referees. The author also wishes to thank Charles Chang and Guiseppe Iarossi for providing data.

Appendix A. Data description, sources and summary statistics (Table A.1)

africa, dummy variable for Sub-Saharan African countries; *aid*, grants and grant equivalents of concessional loans (Chang et al., 1997) deflated by import unit value index (US$) 1985 = 100 (IFS) to real GDP (1985 = base year) (Penn World Tables 5.6), averages over 1980–84, 85–89, 90–93; *bmp*, log of 1 + black-market premium (black-market xrate/official xrate − 1) (World Bank National Accounts, World's Currency Yearbook, average over 1980–84, 85–89, 90–92; *centam*, dummy variable for Central American countries; *cor*, indices of corruption from ICRG (Knack and Keefer, 1995), where 0 indicates least corrupt and 6 most corrupt, averages over 1982–84, 85–89, 90–94; *dem*, ranking of political liberties on a scale from 0 to 6, where 6 is most free (Freedom House, 1997); *ethnic*, index

458   J. Svensson / Journal of International Economics 51 (2000) 437–461

Table A.1
Summary statistics

	Mean	Median	Max	Min	St. dev.
aid	2.31	1.36	17.9	0	2.62
cor	3.36	3.00	6.00	0.62	1.03
ethnic	0.48	0.56	0.93	0	0.30
sxp	16.9	13.3	62.1	1.62	13.0
tt	−0.54	−0.43	2.63	−4.69	1.16
lgdp	7.46	7.51	9.33	5.70	0.75
dem	2.75	2.45	6.00	0	1.78
fgr	4.17	2.00	10.0	0	3.52
bmp	0.38	0.15	4.77	−0.03	0.58
regulation	0	−0.58	8.88	−1.83	1.65

of ethnolinguistic fractionalization, 1960. Measures the probability that two randomly selected people in a country belong to different ethnolinguistic groups (Easterly and Levine, 1997); *fgr*, freedom from government regulations. Component of the Fraser Institute's index of Economic Freedom, from 0 to 10, with 10 least regulations (Fraser Institute, 1997); *lgdp*, log of initial real per capita GDP (Penn World Tables 5.6); *lpop*, log of total population in 100.000 units at the start of sample period (World Bank, 1998); *regulation*, the sum of BMP and FGR after each variable has been standardized; *sxp*, share of exports of primary products in GDP measured in nominal US$, units percentage points at the start of the sample period (World Bank Trade Statistics); *tt*, the average growth rate of dollar export prices times initial share of exports in GDP minus the average growth rate of import prices times initial share of imports to GDP (World Bank, 1998).

Appendix B. Sufficient conditions for the existence of a fixed point

Let θ'_t be a candidate for a fixed point and define

$$\Omega(\theta'_t) = y(\theta'_t) - (n/(n-1))P(\theta'_t). \tag{B.1}$$

Since $\Omega(\theta'_t)$ is continuous, a sufficient condition is that $\Omega(\underline{\theta}) < 0$ and $\Omega(\bar{\theta}) > 0$. Using (1), (4) and (6), Eq. (7) can be written as

$$P(\hat{\theta}_t) = \beta \left[\frac{(n-1)}{n^2} \int_{\underline{\theta}}^{\hat{\theta}} y(\theta_t) dF(\theta_t) + (1 - F(\hat{\theta}_t)) \frac{1}{n} y(\hat{\theta}_t) - \frac{1}{n^2} \int_{\hat{\theta}}^{\bar{\theta}} y(\theta_t) dF(\theta_t) \right], \tag{B.2}$$

where $\beta \equiv \delta/(1-\delta)$. By inserting (B.2) into (B.1) and simplifying we obtain

$$\Omega(\underline{\theta}) = y(\underline{\theta})\left[1 - \frac{\beta}{(n-1)}\right] + \frac{\beta}{n^2}\int_{\theta}^{\bar{\theta}} y(\theta_t)dF(\theta_t) < 0. \qquad (B.3)$$

Hence, condition (i). The other necessary condition is given by the following equation:

$$\Omega(\bar{\theta}) = y(\bar{\theta}_t) - \frac{\beta}{n^2}\int_{\theta}^{\bar{\theta}} y(\theta_t)dF(\theta_t) > 0. \qquad (B.4)$$

A sufficient condition for (B.4) is that condition (ii) is satisfied, in which case the difference between the first two terms is positive.

Appendix C. Proof of Proposition 5.1

The equilibrium with aid is denoted by subscript a. For convenience, time and group subscripts are dropped. Let $y(\theta_1)$ denote the cutoff value of $y(\theta)$ for which (9) no longer binds in the fully CE, i.e. $y(\theta_1) = w_c^{-1}(\varphi) - ny_c$, and $y(\theta_2)$ the corresponding cutoff value in the NE. Comparing with the equilibrium without aid we see that welfare of the social groups in the fully CE is constant $\forall y(\theta_t) \in [y(\underline{\theta}), y(\theta_1)]$, implying that a deviation must occur when $y(\theta_t) > y(\theta_1)$. Moreover, $a^c(\theta_t) = 0 \; \forall y(\theta_t) \in [y(\theta_1), y(\bar{\theta})]$. Hence, the gain of a deviation is not affected by the inclusion of a donor. At the same time $P_a(\theta') \leq P(\theta')$ since

$$P_a(\theta') = \beta\left[\int_{\theta_1}^{\theta_2}[u^c(\theta_t) - u^c(\theta_1)]dF(\theta_t) + \int_{\theta_2}^{\bar{\theta}}[u^c(\theta',\theta_t) - u''(\theta_1)]dF(\theta_t)\right] \qquad (19)$$

is strictly smaller than $P(\theta')$ given in (7), where $u^c(\theta',\theta_t)$ is the utility in the SBE. Hence, $\Omega_a(\theta') > \Omega(\theta')$. Consequently, $\hat{\theta}$ must fall.

Appendix D. Proof of Proposition 5.2

This can be seen by the following two-part argument. First, the gain of a deviation is not affected by the inclusion of a donor (see main text). Second, solving for the equilibrium aid flows in the two institutional settings we have

$$a^c(\theta_t) = w_c^{-1}(\varphi) - \sum_{i=1}^{n} u_i^c(\theta_t), \qquad (D.1)$$

$$a^n(\theta_t) = n\left[w_c^{-1}(n\varphi) - \sum_{i=1}^{n} u_i^n(\theta_t)\right]. \qquad (D.2)$$

Jakob Svensson

There are two opposite forces determining the amount of aid disbursed in (D.1) and (D.2). First, utility is lower in the NE which tends to increase aid flows in the noncooperative setting. Second, a larger amount of aid will be wasted in rent dissipation in the NE which tends to lower aid flows. Using a CES function with constant elasticity of substitution equal to $1/\sigma$ to solve explicitly for the equilibrium aid flows we can show that $a^c(\theta_t) \geq a^n(\theta_t) \; \forall y(\theta_t)$ provided that

$$y_i \geq \left[\frac{(n^{1-1/\sigma} - 1)}{n(n\;1)} \right] \varphi^{-1/\sigma}. \tag{D.3}$$

A sufficient condition for (D.3) is that $\sigma \leq 1$ in which case the term in bracket is negative.

References

Alesina, A., Drazen, A., 1991. Why are stabilizations delayed. American Economic Review 81 (5), 1170–1188.

Benhabib, J., Rustichini, A., 1996. Social conflict and growth. Journal of Economic Growth 1, 125–142.

Boone, P., 1996. Politics and the effectiveness of foreign aid. European Economic Review 40, 289–329.

Boycko, M., Shleifer, A., Vishny, R.W., 1996. Second-best economic policy for a divided government. European Economic Review 40, 767–774.

Burnside, C., Dollar, D., 1997. Aid, policies and growth. Policy Research Working Paper, No. 1777, The World Bank.

Casella, A., Eichengreen, B., 1994. Can foreign aid accelerate stabilization. CEPR Discussion Paper, No. 961.

Chang, C., Fernandez-Ariaa, E., Serven, L., 1997. Measuring aid flows: a new approach. Mimeo, The World Bank.

Easterly, W., Levine, R., 1997. Africa's growth tragedy: policies and ethnic divisions. Quarterly Journal of Economics CXII (4), 1203–1250.

Fraser Institute, 1997. Economic Freedom of the World 1997 Annual Report. The Fraser Institute, Vancouver.

Freedom House, 1997. Index of Economic Freedom, 1997, Heritage Foundation, Washington, DC.

Friedman, J., 1971. A non-cooperative equilibrium for supergames. Review of Economic Studies 38, 1–12.

Klitgaard, R., 1990. Tropical Gangsters, Basic Books.

Knack, S., Keefer, P., 1995. Institutions and economic performance: cross-country tests using alternative institutional measures. Economics and Politics 7 (3), 207–227.

Krueger, A.P., 1974. The political economy of a rent-seeking society. American Economic Review LXIV, 291–303.

Lane, P.R., Tornell, A., 1996. Power, growth and the voracity effect. Journal of Economic Growth 1 (2), 213–241.

Lane, P.R., Tornell, A., 1995. Power and growth. Mimeo, Harvard University.

Mosley, P., 1987. Overseas Aid: Its Defence and Reform, Wheatsheaf, Brighton.

Ranis, G., Mahmood, S.A., 1992. The Political Economy of Development Policy Change, Basil Blackwell, Oxford.

J. Svensson / Journal of International Economics 51 (2000) 437–461 461

Rodrik, D., 1998. Where did all the growth go? External shocks, social conflict and growth collapses. NBER, Working Paper Series, No. 6350.

Rotemberg, J.J., Saloner, G., 1986. A supergame-theoretic model of price wars during booms. American Economic Review 76 (3), 390–407.

Sachs, J.D., Warner, A.M., 1995. Natural resource abundance and economic growth. NBER Working Paper Series, No. 5398.

Soyinka, W., 1996. The Open Sore of a Continent: A Personal Narrative of the Nigerian Crisis, Oxford University Press, New York.

Svensson, J., 1997. When is foreign aid policy credible: aid dependence and conditionality. Journal of Development Economics (forthcoming).

Svensson, J., 1998a. Aid, growth, and democracy. Economics and Politics (forthcoming), The World Bank.

Svensson, J., 1998b. Foreign aid and rent-seeking. Policy Research Working paper, No. 1880, The World Bank.

Tullock, G., 1980. Efficient rent-seeking. In: Buchanan, J.M., Tollison, R.D., Tullock, G. (Eds.), Toward a Theory of the Rent-Seeking Society, Texas A.&M. University Press.

World Bank, 1989. Sub-Saharan Africa: From Crisis to Sustainable Growth. World Bank, Washington, DC.

World Bank, 1998. World Development Indicators, Washington, DC, IBRD.

Available online at www.sciencedirect.com

SCIENCE @DIRECT•

European Journal of Political Economy
Vol. 19 (2003) 161–181

ELSEVIER

European Journal of
POLITICAL
ECONOMY

www.elsevier.com/locate/econbase

The political economy of coffee, dictatorship, and genocide

Philip Verwimp *

Economics Department, Catholic University of Leuven, Naamsestraat 69, Leuven 3000, Belgium
Genocide Studies Program, Yale University, New Haven, CT 06520, USA

Received 17 April 2001; received in revised form 4 April 2002; accepted 5 June 2002

Abstract

The paper presents a political economy analysis of the Habyarimana regime in Rwanda. The analysis shows how, through the producer price of coffee, the dictator buys political loyalty from the peasant population, and how, in periods of economic growth, the dictator increases his level of personal consumption as well as power over the population. The analysis of Habyarimana's policy decisions leads to the conclusion that he was a totalitarian type of dictator. When, at the end of the 1980s, the international price of coffee fell dramatically, the regime switched to severe forms of repression to maintain its hold onto power. Genocide emerges as an outcome of Wintrobe's loyalty-repression model, while foreign aid sustained the dictator's hold onto power.
© 2003 Elsevier Science B.V. All rights reserved.

JEL classification: D72; H30; H56
Keywords: Dictatorship; Coffee; Repression; Genocide; Rwanda

1. Introduction

I cannot cultivate the land the whole year while watching the merchants drive Mercedes.
(a Rwandan peasant in 1990[1])

In colonial times, Rwanda was already a densely populated country. Land was scarce, technology was at a very low level, and human capital was underdeveloped. Labor was the

---

* Economics Department, Catholic University of Leuven, Naamsestraat 69, Louvain 3000, Belgium.
E-mail address: philip.verwimp@econ.kuleuven.ac.be (P. Verwimp).

[1] In *Agriculture Africain*, no. 3, April 1990, authors' translation from French.

162   *P. Verwimp / European Journal of Political Economy 19 (2003) 161–181*

only factor endowment that was abundant and, thus, cheap. The Belgian colonizer found a way to extract wealth from a labor-abundant economy. The colonizer promoted the coffee crop and forced the population to pay taxes (Uwezeyimana, 1996, pp. 51–55). First, the Belgian elite and later the Rwandan elite realized that this was the only way to introduce the monetary economy in the rural areas. The colonizer had to make few investments and bear almost no costs. Habyarimana copied the colonial system and encouraged everybody to grow coffee.[2] Coffee cultivation was heavily subsidized, so that new plants could be obtained almost free of cost. Some fertilizer was also distributed on the condition that it would only be used for the coffee trees. A large administration of coffee monitoring was put in place, with monitors assigned both advisory and policing tasks (Little and Horowitz, 1987). The monitors advised farmers on coffee cultivation practices and at the same time fined farmers who did not maintain their coffee fields. Uprooting coffee trees was forbidden under the Rwandan penal code (June 1978) and fines were levied.[3]

Coffee exports during the Habyarimana regime (1973–1994) accounted for 60–80% of state revenue, depending on the annual output and market prices. Tea cultivation on large plantations became increasingly important as the price of coffee declined in the late 1980s. Farmers were driven off the land with little compensation in order to start state-run tea plantations in Gisovu and Mulindi (Bart, 1993; Uvin, 1998). Leading members of the Akazu (the presidential clan) were in charge of the coffee and tea agencies (Ocir-café and Ocir-thé). As long as the international price of these two export crops was high, the Habyarimana regime could afford to pay a high producer price to farmers. The collapse of these prices in 1987 and 1989 caused the regime to lower the price to farmers and to reduce social services by 40% (Guichaoua, 1992). This double loss hit farmers hard since they were already paying water taxes, health taxes, school fees, and were performing compulsory labor.

In this paper, I use a political economy approach to dictatorship in order to explain the coffee economy. An economy such as Rwanda that entirely depends on the export of coffee faces severe difficulties when the world market price for coffee collapses. The dictator himself may rely on foreign aid to stay in power, but how can he guarantee the loyalty of the coffee-growing farmers? This paper considers the political salience of the coffee economy from the dictator's perspective. Using the loyalty-repression model as set out by Wintrobe (1998), I show how Habyarimana, on the verge of losing power in a single export crop economy, switched to repression and other coercive practices to sustain power. This response explains features of the Rwandan genocide.

2. A short historical overview

The formation of the Rwandan State was the result of century-long expansion of the central territory (ancient Rwanda) in which adjoining territories came under the control of

---

[2] In 1973, then minister of defense Juvenal Habyarimana, assisted by army officers from his home region in northern Rwanda (Gisenyi), became president after a coup d'etat.

[3] The Kenyan coffee sector, by way of comparison, was run differently. Kenyan coffee producers were free to chose to cultivate coffee or not and were not subject to government imposed producer prices. See Bevan et al. (1989).

P. Verwimp / European Journal of Political Economy 19 (2003) 161–181

the King of Rwanda. This process took place in the 18th and 19th centuries, in particular under the reign of King Rwabugiri. The state was characterized by a high degree of organisation in which the king and his advisors decided on all important matters. The inner circle of power was composed of a small group of Tutsi, originating from two clans. The large majority of Tutsi as well as Hutu had no access to power or privilege. The two groups differed in their main economic activity. Hutu were cultivators, whereas Tutsi were cattle-breeders. A significant part of the land was reserved for pastures (Ibikingi).

The advent of colonialism (first by Germany, then by Belgium) brought far-reaching change to the country. The colonizers observed the socio-political composition of the elite and the peasantry, and concluded that the Tutsi were a different race. Attracted by the high stature, facial characteristics, and leading position in society, the coloniser (church and state) concluded that the Tutsi orginated from Northern Africa and were related to the Caucasian race and were thereby genetically predestined to rule. The Hutu on the other hand were considered Bantu people, a black race, predestined to be ruled.

From 1959 to 1962, a Hutu-lead revolution took political power out of the hands of the ruling Tutsi elite. Not only the elite, but also thousands of Tutsi civilians, were driven out of their homes and had to take refuge in neighbouring countries. Grégoire Kayibanda, a Hutu educated in missionary schools, became president and installed the First Republic. Following the revolution, the percentage of Tutsi in the Rwandan population declined sharply. Said to be 17.5% of the population in 1952, Tutsi were counted as 8.4% of the total in 1991.[4]

Habyarimana, minister of defense in the Kayibanda government, took power in a coup d'état in 1973 that removed president Kayibanda from power. The main reason for this coup was that the Kayibanda regime favoured Hutu from Gitarama and other préfectures in the South. Whereas the landed interest of the northern elite (Abakonde) was preserved by the Hutu Revolution, they were not given access to lucrative business opportunities and political power by the Kayibanda regime. According to Pottier (1993), TRAFIPRO, Rwanda's first state-run marketing system, was at the centre of the intrigue. Controlling 27 shops nationwide and 70 buying-up points for coffee (in 1966), TRAFIPRO was accused of running a monopoly and diverting rents to leading politicians in the Kayibanda government. TRAFIPRO was the economic arm of the Gitarama regime (Reyntjens, 1985).

From 1974 to 1976, Habyarimana consolidated his political power. He outlawed political parties and created his own Revolutionary Movement for Development (MRND). According to Prunier (1995), the MRND was a truly totalitarian party: every Rwandan had to be member of the MRND and all bourgmestres and préfets were chosen from among party cadres.[5] Habyarimana institutionalised *Umuganda*, the compulsory communal labour, and had peasants participate in village animation sessions to honor him. He killed 56 businessmen and politicians closely related to the Kayibanda regime. All citizens were under tight administrative control. Every 5 years, the president was reelected with 99% of the vote.

In October 1990, a group of (ca. 7000) Tutsi rebels (former refugees and their sons) attacked Rwanda from Uganda. The following years were marked by a low-intensity civil war and ongoing peace negotiations. In 1993, a peace agreement was reached in Arusha whereby political power would be divided between the rebels and the government.

---

[4] Desforges (1999, p. 40).
[5] Prunier (1995, p. 76).

164   P. Verwimp / European Journal of Political Economy 19 (2003) 161–181

Economic decline, political manipulation of ethnic animosities, and civil war all contributed to the disintegration of Rwandan society in the 1990–1993 period. Christophe Mfizi, close supporter of the president, broke with the MRND in 1992 after discovering state-sponsored massacres in several villages in Northern Rwanda. He wrote that a group called the "zero network" had penetrated the highest levels of government and that

> "this group considers the country as an enterprise where it is legitimate to get out as much profit as possible ... It is this group that has incited ethnic tensions to cover up their own interests ..."[6]

This corresponds to what Bardhan (1997, p. 1396) observed about the political economy of ethnicity, namely, that ethnicity is often used as a device to stake a claim in the process of rent-sharing:

> "As the government has become more important in economic activities, more and more mobilised groups have used ethnicity to stake a claim in the process of rent-sharing."

On April 6, 1994, when president Habyarimana was returning from a meeting in Arusha, his plane was shot down over Kigali airport. His death made the Hutu extremists in his regime turn Rwanda into hell on earth: in no less then 50 days, more then half a million (>500.000) Tutsi and Hutu opponents of the regime were killed. According to Desforges (1999), one of the prominent experts on the subject, the genocide was the result of a plan that had been prepared by the network around Habyarimana.

3. Dictatorship and political economy

3.1. A political economy approach

In a recent review essay, Newbury and Newbury (2000) proposed that one has to study the connection between state activity and peasant agency in the rural areas to understand the history of Rwanda in general and the history of the genocide in particular. Relying on research by Leurquin (1960) and Dorseay (1983), they write that the policies of forced crop cultivation (especially coffee) placed the colonial state directly in the production process. It was the colonial state that encouraged and further developed the penetration of state authority in the rural areas. The theory of political economy is ideally suited to analyse just this: how do the power of the state and the chosen path of economic development interact? In addition, what is the economic underpinning of the relationship between the state and the peasantry?

The advantages of a political economy approach are numerous. Such an approach to dictatorship and genocide allows the researcher to look through the dictator's eyes and to explain the decisions the dictator is making. We do that, assuming that the dictator is rational. Rationality in economics is different from rationality in everyday parlance. It does not mean thoughtful, smart or nice thinking. Rationality means that the dictator will use his

---

[6] Mfizi (1992).

P. Verwimp / European Journal of Political Economy 19 (2003) 161–181   165

available resources as well as possible to attain his goal(s). The dictator's first priority is to stay in power. On dictators in sub-Saharan Africa, see Rowley (2000). Depending on the type of dictator, this can mean increasing power or enjoying the benefits of office (personal consumption). Noneconomists often define rationality differently from economists. Horowitz (1976), for example, states that rational behavior is behavior that benefits a country's economy. Political economists believe that people in general, including politicians and especially dictators, care about their own interests first, i.e., being reelected or seeing their power increase. The dictator judges economic policies by the impact on his personal position and not on the welfare of the whole population. This does not necessarily mean that policies chosen are bad for the population; policies can be beneficial for the population as long as the policies benefit the dictator. This also means that it can be rational for the dictator to implement policies that do not benefit the population.

Whereas the core of the paper explains the functioning of Habyarimana's dictatorship, the analysis also sheds light on features of the 1994 genocide. Most genocide scholars agree that genocide can be explained by the explicit choices made by the regime's elite (for example, Kieran (1996) for Cambodia, Hilberg (1961) for Nazi-Germany, Dadrian (1995) for the Ottoman empire). Genocide scholars can disagree about the motivations of the regime for genocide, about the structure of decision-making among top leaders, about the degree of participation of the population in the killings, and so on. There is however strong consensus among the scholarly community that genocide requires systematic organization and implementation by the top leaders in the regime.

For Rwanda, it has been proposed that the number of people in charge of the organization of the genocide was very small. Desforges (1999) suggests that only a handful of people organized the Rwandan genocide.[7] These people, a small group of persons known as the "zero-network", were at the center of power in Rwanda and were responsible for the small-scale mass murders from 1990 onwards. This makes it possible to use the unitary actor assumption: in order to employ a political economy model of dictatorship, this zero-network can be taken to have acted as a rational unitary agent. If one uses this approach, one can see that political violence and repression, as used by the regime with special brutality from 1990 to 1994, serves someone's interests. The reason the regime uses violence and repression is because it serves the purposes of the regime: to stay in power/increase power.

3.2. Theorizing about bad outcomes

Olson and Mcguire (1996) proposed a theory about how the form of government—democratic rule or dictatorship—affects tax rates, income distribution, and the provision of public goods. Coercion can be used to attain objectives and not just markets. In a market, transactions are voluntary and mutually advantageous. Coase (1960) explained how two parties can bargain on externalities and reach a Pareto-efficient outcome. The externality would be internalised unless the bargaining costs were too high. If transaction or bargaining costs were zero, all externalities would be resolved in a Pareto-efficient manner, because rational parties share maximized joint gains. The Coasean approach includes an awareness that some transaction costs are so high that trade will not occur. When the transaction costs

---

[7] Personal communication with the author, March 4, 1999.

of the trade exceed the gains, the parties do not make the trade, and that too is as it should be. Thus, according to this approach, any status quo resulting from the market is efficient. The logic tells us that as Smith (1776) had suggested, as long as people are free to choose whether to transact, we are automatically in the most efficient of all worlds.

Economists and economic historians after Coase have tried to use the concept of voluntary exchange or Coasean bargains—and the associated transaction costs—to understand government and politics as well as the market.[8] The voluntary exchange approach can be applied to government policies. Political transaction-cost theorists suggest that mutually advantageous bargaining within the political system tends to be bring about socially efficient public policies. Political bargaining, they argue, leads to social outcomes that are Pareto-efficient (see Becker, 1983). If an inefficient policy is chosen, it follows that changing to a more efficient policy must bring net gains, and that there is some distribution of net gains that would leave everyone better off. Again, no matter which government policies are actually chosen, we observe an efficient outcome. Olson (2000, p. 58) concludes:

> "If you start with the assumptions of the Coasean bargain and transaction cost approach and make no logical mistakes, you inevitably keep coming back to the conclusion that the social equilibrium we are in or heading toward is Pareto-efficient, at least to an approximation. Whatever may be thought of the distribution of income that results from bargaining in the market and in the polity, when all bargaining is done it tends to leave society in a situation where it is not possible to make one person better off without making someone else worse off: all the mutually advantageous deals have been made. **The Coasean bargain and transaction cost approach does not lend itself to explaining bad outcomes**" (my emphasis).

In this paper, we are interested in bad outcomes. Economic and political reality offers ample evidence of bad outcomes. War, poverty, famine, and genocide are bad outcomes that have occurred in the past decades and throughout history. As Hirschleifer (1994) has pointed out, people with a sufficient advantage in employing violence will use violence to serve their interests.

4. The Wintrobe model of dictatorship

4.1. The supply of loyalty from the population

Wintrobe (1998) proposes that the loyalty of the population vis-à-vis the ruler is a crucial factor for the survival of a dictatorship, more important than the size of the dictators' budget. Wintrobe considers loyalty a capital asset in the hands of the population, which is accumulated to facilitate political exchange. Citizens and interest groups supply loyalty to the regime because they expect to receive some portion of the gains from political exchange in return. Each citizen accumulates an optimum portfolio of these assets, taking into account the expected rates of return and the risk. A change in either leads the investor to change his or

---

[8] See Olson (2000).

P. Verwimp / European Journal of Political Economy 19 (2003) 161–181   167

her portfolio. The change can be broken down into a substitution and an income effect. Citizens who demonstrate or speak out against the government are offering their loyalty to someone who offers an alternative policy.

The dictator relies on the loyalty of the population, but also uses a certain amount of repression to stay in power. The supply of loyalty (L_s) and the level of repression are related: if repression increases, the risk of dealing with the opposition increases and the expected rate of return from opposition activities decreases. The relative attractiveness of dealing with the dictator or the autocratic regime then increases. Through the substitution effect, the supply of loyalty to the dictator (L_s) is positively related to the level of repression. An increase in repression increases the likelihood that the individual will be the victim of sanctions, even if the individual is loyal. This reduces the individual's wealth and reduces all investment in political loyalty, including to the regime. At low levels of repression, the income effect is small for most individuals and, as a consequence, the substitution effect dominates the income effect. This is important for understanding dictatorial behavior, because it means that a dictator can obtain more loyalty by increasing the level of repression.

L_s, the supply of loyalty function (of the populace), can be expressed as:

$$L_s = L_s(R, P_L, \text{PE}) \qquad \text{with } \partial L_s/\partial R > 0; \ \partial L_s/\partial P_L > 0; \ \partial L_s/\partial \text{PE} > 0. \qquad (1)$$

PE is the performance of the economy, P_L is the price of loyalty received per unit of loyalty supplied, and R is the level of repression.

The supply of loyalty depends on the level of repression and also on the demand for loyalty by the dictator. Loyal citizens expect a return on their loyalty. Wintrobe describes this as a "price" the suppliers receive for each unit of loyalty supplied P_L. If the supply of loyalty to the regime is abundant, the "price" each loyal citizen receives is low, making the production of power cheap for the dictator. The regime will try to keep loyalty cheap because it wants to use its resources for other purposes. Many events, exogenous as well as endogenous can however increase the price of loyalty. The appearance on the political scene of a political challenger, for example, may not only require a higher level of repression, but may also increase the price of loyalty. I assume the supply of loyalty to be positively related to its price. We will return to this issue later.

A further factor that determines the supply of loyalty is the performance of the economy PE. If the rents from political exchange are high, the average citizen will be more inclined to cooperate with the regime. Moreover, a dictator who is able to distribute the rents of a well-performing economy can buy off even the worst opposition. The opposite is also true. If economic performance declines, the rents from political exchange decline and it is less profitable to be loyal to the regime. Ceteris paribus, the supply of loyalty, therefore, decreases.

4.2. A general model of dictatorship

In Wintrobe's model, repression and loyalty form the input factors in a production function for power, $\pi(R, L)$. Not all dictators maximize their power over the population. Some dictators only want enough power to stay in office and to enjoy the benefits of office. Wintrobe calls these kinds of dictators tinpots. Other dictators (totalitarians) want to maximize their power over the population. A general model of dictatorship describes a

Philip Verwimp

dictator as an actor who wants to stay in power and wants to enjoy this power. Most real-world dictators are neither tinpots nor totalitarians, but a combination of these extremes. A general model of a dictator can be written as follows (Wintrobe, 1998, p. 117):

$$Max\ U = U(\pi, C) \tag{2}$$

$$\text{subject to}\ \ B(\pi) = P_\pi \pi (B - C) + C\ \ \text{with}\ P_c = 1 \tag{3}$$

The dictator maximizes utility derived from power and personal consumption. The left-hand side of constraint (3) is the power-into-money function $B(\pi)$, which shows how budgetary resources are obtained. The right-hand side shows how the funds are spent, on personal consumption and power accumulation.

The first order conditions are:[9]

$$\frac{U_c}{U_\pi} = \frac{1}{P_\pi - \pi P'_\pi - B_\pi} = \frac{1}{P_\pi \left[1 - \frac{1}{\varepsilon^\pi}\right] - B_\pi} \quad \text{with}\ \varepsilon^\pi = \frac{\partial \pi}{\partial P_\pi}\frac{P_\pi}{\pi} > 0. \tag{4}$$

Since the left-hand side of Eq. (4) is positive, the right-hand side must also be positive, i.e.:

$$P_\pi \left[1 - \frac{1}{\varepsilon^\pi}\right] - B_\pi > 0$$

The dictator, thus, trades off power and personal consumption. The part of the budget not used for consumption $(B - C)$ is used to attain the desired level of power. The more resources the dictator uses for power, the greater the level of power. The slope of the "money-into-power curve" is positive and it seems reasonable to assume diminishing returns. An increased budget, thus, allows the dictator to buy more loyalty and repression. At high levels of loyalty and repression, the dictator is forced to forge relations with those who are less and less sympathetic to his regime and to employ increasing force to repress hardcore regime opponents. An increase in the budget will, therefore, buy less power at high levels of L and R compared to low L and R (see Section 4.1).

The elasticity of π with respect to money ε^π depends on the political organization of the regime (how flexible are R and L with respect to their prices) and on the productivity of R and L in producing power (π_R and π_L). Wintrobe proposes that the latter depends on the characteristics of the population: if the opposition is weak or the population is docile and apathetic, ε^π will be high. This means that there are no limits to dictatorial power as long as the dictator has access to resources. A dictator can transform resources into power. Wintrobe also argues that with no limit to the dictator's power, resources commanded can always increase, as long as there is property to confiscate, taxes can be increased.

The regime's level of power and the regime's budget are, therefore, simultaneously determined. A primary process for turning power into budgetary resources is the collection

---

[9] I follow here Wintrobe (1998).

P. Verwimp / European Journal of Political Economy 19 (2003) 161–181

of taxes. When the ruler uses tax collection as a way to turn power into budgetary resources, B and π are positively related, that is, $\partial B/\partial \pi \equiv B_\pi > 0$.

Due to the disincentive effect of taxation, the relationship could be reverse at high levels of taxation ($B_\pi < 0$). The slope and shape of $B(\pi)$ depend on economic institutions. It seems reasonable to assume that, initially, it must be positively sloped.

5. Habyarimana and the coffee economy

5.1. The Habyarimana regime

We have seen that the supply of loyalty in Wintrobe's model is influenced by the performance of the economy. In applying the model to the Habyarimana regime, we need to specify the linkages between the political behavior of the dictator and the loyalty of the citizens. We have to do this because the model in Section 4 is a general outline: Wintrobe adds specificity when he describes Nazi-Germany, Stalinist Russia and Apartheid in South Africa. In this section, similar specificity is added for Rwanda. In a coffee economy such as Rwanda, the value of the production of coffee on the world market determines the regime's budget. At the same time, the power of the regime is determined by the loyalty supplied by the population, which in turn depends on the producer price offered to the farmer producer. There is a mutual dependence between power and budget. Specific for Rwanda is that the coffee price and the production of coffee determine the dictator's budget and the supply of loyalty of the population.

Formally,

$$L_s = (R, P_p) \text{ and } B = P_m[K(P_p)] \tag{5}$$

where P_m is the world market price, P_p the price paid to the producer, K the volume of coffee sold, and B is the regime's budget. Since Rwanda is a price-taker in the international coffee market, Habyarimana did not control his budget as much as Wintrobe's dictator. Nevertheless, he could manipulate the producer price of coffee P_p or/and could use nonprice incentives to have farmers plant more coffee trees and, thus, raise the amount K produced. The quantity produced depends on the price paid to the producer. The regime paid a fixed price to the farmer producer and farmers were forbidden to stop cultivating coffee. From the budget $B=P_m K$, the part $P_p K$ is reserved for the producers. The rest of the budget $P_d K$ (with $P_d = P_m - P_p$) finances personal consumption and repression.

Habyarimana can, thus, be portrayed as solving the following problem:

Max $U(\pi, C)$

subject to $P_m[K(P_p)] = P_\pi \pi(P_m[K(P_p)] - C) + C$ with $P_c = 1$ $\tag{6}$

where

$$\frac{U_c}{U_\pi} = \frac{1}{P_\pi - \pi P_\pi' - (P_m[K(P_p)])_\pi} = \frac{1}{P_\pi\left[1 - \frac{1}{\varepsilon^\pi}\right] - (P_m[K(P_p)])_\pi} \tag{7a}$$

Philip Verwimp

with

$$\frac{\partial P_m[K(P_p)]}{\partial \pi} = (P_m[K(P_p)])_\pi. \tag{7b}$$

Eq. (7a) shows the three elements that are important in Habyarimana's calculations:

(1) The marginal effect of power on the dictator's budget. This relates to the economic organization of the regime and is used to answer the question, "how did Habyarimana turn power into money?"
(2) The marginal cost of power accumulation, $P_\pi[1 - (1/\varepsilon^\pi)]$ relates to the political organization of the regime and is used to answer the question, "how did Habyarimana turn money into power?"
(3) Habyarimana's preferences for power versus consumption, U_c/U_π.

5.2. The coffee economy

Fig. 1 shows the course of the international price of other mild arabica coffee and the price that was paid to the peasant producers (in US$ cents per kg). The end of the seventies was marked by a coffee boom that generated large revenues for the government and allowed it to increase the price paid to the producer from 45 Rwandan Francs (RWF) in 1974 to 65 RWF in 1976, and 120 RWF in 1977. According to Uwezeyimana (1996), it was in this period (1976–1980) that the Habyarimana regime established itself among the

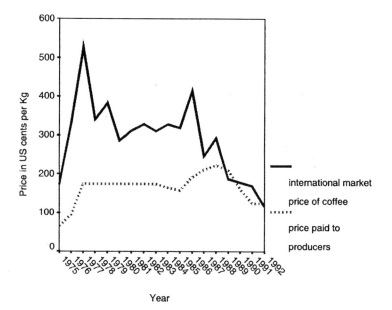

Fig. 1. International price and price paid to producers.

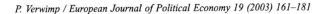
P. Verwimp / European Journal of Political Economy 19 (2003) 161–181   171

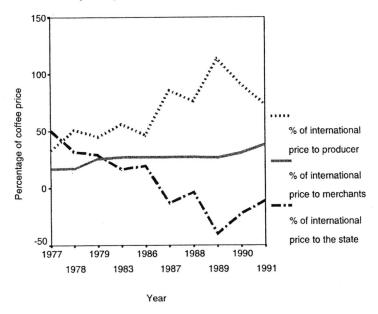

Fig. 2. Percentage of the international price paid to producers, to intermediaries and to the state.

peasant masses. When, toward the end of the 1980s, the international price declined, the regime subsidized the producer price. This is shown in Fig. 2 where the percentage of the international price in the hands of the state turns negative.

5.3. Political power and the coffee economy

5.3.1. The boom of 1976–1979

During the first period (1976–1979), world market prices for coffee were high. The difference between the fixed producer price and the world market price was substantial and the dictator derived large amounts of budgetary resources from coffee exports. In 1975, the world market price for coffee increased significantly. Through its dictatorial power, materialized in the monopoly on coffee trade in Rwanda, the Habyarimana regime fixed the producer price for coffee and extracted large revenues from the coffee sector. P_m remained high for several years. In order to continue the highly lucrative coffee policy, the regime implemented two measures. The regime raised the producer price for coffee, giving farmers an incentive to produce more and at the same time it strengthened monitoring of coffee cultivation. Elements of the latter policy were to make the neglect of coffee trees punishable by law and to provide every commune with a monitor to advise and control farmers' coffee cultivation.[10] It is not coincidence that these measures were

---

[10] Little and Horowitz (1987, 1988).

172   P. Verwimp / European Journal of Political Economy 19 (2003) 161–181

taken in 1978. The very high world market coffee prices allowed the regime's elite to increase both its personal consumption and its power over the population. An increased producer price for coffee (from 60 RFW to 120 RFW) increased the loyalty of the farmer population and at the same time increased coffee production and government coffee revenue.

The state as the monopsony buyer of coffee in Rwanda was not unique in Africa (see Bates, 1981). Governments throughout Africa promoted the cultivation of export crops for taxation purposes: a government-run agency buys the coffee (or another cash crop) from the smallholders for a fixed price. The state agency then processes the coffee and sells it on the international market. The official justification for this institution is to guarantee the farmer's income. The farmer is protected from shocks in the world market by a fixed price. The government however not so much protects the farmer but transfers resources from the agricultural sector to the urban sector. The tax revenue from coffee exports is used to pay for the imports that benefit the urban elite. In the official rhetoric of the Habyarimana regime, the farmer was important.[11] This glorification of the farmer masked the fact that the farmer was only considered important as a producer. The farmer had to produce coffee for export. In order to secure the loyalty of the farmer producer, the price paid to the coffee producer had to be high enough. This means that the dictator is trading off loyalty from farmers against rents. The inclusion of power in the objective function of the dictator expresses the readiness to trade-off power and personal consumption. If Habyarimana were a tinpot dictator, his optimal coffee price would be the price that maximizes the dictator's tax revenue under the constraint that he maintains a minimum level of power (using loyalty and repression). As a totalitarian dictator, he would maximize power and not care about personal consumption. We can determine Habyarimana's type by looking at his policy decisions following a budgetary shock.

Profits from export of coffee during periods with favorable (high) international coffee prices were supposed to be put in a special fund. This fund was called "fond d'égalisation" (price stabilization fund), and was supposed to balance the price paid to the producer when international coffee prices were low. In Rwanda, however, profits from coffee between 1975 and 1977 were directly transferred to the state budget (Tardiff-Douglin et al., 1993). The coffee sector was, therefore, directly linked to the core state functions.

In 1975, Habyarimana abolished all political parties and made all Rwandans members of the MRND (Republican Movement for Development), his single party. From then onwards, the MRND would be used as a vehicle for distributing political rents and to build mass loyalty. Having such a single party to build mass loyalty is, according to Wintrobe, an indicator of a totalitarian type of dictator. In this short period of the coffee-price windfall, we can also observe the workings of the dictator's calculation that turns money into power. When, in 1976 and 1977, the regime's elite were enriched by coffee exports, we notice an increase in repression and loyalty in Rwanda. In 1976, Habyarimana killed 76 dignitaries from the Kayibanda regime by starving them to death.

---

[11] On Habyarimana's speeches to this effect, see Verwimp (2000).

P. Verwimp / European Journal of Political Economy 19 (2003) 161–181   173

Together with the new coffee laws and the increase in the producer price of coffee, this shows that

$$\varepsilon^{\pi} = \frac{\partial \pi}{\partial P_{\pi}} \frac{P_{\pi}}{\pi} \cong 1 \tag{8a}$$

and that the marginal cost of accumulating power was small, or

$$P_{\pi}\left[1 - \frac{1}{\varepsilon^{\pi}}\right] \cong 0 \tag{8b}$$

Eqs. (7a), (8a), and (8b) indicate a set of domestic conditions that favor the accumulation of large amounts of power (ε^{π} high, $\beta_{\pi} > 0$). If, as I contend, the producer price for coffee is not only an important part of the (monetary) income of farmers, but also a key determinant of the political loyalty of the farmers towards the regime, the supply of loyalty from the population to the dictator will increase when the producer price for coffee increases:

$$\partial L_{s}/\partial P_{p} > 0$$

To recapitulate, a number of policy measures indicate that Habyarimana consolidated his power at the time of the coffee price windfall. He did not consume all extra income (as a tinpot dictator would do), but used (most of) the extra budgetary resources to increase the level of loyalty AND the level of repression.

5.3.2. The period of decline, 1986–1989

In 1985, the international quota system for coffee was abolished. The 1986 international coffee trade was liberalized, but nevertheless, the world market price was very high, since Brazil's coffee harvest was lost because of unfavorable weather conditions. The price decreased in 1987, only to improve slightly in 1988 with a one-year reintroduction of the quota system. 1989 and 1990 were very bad years, with declining international prices and declining domestic coffee production. Government tax revenue from coffee production was halved and never restored in the following years.

Survey research on coffee farmers in 1992 has determined the minimum price required to continue the cultivation of coffee. That minimum price was around 120 RWF/kg. With lower world prices, from 1987 onwards, the government subsidized the coffee agency "to secure the income of the farmer", the regime said. From agricultural research, it is known that farmers had other crops, mainly bananas, who give cash income. In his seminal book on Rwandan agriculture, Bart (1993) stresses the importance of bananas and especially banana beer for peasant income. Compared to coffee, bananas are a source of income the whole year round, with a large domestic market. Bananas can be eaten or used for brewing, the leaves are used to cover the soil and bananas require less labor input than coffee. Bananas are also important in social life.[12] Habyarimana, however, wanted to reduce the area for banana cultivation. This is not because he believed occult rituals took place on banana plantations (Pottier, 1993), but because banana cultivation was the main

---

[12] See Bart (1993).

174   *P. Verwimp / European Journal of Political Economy 19 (2003) 161–181*

competitor for coffee in the allocation of land. Bananas were valued on the domestic market and beer was very popular among farmers. The subsidies had a political economy purpose: to maintain the supply of coffee (raising state revenue) and simultaneously keep the loyalty of the farmers. The total amount of subsidies to the coffee sector was high: 3 billion RWF in 1987, 1.6 billion in 1988, 2 billion in 1989, 4.6 billion in 1990, 1 billion in 1991, 2 billion in 1992, and 1 billion in 1993.[13]

As Habyarimana's budget began to decline, he sought new sources of revenue, from raising new taxes to confiscating property. The best example is the removal of several hundred households from their land to allow the regime to grow tea in Northern Rwanda (Mulindi) and in Kibuye (Gisovu). When the world market price of coffee decreased, tea became an important source of foreign exchange for the regime (albeit only for a few years).[14]

In 1990, the price paid to the producer for coffee was dropped from 125 to 100 Rfr. Farmers, however, were no longer interested in growing coffee. Even with a price of 125 Rfr, farmers preferred to grow other crops. Bananas yielded a higher return per acre of land and could be sold on the domestic market. Tardiff-Douglin et al. (1993) reports the price at which farmers said they would destroy their coffee plants (which was forbidden by the regime). At 115 Rfr, 5% would do it. At 100 Rfr, 10% would do it. He relies on a 1992 survey by the Ministry of Agriculture.

Given the culture of respect (and fear) for authority, the percentage of farmers that would uproot their coffee plants was surely much higher. There is other evidence supporting dissatisfaction with government coffee policy. Farmers actually did uproot their coffee trees, in spite of the penalties (Uvin, 1998; Willame, 1995). The only explanation for this is the economic irrationality of the coffee policy from the viewpoint of the farmers. Tardiff-Douglin et al. (1993) reports that a bag of coffee would buy the Rwandan farmer in 1991 only half the goods it bought in 1980. It was especially this real decline in the price of coffee that made coffee cultivation unattractive to the farmer.[15]

Consider now Fig. 3. When an exogenous shock affects the dictator's budget, in this case a drop of the world market coffee price, the equilibrium level of power and budgetary resources at E^* is displaced. A temporary equilibrium is at E_1, where the dictator collects less budgetary resources with the same level of power. Ultimately, E_2 is the new equilibrium because the decrease in budgetary resources results in a reduction in the dictator's power. Any dictator, even a tinpot type, who uses just enough power to stay in office, would be worried about this decline, because he risks being deposed. Therefore, a dictator needs to reduce consumption (to increase power) and increase repression (because loyalty becomes more expensive). This is how Habyarimana responded in the late 1980s.

---

[13] Tardiff-Douglin et al. (1993).

[14] Human Rights Watch (1994) found that the regime sold the present and future earnings from the tea plantation in Mulindi to buy weapons from Egypt for the value of US$6 million.

[15] We can also look at the quality of the coffee as an indication for the decreasing interest of the farmer. At the beginning of Habyarimana's reign, 70% of Rwanda's coffee was of standard quality with some 4% reaching superior quality. Towards the end of the eighties, 70% was of only ordinary quality. See Uwezeyimana (1996, p. 77).

P. Verwimp / European Journal of Political Economy 19 (2003) 161–181

175

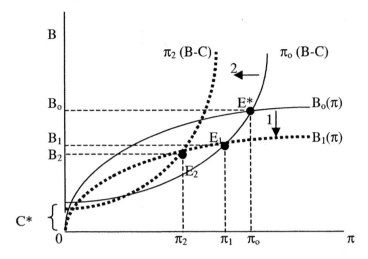

Fig. 3. The effects of a negative exogenous shock on the budget and power of the regime.

With declining coffee prices, he began subsidizing the coffee sector through the state budget and thereby reducing his personal consumption. Through the subsidy, the price paid for loyalty P_p increased, making loyalty more expensive for the dictator. For the effect of the declining budget on consumption, we have the following indirect evidence: in 1988, at the beginning of the coffee crisis, Colonel Mayuya, a top leader in the regime, was murdered.[16] On this, Prunier (1995, p.87) writes that,

"in the late 1980s climate, when political competition for the control of the rapidly shrinking economy was becoming fiercer, the succession plans President Habyarimana seemed to entertain concerning Colonel Mayuya were a grave threat to "le clan de Madame", who might lose control at a time when control was more vital then ever because Mayuya was the President's own man."

Wintrobe points out that a dictator, when confronted with a negative budgetary shock, has an alternative strategy. A dictator, certainly a totalitarian dictator, can increase his resources by confiscating property. This was also a strategy used by Habyarimana, as shown by the fact that he tried to increase taxes in 1989. This caused much resentment from the farmer population, which was already overburdened with all sorts of taxes. At the same time, Habyarimana increased the level of repression or, more accurately, he tried to increase budgetary sources on the one hand and substitute repression for loyalty on the other hand. The increase in repression is documented by the 1993 report of the International Federation of Human Rights Organizations: arbitrary arrest, killing of opposition members by government agents, several massacres of Tutsi, confiscation of property, rape, etc. Given

---

[16] Revealingly, Colonel Mayuya was replaced by Colonel Bagosora as member of the board of directors of the Bank of Kigali in 1988. Bagosora is known to be a major architect of the 1994 genocide.

176   P. Verwimp / European Journal of Political Economy 19 (2003) 161–181

the evidence we have on the level of power of Habyarimana (see also Section 5.3.1), we can conclude that Habyarimana belongs to the class of Wintrobe's totalitarian dictators:

- he did not tolerate a decrease in his level of power,
- his level of power was not at a minimum level but at a maximum level,
- he was aware of his level of power over the population (he did not mistake himself for a tinpot dictator).

6. Extending the approach to explain features of the 1994 genocide

6.1. Existing theories of genocide in Rwanda

From the vast literature on the Rwandan genocide, one can distill five approaches that attempt to explain this historic event. The first and simplest explanation of the Rwandan genocide was given by its perpetrators, the Rwandan ministers, army officers and intellectuals of the genocidal regime. In front of cameras, in diplomatic missions and in public meetings, they said that the country's Hutu majority hated its Tutsi minority and started to kill them spontaneously after the president's plane was shot down. Since the rebels had attacked the country, the government and the population only defended themselves by killing the rebels' accomplices residing inside Rwanda.[17] A second, equally simple, explanation originates from a Malthusian reading of Rwanda. Soon after the genocide, the overpopulation theory of genocide became increasingly popular in certain academic circles. That is, that the demographic density of the country was so great that young men had no access to land and as a consequence became increasingly violent.[18]

These theories have in common that they minimize or "forget" the role of the political elite of the Habyarimana regime. Two of the more interesting, less simplistic theories are developed by Desforges (1999) and Uvin (1998). The former, who has written the standard book on the Rwandan genocide, has shown in great detail how a small group of political leaders used genocide as a political strategy to remain in power. She describes the single party state, the compulsory labor, the manipulation of ethnicity, the lack of international response, the participation and resistance of farmers during the mass murder campaign and much more. Uvin, who is not arguing against Desforges but rather complements her analysis, destroys the myth of "development" that hung around the Habyarimana regime. He shows how international agencies, donors, NGOs, and consultants described Rwanda as a "model" for other developing countries and how painfully wrong this picture was. The Rwandan farmer, Uvin argues, was disempowered, humiliated, frustrated, and infantilized by the top-down state/aid system. He describes how farmers were driven off their land to grow tea on large-scale plantations, how the same people always benefited from foreign aid, how development projects consumed resources and did not reach the poor. This system, according to Uvin, produced structural violence, which in turn facilitates acute violence.

---

[17] Colonel BEMS Bagosora Théoneste, 1995, L' assassinat du Président Habyarimana ou l'ultime opération du Tutsi pour sa reconquête par la force au Rwanda, Yaoundé, October 30. See also Abogenena (1996).

[18] This position, also called demographic entrapment, can be found in King (1994) and Bonneux (1994).

P. Verwimp / European Journal of Political Economy 19 (2003) 161–181   177

6.2. Genocide as a special case in the loyalty-repression model

Just before the outbreak of war, in August 1990, the Habyarimana regime decreased the price paid to the coffee producer from 125 to 100 RWF/kg. This sharp drop was the result of the very expensive subsidy policy to the coffee sector, which proved to be unsustainable. The 1990 coffee season was marked by the highest coffee subsidy ever (US$4 billion). The history of subsidies from 1986 to 1990 again documents the importance of the coffee economy for the regime, both economically and politically.

From a public finance point of view, this cut in subsidies makes sense. The regime needed the money to finance the upcoming civil war. However, there is a clear trade-off with farmer political loyalty. After the outbreak of war, the government increased the producer price for coffee again from 100 to 115 Rfr in 1991. In a political economy analysis, such decisions are not mere coincidence. War not only diminishes the power of the regime (it is proven to be vulnerable), but also increases the need to boost the state budget in order to pay the army. The price was increased again in 1991 out of fear that the farmers would decrease their loyalty to the regime in the face of the RPF attack and continue to uproot coffee trees. From the dictator's point of view, this increase was necessary to maintain both the loyalty of the farmers AND the level of the state budget. Since the world market price for coffee continued to drop, the relative cost to the dictator of paying for the supply of loyalty continued to increase. A power maximizing dictator will, therefore, substitute repression for loyalty. As the budget of the dictator is shrinking, he will look for cheaper ways to increase loyalty and repression. The price paid to the coffee producer was already at its lowest and does not offer further cost-saving opportunities. Repression was made cheaper by training and using unemployed youth as militias. This is one of the strategies used from 1991 onwards.

The civil war offered the regime an excellent occasion to increase its popularity, despite declining coffee prices. I believe one can interpret the whole ideological construction of the Habyarimana regime as a giant effort to increase the supply of loyalty (or at least to keep it constant). That ideology existed already, but the regime used the war to spread extremist propaganda, based on Hutu supremacy and ethnic hatred (Chrétien et al., 1995). A large supply of loyalty by a docile, willing population is the best situation a dictator can have. This keeps the price of loyalty very low. When all Rwandans (and especially the Hutu of course) would feel themselves part of the Habyarimana regime, they would not ask much in return (Prunier, 1995). The fact that a Hutu president is in power, according to this ideology, should already be enough for a Hutu farmer to feel proud. As if the Hutu farmer himself were a member of the government.

Even in the late 1980s and early 1990s, when repression increased substantially, most Hutu could reasonably assume that they would not fall victim to the regime's repressive policies. This means that an increase in repression by the Habyarimana regime was positively related to an increase in the *aggregate* supply of loyalty. The loyalty curve of Tutsi is certainly backward bending, especially from 1990 onwards. On the one hand, the MRND facilitated the exchange of loyalty and rents between the regime and its supporters and on the other hand it facilitated the control and repression from nonsupporters. The Habyarimana regime from 1990 onwards pursued a policy of *immiserization*. Wintrobe (1998, pp. 82–83) believes that a strategy of immiserization may be attractive for the

178   *P. Verwimp / European Journal of Political Economy 19 (2003) 161–181*

tyrannical type of dictator (or, for Rwanda, a dictator who behaves like a tyrant against a part of his population): a high level of repression combined with a low level of loyalty. Looting, confiscating and taxing gives dictators funds to buy off the army and prevents an impoverished population from spending resources (that they no longer have) in political action. The population will be too poor to oppose the dictator.

From Desforges (1999), we know that the regime offered large rewards to the Hutu population to incite them to kill the Tutsi. In the political economy model, this can be understood as a government policy of increasing the price paid for loyalty, in order to obtain a large supply of loyalty from the population. The "price" here is not merely the producer price for coffee, but all kinds of material rewards: appropriating land, looting houses, extracting cash from victims, enslaving a Tutsi woman, distributing free beer.

The decision of the regime in Rwanda to use genocide as a political strategy to survive can be characterized as follows.

• The earnings from the export of coffee had been in decline for the last couple of years. Coffee was no longer an interesting crop to the farmer. Together with decreased earnings, especially in real income terms, the loyalty of the farmer to the regime dissipated.

• The regime tried to hold onto power by using ethnic ideology to legitimize its reign. They were able to increase farmer loyalty by frightening them and depicting the rebels as devils and enemies. The regime substituted other rewards for the share of the coffee price to buy loyalty. In this way, the regime was able to hide its own failures (a failed economy and a failed democratization) and put the blame on one group of people (Tutsi).

• The 1994 genocide in Rwanda can be considered as a double corner solution where maximum loyalty is bought from (and supplied by) one group of people (Hutu) and maximum repression is exercised towards another group of people (Tutsi). We see this in Fig. 4, where L_{sh} is loyalty supplied by Hutu and L_{st} is loyalty supplied by Tutsi.

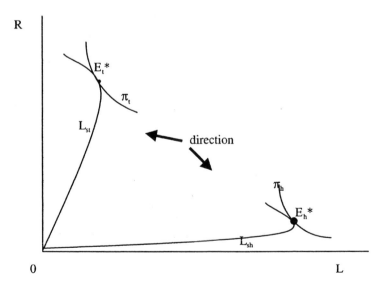

Fig. 4. Genocide as a double-corner solution in the dictatorship model.

P. Verwimp / European Journal of Political Economy 19 (2003) 161–181   179

The dictatorial equilibria are extreme repression against Tutsi and extreme loyalty from Hutu.

The Habyarimana regime did its utmost best to increase the supply of loyalty by the population. A substantial apparatus of ideological indoctrination was at work, including newspapers, radio broadcasting, and training sessions. The regime made use of its budgetary resources to spread its ideology. Ideology was a cheap instrument to increase the supply of loyalty in times of civil war. The legitimacy of the Habyarimana regime in the eyes of the farmer population declined at the end of the 1980s. Ideology was a means to boost and secure this legitimacy again. Blaming the Tutsi was instrumental in masking the regime's responsibility for the economic hardship and the political crisis. The ideology became more extreme as the war and the negotiation process went on (1992–1993), and as the world coffee price continued to decline. At the same time, we notice a sharp increase in the level of repression used by the regime. In addition, the repression was mainly conducted against the Tutsi minority of the population, allowing the Habyarimana regime to increase (or at least maintain) its power over the population without losing the loyalty of most Hutu citizens.

7. Foreign aid

The last element to complete the picture is the level of foreign aid given to the Habyarimana regime. Foreign aid was very important to the regime. From the 1970s to the mid-1980s, foreign aid was approximately as important as earnings from coffee exports, but from the mid-1980s to the mid-1990s, the importance of foreign aid relative to export earnings increased dramatically. The continued supply of foreign aid allowed Habyarimana to sustain his budget, even when coffee prices continued to drop. However, foreign aid could not replace the role of the producer price for coffee. Foreign aid helped to keep the dictator in office during the civil war, but it did not help the farmer. This is consistent with the general picture presented by Easterly (2001).

8. Conclusion

I have linked coffee, dictatorship and genocide in a political economy framework. The mechanism used by the dictator to buy loyalty went through the economy. The loyalty of the population vis-à-vis the dictator is transmitted through the producer price of coffee. In a period of economic growth, the producer price of coffee is increased and personal consumption and the power of the dictator increase. I have shown why Habyarimana was a totalitarian type of dictator. The producer price of coffee was high compared to African standards, but coffee farmers were monitored and penalized for mistreating trees. When at the end of the 1980s, world coffee prices started to drop dramatically, the regime fell into a crisis.

When the regime was unable to pay for political loyalty through the coffee price mechanism, it looked for other mechanisms to maintain its power over the population. The abundance of cheap labor proved ideal: the regime increased repression by mobilizing

P. Verwimp / European Journal of Political Economy 19 (2003) 161–181

unemployed youth. These units targeted Rwanda's Tutsi minority, whereas at the same time the ideological apparatus of the state mobilized Hutu farmers to join the genocidal campaign. Genocide is understood in the framework of Wintrobe's model as a double corner solution in which loyalty of one group is bought by allowing and encouraging extermination of the other. It is not the fall of the coffee price that caused the genocide, but the desire of the ruling elite to stay in power at all cost. Foreign aid helped the dictator to reach his objectives.

Acknowledgements

An earlier version of this paper was presented at the 1999 Annual Meeting of the Public Choice Society, New Orleans, and the 2001 Spring Meeting of Young Economists, Copenhagen. The author thanks Frans Spinnewyn, Ronald Wintrobe, Arye Hillman, Lode Berlage, James Robinson, two anonymous referees, and seminar participants for helpful comments. This research benefited from funding by the Fund for Scientific Research of the regional Government of Flanders (Belgium).

References

Abogenena, J.M., 1996. Bagosora s'explique. Africa International 296 (July–August).

Bardhan, P., 1997. Method in the madness? A political-economy analysis of the ethnic conflicts in less developed countries. World Development 25, 1381–1398.

Bart, F., 1993. Montagne d'Afrique. Terres Paysannes, Bordeaux.

Bates, R., 1981. Markets and States in Tropical Africa. University of California Press, Berkeley.

Becker, G., 1983. A theory of competition among pressure groups for political influence. Quarterly Journal of Economics 98, 371–400.

Bevan, D., Collier, P., Gunning, J.W., 1989. Peasants and Governments: An Economic Analysis. Clarendon Press, Oxford.

Bonneux, L., 1994. Rwanda: a case of demographic entrapment. Lancet 344 (17), 1689–1691.

Chrétien, J.P., Dupaquier, J.-F., Kabanda, M., Ngarambe, J., 1995. Les Médias du génocide. Karthala, Paris.

Coase, R.H., 1960. The problem of social cost. The Journal of Law and Economics 3, 1–44.

Dadrian, V.N., 1995. The History of the Armenian Genocide: Ethnic Conflict from the Balkans to Anatolia to the Caucasus. Berghan Books, Providence, RI.

Desforges, A., 1999. Leave None to Tell the Story. Human Rights Watch, New York.

Dorseay, L., 1983. The Rwandan Colonial Economy 1916–1941, Ph.D dissertation, Michigan State University.

Easterly, W., 2001. The Elusive Question for Growth: Economists' Adventures and Misadventures in the Tropics. MIT Press, Cambridge, MA.

Guichaoua, A., 1992. Le problème des refugies rwandais et des populations Banyarwanda dans la région des Grands Lacs Africains. UNHCR, Geneva.

Hilberg, R., 1961. The Destruction of the European Jews. Quadrangle Books, Chicago, IL.

Hirschleifer, J., 1994. The dark side of the force. Economic Inquiry 32 (January 1994), 1–10.

Horowitz, I.L., 1976. Genocide: State Power and Mass Murder. Transaction Books, New Brunswick.

Human Rights Watch, 1994. Arming Rwanda. Human Rights Watch, New York.

Kieran, B., 1996. The Pol Pot Regime: Race, Power and Genocide in Cambodia under the Khmer Rouge, 1975–1979. Yale Univ. Press, New Haven, CT.

King, M., 1994. Rwanda. Medicus Mundi Bulletin 54.

Leurquin, Ph., 1960. Le niveau de vie des populations rurales du Ruanda-Urundi, Nauwelaerts, Louvain.

II.2.1.3 The political economy of coffee, dictatorship and genocide

P. Verwimp / European Journal of Political Economy 19 (2003) 161–181   181

Little, P.D., Horowitz, M., 1987. Agricultural policy and practice in Rwanda. Human Organisation 46, 254–259.

Little, P.D., Horowitz, M., 1988. Agricultural policy and practice in Rwanda. Human Organisation 47, 271–273.

Mfizi, C., 1992. Reseau Zero, lettre ouverte à Monsieur le Président du MRND. Editions Uruhimbi, Kigali, Juillet-Aout.

Newbury, D., Newbury, C., 2000. Bringing the peasants back in. The American Historical Review 105, 832–877.

Olson, M., 2000. Power and Prosperity: Outgrowing Communist and Capitalist Dictatorships. Basic Books, New York.

Olson, M., Mcguire, M., 1996. The economics of autocracy and majority rule: the invisible hand and the use of force. Journal of Economic Literature 34, 72–96.

Pottier, J., 1993. Taking stock: food marketing reform in Rwanda 1982–1989. African Affairs 92, 5–30.

Prunier, G., 1995. The Rwanda Crisis: History of a Genocide. Columbia Univ. Press, New York.

Reyntjens, F., 1985. Pouvoir et Droit au Rwanda. Musée Royal de Tervuren, Tervuren.

Rowley, C.K., 2000. Political culture and economic performance in sub-Saharan Africa. European Journal of Political Economy 16, 133–158.

Smith, A., 1776. An inquiry into the nature and the causes of the wealth of nations.

Tardiff-Douglin, D., Ngirumwami, J.L., Shaffer, J., Murekezi, A., Kampayana, T., 1993. Apercu sur la politique cafeicole au Rwanda. Kigali.

Uvin, P., 1998. Aiding Violence: The Development Enterprise in Rwanda. Kumarian Press, Connecticut.

Uwezeyimana, L., 1996. Crise du café, faillite de l'etat et implosion sociale au Rwanda. Serie MOCA, Montages et Café, vol. 4. Université de Toulouse, Toulouse.

Verwimp, P., 2000. Development ideology, the peasantry and genocide: Rwanda represented in Habyarimana's speeches. Journal of Genocide Research 2, 325–361.

Willame, J.-C., 1995. Aux sources de l'héctacombe Rwandaise. Cahiers Africains, vol. 14. Karthala et CEDAF, Paris.

Wintrobe, R., 1998. The Political Economy of Dictatorship. Cambridge Univ. Press, Cambridge.

Why Is Rent-Seeking So Costly to Growth?

By KEVIN M. MURPHY, ANDREI SHLEIFER, AND ROBERT W. VISHNY*

Economists from Adam Smith (1776) to Douglass C. North (1981) agree that poor protection of property rights is bad for growth. But why is this problem so severe? Why do Peru (Hernando De Soto, 1989) and Equatorial Guinea (Robert Klitgaard, 1990) fail to grow at all when public and private rent-seeking make property insecure? In this paper, we explore two reasons why rent-seeking, meaning any redistributive activity that takes up resources, is so costly to growth.

First, rent-seeking activities exhibit very natural increasing returns. That is, an increase in rent-seeking activity may make rent-seeking more (rather than less) attractive relative to productive activity. This condition can lead to multiple equilibria in the economy, with "bad" equilibria exhibiting very high levels of rent-seeking and low output.[1]

Second, rent-seeking, particularly public rent-seeking by government officials, is likely to hurt innovative activities more than everyday production. Since innovation drives economic growth, public rent-seeking hampers growth more severely than production.

I. Increasing Returns in Rent-Seeking Activities

The rent-seeking technology *itself* often exhibits increasing returns. Three mechanisms are relevant. First, there may be a fixed cost to setting up a rent-seeking sys-

tem, such as a legal code. Once it is set up, however, lawyers can cheaply sue each other's clients, which they could not do if the code did not exist. Second, rent-seeking may be self-generating in that offense creates a demand for defense. If one feudal lord builds an army, his neighbor does so as well; if a customer hires a lawyer, his supplier must do likewise; and so on. This too, is a form of increasing returns. Third, rent-seekers have a "strength in numbers." If only a few people steal or loot, they will get caught; but if many do, the probability of any one of them getting caught is much lower, and hence the returns to stealing or looting are higher. All these mechanisms, which rely on increasing returns to the aggregate rent-seeking technology, can generate multiple equilibria, some of which have a very high level of rent-seeking and a low level of income.

In this paper, we focus on perhaps an even more generic form of increasing returns to rent-seeking, which arises not from the structure of rent-seeking technology, but instead from interaction of rent-seeking and productive activities. Specifically, as more resources are allocated to rent-seeking, returns to production, as well as to rent-seeking, fall. Over some range, as more resources move into rent-seeking, returns to production may fall faster than returns to rent-seeking do, and so the attractiveness of production *relative* to rent-seeking will fall as well, even though both production and rent-seeking exhibit diminishing-returns neoclassical technologies. When this happens, rent-seeking exhibits general equilibrium increasing returns, in the sense that an increase in rent-seeking lowers the cost of further rent-seeking. Below, we present a simple model that illustrates this idea.

Consider a farm economy, in which each person can engage in one of three activities. He can produce a cash crop for the market, in which case his output is α. He can also

*Murphy and Vishny: Graduate School of Business, University of Chicago, 1101 E. 58th Street, Chicago, IL 60637; Shleifer: Department of Economics, Harvard University, Cambridge, MA 02138. We thank the Bradley Foundation for financial support and Tim Besley for comments.
[1]The idea developed here was briefly described in Murphy et al. (1991). A similar argument was recently made by Daron Acemoglu (1992).

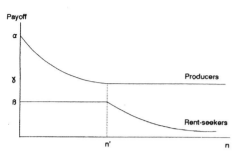

FIGURE 1. PAYOFFS TO PRODUCTION
AND RENT-SEEKING, $\beta < \gamma$

produce a subsistence crop, in which case his output is $\gamma < \alpha$. The subsistence output in not subject to rent-seeking; it cannot be stolen or expropriated. In contrast, market output is subject to rent-seeking. Rent-seeking is the third activity that each person can pursue; if he does, the maximum amount of cash crop he can expropriate is β. Thus, an individual's rent-seeking technology is subject to diminishing returns, in the sense of an upper bound on how much he can grab with limited time and abilities. In this model, rent-seeking drives farmers out of cash-crop production, which is subject to expropriation, and into subsistence production, which is not, with the consequent substantial decline in productivity and living standards, as happened in many African countries (Robert H. Bates, 1987).

An equilibrium in this economy is an allocation of the population between cash-crop production, subsistence production, and rent-seeking. Denote the ratio of people engaged in rent-seeking and market production by n and denote income per capita by y. To study equilibria in this economy, we consider the payoffs to production and rent-seeking as a function of n. These payoffs are presented in Figure 1, which is the essential part of our analysis. At $n = 0$, the returns to market production are α since nothing is expropriated from the farmers, and the returns to rent-seeking are β since the first rent-seeker can take all he can get subject only to the diminishing returns on his technology. As n rises above 0, returns

to market production fall to $\alpha - n\beta$, as farmers get a part of their output expropriated but are still better off than they would be with subsistence production. In this interval, the returns to rent-seeking are still β, since rent-seekers can still get all they are physically able to take.

At some critical level n', the after-transfer returns to market production fall all the way to the subsistence level γ. This is the highest ratio of rent seekers to cash crop producers consistent with rent-seekers getting their full potential output β. The critical level n' is given by $\alpha - n'\beta = \gamma$, or $n' = (\alpha - \gamma)/\beta$, where $\alpha - \gamma$ has the obvious interpretation of the maximum amount that can be taken from a market producer before he switches to subsistence. As the ratio of rent-seekers to cash-crop producers rises above n', rent-seekers begin to crowd each other, since cash-crop producers drop into subsistence production to keep their income level at γ. As a result, for $n > n'$, the return to both cash crop and subsistence producers is given by γ, and the return to each rent-seeker is given by $(\alpha - \gamma)/n < \beta$. In this regime of extreme rent-seeking, rent-seekers crowd each other and operate below their full potentials since they continue to divide a fixed pie between more and more of themselves.

Figure 1 illustrates the fundamental element of this model, namely, that even though all aggregate technologies here exhibit constant returns, the *relative returns* to rent-seeking (relative to entrepreneurship) may be increasing. Specifically, over the range where $0 < n < n'$, the aggregate returns to rent-seeking are constant because the aggregate amount redistributed is limited only by the number of rent-seekers, but aggregate returns to market production are diminishing as more rent-seekers take more wealth away from market producers. As a result, aggregate *relative* returns to rent-seeking over this range are increasing, which, as we shall see, gives rise to multiple equilibria in some cases. To analyze equilibria, we must consider three cases which correspond to the relative positions of the two curves in Figure 1. In case 1, $\beta < \gamma$; in case 2, $\beta > \alpha$; and in case 3, $\gamma < \beta < \alpha$.

VOL. 83 NO. 2 *NEW DEVELOPMENTS IN DEVELOPMENT* *411*

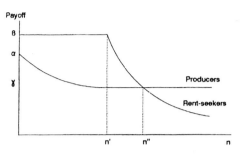

FIGURE 2. PAYOFFS TO PRODUCTION
AND RENT-SEEKING, $\beta > \alpha$

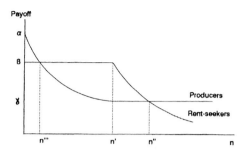

FIGURE 3. PAYOFFS TO PRODUCTION
AND RENT-SEEKING, $\gamma < \beta < \alpha$

Case 1: $\beta < \gamma$.—In this case, which actually corresponds literally to Figure 1, property rights are extremely well protected, and the rent-seeking return is even lower than the return to subsistence production. The equilibrium in this economy is unique: every person produces the cash crop; there are no rent-seekers or subsistence producers. In this sense, well-defined property rights lead to the highest possible output per capita, namely α.

Case 2: $\beta > \alpha$.—This case corresponds to extremely poorly protected property rights, or equivalently, weak diminishing returns to individual rent-seeking. In this case, a first rent-seeker can grab more than a farmer can produce for the market. Figure 2 illustrates the relative position of the returns to rent-seeking and to production in this case and shows that there is only one equilibrium. At this equilibrium, the return to production, driven all the way down to γ, must equal the return to rent-seeking when rent-seekers are crowding themselves [i.e., $\gamma = (\alpha - \gamma)/n$]. That is, in equilibrium, $n'' = (\alpha - \gamma)/\gamma$. (It follows immediately that $n'' > n'$). In this equilibrium, everyone's income is equal to subsistence productivity γ rather than market productivity α.[2]

Case 3: $\gamma < \beta < \alpha$.—In this intermediate case, there are two equilibria, as shown in Figure 3. The first equilibrium corresponds to that in case 1, where everyone is a cash crop producer and income per capita is α. The second corresponds to that in case 2, where rent-seeking is savage, people are split between market production, subsistence production, and rent-seeking, and per capita income is driven down all the way to γ. In the third equilibrium, people are split between market production and rent-seeking (with no subsistence producers), and the return to each activity is β. In this equilibrium, $\alpha - \beta n = \beta$, or $n''' = (\alpha - \beta)/\beta$. (It follows immediately that $n''' < n'$). Entry by rent-seekers drives the returns of market producers down to a rent-seeker's return, yet crowding by rent-seekers has not yet set in. This, however, is not a stable equilibrium, since an incremental increase in n beyond n''' raises returns to rent-seeking above those to market production, and hence invites further increases in resources devoted to rent-seeking. The two stable equilibria, then, are the "good" one with $n = 0$, and the "bad" one with $n = n''$.

Having presented the equilibria in this model, we can briefly discuss what they mean, and how changes in parameter values affect the equilibrium outcome. First, consider the productivity of rent-seeking, β, which captures the quality of property-rights protection in this model. As the above analysis showed, β does not affect the value of output in either equilibrium. However, β obviously affects which case obtains. In par-

---

[2] In this example, the *number* of rent-seekers and cash crop producers is indeterminate; only their ratio is known. With diminishing returns to production, this indeterminacy disappears.

ticular, a very high value of β, corresponding to very poor protection of property rights, eliminates the good equilibrium, whereas a very low level of β, corresponding to good protection of property rights, eliminates the bad equilibrium. This result accords well with intuition.

Holding other parameters constant, raising α increases income in the good equilibrium but also raises the likelihood that this equilibrium exists. A higher α also means a higher ratio of rent-seekers to market producers in the bad equilibrium, since there are more rents to be dissipated per producer before income falls down to γ. Finally, an increase in γ can be interpreted either as the improvement in the subsistence technology or, better yet, as an alternative measure of protection of property rights, since $\alpha - \gamma$ is the maximum amount that could be taken from a producer. An increase in γ does not affect the good equilibrium but raises the income in the bad equilibrium, through two channels. First, raising γ cuts the pie available to rent-seekers and hence drives people out of that activity. Second, raising γ raises the pay in the alternative occupation, namely, subsistence production, which keeps down the amount of crowding in the rent-seeking activity. Reducing how much rent-seekers can take thus raises the living standards in the bad equilibrium.

Of course, the essential point of this model is that the bad equilibrium exists and is characterized by extremely low living standards. If the economy starts out in that equilibrium, it needs to be jump started out of it. To get to the best case, case 1, it is essential to provide enough property-rights protection that β falls below γ (i.e., that the returns to subsistence production exceed those to rent-seeking). A legal system, a rigid culture, or some other form of anti-rent-seeking ideology can play a role (North, 1981); but some protection of subsistence production, as well as raising its productivity, also plays an important role. Whatever strategy for property-rights protection is used, it must be quite radical, since the bad equilibrium is stable and will not be affected by minor improvements of property rights.

This may explain why countries find it so costly to switch out of rent-seeking equilibria and often need a major government or civil-service reform to do so.

As a final implication, the model suggests that an economy that starts out in a good equilibrium can slide into a bad equilibrium as a result of a war, a coup, or social unrest that reduces both productivity and protection of property rights. This may describe what has happened during military instability in Africa or during the collapse of communism in Russia. The model shows how difficult it is to snap out of such equilibria.

II. Rent-Seeking and Innovation

In Section I, rent-seeking reduced output in the economy. However, economic growth often depends critically on investment and innovation. This raises the obvious question: is rent-seeking likely to attack the innovation sector or the production sector more severely? That is, is rent-seeking particularly bad for growth?

To address this question, it is useful to distinguish between private and public rent-seeking. Private rent-seeking takes the form of theft, piracy, litigation, and other forms of transfer between private parties. Public rent-seeking is either redistribution from the private sector to the state, such as taxation, or alternatively from the private sector to the government bureaucrats who affect the fortunes of the private sector. The latter kind of public rent-seeking takes the form of lobbying, corruption, and so on.

Private rent-seeking, such as that described in our model, attacks the productive, rather than the innovative, sector of the economy. Private rent-seekers go after existing stocks of wealth, such as land, output, capital, and so on. Bandits steal crops, lawyers sue deep-pocket corporations, and armies invade rich countries. In contrast, public rent-seeking attacks innovation, since innovators need government-supplied goods, such as permits, licenses, import quotas, and so on, much more so than established producers. To start a new firm, an innovator must get business, building, water, and fire permits, tax documents, import licenses if he needs new machinery, and often dozens of other documents (De Soto, 1989). Innovators' demand for these government-produced goods is high and inelastic, and hence they become primary targets of corruption. In contrast, established producers usually do not need as many government goods, since they have bought them already.

Of course, the government can also try to blackmail the established producers into getting some new licenses and permits. If the government makes no commitments, established and potential producers are in the same boat. Even so, more likely than not, new producers are more vulnerable to public rent-seeking.

First, innovators have no established lobbies and are not part of the government "elite." Whereas the established producers are often part of the government, innovators are outsiders and hence are subject to particularly heavy bribes and expropriations. This problem becomes even worse when the interests of new and established producers are opposed, in which case the government may even stop innovators altogether.

Second, unlike the established producers, innovators are often credit-constrained and cannot as easily find the cash to pay bribes. Human capital is poor collateral. (This also explains why they are less vulnerable to private rent-seeking.) When innovators do not have their own cash to pay bribes and cannot raise the funds to do so for lack of collateral, they can be completely deterred by public rent-seeking from entering and innovating.

Third, innovative projects are typically long-term and involve slow accumulation of capital. This provides rent-seekers plenty of opportunities for future expropriation. In fact, in developing countries with weak protection of property rights, capital is often used in trade, rather than being committed to long-term investments, to avoid expropriation.

Fourth, innovative projects are typically risky, which makes them particularly vulnerable to rent-seeking. For if a project succeeds, the returns are expropriated, whereas if it fails, the innovator bears the cost. Such

ex post rent-seeking raises the risk of innovation.

These problems can be mitigated if the rulers or the bureaucrats can take an equity stake in innovative activities, so that they can effectively accept a bribe without demanding cash, turn innovators into insiders, reduce their own incentives for subsequent expropriation, and bear some of the risk. In some countries, bureaucrats and even political leaders do exactly that, which presumably allows for some innovation. If the politicians had a long horizon, and could collect bribes efficiently, they would always back the innovator over the established producer if innovation increases the wealth in the economy. On the other hand, if innovators destroy more profits than they create (perhaps because they increase consumers' surplus), and if the bureaucrats cannot collect the bribes from consumers' surplus, they might side with established monopolies and stop innovation. Moreover, if corruption must be kept secret, politicians might prefer lower bribes from a clique of insiders to higher bribes from outsiders (Shleifer and Vishny, 1993). Such ruling oligarchies often prevent innovation in Asia (e.g., the government of Ferdinand Marcos in the Philippines), Latin America, and Africa. For these reasons, the possibility of equity holdings rarely cures the adverse effect of public rent-seeking on entrepreneurship.

These arguments suggest that public rent-seeking can put a severe tax on innovative activities and thereby move resources into established production or the public rent-seeking sector. The result would be a sharp reduction in economic growth.

III. Conclusion

This paper has suggested two reasons why countries with productive rent-seeking technologies, such as easy corruption, poor laws, and permissive legal systems, can suffer economically. First, we argued that rent-seeking activity is subject to very natural increasing returns, which means that very high levels of rent-seeking may be self-sustaining. Second, we argued that public rent-seeking in particular may afflict innovative activity the most and hence sharply reduce the rate of economic growth. These arguments add further substance to recently renewed concern about the effect of poor property rights on economic development.

REFERENCES

Acemoglu, Daron, "Reward Structures and the Allocation of Talent," mimeo, London School of Economics, 1992.

Bates, Robert H., *Essays on the Political Economy of Rural Africa*, Berkeley, CA: University of California Press, 1987.

De Soto, Hernando, *The Other Path: The Invisible Revolution in the Third World*, New York: Harper and Row, 1989.

Klitgaard, Robert, *Tropical Gangsters*, New York: Basic Books, 1990.

Murphy, Kevin M., Shleifer, Andrei and Vishny, Robert, "The Allocation of Talent: Implications for Growth," *Quarterly Journal of Economics*, May 1991, *106*, 503–30.

North, Douglass C., *Structure and Change in Economic History*, New York: Norton, 1981.

Shleifer, Andrei and Vishny, Robert W., "Corruption," *Quarterly Journal of Economics*, 1993 (forthcoming).

Smith, Adam, *The Wealth of Nations*, London: W. Strahan and T. Cadell, 1776; reprinted, Chicago: University of Chicago Press, 1976.

European Journal of Political Economy
Vol. 16 (2000) 189–213

European Journal of
POLITICAL
ECONOMY

ELSEVIER

Political culture and economic decline

Arye L. Hillman [a,b], Heinrich W. Ursprung [c,*]

[a] *Department of Economics, Bar-Ilan University, Ramat Gan, 52900, Israel*
[b] *CEPR, London, EC1V 7RR, UK*
[c] *Department of Economics and Statistics, University of Konstanz, Postfach 5560, Box D-138, 78457 Konstanz, Germany*

Received 1 September 1999; received in revised form 1 January 2000; accepted 1 January 2000

Abstract

In societies with a political culture of rent seeking, social norms do not disallow the use of political office for privileged distribution. Societies with such norms tend be characterized by political insiders and outsiders. We describe the attendant contestability of rents in the two domains of rent seeking when insiders seek politically assigned benefits and outsiders seek to re-position themselves as insiders, and show how successive stages of political liberalization result in economic decline. The model is considered against the background of the political liberalization that occurred in the post-socialist societies and the observed tendencies for economic decline, and at times economic collapse, in various of these societies' economies. © 2000 Elsevier Science B.V. All rights reserved.

JEL classification: H11; P30
Keywords: Political culture; Transition; Rent seeking; Political liberalization

According to the head of Russia's central bank, billions of dollars of its foreign exchange reserves have, over a five year period, been secretly administered by an offshore company. The company's existence was first revealed on February 1 (1998) by the country's chief prosecutor, Yuri Shuratov, who had been investigating the high-spending central bank since last August's (1998) financial crash.

---

* Corresponding author. Fax: +49-7531-88-3130.
E-mail address: heinrich.ursprung@uni-konstanz.de (H.W. Ursprung).

219

190   *A.L. Hillman, H.W. Ursprung / European Journal of Political Economy 16 (2000) 189–213*

He resigned ostensibly for health reasons the next day.... A former finance minister, Boris Federov, says he queried the arrangements in 1993, but was told to mind his own business. "They were simply allowing friends to earn handsome profits," he suggests.

The Economist, February 13, 1999.

An anti-corruption law was adopted by the Russian duma (parliament) in November 1997. The law did not designate as illegal the participation of an official figure in a commercial activity for personal benefit. The law did not designate as illegal the use of an official position to divert state resources into private commercial entities for personal benefit, with the involvement to this end of relatives and/or other persons. The law did not designate as illegal the granting privileges to private commercial structures by an official figure for personal benefit.

Observed in the IDEM Foundation, 1998 (see also Levin and Satarov, 2000).

We did not neglect institutional development.

Marcelo Selowsky, Chief Economist, Europe and Central Asian Region, The World Bank, quoted in the periodical Transition 1998, 9, 1–4, published by the World Bank, Washington, DC.

1. Introduction

Socially beneficial competition is efficient in attracting resources to eliminate rents; socially disadvantageous competition is inefficient in attracting resources to the creation and contesting of rents. When rents are politically assigned, political liberalization, by expanding the scope of the latter type of competition, can therefore increase social losses. In a society with a sustained culture of rent seeking, political liberalization can consequently be associated with economic decline.

By a culture of rent seeking, we mean that individuals in a society perceive influence over political allocation to be a primary source of private benefit, and that political behavior is accommodating by assigning privileged private benefit in response to rent-seeking overtures. To acquire wealth and to improve their personal positions in life, individuals therefore focus their attention on seeking beneficial decisions from government.[1]

We shall describe the behavior of the insiders and outsiders in such a rent-seeking society. Insiders have direct access to privileged benefit from political decisions and expend resources in seeking to influence these decisions in their

---

[1] See Tullock (1988).

A.L. Hillman, H.W. Ursprung / European Journal of Political Economy 16 (2000) 189–213 191

favor. The privileged benefits available to the insiders provide incentives for outsiders to compete for insider positions that become available as insiders retire over time (or are retired).

The persons who are in government are distinct from insiders (and outsiders), and seek maximal political gain from allocating benefits among insiders, but are also responsive to discontent of outsiders.

As the society proceeds through successive stages of openness in influence over political allocation, we evaluate the total resources used by insiders contesting politically assigned rents and by outsiders seeking to re-position themselves to become insiders. Under reasonable circumstances, the value of resources used in rent seeking by insiders and outsiders increases with stages of political openness.

Our beginning is in the institutions of political monopoly. Here insiders in the single or monopoly interest group use resources to subjugate outsiders, and outsiders use resources in seeking to become insiders. The replacement of political monopoly by political competition allows a number of insider-groups to compete for politically assigned favors. Outsiders continue to use resources to contest insider positions. A further stage of political openness eliminates the barriers that have sustained the distinction between insiders and outsiders and allows previous outsiders to join any of the now non-exclusive interest groups. In a final stage of political liberalization, political entry barriers altogether disappear; persons who so wish can form their own interest group and the number of competing interest groups can increase.[2]

A further step, which we do not model but can quite naturally follow, is retrogression. If political liberalization makes the population increasingly economically worse off, the population can become increasingly sympathetic to reversion to illiberal regimes under which they were economically better off.

2. Hobbes, Locke and our model of political culture

In common with our model, Hobbes (1651) also associated political liberalization with social disadvantage. Hobbes proposed that, left to themselves in the absence of the authority of government, men and women would devour one other. To protect people from their own base nature, he proposed government by a ''leviathan'', who would have absolute authority and who would own all property and would subjugate all people. By preempting anarchic unproductive contestability of wealth, the leviathan leaves people no alternative but to be productive. Hobbes surmised that rational enlightened people would voluntarily subject themselves and their property to the authority of the leviathan, so as to avoid the anarchy that would otherwise prevail. He thus proposed that people would realize that political liberalization was to their detriment.

---

[2] On entry barriers to political competition, see Tullock (1965).

192   *A.L. Hillman, H.W. Ursprung / European Journal of Political Economy 16 (2000) 189–213*

Hobbes' position contrasts with that of Locke (1690). Locke rejected rule by an authoritarian leviathan, who constrained individual freedom.[3] Men and women are, in Locke's view, born into a natural state of freedom. The only legitimate government is therefore one that is accountable to the people (or more particularly, as he understood, to people of property).

The contrary positions of Hobbes and Locke set the merits of social order against the merits of individual freedom (see Rowley, 1999). Locke's natural state of freedom is inconsistent with the political monopoly of the leviathan[4], but for Hobbes, the political liberalism sought by Locke opens the way to anarchic socially wasteful contestability of wealth.[5]

When positioned within this debate, our model places us with Locke and not with Hobbes. In our model, political liberalization results in economic decline, not because of Hobbesian anarchy *due to absence of government*, but because of the sustained political culture *embedded in the norms of behavior of the government that is present*.

3. Economic decline in transition

Our model describes a general phenomenon of economic decline, but also in particular suggests an answer to the seeming puzzle of decline in post-socialist societies. In the last decade of the 20th century, socialist societies were given the opportunity to undergo change, and a transition from one system to another began. The puzzle lies in poor economic performance throughout the first decade of transition in the face of the external resources and assistance that were provided (see the extensive country studies in Blejer and Škreb, 2000). The decline often went beyond economic living standards; Ellman (1994) documents the unfortunate accompanying decline in health and life expectancy in some post-socialist societies. The scenario could perhaps have been different. Political liberalization could have brought to the fore principled political candidates and socially beneficial policies, while, at the same time, private foreign capital and domestic economic change, with the assistance provided by international organizations and donor countries, could have provided the foundation for economic progress.

Our model stresses the role of a persisting political culture as the explanation for persistent economic deterioration. Other explanations (see the survey by Matveenko et al., 1998) have looked to the role of initial economic conditions.

---

[3] The limitations on individual freedom affect the quality of life, and can affect the continuation of life itself (see Bernholz, 1991).

[4] It is also inconsistent with the coercion of majority rule (see Rowley, 1999).

[5] On behavior under Hobbesian anarchy, including spontaneous emergence of property rights, see for example Tullock (1972), Umbeck (1981), Skaperdas (1992), Wärneryd (1993), Grossman and Kim (1995), and Hirshleifer (1995).

A.L. Hillman, H.W. Ursprung / European Journal of Political Economy 16 (2000) 189–213   193

One alternative answer is "disorganization", or the disruption of traditional supply relationships among the formerly socialist factories (see Blanchard, 1997; Blanchard and Kremer, 1997). Such explanations can be appropriate for explaining outcomes around the point of actual change and informing us why output decline occurred in the early transition. Yet we might suppose, however, that a decade would suffice for initial economic conditions to have declined in significance; for example, a decade might be enough to permit re-organization of intra-factory economic relationships.

A line of argument that addresses the persistence of poor economic performance is that the correct policies were not implemented — which raises the question why this was so, given the extensive policy advice and technical assistance that was provided.[6]

The norms of a rent-seeking society are reflected in personalized allocation as the prime determinant of individual welfare. In such circumstances, not individual merit, but reciprocal personal favors and convincing others of one's deserts are principal avenues for personal gain and advancement. It was thus in the nature of pre-transition socialist society that rent seeking was endemic (see Hillman and Schnytzer, 1986).

Cultural norms are an enduring characteristic of a society. Political culture and associated institutions change slowly (see North, 1990). The ways of thinking about the requisites for personal success also, correspondingly, change slowly. As Levin and Satarov (2000) make clear in their study of the Russian case, and as studies of other post-socialist societies confirm (see Blejer and Škreb, 2000), the former social norms and way of thinking about personal advancement remained embedded in the culture throughout the ongoing transition.

We turn now to the exposition of our model of enduring political culture. We shall subsequently return to the world to which the model relates.

4. A model of political insiders and outsiders

In a total population of size N, the population is partitioned into n_I insiders and n_O outsiders, so that

$$n_O + n_I = N. \tag{1}$$

Insiders are political persons. Outsiders are not. Insiders are positioned to seek personal income and wealth through political assignment, and are for this purpose grouped into associations for collective benefit, or "clubs".[7]

---

[6] The scope of the policy advice can be seen in the different country economic memoranda published by the World Bank during the 1990s.

[7] For an overview of the economic theory of clubs, see Cornes and Sandler (1996).

194   *A.L. Hillman, H.W. Ursprung / European Journal of Political Economy 16 (2000) 189–213*

All persons have active lives of $(T + 1)$ periods. An insider who retires is replaced by an outsider. Outsiders compete for the insider vacancies. An outsider who succeeds in becoming an insider enjoys insider benefits for the remainder of his or her active life.

In the nature of rent seeking, the resources used in the contests among outsiders are expended whether an individual is successful or not in securing a vacant insider position. Each outsider has a unit endowment of potentially productive time,

$$w_O + v_O = 1, \tag{2}$$

where w_O is time spent productively earning income and v_O is time used in seeking to become an insider.

There are two domains of rent seeking. Insiders directly contest benefits from political allocation, and outsiders expend resources in seeking to change their status to insiders. The equilibrium behavior of insiders and outsiders depends on political culture expressed in government responsiveness to rent seeking and on the institutions that specify how rent-seeking contests are conducted and winners are determined.

4.1. Political monopoly

We begin with the institution of political monopoly, with one political "club" of insiders. Members of the single political club or "party" receive benefits that are obtained through the capture of the institutions of the state. The n_O outsiders compete for openings for party membership by choosing allocations in Eq. (2) to maximize lifetime expected utility.

In any period of time, the benefit from being an insider is the difference between insider and outsider utility, and lifetime future benefit at a point in time is the accumulated utility difference over the future period during which an individual is an insider. The n_O outsiders are of different ages. Since the youngest in the population receive the greatest lifetime benefit from party membership, they also have the highest stakes from participation in contests to become insiders.

To describe rent seeking, we require a specification of the contest–success function that designates the identity of a successful rent seeker. For the contests among outsiders seeking insider positions, we adopt a contest–success function that is perfectly discriminating, that is, an outsider who has allocated the most resources to the contest secures the vacant insider position.[8]

Discriminating contests do not have equilibria in pure strategies. This follows readily, since any outsider who makes a pure-strategy choice of a proportion v_O of

---

[8] A discriminating rule assigns success to the highest bidder. A non-discriminating rule provides a probability for success (see Tullock, 1980a). On the distinction between discriminating and non-discriminating contest–success functions, see Hillman and Riley (1989).

A.L. Hillman, H.W. Ursprung / European Journal of Political Economy 16 (2000) 189–213   195

time to allocate to contesting insider membership is defeated by any another outsider who makes a marginally greater outlay. The first contender would then have reason to revise his or her previous decision, either to zero, or to yet a marginally greater outlay than the second contender, who in turn would also have reason to revise his or her initial outlay.

Although no pure-strategy equilibrium exists, mixed-strategy equilibria do exist. Outsiders value success in becoming an insider differently, since individual valuations differ with age of outsiders. In the mixed-strategy equilibria, low-valuation contenders exclude themselves from the contest (see Hillman and Riley, 1989). The actively contesting outsiders who remain maximize expected utility, given by

$$EU_O = (1-t_S)w_O + [\pi_O U_I + (1-\pi_O)(1-t_S)w_O]T. \tag{3}$$

T here is the remaining productive life of an actively contesting outsider, U_I is the per-period utility of an insider, and π_O is the probability of an outsider becoming an insider. A proportional income tax, t_S (the subscript S refers to the state of political monopoly), is levied on the entire population to finance the (net) political allocations to insiders.[9]

The Nash equilibrium solution is for an outsider to choose an outlay less than v_O with probability

$$G(v_O) = \left(\frac{v_O}{T\left(\dfrac{U_I}{1-t_S}\right)} \right)^{\frac{1}{q_z-1}} \tag{4}$$

over the support

$$\left[0, T\left(\frac{U_I}{1-t_S} - 1 \right) \right] \tag{5}$$

where q_z is the number of contenders for insider vacancy z.

Consequently, the expected outlay by an actively contesting outsider follows as

$$Ev_O = \frac{T}{q_z}\left(\frac{U_I}{1-t_S} - 1 \right). \tag{6}$$

The expected *total use of resources by outsiders* seeking to become insiders is then

$$E\Sigma v_O = EV_O = \frac{n_I}{T}q_z Ev_O = n_I\left(\frac{U_I}{1-t_S} - 1 \right). \tag{7}$$

---

[9] We use taxation to describe political redistribution, but the tax is expository. We identify below the types of distribution and political allocation that "taxation" here represents.

196   *A.L. Hillman, H.W. Ursprung / European Journal of Political Economy 16 (2000) 189–213*

Now consider the behavior of insiders. Under political monopoly, insiders expend resources to maintaining outsider subservience. An insider's resource constraint is

$$w_I + v_I = 1. \tag{8}$$

Total resources used by insiders to maintain acquiescence or subservience of outsiders are

$$V_I = \sum_{k=1}^{n_I} v_k = n_I v_I. \tag{9}$$

The resources in Eq. (9) are unproductively used to maintain insider rents.[10] We can suppose that the position of insiders is, in addition, more tenable, the less is appropriated from outsiders, that is, the smaller taxation t_S is.

The resources V_I and taxation t_S determine regime viability, through

$$M = \frac{b}{N} V_I - t_S^2 \geq \hat{M}, \tag{10}$$

where $\hat{M}$ is the minimum popular discontent that is consistent with viability of the single-party insider regime. The discontent of outsiders increases (we assume at an increasing rate) with appropriation of outsider incomes (expressed in taxation t_S). b in Eq. (10) reflects the effectiveness of resource used in countering outsider discontent.

Insiders maximize utility

$$U_I = \left(1 - \frac{V_I}{n_I}\right)(1 - t_S) + \left[\frac{[N - EV_O - V_I] t_S}{n_I}\right], \tag{11}$$

subject to the minimum popularity constraint (Eq. 10) and individual resource constraints (Eq. 8). The first term in Eq. (11) is net-of-tax taxable income of insiders (insiders' taxable income consists of the proceeds of their productive activities, net of the resources per insider contributed to the common cause of containing discontent of outsiders). The second term is the income transfer received by an insider from outsiders: the tax is levied on an economy-wide base of $[N - EV_O - V_I]$ and the proceeds are distributed among the n_I insiders. The solution, using Eq. (7), is the equilibrium tax rate[11]

$$t_S = \frac{1+b}{3} + \sqrt{\left(\frac{1+b}{3}\right)^2 - \frac{\varphi}{3}}, \tag{12}$$

where $\varphi = b(n_O/N) + \hat{M}$.

---

[10] Inefficiency here is reflected in resources not productively used. The same considerations arise with inefficiency due to deadweight losses, which are not present in this model. See also McGuire and Olson (1996) on the efficiency incentives of a ruler as residual claimant.

[11] For interior solutions, $t_S < 1$, and we therefore assume $b < 2$.

A.L. Hillman, H.W. Ursprung / European Journal of Political Economy 16 (2000) 189–213   197

The *total expected unproductive use of resources in the society* is

$$V_S = EV_O + V_I = Nt_S. \tag{13}$$

The revenue function for transfers between outsiders and insiders has Laffer-type properties, expressed in:

$$S_S = (N - V_S)t_S = (1 - t_S)t_S N. \tag{14}$$

The equilibrium is described in Fig. 1. We express the constraint indicating maximum sustainable political discontent, given in Eq. (10), as

$$V_I = \frac{N}{b}(\hat{M} + t_S^2). \tag{15}$$

The indifference map of insiders between V_I and taxation t_S can be expressed as

$$V_I = Nt_S + n_I\left(1 - \frac{\bar{U}_I}{1 - t_S}\right), \tag{16}$$

where $\bar{U}_I$ is a constant level of insider utility. The unique equilibrium solution for the tax rate is t_S^*, which via Eq. (15) specifies insiders' utility-maximizing allocations V_I to the collective objective of sustaining the monopoly insider regime.

4.2. Competition for political influence

We now introduce a regime change where competing interest groups, replace the political monopoly. Each of the m interest groups has equal ex-ante access to influence over political allocation of transfers offered to insiders by the government. Members of interest groups cooperatively contribute personal resources to their collective aim of enriching themselves by influence over political allocation. The utility of an insider in interest group j is

$$U_j = (1 - t_C)w_j + \rho_j \frac{S_C}{n_j}, \tag{17}$$

where the subscript C refers to the regime of competition for influence over political allocation and n_j denotes the size of interest group j.

ρ_j in Eq. (17) is the share of government benefits obtained by interest group j. The share is determined by two characteristics of an interest group. A larger size is beneficial politically, because of the greater number of votes that the interest group can offer. The interest group at the same time also benefits from greater resources

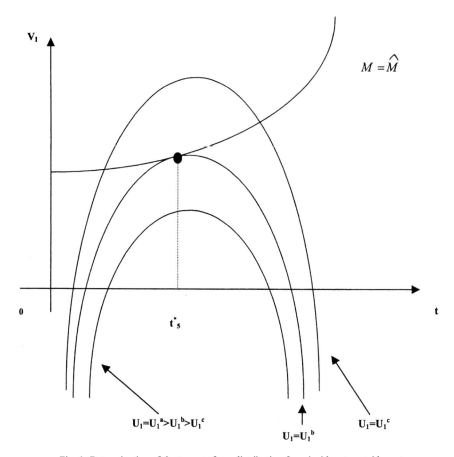

Fig. 1. Determination of the tax rate for redistribution from insiders to outsiders.

available to influence political allocation decisions.[12] An interest group's share of lobbying outlays and the relative size of the interest group establish ρ_j as

$$\rho_j = \theta \frac{V_j^\alpha}{\sum_1^m V_k^\alpha} + (1 - \theta) \frac{\Psi_j}{\sum_1^m \Psi_k}, \tag{18}$$

where $\Psi_j = \beta(n_j - \hat{n})$ and $\alpha \leq 1$.

---

[12] See Potters et al. (1997) for a model of the ways that votes and political expenditures combine to influence political support.

A.L. Hillman, H.W. Ursprung / European Journal of Political Economy 16 (2000) 189–213   199

We obtain the total resources V_I allocated by insiders to seeking political influence by summing over allocations V_j that maximize the utility U_j of a member of interest group j. We obtain

$$V_j^* = \frac{\varepsilon S_C}{(1 - t_C) m},$$
(19)

where $\varepsilon = \alpha \theta [(m - 1)/m]$ measures competitiveness of the quest for political influence (ε is increasing in θ, α, and m, which are all dimensions of political competitiveness). The total resources used by all insiders in all interest groups are

$$V_I = m V_j^* = \frac{\varepsilon S_C}{1 - t_C},$$
(20)

which is increasing in ε.

Interest groups also decide on their size. This decision is made by balancing two consequences of group size. A larger membership provides greater political effectiveness as a constituency to be courted for its votes. A larger membership also gives rise to the need to share politically assigned benefits with more persons. The utility-maximizing number of insiders in an interest group is the solution to $\max_{n_j} U_j(V_j^*)$, which is

$$n_j = \bar{n} = \left\{ \frac{m - \alpha \theta (m - 1)}{(m - 1)(1 - \alpha)\theta + 1} \right\} \hat{n},$$
(21)

where

$$\frac{\partial \bar{n}}{\partial m} < 0, \qquad \frac{\partial \bar{n}}{\partial \theta} < 0, \qquad \frac{\partial \bar{n}}{\partial \alpha} > 0.$$
(22)

That is, interest groups have fewer members, the greater the number of competing groups. The size of an interest group also increases with the political benefit $(1 - \theta)$ of a larger constituency of voters. Interest groups are also larger, the greater the benefit, reflected in the magnitude of α, from allocating resources to increase political influence.

Let us now turn to the behavior of the government. Under political monopoly, we described a single insider group as having captured government. Here, m interest groups seek to influence political allocation. The government responds to this competitive rent seeking by choosing redistribution from outsiders to insiders. The government's budget constraint is

$$[(n_O - E V_O) + (n_I - V_I)] t_C = S_C.$$
(23)

Using (Eqs. (7), (17), and (20), and noting that, in equilibrium, $\rho = (1/m)$, the government budget constraint can be expressed as

$$S_C = t_C (1 - t_C) N,$$
(24)

which, as Eq. (14), has the form of a Laffer curve.

200   *A.L. Hillman, H.W. Ursprung / European Journal of Political Economy 16 (2000) 189–213*

Under political monopoly, the objective was the minimal acquiescence that maintained subservience of outsiders. Now the government seeks to maximize political popularity. We retain the popularity function of political monopoly. The government under democracy chooses t_C to maximize

$$M = \frac{b}{N} V_1 - t_C^2,$$ (25)

where b indicates political sensitivity to rent seeking.

The rate of taxation t_C determines total transfers from outsiders to insiders. From Eq. (20), the government's objective can be re-expressed as maximization of

$$M = b\varepsilon t_C - t_C^2$$ (26)

and the chosen tax rate is

$$t_C = \frac{\varepsilon b}{2}.^{13}$$ (27)

Insiders again retire and outsiders contest the vacancies. Insiders make contributions of resources to the rent seeking activities of their respective interest groups, and the total resources so used by insiders follow from Eqs. (20) and (24) as

$$V_1 = \frac{b\varepsilon^2 N}{2}.$$ (28)

The combined resources used in rent-seeking activities by insiders and outsiders are then from Eq. (13)

$$V_C = EV_0 + V_1 = Nt_C.$$ (29)

We are now in a position to compare the resources unproductively used in rent seeking under the two regimes of political monopoly and competition for political influence. We base the comparison on the following assumptions.

A. Maximized popularity achieved by democratic government exceeds the minimum popular support required to maintain the authoritarian regime of political monopoly.

We also require an assumption regarding the location of the economy on its Laffer curve; for this purpose, we assume that taxation has not driven the economy to the revenue-inefficient segment, so that

B. The economy, in regimes of political monopoly and political competition, is situated on the upward sloped segment of the Laffer curve.

---

[13] Notice that for $b < 2$ (cf. note 11) we have $t_C < 1$.

A.L. Hillman, H.W. Ursprung / European Journal of Political Economy 16 (2000) 189–213   201

To distinguish the regimes of political monopoly and competition for political influence, we require that there be sufficient political competition. Using the measure ε defined in Eq. (19), we assume

C. *There is sufficient competition for political influence.*

A, B, and C allow us to conclude that

Proposition 1. *In the change from political monopoly to competition for political influence, the tax rate increases, total redistribution from outsiders to insiders increases, and the total resources used unproductively in rent seeking by insiders and outsiders increase.*

For the proof, see Appendix A. An intuitive explanation for Proposition 1 is as follows. The increased popularity of the government in the regime of competition for political influence is achieved with greater largesse to insiders, whose activities evoke a higher tax rate, and with the economy on the upward sloping segment of the Laffer curve, the outcome is greater redistribution.

Since being an insider is now more attractive, outsiders have a greater incentive to expend resources in seeking to become insiders. The enhanced incentive of an outsider to use resources in seeking to become an insider also reflects the increased unattractiveness of productive activity for outsiders, because of the higher tax rate on income from productive activity. That is, outsiders confront a substitution effect on resource allocation.

Insiders and outsiders thus expend more resources in unproductive rent-seeking activities, and, as Proposition 1 states, real output in the economy declines.

4.3. The end of insider privilege

After the above liberalization from political monopoly, the population has remained divided between insiders and outsiders. Further liberalization in access to political influence can end the insider–outsider distinction, and permit everybody to join one of the m interest groups.

If there are no longer outsiders and insiders, no resources are expended in seeking to change status from outsider to insider. However, with the political culture of rent seeking retained, government remains responsive to private quests for political favors, and the incentive remains for interest groups to seek to influence political allocation (which is the raison d'être for the continued existence of the interest groups). Individuals continue to contribute personal resources to their respective interest groups. Everyone thereby participates in direct political activity through an interest group association.

The government again chooses a rate of taxation to maximize political popularity, and the revenue is distributed among the interest groups. The government's budget constraint is (the subscript L refers to the further political liberalization)

$$wt_L N = S_L .\tag{30}$$

From Eq. (20), per-capita income in the economy derived from productive activity is

$$w = 1 - \frac{V_1}{N} = 1 - \frac{\varepsilon S_L}{(1 - t_L) N}. \tag{31}$$

Substituting Eq. (31) into Eq. (30) yields the total value of government transfers available for distribution as

$$S_L = \frac{t_L(1 - t_L) N}{1 - (1 - \varepsilon) t_L}, \tag{32}$$

and using Eq. (20) again, the total value of resources unproductively used in rent-seeking activities in the economy is

$$V_L = \frac{\varepsilon t_L N}{1 - (1 - \varepsilon) t_L}. \tag{33}$$

When we evaluate V_L, at interior solutions for the tax rate t_L, we conclude that

Proposition 2. *Liberalization of access to political influence that ends insider privilege increases the tax rate. With sufficient competition for political influence (ε sufficiently high) and with bounded sensitivity of government popularity to insider rent seeking, total redistribution increases, and total unproductive use of resources in rent seeking increases.*[14]

The proof is in Appendix B. To understand Proposition 2, we begin with the observation that the end of privileged exclusivity of insiders in seeking politically assigned benefits has increased the number of members in each of the m interest groups. This does not change an interest group's equilibrium total political outlays for a given aggregate rent-seeking prize S that is to be shared among the interest groups.[15] When the tax rate increases, political support declines (taxes per se are unpopular). The increased taxes also increase the value of the political prizes available to the (now non-exclusive) interest groups, which increases political popularity, and by more so than the popularity lost by the tax increase (otherwise in the new equilibrium, the tax rate would not have been increased). In a regime of political insiders and outsiders, increasing the tax rate from the equilibrium value would lead outsiders to increase their efforts to become insiders, so reducing the tax base, which is composed of income that has been earned from productive activity. This disincentive for government to increase the tax rate is no longer present, since there are now no outsiders — and in the new regime the tax rate consequently increases.

---

[14] The parameter b can assume values such that $S_L > S_C$ and $V_L > V_C$.

[15] This is so, since in contests where the prize is shared and where total outlays are cooperatively determined, the total resources used by members of an interest group to influence political allocation depend only on the value of the prize, and are independent of the size of the interest group (see Eq. 19).

A.L. Hillman, H.W. Ursprung / European Journal of Political Economy 16 (2000) 189–213   203

The increase in the value S of the total prize offered for redistribution can be seen to depend upon the weight b of rent seeking in the political-popularity function. A larger value of b encourages use of resources in rent seeking and so reduces the tax base of income from productive activity from which S is obtained. Therefore, if S is to increase, b cannot be too large. Nor can b too small, for then there is, in the limit, no point to rent seeking.

Proposition 2 describes the outcome of a negative-sum rent-seeking game for society at large (see also Tullock, 1980b). Rent-seeking prizes are financed by the entire population, which dissipates resources in competing for a share of the politically assigned prizes. All members of society are therefore placed in a prisoners' dilemma. Everybody would have a higher expected utility if, in the function describing the behavior of government, b was equal to zero, that is, if government was unresponsive to rent seeking. M would then be maximized by t_L equal to zero, and the aggregate rent-seeking prize S would be zero.

When the population is divided into political insiders and outsiders, the privileged insiders have a self-interest in perpetuating the political culture that maintains b positive. When everyone is free to join an interest group, the political culture is mutually disadvantageous for the entire population.

4.4. Free entry of interest-group coalitions into contests for political favor

A further step in liberalization of competition for political influence allows any group of individuals to form a coalition to approach the government to seek politically assigned benefits. The number of interest groups m is then no longer fixed but variable. The consequence of this next step in liberalization in influence over government is

Proposition 3. *Beginning from the equilibrium of Proposition 2, let individuals be free to form new interest groups. Let the number of competing interest groups as a consequence increase. Total resources used unproductively in rent seeking then increase, and real income in the economy declines further, provided that there is sufficient political competition (i.e., that ε is sufficiently high), and that b is not too large.*[16]

The proof is in Appendix C. Proposition 3 reflects the increased competition among the greater number of interest groups. Again, society is engaged in a negative-sum game, with now greater real losses because of greater competition in rent seeking, and everyone in society would gain from the end of the political culture of rent seeking.

---

[16] Again, if b is too large, the incentives to use resources in rent seeking erodes the tax base, and there is little or nothing to transfer. Hence the proposition requires that b not be excessively large.

Arye L. Hillman and Heinrich W. Ursprung

5. Bribery and corruption

A question that we can now raise is: why, after the end of political monopoly, is b still positive? That is, since the positive weight on political response to rent seeking underlies economic decline, why is government responsive to the unproductive rent seeking of private agents?

One interpretation of $b > 0$, consistent with political competition in more mature democracies, is that interest groups provide ''political support''.[17] In these circumstances, the resources used in rent seeking take the form of time spent gaining political access to state a case, and then the time and resources used to promote the electoral success of preferred candidates. The quotations at the beginning of this paper, and other indications, suggest however that money rather than real resources is used to seek favorable political allocation in post-socialist economies.[18] Monetary bribes are not in themselves a source of social loss, since money changing hands does not in itself mean that real resources are wastefully employed.

Our model has not identified the people in government who would receive any such monetary bribes. Government has been placed outside of the population of N insiders and outsiders. With persons in government outside the population, bribery requires no amendment to the conclusions. This is so, since the value of real resources available for consumption by the N insiders and outsiders is independent of whether V_I is lost in the form of resources directly dissipated in rent seeking, or whether V_I is an external monetary transfer used for real consumption outside the population (and perhaps outside the country).

A simple amendment to the model places persons in government within the population of N and introduces another domain of rent seeking. The new contests are for the monetary transfers received by political decision-makers. Social loss is then re-computed within the extended hierarchy of rent-seeking contests.[19] For example, let β be the share of V_I that is a personal monetary transfer to persons in government: βV_I is then the prize in rent-seeking contests to become these persons. In the now three-tiered hierarchy of contests, (1) outsiders are seeking to become insiders, (2) insiders are seeking to influence political allocation decisions, and (3) individuals are at the same time seeking to achieve positions in government to which bribes βV_I accrue.

Corruption of persons in government in accepting monetary bribes thus adds a third stage to rent dissipation. In discriminating contests, the value of the bribes is

---

[17] In representative democracy, interest groups can be expected to have political weight that belies the numbers of their members (see for example Sandler, 1992).

[18] See McChesney (1997) on political rent extraction. Ursprung (1990) describes political competition where candidates for elected office personally keep for themselves some part of the campaign contributions they receive.

[19] For an exposition of rent seeking within a hierarchy of beneficiaries who benefit from lower echelon corruption, see Hillman and Katz (1987).

A.L. Hillman, H.W. Ursprung / European Journal of Political Economy 16 (2000) 189–213 205

on average dissipated in unproductive rent seeking, and again, no changes are required in Propositions 1–3.

6. Realities of decline and collapse

As we have observed, and as predicted by our model, political liberalization in post-socialist economies was accompanied, in different instances and degrees, by economic decline. The Ukraine experienced ongoing economic deterioration within a political culture of rent seeking (see Kaufman, 1997; Åslund, 2000). In Belarus, economic decline culminated in retrogression to an illiberal regime (see Nuti, 2000).[20] Collapse occurred in 1997 in Bulgaria and in Albania (on Bulgaria, see Koford, 2000; on Albania see Muço, 1998, who describes insider–outsider transfers that took place through Albanian pyramid investment schemes, with apparent state mediation). In Russia, the institutions of government were used to bestow privileged political favors on insiders (see Levin and Satarov, 2000) and economic collapse occurred in the summer of 1998 (when the government defaulted on domestic-currency denominated bonds).

Not all the stages of political liberalization described in the model were attained when collapse took place. In general, at the time of collapse, the insider–outsider distinction remained present.

The contestability of wealth has often taken place in an interface, which we have not modeled, between criminal activity and political allocation. The occupations most dangerous to life in Russia have been those of banker, businessman, and politician (see Kisunko, 1996). Under these conditions, the social costs of extortion (see Konrad and Skaperdas, 1998) and organized criminal activity (see Fiorentini and Peltzman, 1996) complement the social losses due to rent seeking.

In considering the relation of our model to observed behavior, it is also important to note that our concept of "taxation" is symbolically representative of means of redistribution and rent assignment, and is not taxation as understood as the collection of government revenue for disbursement. Tax-revenue collection was lax in Russia and in other transition economies.[21]

---

[20] The International Herald Tribune reported on November 26, 1998 (thanksgiving): "Amid severe food shortages, the Belarus government is imposing rationing for milk, meat, matches, and other goods. Officials in the capital, Minsk, have limited shoppers to 2 cartons of milk, 2 kg (4.4 lb) of meat or poultry, 400 g (11 oz) of cheese, 10 boxes of matches, and 300 g of chocolate." Such rationing is of course reminiscent of Soviet times.

[21] Since taxes are public income, the prediction, from a rent-seeking perspective, is that where possible, taxes will be converted to private income. Consistently, in Russia the interest rate on tax arrears has been less than the market bank rate of interest, and tax liability has been incurred only when monetary payment has been received for goods and services rendered, under conditions where (as a consequence) the majority of transactions take place by barter (see Conrad, 1998).

206   *A.L. Hillman, H.W. Ursprung / European Journal of Political Economy 16 (2000) 189–213*

The list of means of rent assignment and redistribution represented by "taxation" in the model is extensive. The list can begin with exclusive privileged private transactions with non-privatized state factories, which create private rents by permitting sale of inputs and purchase of outputs at arbitrary prices. When privatization takes place, insiders purchase state assets at privileged prices or secure privileged allotments of stock. When workers receive stock allocations, insiders secure the stock from workers at preferential prices. Insiders who control share registries allocate stock to themselves and annul ownership of others. Privileged export quotas are assigned in combination with domestic price subsidization, and foreign-imposed export quotas are likewise assigned by privilege. Exclusive import rights are assigned. Taxes are withheld or are simply not paid, not as surreptitious tax evasion but as privileged (although formally de jure illegal) dispensation. Privileged private banks service the government. Directed subsidies and credits are provided from state banks or from the central bank for the benefit of private agents. Insider-information about impending devaluations permits foreign exchange reserves, including funds made available from international-agency assistance, to be "privatized" for personal gain.

These mechanisms for insider benefit require active participation by government as the patron and designator of privilege. Privileged distribution also takes place in consequence of state passivity (or using the terminology of Abel and Bonin, 1994, by "state desertion"). Assets of banks (depositors' savings) are illegally appropriated because of absent or inadequate regulation. Payments for fictitious imports are made through false invoicing, and taxes are evaded by retention abroad of export proceeds. Where the state has remained a shareholder in the exporting firm, revenue due to the state is appropriated. Insiders are permitted to decapitalize state firms. Large-scale smuggling is condoned. Or there is state passivity (or state complicity) in the face of pyramid "investment" schemes offered to a naive public.[22]

7. The economic structure

We have emphasized political allocation as the source of private benefit;[23] economic activity in our model has been described through individual time-allocation decisions. More elaborate descriptions of economic structure are consistent with our model of political allocation. Nekipelov (1998) observes that the market infrastructure of Russia during the first decade of transition should be viewed as

---

[22] On these mechanisms of insider benefit, see also Gelb et al. (1996, 1998).

[23] Our focus on rents has downplayed market incomes. Brainerd (1998) reports on market income disparities between "winners" and "losers" during the Russian transition. The inequalities are made wider by the politically assigned insider rents that are not reported in official market statistics and household survey data.

A.L. Hillman, H.W. Ursprung / European Journal of Political Economy 16 (2000) 189–213   207

"little more than Potemkin's village". Gaddy and Ickes (1998) elaborate on Nekipelov's theme, and describe an economy that consists of a natural-resource sector that has positive value-added and a manufacturing sector that destroys value.[24] The negative value-added manufacturing sector is a means of internal distribution that provides employment and income for the general population. The political insiders who contest and claim the natural-resource wealth accept the transfer mechanism as necessary for preserving outsider acquiescence and social stability.[25] As is the case with the political culture, the economic structure of negative-value-added manufacturing is a carry-over from the prior industrial system that was sustained by subsidized (below world-price) inputs.

8. Solutions

It is natural to contemplate solutions. A direction that a solution can take is constitutional restraint to bound political discretion. A constitutional solution may however offer little promise of change for contemporary generations. The constitution that is sought will require detachment in time, so as to permit future social altruism to overcome contemporary personal and political self-interest (see Buchanan, 1975). A constitutional solution thus requires a population with patience.[26]

An attempt can also be made to change behavioral norms through education (see Guttman et al., 1992). Personal example of the leadership offers another direction. One can hope for spontaneous national moral revival (see Grossman and Kim, 2000).

We can observe that some of the prizes for rent seeking have been supplied by international agencies seeking to preserve "stability" in the post-socialist society. Rent-seeking behavior may be abated if rent-seeking prizes are restrained.

As a concluding remark, we note that our model has portrayed all outsiders as wishing to become insiders. We require however only that the insider vacancies are contestable. This is compatible with the personal choice that people make to remain political outsiders, and recognizes that many people in the population of outsiders find participation in contests to become political insiders ethically distasteful. Outsiders can contemplate other responses. If they are geographically concentrated, they might attempt to escape by secession (see Buchanan and Faith, 1987), or they might seek to escape by emigration (on emigration of outsiders, see Epstein et al., 1999). They might also seek to resist by civil disobedience (see Grossman and Kim, 1995; Falkinger 1999).

---

[24] The monetary value of manufacturing output is artificially inflated by declarations of value that are not put to the test of market valuation; barter is prominent and monetary exchange is not, because barter sustains the artificially inflated declarations of value.

[25] See Grossman (1995) for a model with such voluntary redistribution incentives.

[26] See also Buchanan (1993) on attributes of the constitution.

208   A.L. Hillman, H.W. Ursprung / European Journal of Political Economy 16 (2000) 189–213

Acknowledgements

In revising this paper, we have benefited from the helpful insights of Martin McGuire. We have also benefited from the comments of participants at the Conference on Financial Instability and Longer-Term Prospects for Economic Transformation in Russia, sponsored by the Education and Research Consortium, Moscow, in December 1998, and the Conference on Political Culture, Economic Policy, and Economic Performance, at the Tinbergen Institute, Erasmus University, Rotterdam, in February 1999. We acknowledge the support of the Max Planck Prize in undertaking this joint research.

Appendix A. Proof of Proposition 1

The tax rates t_S and t_C are determined in Eqs. (12) and (27), respectively. Since t_C is an increasing function of ε, t_C can only exceed t_S if the condition $t_C(\varepsilon = 1) > t_S$ is satisfied, and does so for ε sufficiently close to unity. Using Eqs. (12) and (27) we arrive at

$$t_C(\varepsilon = 1) > t_S \Leftrightarrow \frac{n_O}{N} + \frac{\hat{M}}{b} < \frac{15}{4}. \tag{A1}$$

The equilibrium level of political support M_C in regime C is given by (see Eqs. (25), (27) and (28))

$$M_C = \frac{b^2 \varepsilon^2}{4}. \tag{A2}$$

For $M < M_C$, we thus have

$$\frac{\hat{M}}{b} < \frac{b\varepsilon^2}{4} \tag{A3}$$

and since $b < 2$ (see note 11), condition (A1) is satisfied

$$\frac{n_O}{N} + \frac{\hat{M}}{b} < \frac{n_O}{N} + \frac{b\varepsilon^2}{4} < \frac{6}{4} < \frac{15}{4}. \tag{A4}$$

Comparing rent-dissipation under the two regimes with the help of Eqs. (13) and (29) immediately yields

$$t_C < t_S \Leftrightarrow V_C < V_S. \tag{A5}$$

The relationship between the size of the state sector as defined by S and the tax rate (see Eqs. (14) and (24) for the regimes S and C, respectively) represents a Laffer curve with a maximum at $t = 1/2$

$$S_K = t_K(1 - t_K)N, \quad K = S,C. \tag{A6}$$

A.L. Hillman, H.W. Ursprung / European Journal of Political Economy 16 (2000) 189–213   209

Thus, as long as $t_C < 1/2$, i.e. as long as we are on the upward-sloping side of the Laffer curve (Eq. (A6)) we have

$$t_C > t_S \Leftrightarrow S_C > S_S \tag{A7}$$

which completes the proof.

Appendix B. Proof of Proposition 2

Substituting Eq. (33) in Eq. (25) yields

$$M_L = b\varepsilon \frac{t_L}{1 - (1 - \varepsilon)t_L} - t_L^2. \tag{A8}$$

Comparing this expression with Eq. (26), we arrive at the common government objective function for the regimes C and L

$$M_K = b\varepsilon \frac{t_K}{1 - (1 - \delta\varepsilon)t_K} - t_K^2, \quad \text{where } \delta = \begin{cases} 1, \text{ for } K = \text{L} \\ 1/\varepsilon, \text{ for } K = \text{C} \end{cases}. \tag{A9}$$

Since we envisage interior solutions of t_L, we derive the first-order condition for political-support maximization

$$\frac{\partial M_K}{\partial t_K} = \frac{\varepsilon b}{\left[1 - (1 - \delta\varepsilon)t_K\right]^2} - 2t_K = 0 \tag{A10}$$

and apply the implicit function rule to obtain

$$\frac{\partial t_K}{\partial \delta} = \frac{\varepsilon^2 b t_K}{\left[1 - (1 - \delta\varepsilon)t_K\right]^3} \bigg/ \frac{\partial^2 M}{\partial t_K^2} \tag{A11}$$

which is negative given that the second-order condition of political-support maximization is satisfied. A regime change from C to L is associated with a decrease in δ from $1/\varepsilon > 1$ to 1. We thus have $t_L > t_C$.

To compare S_L with S_C we use Eqs. (24) and (27) to arrive at

$$\frac{dS_C}{d\varepsilon} = \frac{bN}{2}(1 - b\varepsilon). \tag{A12}$$

Differentiating S_L with respect to ε yields

$$\frac{dS_L}{d\varepsilon} = \frac{\partial S_L}{\partial \varepsilon} + \frac{\partial S_L}{\partial t_L} \frac{\partial t_L}{\partial \varepsilon} \tag{A13}$$

and using Eqs. (32) and (A10) to compute the partial derivatives we obtain

$$\frac{dS_L}{d\varepsilon} = -\frac{t_L^2(1 - t_L)N}{Z^2} + \frac{bN}{Z^2}(1 - 2t_L + (1 - \varepsilon)t_L^2)\frac{(1 + \varepsilon)t_L - 1}{2\varepsilon(1 - \varepsilon)b - 2Z^3}, \tag{A14}$$

Arye L. Hillman and Heinrich W. Ursprung

where $Z = 1 - (1 - \varepsilon)t_L$. At $\varepsilon = 1$ we have $t_L = t_C = b/2$ since the first-order condition in Eq. (A10) coincides for the two regimes. Thus,

$$\frac{dS_L}{d\varepsilon}(\varepsilon = 1) = \frac{bN}{8}(4 - 10b + 5b^2). \tag{A15}$$

Combining Eqs. (A12) and (A15), we arrive at

$$\frac{dS_C}{d\varepsilon}(\varepsilon = 1) - \frac{dS_L}{d\varepsilon}(\varepsilon = 1) = \frac{b^2 N}{8}(6 - 5b) > 0 \Leftrightarrow b < 6/5. \tag{A16}$$

For $b < 6/5$ and ε sufficiently close to unity we thus obtain $S_L > S_C$ since $S_L(\varepsilon = 1) = S_C(\varepsilon = 1)$.

To compare the extent of rent dissipation under the two regimes, we proceed just as above and compute, using Eqs. (27) and (29),

$$\frac{dV_L}{d\varepsilon} = \frac{bN}{2}. \tag{A17}$$

We then use Eqs. (33) and (A10) to compute the expression

$$\frac{dV_L}{d\varepsilon} = \frac{\partial V_L}{\partial \varepsilon} + \frac{\partial V_L}{\partial t_L}\frac{\partial t_L}{\partial \varepsilon} \tag{A18}$$

and arrive at

$$\frac{dV_L}{d\varepsilon} = \frac{t_L(1 - t_L)N}{Z^2} + \frac{\varepsilon N}{Z^2}\frac{[(1 + \varepsilon)t_L - 1]b}{2\varepsilon(1 - \varepsilon)b - 2Z^3}. \tag{A19}$$

At $\varepsilon = 1$, we again have $t_L = t_C = b/2$ and thus obtain

$$\frac{dV_L}{d\varepsilon}(\varepsilon = 1) = \frac{bN}{2}\left(2 - \frac{3}{2}b\right). \tag{A20}$$

Comparing Eq. (A17) with Eq. (A20), we arrive at

$$\frac{dV_L}{d\varepsilon}(\varepsilon = 1) < \frac{dV_C}{d\varepsilon} \Leftrightarrow b > \frac{2}{3}. \tag{A21}$$

For $b > 2/3$ and ε sufficiently close to unity we thus obtain $V_L > V_C$ and the proof is complete.

Appendix C. Proof of Proposition 3

Since the number of interest groups m appears only in the parameter ε, we consider the consequences of an increase in political competitiveness

A.L. Hillman, H.W. Ursprung / European Journal of Political Economy 16 (2000) 189–213 211

$\varepsilon = \alpha\theta(m - 1)/m$. Assuming again an interior equilibrium $t_L \in (0,1)$, the first-order condition (Eq. A10) is satisfied and we obtain

$$\frac{dt_L}{d\varepsilon} = \frac{[(1 + \varepsilon)t_L - 1]b}{2\varepsilon(1 - \varepsilon)b - 2Z^3}. \tag{A22}$$

At $\varepsilon = 1$, using $t_L(\varepsilon = 1) = b/2$, we have $dt_L/d\varepsilon(\varepsilon = 1) = b(1 - b)/2$ for $b < 1$ and thus $dt_L/dm > 0$ for ε close to unity and $b < 1$.

Turning, finally, to rent dissipation, we see immediately from Eq. (A20) that

$$\frac{dV_L}{d\varepsilon}(\varepsilon = 1) = \frac{bN}{2}\left(2 - \frac{2}{3}b\right) > 0 \Leftrightarrow b < \frac{4}{3}. \tag{A23}$$

Thus, for $b < 4/3$ and ε sufficiently close to unity, $dV_L/dm > 0$, which completes the proof.

References

Abel, I., Bonin, J., 1994. State desertion and credit market failure in the transition. Acta Oeconomica 46, 97–122. In: Abel, I., Siklos, P.L., Szekely, I. (Eds.), Money and Finance in the Transition to a Market Economy. Edward Elgar, Cheltenham.

Åslund, A., 2000. Problems with economic transformation in Ukraine. In: Blejer, M.I., Škreb, M. (Eds.), Transition: The First Decade. Kluwer Academic Publishing, Boston.

Bernholz, P., 1991. The constitution of totalitarianism. Journal of Institutional and Theoretical Economics 147, 424–440.

Blanchard, O., 1997. The Economics of Post-Communist Transition. Oxford Univ. Press, New York.

Blanchard, O., Kremer, M., 1997. Disorganization. Quarterly Journal of Economics 112, 1091–1126.

Blejer, M.I., Škreb, M. (Eds.), Transition: The First Decade. Kluwer Academic Publishing, Boston.

Brainerd, E., 1998. Winners and losers in Russia's economic transition. American Economic Review 88, 1094–1116.

Buchanan, J.M., 1975. The Limits of Liberty: Between Anarchy and Leviathan. University of Chicago Press, Chicago.

Buchanan, J.M., 1993. How can constitutions be designed so that politicians who seek to serve the public interest can survive? Constitutional Political Economy 4, 1–6.

Buchanan, J.M., Faith, R., 1987. Secession and the limits of taxation: towards a theory of internal exit. American Economic Review 77, 1023–1031.

Conrad, R., 1998. Reforming the Russian tax system, Paper presented at the Conference on Financial Instability and Longer-Term Prospects of Economic Transformation in Russia, Moscow.

Cornes, R., Sandler, T., 1996. The Theory of Externalities, Public Goods, and Club Goods. Cambridge Univ. Press, Cambridge, MA.

Ellman, M., 1994. The increase in death and disease under katastroika. Cambridge Journal of Economics 18, 329–355.

Epstein, G., Hillman, A.L., Ursprung, H.W., 1999. The king never emigrates. Review of Development Economics 3, 107–121.

Falkinger, J., 1999. Social instability and the distribution of income. European Journal of Political Economy 15, 35–51.

Fiorentini, G., Peltzman, S. (Eds.), The Economics of Organized Crime. Cambridge Univ. Press, New York.

212   *A.L. Hillman, H.W. Ursprung / European Journal of Political Economy 16 (2000) 189–213*

Gaddy, C.G., Ickes, B.W., 1998. Russia's virtual economy. Foreign Affairs 77, 53–67.

Gelb, A., Hillman, A.L., Ursprung, H.W., 1996. Rents and the transition, World Development Report background paper, the World Bank, Washington, DC, revised as Rents as distractions: why the exit from transition is prolonged, In Baltas, N.C., Demopoulos, G., Hassid, J. (Eds.), 1998. Economic Interdependence and Cooperation in Europe, Springer, 21–38.

Grossman, H.I., 1995. Robin Hood and the distribution of income. European Journal of Political Economy 11, 399–410.

Grossman, H.I., Kim, M., 1995. Swords or plowshares: a theory of security to the claims to property. Journal of Political Economy 102, 1275–1288.

Grossman, H.I., Kim, M., 2000. Predation, moral decay, and moral revivals. European Journal of Political Economy 16, 173–187, This issue,.

Guttman, J., Nitzan, S., Spiegel, U., 1992. Rent seeking and social investment in taste change. Economics and Politics 4, 31–42.

Hillman, A.L., Katz, E., 1987. Hierarchical structure and the social costs of bribes and transfers. Journal of Public Economics 34, 129–142. In: Fiorentini, G., Zamagni, S. (Eds.), The Economics of Corruption and Illegal Markets. Edward Elgar, Cheltenham.

Hillman, A.L., Riley, J., 1989. Politically contestable rents and transfers. Economics and Politics 1, 17–39. In: Bhagwati, J., Rosendorff, P. (Eds.), Readings in the Political Economy of Trade Policy. MIT Press, Cambridge, MA, p. 2001.

Hillman, A.L., Schnytzer, A., 1986. Illegal activities and purges in a Soviet-type economy: a rent-seeking perspective. International Review of Law and Economics 6, 87–99.

Hirshleifer, J., 1995. Anarchy and its breakdown. Journal of Political Economy 103, 26–52.

Hobbes, T., 1651. Leviathan. .

IDEM Foundation, 1998. Russia versus Corruption: Who Will Win? Council of Foreign and Defense Policy, Moscow.

Kaufman, D., 1997. The missing pillar of a growth strategy for Ukraine, HIID discussion paper, Harvard University.

Kisunko, G., 1996. Economic crime in Russia. In: Transition 7 7–8 The World Bank, Washington, DC, pp. 13–16.

Koford, K., 2000. Citizen restraints on Leviathan government: transition politics in Bulgaria. European Journal of Political Economy 16.

Konrad, K., Skaperdas, S., 1998. Extortion. Economica 65, 461–477.

Levin, M., Satarov, G.A., 2000. Corruption and institutions in Russia. European Journal of Political Economy 16.

Locke, J., 1690. Two Treatises of Government. .

Matveenko, V., Vostroknoutov, K., Bouev, M., 1998. Transformation decline and preconditions for growth in Russia, EER Consortium Moscow, Russian Economics Research Program, working paper, 98-03.

McChesney, F.S., 1997. Money for Nothing. Harvard University Press, Cambridge, MA.

McGuire, M.C., Olson, M., 1996. The economics of autocracy and majority rule: the invisible hand and the use of force. Journal of Economic Literature 34, 72–96.

Muço, M., 1998. The Financial System in Albania. National Bank of Albania, Tirana.

Nekipelov, A., 1998. Setting Russia's economy on a new path. In: Transition 9 5–12 The World Bank, Washington, DC.

North, D., 1990. Institutions, Institutional Change, and Economic Performance. Cambridge Univ. Press, New York.

Nuti, D.M., 2000. Belarus: a command economy without central planning. In: Blejer, M.I., Škreb, M. (Eds.), Transition: The First Decade. Kluwer Academic Publishing, Boston.

Potters, J., Sloof, R., van Winden, F.A.A., 1997. Campaign expenditures, contributions, and direct endorsements: the strategic use of information and money to influence voter behavior. European Journal of Political Economy 13, 1–31.

A.L. Hillman, H.W. Ursprung / European Journal of Political Economy 16 (2000) 189–213   213

Rowley, C.K., 1999. Constitutional political economy and civil society. In: Mudambi, R., Navarra, P., Sobbrio, G. (Eds.), Rules and Reasons: Constitutional Issues in Modern Democracies. Cambridge Univ. Press, New York.

Sandler, T., 1992. Collective Action. University of Michigan Press, Ann Arbor.

Skaperdas, S., 1992. Cooperation, conflict, and power in the absence of property rights. American Economic Review 82, 720–739.

Tullock, G., 1965. Entry barriers in politics. American Economic Review 55, 458–466.

Tullock, G. (Ed.), Explorations in the Theory of Anarchy. Center for the Study of Public Choice, Blacksburg.

Tullock, G., 1980a. Efficient rent seeking. In: Buchanan, J.M., Tollison, R.D., Tullock, G. (Eds.), Toward a Theory of the Rent Seeking Society. Texas A&M Press, College Station, pp. 97–112.

Tullock, G., 1980b. Rent seeking as a negative sum game. In: Buchanan, J.M., Tollison, R.D., Tullock, G. (Eds.), Toward a Theory of the Rent Seeking Society. Texas A&M Press, College Station, pp. 16–36.

Tullock, G., 1988. The Economics of Rent Seeking and Privilege. Kluwer Academic Publishing, Boston.

Umbeck, J., 1981. Might makes right: a theory of the foundation and initial distribution of property rights. Economic Enquiry 19, 38–59.

Ursprung, H.W., 1990. Public goods, rent dissipation, and candidate competition. Economics and Politics 2, 115–132.

Wärneryd, K., 1993. Anarchy, uncertainty, and the emergence of property rights. Economics and Politics 5, 1–14.

The Economic Journal, 116 (January), 1–20. © Royal Economic Society 2006. Published by Blackwell Publishing, 9600 Garsington Road, Oxford OX4 2DQ, UK and 350 Main Street, Malden, MA 02148, USA.

INSTITUTIONS AND THE RESOURCE CURSE*

Halvor Mehlum, Karl Moene and Ragnar Torvik

Countries rich in natural resources constitute both growth losers and growth winners. We claim that the main reason for these diverging experiences is differences in the quality of institutions. More natural resources push aggregate income down, when institutions are grabber friendly, while more resources raise income, when institutions are producer friendly. We test this theory building on Sachs and Warner's influential works on the resource curse. Our main hypothesis – that institutions are decisive for the resource curse – is confirmed. Our results contrast the claims of Sachs and Warner that institutions do not play a role.

One important finding in development economics is that natural resource abundant economies tend to grow slower than economies without substantial resources. For instance, growth losers, such as Nigeria, Zambia, Sierra Leone, Angola, Saudi Arabia and Venezuela, are all resource-rich, while the Asian tigers: Korea, Taiwan, Hong Kong and Singapore, are all resource-poor. On average resource abundant countries lag behind countries with less resources.[1] Yet we should not jump to the conclusion that all resource rich countries are cursed. Also many growth winners such as Botswana, Canada, Australia, and Norway are rich in resources. Moreover, of the 82 countries included in a World Bank study, five countries belong both to the top eight according to their natural capital wealth and to the top 15 according to per capita income (World Bank, 1994).

To explain these diverging experiences this article investigates to what extent growth winners and growth losers differ systematically in their institutional arrangements. As a first take we plot in Figure 1 the average yearly economic growth from 1965 to 1990 versus resource abundance in countries that have more than 10 % of their GDP as resource exports. In our data set this group consists of 42 countries. Panel (a) is based on data from all 42 countries and the plot gives a strong indication that there is a resource curse. In panel (b) and (c), however, we have split the sample in two subsamples of equal size, according to the quality of institutions (a measure to be discussed below). Now the indication of a resource curse only appears for countries with inferior institutions – panel (b); while the indication of a resource curse vanishes for countries with better institutions –

---

* We are grateful to two anonymous referees and editor Andrew Scott for their constructive suggestions. We also thank Jens Chr. Andvig, Carl-Johan Lars Dalgaard, James A. Robinson and a number of seminar participants for valuable comments.

[1] This is documented in Sachs and Warner (1995, 1997a, b), Auty (2001). See also Gelb (1988), Lane and Tornell (1996) and Gylfason et al. (1999). Stijns (2002), however, argues that these results are less robust than the authors claim. It should furthermore be noted that concerns about specialising in natural resource exports was raised by economists well before the recent resource curse literature. Notably, Raol Prebisch and Hans Singer argued more than fifty years ago that countries relying on exports of primary goods would face sluggish growth of demand and declining terms of trade.

(a)

All resource rich countries

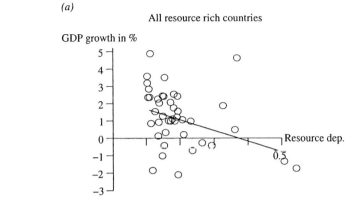

(b)

With bad institutions

(c)

With good institutions

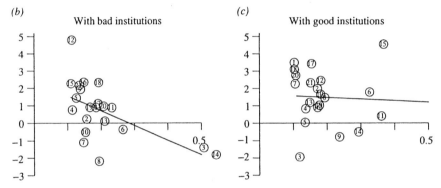

Fig. 1. *Resources and Institutions (a) all resource rich countries (b) with bad institutions*
(c) with good institutions

panel (c).[2] This basic result survives when we control for other factors in the empirical section of the article.

On this basis we assert that the variance of growth performance among resource rich countries is primarily due to how resource rents are distributed via the institutional arrangement.[3] The distinction we make is between producer friendly

[2] The regression for the total sample of 42 countries in panel (a) gives a correlation of $R^2 = 0.11$ and a significant slope of -6.15. The regression for the 21 coutries with worst institutional quality in panel (b) gives an R^2 of 0.35 and a significant slope of -8.46. The regression for the 21 countries with the best institutional quality in panel (c) gives an R^2 of 0.00 and an insignificant slope of -0.92.

The countries in panel (b) are numbered as follows: 1 Bolivia, 2 El Salvador, 3 Guyana, 4 Guatemala, 5 Philippines, 6 Uganda, 7 Zaire, 8 Nicaragua, 9 Nigeria, 10 Peru, 11 Honduras, 12 Indonesia, 13 Ghana, 14 Zambia, 15 Morocco, 16 Sri Lanka, 17 Togo, 18 Algeria, 19 Zimbabwe, 20 Malawi, 21 Dominican Rep. The countries in panel (c) are numbered as follows: 1 Tunisia, 2 Tanzania, 3 Madagascar, 4 Jamaica, 5 Senegal, 6 Gabon, 7 Ecuador, 8 Costa Rica, 9 Venezuela, 10 Kenya, 11 Gambia, 12 Cameroon, 13 Chile, 14 Ivory Coast, 15 Malaysia, 16 South Africa, 17 Ireland, 18 Norway, 19 New Zealand, 20 Belgium, 21 Netherlands.

[3] In focusing on the decisive role of institutions for economic development we are inspired by North and Thomas (1973), Knack and Keefer (1995), Engerman and Sokoloff (2000) and Acemoglu *et al.* (2001).

institutions, where rent-seeking and production are complementary activities, and grabber friendly institutions, where rent-seeking and production are competing activities. With grabber friendly institutions there are gains from specialisation in unproductive influence activities, for instance due to a weak rule of law, malfunctioning bureaucracy, and corruption. Grabber friendly institutions can be particularly bad for growth when resource abundance attracts scarce entrepreneurial resources out of production and into unproductive activities. With producer friendly institutions, however, rich resources attract entrepreneurs into production, implying higher growth.

Our approach contrasts the rent-seeking story that Sachs and Warner (1995) considered but dismissed in favour of a Dutch disease explanation. The rent-seeking hypothesis they explored states that resource abundance leads to a deterioration of institutional quality in turn lowering economic growth. Sachs and Warner found that this mechanism was empirically unimportant. However, the lack of evidence for institutional decay caused by resource abundance is not sufficient to dismiss the role of institutions. Institutions may be decisive for *how* natural resources affect economic growth even if resource abundance has no effect on institutions. We claim that natural resources put the institutional arrangements to a test, so that the resource curse only appears in countries with inferior institutions.

This hypothesis is consistent with observations from several countries. Botswana, with 40% of GDP stemming from diamonds, has had the world's highest growth rate since 1965. Acemoglu *et al.* (2002) attribute this remarkable performance to the good institutions of Botswana. (Among African countries Botswana has the best score on the Groningen Corruption Perception Index.) Another example is Norway – one of Europe's poorest countries in 1900, but now one of its richest. The growth was led by natural resources such as timber, fish and hydroelectric power and more recently oil and natural gas. Norway is considered one of the least corrupt countries in the world. Similarly, in the century following 1850 the US exploited natural resources intensively. David and Wright (1997) argue that the positive feedbacks of this resource extraction explain much of the later economic growth.[4]

There are also many examples of slow growth among resource rich countries with weak institutions. Lane and Tornell (1996) and Tornell and Lane (1999) explain the disappointing economic performance after the oil windfalls in Nigeria, Venezuela, and Mexico by dysfunctional institutions that invite grabbing. Ades and Di Tella (1999) use cross-country regressions to show how natural resource rents may stimulate corruption among bureaucrats and politicians. Acemoglu *et al.* (2004) argue that higher resource rents make it easier for dictators to buy off political challengers. In the Congo the 'enormous natural resource wealth including 15% of the world's copper deposits, vast amounts of diamonds, zinc, gold, silver, oil, and many other resources [. . .] gave Mobutu a constant flow of income to help sustain his power'. (p. 171) Resource abundance increases the political benefits of buying votes

---

[4] See also Clay and Wright (2003) for a study of the California Gold Rush and the establishment of private institutions to regulate property rights and access to a non-renewable resource.

through inefficient redistribution. Such perverse political incentives of resource abundance are only mitigated in countries with adequate institutions. On this our approach complements recent political economy papers such as Acemoglu and Robinson (2002), Robinson et al. (2002) and Acemoglu et al. (2004).

Other examples of slow growth among resource rich countries are the many cases where the government is unable to provide basic security. In such countries resource abundance stimulate violence, theft and looting, by financing rebel groups, warlord competition (Skaperdas, 2002), or civil wars. In their study of civil wars Collier and Hoeffler (2000) find that 'the extent of primary commodity exports is the largest single influence on the risk of conflict' (p. 26). The consequences for growth can be devastating. Lane (1958) argues that 'the most weighty single factor in most periods of growth, if any one factor has been most important, has been a reduction in the resources devoted to war' (p. 413).

Our main focus in the theoretical part of the article is the allocation of entrepreneurs between production and unproductive rent extraction (grabbing). Clearly grabbing harms economic development. Depending on the quality of institutions, however, lootable resources may or may not induce entrepreneurs to specialise in grabbing. In the empirical part we build on Sachs and Warner (1997a), whose result that natural resource abundance affects growth negatively has earlier been shown to be rather robust when controlling for other factors: see Sachs and Warner (1995, 1997a, b, 2001). We extend these growth regressions by allowing for the growth effects of natural resources to depend on the quality of institutions. Our main finding is that the resource curse applies in countries with grabber friendly institutions but not in countries with producer friendly institutions.

This finding is consistent with our model but is in contrast to earlier resource curse models, such as the Dutch disease models by van Wijnbergen (1984), Krugman (1987) and Sachs and Warner (1995),[5] and the rent-seeking models by Lane and Tornell (1996), Tornell and Lane (1999) and Torvik (2002). All these models imply that there is an unconditional negative relationship between resource abundance and growth.

1. Grabbing Versus Production

In the model the total number of entrepreneurs is denoted by $N = n_P + n_G$, where n_P are producers while n_G are grabbers. Grabbers target rents from natural resources R and use all their capacity to appropriate as much as possible of this rent. To what extent grabbing succeeds depends on the institutions of the country. In the model the institutional quality is captured by the parameter λ, which reflects the degree to which the institutions favour grabbers versus producers. Formally λ measures the resource rents accruing to each producer relative to that accruing to each grabber. When $\lambda = 0$, the system is completely grabber friendly such that grabbers extract the entire rent, each of them obtaining R/n_G. A higher λ implies a more producer friendly institutional arrangement. When $\lambda = 1$, there are no gains

---

[5] See Torvik (2001) for a discussion of the Dutch disease models.

from specialisation in grabbing as both grabbers and producers each obtain the share R/N of resources. In other words, $1/\lambda$ indicates the relative resource gain from specialising in grabbing activities. In countries where λ is low, this relative gain is large. Clearly, in this case rent appropriation and production are competing activities. In countries where λ is higher, however, rent appropriation and production may become complementary. The higher is λ, the lower is the resource gain from specialising in grabbing and the less willing are entrepreneurs to give up the profits from production to become grabbers.

The pay-off π_G to each grabber is a factor s times R/N

$$\pi_G = sR/N \qquad (1)$$

while each producer's share of the resource rent is $\lambda sR/N$. The factor s is decreasing in λ since each grabber gets less the more producer friendly the institutions. There is also a positive effect on s from less competition between grabbers. Hence, the value of s is an increasing function of the fraction of producers $\alpha = n_P/N$ and a decreasing function of the institutional parameter λ. The sum of shares of the resource rent that accrue to each group of entrepreneurs, cannot exceed one. Hence, the following constraint must hold

$$(1 - \alpha)s + \alpha\lambda s \leq 1. \qquad (2)$$

To err on the safe side we assume that sharing of the resource rents does not imply direct waste. When no rents are wasted in the sharing, the condition (2) must hold with equality, implying that

$$s = s(\alpha, \lambda) \equiv \frac{1}{(1 - \alpha) + \lambda\alpha}. \qquad (3)$$

In fact, $s(\alpha, \lambda)$ is a much used contest success function in the rent-seeking literature and is a special case of the function used by Tullock (1975).

The profits of a producer π_P is the sum of profits from production π and the share of the resource rents $\lambda sR/N$. Hence,

$$\pi_P = \pi + \lambda s(\alpha, \lambda)R/N. \qquad (4)$$

In order to determine profits from production, π, we now turn to the productive part of the economy. Since we are interested in how natural resources affect incentives to industrialise we embed our mechanism in a development model with joint economies in modernisation. We follow Murphy *et al.* (1989) simple formalisation of Rosenstein-Rodan's (1943) idea about demand complementarities between industries.

There are L workers and M different goods; each good can be produced in a modern firm or in a competitive fringe. In the fringe the firms have a constant returns to scale technology where one unit of labour produces one unit of the good. Hence, the real wage in the fringe and the equilibrium wage of the economy is equal to unity. A modern firm applies an increasing returns to scale technology. Each modern firm is run by one entrepreneur and requires a minimum of F units of labour. Each worker beyond F produces $\beta > 1$ units of output. Hence, the marginal cost is $1/\beta < 1$.

Assuming equal expenditure shares in consumption, inelastic demand and Bertrand price competition, it follows that:

(i) all M goods are produced in equal quantities y and all have a price equal to one. Hence total production is My.

(ii) each good is either produced entirely by the fringe or entirely by one single modern firm.

To see this, observe that the fringe can always supply at a price equal to unity. Price competition à la Bertrand implies that the modern firm sets a price just below the marginal cost of its competitors. A single modern firm in an industry only competes against the fringe and the price is set equal to one. If a second modern firm enters the same industry competition drives the price down to $1/\beta$, implying negative profits for both. Hence, only one modern firm will enter each branch of industry.

Profits from modern production are therefore

$$\pi = \left(1 - \frac{1}{\beta}\right)y - F. \tag{5}$$

Total income Y consists of resource rents, R, in addition to the value added in production, yM. Total income Y is also equal the sum of wage income, L, and the sum of profits to producers and grabbers:

$$Y = R + My = N[\alpha\pi_P + (1 - \alpha)\pi_G] + L. \tag{6}$$

Inserting in (6) from (1) and (4) it follows when taking into account the no waste condition (3) that

$$Y = R + My = L + R + n_P\pi. \tag{7}$$

Combining the latter equality with (5), and solving for y, we get[6]

$$y = \frac{\beta(L - n_P F)}{\beta(M - n_P) + n_P}. \tag{8}$$

In an economy without modern firms, total income is equal to $L + R$. In a completely industrialised economy ($n_P = \alpha N = M$) total income equals $\beta(L - MF) + R$. We assume that the income in a completely industrialised economy is higher than in an economy without modern firms, implying that the marginal productivity in modern firms β is sufficiently high:

$$\beta(L - MF) + R > L + R \iff \beta > \frac{L}{(L - MF)}. \tag{9}$$

---

[6] Assuming that the natural resource R consists of the same basket of goods that are previously produced in the economy, or (more realistic) that the natural resource is traded in a consumption basket equivalent to the one the country already consumes. This simplifies the analysis as production of all goods will be symmetric as in Murphy *et al.* (1989). For analysis of demand composition effects of natural resources, the cornerstone in the 'Dutch disease' literature, see for example van Wijnbergen (1984), Krugman (1987), Sachs and Warner (1995) and Torvik (2001). For rent-seeking models with demand composition effects, see Baland and Francois (2000) and Torvik (2002).

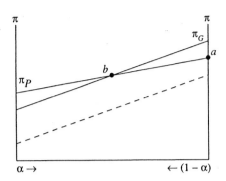

Fig. 2.   *Resources and Rent Seeking*

We also assume that there always is a scarcity of producing entrepreneurs, implying that $N < M$. By inserting from (8) in (5) it follows that π can be written as a function of the number of productive entrepreneurs

$$\pi = \pi(n_P). \tag{10}$$

We can show that as a result of (9) $\pi(n_P)$ is everywhere positive and increasing in the number of producers $n_P = \alpha N$.[7] The total profits (including resource rents) to each producer are

$$\pi_P = \pi(\alpha N) + \lambda s(\alpha, \lambda) R/N. \tag{11}$$

Or equivalently, using (1),

$$\pi_P = \pi(\alpha N) + \lambda \pi_G. \tag{12}$$

The equilibrium allocation of entrepreneurs, between production and grabbing, is determined by the relative profits of the two activities from (1) and (11). Both profit functions π_G and π_P are increasing in the fraction of producers α. This is illustrated in Figure 2, where the dashed curve represents a lower π_G-curve. The π_G-curve is high relative to the π_P-curve if the institutional quality λ is low, the resource rent R is high, or the number of entrepreneurs is low. In the following we assume that the number of entrepreneurs and the profitability of modern production are sufficiently high to rule out the possibility of equilibria without a single producer. Formally,

$$\frac{R}{N} \leq \pi(0). \tag{13}$$

This condition states that some entrepreneurs find it worthwhile to produce rather than to grab, even in cases where institutions are completely grabber friendly. It follows by inserting $\alpha = 0$ and $\lambda = 0$ in the inequality $\pi_P \geq \pi_G$.

Now the economy may be in one of the following two types of equilibria:

---

[7] Since π is positive entrepreneurs will always choose to be active either as producers or grabbers.

(a) *Production equilibrium,* where all entrepreneurs are producers ($\pi_P \geq \pi_G$ and $\alpha = 1$), is illustrated by point a in Figure 2. In this case π_G is represented by the dashed curve in the Figure.

(b) *Grabber equilibrium,* where some entrepreneurs are producers and some are grabbers ($\pi_P = \pi_G$ and $\alpha \in (0, 1)$), is illustrated by point b in Figure 2. In this case π_G is drawn as a solid curve in the Figure.

It follows from (7) that in the production equilibrium total income is

$$Y = N\pi(N) + R + L. \tag{14}$$

In the grabber equilibrium the basic arbitrage equation $\pi_P = \pi_G$ can, when using (12), be expressed as

$$\pi_P(1 - \lambda) = \pi(\alpha N). \tag{15}$$

The left-hand side of (15) is the excess resource rents that a grabber has to give up if he switches to become a producer. The right-hand side of (15) is the profit from modern production that is the gain achieved by switching. Total income in the grabber equilibrium can be found by combining (15) and (6)

$$Y = \frac{N}{1 - \lambda}\pi(\alpha N) + L. \tag{16}$$

Note that (13) implies that the π_P-curve starts out below the π_G-curve. It follows from (12), since $\pi > 0$, that when institutional quality is high relative to resource rents, the equilibrium is a production equilibrium;[8] and when institutional quality is low relative to the resource rents, the equilibrium is a grabber equilibrium. There will be an institutional threshold $\lambda = \lambda^*$ that determines in which of the two equilibria an economy ends up. From the definitions of the equilibria the institutional threshold λ^* is implicitly defined by $\pi_G = \pi_P$ and $\alpha = 1$. Inserting from (3), (11) and (12) we get

$$\lambda^* \equiv \frac{R}{R + N\pi(N)} \tag{17}$$

and we have the following Proposition:

PROPOSITION 1. *When institutional quality is high, $\lambda \geq \lambda^*$, the equilibrium is a production equilibrium. When the institutional quality is low, $\lambda < \lambda^*$, the equilibrium is a grabber equilibrium.*

This Proposition shows how natural resources put the institutional arrangement to a test. The higher the resource rents R relative to the potential production profits $N\pi(N)$, the higher is the institutional quality threshold λ^*. Accordingly, more resources require better institutions to avoid the grabber equilibrium.

The economic effects of higher resource rents in the two equilibria are quite different as the following Proposition shows:

---

[8] Clearly, irrespective of R, entrepreneurs in a country with $\lambda \geq 1$ will never enter into grabbing.

PROPOSITION 2. *More natural resources is a pure blessing in a production equilibrium – a higher R raises national income. More natural resources is a curse in a grabber equilibrium – a higher R lowers national income.*

Proof. That national income goes up with R in the production equilibrium follows directly from (14). The impact of a higher R in the grabber equilibrium follows when inserting from (1) and (11) in the equilibrium condition $\pi_P = \pi_G$ and implicitly differenting α with respect to R

$$\frac{\partial\alpha}{\partial R} = \frac{\overbrace{\left(\dfrac{\partial\pi_P}{\partial R} - \dfrac{\partial\pi_G}{\partial R}\right)}^{-}}{\underbrace{\left(\dfrac{\partial\pi_G}{\partial\alpha} - \dfrac{\partial\pi_P}{\partial\alpha}\right)}_{+}} < 0.$$

The sign of the numerator follows directly from the definitions of π_P and π_G. The sign of the denominator follows as π_G as a function of α crosses π_P from below (Figure 1 and (13)). Knowing that α is decreasing in R the Proposition is immediate from (16). ∎

The result that more resources reduce total income may appear paradoxical. There are two opposing effects: *the immediate income effect* of a higher resource rent R is a one to one increase in national income; *the displacement effect* reduces national income as entrepreneurs move from production to grabbing. The resource curse follows as the displacement effect is stronger than the immediate income effect. An entrepreneur who moves out of production forgoes the profit from modern production $\pi(n_P)$, but obtains an additional share of the resource rent equal to $(1 - \lambda)sR/N$. In equilibrium (15) these two values are equal. With more natural resources the additional resource rents to grabbers obviously go up. Hence, producers are induced to switch to grabbing until a new equilibrium is reached. It is a well-known result from the rent-seeking literature that a fixed opportunity cost of grabbing implies that a marginal rise in rents is entirely dissipated by more grabbing activities. Hence, in these models the displacement effect exactly balances the immediate income effect. In our case, however, the positive externality between producers implies that the opportunity cost of grabbing declines as entrepreneurs switch from production to grabbing. The declining opportunity cost magnifies the displacement effect and explains why the displacement effect eventually is stronger than the immediate income effect.[9]

The extent of rent dissipation also depends on the quality of institutions:

PROPOSITION 3. *In the grabber equilibrium (i.e. $\lambda < \lambda^*$) more producer friendly institutions (higher values of λ) increase profits both in grabbing and production, and thus leads to higher total income. In the production equilibrium (i.e. $\lambda \geq \lambda^*$) a further increase in λ has no implications for total income.*

---

[9] In our model resource rents in each period are exogenous. Of course, if more grabbers also mean that resources are increasingly overexploited, the effect of more grabbers may be even worse than predicted by the model. For a political economy model of overexploitation of natural resources, see Robinson *et al.* (2002).

Proof. The first part is evident from (15). The last part is evident from (14).■

Interestingly, worse opportunities for grabbers raise their incomes. The reason is that a higher value of λ induces entrepreneurs to shift from grabbing to production. As a consequence, the national income goes up, raising the demand for modern commodities, and thereby raising producer profits even further. In the new equilibrium profits from grabbing and from production are equalised at a higher level.

The extent of grabbing is also determined by the total number of entrepreneurs as stated in the following Proposition:

PROPOSITION 4. *In the grabber equilibrium a higher number of entrepreneurs N raises the number of producers n_P, lowers the number of rent-seekers n_G, and leads to higher profits in both activities.*

Proof. By differentiating the equilibrium condition $\pi_P = \pi_G$, and reasoning as in the proof of Proposition 2, it follows that $\partial\alpha/\partial N > 0$. Hence, as $n_P = \alpha N$, the value of n_P unambiguously increases with N. From (15) it follows that the common level of profits in grabbing and production must go up. Finally, it follows, when plugging (3) into (1), that $\pi_G = R/(n_G + \lambda n_P)$. Now, since both n_P and π_G increase, the number of grabbers n_G must decline.   ■

The Proposition states that a higher number of entrepreneurs is a double blessing. Not only do all new entrepreneurs go into production but their entrance also induces existing grabbers to shift over to production. The reason is the positive externality in modern production. The Proposition also states that grabbing is most severe – both absolutely and relatively – in economies where the total number of entrepreneurs is low. These results are important for the dynamics to which we now turn.

The growth of new entrepreneurs is assumed to be a fixed inflow θ of new entrepreneurs minus the exit rate δ times the number of entrepreneurs N, expressed as $dN/dt = \theta - \delta N$. When this is the case the number of entrepreneurs will grow until it reaches the long-run steady state level equal to $\bar{N} = \theta/\delta$. Countries that have little natural resources or good institutions, will in the long run end up in a production equilibrium. Using the definition of the institutional threshold λ^* in (17) we define a resource threshold R^* such that

$$\lambda = \lambda^* \equiv \frac{R}{R + \bar{N}\pi(\bar{N})} \iff R = \frac{\lambda}{1-\lambda}\bar{N}\pi(\bar{N}) \equiv R^*(\bar{N}, \lambda). \tag{18}$$

A country with institutional quality λ and with long run number of entrepreneurs $\bar{N}$ will end up in a production equilibrium if and only if $R < R^*(\bar{N}, \lambda)$. This condition assures that the resource rents (relative to the quality of institutions) are not high enough to make grabbing attractive when the total number of entrepreneurs has reached its steady state level $\bar{N}$. Countries with more resources, $R > R^*(\bar{N}, \lambda)$, are not able to avoid the grabber equilibrium in the long run.

To see how the dynamics work consider Figure 3 where we measure the number of productive entrepreneurs n_P on the horizontal axis and the value of resources R on the vertical axis. From (1), (3), and (15) it follows that in a grabber equilibrium the long-run relationship between R and n_P is

$$R = \frac{\bar{N}}{1-\lambda}\pi(n_P) - n_P\pi(n_P). \tag{19}$$

In the producer equilibrium, however, n_P is by definition equal to $\bar{N}$. Thus the long-run relationship in Figure 3 has a kink for $n_P = \bar{N}$. The kink defines the separation between the grabber and the producer equilibrium and is thus given by R^*. The long-run relationship between R and n_P is given by the bold curve in Figure 3.

In the Figure we have also drawn iso-income curves. Each curve is downward sloping as more natural resources are needed to keep the total income constant when the number of producers declines. For a fixed total income $Y = Y_i$, an iso-income curve is from (7) given by

$$R = -L - n_P\pi(n_P) + Y_i. \tag{20}$$

By comparing this expression with (19) we see that the iso-income curves are steeper than the long-run equilibrium curve, as depicted in Figure 3.

We are now ready to illustrate the implications of resource abundance and institutions on income growth. We first focus on two countries, A and B, that have the same quality of *institutions* (the same λ) and by construction the same initial *income* level. Country A has little resources, but a high number of producers, while country B has more resources and fewer producers. Country A, that starts out in point a, ends up in point d, while country B, that starts out in point b, ends up in point b'.

As seen from the Figure the resource rich country B ends up at a lower income level than the resource poor country A. The reason is that country A because of its

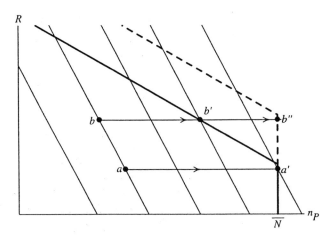

Fig. 3.   *Resources and Rent Seeking*

lack of resources, ends up in the production equilibrium, while country B because of its resource abundance ends up in the grabber equilibrium. Accordingly, over the transition period growth is lowest in the resource rich country. This is a specific example of a more general result. As proved in Proposition 2, country B would increase its growth potential if it had less resources.

Assume next that country B instead had more producer friendly institutions and thus a higher λ than country A. As country B now is more immune to grabbing, it can tolerate its resource abundance and still end up in the production equilibrium. As a result, the long-run equilibrium curve for country B shifts up, as illustrated by the dotted curve in Figure 3. With grabber friendly institutions (low λ) country B converges to point b', while with producer friendly institutions (high λ) country B converges to point b''. Income is higher in b'' than in b'. Over the transition period growth is therefore highest with producer friendly institutions. Moreover with more producer friendly institutions, the resource rich country B outperforms the resource poor country A, eliminating the resource curse.

2. Empirical Testing

Our main prediction is that the resource curse – that natural resource abundance is harmful for economic development – only hits countries with grabber friendly institutions. Thus countries with producer friendly institutions will not experience any resource curse. Natural resource abundance does therefore hinder economic growth in countries with grabber friendly institutions but does not in countries with producer friendly institutions.

This prediction challenges the Dutch disease explanation of the resource curse, emphasised in the empirical work by Sachs and Warner (1995, 1997a). They dismiss one rent-seeking mechanism by showing that there is at most a weak impact of resource abundance on institutional quality. Hence, resource abundance does not cause a deterioration of institutions. They do not, however, consider our hypothesis that a poor quality of institutions is the cause of the resource curse and that good enough institutions can eliminate the resource curse entirely. If our hypothesis is supported by the data, the role of institutions is confirmed and the Dutch disease story is less palatable.

In order to test our hypothesis against Sachs and Warner's we use their data and methodology. All the data are from Sachs and Warner and are reproduced in the appendix. For a complete description of the data sources we refer to Sachs and Warner (1997b). Our sample consists of 87 countries, limited only by data availability. We use Sachs and Warner's *Journal of African Economies* article (1997b) rather than the Harvard mimeo (1997a). The reason is that the data series in the *Journal of African Economies* article covers a longer period, a larger number of countries and contains a more suitable measure of institutional quality.[10]

[10] The data used in both papers can be downloaded from Centre for International Development at http://www.cid.harvard.edu/ciddata/ciddata.html

In the Appendix we have reported our main regression using the data from (1997a). The results differ only marginally from the results reported below.

The dependent variable is: *GDP growth* – average growth rate of real GDP *per capita* between 1965 and 1990. Explanatory variables are: *initial income level* – the log of GDP per head of the economically active population in 1965; *openness* – an index of a country's openness in the same period; *resource abundance* – the share of primary exports in GNP in 1970; *investments* – the average ratio of real gross domestic investments over GDP, and finally *institutional quality* – an index ranging from zero to unity.

The institutional quality index is an unweighted average of five indexes based on data from Political Risk Services: a rule of law index, a bureaucratic quality index, a corruption in government index, a risk of expropriation index and a government repudiation of contracts index.[11] All these characteristics capture various aspects of producer friendly versus grabber friendly institutions. The index runs from one (maximum producer friendly institutions) to zero. Hence, when the index is zero, there is a weak rule of law and a high risk of expropriation, malfunctioning bureaucracy and corruption in the government; all of which favour grabbers and deter producers.

Our first regression confirms Sachs and Warner's (1995, 1997a) results on convergence, openness and natural resource abundance.[12]

In regressions 2 and 3 we successively include institutional quality and investment share of GDP, which both have a positive impact on growth. When investment is included, however, institutional quality no longer have a significant effect.

So far our estimates have added nothing beyond what Sachs and Warner showed. Regression 4, however, provides the new insights to the understanding of the resource curse. In this regression we include the interaction term that captures the essence of our model prediction:

$$interaction\ term = resource\ abundance \times institutional\ quality.$$

Our prediction is that the resource abundance is harmful to growth only when the institutions are grabber friendly. Therefore we should expect that the interaction term has a positive coefficient. This is indeed what we find. The effect from the interaction term is both strong and significant (with a p-value of 0.019).

The growth impact of a marginal increase in resources implied by regression 4 is

$$\frac{d(growth)}{d(resource\ abundance)} = -14.34 + 15.40(institutional\ quality).$$

We see that the resource curse is weaker the higher the institutional quality. Moreover, for countries with high institutional quality (higher than the threshold $14.34/15.40 = 0.93$) the resource curse does not apply. As shown in the Appendix, 15 of the 87 countries in our sample have the sufficient institutional quality to neutralise the resource curse.

---

[11] A more detailed description of the index is provided by Knack and Keefer (1995).

[12] The minor differences in the estimated coefficients between our regression and Sachs and Warner's are caused by different starting years (ours is 1965, while theirs is 1970) and that they exclude outliers. In the Appendix we include regression results that exactly reproduce Sachs and Warner (1997a) using their data.

As mentioned in the introduction there are five countries that belong both to the top eight according to their natural capital wealth and to the top 15 according to *per capita* income. Of these countries US, Canada, Norway and Australia have an institutional quality above the threshold. The fifth, Ireland, follows close with an index value of 0.83.

Our results are also confirmed in the regressions contained in the Appendix where we use exactly the same data and countries as Sachs and Warner (1997*a*). As they did, we there use the rule of law as an indicator of the institutional quality.

One concern is that resource abundance might be correlated with some measure of underdevelopment not included in our analysis. For instance, underdevelopment can be associated with specialisation in agricultural exports, and this may drive the empirical results. Our mechanism of resource grabbing is less likely to apply in agrarian societies, as land is less lootable and taxable than most natural resources. Therefore we investigate how the results are affected by using an alternative resource measure that concentrate on lootable resources. In Regression 1 in Table 2 we use *mineral abundance* – the share of mineral production in GNP in 1971 from Sachs and Warner (1995).

The regression shows that the direct negative effect of natural resources becomes stronger and that the interaction effect increases substantially. Since resources that are easily lootable appear to be particularly harmful for growth in countries with weak institutions, our grabbing story receives additional support. A more detailed exploration of how different types of resources, in combination with institutions, affect economic growth has been done by Boschini *et al.* (2004). They use four different measures of resource abundance and show that institutions are more decisive the more appropriable the natural resources.

A possible worry is that the resource curse mechanism might be purely an African phenomenon and that it does not apply to other countries. In regression 2 in Table 2 we exclude African countries from the analysis. As seen the coefficients keep their signs, while their values are somewhat reduced. We conclude from this that the effects that we have identified in Table 1 are not solely related to African experiences and that they are not artefacts stemming from systematic differences between African and Non-African countries.

Another worry is that our estimates may be biased by leaving out important explanatory variables. In regression 3 in Table 2 we investigate whether our results survive when we control for the level of education by the secondary school enrolment rate – *secondary* – from Sachs and Warner (1995). Compared to the estimates in regression 4 in Table 1, the coefficients on resource abundance increase marginally. Moreover, there seems to be no clear connection between the secondary school enrolment rate and growth in our sample. In regressions 4 and 5 in Table 2 we control for ethnic fractionalisation – *ethnic* – and language fractionalisation – *lang* – from Alesina *et al.* (2003). Controlling for these variables again only changes the results marginally. This indicates that the growth disruptive effects that we identify are due to resources and institutions rather than ethnic conflicts. In regression 6 we include all three variables above. As seen, our estimated coefficients are quite stable and remain significant.

Table 1

Regression Results I

Dependent variable: GDP growth.

	Regression 1	Regression 2	Regression 3	Regression 4
Initial income level	−0.79*	−1.02*	−1.28*	−1.26*
	(−3.80)	(−4.38)	(−6.65)	(−6.70)
Openness	3.06*	2.49*	1.45*	1.66*
	(7.23)	(4.99)	(3.36)	(3.87)
Resource abundance	−6.16*	−5.74*	−6.69*	−14.34*
	(−4.02)	(−3.78)	(−5.43)	(−4.21)
Institutional quality		2.2*	0.6	−1.3
		(2.04)	(0.64)	(−1.13)
Investments			0.15*	0.16*
			(6.73)	(7.15)
Interaction term				15.4*
				(2.40)
Observations	87	87	87	87
Adjusted R²	0.50	0.52	0.69	0.71

Note: The numbers in brackets are t-values. A star (*) indicates that the estimate is significant at the 5-% level.

Table 2

Regression Results II

Dependent variable: GDP growth.

	Regression 1	Regression 2	Regression 3	Regression 4	Regression 5	Regression 6
Initial income level	−1.33*	−1.88*	−1.33*	−1.34*	−1.36*	−1.45*
	(−6.26)	(−7.95)	(−5.90)	(−6.97)	(−6.13)	(−5.45)
Openness	1.87*	1.34*	1.60*	1.59*	1.63*	1.56*
	(3.77)	(3.20)	(3.47)	(3.73)	(3.76)	(3.36)
Resource abundance		−10.92*	−16.35*	−13.70*	14.78*	−16.25*
		(−3.16)	(−3.71)	(−4.00)	(−4.26)	(−3.60)
Mineral abundance	−17.71*					
	(−3.16)					
Institutional quality	−0.20	1.83	−0.90	−1.15	−1.18	−0.78
	(−0.22)	(−1.35)	(−0.69)	(−0.96)	(−0.94)	(−0.56)
Investments	0.15*	0.11*	0.15*	0.15*	0.15*	0.14*
	(6.25)	(4.09)	(5.56)	(6.51)	(6.76)	(4.91)
Interaction term	29.43*	11.01	18.31*	15.86*	16.84*	19.01*
	(2.66)	(1.84)	(2.34)	(2.45)	(2.55)	(2.41)
Secondary			−0.60			−0.57
			(−0.44)			(−0.41)
Ethnic frac.				−0.88		−0.77
				(1.69)		(1.12)
Language frac.					−0.36	−0.11*
					(0.75)	(0.18)
Africa exluded	no	yes	no	no	no	no
Observations	87	59	76	86	84	74
Adjusted R²	0.63	0.79	0.70	0.71	0.70	0.70

Note: The numbers in brackets are t-values. A star (*) indicates that the estimate is significant at the 5-% level.

In our regressions there may be problems of reverse causality. Sachs and Warner (1997a, 2001) address the aspect of reverse causality between the measure of growth and the measure of natural resource abundance. They find no evidence of this. Another possibility is that the quality of institutions itself is determined by GDP. This aspect of reverse causality is addressed in Acemoglu et al. (2001). They show, by using settler mortality as an instrument for institutional quality, that the effect of institutions on income becomes stronger. Furthermore, Boschini et al. (2004) show (for a somewhat different time period than ours) that the interaction effect between resources and institutional quality is also strong and significant when institutional quality is instrumented by using the fraction of the population speaking an European language and by latitude. When Boschini et al. (2004) instrument for institutions, using settler mortality, the sample becomes smaller. The signs of the estimated coefficients remain, but some become insignificant.[13]

A final concern may be that we test our main prediction by applying Barro-type growth regressions. We could have worked with level regressions with income at the end of the period as the dependent variable – an approach similar to those of Hall and Jones (1999) and Acemoglu et al. (2001). To apply level regressions in our case requires another measure of resource abundance. We measure resource abundance relative to GDP. All else being equal, countries with high GDP would appear as resource scarce, while countries with a low GDP would appear as resource abundant. In regressions controlling for initial income this problem does not arise. Clearly, using level regressions and controlling for initial income is in effect a growth regression.

3. Concluding Remarks

Countries rich in natural resources constitute both growth losers and growth winners. We have shown that the quality of institutions determines whether countries avoid the resource curse or not. The combination of grabber friendly institutions and resource abundance leads to low growth. Producer friendly institutions, however, help countries to take full advantage of their natural resources. These results contrast the claims of Sachs and Warner that institutions are not decisive for the resource curse.

Our results also contrast the most popular Dutch disease explanations of the resource curse, that emphasise how natural resources crowd out growth generating traded goods production. Why should the crowding out of the traded goods sector be directly related to institutional quality? In particular it is hard to argue that the Dutch disease is closely related to the rule of law. In the Appendix we use the rule of law as our measure of institutional quality confirming our results. We take this as further evidence that the dangerous mix of weak institutions and resource abundance causes the resource curse.

---

[13] Institutions may also be endogenous with respect to natural resources, as argued for instance by Ross (2001a, b). Resource abundance may give politicians incentives to destroy institutions in order to be able to grab the resource rents, or to suppress democracy for the same reason. Note that this multicollinearity is not a major concern for the empirical results as the correlation between institutions and resource abundance is weak, see Sachs and Warner (1995).

University of Oslo and International Peace Research Institute, Oslo
University of Oslo and International Peace Research Institute, Oslo
Norwegian University of Science and Technology

Submitted: 18 March 2003
Accepted: 11 March 2005

Appendix

Regression Results with Sachs and Warners (1997a) Data.

In this Appendix we report the regression result when we use the data that Sachs and Warner (1997a) used. The first column exactly replicates their result. The second column reports our regression 4 with their data. Observe that rule of law has taken the place as our indicator of institutional quality, both as a stand alone variable and in the interaction term. When interpreting the results keep in mind that the rule of law index runs from 0–6 while the institutional quality index runs from 0 to 1.

Table 3

Regression Results. Dependent variable is GDP growth

	Sachs and Warner's regression	Regression 4 (alternative)
Initial income level	−1.76*	−1.82*
	(−8.56)	(−8.96)
Openess	1.33*	1.53*
	(3.35)	(3.82)
Resource abundance	−10.57*	−16.36*
	(−7.01)	(−5.06)
Rule of law	0.36*	0.18
	(3.54)	(1.32)
Investments	1.02*	0.95*
	(3.45)	(3.28)
Interaction term		1.96*
		(2.01)
Observations	71	71
Adjusted R^2	0.72	0.74

Note: The numbers in brackets are t-values. A star (*) indicates that the estimate is significant at the 5-% level.

The data are downloaded from Centre for International Development at http://www.cid.harvard.edu/ciddata/ciddata.html. A short description of the data is as follows (For a complete description, consult Sachs and Warner 1997a): *initial income level* – natural log of real GDP divided by the economically-active population in 1970. *GDP growth* – average annual growth in real GDP divided by the economically active population between 1970 and 1990. *resource abundance* – share of exports of primary products in GNP in 1970. *openness* – the fraction of years during the period 1970–1990 in which the country is rated as an open economy. *investments* – log of the ratio of real gross domestic investment (public plus private) to real GDP averaged over the period 1970–1989. *rule of law* – an index constructed by the Center for Institutional Reform and the Informal Sector which reflects the degree to which the citizens of a country are willing to accept the established institutions to make and implement laws and adjudicate disputes. Scores 0 (low) – 6 (high). Measured as of 1982. *interaction* – variable constructed by multiplying rule of law with resource abundance.

Table 4

Dataset Used in the Main Regression

COUNTRY	IQ	LGDPEA	SXP	OPEN	INV	GDP6590
BOLIVIA	0.23	7.82	0.18	0.77	15.34	0.85
HAITI	0.26	7.40	0.08	0.00	6.64	−0.25
EL SALVADOR	0.26	8.15	0.16	0.04	8.19	0.19
BANGLADESH	0.27	7.68	0.01	0.00	3.13	0.76
GUATEMALA	0.28	8.16	0.11	0.12	9.19	0.71
GUYANA	0.28	8.06	0.51	0.12	20.23	−1.47
PHILIPPINES	0.30	7.78	0.13	0.12	16.50	1.39
UGANDA	0.30	7.10	0.27	0.12	2.52	−0.41
ZAIRE	0.30	6.93	0.15	0.00	5.20	−1.15
NICARAGUA	0.30	8.45	0.19	0.00	12.19	−2.24
MALI	0.30	6.71	0.08	0.12	5.89	0.82
SYRIA	0.31	8.37	0.08	0.04	15.31	2.65
NIGERIA	0.31	7.09	0.14	0.00	15.06	1.89
PERU	0.32	8.48	0.15	0.12	17.49	−0.56
HONDURAS	0.34	7.71	0.23	0.00	13.40	0.84
INDONESIA	0.37	6.99	0.11	0.81	21.57	4.74
CONGO	0.37	7.60	0.08	0.00	9.24	2.85
GHANA	0.37	7.45	0.21	0.23	5.05	0.07
SOMALIA	0.37	7.51	0.09	0.00	9.85	−0.98
JORDAN	0.41	8.04	0.09	1.00	16.80	2.43
PAKISTAN	0.41	7.49	0.03	0.00	9.57	1.76
ZAMBIA	0.41	7.66	0.54	0.00	15.98	−1.88
ARGENTINA	0.43	8.97	0.05	0.00	16.87	−0.25
MOROCCO	0.43	7.80	0.11	0.23	11.22	2.22
SRI LANKA	0.43	7.67	0.15	0.23	10.93	2.30
TOGO	0.44	6.82	0.19	0.00	18.35	1.07
EGYPT	0.44	7.58	0.07	0.00	5.13	2.51
ALGERIA	0.44	8.05	0.19	0.00	27.14	2.28
PARAGUAY	0.44	7.88	0.10	0.08	15.53	2.06
ZIMBABWE	0.44	7.58	0.17	0.00	14.87	0.86
MALAWI	0.45	6.68	0.21	0.00	11.29	0.92
DOMINICAN REP	0.45	7.85	0.13	0.00	17.75	2.12
TUNISIA	0.46	7.81	0.10	0.08	14.54	3.44
TANZANIA	0.46	6.58	0.17	0.00	11.60	1.93
MADAGASCAR	0.47	7.63	0.12	0.00	1.39	−1.99
JAMAICA	0.47	8.32	0.14	0.38	18.85	0.78
SENEGAL	0.48	7.69	0.14	0.00	5.11	−0.01
BURKINA FASO	0.48	6.52	0.04	0.00	9.49	1.26
URUGUAY	0.51	8.67	0.09	0.04	14.34	0.88
TURKEY	0.53	8.12	0.04	0.08	22.52	2.92
COLOMBIA	0.53	8.19	0.09	0.19	15.66	2.39
GABON	0.54	8.35	0.33	0.00	28.18	1.73
MEXICO	0.54	8.82	0.02	0.19	17.09	2.22
SIERRA LEONE	0.54	7.60	0.09	0.00	1.37	−0.83
ECUADOR	0.54	8.05	0.11	0.69	22.91	2.21
COSTA RICA	0.55	8.52	0.19	0.15	17.26	1.41
GREECE	0.55	8.45	0.04	1.00	24.57	3.17
VENEZUELA	0.56	9.60	0.24	0.08	22.16	−0.84
KENYA	0.56	7.14	0.18	0.12	14.52	1.61
GAMBIA	0.56	7.17	0.36	0.19	6.05	0.35
CAMEROON	0.57	7.10	0.18	0.00	10.59	2.40
CHINA	0.57	6.94	0.02	0.00	20.48	3.35
INDIA	0.58	7.21	0.02	0.00	14.19	2.03
NIGER	0.58	7.12	0.05	0.00	9.37	−0.69
TRINIDAD & TOBAGO	0.61	9.39	0.08	0.00	13.10	0.76
ISRAEL	0.61	8.95	0.04	0.23	24.50	2.81
THAILAND	0.63	7.71	0.09	1.00	17.56	4.59

Table 4

Continued

COUNTRY	IQ	LGDPEA	SXP	OPEN	INV	GDP6590
CHILE	0.63	8.69	0.15	0.58	18.18	1.13
BRAZIL	0.64	8.16	0.05	0.00	19.72	3.10
KOREA. REP.	0.64	7.58	0.02	0.88	26.97	7.41
IVORY COAST	0.67	7.89	0.29	0.00	10.06	−0.56
MALAYSIA	0.69	8.10	0.37	1.00	26.16	4.49
SOUTH AFRICA	0.69	8.48	0.17	0.00	18.53	0.85
BOTSWANA	0.70	7.10	0.05	0.42	24.61	5.71
SPAIN	0.76	8.87	0.03	1.00	25.05	2.95
PORTUGAL	0.77	8.25	0.05	1.00	22.99	4.54
HONG KONG	0.80	8.73	0.03	1.00	20.79	5.78
ITALY	0.82	9.07	0.02	1.00	25.90	3.15
TAIWAN	0.82	8.05	0.02	1.00	24.44	6.35
IRELAND	0.83	8.84	0.15	0.96	25.94	3.37
SINGAPORE	0.86	8.15	0.03	1.00	36.01	7.39
FRANCE	0.93	9.37	0.03	1.00	26.72	2.58
U.K.	0.93	9.38	0.03	1.00	18.12	2.18
JAPAN	0.94	8.79	0.01	1.00	34.36	4.66
AUSTRALIA	0.94	9.57	0.10	1.00	27.44	1.97
AUSTRIA	0.95	9.18	0.04	1.00	25.89	2.91
GERMANY. WEST	0.96	9.41	0.02	1.00	25.71	2.37
NORWAY	0.96	9.30	0.10	1.00	32.50	3.05
SWEDEN	0.97	9.56	0.05	1.00	22.38	1.80
NEW ZEALAND	0.97	9.63	0.18	0.19	23.79	0.97
CANADA	0.97	9.60	0.10	1.00	24.26	2.74
DENMARK	0.97	9.47	0.10	1.00	24.42	2.01
FINLAND	0.97	9.21	0.07	1.00	33.81	3.08
BELGIUM	0.97	9.27	0.11	1.00	22.26	2.70
U.S.A.	0.98	9.87	0.01	1.00	22.83	1.76
NETHERLANDS	0.98	9.38	0.15	1.00	23.32	2.27
SWITZERLAND	1.00	9.74	0.02	1.00	28.88	1.57

The variables are: IQ – an index of institutional quality,
LGDPEA – the log of GDP per head of the economically active population in 1965,
SXP – the share of primary exports in GNP in 1970, OPEN – an index of a country's openness
INV – the average ratio of real gross domestic investments over GDP
GDP6590 – average growth rate of real GDP per capita between 1965 and 1990
For more details, see Sachs and Warner (1997a)

References

Acemoglu, D., Johnson, S. and Robinson, J. A. (2001). 'The colonial origins of comparative develop-ment: an empirical investigation', *American Economic Review*, vol. 91, pp. 1369–401.

Acemoglu, D., Johnson, S. and Robinson, J. A. (2002). 'An African success: Botswana', in (D. Rodrik ed.) *Analytic Development Narratives*, Princeton: Princeton University Press.

Acemoglu, D. and Robinson, J. A. (2002). 'Economic backwardness in political perspective', NBER Working Paper No. 5398.

Acemoglu, D., Robinson, J. A. and Verdier, T. (2004). 'Kleptocracy and divide-and-rule: a theory of personal rule', *Journal of the European Economic Association*, vol. 2, pp. 162–92.

Ades, A. and Di Tella, R. (1999). 'Rents, competition, and corruption', *American Economic Review*, vol. 89, pp. 982–93.

Alesina, A., Devleeschauwer, A., Easterly, W., Kurlat, S. and Wacziarg, R. (2003). 'Fractionalization', *Journal of Economic Growth*, vol. 8, pp. 155–94.

Auty R. M. (2001). *Resource Abundance and Economic Development*, Oxford: Oxford University Press.

Boschini, A. D., Pettersson, J. and Roine, J. (2004). 'Resource curse or not: a question of appropria-bility', Working Paper, Department of Economics, Stockholm University.

20   THE ECONOMIC JOURNAL   [JANUARY 2006]

Baland, J.-M. and Francois, P. (2000). 'Rent-seeking and resource booms', *Journal of Development Economics*, vol. 61, pp. 527–42.

Clay, K. and Wright, G. (2003). 'Order without law? Property rights during the California gold rush', John M. Ohlin Program in Law and Economics Working Paper 265, Stanford Law School.

Collier, P and Hoeffler, A. (2000). 'Greed and grievance in civil war', World Bank Policy Research Paper 2355.

David, P. A. and Wright, G. (1997). 'Increasing returns and the genesis of American resource abundance', *Industrial and Corporate Change*, vol. 6, pp. 203–45.

Engerman, S. L. and Sokoloff, K. L. (2000). 'Institutions, factor endowments, and paths of development in the New World', *Journal of Economic Perspectives*, vol. 14(3), pp. 217–32.

Gelb A. (1988). *Windfall Gains: Blessing or Curse?*, Oxford: Oxford University Press.

Gylfason, T., Herbertsson, T. T. and Zoega, G. (1999). 'A mixed blessing: natural resources and economic growth', *Macroeconomic Dynamics*, vol. 3, pp. 204–25.

Hall, R. E. and Jones, C. I. (1999). 'Why do some countries produce so much more output per-worker than others?', *Quarterly Journal of Economics*, vol. 114, pp. 83–116.

Knack, S. and Keefer, P. (1995). 'Institutions and economic performance: cross-country tests using alternative institutional measures', *Economics and Politics*, vol. 7, pp. 207–27.

Krugman, P. (1987). 'The narrow moving band, the Dutch disease, and the competitive consequences of Mrs. Thatcher: notes on trade in the presence of dynamic scale economies', *Journal of Development Economics*, vol. 37, pp. 41–55.

Lane, F. C. (1958). 'Economic consequences of organized violence', *Journal of Economic History*, vol. 58, pp. 401–17.

Lane, P. R. and Tornell, A. (1996). 'Power, growth and the voracity effect', *Journal of Economic Growth*, vol. 1, pp. 213–41.

Murphy, K., Shleifer, A. and Vishny, R. (1989). 'Industrialization and the big push', *Journal of Political Economy*, vol. 97, pp. 1003–26.

North, D.C. and Thomas, R.P. (1973). *The Rise of the Western World: a New Economic History*, New York: Cambridge University Press.

Robinson, J. A., Torvik, R. and Verdier, T. (2002). 'Political foundations of the resource curse', CEPR Discussion Paper No. 3422.

Rosenstein-Rodan, P. (1943). 'Problems of industrialisation of Eastern and South-Eastern Europe', ECONOMIC JOURNAL, vol. 53(210/211), pp. 202–11.

Ross, M. L. (2001a). *Timber Booms and Institutional Breakdown in Southeast Asia*, New York: Cambridge University Press.

Ross, M. L. (2001b). 'Does oil hinder democracy?', *World Politics*, vol. 53, pp. 325–61.

Sachs, J. D. and Warner, A. M. (1995). 'Natural resource abundance and economic growth', NBER Working Paper No. 5398.

Sachs, J. D. and Warner, A. M. (1997a). 'Natural resource abundance and economic growth - revised version', Working Paper, Harvard University.

Sachs, J. D. and Warner, A. M. (1997b). 'Sources of slow growth in African economies', *Journal of African Economies*, vol. 6, pp. 335–76.

Sachs, J. D. and Warner, A. M. (2001). 'The curse of natural resources', *European Economic Review*, vol. 45, pp. 827–38.

Skaperdas, S. (2002). 'Warlord competition', *Journal of Peace Research*, vol. 39, pp. 435–46.

Stijns, J. P. (2002). 'Natural resource abundance and economic growth revisited', Working Paper, Department of Economics, UC Berkeley.

Tornell, A. and Lane, P.R. (1999). 'The voracity effect', *American Economic Review*, vol. 89, pp. 22–46.

Torvik, R. (2001). 'Learning by doing and the Dutch disease', *European Economic Review*, vol. 45, pp. 285–306.

Torvik, R. (2002). 'Natural resources, rent seeking and welfare', *Journal of Development Economics*, vol. 67, pp. 455–70.

Tullock, G. (1975). 'On the efficient organization of trials', *Kyklos*, vol. 28, pp. 745–62.

van Wijnbergen, S. (1984). 'The "Dutch disease": a disease after all?', ECONOMIC JOURNAL, vol. 94, pp. 41–55.

World Bank (1994). 'Expanding the measure of wealth: indicators of environmentally sustainable development', Environmentally sustainable development studies and monographs series no. 7.

Review of Development Economics, 3(2), 107–121, 1999

The King Never Emigrates

Gil S. Epstein, Arye L. Hillman, and Heinrich W. Ursprung*

Abstract

This paper uses a locational model of rent-seeking to describe incentives to emigrate. A country is considered in which how a person fares in privileged income redistribution is determined by proximity to a king. Contests for privilege determine whether the more or the less productive in the population are located closer to the king. A distinction is drawn between contests for privilege that are "easy" and "difficult." When contests are "easy," the more productive are furthest from the king and emigrate first. When contests are "difficult," the least productive emigrate first. In either case, the population begins to unravel.

1. Introduction

Emigration decisions can be categorized by a push–pull distinction (Zimmermann, 1994a). That is, people may emigrate because they are pushed by adversity from their original country, or they may be pulled to a new country by the advantages the new location offers. Or there may of course be a combination of both influences present.

When people are pushed, emigration is involuntary. Pull suggests voluntary relocation. This paper is concerned with involuntary push emigration. We present a model which describes how emigration is tied to privileged endogenous income redistribution. Because of the privileged redistribution, people who could in principle be better off in their own countries nonetheless find themselves compelled to emigrate.

The privilege that determines the extent to which a person gains or loses from redistribution of income is contestable. We model a rent-seeking contest (see the survey of rent seeking by Nitzan (1994)) where the contest is locational and offers multiple prizes (some negative) depending on a person's equilibrium distance from the king. Time and resources are used in ingratiating oneself with the king. People differ in their productive abilities, and hence in their opportunity costs of using time and resources in ingratiating activities.

We wish to establish who under these circumstances has the greater incentive to emigrate, the more productive or the less productive of the king's subjects. The answer is established by the outcome of the domestic contest for privilege. Those furthest from the king are the least privileged, and have the greater incentive to emigrate.

If the most productive in the population finish the contest furthest from the king, they emigrate (if they can), so depriving the king of the most useful segments of his tax base. If the less productive finish the contest furthest from the king, it is they who emigrate (if they can). In the first case we have an instance of the phenomenon that has been described as a "brain drain." In the second case, the recipient countries find themselves host to unskilled (and perhaps illegally present) foreign labor.

---

* Epstein and Hillman: Bar-Ilan University, Ramat Gan 52900, Israel and CEPR. E-mail: epsteig@ashur.cc.biv.ac.il. Ursprung: Faculty of Economics and Statistics, University of Konstanz, Germany. * Arye Hillman and Heinrich Ursprung acknowledge the support of the Max Planck Research Prize. This paper was presented at the European Public Choice Society Annual Meetings, Göteborg, 1998, and at the CEPR conference "Trade and Factor Mobility", Venice, 1997. We are grateful to Mario Ferrero and Annemarie ter Veer for helpful comments. We have also benefited from the helpful comments of the referees.

In a rent-seeking contest, contest–success functions specify how winners are designated. In a standard Tullock contest–success function (Tullock, 1980), the probability of winning a contest increases with a person's rent-seeking effort or outlays relative to effort or outlays of others. Applying the Tullock function to our contest for privilege yields an equilibrium consistent with comparative advantage in the population. That is, the least productive, who have lower opportunity costs of spending time to make themselves liked by the king, end up closer to the king. The most productive end up furthest from the king, and provide the tax base for the privileged redistribution. Hence, when emigration is possible, the king then loses the best segments of his tax base.

We also use a second, novel, contest–success function that can be interpreted as representing "difficult" contests. The idea of "difficulty" is that rent-seeking effort by others is very spoiling of the effect of any person's own effort. That is, people countervail each other in their rent-seeking efforts. Also, there is an advantage to being able to make larger rent-seeking outlays. Resources are quickly eaten up in these "difficult" contests. Such contests for privilege conclude with the more productive members of the population closer to the king. The ranking of people along a scale of privilege is thus reversed from the outcome of the more standard rent-seeking contest.

The Tullock contest is "easy" for participants, since people in effect buy lottery tickets, and the more they spend relative to others the more they will win. There is still "spoiling" in the standard Tullock contest, in that the more others spend, the smaller one person's privileged allocation. It is the magnitude of the spoiling which distinguishes the easy from the difficult contests.

The contest–success functions can be thought of as expressing political culture. When rent seeking is easy, the king is open to rent-seeking overtures. When rent seeking is difficult, the institutions of the society spoil the effectiveness of rent-seeking overtures, and the more productive have an advantage over the less productive.

Although our model is set in terms of a king, we do not literally intend the model to apply only to a male absolute monarch. There could just as well be a queen, or a dictator, or a military junta. The characteristic element is that a ruler dispenses privilege to those who are "closest" to the "throne." The model is, in its general intent, a portrayal of the nondemocratic institutions of various developing countries where proximity to an autocratic ruler influences a person's economic fortune (see Gordon Tullock (1987) on autocracy). In particular, in less developed countries where support from the military has sustained autocratic government, there is documented evidence of rent allocations that reflect privileged proximity to the countries' rulers (Kimyeni and Mbaku, 1995).

For exposition, we model taxation as the means of redistribution. The mechanisms of privileged redistribution encompassed by our model are, however, in practice considerably more extensive. Monopolies are awarded to designated families. Or families (often the ruler's own relatives) receive import licenses, import or export quotas, or allocations of otherwise restricted foreign exchange. Government (or private) banks are instructed to provide subsidized credit or to forgive loans. Privatization takes place under privileged conditions of sale. Protection against import competition is provided to local production facilities owned by favored people (or relatives). Privileged families are permitted to send their children to superior local education facilities, often abroad. Our model encompasses "crony capitalism," where privileged access to capital is provided to people "close" to the government. In the model, in the absence of privileged redistribution, the entire population earns incomes (or has utility levels) in excess of foreign alternatives, and no-one has an incentive to emigrate. It is only because of privileged redistribution that some people's incomes are below the income attainable abroad, so that emigration incentives arise. If the king were to dispense altogether with privilege, no-one would wish to emigrate.

The emigrants who leave will wish to avoid alternative locations where a similar political culture of privilege prevails. Besides losing some of their human capital when they emigrate, people also enter the new country with a comparative disadvantage in the seeking of privilege relative to a pre-existing population, precisely because they are newcomers. We do not model where the immigrants choose to go, but our model suggests that the countries of immigration will have political cultures where privilege is less important in determining incomes than in the countries the emigrants have left.

2. A General Model of Endogenous Privilege

The King and his Subjects

The king is the source of authority and dispenses privilege in accord with proximity of the population to the throne. *Ex post*, after the designation of privilege, the population is ranked along a line. An individual j is located at the position d_j on the line, where $d_j \in [0,1]$. The measure 0 is the furthest from the king, the measure 1 the closest. An individual's position on the line is determined endogenously by the individual's investment in the quest for privilege in a contest where the remainder of the population is likewise seeking to position itself favorably in close proximity to the king. The real income I_j of individual j consists of net earnings from productive activity w_j^n plus a transfer from the king s_j:

$$I_j = w_j^n + s_j. \tag{1}$$

Each individual has an endowment of labor time normalized to unity which is allocated between productive activity A_j and time L_j spent in privilege-seeking activities:

$$A_j + L_j = 1. \tag{2}$$

The population differs in relative production efficiency, and thereby in individual comparative advantage between productive and privilege-seeking activity. Individual j's productive efficiency is a_j. There are N individuals in the population, who are ranked in accord with exogenous efficiency in productive activity:

$$a_1 < a_2 < \ldots < a_N. \tag{3}$$

We shall be interested in who emigrates, characterized with respect to individuals' productive efficiency.

We shall assume a competitive economy, not because we believe that the types of economies we are modeling encourage competition, but because we will encompass all rents and redistribution in taxes and transfers. So we consider competitive firms as producing output under conditions of constant returns to scale, and using only labor inputs. The wage is competitively determined per efficiency-unit of labor supplied. An individual j's gross income from productive activity is

$$w_j^g = a_j A_j. \tag{4}$$

Income from productive activity is subject to a proportional income tax, leaving net-of-tax productive income of individual j as[1]

$$w_j^n = (1 - \gamma) w_j^g = (1 - \gamma) a_j A_j. \tag{5}$$

The total tax proceeds received by the king are consequently

$$T = \gamma \sum_{i=1}^{N} a_i A_i.$$
(6)

The tax receipts are distributed at the king's largesse in accord with *ex post* proximity d_j to the throne. The *ex post* redistribution to individual j is

$$s_j = \alpha d_j \geq 0,$$
(7)

so that closer, more privileged individuals receive a higher transfer from the king. The king's total transfers are thus

$$S = \sum_{i=1}^{N} s_i = \alpha \sum_{i=1}^{N} d_i.$$
(8)

The king keeps for himself a sum

$$\Omega \geq 0.$$
(9)

The king's budget constraint is accordingly

$$T - S = \gamma \sum_i a_i A_i - \alpha \sum_i d_i = \Omega.$$
(10)

The redistribution of income subject to this budget constraint partitions the population between those for whom taxes exceed the transfer received from the king, and those who are net beneficiaries of the king's transfers.

The Determination of Privilege

The relative position of an individual (or family) in the hierarchy of privilege is improved by expending resources L_j in ingratiating themselves with the king, and deteriorates with resources L_i expended with the same objective by all others:

$$d_j = g(L_1, \ldots, L_j, \ldots, L_N), \quad \frac{\partial d_j}{\partial L_j} > 0, \quad \frac{\partial d_j}{\partial L_i} < 0 \quad \text{for } i \neq j.$$
(11)

This is then *a multi-prize contest* for N prizes $\{s_1, s_2, \ldots, s_N\}$ assigned to the N members of the population. All prizes are allocated, and the value of the prizes increases with proximity to the king.[2] The proximity is determined by equation (11) where the population chooses its allocations L_j as Nash equilibria. The expected transfer for individual j is accordingly

$$s_j = a d_j = \alpha g(L_1, \ldots, L_N) \geq 0.$$
(12)

The Individual's Optimization Problem

Individuals are thus taxed on income earned from productive activity, and receive a transfer based on privilege. Faced with these circumstances, an individual's optimizing behavior requires choice of allocation of resources available to him between productive and privilege-seeking activity to maximize income:

$$I_j = w_j^n + s_j = (1 - \gamma) a_j (1 - L_j) + \alpha g(L_1, \ldots, L_N).$$
(13)

So, with the individual allocating some time to each activity, allocation of his or her resources satisfies

$$\frac{\partial I_j}{\partial L_j} = -(1-\gamma)a_j + \alpha\frac{\partial g}{\partial L_j} = 0 \tag{14}$$

and

$$\frac{\partial^2 I_j}{\partial L_j^2} = \alpha\frac{\partial^2 g}{\partial L_j^2} < 0. \tag{15}$$

Equation (15) equates the marginal opportunity cost of not being productive with the expected benefit from allocating resources to seeking influence with the king. The function g is evidently required to be strictly concave at the equilibrium point if (15) describes optimal behavior.

3. An Easy Contest–Success Function

Our contest for privileged proximity to the king requires a contest–success function (Hirshleifer, 1989). Given a Tullock function (Tullock, 1980), success improves the more an individual has allocated to the contest relative to the total value of resources allocated:

$$d_j = g(L_1,\ldots,L_N) = \frac{L_j}{\sum\limits_{i=1}^{N} L_i}. \tag{16}$$

To analyze behavior, notice that from (7) and (16)

$$s_j = \alpha\frac{L_j}{\sum\limits_i L_i}. \tag{17}$$

Summing over all the population yields

$$\sum_i s_i = S = \alpha. \tag{18}$$

Thus the income distributed via the political system is here given. Equation (13) can be rewritten as

$$I_j = w_j^n + s_j = (1-\gamma)a_j(1-L_j) + S\frac{L_j}{\sum\limits_i L_i}, \tag{19}$$

demonstrating that we have a rent-seeking game in which rent seekers have different opportunity costs of rent seeking. The first-order conditions (14) then take the following form:

$$-1(1-\gamma)a_j + \frac{\sum\limits_{i\neq j} L_i}{\left(\sum\limits_i L_i\right)^2}S = 0 \quad \text{for } j=1,\ldots,N. \tag{20}$$

This implies the N conditions

$$\frac{L-L_1}{a_1} = \frac{L-L_2}{a_2} = \ldots = \frac{L-L_N}{a_N} = \frac{(1-\gamma)L^2}{S}, \quad \text{where } L = \sum_i L_i \tag{21}$$

which solve for

$$L_j = \left[\frac{\sum_i a_i - a_j(N-1)}{\left(\sum_i a_i\right)^2}\right]\left[\frac{S(N-1)}{1-\gamma}\right]. \tag{22}$$

This, however, constitutes an equilibrium only if L_j is positive for all j. If some individual political contributions L_j as given by equation (22) are negative (i.e. if $L_i > 0$ for $i = 1, \ldots, K-1$ and $L_i < 0$ for $i = K, \ldots, N$), the equilibrium is characterized as follows: the first $(K-1)$ rent-seekers are active and their political contributions are given by equation (22) in which N now needs to be replaced by $(K-1)$, and the last $(N-K+1)$ individuals remain passive ($L_i = 0$ for $i = K, \ldots, N$).[3] We thus have the following attributes of behavior:

(1) If some people do not actively participate in privilege-seeking, these individuals are the most productive ones in the society.
(2) The more productive an active rent seeker, the more resources he or she allocates to productive activity and the less to seeking privilege.
(3) The more productive are the competitors in the quest for privilege, the more resources an active rent seeker allocates to the political contest.
(4) The more the king taxes productive activity and/or the greater the benefits he provides from privileged proximity, the fewer resources are allocated to productive activity and the more to seeking privilege.

It follows that the ranking on $\{a_1, \ldots, a_N\}$ is therefore inversely related to the individuals' endogenous ranking $\{d_1, \ldots, d_N\}$. Those close to the king are those who are less efficient in production and have a comparative disadvantage in productive activity. The most productive individuals enjoy no privileges whatsoever.

Migration

In the absence of the redistributional policy, the population receives its competitively determined value of marginal product. An individual j who emigrates receives in foreign employment a proportion $\beta(a_j)$ of the value of his or her marginal product. Under these circumstances, if the technologies abroad are the same and product prices are the same, no member of the population will emigrate. We use this as a benchmark case.

When the king has imposed his redistribution system, an individual's *ex ante* income is the sum of gross income from productive activity and his or her net tax, given by:

$$I_j = a_j(1-L_j) + \{ad_j - \gamma a_j(1-L_j)\}. \tag{23}$$

A person who emigrates receives an income

$$I_j^f = \beta(a_j)a_j, \tag{24}$$

and hence individual j will emigrate if $I_j < I_j^f$; i.e. if

$$a_j(1-L_j) + \{ad_j - \gamma a_j(1-L_j)\} < \beta(a_j)a_j. \tag{25}$$

Consider now the Nth individual. This person is the most productive, and is furthest from the king. For $\beta(a_N)$ sufficiently high, he will certainly emigrate, and suppose that he does. This now reduces the population to $(N-1)$. The Nth person's departure is a loss for the tax base. Indeed the best individual tax base has departed. Moreover, all individuals for whom equation (25) is satisfied will depart. If M individuals leave, then it is the M most productive, and the M highest net tax payers, who will have emigrated. However, if these M individuals have left, the king's budget constraint is no longer sustainable. To balance his budget, he must increase the tax rate on productive activity, or reduce the base transfer, or reduce his own appropriation. This is, of course, a situation that is common for rulers and governments. At this point, we must ask ourselves about the king's objective function.

Suppose that privilege is the source of the king's tenure. Then he may be reluctant to reduce S, and prefer rather to increase the rate of taxation. In this case, the formerly indifferent productive individuals now leave. There is more averse selection. When will emigration cease? If individual N has emigrated, then for individual j who has remained, since individual N was part of the tax base:

$$I_j(L_1,\ldots,L_{N-1}) < I_j(L_1,\ldots,L_N). \tag{26}$$

Now suppose that all individuals $\{j+1,\ldots,N\}$ have emigrated. Then individual j will also emigrate if

$$I_j(L_1,\ldots,L_j) < \beta(a_j)a_j. \tag{27}$$

Using (25), this relation can be equivalently expressed as

$$a_j(1-\gamma-\beta(a_j)) + \left[\alpha\frac{L_j}{\sum_{i=1}^{j}L_i} - a_j(1-\gamma)L_j\right] < 0. \tag{28}$$

Emigration will cease when the left-hand side of equation (28) is nonnegative. The critical tax rate γ_c which makes individual j indifferent between staying and leaving (i.e. the tax rate which renders the left of (28) equal to zero) amounts to

$$\gamma_c = 1 - \beta(a_j) - \left[(1-\gamma)L_j = \frac{S}{a_j}\frac{L_j}{\sum_{i=1}^{j}L_i}\right]. \tag{29}$$

Notice that the terms in the square bracket do not depend on γ, since, according to equation (22), the terms $(1-\gamma)$ cancel. In the symmetric case ($a_i = a$ for all i) it is straightforward to show that the $\gamma_c(j)$ function is negatively sloped (in the general case, the shape of this function depends on the distribution of the individual productivities and the characteristics of $\beta(a_j)$). We use this result to illustrate the relationship between γ_c and the number j of remaining subjects in Figure 1. The tax rate γ_{BC} which balances the king's budget constraint (cf. equation (10)) is implicitly given by

$$T = \gamma\sum_{i=1}^{j}a_i(1-L_i(\gamma)) = S + \Omega. \tag{30}$$

In the symmetric case, γ_{BC} also varies negatively with the number j of subjects left;[4] and we again use this result to illustrate the function $\gamma_{BC}(j)$ in Figure 1.

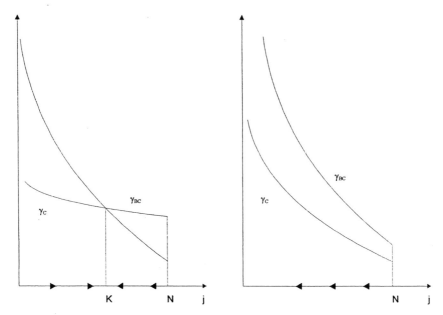

Figure 1. The King Loses Some Subjects or All

The first panel of Figure 1 depicts a situation in which the king loses some subjects by opening up the country to emigration, but emigration does not completely deplete the country of people. For all population sizes between $(K + 1)$ and N, the critical tax γ_c rate that makes the most productive individual indifferent between emigrating and staying, is lower than the tax rate that the king requires to balance his budget. Thus all individuals $N, N - 1, \ldots, K + 1$ will eventually leave. Individual K's critical tax rate is equal to the tax rate that balances the budget for K subjects, and this person therefore does not have an incentive to leave. The second panel depicts a situation in which the king loses all of his subjects.

More interesting is the situation depicted in Figure 2. Here we have two equilibrium population sizes, a stable equilibrium at K and an unstable one at L. After the country is opened to emigration, the $(N - K)$ most productive people emigrate and the king is left with K subjects. Even if the population size is subject to some exogenous noise, this does not jeopardize the viability of the kingdom if the safety margin of $(K - L)$ individuals is sufficiently large. If, however, the king is greedy and increases his appropriation from Ω_0 to Ω_1, the graph of the γ_{BC} function shifts upwards and the safety margin shrinks to $K' - L'$, which may not be compatible with guaranteed viability of the population. Greed and viability of the population are thus potentially incompatible.

Faced with an exodus of his subjects, the king has two alternatives to increasing the tax rate. He can reduce his own consumption Ω, or reduce the base benefit S for the privilege of proximity. That is, he can reduce his own personal income, or he can reduce the privilege dispensed by his patronage. The first, however, may not be personally satisfactory for the king, and the second implies in the limit that he ceases being a king.

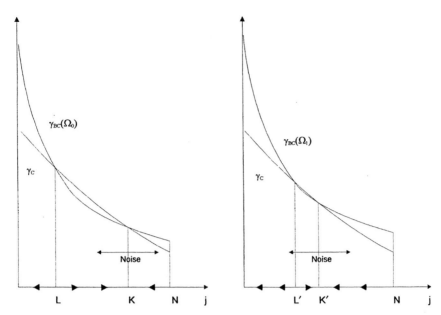

Figure 2. Two Equilibrium Population Sizes

4. Inherited Noncontestable Privilege

In the previous section we assumed that heterogeneity among the population is due to different productivities that translate into different opportunity costs of lobbying and thus to different endogenous equilibrium privileges. Yet often privileges are inherited and thus exogenous. For reference, we consider now a situation where this is the case. Let productivities be identical ($a_i = a$ for all i), but let differences in privilege ($d_1 < d_2 < \ldots < d_N$) translate into different effectiveness of royal persuasion. In that case

$$I_j = (1-\gamma)(1-L_j) + S\left(\frac{d_j L_j}{\sum_i d_i L_i}\right). \tag{31}$$

If all individuals are politically active ($L_i > 0$) we obtain:

$$L_j = \frac{\left(\prod_{i \neq j} d_i\right)\Sigma_{-j}}{\Sigma^2}\frac{(N-1)S}{1-\gamma} > 0, \tag{32}$$

where Σ denotes the sum over all products of $(N-1)$ different d_js and Σ_{-j} equals Σ minus $(N-1)$-times the product which does not contain d_j.[5] If the distribution of privilege is not sufficiently equal to induce all individuals to be politically active, the equilibrium is characterized as follows. The least privileged individuals will remain passive ($L_i = 0$ for $i = 1, \ldots, K$) whereas the remaining $N - K$ individuals will set their respective contributions L_j according to equation (32) in which N now needs to be replaced by the number $N - K$ of active rent-seekers.[6]

From (32) it follows that $L = \Sigma L_i$ is a linear function of $S/(1 - \gamma)$:

$$L = x(d_1, \ldots, d_N) \frac{S}{1 - \gamma}. \tag{33}$$

The king appropriates a given fraction κ of the total rent S. The budget constraint of the king is thus

$$(1 + \kappa)S = \gamma(N - L). \tag{34}$$

With the king maximizing his income $\Omega = \kappa S$ under the budget constraint, his optimal tax rate is

$$\gamma = \left[1 + \sqrt{\frac{x}{(1 - \kappa)}}\right]^{-1}. \tag{35}$$

An Example

To demonstrate the model, we provide a simple numerical example. We take $(d_1, d_2, d_3, d_4) = (0.6, 0.7, 0.9, 1)$, $\kappa = 0.1$, and the income any domestic subject can earn abroad by emigrating is $I_a = 0.46$. In a country from which emigration is not possible, the king thus has four subjects. In equilibrium the income-maximizing income-tax rate here is 0.56 and the corresponding size S of the budget that is redistributed among the population is 1.16. The least privileged subject's lobbying outlay amounts to $L_1 = 0.10$ and his income is $I_1 = 0.44$. The other subjects' lobbying outlays and incomes are $L_2 = 0.39$, $L_3 = 0.61$, $L_4 = 0.65$ and $I_2 = 0.47$, $I_3 = 0.59$, $I_4 = 0.64$.

How does the situation change if emigration becomes feasible? First of all, the least privileged subject will leave. The king is left with three subjects and recalculates his income-maximizing income-tax rate. He arrives at $\gamma = 0.57$, which entails a small increase. Since the tax base is smaller, however, the sum S decreases to 0.88. The subjects react by reducing their lobbying outlays to $L_2 = 0.32$, $L_3 = 0.48$, and $L_4 = 0.50$. Since the person who emigrated can no longer be exploited, everyone is worse off (with the exception of the emigrant, of course): $I_2 = 0.456$, $I_3 = 0.54$ and $I_4 = 0.58$. As it turns out, the income of subject 2, who is the least privileged among those who are left, now also falls under the threshold value of 0.46 and she, too, emigrates. The king is left with only two subjects, and sets an income-tax rate of 0.60, which yields $S = 0.65$. As a consequence, the two subjects who are left reduce again their lobbying efforts ($L_3 = L_4 = 0.40$). The tax base declines again, and their incomes drop even more: $I_3 = 0.465$ and $I_4 = 0.49$. Despite this last decrease in income, both subjects are still better off at home than by emigrating and, as a consequence, they will stay. We arrive at a migration equilibrium with the equilibrium size of the kingdom of $N = 2$.

Assume now the same parameters with the exception of the appropriation parameter κ which we reduce to 0.05; i.e. we assume now a political system that allows the king to appropriate only 5% of the tax revenue instead of 10% as before. This does not significantly change the tax-rate; however, the size S of the income available for redistribution increases compared with the system above. S increases from 1.16 to 1.19. This increases the incentives to lobby. The lobbying outlays now amount to $L_1 = 0.10$, $L_2 = 0.39$, $L_3 = 0.62$, and $L_4 = 0.66$. The incomes also increase: $I_1 = 0.44$, $I_2 = 0.48$, $I_3 = 0.60$, and $I_4 = 0.65$. Just as before, however, the least privileged subject decides to emigrate because his income falls short of the income he can earn abroad. Being left with three subjects, the king increases the tax rate but has to reduce the size of the total rent distributed: $S = 0.90$. This gives rise to a reduction of lobbying and a decrease of the incomes: $L_2 = 0.32$, $L_3 = 0.48$, $L_4 = 0.51$, $I_2 = 0.462$, $I_3 = 0.55$, and $I_4 = 0.59$. Despite the reduction in income (which is a consequence of the fact that the emigrant can no longer be exploited), all three subjects are still better off at home than by emigrating. We arrive at a migration equilibrium with an equilibrium number of subjects which is larger than in the case above. We conclude:

In a country where privilege is inherited and emigration is possible, the more appropriative the political system, the more people will emigrate.

5. Difficult Contests for Privilege

We now turn to consider an institutional structure where privilege is endogenous, but the seeking of privilege is a difficult activity. Consider in place of the Tullock contest–success function the following:

$$d_j = g(L_1, \ldots, L_N) = \varphi \frac{\sqrt{L_j}}{\prod_{i \neq j} L_i}, \tag{36}$$

where the parameter φ is chosen sufficiently small for all distances d_i to be contained in the unit interval.[7] From equations (7) and (8) we know that $s_j = (d_j/\Sigma d_i)S$. Using equation (36) we obtain

$$s_j = \frac{L_j^{1.5}}{\sum_i L_i^{1.5}} S, \quad \text{where} \quad S = \frac{\alpha}{\prod_i L_i} \sum_i L_i^{3/2}. \tag{37}$$

Again the individual optimization problem is to maximize

$$I_j = w_j^n + s_j = (1 - \gamma)\alpha_j(1 - L_j) + \alpha d_j. \tag{38}$$

In the case where the individual maximizes expected income given S, the problem reduces to that of a Tullock nondiscriminating contest–success function with the total income transfer fixed. As we can see from equation (37), S is a function of the levels of lobbying L_i of the population. With S not taken as given, we no longer have the Tullock problem because of the dependence of S on $(L_1, \ldots, L_N)$. The lobbying competition determines the total value of income transfers rather than S fixed as above.

If the absolute distance of all individuals is far from the king, the total sum of transfers will be low. However, as the levels of lobbying of the population increase, the absolute distance increases and the level of transfers thus decreases. This is consistent with our conception of a "difficult" contest.

An individual's income is now given by

$$I_j = (1 - \gamma)a_j(1 - L_j) + \alpha \varphi \frac{L_j^{1/2}}{\prod_{i \neq j} L_i}. \tag{39}$$

Hence

$$\frac{\partial I_j}{\partial L_j} = -a_j(1-\gamma) + \frac{\alpha\varphi}{2L_j^{1/2}\prod_{i\neq j}L_i} = 0 \tag{40}$$

and

$$\frac{\partial^2 I_j}{\partial L_j^2} = -\frac{\alpha\varphi}{4L_j^{3/2}\prod_{i\neq j}L_i} < 0. \tag{41}$$

Individual j's reaction function is

$$L_j = \left[\frac{\alpha\varphi}{2(1-\gamma)a_j\prod_{i\neq j}L_i}\right]^2. \tag{42}$$

That is, the reaction function is negatively sloped. The Nash solution for choice of privilege-seeking activity is

$$L_j = \left[\frac{a_j^{2N-3}}{\prod_{i\neq j}a_i^2}\frac{\alpha}{2(1-\gamma)}\right]^{\frac{2}{2N-1}}. \tag{43}$$

For two individuals i and j with different productivities:

$$\frac{L_j}{L_i} = \left[\frac{a_j}{a_i}\right]^2. \tag{44}$$

Hence, we conclude:

In "difficult" contests, more productive individuals allocate relatively more resources to the seeking of privilege, and are on average closer to the king.

The "difficult" contest has thus resulted in a switch, relative to the easy contest, in the correlation between productivity and proximity to the king. The more productive can allocate smaller quantities of resources to productive activity, and still have more resources available for the contest for privilege. This was also the case in the easy contest. However, in the difficult contest, the strength of the opposition and the marginal benefit from allocating resources to the contest are magnified. The potential income of more productive individuals is higher than that of the less productive: the more productive earn more income if they choose productive activity; but they also lose more if they find themselves in that part of the population that is taxed. Their greater incentive to engage in political activity is due to the greater income they avoid losing if close to the king. And under the conditions of the difficult contest, the equilibrium places then closer to the king. It is now the least productive who emigrate when emigration is possible.

6. Concluding Observations

In this paper we have been interested in why people are led to leave their home countries. This contrasts with much of the international migration literature, which has been concerned with issues that arise in the host country; see the survey by Hillman and

Weiss (1999) and, for example, Gang and Rivera-Batiz (1994), Zimmermann (1994a,b), Djajic (1997), Mazza and van Winden (1996), and Epstein et al. (1999).

Also, when looking at emigration, it is generally supposed that people have left their homes voluntarily, in response to higher incomes attainable in the host countries. This is in particular so when immigration is considered in the context of the theory of international factor mobility (Wong, 1995). Or Stark and Taylor (1991) consider voluntary migration as a response to relative deprivation. We have, in contrast, focused attention on cases where emigration is an *involuntary response* to the local political culture. People in our model would be better off in their home countries, and they would not emigrate, if they were not disadvantaged by domestic privilege. Thus, while migration in general takes place from low to high income countries, our model suggests that we should also look to certain types of economic, and political, regimes that "push" parts of their population to emigrate.

Our emphasis has been on the role of institutions. Democratic collective decision-making institutions in general make rent-seeking contests more "difficult" and assign a lower weight to privilege in personal success, than do the personalized institutions of autocracy where the ruler's decisions are important for people's well-being. The contestable privilege that is often inherent in autocracy is tied to emigration, and to impediments to economic development.[8]

Historically, patterns of migration have tended to be from countries with autocratic regimes and privilege, to democracies where privilege has a smaller role in determining personal incomes. This is reflected in the movement of people from the old to the new world, including the mass migrations following the failures of the 1848 revolutions in Europe. The historical migrations of Jews within Europe and the high proportion of Jews in the emigrations from Europe also attest to movements of people not favored by proximity to "kings." In more contemporary times, we likewise observe emigration from countries where well-being depends more on privileges to favored cliques, tribes and families than on individuals' own productive activities.

References

Djajic, Slobodan, "Illegal Immigration and Resource Allocation," *International Economic Review* 38 (1997):97–117.

Epstein, Gil S., Arye L. Hillman, and Avi Weiss, "Creating Illegal Immigrants," *Journal of Population Economics* 12 (1999):3–21.

Fabella Raul V. (1995) "The Social Cost of Rent Seeking under Countervailing Opposition to Distortionary Transfers," *Journal of Public Economics* 57 (1995):235–247.

Gang, Ira N. and Francisco L. Rivera-Batiz, "Labor Market Effects of Immigrants in the United States and Europe: Substitution Versus Complementarity," *Journal of Population Economics* 7 (1994):157–75.

Gradstein, Mark, "Intensity of Competition, Entry and Entry Deterrence in Rent Seeking Contests," *Economics and Politics* 7 (1995):79–91.

Hillman, Arye L. and Eliakim Katz, "Risk-Averse Rent Seekers and the Social Cost of Monopoly Power," *Economic Journal* 94 (1984):104–10.

Hillman, Arye L. and John Riley, "Politically Contestable Rents and Transfers," *Economics and Politics* 1 (1989):17–39.

Hillman, Arye L. and Avi Weiss, "Beyond International Factor Movements. Cultural Preferences, Endogenous Policies, and the Migration of People: an overview," in Jaime de Melo, Riccardo Faini, and Klaus F. Zimmermann (eds.) *Trade and Factor Mobility*, Cambridge: Cambridge University Press, 1999.

Hirshleifer, Jack, "Conflict and Rent Seeking Success Functions: Ratio vs Difference Models of Relative Success," *Public Choice* 63 (1989):101–12.

Kimyeni, Mwangi S. and John Mukum Mbaku, "Rents, Military Elites, and Political Democracy," *European Journal of Political Economy* 11 (1995):699–708.

Mazza, Isodoro and Frans van Winden, "A Political Economic Analysis of Labor Migration and Income Redistribution," *Public Choice* 88 (1996):333–63.

McGuire, Martin and Mancur Olson, "The Economics of Autocracy and Majority Rule: The Invisible Hand and the Use of Force," *Journal of Economic Literature* 34 (1996):72–96.

Nitzan, Shmuel, "Modeling Rent-Seeking Contests," *European Journal of Political Economy* 10 (1994):41–60.

Olson, Mancur, *The Rise and Decline of Nations*, New Haven: Yale University Press, 1982.

Stark, Oded and Edward J. Taylor, "Migration Incentives, Migration Types: The Role of Relative Deprivation," *Economic Journal* 101 (1991):1163–78.

Tullock, Gordon, "Efficient rent seeking," in J. M. Buchanan, R. D. Tollison, and G. Tullock (eds.) *Toward a Theory of the Rent Seeking Society*, Texas: A&M Press, 1980, pp. 97–112.

———, *Autocracy*, Boston: Kluwer Academic, 1987.

Ursprung, Heinrich W., "Public Goods, Rent Dissipation, and Candidate Competition," *Economics and Politics* 2 (1990):115–32.

Wong, Kar-Yiu, *International Trade in Goods and Factor Mobility*, Cambridge, MA: MIT Press, 1995.

Zimmermann, Klaus F., "European Migration: Push and Pull," in *Proceedings of the World Bank Annual Conference on Development Economics*, 1994a, pp. 313–42.

———, "Immigration Policies in Europe: An Overview," in Horst Siebert and J .C. B. Mohr (eds.) *Migration: A Challenge for Europe*, Tübingen: Paul Siebeck, 1994b.

Notes

1. There are no deadweight losses associated with taxation in this model, and we do not ask questions about how the presence of deadweight losses affects the structure of taxation chosen by the ruler. On these questions, see McGuire and Olson (1996).

2. We assume risk neutrality; an extension to risk aversion is straightforward (Hillman and Katz, 1984). Also, the prizes are depicted as providing private rather than public-good type collective benefit to a group. The model can be restated in terms of the standard conditions of collective rent-seeking and collective prizes (Ursprung, 1990; Nitzan, 1991; Gradstein, 1993). Our basic collective unit is, however, the individual or family as the potential beneficiary of privilege, and we can assume that all costs and benefits are perfectly internalized—although intra-family squabbles are not unknown.

3. A sketch of the proof of this result runs as follows (see also Hillman and Riley, 1989). L_K, as computed by equation (22), is negative if and only if $\Sigma_i a_i < (N-1)a_K$, which implies

$$\sum_{i=1}^{K-1} a_i - (K-2)a_K < (N-K)a_K - \sum_{i=k+1}^{N} a_i < 0.$$ For $L_K = \ldots = L_N = 0$, the sum $L = \sum_{i=1}^{K-1} L_i$ of all con-

tributions amounts to $(K-2)S/(1-\gamma)\sum_{i=1}^{K-1} a_i$. The income of individual K then amounts to

$I_K = (1 - \gamma)(1 - L_K)a_K + L_K S/(L + L_K)$, and to K's marginal income at $L_K = 0$ to

$(1-\gamma)\left[\sum_{i=1}^{K-1} a_i - (K-2)a_K\right]\Big/(K-2)$. This expression is negative because of the above inequality.

Moreover, the second derivative of $I_K(L_K)$ is also negative which shows that L_K needs to be zero. However, if L_k is zero, then all other political contributions L_i are also zero for $i = K+1, \ldots, N$.

Notice, also, that if $L_j \geq 0$ for all j, the constraint $I_j \geq (1 - \gamma)a_j$ is automatically satisfied (because

this inequality is equivalent to $S/\Sigma L_i \geq (1 - \gamma)a_j$ and ΣL_i amounts to $(K-2)S/(1-\gamma)\sum_{i=1}^{K-1} a_i$; thus

we have $\sum_{i=1}^{K-1} a_i \geq (K-2)a_j$ which implies $L_j \geq 0$ and vice versa).

4. This result can easily be derived by applying the implicit function rule and the information that the king stays on the upward-sloping side of the Laffer curve; i.e. $\partial T/\partial \gamma > 0$.

5. Thus we have for $N = 2$

$$L_1 = \frac{d_2(d_1 + d_2 - 1(d_2))}{(d_1 + d_2)^2} \frac{S}{1-\gamma} = \frac{d_1 d_2}{(d_1 + d_2)^2} \frac{S}{1-\gamma}$$

and $L_1 = L_2$. For $N = 3$ we have

$$L_1 = \frac{d_2 d_3 (d_1 d_2 + d_1 d_3 + d_2 d_3 - 2(d_2 d_3))}{(d_1 d_2 + d_1 d_3 + d_2 d_3)^2} \frac{2S}{1-\gamma} = \frac{d_2 d_3 (d_1 d_2 + d_1 d_3 - d_2 d_3)}{(d_1 d_2 + d_1 d_3 + d_2 d_3)^2} \frac{2S}{1-\gamma}$$

and analogous expressions for L_2 and L_3. For $N = 4$ we have

$$L_1 = \frac{d_2 d_3 d_4 (d_1 d_2 d_3 + d_1 d_2 d_4 + d_1 d_3 d_4 - 2 d_2 d_3 d_4)}{(d_1 d_2 d_3 + d_1 d_2 d_4 + d_1 d_3 d_4 + d_2 d_3 d_4)^2} \frac{3S}{1-\gamma}$$

and analogous expressions for L_2, L_3, and L_4.

6. A sketch of the proof runs as follows (see also Gradstein, 1995). Assume that using equation (32) for N active rent-seekers yields $L_1 < 0$; i.e. $\Sigma_{-1} = \Sigma - (N-1) \prod_{k \neq 1} d_K < 0$ or, alternatively,

$$\left(d_1 \Sigma^{N-2}\right) \Big/ \left[(N-2) \prod_{k \neq 1} d_K\right] < 1,$$ where Σ^{N-2} indicates that the sum contains products of $(N-2)d_i$ $(i \neq 1)$. If the first (i.e. the least privileged) individual stays politically passive, the weighted lobbying contributions of the remaining $N - 1$ individuals add up to $L = \sum_{i \neq 1} d_i L_i = \left[(N-2)S \prod_{k \neq 1} d_K\right] \Big/ \left[(1-\gamma)\Sigma^{N-2}\right]$. It is easy to see that it is indeed optimal for the first individual to remain passive under these circumstances. Differentiating his or her income, $I_1 = -(1 - \gamma)(1 - L_1) + d_1 L_1 S(d_1 L_1 + L)$, yields, at $L_1 = 0$:

$$(1-\gamma)\left[\frac{d_1 \Sigma^{N-2}}{(N-2)\prod_{K \neq 1} d_K} - 1\right],$$

which, given the above assumption, is negative. Moreover, the second derivative of I_1 with respect to L_1 is negative, too, indicating that $L_1 = 0$ is optimal. This procedure can be repeated as long as equation (32) yield negative L_i.

7. Note that the difficulty of the contest is encompassed by the character of the contest–success function. An alternative approach, not appropriate in the conditions we describe, pre-identifies gainers and losers, and sets difficulties before the potential gainers because of the countervailing resources expended by those seeking to protect their incomes (the potential losers). See, for example, Fabella (1995).

8. See also Olson (1982) on the decline of nations.

Available online at www.sciencedirect.com

SCIENCE ⓓ DIRECT®

European Journal of Political Economy
Vol. 20 (2004) 755–767

ELSEVIER

European Journal of
POLITICAL
ECONOMY

www.elsevier.com/locate/econbase

Immigration as a challenge to the Danish welfare state? ☆

Peter Nannestad *

Department of Political Science, Aarhus University, Universitetsparken, DK-8000 Aarhus C, Denmark

Received 9 February 2004; received in revised form 10 February 2004; accepted 11 February 2004
Available online 23 April 2004

Abstract

In a universalistic, tax-financed welfare state such as that of Denmark with strong redistribution, gains and losses from migration may be asymmetrically distributed between immigrants and natives. The redistributive welfare state both weakens the incentives of immigrants to enter the labor market and creates barriers to entry to the labor market. As a consequence, immigrants as a group are net beneficiaries of the welfare state even after extended periods of stay in the country. While soaring dependency ratios are expected in the future due to an aging native population, immigration has so far added to rather than ameliorated this problem. The Danish experience would seem to suggest that unchecked immigration and a redistributive welfare state are difficult to reconcile.
© 2004 Elsevier B.V. All rights reserved.

JEL classification: I38; J11; J15
Keywords: Immigration; Welfare state; Redistribution

1. Introduction

As is the case in many other western countries, the Danish welfare state will be facing a new challenge in the near future. In a few years time, the war and postwar "baby boom" generation will begin to retire from the labor market. Due to a secular drop in fertility rates that began with this very same generation, the "baby boomers" leaving the labor force will not be fully replaced by the generation of their children. Increased life expectancy, as well as a trend towards earlier retirement,[1] tends to exacerbate the situation still further. So

---

☆ Invited lecture, European Public Choice Society, Aarhus, 2003.
* Tel.: +45-8942-1257.
E-mail address: pnannestad@ps.au.dk (P. Nannestad).
[1] While the official retirement age in Denmark was 67 years in 1998, the average actual retirement age was 61 years (Statistics Denmark, 1999).

756   P. Nannestad / European Journal of Political Economy 20 (2004) 755–767

does the trend towards later entry into the labor force, due mainly to prolonged education, and the trend towards enjoying more leisure at the expense of working hours. As a consequence, dependency ratios will begin to soar in the near future, putting a squeeze on the Danish welfare state: on the one hand, demands for the benefits and services of the welfare state are bound to increase, due to the increase in the number of the elderly, old and very old. On the other, financing the welfare state will become more burdensome, due to the reduction in the size of the labor force.

In this situation, immigration might seem to suggest itself as a natural remedy. Since immigrants are normally young, and since their fertility rates are normally higher than in the country of destination, immigration will to some extent be able to counteract the aging of the native population and the reduction in the size of the labor force both in the short and in the longer run. At the same time, migrating from a less developed country to Denmark will raise the utility of the migrant by the difference between the net present value of utility in the home country and in Denmark. Since this difference will in most cases be sizeable, recruiting immigrants from nonwestern countries[2] should not pose serious problems. Thus, immigration is sometimes proposed as a partial solution to the demographic problem that Denmark will face in the near future and as a solution that will be beneficial to both native Danes and immigrants (e.g., Rasmussen, 1997; Rasmussen, 2000).

While immigration may indeed contribute to a more balanced age distribution in the Danish population, it will not necessarily decrease dependency ratios or defuse the waiting "pension bomb." Quite to the contrary: during the last two decades, immigration to Denmark from nonwestern countries has gradually developed into a challenge of its own for the Danish welfare state.

I shall be concerned primarily with migration from nonwestern countries to Denmark. For the last 25 years, this has been the dominant category of immigration. I shall propose that the redistributive policies of the welfare state are the main reason why immigration from nonwestern countries is part of the problem of demographic change posed for the Danish welfare state rather than part of the solution. So far, the Danish welfare state has proven itself to be less than well suited to successfully integrating immigrants from nonwestern countries into the labor force. On the one hand, its redistributive policies tend to weaken immigrants' economic incentives for labor market participation; on the other, barriers are created to entry of immigrants into the labor market. The redistributive Danish welfare state contributes to a situation where sizeable numbers of immigrants from nonwestern countries over prolonged periods of time do not gain access to the labor market but claim social benefits instead, thus contributing to soaring dependency ratios. While large immigrant groups gain from migration even under these conditions, native Danes do not.[3]

---

[2] In the following, western countries are the Nordic countries, EU countries, Switzerland, Iceland, Canada, USA, Australia and New Zealand. All other countries are classified as nonwestern. Furthermore, nonwestern will be considered roughly equivalent to less developed.

[3] For a theoretical analysis of the distribution of welfare gains from migration in a redistributive welfare state, see, for example, Wellisch and Walz (1998) and Hansen (2003).

P. Nannestad / European Journal of Political Economy 20 (2004) 755–767   757

The discussion will proceed as follows. I shall begin with a short overview of postwar immigration to Denmark and characteristics of the immigration flows during the last two decades. I shall then discuss aspects of the role of the Danish welfare state in relation to labor market integration of immigrants and present some empirical findings on labor market integration of immigrants and on the impact on public finances. I then turn to prospects of second-generation immigrants in the Danish labor market, which links back to the question whether immigration may eventually help solve the problem of the welfare state of rising dependency ratios.

2. Postwar immigration to Denmark

During the early post-World War II period, there was net emigration of Danish citizens, mainly to Canada and Australia. Until the late 1950s, unemployment stood at fairly high levels in Denmark compared to most other western European countries, making emigration attractive. Immigration to Denmark was limited and originated mainly from other Nordic and western European countries.[4]

During the 1960s and until 1974, Denmark experienced a period of full employment bordering on excess demand for labor. While this kept net migration of Danes at a low level, a minor guest worker scheme was introduced to relieve labor shortages in certain sectors of the economy. Guest workers were recruited mainly from Turkey, Yugoslavia and Pakistan. The numbers were very modest. Between 1965 and 1967, the number of foreign citizens from Turkey and Yugoslavia was below 500 for each group. In 1974, there were 6779 citizens from Yugoslavia, 8138 from Turkey and 3733 from Pakistan in Denmark. These were outnumbered by citizens from the Nordic countries, USA and the EU (50,669). Citizens from these western countries made up about 56% of the total number of foreign citizens in Denmark in 1974 (Larsen and Matthiessen, 2002).

In the wake of the first oil price crisis, the recruitment of guest workers ceased in 1973 as part of a general stop to immigration.[5] However, guest workers already in the country were allowed to stay and were given the option to apply for permission to bring in close family. Thus, family reunification became one of the ways around the formal Danish immigration stop. The other way of immigrating was to claim asylum in accordance with the Geneva Convention. In neither case was the right of abode contingent on secured employment.

Family reunification was initially the most important access route to Denmark for would-be immigrants. However, from the early 1980s, asylum became an important vehicle of immigration as well. Yearly statistics for the period 1988–2001 show that between 15% and 27% of the total number of resident permits to foreigners were given to asylum seekers,[6] while between 25 and 33% were due to family reunification.

---

[4] Since 1954, there has been free labor mobility between the Nordic countries.

[5] This immigration stop remains formally in effect. It never applied to citizens from other Nordic countries and from the EU, however.

[6] In 1995, the percentage was 53.7%. This was due to a large number of refugees from ex-Yugoslavia who had initially been given a special temporary protection status, which in 1995 was converted to regular asylum status (Larsen and Matthiessen, 2002).

758   *P. Nannestad / European Journal of Political Economy 20 (2004) 755–767*

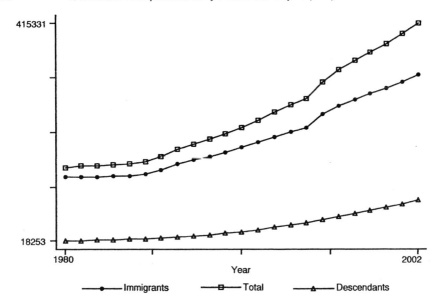

Fig. 1. Immigrants and descendants in Denmark, 1980–2002. Source: Larsen and Matthiessen (2002, p. 37).

From 1980 to 2001 the number of immigrants and descendants[7] in Denmark rose from 152,958 to 415,331 persons, or from 3.0% to 7.7% of the total population (Fig. 1). While the number of immigrants and descendants from western countries has remained almost constant at about 100,000 persons, the number of immigrants and descendants from nonwestern countries has increased strongly. The five largest ethnic groups in Denmark today are—in order—immigrants and descendants from Turkey, ex-Yugoslavia, Iraq, Lebanon (Palestinians), Pakistan and Somalia.

The group of immigrants and descendants from nonwestern countries differs quite markedly from the native Danish population with respect to their age distribution. The proportion younger than 45 years is somewhat higher in the population of nonwestern immigrants and their descendants than in the native Danish population, while a higher proportion in the native Danish population than in the immigrant population is above 50 years of age. Nevertheless, the impact of the immigrants and their descendants on the age distribution of the whole population in Denmark has remained marginal. Unsurprisingly, immigration in the orders of magnitude experienced during the last 20 years is still far below the levels that would be needed in order to decisively counteract the aging of the native Danish population.

More importantly, the group of immigrants and descendants from nonwestern countries also differs markedly from the native Danish population with respect to educational

---

[7] Statistics Denmark classifies a person as an immigrant if (s)he was born outside Denmark to parents none of whom were Danish citizens and born in Denmark. A person is classified as descendant if (s)he was born in Denmark to parents none of whom were Danish citizens and born in Denmark (Larsen and Matthiessen, 2002, p. 28).

P. Nannestad / European Journal of Political Economy 20 (2004) 755–767   759

achievement levels and skills. In a survey in 1999, 11% of immigrants and descendants in the age group 16–70 years from Turkey reported having completed or being enrolled in vocational education or a theoretical education program beyond the secondary level. The corresponding figures were 10% for immigrants and descendants from Pakistan, 21% for immigrants and descendants from Lebanon and 18% for immigrants and descendants from Somalia. In comparison, 54% of the native Danish population aged 16–70 years had completed or were enrolled in a vocational education or a theoretical education program beyond the secondary level (Larsen, 2000).[8] In an increasingly knowledge-based economy, the market value of immigrants with weak educational backgrounds will tend to be low.

In sum, the last 20 years' migration from nonwestern countries to Denmark has consisted mainly of (i) younger and (ii) less well-educated immigrants, compared to the native Danish population. In the next section, we shall look at some consequences for the Danish welfare state of this development.

3. Immigrants between the welfare state and the labor market

The Danish welfare state belongs to the group of universalistic welfare states (Esping-Andersen, 1990). Most social rights (access to welfare services and social transfers) depend only on legal residence in the country, not, for example, on labor market participation or citizenship. Benefits are mostly tax financed. There are few contributory schemes.[9] As a consequence, legal immigrants become a financial liability on the welfare state, unless they are integrated into the labor market at once and thus are able to provide for themselves. This was typically the case with the immigrants who arrived during the few years of the Danish guest worker scheme in the 1960s and early 1970s.

In addition to broad coverage, transfer payments in the Danish welfare state are also quite generous relative to minimum wages in the labor market. Thus, the welfare state weakens economic incentives for labor market participation, especially for low-skilled, low-paid individuals. While the net present value of social benefits may be a little lower than the net present value of earnings from labor even for unskilled immigrant workers in Denmark, the difference to the net present value of earnings in their homelands will normally still be large. Due to their relatively low educational achievement levels, this applies to a rather large proportion of the population of immigrants and descendants from nonwestern countries in Denmark. Through the same mechanism, the welfare state may also weaken immigrants' incentives to invest in acquiring the necessary preconditions for labor market participation, such as minimum levels of language and social skills.

Besides weakening economic incentives, the welfare state also contributes to creating barriers for the entry of (especially) low-skilled immigrants into the labor market. High levels of social transfer payments exert upward pressures on minimum wages. In turn, a high minimum wage tends to reduce the number of low-skilled jobs and to price low-

---

[8] Figures for immigrants and descendants are standardized so as to make the respective groups equal to the native Danish population with respect to gender and age distributions.

[9] One of these is unemployment benefits. However, even with this scheme, contributions cover only a minor fraction of total expenditures. The remaining part is tax financed.

760   P. Nannestad / European Journal of Political Economy 20 (2004) 755–767

Table 1
Labor marked participation rates among immigrants and descendants 16–66 years old, as well as among native Danes, 2001[a]

Country of origin	Labor market participation rate (%)
Ex-Yugoslavia	48
Iran	47
Lebanon (Palestinians)	26
Pakistan	47
Poland	60
Somalia	14
Turkey	50
Vietnam	56
Other nonwestern countries	46
Nonwestern, total	46
Native Danes	76

[a] Source: Schultz-Nielsen (2002a, p. 87).

skilled, low-productive immigrants out of the labor market, since immigrants cannot compensate for lack of skills and low productivity by accepting wages below the going minimum rate.[10] By a similar logic, the welfare state contributes to the exclusionary effects of discrimination by employers against nonwestern immigrants and their descendants.[11]

Further, a welfare state like that of Denmark necessitates high taxes.[12] Since most government revenue in Denmark is raised by means of taxes on income and on consumption, a considerable tax wedge is created that adversely affects private demand for various kinds of domestic services, thus closing still another potential labor market access route for low-skilled immigrants.

Finally, the combination of generous welfare provisions and a high tax pressure that characterizes the Danish welfare state may lead to an adverse selection problem in the case of immigration. While immigrants as a whole are probably favorably self-selected (Chiswick, 2000), the Danish welfare state may be most attractive to immigrants with a relatively low market value.[13]

---

[10] Minimum wages in Denmark are not fixed by law, but by collective agreements in the labor market. That does not make them less binding, however.

[11] Discriminatory hiring practices certainly do occur, although they are hardly the most important barrier facing nonwestern immigrants and their descendants in the Danish labor market (Schultz-Nielsen, 2002b, pp. 118–124). From an economic point of view, employers using discriminatory hiring practices impose a negative externality on the groups discriminated against. If left to themselves, discriminating employers and discriminated-against groups could solve the problem by having the discriminated-against groups pay the employers to discontinue using discriminatory hiring practices. That would normally mean accepting lower wages. This solution will in most cases be prevented by the high Danish minimum wage. Thus, discrimination will result in exclusion from the labor market instead. The role played by the high Danish minimum wages and thus—indirectly—by the Danish welfare state in bringing about this effect does not of course make discrimination any more acceptable from a moral point of view.

[12] In 2002, Danish taxes were 49.2% of GNP (Ministry of Finance, 2003).

[13] Borjas (1998) shows how the interstate dispersion in welfare benefits in the US affects the geographical clustering of immigrants with immigrant welfare recipients more heavily concentrated in states offering high benefits than states that offer less welfare benefits.

P. Nannestad / European Journal of Political Economy 20 (2004) 755–767   761

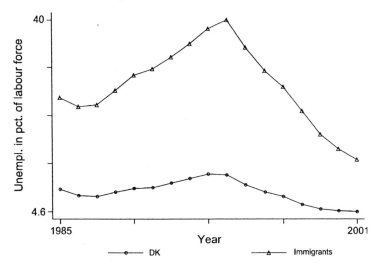

Fig. 2. Unemployment rates (in percent of those in the labor force) among immigrants and descendants 16–66 years old, as well as among native Danes, 1985–2001.[14]

The combined effects of the Danish welfare state on labor market integration of nonwestern immigrants must therefore be expected to be negative, at least in the short run. Empirical evidence suggests that this is the case. Table 1 shows labor market participation rates for nonwestern immigrants (including descendants) and for native Danes in 2001.

Two patterns stand out clearly. In the first place, labor market participation rates among nonwestern immigrants and descendants are considerably lower than in the native Danish population. Secondly, these rates also vary significantly among ethnic groups in the nonwestern immigrant population. In particular, Somalians and Palestinians exhibit very low levels of labor market activity. However, even the groups with the highest levels of labor market participation rates—the Poles and the Vietnamese—do not reach the rates in the native Danish population.

Table 1 does not tell the whole story, however. Unemployment rates also differ markedly between native Danes and nonwestern immigrants and their descendants, as shown in Fig. 2. Combining Table 1 and Fig. 2, it turns out that not only were 54% of nonwestern immigrants and descendants outside the labor force in 2001, but an annual average of 14.2% of those actually in the labor force were unemployed (as against 4.6% among native Danes in the labor force) and hence on social benefits. While the time trends in unemployment rates are approximately the same for both native Danes and nonwestern immigrants and descendants, representing primarily the impact of the business cycle on unemployment in both groups, it appears that the economic boom since the second half of the 1990s led to a somewhat steeper decline in the unemployment rates of nonwestern immigrants and their descendants than in the rates of native Danes. Nevertheless, the unemployment rate among nonwestern immigrants

---

[14] Source: Schultz-Nielsen (2002a, pp. 114–115).

Table 2
Net transfers to the public sector in Dkr. (1997 prices) per person[a]

	1991	1995	1996	1997	1998
Native Danes	14.900	16.500	19.000	22.700	24.500
Immigrants and descendants from nonwestern countries	− 48.000	− 62.600	− 63.700	− 58.200	− 50.500

[a] Source: Wadensjö and Orrje (2002, p. 72).

and their descendants still remains about three times the unemployment rate among native Danes in the labor force.

The financial and distributional consequences of the generally poor labor market integration of nonwestern immigrants and descendants can be seen in Table 2. This table shows static estimates of the size of net transfers per person to the public sector from native Danes and nonwestern immigrants and their descendants, respectively, for selected years in the 1990s.

As can be seen, the average net transfer from nonwestern immigrants and descendants to the Danish public sector is negative for all years included in the analysis. During the 1990s, immigrants from nonwestern countries and their descendants as a group were net beneficiaries of the welfare state, while native Danes were net contributors.[15] Total net transfers from the public sector to immigrants from nonwestern countries and their descendants varied between 0.54% and 0.91% of GDP (Wadensjö and Orrje, 2002, p. 75). There was thus a sizeable redistribution from native Danes to nonwestern immigrants and their descendants in all the years analyzed.

The slight decline in the size of negative transfers from nonwestern immigrants and descendants to the public sector in 1997 and 1998 as compared to earlier years primarily reflects a decline in their unemployment rates as shown in Fig. 2. Much the same is true for the increase in the size of positive net transfers to the public sector from native Danes.

One of the reasons for the rather high cost of immigrants from nonwestern countries and their descendants to the Danish welfare state in the past could be that large-scale immigration from nonwestern countries to Denmark is a relatively recent phenomenon. It may be argued that with increasing length of stay, nonwestern immigrants will turn from net beneficiaries of the welfare state to net contributors as the integration process, especially in the labor market, progresses. Thus, the high costs of immigrants from nonwestern countries may be a transient phenomenon. However, results reported by Wadensjö and Orrje (2002, pp. 73–74) indicate that for immigrants from nonwestern countries with up to 10 years of stay in Denmark, differences in the size of their (negative) net transfers to the public sector per person are actually fairly small. In addition, even though (negative) net transfers to the public sector from those with 10 or more years of stay in Denmark tend to become smaller, they are still negative and quite substantial. Thus,

---

[15] These differences persist even when controlled for the impact of age, gender and family status. Differences in distributions over these variables do not explain differences in the size and direction of net transfers to the public sector per person between the groups of native Danes and of nonwestern immigrants and descendants (Wadensjö and Orrje, 2002, p. 80).

P. Nannestad / European Journal of Political Economy 20 (2004) 755–767   763

even after 10 years (or even longer) of stay in Denmark, immigrants form nonwestern countries and their descendants as a group have so far remained net beneficiaries of the welfare state.

4. As time goes by...

At present, immigrants and descendants from nonwestern countries as a group are an economic liability on the Danish welfare state and have been so for more than a decade at least. The question is whether they will also remain a liability in the future. Must they be expected to add to the upcoming challenges to the welfare state due to the aging of the native Danish population, or can they be expected to contribute to alleviating this problem by boosting the size of the labor force?

According to an optimistic scenario, cherished mainly in some political and media circles, things are going to straighten out by themselves. As time goes by and the group of first-generation immigrants dies out, so a popular argument runs, it will be replaced by second- and third-generation immigrants. These subsequent immigrant generations are born and raised in Denmark and will hence have largely adapted to the behavior of native Danes, especially with respect to educational choices and labor market participation.

This optimistic scenario is premised on two assumptions. The first is that the initial generation of immigrants is going to die away with the passing of time. The second is that second-generation immigrants will become like native Danes with respect to educational background, skills and labor market participation rates. The validity of both assumptions can be doubted.

The idea that the group of first-generation immigrants will gradually die away seems to be based on a fallacious analogy between biological and immigrant generations. Biological generations do inevitably die away with time. In contrast, the group of first-generation immigrants in Denmark will die away only if there is a total stop to all immigration. In the absence of such a total stop, the pool of first-generation immigrants can renew and replenish itself indefinitely through ongoing immigration instead of dying away, even though the earliest first-generation immigrants (the guest workers of the 1960s) eventually must die away.

In this context, certain behavioral patterns among second-generation immigrants may become crucial. If large proportions of second-generation immigrants from nonwestern countries prefer to find their spouses in their parents' country of origin and to bring them to Denmark under the rules for family reunification, second-generation immigrants will contribute to maintaining the numbers of first-generation immigrants in Denmark.

Available data indicate a strong tendency to find spouses in the parents' country of origin among second-generation immigrants from nonwestern countries and among immigrants from nonwestern countries who have come to Denmark as children and have grown up in this country.[16] In 1998, 79% of the married males and 69% of the

---

[16] Third-generation immigrants from nonwestern countries living in Denmark have not yet reached marriage age.

764   *P. Nannestad / European Journal of Political Economy 20 (2004) 755–767*

married females in these groups were married to a person from their or their parents' country of origin. Among Turks, the figures were 89% for married males and 81% for married females. It can also be seen that about 30% of all married males and close to 50% of all married females among immigrants from nonwestern countries have come to Denmark by means of marriage to and family (re)unification with (normally) a person from the same country already living in Denmark (Larsen and Matthiessen, 2002, pp. 56–60).

There is thus little empirical evidence to suggest that one should expect to see the group of (poorly integrated) first-generation immigrants from nonwestern countries being gradually replaced by (much better integrated) second- and third-generation immigrants. Unless the patterns of marital choice change rather dramatically, second-generation immigrants from nonwestern countries will contribute to continuously replenishing the pool of first-generation immigrants from nonwestern countries in Denmark.[17] This, in turn, may have a negative impact on the integration of third-generation nonwestern immigrants through intergenerational transmission mechanisms.

The other crucial assumption in the optimistic scenario is that second-generation immigrants from nonwestern countries will on average come to approach the labor market performance of native Danes. This is equivalent to assuming that there is no (negative) intergenerational transmission from first-generation immigrant parents to their second-generation immigrant offspring.

A large-scale study of the transition from school to work among second-generation immigrants in Denmark aged 18–35 years (Nielsen et al., 2001) demonstrates strong intergenerational transmission effects. It is demonstrated, for example, that the parents' attachment to the labor market has an effect on the descendants' probability of obtaining a qualifying education and a stable position in the labor market. The study concludes that assimilation of second-generation immigrants is not a process that is guaranteed to take place over time under all circumstances. It "...is also dependent on the employment success of the parent generation, and if the parents are not successfully integrated into the labor market, this result may carry over to the children" (Nielsen et al., 2001, p. 30), and as has been noted, immigrant parents from nonwestern countries are as a group not at all successfully integrated into the Danish labor market.

The same study also shows that there is still a huge gap in educational levels between native Danes and second-generation immigrants. Among native Danes aged 18–35 years in 1997, 65% of the males and 62% of the females had completed a formal education; among second-generation immigrants, the corresponding figures were 33% for males and 35% for females (Nielsen et al., 2001, p. 34).[18] While part of this difference may be

---

[17] Since considerable social and cultural as well as material interests are invested in these patterns of marital choice, change is unlikely to be allowed quickly. With regard to material aspects, Wikan (2002, p. 216) relates that young marriageable Muslim girls are colloquially referred to as "visa" or "gilded paper" in some immigrant circles in Norway.

[18] In a study of the educational attainment of the children of the Danish guest worker immigrants Jakobsen and Smith (2003) find similar results when looking at second-generation immigrants from Turkey, Pakistan and ex-Yugoslavia. It turns out that the problems are most severe with second-generation immigrants form Turkey. Immigrants from Turkey and their descendants make up the largest group of nonwestern immigrants in Denmark.

P. Nannestad / European Journal of Political Economy 20 (2004) 755–767   765

attributable to differences in the age distributions in the two groups, other studies show the same picture. Already in primary school, the achievement levels are lower for children with immigrant background than for native Danish children (Nannestad, 2003). Even worse, the achievement levels of second-generation immigrant children in Danish and mathematics are not better than the achievement levels of first-generation immigrant children (Ministry of Education, 2003). Among the pupils who finished primary school in 1995, 40% of those with a nonwestern immigrant background had not completed and were not enrolled in a qualifying educational program 6 years later, while the corresponding figure was 10% among native Danish pupils (Dansk Arbejdsgiverforening, 2003). Against this backdrop, the future prospects of a sizeable proportion of second-generation immigrants from nonwestern countries in the Danish labor market look bleak indeed.

It thus does not seem very likely that with the mere passing of time immigrants from nonwestern countries and their descendants in Denmark will as a group cease to be net beneficiaries of the welfare state and turn into net contributors instead. If this holds true, rather than assisting to resolve the problems, immigration will in fact be contributing to the challenges that the welfare state will be facing in the next decades due to an aging population of native Danes.

5. Conclusion

In the world described by the long-run neoclassical trade theory of the Heckscher–Ohlin type, consequences of trade and migration between countries with different factor endowments are in general equivalent. However, when the institutions of a universalistic, tax-financed welfare state with strongly redistributive goals are superimposed, asymmetrically distributed gains and losses from migration can arise. While migrants from poor countries will still reap benefits from migration, the native population in the receiving country will experience a loss (Wellisch and Walz, 1998; Hansen, 2003). The Danish welfare state exhibits that pattern with respect to immigration from nonwestern countries. The type of immigration that has been dominant since the early 1980s has resulted in the buildup in Denmark of a pool of immigrants from nonwestern countries and descendants of immigrants, characterized by being younger and less well educated than the rest of the population.

Immigrants from nonwestern countries and their descendants have been net beneficiaries of the Danish welfare state for a long period due, primarily, to lower labor market participation rates and higher unemployment rates compared to both immigrants from western countries and native Danes. While this may in principle change with the passing of time, as of now, there is little evidence to suggest that immigrants from nonwestern countries and their descendants will approach a position in the labor market that is comparable to the position of immigrants from western countries and native Danes. Typically, immigrants from nonwestern countries are still net beneficiaries of the welfare state even after more than 10 years of stay in the country. The educational achievements of second-generation immigrants from nonwestern countries suggest that a considerable part will end up in the group of unskilled workers that faces ever decreasing demand in the Danish labor market.

766 *P. Nannestad / European Journal of Political Economy 20 (2004) 755–767*

The institutions of the Danish welfare state may well contribute to creating and perpetuating problems with the position of nonwestern immigrants and their descendants in the Danish labor market. The influence of the welfare-state institutions is felt both on the supply and the demand sides. On the supply side, generous social benefits and small differences between the level of social benefits and minimum wages weaken economic incentives for labor market participation, especially among low-skilled low-wage labor. On the demand side, generous social benefit levels exert upward pressure on minimum wages, thus reducing demand for low-skilled, low-productive labor, and a sizeable tax wedge all but eliminates private demand for domestic services.

Thus, due not least to the redistributive welfare state, immigration from nonwestern countries to Denmark has so far not been advantageous to the native Danish population from an economic point of view, and there is not much to suggest that this picture is going to change in the foreseeable future.

References

Borjas, G.J., 1998. Immigration and welfare magnets. NBER working paper no. 6813. National Bureau of Economic Research, Cambridge, MA.

Chiswick, B., 2000. Are immigrants favorably self-selected?: An economic analysis. IZA Discussion paper 131. IZA, Bonn.

Dansk Arbejdsgiverforening, 2003. 4 ud af 10 unge indvandrere uden uddannelse (Four out of ten young immigrants without any qualifying education). ArbejdsMarkedsPolitisk Agenda, Sept. 11, 6.

Esping-Andersen, G, 1990. The Three Worlds of Welfare Capitalism. Polity Press, Cambridge, UK.

Hansen, J.D., 2003. Immigration and income distribution in welfare states. European Journal of Political Economy 19, 713–735.

Jakobsen, V., Smith, N., 2003. The educational attainment of the children of the Danish "guest worker" immigrants. IZA Discussion paper 749. IZA, Bonn.

Larsen, C., 2000. Uddannelse og danskkundskaber (Education and Danish language proficiency). In: Mogensen, G.V., Matthiessen, P.Chr. (Eds.), Indvandrerne og arbejdsmarkedet (Immigrants and the Labour Market). Spektrum, Copenhagen, pp. 160–197.

Larsen, C., Matthiessen, P.Chr., 2002. Indvandrerbefolkningens sammensætning og udvikling i Danmark (The composition and development of the immigrant population in Denmark). In: Mogensen, G.V., Matthiessen, P.Chr. (Eds.), Indvandrerne og arbejdsmarkedet (Immigrants and the Labour Market). Spektrum, Copenhagen, pp. 25–79.

Ministry of Education, 2003. Social baggrund påvirker karakterer (Social background influences examination scores). Undervisningsministeriets Nyhedsbrev (Newsletter of the Ministry of Education) 17 (14), 3.

Ministry of Finance, 2003. Økonomisk redegørelse, maj 2003 (Economic report, May 2003). Schultz, Copenhagen.

Nannestad, P., 2003. It's not the economy, stupid!: Municipal school expenditures and school achievement levels in Denmark. Paper presented at the annual meeting of the European Public Choice Society, Aarhus. (http://www.econ.au.dk/EPCS/Papers/Nannestad.pdf).

Nielsen, H.S., Rosholm, M., Smith, N., Husted, L., 2001. Intergenerational transmissions and the school-to-work transition of 2nd generation immigrants. IZA Discussion paper 216. IZA, Bonn.

Rasmussen, H.K., 1997. No Entry: Immigration Policy in Europe. CBS Press, Copenhagen.

Rasmussen, H.K., 2000. Dem og os (Them and Us). Tiderne skifter, Aarhus.

Schultz-Nielsen, M.L., 2002a. Indvandrernes tilknytning til arbejdsmarkedet 1985–2001 (The absorption of immigrants into the labour market 1985–2002). In: Mogensen, G.V., Matthiessen, P.Chr. (Eds.), Indvandrerne og arbejdsmarkedet (Immigrants and the Labour Market). Spektrum, Copenhagen, pp. 80–117.

Schultz-Nielsen, M.L., 2002b. Hvorfor er så mange indvandrere uden beskæftigelse? (Why are so many immi-

P. Nannestad / European Journal of Political Economy 20 (2004) 755–767   767

grants without employment?). In: Mogensen, G.V., Matthiessen, P.Chr. (Eds.), Indvandrerne og arbejdsmar-kedet (Immigrants and the Labour Market). Spektrum, Copenhagen, pp. 118–159.

Statistics Denmark, 1999. Statistical Ten-year Review 1999. Danmarks Statistik, Copenhagen.

Wadensjö, E., Orrje, H., 2002. Immigration and the Public Sector in Denmark. Aarhus Univ. Press, Aarhus.

Wellisch, D., Walz, U., 1998. Why do rich countries prefer free trade over free migration?: The role of the modern welfare state. European Economic Review 42, 1595–1612.

Wikan, U., 2002. Generous Betrayal. University of Chicago Press, Chicago.

Part 3

Political and Legal Institutions

Public Choice 49: 249-263 (1986).

Rent-seeking aspects of political advertising

ROGER D. CONGLETON*

Department of Economics, Clarkson University, Potsdam, NY 13676

1. Introduction

Political contests have all the usual characteristics of rent-seeking games characterized in the recent volume edited by Buchanan, Tollison and Tullock (1980). That is to say, resources are committed to a distributive contest where the social pie is not necessarily enlarged but rather divided up (a policy enacted) via a 'winner take all' apportioning. Since political advertising is one method of influencing electoral outcomes, we might expect competitive political advertising to exhibit rent-seeking losses of the usual sort. The extent of the rent-seeking losses associated with political advertising depends upon the extent to which advertising affects voter perceptions of the relative merits of electoral alternatives. Political proponents may well completely dissipate any electoral rents at stake through their advertising efforts, yet still increase social welfare if political advertisments provide sufficiently valuable information to the electorate. On the other hand, if advertising has no effect on voter perceptions or provides information of dubious value then rent dissipating advertising may generate substantial rent-seeking losses.

Conceptually, every electoral process consists of three stages: (1) the preelectoral stage in which referendum proposals are considered, (2) the electioneering stage in which political advocates attempt to pursuade voters of the merits of the positions or candidates at issue, and (3) the final stage in which the votes are actually cast and tabulated. While all three stages are clearly interdependent (see Tullock, 1967), this paper focuses on stage two of the process. The selection of candidates or policy positions and the voting rule by which votes are tabulated are assumed to have taken place prior to

* A previous version of this paper was presented at the Public Choice Meetings in New Orleans. The author would like to thank Paul Rubin, Gordon Tullock and the session participants for their numerous helpful suggestions, many of which have been incorporated into this paper.

the advertising phase of the election and remain fixed during the advertising campaign.

To explore the extent to which political advertising may have a dead-weight loss associated with it, we examine situations where two policy proponents attempt to determine the outcome of a referendum by influencing the vote of an undecided group of voters. Two advertising environments are examined: (1) a setting in which every message sent by an advertiser will reach and influence members of the undecided group, and (2) a setting in which additional messages merely influence the probability that members of the targeted group will confront the message sent. Our analysis suggests that rent-seeking losses will tend to be larger within the perfect advertising environment than in the second setting.

The paper is organized as follows. Section 2 characterizes the effects of advertising on the targeted group voters. Section 3 analyses the optimal advertising efforts of two groups of political advocates directed at the decisive undecided group given a perfect advertising medium. Section 4 explores the implications of an imperfect advertising medium. Section 5 summarizes the paper and suggests possible policy implications.

2. Advertising and voter perceptions

Let there be three homogeneous groups of voters who differ in their assessment of a proposed policy change. One group is unalterably in favor of the proposed policy change, another is opposed to the change, and the third is as yet undecided about the merits of the proposed policy change. If neither of the pro-change and anti-change groups is sufficiently large to determine the electoral outcome, then the final evaluation of the undecided group will be decisive. Political advertising represents one method of influencing the deliberations of the undecided group.

Following Kramer (1971), we assume that voters are principally concerned with the likely range of their own post-election wealth. Expected utility is assumed to be a linear function of the mean and variance of the perceived wealth distribution.

$$U^e = e(W) - B\, v(W) \tag{1}$$

Where $e(W)$ and $v(W)$ are the respective mean and variance of the distribution of voter wealth associated with a particular electoral outcome, and B is a parameter representing the degree of risk aversion exhibited. Similar linear indices of the value of risky assets are widely used in the finance literature in a different context.

To simplify exposition, we assume that the level of wealth associated with current policy has a value of zero and is known with certainty, but that assessment of the level of wealth associated with the proposed policy change is problematic. This normalizes the utility function so that the expected utility of the *status quo* is zero, and is broadly consistent with the observation that risk averse voters are naturally predisposed toward the *status quo*. Proposed changes that generate the same average wealth as current policy will be rejected in favor of the *status quo* because of the greater uncertainty associated with new policies.

In this context, political advertising is effective if it alters the perceived mean and variance of the distribution of possible wealth levels associated with the proposed policy change. Thus, advertising does not have to change tastes to be effective. It is sufficient that advertising have an impact on voter expectations about the likely consequences of the policy choices at issue. While there are a good many possible ways to represent the manner in which advertising influences voter perceptions (see Tullock, 1967; Crain and Tollison, 1976; Nelson, 1976; or Kau, Keenan and Rubin, 1982), this paper utilizes a mechanism analogous to Bayes' law. A Baysesian mechanism has the desireable property that both the message sent and the number of times the message is heard have effects on voter perception in so far as new posterior probabilities are determined. Undecided voters are assumed to have priors and likelihood functions consistent with being 'open minded sceptics'. That is to say, they have diffuse priors over the range of interest, and likelihood functions that assign a slightly greater probability to a particular message being heard if it is true than if it is false, but regard false messages as only slightly less likely. Exposure to a political message is treated as if it were an experimental observation. Posterior probabilities are calculated according to Bayes' Law.

Let the probability of hearing a particular message if it is true be T and the probability of hearing some other message be F, where T is greater than F. Let W_i be a particular post election wealth level, w_i be the message that W_i will in fact obtain and n_i be the number of w_i messages confronted by a voter. A sequence of messages concerning W_i and W_j will yield the following posterior probability that W_i obtains.

$$P(W_i \mid n_i, n_j) = \frac{1}{1 + (M-2)(F/T)^{n_i} + (F/T)^{(n_i - n_j)}} \tag{2}$$

Inspection reveals that:

$$\delta P(W_i)/\delta n_i > 0 \qquad \delta(W_i)/\delta n_j < 0$$

The probability that a particular wealth level, W_i, will occur following a particular electoral outcome rises with the number of w_i messages con-

fronted and falls with the number of other messages heard, other things being equal. On the other hand, the relationship between messages confronted
and utility is more complex. Bayesian adjustment implies that voter perceptions will converge to a single value if a single message is repeated endlessly.
In this case, the variance of the distribution of wealth associated with a particular policy approaches zero. However, in cases where several different
messages are confronted, the perceived variance of post election wealth will
increase if the messages are sufficiently diverse. For example, an extremely
positive message may increase the expected wealth associated with adoption
of the new policy yet increase the perceived risk sufficiently to *reduce* utility.
The task of political advertisers is not an easy one.

3. Optimal advertising with a perfect advertising medium

Advertisers face the dual problem of choosing a message to transmit and the
number of times that the message should be transmitted to the targeted
group of voters. The pro-change group[1] will be inclined to send messages
that lead undecided voters to prefer the proposed policy change to the *status
quo*. The group favoring the *status quo* will attempt to convince voters that
they will be worse off if the proposed policy change is enacted. In order to
maximize rents, each politically active group must accomplish their goal at
least cost.

Let N' and N'' be the value of a negative electoral outcome for the anti
and pro change coalition respectively. Let Y' and Y'' be similar values for
passage of the proposal. Clearly $N' > Y'$ and $Y'' > N''$ given the policy
positions of the two groups. The rent or net advantage realized by politically
active groups is simply the difference between their respective evaluations
of the alternatives less the cost of resources devoted to influencing the electoral outcome.

$$R' = Y' - N' - c(n') \tag{3a}$$

$$R'' = Y'' - N'' - c(n'') \tag{3b}$$

Given fixed evaluations of the electoral alternatives by the politically active
groups, maximizing rents requires minimizing the cost of bringing undecided voters around to the appropriate points of view.

Figure 1a represents the optimal advertising campaign for the group opposing the proposed change. Their task is to ensure that voters assign a
negative expected utility to the proposed electoral change. The upward sloping lines represent utility levels that the undecided group would assign to the
proposed change after hearing n_j messages that W_j will obtain, other things

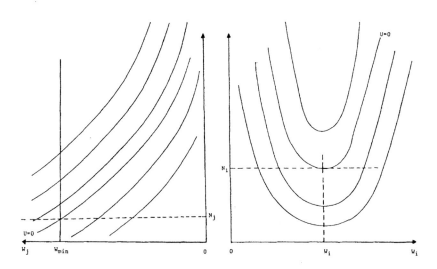

Figure 1a.   Figure 1b.

being equal. Extremely negative messages lower utility by both decreasing the mean and increasing the variance of the distribution of wealth associated with the referendum proposal. A similar result can be obtained with less extreme messages if the message is repeated a few more times. For the anti-change group extremism and message repetitions are substitutes. Since it is no more costly to transmit extreme messages than moderate messages, iso-cost lines are horizontal. Thus, the optimal advertising campaign is the combination of message and broadcasts found at the point where the zero iso-utility line touches the lowest iso-cost line. This occurs at the point where the $U = 0$ iso-utility curve crosses the vertical line representing the minimum plausible outcome, W_{min}. Extremism is cost effective for the anti-change group since it both increases uncertainty and reduces the mean of the distribution of wealth associated with the proposed policy change.

The pro-change coalition can not rely upon a similarly extreme positive message because such extremism may not increase the mean sufficiently to offset the now undesireable effect of higher variance. Proponents of the *status quo* benefit by making the alternative seem risky, but those favoring change must assure voters that risks are relatively small. This constraint does not imply that pro-change messages should accurately represent the likely outcome, but simply that the messages can not present the pro-change case in the most glowing terms imaginable. Causal observation affirms this assymetry. While opponents of policy changes often emphasize that the proposed policy revision implies the 'end' of civilization in one manner or another, proponents rarely promise nirvana.[2] Figure 1b illustrates the optimal advertising campaign for the coalition favoring adoption of the new policy. The iso-utility lines confronted by the pro-change coalition are U-shaped. Over part of the range, number of messages and extremism are substitutes. After the point where the variance effect dominates the effect on the perceived mean of the wealth distribution, a complementary relationship exists. The optimal level of extremism is found at the bottom of the $U = 0$ curve, at the point where the marginal increase in the mean is just offset by the risk adjusted change in the variance. The minimum cost effective advertising campaign requires a number of messages just larger than that required to reach the zero iso-utility curve. While the optimal message may suggest that the policy yields a substantial increase in voter utility, claims are below the highest imaginable.

Obviously, it is not possible for both advertisers to achieve their intended goal. Voters can not simultaneously assign an expected utility to the proposal that is greater and less than zero. There is no Nash equilibrium in an advertising game where advertisers utilize a perfect medium. The deterministic link between advertising and voter response implies that any campaign undertaken by one group may be defeated by the other with a suitable change in strategy. For example, adoption of a winning campaign by the pro-change group implies that the iso-utility curves of the anti-change group shift up and to the left of those in Figure 1a. As a consequence, the previous combination of message and broadcasts will no longer achieve the desired result. A successful campaign now requires additional broadcasts. Adoption of this strategy by the anti-change group would, in turn, shift the iso-utility curves faced by the pro-change group upward and to the left. As a result, the pro-change group will find that a successful advertising campaign now requires more broadcasts and a somewhat more modest message. A sequence of Cournot adjustments by political proponents will tend toward more and more expensive advertising campaigns, completely dissipating the rents at issue.

Tables 1 and 2 below simulate the effects of message extremism and repetition on a representative undecided voter. Table 1 illustrates the effect of extreme messages in a setting where there are just five possible outcomes and hence messages that might be sent concerning the consenquences of the proposed change. In particular, the policy may yield much better results than the *status quo*, w = + 2, might be moderately better than the *status quo*, w = + 1, might be about the same as the *status quo*, w = 0, or it may be moderately, w = − 1, or extremely worse, w = − 2, than the current situation. At the top of each cell are two numbers representing the mean and variance perceived by the voter after confronting 5 identical messages from each coalition.[3] Thus, the upper righthand cell represents the expectations resulting from a series of five messages of W = + 2 from the pro-change group and 5 messages of W = − 2 from the anti-change group.

Note that extreme messages $w = +2$ or $w = -2$ have the greatest impact on the voter's expected wealth regardless of the message sent by the other group. On the other hand, as both messages move toward extremes, the estimated variance of the associated distribution of policy outcomes increases. The net effect of a particular combination of messages will depend upon the extent of voter risk aversion.

Evidence of the overall effect of the advertising campaign is given by the two numbers in parentheses in each cell. These characterize the utility level realized by voters at risk aversion varies. The lower numbers characterize a more risk averse population of voters than the upper numbers. The upper number is obtained by setting risk aversion parameter B in equation 1 equal to 0.10. The lower number is calculated by setting B equal to 0.25. Since the utility level of the *status quo* has been assigned a value of zero, voters will favor the proposed change if their utility level exceeds zero.

Table 1 illustrates three significant points. (1) Given equally extreme messages, the anti-change coalition can always defeat the pro-change coalition if voters are risk averse, other things being equal.[4] Equally extreme messages offset each other in terms of expected value, but increase the estimated variance of the distribution of outcomes believed to be associated with the proposed change in policy. This makes the proposal less attractive to an open minded sceptic than the *status quo*. Utility levels along the left-to-right diagonal yield uniformly negative values for the utility.[5] (2) Increases in voter risk aversion make successful adoption of a new proposal less and less likely. In the case where B = 0.25 the proposal will gain support only if both 'sides' agree that the proposed change will be advantageous. (3) Coalition efforts to gain voter support for their position tends to cause them to send extreme messages. The Nash equilibrium message of the game characterized by Table 1 is (2, −2) with the proposed change being defeated.

Table 2 illustrates the impact of increased advertising on the open minded but sceptical voter characterized above. Table 2 represents the effects that a series of $w = +2$ messages and $w = -2$ messages have on the previously characterized undecided voter. Each cell contains values for the perceived mean and variance of electoral outcomes and, in parentheses, values for associated utilities. The latter are calculated using equation 1 and B = 0.10 and are thus comparable to those of the less risk averse voter in Table 1. A simultaneous increase in message repetitions by both groups does not affect the mean wealth associated with the proposed policy, but does affect the perceived variance of that wealth by making voters believe that extreme outcomes are somewhat more likely. As a consequence, risk averse voters will be even less inclined to support the proposed change than they would have at lower exposure levels. A simultaneous increase in advertising expen-

Table 1.

	−2	−1	0	+1	+2
+2	0.0 2.9 (−.29) (−.74)	.23 2.2 (+.01) (−.32)	.47 1.8 (+.29) (+.03)	0.7 1.7 (+.53) (+.27)	1.3 1.6 (+1.14) (+.90)
+1	−.23 2.2 (−.45) (−.78)	0.0 1.5 (−.15) (−.38)	.23 1.24 (+.11) (−.08)	.65 .92 (+.56) (+.42)	0.7 1.7 (+.53) (+.27)
0	−.47 1.8 (−.65) (−.92)	−.23 1.24 (−.35 (−.54)	0.0 0.70 (−.07) (−.18)	.23 1.24 (+.11) (−.08)	0.47 1.8 (+.29) (+.03)
−1	−.70 1.7 (−0.87) (−1.14)	−.65 .92 (−.74) (−.88)	−.23 1.24 (−.35) (−.54	0.0 1.5 (−.15) (−.38)	0.23 2.2 (+.01) (−.32)
−2	−1.3 1.6 (−1.5) (−1.7)	−.70 1.7 −.87) (−1.14)	−.47 1.8 (−.65) (−.92)	−.23 2.2 (−.45) (−.78)	0.0 2.9 (−.29) (−.74)

Each cell has numbers for the mean and variance of W after receiving five messages from each coalition of $W = W_i$. Below the mean and variance are two numbers in parentheses reflecting the utility levels associated with a vote in favor of the proposal calculated from: (i) $U = \text{mean}(w) - 0.1\text{var}(w)$ and (ii) $U = \text{mean}(w) - 0.25\text{var}(w)$.

Table 2.

w = +2 messages			
	0	5	10
w = −2 messages 0	0.0 2.00 (−.50)	0.61 2.24 (+.05)	1.30 1.61 (0.89)
5	−0.61 2.24 (−1.17)	0.0 2.94 (−.735)	0.86 2.66 (+.195)
10	−1.30 1.61 (−.170)	−0.86 2.66 (−1.52)	0.0 3.58 (−.895)

Each cell has values for the mean value of W, the variance of W and the utility of voting for the policy alternative calculated as $U = \text{mean}(w) - .10\,\text{var}(w)$ after a sequence of $w = +2$ and $w = -2$ messages.

ditures reinforces the *status quo's* electoral support.

Together, Tables 1 and 2 suggest that interaction between political advertisers is likely to result in increasing numbers of relatively extreme messages. The former suggests that competitive advertising efforts will tend to dissipate electoral rents. The latter suggests that, ignoring cases in which the true distrubution of outcomes is bimodal, the information provided by their efforts will be biased and tend to increase uncertainty. Political advertising may generate external costs rather than benefits. The rent-seeking losses of political advertising in this case will exceed the sum of the two advertising budgets.

4. Political advertising with an imperfect medium

We now turn to an examination of the choice faced by political proponents in a less perfect advertising environment. In this setting additional messages do not necessarily reach and influence voters, but rather increase the probability that voters will confront the message distributed. In the previous case, the absence of a Nash equilibrium implied that advertising efforts would escalate toward levels where all rents were dissipated. In this case, advertisers will find advertising a less effective tool and tend to devote fewer resources to advertising. As a consequence, a Nash equilibrium does exist and the escalation of the first setting is not a concern. Thus, the necessity of using an imperfect advertising medium may reduce rent-seeking losses associated with political contests.

Let us assume that advertisers have established the most effective message to broadcast and at this point primarily concerned with determining the optimal number of times to transmit the message. This choice can be represented as an attempt to maximise the expected rents of the advertising campaign. For the coalition in favor of the proposed change, the net benefit of advertising can be represented as:

$$R'' = P(Y, N)Y'' + (1 - P(Y, N))N'' - YC \qquad (4)$$

with: $P_Y > 0, P_N < 0, P_{YY} < 0,$

$P_{NN} < 0,$ and $P_{YN} < 0.$

Where Y is the number of messages sent by those favoring the change, N the number sent by those opposed and $P(Y, N)$ is the resulting probability of successfully passing the referendum. The probability of successfully enacting a policy change increases as the number of messages sent increases, but at a decreasing rate. On the other hand, the probability of adoption falls as the number of messages sent by the opposition increases, but at a decreasing rate. If we assume that advertisements are purchased in a competitive market at a cost of C per broadcast, YC will be the cost of the advertising campaign. Y'' and N'' represent the value to the pro-change coalition of successful passage and defeat respectively.

First order conditions for maximizing the coalition rents through advertising can be obtained by differentiating equation 4 with respect to the number of broadcasts, Y, and setting the result equal to zero.

$$P_Y (Y'' - N'') = C \tag{5}$$

Advertising should be undertaken up to the point where the expected marginal improvement in the electoral outcome equals the marginal cost of the improvement. The properties of function P imply the existance of a unique optimum advertising level for each combination of rents at stake, advertising costs, and advertising strategy by the opposition. The implicit function theorem suggests that this relationship can be written as a function of these other variables.

$$Y^* = f(N, C, Y' - N') \tag{6.0}$$

The implicit function differentiation rule can be used to determine the qualitative effects of these variables on the optimal advertising level.

$$Y_{(Y' - N')}^* = -[P_Y]/[P_{YY}] < 0 \tag{6.1}$$

$$Y_C^* = 1/[P_{YY}] < 0 \tag{6.2}$$

$$Y_N^* = -[P_{YN}]/[P_{YY}] < 0 \tag{6.3}$$

These derivatives imply that the net benefit maximizing level of advertising increases as rents and as the marginal cost of sending a message decreases. Public policies that affect the level of rents at issue or change the cost of broadcasting campaign messages will directly affect the level of advertising undertaken. The last partial derivative suggests that optimal advertising *decreases* as level of advertising undertaken by the opposition increases. The last result obtains because the efficacy of each broadcast diminishes as a consequence of advertising by the opposition.

Equation 6.0 can be regarded as a reaction function that determines the pro-change coalition's optimal response to an advertising level of the anti-change coalition given the cost of advertising and electoral rents. A similar reaction function can be derived for the opposition in an analogous manner:

$$N^* = g(Y, C, (N - Y')) \tag{7}$$

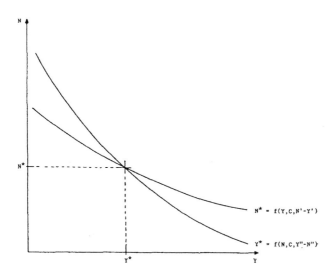

Figure 2.

where $N' - Y'$ is the rent that the opposing group seeks to protect by campaigning against the proposed change. Equation 6.3 implies that both reaction functions will be downward sloping in the NxY plane. A Nash
equilibrium occurs when a particular Y^*, N^* combination simultaneously
satisfies both equations 6a and 7. Figure 2 illustrates the case where the
resulting equilibrium is dynamically stable in the sense that a sequence of
Cournot adjustments will converge to the intersection of the two curves.[6]
In other situations Cournot adjustments will cause one of the advertisers to
drop out of the political contest. In either case, the optimal response to an
increase in advertising by the opposition is not a reciprocal increase but
rather a decrease in advertising effort. The absence of escalating tendencies
suggests that rent-seeking losses will be smaller in this setting than in the
previously explored perfect advertising setting.[7]

   The extent of the rent-seeking losses that do occur can be calculated by
contrasting the above Nash equilibrium with the socially net-benefit maximizing levels of advertising. If we assume that electoral rents are concentrated in the politically active coalitions, then the expected social net-benefit
of advertising can be summarized as:

$$NB = P(Y, N)(Y'' - N'') + (1 - P(Y, M))(N' - Y') - $$
$$- (Y + N)C + V(Y, N) \tag{8}$$

Where $V(Y, N)$ is the value of advertising to the targeted group of voters and the other variables are as previously defined. Social net-benefits consist of expected coalition rents, less advertising costs, plus any benefits accruing outside the coalitions as a consequence of advertising expenditures. Differentiating with respect to Y and N, and setting the result equal to zero yields the following first order conditions:

$$P_Y [Y'' - N'') + (Y' - N')] + V_Y = C \tag{8.1}$$

$$P_N [(Y'' - N'') + (Y' - N')] + V_N = C \tag{8.2}$$

Equations 8.1 and 8.2 suggest that a coalition send messages up to the point where marginal social benefit of the message equals its marginal social cost. Equation 8.1 bears a close resemblance to equation 5 above. They differ in that the condition for the socially optimal number of messages requires internalization of external costs imposed on the opposition coalition and of any external benefits (or costs) realised by the undecided coalition. In the special case where the contest of interest is a zero sum game, the term in brackets becomes zero, and maximizing social net-benefits requires messages to be sent as long as their marginal value to the undecided coalition exceeds their marginal cost. In a setting where gains of one group exceed the losses of the other, the term in the group with fewer rents at stake will be negative. Efficiency requires this group to send even fewer messages than might be justified on purely informational grounds. The coalition with the larger rents at stake should send a few more messages than justifiable on purely informational grounds.

Only in the case where the external cost imposed on competing advertisers *exactly* equals the gains to the electorate will competitive advertising generate the social net-benefit maximizing level of advertising. To the extent that our previous analysis of advertising messages obtains, messages are likely to generate costs rather than benefits to voters at the margin. In this case, the absence of terms representing costs imposed on political competitors and targeted voters implies that political advertisers tend to overadvertise and generate rent-seeking losses. The extent of the rent-seeking loss may be characterized as the difference equation 8.0 evaluated at the socially optimal level and equation 8.0 evaluated at the level that would be chosen in a private contest. In the case where the political contest is a zero sum game and the information of no particular value, the dead weight loss of political advertising will once again be the sum of the two advertising budgets plus any external losses imposed on voters.

5. Conclusion

This paper has demonstrated that advertising by policy proponents can generate rent-seeking losses of the sort often associated with distributional games. In particular, political advertising that fails to provide substantial benefits to individuals not directly involved in the political contest will generally have a rent-seeking waste associated with it. Our analysis of the effects of political advertising on the electorate and on electoral results suggests that such rent-seeking losses are likely to be the case. In addition to the usual resources costs of rent-seeking activities, political advertising may impose negative externalities on voters by providing biased appraisals of the likely outcomes of policy proposals and the risks involved. In the cases examined in this paper, political advertising *increased* uncertainty about proposed policy changes and so reduced the likelihood that generally useful reforms would be adopted. For the most part, competitive advertising efforts tended to offset each other which implied that a voter's initial predilections toward the alternatives at issue were the decisive factor. Yet, the prisoners' dilemma nature of the advertising game implies that political advertisers can not readily escape from the necessity of expensive advertising campaigns.

While it is only with great hesitation that one should draw policy conclusions from highly abstract models like those developed above, some conclusions seem sufficiently general to be worth the risk. First, imposing ceilings on advertising below the levels that would have otherwise been chosen will clearly reduce the dead weight loss of political advertising in either environment. On the other hand, it will bias electoral results in favor of the *status quo*. Equal numbers of messages allow policy proponents to send messages which, on balance, increase the perceived risk associated the policy change at issue. This in turn reduces the inclination of risk averse voters to support the proposed revision. Second, a rule which limits political advertising methods to less perfect instruments tends to reduce advertising effort. Such rules do not change the inherent advantage that the *status quo* has over proposed policy changes as a simple matter of voter risk aversion, but do increase the likelihood that modestly useful policy revisions could be adopted by referendum. Third, an advertising tax can be used to influence the extent of political advertising and any dead weight loss associated with it. In both environments, advertisers were affected by the cost of sending messages.[8] Any of these three steps would, in the context of the models analysed above, reduce advertising expenditures and rent-seeking losses associated with the electoral process.

262

NOTES

1. For the purposes of this paper, we assume that the usual public goods problems of collective action have been overcome by the politically active coalitions. While these problems do play a role in determining both the referendum agenda and the financial strength of a particular group, explicit consideration of these aspects of political advertising is left for future research.

2. In a setting where voter evaluations of the *status quo* are open to change advertisers will face symmetric constraints. The pro-change coalition will find extreme negatism to be cost-effective, while, the anti-change group will find that making extreme claims for the *status quo* is counterproductive. In complex settings where the range of possible messages is restricted by prior commitments or other constraints not considered here, the optimal number of message repetitions will tend to increase since the optimal message may no longer be a feasable message.

3. Numbers for the mean and variance of the posterior distribution are calculated using diffuse priors, and likelihood functions that assign a probability of 0.24 to hearing a message that is actually correct, $P(W_i | w_i) = 0.24$, and a probability of 0.19 to all other messages, $P(W_i | w_j) = 0.19$.

4. The complete dominance of the *status quo* in the simulation is partially an artifact of the assumed diffuse priors of the group of undecided voters. If voters are not truly undecided in the sense characterized above, then the initial advantage of the *status quo* may be eroded or eliminated. If voters have an initial predisposition against the *status quo* or favoring the alternative, then new policies may more readily defeat the *status quo*. This may be the case if recent experience has been tumultuous or if an especially attractive policy is proposed.

5. This is not to say that extreme *policies* are necessarily desireable. An important consideration in the pre-electioneering stage is to place the optimal candidate or position on the ballot. The choice of an optimal candidate or position is analogous to the choice of message discussed above. The position chosen will maximize rents for the politically active group subject to the constraint of being sufficiently attractive to the undecided group (in conjunction with the advertising campaign) that the policy is adopted. In the context of the model explored here, the choice of the proposition on to be on the ballot is in effect the choice of a pre-advertising (*a priori*) probability distribution of wealth associated with successful passage of the proposal. The optimal policy position involves a tradeoff between realizable rents and attendant advertising costs associated with a successful campaign. Thus, extremists may loose even if they run an effective advertising campaign because of initial predilections against their espoused positions. Our focus on advertising is not meant to imply that advertising alone is decisive.

6. The Nash equilibrium illustrated would also result if political advertisers made a once and forever adoption of what Case (1979) calls robust strategies.

7. This is not to say that advertising budgets in successive campaigns would tend to decrease. Changes in the cost of sending messages and/or the level of rents at issue will dictate the time path of advertising expenditures through time. For example, an upward trend in rents at issue would imply an upward trend in advertising budgets as both reaction functions shift outward through time.

8. The appropriate remedial Pigovian tax can be calculated for the prochange group by subtracting equation 5 from equation 8.1. A similar computation can be performed for the messages from those favoring the *status quo*.

$$T_Y = P_y (W'' - W') - V_y \tag{9.1}$$

$$T_N = P_n (Y' - N') - V_n \tag{9.2}$$

These taxes would cause policy proponents to make the appropriate internalized of costs and benefits imposed on others. Imposition of Pigovian taxes would shift both reaction curves so that they intersect at social net-benefit maximizing levels.

Unfortunately, the cost-benefit analysis required to properly tax political opponents is difficult to undertake, and probably would create an even less attractive rent-seeking game over who gets to perform the analysis. Failing the appropriate cost benefit analysis, a modest excise tax on political messages seems to be the best tax that might be hoped for. An excise tax would increase the cost of political advertising and thereby reduce the number of messages sent by each coalition and hence the level of rent-seeking losses.

REFERENCES

Buchanan, J.M., Tollison, R.D., and Tullock, G., Eds. (1980). *Towards a theory of the rent-seeking society*. College Station: Texas A&M Press.
Case, J.H. (1979). *Economics and the competitive process*. New York: New York University Press.
Corcoran, W.J. (1984). Long-run equilibrium and total expenditures on rent seeking. *Public Choice* 43: 89–94.
Crain, W., and Tollison, R. (1976). Campaign expenditures and political competition. *Journal of Law and Economics* (April): 177–188.
Kau, J.B., Keenan, D., and Rubin, P.H. (1982). A general equilibrium model of congressional voting. *Quarterly Journal of Economics* (May): 271–293.
Kramer, G. (1971). Short-term fluctuations in U.S. voting behavior. *American Political Science Review* 65: 131–143.
Nelson, P. (1976). Political information. *Journal of Law and Economics* (August): 315–336.
Tullock, G. (1967). *Towards a mathematics of politics*. Ann Arbor: University of Michigan Press.

RENT EXTRACTION AND RENT CREATION IN THE ECONOMIC THEORY OF REGULATION

*FRED S. MCCHESNEY**

I. Introduction

THE economic theory of regulation has advanced considerably since Stigler's seminal piece explained government's ability to create rents by cartelizing private producers.[1] Because political action can redistribute wealth generally, it is now seen that private interest groups other than producers also have an incentive to organize, both to obtain the gains and to avoid the losses from a whole menu of government enactments.[2] The configuration of winners and losers depends on many factors, and it changes as the underlying demands for and costs of regulation shift. New technology, for example, may render existing government regulations undesirable to their prior beneficiaries or make current regulations useful to groups previously not benefited. Finally, "government" itself has come to be treated, not as a unit, but as a complicated network of individuals, each with an incentive to maximize his own interest.

The original economic theory of regulation thus has evolved into a more complex description of the various ways government regulatory power can be turned to private ends. Two limitations of the current economic

* John M. Olin Visiting Fellow in Law and Economics, University of Chicago Law School; Associate Professor, Emory University School of Law. Many persons commented helpfully on earlier drafts of this paper, including participants in presentations at Emory University, Clemson University, the Federal Trade Commission, Holy Cross College, and the annual meetings of the Western Economic Association (July 1985) and the Public Choice Society (March 1985). My colleague David Haddock provided especially helpful comments. Henry Butler, Frank Easterbrook, Ernest Gellhorn, Mark Moran, Timothy Muris, Steven Salop, David Schap, and an anonymous referee also contributed much useful criticism.

[1] George J. Stigler, The Theory of Economic Regulation, 2 Bell J. Econ. 3 (1971).

[2] Sam Peltzman, Toward a More General Theory of Regulation, 19 J. Law & Econ. 211 (1976); Gary S. Becker, A Theory of Competition among Pressure Groups for Political Influence, 98 Q. J. Econ. 371 (1983).

[*Journal of Legal Studies*, vol. XVI (January 1987)]

101

model are noteworthy, however. First, despite the growing realization that "government" is not a monolith, the role of the politician has not been integrated satisfactorily into the model. The politician has remained a "mystery actor,"[3] a passive broker among competing private rent seekers.[4] Second, the economic theory, even in its post-Stiglerian form, remains one of rent creation. Observers note that creation of rents does not seem to explain many of the regulatory statutes that legislators have enacted.[5] But the opportunities for political gains from activities other than rent creation have not been considered.

This article focuses specifically on politicians. It views them, not as mere brokers redistributing wealth in response to competing private demands, but as independent actors making their own demands to which private actors respond. The conceptual reversal of roles in turn forces consideration of the ways other than rent creation that politicians can gain from private parties. A model is developed to show how politicians reap returns first by threatening and then by forbearing from extracting private rents already in existence. These private rents, as opposed to politically created rents, represent returns to their owners' entrepreneurial ability and firm-specific private investments.[6]

Political office confers a property right, not just to legislate rents, but to impose costs. A politician can gain by forbearing from exercising his right to impose burdensome restrictions on private actors. The passage of sharply focused taxes and regulations will reduce the returns that private capital owners receive from their skills and investments. In order to protect these returns, private owners have an incentive to strike bargains with legislators, as long as the side payments to politicians are lower than

---

[3] Robert D. Tollison, Rent Seeking: A Survey, 35 Kyklos 575, 592 (1982).

[4] For example, Robert E. McCormick & Robert D. Tollison, Politicians, Legislation, and the Economy (1981).

[5] "The 'consumerist' measures of the last few years . . . are not an obvious product of interest group pressures, and the proponents of the economic theory of regulation have thus far largely ignored such measures." Richard A. Posner, Theories of Economic Regulation, 5 Bell J. Econ. 335 (1974). Migué also discusses regulations that are "difficult to reconcile with the economic theory of regulation." Jean-Luc Migué, Controls versus Subsidies in the Economic Theory of Regulation, 20 J. Law & Econ. 213, 214 (1977).

[6] Technically, some of the returns to private individuals are true economic rents (for example, the returns to entrepreneurial capacity), while others are more properly termed "quasi rents" (the returns to any fixed-cost investment). See Milton Friedman, Price Theory: A Provisional Text 115–18 (1962). Often, however, the differences are of little operational significance. See, for example, Donald N. McCloskey, The Applied Theory of Price 294 (1985) ("Producers' Surplus Is Economic Rent Is Quasi-Rent Is Supernormal Profit"). It is not the type of rent but its source that is of interest in this article. For expositional clarity, therefore, all profits created politically are described here as "political rents," while the returns to private capital are referred to as "private rents." Also, the term "capital" is used here to refer to both human (including entrepreneurial) and other types of capital.

the expected losses from compliance with the threatened law. (The payments need not be bribes; they might be contributions to political campaigns or in-kind donations of service and property, for example.)

A politician thus can gain by forbearing—for a price—from exercising his right to impose costs on private actors that would reduce rents from capital they have created or invested themselves. Though the strategy has not been recognized heretofore, one in fact observes private producers being compelled to pay legislators to prevent private rents from being extracted. In a static sense the payments might seem to be simple transfers. But the transfers required to protect returns to private investments create disincentives to invest in valuable specific capital in the first place. The short-run view ignores the longer-run adverse consequences of threatened rent extraction for overall levels of wealth. In the end, the article suggests, existing estimates of the welfare costs of government regulation overlook the costs of inducing government *not* to regulate.

II.   RENT EXTRACTION AND THE ECONOMIC THEORY OF REGULATION

A.   *Legislative Creation of Political Rents*

The original (Stiglerian) interpretation of regulation is the traditional cartel model, but one in which government imposes and enforces the anticompetitive restrictions. If expected political rents net of the costs of organizing and procuring favorable legislation are positive, then producers will demand—pay for—regulation. Deadweight consumer loss is measured by the welfare triangle. Producers stand to gain the rent rectangle, but political competition for it produces additional social loss from rent-seeking.[7]

Industry-wide cartelization is not the only way politicians can create rents. More recent theoretical[8] and empirical[9] contributions have noted

---

[7] Gordon Tullock, The Welfare Costs of Tariffs, Monopolies, and Theft, 5 W. Econ. J. 224 (1967); Richard A. Posner, The Social Costs of Monopoly and Regulation, 83 J. Pol. Econ. 807 (1975).

[8] For a diagrammatic presentation of the theory, see Fred S. McChesney, Commercial Speech in the Professions: The Supreme Court's Unanswered Questions and Questionable Answers, 134 U. Pa. L. Rev. 45, 74–100 (1985).

[9] For example, Howard P. Marvel, Factory Regulation: A Reinterpretation of Early English Experience, 20 J. Law & Econ. 379 (1977); R. H. Coase, Payola in Radio and Television Broadcasting, 22 J. Law & Econ. 269 (1979); Michael T. Maloney & Robert E. McCormick, A Positive Theory of Environmental Quality Regulation, 25 J. Law & Econ. 99 (1982); B. Peter Pashigian, The Effect of Environmental Regulation on Optimal Plant Size and Factor Shares, 27 J. Law & Econ. 1 (1984); Ann P. Bartel & Lacy Glenn Thomas, Direct and Indirect Effects of Regulation: A New Look at OSHA's Impact, 28 J. Law & Econ. 1 (1985).

that regulation can create Ricardian (inframarginal) rents if it raises costs of some firms more than those of others. This "cost-predation" strategy differs from Stiglerian cartelization in that only some firms in the industry gain while others lose. Industry cooperation to obtain rents for all firms is replaced by rivalry among industry subgroups to benefit some firms at others' expense.

The cooperation and rivalry models of regulation are the same, however, in that both focus on private purchase of rents. Politician-brokers respond to private demands for rents with a supply of regulation but do not actively enter the market for rents with their own demands.[10] This is perhaps in keeping with the consumer-sovereignty model of private markets, but the applicability of that model to the political market is questionable. Clearly, a politician himself actively seeks votes, campaign contributions, and other forms of recompense, contracting to receive a supply of goods or services from private parties in response to his own demands.[11]

Modeled just as a broker among competing private demands, the politician has not been well integrated into the economic theory of regulation. His role thus far has been "subsumed,"[12] with little explicit consideration given to the ways in which the politician himself benefits from creating rents for private parties. More important, no attention has been paid to ways other than rent creation that a politician can obtain benefits from private individuals.

A politician has alternative ways to engage private parties in exchange. He may demand votes or money and offer the rent rectangle as consideration, as in the orthodox economic theory of regulation. But a politician may also make his demands on private parties, not by promising benefits, but by threatening to impose costs—a form of political blackmail. If the expected cost of the act threatened exceeds the value of the consideration that private parties must give up to avoid legislative action, they will surrender the tribute demanded of them. With constant marginal utility of wealth, a private citizen will be just as willing to pay legislators to have rents of $1 million created as he will to avoid imposition of $1 million in losses.

---

[10] "Regulation is . . . an instrument of wealth transfer—the extent of which is determined in a political market—where interest groups demand regulation and politician-regulators supply it." Migué, *supra* note 5, at 214.

[11] For one of the few models based on political demands being made of private individuals, see William P. Welch, The Economics of Campaign Funds, 17 Pub. Choice 83, 84 (1974) ("[t]he politician demands funds in exchange for political influence").

[12] Robert E. McCormick, The Strategic Use of Regulation: A Review of the Literature, in The Political Economy of Regulation: Private Interests in the Regulatory Process 14 (Robert A. Rogowsky & Bruce Yandle eds. 1984).

Once the politician is seen as an independent actor in the regulatory process, his objective function cannot be treated as single valued. He will maximize total returns to himself by equating at the margin the returns from votes, contributions, bribes, power, and other sources of personal gain. All these, in turn, are positive functions not only of private benefits he confers but also of private costs he agrees not to impose.

The political strategy of cost forbearance can assume several forms. Perhaps most obvious is the threat to deregulate an industry previously cartelized. Expected political rents created by earlier regulation are quickly capitalized into firm share prices. If politicians later breach their contract and vote unexpectedly to deregulate, shareholders suffer a wealth loss. Rather than suffer the costs of deregulation, shareholders will pay politicians a sum up to the amount of wealth threatened to have them refrain from deregulating. In fact, one routinely observes payments to politicians to protect previously enacted cartel measures.[13]

Subsequent payments to avoid postcontractual opportunism by politicians must be distinguished from contractual payments to guarantee rent permanence ex ante. Both politicians and rent recipients gain when the durability of regulation is increased by holding legislators to longer contracts. But new arrivals on both sides succeed to the interests of the original contracting parties. A legislator not party to the original bargain has less incentive to abide by the political rent-creation deal struck by his predecessors unless he too is compensated. Guaranteed rent durability is thus impossible. Among firm owners, subsequent purchasers of shares with expected rents capitalized into their prices are vulnerable to rent extraction on the part of opportunistic politicians. Payments to political newcomers to secure performance of previously negotiated contracts earn no rents. Rather, they protect against windfall losses that new legislators could otherwise impose.

B. Political Extraction of Private Rents

The durability problem for politically created rents has been discussed elsewhere[14] and is not the focus of this article. But recognition of the rent-

---

[13] Dairy interests pay handsomely for the continuation of congressional milk-price supports. Larry J. Sabato, PAC Power: Inside the World of Political Action Committees 133, 137 (1984). Physician and dentist "political action committees" (PACs) contribute large sums for continuation of self-regulation. *Id.* at 134–35.

[14] Since more durable rent contracts are in the interest of both private parties and politicians, the intervention of third-party institutions predictably would be sought to hold legislators to their deals. The judiciary, for example, may help guarantee congressional rent-creation contracts, since courts can overrule legislators' attempted revisions of earlier contracts by holding the changes unconstitutional. William M. Landes & Richard A. Posner,

extraction opportunities that capitalized cartel rents represent to politicians suggests that similar strategies may offer gains to politicians when other sorts of rents exist. In particular, it leads one to focus on the capital value of privately created rents and predictable political responses to their existence.

1. The Model

Figure 1 depicts an industry in which producers have differing amounts of entrepreneurial capacity or some firm-specific, fixed-cost asset. The industry supply curve in the absence of regulation (S_0) thus is upward sloping. Returns to entrepreneurship and specific assets come as rents out of producers' surplus, $0AD$. Regulatory measures could be identified that would increase costs for all firms, but more for marginal firms, moving the industry supply curve to S_1.[15] To inframarginal producers regulation is advantageous (that is, they would pay politicians to effect it) as long as there is a net increase in rents. In Figure 1, area I is greater than area II ($CDEF > ABC$): the gains from higher prices exceed the losses due to fewer sales. The capitalized value of the increased rent flow defines the maximum payment producers would make to politicians in return for regulation.[16]

But rent creation by a governmentally mandated shift from S_0 to S_1 is not the only option open to politicians. *Existing* private rents rewarding specific assets are greater than the rents that can be created by regulation: $0AD > CDEF$ (area I). Regulatory measures can also be identified that

---

The Independent Judiciary in an Interest-Group Perspective, 18 J. Law & Econ. 875 (1975); Robert D. Tollison & W. Mark Crain, Constitutional Change in an Interest-Group Perspective, 8 J. Legal Stud. 165 (1979). Executive veto of attempted changes in legislative deals is another way to increase the amounts private parties would spend for rent creation. W. Mark Crain & Robert D. Tollison, The Executive Branch in the Interest-Group Theory of Government, 8 J. Legal Stud. 555 (1979). But neither guarantee system is perfect "since there will be some expectation that an independent judiciary will not support all past legislative contracts," Tollison & Crain, *supra*, at 167, and because newcomers to both the legislature and the executive office have less stake in continuing bargains made by their predecessors, Crain & Tollison, *supra*, at 561–66.

[15] For an empirical demonstration of the harm to marginal firms from minimum-wage and union-pay increases, for example, see David E. Kaun, Minimum Wages, Factor Substitution and the Marginal Producer, 79 Q. J. Econ. 478 (1965); and Oliver E. Williamson, Wage Rates as a Barrier to Entry: The Pennington Case in Perspective, 82 Q. J. Econ. 85 (1968). For discussion of other regulatory measures with different effects on firms, see the sources cited in note 9 *supra*.

[16] Maximizing payments to politicians would require, inter alia, that all producer beneficiaries be induced to pay and that consumer-voters exert no counterinfluence on the amount of regulation imposed. Relaxing these assumptions would not alter the fundamental implications of the rent-extraction model proposed here. See, for example, Becker, *supra* note 2; and Peltzman, *supra* note 2.

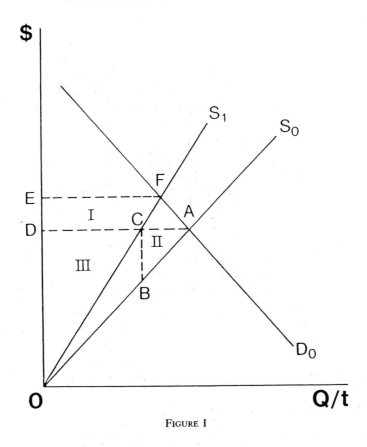

FIGURE 1

would expropriate the producers' surplus, as explained below. Once such regulation is threatened, the price that producers would pay politicians in return for governmental nonaction would exceed any payment for rent-creating regulation.

Faced, then, with a choice between the two strategies, a regulator would maximize the benefits to himself by threatening to expropriate the existing private rents rather than by creating new political rents.[17] As with threatened deregulation of government cartels, payments must be made to protect rents. But unlike the cartel case, where rents were created by government itself, a legislator threatening to expropriate private rents is paid to let firms earn returns on capital they have created or invested for themselves. "Milker bills" is one term used by politicians to describe legislative proposals intended only to squeeze private producers for pay-

---

[17] The conditions under which rent extraction is politically preferable to rent creation are explored further below.

ments not to pass the rent-extracting legislation. "Early on in my association with the California legislature, I came across the concept of 'milker bills'—proposed legislation which had nothing to do with milk to drink and much to do with money, the 'mother's milk of politics.' . . . Representative Sam, in need of campaign contributions, has a bill introduced which excites some constituency to urge Sam to work hard for its defeat (easily achieved), pouring funds into his campaign coffers and 'forever' endearing Sam to his constituency for his effectiveness."[18] Milked victims describe the process simply as blackmail and extortion.[19] The threats are made quite openly. One reads, for example, that "House Republican leaders are sending a vaguely threatening message to business political action committees: Give us more, or we may do something rash."[20]

The producers' surplus compensating firm-specific capital is inframarginal, but this does not mean that its potential expropriation by politicians has no allocative consequences. Even if politicians eventually allow themselves to be bought off, their minatory presence reduces the expected value of entrepreneurial ability and specific-capital investments. The possibility that government may reduce returns to their capital unless paid off reduces firms' incentives to invest in the first place. It also induces inefficient shifts to investment in more mobile or salvageable (that is, less firm specific) forms of capital as insurance against expropriation. In either event, the allocative losses from politicians' ability to extract the returns from private capital are measured by investments that are never made in the industry threatened.

In effect, an important similarity between capital expropriations in less-developed countries and "mere" regulation in developed nations has been overlooked. In both cases the very presence of a threatening government will reduce private investment.[21] The resulting welfare losses would be measured by the value of specific capital and other investments that firms would have made, but for the fear of subsequent expropriation and

[18] W. Craig Stubblebine, On the Political Economy of Tax Reform 1, 2 (paper presented at the meeting of the Western Economic Ass'n 1985).

[19] One PAC director describes congressional "invitations" to purchase tickets to political receptions as "nothing but blackmail." Sabato, *supra* note 13, at 86. Likewise, "[t]he 1972 reelection effort for President Richard Nixon included practices bordering on extortion, in which corporations and their executives were, in essence, 'shaken down' for cash donations." *Id.* at 5.

[20] Brooks Jackson, "House Republicans Are Pressing PACs for Contributions," Wall St. J., June 27, 1985, at 36, col. 2. Further instances of how politicians pressure PACs for money are given in Sabato, *supra* note 13, at 111–14.

[21] The effects of Third World government expropriations of private capital in diminishing the amount of investment made are analyzed in Jonathan Eaton & Mark Gersovitz, A Theory of Expropriation and Deviations from Perfect Capital Mobility, 94 Econ. J. 16 (1984).

the cost of purchasing protection from politicians. The consequences are like those of ordinary theft: "One way of minimizing loss by theft is to have little or nothing to steal. In a world in which theft was legal we could expect this fact to lead to a reduction in productive activities."[22]

Rent extraction can succeed only to the extent that threats to expropriate private rents are credible. With any given firm or industry, producers and politicians may be locked in a "chicken" game: since legislators seemingly gain nothing if they actually destroy private capital, capital owners may be tempted to call politicians' bluff by refusing to pay. But a politician's demonstrated willingness actually to expropriate private rents in one situation provides a lesson for other firms or industries that will induce them to pay in their turn. To make credible expected later threats to destroy others' capital, politicians may sometimes have to enact legislation extracting private rents whose owners do not pay.[23] (And as discussed below, legislators can always enact statutes now and sell repeal later.)

The credibility and thus the political attraction of rent-extraction strategies also depend on the strength of constitutional rules that protect private property and contract rights against governmental taking. Legislative threats to expropriate returns to private capital will elicit fewer payments to politicians the more likely it is that capital owners later can have any legislation voided constitutionally in the courts. The level of constitutional scrutiny of legislative expropriations involving private contract and property rights has declined throughout the twentieth century.[24] The scope for credible legislative threats against private capital has expanded apace. In effect, as courts have retreated from affording constitutional protection against legislative takings, potential private victims have been forced to employ more self-help remedies by buying off politicians rather than submit to rent-extracting regulation.

2. Private Rent Extraction versus Political Rent Creation

Extraction of private rents and creation of political rents need not be mutually exclusive; maximum gains to politicians may involve a combina-

---

[22] Tullock, *supra* note 7, at 229 n.11.

[23] The situation is thus a form of the "Samaritan's dilemma," in which a politician must convince private producers that he is willing to suffer losses in the short run in order to reap longer-run gains whose present value exceeds that of any immediate losses. See James M. Buchanan, The Samaritan's Dilemma, in Altruism, Morality, and Economic Theory 71 (Edmund S. Phelps ed. 1975). Of course, to the extent that the political threats are convincing, private parties are more likely not to call a legislator's bluff, and he therefore will not actually suffer any short-run loss.

[24] Richard A. Epstein, Takings: Private Property and the Power of Eminent Domain (1985); Terry L. Anderson & P. J. Hill, The Birth of a Transfer Society (1980).

tion of the two. In Figure 1, for example, politicians could create rents in area I (*CDEF*) by imposing regulation while threatening at the same time to expropriate the remaining producers' surplus in area III (*0DC*). The maximum private payment forthcoming from this combined tactic, I + III (*0EF*), would exceed that from merely threatening rent expropriation without regulation (*0AD*). But a combined strategy of rent creation and rent extraction is not necessarily optimal to politicians. Political rent creation (of either the Stiglerian or the inframarginal sort) requires restriction of output, which itself reduces the current stock of expropriable producers' surplus. Ceteris paribus, greater rent creation therefore means more forgone rent extraction. Particularly because the political processes of creating or extracting rents are not costless to legislators, the gains may justify using only one or the other strategy in a particular market.

The relative gains from the two strategies, and thus the optimal political mix of created and extracted rents, will depend on industry supply and demand conditions. The more inelastic industry demand is, the greater the relative attraction of political rent creation. Likewise, if industry supply is perfectly elastic, there is no producers' surplus and so no opportunity for rent extraction. On the other hand, when industry demand is perfectly elastic, extraction of private rents is the only plausible political strategy. Similarly, a large stock of specific (nonsalvageable) capital increases the relative attraction to politicians of private rent extraction. Of course, producers themselves would rather buy new rents than pay to protect their own existing rents. But in some markets, rent-creation opportunities may be slight as compared to the opportunities for extraction of returns to entrepreneurship and private capital. For example, ease of new entry into an industry may make rent-creating cartelization futile. At the same time, the presence of large specific-capital stocks would make the same industry vulnerable to rent extraction.

Information concerning demand and supply elasticities, entry costs, and the size and mobility of capital stocks is costly to politicians. The specter of rent extraction naturally will induce private owners of expropriable capital to try to hide the size of their capital stocks, which increases the costs to politicians of discovering how much producers would pay to avoid expropriation.[25] But political threats to act have the effect of instituting an auction market among private parties. "[L]egislatures work on the presence or absence of opposition. Legislation for which the claim can be made that some group will benefit, if only modestly, and which induces no opposition is almost certain to pass. Thus, introduction of a

---

[25] See J. Patrick Gunning, Jr., Towards a Theory of the Evolution of Government, in Explorations in the Theory of Anarchy 22 (Gordon Tullock ed. 1972).

milker bill which does not generate the expected opposition to its passage, as evidenced by resources devoted to lobbying for its defeat, indeed will pass. By contrast, milker bills which generate the anticipated opposition will fail. Contrasting these outcomes usually makes an effective case for generating the lobbying resources."[26] An auction not only drives competitive bids for legislative favors higher but also reveals which firms stand to gain and which to lose and the magnitude of the respective effects.

The auction thus provides valuable information whether regulatory action or inaction will be more lucrative to politicians themselves; it helps to identify the likely payors and to set the amounts of the compensation to be paid. Particularly since legislators may not know the size of the rents potentially expropriable, they may prefer to make good their threat in order to elicit bids revealing the true size of the private capital stock. Actual enactment of legislation raises to unity the probability of rent-destroying measures being imposed, unless firms buy legislative repeal. Legislation that would destroy rents can be enacted with a delayed effective date to allow firms to mobilize and bid to remove or alter the statute.[27]

Because the maximum gains to legislators depend on knowledge of elasticities and the size of private rents, there may also be gains from specialization in identifying industries with expropriable producers' surplus and in determining how best to extract it. If so, legislators predictably would delegate cost-imposing functions to specialized bureaucratic agencies. By threatening or actually imposing costs, these outside agents create a demand for politicians to mitigate the costs. Use of specialized agencies to impose costs has a second advantage to politicians. While they may act at the behest of elected officials, bureaucrats will be perceived by at least some rationally ignorant voters as independent. Information about the regulatory process is costly to obtain, and so it may appear that misguided agencies rather than politicians themselves are responsible for the costs threatened.[28] Designation of institutions like the

[26] Stubblebine, *supra* note 18, at 2.

[27] This was the pattern observed, for example, with the amendments to the Clean Air Act in the early 1970s, when the Department of Transportation repeatedly delayed and altered standards on auto emissions in response to auto-firm lobbying.

[28] The rent-extraction model thus sheds light on the recurring controversy whether bureaucratic agencies "run amuck," free of congressional or other constraints. The most recent study of the Federal Trade Commission (FTC), for example, concludes that "the Commission remains largely unconstrained from without." Kenneth W. Clarkson & Timothy J. Muris, Commission Performance, Incentives and Behavior, in The Federal Trade Commission since 1970: Economic Regulation and Bureaucratic Behavior 282 (1981). But Weingast and Moran present evidence of systematic congressional influence over FTC actions. Barry R. Weingast & Mark J. Moran, Bureaucratic Discretion or Congressional Control? Regulatory Policymaking by the Federal Trade Commission, 91 J. Pol. Econ. 765 (1983). The rent-extraction model suggests that neither view may fully capture the essence

Federal Trade Commission (FTC) and the Securities and Exchange Commission as "independent agencies" may further the perception in some voters' eyes that politicians are less responsible for their activities.[29]

C.   Methods of Extracting Private Rents

Having located private capital stocks whose returns will come out of producers' surplus, how can legislators extract that surplus? Two general strategies represent threats to private producers: reductions in price and increases in cost.[30]

1.   Legislative Threats to Reduce Prices

Consider, for example, firms' fixed-cost investments in brand-name capital or reputation.[31] All firms may produce otherwise equivalent products, but some will have incurred greater costs in past periods (for example, by advertising) to make their names and quality familiar to consumers. Advertising creates a capital stock, returns from which are taken over time.[32] Once created, the capital is specific to the firm and enables the firm in a later period to incur lower costs to guarantee the quality of the goods or services that it sells. Rival firms without brand-name capital must incur higher costs in that same period to make their names and product quality as well-known and trustworthy to consumers.

This is shown in Figure 2 for two representative firms. Industry supply

---

of Congress-agency relations. A politician has less incentive to monitor specialized agencies ex ante while they consider and adopt cost-imposing measures more cheaply than Congress itself could. There is more incentive for legislative surveillance of agency action ex post, in order to locate opportunities for alleviating those costs (for a fee). For a discussion and evidence of politicians' intervention to remove the costs imposed by bureaucrats' antitrust investigations and prosecutions, see Roger L. Faith, Donald R. Leavens, and Robert D. Tollison, Antitrust Pork Barrel, 25 J. Law & Econ. 329 (1982).

[29] Further, the appearance may not be purely illusory. Congressional monitoring of agencies is costly. See Isaac Ehrlich & Richard A. Posner, An Economic Analysis of Legal Rulemaking, 3 J. Legal Stud. 257 (1974). Some of what agencies do, therefore, will not be known to a legislator until constituents bring it to his attention.

[30] The purpose here is to illustrate how politicians acting collectively can induce private payments not to extract rents. This admittedly leaves unaddressed public-choice problems of achieving collective political action: how to assemble political coalitions when each politician maximizes his own interest, how to divide the gains from rent extraction among individual politicians, the role of the committee system in rent extraction, and so forth.

[31] Benjamin Klein & Keith B. Leffler, The Role of Market Forces in Assuring Contractual Performance, 89 J. Pol. Econ. 615 (1981); L. G. Telser, A Theory of Self-enforcing Agreements, 53 J. Bus. 27 (1980).

[32] See, for example, Yoram Peles, Rates of Amortization of Advertising Expenditures, 79 J. Pol. Econ. 1032 (1971); Robert Ayanian, Advertising and Rate of Return, 18 J. Law & Econ. 479 (1975).

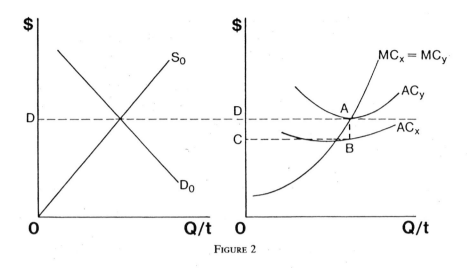

FIGURE 2

and demand (from Figure 1) establish the equilibrium price, $0D$. Firm X has been in business and advertised for years; firm Y has just started business. Both firms provide identical products of equivalent quality at the same production cost ($MC_X = MC_Y$). But customers cannot evaluate product quality prior to purchase; hence there is uncertainty. Both firms guarantee quality, but in different ways. Firm X relies on its investment in brand-name capital in prior periods, its customers paying a premium for the credible guarantee of quality that the reputation capital provides. To offer an equivalent guarantee, firm Y must incur other fixed costs in the current period, such as having an independent laboratory test its product quality and publicize the fact that it is just as good as X's, making its average costs higher ($AC_Y > AC_X$). The premium (AB) that firm X's customers pay for the reputational guarantee earns rents ($ABCD$).

But X's rents can be reduced or destroyed by government intervention. Politicians can pass legislation to have administrative agencies guarantee quality or truthful information by imposing minimum quality standards or mandatory information-disclosure regulations. Government agents then would police the market for quality and truth, substituting both for the brand-name capital invested earlier by firm X and for the current testing that firm Y would have commissioned to guarantee quality. To the extent it substitutes for private reputation capital, government regulation destroys the premium value of firm X's private capital while relieving the nonreputational firm, Y, of the need to incur new costs to warrant its own quality.

The threatened government intervention would lower price and increase the elasticity of industry supply, eradicating the producers' surplus available to compensate firms for their earlier fixed-cost investments. Rather than have politicians depreciate their capital stock, firm X would pay up to *ABCD* per period for nonintervention in the market. Even if regulation "only" substitutes for activities currently provided privately, it reduces the expected returns to private-reputation investments and so over time the amount of investment. Note also that in the new equilibrium firm Y would earn no rents from the regulation and so would offer politicians nothing for it. The only gains to politicians in this case come from threatening to extract X's rents.

The history of the FTC's "Used Car Rule" provides an example of the gain to politicians from threatening this type of regulation and later removing the threat for a fee. In 1975, Congress statutorily ordered the FTC to initiate a rulemaking to regulate used-car dealers' warranties.[33] The FTC promulgated a rule imposing costly warranty and auto-defect disclosure requirements, creating the opportunity for legislators to extract concessions from dealers to void the burdensome measures. In the meantime, in fact, Congress had legislated for itself a veto over FTC actions.[34] On promulgation of the rule, used-car dealers and their trade association descended on Congress, spending large sums of money for relief from the proposed rule's costs.[35] When the concessions were forthcoming, Congress vetoed the very rule it had ordered.[36]

It is noteworthy that conditions in the used-car industry conform closely to those hypothesized as conducive to a strategy of rent extrac-

---

[33] The Magnuson-Moss Warranty–Federal Trade Commission Improvement Act of 1975 included an order to the FTC to initiate within one year "a rulemaking proceeding dealing with warranties and warranty practices in connection with the sale of used motor vehicles." 15 U.S.C. § 2309(b). For the FTC's initial rule, see 16 C.F.R. § 455 (1982).

[34] Since Congress has always been able to annul any agency rule or regulation statutorily, the question arises why it would want a veto. Statutes to change agency action require the president's signature. If the president must sign the statute, he then is able to exact payment for his participation in rent-protecting legislation, lowering the payments available to Congress. In eliminating the executive role, the legislative veto is hardly a check on agency action. It is an attempt to avoid splitting fees with the executive. Indeed, if Congress has a veto, it then has an incentive to fund even more rent-threatening activities by independent agencies, ceteris paribus.

[35] One study, cited in Sabato, *supra* note 13, at 134, found that, "[o]f the 251 legislators who supported the veto resolution and ran again in 1982, 89 percent received contributions from NADA [National Auto Dealers Association], which averaged over $2,300. This total included 66 legislators who had not been backed by NADA at all in 1980, before the veto resolution vote. Just 22 percent of the 125 congressmen who voted against NADA received 1982 money, and they averaged only about $1,000 apiece."

[36] See the FTC announcement of the veto published at 47 Fed. Reg. 24542 (June 7, 1982). When the Supreme Court later invalidated the legislative veto, INS v. Chadha, 462 U.S. 919 (1983), and thus Congress's overruling of the FTC's rule, Process Gas Consumers Group v. Consumer Energy Council, 463 U.S. 1216 (1983), the FTC recalled its proposed rule and essentially gutted it. See 16 C.F.R. § 455 (1985).

tion. As Stigler himself notes,[37] cartelization of the used-car industry would be difficult: start-up costs are low; there are no entry barriers (for example, licensing requirements); and units of the product have different qualities, making enforcement of cartel pricing difficult. By comparison, the industry is susceptible to a strategy of rent extraction. Quality uncertainty (the risk of getting Akerlof's "lemon")[38] is a problem, leading sellers to invest in reputation capital.[39] By requiring and policing seller disclosure of warranty and defect information, government would have substituted for sellers' investments in quality-assuring reputation. Rather than suffer the capital losses that regulation would entail, firms predictably would—and did—compensate legislators not to intervene.

2. Legislative Threats to Raise Costs

Just as proposals to institute price-lowering regulation imperil private rents, so do regulations that threaten to increase costs. Consider the situation portrayed in Figure 3, in which legislators threaten to impose an excise tax or other per-unit cost of $0C$. Rather than suffer a net loss in producers' surplus, area I − area II ($0AEC - BDFE$), firms earning rents will offer to compensate legislators to refrain from imposing the costs.

There are many examples of payments to politicians to purchase governmental inactivity in taxation.[40] Recently, the excise tax on beer has generated substantial revenue for legislators in return for their inactiv-

---

[37] Stigler, *supra* note 1, at 9–10.

[38] George A. Akerlof, The Market for "Lemons": Quality Uncertainty and the Market Mechanism, 84 Q. J. Econ. 488 (1970).

[39] "Both intuition and empirical data suggest that the used-car market attracts lemons. . . . A number of market mechanisms serve to alleviate these problems. The most visible solutions take the form of dealer guarantees and warranties, which recently have been beefed up with extended coverage backed by national insurers. Indirectly, dealers invest in brand-name maintenance (local television ads, for instance), which makes it more costly for them to renege on a reputation for quality. The reputation of the parent automakers is also laid on the line. All four domestic car manufacturers have certified the quality of the better used cars sold by their dealers. Two generations of Chevrolet dealers, for example, have designated better used cars with an 'OK' stamp of the dealer's confidence in the car's marketability." Can Regulation Sweeten the Automotive Lemon? Reg., September/December 1984, at 7, 8.

[40] "[M]embers of the tax-writing committees nearly tripled their take from political action committees during the first six months of this year, to $3.6 million, compared to the like period in the past two-year election cycle. . . . [T]he money is pouring in from . . . insurance companies that want to preserve tax-free appreciation of life insurance policy earnings, from horse breeders who want to keep rapid depreciation of thoroughbreds, from drug companies seeking to keep a tax haven in Puerto Rico, and from military contractors seeking to retain favorable tax treatment of earnings from multiyear contracts." Brooks Jackson, Tax-Revision Proposals Bring Big Contributions from PACs to Congressional Campaign Coffers, Wall St. J., August 9, 1985, at 32, col. 1.

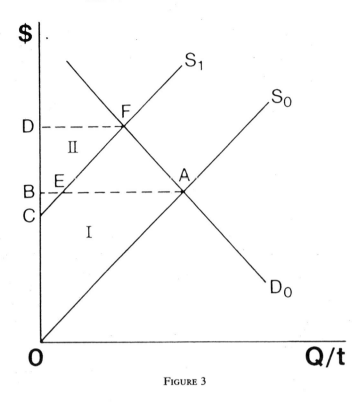

FIGURE 3

ity.[41] Of course, excise taxes are just one cost that politicians can threaten to impose on private firms. Other recent threats include proposals to require financial institutions to start costly reporting and withholding of taxes from depositors' interest and dividends (a measure that was passed and then repealed) and proposals to impose "unisex" premiums and benefit payments on insurance firms. Both episodes are difficult to explain using the standard economic model, as they consumed considerable political time but ended with no regulation at all being imposed. But even if the regulation was never actually imposed, each measure would be attractive politically as a device that might ultimately elicit private payments to

---

[41] One report notes that "there hasn't been an increase in the 65-cent-a-case federal tax on beer since the Korean War, and nobody is seriously proposing one right now." Yet the industry has organized a coalition of brewers and wholesalers to compensate key members of Congress anyway: "Members of House and Senate tax-writing committees regularly drop by the coalition's monthly meetings to talk about budget and tax trends, [and] pick up $2,000 appearance fees." Though new beer taxes "haven't . . . generated much interest in Congress," the president of the brewers' trade association says they "want to be prepared." Brooks Jackson, Brewing Industry Organizes Lobbying Coalition to Head off Any Increase in U.S. Tax on Beer, Wall St. J., July 11, 1985, at 48 col. 1.

legislators *not* to impose the threatened costs—which in fact each one did.[42]

III. CONCLUSION

This article extends the economic theory of regulation to include the gains available to elected politicians from alleviating costs threatened or actually imposed on private actors by legislators themselves and by specialized bureaucratic agencies. Status as a legislator confers a property right not only to create political rents but also to impose costs that would destroy private rents. Their ability to impose costs enables politicians credibly to demand payments not to do so. Even when politicians eventually eschew intervention, the mere threat and the payments required to remove it distort private investment decisions.

The model of rent extraction set out here in no way undermines the orthodox model of rent-creating regulation; rather it supplements it by recognizing alternative sources of political gains. Indeed, Stigler's original article foreshadowed a complementary rent-extraction model: "The state—the machinery and power of the state—is a potential resource *or threat* to every industry in the society. With its power to prohibit or compel, *to take* or give money, the state can and does selectively help *or hurt* a vast number of industries. . . . Regulation may be actively sought by an industry, *or it may be thrust upon it*" (emphasis added).[43] Conditions that make political rent creation relatively unattractive to politicians make private rent extraction more attractive. The relative attraction of rent extraction has also increased as constitutional protection of private rights has diminished.

Many of the insights from the rent-creation model of regulation will doubtless prove useful in further explorations of rent extraction. For example, the problem of double-dealing by opportunistic politicians that was discussed above in connection with deregulation raises equivalent issues for contracts with legislators not to extract private rents. As with rent creation, the rent-extraction model will be enriched by consideration of the need to assemble coalitions to obtain rent protection, the problems created by changes in coalitions' composition and power, and similar

---

[42] The banking industry contributed millions of dollars to politicians in 1982 to obtain repeal of the statutory provision requiring banks to withhold taxes on interest and dividends. There are no precise figures on contributions to politicians to stop legislation banning gender-based insurance-rate and benefit schedules, but their magnitude may be inferred from the American Council of Life Insurance's media budget of nearly $2 million in 1983 and 1984 to defeat the legislation. Sabato, *supra* note 13, at 125.

[43] Stigler, *supra* note 1, at 3.

issues that arise once "government" is recognized as a collectivity of rational, maximizing individuals.

For the moment, however, it is sufficient to note that the problems of political opportunism and the imperfections in private-capital protection create disincentives for capital owners to buy off legislators. Yet several instances have been presented here in which private actors in fact have paid significant sums to induce government not to impose costs. Despite the political impediments to contract, then, the evident willingness of capital owners to purchase protection indicates that appreciable capital stocks are credibly imperiled by regulations that are never actually enacted.

If so, one cost of government regulation has been missed. Heretofore, the economic model has identified several different costs of government regulation: deadweight consumer loss, resources expended as private parties seek rents,[44] costs of compliance with regulation,[45] and diversion of resources to less valuable but unregulated uses.[46] To these should be added the costs of protecting private capital even when politicians ultimately are persuaded not to regulate. There is no such thing as a free market.

---

[44] Posner, *supra* note 7. See also Franklin M. Fisher, The Social Cost of Monopoly and Regulation: Posner Reconsidered, 93 J. Pol. Econ. 410 (1985); W. P. Rogerson, The Social Costs of Monopoly and Regulation: A Game-theoretic Analysis, 13 Bell J. Econ. 391 (1982).

[45] Tullock, *supra* note 7.

[46] James Alm, The Welfare Cost of the Underground Economy, 24 Econ. Inquiry 243 (1985).

Rigging the Lobbying Process: An Application of the All-Pay Auction

By Michael R. Baye, Dan Kovenock, and Casper G. de Vries[*]

Why do politicians frequently "announce" that they have narrowed down a set of potential recipients of a "prize" to a slate of finalists?[1] In general, does the slate of finalists comprise the "best" candidates, and does the best candidate always win?[2] This paper provides answers to these questions. Our model of the political process is one of rent-seeking, which takes the (perhaps overly jaded) view that persons with power award political prizes on the basis of self-interest.

In a world where a politician can explicitly auction off a prize to the high bidder, the standard auction literature can be used to analyze political behavior. The justice system, however, precludes politicians from explicitly selling the prize to the highest bidder; thus politicians cannot let it become public knowledge that they are in the business of selling political favors.

An interesting institution has emerged in political markets to overcome this constraint: lobbying. Lobbyists make *implicit* payments to the politician, through campaign contributions or "wining-and-dining." If these up-front payments were rebated to those failing to receive the prize, it would be clear that the politician was selling favors. It is natural, therefore, for a political institution to arise such that lobbyists "ante up" before the prize is awarded, and these up-front payments are not refunded to those failing to win the prize. This view of lobbying has a structure isomorphic to the all-pay auction, which differs from standard auctions in one principal respect: all bids are forfeited by the bidders.

Before we describe our model of the lobbying process, it is useful to provide an overview of the existing literature and to contrast it with the present analysis. The case in which more than two lobbyists value the prize identically was first analyzed by Hervé Moulin (1986), who characterizes the symmetric equilibrium to the all-pay auction. Similar analysis is provided by Arye Hillman (1988), who argues that the equilibrium is unique. It turns out, however, that the symmetric equilibrium is not unique; in fact there is a *continuum* of equilibria (in Baye et al. [1990], we provide a full characterization of the equilibria.)

The case in which some lobbyists value the prize more than others has been analyzed by, among others, Hillman and John Riley (1989), who argue that equilibrium involves only the top two lobbyists. In this *Review*, Tore Ellingsen (1991) has considered the interesting case in which one lobbyist values the prize more than $n-1$ competitors with common valuations (see his proposition 1), and he demonstrates the existence of n equilibria. Baye et al. (1990) have shown, however, that there actually exists a continuum of equilibria in this case. Moreover, the expected revenue earned by the politician differs across this continuum of equilibria; there is *not* revenue equivalence across the equilibria.

The present analysis provides a simple closed-form expression for expected revenues that is valid for *all* equilibria. Our

*Baye: Department of Economics, Pennsylvania State University, University Park, PA 16802; Kovenock: Department of Economics, Purdue University, West Lafayette, IN 47907; de Vries: Department of Economics, Erasmus Universiteit Rotterdam, P.O. Box 1738, 3000 DR Rotterdam, The Netherlands. We are grateful to Donald Deere, Tom Gresik, Tim Gronberg, Bill Nielson, Guoqiang Tian, Steve Wiggins, and three anonymous referees for suggestions that led to improved content and exposition.
[1] The International Olympic Committee, for instance, selected six cities as "finalists" for the 1996 Summer Olympics: Belgrade, Manchester, Toronto, Melbourne, Athens, and Atlanta.
[2] Atlanta won the bid for the 1996 Olympics.

American Economic Review 83, 289–294

Michael R. Baye, Dan Kovenock, and Casper G. de Vries

technique does not require an explicit calculation of the Nash-equilibrium mixed strategies. Consequently, our results provide a framework with which one may reexamine the implications of the equilibria missed for previous results, without explicitly calculating the (uncountable infinity) of equilibria.

The objective of the present paper is to take into account the continuum of equilibria and to determine the amount of rents the politician can expect to earn given such a political institution. To answer this question, we model the political process as a two-stage game of complete information. In stage 1 the politician takes the political institution of lobbying as given but is free to constrain the process by "narrowing down" the slate of candidates to a set of "finalists." In stage 2, the finalists compete in an all-pay auction: the lobbyist giving the greatest bribe wins the prize, while the others receive nothing for their payments. We solve this decision problem by backwards induction, solving first for the Nash-equilibrium payments that accrue to the politician in the second-stage lobbying game given an arbitrary set of lobbyists. We then solve for the optimal first-stage decision of the politician, which involves the selection of the set of "finalists" that maximizes expected political rents. We will show that, under plausible circumstances, the politician has a perverse incentive to preclude lobbyists most valuing the prize from participating in the second-stage lobbying game. Intuitively, this precommitment may take the form of announcing prior to any lobbying that "five states have been selected as finalists for the site of a new military base." We will refer to this precommitment as the *exclusion principle*. The exclusion principle has obvious implications for efficiency; states deriving the greatest economic benefit from a military base (and hence having the highest valuation of the prize) may be excluded a priori from the announced set of finalists.

I. The Model

Consider a politician who must determine which of $n > 2$ lobbyists will receive a prize. The value of the prize to lobbyist i is $v_i > 0$,

where the v_i's are common knowledge and ordered such that $v_1 \geq v_2 \geq \cdots \geq v_n$.

The politician does not care which lobbyists wins the prize but does care about how much money he has available in his campaign chest. Accordingly, he decides to award the prize to the lobbyist who gives him the greatest up-front, nonrefundable *implicit* bribe. The objective of the politician is to select a set of lobbyists (the set of finalists) that maximizes his expected rents, $W = E\sum_{i=1}^n b_i$, where b_i is the bribe paid by player i.

Given a set of "finalists," lobbying is an all-pay auction: the payoff to lobbyist i if he offers a bribe of b_i is $\pi_i = v_i - b_i$ if b_i is the highest of all n bribes. However, if some other lobbyist offers a higher bribe, lobbyist i's payoff is $\pi_i = -b_i$. We assume that when multiple lobbyists submit the highest bribe, the prize is awarded to one of them at random. Thus, the payoff of lobbyist i is given by

$$(1) \quad \pi_i(b) = \begin{cases} v_i - b_i & \text{if } b_i > b_j \ \forall \ i \neq j \\ \dfrac{v_i}{M} - b_i & \text{if } i \text{ ties } M - 1 \text{ others} \\ & \text{for high bid} \\ -b_i & \text{if } b_i < b_j \text{ for some} \\ & j \neq i. \end{cases}$$

This payoff structure is standard in the lobbying literature (cf. Hillman, 1988). It can also be viewed as the limiting case of an alternative payoff structure suggested by Gordon Tullock (1980) that is also used in this literature (see Baye et al., 1989). In Section II we characterize the expected payments by lobbyists in the second-stage lobbying game. These results are used in Section III to determine the politician's rent-maximizing selection of the set of "finalists."

II. The Lobbying Game

We first sketch a proof of the nonexistence of a pure-strategy Nash equilibrium for the all-pay auction. Consider the two-player case and suppose (b_1, b_2) did comprise a pure-strategy Nash equilibrium (without loss of generality, suppose $b_1 \geq b_2$). If $b_1 < v_2$, player 2 could deviate to earn a higher payoff by increasing b_2 slightly above b_1 to win the prize. If $b_1 \geq v_2$, player 2's best reply to b_1 is zero; but with $b_2 = 0$, it pays player 1 to deviate from b_1 by lowering the bid to (small) $\varepsilon > 0$, contradicting the hypothesis that $b_1 \geq v_2$.

It is known, though, that there does exist an equilibrium in mixed strategies, in which lobbyists randomize their bribes (cf. Partha Dasgupta and Eric Maskin, 1986; Moulin, 1986; Hillman and Riley, 1989; Baye et al., 1990). Moreover, with more than two players, there generally exists a continuum of possible equilibria (Baye et al., 1990). As our focus centers around the politician's rent-maximizing selection of finalists, we need only characterize the expected total bribes that accrue in a given Nash equilibrium of the lobbying game. The innovation is that the techniques employed below do not rely on the algebraic form of the mixed strategies used by the lobbyists in equilibrium and, thus, are valid even in the presence of a continuum of Nash equilibrium mixed strategies.

The following theorem is the key ingredient that enables us to determine the set of finalists that maximizes the politician's rents. The novelty of the result is that it is valid for *each* equilibrium in the continuum of possible Nash equilibria and thus can be used for purposes beyond the present paper. For example, the formula allows one to strengthen the results of Ellingsen (1991), which are based on a finite subset of equilibria.

THEOREM 1: *Let* $v_1 \geq v_2 \geq \cdots \geq v_n$ *denote the valuations of lobbyists* $\{1, 2, \ldots, n\}$ *in the stage-2 lobbying game. Let* $E_1 b_1$ *denote the expected bid of a lobbyist with the highest valuation. Then in any Nash equilibrium,*

$$(2) \qquad W = \frac{v_2}{v_1} v_2 + \left[1 - \frac{v_2}{v_1} \right] E_1 b_1 \leq v_2.$$

PROOF:

Let $F_i(b_i)$ denote the cumulative distribution function of lobbyist i in an arbitrary

(mixed-strategy) Nash equilibrium, and let S_i denote the support of the distribution. Lobbyist i must earn constant (expected) profits almost everywhere (a.e.) in S_i. For lobbyist 1 this constant must equal $v_1 - v_2$, and for lobbyists $2, 3, \ldots, n$, this constant is zero (see Baye et al., 1990).[3] Hence, the following conditions must hold:

$$(3) \quad \pi_1(b_1) = \prod_{i \neq 1}^{n} F_i(b_1)[v_1 - b_1]$$

$$+ \left[1 - \prod_{i \neq 1}^{n} F_i(b_1) \right][-b_1]$$

$$= v_1 - v_2 \qquad \text{a.e. on } S_1$$

and

$$(4) \quad \pi_i(b_i) = \prod_{j \neq i}^{n} F_j(b_i)[v_i - b_i]$$

$$+ \left[1 - \prod_{j \neq i}^{n} F_j(b_i) \right][-b_i] = 0$$

$$\text{a.e. on } S_i, i \neq 1.$$

Let $p_i(b_i) \equiv \prod_{j \neq i}^{n} F_j(b_i)$ denote the probability that lobbyist i wins the prize, conditional on his bid and the strategies employed by the other $n - 1$ lobbyists in a Nash equilibrium.[4] Then, since equations (3) and (4) hold almost everywhere in their respective supports, taking the expectations of these equations and manipulating reveals that

$$(5) \qquad P_1 v_1 - E_1 b_1 = v_1 - v_2$$

and

$$(6) \qquad P_i v_i - E_i b_i = 0 \qquad \forall i \neq 1$$

where E_j denotes the expectation with respect to lobbyist j's (equilibrium) mixed

---

[3]Note that when lobbyist 2's valuation equals that of lobbyist 1, $v_1 - v_2 = 0$.

[4]We can rule out mass points for any agent at a bid $b > 0$ (see Baye et al., 1990).

strategy and $P_j \equiv E_j p_j(b_j)$. Summing over equations (5) and (6), we then obtain

(7) $\quad W \equiv \sum_{j=1}^{n} E_j b_j$

$$= (P_1 - 1)v_1 + \sum_{i \neq 1} P_i v_i + v_2.$$

Applying the fundamental theorem of integral calculus to $\sum_{j=1}^{n} P_j$, it follows that $\sum_{j=1}^{n} P_j = 1$. Furthermore, if $v_2 > v_i$, $i > 2$, then $P_i = 0$ (see Baye et al., 1989, 1990). Hence,

(8) $\quad W = (P_1 - 1)v_1 + (2 - P_1)v_2.$

Rearranging (5), we find

$$P_1 = \frac{v_1 - v_2 + E_1 b_1}{v_1}$$

which, inserted into (8), yields our results.

Two implications of Theorem 1 are worth noting. First, if two or more players most value the prize at some common level, v, the expected rents accruing to the politician equal v; there is full rent dissipation. Secondly, if $v_1 > v_2$, then the expected rents accruing to the politician are strictly *less* than v_2, since $E_1 b_1 < v_2$ in any Nash equilibrium. In other words, regardless of whether there is a unique equilibrium[5] or a continuum of equilibria,[6] in every equilibrium there is *under*dissipation of rents. In the following section, this result will be used to establish when it pays a politician to preclude some lobbyists from competing in the lobbying game. First, however, we state the following lemma from Hillman and Riley (1989).

LEMMA 1: *Suppose that the valuations of the lobbyists in the stage-2 lobbying game are such that $v_1 \geq v_2 > v_3 \geq v_4 \cdots \geq v_n$. Then in the unique Nash equilibrium, $Eb_1 = v_2/2$.*

[5]The equilibrium is unique when $v_2 > v_3$.
[6]There is a continuum of equilibria when $v_2 = v_3$.

Theorem 1 and Lemma 1 together imply that, when two players value the prize strictly more than all other players, the expected rents accruing to the politician in the stage-2 lobbying game are

(9) $\quad W(v_1, v_2) = \left[1 + \dfrac{v_2}{v_1}\right]\dfrac{v_2}{2}.$

Note that, when $v_1 > v_2 > v_3$, expected rents are increasing in v_2 but decreasing in v_1. Intuitively, as player 1's valuation increases, the playing field becomes more unequal. Hence, player 2 reduces his expected payment to the politician, and total expected rents decline.

It is important to note that the formula in equation (9) is based on specific configurations of valuations and does not hold in general (it does not hold when $v_1 > v_2 = v_3$). The reason is that, when $v_1 > v_2 = v_3$, Eb_1 in equation (2) varies depending upon which of the continuum of equilibria is played, and thus, the politician's expected rents depend upon which equilibrium the lobbyists play. This point has not been addressed in the existing literature, and it plays a crucial role in our analysis.

III. Selecting the Finalists

Since there exists a continuum of expected political rents for some configurations of valuations, our next task is to characterize properties of the maximum expected political rents that can be extracted from the lobbyists.

PROPOSITION 1: *If $\{\hat{1}, \ldots, \hat{m}\}$ is a rent-maximizing set of finalists (with valuations $\hat{v}_1 \geq \cdots \geq \hat{v}_m$), then expected rents are*

(10) $\quad W(\hat{v}_1, \hat{v}_2) = \left(1 + \dfrac{\hat{v}_2}{\hat{v}_1}\right)\dfrac{\hat{v}_2}{2}.$

PROOF:

We must show that if $\{\hat{1}, \ldots, \hat{m}\}$ is a set of finalists that maximizes expected rents (and the corresponding valuations are $\hat{v}_1 \geq \cdots \geq$

$\hat{v}_m$), then expected rents are $W(\hat{v}_1, \hat{v}_2)$. This is clearly true if $m = 2$; hence, suppose $m > 2$. If $\hat{v}_1 = \hat{v}_2 \equiv \hat{v}$, equation (2) reveals that $W = \hat{v} = W(\hat{v}_1, \hat{v}_2)$. If $\hat{v}_1 > \hat{v}_2 > \hat{v}_3$, equation (9) shows again that $W = W(\hat{v}_1, \hat{v}_2)$. Finally, if $\hat{v}_1 > \hat{v}_2 = \hat{v}_3 \equiv \hat{v}$, expected rents increase by excluding player $\hat{1}$, since by Theorem 1 $W(\hat{v}_1, \hat{v}_2) < \hat{v}_2 = W(\hat{v}_2, \hat{v}_3)$. However, this contradicts the hypothesis that the set $\{\hat{1}, \ldots, \hat{m}\}$ maximizes expected rents. Hence, we conclude that any rent-maximizing set of finalists generates expected rents of $W(\hat{v}_1, \hat{v}_2)$.

Thus, while equation (9) does not hold for all possible configurations of values, it does hold when the set of finalists is selected so as to maximize expected rents [equation (10)]. This result allows us to determine the set of finalists that maximizes the politician's expected rents. Specifically, since equation (10) is decreasing in the highest valuation and increasing in the second-highest valuation, it never pays to exclude a player with a valuation that lies between the valuations of any two lobbyists who are in the set of finalists. Thus, the expected rent-maximizing set of finalists is determined by considering all pairwise combinations of adjacent lobbyists until lobbyists k and $k+1$ are found such that

$$W(v_k, v_{k+1}) = \max_i W(v_i, v_{i+1}).$$

To realize these rents, the politician must exclude players with valuations greater than v_k from the set of finalists. Formally, we have shown the following:

PROPOSITION 2: *Suppose* $v_1 \geq v_2 \geq v_3 \geq \cdots \geq v_n$. *Then the politician maximizes expected rents by constructing a set of finalists that excludes lobbyists with valuations strictly greater than* v_k, *where* k *is such that*

$$\left(1 + \frac{v_{k+1}}{v_k}\right)\frac{v_{k+1}}{2} \geq \left(1 + \frac{v_{i+1}}{v_i}\right)\frac{v_{i+1}}{2} \quad \forall\, i.$$

In order to highlight the implications of our results, consider the following two corollaries.

COROLLARY 1: *Suppose* $v_1 = v_2 \geq v_3 \cdots \geq v_n$. *Then the politician does not gain by constructing an agenda that excludes some lobbyists from the lobbying game.*

COROLLARY 2: *Suppose* $v_1 > v_2 = v_3 \geq \cdots \geq v_n$. *Then the politician maximizes expected rents by excluding the lobbyist with the highest valuation from the set of finalists.*

It may also be optimal for a politician to exclude more than one lobbyist from the stage-2 game. For instance, suppose $v_1 > v_2 > v_3 = v_4 \geq \cdots \geq v_n$. Then the politician maximizes expected rents by constructing an agenda that excludes lobbyists 1 and 2 from the set of finalists whenever

$$\left(1 + \frac{v_2}{v_1}\right)\frac{v_2}{2} < v_3.$$

These results demonstrate the *exclusion principle*: a politician may benefit from precluding the lobbyists valuing the prize the most from participating in the lobbying process.

We conclude with a numerical example to aid in elucidating our findings. Suppose $v_1 = 50$, $v_2 = 40$, and $v_3 = 38$. The theorem and lemma imply that the politician earns $W = 36$ if he does not constrain the lobbying process or limits lobbying to only players 1 and 2. However, if the politician announces that players 2 and 3 are the finalists, then the expected payments to the politician are $W(40, 38) = 37.05$. Thus it pays the politician to exclude lobbyist 1, who values most the prize, from participating in the lobbying game.

IV. Conclusions

This paper has examined an interesting principle arising in all-pay auctions: the exclusion principle. This principle states that a politician wishing to maximize political rents may find it in his best interest to exclude certain lobbyists from participating in the lobbying process—particularly lobbyists valuing most the political prize. In addition to pointing out the exclusion principle, our

Theorem 1 characterizes expected revenue for the entire continuum of equilibria that can arise in $n > 2$-player all-pay auctions with arbitrary valuations of the prize. This is in contrast to the results of Ellingsen (1991), Hillman (1988), Hillman and Riley (1989), and Hillman and Dov Samet (1987), among others, which are valid only for a subset of possible equilibria.

REFERENCES

Baye, Michael R., Kovenock, Dan and de Vries, Casper G., "The Economics of All-Pay, Winner-Take-All Contests," Texas A&M University Working Paper No. 89-21, 1989.

_____, _____ and _____, "The All-Pay Auction with Complete Information," CentER Working Paper No. 9051, Tilburg University, 1990.

Dasgupta, Partha and Maskin, Eric, "The Existence of Equilibrium in Discontinuous Economic Games, I: Theory," *Review of Economic Studies*, January 1986, *53*, 1–26.

Ellingsen, Tore, "Strategic Buyers and the Social Cost of Monopoly," *American Economic Review*, June 1991, *81*, 648–57.

Hillman, Arye L., *The Political Economy of Protectionism*, New York: Harwood, 1988.

_____ and Riley, John, "Politically Contestable Rents and Transfers," *Economics and Politics*, Spring 1989, *1*, 17–39.

_____ and Samet, Dov, "Dissipation of Contestable Rents by Small Numbers of Contenders," *Public Choice*, 1987, *54* (1), 63–82.

Moulin, Hervé, *Game Theory for the Social Sciences*, 2nd Ed., New York: New York University Press, 1986.

Tullock, Gordon, "Efficient Rent Seeking," in J. M. Buchanan, R. D. Tollison, and G. Tullock, eds., *Toward a Theory of the Rent Seeking Society*, College Station: Texas A&M University Press, 1980, pp. 97–112.

Caps on Political Lobbying

By Yeon-Koo Che and Ian L. Gale*

The cost of political campaigns in the United States has risen substantially in recent years. For example, real spending on congressional election campaigns doubled between 1976 and 1992 (Steven D. Levitt, 1995). There are many reasons why increased campaign spending might be socially harmful. First, increased spending means increased fund-raising, which may keep politicians from their legislative duties.[1] Second, a lobbyist who makes a large campaign contribution may have undue influence on electoral outcomes, on the shaping of legislation, or on the outcome of regulatory proceedings.[2] That is, the socially preferred candidate or legislation may not prevail. Likewise, a lobbyist involved in a regulatory matter or a competition for a government contract may benefit unduly from a legislator's intervention.[3] Third, a perception that campaign contributions purchase influence may lead to increased tolerance of corruption in the private sector.

A desire to control campaign spending has spawned many initiatives to limit both campaign contributions and spending, beginning with the passage of the Federal Election Campaign Act (FECA). Political action committees can contribute at most $5,000 per election to a candidate, while individuals can contribute at most $1,000. (Restrictions have also been put on in-kind contributions, making it more difficult to circumvent these limits.)[4] While direct restrictions on campaign spending have proven difficult to implement, recent initiatives aim to impose voluntary spending limits and stricter limits on contributions.[5]

Despite the existing legislation and the proposals to limit contributions, little is known about the impact of contribution limits on aggregate expenditures. While it is intuitively appealing that aggregate expenditures would drop, we challenge that intuition here. We study a lobbying game and show that a cap on individual lobbyists' expenditures may have the perverse effect of increasing aggregate expenditures and lowering total surplus. This result suggests that a cap on campaign contributions may increase aggregate contributions.[6]

---

* Che: Department of Economics, University of Wisconsin, Madison, WI 53706 and Yale Law School, New Haven, CT 06520; Gale: Department of Economics, Georgetown University, Washington, DC 20057. We thank three anonymous referees for numerous valuable comments.

[1] The following quotation makes this point: "Critics maintain that high campaign costs force candidates to devote an inordinate amount of time to raising money. They also hold that special interest groups seeking to exercise influence by satisfying the candidates' need for campaign funds threaten the integrity of the election and governmental processes." (Herbert E. Alexander and Monica Bauer, 1991 pp. 1–2.)

[2] The empirical evidence of a link between campaign contributions and roll-call votes in the House of Representatives and Senate is mixed (Levitt, 1995). There is evidence that lobbyists' influence is felt before legislation reaches the floor, however. Richard L. Hall and Frank W. Wayman (1990) examined committees of the House of Representatives, finding a significant relationship between campaign contributions and members' efforts to shape legislation at the committee stage. Thomas Romer and James M. Snyder, Jr. (1994) found a significant relationship between committee assignments and political action committee (PAC) contributions. In particular, they found that seniority is rewarded, suggesting that contributors target influential members. John R. Wright (1990) studied committee voting and found that campaign contributions facilitate subsequent lobbying.

[3] In one legendary case, five senators met with officials of the Federal Home Loan Bank Board on behalf of a banker who had contributed $1.3 million to the senators and their parties (Alexander, 1991 pp. 116–17).

[4] Recent legislation restricted the types of gifts that members of Congress may accept (*Congressional Quarterly*, 1995a).

[5] Mandatory spending limits were struck down by the Supreme Court in *Buckley v. Valeo*, 424 U.S. 1 (1976). The FECA was then amended to incorporate public funding for presidential candidates who voluntarily accept spending limits. Some recent proposals include voluntary spending limits for congressional campaigns and stricter contribution limits (*Congressional Quarterly*, 1996).

[6] Lobbying organizations provide a large and growing fraction of total campaign contributions. For example,

American Economic Review **88**, 643–651

Yeon-Koo Che and Ian L. Gale

The next section presents the model and describes the equilibrium when lobbyists are unconstrained. We then solve for the equilibrium when lobbyists face a cap on individual expenditures. When a cap constrains the high-valuation lobbyist, a lobbyist with a lower valuation for the political prize becomes relatively more aggressive. As a consequence, total lobbying expenditures may rise. Since the high-valuation lobbyist's probability of winning the prize drops, the cap reduces total surplus if private and social valuations coincide. Concluding remarks are contained in the final section.

I. The Model

Two risk-neutral lobbyists seek a political prize.[7] The prize could be a government contract, a military base, or a license to produce a good or service. An incumbent politician determines who will receive the prize. Ethics legislation prevents the open sale of political prizes, so the politician will award the prize to the lobbyist who spends more. We do not model the politician's objective function explicitly, but two interpretations of her behavior are possible.[8] First, the politician may be self-interested. A self-interested politician wishes to extract rents from the lobbyists. Although she cannot sell the prize openly, the politician may accept campaign contributions or in-kind contributions.[9] Second, the politician may be benevolent. In this case, the politician wishes to award the prize to the lobbyist who will add

more to social welfare. A benevolent politician will award the prize to the lobbyist who spends more, if she does not know the individual valuations, since a lobbyist with a higher valuation will spend more, on average.[10] (Recent legislation requires lobbyists to disclose their lobbying expenditures for each issue on which they lobby members of Congress.)[11]

Gordon Tullock (1980) considered lobbying in a setting where an individual's probability of winning a political prize depended directly on his lobbying expenditures.[12] The case known as the ''all-pay auction'' has been analyzed by Arye L. Hillman and John G. Riley (1989) and Michael R. Baye et al. (1993, 1996). In an all-pay auction, bidders submit nonnegative bids simultaneously and the prize is awarded to the highest bidder. The novel feature is that all bidders pay their bids, which is appropriate here since a lobbyist's contributions are not typically returned if his efforts are unsuccessful. The all-pay auction is also appropriate for other rent-seeking games such as labor-market tournaments, as well as for research and development contests.

We analyze the all-pay auction when bidders face an exogenous cap on bids. In keeping with the all-pay terminology, we refer to the politician as ''the seller'' and to the lobbyists as ''the bidders.'' Bidder i's valuation of the prize is v_i, and $v_1 > v_2 > 0$.[13] If bidder i wins with a bid b_i his payoff is $v_i - b_i$, whereas his payoff is $-b_i$ if he loses. (If they tie, the bidders are equally likely to win.) The rules of the game and the payoffs are known by the bidders, who maximize their individual expected payoffs. We look for a Nash equilibrium in

---

PACs contributed nearly half of all money spent by incumbents in the 1992 elections for the House of Representatives (Levitt, 1995).

[7] Another interpretation of the model is that the lobbyists are candidates for political office, and the candidate who spends more will win.

[8] A complementary view is that lobbying is directly informative (see David Austen-Smith and Wright [1992] or Austen-Smith [1995]). The information might concern the impact on constituents of pending legislation, and it could take the form of technical research or public opinion surveys, for example.

[9] Even if the politician wished to hold a standard auction rather than an all-pay auction, it might be difficult to commit to return contributions from unsuccessful lobbyists, or for lobbyists to commit to make a contribution if awarded the prize.

[10] In Robert W. Helsley and Arthur O'Sullivan (1994), contributions to a referendum campaign signal the private valuations of the competing lobbies, so citizens' votes depend on which lobby contributes more to the referendum campaign.

[11] See *Congressional Quarterly*, 1995b.

[12] Tullock supposed that lobbyist i's probability of winning the political prize is $b_i^R / (\sum_{j=1}^n b_j^R)$, where b_j is the amount lobbyist j spends and R is a constant. In the all-pay auction, $R = \infty$.

[13] In the case of a political prize that may not be awarded until after the next election, the valuations could incorporate the probability that the politician will be reelected.

bidding strategies. The bids accrue to the seller.

Absent a cap on bids, bidder 1 wins the prize with probability $1 - (v_2/2v_1) > \frac{1}{2}$ in equilibrium and the seller's expected revenue is $v_2(v_1 + v_2)/2v_1 < v_2$.[14] Bidder 2 will bid less than v_2, since he forfeits his bid even if he loses. Bidder 1 will take advantage of bidder 2's passivity by bidding less than v_2 himself, resulting in expected revenue strictly below v_2.[15] A cap on bids can attenuate bidder 1's ability to "preempt" bidder 2, which may increase bidding competition and raise the seller's expected revenue.

II. Equilibrium with a Cap on Bids

We now show the impact of an exogenous cap on bids. Let m denote the maximum allowable bid. We consider $m < v_2$ since a larger cap has no effect. There is a unique equilibrium in essentially all cases. That is, there is a unique pair of cumulative distribution functions for equilibrium bids. We focus on these cases first, followed by the nongeneric cases of $m = v_1/2$ and $m = v_2/2$. For small values of m, the equilibrium is in pure strategies. For larger values, it is in mixed strategies, although it still differs qualitatively from the equilibrium in the absence of a cap. (There are mass points at bids other than zero and there are gaps in the support of the equilibrium bids.) Let $F_i(z) \equiv \text{prob}(b_i \leq z)$ denote the cumulative distribution function for bidder i's bids in equilibrium.

Three lemmas provide necessary conditions for the distributions of equilibrium bids. The first lemma, which is stated without proof, shows that there cannot be mass points in the interval $(0, m)$. A sketch of the proof follows. If both bidders have mass points at a particular bid between zero and m, then each has an incentive to move the mass higher, since the (conditional) probability of winning would then jump up. (The same argument holds if both have mass points at zero.) If exactly one bidder has a mass point at the bid, then the other bidder will not place density immediately below that bid, since it would be preferable to move such density above the mass point. But it is profitable to move the mass lower if the other bidder has no density just below the mass point. Since there is an incentive to change bids in both cases, there cannot be mass points in $(0, m)$ in equilibrium. Proposition 1 of Hillman and Riley (1989) contains a proof for the case without a cap on bids (i.e., $m = \infty$).

LEMMA 1: *Neither bidder has a mass point at any bid* $b \in (0, m)$. *At most one bidder has a mass point at zero.*

An implication of Lemma 1 is that bidder i's expected payoff from a bid $b \in (0, m)$ is $v_i F_j(b) - b$, since there is zero probability that bidder j will also bid b. Another implication is that there cannot be a pure-strategy equilibrium here unless both bidders bid m. We now determine the lower limit of bids made in equilibrium. The proofs of the next two lemmas are in the Appendix.

LEMMA 2: *If* $m \in (v_2/2, v_2)$, *both bidders have an infimum bid of zero. If* $m < v_2/2$, *both have an infimum of* m.

Lemma 2 implies that the equilibrium bids are $b_1 = b_2 = m$ when $m < v_2/2$. We now show that there is a gap in the set of possible equilibrium bids when $m \in (v_2/2, v_2)$, and that both bidders have mass points at the cap.

LEMMA 3: *Suppose that* $m \in (v_2/2, v_2)$. *There exists a constant* b' *such that both bidders place nonzero density on every* $b \in (0, b']$ *and zero density on every* $b \in (b', m)$. *Both bidders have mass points at* m.

The lemmas provide necessary conditions for equilibrium distribution functions. We now

---

[14] An implication of Lemma 1, which follows, is that the equilibrium is in mixed strategies. Thus, bidder 2 has a nonzero probability of winning.

[15] Suppose that bidder 1 wins with (*ex ante*) probability $\pi < 1$. By the standard revealed preference argument, his expected payment, e, satisfies $\pi v_1 - e \geq v_1 - v_2$ since he could win with probability one by bidding v_2. Thus, $e \leq \pi v_2 - (1 - \pi)(v_1 - v_2) < \pi v_2$. At the same time, bidder 2 will not pay more than $(1 - \pi)v_2$ for a probability $(1 - \pi)$ of winning, so the seller's expected revenue is strictly below v_2. By contrast, if the seller could hold an oral auction, she could raise revenue of v_2. This last observation coincides with our result that changing the structure of the auction by imposing a cap may increase expected revenue.

find the unique pair that satisfies these conditions. Consider $m \in (v_2/2, v_2)$. We first determine the distribution functions that make the bidders indifferent among all bids in $(0, b'] \cup \{m\}$, as required by Lemma 3. We then find the equilibrium value of b'.

Since bidder 1 must be indifferent among all bids in $(0, b'] \cup \{m\}$, each bid in that set must yield the same expected payoff. That is,

$$(1) \quad v_1 F_2(b) - b$$

$$= v_1 \lfloor F_2(b') + (1 - F_2(b'))/2 \rfloor - m,$$

for all $b \in (0, b']$. The left-hand side gives the expected payoff from bidding $b \in (0, b']$, while the right-hand side corresponds to a bid of m. (When bidder 1 bids m, there is probability $1 - F_2(b')$ that bidder 2 also bids m. The tie is broken in bidder 1's favor with probability $\frac{1}{2}$.) Similarly, a bid $b \in (0, b']$ yields bidder 2

$$(2) \quad v_2 F_1(b) - b$$

$$= v_2 [F_1(b') + (1 - F_1(b'))/2] - m.$$

We now use (1) and (2) to show that bidder 2 has mass at zero. Straightforward algebra implies

$$(3) \quad v_1[1 - F_2(b)] = v_2[1 - F_1(b)],$$

for all $b \in (0, b']$.[16] Lemma 1 states that the bidders cannot both have mass points at zero, so either $F_1(0) = 0$ or $F_2(0) = 0$. Since $v_1 > v_2$, (3) implies $1 - F_2(0) < 1 - F_1(0)$, so $F_1(0) = 0$ and $F_2(0) = 1 - (v_2/v_1)$.[17]

The distribution functions can now be specified for bids above zero. Bidder 2's equilibrium expected payoff is zero, since a bid of zero yields $v_2 F_1(0) = 0$, so (2) implies

$$(4) \quad v_2 F_1(b) - b = 0,$$

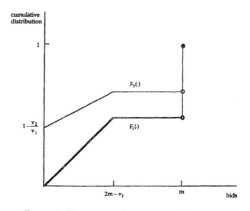

cumulative
distribution

FIGURE 1. EQUILIBRIUM DISTRIBUTION FUNCTIONS

for all $b \in (0, b']$. Thus, bidder 1's distribution function satisfies $F_1(b) = b/v_2$ in that range. Lemma 3 implies $F_1(b) = F_1(b') = b'/v_2$ for $b \in (b', m)$. Finally, $F_1(m) = 1$, by definition.

Bidder 1's equilibrium expected payoff is $v_1 F_2(0) = v_1 - v_2 > 0$.[18] A bid $b \in (0, b']$ therefore gives bidder 1 an expected payoff of

$$(5) \qquad v_1 F_2(b) - b = v_1 - v_2,$$

so $F_2(b) = 1 - (v_2 - b)/v_1$ for $b \in [0, b']$. Finally, $F_2(b) = 1 - (v_2 - b')/v_1$ for $b \in (b', m)$. Equation (2) now implies that $b' = 2m - v_2$. The equilibrium distribution functions are graphed in Figure 1.

All bids made by bidder 1 yield an expected payoff of $v_1 - v_2$, by construction, while all bids made by bidder 2 yield zero. All other feasible bids are inferior to a bid of b' since a bid in (b', m) wins with the same probability as a bid of b', but is more costly. Thus, we have found the equilibrium bidding strategies.

---

[16] Rearranging (1) yields $m - b = v_1[(1 + F_2(b'))/2] - v_1 F_2(b)$, so $m - b' = v_1[(1 - F_2(b'))/2]$. Adding these two equations yields $2m - b - b' = v_1[1 - F_2(b)]$. Repeating the exercise for bidder 2 yields $2m - b - b' = v_2[1 - F_1(b)]$.

[17] Since (3) holds only for $b > 0$, we use the fact that $\lim_{b \downarrow 0} F_i(b) = F_i(0)$.

[18] This holds since an infinitesimal bid gives him an expected payoff of $\lim_{b \downarrow 0} v_1 F_2(b) - b = v_1 F_2(0) = v_1 - v_2$. Absent a cap, bidder 1 could guarantee a victory by bidding v_2, again yielding $v_1 - v_2$. The cap prevents us from making that direct inference here.

VOL. 88 NO. 3   CHE AND GALE: CAPS ON POLITICAL LOBBYING   647

We can now determine the seller's expected revenue. Note first that bidder 1's (*ex ante*) probability of winning the prize is

(6) $\displaystyle\int_0^{b'} \frac{1}{v_2} F_2(b)\,db + \left[1 - \frac{b'}{v_2}\right]$

$\times \left[F_2(b') + \dfrac{1 - F_2(b')}{2}\right]$

$= 1 - (v_2/2v_1).$

The integral gives the probability that bidder 1 wins, conditional on bidding in $(0, b']$. [The density is $1/v_2$, and a bid b wins with probability $F_2(b)$.] The second term corresponds to the case in which he bids m. Bidder 1's expected payment is the difference between his gross and net expected payoffs:

(7) $v_1[1 - (v_2/2v_1)] - [v_1 - v_2] = v_2/2.$

Using the same approach, bidder 2's expected payment can be expressed as $(v_2/v_1)(v_2/2)$. The seller's expected revenue is the sum:

(8) $v_2(v_1 + v_2)/2v_1.$

Now consider $m < v_2/2$. Lemma 2 implies that both bidders must bid m in any equilibrium. Bidding m is clearly equilibrium behavior. If $b_i = m$, then $b_j = m$ yields an expected payoff of $v_j/2 - m > 0$. A higher bid is not feasible while a lower bid loses with probability one, yielding a nonpositive expected payoff. In equilibrium, each bidder wins with probability $\frac{1}{2}$, and the seller's expected revenue is $2m$. We now summarize the results.

PROPOSITION 1: *If $m \in (v_2/2, v_2)$, bidder 1 wins with probability $1 - (v_2/2v_1)$, and the seller's expected revenue is $v_2(v_1 + v_2)/2v_1$. If $m < v_2/2$, bidder 1 wins with probability $\frac{1}{2}$, and the expected revenue is $2m$.*

A cap $m \in (v_2/2, v_2)$ leaves the seller's expected revenue the same as it is without a cap. If $m \in (v_2(v_1 + v_2)/4v_1, v_2/2)$, the expected revenue is $2m > v_2(v_1 + v_2)/2v_1$, so it exceeds the revenue without a cap. The cap is small enough here to remove bidder 1's ability to

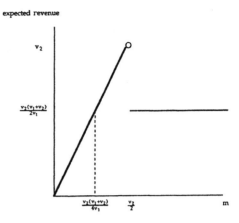

FIGURE 2. EXPECTED REVENUE

preempt, but it is large enough that the increase in bidder 2's aggressiveness outweighs the decrease in bidder 1's. For lower m, the expected revenue is strictly lower with a cap than without. Expected revenue is graphed in Figure 2, as m varies.

Total surplus is (weakly) lower with a cap than without. When $m > v_2/2$, bidder 1's probability of winning is the same as without the cap, so total surplus is unchanged. When $m < v_2/2$, however, bidder 1 wins with probability $\frac{1}{2} < 1 - (v_2/2v_1)$, making total surplus strictly lower than without a cap.

We now consider the nongeneric cases of $m = v_1/2$ and $m = v_2/2$. If $m = v_2/2$, then there is an equilibrium in which $b_1 = b_2 = m$. There is also a continuum of equilibria in which bidder 2 places mass of v_2/v_1 or more on m and the remainder on zero, while bidder 1 always bids m.[19] If $m = v_1/2$, then there is an equilibrium of the form described in Lemma 3, but there is also an equilibrium in which bidder 1 randomizes between zero and m, while bidder 2 always bids m.[20]

---

[19] The proof of Lemma 2 showed that an infimum bid in $(0, m)$ was inconsistent with equilibrium, so only zero and m can be infimum bids here. The bidders can have different infimum bids only if one always bids m while the other randomizes between zero and m.

[20] The latter equilibrium requires $m = v_1/2 \le v_2$, or else bidder 2 is not optimizing. (The cap does not bind if $m =$

The qualitative results from these cases mirror the earlier results. Bidder 1's probability of winning is lower in these equilibria than in the case without a cap, so total surplus is again lower. The equilibria for $m = v_2/2$ again show that expected revenue can be higher with a cap than without.

III. Concluding Remarks

We have shown that an exogenous cap on bids in an all-pay auction (weakly) reduces the probability that the high-valuation bidder wins and increases the seller's expected revenue. When lobbying is seen as an all-pay auction, the results imply that limits on individual expenditures may increase total expenditures and lower total surplus. A cap on campaign contributions may therefore have the perverse effect of increasing aggregate contributions while lowering total surplus.

This paper also contributes to auction theory. We have characterized the equilibrium of the all-pay auction in the presence of an exogenous cap on bids. The results are applicable to a range of contests in which a limit is imposed on effort or expenditure, or in which contestants are constrained because of limited endowments. For instance, caps may increase total expenditures and lower total surplus in a war of attrition that would exhibit preemption in the absence of caps.[21] Limiting individual expenditures on research and development could increase total expenditures, and shorten the expected time to innovation. We conclude with a further discussion of robustness and implications of the results.

A. *Additional Bidders*

Suppose that there are $n > 2$ bidders, with valuations $v_1 > v_2 > \cdots > v_n$. In the absence of a cap, only the two bidders with the highest valuations make nonzero bids, so the expressions for expected revenue and total surplus are unchanged (Hillman and Riley, 1989; Baye et al., 1993, 1996). Now suppose that there is a cap satisfying $v_k/k > m > v_{k+1}/(k + 1)$ for some $k < n$. There is an equilibrium with expected revenue of km. Bidding m gives a strictly positive expected payoff to bidders $1, 2, \ldots, k$. Any other feasible bid loses with probability one. At the same time, bidders $k + 1, k + 2, \ldots, n$ have no incentive to submit a nonzero bid.[22] Thus, expected revenue may again rise relative to the case without a cap. Total surplus is strictly lower than without a cap.

B. *Incomplete Information*

The results do not rely crucially on the assumption of complete information. Rather, the *ex ante* asymmetry in valuations generates the properties discussed above. While explicit handicapping of the high-valuation bidder may increase expected revenue in a first-price auction (Roger B. Myerson, 1981), a *symmetric* cap has that effect here. Thus, symmetric limits on effort or expenditure can substitute for handicapping of favorites in tournaments and contests.

C. *Socially Wasteful Lobbying*

Lobbying expenditures take forms other than campaign contributions. For example, lobbyists spend money on public opinion surveys, and on print, radio, and television advertisements. They spend money encouraging citizens to participate in letter-writing campaigns. They also make in-kind contributions to politicians. Moreover, the value that a politician places on an in-kind contribution may be less than the expenditure involved. These observations suggest that not all lobbying expenditures accrue to politicians.

$v_1/2 > v_2$, so this case does not arise.) This equilibrium is unappealing in the sense that mass is put on a bid that is weakly dominated. Bidder 1 is indifferent between zero and m, but if bidder 2 might tremble and not bid m, then a bid of m would strictly dominate a bid of zero for bidder 1. The same point holds for the equilibria in which bidder 2 randomizes between zero and m.

[21] These preemption results are discussed in Drew Fudenberg and Jean Tirole (1991), for example.

[22] The identity of the active bidders is not uniquely determined if $v_{k+1}/k > m > v_{k+1}/(k + 1)$, since there is an equilibrium in which bidder $k + 1$ bids m while bidder k bids zero.

Our results do not depend critically on the assumption that bids accrue to the seller. Suppose that a fraction τ of each dollar spent on lobbying is effectively wasted, $0 < \tau < 1$. In the case of a political campaign, contributions enhance the politician's reelection chances, but the value to her of a contribution equal to b is only $(1 - \tau)b$. With two bidders and a cap $m < v_2/2$, expected revenue is $2(1 - \tau)m$, and total surplus is $(v_1 + v_2)/2 - 2\tau m$. There are now two ways that the cap can lower total surplus. In addition to increasing the probability that the prize goes to the low-valuation bidder, the cap may also increase the deadweight loss associated with the wasting of resources. In the region where the cap increases expected revenue, the amount of waste is higher with the cap than without, since waste increases with total expenditures.

D. Divergence of Private and Social Valuations

Whether the private and social valuations of the political prize are congruent in any particular context is important. Suppose that one bidder represents a corporation or a closely held business while the other represents a diffuse group, such as consumers. Free-riding among members of the latter group may lead to an understatement of their individual valuations and a consequent lowering of their probability of winning. Imposing a cap and increasing the group's probability of winning may therefore increase total surplus. Similar points hold if the groups differ in both valuations and costs of lobbying.

E. Empirical Implications

Aggregate spending on congressional races has doubled since passage of the FECA, which placed controls on campaign contributions. While consistent with the prediction of this paper, such evidence is not definitive since there have been other developments in the intervening years. It is also unclear how tightly the contribution limits bind since there are indirect ways to contribute. (For example, "soft money" can be funneled to political parties.) Thus, a careful empirical analysis is needed.

There are related studies the conclusions of which are consistent with the predictions of this paper. Several researchers have found that close electoral contests induce greater contributions (see James F. Herndon, 1982; Keith T. Poole et al., 1987, for example). To the extent that caps on campaign contributions make elections close, this finding is consistent with the prediction of our paper.

APPENDIX

PROOF OF LEMMA 2:

Let $b^* \equiv \inf\{z \mid F_1(z) > 0\}$ denote the infimum of bidder 1's bids. We first show that only zero or m can be infimum bids in equilibrium. Suppose instead that bidder 1's infimum bid is $b^* \in (0, m)$. If bidder 2 makes a bid in $(0, b^*)$, he loses with probability one. Since a bid of zero is better, bidder 2 must have zero density in $(0, b^*)$.[23] This means that bidder 1 could profitably move density in $(b^*, b^* + \varepsilon^*)$ arbitrarily close to zero. For $b \in (b^*, b^* + \varepsilon^*)$, the payment would drop by b. The probability of winning would drop by only $F_2(b) - F_2(0) = F_2(b) - F_2(b^*) < F_2(b^* + \varepsilon^*) - F_2(b^*)$, however. This last term is of order ε^*, by Lemma 1. It follows that moving the density raises bidder 1's expected payoff, for some $\varepsilon^* > 0$. Since a profitable deviation exists, an infimum bid of $b^* \in (0, m)$ cannot occur in equilibrium. The symmetric argument shows that bidder 2 cannot have an infimum in $(0, m)$ either, so only zero and m are possible infimum bids in equilibrium.

The remainder of the proof comprises two cases. Suppose first that $m \in (v_2/2, v_2)$. We employ a proof by contradiction to show that both bidders have an infimum of zero. Suppose instead that $b^* = m$, which implies that bidder 1 bids $b_1 = m$. Bidder 2 will bid zero or m, or he will randomize between the two, since a bid of zero strictly dominates any $b \in (0, m)$. Bidding zero is inconsistent with

---

[23] This condition on the density function holds for *almost every* bid in the interval $(0, b^*)$. That is, it can be violated on a set of measure zero without changing the result. In the interest of brevity, we leave this qualification understood throughout the paper.

equilibrium since $b_1 = m$ is not optimal if $b_2 = 0$. Bidding m or randomizing between zero and m can only be optimal for bidder 2 if $v_2/2 - m \geq 0$, since a bid of m results in a tie. This restriction on m contradicts $m \in (v_2/2, v_2)$, so $b^* = m$ cannot occur in equilibrium here. An analogous argument shows that bidder 2 cannot have an infimum bid of m, so the common infimum is zero.

Now suppose that $m < v_2/2$. We employ a proof by contradiction to show that both bidders have an infimum of m. Bidding m guarantees at least a tie, so bidder i must receive an expected payoff of at least $v_i/2 - m > 0$. Suppose that bidder i has an infimum bid of zero. Since his infimum is zero, a bid near zero must be as good as a bid of m for bidder i. But if bidder j does not have mass at zero, then bidder i receives less than $v_i/2 - m$ if he bids near zero. (The probability that bidder i wins would be arbitrarily small for bids that are arbitrarily close to zero.) Bidder j must therefore have mass at zero. Since bidder j's infimum is also zero, the same argument implies that bidder i must have mass at zero. The bidders cannot both have mass at zero, by Lemma 1, so the infimum must equal m for both bidders.

PROOF OF LEMMA 3:

We first show that both bidders have mass points at m. Lemma 2 shows that the common infimum is zero, while Lemma 1 shows that at least one bidder has no mass at zero. Suppose, in particular, that bidder i does not have mass at zero. Then, if bidder j bids arbitrarily close to zero, his expected payoff is strictly below $v_j - m > 0$. Since his infimum is zero, a bid near zero must be as good as a bid of m for bidder j. But if bidder i does not have mass at m, then a bid of m would yield bidder j an expected payoff of $v_j - m$. Bidder i must therefore have mass at m. We conclude that at least one bidder has mass at m, since at least one bidder has no mass at zero.

Suppose, in particular, that bidder i has mass $\alpha > 0$ at m. If bidder j has nonzero density in $(m - \varepsilon', m)$, he could profitably move it to m, for some $\varepsilon' > 0$. For $b \in (m - \varepsilon', m)$, the payment would rise by only $m - b < \varepsilon'$, but the probability of winning would rise by at least $\alpha/2$, since bidder j would now tie if bidder i bids m. Since mov-

ing the density up raises bidder j's expected payoff, bidder j must have zero density in $(m - \varepsilon', m)$. If bidder j has no mass at m, then bidder i could profitably take mass from m and move it lower. We conclude that both bidders have mass points at m.

The presence of mass points at m for both bidders implies that both bidders have zero density in $(m - \varepsilon'', m)$, for some $\varepsilon'' > 0$. This demonstrates the existence of $b^* \in [0, m]$ such that both bidders have zero density in (b^*, m). Let b' denote the smallest $b^* \in [0, m]$ such that both bidders place zero density on every bid in (b^*, m).[24] We now show that both bidders place nonzero density on every $b \in (0, b']$. By the argument used in the proof of Lemma 2, if bidder i has zero density in an interval $(s, t) \subset (0, b']$, then so must bidder j. But if both bidders have zero density in (s, t), then either bidder could profitably move density from $(t, t + \varepsilon^*)$ down to s, for some $\varepsilon^* > 0$. Thus, both bidders must have nonzero density on every $b \in (0, b']$.

REFERENCES

Alexander, Herbert E. and Bauer, Monica. *Financing the 1988 election*. Boulder, CO: Westview Press, 1991.

Austen-Smith, David. "Campaign Contributions and Access." *American Political Science Review*, September 1995, 89(3), pp. 566–81.

Austen-Smith, David and Wright, John R. "Competitive Lobbying for a Legislator's Vote." *Social Choice and Welfare*, July 1992, 9(3), pp. 229–57.

Baye, Michael R.; Kovenock, Dan and de Vries, Casper G. "Rigging the Lobbying Process: An Application of All-Pay Auctions." *American Economic Review*, March 1993, 83(1), pp. 289–94.

———. "The All-Pay Auction with Complete Information." *Economic Theory*, August 1996, 8(2), pp. 291–305.

---

[24] In fact, $b' \in (0, m)$. The preceding paragraph shows that $b' \neq m$. If $b' = 0$, then both bidders must have mass points at zero, by Lemma 2. This contradicts Lemma 1, so $b' \neq 0$.

VOL. 88 NO. 3   *CHE AND GALE: CAPS ON POLITICAL LOBBYING*   *651*

Congressional Quarterly. "House Votes to Toughen Gift Restrictions." November 18, 1995a, *53*(45), pp. 3516–19.

———. "Bill Would Open Windows on Lobbying Efforts." December 2, 1995b, *53*(47), pp. 3631–33.

———. "Hoekstra Proposes Legislation to Make Overhaul GOP Issue." February 3, 1996, *54*(5), p. 281.

Fudenberg, Drew and Tirole, Jean. *Game theory.* Cambridge, MA: MIT Press, 1991.

Hall, Richard L. and Wayman, Frank W. "Buying Time: Moneyed Interests and the Mobilization of Bias in Congressional Committees." *American Political Science Review*, September 1990, *84*(3), pp. 797–820.

Helsley, Robert W. and O'Sullivan, Arthur. "Altruistic Voting and Campaign Contributions." *Journal of Public Economics*, September 1994, *55*(1), pp. 107–19.

Herndon, James F. "Access, Record, and Competition as Influences on Interest Group Contributions to Congressional Campaigns." *Journal of Politics*, November 1982, *44*(4), pp. 996–1019.

Hillman, Arye L. and Riley, John G. "Politically Contestable Rents and Transfers." *Econom*-ics and Politics, Spring 1989, *1*(1), pp. 17–39.

Levitt, Steven D. "Congressional Campaign Finance Reform." *Journal of Economic Perspectives*, Winter 1995, *9*(1), pp. 183–93.

Myerson, Roger B. "Optimal Auction Design." *Mathematics of Operations Research*, February 1981, *6*(1), pp. 58–73.

Poole, Keith T.; Romer, Thomas and Rosenthal, Howard. "The Revealed Preferences of Political Action Committees." *American Economic Review*, May 1987 (*Papers and Proceedings*), *77*(2), pp. 298–302.

Romer, Thomas and Snyder, James M., Jr. "An Empirical Investigation of the Dynamics of PAC Contributions." *American Journal of Political Science*, August 1994, *38*(3), pp. 745–69.

Tullock, Gordon. "Efficient Rent Seeking," in James M. Buchanan, Robert D. Tollison, and Gordon Tullock, eds., *Toward a theory of the rent seeking society.* College Station, TX: Texas A&M University Press, 1980, pp. 269–82.

Wright, John R. "Contributions, Lobbying and Committee Voting in the U.S. House of Representatives." *American Political Science Review*, June 1990, *84*(2), pp. 417–38.

The Economic Journal, 114 (*January*), 69–82. © Royal Economic Society 2004. Published by Blackwell Publishing, 9600 Garsington Road, Oxford OX4 2DQ, UK and 350 Main Street, Malden, MA 02148, USA.

INVERSE CAMPAIGNING*

Kai A. Konrad

It can be advantageous for an 'office motivated' party A to spend effort to make it public that a group of voters will lose from party A's policy proposal. Such effort is called inverse campaigning. The inverse campaigning equilibria are described for the case where the two parties can simultaneously reveal information publicly to uninformed voters. Inverse campaigning dissipates the parties' rents and causes some inefficiency in expectation. Inverse campaigning also influences policy design. Successful policy proposals hurt small groups of voters who lose a lot and do not benefit small groups of voters who gain a lot.

Policy reform proposals are often debated publicly. Information processed in this debate may change the voters' attitudes towards the reform. This information is often of a particular type. Consider, for instance, the debate on tax reform. Often, the advocates of a tax reform do not identify the set of voters who gain but do point out that the reform will eliminate some 'undeserved' large benefits of a minority group, or close some 'tax loophole' that benefits a minority group of voters.[1] They point to a group of voters who will lose from the reform. Similarly, the party that opposes the reform identifies small interest groups which will receive large benefits from the reform and accuses the reform advocates of favouring a small minority at the expense of the large majority. For instance, the Democratic National Platform (2000, p. 5) criticised the tax reform suggested by the Republicans as follows: 'The Bush tax slash ... is bigger than any cut Newt Gingrich ever dreamed of. It would let the richest one percent of Americans afford a new sports car and middle class Americans afford a warm soda'. A particular voter in the remaining 99% segment may benefit or lose from the tax cut, depending on the allocation of the reduction in spending among the different categories of public expenditure that is not known. However, these voters can correctly calculate that they will make a loss in expected value terms.

I will call this type of information policy *inverse campaigning*. Inverse campaigning differs from ordinary campaigning where parties use resources to tell the voter how beautiful, moral, and competent they are (positive campaigning) or where they use them to tell the voter how bad, ugly, and incompetent the opponent is (negative campaigning).[2] An example that illustrates a possible rationale for inverse campaigning is as follows. Suppose a party X proposes a policy. Suppose there are 100 voters. If the policy proposal is carried out, 51 voters gain one unit and 49 voters lose one unit. Suppose further that each voter knows this distribution of gains and

---

* I thank Helmut Bester, Amihai Glazer, Daniel Krähmer, Frode Meland and participants in seminars at UCL, Bonn, Bergen and Frankfurt and two anonymous referees for valuable comments. The usual caveat applies.
[1] See, e.g., page 19 of the agreement between German Social Democrats and the Green Party (http://www.spd.de/servlet/PB/show/1023294/Koalitionsvertrag.pdf2002).
[2] For a discussion of positive and negative campaigning see, e.g., Skaperdas and Grofman (1995) and Harrington and Hess (1996).

[69]

losses, but does not know whether he belongs to the group of winners or to the group of losers. In the absence of information, all voters will vote for party X, because this choice maximises each voter's expected payoff. Consider now a party Y which opposes this policy proposal. Suppose party Y identifies three voters a_1, a_2 and a_3 who gain if the policy proposal is carried out, and informs the public that these voters will be among the winners. Once this has happened, all remaining uninformed voters will update their probability beliefs and their expected gains from the policy proposal fall from $+2/100$ to $-1/97$. Accordingly, the three informed voters will vote for party X, but all 97 uninformed voters will vote for party Y.

The central idea in this example that motivates party Y to engage in inverse campaigning is as follows. It is difficult and costly for a voter to calculate whether he or she gains or loses from a particular policy reform. This has frequently been recognised in the literature on policy reform and it results from the complexity of many policy proposals and their various general equilibrium repercussions. If it becomes known that the reform affects a well-defined group, the information is also valuable to the voters who do not belong to this group: if the reform takes from a group, the redistributional impact of the reform is more likely to benefit the majority of voters who do not belong to this group. Similarly, if the uninformed majority learns that the reform shifts massive benefits to a small minority group, it becomes more likely that the reform will be less advantageous to this majority of voters.

A further aspect is that this mechanism will have some impact on the design of the reform. If a party chooses a reform that makes it easy for the opposition to identify a minority group that gains much by this reform, the reform is unlikely to receive majority support. However, by choosing a reform that inflicts substantial losses on a well determined minority group the party can increase the likelihood of adoption.

The importance of the group of incompletely informed voters has been shown in a number of contexts. Feddersen and Pesendorfer (1996) explain why incompletely informed voters may abstain from voting even if they have some expectations about the benefits and costs of the different policy proposals. It is important for their result that the uninformed and informed voters' preferences are aligned. This is the case, for instance, if all voters gain or all voters lose from a reform proposal. In contrast, the mechanism in this paper focusses on reforms where there is a conflict of interests between voters about the policy proposal, for instance, for redistributive reforms. Fernandez and Rodrik (1991) develop a theory of structural conservativism that is based on a statistical phenomenon similar to the one in this paper. They explain why the majority of voters – the *ex ante* uninformed – may first oppose a reform and why a majority of voters – the *ex post* informed voters who learn that they will gain from the reform – may then favour the reform once it has been adopted and all the voters have learned whether they belong to the winners or losers.[3] They explain the time inconsistent preferences of voter

---

[3] This learning effect is also crucial for the results in Glazer and Konrad (1993) who show that groups of voters may oppose a welfare enhancing reform if, when the reform is adopted, they lose control over future projects.

majorities which have a status-quo preference.[4] Their results also rely on the decisiveness of the group of incompletely informed voters. However, they consider the information status of voters prior to the election to be exogenous and do not consider whether and how the information status and their voting decision can be influenced by strategic information revelation.

In this paper time consistency is not an issue. I consider the parties' campaign incentives and show that they have an incentive to strategically reveal information publicly about who benefits or loses from policy adoption. I analyse the way two parties' incentives interact. The focus is on whether parties or candidates can manipulate the voting outcome in their favour by giving information to small groups of voters, what kind of information campaigns they use, what the welfare properties of the campaign equilibrium are and what inverse campaigning implies for the design of policy proposals.[5]

Section 1 establishes a framework in which inverse campaigning can be studied. Section 2 analyses one party's unilateral incentive to disclose information. Section 3 turns to the problem of simultaneous information disclosure. Section 4 discusses extensions and implications of the main result for the design of policy reform, and Section 5 summarises the results.

1. The Framework

Suppose there are two parties X and Y. Party X is committed to implementing a particular reform. Party Y is committed to abstaining from this reform. The share $\frac{1}{2} + e$ of voters benefits from the reform that party X proposes and each of these voters has a benefit equal to some $t > 0$. These voters are called 'type-x voters'. The share $\frac{1}{2} - e$ of voters loses from this reform, and the loss of each voter in this group is the same size t as a winner's gain. These voters are called 'type-y voters'.

The reform could be a complex change in the system of taxes or transfers with general equilibrium repercussions. The consequences of such reform for a single individual are difficult and costly to calculate. With a continuum of voters, rational voters are not willing to spend anything on information acquisition. I assume that all voters are therefore uninformed about their type, but that they know the distribution of types. The analysis could be carried out for the case in which some groups of voters know the effect of the reform for their individual payoffs at some cost in terms of complexity and notational effort. As long as this share of voters is small, or if the share of winners and losers from the reform is sufficiently similar in size, the results obtained here generalise to these cases. I discuss this in Section 4.

Analytically the type uncertainty is described as follows. The set of voters is V, and has a measure $p(V) = 1$. A subset V_x of voters is of type x. This subset has a measure of $p(V_x) = \frac{1}{2} + e$ and, without loss of generality, $e \geq 0$ (otherwise 'not

---

[4] The literature on policy reform is vast. Some of this literature is surveyed in Rodrik (1996). Much emphasis has been given to the issue of time consistency. However, there seems to be little research on the role played by strategic information production for policy adoption.

[5] A small literature in industrial organisation considers the consequences of consumers' information status with respect to experience goods; see, e.g., Bergemann and Välimäki (1996). The inverse campaigning idea could be applied there to study firms' incentives to inform customers.

implementing the reform' and 'implementing the reform' switch roles). All other voters are of type y and constitute the set V_y that is of measure $p(V_y) = \frac{1}{2} - e$. Voters know the distribution of types, but do not know their own type. Accordingly, without any further information, each voter considers the probability ξ of being of type-x as $\xi = \frac{1}{2} + e$.

Parties are office motivated. They care about winning more than 50% of the votes (as in presidential elections or the competition between two candidates more generally). Let θ_Y and $\theta_X = 1 - \theta_Y$ be the shares of voters voting for party Y and party X, respectively. Then party Y's benefit is

$$\Psi(\theta_Y) = \begin{cases} 1 & \text{if } \theta_Y > 1/2 \\ 1/2 & \text{if } \theta_Y = 1/2 \\ 0 & \text{if } \theta_Y < 1/2 \end{cases} \tag{1}$$

and party X's benefit is $1 - \Psi(\theta_Y)$, where the benefit of winning is normalised to 1.

The sequence of actions is as follows. In STAGE 0 nature assigns a type to each voter. That is, each voter becomes an element of V_x or V_y. All this is common knowledge to the parties and the voters, but voters do not know their own type.

Given a continuum of voters, each voter has a negligible impact on the election outcome and has no incentive to invest resources in becoming informed. Parties' incentives to invest in information on voters' types, however, can be considerable: as will be shown, parties can affect the election outcome by collecting information on very small groups of voters. The information acquisition decision is made in STAGE 1. Parties X and Y can choose respectively sets A and B that are measurable subsets of V and then inform the voters in these sets about their types. For simplicity, if a party chooses a subset I with measure $p(I)$, this is not a pure random selection; the party can determine how big the share of voters in I is that belongs to V_x or to V_y, that is, they can choose how many x-types or y-types they would like to identify and reveal.[6] The party's cost of information acquisition for a set I of voters is proportional to the number of voters who become informed about their type, that is, the cost is $cp(I)$. Accordingly, the payoff of party Y becomes

$$G_Y(A, B) = \Psi[\theta_Y(A, B)] - cp(B), \tag{2}$$

where A is the set of voters whose types are identified by party X, B is the set chosen by party Y, and θ_Y is the share of voters who will choose party Y given these choices about information acquisition. The function $\theta_Y(A,B)$ will be determined later. The payoff of party X is determined analogously.

In STAGE 2 the choices of sets A and B and the measures $p(A \cap V_x)$, $p(A \cap V_y)$, $p(B \cap V_x)$ and $p(B \cap V_y)$ are publicly observed and the voters who are in these sets also learn their individual types. Accordingly, some voters know their individual types and some other voters know that they belong to the set $V \setminus (A \cup B)$ and can

[6] Alternatively, one could assume that each party first chooses a set I of voters whose types are then determined and then chooses which subset of voters from I the party will inform in public about their types. This revelation choice is an additional complication because the voters' out-of-equilibrium expectations could be conditional on these choices and this could generate further equilibria.

update their prior beliefs about their probabilities of being type x or type y accordingly.

In STAGE 3 voters vote sincerely; voters who know their types vote for the party whose programme they prefer and voters who do not know their types vote for the party whose programme maximises their expected payoff.

Before proceeding to describe the equilibria with information acquisition, it is instructive to show the outcome where there is no access to information, i.e., if $A \cup B \equiv \emptyset$. In this case each voter is uninformed and maximises an expected payoff that is equal to $t(\frac{1}{2} + e) - t(\frac{1}{2} - e) = 2et$ if party X is elected and equal to 0 if party Y is elected. Accordingly, all voters vote for party X if $e > 0$. We state this benchmark case as

PROPOSITION 1. *If all voters are uninformed, all voters vote for the party that maximises the expected payoff of the uninformed voter. If $e > 0$ all vote for party X.*

2. Unilateral Inverse Campaigning

Let $e > 0$. Suppose only party Y can acquire information, i.e., $A = \emptyset$. The case in which only party X can acquire information is uninteresting for $e > 0$, because in this case party X wins all the votes if all parties abstain from information acquisition. The general case in which all parties simultaneously acquire and reveal information is considered in Section 3.

The mapping between a choice of a set B of voters and voters' choices is as follows. All voters from the set B become fully informed about their types and vote according to their types. All other voters remain incompletely informed about their types. However, they do update their beliefs. Their beliefs about the probability of being of type y are updated as follows. For any subsets $A, B \in V$ define

$$A_x \equiv A \cap V_x, \quad A_y \equiv A \cap V_y, \quad B_x \equiv B \cap V_x, \quad B_y \equiv B \cap V_y. \tag{3}$$

Let party Y choose set B. Given that $\xi = \frac{1}{2} + e$ was a voter's probability of being of type x in the absence of information, using Bayes Rule, for $i \notin B$ the updated probability $(1 - \tilde{\xi}(B))$ of being of type y becomes[7]

$$1 - \tilde{\xi}(B) \equiv 1 - \frac{\xi - p(B_x)}{1 - p(B)} = \frac{\frac{1}{2} - e - p(B_y)}{1 - p(B)} \tag{4}$$

and i votes for Y if this probability is larger than 1/2. For the case of equality, where only one party acquires information, adopting the following tie-breaking rule in this Section is without loss of generality and makes the analysis as simple as possible. This rule is that a voter who is indifferent votes for party Y.

Party Y will not choose to identify voters who, if informed, prefer party Y. More formally:

---

[7] Both parties and voters are fully informed about e, and all new information about A and B is shared among all players. This simplifies the analysis because Bayesian updating then strictly follows (4), and equilibria can be ruled out that could be based on out-of-equilibrium beliefs of voters if parties had, or gained, superior information and could select the information they reveal.

PROPERTY 3.1. *Party Y will choose some B with $p(B_y) = 0$.*

For a proof I show that any B with $p(B_y) > 0$ is strictly dominated by $\hat{B} = B\backslash B_y$. To see this note first that $\hat{B}$ has a lower information cost than B by $cp(B_y)$. It is, therefore, sufficient to show that $\Psi(B) \leq \Psi(\hat{B})$.

(i) If B yields $1 - \tilde{\xi}(B) < 1/2$, then $\Psi(B) = 0$. But $\Psi(\hat{B}) \geq 0$.
(ii) If B yields $1 - \tilde{\xi}(B) = 1/2$, then the total number of voters voting for Y is not lower if the party chooses $\hat{B}$. The reason is as follows. $1 - \tilde{\xi}(B) = 1/2$ implies $1 - \tilde{\xi}(\hat{B}) > 1/2$ by (4). Hence, all uninformed voters vote for party Y if party Y chooses $\hat{B}$. Moreover, for a choice of $\hat{B} = B\backslash B_y$, the set $V\backslash\hat{B}$ of uninformed voters includes B_y. Accordingly, $\Psi(\hat{B}) = 1 \geq \Psi(B)$.
(iii) If $1 - \tilde{\xi}(B) > 1/2$, this implies that $1 - \tilde{\xi}(\hat{B}) > 1/2$ and the same reasoning as in (ii) applies.

Summarising, $\Psi(\hat{B}) \geq \Psi(B)$ and $cp(\hat{B}) < cp(B)$ if $p(B_y) > 0$.

Property 3.1 suggests that party Y does not benefit from informing type-y voters. It chooses a set B such that $p(B) = p(B_x)$. It will inform only type-x voters about their type. Intuitively, Y wins if, and only if, the incompletely informed voters are decisive and vote for party Y. Identifying voters who gain from the reform (type-x voters) is useful for party Y because uninformed voters consider it more likely that they will lose from the reform if more voters who gain are identified. However, identifying reform losers (type-y voters) is counterproductive for party Y as the remaining uninformed voters consider it less likely that they belong to the losers of the reform.

A second, more straightforward observation is

PROPERTY 3.2. *Any two sets B, B' with $p(B_y) = p(B'_y) = 0$ and $p(B) = p(B')$ yield the same θ_Y.*

Property 3.2 states that which particular subset of voters from the subset V_x of type-x voters is chosen and informed by party Y does not matter for the voting outcome. Only the size of the set B_x of voters of type x that are informed matters for the voting outcome. The reason is that these voters will vote for x in any case, and all other voters update according to (4), but this updating is based only on the measure of the set of B_x voters who are informed and not on the particular set.[8]

Party Y's optimal campaign policy is therefore characterised by the optimal measure p of voters from the set V_x whose type is revealed. To find the optimal p, four ranges of p have to be distinguished. For $p < 2e$, the uninformed voters are decisive and vote for X. For $p \in [2e, 1/2)$ the uninformed voters are decisive and vote for Y. Note that this range is non-empty only if $e < 1/4$. For $p = 1/2$, there is a tie with $\theta_Y = \theta_X = 1/2$. For larger p, there is a majority of voters who know they are of type x. The maximum payoff therefore is attained at $p = 2e$ (and at a slightly

---

[8] This property depends on the fact that all voters in the respective sets V_x and V_y are homogeneous. In Section 4 generalisations will be discussed with a continuum of fully heterogeneous voters. It will become clear from this discussion that, for heterogeneous sets V_x and V_y, party Y prefers to identify groups of voters who gain most strongly from party X's policy proposal.

larger p for other tie-breaking rules) or at $p = 0$. The choice $p = 2e$ yields higher payoff than $p = 0$ if

$$2ec < 1. \tag{5}$$

The inequality (5) describes that the minimum cost of informing a sufficient number of voters needed to change the decision of the remaining uninformed voters (left hand side of (5)) is smaller than the benefit from being elected that was normalised to unity (right hand side of (5)). Even for extremely high information cost, this condition can easily be fulfilled if e is not much different from 0, that is, if the set of beneficiaries of the reform is approximately $1/2$. We summarise this as

PROPOSITION 2. *Suppose only party Y can make use of inverse campaigning. Let $e <$ $1/4$. If $2ec < 1$, a situation in which party Y reveals information about a set $B \subset V_x$ of voters of type x with $p(B) = 2e$ is a perfect Bayesian equilibrium.*

To make this intuitive, recall the finite numbers example in the introduction where there are 51 voters of type x and 49 voters of type y and in which case e equals 1%. If no voters are informed, party X wins: all voters vote for X, because each has a 51:49 chance of being of type x. If party Y reveals the types of two type-x voters, these two voters will vote for X, but the remaining 98 uninformed voters change their beliefs. Their chances of being of types x or y are now 49:49, and, given the tie-breaking rule, they will all vote for Y. The minimum percentage of type-x voters who need to be informed to cause this reversal of the uninformed voters' decision is 2%, or $2e$. Party Y would not want to incur unnecessary cost to inform even more voters. Further, the cost condition states that party Y's cost of informing two voters is lower than the gain from winning. Finally, if $e > 1/4$, in the finite numbers example this translates into a distribution with more than 75 voters of type x and less than 25 voters of type y. Party Y would have to inform more than 50 voters that they are of type x to make the uninformed vote for Y. But then the uninformed voters are a minority and the informed majority votes for X. Hence, party Y could not change the outcome by inverse campaigning.

In this Section an asymmetric situation was considered in which party X had an advantage in the uninformed situation ($e > 0$) but party Y was allowed to acquire and disseminate information about voters' actual types/preferences. This analysis was carried out mainly in order to reveal the intuition about why a party might want to inform groups of voters that they are better off by voting against this party. This type of effort was called *inverse campaigning.*

It is more plausible for both parties to have similar opportunities of acquiring and disseminating information, and I turn to this case next.

3. Simultaneous Campaigning

Depending on the distribution of the voters' types and the comparison between the cost of information acquisition and dissemination and the benefit of being elected, there are many cases that could be considered if both parties can acquire and disseminate information. I concentrate on the case that is perhaps most relevant for which

$$\frac{1}{2e} > c, \tag{6}$$

and for which the cost of information acquisition is in the range

$$c > \frac{4}{1 - 8e}. \tag{7}$$

The other cases can be considered briefly when discussing these conditions. The two inequalities together imply $0 \leq e < 1/16$, i.e., that the two alternatives proposed by the two parties split the voter population approximately evenly into winners and losers. If e is large, then party Y has a considerable disadvantage. As with unilateral inverse campaigning, inverse campaigning will break down if one party's advantage is too large.

Conditions (6) and (7) show that the cost of informing voters is not negligible but that it is also not prohibitively high. These assumptions are important for eliminating cases in which information acquisition does not take place because it is prohibitively costly or in which information acquisition is very inexpensive. The first inequality is identical with (5): if $1/(2e) > c$ does not hold, there will be no campaigning and party X will win. Note, however, that $1/(2e) > c$ always holds if e is sufficiently small, that is, if neither party has a considerable advantage. Further, if $c > 4/(1 - 8e)$ does not hold, then a party's gain from winning is higher than the cost of informing about a quarter of all voters. In this case the equilibria will be in mixed strategies and the results derived below will partially carry over to this case, although parties may also use other strategies than inverse campaigning.[9]

We first note:

PROPOSITION 3. *If $e \geq 0$ is sufficiently small, no equilibrium in pure strategies exists.*

For a proof of the nonexistence of a pure-strategy equilibrium suppose that (A, B) characterises an equilibrium in pure strategies. Note first that $p(A) = 0$ cannot hold in the equilibrium. If party X chooses some A with $p(A) = 0$, then by $1/(2e) > c$, Y can optimally choose some B with $p(B_y) = 0$ and $p(B_x)$ slightly above $2e$, because this makes B win the election and has the lowest cost among the choices that make Y win. But this makes A with $p(A) = 0$ suboptimal for party X. Suppose now $p(A) > 0$. Party Y's optimal reaction to this A is either some appropriately chosen $B(A)$ with $p(B_x) > 0$ that makes Y win with certainty or $p(B) = 0$. For both these cases, the choice of A is not an optimal answer to $B(A)$: if $p[B(A)] = 0$ then some $\hat{A}$ with $p(\hat{A}_y) = \delta$ for small non-negative δ dominates A and if $B(A)$ makes Y win with certainty then some $\hat{A}$ with $p(\hat{A}) = 0$ dominates A.

[9] If the second inequality in (7) is violated, the total size of the voter population induces a cap on inverse campaigning, and some of the equilibria are similar to contest equilibria as in Che and Gale (1998).

Hence, some A with $p(A) > 0$ can also not be X's pure equilibrium strategy and this shows that there can be no pure-strategy equilibrium.

Here, and in what follows, I adopt the rule that uninformed voters who are indifferent because they think that they are equally likely to be type x or type y, randomise and vote for party X or party Y with equal probabilities. While it does not matter for the qualitative results, this tie-breaking rule simplifies the analysis of the case where the two parties simultaneously choose inverse campaigning effort. This tie-breaking rule leads to a unique voting outcome for all given choices of A and B. All voters $i \in A \cup B$ vote according to their type. All voters who are not in this set update their beliefs and vote accordingly.

Before we characterise an equilibrium we notice two properties:

PROPERTY 4.1. *None of the parties will choose some set I of voters with $p(I) > \frac{1}{4} - 2e$.*

This property is an implication of the cost condition $c > 4/(1 - 8e)$. The choice of some I with $p(I) \geq \frac{1}{4} - 2e$ has a higher cost than the maximum gain from winning.

PROPERTY 4.2. (*Inverse campaigning*) *If A and B are in the equilibrium support of parties X and Y, respectively, then $p(A_x) = p(B_y) = 0$.*

This property states that party X acquires information only to identify type-y voters and to reveal their type and party Y acquires information only to identify type-x voters and to reveal their type. Accordingly, if a party uses resources in order to inform voter groups and the public about the implications of the reform, the party informs interest groups who then oppose this party's programme.

A proof of Property 4.2 is in the Appendix. The intuition for this property is as follows. The decisive group of voters is the group of incompletely informed voters who have to vote on the basis of expectations about whether they benefit or lose from the reform. For party X it is important to change the prior beliefs of this group favourably. If party X reveals that some group of voters is of type y, the size of the decisive group of voters will be reduced and the newly informed voters will vote for party Y. But the group of incompletely informed voters is still decisive and the fact that some measure of type-y voters has been identified and eliminated from the set of incompletely informed voters will make it more likely that a voter in this incompletely informed group belongs to the voters of type x who prefer party X. Hence, party X benefits from informing and revealing voters of type y. Conversely, party X is harmed if party X reveals that some group of voters is of type x. Incompletely informed voters will then revise their probability estimates and will consider it less likely that they are of type x. The analogous reasoning explains why it is not in party Y's interest to inform incompletely informed voters of type y of their type.

The following proposition characterises an equilibrium for a broad range of parameters as shown in (6) and (7).

PROPOSITION 4. *Suppose both parties can make inverse campaigning effort. A perfect Bayesian equilibrium in mixed strategies exists that is described by choices of sets A and B made by parties X and Y, respectively, such that $p(A_x) = 0$ and $p(B_y) = 0$ for all A in the*

*equilibrium support of X and all B in the equilibrium support of Y, and with $p(A)$ and $p(B)$
distributed according to cumulative distribution functions F_X and F_Y with*

$$F_X[p(A)] = \begin{cases} 2ec + cp(A) & \text{for } p(A) \in [0, 1/c - 2e] \\ 1 & \text{for } p(A) > 1/c - 2e \end{cases} \tag{8}$$

and

$$F_Y[p(B)] = \begin{cases} 2ec & \text{for } p(B) \in [0, 2e] \\ cp(B) & \text{for } p(B) \in [2e, 1/c] \\ 1 & \text{for } p(B) > 1/c. \end{cases} \tag{9}$$

The equilibrium payoffs are $2ec$ for party X and 0 for party Y.

For a proof that (8) and (9) establish an equilibrium in mixed strategies, given Properties 4.1 and 4.2 it is sufficient to show that these probability distribution functions establish mutually optimal responses. To see this, consider first the payoff of party Y for different choices $p(B)$. Y wins if $(\frac{1}{2} - e) - p(A_y) > (\frac{1}{2} + e) - p(B_x)$ or, equivalently, if $p(B_x) - 2e > p(A_y)$. If X chooses the mixed strategy as in (8), then party Y wins with probability $F_X[p(B_x) - 2e]$. Party Y's payoff from some choice B with $p(B_y) = 0$ is equal to

$$F_X[p(B_x) - 2e] - cp(B_x). \tag{10}$$

This can be seen as follows. As the benefit of being elected is normalised to 1, the expected benefit of being elected is equal to the probability that Y wins the election. For a choice $p(B) = p(B \cap V_x) = p(B_x)$, this probability is given by (8) as $F_X[p(B_x) - 2e]$. The second term in (10) is the campaign cost. The payoff in (10) is equal to zero if $p(B_x) \in \{0\} \cup [2e, 1/c]$ and smaller than zero for all B with $p(B_x)$ outside this range. Hence, any mixed strategy by Y with support $\{0\} \cup [2e, 1/c]$ is an optimal response to F_X as defined in (8). Similarly, party X wins if $(1 + e) - p(B_x) > (1 - e) - p(A_y)$, or, equivalently, if $p(A_y) > p(B_x) - 2e$. This is the case with probability $F_Y[p(A_y) + 2e]$ if party Y chooses the mixed strategy described by (9). Party X's payoff from choosing some set A_y of y-types becomes

$$F_Y[p(A_y) + 2e] - cp(A_y). \tag{11}$$

This payoff is equal to $2ec$ for all A for which $p(A_x) = 0$ and $p(A) \in [0, 1/c-2e]$ and smaller than $2ec$ for all other A.

The mixed strategy equilibrium that is characterised in Proposition 4 follows straightforwardly from the theory of all-pay auctions, as in Hillman and Riley (1989) and Baye *et al.* (1996). They also show that the equilibrium cumulative density functions in the two-player all-pay auction are unique for the case $e = 0$, and their line of reasoning extends to small $e > 0$. The important element of the proof of Proposition 4 is therefore property 4.2 which makes sure that parties choose A and B from disjunct sets. This ensures that the parties' payoffs are functions of the measures of A and B and not of the sets A or B themselves, and this turns the problem into a simple all-pay auction.

The main result can be summarised as follows. If neither party is particularly disadvantaged by its commitment to support or to oppose a particular policy reform, and if voters are uncertain whether they belong to the winners or losers of the reform, then parties may have an incentive to change the decisions of incompletely informed voters who maximise their expected payoff by revealing how the reform will affect some minority groups of voters. A party will typically publicly identify groups that have good reason to oppose this party's proposal in order to change the prior beliefs of the remaining group of incompletely informed voters favourably. Proposition 4 also implies that the sum of the parties' expected rents in the equilibrium is equal to $2ec$ and that these fully accrue to the party that would be elected in the absence of campaigning. Hence, much of the parties' rent is dissipated in the inverse campaigning effort. For the case of symmetry ($e = 0$), all rents are fully dissipated by these activities.

4. Generalisations and Implications

4.1. *Ex ante Informed Voters*

In the previous Sections, I assumed that all voters are uninformed unless one of the parties informs them about their types. For some reforms some sets of voters may know the direction of the impact of the reform even in the absence of campaigning. However, for some other sets of voters, the impact of the reform may be unclear. In this case the results in the paper continue to hold as long as the set of voters who know they gain is not much smaller or larger than the set of voters who know that they lose. Suppose, for instance, the sets are of precisely equal size. Then these *ex ante* informed voters neutralise each other perfectly, and the aggregate set of these voters has no impact on the election outcome. Hence, the election outcome is determined by the set of *ex ante* uninformed voters. The incentives for influencing the voting outcome by inverse campaigning are even stronger in this case. The reason is that the sets A or B needed to change the incompletely informed voters' decisions are even smaller, because there are fewer incompletely informed voters.

4.2. *Skewed Payoff Distributions*

One could expect that voters' gains and losses from reform are not a binary variable and that the distribution of gains and losses for many reforms is skewed. This complicates the analysis but strengthens the incentives for inverse campaigning. In this case, the parties are no longer indifferent to the subset of voters of the opposite type that they prefer to identify. Consider the example of a purely redistributive tax reform that leaves aggregate income unchanged. Uninformed voters will like a reform if a set of, say, 10% of voters is identified who all lose one unit because this increases the expected payoff for uninformed voters. However, they will like the reform even better if a set of 1% of voters is identified who lose 100 units each. The increase in their expected payoff from this latter information is much stronger than for the former information, even though the set of voters who become informed is much smaller. If campaign costs are proportional to the size of the set of voters whose type is identified, then parties will prefer to identify sets of voters whose stakes in the reform are high. Inverse campaigning towards voters who have high stakes in the reform is more effective.

4.3. Design of Policy Reform

The insight about skewed payoffs and the effectiveness of inverse campaigning has some implications for the optimal design of policy reforms. Suppose a party X designs a policy reform proposal that is purely redistributive and does not change aggregate rents. It is useful for party X if there is a small minority group A that incurs major per capita losses from the reform. Party X can publicly identify this group. This campaigning is very effective. Its cost is low, given that the set A is small, and the size of the set of decisive voters is also not reduced by much. However, because each voter in A loses much if the reform is enacted, the gains of the uninformed voters must be high. The more each voter in set A loses, the larger the increases in the expected gains of the uninformed voters. Conversely, it is dangerous for party X if the reform generates large *per capita* benefits for some small group. The opponent of party X will identify this group of reform winners. This information will lower the expected gain from the reform for the large set of incompletely informed voters and will make it more likely they will oppose the reform.

Accordingly, with inverse campaigning, a policy proposal for redistribution is more likely to succeed if there are no small groups of voters who gain much, but there are rather small groups who lose much. Parties may take this into account when designing redistributional policies.

Inverse campaigning is only one of many explanations for the precise form of legislation that may reinforce or counteract each other. It is interesting to note, for instance, that the implications of inverse campaigning for policy choices in a voting context are the reverse of the predictions of Olson's (1965) logic of collective action in a lobbying context. He suggests that small interest groups with high stakes successfully influence policy outcomes to their benefit.

5. Summary and Discussion

This paper considers the question why parties or candidates in a two-party system use resources for inverse campaigning: they inform the public that small interest groups gain by a victory of their competitor, so that these interest groups also vote for their competitor. The intuitive reason for this behaviour is that the information about other voters' gains or losses from a policy reform changes the perceptions and expectations of uninformed voters about whether they will gain or lose from this reform.

What are the crucial assumptions for this puzzling result and how plausible is inverse campaigning for different types of policy reform? First, it is important for the voters to be uncertain about what a policy reform means for them personally. This assumption is probably fulfilled for many reform proposals and for a large set of voters in a complex environment where voters have very little incentive to use resources to learn whether they gain or lose from a reform. Second, it is important for the parties to be able to acquire information about the groups of voters which win or lose by the reform, and to be able to disseminate this information. Parties then can indeed influence the election outcome favourably by inverse campaigning. Third, it was assumed here that the shares of winners and losers and the size of their losses or gains are given. Hence, the revelation of information about a group of winners does not affect the expected quality of a policy proposal as such. Some policy proposals are more likely to meet this condition than others. For instance, implementing a reform that has considerable allocative effects may increase or decrease efficiency, and there may also be uncertainty about the aggregate efficiency gains of a reform. Searching for, and finding, individuals who benefit may then be an indication of the proposal's good quality. If this type of uncertainty is sufficiently important, it weakens the incentives for inverse campaigning. For instance, in a world in which the benefits of a policy proposal are perfectly positively correlated across all voters, identifying some voters who benefit from the proposal will make other voters revise upwards their expectations about what the proposal will mean to them. However, there are many policy proposals that have reasonably well known efficiency effects in the aggregate but for which it may be difficult to determine who wins and who loses. A situation where what is considered good news for one group of voters is bad news for other voters is the context in which inverse campaigning is most likely to play a role.

WZB and Free University of Berlin

Date of receipt of first submission: July 2002
Date of receipt of final typescript: March 2003

Appendix

Proof of Property 4.2. Consider some A with $p(A) < \frac{1}{4} - 2e$. Suppose B with $p(B_y) > 0$ is an optimal answer to this A. Note first that any B with $p(A_y \cap B_y) > 0$ is suboptimal for party Y as it is dominated by $B \backslash (A_y \cap B_y)$ which generates the same information for voters and has lower cost for party Y. I therefore restrict consideration to B with $p(B_y) > 0$ and $p(A_y \cap B_y) = 0$. I show that $\hat{B} = B \backslash B_y$ dominates B.

First, $\hat{B}$ has an information cost that is lower by $cp(B_y)$.

Second, the expected gain from becoming elected is not reduced by $\hat{B}$, compared to B, that is, $\Psi(B) \leq \Psi(\hat{B})$. To show this, note that, by Property 4.1, at least some votes by the set of incompletely informed voters are required for winning the election. Y cannot win without at least some support by incompletely informed voters. Incompletely informed voters vote for Y if their probability of being of type y is larger than $1/2$. Their beliefs $(1 - \tilde{\xi})$ about this probability are updated for given A and B according to Bayes Rule such that

$$1 - \tilde{\xi} = \frac{1 - (\frac{1}{2} - e) - p(A_y \cup B_y)}{1 - p(A_y \cup B_y) - p(A_x \cup B_x)}.$$

This term is decreasing in $p(B_y)$, as $\frac{1}{2} + e \geq \frac{1}{2} > p(A_x \cup B_x)$ by Property 4.1. Now consider three cases. First, if $1 - \tilde{\xi}(A, B) < \frac{1}{2}$, then $\Psi(A, B) = 0 \leq \Psi(A, \hat{B})$. That is, the election outcome under $\hat{B}$ cannot be worse than under B if party Y loses for sure when it

Kai A. Konrad

chooses B. Second, if $1 - \tilde{\xi}(A, B) = \frac{1}{2}$, then party X gets half of the uninformed votes, and, depending on $p(A_x)$ and $p(B_y)$, this may, but need not, be enough to win. However, if party Y chooses $\hat{B}$ in this case, then $1 - \tilde{\xi} > \frac{1}{2}$ and party Y wins for sure. The same reasoning applies if $1 - \tilde{\xi}(A, B) > \frac{1}{2}$. A choice of $\hat{B}$ also leads to a sure election victory. But if $(B \backslash B_y)$ dominates B for any given A, then it also dominates B for any random mixture of As.

Now consider some choice B by party Y with $p(B_y) = 0$ and show that any A with $p(A_x) > 0$ is also suboptimal for party X given this choice B by party Y. For a proof, note first that $p(A_x) < \frac{1}{4} - 2e$ and $p(B_x) < \frac{1}{4} - 2e$ by Property 4.1. Suppose some A with $p(A_x) > 0$ is optimal. Then $\hat{A} = A \backslash A_x$ dominates A. To see this first note that $\hat{A}$ always has an information cost that is lower than the cost for A by $cp(A_x)$. But, in addition, the expected election benefit is not higher for A than for $\hat{A}$ for the following reason. By $p(A_x \cup B_x) < \frac{1}{2} - 4e$ and $p(A_y \cup B_y) < \frac{1}{2} - 4e$, the group of incompletely informed voters is decisive. The probability for being type x is updated according to

$$\tilde{\xi} = \frac{(1+e) - p(A_x \cup B_x)}{1 - p(A_y \cup B_y) - p(A_x \cup B_x)},$$

and this term is strictly decreasing in $p(A_x \cup B_x)$, as $1 + e \geq \frac{1}{2} > p(A_y \cup B_y)$ by Property 4.1. For $\tilde{\xi}(A, B) < \frac{1}{2}$ the party X loses the election if it chooses A, and a choice $\hat{A}$ can only increase election probabilities. For $\tilde{\xi}(A, B) = \frac{1}{2}$ the choice of $\hat{A}$ turns the possible victory into a sure victory and for $\tilde{\xi}(A, B) > \frac{1}{2}$ the party Y's election victory is certain for both the choice of A and the choice of $\hat{A}$. Again, the argument extends to a random selection of B, and this concludes the proof.

References

Baye, M. R., Kovenock, D. and deVries, C. (1996). 'The all-pay auction with complete information', *Economic Theory*, vol. 8, pp. 291–305.
Bergemann, D. and Välimäki, J. (1996). 'Learning and strategic pricing', *Econometrica*, vol. 65, pp. 1125–49.
Che, Y.-K. and Gale, I. L. (1998). 'Caps on political lobbying', *American Economic Review*, vol. 88, pp. 643–51.
Democratic National Convention (2000). *The 2000 Democratic National Platform: Prosperity, Progress, and Peace*, Washington D.C.: Democratic National Convention Committee, Inc.
Feddersen, T. J. and Pesendorfer, W. (1996). 'The swing voter's curse', *American Economic Review*, vol. 86, pp. 408–24.
Fernandez, R. and Rodrik, D. (1991). 'Resistance to reform: status quo bias in the presence of individual-specific uncertainty', *American Economic Review*, vol. 81, pp. 1146–55.
Glazer, A. and Konrad, K. A. (1993). 'The evaluation of risky projects by voters', *Journal of Public Economics*, vol. 52, pp. 377–90.
Harrington, J. E. Jr. and Hess, G. D. (1996). 'A spatial theory of positive and negative campaigning', *Games and Economic Behavior*, vol. 17, pp. 209–29.
Hillman, A. and Riley, J. G. (1989). 'Politically contestable rents and transfers', *Economics and Politics*, vol. 1, pp. 17–40.
Olson, M. (1965). *The Logic of Collective Action*, Cambridge: Harvard University Press.
Rodrik, D. (1996). 'Understanding economic policy reform', *Journal of Economic Literature*, vol. 34, pp. 9–41.
Skaperdas, S. and Grofman, B. (1995). 'Modeling negative campaigning', *American Political Science Review*, vol. 89, pp. 49–61.

KYKLOS, Vol. 28 – 1975 – Fasc. 4, 745–762

ON THE EFFICIENT ORGANIZATION
OF TRIALS

Gordon Tullock*

Since Aristotle, economists have realized that efficient functioning of the economy requires the existence of firm property rights. This is even true of socialists, although the property they have in mind is somewhat different. The theft of state property is, after all, one of the more severe (and, apparently, also one of the commoner) offenses in Russia. The fulfillment of a contract and the enforcement of various rules which prevent people from inflicting negative externalities on each other are also part of orthodox economics. All of this assumes, usually implicitly rather than explicitly, that there is some kind of enforcement mechanism which will see to it that the rules are carried out.

This enforcement mechanism can be analyzed in two parts: first, a mechanism that decides who has broken the rule, contract, and/or trespassed on other people's property; second, the actual apparatus of force which compels the person violating the rule to stop violating it or which imposes some kind of sanction upon him if the violation has occurred in the past. This article is concerned with the first of these mechanisms, *i.e.*, the actual court process. In spite of the very general title, I will actually confine myself to a comparison of only two different procedures and will, in fact, assume a rather simplified model even of those two[1].

Among Western countries there are two basic court methods. One, which descends from the Roman law, is used by most Continental countries; and the other, which descends from medieval precedents, is used in the Anglo-Saxon countries. There are a number of differ-

* Virginia Polytechnic Institute and State University.

1. A more general discussion of the problem will, eventually, be presented in a book on which I am now working.

GORDON TULLOCK

ences between these two methods, but only one will be discussed in this article. The Anglo-Saxon procedure is called the adversary system, because the proceeding is dominated by the two parties to the litigation with, in some cases, one of the parties being the state in the form of a prosecuting attorney. It descends from trial by battle in which the government official present at the trial simply refereed the contest. Under modern circumstances, the evidence and arguments are presented by the two sides and a government official, board of officials, or a group of conscripted private citizens (called jurors) decides which one has won.

The other system, used on the Continent, is usually called the inquisitorial system. In this system, the judges or judge in essence are carrying on an independent investigation of the case, and the parties play a much more minor role. It is the thesis of this article that the Roman jurists were right and the medieval feudal lords, who established the adversary system, were wrong in their choice of trial procedure. But that is simply to warn the reader. The line of reasoning used in this article will not rigorously prove this proposition[2]. Further empirical research will be necessary in order to prove that the inquisitorial system is superior to the adversary system. In this article, I shall merely establish a theoretical structure for the analysis of the two systems, and present a fairly strong argument that the inquisitorial system is better.

In practice, of course, the inquisitorial system of necessity has some adversary elements, since the parties are given some role in court; and the adversary system has some inquisitorial elements, because the judge (and, in some rare cases, the jury) also engage in some direct investigation of the case. The judge, for example, may ask questions of the witnesses on occasion.

Consider the situation of a party in the adversary-type proceedings. He can invest various amounts of resources in hiring lawyers, investigating the facts, testifying himself – either truthfully or falsely, *etc.* Since he knows a good deal about the facts of the case and can make an estimate of the resources the other party will invest in his case, he should have an idea of the likely probability of success for

2. See, GORDON TULLOCK, *The Logic of the Law,* New York, Basic Books, Inc., 1971, for a 'commonsense' argument for the European system as opposed to the Anglo-Saxon system.

746

ON THE EFFICIENT ORGANIZATION OF TRIALS

Figure 1

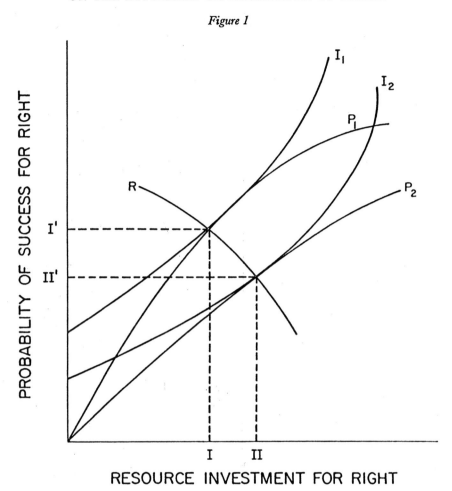

RESOURCE INVESTMENT FOR RIGHT

various investments of resources. On *Figure 1*, line P_1 shows for one party, Mr. Right, the probability of success for various resource commitments in a particular litigation.

We assume, as we shall throughout this article, that there are two parties, Mr. Right and Mr. Wrong, and that, as their names suggest, Mr. Right in fact is the one who (if we had divine justice) would win. Line P_1 then shows the probability of success that he can purchase by each investment of resources in his case. The investment exhibits declining marginal productivity, as we would anticipate. R's tastes are depicted by a set of indifference curves and his bliss point is in

747

the upper left-hand corner, with a certainty of success and a zero resource investment. He chooses the resource commitment where his highest possible indifference curve is tangent to the production function line, with the result that he invests I resources and obtains a probability of success of I', as shown on the diagram.

The evidence available for the case is more or less unchanging, but the resources the other party may put in are subject to adjustment. Suppose that Mr. Right, instead of assuming that Mr. Wrong would put in the number of resources which generated curve P_1, thought Mr. Wrong would put in more resources, and hence that there was a lower probability of success with each investment by Mr. Right. This would produce curve P_2. Mr. Right is forced to be satisfied with the lower indifference curve I_2. Under these circumstances, he would invest II resources and obtain II' possibility of success.

Note that, although in this case an increase in resources invested by Wrong leads Right to both increase his resources *and* reduce his likelihood of success, this is not general. In cases in which the resource commitment or evidence is very one-sided, an increase in resources by the party in the stronger position may change the situation so that the other side will reduce his resource commitments and take the corresponding increased probability of losing the suit (see *Figure 3* below). It depends on the payoff to the marginal dollar of resources invested and, where it is less than $1, there is a motive for reducing instead of increasing resources.

If we consider all possible resource commitments by Mr. Wrong, each would be accompanied by a risk-production function, like P_1 or P_2, for Mr. Right and Mr. Right would have an indifference curve tangent to it at some point. A line could be drawn connecting all such points. A segment of such a line is shown as R in *Figure 1*. It is the reaction curve of Mr. Right to possible investments of resources by Mr. Wrong. In *Figure 2*, reaction curves for both of the parties are shown. On the vertical axis are the resources invested by R and on the horizontal are those invested by W. Granting declining marginal returns and that the evidence is reasonably close to equal, the two curves will have the shape shown and will intersect as shown in the figure. The point of intersection is the equilibrium of the model, which would occur with Mr. Right investing R resources and Mr. Wrong investing W.

748

ON THE EFFICIENT ORGANIZATION OF TRIALS

Figure 2

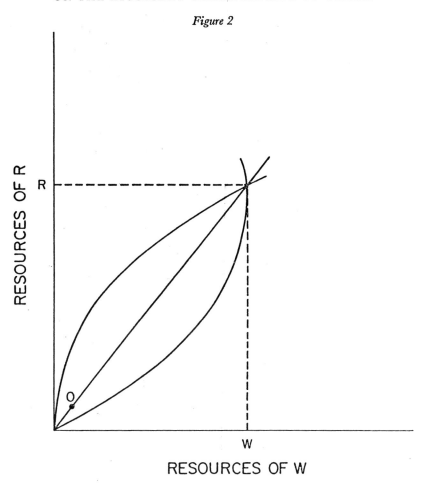

RESOURCES OF R

R

O

W

RESOURCES OF W

In *Figure 3*, I have shown by line *P* the situation in which the evidence happens to be very strong for Mr. Right, and hence that he can purchase a high probability of success with a relatively modest investment of resources. Line P_1 goes up very steeply and is, of course, tangent to a very high indifference curve with a relatively low resource investment and a high probability of success. It might be, however, that the evidence is positively misleading, and hence that Mr. Right would have a great deal of difficulty in raising his probability. Line P_2 shows these circumstances, and the indifference curve tangent to it, I_2, which is a low one, shows the best that Mr. Right could do under these circumstances. It will be observed that Mr.

749

Figure 3

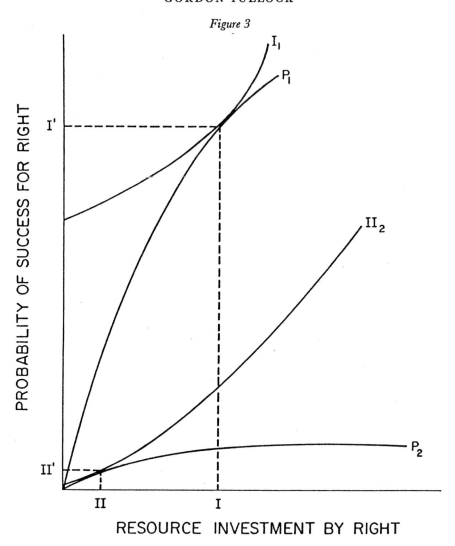

RESOURCE INVESTMENT BY RIGHT

Right would choose to put fewer resources into his suit in the unfavorable case than in the very favorable case; but this is simply an
artifact of the particular lines I have drawn. The reaction curves for
the later case are shown on *Figure 4*, and the equilibrium point is,
of course, very near to the horizontal axis.

Looked at from the economic point of view, it is immediately
obvious from *Figure 2* that the outcome is not apt to be optimal.
I have drawn a line from the equilibrium point to the origin and put

750

366

ON THE EFFICIENT ORGANIZATION OF TRIALS

Figure 4

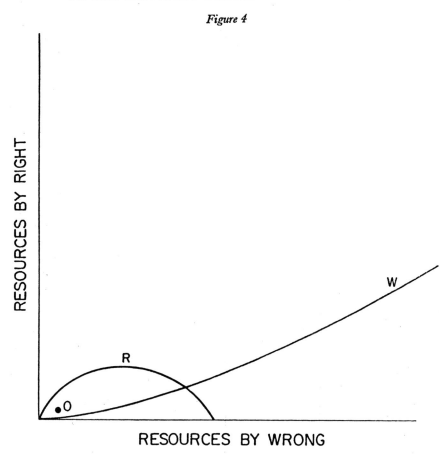

a point O on it. Point O has the same probability of success for the two parties, but with a much lower investment of resources. Clearly, it dominates the equilibrium solution. This is also true of point O on *Figure 4*. The only question is whether O is possible. As a brief digression, our diagram can also be used to deal with the international problem of arms races. The equilibrium would be the point reached in an arms race *without* agreement, and point O the result of an arms agreement, if there were no cheating anticipated[3].

3. This analysis was originally developed using other techniques; but in my book, *The Social Dilemma: The Economics of War and Revolution*, Blacksburg, Va., Center for Study of Public Choice, 1974, I use diagrams almost identical to those in this article to deal with the problem.

751

GORDON TULLOCK

I should now like to introduce a game I have invented and which is helpful in analyzing court proceedings. Suppose that a sum of money is put up for a prize for a particular form of lottery. The lottery has only two contestants and each of them may buy as many tickets for the lottery as he wishes for $1 each. One ticket is drawn at random, and the owner of that ticket receives the prize. Note that the payments for the tickets are not added on to the prize. The payoff to this game for our two parties is shown in the set of equations (1).

$$V_R = D \cdot \frac{R}{R+W} - R$$

$$V_W = D \cdot \frac{W}{R+W} - W \tag{1}$$

The *ex ante* value for Right, for example, is the prize (D) times the probability that the ticket purchased by Right will be drawn $[R/(R+W)]$, minus the amount of money put in by Right (R). Wrong's value is symmetric. It is obvious that we could solve this equation set, although in the real world we would want to add in risk aversion.

This set of equations, of course, would generate a set of lines of the same nature as those drawn on *Figure 1* and a set of reaction functions similar to those shown on *Figure 2*. The probability of success is a function of resources, depends also on the resources put in by the other party, and exhibits declining marginal returns. The indifference curves would also be of the same shape as in our normal trial.

This game can be changed so that it maps many different types of trial institutions. For example, in England the defeated party pays the winning party's attorney fees. It is easy to alter the above equations to take that into account. However, we are interested only in one particular type of alteration here. The equations as given are egalitarian, *i.e.*, they indicate that two parties, in the nature of things, have the same inherent likelihood of winning. In the real world, the physical evidence available in a case means that it is rare that two parties have exactly the same probability of winning. This can be very easily dealt with by adjusting the equation in a variety of ways.

For example, we might alter the rules of the game so that Mr. Right can purchase two lottery tickets for $1, whereas Mr. Wrong

752

ON THE EFFICIENT ORGANIZATION OF TRIALS

must still pay \$1 for each one. This would increase the value for Mr. Right. Indeed, there are many complications of this sort that can easily be put into the game; but since we do not know a great deal about the real world parameters of trials, it seems that there is no great reason for us to be extremely complex in our discussion of the matter. No doubt the payoff to various conditions which may make the trial less than completely equal – such as evidence in favor of one side – is quite complex; but, for the moment, let us use a very simple function. A variant of the game, in which the number of tickets Mr. Right can buy for \$1 is R times some function of the evidence (E), is shown in equation set (2).

$$V_R = D \cdot \frac{f(E)R}{f(E)R + W} - R$$

$$V_W = D \cdot \frac{W}{f(E)R + W} - W \tag{2}$$

In order to make it easier to deal with some matters to which we will turn shortly, I should like to further simplify these equations and change them from statements as to the payoff of the game to the probability of success. This permits us to drop part of the equation, as in equation set (3).

$$P_R = \frac{f(E)R}{f(E)R + W}$$

$$P_W = \frac{W}{f(E)R + W} \tag{3}$$

Note that the reason I have attached the evidence function to R instead of to both R and W is simply that they would be different functions, and, without any knowledge of their exact shape, it seems a waste of time to make the matter more complicated than is necessary.

In this form, the equation shows in a particularly pure form the externality associated with adversary proceedings. It will be noted that in each case the investment of resources by one party generates damage to the other party of exactly the same size as the benefit to himself. We have perfect 100 percent externality here. If I increase

753

the likelihood that I will win by 1 percent, I automatically reduce the likelihood that you will win by 1 percent. Under the circumstances, the likelihood that I will choose the resource investment which is socially optimal is, to put the matter mildly, slight.

In this connection, I have collected a little empirical information, unfortunately, by the crudest of all possible methods, *i.e.*, asking practicing lawyers. For what it may be worth, practicing attorneys with whom I have discussed the matter agree that in a law suit between two private parties, each party will normally pay in legal expenses about one-third of the amount at issue. This means, as the reader can readily observe, that if there is $1,000 at issue, $666 will be expended in the decision process; there are also court costs. Clearly, this is a highly expensive proceeding, although the fact that it is very expensive does not, in and of itself, prove that it is not efficient.

So far, we have discussed almost exclusively the adversary proceeding rather than the inquisitorial, and hence I have not fulfilled my promise that the two will be compared. In order to make a comparison, I would like to introduce another set of equations, set (4).

$$P_R = \frac{f(E)\,R}{f(E)\,R + W} + g(E, J)$$

$$P_W = \frac{W}{f(E)\,R + W} - g(E, J)$$

(4)

This is, of course, the same as set (3), except that another term has been added on at the right. This term shows the investment of resources in the actual judging process, something which, up to now, we have not considered. This function is assumed to improve Mr. Right's chances as the evidence (E) becomes better and as the resources invested in judging (J) are increased.

With this modification, we can now deal somewhat more generally with the problem. It is clear that increasing the skill or diligence of the decisionmakers will increase the likelihood of accuracy. However, this particular change is not subject to the kind of externality we were discussing earlier. The difference can perhaps best be seen from considering a rather unusual way of investing resources in a trial. Suppose that instead of permitting the parties to decide how

754

ON THE EFFICIENT ORGANIZATION OF TRIALS

much they were going to invest in legal fees for their own attorneys, we let them decide how much they would like to put in to hire a judge. Each one could put in whatever he wished, and then the authorities would purchase for this trial the best judge that could be obtained for the sum of the two contributions. Of course, they would not tell the judge which of the two parties had put up the most money.

Unless we assume that in making selection of judges we are random or, perhaps, systematically perverse, surely a better judge would be hired if there were more resources available[4]. If, then, with larger amounts of money we get a decisionmaker who is better qualified and more likely to reach the right conclusion, it will be contrary to the interests of Mr. Wrong to have a very good judge and he would tend to put no money at all into the pot. Mr. Right, on the other hand, would want the best judge available and would be willing to make a suitable payment. Presumably the amount he would be willing to pay would be less if the case looked to him to be an easy one, and hence suitable for a rather poorly qualified judge, than if the case looked to him to be a difficult one.

The interesting feature of this little *Gedankenexperiment*, however, is not Mr. Right's investment but Mr. Wrong's. Mr. Wrong would have no motive to try to improve the quality of judiciary, because the better the judiciary, the worse off he is going to be. Whereas he might have very strong motives to hire excellent attorneys and put a lot of money into his legal defense under the adversary system, under this system he would have no motive for investment at all.

PETER BERNHOLZ, when this paper was given orally in Basel, suggested that a good judge in essence changes the production function of the initial parties, as shown on *Figure 1*, in the sense that he raises the production function for Mr. Right and lowers the production function for Mr. Wrong. Thus, each improvement in the quality of the judge tends to move cases in the proper direction.

The point of this article has been to compare the European-type procedure (inquisitorial) with that used in Anglo-Saxon countries (adversary). It can be seen that the basic difference between these

---

4. Needless to say, it might be wiser to hire a board of judges rather than an individual, a technical specialist rather than a legal specialist, *etc.*

755

two is the amount of resources put on the two parts of our set of equations. The adversary proceeding puts almost all of its resources on R and W in (4); and the inquisitorial proceeding puts almost all of them on J. We have, so far, been simplifying the situation when we talk about the adversary proceedings by assuming that $g(E, J)$ is zero, and we could take the complementary simplification and assume that, in Europe, R and W are zero.

In practice, of course, there is at least some resource investment in the judicial process in the adversary proceedings, and the parties do have some things they can do that will affect the outcome in inquisitorial proceedings, so it is a matter of emphasis rather than a matter of absolute exclusion of one of the two factors. Nevertheless, in general the conclusions we draw from our simplified model will not be much wrong.

The basic difference between the two, as will be seen, is the W which appears in all of the equations. In essence, a great deal of the resources in the adversary proceedings are put in by someone who is deliberately attempting to mislead. Assume, for example, that in the average American court case 45 percent of the total resources are invested by each side and 10 percent by the government in providing the actual decisionmaking apparatus. This would mean that 55 percent of the resources used in the court are *aimed* at achieving the correct result, and 45 percent at reaching an incorrect result. Under the inquisitorial system, assume that 90 percent of the resources are put up by the government which hires a competent board of judges (who then carry on an essentially independent investigation) and only 5 percent by each of the parties. Under these circumstances, 95 percent of the resources are contributed by people who are attempting to reach the correct conclusion, and only 5 percent by the saboteur. Normally, we would anticipate a higher degree of accuracy with the second type than with the first. Surely, the same degree of accuracy could be obtained with less resources, also.

This line of reasoning is so simple that I always find it difficult to understand why the Anglo-Saxon court system has persisted. Its origins, from trial by battle, are obvious enough and, at a time when the law quite literally was the will of the stronger, it was indeed quite rational. Its persistence can perhaps be explained in terms of the inertia of established custom, but customs do change.

756

ON THE EFFICIENT ORGANIZATION OF TRIALS

There is, of course, an immensely powerful interest group dependent upon the preservation of the present situation in Anglo-Saxon courts. The number of lawyers per capita in Anglo-Saxon countries (and, in particular, the United States) is a high multiple of the number needed in the systems using the inquisitorial system. We also probably have more judges per capita than such countries as Switzerland or Sweden in spite of the greater emphasis put on judicial decisionmaking in those countries. The higher inherent accuracy of their court system means that there are fewer cases brought before the courts; and, once the case is brought before the court, the judge makes the decisions as to how much time will be spent on it, rather than the parties, with the result that cases are frequently disposed of quite quickly with good accuracy.

It is likely that a change from our system to the Continental system would, quite literally, eliminate about 90 percent of the demand for lawyers. This statement is not, of course, made under the assumption that our lawyers spend all of their time in court; indeed, they spend relatively little of their time in court. The advice they give, however, is very heavily affected by the type of judicial proceeding they anticipate if a court case does arise. Further, they spend much time negotiating cases and preparing for cases. All of this is immensely less expensive in Europe.

A fall of 90 percent in the demand for lawyers, of course, quite literally would impoverish the present profession. Immense numbers of lawyers would be fighting for a very limited amount of business, many of them becoming vacuum clearner salesmen, law schools would be compelled to close, immense bodies of accumulated personal capital would cease to be of any relevance, and, altogether, the legal profession would suffer a major disaster[5]. Under the circumstances, the opposition of the lawyers to the type of legal system used on the Continent is understandable. Nevertheless, although I have started with two reasons why one might anticipate that there would be opposition to changing which are not intellectually respectable, the lawyers defending our current system do offer some arguments for it. The first I usually encounter in talking to the average American

5. It is my personal opinion that the social benefits would be large enough so that a Pareto optimal move is available, *i.e.*, we could fully compensate them for this loss and still make a gain.

lawyer is an expression of incredulity that any other system exists. They will also (and consistently) normally tell me a few myths about European procedure, such as, that the defendant is compelled to prove his innocence rather than the prosecution being compelled to prove his guilt; but, once one has penetrated through this smoke screen, there is an intellectually possible defense of our system.

The point of this defense is that the judge may be undermotivated, and hence will not work hard enough. The two sides, whatever else may be said about them, are strongly motivated; hence, they can be expected to put a great deal of resources into reaching the decision. The judge has nothing personal riding on it and may not put in many resources, and hence may not reach a good decision according to this argument[6].

To deal with this situation, we should begin by talking a little bit about the factual problem of accuracy. Legal research has almost completely and totally shunned the question of how often the courts go wrong. However, I have been able to put together some evidence on accuracy, mainly by taking data generated for other purposes and interpreting them in terms of accuracy. For example, a research group in Oxford arranged, in 28 cases, to have a regular jury impaneled and then a jury of 12 men drawn from the regular jury list sit in the front of the spectators row and listen to the cases; afterwards, they go off to deliberate and vote on them[7]. This was done, as I said, for 28 cases; in 21 of the cases, the two juries agreed, in 7 they disagreed. It is surely true that one of the two juries was wrong in the 7 cases on which they disagreed, and this provides for a minimum of one-eighth of the decisions of juries being in error[8].

Obviously this research design is far from perfect, in particular, the jury which is not going to have its decision count presumably

6. For a discussion of the general problem of the undermotivation of government officials, see, GORDON TULLOCK, 'Public Decisions as Public Goods', *Journal of Political Economy*, Vol. 79 (1971), July/August, pp. 913–918.

7. See, PETER EVANS, '"Shadow" jurors disagreed with one court verdict in four, penal research report says', *The (London) Times*, 18 December 1974, p. 4. This is a resume of the following book: SARAH McCABE and ROBERT PURVES, *The Shadow Jury at Work*, Oxford, Basil Blackwell, 1974.

8. Actually, the percent of error necessary to provide for the difference of opinion in one-quarter of the cases is slightly higher than one-eighth, because there should be at least some cases in which both juries are wrong.

ON THE EFFICIENT ORGANIZATION OF TRIALS

puts less effort into it than the one that will have its decision count. Nevertheless, it is some evidence.

The University of Chicago Jury Project made an experiment which can be regarded as a test of the accuracy of courts in general, in which a questionnaire was circulated to judges, and they were asked to mark down their decision and the decision of the jury in cases they had heard[9]. Once again, if the judge and jury disagree, one of them must be wrong; and rough calculations indicate an error term for these two decisionmaking bodies of about the same order of magnitude[10]. As a third test, the University of Chicago Jury Project made up tapes of two law cases and then played them for a number of experimental 'juries'[11]. In this case, the difference between the juries was very much larger than can be explained by a one-eighth error term, but I believe the two cases used for this were harder than normal.

All of this does not indicate, of course, that the inquisitorial system would be better than the adversary system. An error term of one-eighth is high; but it might conceivably be true that the inquisitorial system has an even higher one. Still, it is surely true that we can do a good deal to improve. Unfortunately, I know of absolutely no empirical evidence on the accuracy of European courts.

One of the problem in research of this type, of course, is that the courts have the power to prevent themselves from being investigated, and they do not want to be investigated. In general, we take the view that people who try to avoid investigation do so because the investigation would turn up things that are not to their credit; but it must be admitted that courts may have a valid reason for not wanting to be investigated. It is possible to argue that the judicial system works

9. See, HARRY KALVEN, Jr., and HANS ZEISEL, *The American Jury*, Boston, Little, Brown & Company, 1966, pp. 12–193.

10. The data are published in a form that makes it impossible to do anything more than very rough calculations.

11. For examples, see: RITA JAMES SIMON, 'Status and Competence of Jurors', *American Journal of Sociology*, Vol. 64 (1959), pp. 563–570; 'Trial by Jury: A Critical Assessment', in: *Applied Sociology: Opportunities and Problems*, ed. by A. W. GOULDNER and S. M. MILLER, New York, The Free Press, 1965, pp. 294–307; and 'Jurors' Evaluation of Expert Psychiatric Testimony', in: *The Sociology of Law: Interdisciplinary Readings*, ed. by RITA JAMES SIMON, San Francisco, Chandler Publishing Co., 1968, pp. 314–328.

759

better if it is surrounded by myths and magic than if everyone concerned knows that the court regularly makes mistakes.

Regardless of this, we now turn to a second issue, which is how hard judges work. Once again, the judges have prevented serious investigation of this matter, but there are a few scattered bits of evidence[12]. It seems fairly certain that judges and juries are not particularly highly motivated in law cases, and hence there is something to be said for the view that leaving everything to them would be undesirable. It should be pointed out that there are various methods used in Europe to provide stronger motives for judges than are provided under the Anglo-Saxon system. The judicial career is organized with promotion, regular transfers, *etc.* This would normally motivate judges under this system more than the judge under the Anglo-Saxon system. Certainly the jurors, who are conscripted amateurs, have practically no motives to work hard and, indeed, do not.

In fact, there is no reason to believe that judges and juries under either system are motivated to the optimal extent, and further research should be undertaken for the purpose of developing institutions which will give them a better motivation. For the moment, however, it should be pointed out that the undermotivation is more extreme with respect to the jury and the Anglo-Saxon judge than with respect to the European judge. It is true that in Anglo-Saxon adversary proceedings the parties have every motive to put great resources into presenting their case; but this case is to be presented

12. For example, ROBERT GILLESPIE cites an official study of 'all 336 U.S. District Judges, who were asked to keep time diaries of their judicial aticities over the approximately 95 working days from October 1969 through February 1970'. Only about two-thirds of the judges actually filled out the form, presumably the most energetic two-thirds. There is, I think, no possibility that the underestimated their workload. It works out to an average of 4.2 hours per day for 'judicial activities'. See, ROBERT W. GILLESPIE, 'Measuring the Demand for Court Services: A Critique of the Federal District Courts Case Weight', *Journal of the American Statistical Association*, Vol. 69 (1974), March, pp. 38–53. Other studies with which I am familiar produce about the same picture. It should, of course, be noted that all of the more detailed studies have turned up individual judges who work very hard, apparently because they treat their job as a hobby. The situation is rather similar to academic life, where the bulk of the faculty do not work very hard; but a certain number of people, who are deeply interested in their subject matter, do.

760

ON THE EFFICIENT ORGANIZATION OF TRIALS

before a group of people who, in the case of the jury, are amateurs and of only average intelligence; in any event, they are not motivated particularly to hard intellectual labor to understand the case. As a result, the parties' arguments are unlikely to be designed in such a way as to put great strain on the minds of the listeners, even if the situation is such that truth can only be obtained *with* a great strain.

Still, the lack of motivation for the public officials concerned is a defect in both court systems. It is not obvious that it is less of a defect for the Anglo-Saxon than for the European system, but it is clear that public officials play a larger role in the European system. Thus, it is at least conceivable that the undermotivation of the judges more than counterbalances the overinvestment of resources by the parties, with which this article has been mainly concerned.

It will not have escaped the reader of this article that, personally, I favor the European system. It seems to me the theoretical arguments in its favor are much stronger than those against it. But I cannot be sure. The whole field of legal research has been dominated by essentially unscientific techniques. This has been particularly true of the comparison of these methods of reaching decisions in law suits. This article has been an effort to set the matter on a sound theoretical basis. Without further research, particularly empirical research, it is not possible to be certain that the Continental system is better than the Anglo-Saxon, but the presumption is surely in that direction.

SUMMARY

An economic model of the Anglo-Saxon adversary court system is presented. Under this system, the parties control a good many of the resources invested in the procedure through their attorneys, and the outcome is in part a resultant of this investment of resources, as well as the evidence. Investment of resources by either party generates a pure externality on the other, and hence the system generates an overinvestment of resources in trials. The inquisitorial court system in use on the Continent of Europe, on the other hand, puts much more emphasis on the control of proceedings by the judge or board of judges and gives the parties less control over the resource investment. *A priori*, this would seem to be more efficient, but the possibility of undermotivation of judges is a real problem. Of course, this problem also applies to the adversary system of trials used in the Anglo-Saxon countries. Although the *a priori* arguments would appear to favor the Continental system, further empirical research is necessary. The article also includes a brief summary of what little empirical evidence there is on the func-

761

GORDON TULLOCK

tioning efficiency of courts, confined entirely to the Anglo-Saxon system, because, so far as the author knows, that is the only place in which any statistics of value have been collected.

ZUSAMMENFASSUNG

Im vorliegenden Aufsatz wird ein ökonomisches Modell des angelsächsischen Gerichtssystems dargestellt. Bei diesem System kontrollieren die Parteien eine Menge von Ressourcen, die durch ihre Anwälte in das Verfahren investiert werden. Das Ergebnis wie auch die Klärung des Tatbestandes sind zum Teil ein Resultat dieser Investitionen. Der Mitteleinsatz einer Partei ruft eine reine Externalität für die andere hervor, daher führt dieses System zu einer Überinvestition von Mitteln in Verhandlungen. Das Gerichtssystem dagegen, das auf dem europäischen Kontinent gebräuchlich ist, legt wesentlich mehr Gewicht auf die Kontrolle des Verfahrens durch den Richter oder den Richterstab und erteilt den Parteien weniger Kontrolle über den Mitteleinsatz. *A priori* scheint dies effizienter zu sein, doch besteht in der möglicherweise zu geringen Motivation der Richter ein ernstes Problem. Natürlich gilt dieses Problem auch für das Verhandlungssystem der angelsächsischen Länder. Obwohl die *a priori* Argumente dem kontinentalen System den Vorzug zu geben scheinen, sind weitere empirische Untersuchungen notwendig. Der Artikel enthält ferner eine kurze Zusammenstellung der wenigen vorhandenen empirischen Zeugnisse hinsichtlich der Arbeitseffizienz von Gerichten, die sich ausschliesslich auf das angelsächsische System bezieht, da nach Wissen des Autors nur über dieses System verwertbare Statistiken bestehen.

RÉSUMÉ

Cet article présente un modèle économique du système anglo-saxon de jugement accusatoire. Dans ce système, les parties contrôlent une bonne part des ressources investies dans la procédure du fait de leurs avocats; l'issue de cette procédure, tout comme les témoignages, résultent en partie de cet investissement. Les ressources investies par l'une des parties engendrent un pur effet externe sur l'autre, un tel système entraine donc un surinvestissement des ressources dans les procès. Par contre, le système inquisitoire en vigueur sur le continent européen met plus l'accent sur le contrôle des débats par les juges et diminue le contrôle des parties sur les ressources investies. *A priori*, celà pourrait sembler plus efficace, mais il ne faut pas exclure la possibilité d'un manque de motivation de la part des juges. Bien sûr, il existe la même possibilité dans le système accusatoire utilisé dans les pays anglo-saxons. Bien que les arguments *a priori* semblent donner l'avantage au système continental, une recherche empirique plus approfondie est cependant nécessaire. L'article contient également un bref résumé des quelques rares études consacrées à l'efficacité du fonctionnement des tribunaux; ces études sont limitées au système anglo-saxon qui est le seul, à la connaissance de l'auteur, à avoir fait l'objet de statistiques sérieuses.

762

Public Choice **100**: 271–288, 1999.

© 1999 *Kluwer Academic Publishers. Printed in the Netherlands.*

271

Legal expenditure as a rent-seeking game[*]

AMY FARMER[1,2] & PAUL PECORINO[3]

[1]*Department of Economics, University of Tennessee, Knoxville, TN 37996, U.S.A.,* [2]*present address: Department of Economics, University of Arkansas, U.S.A.,* [3]*Department of Economics, Finance and Legal Studies, University of Alabama, Box 870224, Tuscaloosa, AL 35487, U.S.A.*

Accepted 26 January 1998

Abstract. Legal expenditures at a civil trial constitute an interesting type of rent-seeking contest. In civil litigation there is a natural interaction between the objective merits of the case and the outcome of the contest. Institutions such as fee shifting do not generally have a counterpart in other rent-seeking contests. The endogenous decision to participate in the rent-seeking contest corresponds to the decision by the plaintiff to bring a case, and the decision by the defendant to defend it. The desirability of fee shifting is very sensitive to the value of the parameter which describes the legal technology.

1. Introduction

There are several reasons why legal expenditures at a civil trial constitute an interesting and distinct type of rent-seeking contest. First, in civil litigation, there is a natural interaction between the objective merits of the case and the outcome of the contest. In addition, in the context of legal spending, we can analyze institutions such as fee shifting which do not generally have a counterpart in other rent-seeking contests. Finally, the endogenous decision to participate in the rent-seeking contest corresponds to the decision by the plaintiff to bring a case, and the decision by the defendant to defend the case. In this paper we analyze how the legal technology, the use of fee shifting, and the objective merits of the case interact with the endogenous participation decisions of the plaintiff and defendant.

In the United States, there has been much recent debate about switching from the American rule to the English rule for the allocation of lawyer fees at trial. Under the American rule, both parties to the dispute bear their own legal costs, while under the English rule, the losing party at trial pays the lawyer fees of the winning party.[1] It has been argued that use of the English rule will discourage nuisance suits, and might therefore reduce total costs

---

[*] We would like to thank William F. Shughart II for helpful comments on the paper.

associated with the civil litigation system. It is a widely accepted theoretical result, however, that the use of the English rule will raise spending on those cases which do proceed to trial.

The total effects of switching from the American rule to the English rule are wide ranging, and extend well beyond those analyzed in our paper. However, even when viewed narrowly through the lens of our model, we find that the apparent desirability of each rule is extremely sensitive to the key parameter of our legal technology. For both the American and English rules, there are values of this parameter (different for each rule) with the following properties: the plaintiff only files suits in which the objective merits of the case favor her, and the defendant only defends cases in which he is favored by the objective merits of the case.[2] As a result, only "meritorious" suits are filed, and no trials occur. Of course, for most parameter values, the equilibrium of the game does not have such attractive properties.

The topic of this paper spans both the rent-seeking literature and the law and economics literature on endogenous spending at trial. With few exceptions, little work has been done linking the two literatures. The literature on rent-seeking contests is huge, and so our discussion of it is necessarily incomplete. Tullock (1980a) initiated the literature on rent-seeking contests, though the concept of rent seeking originates in the papers of Tullock (1967) and Krueger (1974).[3] Tollison (1982) and Nitzan (1994) provide surveys of the literature and Buchanan, Tollison and Tullock (1980a) and Rowley, Tollison and Tullock (1988) are notable collections of papers on the topic. In discussing the objective merits of the case, we introduce into the contest success function what is termed "bias" in the rent-seeking literature. This is first discussed by Tullock (1980a) with analytical results given in Gradstein (1995).[4]

In our model, "rent seeking" consists of legal expenditures at trial. Katz (1988) provides microfoundations for the effect of legal expenditure at trial by developing a model in which legal expenditure produces legal arguments.[5] These arguments influence the outcome at trial, but noise in the system makes the outcome at trial stochastic. As an example of a type of reduced form spending function which is consistent with his model, Katz presents the following: $P(X,Y) = \frac{e^M X^\alpha}{e^M X^\alpha + Y^\beta}$, where P is the probability the plaintiff prevails at trial, X and Y are legal expenditures by the plaintiff and defendant respectively, and M reflects the objective merits of the case. When $M > 0$, the merits favor the plaintiff, when $M < 0$, they favor the defendant, and for $M = 0$, they favor neither party. The parameters α and β reflect the technologies by which legal arguments are produced. If $\alpha, \beta < 1$, there are decreasing returns to scale in the production of legal arguments and if $\alpha, \beta > 1$, there are increasing returns to scale in the production of legal arguments.

Katz does not explore the properties of this specific function, but we shall do so below under the assumptions that the plaintiff and defendant have access to identical technologies for the production of legal arguments ($\alpha = \beta$). As a result, we will have a standard rent-seeking function except that our "bias" (represented by the e^M term) reflects the objective merits of the case. Our analysis will allow us to determine which cases the plaintiff will bring and which cases the defendant will defend, as functions of the merits of the case, the legal rule in use, and the technology parameter α. We can also relate the level of legal spending ("rent dissipation") to the legal technology and the use of fee shifting arrangements. We show that once the endogenous participation decisions of the plaintiff and defendant are taken into account, the relationship between the technology parameter, α, and legal spending is not monotonic.

The next section provides an overview of the structure of the game, while Section 3 follows with an analysis of the American rule. Some of the results under the American rule have analogs in the rent-seeking literature, but our interpretation of the "bias" term allows for an interesting analysis of the conditions under which a credible threat to litigate exists for both the plaintiff and the defendant. In Section 4 we examine the English rule under which the loser of the contest pays the costs of both parties to the dispute. This fee-shifting element is generally not present in the existing rent-seeking literature. Again, we are able to analyze the relationship between case quality and the credibility of a threat to proceed to trial under the English rule. Section 5 concludes the paper.

2. The structure of the model

For both the American rule and the English rule, the game will have the following general structure:

1. The risk neutral Plaintiff chooses whether or not to file suit costlessly. If a suit is not filed, the game ends. If she does file suit, the case proceeds to stage 2.
2. The risk neutral Defendant chooses whether or not to defend the case. If he does not defend the case, he pays the plaintiff the default judgment J, and the game ends. If he decides to defend the case, it proceeds to trial.
3. At trial, both the plaintiff and defendant choose their level of spending on legal assistance X and Y respectively. Combined with the objective merits of the case, these expenditures determine the probability that the defendant is found liable. If the defendant is deemed liable, he pays the plaintiff J. Legal costs are then allocated according to the rule in place. Under the American Rule, each party pays their own legal expenditures.

Under the English Rule, the loser must pay the expenditures of both parties, $X + Y$.

To solve the model, we need to first examine the outcome at trial should it occur. Using standard backward induction we can then solve for the decisions of both parties to bring and defend cases. As in most of the literature on endogenous expenditure at trial, we ignore the possibility of pretrial settlement, except that the defendant is free to pay the default judgment J at stage 2.[6] In addition, the size of the judgment J is not affected by legal expenditure. We first solve the model under the assumption that the American Rule is in place, and then in Section 4 we analyze the English Rule.

3. The American rule

We discuss stage 3 first, with the interior solution analyzed in Section 3.1. Even at stage 3, both players retain the option of spending zero rather than playing the interior Nash solution. The participation constraints of both players are analyzed in Section 3.2. When only one player has his or her participation constraint violated, we consider preemptive strategies by the remaining player. These are discussed in Section 3.3. Stages 1 and 2 are analyzed in Section 3.4, and the relationship between case quality, legal expenditure and the legal technology is discussed in Section 3.5.

3.1. *Trial expenditures: The interior solution*

Once both parties arrive at trial, they must choose their levels of legal expenditures. These choices depend upon the legal technology which converts expenditures are into a probability of victory. Assume that this technology converts expenditures X and Y into the following probability that the plaintiff wins:

$$P = \frac{e^M X^\alpha}{e^M X^\alpha + Y^\alpha},\tag{1}$$

where M represents the exogenous merits of the case and α reflects the effectiveness of legal expenditures.[7] The objective merits favor the plaintiff when $M > 0$, the defendant when $M < 0$, and neither party when $M = 0$. This function represents a special case of the Katz (1988) model, and is a standard rent-seeking function with bias (see Tullock [1980] and Gradstein [1995]). Given this function, the plaintiff must choose X to maximize her expected award at trial. Since the outcome of a trial will be an award of J with a probability of P, the objective is to

$$\max_{x} \left(\frac{e^M X^\alpha}{e^M X^\alpha + Y^\alpha} \right) J - X. \tag{2}$$

The first order condition to this problem implies

$$\alpha e^M X^{\alpha-1} Y^\alpha J = (e^M X^\alpha + Y^\alpha)^2. \tag{3}$$

Similarly, the defendant chooses Y to minimize his expected payment. This problem may be expressed as

$$\max_{Y} - \left(\frac{e^M X^\alpha}{e^M X^\alpha + Y^\alpha} \right) J - Y. \tag{4}$$

The first order condition from this problem implies

$$\alpha e^M Y^{\alpha-1} X^\alpha J = (e^M X^\alpha + Y^\alpha)^2. \tag{5}$$

Equations (3) and (5) may be solved simultaneously for X and Y to get

$$X^* = Y^* = \frac{\alpha e^M J}{(1 + e^M)^2}, \tag{6}$$

where the '*' denotes value of the variables at the interior Nash equilibrium.

At an interior solution under the American Rule, the expenditure of each party is equal regardless of the merits of the case. This symmetric spending in rent-seeking games with "bias" is first discussed in Tullock (1980a). The American rule is neutral with respect to the probable trial outcome since $X^* = Y^*$, and the resulting equilibrium probability that the plaintiff prevails is $\frac{e^M}{1+e^M}$. If instead, for example, the favored party spent more at trial, then the endogenity of spending would reinforce the favored party's initial advantage. In addition, total spending by the two parties is the highest when $M = 0$ (see Gradstein, 1995). In other words, for each value of α, the parties spend the most in cases which are close based on the objective merits. Also, as is standard, spending at trial is increasing both in the productivity parameter α and the size of the judgment J.

From (6), when $\alpha = 2$ and $M = 0$, total spending at trial just equals the amount of the judgment J. For $\alpha < 2$ (and $\alpha = 2$, $M \neq 0$), the total level of spending by the two parties will be less than J. When $\alpha > 2$, there is the possibility that total spending will exceed the judgment, but as developed below, when $\alpha > 2$, the participation constraint of at least one of the players will be violated. Thus, in equilibrium, total spending at trial never exceeds the amount of the judgment J.

3.2. *Participation constraints*

The solutions in (6) may not constitute an equilibrium; they must be checked against the possibility of a corner solution in which one or both players prefers an expenditure of zero to the interior Nash equilibrium. In other words, each player has a participation constraint which ensures that playing the game is at least as profitable as not playing (spending 0).

As an alternative to the interior Nash solution, the plaintiff may spend nothing and earn a payout of zero. Thus, the participation constraint for the plaintiff requires that $P^* J - X^* > 0$, where '*' denotes the interior equilibrium values of the variables. Using (1) and (6) this condition may be reduced to

$$e^M \geq \alpha - 1. \tag{7}$$

Let M' be the critical value of M such that (7) holds as an equality; thus for $M < M'$, the plaintiff's participation constraint is violated.

The participation constraint for the defendant requires that $P^* J + Y^* < J$ (i.e., the expected payment at the interior solution is less than the judgment J). Using (1) and (6), this condition may be expressed as

$$\frac{1}{e^M} \geq \alpha - 1. \tag{8}$$

Let M'' be the critical value of M such that (8) holds as an equality; thus for $M > M''$, the defendant's participation constraint is violated.

We will analyze the participation decisions of the plaintiff and the defendant for three cases: $\alpha \leq 1$, $1 < \alpha \leq 2$, and $\alpha > 2$.

From (7) and (8), we can see that when $\alpha \leq 1$ the participation constraints for both the plaintiff and the defendant are always satisfied regardless of case quality. For $1 < \alpha \leq 2$, there are values of M such that $M < M' \leq 0$ where the plaintiff's participation constraint is violated. Similarly there are values of M such that $M > M'' \geq 0$, where the defendant's participation constraint is violated. Note that the constraints are never both violated simultaneously. When $\alpha = 2$, $M' = 0$ so that the plaintiff prefers the interior equilibrium only when $M \geq 0$, i.e., when (except for $M = 0$) the objective merits favor her. Similarly, $M'' = 0$, so that the defendant prefers the interior equilibrium only when $M \leq 0$, where (except for $M = 0$) the objective merits favor him.

For cases in which a participation constraint is violated, the interior Nash equilibrium does not exist. These cases can be problematic and have been discussed at length in the rent-seeking literature.[8] One way to obtain an equilibrium in such a game is to appeal to a Stackelberg solution in which one player has a first mover advantage. Of course, the issue of which player has

Table 1. The American rule

	$\alpha \leq 1$	$1 < \alpha \leq 2$	$\alpha = 2$	$\alpha > 2$
Plaintiff	None	$M < M' < 0$	$M < M' = 0$	$M < M'$, $M' > 0$
Defendant	None	$M > M'' > 0$	$M > M'' = 0$	$M > M''$, $M'' < 0$

Values of M for which participation constraints are violated under the American rule.

the first move can itself be problematic. Because we consider the objective merits of the case (or "bias") in our rent seeking function, for $1 < \alpha \leq 2$ our model exhibits a feature not generally present in discussions of this issue; at most only one player wishes to defect from the interior Nash equilibrium. There is always at least one player who weakly prefers the interior solution to spending 0. When only *one player* is willing to play the interior solution, that player is favored by the objective merits of the case. We assume this player gains the initiative in a Stackelberg game in which he or she may play a preemptive strategy which we analyze in Section 3.3.

When $\alpha > 2$, we have $M' > 0$, so that there are cases in which the objective merits favor the plaintiff, but where her participation constraint is nonetheless violated. Similarly, for the defendant, $M'' < 0$ so that his participation constraint is violated in some cases where the objective merits favor him. Thus for $\alpha > 2$, at least one player must have his or her participation constraint violated, and there are some cases where $M'' < M < M'$ so that both constraints are violated. These later cases, which are particularly problematic, are discussed below. The results of this section are summarized in Table 1.

3.3. *Preemptive strategies*[9]

When $\alpha < 1$, the participation constraints for both players are always satisfied. For $1 < \alpha \leq 2$, there are some cases which favor the plaintiff and for which the defendant's participation constraint is violated. No Nash equilibrium exists in this case, but it is only the defendant who wishes to defect from the interior Nash equilibrium. As a result, we assume the plaintiff gains the initiative in a Stackelberg game, allowing her to set her legal expenditure at a preemptive level. The preemptive level of expenditure is the lowest level of spending for the plaintiff such that the optimal expenditure by the defendant, moving second, will be 0. This requires that

$$\frac{-e^M (X^s)^\alpha}{e^M (X^s)^\alpha + (Y^s)^\alpha} J - Y^s = -J, \tag{9}$$

where the 's' denotes the values associated with this Stackelberg equilibrium, and Y^s is the optimal interior response by the defendant to the plaintiff's level of expenditure. The defendant's reaction function is implicitly defined by equation (5). Using (5) plus (9), the plaintiff can find the preemptive level of expenditure.

Similarly, for $1 < \alpha \leq 2$ there will be some cases which favor the defendant, but where the plaintiff's participation constraint will be violated. In these cases, the defendant will have the initiative in a Stackelberg game and will be able to play a preemption game against the defendant. Such a strategy requires

$$\frac{e^M (X^s)^\alpha}{e^M (X^s)^\alpha + (Y^s)^\alpha} J - X^s = 0, \tag{10}$$

where X^s is the plaintiff's optimal interior response to the defendant's level of expenditure. The plaintiff's reaction function is implicitly defined by (3). Combining (3) plus (10) will yield the level of the preemptive expenditure for the defendant.

As developed below, cases in which the preemptive strategies would be relevant will be dropped at either stage 1 or stage 2, so we will not derive explicit solutions for the preemptive strategies (see Pérez-Castrillo and Verdier (1992)).

Similarly, for $\alpha > 2$ there are high values of M where only the defendant's participation constraint is violated, and low values for which only the plaintiff's participation constraint is violated. For these cases, the preemptive strategies discussed above apply. However, for $\alpha > 2$, there exists a range of cases where $M'' < M < M'$ in which the participation constraints of both players are violated. These cases are problematic in that there is no presumption that either player has the initiative and can play a preemptive strategy. We will discuss these cases further below. Note that these problematic cases are drawn from the center of the distribution of M.

3.4. Stages 1 and 2

Consider games where at most only one of the two players' participation constraints is violated. The case where both constraints are violated is discussed in Section 3.5.3. Neither the plaintiff nor the defendant commits to any expenditure by proceeding to trial; they both may spend 0 at stage 3. As a result, the participation constraints at stages 1 and 2 are the same as those derived earlier for stage 3.

3.4.1. Stage 2

If in looking ahead to stage 3, the defendant sees that his participation constraint will be satisfied, he will take the case to trial. If his participation constraint will be violated, he would spend 0 on his defense, and pay the judgment J at stage 3 (because the plaintiff will play a preemptive strategy). If he elects not to defend the case, he pays the default judgment J at stage 2. We assume that since the defendant is indifferent, he will end the case at stage 2 and pay the default judgment J. This strategy is strictly preferred if there are even small fixed costs of proceeding to trial.[10]

3.4.2. Stage 1

If the plaintiff looks ahead to stage 3 and sees that her participation constraint will be satisfied, she files the case. If her constraint will be violated, she would spend zero at trial and earn a payout of zero (because the defendant will play a preemptive strategy). We assume that these cases are not filed (the game ends at stage 1), and that the plaintiff earns a payoff of zero. If there are even small costs of filing a case, this strategy is strictly preferred to proceeding to stage 2 (and eventually to trial).

3.5. Case quality, legal expenditure and lawyer productivity

In analyzing the relationship between case quality and legal expenditure, it will be helpful to discuss separately three ranges for the parameter α.

3.5.1. $\alpha \leq 1$

As discussed earlier, the participation constraints for both participants are always satisfied in this range, so that all cases are filed, and all cases proceed to trial. Thus from (6), higher values of α within this range guarantee higher levels of legal expenditure. To get a sense of the level of expenditure implied throughout this range note that with $\alpha = 1$ and $M = 0$ total spending by the plaintiff and defendant combined equals half of the judgment. This set of parameter values gives the highest level of total expenditure for $\alpha \leq 1$.

3.5.2. $1 < \alpha \leq 2$

For cases which reach trial in this range, total spending is clearly higher than for $\alpha \leq 1$, but not all cases will be filed, and not all cases which are filed will be defended. Thus, the relationship between α and total expenditure may not be monotonic within this range. When $\alpha = 2$ total legal expenditures drop to zero, except for cases where $M = 0$, where total spending equals J (i.e., the "rent" is just exhausted).[11] The defendant is only willing to defend cases where $M \geq 0$ (i.e., the objective merits favor him), and the plaintiff is only willing to file cases where $M \geq 0$ (the objective merits favor her).

280

Thus, for $\alpha = 2$ (and except for $M = 0$), only meritorious cases are filed, but none reach trial and legal expenditure is zero. If as a normative matter we want "meritorious" ($M > 0$) cases for the plaintiff filed and "meritorious" ($M < 0$) cases for the defendant not to be filed (and defended if they are filed), then for $\alpha = 2$, the American rule works as well as possible.

For $1 < \alpha < 2$, $M' < 0$ so that the plaintiff will file all cases in which she is favored by the objective merits of the case and some cases in which the objective merits favor the defendant. Similarly, since $M'' > 0$ the defendant will defend all cases in which he is favored by the objective merits and some cases in which the objective merits favor the plaintiff. The cases not filed by the plaintiff are her weakest (i.e., from the left tail of the distribution of M), and those not defended by the defendant are his weakest (i.e., from the right tail of the distribution of M). This means that cases which reach trial are drawn from the center of the distribution of M with this "center" shrinking to a single point as α approaches 2.

3.5.3. $\alpha > 2$

In this range, *at least* one of the players will have their participation constraint violated. When only one player has his or her constraint violated, we proceed as earlier, where the remaining player gains the initiative and will play a preemptive strategy at stage 3. As before, the objective merits of the case will favor the player whose participation constraint is satisfied, and the case will not reach trial (the game will end at either stage 1 or 2). The problem arises for cases in which $M'' < M < M'$. These games have no equilibrium in the Nash game, and *a priori*, we have no way of knowing which player might have the initiative in a Stackelberg game.[12] The ability to commit to a preemptive level of legal expenditure might arise if, for example, one of the players faced repeated litigation, and was able to establish a reputation.

Regardless of which player might gain the initiative, the outcome may have problematic features. If the plaintiff can commit to a preemptive level of expenditure, then she will file (and win a default judgment) in some cases in which the objective merits favor the defendant. Similarly, if the defendant can commit to a preemptive level of expenditure, he will do so (and discourage the plaintiff from filing) in some cases in which the objective merits favor the plaintiff.

4. The English rule

Sections 4.1–4.3 analyze stages 3, 2 and 1 respectively. In Section 4.4 we analyze the relationship between case quality, legal expenditure and the parameter α.

4.1. *Stage 3*

Under the English rule, the losing party at trial pays the lawyer fees of the winning party. In stage 3, the plaintiff's problem now is to

$$\max_{X} \left(\frac{e^M X^\alpha}{e^M X^\alpha + Y^\alpha} \right) (J + X + Y) - (X + Y). \tag{11}$$

The first order condition to this problem implies

$$\left(\frac{\alpha e^M X^{\alpha-1}}{e^M X^\alpha + Y^\alpha} \right) (J + X + Y) = 1. \tag{12}$$

Similarly, the defendant will

$$\max_{Y} - \left(\frac{e^M X^\alpha}{e^M X^\alpha + Y^\alpha} \right) (J + X + Y). \tag{13}$$

The first order condition to this problem implies

$$\left(\frac{\alpha Y^{\alpha-1}}{e^M X^\alpha + Y^\alpha} \right) (J + X + Y) = 1. \tag{14}$$

Use (12) and (14) to get the interior Nash solution for spending by the plaintiff and defendant in this game:

$$X = \left(\frac{\alpha}{1 - \alpha} \right) J \left(\frac{(e^M)^{1/1-\alpha}}{1 + (e^M)^{1/1-\alpha}} \right), \tag{15}$$

$$Y = \left(\frac{\alpha}{1 - \alpha} \right) J \left(\frac{1}{1 + (e^M)^{1/1-\alpha}} \right). \tag{16}$$

Note that relative spending $X/Y = (e^M)^{(1/1-\alpha)}$. In contrast to the American Rule, spending by both parties is not identical. The English rule is not "neutral" with respect to the trial outcome in the sense that the party favored by the merits will spend more than his or her opponent, and will enjoy a higher probability of success at trial than under the American rule.[13] From (1), (15) and (16), the equilibrium probability of success for the plaintiff at trial is given by

$$P^* = \frac{e^{\frac{M}{1-\alpha}}}{1 + e^{\frac{M}{1-\alpha}}}.$$

As with the American Rule, spending rises as the legal technology becomes more productive. Total spending approaches infinity as α approaches 1, and for values of $\alpha \geq 1$, the Nash equilibrium does not exist, even if we ignore the participation constraints of the two parties to the dispute (Plott (1987)). Thus in what follows, we only consider $\alpha < 1$. Under the American rule, spending is highest when the merits of the case are equal. From (15) and (16), note that total spending under the English rule equals $(\alpha/(a - \alpha)J$, and is independent of the merits of the case. It is also straightforward to show that for cases which reach trial, spending is always higher under the English rule compared with the American rule.[14] This is a standard result in the literature on endogenous legal expenditure (Braetigam, Owen and Panzar (1984)).

Once the case has reached the trial stage, the losing party must pay the legal fees of the victorious party. If the plaintiff never files the case (the game ends at stage 1), or if the defendant pays the default judgment (the game ends at stage 2), fee shifting is not an issue since no spending has occurred through those stages of the game. Thus, in contrast with the American rule, the participation constraints of the plaintiff and defendant will differ depending on the stage of the game. At stage 3, the plaintiff's participation constraint requires $P^* J - (1 - P^*)(X^* + Y^*) > -Y^*$, where '*' denotes the interior Nash solution. The right hand side reflects the fact that the plaintiff must pay the defendant's legal fees, even if she decides to spend nothing herself. It can be shown for $\alpha < 1$ that the participation constraint for the plaintiff is always satisfied; having proceeded to stage 3, the plaintiff always prefers the interior Nash solution to the corner solution of zero expenditure.

Similarly, for the defendant, the participation constraint at stage 3 requires that $P^*(J + X^* + Y^*) < J + X^*$. Again, this constraint is always satisfied for $\alpha < 1$.

4.2. Stage 2

Once the plaintiff has filed the case, the defendant must decide whether to pay the default judgment J, or to proceed to trial. Thus at stage 2, the defendant's participation constraint requires that $P^*(J + X^* + Y^*) < J$. Using (1), (15) and (16), this may be expressed as

$$e^M \leq \left(\frac{1 - \alpha}{\alpha}\right)^{1-\alpha}. \tag{17}$$

Again, letting M'' be the value of M such that (17) holds as an equality, for cases with $M > M''$ the defendant would strictly prefer to pay the default judgment at stage 2 rather than proceed to trial. For $\alpha < 1/2$, we have $M'' > 0$, so the defendant will drop some of his weakest cases in which the objective merits favor the plaintiff. However, there are some stronger cases for the defendant which he will bring to trial but where the objectives merits

Table 2. The English rule

	$\alpha < 1/2$	$\alpha = 1/2$	$\alpha > 1/2$
Plaintiff	$M < M' < 0$	$M < M' = 0$	$M < M'$, $M' > 0$
Defendant	$M > M'' > 0$	$M > M'' = 0$	$M > M''$, $M'' < 0$

Values of *M* for which participation constraints are violated under the English rule.

favor the plaintiff (i.e., $0 < M < M''$). For $\alpha = 1/2$, the defendant will only take cases to trial in which $M \leq 0$ (i.e., cases in which he is favored by the objective merits). For $\alpha > 1/2$, we have $M'' < 0$, so there are some cases where the objective merits favor the defendant, but where his participation constraint is nonetheless violated.

4.3. *Stage 1*

Under the American rule, the order of moves before trial is not crucial, since neither party is committing to any costs by proceeding to trial. By contrast, under the English rule, by proceeding to trial each party incurs potential liability for the other's legal expenditures. Thus our structure does give the plaintiff a meaningful first mover advantage. This will be important in cases where both players' participation constraints would otherwise be violated.[15] We will discuss this case later, but for now we assume that the defendant's participation constraint is satisfied, and derive which cases the plaintiff is willing to file.

The participation constraint for the plaintiff is $P^*(J + X^* + Y^*) - (X^* + Y^*) > 0$. Using (1), (15) and (16), this may be expressed as

$$e^M \geq \left(\frac{\alpha}{1 - \alpha}\right)^{1-\alpha}. \tag{18}$$

Again, M' is the value of M such that (18) holds as an equality. The plaintiff will only bring cases for which $M > M'$. For $\alpha < 1/2$, $M' < 0$, so the plaintiff will drop some of her weakest cases in which the objective merits favor the defendant. However, there are other (stronger) cases where the objective merits favor the defendant, but which the plaintiff will bring to trial (i.e., $M' < M < 0$). For $\alpha = 1/2$, the plaintiff will only bring cases in which $M \geq 0$ (i.e., the objective merits favor her). For $\alpha > 1/2$, $M' > 0$, so that there are some cases in which the objective merits favor the plaintiff, but for which she will not file suit (assuming she believes that the defendant will force the case to trial). The results of this section are summarized in Table 2.

4.4. *Case quality and legal expenditure*

There are two relevant ranges of the parameter α to consider: $\alpha \leq 1/2$ and $1/2 < \alpha < 1$.

4.4.1. $\alpha \leq 1/2$

In this range, (17) and (18) cannot be violated simultaneously; at least one participation constraint must be satisfied. Furthermore, if only one participation constraint is satisfied, that player is favored by the objective merits of the case. This is analogous to the American rule for the range $1 < \alpha \leq 2$ in which some cases are either not filed or not defended, and these are the "right" cases in the sense that the case is not pursued by the party who has the weak case ($M < 0$ for the plaintiff and $M > 0$ for the defendant). The cases which do not reach trial are from the tails of the distribution of M, while cases which proceed to trial are from the center of the distribution. For $\alpha = 1/2$, we have the same attractive equilibrium features as under the American rule for $\alpha = 2$; the plaintiff only brings cases in which she is favored by the objective merits ($M \geq 0$), and the defendant only defends cases in which he is favored by the objective merits ($M \leq 0$). Except for $M = 0$, no cases reach trial, and the associated legal expenditures are avoided. Note that for $\alpha = 1/2$, total spending by the parties at trial (should it occur) just equals the amount of the judgment J (as under the American rule with $\alpha = 2$ and $M = 0$).

Note again that we are not guaranteed a monotonic relationship between α and legal expenditure. As α rises towards 1/2, spending increases on those cases which reach trial, but fewer cases reach trial.

4.4.2. $\alpha > 1/2$

As with $\alpha > 2$ under the American rule, in this range, there are cases in which $M'' < M < M'$, where $M'' < 0$ and $M' > 0$ (i.e., the participation constraints of both players are violated). This poses the same set of problems discussed in Section 3.5.3, except that now the structure of our game does give the plaintiff a meaningful first mover advantage. If the defendant's participation constraint is violated, the plaintiff should file the case even if her own participation constraint would otherwise be violated (meaning she would not file if the case would be brought to trial). Because $M'' < 0$, this means there are some cases in which the objective merits favor the defendant, but where the plaintiff files suit and the defendant pays the default judgment.

That our particular structure gives the plaintiff a first mover advantage is of course arbitrary. Actually, there is a disadvantage to moving last since this party has the last chance to prevent the case from proceeding to trial. If the plaintiff moved last, then the defendant would have the advantage, and as a result, the plaintiff would fail to file some cases where $M > 0$. Regardless of which player is able to commit to trial first, the result is problematic in that this player can use this advantage to "win" cases in which the objective merits favor the other party.

5. Conclusion

What can we say about the relative merits of the English and American rules? The answer is very sensitive to the value of the parameter α. If $\alpha \geq 1$, the interior Nash equilibrium under the English rule does not exist for any finite level of legal expenditure. Clearly the English rule is undesirable in this range. No cases reach trial, but whichever party has first mover advantage will be able to prevail in all cases, even when the objective merits do not justify it. The American rule functions well in the range $1 < \alpha \leq 2$, and for $\alpha = 2$, the plaintiff only files meritorious cases, the defendant pays the default judgment J, and legal expenditure is zero! In general, once the participation constraints are taken into account, there is not a monotonic relationship between total spending and α, though spending does monotonically increase as α increases from 0 to 1. This is because for $\alpha \leq 1$ under the American rule, all cases are filed by the plaintiff and defended by the defendant. For $1 < \alpha \leq 2$, the plaintiff fails to file some of her weaker cases, and the defendant does not defend some of his weak cases. For $\alpha > 2$, there is a range of problematic cases in which the participation constraints of both players are violated. For the English rule, $\alpha = 1/2$ has the same attractive properties as $\alpha = 2$ under the American rule. Similarly, the outcomes for $\alpha \leq 1/2$ and $1/2 < \alpha < 1$ roughly correspond to the ranges $1 < \alpha \leq 2$ and $\alpha > 2$ respectively under the American rule. For $\alpha < 1/2$, fewer cases reach trial under the English rule, but spending on those cases is higher than under the American rule. Thus we are unable to compare total legal expenditures under the two rules in this range.

What can American experience under the American rule tell us about what range for α is empirically relevant? Under the American rule with $\alpha \leq 1$, all cases are filed by the plaintiff and defended by the defendant, regardless of the merits of the case. This seems counterfactual. As Eisenberg and Farber (1997:S98) among others point out, most potential lawsuits are never filed. This suggests that the range $1 < \alpha < 2$ is empirically relevant. Tullock (1980b: 15) puts combined legal fees for the plaintiff and defendant in the U.S. at about 2/3 of the judgment, while the figures in Spier (1992: footnote 1) indicate that these fees total about 1/2 of the judgment. This too suggests that $1 < \alpha < 2$ is the empirically relevant range.[16] To the extent this is true, switching to the English rule will not produce desirable outcomes. However, we must be cautious in drawing strong conclusions at this point. We have analyzed legal expenditure in the context of a standard rent-seeking technology, but the actual legal technology may differ.[17] One simple modification of our technology might allow for certain fixed costs of trial which do not directly affect the probable trial outcome. For example, there may be psychic costs incurred in the litigation process, which do not affect the probability of success at trial. Once such costs are considered, even for $\alpha \leq 1$ under the American rule, not all cases will be filed by the plaintiff, nor will all cases filed be brought to trial by the defendant. As a result, the observation that not all potential cases are filed does not necessarily imply values of α which lead to explosive spending under the English rule. In addition, to the extent that only "reasonable fees" are assessed to the losing party, there may be limits on fee shifting in practice. As a result, spending under the English rule may be lower than predicted by our model and nonexplosive in general.[18]

Even our simple model suggests that we need to know a good deal about the legal (or rent seeking) technology in evaluating fee shifting arrangements. In addition, to fully evaluate such arrangements, we must consider a model with pretrial settlement, which might include asymmetric information, among other features.

Notes

1. Under US antitrust law, plaintiffs can sue to recover their "reasonable" legal fees from the defendant if the plaintiff wins on the merits.
2. Throughout the paper, the pronoun she will refer to the plaintiff and the pronoun he will refer to the defendant.
3. In a typical rent-seeking contest, players compete to receive a rent from the government. In a legal case, the "rent" to be transferred represents a payment from one player (the defendant) to the other player (the plaintiff). Appelbaum and Katz (1986) analyze a rent-seeking contest in which the losing players pay for the rent received by the winner. It turns out, however, that the mathematics of our game are closer to the mathematics of the traditional rent-seeking game than they are to those of Appelbaum and Katz (1986).
4. Other types of asymmetries in rent-seeking contests are addressed by Paul and Wilhite (1990), Allard (1988) and Leininger (1993).
5. Other papers which model endogenous legal expenditure include Tullock (1975, 1980b) Braeutigam, Owen and Panzar (1984), Plott (1987), Hause (1989) and Hughes and Wolgom (1996).
6. Hause (1989) is an exception in that he jointly considers the problems of endogenous expenditure at trial, and settlement.
7. Underlying this is the returns to scale in the production of legal arguments. See the discussion of Katz (1988) in the introduction.
8. See Corcoran (1984), Tullock (1984, 1985), Corcoran and Karels (1985), and Higgins, Shughart and Tollison (1985).
9. Pérez-Castrillo and Verdier (1992) prove that a preemptive strategy is optimal for a Stackelberg leader in a standard rent-seeking game with entry. A proof that such a strategy in optimal in our game is available from the authors upon request.

10. By fixed costs we mean costs which do not directly affect the probable outcome at trial (i.e., they do not appear in equation 1), such as the opportunity cost of time, or psychic costs of being involved in a lawsuit.

11. If M is distributed continuously, then $M = 0$ is a measure zero event.

12. Our specification that the plaintiff moves in stage 1 and that the defendant moves in stage 2 does not give a first mover advantage to the plaintiff because even after she files the case, she is not committed to any particular level of expenditure at stage 3, and an expenditure of zero is still possible.

13. This property of the English rule is noted by Hughes and Woglom (1996).

14. Given α, spending is maximized under the American rule for $M = 0$. From (6), with $M = 0$, total spending is $\alpha J/2$ under the American rule. This is always less than $(\alpha/1 - \alpha)J)$, total spending under the English rule (recall our restriction $\alpha < 1$).

15. By that we mean that the plaintiff would not file the case unless she knew that the defendant would pay the default judgment.

16. Recall that under the American rule for $\alpha = 1$ and $M = 0$, the model indicates that total expenditure is 50% of the judgment. For $\alpha = 1$ and $M \neq 0$ expenditure is less than 50%. Thus the empirical observation that 50% of the judgment is consumed by legal fees is consistent with a value of $\alpha > 1$. As per the earlier discussion of the Katz (1988) model, this range implies increasing returns to scale in the production of legal arguments.

17. See Hirshleifer (1989) for an alternative form of the contest success function.

18. The absolute ability of the losing party to pay the shifted fees may also put a damper on spending in practice.

References

Allard, R.J. (1988). Rent seeking with non-identical players. *Public Choice* 57: 3–14.

Appelbaum. E. and Katz, E. (1986). Transfer seeking and avoidance: On the full social cost of rent seeking. *Public Choice* 48: 175–181.

Braeutigam, R.B., Owen, B. and Panzar, J. (1984). An economic analysis of alternative fee shifting systems. *Law and Contemporary Problems* 47: 173–185.

Buchanan, J.M., Tollison, R.D. and Tullock, G. (Eds.) (1980). *Toward a theory of the rent-seeking society.* College Station, Texas: Texas A&M University Press.

Corcoran, W.J. (1984). Long-run equilibrium and total expenditures in rent-seeking. *Public Choice* 43: 89–94.

Corcoran, W.J., and Karels, G.V. (1985). Rent-seeking behavior in the long-run. *Public Choice* 46: 227–246.

Eisenberg, T. and Farber, H.S. (1997). The litigious plaintiff hypothesis: Case selection and resolution. *Rand Journal of Economics* 28: S92-S112.

Gradstein, M. (1995). Intensity of competition, entry and entry deterrence in rent seeking contests. *Economics and Politics* 7: 79–91.

Hause, J.C. (1989). Indemnity, settlement, and litigation, or I'll be suing you. *Journal of Legal Studies* 18: 157–179.

Higgins, R.S., Shughart, W.F. II and Tollison, R.D. (1985). Free entry and rent seeking. *Public Choice* 46: 247–258.

Hirshleifer, J. (1989). Conflict and rent-seeking success functions: Ratio vs. difference models of relative success. *Public Choice* 63: 101–112.

Hughes, J.W., and Woglom, G.R.. (1996). Risk aversion and the allocation of legal costs. In D. Anderson (Ed.), *Dispute resolution: Bridging the settlement gap*, 167–192. Greenwich, Connecticut: JAI Press.

Katz, A. (1988). Judicial decisionmaking and litigation expenditure. *International Review of Law and Economics* 8: 127–143.

288

Krueger, A.O. (1974). The political economy of the rent-seeking society, *American Economic Review* 64: 291–303.

Leininger, W. (1993). More efficient rent-seeking – A Münchhausen Solution. *Public Choice* 75: 43–62.

Nitzan, S. (1994). Modeling rent-seeking contests. *European Journal of Political Economy* 10: 41–60.

Paul. C. and Wilhite, A. (1990). Efficient rent seeking under varying cost structures. *Public Choice* 64: 279–290.

Pérez-Castrillo, J. and Verdier, T. (1992). A general analysis of rent-seeking games. *Public Choice* 73: 335–350.

Plott, C.R. (1987). Legal fees: A comparison of the American and English rules. *Journal of Law, Economics and Organization* 3: 185–192.

Rowley, C.K., Tollison, R.D. and Tullock, G. (Eds.) (1988). *The political economy of rent seeking*. Boston: Kluwer.

Spier, K. (1992). The dynamics of pretrial negotiation. *Review of Economic Studies* 59: 93–108.

Tollison, R.D. (1982). Rent seeking: A survey. *Kyklos* 35: 575–602.

Tullock, G. (1967). The welfare costs of tariffs, monopolies and theft. *Western Economic Journal* 5: 224–232.

Tullock, G. (1975). On the efficient organization of trials. *Kyklos* 28: 745–762.

Tullock, G. (1980a). Efficient rent seeking. In J.M. Buchanan, R.D. Tollison and G. Tullock (Eds.), 97–112. *Toward a Theory of the Rent-Seeking Society*. College Station, Texas: Texas A&M University Press.

Tullock, G. (1980b). *Trials on trial*. New York: Columbia University Press.

Tullock, G. (1984). Long-run equilibrium and total expenditures in rent-seeking: A comment. *Public Choice* 43: 95–97.

Tullock, G. (1985). Back to the bog. *Public Choice* 46: 259–263.

ELSEVIER   International Review of Law and Economics 22 (2002) 193–216

International
Review of
Law and
Economics

Rent-seeking through litigation: adversarial and inquisitorial systems compared

Francesco Parisi*

School of Law, George Mason University, 3401 North Fairfax Drive, Arlington, VA 22201, USA

Accepted 24 May 2001

Abstract

This paper compares the adversarial system of adjudication, dominant in the common law tradition, with the inquisitorial system, dominant in the civil law tradition, using a rent-seeking, Nash equilibrium, model of litigation expenditure in which the litigants simultaneously choose their levels of effort with the goal of maximizing their returns from the case. The choice between the two systems is modeled as a continuous variable showing the equilibrium solutions of the game and their implications for procedural economy. The results are then utilized to characterize the optimal levels of adversarial and inquisitorial discovery with respect to the social benefits of truth-finding and correct adjudication, and the private and administrative costs of litigation.
© 2002 Elsevier Science Inc. All rights reserved.

> [A] common law trial is and always should be an adversary proceeding.
>
> Hickman v. Taylor (1947), 329 U.S. 495, 516 (Jackson, J., concurring)

Scholars of comparative civil procedure often contrast American and continental European legal systems by reference to the distinctive functions fulfilled by judges and lawyers in the two legal traditions. A distinction is often drawn between "adversarial" and "inquisitorial" procedural systems. The two opposing paradigms refer to the different roles played by the judge in the conduct of a civil case.

In a typical inquisitorial proceeding, the trial is dominated by a presiding judge, who determines the order in which evidence is taken and who evaluates the content of the gathered evidence. In those proceedings, the court determines the credibility and relative weight of each

* Tel.: +1-703-993-8036.
E-mail address: parisi@gmu.edu (F. Parisi).

0144-8188/02/$ – see front matter © 2002 Elsevier Science Inc. All rights reserved.
PII: S0144-8188(02)00089-3

piece of evidence without being constrained by strict rules in that respect. By contrast, in a typical adversarial system, the case is organized and the facts are developed by the sole initiative of the parties. The process develops through the efforts of the litigants before a passive decision maker who reaches a decision on the sole basis of the evidence and motions presented by the litigants.

Law and economics scholars have occasionally examined the various methods of discovery in a comparative perspective. The discussion has often invoked alternative ideological paradigms. Most notably, in a well-known debate, Posner (1988) and Tullock (1988) have taken opposite sides on this issue, defending respectively the adversarial and the inquisitorial systems, on a variety of grounds. Posner argues that the adversarial system is preferable because it allows the parties who bear the costs and benefits of the litigation to shape the litigation. Alternatively, the inquisitorial method shifts power to judges, and thus promotes an expansion of the public sector as well. Posner contends that it is doubtful whether such a shift would improve the performance of our judicial system.

In this paper I consider the strategic implications of these procedural alternatives, showing the impact of a change in the extent of the inquisitorial role of the judge on parties' incentives to expend in litigation. In Part I, I consider the key differences between the conduct of a case in an adversarial procedural system and an inquisitorial system. The analysis evaluates some general features of alternative modes of discovery. The results can be extended to both civil and criminal procedure, notwithstanding the different goals and concerns associated with civil and criminal adjudication. In Part II, I show the impact of the two procedural rules on the equilibrium expenditures on litigation for the two parties. The results suggest that both an increase in the weight attached to the judge-obtained evidence and an increase in judicial scrutiny of the adversary's arguments and evidence will have a negative impact on the equilibrium levels of litigation expenditures undertaken by the litigants. In Part III, I depict the optimal weight to be attached to the inquisitorial efforts of the judge as the value that maximizes the social benefits from truthful adjudication net of the private and administrative costs. The comparative statics of the model show how the optimal weights placed on the adversarial and inquisitorial components of the process vary with some key features of the cost and benefit functions. The results indicate that the optimal weight attached to the adversarial component of the process is positively related to the visibility and social relevance of the litigated case and to the judicial scrutiny applied by the court to the parties' evidence, while it is negatively related to the private cost of litigation for the parties, the relative efficiency of the court in obtaining and evaluating evidence, and the number of litigants competing for the adjudication of a fixed award. Part IV offers a few concluding remarks about the costs of the adversary system.

1. The adversarial and inquisitorial systems compared

The distinction between adversarial and inquisitorial systems finds its origin in twelfth century European law. Adversarial processes could only be initiated by the action of a private party (the so-called *processus per accusationem*), while inquisitorial proceedings could be triggered *ex officio* by the judicial system (the so-called *processus per inquisitionem*).

F. Parisi / International Review of Law and Economics 22 (2002) 193–216   195

The meaning of the distinction evolved in later medieval times to include other features generally associated with the two procedures.[1] Most notably, the distinction came to refer to the general role of the judge in the fact-finding phase of the trial. In medieval times, the judge was generally conceived as an official truth seeker. In a well-known *dictum*, fourteenth century jurist Bartolus from Sassoferrato argued that, with or without a proposal by a party, courts could produce and examine witnesses for the purpose of truthful discovery.[2] Along similar lines, Baldus de Ubaldis, a jurist who wrote during the second half of the 14th century, argued that, because of their institutional role as cognitional judges, medieval courts were at liberty to hear those witnesses whose depositions they considered necessary for establishing the facts at issue.[3] Production and evaluation of the evidence were the sole prerogatives of the judge who could summon witnesses to assist the court's fact-finding efforts. In this context, Baldus further argued that it was not part of the prerogatives of the individual litigants to examine the witnesses or to produce them.[4]

Historically, the procedural systems of the common law tradition developed away from the inquisitorial models, adopting the adversarial paradigm of adjudication in both criminal and civil legal proceedings. In common law proceedings the presentation of evidence became the exclusive task of the parties. As pointed out by Damaska (1997) this is not surprising, given the absence from England of an official apparatus capable of routine judicial investigations. In spite of much legal evolution, the ancient roots of the adversarial trial are still evident in the current rules of procedure.[5] The role of the victim in the trials against the accused is replicated in modern times through the adversarial process, with a public accuser carrying out the victim's task in the accusation of the wrongdoer.

Nineteenth century classical liberal ideas allowed the adversarial model to outlive its historical origins. Adversarial procedure was defended for its closer proximity to "dialectical" models, with emphasis on assertion and refutation, and yet attacked by enlightened rationalists, generally skeptical of information provided by biased and self-interested actors.[6] In the evolved conception of the adversarial procedure, the parties' attorneys became responsible for discovering and presenting evidence for their clients and for challenging the evidence presented by their opposition.[7] Similarly, the parties bore the full responsibility for presenting the law: legal theories were formulated by the parties' attorneys and expressed in oral and written arguments. In this setting the judge played the role of a neutral and passive arbiter, ruling, often without explanation, on objections and contentions moved by the parties. Even relatively active judges were limited in the scope of their action, compared with the role played by the typical judge serving in a civil law jurisdiction.[8]

In the current legal usage, the distinction between inquisitorial and adversarial proceedings continues to refer to the general differences in approach between the civil law and common law procedural systems.[9]

In a typical common law trial, the process is party-controlled. The case is organized and the facts are developed by the sole initiative of the parties.[10] The process develops through the efforts of the litigants before a passive decision maker who reaches a decision on the sole basis of the evidence and motions presented by the parties. In an adversarial system of legal procedure, the judge thus enjoys limited initiative in the process. While the judge has some discretion over the nature and extent of his or her participation, in no case may he or she contribute to the fact-elucidation efforts of the parties. The truth of the case cannot be searched directly by the judge, but shall instead emerge out of the adversarial dynamic of the process, with a partisan presentation of the facts.[11]

In a typical civil law trial, judicial officials perform a more active role which is not limited to the examination of the evidence presented by the parties or to the execution of the parties' motions. The control over the process is shifted from the parties to the court, which enjoys greater discretion in the evaluation of the evidence and may guide the discovery process with bench requests. In these systems, the presiding judge determines the order in which evidence is taken and is free to weigh up the relative value of conflicting evidence, acting independently of the proposals and motions of the parties (Ullmann, 1946). The inquisitorial character of the procedure generally implies that judges are generally not bound by any formal rule in the evaluation of the facts but are to decide on the basis of their "internal conviction" (*intime conviction*).[12] Accordingly, in several civil law jurisdictions, the court determines the credibility and relative weight of each piece of information without being guided by formal rules of evidence.[13] In this respect, the court is vested with a large degree of initiative to shape the course of the litigation. Concepts such as "plaintiff's case" or "defendant's case" are unknown to the procedural systems of the civil law tradition.[14] In a typical civil law court, the judge contributes to ascertaining the facts and identifying potentially relevant evidence, and actively screens and evaluates the evidence presented by the parties.[15] The civil law judge has authority to investigate the facts on his own initiative, exercising the power by asking supplemental questions when the advocates have concluded their questioning, and often conducting the primary examination of witnesses.[16]

In an inquisitorial proceeding, the direct involvement of the judge in the gathering of evidence often avoids the consolidation of two contrary point of views resulting from an independent partisan search and presentation of the facts. In contrast, an adversarial process often leads to two clashing positions. As pointed out by Damaska (1997) this format is often conducive to an exacerbation of the differences and a neglect of the common grounds: "Neutral information tends to be short-changed. . . . the world presented to the triers of fact is illuminated by two narrow beams of light."[17] Froeb and Kobayashi (2000) have further analogized the fact-finding process in an adversarial system to an "extremal" estimator based on the difference between the most favorable pieces of evidence produced by each party.[18] This, in turn, yields an important testable proposition: with the judge's involvement vanishing, the litigants' differences will surface more noticeably, and greater overall expenditures in litigation will obtain.

In a typical civil law case, the active participation of the judge in the gathering and evaluation of evidence further creates a blurring of the distinction between pretrial and trial. As pointed out by Adams (1998), this implies that in civil law jurisdictions, trial is not a single continuous event. Rather there are several hearings in which the court meets with the litigants to gather and evaluate the evidence of the case. The ongoing involvement of the judge in the discovery process has important implications for procedural economy.

In a two-stage process, the parties tend to gather and disclose all the evidence that may in some way relate to the litigated case. Evidence that is not gathered and disclosed in the pretrial phase often becomes inadmissible at trial. Given the likely uncertainty over the usefulness and relevance of each piece of information in the later trial phase, the litigants tend to introduce much more evidence than is actually utilized in the trial phase. The litigants compete in the adversarial supply of information, in order to dominate the opponent in the

F. Parisi / International Review of Law and Economics 22 (2002) 193–216   197

subsequent presentation of their case. Such advantage may indeed prove very valuable in jury trials, where a lay jury decides, in the absence of a professional judge, which facts have been proved.

In a one-stage process, instead, the judge guides and actively participates in the discovery process, indicating the issues and factual questions that he would like to investigate. In doing so, the court confines the scope of the adversarial supply of information by the parties to those issues that appear more obscure to him. The judge will discourage the litigants from dissipating their efforts and resources to prove a factual circumstance that has been rendered irrelevant by other findings of the court. The parties have an opportunity to get some preliminary feedback from the judge as to the likely relevance of costly information, thus avoiding expenditures in discovery that may later prove unnecessary or irrelevant.

2. Rents, rent-dissipation, and rational litigation

The dichotomous distinction between adversarial and inquisitorial proceedings obviously embraces several dimensions of the legal process, summarizing them within two discrete categories. This approach has been criticized by scholars of comparative law who observe that there are too many elements that these legal terms attempt to consider.[19] The legal systems of the world, although historically interrelated, have assumed different forms and procedural connotations that render the dichotomous distinction inapt.[20] The following analysis considers the adversarial nature of the process as a continuous variable.[21] This enables us to consider the range of real world alternatives without artificial and arbitrary dichotomies.

In the model developed in the present section, I follow the conventional wisdom (Posner, 1973; Damaska, 1983), which models the dispute resolution process as a simulation of, and substitute for, the private conflict between two parties. This leads to the central image of proceedings as a contest of two sides before a judge or arbiter. According to this line of thinking, the task is then to consider alternative procedural arrangements as instrumental to the most efficient resolution of the parties' conflict. For example, if the judge were permitted to conduct independent inquiries into the facts of the case, the discovery process would logically cease to be a mere party contest and the return to private litigation efforts would be reduced accordingly.

In this setting, I classify procedural systems according to the allocation of control over the process and the relative dominance of inquisitorial and adversarial formats. The variable I captures the weight attached to the inquisitorial (i.e., non-adversarial) findings in determining the size of the award. Greater values of I indicate that the judge, as opposed to the litigants, has greater control over the process, or that the evidence obtained directly by the judge is, *ceteris paribus*, given greater weight than the evidence provided by the parties. I use the subscripts A and I to identify the returns from the adversarial and inquisitorial components of the litigation.

In this model, legal expenditure at trial is endogenous.[22] In this section, I consider how the equilibrium expenditures in litigation vary with the institutional choice of I. E_J is the judicial effort exerted by the court in independent investigation and examination of independently obtained evidence. This level of effort will depend positively on the level of I. S

Francesco Parisi

denotes the level of scrutiny to which the evidence provided by the parties is subjected. S is considered a parameter for our analysis, and is not chosen by the judge. The level of S may denote procedural safeguards against the admission of certain types of evidence, like hearsay. As S increases, the likelihood than any piece of evidence submitted by the parties will be discarded increases, and so the equilibrium level of expenditures by the parties will decrease.

Following Posner (1973, 1999), I set the probability of prevailing in litigation as a function of relative party expenditures. Equilibrium is achieved via independent spending decisions by the litigants. In this model, a relative increase in litigation spending reduces the opponent's expected return from the case.[23] More specifically, the parties' total expected return R^e depends upon the following two components: (i) the merits of the disputed case, R_I, as ascertained through the inquisitorial discovery; (ii) the disputed case, R_A, captured through the adversarial efforts of the parties $E_{p,d}$. A shift in the weight attached to the inquisitorial and adversarial components of the process may change the expected return from the parties' case. The total marginal effect of a procedural change for all parties is zero-sum.[24] Note that R_I and R_A represent plaintiff awards. The former represents the award level that would be given if no adversarial effort is exerted, and the judge's decision is made only on the basis of independently gathered evidence. The latter is the award amount that results from the parties' evidence. The plaintiff's adversarial award amount will depend on R_A and on the relative amount of effort he spends in litigation.

The return from the non-adversarial component is a function of the underlying merits of the plaintiff's case as well as the judicial discovery efforts, E_J. The returns from the adversarial component, instead, are a proportional share function of the parties' respective efforts, and the residual value of the case which depends on the adversarial evidence and the level of scrutiny that evidence is subjected to by the court. An adversary's expected return from the case is a weighted average of the inquisitorial and adversarial components, with the institutional choice variable I determining the weights. The same functional form could be used to characterize a winner-takes-all system where the parties' respective probabilities of success are proportional to their shares of effort.

For two litigants (plaintiff, defendant), the respective objective is to maximize their expected return from litigation. For the typical case of a zero-sum judgment, the plaintiff will try to maximize the net judicial award, while the defendant will try to minimize the total loss from litigation. The plaintiff's objective could thus be to maximize:

$$R_p^e = IR_I(E_J) + (1 - I)R_A(S)\frac{E_p}{E_p + E_d} - CE_p \tag{2.1}$$

Symmetrically, the defendant wishes to minimize the sum of the expected judgment and his litigation costs. This objective can be represented as maximizing:

$$R_d^e = -IR_I(E_J) - (1 - I)R_A(S)\frac{E_p}{E_p + E_d} - CE_d \tag{2.2}$$

Given the zero-sum constraint, the effect of a change in procedure, I, on the parties' expected payoffs will have opposite signs for the two litigants.[25]

F. Parisi / International Review of Law and Economics 22 (2002) 193–216   199

The first-order conditions for the optimal levels of efforts, E_p^* and E_d^*, for each party will be respectively:

$$H_p = \frac{\partial R_p^e}{\partial E_p} = (1 - I)R_A(S)\frac{E_d}{(E_p + E_d)^2} - C = 0 \tag{2.3}$$

$$H_d = \frac{\partial R_d^e}{\partial E_d} = (1 - I)R_A(S)\frac{E_p}{(E_p + E_d)^2} - C = 0 \tag{2.4}$$

We can verify that $\partial H_1/\partial E_1$ and $\partial H_2/\partial E_2$ are non-zero by explicitly solving for the optimal values of E_1^* and E_2^*. This, in turn, allows us to characterize the litigants' respective reaction functions as:

$$E_p^* = \sqrt{\frac{(1 - I)E_dR_A(S)}{C}} - E_d \tag{2.5}$$

$$E_d^* = \sqrt{\frac{(1 - I)E_pR_A(S)}{C}} - E_p \tag{2.6}$$

In equilibrium, $E_p^* = E_d^*$, such that

$$E_p^{**} = E_d^{**} = \frac{(1 - I)R_A(S)}{4C} \tag{2.7}$$

For the special, yet most common, case of two litigants, the total expenditure in litigation, at cost C, for the adjudication of the adversarial portion of the award will be given by:

$$L = C(E_p^{**} + E_d^{**}) = \frac{(1 - I)R_A(S)}{2} \tag{2.8}$$

This implies that in a symmetric two-litigant case, parties will exert litigation effort in proportion to the value of the adversarial component of the case and the weight assigned to adversarial evidence in the decision-making process. In a purely adversarial system ($I = 0$) the parties will spend a full half of the value of the case in litigation.

For the more general case of N litigants, it is necessary to distinguish two main cases: (a) N litigants competing for the adjudication of a mutually exclusive award, where the returns from the adversarial efforts are a proportional share function of the parties' respective efforts;[26] and (b) N litigants litigating as joint actors in a joint or class action claim. In the first case, the individual maximization problem of (2.1) can be recast as:

$$R_i^e = IR_{I(i)}(E_J) + (1 - I)R_A(S)\frac{E_i}{\sum_{i=1,\dots,N}E_i} - CE_i \tag{2.9}$$

We can replicate the steps (2.3) through (2.7) to obtain the Nash expenditures in discovery for the general case of N litigants. The individual expenditure in discovery, E_i^{**}, and the total private cost of discovery for the N litigants at unitary cost, C, become respectively:

$$E_i = \frac{(1 - I)R_A(S)(N - 1)}{CN^2} \quad \text{and} \quad L = \frac{(1 - I)R_A(S)(N - 1)}{N} \tag{2.10}$$

This implies that in the more general case of N litigants with competing claims over a fixed award, a share equal to $(N - 1)/N$ of the value of the adversarial case from the perspective

200   F. Parisi / International Review of Law and Economics 22 (2002) 193–216

of the parties (i.e., an amount ranging from at least one half and up to the full value of the disputed case) will be dissipated through litigation.

Different results obtain in the case of joint or class actions, where more joint plaintiffs or joint defendants litigate, as a group, for the adjudication of R_A. If the two groups have successfully corrected the collective action problems in pursuing their common cause, then the plaintiffs' and defendants' teams will behave as two individual agents, facing an optimization problem similar to (2.1). Conversely, if the collective action of the various actors is affected by free-riding, the private incentives to litigate may be undermined. Thus, the total private expenditures in adversarial discovery may decrease with an increase in the number of joint claimants.

For the general case of multiple litigants with competing claims, we can further study the behavior of the Nash values of aggregate private expenditure L, characterizing it more compactly as:

$$L \equiv C \sum_{i=1,\dots,N} E_i^{**} = \ell(I, E_J, R_A, N) \tag{2.11}$$

Having verified that (2.2) and (2.3) are non-zero,[27] we can use the Implicit Function Theorem to study how the equilibrium value of L varies with (i) the institutional weight attached to the inquisitorial findings and (ii) the judicial scrutiny applied to the evidence submitted by the parties; (iii) the value of the disputed case which rests on the findings from the adversarial discovery; (iv) the number of litigants competing for the adjudication of a mutually exclusive award. These calculations, which have been omitted for the sake of brevity,[28] respectively yield:

$$\frac{\partial L}{\partial I} = \frac{-H_I}{H_E} < 0 \tag{2.12}$$

$$\frac{\partial L}{\partial S} = \frac{-H_S}{H_E} < 0 \tag{2.13}$$

$$\frac{\partial L}{\partial R_A} = \frac{-H_A}{H_E} > 0 \tag{2.14}$$

$$\frac{\partial L}{\partial N} = \frac{-H_N}{H_E} > 0 \tag{2.15}$$

where H_E, H_I, H_S, H_A and H_N are the partial derivatives of (2.2) with respect to E_p, I, S, R_A, and N, respectively.

The comparative statics of this problem yield interesting and unambiguous results. The result of (2.12) suggests that the total amount of litigation expenditure rises with an increase in weight accorded to adversarially produced evidence. This should not be surprising, since the evidence that is privately produced in an adversarial system is given more decisional weight and therefore is likely to generate higher returns for the litigants.

Likewise, (2.13) indicates that the parties' total expenditure in discovery is reduced with an increase in the scrutiny used by the judge in the fact-finding process. With an increase in judicial scrutiny, the evidence that is privately produced by the parties is more likely to

F. Parisi / International Review of Law and Economics 22 (2002) 193–216

be discarded and thus yields lower returns. Notice that this result depends on the same level of scrutiny being used with both parties' evidence. A different definition of judicial activism which is not result-neutral may alter our results.

In (2.14) we learn that the expenditure in discovery and litigation is exacerbated by an increase in the value of the case which rests on the findings from adversarial evidence. For pure wealth-maximizers, there will be a straightforward relationship between the value of the case, R_A, and the equilibrium expenditure in litigation. Risk aversion would add a concave curvature to such a relationship. Finally, (2.15) indicates that the total expenditure in discovery increases with the number of litigants competing for the adjudication of a mutually exclusive award. This result is a mere restatement of the explicit relationship between number of litigants and total expenditure, identified in Eq. (2.10). The total share of the judicial award that is expended in litigation increases monotonically with the number of litigants at a rate $(N-1)/N$. Thus, under conditions of symmetry and linear production functions for the litigants, total expenditures would range from a minimum of one half to the full value of the litigated case from the perspective of the parties.[29]

3. Truth-finding, litigation costs and optimal procedures

In the previous discussion, we considered the different costs associated with the inquisitorial and adversarial procedures.

Duplication of costs is not the only effect of adversarial procedures. In an adversarial system, the strategic interaction of the parties creates additional costs (and potential benefits) that are not the mere consequence of the uncoordinated efforts of the litigants. In this respect, the claim that the inquisitorial system is more efficient merely because it involves only one searcher of truth (the judge) instead of two or more searchers (the parties and their counsels) overlooks an important dimension of the problem.

The strategic nature of the parties' choices produces a systematic discrepancy between the private and social incentives to gather evidence. The parties' (privately) optimal level of discovery and adversarial activity may be inconsistent with the judge's optimal choice of inquisitorial efforts.[30] Since the damage award the parties gain is a zero-sum result, the efforts of the litigants yield offsetting benefits from a private standpoint but may yield positive net benefits from a social standpoint if adversarial evidence contributes to a correct decision. Furthermore, the efforts of the litigants often shed light on the weaknesses and flaws of the evidence presented by their opponents.[31]

The above considerations should be further examined in light of the concerns that public choice theory may raise regarding the judges' ability to identify the optimal level of inquisitorial efforts (i.e., the formidable weighing of costs and benefits of judicial action). We shall proceed assuming that judges attempt to optimize social benefit from correct decisions, and have a varying degree of efficiency, ϕ, in acquiring and processing information.

In this section, I explore the implications of the divergence between private incentives and social incentives in the discovery of a case, extending the previous analysis to additional variables. I treat the choice of the inquisitorial share of the process as endogenous and characterize the optimal level of inquisitorial effort as that which maximizes the net social benefits from litigation. The relevant welfare function, W, includes the social benefits from accurate discovery and adjudication, B,[32] and the social cost of litigation, given by the sum of the private cost and public cost of the discovery process.

In what follows, I set up the social net benefit function which depends on I, the institutional weight placed on inquisitorial findings, the parties' and judge's levels of effort, and model parameters. I derive I^*, the optimal "mix" of adversarial and inquisitorial systems. The stylized representation of the cost and benefit functions allows us to perform comparative statics exercises to study how the optimizing value I^* varies with a change in the exogenous variables, such as the level of judicial scrutiny, S, the cost of private production of evidence, C, the efficiency of the judicial system, ϕ, and the social relevance and visibility of the litigated case, V.

I assume that social benefit results from accurate decisions, such as correct interpretations of legislation or proper application of precedent or general principles of law. Social cost is simply the sum of private and judicial costs, so that the problem faced by society in setting the value of I is

$$\max W = B[E_p, E_d, E_J, S, V] - C(E_p + E_d) - C_J(E_J, \phi) \tag{3.1}$$

where the effort levels of the parties to the litigation are the Nash equilibrium levels of effort obtained above, and judicial effort is chosen to maximize social welfare.

The benefits from accurate decision making increase directly with the social relevance and visibility of the case. To keep things simple, I have assumed that the administrative and private cost functions do not depend on the social relevance and visibility of the case.

In order to find the optimal level of inquisitorial procedure for our welfare function, we can study the first-order conditions of (3.1) with respect to I. Assuming complete symmetry between the two parties to the litigation, we can define:

$$\frac{\partial B}{\partial E_{adv}} \equiv \frac{\partial B}{\partial E_p} = \frac{\partial B}{\partial E_d} \quad \text{and} \quad \frac{\partial E_{adv}^*}{\partial I} \equiv \frac{\partial E_p^*}{\partial I} = \frac{\partial E_d^*}{\partial I}$$

This yields the first-order condition:

$$F = 2\left(\frac{\partial B}{\partial E_{adv}} - C\right)\frac{\partial E_{adv}}{\partial I} + \left(\frac{\partial B}{\partial E_J} - \frac{\partial C_J}{\partial E_J}\right)\frac{\partial E_J}{\partial I} = 0 \tag{3.2}$$

Notice that since adversarial effort decreases and judicial effort increases as I rises, the two terms in parentheses in (3.2) must have the same sign. In other words, at the socially optimal value of I, either the adversaries and the judge are inputting too much effort from the social perspective, or they are inputting too little effort, or both the parties and the judge are exerting the socially optimal level of effort. To see why this is the case, consider the possibility that the parties are inputting too much effort from the social perspective, while the judge exerts too little effort. The socially optimal level of I could then be increased, resulting in less adversarial and more judicial effort, and thus social welfare would increase.

Under our assumption that the judge exerts effort to maximize social welfare, both terms in parentheses above must equal 0, so that the adversarial parties and the judge input the correct levels of effort from the social perspective. Essentially, our assumption about the behavior of the judge is equivalent to giving the social decision-maker two instruments, I and E_J, instead of just one. Under different assumptions about how judicial effort is set, such as self-serving

F. Parisi / International Review of Law and Economics 22 (2002) 193–216   203

behavior by the judge or incomplete information about the relevance or underlying truth-value of the case, it is possible that no level of I would achieve optimal effort exertion by the parties and the judge. The level of I would then be set to achieve a second-best solution, in which net marginal social costs from the distortions in the parties' and the judiciary's effort are equalized.

After verifying that $\partial F/\partial I$ is strictly negative, we can assume the existence of the welfare-maximizing value I^*. I further assume that when one party's level of effort increases, the effect of this change on the marginal social benefit from that party's effort is (negative and) greater in magnitude than the effect of this change on the marginal social benefit of its opponent's effort.[33] This assumption is quite innocuous and insures that social benefit cannot increase indefinitely as any party's level of effort continues to increase. This interior solution indicates that neither the pure inquisitorial system nor the pure adversarial system are likely to represent the social optimum. This may explain the gradual convergence of both procedural traditions towards mixed solutions. In common law jurisdictions, for example, the creation of very rigorous rules of evidence constrains the adversarial efforts of the parties and limits the wealth dissipation occasioned by adversarial litigation.[34] In civil law jurisdictions an increasing number of procedural choices are left, as a matter of judicial practice, to the motions of the litigants.

Having determined the existence of a maximum, we can proceed to study the comparative statics of the model. I will invoke the usual assumptions regarding the curvature of the cost functions (increasing marginal costs), and the curvature of the benefit function (decreasing marginal benefits).[35] I assume that all second partials are non-positive, so that the benefit function is concave. Regarding cross partials, I assume that increases in E_p raise the marginal benefit of E_d, increases in E_J raise the marginal benefit of E_p and E_d, and so on. This is because the efforts exerted by the judge and the parties are complementary in the sense that they shed light on the same truth. As the judge expends more effort in fact-finding, he is more likely to find evidence that confirms correct evidence presented by the parties, or negates bad evidence submitted by the parties. Thus, additional judicial effort increases the truth-finding benefit of the parties' effort. Similarly, increases in S cause the marginal truth-finding benefit of the parties' effort to increase. Recall that parties will exert less effort in litigation when S is higher, because their evidence is more likely to be thrown out. Thus, increasing S makes the parties less willing to input effort, even as it makes their efforts more valuable to society.[36] The level of scrutiny has no effect on the marginal social benefit of additional judicial fact-finding, since scrutiny is only directed at the parties' evidence. Finally, I assume that more visibility increases the marginal benefits of the parties' and the judge's effort. This is because mistakes in the formation or application of the law are more costly if they are known to more third parties and can thus affect more future dealings between such parties.

Under these assumptions, I use the Implicit Function Theorem to study how I^* varies with the other arguments of the welfare function (3.1). We can start by studying the impact of an increase in judicial scrutiny, S, on the optimal level of inquisitorial proceedings, I^*. Given our assumptions we can derive:

$$\frac{\partial F}{\partial S} = \frac{\partial^2 B}{\partial E_p \partial S}\frac{\partial E_p}{\partial I} + \frac{\partial^2 B}{\partial E_d \partial S}\frac{\partial E_d}{\partial I} + \left(\frac{\partial B}{\partial E_p} - C\right)\frac{\partial^2 E_p}{\partial I \partial S} + \left(\frac{\partial B}{\partial E_d} - C\right)\frac{\partial^2 E_d}{\partial I \partial S} \quad (3.3)$$

Since scrutiny increases the public marginal benefit of the parties' effort, and in equilibrium the parties will be exerting socially optimal effort levels, (3.3) is negative. Given that the

204   *F. Parisi / International Review of Law and Economics 22 (2002) 193–216*

second-order condition is strictly negative, we can determine that

$$\frac{\partial I^*}{\partial S} = \frac{-F_S}{F_I} < 0 \tag{3.4}$$

This indicates that with an increase in judicial scrutiny, the optimal institutional weight attached to the inquisitorial findings should diminish.[37] This result can be explained considering that, in the present context, judicial scrutiny and inquisitorial proceedings are substitutes. Litigants will consider an increase in the weight attached to inquisitorial evidence as qualitatively similar to an increased scrutiny by the court of the evidence they present. In either case, the private discovery of the parties becomes less valuable and the total private expenditures in litigation diminish.

Although this section explicitly considers only two parties to the case, the effect of changes in the number of litigants could be studied by extending (3.1) to include additional parties in both the social benefit function and the private cost function. As N increases, private incentives to engage in litigation expenditures will increase, as found in the previous section. Thus, we would find that the optimal I^* increases with the number of litigants, because the marginal social benefit of each party's expenditure falls as all parties spend more.

This suggests that greater reliance should be placed on court-obtained evidence in multiple-litigant cases, given the greater rate of dissipation of private resources in adversarial discovery. As shown in Section II, when more than two parties are competing for the appropriation of a fixed judicial award, the portion of the award that will be dissipated increases relative to the two-litigant case. Thus, an increased weight on inquisitorial evidence in multiple-party cases will minimize the social cost of litigation.

This result does not apply to the case of joint or class actions, where the multiple plaintiffs—having coordinated their collective action—should be viewed as a single entity, keeping N invariant. Likewise, this result does not apply (and the normative conclusions may indeed be reversed) for the case of multiple joint litigants with imperfect internal coordination. In this latter case, free-riding may indeed affect the private incentives to procure evidence, and a lower value of I (and consequential greater value of the "adversarial case") may be necessary to offset the diminished private incentives.

Additionally, we allowed only the private expenditure in litigation to vary with the number of litigants. If the administrative costs of adjudicating multiple-party cases were to increase at a faster rate than the total private costs of discovery, our result would no longer hold.

Proceeding in our analysis, we can study the effect of a change in the private cost of discovery and litigation on the choice of the optimal amount of inquisitorial procedures.

$$\frac{\partial F}{\partial C} = -\left(\frac{\partial E_p}{\partial I} + \frac{\partial E_d}{\partial I}\right) > 0 \tag{3.5}$$

Hence

$$\frac{\partial I^*}{\partial C} = \frac{-F_C}{F_I} < 0 \tag{3.6}$$

The results in (3.6) suggests that more reliance on court-obtained evidence should be placed with an increase in the private cost of discovery and litigation for the parties. In this case, higher

F. Parisi / International Review of Law and Economics 22 (2002) 193–216   205

private costs will reduce the privately optimal choice of discovery, and will also reduce the socially optimal level of litigation effort by the parties. Contrast this with a case in which private litigation costs are higher but this does not increase the social cost of litigation. For example, richer individuals have a higher value of time and thus it is more costly for them to pursue litigation. Nevertheless, the social cost of their time may not be greater than that of poorer individuals. In such a case, our results could be reversed. A lower value of I may become necessary to offset the diminished private incentives to procure evidence.

This result raises a question as to whether the judicial process is likely to become increasingly biased in favor of the rich against the poor. In general this may not be the case, once the mixed procedural system that results from Eq. (3.2) is compared to its alternatives. A pure adversary system depends to a much greater degree on effective advocacy.[38] The market for legal services ensures that those who are able to pay higher professional fees can attract more effective advocates.[39] A procedure which gives lesser weight to the adversarial efforts of the parties will, at the limit, facilitate access to the justice system for indigent individuals.

In the present model, the adversarial share of the judicial award, R_A, depends only on the procedural variable S, denoting judicial scrutiny of evidence presented by the parties. If the adversarial portion of the judgment was allowed to vary autonomously, an additional partial derivative would be necessary to study the effect of a change in R_A on the optimal choice of the institutional variable, I. The results would be quite intuitive. An increase in the value of the unsettled portion of the litigated case, R_A has an impact on the Nash levels of efforts found in (2.7). Given the presence of R_A solely in the numerator of the Nash values, a greater use of inquisitorial proceedings may be appropriate with an increase in the value of R_A. The result is consistent with the fundamental idea that the value of the rent dissipated through litigation is proportional to the value of the unsettled portion of the dispute.[40]

Analogous, unambiguous, results can be reached with respect to the other exogenous arguments of (3.1). I begin by considering the effects of notoriety, visibility and the social, political, or moral importance of the disputed issue, V. The effect of an increase in the visibility and social relevance of the case, V, on the optimal level of inquisitorial proceedings, I^*, can be studied by finding $\partial F/\partial V$. If we assume that $\partial E_{\text{adv}}/\partial I$ and $\partial E_{\text{adv}}/\partial I$ do not depend on V, we obtain:

$$\frac{\partial F}{\partial V} = 2\frac{\partial^2 B}{\partial E_{\text{adv}}\partial V}\frac{\partial E_{\text{adv}}}{\partial I} + \frac{\partial^2 B}{\partial E_J\partial V}\frac{\partial E_J}{\partial I} \tag{3.7}$$

Given our assumptions about the signs of cross partial derivatives and the effect of changes in I on the effort levels of the parties and the judge, the sign of (3.7) is theoretically ambiguous. This sign depends on whether visibility makes the parties' or the judge's effort relatively more beneficial to society. If, for example, we assume that the cross partial derivatives in (3.7) are roughly of the same size, then we would obtain:

$$\frac{\partial I^*}{\partial V} = \frac{-F_V}{F_I} < 0 \tag{3.8}$$

In other words, since visibility increases the marginal benefits from both the parties' and the judge's efforts, but lowering I increases the parties' effort more than it diminishes the judge's effort, the optimal level of I falls when visibility increases. Note that an increase in the visibility of the case affects the benefits from accurate adjudication. High profile and notorious cases have a greater impact on the general community. The accuracy of the adjudication process is thus more critical in such cases. The social sense of justice may be more seriously offended by the wrongful decision of a publicly known case. In addition, the creation of an erroneous legal rule can affect the incentives of private parties to invest or to enter into beneficial contracts. Due to the importance of precedent in many legal systems, incorrect rules formulated by the court tend to cause persistent error in the adjudication of other cases. Many of these adverse effects of wrong decisions are exacerbated by high visibility and publicity. The reader should note that the current model treats visibility, V, as analytically independent of R_A, which represents only the portion of the case the adjudication of which rests on the adversarial evidence provided by the parties. By relaxing this simplifying assumption, and creating some interaction between the visibility of the case, V, and the value of the unsettled share of the judgement, R_A, more ambiguity in signing (3.7) would be generated.

A similar conclusion holds with respect to cases involving important moral, political or social issues. An increase in the moral or social importance of the litigated issue increases the importance of an accurate adjudication. To the extent that a precise assessment of the factual circumstances is relevant for the outcome of such issues, the accuracy of the discovery and adjudication process becomes more critical in the resolution of this group of disputes. Put differently, the forward-looking function of judicial decision making may be more seriously compromised by the wrongful decision of a politically or socially important issue.

An alternative interpretation of (3.8) would consider the different benefits associated with accurate adjudication in criminal and civil cases. Higher competition in providing evidence and greater adversarial scrutiny of the evidence offered by the other party lessen the possibility of convicting an innocent person and increase the possibility that the guilty may escape conviction. By keeping the barriers to conviction high, as mandated by the adversary system, the costs associated with wrongful convictions are minimized. As observed by Damaska (1983), where this is recognized, proponents of the adversary system accord decisive weight to liberal values. Type I and Type II errors in adjudication are regarded as having socially different costs, thus making it preferable to let a larger number of the guilty go free than to convict a smaller number of innocent persons.[41]

The above argument explains the stronger emphasis on adversarial proceedings in criminal rather than civil cases. Unlike the criminal law scenario, Type I and Type II judicial errors have symmetric social costs in most civil law disputes. Assuming non-systematic bias, errors of either type only bring about a transfer of wealth between the litigants and the incentives of the parties remain unaltered. If litigants are risk averse, some social loss is occasioned due to the parties' uncertainty, and such loss would have to be balanced against the additional litigation costs that would be induced by a greater use of adversarial proceedings.

Finally, I consider the effect of a change in ϕ, the parameter measuring judicial efficiency in fact-finding, on the optimal level of inquisitorial proceedings, I^*. In this case the result is straightforward. The variable ϕ captures the direct and indirect changes in the administrative cost of non-adversarial discovery. Actually ϕ denotes the level of administrative inefficiency: higher levels of ϕ imply higher marginal social cost of judicial discovery. The effect of a change in ϕ on the choice of optimal level of non-adversarial discovery, I^*, can be studied by

F. Parisi / International Review of Law and Economics 22 (2002) 193–216   207

deriving:

$$\frac{\partial F}{\partial \phi} = -\frac{\partial^2 C_J}{\partial E_J \partial \phi}\frac{\partial E_J}{\partial I} < 0 \tag{3.9}$$

This means that

$$\frac{\partial I^*}{\partial \phi} = \frac{-F_\phi}{F_I} < 0 \tag{3.10}$$

This indicates that more non-adversarial discovery may be appropriate with an increase in the efficiency of the courts in the procurement and evaluation of evidence, other things being equal. The last result is self-explanatory. If the court system has a comparative advantage in the use of specialized technology or information, greater court involvement in the discovery process may be desirable.[42] Conversely, if the specialized or trade-specific nature of the evidence renders the judicial involvement too costly or inefficacious, greater reliance on the adversarial efforts of the litigants may be appropriate.

4. Costs of the adversarial system

While practitioners from both civil and common law jurisdictions appear to be content with their procedural system, legal scholars continue their debate on the theoretical and policy implications of alternative discovery systems. Comparative scholars suggest that inquisitorial and adversarial systems have gradually converged towards mixed solutions, but procedural differences still remain marked. In the intellectual debate, different rationales have been invoked in support of one or the other procedural systems, including private autonomy of the litigants and historical tradition (for the case of adversarial procedure), and neutral truth-finding and economy in adjudication (for the case of inquisitorial procedure).

Adversarial civil procedure is viewed as consistent with the principles of personal liberty and equality that so strongly permeate the American ideal of justice,[43] and is often lauded as vital to the protection of American democracy and freedom.[44] According to Damaska (1983), the adversary system is lauded because of its competitive style of presenting evidence and argument, which is thought to produce a more accurate result than its inquisitorial alternative, with the judge monopolizing the discovery process. Along similar lines, Hazard (1978) observed that a judge who is involved in the discovery process can hardly keep an open mind and lacks sufficient incentives to do a proper job in the finding of facts.[45] In this setting, firm adherence to the adversarial approach is viewed as the best antidote against possible invasions of the personal autonomy of the parties by the constituted judicial authority.[46]

In this setting, it is often believed that the contrast between the adversarial and the inquisitorial procedural systems stems from two antithetic views about the role of government in society, contemplating, respectively, a "reactive" and a "proactive" system of government.[47] According to this view of the adversarial proceeding, the judge should come into action only to resolve disputes between the contending parties.

This paper has examined some of the features associated with adversarial judicial process, contrasting it with the results obtained under the non-adversarial procedure adopted in the civil law tradition. The results obtained in Parts II and III of this paper challenge the common idealization of adversary procedure.[48] The arguments in favor of the adversary procedure analogize the efforts of the litigants to the competition that takes place in the market for goods. The analogy between the adversary procedure and a competitive market, however, underestimates the rent-seeking dynamic of the litigation process.

For the most part, litigants compete over the division of a fixed resource (represented by the value R_A in our model). Unlike the efforts of two competitors in the marketplace, the efforts of two litigants are not capable of increasing the value of the litigated asset, R_A, and often cause a dissipation of a good portion of its net value. Indeed, the analogy between the adversary procedure and a competitive auction fails to consider the fact that, unlike an auction (in which only the highest bidder is bound to pay), litigation creates positive rent-seeking costs for each litigant. In litigation, each party has to bear the full private cost of his or her rent-seeking activity, even though only the prevailing party captures the residual value of the litigated asset, R_A. In this respect, the analogy should be revisited in light of the rent-seeking element of real world litigation. A more appropriate analogy could be drawn between litigation efforts and the advertising efforts of two competitors. Most advertising expenditures, presumably, are mutually offsetting, just like most litigation expenditures in an adversary system. Indeed, we could argue that litigation expenditures are to judicial decisions as advertising expenditures are to consumer decisions.

As illustrated earlier, the rent-seeking analysis unveils an important characteristic of the adversarial system, namely the exacerbation of the incentives for rent dissipation through litigation. The paper suggests that the adversary system conduces rent-seeking because the expenditures of each party are determined by the private rather than the social cost of winning. The comparative statics of the problem reveal that the rent dissipation problem is exacerbated with an increase in the value of the unsettled component of the disputed case, and an increase in the number of litigants with competing claims on a fixed award. Conversely, the dissipation is reduced with an increase in the involvement of the judge in the fact-finding process. The judge who gathers the facts soon comes to know the case as well as the involved parties, and will be able to concentrate its subsequent fact-finding efforts toward more important and still unresolved factual issues. As shown in this paper, the weight attached to the adversarial discovery affects the degree to which parties' efforts can influence the outcome of the case. Thus, the judge's direct involvement in the fact-finding has obvious implications for procedural economy, reducing the marginal incentives for the parties' adversarial efforts, and possibly facilitating the settlement of the case.

In this context, several arguments can be formulated to complement the classical hands-off approach to adjudication. Just as legal systems play an important role in correcting economic market failures, so a judge may play a valuable institutional role in redressing the rent-dissipating competition of the parties during a trial.[49] This conclusion poses the difficult question as to how far the judge can go in his intervention without negatively affecting the incentives of the litigants and the successful functioning of the adversary system.[50]

Undoubtedly, in a world characterized by contentious litigation and discovery, the minimization of the rent-seeking component represents only one argument in a more complex social welfare function. The normative analysis of this paper has examined some trade-offs between the costs and benefits of adversarial discovery and litigation. Most importantly, adversarial

F. Parisi / International Review of Law and Economics 22 (2002) 193–216   209

efforts may have a direct social value, insofar as they make the tribunal better informed about the case and therefore increase the likelihood of a correct decision. The social benefits from accurate decision making may further vary with the degree of visibility of the case and the social or political relevance of the litigated issue. Likewise, the private and social costs of litigation may be affected by a change in the relative costs of discovery for courts and private litigants.

The analysis could usefully be enriched by other important institutional considerations in order to yield a valid assessment of the respective merits of each procedure. For example, rent-seeking expenditures will be factored in the parties' decision to pursue litigation. The more costly litigation is, the less of it there will be. If there are negative externalities, from high levels of litigation, rent-seeking expenditures would generate a social benefit, given the reduction in the number of litigated cases. Furthermore, it is conceivable that the parties' acceptance of the judgment is facilitated where the parties are permitted to exercise greater control over discovery and procedure.

These theoretical results should be further examined in light of empirical data. Most of the empirical studies compare the efficiency of the adversary system with the inquisitorial alternative by testing the relative efficacy of those procedures in overcoming the decision-maker's bias and inducing reliable truth-finding.[51] Additional empirical evidence will be necessary to test the predictions of this paper regarding the different levels of litigation expenditure under the two procedural regimes.

One final consideration, which has been only briefly sketched in the preceding analysis, should examine the conditions under which an adversarial procedure guarantees an equal and effective representation to the parties. The conclusions of this paper should not be read to endorse ad hoc balancing between the inquisitorial and adversarial components of the process as a way to compensate for parties' differential wealth or access to legal representation. In cases involving indigent individuals, it may be better to pursue equal access to justice through counterbalancing procedures other than an increased role for judges in discovery. Given the availability of more neutral and cost-effective means for promoting equal representation, the determination of the optimal level of inquisitorial efforts should be based on the objective values indicated above and should not be influenced by the need to provide legal aid to unrepresented parties.

Notes

1. In a recent paper, Glaser and Shleifer (2001) have suggested that the inquisitorial system developed in France as an instrument for the protection of law enforcers from coercion by litigants through either violence or bribes. The higher the risk of coercion, the greater the need for protection and control of law enforcers by the state. According to the authors, this explains why, in the twelfth and thirteenth centuries, the relatively more peaceful England developed trials by jury, while the less peaceful France relied on state-employed judges for both collecting evidence and making decisions. Despite considerable legal evolution, these initial design choices have persisted for centuries, explaining many differences between common and civil law procedural traditions.

2. Bartolus a Saxoferrato (1313–1357), Comment to C. 9.42.2, no. 2, fol. 124: "Judex tamen potest ex officio suo testes producere ad inquirendam veritatem."

210   *F. Parisi / International Review of Law and Economics 22 (2002) 193–216*

3. Baldus de Ubaldis (1327–1400), most notably, in Comment to C. 4.20.19, no. 3, fol. 53: "In examinandis testibus officium judicis debbe esse curiosum, id est, judex debet esse solicitus et ad curam judicis pertinet hoc scil. examinare, unde hoc non est in potestate parties."

4. Baldus de Ubaldis (1327–1400), Comment to C. 1.3.8, no. 8, fol. 37: "Pone, quod testes non sunt producti, sed judex ex mero officio recipit eos."

5. Damaska (1997) observes: "The interaction with the accused constantly injected disputational, 'altercating' notes into proceedings—long before the admission of lawyers to felony trials gave rise to the adversary criminal trial as we now know it." (p. 118).

6. On the theoretical underpinning of this debate, see, more extensively, Damaska (1997, p. 101).

7. Hazard and Taruffo (1993) observe that: "The advocate conducts the pretrial discovery against the opposing party. This involves taking the depositions of potential witnesses, including the opposing party, and identifying and inspecting relevant documents in the opposing party's possession. In complicated business litigation, thousands of such documents must be reviewed and analyzed. Discovery may require weeks or months of the advocate's effort, sometimes over the course of years before the anticipated trial date." (p. 88).

8. This paper considers the adversary common law process as it relates to civil proceedings. The dogma of adversarial discovery is equally applicable to the criminal proceedings in common law jurisdictions: "The principles announced today deal with the protection which must be given to the privilege against self-incrimination. .... It is at this point that our adversary system of criminal proceedings commences, distinguishing itself at the outset from the inquisitorial system recognized in some countries." (Miranda v. Arizona, 1966, 384 U.S. 436, 477).

9. More generally, see Pound (1906), Cappelletti and Perillo (1965), Damaska (1986), Gerber (1986), Herzog (1967), Kaplan (1960), Kaplan et al. (1958), Taruffo (1979) for a comparative analysis of the different approaches to the administration of justice in the civil law and common law traditions.

10. See Chayes (1976) for a stylized description of the role of the judge in U.S. litigation.

11. See Landsman (1983) for a more detailed description of the adversarial system and a discussion of its development in the United States.

12. See, e.g., Article 427 of the French Code of Criminal Procedure.

13. According to Weigend (1983), comparative legal scholars usually consider the French criminal procedure as the prototype of the inquisitorial model, where judges enjoy full discretionary power in the examination of the evidence. The same principles apply in the Japanese and Spanish systems, even though evidence is presented by the parties. Japanese criminal procedure law originally followed the model of the French and German codes, but after Word War II, American procedural principles were superimposed on its inquisitorial structure.

14. Langbein (1985) describes the concepts of "defendant's case" and "plaintiff's case" as traffic rules for the for the partisan presentation of evidence to an ignorant and passive trier of facts.

15. For a description of the German inquisitorial approach, see Langbein (1985).

F. Parisi / International Review of Law and Economics 22 (2002) 193–216   211

16. The civil law judge often takes initiative for gathering additional evidence, and reviews the evidence presented by the parties in detail—recapitulating it prior to reaching a decision. In most jurisdictions this authority is conservatively exercised. Hazard and Taruffo (1993) observe that, in practice, neither system fully corresponds to its theoretical model: "In the civil law system the judge has dominant authority to determine the legal theory to be applied, but the judge is highly dependent on the parties for presentation of the evidence. Common law judges have authority to initiate inquiry into the evidence but rarely exercise it. In this sense, both systems depend on adversary presentations so far as the facts are concerned, notwithstanding the theoretical differences between their conceptions of the judge's role." (p. 86).

17. See Damaska (1997, p. 100).

18. Froeb and Kobayashi (2000) suggest that the advantage of the adversarial regime of judicial decision-making is the superior information of the parties while the advantage of an idealized inquisitorial regime is its neutrality. The authors characterize the properties of the estimators utilized under the two evidence regimes, analogizing the decision making process under an adversarial system to an "extremal" estimator based on the difference between the most favorable pieces of evidence produced by each party; conversely, the inquisitorial system is analogized to an unbiased sample mean. The authors find that neither regime dominates the other. In a previous paper, Froeb and Kobayashi (1996) consider an additional critique often moved to the adversarial process, namely the use of juries and lay fact finders. The authors suggest that the criticisms of the jury process based on jury bias is often overstated, and stress the importance of competitively produced evidence in legal decision-making.

19. See, for example, Damaska (1986, pp. 3–6).

20. Until recent years, comparative legal scholars have refused to theorize on the respective merits of the two systems. The analysis involved too many legal dogmas and intellectual beliefs and any comparative evaluation would have appeared, on the whole, quite suspect. Even on purely methodological grounds, differences of opinion dominate. Jorg, Field, and Brants (1995). While agreeing that real world adversarial and inquisitorial systems of (criminal) procedure are converging and do not follow their ideal types, Jorg et al. observe that the systems' basic ideologies about truth seeking are different enough that they could never converge entirely, nor present an entirely continuous set of systems.

21. In a recent paper, Posner (1999, p. 16) argues that the use of amateur judges (the jurors) in the typical adversarial proceeding makes it difficult to situate the adversarial system on a continuum with the inquisitorial. For the purpose of this paper, I will consider the features of the adversary system as independent of the use of a jury. This will allow us to use a single continuous variable to characterize the adversarial or inquisitorial nature of the process.

22. Braeutigam, Owen, and Panzar (1984) have utilized a similar approach to study the different equilibrium expenditures at trial under the English and American rules, for the recovery of legal fees. Hause (1989) followed the same approach considering asymmetric beliefs and probabilities. Most recently, Farmer and Pecorino (1997) have modeled

endogenous legal expenditures utilizing a rent-seeking framework for the study of the institution of fee shifting.

23. With similar consequences, in Posner (1973), a relative increase in litigation spending merely reduced the opponents' probability of winning. For further examples of rent-seeking functions, see Tullock (1996), Congleton (1980), Tollison and Congleton (1995).

24. The zero-sum constraint implies that, setting aside costs of litigation, $\partial R_p / \partial I + \partial R_d / \partial I = 0$. The implicit relationship between R_I, R_A, and I, allows for a fixed share coefficient of the type $J = IR_I + (1 - I)R_A$, but is not limited to it. Indeed, there may be a correlation between the judgment level J and the degree of adversary litigation. The variability of total J with respect to I may indeed be necessary to account for the (fragmentary) evidence offered by comparative legal scholars regarding the different measures of pecuniary judicial awards in the American and European legal traditions.

25. In this section, the choice of procedure is treated as an institutional variable and not as a choice variable for the litigants. In the following section, the normative analysis will consider the optimal procedural choice, treating I as an institutional choice variable.

26. Again, the same results hold in a winner-takes-all system where the parties' respective probabilities of success are proportional to their shares of effort.

27. Similar results are obtained studying the sign of the second derivative of (2.8) which represents the multiple-agent version of (2.2) and (2.3).

28. These results could be obtained with equal simplicity by inspection of (2.9).

29. The result of (2.14) holds only if the N litigants compete for the adjudication of a mutually exclusive benefit. If the various actors litigate a joint claim with a common award, free-riding may undermine their private incentives to litigate. Thus, the opposite result $\partial L / \partial N = -H_N / H_E < 0$ may hold if the N actors are litigating a common cause in the presence of free-riding.

30. Most recently, Posner (1999) recognizes this point observing that: "privatizing the search (as in the adversarial system) may result in too much or too little evidence from a social standpoint ... whereas in principle ... the inquisitorial judge can continue his search for evidence until he reaches the point at which marginal cost and marginal benefit intersect and he can stop right there."

31. On this point, see also Palumbo (1998) and Posner (1999).

32. The present model contemplates civil disputes. In extending it to other categories, one should keep in mind that the objective benefit function, B, is likely to differ between civil and criminal cases, in that inaccurate decisions may be socially more costly for criminal cases than civil cases. Thus, *ceteris paribus*, adversarial proceedings may be more appropriate in criminal cases. This conclusion is at odds with the comparative findings of Damaska (1997) who notes that, in spite of its inquisitorial tradition, Continental civil law systems tend to give a relatively greater control to the parties in civil cases, preserving the original inquisitorial approach in criminal proceedings. The author (Damaska, 1997, p. 112) explains this paradox on the basis of the greater need for expeditious adjudication of criminal cases.

F. Parisi / International Review of Law and Economics 22 (2002) 193–216

33. In addition to our assumption about how judicial effort is chosen, we need to assume that

$$\left| \frac{\partial^2 B}{\partial E_p^2} \right| = \left| \frac{\partial^2 B}{\partial E_d^2} \right| > \left| \frac{\partial^2 B}{\partial E_p \partial E_d} \right|.$$

34. Posner (1999, p. 17) considers Rule 403 of the Federal Rules of Evidence and hearsay rules as examples of evidence law limiting the cost of discovery in an adversary system. The author further observes that the more limited weight given to party obtained evidence by inquisitorial systems allows greater flexibility in the continental European rules of evidence.

35. This ensures that the existence of a positive term in the second-order condition does not undermine its overall negative sign in the neighborhood of I^*, so that the first-order condition identifies a maximum in the welfare function (3.1).

36. In the previous section, we assumed that the parties choose their effort levels independently of the level of judicial effort. In other words, both the parties' and the judge's effort levels depend on I, with opposite signs, but they do not depend directly upon each other. Practically, this is equivalent to assuming that private and judicial expenditures in discovery are strategic substitutes. This assumption is plausible if an increase in judicial inquisition decreases the private returns on the parties' evidence. If we were to assume that judicial and private efforts were strategic complements, lesser weight to adversarial evidence would be necessary to confine the excessive expenditures in litigation. Furthermore, in an adversarial system, sufficiently high coefficients of complementarity may generate total expenditures that exceed the value of the case. In those situations, the participation constraint of the parties would be violated and, given an exit option for the parties, litigation would not be undertaken in equilibrium.

37. This result is complementary to the common concern that judicial activism risks compromising the outcome-neutrality of the judicial process (see Wechsler, 1959). But see Hasnas (1995, p. 201), stating that: "[T]he frequent condemnation of the judiciary for 'undemocratic judicial activism' ... is merely a reflection of the public's belief that the law consists of a set of definite and consistent 'neutral principles' which the judge is obligated to apply in an objective manner ... [even] in the face of overwhelming evidence to the contrary." Hasnas calls this a fiction and labels it "the myth of the rule of law." Other scholars share this concern, suggesting that when a judge becomes too enamored with the merits of a case, he may be induced to evaluate the evidence or the legal basis of the case through colored lenses, extending procedural advantages to one party or giving lesser weight to the evidence provided by the opposing party: "the deference accorded admissibility determinations and the existence of inconsistent rules regarding the admissibility of certain [social science] theories allows judges leeway to engage in judicial activism." Because "many social science theories generally favor one side," a judge with a personal bias can make results-oriented admissibility decisions (Etlinger, 1995, p. 1278).

38. "In our adversary system the strength with which each side is able to present its case depends in large part on the freedom to ascertain and present to the trier of fact all relevant evidence." (van Kessel, 1992, p. 420).

214   F. Parisi / International Review of Law and Economics 22 (2002) 193–216

39. The market for legal services can also provide "litigation-biased expert witnesses that American lawyers recruit and pay to bolster preordained results." (Langbein, 1988, p. 764).

40. An increase in the value of R_A, however, may be correlated to the general visibility of the case, V. This may create some indeterminacy in our results. High stake cases, being more visible by the general public, could benefit from a more adversarial procedure, insofar as such procedure makes the tribunal better informed about the case and therefore increases the likelihood of a correct decision. Thus, high stake cases may justify greater litigation expenditures given the greater social benefits of a correct decision. The point was noted by Judge Richard Posner whose comments on an earlier draft have been very valuable for the development of this section.

41. For further analysis, see Damaska (1983, p. 26).

42. Consistent with this predicament, Erichson (1999) examines recent developments in mass tort litigation, suggesting that there has been an evolutionary shift in the direction of inquisitorial justice systems such as those of certain civil law countries. Court-appointed experts and judicial inquiry into settlement class actions resemble inquisitorial tools.

43. See Hazard and Taruffo (1993, p. 101).

44. For a more extensive discussion of the merits of the adversary system, see Hazard and Taruffo (1993, pp. 101–104).

45. See Hazard (1978, p. 121).

46. See the Jackson opinion in Hickman v. Taylor (1947), 329 U.S. 495, 516.

47. See, e.g., Goldstein (1974).

48. See also Sward's (1988) "demystifying" of the adversarial ideology, in which she endorses a more inquisitorial approach as a means of increasing the efficiency of American adjudication.

49. For further discussion, see Fuller (1961, p. 41).

50. For a more extensive discussion, see Damaska (1983, pp. 25–26).

51. Those studies often suggest that, since the adversary model requires the judge to listen passively to both sides of the case before making a decision, he would be less likely to become prematurely biased and draw a conclusion too early (see Damaska, 1983; Thibaut & Walker, 1975; Sheppard & Vidmar, 1980).

Acknowledgments

I am indebted to Richard Posner, Ugo Mattei, Roger Congleton, Joyce Sadka, and an anonymous referee for extensive comments on earlier drafts. This article is dedicated to my third child, Elvira Caterina.

References

Adams, M. A. (1998). Civil procedure in the USA and civil law countries. In P. Newman (Ed.), *The new Palgrave dictionary of economics and the law*. London, UK: Macmillan Reference Ltd.

F. Parisi / International Review of Law and Economics 22 (2002) 193–216   215

Braeutigam, R. B., Owen, B., & Panzar, J. (1984). An economic analysis of alternative fee shifting systems. *Law and Contemporary Problems, 47,* 173–185.

Cappelletti, M., & Perillo, J. (1965). *Civil procedure in Italy.* The Hague: Martinus Nijhoff Publisher.

Chayes, A. (1976). The role of the judge in public litigation. *Harvard Law Review, 89,* 1281.

Congleton, R. D. (1980). Competitive process, competitive waste, and institutions. In J. M. Buchanan, R. D. Tollison, & G. Tullock (Eds.), *Toward a theory of the rent-seeking society.* College Station, TX: Texas A&M University Press.

Damaska, M. (1983). *Adversary system. Encyclopedia of crime and justice.* New York, NY: Macmillan Publishing.

Damaska, M. R. (1986). *The faces of justice and state authority. A comparative approach to the legal process.* New Haven, CT: Yale University Press.

Damaska, M. R. (1997). *Evidence law adrift.* New Haven, CT: Yale University Press.

Erichson, H. M. (1999) Mass tort litigation and inquisitorial justice. *Georgetown Law Journal* 87.

Etlinger, L. (1995). Note: Social science research in domestic violence law: A proposal to focus on evidentiary use. *Albany Law Review, 58,* 1259.

Farmer, A., & Pecorino, P. (1997, July). *Legal expenditures as a rent-seeking game.* Unpublished manuscript.

Froeb, L., & Kobayashi, B. H. (1996). Naive, biased, yet Bayesian: Can juries interpret selectively produced evidence? *Journal of Law, Economics and Organization, 12,* 257–277.

Froeb, L., & Kobayashi, B. H. (2000). *Evidence production in adversarial vs. inquisitorial regimes.* Vanderbilt Law School, Joe C. Davis Working Paper No. 99-13.

Fuller, L. L. (1961). In H. J. Berman (Ed.), *The adversary system: Talks on American law.* New York: Random House, Vintage Books.

Gerber, D. J. (1986). Extraterritorial discovery and the conflict of procedural systems: Germany and the United States. *American Journal of Comparative Law, 34,* 745–766.

Glaser, E. L., & Shleifer, A. (2001). *Legal origins.* Harvard Institute of Economic Research Paper No. 1920.

Goldstein, A. (1974). Reflections on two models: Inquisitorial themes in American criminal procedure. *Stanford Law Review, 26,* 1009–1025.

Hasnas, J. (1995). The myth of the rule of law. *Wisconsin Law Review, 1995,* 199.

Hause, J. C. (1989). Indemnity settlement, and litigation, and litigation, or I'll be suing you. *Journal of Legal Studies, 18,* 157–179.

Hazard, G. C., Jr., & Taruffo, M. (1993). *American civil procedure: An introduction.* New Haven, CT: Yale University Press.

Herzog, P. E. (1967). *Civil procedure in France.* The Hague: Martinus Nijhoff Publisher.

Hickman v. Taylor (1947), 329 U.S. 495.

Jorg, F., & Brants (1995). Are inquisitorial and adversarial systems converging? In Harding, Fennell, Jorg, & Swart (Eds.), *Criminal justice in Europe. A comparative study.* Oxford, Clarendon Press.

Kaplan, B. (1960). Civil procedure—Reflections on the comparison of systems. *Buffalo Law Review, 9,* 409.

Kaplan, B., von Mehren, A. T., & Schaefer, R. (1958). Phases of German civil procedure, Parts I and II. *Harvard Law Review, 71,* 1193 and 1443.

Landsman, S. A. (1983). A brief survey of the development of the adversary system. *Ohio State Law Journal, 44,* 713.

Langbein, J. H. (1985). The German advantage in civil procedure. *University of Chicago Law Review, 52,* 823.

Langbein, J. H. (1988). Trashing the German advantage. *Northwestern University Law Review, 82,* 763.

Miranda v. Arizona (1996), 384 U.S. 436.

Palumbo, G. (1998, June). *Optimal "excessive" litigation in adversarial systems.* ECARE, Université Libre de Bruxelles, Working Paper No. 98-01.

Pound, R. (1906). *The causes of popular dissatisfaction with the administration of justice* (pp. 395–408). Report of the 29th Annual Meeting of the American Bar Association. Philadelphia: Dando.

Posner, R. A. (1973). An economic approach to legal procedure and judicial administration. *Journal of Legal Studies, 2,* 399.

Posner, R. A. (1988). Comment: Responding to Gordon Tullock. *Research in Law and Policy Studies, 2,* 29.

Posner, R. A. (1999, February). *An economic approach to the law of evidence.* Chicago Working Papers in Law & Economics No. 66 (2nd Series).

Sheppard, B. H., & Vidmar, N. (1980). Adversary pretrial procedures and testimonial evidence: Effect of lawyer's role and Machiavellianism. *Journal of Personality and Social Psychology, 39*, 320–332.

Sward, E. E. (1988). Values, ideology and the evolution of the adversary system. *Indiana Law Journal, 64*, 301.

Taruffo, M. (1979). *Il processo civile "adversary" nell'Esperienza Americana.* Padua, Italy: Cedam Publishing.

Thibaut, J. W., & Walker, L. (1975). *Procedural justice: A psychological analysis.* Hillsdale, NJ: Laurence Erlbaum Associates.

Tollison, R. D., & Congleton, R. D. (1995). *The economic analysis of rent-seeking.* Aldershot, UK: Edward Elgar Publishing Ltd.

Tullock, G. (1988). Defending the Napoleonic code over the common law. *Research in Law and Policy Studies, 2*, 3–27.

Tullock, G. (1996). *The case against the common law* (1 Blackstone Commentaries Series). Durham, NC: Carolina Academic Press.

Walter, U. (1946). Medieval principles of evidence. *Law Quarterly Review, 62*, 78. Reprinted in Walter Ulmann, Law and Jurisdiction in the Middle Ages, (London: Variorum Reprints, 1988).

van Kessel, G. (1992). Adversary excesses in the American criminal trial. *Notre Dame Law Review, 67*, 403.

Wechsler, H. (1959). Toward neutral principles of constitutional law. *Harvard Law Review, 73*, 1.

Weigend, T. (1983). *Criminal procedure. Encyclopedia of crime and justice.* New York, NY: Macmillan Publishing.

The Economic Journal, 115 (*July*), 583–601. © Royal Economic Society 2005. Published by Blackwell Publishing, 9600 Garsington Road, Oxford OX4 2DQ, UK and 350 Main Street, Malden, MA 02148, USA.

COMPARATIVE ANALYSIS OF LITIGATION SYSTEMS: AN AUCTION-THEORETIC APPROACH*

Michael R. Baye, Dan Kovenock and Casper G. de Vries

A simple auction-theoretic framework is used to examine symmetric litigation environments where the legal ownership of a disputed asset is unknown to the court. The court observes only the quality of the case presented by each party, and awards the asset to the party presenting the best case. Rational litigants influence the quality of their cases by hiring skilful attorneys. This framework permits us to compare the equilibrium legal expenditures that arise under a continuum of legal systems. The British rule, Continental rule, American rule, and some recently proposed legal reforms are special cases of our model.

Why is the US internationally scorned as the 'litigious society?' Are judicial reforms, such as those proposed by the President's Council on Competitiveness, justified or misguided? More generally, can one rank the legal expenditures induced by legal systems such as the American, British, and Continental rules, and if so, do systems that result in lower expenditures per trial necessarily reduce the social cost of litigation? This paper uses an auction-theoretic framework to address these and other questions.

Our article is motivated in part by the growing policy debate over the need for reform of the American justice system.[1] For instance, as early as 1991 the President's Council on Competitiveness (chaired at that time by Vice President Dan Quayle), proposed to modify the American legal system (in which all litigants pay their own legal expenditures) by requiring that the loser reimburse the winner for legal fees up to the amount actually spent by the loser.[2] The rationale for the proposed 'Quayle system' was that it would reduce legal expenditures and the number of cases brought to court, since every dollar the loser paid its attorneys would ultimately result in two dollars paid by the loser. Other legal systems (such as the British and Continental rules), also require losers to compensate winners for a portion of their legal costs.[3]

More recently, the 2004 edition of the *Economic Report of the President* devoted an entire chapter to the issue of tort reform, and noted that Americans collectively

---

* A preliminary version of this article, entitled 'Fee Allocation of Legal Services in Litigation', was presented at the Tinbergen Institute Conference on Contests. We are grateful to Yeon-Koo Che, Paul Klemperer, David de Meza, John Morgan, and the referees for comments that have substantially improved this paper. Kovenock has benefitted from the financial support of the Wissenschaftszentrum Berlin fur Sozialforschung. Baye thanks his colleagues at Trinity College Cambridge, Nuffield College Oxford and the University of Bonn for their hospitality during visits when this revision was completed.

[1] A number of recent papers provide important insights into the impact of reforms designed to deter frivolous suits (Che and Earnhart, 1997; Bebchuk and Chang, 1996; Polinsky and Rubinfeld, 1996, 1998) or affect settlement incentives (Spier,1994; Gong and McAfee, 2000).

[2] This was proposed in the Council's *Agenda for Civil Justice Reform in America*,1991.

[3] Under the 'classic' interpretation of the British system; see, for example, Hughes and Snyder (1995), the loser pays its own legal costs and, in addition, reimburses the winner for all of its costs. The Continental system requires the loser to pay its own legal costs, plus a fixed fraction of the winner's legal fees. Note that under this interpretation, the British system may be viewed as a limiting case of the Continental system.

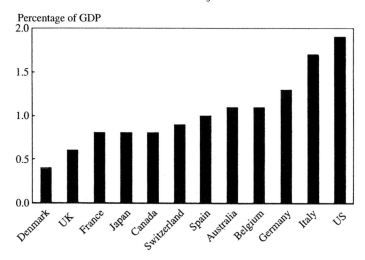

Fig. 1. *Tort Expenditures as a Percentage of GDP.*
Source: Economic Report of the President, 2004

spend more than twice as much on tort expenditures than they spend on new automobiles. As shown in Figure 1, these litigation expenditures (as a percentage of GDP) are over 3 times greater than those in the UK, and are significantly higher than those in other industrialised countries. The *per capita* number of suits filed in the US is also comparatively high. On an annual basis, 3.3 tort suits are filed in the US for each 1,000 inhabitants, compared to only 1.2 per 1,000 in England (see Posner, 1997).

In modelling litigation, simplifying assumptions are typically made to facilitate the analysis. One approach, common to the literature on pre-trial negotiation and settlement, assumes that legal expenditures during a trial do not have any effect on the trial's outcome. For instance, Spier (1992) assumes that it is costly for a plaintiff to go to court but that these costs do not influence the court's decision. In her model, the plaintiff always wins, but the amount won is a random variable from a distribution $f(v)$ with a strictly increasing hazard rate, $f/(1 - F)$. Reinganum and Wilde (1986) and Schweizer (1989) consider models in which both the plaintiff and defendant might win but the probability of winning is exogenous and independent of the legal expenditures of the parties. While these modelling assumptions are useful for understanding why parties in a dispute have an incentive to settle out of court rather than going to trial, they do not permit a comparative analysis of the equilibrium legal expenditures that arise in situations where parties can improve their chances of winning a trial by hiring better attorneys or experts.

Another approach, called the optimism model (Hughes and Snyder, 1995), assumes that each party has exogenous beliefs regarding the merits of their case. These beliefs determine not only whether the parties settle, but also the expected payoff to each party from a trial. Hughes and Snyder conclude that, for exogenously given legal expenditures per trial and exogenous subjective probabilities of winning a case, the British rule leads to lower total legal outlays than the American system.

Our analysis differs from this existing literature in that we endogenise parties' decisions to go to trial as well their expenditures on legal representation. Specifically, we examine a non-cooperative game where parties in the dispute rationally choose whether to settle or go to trial. In the absence of pre-trial settlement, the parties go to court and can influence the observable merit of their respective sides of the case (and thus their probabilities of winning) by purchasing legal services. Thus, unlike the existing literature which assumes either that there is an *a priori* 'correct' verdict or that the probability of winning is independent of the quality of legal services purchased by the litigants, we examine the *equilibrium* expenditures that arise under various legal systems. Equilibrium requires, among other things, that expenditures on legal services be based on rational beliefs regarding the probability of winning: Subjective beliefs are correct in equilibrium.

As we will see, these modelling differences enable us to use auction-theoretic tools to examine how rational litigants respond to the incentives created by various fee-shifting rules.[4] In addition, we are able to examine the impact of asymmetric information on equilibrium litigation expenditures and outcomes under a continuum of legal settings, including the Quayle system. This is in contrast to existing work that provides pair-wise comparisons of the American and British rules (Shavell, 1982; Braeutigam *et al.*, 1984), or models such as those by Cooter and Rubinfeld (1989) and Hause (1989) which are based on different informational and/or rationality assumptions.

Our simple model also sheds light on two competing views of the justice system. One view, held by many Americans, is that winners and losers in court cases are determined by how much the parties spend on high-priced attorneys – not on the intrinsic merits of the case. At the other extreme is the view that the amount paid to an attorney is irrelevant; all that matters is the quality of the case presented at trial. We show that these two views need not be inconsistent.

More specifically, we examine the symmetric equilibrium of a litigation game where

(1) legal expenditures increase the quality of the case presented;
(2) the party putting forth the best case wins, and
(3) litigation costs are neither subsidised nor taxed in the aggregate.

We then show that, taking into account the expected payoffs that arise conditional on litigation, there is a sort of 'prisoner's dilemma' that induces litigation even though, collectively, players would be better-off not doing so. More specifically, we show that 'strong' players have incentives to litigate and 'weaker' types have incentives to settle (concede) when our litigation game is preceded by binary decisions to litigate or settle.

Section 1 presents a parameterised litigation model that subsumes the American, British, and Continental systems as special cases. Novel systems like the Quayle

---

[4] As noted by Klemperer (2003), auction theory is a powerful tool for analysing a host of economic problems, including litigation.

system, the Matthew system (where the winner pays the loser an amount that is proportional to the winner's legal expenditures), and the Marshall System (where the winner graciously picks up the loser's legal bill), all obtain as special cases. We show that, in any litigation environment where the best case wins, players have symmetric access to 'quality' legal representation, and where legal expenditures increase the quality of the case presented to the court, the player spending the most on attorneys always wins.

Section 2 uses auction-theoretic tools to characterise the equilibrium legal expenditures and payoffs at trial that arise for the parameterised class of legal systems. We find that, conditional on going to trial, the American system results in lower expected legal expenditures per trial than either the Continental or British system, and furthermore, that the Quayle system leads to precisely the same expected legal expenditures as the American system. These results are used in Section 3 to examine incentives to litigate in the first place. We show that settlement is more prevalent in the British and Continental systems than under the American or Quayle system. Taking into account both litigants' incentives to go to trial rather than settle as well as their expected legal expenditures conditional on going to trial, we find that the British system results in the lowest expected legal expenditures while the American and Quayle systems result in the highest. Finally, Section 4 points out some of the limitations of our model and discusses extensions. The Appendix provides proofs for various assertions contained in the text, and shows how the results change when 'luck' can also influence decisions at trial.

1. An Auction-Theoretic Model of Litigation

Two parties are unable to settle a dispute regarding the ownership of an indivisible asset. Each party i values the asset at v_i, and these valuations are independent random draws from a continuous density f with distribution function F.[5] Each party's valuation is private information, unobserved by the other party and the court. The distribution of valuations is assumed to be common knowledge.

The legal ownership of the asset in dispute is unknown. The role of the court is to examine the evidence presented at trial and, based on the evidence, award the asset to one of the parties. It is costly for the parties to gather evidence and present their case. We assume that the quality of the case presented by a party (q_i) is a function of her expenditures on legal services. The court observes only the quality of the case presented by each party (q_1 and q_2).

The litigation environment requires the two parties to commit simultaneously to legal expenditures, $e_i \geq 0$. Of course, different litigation systems have different implications for ultimate payoffs of the parties. For instance, the American system requires the winner and loser to pay their own legal expenditures, while the British system requires the loser to reimburse the winner for her legal expenditures. To capture the effects of different legal environments, assume that the payoff to party

---

[5] The analysis can be extended to the case of correlated values and/or the case where litigants receive affiliated signals of values; see Baye *et al.* (1998). Obviously, this different information structure changes some of the results, since revenue equivalence does not generally hold in the case of affiliation.

i depends on whether she wins or loses the trial as well as the fee-shifting rules implied by the justice system:

$$u_i(e_i, e_j, v_i) = \begin{cases} v_i - \beta e_i - \delta e_j & \text{if party } i \text{ wins} \\ -\alpha e_i - \theta e_j & \text{if party } i \text{ loses.} \end{cases} \tag{1}$$

Here, $(\beta, \alpha, \delta, \theta)$ are fee-shifting parameters that summarise the amount of legal expenditures borne by each party in the event of a favourable or unfavourable judgement. We assume that $(\beta, \alpha) > 0$. This implies that, given the judicial decision, a party's utility is decreasing in her legal expenditures. In contrast, the parameters (δ, θ) may be positive or negative, depending upon whether the winner and loser pay or receive a transfer based on the other party's legal expenditures. This formulation permits us to examine a variety of legal environments. For instance, when $\beta = \alpha = 1$ and $\delta = \theta = 0$, the model captures the American system where each party pays her own legal expenses regardless of the outcome. The case where $\alpha = \theta = 1$ and $\beta = \delta = 0$ corresponds to the British system, where the loser pays its own legal costs as well as those of the winner.[6]

To complete the model, we assume that the court's decision is influenced by the quality of the case presented by each party. The quality of party i's case, in turn, is a continuous, strictly increasing function of her legal expenditures. We focus on environments where parties are endowed with symmetric technologies for producing a favourable case. In other words, neither party has a distinct advantage with respect to the evidentiary or legal merits of her claims to the disputed asset, nor access to an attorney capable of making superior legal argument on her behalf. This is a strong assumption; obviously, in some legal environments one party may have a stronger claim to the asset than the other party.[7] Nonetheless, the symmetric case is a natural benchmark, and as discussed below, permits one to make *ceteris paribus* comparisons of the expenditures induced by different fee allocation mechanisms.

More formally, let q_i denote the quality of party i's case and ϕ denote the production function that maps each player's legal expenditures into that player's case quality. We assume

(A1) *Monotonic Legal Production Function* The quality of the case presented by player i is given by $q_i = \phi(e_i)$, where ϕ is a continuous and strictly increasing function of player i's expenditures on legal services.

Notice that we are taking an agnostic position with respect to any notion of the 'truth' underlying the case. Our motivation for this is three-fold. First, 'truth' is typically unobservable; all the court can do is to evaluate observable evidence presented at trial. Second, in many disputes regarding ownership, each side believes that they have the legal right to the item in dispute. Each

---

[6] For notational convenience, we will use the notation $\beta = 0$ and $\alpha = 0$ to refer to the cases where $\lim \beta \to 0$ and $\lim \alpha \to 0$, respectively.

[7] An interesting (but complicated) extension would be to allow for such asymmetries. One possible justification for the symmetry assumption is the evidence provided by Waldfogel (1998) which suggests that the pretrial adjudication process tends to weed out parties with observable asymmetries, so that parties actually going to trial tend to be fairly symmetric.

side presents arguments supporting a decision in their favour, and the court's role is to weigh the case presented by the parties and render its decision. Third, since our objective is to compare the amount spent for legal services under various fee-shifting rules, it is important to restrict attention to environments where legal expenditures do not distort the truth. While situations do arise where a party expends hefty legal expenditures to win a case 'wrongfully', a comparative analysis of fee-shifting rules in such environments would be misguided. In particular, if one fee-shifting system resulted in lower expenditures than another system but resulted in more 'incorrect' judicial decisions, the relative merits of the two systems would depend on the social trade-off (if any) between 'justice' and legal costs. Our focus on the expected expenditures arising under different systems is meant to provide a positive analysis of the outlays induced by different systems – not a general normative analysis of which system is 'best'.

Since we are assuming that the true ownership of the item in dispute is unknown, 'justice' or 'fairness' reduces to the situation where the court weighs the observable evidence presented at trial, and awards the asset to the party with the most meritorious case. For example, consider a divorced couple engaged in a nasty custody battle over a child and suppose that there is no *a priori* basis for determining the 'correct' or 'incorrect' decision (both parent's work and are on good terms with the child). All the court can do is evaluate the arguments presented by each side at trial, and award custody to the party presenting the best case. Thus, the assumption that the 'best case wins' does not mean that absolute 'truth' is realised but rather that the court awards custody to the most deserving party, given the evidence presented at trial.

(A2) *Best Case Wins* If party i presents the best case ($q_i > q_j$), party i wins with probability one. If the two parties' cases are of identical quality ($q_i = q_j$), each party wins with probability $1/2$.

This assumption rules out, for example, 'jury nullification' whereby the court relies on non-trial evidence or other 'unobservables' to rule against the party presenting the most meritorious case at trial; the Appendix relaxes this assumption.

Finally, we focus on environments where the two litigants' legal expenditures are neither subsidised nor taxed by an outside party. Thus, while the loser and/or winner might be required to reimburse the other party for some portion of her legal expenditures, the sum of the expenditures of the two litigants exactly equals the aggregate amount spent on legal services. We formalise this assumption as

(A3) *Internalised Legal Costs* There are no subsidies or taxes; all legal expenses are borne by the litigants.

Note that assumption A3 implies that $\alpha + \delta = \beta + \theta = 1$, so $\delta = (1 - \alpha)$ and $\theta = (1-\beta)$. By A2, party i wins if $q_i > q_j$, loses if $q_j > q_i$, and wins with probability $1/2$ if $q_i = q_j$. Substituting these relations into (1) and noting that A1 implies that $q_i \geq q_j$ if and only if $e_i \geq e_j$ yields:

PROPOSITION 1 *Suppose assumptions* A1 *to* A3 *hold. Then the payoff functions for the two parties are given by*

$$u_i(e_i, e_j, v_i) = \begin{cases} v_i - \beta e_i - (1-\alpha)e_j & \text{if } e_i > e_j \\ v_i/2 - e_i & \text{if } e_i = e_j \\ -\alpha e_i - (1-\beta)e_j & \text{if } e_j > e_i. \end{cases} \quad (2)$$

Two aspects of Proposition 1 are worth noting. First, in symmetric environments where legal expenditures enhance the quality of the case presented and the best case wins, the party spending the most on legal services always wins. Outcomes where parties appear to 'buy justice' by hiring superior (and more costly) attorneys are, in fact, consistent with the court determining the winner based purely on the observable evidence presented at trial. While our focus on trial environments that are symmetric in the eyes of the court and where the best case wins is not without loss of generality, it is the natural benchmark to use in comparing the relative merits of different fee-shifting rules.

Second, the form of payoff functions in Proposition 1 permits us to vary the fee-shifting parameters to capture a variety of different litigation rules as special cases. For instance, the following litigation rules are included as important special cases:

American System ($\alpha = \beta = 1$)[8] Each party pays their own legal expenses, and the party presenting the highest quality case wins.

Continental System ($\alpha = 1$; $\beta \in (0,1)$) The loser pays his own costs and, in addition, pays a fraction $(1-\beta)$ of the winner's expenses.

British System ($\alpha = 1$; $\beta = 0$)[9] Technically, this is the limit of the Continental System as β tends to zero. Here, the party presenting the best case wins, and the loser pays her own legal expenses and virtually all of those of the winning party.

In addition to these well-known systems, our parameterisation permits us to examine more exotic systems, such as ones we call the Quayle, Marshall, and Matthew systems:

Quayle System ($\alpha = 2$; $\beta = 1$)[10] The loser pays his own costs and reimburses the winner up to the level of the loser's own costs.

---

[8] We have adopted this terminology from the economics and legal literatures, which uses the terms 'American System' and 'American Rule' to refer to legal environments where each party pays his or her own legal expenses. It is important to note, however, that in practice it is not this black and white. Kritzer (2002) notes that many US jurisdictions have adopted 'one-way' fee-shifting regimes, whereby a successful *plaintiff* may recover a fraction of its attorneys' fees from the losing defendant but a winning defendant cannot recover its legal expenses. One such example stems from the *Equal Access to Justice Act*, which allows a successful nongovernmental party to recover a fraction of its legal outlays in cases involving federal agencies.

[9] Once again, we adopt this terminology from the relevant literatures which use the terms 'British System' and 'English Rule' to refer to environments where the loser pays the winner's legal expenses. Even in England, this rule is not generally applied in its pure form (Kritzer, 2002; Davis, 1999).

[10] As noted in introduction, we call this parameterisation the 'Quayle system' because Dan Quayle chaired the President's Council on Competitiveness, which recommended that the US adopt this mechanism in its *Agenda for Civil Justice Reform in America* (1991). Smith (1992) analysed this system in a model where parties' subjective probabilities of winning may not be consistent, and in which the determination of legal expenditures is exogenous.

Marshall System ($\alpha = 0$; $\beta = 1$).[11] Technically, this is the limit of the Continental system as α tends to zero. The Marshall system is the reverse of the British system: The *winner* pays her own costs and, in addition, reimburses the loser for all of its legal costs.

Matthew System ($\alpha = 1$; $\beta \in (1, \infty)$).[12] The winner is required to 'go the extra mile' and transfer an amount to the loser that is proportional to the winner's legal expenditures. This is, in a sense, the reverse of the Quayle system which requires the *loser* to transfer an amount to the winner. The payoffs for the Matthew system are similar to the Continental rule, except $\beta > 1$.

The auction-like structure of the these payoffs, and more generally the payoffs in (2), permits us to use auction-theoretic tools to analyse this parameterised class of legal systems. For the remainder of the analysis, we also assume:

(A4) *Regulatory Conditions on the Distribution of Valuations* The density of valuations is bounded, continuous and strictly positive on its support, $[0, \bar{v}]$, where $0 < \bar{v} < \infty$.

2. Legal Outlays at Trial

This Section characterises the equilibrium expenditures on legal services that arise when both parties opt to litigate their dispute in court. The first subsection provides closed-form expressions for the equilibrium expenditures that arise at trial, while the second subsection shows how the cost of litigation per trial varies across different legal systems.

2.1. Equilibrium Legal Outlays

Let $e_i(v_i)$ denote the legal expenditures of a party who values the item in dispute at v_i. If legal expenditures are a strictly increasing function of the amount a litigant stands to gain by winning ($e_i'(v_i) > 0$) then e_i^{-1} exists and the expected payoff $EU(e_i, v_i)$ of a party who expends e_i on legal services is:

$$EU(e_i, v_i) = \int_0^{e_j^{-1}(e_i)} [v_i - \beta e_i - (1 - \alpha)e_j(v_j)]f(v_j)dv_j$$
$$+ \int_{e_j^{-1}(e_i)}^{\bar{v}} [-\alpha e_i - (1 - \beta)e_j(v_j)]f(v_j)dv_j. \tag{3}$$

The first term represents the payoffs arising when player i puts forth a higher-quality case than player j and thus wins the item valued at v_i, while the second term

---

[11] We call this the Marshall System in honour of George Catlett Marshall who, as US Secretary of State, organised the *European Recovery Program* (better known as the *Marshall Plan*). He is not to be confused with Thurgood Marshall or John Marshall, both of whom served on the US Supreme Court.

[12] We call this the Matthew system because Matthew 5: 39–41 states: 'But I say unto you, that ye resist not evil: but whosoever shall smite thee on thy right cheek, turn to him the other also. And if any man will sue thee at the law, and take away thy coat, let him have thy cloak also. And whosoever shall compel thee to go a mile, go with him twain.' Loosely translated: if you are forced to spend $1 defending yourself in court, go the extra mile and pay an additional amount to your adversary.

represents the payoff from losing. Notice that the expected payoff from litigation critically depends on the fee-shifting rules of the legal system.

Differentiating with respect to e_i gives the first-order condition for player i's optimal level of legal expenditures, given the level e_j of the rival. Using standard auction-theoretic methods (see the Appendix for a detailed proof) we obtain:

PROPOSITION 2 *Suppose the litigation environment satisfies* (A1) *to* (A4). *In the unique symmetric equilibrium in differentiable strategies, the legal expenditures of a party who values the item in dispute at v is*

$$e(v) = [\alpha - (\alpha - \beta)F(v)]^{-2} \int_0^v sf(s)[\alpha - (\alpha - \beta)F(s)]\mathrm{d}s. \qquad (4)$$

Notice that under assumptions A1 to A4, the item in dispute is always awarded to the party presenting the best case and, furthermore, the allocation of the item is efficient, since it is always awarded to the party valuing it most highly (this follows from the symmetry and monotonicity of the equilibrium expenditures in (4); see the Appendix).

As a corollary to Proposition 2, one may obtain closed form expressions for the equilibrium legal expenditures that arise under various legal systems by simply substituting specific parameter values for (α, β) into the general expression in Proposition 2. These are presented in Table 1.

2.2. *The Cost of Litigation per Trial*

Proposition 2 permits us to compare the expenditures arising under several of the litigation systems in Table 1. To see this, note that the only differences in the American, British, Continental, and Matthew systems is β, as $\alpha = 1$ for all of these systems. It is straightforward to establish that the equilibrium expenditures of a litigant who values the item at $v \in (0, \bar{v})$, given in (4), are strictly decreasing in β. Thus, other things equal, litigants spend less *per trial* in systems where β is higher. The intuition is that legal systems with higher βs require the winner to pay a greater

Table 1

Equilibrium Legal Expenditures

Legal system	α, β	Expenditures $(e(v))$
American	$\alpha = 1, \beta = 1$	$\int_0^v sf(s)\mathrm{d}s$
British	$\alpha = 1, \beta = 0$	$\dfrac{\int_0^v sf(s)[1 - F(s)]\mathrm{d}s}{[1 - F(v)]^2}$
Continental	$\alpha = 1, \beta \in (0,1)$	$\dfrac{\int_0^v sf(s)[1 - (1 - \beta)F(s)]\mathrm{d}s}{[1 - (1 - \beta)F(v)]^2}$
Marshall	$\alpha = 0, \beta = 1$	$\dfrac{\int_0^v sf(s)F(s)\mathrm{d}s}{F(v)^2}$
Quayle	$\alpha = 2, \beta = 1$	$\dfrac{\int_0^v sf(s)[2 - F(s)]\mathrm{d}s}{[2 - F(v)]^2}$
Matthew	$\alpha = 1, \beta \in (1,\infty)$	$\dfrac{\int_0^v sf(s)[1 - (1 - \beta)F(s)]\mathrm{d}s}{[1 - (1 - \beta)F(v)]^2}$

Michael R. Baye, Dan Kovenock, and Casper G. de Vries

share of her own legal expenditures. This reduces the benefits of winning and therefore induces parties to spend less on attorneys. Furthermore, an increase in β increases the payoff to the loser by reducing the amount of the winner's expenses the loser is required to pay. In fact, when β increases above unity, the loser actually receives a direct payment from the winner. In short, an increase in β reduces the benefit of winning relative to losing, and this leads to less vigorous legal battles in court.

Since β is highest under the Matthew system and lowest under the British system, it follows that, regardless of her valuation, a litigant will spend more under the British system than under the Continental, American, or Matthew systems. To summarise:

PROPOSITION 3   *Under assumptions* A1 *to* A4, *the equilibrium expenditures of a litigant who values the item at* $v \in (0, \bar{v})$ *can be ordered as follows:*

$$e(v)^{British} > e(v)^{Continental} > e(v)^{American} > e(v)^{Matthew}.$$

Unfortunately, Proposition 3 does not provide a complete ranking of all of the legal systems in Table 1. This stems from the fact that the equilibrium expenditure functions under the American system and the Quayle system cross, as do expenditures under the American system and Marshall system. In situations where the expenditure functions cross, unambiguous expenditure rankings are not possible. To see this, consider the special case where the distribution of values is uniformly distributed on the unit interval ($F(v) = v$ for $v \in [0,1]$). In this case, equilibrium expenditures under the American and Marshall systems are given by

$$e^A(v) = \frac{1}{2}v^2$$

and

$$e^M(v) = \frac{1}{3}v,$$

respectively. These functions cross at $v = 2/3$: Litigants with valuations below $2/3$ spend less under the American system, while those with valuations above $2/3$ spend more under the American system.

It is possible, however, to rank the *expected* legal outlays induced by legal systems unambiguously with arbitrary fee-shifting parameters. Indeed, the expected legal outlays induced by a litigation system are independent of α and decreasing in β. A simple and elegant way of seeing this is to apply arguments based on the Revenue Equivalence Theorem (RET).[13]

Let $U(v)$ denote the expected utility of a litigant of type v in the unique symmetric equilibrium in differentiable strategies, and $P(v)$ denote the corresponding probability she wins the suit. Note that, since the litigant with the higher valuation always wins, $P(v) = F(v)$ for all $v \in [0, \bar{v}]$. Hence, the expected utility of a litigant of

---

[13] In Baye *et al.* (2000) we provide an alternative analytic proof that expected legal outlays are independent of α and decreasing in β by direct integration of (4) with respect to the density f. Paul Klemperer, in private communication and subsequently in Klemperer (2003), suggested a proof based on the Revenue Equivalence Theorem (RET). We are indebted to Paul Klemperer for this insight and use the RET approach in what follows.

type v is the probability she wins the suit times her valuation of the item in dispute, less her expected net payment. Since the internalisation of legal costs (A3) implies that the expectation of net payments across all types is simply $E[e(v)]$,

$$E[U(v)] = E[F(v)v] - E[e(v)].\tag{5}$$

Note that, by standard results in mechanism design (Klemperer, 1999), $U(v) = U(0) + \int_0^v F(x)\mathrm{d}x$. Hence

$$E[U(v)] = U(0) + E\left[\int_0^v F(x)\mathrm{d}x\right].\tag{6}$$

Furthermore, since the litigant with the higher valuation always wins, the expected utility of a litigant with the lowest possible valuation is $U(0) = -(1 - \beta)E[e(v)]$. Substituting this expression for $U(0)$ in (6) and taking expectations yields

$$E[U(v)] = -(1 - \beta)E[e(v)] + \int_0^{\bar{v}}\left[\int_0^v F(x)\mathrm{d}x\right]f(v)\mathrm{d}v.\tag{7}$$

Equating (5) and (7) and integrating reveals that

$$E[e(v)] = \frac{1}{\beta}\int_0^{\bar{v}} vf(v)[1 - F(v)]\mathrm{d}v.$$

To summarise:

Proposition 4 *Under assumptions A1 to A4, a litigant's expected equilibrium legal expenditures at trial are given by*

$$E[e(v)] = \frac{1}{\beta}\int_0^{\bar{v}} vf(v)[1 - F(v)]\mathrm{d}v.\tag{8}$$

Thus, while a litigant's actual legal expenditures generally depend on both α and β, her *expected* legal expenditures are independent of α. The above proof essentially utilises a version of the RET that applies to litigation systems in which the expected utility of a litigant with the lowest possible valuation is non-zero (as is the case in the British legal system). The RET implies that equilibrium expected utility depends on the underlying litigation parameters only through their effect on the expected utility of a litigant with the lowest possible valuation. Regardless of the magnitude of α, a litigant with the lowest possible valuation knows she will lose for sure, and thus in equilibrium spends nothing on legal services. Hence, the expected utility of a litigant with the lowest possible valuation is simply $-(1 - \beta)$ times the expected equilibrium expenditures induced by the litigation system. These observations induce the structure of (7), which when combined with (5), implies that expected equilibrium expenditures are independent of α, but are strictly decreasing in β.

In addition, since total expected legal expenditures per trial are given by $TC = 2E[e(v)]$, Proposition 4 implies that total expected legal expenditures per trial are not only independent of α, but are strictly decreasing in β. Thus we immediately have the following result as corollary to Proposition 4:

PROPOSITION 5 *Under assumptions A1 to A4, total expected legal expenditures per trial are given by*

$$TC(\beta) = \frac{2}{\beta} \int_0^{\bar{v}} vf(v)[1 - F(v)]\mathrm{d}v.$$

Thus, regardless of the value of α, legal systems with higher βs result in unambiguously lower total expected legal expenditures per trial. In particular:

$$TC^{British} > TC^{Continental} > TC^{American} = TC^{Marshall} = TC^{Quayle} > TC^{Matthew}.$$

Since the American, Marshall and Quayle systems all have the same β, they result in the same expected legal expenditures at trial. As we show in the Appendix, this result critically depends on our assumption (A2); if random effects also influence the court's decision, the Marshall, Quayle, and Matthew systems will result in different expected expenditures at trial.[14]

Proposition 5 reveals that, conditional on both players litigating, expected legal expenses per trial are highest under the British system and lowest under the Matthew system. In fact, Proposition 5 implies that by choosing β arbitrarily large in the Matthew system, one can make total expected legal expenditures arbitrarily small. Thus, one might be tempted to conclude that, given the assumptions of the model, the Matthew system is the 'optimal' litigation system; after all, the judicial outcome is both efficient and just (in the sense that the party presenting the best case always wins), and furthermore, the system can be devised in a manner that 'minimises' legal expenditures on a per-trial basis. This reasoning is incomplete, however, as the following analysis reveals.

By assumption A3, litigation costs are internalised, so total expected legal expenditures equal the total expected utility loss from litigation. Thus, the expected payoffs from litigating (denoted EU) are higher in legal systems where expected expenditures per trial are lower. It follows from Proposition 5 that

PROPOSITION 6 *Under assumptions A1 to A4, the expected payoffs of litigants can be ordered as follows:*

$$EU^{British} < EU^{Continental} < EU^{American} = EU^{Marshall} = EU^{Quayle} < EU^{Matthew}.$$

More generally, the expected payoffs of the litigants are independent of α and strictly increasing in β.

Together, Propositions 5 and 6 illustrate an important trade-off. On the one hand, legal systems with higher βs result in lower expected equilibrium legal expenditures per trial, and the Matthew system results in the lowest possible expected expenditures per trial. On the other hand, legal systems with higher βs result in higher expected payoffs from litigation, thus making it more attractive for parties to bring suits in the first place. Thus, while the Matthew system results in lower expenditures per trial, adopting such a system would likely increase the number of cases brought to trial.

[14] We are indebted to an unusually insightful referee for pointing this out and for providing a sketch of the treatment we provide in the Appendix.

Factoring in the increased number of trials, it is not at all clear which legal system results in the lowest expected total legal expenditure from an *ex ante* standpoint. Furthermore, for litigation systems in which expected payoffs are negative at trial, it is not at all clear rational players would opt to litigate in the first place. We address these two important issues in the next Section.

3. Why Litigate in the First Place?

The total expected expenditures induced by a given legal system depend not only on the expected expenditures per trial under each system but also on the number of trials induced by each system. *Ceteris paribus*, systems that generate lower expected expenditures per trial provide greater expected payoffs from litigation and, therefore, result in more cases being brought to trial. The ranking across legal systems of the *ex ante* expected total costs of litigation depend upon this trade off. We now provide a simple model that captures these basic forces, and also show that litigation results in a sort of 'prisoner's dilemma' when one endogenises players' decisions to litigate or settle in the first place.

To illustrate these issues, consider a two stage game where in the first stage, players simultaneously but independently make a decision whether to litigate or to concede. If both players decide to litigate, they enter a second stage in which they simultaneously decide how much to spend on legal effort (the game analysed above). If one party concedes while the other opts for litigation, the litigating party is awarded the item in summary judgement. If both parties concede, the payoffs to the parties depend on the nature of the dispute. For example, if the item in dispute is a parcel of land, the absence of clearly defined property rights might result in the land remaining fallow and each party receiving a payoff of $U^C(v_i) = 0$. Alternatively, property rights in this case might be allocated on the basis of a coin flip or an unmodelled administrative process which – from the standpoint of the disputants – resembles a fair randomising device. In this case party i's expected payoff is $U^C(v_i) = v_i/2$.

The expected payoff to player i (with value v_i) from entering the litigation stage depends on the set of values v_j for which player j chooses to litigate, the beliefs that player j has about the set of values for which player i litigates, the beliefs of player i concerning these beliefs of player j, and so on. If players have common beliefs regarding the distribution of litigants' valuations in the litigation stage (so that the environment is symmetric and our previous results apply), the incentives of the two parties in the first stage of the game are as illustrated in the matrix.

		Player j	
		Litigate	Concede
Player i	Litigate	$U^L(v_i, F^*), U^L(v_j, F^*)$	$v_i, 0$
	Concede	$0, v_j$	$U^C(v_i), U^C(v_j)$

Michael R. Baye, Dan Kovenock, and Casper G. de Vries

Here $U^L(v_i, F^*)$ and $U^L(v_j, F^*)$ refer to the expected payoffs to i and j, respectively, from entering the litigation game described in the sections above when the distribution of valuations of those opting to litigate is F^*.[15] Note that, due to the asymmetric information, player i knows v_i but perceives that v_j is a random draw from F^*. We will show that there exists a symmetric perfect Bayesian equilibrium with a cut-off value $\hat{v}$, such that each player litigates if and only if his realised value is greater than or equal to his respective cut-off value, and thus $F^*(v) = [F(v) - F(\hat{v})]/[1 - F(\hat{v})]$.

Note first that if $U^C(v_i) < v_i$, player i has an incentive to litigate if he expects his rival to concede. This implies, among other things, that there does not exist an equilibrium in which all types of players concede, so that $\hat{v} < \bar{v}$. Since player valuations are private information, this implies that, in a symmetric equilibrium, a positive fraction of players will be engaged in litigation games of the sort examined in Sections 1 and 2. Expressed differently, even if litigation is socially inefficient (due to wasteful expenditures on attorneys), one would expect to observe a positive level of litigation. Furthermore, if $U^L(v_i, F^*) \geq 0$ for all i, endogenising players' decisions to litigate in the first place leads to a sort of 'prisoner's dilemma'.

To illustrate, consider the special case where $U^C(v_i) = v_i/2$. Suppose there exists a symmetric equilibrium in which players with valuations $v \geq \hat{v}$ choose to litigate and those with valuations below $\hat{v}$ do not. Hence,

$$U^L(v_i, F^*) = U^L\{v_i, [F(v) - F(\hat{v})]/[1 - F(\hat{v})]\}$$
$$\equiv E U^L(v_i|\hat{v}).$$

In this case, a player with a valuation $\hat{v}$ is indifferent between litigating and not, so $\hat{v}$ must satisfy

$$[1 - F(\hat{v})]EU^L(\hat{v}|\hat{v}) + F(\hat{v})\hat{v} = \frac{1}{2}\hat{v}F(\hat{v}), \tag{9}$$

where $EU^L(\hat{v}|\hat{v})$ refers to the expected payoff of a player whose valuation is $\hat{v}$, given that it is common knowledge that each player litigates if and only if his value is greater than or equal to $\hat{v}$. Rearranging this expression yields

$$EU^L(\hat{v}|\hat{v}) = \frac{-\hat{v}F(\hat{v})}{2[1 - F(\hat{v})]}. \tag{10}$$

For a given $\hat{v}$, we know from Proposition 6 that the left-hand side of (10) depends only on β and F, and furthermore, is increasing in β. It follows that $\hat{v}$ is a decreasing function of β, and thus there exists a symmetric perfect Bayesian equilibrium where players with valuations below $\hat{v}$ concede while those with higher valuations go to trial and play a game analogous to that described in Sections 1 and 2.

[15] Note that, while the results in the previous section assume valuations are drawn from a common distribution F on $[0, \bar{v}]$, it is trivial to extend the results to the case where the support is $[\underline{v}, \bar{v}] \subset R_+$. All we require here is that, given an initial distribution of values, F, each litigant perceives that valuations (conditional on litigation) are *iid* draws from some distribution, F^*. As shown below, there exists an equilibrium in which F^* is a simple truncation of F.

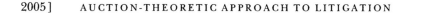

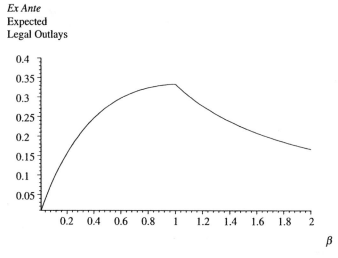

Fig. 2.   *Expected Expenditures at Trial and the Incentive to Litigate.*

Imposing additional structure enables one to solve explicitly for the set of types who will rationally engage in litigation. For instance, suppose v is uniformly distributed on $[0,1]$ (so that $F(v) = v$) and $\alpha = \beta$. Straightforward calculations (see the Appendix) reveal that the *ex ante* expected legal outlays – taking into account both the incentives to litigate and expected expenditures per trial – are maximised when $\beta = 1$. The relationship between expected expenditures and β is shown in Figure 2. In this case, taking into account not only *ex post* expenditures per trial but also the incentives to litigate in the first place, the *ex ante* expected legal expenditures are maximised under the American System ($\alpha = \beta = 1$). Under this system, litigation dominates conceding for any player with valuation $v > 0$, and total expected expenditures are

$$2\mathrm{E}[e(v)] = 2\mathrm{E}\left[\int_0^v sf(s)\mathrm{d}s\right]$$
$$= 2\int_0^1 \frac{1}{2}v^2\mathrm{d}v = \frac{1}{3}.$$

We may conclude that, for this parameterisation with endogenous litigation choice, the American system results not only in more litigation but in greater *ex ante* expected legal outlays than in a system in which $\beta < 1$. Furthermore, all types litigate under the American system, so increases in β above 1 do not increase the incidence of litigation. Since total legal expenditures conditional upon litigating decrease in β, the American legal system leads to the highest possible *ex ante* total expected legal expenditures.

Since the expected legal expenditure of the litigant with the lowest valuation is invariant with respect to α, any legal system satisfying (A1) to (A4) and $\beta = 1$ will generate the same *ex ante* expected legal expenditure as the American system.

Hence, in particular, the Quayle System also results in higher *ex ante* expected expenditures than legal systems where $\beta \neq 1$.

In concluding this Section, we stress that these findings are based on a specific parameterisation of a discrete two stage game in which any attempts to settle the case out of court must occur in the first stage. The second stage represents the point at which there is insufficient time for further settlement discussions, and players must commit (through the irreversible payments to attorneys required at this stage) to the court's mechanism for resolving the dispute. One may readily extend the settlement stage to include multiple periods, so long as there exists a 'drop dead date' at which players must *simultaneously* commit *all* legal expenditures. An interesting extension of our model would be to examine settlement and litigation with flow expenditures in continuous time or to extend the model to allow for pre-emption by one of the parties.

4. Discussion

Our auction-theoretic framework considered a symmetric litigation environment in which the legal ownership of the disputed asset is unknown to the court. The court observes only the quality of the case presented by each party and awards the asset to the party presenting the best case (justice is always served). Litigants can influence the quality of their case by hiring skilful attorneys. The class of litigation systems considered includes standard systems (such as the American, British, and Continental systems), as well as more exotic ones (which we call the Quayle, Marshall and Matthew systems). Equilibrium legal expenditures per trial are increasing in the proportion of the winner's attorney fees that must be paid by the loser, while the expected payoffs of the litigants are a decreasing function of this proportion. This results in a trade-off: litigation systems with lower equilibrium legal expenditures per trial (such as the American, Quayle and Matthew systems) provide a greater incentive for parties to sue than systems that entail higher equilibrium legal expenditures (such as the British and Continental systems). Expected legal expenditures per trial, as well as litigation incentives, are independent of the proportion of the loser's legal fees paid by the winner and loser.

Notice that if one's objective is solely to reduce wasteful expenditures on attorneys, one might contemplate imposing a tax on legal expenditures. This can easily be analysed within our framework by altering assumption (A3) to permit taxes on legal services. For example, suppose a proportional tax rate of, say, τ, is imposed on the parties' legal expenditures. Given the payoff structure in (1), the invariance of expected utility with respect to affine transformations implies that the ultimate effect is to reduce each litigant's valuation of the disputed item by the same factor. In particular, for any tax rate τ imposed on the parties' litigation expenditures, the incentives confronting a player with valuation v are equivalent to a no-tax regime in which the disputed item's value is $v_\tau \equiv v/(1 + \tau)$. Thus, it follows that for any given τ, the rankings derived in Propositions 3 to 6 still apply.

Importantly, however, even a casual reading of the literature makes it clear that the 'best' legal system is not necessarily the one that minimises expected legal expenditures. Indeed, equity, equal access to the law, fairness, and a host of other factors (such as the probability of a wrong verdict) are also important considerations. Furthermore, different legal systems induce different asymmetries; in some jurisdictions, a defendant is presumed innocent until proven guilty, while in others the burden is on the defendant. Even within a given country, some types of cases have different burdens of proof, ranging from 'beyond reasonable doubt' to merely a 'preponderance of the evidence'. In short, alternative legal systems have a plethora of advantages and disadvantages, and are far more complex than those analysed in any theoretical model. Our analysis of the expected expenditures arising under different legal systems is but one small piece of a much larger puzzle.

With these caveats, our analysis suggests that a movement from the American system to the Quayle system would neither reduce expected legal expenditures on a per-trial basis nor reduce the incentives for parties to litigate. To the extent that America's reputation for being a litigious society is based on the sheer number of suits brought to trial,[16] a movement toward the Continental or British system might reduce the number of suits and the strain on the court system. Furthermore, while our analysis suggests that such a move would result in higher expected legal costs on a per-trial basis, under plausible conditions the *ex ante* legal expenditures (taking into account both incentives to litigate and expected expenditures to trial) would be lower.

Unfortunately, there are relatively few empirical studies that shed definitive light on whether these predictions are consistent with the evidence. As Kritzer (2002) notes, cross-country comparisons, such as studies comparing litigation expenditures in the US with those in Britain, are problematic because of other substantive differences between the countries.[17] Snyder and Hughes (1990) attempt to avoid these problems by using data from a 'natural experiment' within the US in which Florida shifted from the American system to the British system for resolving medical malpractice suits. They provide evidence that is consistent with the predictions of our model: The shift from the American to the British system significantly reduced the incidence of litigation, but increased expenditures at trial by over 61.3%. Further empirical research in this area, perhaps combining our theoretical framework with empirical auction techniques, might be a fruitful avenue for future research.

Finally, it is also important to stress that our findings are based on a stylised model that incorporates a number of simplifying assumptions. For instance, our assumption (A1) restricts attention to environments where neither party has an advantage with respect to the evidentiary or legal merits of her claims to the disputed asset, nor access to an attorney capable of making superior arguments on her behalf. While the empirical evidence provided by Waldfogel (1998) suggests that the pre-trial adjudication process tends to weed out cases with observable asymmetries, one can certainly imagine trials in which one party has a distinct advantage with respect to the intrinsic legal merits. An interesting extension would

---

[16] Branham (1998) reports that product liability suits are, on a per-capita basis, 8 times more prevalent in the US than in the UK.

[17] For example, contingency fees – the practice whereby attorneys do not bill clients for attorney's fees but instead receive a fraction of any winnings – are common in the US but absent in most other countries (Davis, 1999).

be to capture differences in intrinsic merit by allowing for asymmetric legal production functions.

Our analysis also ignores the impact of budget constraints. One undesirable feature of the British system is that it might make courts a playing field for only the wealthy. Under the British system, the prospect of having to pay the winner's legal expenses might preclude the poor from seeking justice through the court system. This may explain why there are significant differences across countries in government subsidies designed to aid low-income litigants. For example, Houseman (2003) notes that, as a fraction of GDP, Britain's expenditures on civil legal aid is about 12 times greater than that in the US. The simple auction-theoretic litigation framework set forth in this paper, coupled with recent work by Che and Gale (1998) on auctions with budget-constrained players, may serve as a useful starting point for a more complete analysis of these issues.

Indiana University
Purdue University
Erasmus University Rotterdam and Tinbergen Institute

Date of accept of first submission: February 2002
Date of accept of final type script: August 2004

A Technical Appendix is available for this paper at http://www.res.org.uk/economic/ta/tahome.asp

References

Baye, M. R., Kovenock, D. and de Vries, C. G.(1998). 'A general linear model of contests', mimeo, Purdue University.
Baye, M. R., Kovenock, D. and de Vries, C. G. (2000). 'Comparative analysis of litigation systems', Discussion Paper, Tinbergen Institute, TI 2000-103/2.
Bebchuk, L. A. and Chang H. F. (1996). 'An analysis of fee-shifting based on: the margin of victory: on frivolous suits, meritorious suits and the role of Rule 11', *Journal of Legal Studies*, vol. 25, pp. 371–403.
Braeutigam, R., Owen, B. and Panzar, P. (1984). 'An economic analysis of alternative fee shifting systems', *Law and Contemporary Problems*, vol. 47, pp. 173–85.
Branham, C. W. (1998). 'It couldn't happen here: the English rule but not in South Carolina', *South Carolina Law Review*, vol. 49, p. 971.
Che, Y.-K. and Earnhart, D. (1997). 'Optimal use of information in litigation: does withholding information deter frivolous suits?', *Rand Journal of Economics*, vol. 28, pp. 120–34.
Che, Y.-K. and Gale, I. (1998). 'Standard auctions with financially-constrained buyers', *Review of Economic Studies*, vol. 65, pp. 1–21.
Coddington, E. A. and Levinson, N. (1955). *Theory of Ordinary Differential Equations*, NewYork: McGraw-Hill.
Cooter, R. and Rubinfeld, D. L. (1989). 'Economic analysis of legal disputes and their resolution', *Journal of Economic Literature*, vol. 27, pp. 1067–97.
Davis, W. K. (1999). 'The international view of attorney fees in civil suits: why is the US the "odd man out" in how it pays its lawyers', *Arizona Journal of International and Comparative Law*, vol. 16, p. 361.
Gong, J. and McAfee, R. P. (2000). 'Pre-trial negotiation, litigation and procedural rules', *Economic Inquiry*, vol. 38, pp. 218–38.
Hause, J. C. (1989). 'Indemnity, settlement, and litigation, or I'll be suing you', *Journal of Legal Studies*, vol. 18, pp. 157–79.
Houseman, A. W. (2003). 'Civil legal aid in the US: an overview of the program in 2003', Center for Law and Social Policy Working Paper, September.

Hughes, J. W. and Snyder, E. A. (1995). 'Litigation and settlement under the English and American rules: theory and evidence', *Journal of Law and Economics*, vol. 38, pp. 225–50.

Klemperer, P. (1999). 'Auction theory', *Journal of Economic Surveys*, vol. 13(3), pp. 227–86.

Klemperer, P. (2003). 'Why every economist should learn some auction theory', in (M. Dewatripont, L. Hansen, and S. Turnovsky, eds.), *Advances in Economics and Econometrics: Theory and Applications*, Vol. I, pp. 25–55, Cambridge: Cambridge University Press.

Kritzer, H. M. (2002). 'Lawyer fees and lawyer behavior in litigation: what does the empirical literature really say?'. *Texas Law Review*, vol. 80, pp. 1943–83.

Matthews, S. A. (1995). 'A technical primer on auction theory I: independent private values', Discussion Paper no. 1096, Northwestern University.

Myerson, R. B. (1981). 'Optimal auction design', *Mathematics of Operations Research*, vol. 6, pp. 58–73.

Polinsky, A. M. and Rubinfeld, D. L. (1996). 'Optimal awards and penalties when the probability of prevailing varies among plaintiffs', *Rand Journal of Economics*, vol. 27, pp. 269–80.

Polinsky, A. M. and Rubinfeld, D. L. (1998). 'Does the English rule discourage low-probability-of-prevailing plaintiffs?', *Journal of Legal Studies*, vol. 27, pp. 519–35.

Posner, R. A. (1997). 'Explaining the variance in the number of tort suits across US states and between the US and England', *Journal of Legal Studies*, pp. 26, pp. 477–90.

Reinganum, J. and Wilde, L. L. (1986). 'Settlement, litigation, and the allocation of litigation costs', *Rand Journal of Economics*, vol. 17, pp. 557–66.

Schweizer, U. (1989). 'Litigation and settlement under two-sided incomplete information', *Review of Economic Studies*, vol. 56, pp. 163–78.

Shavell, S. (1982). 'Suit, settlement, and trial: a theoretical analysis under alternative methods for the allocation of legal costs'. *Journal of Legal Studies*, vol. 11, pp. 55–81.

Smith, B. L. (1992). 'Three attorney fee-shifting rules and contingency fees: their impact on settlement incentives', *Michigan Law Review*, vol. 90(7), pp. 2154–89.

Snyder, E. A. and Hughes, J. W. (1990). 'The English rule for allocating legal costs: evidence confronts theory'. *Journal of Law, Economics, and Organization*, vol. 6(2), pp. 345–80.

Spier, K. (1992). 'The dynamics of pre-trial negotiation', *Review of Economic Studies*, vol. 59, pp. 93–108.

Spier, K. (1994). 'Pre-trial bargaining and the design of fee-shifting rules'. *Rand Journal of Economics*, vol. 25, pp. 197–214.

Waldfogel, J. (1998). 'Reconciling asymmetric information and divergent expectations theories of litigation', *Journal of Law and Economics*, vol. 41, pp 451–76.

Part 4

Institutions and History

RENT SEEKING, NONCOMPENSATED TRANSFERS, AND LAWS OF SUCCESSION*

JAMES M. BUCHANAN
Center for Study of Public Choice

[Men] will spend years in degrading subserviency to obtain a niche in a will; and the niche, when at last obtained and enjoyed, is but a sorry payment for all that has been endured. [ANTHONY TROLLOPE, *Doctor Thorne* (Oxford University Press, 1980), p. 246]

I. INTRODUCTION

MY purpose in this paper is to analyze inefficiencies that may emerge from the noncompensated transfer of valued rights among persons. This source of inefficiency has not, to my knowledge, been fully incorporated either in the economic theory of property rights or in orthodox tax analysis. My discussion is based on the elementary fact that all noncompensated transfers are rents to the recipients. Implications for the emergence of rent-seeking behavior follow straightforwardly. The now-familiar propositions to the effect that rent seeking may dissipate economic value can be applied to a variety of transfer settings, only a few of which are explored in this paper.[1] To the extent that the efficiency criterion is the relevant norm, direct implications may be drawn for policy with respect to the laws or rules for succession.

In a broad and very general sense, the resource-wasting struggles for

* I am indebted to my colleagues Geoffrey Brennan, Dwight Lee, and John Pettengill and to William Landes for helpful comments. The paper is also strictly "Tullockian" in character, although Gordon Tullock was not in Blacksburg during its writing. Indeed, a junior colleague, on hearing the argument orally, said that Tullock must have made its central point. That he did not do so indicates that Tullock may, indeed, have a "blind spot" when he discusses inheritance.

[1] The seminal papers are those by Gordon Tullock, The Welfare Costs of Tariffs, Monopolies, and Theft, 5 Western Econ. J. 224 (1967); Anne O. Kreuger, The Political Economy of the Rent-seeking Society, 64 Am. Econ. Rev. 291 (1974); and Richard A. Posner, The Social Costs of Monopoly and Regulation, 83 J. Pol. Econ. 807 (1975). These papers are reprinted, along with others, in the volume edited by James Buchanan, Robert Tollison, & Gordon Tullock, Towards a Theory of the Rent-seeking Society (1980).

[*Journal of Law & Economics*, vol. XXVI (April 1983)]

71

access to noncompensated transfers of value (and power) have long been recognized. For example, quasi-economic arguments have been made for hereditary succession and tragically wasteful conflict for highly valued prizes has long been the stuff of classic fiction. Nonetheless, a more explicit analysis that takes rent-seeking behavior as its central organizing element seems to be warranted.

In Section II, I discuss the meaning of noncompensated transfers. Section III analyzes the model in which the power to transfer is totally unrestricted. Section IV discusses rules or laws of succession that restrict the choice options of potential donors. In Section V, I explore briefly the elements of what might be required for a transfer policy that combines the norms of economic efficiency and intergenerational equity. Section VI discusses the problem of succession in attenuated-rights settings. A few conclusions are offered in Section VII. In an Appendix to the paper, I use a highly simplified construction to demonstrate conceptually how an efficient transfer restriction might be determined.

II. COMPENSATED AND NONCOMPENSATED TRANSFERS

The rentlike attribute of noncompensated transfers cannot be questioned, but the significance of such transfers of value among persons may be subject to challenge. A strictly "economic" approach to interpersonal and particularly intrafamily relationships might suggest that many of the transfers of valued assets or claims, which do not seem to be explicitly compensated, may represent only one side of a complex exchange in which a reciprocal transfer of value has been or is expected to be made. Transfers that take the form of gifts or bequests are, on their face, noncompensated. Some part of such transfers may, nonetheless, represent payment by the apparent donor for reciprocal services that have been or are to be rendered by the designated donee. A person may will his estate to an identified legatee in exchange for services that the legatee agrees to perform prior to the death of the legator.

To the extent that gifts and bequests are literally payments for equal values received in exchange, no matter how complex the process of exchange may be, there is no net transfer of value among persons involved and there is no incentive for the emergence of rent-seeking behavior. Hence, for purposes of the analysis in this paper, fully compensated transfers of value can be neglected. It should be noted, however, that noncompensated elements may remain even in those cases where prospective donees make some reciprocal transfers of value to the donor. If the "terms of trade" offered to prospective donees are favorable, rent seeking will emerge among prospective entrants as in those settings where no part of the transfer is offset by a reciprocal flow of services. The analysis, as such, applies only to noncompensated transfers or that portion of total transfers that is noncompensated. The distinction between compensated and noncompensated transfers must, of course, be made in any attempts to formulate a legal-political policy for restricting interpersonal transfers of value.

Noncompensated transfers that become rents to potential recipients will motivate rent-seeking behavior, but there is no necessary linkage between such behavior, in itself, and inefficiency in resource use. In the familiar rent-seeking examples, the payment of direct money bribes to those who hold decisive powers of control over access to artificially scarce rental opportunities (for example, import quotas) may reflect minimal resource wastage, at least by comparison with a situation where direct bribes are not possible while the rental opportunities remain. In all such cases, however, those persons who control access to the opportunities are, in a sense, ensuring that the transfers of value will, in fact, be directly compensated. Rent seeking becomes wasteful only in those situations where those who control access to rents do not or cannot ensure direct compensation. In the familiar examples, rent seeking becomes wasteful because standards of moral-legal behavior make direct bribes inappropriate. In the cases to be analyzed here, direct compensation, in effect, would negate the transfer of value away from the person who controls access. The objective sought for may be that of accomplishing a net transfer of value. Hence, a prospective donor will explicitly eschew relationships that convert noncompensated into compensated transfers. In so doing, the donor ensures that the rent seeking that emerges will represent allocative inefficiency.

III.   Unrestricted Powers of Transfer

Consider first a setting in which a single individual is sole owner of a nonhuman asset that commands a value in the market. This asset may be marketed costlessly and instantaneously at any time. Further, assume that income from the asset can be costlessly converted into additions to the capital stock and vice versa. There are no restrictions on consuming or "eating up" either the income from the asset or the capital value itself. There are no restrictions on the owner's power and authority to transfer title of the asset to other persons. There are no taxes on such transfers, whether by gift or bequest.

In this model, there is no incentive for the owner of the asset to depart from present-value maximization as a norm for managing the flow of income from the asset and the capital value of the asset itself. Regardless of the owner's rate of time preference, sustained maximization of the remainder value of the asset is dictated by simple precepts of rationality. Moreover, since there are no restrictions, either direct or indirect, on the transfer of value to other persons, the owner of the asset accumulates (or decumulates) value in accordance with nondistorted maximization of his own utility. The ultimate amount and direction of the capital value that is transferred to others will depend on the arguments within the owner's utility function. The trade-offs among these arguments that he confronts are not distorted in any way by elements exogenous to the potential transfers.

There is no attenuation of ownership rights in this setting. The orthodox theory of property rights, or of welfare economics for that matter, suggests that the efficiency norm will be fully satisfied under these conditions. The potential donor will make capital accumulation (decumulation) decisions in the knowledge that an additional dollar projected for transfer to another person will involve an opportunity cost of precisely one dollar in current consumption. This orthodox analysis, however, has overlooked (at least to my knowledge) a possibly important source of inefficiency. The implications of the fact that transfers (gifts or bequests) are net rents to the persons who receive them has not been incorporated in the standard analytics. Because receipt of such values are rents, we should predict the emergence of rationally motivated rent-seeking behavior in all settings where there remains any uncertainty about the identity of the potential recipients. If, as in the model described here, the initial owner of the capital asset or value retains unrestricted freedom to select the potential recipient of the transfer or transfers, rent-seeking competition will arise among all those persons who place a positive value on the prospect of being among the recipient group. A substantial portion of the investment of effort, time, and resources in this rent-seeking activity will be socially wasteful.

The magnitude of net resource waste involved is not easy to estimate, either conceptually or empirically. Early contributors to the analysis of rent seeking, and notably Gordon Tullock[2] and Richard Posner,[3] implicitly or explicitly suggested that rent-seeking investment would be extended to the point where all net rents are dissipated. More recent developments in the theory, again by Gordon Tullock,[4] suggest that total investment in rent seeking may exceed, be equal to, or fall short of the

[2] Tullock (1967), *supra* note 1.

[3] Posner, *supra* note 1.

[4] Gordon Tullock, Efficient Rent Seeking, in Towards a Theory of the Rent-seeking Society (1980).

value of the net rents to be transferred. The magnitude here depends critically on the precise characteristics of the institutional setting within which the transfers are made and on the procedures within the rent-seeking interaction itself.

An example may be helpful. Suppose that it is widely known that a potential donor plans to make a gift of $1 million at a specified date, say, January 1984, to a "deserving" person. It is assumed that his choice of this amount will not be affected by any activity of the potential rent seekers. How much rent seeking will take place?

The answer will depend on the setting. Assume that the "players" in the game can be identified in advance. They may be, for example, the ten direct lineal descendants (sons and daughters) of the man who promises to make the gift of $1 million to one of them on the date specified. Rent seeking involves the equivalent in this model to the purchase of chances to win in a lottery with an open-ended number of tickets. It is as if the ten bidders are offered tickets at $1.00 each, with the option that each may purchase as many tickets as desired, tickets which, once purchased are put into the urn making the chances for winning directly proportional to the number of tickets purchased.[5]

Many other variants of the transfer "game" might be developed, either in terms of abstracted models with explicit numerical payoffs and outlays or in terms of more general formulations. In the setting where individual powers to transfer are unrestricted, the above simplification may not seem adequately descriptive. The set of potential entrants may not be defined. The man who promises the $1 million may have ten direct heirs, who may expect to occupy a favored place among potential donees, but he remains free to make the gift, in whole or in part, to persons other than his own children. Differentially valued prospects for qualifying as a potential donee and for success in the final transfer process will be predicted to motivate differentially valued investments in rent seeking.

It becomes intuitively clear that the ratio between the predicted total resource investment in rent seeking and the size of the expected transfer will be determined by the particular characteristics of the institutional setting. The two children of the wealthy recluse who has no close relatives and no friends would be predicted to invest less, relative to the size of the expected transfer, than would the many children and other relatives and friends of the gregarious wealthy *padrone* of the whole community. In

---

[5] Variations of this precise game are analyzed in some detail by Gordon Tullock in his paper, Efficient Rent Seeking, *id*. In the particular example here, where there is a potential prize of $1 million and ten potential recipients, each member of the group will tend to invest roughly $90,000, for a total outlay of $900,000 in pursuit of the single prize of $1 million.

the first case, total rent-seeking effort may dissipate a relatively small proportion of the transfer value; in the second case, rent seeking may more than dissipate the expected total value of the transfer ultimately made.

For purposes of my general argument, the ratio between total rent-seeking investment and the value of the interpersonal transfer is irrelevant. (See App. for a simplified analysis that shows how this ratio is important in particular problems.) Once the probable emergence of wasteful rent seeking is acknowledged in all settings of unrestricted transfer power, the efficiency basis for the argument against any and all restrictions on the transfer power vanishes. The central proposition of the orthodox argument must, of course, be accepted. Any restriction on the donor's freedom of disposition over his asset values will introduce distortions in his choice, and these distortions will reduce the value of the donor's surplus that he expects to secure from transfer activity. But missing from this traditional argument is any recognition of the possibly offsetting reductions in rent seeking that restriction on the transfer power may induce.

Critics will have noted what may seem to be several qualifications of the analysis to this point. I have implicitly assumed that the potential legator or donor is either not interested in or informed about the rent-seeking activity that his own expected behavior in giving or bequeathing may stimulate. Whether or not such an assumption is appropriate depends, in part, on the ultimate motivation for making interpersonal transfers. If bequests emerge more or less as residual by-products of life-cycle uncertainties and unavoidable transactions costs of estate planning, and particularly if the maintenance of control over valued assets yields utility directly, potential legators may be unconcerned about rent seeking.

If, on the other hand, transfers are motivated by donor interests in the prospective utilities of identified recipients, any wasteful rent seeking on the part of those whose utilities are relevant will be undesirable to the prospective donor. Efforts will be exerted to arrange transfers in such a way as to minimize such rent-seeking activities. The prospective donor will not, however, be concerned about rent seeking on the part of persons whom he has not internally identified as being among those whose utilities matter to him. At the same time, for reasons to be noted, the prospective donor may seek to avoid advance identification of those whom he has targeted as potential recipients. In this setting, rent seeking may be widely observed even if utility interdependence remains a primary motivation for transfer activity.

Rent seeking will tend to be eliminated only in those settings where utility interdependence is strong, where there is a well-identified group of potential recipients, and where the prospective donor can readily monitor the behavior of the potential recipients. This interaction is essentially that which is analyzed by Gary Becker.[6] Rent seeking, on the part of a potential legatee, will not emerge because he will know, in advance, that any effort to increase his own distributional share will be self-defeating. The potential legator retains ultimate allocative power; his distributive choice is unaffected by rent seeking. Such activity becomes totally unproductive to any prospective donee. The informational as well as the interdependence requirements for ensuring such results seem strong indeed.

A second qualification involves the possibility that rent-seeking activity on the part of potential recipients of transfers may, in itself, yield value or utility to the person who proposes to make the ultimate transfer, even if, as we have assumed here, the donor does not enter into either the explicit or an implicit exchange with his potential donees. That is to say, even if the transfer itself is uncompensated, rent-seeking behavior may increase the utility of the donor. For example, whether or not it may be so intended by the rent seekers, their activity may yield valued information to the donor. To the extent that it does so, this increase offsets some part of the resource waste that rent seeking involves. However, it must also be recognized that rent seeking, as he observes it, may actually reduce the utility of the donor, hence adding to the loss of value that rent seeking embodies.

A third qualification to the argument involves the "relative wastefulness" of the rent-seeking activity that any prospective transfer of value generates. To the extent that such activity takes a form that may yield unanticipated utility gains to participants, notably in subsequent periods, the "social waste" is reduced. When the problems analyzed here are considered in a context of institutional and family history, and when it is acknowledged that at least some adjustments have been made to minimize the overt and apparent inefficiencies, the question of the direction or channels through which rent seeking has been allowed to accrue would surely warrant further examination.

A potential donor can effectively close off rent seeking by making unannounced and unanticipated gifts. Totally unanticipated transfers are, of course, equivalent to lump-sum payments that cannot, by definition, induce behavioral changes that will modify the expected value of the individual transfers. In such event, the prospective donor would also attempt to remain secretive about the amount of total value to be transferred to others. In actuality, concealment is difficult to achieve, even if

[6] Gary Becker, Altruism in the Family and Selfishness in the Marketplace, 48 Economica 1 (1981).

desired, and, in addition, it would be hard for a donor to succeed in making a totally unanticipated gift to a person whose utility level really matters for his own utility.[7]

IV.   SUCCESSION WITHIN RIGIDLY DEFINED RULES: RESTRICTIONS ON POWERS OF TRANSFER

Rent seeking will tend to be eliminated where the donors' *discretion* over selection of the beneficiary is absent, even if the donor is allowed to carry out transfers. So long as there exist well defined and widely known enforceable rules or laws that determine the identity of the potential recipients, independent of the choice of the donor, there is no profit to be gained from engaging in rent seeking.[8]

Such a rule as primogeniture comes to mind as perhaps the most obvious example. If the firstborn is designated by law as the necessary legatee of any capital transfer by a potential legator with offspring (and if there is a comparable well-defined equivalent for potential donors without direct offspring), there would be no purpose to be served by others than the firstborn making efforts to change the direction of the intergenerational transfers.

Primogeniture is, of course, only one among many possible sets of rules for succession that might serve the same efficiency-enhancing objective. The rule for equal division among direct heirs would work equally well, provided that the rule is well defined and known in advance by everyone who might be potentially concerned. It is the *predictability* of the rules for succession rather than any intrinsic content of the rules themselves that is relevant for the elimination of rent-seeking behavior.

There may, however, be serious difficulties in the implementation of the predictability norm, even if the efficiency criterion is dominant in any reform proposals. A set of rules or laws of succession that seems definitive on its face may be subject to varying legal interpretation which will, of course, guarantee investment in litigation. Such investment reflects socially wasteful rent seeking, even if it is now directed toward a different object from that which occurs when discretionary power remains with the potential donor of transfers. With nominally explicit rules or laws for succession, rent seeking is redirected from efforts to modify

---

[7] To the extent that an implicit exchange is present, in which the prospective donee modifies his or her behavior in order to increase the utility of the prospective donor, there is an incentive for the transfer of value to be announced but not made.

[8] Gordon Tullock comes close to recognizing the point here in his discussion of bias in selectivity processes as a means of reducing rent seeking. See *supra* note 4. It is somewhat surprising, therefore, that, in his earlier paper on inheritance, Tullock seems to have altogether missed the point. Gordon Tullock, Inheritance Justified, 14 J. Law & Econ. 465 (1971).

donor choices to efforts to influence the judicial interpretation of the rules. Adjudication in the courts becomes the institutionalized form. Observed experiences in modern legal structures when persons die intestate, where there presumably exist quite explicit laws for succession, suggest that this source of inefficiency may be large.[9]

Donor Precommitment through Wills and Testaments. The relationship between pretransfer rent-seeking behavior and predictability or the absence thereof in the rules for succession suggests that, even in the absence of overt legal restrictions on the transfer powers, rent seeking may be eliminated by precommitment behavior of the potential donor. The wealthy person who observes the rent seeking among his potential heirs may seek to eliminate this activity, once and for all, by precommitting himself through the making of an irrevocable will, provided that this action is sufficiently publicized and provided that potential heirs believe that the assignment of succession is indeed irrevocable. Irrevocability is the essential requirement here. If it is known that wills, once made, can be amended at the behest of the makers, there may be minimal effects on rent seeking produced by resort to the instruments of wills and testaments.[10]

Even with effective precommitment, however, rent-seeking behavior of the second sort may still be predicted to emerge. Efforts will continue to be made, and perhaps on an accelerated scale, to modify the legal interpretations of the assignments of assets made through wills, no matter how specific the apparent terms of the documents might appear to be.[11]

V. Toward a Policy for Interpersonal Transfers

The analysis suggests directions for institutional reform if the objective is that of increasing efficiency in resource use. If we ignore posttransfer

[9] Frank H. Easterbrook has discussed the relative importance of what I have here called rent seeking in the whole process of litigation. He suggests that, since litigating parties' interests are primarily in what he calls the stakes-dividing function of litigation, there may be inefficient overinvestment in litigation. See Frank H. Easterbrook, Insider Trading, Secret Agents, Evidentiary Privileges, and the Production of Information, Sup. Ct. Rev. 309 (1981), see especially 358–60.

[10] Noncompensated transfers may or may not emerge from nonreciprocal promises. In their analysis of the latter, Goetz & Scott introduce a possible source of inefficiency that arises from behavioral adjustments made by prospective donees in expectations of transfers that are not finally made. Legally enforceable precommitments to transfer would serve to eliminate this source of inefficiency as well as the rent-seeking source stressed here. See Charles J. Goetz & Robert E. Scott, Enforcing Promises: An Examination of the Basis of Contract, 99 Yale L. J. 1261 (1980).

[11] There are important normative implications to be drawn from the analysis relating to the comparative tax treatment of gifts and bequests. Geoffrey Brennan has a paper in process on this aspect of the issue.

litigation, there are two major sources of allocative distortion, one within the pretransfer choice of the potential donor, the other within the pretransfer choice of the potential donees. The efficiency objective would be the minimization of the loss of value generated by the two sources combined. As noted, the imposition of restrictions on the powers to transfer may substantially eliminate incentives for potential donees to engage in wasteful rent seeking, but it does so at the expense of introducing necessary distortions in the choice calculus of the potential donor. Minimal violation of the efficiency norm, considering the two separate sources of waste, would seem to exist when the rules of succession restricting the transfer power correspond with or map reasonably well with the set of transfer results that might emerge from unrestricted exercise of such power. If a person would, under unrestricted transfer power, plan to divide his patrimony equally among his direct heirs, an explicit law of succession requiring him to do precisely this would minimally affect his choice between current consumption and capital accumulation (decumulation). Any rigid set of rules for succession, sufficiently rigid to affect the level of rent seeking, will, in some individual cases, seriously distort the capital accumulation (decumulation) choices of prospective donors. The person who is totally alienated from his children would, under such rules as primogeniture or equal division, have a strong incentive to consume all of his capital value before any transfer is made. At best, the correspondence or mapping that might be indicated for an economically efficient transfer policy would reflect some average or representative person's desired plan for transfers. Differing societies or even the same society at differing stages of its history may embody differing preferred patterns of transfer for their average or representative donors.

Economic efficiency rarely occupies a position as the exclusive or even overriding norm or objective for policy reform. Competing norms intrude, and particularly in the case of transfer arrangements. Norms of intergenerational justice or equity may be as significant as or even more significant than those of efficiency. I shall not discuss such norms in detail in this paper, but it will perhaps be useful to evaluate briefly the transfer institutions identified above against the entitlement norm and against nonentitlement norms generally.

Consider, first, Robert Nozick's entitlement theory of justice, which holds that persons possess assets justly if these have been justly acquired.[12] Transfers by gift or bequest qualify as just acquisitions. They do so because persons who hold assets justly *voluntarily* transfer ownership rights to others of their own choosing. It seems evident, however, that

[12] Robert Nozick, Anarchy, State and Utopia (1974).

this argument for justice in holdings or entitlements could not readily be extended to apply to assets received through an *involuntary* transfer implemented as a result of a strict rule or law of succession. It would seem to follow, therefore, that any restrictions on the powers to transfer that might be dictated by a recognition of the rent-seeking incentives would be inconsistent with Nozick's entitlement theory of justice.

Most nonentitlement norms for justice are consistent with restrictions on the powers to transfer but would be inconsistent with those rules of succession (such as primogeniture or equal division) that reflect overt discrimination in favor of genetically identified potential beneficiaries. Exclusive concentration on the furtherance of these norms for intergenerational equity, in total disregard for those of efficiency, might lend support to a policy that would prohibit altogether interpersonal transfers. Incorporation of the rent-seeking analysis into the evaluation of alternative arrangements lend at least limited efficiency-based support to those who advance the nonentitlement norms, in that the efficiency costs of imposing restrictions on transfer powers are demonstrated to be less than might otherwise have been assumed. But there are perhaps relatively few persons who would argue exclusively in terms of intergenerational norms of justice to the total neglect of efficiency considerations.

The norm for economic efficiency and the norm for intergenerational equity might be appropriately combined or balanced by a set of arrangements that would allow potential donors to retain powers of transfer in a quantitatively limited sense. The amount of value transferred might be restricted, in total and/or per person terms. Such institutional arrangements would distort to some extent the donor's choices concerning capital accumulation (decumulation), but often less so than in the case of specifically directed transfers. The arrangements suggested would also stimulate investment in rent seeking by potential donors, but again less investment than would be forthcoming under quantitatively and directionally restricted powers of transfer. These arrangements, while not fulfilling the norm for intergenerational equity to the extent desired by many persons, would at least mitigate the gross and apparent injustices in holdings that would emerge from either totally unrestricted transfers or from strict rules of succession that embody overt discrimination.

VI.   Rent Seeking in Attenuated Rights Settings

In the preceding parts of this paper I have explicitly confined the discussion to settings in which potential donors of transfer values retain full ownership rights over all domains of possible usage other than noncompensated transfers to other persons. Owners of valued assets have been presumed to be able to sell such assets freely to others in the economy and/or to convert values readily into direct consumption of any goods or services that may be desired. In these nonattenuated rights settings, rent seeking emerges among potential beneficiaries of noncompensated transfers.

The motivation for rent seeking may, however, be even greater in those institutional settings where the initial "ownership" rights are attenuated in other ways than those involving the transfer authority. With nonattenuated rights, the owner of an asset might, in response to a restriction on the transfer power, convert value into direct consumption. In doing so, he can insure that a lower value is available for transfer than otherwise. Suppose, however, that the nominal owner of an asset or enterprise cannot convert the capital value into current consumption. He does not have the option of "eating up" his capital. Rent seekers will, in this case, operate with an expectation that becomes almost literally like the fixed-prize lottery. In our earlier example, we referred to the person who planned to bequeath $1 million, but the setting was such that rent seekers would know that the donor could, at any time, modify the total to be bequeathed, even to the extent of eliminating all bequests. Contrast this setting with that now examined; the current owner of the capital value enjoys the income from the asset, but he is required to transmit the capital value intact in the form of bequest. It seems evident that the amount of rent seeking in the second case will exceed that in the first.

As a further constraint on the initial owner's rights, suppose that he is not allowed to bequeath the asset at all, even though he must maintain its capital value. He cannot designate his heir or successor. In this model, unless there are strict rules for succession, rent seeking will perhaps be at its maximum. This model approaches the classically familiar case of succession in nonhereditary dictatorships. There are, of course, notorious examples in which the values inherent in political authority have been transformed into Swiss bank accounts, in which cases the dictator can indeed designate his legatees. To the extent that such indirect exercise of "ownership" rights is not possible, rent-seeking activity takes on maximal proportions.

VII. Conclusion

The dictator example should not, however, be allowed to distract attention from the ubiquity of this setting. To the extent that positions in the upper echelons of modern bureaucracies carry with them elements of reward that are understood to embody rents, behavior that has been discussed at some length in the orthodox rent-seeking analysis will emerge. The orthodox analysis has, however, implied, at least implicitly, that rent seeking generates social waste only in settings where *artificial* scarcities are created, for the most part by political agency.[13] The creation and dispensation of access to such artificially created rents will, indeed, bring forth inefficient rent-seeking behavior. What I have suggested in this paper is that rent seeking emerges as wasteful activity in any uncompensated transfer of value, and notably with respect to gifts and bequests among persons.

The rents involved in uncompensated transfers are not themselves "artificial" in the usual meaning of this term. The value embodied in the gift or bequest that a person plans to make may represent accumulation from a stream of returns that have been earned solely in competitive markets; there need be not one whit of monopoly rent or profit involved. To the set of potential recipients, however, any such value becomes precisely analogous to a rental opportunity that has been artificially created. The frugal rich man whose fortune must be transferred by gifts or bequests stands before his potential heirs in precisely the same relationship as Queen Elizabeth before her courtiers when she announced the possible assignment of a playing-card monopoly.

As I noted in my introductory essay to the volume, *Towards a Theory of the Rent-seeking Society*, rent seeking and profit seeking are behaviorally equivalent. The latter is socially efficient because it facilitates the flow of resources to their highest valued uses. Profit seeking (and loss avoidance), *as a process*, creates value in itself. By contrast, rent seeking is socially inefficient because the process in itself creates no value while utilizing scarce resources. The analysis of this paper suggests that any value that is to be transferred without compensation exists independently of the investment in attempts to redirect its disposition. No value can be created by such attempts. In terms of the efficiency norm, therefore, the identification of the succession in the ownership of valued assets is totally irrelevant.

Finally, a point about significance. I should not claim that this paper "discovers" a source of inefficiency that is quantitatively important in the aggregate transfers of value among persons. The rent-seeking ratio may be relatively small in many of the institutional settings within which transfers take place, although further empirical and institutional analysis would

---

[13] I can directly cite my own confusion here. In the concluding paper in Toward a Theory of the Rent-seeking Society (*supra* note 1), I stated: "Rent-seeking, as such, is totally without allocative value, although, of course, *the initial institutional creation of an opportunity for rent seeking ensures a net destruction of economic value*" (at 359, italics added). This statement is ambiguous in its implication that wasteful rent seeking emerges only when value is initially destroyed by the creation of monopoly rents.

be required to make serious estimates. I consider this paper more as a "tidying up" of the analysis of transfers than as a new motivation for ultimate policy reform. The theory of rent seeking remains novel; it is therefore not at all surprising that its range of applications has not been exhausted.

APPENDIX

My purpose in this Appendix is limited to the demonstration that, in the presence of rent seeking, quantitative restrictions on the unlimited rights-or powers to make uncompensated transfers can increase rather than decrease allocative efficiency. Through a highly simplified abstract example I shall compare the losses stemming from reductions in donor's surplus and those embodied in rent seeking. The example suggests that the efficient or optimal degree of quantitative restriction depends directly on the elasticity of demand for making transfers and on the size of the rent-seeking ratio.

Consider Figure 1, which is drawn in unit squares of value for expositional clarity. The donor's demand for making transfers is shown by D, drawn with a negative slope of unity. If there are no restrictions, 4 units of value will be transferred to recipients. There will be a donor's surplus of 8 units generated in the transfer process. In the presumed absence of rent seeking, the donor's cost of 4 units of value will just be matched by the recipient's gain of 4 units. Under these conditions it is clear that any restriction on the transfer power will reduce efficiency. If these restrictions take the form of quantitative limits on amounts transferred, the welfare losses can be measured by the familiar welfare triangles.

Assume now that the rent-seeking ratio is one-half. This ratio measures the relationship between total outlay on rent seeking and the net value of the transfer made. In this setting, if there are no quantitative restrictions on the power to transfer, there will be a net value of only 6 units generated. There will be a resource investment of 2 units in the attempts to qualify as recipients of the 4 units of value transferred. By comparison, consider a restriction that allows the donor to transfer a maximum of only 3 units. In this case, donor's surplus is reduced by ½ unit, but rent seeking is also reduced by ½. There are still 6 units of value generated as before; the restriction does not generate allocative inefficiency.

The "optimal" or "efficient" degree of restriction is at 3½ units. Note that, in this setting, the donor's surplus is reduced by only ⅛ unit below that which is enjoyed without restriction. But rent seeking is reduced by ¼ unit. There is a net efficiency gain of ⅛ unit of value in moving from totally unrestricted transfers to the quantitative restrictions that allow gifts or bequests of only 3½ units to be made.

If the quantitative restrictions should take the form of a tax on transfers (and if we can make the *highly questionable assumption* that access to governmental revenues does not itself set off further rent seeking) note that the optimal restriction under the simplified conditions specified is a tax of 50 percent of net transfer, or a tax of 33.3 percent of gross transfer, inclusive of tax.

The optimal degree of restriction clearly depends on the size of the rent-seeking ratio. If this ratio falls to ¼, the optimal degree of restriction is reduced. In terms of tax rates, under the assumptions noted, the rate that will generate the efficient

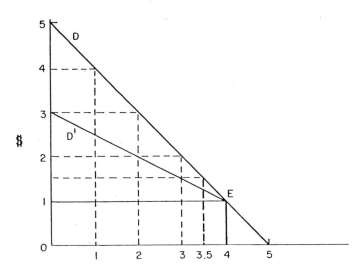

DOLLARS OF TRANSFER

FIGURE 1

restriction becomes 25 percent of net transfer, or 20 percent of transfer value gross of tax.

As the construction of Figure 1 indicates, the efficient degree of restriction will also depend on the elasticity of demand for making transfers. If we examine demand curves of differing slopes, it is relatively easy to see that there is a direct relationship between demand elasticity and restrictiveness. With demand curve, D', for example, the optimal restrictiveness is to limit transfers to 2½ units of value rather than 3½ units as in the earlier case. Note, however, that the tax rate required to produce this result is the same in both cases, 50 percent of net transfer value, or 33.3 percent of gross value, if the rent-seeking ratio is ½.

In somewhat more formal terms, the necessary condition for a maximally efficient level of transfers is given by

$$\frac{\delta U_d}{\delta t} = \frac{\delta R}{\delta t},$$

where the left-hand side defines the change in donor's surplus (converted into a numeraire) as transfer values increase and the right-hand side defines the change in rent seeking (valued in the numeraire) as transfers (t) increase. Unrestricted transfer power will produce a solution where, $\delta U_d/\delta t = 0$, which will be optimal only if, also, $\delta R/\delta t = 0$.

ELSEVIER

Journal of Economic Behavior & Organization
Vol. 44 (2001) 169–176

JOURNAL OF
Economic Behavior
& Organization

www.elsevier.com/locate/econbase

A model of institutional formation within a rent seeking environment

Kevin Sylwester*

*Department of Economics, Southern Illinois University Carbondale,
Mailcode 4515, Carbondale, IL 62901, USA*

Received 9 November 1998; received in revised form 10 January 2000; accepted 18 January 2000

Abstract

This paper presents a game theoretic model in which some fraction of output is appropriated from entrepreneurs. Entrepreneurs are able to form a league to prevent this appropriation, but this might not be individually rational because of either the free rider problem or coordination failure. The model also shows that poorer countries are less able to form this league and so might not be able to develop institutions establishing property rights. © 2001 Elsevier Science B.V. All rights reserved.

JEL classification: O10; H41

Keywords: Rent Seeking; Institutions; Property rights

1. Introduction

Although most economic models assume that agents can costlessly retain their property, this assumption has seldom held. Merchants and property owners have often been subject to theft or to other external threats to their possessions. In addition to illegal transfers of property, legal appropriation is also common. Agents engaged in rent seeking hire lawyers and lobbyists to redistribute wealth through laws and government regulations or to protect their property from government confiscation. North (1990) and Eggertsson (1990) focus upon how various institutions can promote or deter productive activities. But why should a society have institutions that lead to rent seeking and redistributive as opposed to productive activities? Why have some communities been able to form protective leagues or institutions that promote growth whereas others have not been as fortunate?

This paper attempts to answer these questions by presenting a model in which producers lose a fraction of their output to rent seekers. (See Tollison (1992) and Tollison (1982) for

---

* Tel.: +1-618-453-5347; fax: +1-618-453-2717.
E-mail address: ksylwest@siu.edu (K. Sylwester).

surveys on the rent seeking literature.) Agents can form an institutional structure (which is denoted as a coalition in the paper) to protect their property, but the free rider problem and coordination failure can prevent the coalition from forming. Thus, this paper focuses upon some of the problems of acting collectively as discussed in Olson (1965) and Olson (1982). This coalition can be viewed not only as a physical fortification but as the emergence of a social contract or constitution as in Buchanan (1975). In this setting, the formation of the coalition is contractarian in approach in that agents come together to form a collective and contrasts that of Olson (1993) in which property rights are either established by an autocrat or by several individuals when no one agent is strong enough to dominate the others. Of course, other collective institutions such as guilds and cartels seek to diminish competition in order to protect rents and are more formally considered in Olson (1982). The coalition in this paper is viewed as more encompassing of an entire community or society.

This model differs from other models of predation in two respects. First, there is no common property or tragedy of the commons as in Tornell (1997), Benhabib and Rustichini (1996), Hirshleifer (1991), and De Meza and Gould (1992). A more important difference is that agents have the opportunity to work collectively although this is not assumed. In Grossman and Kim (1995,1996a); Grossman (1991,1994), and Usher (1989), protecting property is a private endeavor. These models do not include a technology in which agents can band together for mutual protection. Grossman and Kim (1996b); Freeman (1993), and Shavell (1991) present models in which agents act collectively to protect property but these models do not consider any deterrents to act collectively. Collective action is assumed. Finally, Skogh and Stuart (1982) consider how the rise of a criminal code can lower theft and promote productive activity relative to anarchy but they also do not consider issues such as the free rider problem and coordination failure as to why this code fails to develop.

The model is presented in section two and equilibria are determined in section three. Section four presents comparative statics and implications. A conclusion follows.

2. The Model

There is a two stage game involving two sets of agents.[1] These agents take actions consistent with rational beliefs as to what the other agents will do. All parameters are common knowledge. Part one of this section describes the agents. Part two describes the two stages.

2.1. Agents

The first set comprises an identical group of agents which I denote as entrepreneurs. An extension with heterogeneous agents is available from the author. Each agent has density equal to one and the total density of the group is $N > 0$. Let $g > 0$ denote the level of output that each agent produces.

---

[1] The model could be changed so as to contain only one set of agents and such a version is available from the author. The model is more tractable having two sets of agents and the primary conclusions of the paper remain.

K. Sylwester / J. of Economic Behavior & Org. 44 (2001) 169–176   171

The second set consists of a continuum of heterogeneous agents. These agents also produce output but in a different sector (e.g. a traditional sector) of the economy than do entrepreneurs. This continuum lies along some distribution B within the range $[0, b^H]$ where $0 < b^H < \infty$. Each agent, j, has density one. b is an element of B and denotes agent j's level of production where the "j" is understood. This group of agents has the option to appropriate output from entrepreneurs. If an agent chooses to appropriate output, he does not produce output himself. I denote an agent who appropriates output as a bandit although this should not be interpreted to mean that appropriation is necessarily an illegal activity.

The payoff for each agent is the amount of output that he acquires.

2.2. Stages

2.2.1. Stage 1: Agents choose whether or not to become bandits

Each agent in the traditional sector decides whether or not to become a bandit. Each bandit appropriates the fraction z of output from all entrepreneurs with $0 < z < 1$.[2] The parameter z denotes the return to rent seeking. If appropriating output is not an illegal activity, a low z could denote a political system where those in the traditional sector have little power and so cannot acquire transfers from other agents. The return to banditry (Ban) with no coalition is $\text{Ban} = zNg$. With mass S bandits, the return for an entrepreneur is $(1 - Sz)g$. I only consider cases where $S < 1/z$ so that an entrepreneur does not lose all of his output.

2.2.2. Stage 2: Forming the coalition

Each entrepreneur has the option of joining a coalition which collects contributions from its members in order to provide protection from bandits. Agents noncooperatively decide whether or not to join the coalition. For expositional purposes, I assume that not more than one coalition exists.[3] The coalition cannot exclude any agent who wants to join. The total cost of the coalition is $F[E^c, S, \psi]$ which can be thought of as the cost of building fortifications or as enforcement costs under a legal system. E^c denotes the mass of coalition members. $F[*, *, *]$ is increasing with both E^c and S. As the mass of coalition members increases, coordination costs increase. With more bandits, more resources are required to protect output. The parameter ψ captures factors such as the efficiency of the bureaucracy in fighting rent seeking or the technology of protecting coalition members from theft. I assume $F[1, S > 0, *] > g$ which implies that no agent can afford to pay for the coalition if he is the lone member of the coalition. I also assume that $F[E^c, S, \psi]/S$ is increasing with S. Each member of the coalition pays an equal share of the cost and so makes a payment (P) of $P = F[E^c, S, \psi]/E^c$. The coalition cannot price discriminate among agents. An Appendix A shows that the conclusions of the model continue to hold under a voluntary payment scheme.

Provided a coalition forms, a coalition member retains all of his output and so is completely protected. For those entrepreneurs not in the coalition, each retains $g(1 - Sz\delta)$. The

---

[2] The model does not assume that predation is costly in that no output is destroyed during the transfer from entrepreneur to bandit, but the model could be extended so as to allow for lost output and still retain its general conclusions.

[3] Having more than one coalition will not affect the primary conclusions of the paper.

Kevin Sylwester

parameter $0 \leq \delta \leq 1$ measures the degree of exclusion. If $\delta = 1$, agents outside the coalition are completely excluded from the benefits provided by the coalition. If $\delta = 0$, there is no exclusion and the coalition is a public good. The parameter δ denotes such factors as the ability of the society to ostracize nonparticipants as well as the technology of protection. For example, δ may be "high" if the coalition denotes a protective league in which noncontributors can be kept outside the walls of a fort or castle.

As stated, the coalition cannot deny entry to any agent nor can it price discriminate. The technology of the coalition is discrete in that no protection arises if it is not fully funded. Under these assumptions, the objective of the coalition becomes trivial and is to fully protect all agents who make a payment of P and join. The extensions mentioned above are interesting issues but are beyond the scope of this paper.

3. Decision rules and equilibria

In this section, I use backward induction to solve the model for pure strategy, subgame perfect equilibria. Agents act noncooperatively and view their actions as negligible in determining outcomes.

In stage two, S is given. An agent joins the coalition if the return to joining outweighs the return from free riding: $g - P \geq g(1 - Sz\delta)$. Dividing by g, $1 - F[E^c, S, \psi]/gE^c \geq (1 - Sz\delta)$. Given E^c and S, this inequality holds for all entrepreneurs if and only if the inequality holds for any entrepreneur. Thus, either all entrepreneurs join the coalition or no one joins and only one of these two extremes is realized. For a coalition to exist in which all entrepreneurs join, the above inequality must hold for $E^c = N$ given S. As assumed above, this inequality does not hold for $E^c = 1$ for any $S > 0$.

In stage one, the return to banditry is dependent upon the mass of coalition members: $\text{Ban} = z\delta(N - E^c)$. From above, either all entrepreneurs join the coalition or no entrepreneurs join. If all entrepreneurs join, then $N = E^c$ and $\text{Ban} = 0$. The only agents that become bandits are those for which $b = 0$ since they are indifferent to becoming bandits or to remaining in the traditional sector. [4] No agent for which $b > 0$ becomes a bandit. Instead, these agents produce output. If no entrepreneurs join the coalition, then all entrepreneurs are unprotected. Agents in the traditional sector become bandits until the return to banditry equals the return to working in the traditional sector. For the marginal bandit, $b = zNg$.

Therefore, there are potentially two equilibria. An equilibrium that always exists is one in which no entrepreneurs join the coalition and in which there are mass S^{**} bandits where S^{**} is determined by the mass of agents for which $b \leq zNg$. Entrepreneurs do not join the coalition because a coalition with $E^c = N$ is not individually optimal given S^{**} or because of coordination failure. Since no agent can afford to pay for the coalition himself, no agent wants to be the lone member of the coalition and so will never join by himself. The other equilibrium consists of all entrepreneurs joining the coalition and for S to equal the mass of agents for which $b = 0$. I denote this mass as S^* and $S^* < S^{**}$ since $0 < zNg$. The following proposition summarizes the possible equilibria of the model.

---

[4] I assume that all agents for which $b = 0$ become bandits even though they are indifferent when $E^c = N$. These agents can be thought of as permanent bandits.

K. Sylwester / J. of Economic Behavior & Org. 44 (2001) 169–176   173

Proposition 1. *Consider the following inequality:*

$$1 - \frac{F[N, S, \psi]}{Ng} \geq 1 - z\delta Sa \tag{1}$$

Regardless of (1), an equilibrium always exists where $E^c = 0$ and $S = S^{**}$. If (1) holds for $S = S^*$, then an equilibrium with a coalition exists where $E^c = N$ and $S = S^*$. If (1) does not hold for $S = S^*$, then (1) does not hold for $S = S^{**}$ and the only equilibrium is for $E^c = 0$ and $S = S^{**}$.

Given a coalition, there are S^* bandits. Eq. (1) says that joining the coalition is individually optimal if all other entrepreneurs join given S bandits. Hence, an equilibrium with a coalition exists provided (1) holds with $S = S^*$. Since $F[N, S, \psi]/NgS$ is increasing with S, then (1) does not hold for $S = S^{**}$ if (1) does not hold for $S = S^*$. Therefore, if (1) does not hold for $S = S^*$, the only equilibrium is for $S = S^{**}$ and $E^c = 0$. A coalition having only a subset of entrepreneurs does not exist in equilibrium since all agents join the coalition if any agent finds it optimal to join.

A special case occurs if $\delta = 0$. No coalition forms in equilibrium since the payoff from not joining the coalition (g) is higher than the payoff from joining the coalition $(g - P)$ for all agents. No agent joins the coalition since nonmembers receive the same protection as members. It is this case that most resembles the argument from Olson (1965). Moreover, no agent can afford to be the lone member of the coalition with $g < F[1, S > 0, *]$. Thus, an equilibrium with a coalition does not exist with $\delta = 0$.

4. Comparative statics and implications

The parameters of the model are g, B, z, N, F, ψ, and δ. The first four parameters determine S^{**}, the mass of bandits in the absence of a coalition. S^{**} is increasing with z since the return to banditry increases as bandits take a higher fraction of output from entrepreneurs. S^{**} is also increasing with Ng, the aggregate income of entrepreneurs. Multiplying each element of B by some constant greater than one lowers S^{**} since there is less incentive to become a bandit when the return in the traditional sector increases. However, multiplying g and each element of B by the same constant does not affect S^{**} because it does not affect the relative return of producing output to become a bandit. S^{**} is only affected when g and B grow at unequal rates. If g grows faster than the elements of B, S^{**} increases.

Given S, the parameters $g, N, F[*, *, \psi]$, and δ determine whether or not a coalition with an equilibrium exists. As ψ increases, the cost of the coalition rises implying that there are fewer values of S for which (1) holds. The effect of N upon the per agent cost of the coalition is ambiguous. A large entrepreneurial sector raises the aggregate cost of forming a coalition but also lowers the per agent cost given $F[N, *, \psi]$.

The inequality in (1) holds for more values of S as g becomes larger. As per capita income grows, the relative cost of joining the coalition decreases. This implies that higher income countries are better able to develop institutions that protect property than are poorer countries. North (1990) as well as others have argued that effective institutions promote economic growth. This model suggests that causality can run in the opposite direction as well, from income levels to the creation of effective institutions. Therefore, one might expect

174   K. Sylwester / J. of Economic Behavior & Org. 44 (2001) 169–176

to see countries with better institutions grow faster over time (as argued elsewhere), but one would also expect to see that at a point in time higher income countries are more likely to develop institutions to protect property. This might be one reason why poor countries are not converging to high income nations as implied by many neoclassical growth models (see Quah (1993)). In fact, using the same aggregate production function for both high and low income nations (so that the only difference between the two is the capital to labor ratio) may not be reasonable if various institutional environments hold different implications for the marginal returns to inputs.

A lower δ makes free riding more attractive and creates a disincentive for agents to join the coalition thereby further separating socially optimal and individually optimal outcomes. Suppose (1) holds with $\delta = 1$. Then, entrepreneurs will form a coalition given S bandits if they could act collectively. This is the outcome in Grossman and Kim (1996b) where collective action is assumed to occur. If (1) does not hold with $\delta = 1$, then entrepreneurs as a group tolerate banditry and concerns such as coordination failure or the free rider problem become irrelevant. However, suppose (1) holds in country A with $\delta_A = 1$ but does not hold in country B with $\delta_B < 1$ but which is otherwise identical to A. Without agents being able to act collectively, the free rider problem prevents the coalition from forming in B even though an entrepreneur would prefer to join a coalition as opposed to having no coalition at all.

A limiting case occurs when $\delta_B = 0$. Then, all entrepreneurs in B can be protected by the coalition even if the coalition is small. Consequently, the aggregate cost of the coalition is lower in B and so it is less expensive for B to protect all of its entrepreneurs than can A where nonmembers are excluded. In this sense, country B has a superior "protection technology" since it entails lower aggregate costs for society. However, it is not individually optimal for an entrepreneur in B to "use the superior technology" (i.e. join the coalition) and so having a superior protection technology may not lead to a better outcome for society. This implies that when designing a system of property rights or of physical protection, avoiding the free rider problem by excluding or punishing noncontributors might entail higher costs for society along other dimensions.

However, not all agents are better off with a coalition. Agent j in the traditional sector receives b from producing. If $b < zNg$, then his income is higher without a coalition. Since the poorest agents have higher income and richer agents lose income, income inequality declines without a coalition. In this case, a trade-off exists between maximizing output and lowering income inequality. [5] Moreover, a fall of this institutional structure (possibly brought about by some political upheaval) would result in a loss of aggregate output as well as a fall in the level of income inequality between the two groups.

5. Conclusion

Spending resources to appropriate property negatively affects aggregate production although agents find it in their private interest to engage in rent seeking. By forming a

---

[5] This result stems from the assumption that a coalition only comprises entrepreneurs and is designed to protect their wealth. This assumption is relevant in cases where those with the highest incomes (taken here to be the entrepreneurs) also have the political power to shape property rights in their interests.

K. Sylwester / J. of Economic Behavior & Org. 44 (2001) 169–176   175

coalition, a community can deter predation and thereby increase aggregate output (although this might not benefit all agents). However, coordination failure or the free rider problem can prevent the creation of a coalition. In addition, the model implies that poor countries are less able to develop institutional structures that protect property than are higher income communities and so causality between the institutional and economic environments runs in both directions.

Acknowledgements

I would like to thank Rody Manuelli, Steve Durlauf, Larry Samuelson and four anonymous referees for their suggestions. All errors are mine.

Appendix A

In the text, the cost of joining the coalition is the same for each agent. This appendix considers an environment in which each agent voluntarily contributes an amount to fund the cost of the coalition thereby showing that the results of this paper do not rely upon the specific payment scheme constructed above.

Consider the game of deciding how much to contribute to the coalition. A strategy for each coalition member, denoted by c, is a fraction $p(c)$ (where $0 \leq p(c) \geq 1$) of his revenue to contribute to paying for the coalition. For a coalition to be funded,

$$F[E^c, S, \psi] \leq g \sum p(c)$$

where the summation runs across all members of the coalition. But an agent should decrease his contribution if there are more than enough funds so,

$$F[E^c, S, \psi] = g \sum p(c)$$

in equilibrium. For an agent to join the coalition, the return from doing so must be greater than the return from free riding: $g - gp(c) \geq g(1 - Sz\delta) \to 1 - p(c) \geq 1 - Sz\delta$. Provided that the coalition is funded, all entrepreneurs join if $\delta > 0$ since $p(c)$ is allowed to be arbitrarily close to zero and each agent takes $F[*, *, *]$ as given. So with $\delta > 0$, all agents join the coalition provided the costs of the coalition are met.

When can a coalition exist? A coalition can form given S if there exists some set $\{p(c)\}_{c \in [0, N]}$ with $1 - p(c) \geq 1 - Sz\delta$ for all $c \in [0, N]$ such that,

$$g \sum p(c) = F[N, *, *]$$

Suppose all agents choose the same rate, $p(c) = p$ for all $c \in [0, N]$ where p solves $F[N, S^*, *] = gNp$. This is the case in the text. If $1 - p > 1 - z\delta S^*$, then an equilibrium with a coalition exists in the text and so there is a trivial voluntary payment scheme that can support a coalition, namely $p(c) = p$ for all agents.

176   *K. Sylwester / J. of Economic Behavior & Org. 44 (2001) 169–176*

On the other hand, if there exists a voluntary payment scheme $\{p(c)\}_{c \in [0,N]}$ such that $1 - p(c) \geq 1 - z\delta S^*$ for all $c \in [0, N]$ and

$$g \sum p(c) = F[N, S^*, *]$$

then a coalition exists with $p(c) = p$ for all agents, which is the case in the text. This is true because p also solves $F[*, *, *] = gNp$. Moreover, $p \leq \max\{p(c)\}$ with equality only if $p(c) = p$ for all agents. So if joining the coalition is individually optimal when contributing $\max\{p(c)\}$, it is individually optimal for an agent contributing $p \leq \max\{p(c)\}$. If all agents contributed less than p, then the coalition would be underfunded and would not exist.

In summary, a coalition exists in equilibrium given $p(c) = p$ for all agents if and only if there is at least one voluntary payment scheme which supports a coalition.

References

Benhabib, J., Rustichini, A., 1996. Social conflict and growth. Journal of Economic Growth 1, 125–142.

Buchanan, J., 1975. The Limits of Liberty: Between Anarchy and Leviathan. The University of Chicago Press, Chicago.

De Meza, D., Gould, J.R., 1992. The Social efficiency of private decisions to enforce property rights. Journal of Political Economy 100, 50–68.

Eggertsson, T., 1990. Economic Behavior and Institutions. Cambridge University Press, New York.

Freeman, S., 1993. Underdevelopment and the Enforcement of Property Rights. Working Paper no. 9302, Department of Economics, University of Texas.

Grossman, H., 1991. A general equilibrium model of insurrections. American Economic Review 81, 912–921.

Grossman, H., 1994. Production, appropriation and land reform. American Economic Review 84, 705–712.

Grossman, H., Kim, M., 1995. Swords or plowshares? A theory of the security of the claims to property. Journal of Political Economy 103, 1275–1288.

Grossman, H., Kim, M., 1996a. Predation and accumulation. Journal of Economic Growth 1, 333–350.

Grossman, H., Kim, M., 1996b. Inequality, Predation, and Welfare. NBER Working Paper no. 5704.

Hirshleifer, J., 1991. The paradox of power, economics. Economics and Politics 3, 177–200.

North, D., 1990. Institutions, Institutional Change, and Economic Performance. Cambridge University Press, New York.

Olson, M., 1965. The Logic of Collective Action. Schocken Books, New York.

Olson, M., 1982. The Rise and Decline of Nations. Yale University Press, New Haven.

Olson, M., 1993. Dictatorship, democracy, and development. American Political Science Review 87, 567–576.

Quah, D., 1993. Galton's fallacy and tests of the convergence hypothesis. Scandinavian Journal of Economics 95, 427–443.

Shavell, S., 1991. Individual precautions to prevent theft: private versus socially optimal behavior, international review of law. International Review of Law and Economics 11, 123–132.

Skogh, G., Stuart, C., 1982. A contractarian theory of property rights and crime. Scandanavian Journal of Economics 84, 27–40.

Tollison, R.D., 1982. Rent seeking: a survey. Kyklos 35, 575–602.

Tollison, R.D., 1992. Rent Seeking. In: Mueller, D.C. (Ed.), Perspectives on Public Choice: A Handbook. Cambridge University Press, New York.

Tornell, A., 1997. Economic growth and decline with endogenous property rights. Journal of Economic Growth 2, 219–250.

Usher, D., 1989. The dynastic cycle and the stationary state. American Economic Review 79, 1031–1044.

Soc Choice Welfare 26:183–189 (2006)
DOI 10.1007/s00355-006-0079-1

ORIGINAL PAPER

J. Atsu Amegashie

The 2002 Winter Olympics scandal: rent-seeking and committees

Received: 21 April 2004 / Accepted: 16 December 2004 / Published online: 23 March 2006
© Springer-Verlag 2006

Abstract In the wake of a judging controversy at the Winter 2002 Olympic games, the governing council of the International Skating Union scrapped its judging system, replacing it with a new system which uses scores from only some of the judges, selected randomly. This means that the composition of the awarding committee is unknown. I examine rent-seeking expenditures when the composition of the committee is unknown relative to the case when it is known. When the composition of the committee is unknown, I find that rent-seeking expenditures directed towards each committee member may fall but aggregate rent-seeking expenditures will not fall. I find the counter-intuitive result that there may be no change in the rent-seeking effort directed at each committee member, even if it is known that some of the members will not be part of the final awarding committee. The results hinge on whether there is full rent dissipation or rent under-dissipation when the composition of the committee is known.

1 Introduction

"In the wake of a judging controversy that shook the foundations of the sport of figure skating at the 2002 Winter Olympics in Salt Lake City, USA, the governing council of the International Skating Union (ISU) voted ... to scrap its judging system, replacing it with a new point system and using scores from only some of the judges, selected randomly.... ISU President Ottavio Cinquanta said the changes mark a 'total revolution' that will reduce the possibility of bloc judging, in which judges from different countries agree to support each other's skaters. ... [i]nstead of nine judges on the panel, there would be fourteen. A computer would randomly pick seven of those fourteen judges, whose marks would decide who wins. No one – not even the judges –

J. A. Amegashie (✉)
Department of Economics, University of Guelph, Guelph, ON, N1G 2W1, Canada
E-mail: jamegash@uoguelph.ca

would know which marks count and which do not... [t]he decision by the ISU Council comes in the wake of the controversial judging of the pairs competition at the Salt Lake Olympics, where a Russian pair who stumbled triumphed over the Canadian pair that did not. The ISU and the International Olympic Committee eventually decided to award a second set of gold medals to Canadians Jamie Sale and David Pelletier...."[1]

In this paper, I examine the effect of the random selection of judges on the rent-seeking efforts of the various countries. I do not examine how this change affects bloc judging. Instead, I investigate whether rent-seeking expenditures, if the composition of the awarding committee is known, are higher than expenditures when the composition of the awarding committee is unknown. The magnitude of individual and aggregate rent-seeking expenditures may be used as a proxy for bloc judging in so far as a judge's decision to participate in bloc judging is influenced by the rent-seeking efforts directed towards that judge. In other words, the propensity to engage in bloc judging is positively related to rent-seeking efforts directed at a given judge. Indeed, Jamie Sale and David Pelletier were awarded gold medals after a French judge, Marie-Reine Le Gougne, admitted she had been pressured into voting for the Russians. If the judges are under less rent-seeking pressure, then they are likely to reach the correct decision. I therefore assume that a goal of the ISU is to minimize rent-seeking pressure on judges.

We may formalize the preceding argument as follows: Suppose skater i has valuation, $W_i > 0$, for winning the prize. A skater with a higher valuation could also be thought of as one with a higher ability in the skating contest (see Baye et al. 1996; Clark and Riis 1998 for reviews). Therefore, suppose that a judge, say judge k, is likely to reach a "correct" decision if she were to vote with probability $\frac{W_i}{W_i + \sum_{j \neq i} W_j}$ for skater i. This function may be the outcome of the equilibrium efforts in the skating contest. For example, suppose there are only two skaters competing and e_i is the skating effort of player i. Then if $e_i/(e_i + e_j)$ is the success probability of skater i (used by a given judge), it can be shown that, in equilibrium, this judge will vote for skater i with probability $W_i/(W_i + W_j)$, if the cost function of skating effort is linear (i.e., $c(e_i) = e_i$).[2]

Let x_{ik} be the lobbying effort directed at judge k on behalf of skater i. Taking into account lobbying efforts, suppose judge k votes for skater i, with probability $p_{ik} = \theta \frac{W_i}{W_i + \sum_{j \neq i} W_j} + (1 - \theta) \frac{x_{ik}}{x_{ik} + \sum_{j \neq i} x_{jk}}$, where $0 \leq \theta \leq 1$. Thus, the judge's decision is a weighted function of lobbying efforts and skating efforts. Then as x_{ik} increases, judge k is more likely to deviate from the "correct" decision because the *relative* contribution of the rent-seeking (lobbying) component of the judge's decision-making increases (i.e., $\partial p_{ik}/\partial x_{ik} > 0$). Hence, reducing rent-seeking effort may move the judges towards the "correct" decision.

I assume that the rent-seekers or the contestants in the lobbying contest are the officials of the various countries represented by the skaters. I assume that each judge does not necessarily vote for the contestant who expends the highest

---

[1] This paragraph appeared in an article at a CNN website on February 18, 2002 at http://sportsillustrated.cnn.com/olympics/2002/figure_skating/news/2002/02/18/skating_reforms/. The article was not attributed to any author.
[2] See, for example, Nti (1999) for a review.

lobbying effort. Hence, voting by a judge is probabilistic (not deterministic). As noted by Coughlin (1992, p. 21) "deterministic voting models are most appropriate with candidates who are well-informed about the voters and their preferences.... [p]robabilistic voting models... are most appropriate in elections in which candidates have incomplete information about voters' preferences and/or there are some random factors that can potentially affect voters' decisions...." In my model, the contestants are the candidates and the committee members (i.e., the judges) are the voters. Hence, one could interpret my model as one in which the contestants do not know the exact preferences of the committee of judges or that some random factors affect the decisions of the judges.

There has been a wide literature on committees and collective decision_making since the seminal works of Arrow (1963); Black (1958); Buchanan and Tullock (1962). The relationship between rent–seeking[3] and committees was first examined by Congleton (1984). He showed that a rent awarded by a committee will generate less rent-seeking expenditures than a similar rent awarded by a single administrator. Amegashie (2002, 2003) shows that the result of Congleton (1984) is not robust.

The main results of this paper are as follows: When the composition of the committee is unknown, I find that rent-seeking expenditures directed towards each committee member may fall but aggregate rent-seeking expenditures might increase. I find the counter-intuitive result that there may be no change in the rent-seeking effort directed at each committee member, even if it is known that some of the members will not be part of the final awarding committee. The results hinge on whether there is full rent dissipation or rent under-dissipation when the composition of the committee is known.

2 The model

Suppose a committee of size S will be chosen to award a rent which is commonly valued at $V > 0$ by $N \geq 2$ risk-neutral and identical contestants. Suppose the committee will be chosen from M potential members, where $M \geq S$. If $M = S$, then the composition of the committee is known by the contestants. If $M > S$, then the contestants do not know which of the M members will actually be members of the committee. As in the case of the ISU's rules above, we assume that the contestants have to expend rent-seeking efforts before the composition of the awarding committee is revealed.

Let $P_i(S)$ be the probability that the i-th contestant will win the prize, if the composition of the committee is known and is of size S. Define $P_i(S, M)$ as the probability that the i-th contestant will win the prize, if the composition of the committee is unknown (i.e., S members will be chosen from M members). Let x_{ik} be the rent-seeking effort of the i-th contestant directed at the k-th committee member, $k = 1, 2, ..., M - 1, M$, and $i = 1, 2, ..., N - 1, N$. I assume that $P_i(S)$ and $P_i(S, M)$ are continuous, twice differentiable functions and are increasing in x_{ik} but decreasing in x_{jk}, $i \neq j$.

---

[3] See Nitzan (1994) for a survey of the rent-seeking literature and Epstein and Nitzan (2003a,b) for some recent rent-seeking models.

In what follows, we assume that all potential committee members are identical. For example, they have the same sensitivity to rent-seeking expenditures.[4] This assumption allows us to focus on the effect of random selection of committee members.

First, consider the case where the composition of the committee is known (i.e., $S = M$). The i-th contestant chooses his rent-seeking efforts to maximize

$$\pi_i(S) = P_i(S)V - \sum_{k=1}^{S} x_{ik} .\tag{1}$$

The first-order conditions are:

$$\partial \pi_i(S)/\partial x_{ik} = V\left(\partial P_i(S)/\partial x_{ik}\right) - 1 = 0 \tag{2}$$

$\forall i \neq j$ and $k \neq h$. In a symmetric Nash equilibrium, $x_{ik} = x_{jk} = x \ \forall \ i \neq j$ and $k \neq h$.[5] Putting these into the first-order conditions above gives the Nash equilibrium effort per contestant per committee member. Denote this value by x^*. The equilibrium payoff is $(1/N)V - Sx^* \geq 0$. Therefore, we require $x^* \leq V/NS$.

Now consider the case where the composition of the committee is unknown (i.e., $M > S$). There are $m \equiv M!/S!(M-S)!$ ways of selecting S members from M members. Following the ISU's rules, we assume that each of these combinations is equally likely. The i-th contestant chooses his rent-seeking efforts to maximize

$$\pi_i(S, M) = P_i(S, M)V - \sum_{k=1}^{M} x_{ik} .\tag{3}$$

Given that the size of the awarding committee is S in each of the m possible cases, we can write $P_i(S, M) = \frac{1}{m}\sum_{g=1}^{m} P_{ig}(S)$, where P_{ig} is the probability that the i-th contestant will win the prize if the g-th committee of size S is chosen. However, given that the M potential committee members are identical, we can also write $P_{ig}(S) = P_i(S) \ \forall \ g$. Hence, we can write $P_i(S, M) = \frac{1}{m}\sum_{g=1}^{m} P_i(S) = P_i(S)$.

Using Eq. 3, the first-order conditions are

$$\partial \pi_i(S, M)/\partial x_{ik} = V\left(\partial P_i(S)/\partial x_{ik}\right) - 1 = 0 \tag{4}$$

$\forall i \neq j$ and $k \neq h$. In a symmetric Nash equilibrium, $x_{ik} = x_{jk} = x \ \forall \ i \neq j$ and $k \neq h$. Putting these into the first-order conditions in Eq. 4 above gives the Nash equilibrium effort per contestant per committee member. Denote this value by $\hat{x}$. The equilibrium payoff is $(1/N)V - M\hat{x} \geq 0$. Therefore, we require $\hat{x} \leq V/NM$. Comparing Eqs. 2 and 4, it is straightforward to see that $x^* = \hat{x}$. However, this will only hold subject to a non-negative payoff condition for each player. I shall elaborate below.

---

[4] See Amegashie (2002) for a model in which committee members have different sensitivities to rent-seeking and an explicit function for $P_i(S)$ is specified.
[5] We assume that the second-order conditions for a maximum hold.

It is important to note that no player has the incentive to deviate from the symmetric equilibrium above. A similar result was obtained in Amegashie (2002). This is because, in equilibrium, if the i-th player were to deviate by increasing his rent-seeking effort on committee member h and reduce his effort on member k, his probability of success will not change because $\partial P_i(S)/\partial x_{ik} = \partial P_i(S)/\partial x_{ih} = 1/V$, $\forall h \neq k$. The continuity of the success probabilities stems from the assumption that a committee member does not necessarily vote for the contestant who exerts the highest rent-seeking effort. If each committee member voted for the contestant who lobbies him the most, then the symmetric equilibrium above will not hold. The success probabilities will be discontinuous functions and each contestant will target a subset of committee members (i.e., majoritarian coalitions).[6]

Now suppose $x^* = V/NS$. This means that there is full rent dissipation when the composition of the committee is known. In general, there will be full rent dissipation if the number of contestants is sufficiently large (i.e., N is large) and/or the sensitivity of the judges to rent-seeking expenditures is sufficiently high (i.e., $\partial P_i(S)/\partial x_{ik}$ is high). For an example, consider Eq. 4 in Amegashie (2002), where the Tullock probability function is used and the size of the committee is 3. It is easy to show that, given $S = M = 3$ and committee members have the same sensitivity to rent-seeking efforts (i.e., $\alpha = \beta = \gamma > 0$), aggregate rent-seeking expenditure is $\alpha\left(1 - \frac{1}{N^2}\right)V$. Then aggregate rent-seeking expenditure is equal to V, if α and/or N is sufficiently high.

If $x^* = V/NS$, then $\hat{x} \neq x^* = V/NS$. To see this, recall that we require that $\hat{x} \leq V/NM$. However, given $M > S$, we know that $V/NM < V/NS$. Hence, the optimal solution is $\hat{x} \leq V/NM < x^*$. Therefore, in a symmetric equilibrium, $\partial \pi_i(S, M)/\partial x_{ik} = V\left(\partial P_i(S)/\partial x_{ik}\right) - 1 > 0$ at $x_{ik} = \hat{x} < x^* \forall i$. In this equilibrium, $\partial P_i(S)/\partial x_{ik} = \partial P_i(S)/\partial x_{ih} \forall h \neq k$. Hence, as argued before, no player has the incentive to deviate. Aggregate expenditure is $NM\hat{x} \leq V$. This leads to the following proposition:

Proposition 1: *When the composition of the awarding committee is known and there is full rent dissipation (i.e., if $x^* = V/NS$), then there could also be full rent dissipation when the composition of the committee is unknown but the rent-seeking effort per committee member is higher when the composition of the committee is known.*

Now, suppose $x^* < V/NS$ (i.e., rent under-dissipation). Then it is possible to have $\hat{x} = x^* \leq V/NM < V/NS$. Aggregate expenditure is $NMx^* \leq V$, when the composition of the committee is unknown and is $NSx^* < V$ when the composition is known, where $NMx^* > NSx^*$. This gives the following proposition:

Proposition 2: *When the composition of the awarding committee is known and there is rent under-dissipation, then (a) there could be full rent dissipation when the composition of the committee is unknown, and (b) the rent-seeking effort per committee member is never smaller when the composition of the committee is known.*

---

[6] See Congleton (1984), Myerson (1993) and Amegashie (2003).

3 Discussion and conclusion

Propositions 1 and 2 imply that holding the size of the awarding committee fixed,[7] the new ISU rule will (at best) reduce and will (at worst) not increase the rent-seeking expenditures directed at each member of the panel of judges but it will not reduce aggregate rent-seeking expenditures. The former objective is probably the goal of the ISU.

Notice when the composition of the committee is known and there is rent under-dissipation, there is full rent dissipation when the composition of the committee is unknown and the number of potential members, M, is sufficiently large. The intuition is simple. If the contestants have a positive surplus when the composition of the committee is known, they simply dissipate part or all of their surpluses when extra potential committee members are added. This also accounts for the counter-intuitive result that there may be no change in the rent-seeking effort directed at each committee member, even if it is known that some of the members will not be part of the final awarding committee (i.e., $x^* = \widehat{x}$ is possible).

It is important to note that our propositions will not significantly change if the contestants are not identical (i.e., if the Vs are different). This is because our key argument which enabled us to write $P_i(S, M) = \frac{1}{m} \sum_{g=1}^{m} P_i(S) = P_i(S)$ hinges on the assumption of identical judges not on identical contestants. It also hinges on the assumption that the size of the awarding committee is the same in each of the m possible scenarios.

The paper has offered some insights into rent-seeking expenditures under committee administration when the composition of the committee is unknown relative to the case where it is known. The analysis was applied to the recent changes by the ISU with regard to the selection of its panel of judges. The new rule *may* reduce rent-seeking effort directed towards each panel member but will not reduce aggregate rent-seeking expenditures. However, the results hinge crucially on whether there is full rent dissipation or rent under-dissipation when the composition of the committee is known.

Acknowledgement My thanks are due to an anonymous referee for the helpful comments.

References

Amegashie JA (2002) Committees and rent-seeking effort under probabilistic voting. Public Choice 112:345–350
Amegashie JA (2003) The all-pay auction when a committee awards the prize. Public Choice 116:79–90
Arrow KJ (1963) Social choice and individual values, 2nd edn. Wiley, New York
Baye MR, Kovenock D, de Vries CG (1996) The all-pay auction with complete information. Econ Theory 8:291–305
Black D (1958) The theory of committees and elections. Cambridge Univ. Press, London
Buchanan JM, Tullock G (1962) The calculus of consent. Univ. of Michigan Press, Ann Arbor
Clark DJ, Riis C (1998) Competition over more than one prize. Am Econ Rev 88:276–289
Congleton RD (1984) Committees and rent-seeking effort. J Public Econ 25:197–209

---

[7] In Amegashie (2002, 2003) and Congleton (1984), the size of the awarding committee is varied. To focus on only the effect of random selection of judges, I keep the size of the committee fixed.

Coughlin PJ (1992) Probabilistic voting theory. Cambridge Univ. Press, Cambridge
Epstein GS, Nitzan S (2003a) Political culture and monopoly price determination. Soc Choice
     Welf 21:1–19
Epstein GS, Nitzan S (2003b) Reduced prizes and increased effort in contests. Soc Choice Welf,
     (in press)
Myerson RB (1993) Incentives to cultivate favored minorities under alternative electoral systems.
     Am Polit Sci Rev 87:856–869
Nitzan S (1994) Modelling rent-seeking contests. Eur J Polit Econ 10:41–60
Nti KO (1999) Rent-seeking with asymmetric valuations. Public Choice 98:415–430

14

·········

Mercantilism as a
Rent-Seeking Society

by

BARRY BAYSINGER, ROBERT B. EKELUND, JR.,

and ROBERT D. TOLLISON

> The proposal of any new law or regulation of commerce which comes from this order [merchants and manufacturers], ought never to be adopted till after having been long and carefully examined, not only with the most scrupulous, but with the most suspicious attention. It comes from an order of men, whose interest is never exactly the same with that of the public, who have generally an interest to deceive and even to oppress the public, and who accordingly have, upon many occasions, both deceived and oppressed it. —Adam Smith, *Wealth of Nations*

MERCANTILIST economic doctrines are typically summarized in terms of the central tendencies found in the literature of the period, roughly dated from 1500 to 1776. Among the most often-stressed tenets of the mercantilists are the equation of specie with wealth, regulation of the trade sector to produce specie inflow, and emphasis upon population growth and low wages. Absolutist historians of economic thought tend to stress the presence of grave errors in mercantilist logic, which were exposed by David Hume, Adam Smith, and the classical economists generally. The primary example of such faulty reasoning was, of course, the failure of the mercantilists to recognize the self-regulating nature that the "specie-flow mechanism" imposed on the mercantilist objective of a perennial trade surplus.[1] Relativist histo-

---

[1] Keynes defended the mercantilists on the grounds that a favorable balance of trade was the only feasible means available to a country at that time of lowering domestic

In: James M. Buchanan, Robert D. Tollison, and Gordon Tullock (Eds.),
Toward a Theory of the Rent-Seeking Society. Texas A&M University Press,
College Station, 235–268

rians of thought tend to view the mercantilists more charitably. Writers in the German Historical School, such as Gustav Schmoller, and their English disciples argued that mercantilist policies were very rational for a period in which the attainment of state power was the overriding goal of the polity.

Methodological preferences aside, the major students of mercantilism seem to organize their interpretations of this period and its writers around a paradigm that stresses that certain regulatory implications follow from a balance-of-trade and specie-accumulation objective.[2] Adam Smith, perhaps the keenest student of the mercantilists, suggests a different view. He argues (in Mark Blaug's words) that "mercantilism is nothing but a tissue of protectionist fallacies foisted upon a venal Parliament by 'our merchants and manufacturers,' grounded upon 'the popular notion that wealth consists in money.'"[3] In this view causation is reversed in the mercantilist paradigm, that is, the balance-of-trade objective is seen as flowing from the effective demand for regulatory rents by domestic economic agents.

We will develop such an interpretation of mercantilism in this paper.[4] In doing so, we will concentrate on the gains to economic agents in using the state for profits, and we will use concepts from modern developments in the theory of the rent-seeking society to explain mer-

---

interest rates and increasing home investment and employment. See J. M. Keynes, *General Theory of Employment, Interest and Money* (New York: Harcourt, Brace and World, Inc., 1936), chapter 15. Heckscher argued in rebuttal that unemployment in mercantilist times was essentially voluntary and not sensitive to changes in aggregate demand. See Eli Heckscher, *Mercantilism*, trans. Mendel Shapiro, 2 vols. (London: George Allen and Unwin Ltd., 1934).

[2] The two great writers on mercantilism were, of course, Heckscher, *Mercantilism*, and Jacob Viner, *Studies in the Theory of International Trade* (New York: Augustus M. Kelley, Publishers, 1967; first published, 1937).

[3] Mark Blaug, *Economic Theory in Retrospect* (Homewood, Ill.: Richard D. Irwin, Inc., 1968), p. 11.

[4] In other work on the general topic of mercantilism, two of the present authors have (1) expanded the theory of the emergence of the modern corporation (R. B. Ekelund and R. D. Tollison, "Mercantilist Origins of the Corporation," *Bell Journal of Economics* (forthcoming); (2) developed a cartel interpretation of mercantile French business organization (Ekelund and Tollison, "A Cartel Theory of French Mercantilism," unpublished manuscript, 1979); and (3) analyzed the role of the justices of the peace and the mercantile judiciary in the domestic regulation of mercantile England (Ekelund and Tollison, "Economic Regulation in Mercantile England: Heckscher Revisited," *Economic Inquiry*, forthcoming).

Mercantilism as a Rent-Seeking Society   237

cantilist doctrine and policy.[5] Methodologically, we will not evaluate mercantilist economics from the standpoint of modern economic theory (à la Keynes); we will simply try to explain the doctrines of the mercantilists in terms of the larger rent-seeking society in which they lived. In other words, we are engaging in an exercise in positive economics, not arguing that the mercantilists were good economists from the standpoint of modern economic theory.

The model developed in this paper explains the rise and fall of mercantilism in the positive terms of costs and benefits accruing to the participants in the often deadly game of mercantile rent seeking. Merchants, monarch, and the public (as represented by democratic institutions, legislative and judicial) are featured as self-interested protagonists in institutional change. Focusing upon specific examples of rent seeking in England and France, as well as upon the comparative institutional frameworks in these countries, we seek to explain with our theory (1) why mercantilism declined in England at the same time it was being strengthened in France, and (2) how an analysis of self-interested forces reacting to shifting costs and benefits to rent seeking presents a more satisfying explanation of mercantilism than the well-known alternatives.

With respect to the latter point, there appear to be two wholly consistent views of mercantilism in the literature. The first view, espoused and promulgated to a large extent by the historians (with modified and improved versions by Jacob Viner and Eli Heckscher), emphasizes mercantilism as a concerted policy of nationalism or state-building, stressing an exogenously determined economic policy divorced from the endogenous interplay of self-interested forces. Thus, a policy of taxing the import and subsidizing the export of "finished" goods is seen as a method of state-building or of accumulating specie or promoting domestic employment, rather than as the simple product of rent maximization by parties to the resulting income distribution. "Mercantile policy," in this view, achieved a life of its own, and

---

[5] In particular, we refer to the work of George J. Stigler, "The Theory of Economic Regulation," *Bell Journal of Economics and Management Science* 2 (Spring, 1971): 3–21; Gordon Tullock, "The Welfare Costs of Tariffs, Monopolies, and Theft," chapter 3 in this volume; Anne O. Krueger, "The Political Economy of the Rent-Seeking Society," chapter 4 in this volume; and Richard A. Posner, "The Social Costs of Monopoly and Regulation," chapter 5 in this volume.

the underlying forces that produced it (which, to us, is the important matter) remain unexplored and, worse, unexplained.

A second tactic of historians of thought in dealing with the mercantile era, which does not compete with the first view, has been to argue, at least implicitly, that the achievement of laissez-faire was the product of the subjective philosophical forces of the times. Here, we encounter "anticipatory" works on individualism and the natural ordering of economic phenomena, ranging from the writings of John Hales, John Locke, William Petty, and Richard Cantillon through those of Bernard Mandeville, David Hume, and the Physiocrats. Indeed, most common references imply that the intellectual case for free trade (Adam Smith, David Ricardo, and earlier writers) made such an impression on legislators that they quickly transformed the policy proposals of these authors into practice.

Although the latter of these positions may possess merit as an auxiliary, supporting explanation of the mercantile era, the former in our view obfuscates an understanding of the period, and, especially, of its tortuous evolution to laissez-faire. Although neither position is inconsistent with our own, we reject both these interpretations of mercantilism and of the movement to a free economy in England as a primary explanation for the emergence of liberalism. They are simply incomplete. Rather, we seek explanations in terms of institutional changes (e.g., the growth of the rule of law), which altered the costs and benefits of regulation to rent seekers. The emergence of a modern theory of rent seeking greatly facilitates such a re-evaluation.

We begin in the next section by presenting a model of the use of the state for profit in the mercantilist era. We stress the importance of institutional developments to the relative profitability of rent seeking in these times. In particular, our model stresses the role of an unfettered monarchy as an almost perfect setting for the creation of regulatory rents and state interference in the mercantile economy. Additionally, the rise of representative democracy and the consequent struggle over the power to supply legislation may be viewed as the primary reasons for a fall in relative rates of return to political investments (e.g., lobbying) under mercantilism and for the demise of mercantilism and the rise of a free economy in England.[6] In the subse-

---

[6] On the latter point see the hint of a suggestion by Friedrich A. Hayek, *The Constitution of Liberty* (Chicago: University of Chicago Press, 1960), p. 163.

Mercantilism as a Rent-Seeking Society   239

quent three sections, we apply our model to the mercantile economies of England and France. Our purpose in these sections is to show how well the rent-seeking model elucidates the doctrines and policies of these economies relative to the paradigm of mercantilism as a confused collection of ideas centered around the concept of specie accumulation. We also seek to show how our model is useful in interpreting differences in English and French mercantilism. Some concluding remarks are offered in a final section.

Rent Seeking in the Mercantile Economy

The central purpose of our model will be to explain the record of the mercantile era as individual rent-seeking behavior in a variety of institutional settings. Our positive model seeks to explain the development of the mercantile state and its evolution into modified laissez-faire, as the result of consistent individual behavior under slowly changing institutional constraints. The blend of methodological individualism and slowly changing institutional constraints is central to our main thesis concerning the rise and fall of mercantilism. If we define the mercantilist era as a collection of economic phenomena, then we may explain these phenomena using the standard theory of choice, without recourse to historical or dialectical explanation. Given the standard (timeless) assumptions of individual choice theory, the model of rent seeking simplifies into a specification of the constraints that modify economic behavior. Once the model is developed, we may turn to the historical record and seek the institutional features that served as constraints to explain observed phenomena.

THE RISE OF MERCANTILISM

We assume for purposes of initial exposition that monopolies are created by the rent-seeking activities of individuals, rather than spontaneously appearing or being independently created by governmental authorities. At some point, emergent competition is the rule in the production of goods and services, and there exists a state or government with authority to order society as it chooses within the limits of feasible production possibilities (which include enforcement costs). In this context we imagine individuals who see potential gains accruing from the sole rights to produce particular goods and services. These

FIGURE 14.1

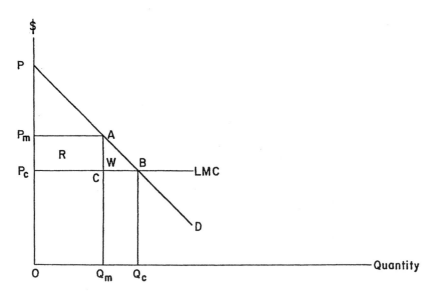

individuals will attempt to subvert the forces of the market and to monopolize the production of goods and services by having the state limit production to themselves by fiat. The process may be simply illustrated by figure 14.1.

It is clear that the entire triangle, $P_c PB$, is a measure of surplus in the case of competitive organization, a surplus to which no one has a property right. It exists because of technological conditions that preclude producers from perfect price discrimination. The entire area belongs to no one, yet consumers and producers can both attempt to claim it. This situation is further illustrated in figure 14.2.

From the point of view of the contenders for the surplus, the problem is not one of efficiency. Monopolists seek to achieve a position on the contract curve close to P_m, and consumer forces to seek a position toward P_c. There is nothing in the theory of choice that assigns preference to either position; both are on the contract locus.[7] Thus, the issue of dynamic monopoly creation is (net of the welfare triangle) a matter of bilateral monopoly.

It stands to reason that in such matters the two parties will retain

---

[7] Figure 14.2 adjusts for the monopoly welfare loss involved if the market solution is P_m.

Mercantilism as a Rent-Seeking Society   241

FIGURE 14.2

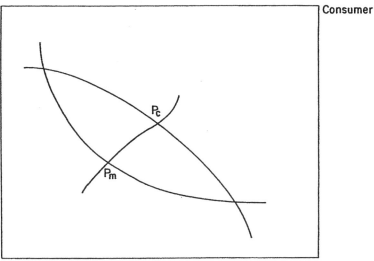

Consumer

Monopolist

brokers (lobbyist-lawyers) to assure a favorable outcome, and each will devote resources equal to an epsilon below the potential gains in their efforts. That producers are better able to effect the P_m solution is well known but is no more undesirable (net of the welfare triangle) than the technological constraints precluding perfect price discrimination. The social waste of monopoly thus involves the traditional welfare triangle, which measures both the portion of consumers' surplus that is lost to society because some individuals refrain from purchasing the monopolized output at higher prices (area W in figure 14.1) and also the use of lobbyist-lawyer resources to effect a pure transfer (area R in figure 14.1).[8]

If an incipient monopolist is successful in his dealings with government, he will be able to impose the classic monopoly solution of $P_m Q_m$ in figure 14.1, receiving a return on his rent-seeking investment of $P_m A C P_c$. With the gain in rents so depicted, we expect several other features of the rent-seeking society to be present. There is no reason to believe that only one individual will discover the gains from seeking

[8] On the static welfare loss from monopoly, see Arnold C. Harberger, "Monopoly and Resource Allocation," *American Economic Review* 44 (May, 1954): 77–87. For the original statement of the rent-seeking welfare loss from monopoly, see Tullock, "The Welfare Costs of Tariffs, Monopolies, and Theft."

monopoly rights sponsored by the state. We thus expect numerous rent seekers to compete for these rights, and that in the long run this competition will dissipate the returns from using the state as a source of profit.[9] Also, as the above discussion intimates, we expect those who stand to lose from the monopolization of an activity to have an interest in preventing such losses. Consumers stand to lose P_mACP_c, the rent gained by the successful monopolist, plus the deadweight welfare loss, *ABC*. In a costless world consumers would invest resources to retain this surplus, but we will abstract from such behavior here, because of the well-known transaction costs in organizing consumer efforts to resist government action in raising prices.[10]

But what about the remaining party in the rent-seeking society, that is, the state authority holding the power to grant monopoly rights? The interest of the rent seekers is clear, but what are the interests of the supplier of monopoly rights? One may conceive of a range of possibilities. At one extreme we may picture the state as a unified, revenue-seeking leviathan, where fiscal needs (defense, court expenses, and so forth) prompt the sale of protective legislation. For example, to "the mercantilist politician, the state was more or less the leviathan, absolute and all powerful."[11] In the rent-seeking society this case corresponds to an absolute monarchy. Entry into the business of granting monopoly rights is completely limited in this case because—in the extreme case at least—the monarch rules by divine right, the supply of which is very inelastic. This type of institutional arrangement tilts the bargaining power in the market for monopoly strongly in favor of the crown. If enforceable monopoly rights cannot be bought elsewhere in the dominion, the king should be able to price-discriminate effectively in the award of such rights. Most of the consumer surplus in figure 14.1 will end up in the king's coffers under these circumstances.

As we will develop more fully in the next two sections, revenue seeking was an important aspect of European history in the early mercantilist era. For example, one historian of the period characterizes

[9] See Posner, "The Social Costs of Monopoly and Regulation," for this argument.

[10] On this point see especially James M. Buchanan and Gordon Tullock, "The 'Dead Hand' of Monopoly," *Antitrust Law and Economics Review* 1 (Summer, 1968): 85–96.

[11] C. H. Heaton, "Heckscher on Mercantilism," *Journal of Political Economy* 45 (June, 1937): 392.

Mercantilism as a Rent-Seeking Society   243

mercantilism "as a negative and restrictive factor, which had its principal source, not in any deliberate plan of promoting economic progress, but in the fiscal exigencies of short-sighted and inpecunious government."[12] C. H. Heaton, reflecting on this appraisal, concurs, adding that "rarely in framing government policy did a government have the deplorable condition of the exchequer far out of mind, and every 'projector' who presented a scheme to his ruler stressed the benefit that would directly or indirectly flow into the royal coffers."[13] Further evidence comes from Heckscher: " . . . one of the most important features of economic policy if not the most important of all [was] what is called in French *fiscalisme*. . . . The state, by its intervention, wanted to create large sources of revenue for itself. . . . The state exploited for its own ends the monopolistic advantages which the guilds had secured for their members or the owners of private producers had received for themselves."[14]

In general, then, we may analyze the situation faced by the monarchical state authority and potential rent seekers in the context of an Edgeworth-box diagram. Given royal prerogative, consumer interests are effectively left out of consideration. Hence, under competitive organization, with the crown at one corner of an Edgeworth box and "projectors" at the other, the solution is off the contract curve, and each party stands to gain from cooperation. The remaining issue is merely the location of the solution on the contract curve. With a unified state authority the ease with which mutual interests were recognized and realized was relatively great.

In sum, we posit that the pursuit of special favor by individuals was the driving force behind the rent-seeking activities that flourished during the mercantile era. "The incentive rarely came from a whole class, for a class was too unwieldy, too class-unconscious, and too much torn by conflicting factors or interests to have one will or voice. Action came from individuals or compact groups who saw an opportunity to profit by protection or promotion."[15] The ascension of mercantilism in the early part of the era is readily explained by the institutional setting

[12] R. H. Tawney (ed.), *Studies in Economic History: The Collected Papers of George Unwin* (London: Royal Economic Society Reprint, 1958), p. lxiv.

[13] Heaton, "Heckscher on Mercantilism," pp. 375–376.

[14] Heckscher, *Mercantilism*, I, 178.

[15] Heaton, "Heckscher on Mercantilism," p. 387.

facing the participants in the process of monopolization. Since the transaction costs required for seeking rents were low with a unified state authority (the monarch), the flowering of mercantilism during this period is explained. That is, since the cost of seeking monopolies was relatively low under absolute monarchy, other things equal, we expect to observe relatively more of this activity in this institutional milieu.

THE DECLINE OF MERCANTILISM

At the other extreme from the rent-seeking leviathan was the rise of representative democracy. This historical development in England was embodied in a struggle over the power to supply legislation in a rent-seeking context. This struggle ultimately led to the demise of English mercantilism because of the profound changes that took place in the institutional environment. Under the assumption that self-interest is independent of time, the source of the fall of mercantilism must be found in the changing cost-benefit structure facing potential rent seekers. We have thus far suggested that mercantilism arose because the relative costs of negotiating favored treatment with a state in which authority was vested in a central figure were low. Prior to the centralization of authority, rent seekers had to deal with a multitude of feudal rulers, which made the costs of negotiating and enforcing exclusive rights relatively higher. The correlated rise of mercantilism and central monarchies was thus the result of changed cost conditions, and the fall of widespread mercantile activity in England may be explained as a manifestation of changes in the bargaining environment, which occurred as the result of political upheaval.

In seeking an explanation for the decline of English mercantilist policies within the rent-seeking paradigm, we follow Friedrich Hayek when he notes that "it was finally in the dispute about the authority to legislate in which the contending parties reproached each other for acting arbitrarily—acting, that is, not in accordance with recognized general laws—that the cause of individual freedom was inadvertently advanced." [16] Throughout his discussion of the emergence of the rule of law in England, Hayek stresses that economic freedom came about as a by-product of a struggle for the power to supply legislation. In this

---

[16] Hayek, *The Constitution of Liberty*, p. 163.

Mercantilism as a Rent-Seeking Society   245

struggle several important institutional changes occurred, which dramatically affected relative rates of return on rent-seeking investments. We seek to explain the deregulation of mercantile society in terms of these changes.

As the power of the monarchy in England declined, the movement toward representative democracy shifted the locus of rent-seeking activity to new forums, primarily the legislature and the judiciary, with predictable implications for the decline of the rent-seeking society of mercantilism. For example, the costs of lobbying a representative body are higher than the costs of lobbying a unified monarchy for monopoly charters because there are many decision makers rather than one. The rational rent seeker will reduce his bid for a monopoly right when lobbying costs rise. Moreover, the uncertainty costs facing the rent seeker will rise under representative government. Logrolling in the legislature will mask current votes to some extent, making current legislative outcomes more uncertain. There will be turnover among politicians and uncertainty about the durability of legislation from session to session of the legislature.[17] For these and other reasons, the costs of lobbying to rent seekers will rise under representative democracy, and we would therefore expect to see a decline of government interference in the economy because of these higher costs.

With respect to the mercantile judiciary in England, there was an important jurisdictional competition between the common law courts and those supporting the king's interests. The common law courts evolved a doctrine that held that royal monopoly and prerogative were illegal, whereas the special interests sanctioned by Parliament were legitimate. The king's courts obviously disagreed with this doctrine. The net result was a legal conflict in which one court system would rule that a monopoly right was valilid and the other that it was invalid. There was, in effect, no legal basis for a completely valid monopoly right under these conditions. So, even if a rent seeker could obtain a monopoly grant from the king or Parliament, he had no guarantee that it could be sustained against interlopers. Seeking monopoly through the shelter of the state was clearly going to be a less profitable activity under these circumstances.

[17] For further discussion of the durability of special-interest legislation, see William M. Landes and Richard A. Posner, "The Independent Judiciary in an Interest-Group Perspective," *Journal of Law and Economics* 18 (December, 1975): 875–901.

246   *Applications of Rent-Seeking Theory*

As we shall outline in the next sections, a great struggle evolved in England between the king and Parliament and between the king's courts and the common law courts allied to parliamentary interests. This struggle, which had important religious and political bases, was also a struggle over who was to run and to profit from the rent-seeking economy of English mercantilism. This conflict over authority to legislate and to adjudicate legal disputes meant that the costs of seeking monopoly protection from the state ultimately exceeded the potential benefits for rent seekers, and state interference in the economy consequently declined.[18]

SUMMARY

Our argument here is that the theory of the rent-seeking society is a more useful paradigm for explaining the rise and fall of mercantilism than the usual specie-accumulation interpretation. The rent-seeking paradigm rationalizes the emergence of the social order of mercantilism and its demise in terms of individual behavior in the face of varying institutional arrangements, rather than in terms of such arguments as that mercantilism was a highly irrational social order.

Mercantilism as a Rent-Seeking Society: Some Historical Evidence

Although historians of economic thought are wont to label the period 1500 to 1776 as (roughly) the "mercantile period," this convenient generalization fails when one considers rent seeking as a primary feature of the mercantile economy. The battle for property rights (i.e., the right to rent seek) arose in an environment where industrial and constitutional interests were emerging in the context of ongoing monarchies. This process, though historically complex, is clearly discernible, under vastly different institutional structures, in England, France, the Netherlands, and Spain between the thirteenth and eighteenth centuries.

It is instructive to contrast some of the central features of the institutional structures of England and France vis-à-vis the fisc in those

---

[18] See Ekelund and Tollison, "Economic Regulation in Mercantile England: Heckscher Revisited," for a more detailed discussion of the role of legislative and judicial conflict in explaining the demise of English mercantilism.

Mercantilism as a Rent-Seeking Society   247

countries before proceeding to some historical evidence that illustrates our theory of the rise and fall of mercantilism. In the first place, French and English monarchs differed greatly in their power to tax over this long period, and the "mercantile" systems of venality, which the power to tax (or lack thereof) created, were accordingly vastly different. The "French system" was absolutist in the sense that, from the time of Charles VII and the Ordinance of 1439 the Estates General gave the king the absolute power to tax without popular consent, a power that molded the form of rent-seeking in French society for over three hundred years.

In contrast, there were early consensual constraints on the English monarch's ability to tax. (England's Parliament was already well established when France's first Estates General met in 1302.)[19] These elements of parliamentary consent were not absolute until the revolutionary period of the mid-seventeenth century, largely engendered by conflict between monarch and the House of Commons over authority to collect rents to support armed struggles. As noted previously, costs and benefits of regulation were changing over this period (late sixteenth and early seventeenth centuries), and these changes led to the fall of a predominantly rent-seeking society in England.

MERCANTILE MONARCHY IN ENGLAND

The process of rent seeking described in the last section of this paper was a prominent feature of English government for centuries before 1649 and the execution of Charles I. The conduct of the wool trade in fourteenth-century England provides a very clear example of this process, which, during the reign of the three Edwards, precipitated constitutional crisis, presaging those of the seventeenth century. The first crisis was over the taxation of wool.

The wool trade of medieval England included a large number of competitively organized wool producers, a smaller number of large-scale producers (mostly monasteries), and an even smaller number of wool exporters. An export monopoly was fostered by the combined

[19] Martin Wolfe, *The Fiscal System of Renaissance France* (New Haven: Yale University Press, 1972), pp. 10, 33. For an interesting examination of fiscal policy and alterations in population and property rights as causal factors in the emergence of efficient economic organization, see Douglass C. North and Robert P. Thomas, *The Rise of the Western World* (Cambridge: Cambridge University Press, 1973). Our analysis of mercantilism is broadly in the spirit of their investigation.

rent-seeking interests of large merchants and exporters in bilateral negotiation with the king. The mechanism through which these activities took place was an "assembly of merchants" called by the king as early as the late thirteenth century for the purpose of advice and consent on the matter of export and other taxation, especially on wool. This body, which rivaled Parliament in its functions, was willing to consent to taxation, given that monopoly and other privileges could be exacted from the crown.[20] In short, merchants would accept the costs of taxation and regulation so long as the benefits conferred by regulation exceeded these costs.

The ability of merchants to shift the incidence of the wool tax, both backward to wool growers, large and small, and forward to foreign consumers (depending, of course, upon elasticity of demand), forced a polarization of parliamentary interests, which came to recognize the deleterious effects of higher wool prices. This interest group was composed of lay and ecclesiastical magnates (the large wool producers) and the knights of the shire, who represented more than a million small freeholders in Commons. Parliament's fight for the abolition of the tax was thus premised upon their objection to the income-reducing effects of the regulation of the wool market by the king (Edward I) and the wool merchants. Significant constitutional crises, which occurred in the 1290's and 1330's, resulted principally because of realigned and eventually shared interests between Parliament and the merchants. The costs of monarchial regulation (taxes) exceeded the benefits (entry-restricted monopoly) only so long as the king did not impose *new* taxes on the wool merchants. When this did in fact occur, owing to war and other pressures on the English fisc, wool merchants clearly recognized that the bilateral form of rent seeking was one-sided and unprofitable. Merchant voices thus joined those of Parliament calling for *abolition* of the tax.[21]

[20] Eileen Power, *The Wool Trade in English Medieval History* (London: Oxford University Press, 1941), p. 71.

[21] The alienation of merchants was furthered when the king shifted his favor to a group of "rogue financiers," less than thirty in number, who advanced money to the crown on wool granted to him. Power notes that the "king was . . . compelled to impose an embargo on general export for a time (sometimes a whole year) in order to enable his financiers to dispose of the wool on his behalf. And every time this happened a virtual monopoly of a financial group was established" (ibid., p. 83). The result was the dissolution of the larger group of merchant exporters, with those "shut out" becoming disposed (in their self-interest) to urge Parliament to impose constraints on the king.

Mercantilism as a Rent-Seeking Society   249

Though Parliament was unsuccessful in abolishing the periodically imposed ("extraordinary") wool tax ("maltote"), the increased demand of the sovereign for funds at the outbreak of the Hundred Years War (1336) was met by a tax, but with domestic price controls on wool as quid pro quo.[22] In 1350 Parliament finally gave up on the issue of abolishing the tax, but got control over it and converted it into a parliamentary subsidy for specified time periods. A quasi-monopoly of the wool trade (the English Company of the Staple) remained, and as Power reports, " . . . it is by virtue of this monopoly alone that they were able to shoulder the subsidy," the latter contingent on the will and consent of Parliament.[23]

A MERCANTILE PATTERN OF RENT SEEKING

The pattern and effects of mercantile monarchy, as developed in our theory of rent seeking, may be seen in the early history of the medieval wool trade. Again and again in the mercantile period—most significantly in the sixteenth and seventeenth centuries—Parliament was strengthened to limit and oppose the crown's ability to regulate. In England the rent-seeking proclivities of the crown were strengthened by a legislative constraint on its possible revenues. Extraordinary expenditures, which arose with ever-increasing frequency in order to conduct wars, meant that English monarchs were always in need of funds. (The French crown was often in similar need, but it did not face the same constraints, as we shall see in a later section.) The crown's reaction to this situation was initially to offer special favors, monopoly-entry control, to growing national industries (large exporters were often fewer in number, organized with lower transactions costs, and more easily controlled), who, in return, submitted to taxation.

Reactions to this state of affairs were twofold, and both eventually brought about the decline of monarchial rent seeking and an increase in costs to legislative supply of regulation. First, Parliament, which represented "society's" and, ultimately, merchants' interests, grew restive at the rent-seeking franchises of the king. As the mercantile period wore on, this restiveness became more pronounced. Second, and more important perhaps, the absolutism of the English monarchy

---

[22] At this point the wool merchants were still sanguine about the export monopoly franchise, since the prospect of passing the tax forward still existed (ibid., p. 81).

[23] Ibid., p. 85.

was more and more eroded with the aid and action of the merchant classes themselves. Great uncertainty crept in as merchants grew wary of the net benefits of a regulatory alliance with the king. Specifically, this uncertainty of benefits drove merchants to support parliamentary interests, which reduced the powers of the monarch in economic as well as in legal and religious matters. Thus, the caprice of monarchial power, which led to uncertainty among merchants, landowners, and freeholders, resulted in the emergent constitutional solution of the late sixteenth and seventeenth centuries.

THE DECLINE OF ENGLISH MERCANTILISM

We must now amplify and further illustrate the pattern of rent-seeking discerned in the medieval wool trade and described by our theory. Here, we focus upon a "high period of mercantile monarchy," followed by its fall in 1640 or so. Roughly, our treatment extends from the reign of Elizabeth I (the last Tudor monarch) through those of James I and Charles I (the first two Stuarts).

The constraints on regulatory supply and demand between the death of Henry VIII (1547) and the execution of Charles I (1649) were in kind very much like those of the earlier period. The monarch still required the consent of the taxed in order to obtain revenue. He still depended, in other words, upon the good will and self-interest of the wealthy gentry and landowners in order to function, especially when he had to meet "extraordinary" expenses. Over this period the three major checks upon the crown's power and rent-seeking activities were (1) private local interests composed of increasingly wealthy city merchants and magistrates, (2) the common law courts, and (3) the House of Commons. The latter two institutions were increasingly representative of and peopled by the wealthy merchants from whom the king wished to extract rents.[24]

---

[24] Here, we must emphasize that we are not trying to explain the decline of rent seeking solely in terms of the rise of constitutional democracy, though we argue that it is a major causal factor in explaining mercantile policies. Technological growth and an emergent factory system, a familiar *deux ex machina*, may have (for example) fostered powerful interests (such as wool buyers or household producers), which arose to compete with the large wool producers and exporters for rents in Parliament, thereby dissipating them. North and Thomas, *The Rise of the Western World*, emphasize still other changes as the grounds for economic development and the emergence of property rights. While their arguments concern somewhat more fundamental causal features of development, they do not emphasize, as we do, the role of rent seeking in the decline of mercantilism.

Mercantilism as a Rent-Seeking Society 251

The actual means of rent seeking and the king's ability to enforce it were likewise in transition, being eroded by self-interested forces and developments in constitutional law. Basically the crown had to depend upon three means of imposing industrial regulation: (1) enactment of regulation by statutes of Parliament, (2) royal proclamations and letters patent, and (3) orders of privy council or decrees instituted by privy council sitting in Star Chamber (the king's court). Developments of the period 1547–1640 led to the utter supremacy of Parliament in imposing regulation. The concept of the "crown in council" as ultimate authority—the great Tudor contribution to administrative government—was also swept away by the events of these years, though the "council" form of executive administration survives and, indeed, is enshrined in the forms of most contemporary representative governments.[25] During this period, self-interested forces successfully opposed every attempt of the crown to impose and enforce industrial regulation. We now turn to a few examples of these forces.

EXAMPLES, 1563–1597

The reign of Elizabeth I (1558–1603) is regarded by many as the high time of successful mercantile policy. Historical facts do not appear to justify this view, however. To echo a modern directive, regulation should be judged not on the basis of its aims or intent, but on grounds of its effects.[26] In fact, Elizabeth opened her reign with a great deal of patent granting and lusty rent seeking from industry, but closed it by meekly admitting that patent monopoly was a dangerous innovation contrary to common law.

In common with successful French systems of regulation, the English monarch would have liked to have controlled industry locally through the guild system and crown representatives like local magistrates, justices of the peace, and their subordinates. Much regulation to this end was imposed during the reign of Elizabeth. In 1563 a Statute of Artificers was passed commanding craftsmen to serve a seven-year apprenticeship and regulating wages in all occupations

[25] Bureaucratic reforms in Tudor administration are treated exhaustively in G. R. Elton, *The Tudor Revolution in Government: Administrative Changes in the Reign of Henry VIII* (Cambridge: Cambridge University Press, 1966).

[26] The growing literature of the "effects and effectiveness" of regulation dates to George Stigler and Claire Friedland, "What Can Regulators Regulate? The Case of Electricity," *Journal of Law and Economics* 5 (October, 1962): 1–23.

then existing.[27] In 1596–1597, by an act of the privy council, Elizabeth attempted to fix the prices of grain, bread, ale, beer, and malt, and, for a time, those of building materials, bricks, and the wholesale price of coal. The crown's response to new and growing industries, such as tobacco pipe makers, gun makers, and spectacle makers, and to the nascent manufacturing towns they supported, was to incorporate these industries (an attempt to bring them under the umbrella of guild regulation) and to enact statutes aimed at keeping industry from moving from old towns to the country, where many regulations did not apply.

THE LOCAL REACTION TO REGULATION

Such regulations yielded Elizabeth very meager results, except to implant in the minds of most of those she attempted to regulate the notion that self-interest and progress demanded nonregulation. Reasons for the failure to impose price and wage controls could not be more clear. It was a question of unpaid enforcers (local justices of the peace), or highly self-interested magistrates (industrial merchants harmed by regulations) attempting to enforce a system of regulation that injured the influential majority of those it affected. The opportunity cost structure for regulatory enforcement was changing drastically. As John U. Nef has noted, "During the eighty-five years which followed the accession of Elizabeth and culminated in the civil war, the privy council was not able to strengthen the royal authority for enforcing industrial legislation by introducing new, disinterested officials into the local administration to help the justices of the peace in performing the increasingly heavy duties imposed on them by the new enactments."[28] Heckscher goes even further on the matter, noting that "neither before nor after 1688 was there in England a paid *ad hoc* bureaucracy to supervise the enforcement of industrial legislation which Colbert had been at pains to create in France."[29]

As mentioned above, the statutes regulating wages applied only

[27] See the discussion of the statute in Heckscher, *Mercantilism*, I, 227 ff.

[28] John U. Nef, *Industry and Government in France and England, 1540–1640* (Ithaca: Cornell University Press, 1957; first published, 1940), p. 36. We question the extent to which local officials were disinterested (see Ekelund and Tollison, "Economic Regulation in Mercantile England: Heckscher Revisited").

[29] Heckscher, *Mercantilism*, I, 263. Professor Hartwell has recently amplified Heckscher's point, contrasting his view to the character of nineteenth-century administration. See R. Max Hartwell, "Capitalism and the Historians," in *Essays on Hayek*,

Mercantilism as a Rent-Seeking Society   253

to existing industries. It takes little imagination to predict what happened, given this loophole in the law. Large numbers of new industries forming between 1575 and 1620 were simply exempt from the laws. Other industries such as textiles, which were undergoing a transition to large-scale manufacturing, simply evaded the laws altogether by moving to the countryside (where the laws did not apply), by importing cheap unskilled labor from the country, or by "letting" or "putting out" the finishing of textiles to large numbers of workmen in their homes. Outright disobedience of the law was facilitated by self-interested local magistrates and justices of the peace and by decisions of the common law courts limiting the applicability of local regulations over industry.[30]

MONOPOLY REGULATION

Apart from the attempt to impose local industrial regulation, which was virtually swept away by parliamentary acts of 1575–1576 and 1623–1624, there was no dearth of attempts by industrial rent seekers and crown to institute monopolies over specific branches of trade. But in these cases, the self-interest of those left out (potential competitors) and eventually of those protected—together with the common law judges and a House of Commons pliant to the wishes of merchant-capitalists—combined to overthrow and render ineffective monopolies created by patents, royal decree, or proclamation of the crown's privy council. Examples are numerous, and here we might note the attempted monopolization of the saltpeter, gunpowder, salt, and paper industries and the attempt of the queen to tax mines and mineral extraction, most of which failed to provide any rents to the crown.[31]

On familiar grounds of national defense, Elizabeth claimed exclu-

---

ed. Fritz Machlup (New York: New York University Press, 1976), p. 84. Hartwell's interpretation of Heckscher is certainly correct with respect to England and perhaps the Netherlands, but this was not the case in France and Spain, as we shall see. Moreover, Hartwell does not provide a cogent explanation for the *origins* of bureaucratic control in nineteenth-century administration.

[30] The classic judicial decisions of Sir Edward Coke in the Tolley case and others were of singular importance in bringing about legal limits on crown regulation. See D. O. Wagner, "Coke and the Rise of Economic Liberalism," *Economic History Review* 6 (March, 1935): 30–44.

[31] See Nef, *Industry and Government in France and England*, pp. 88–112.

sive rights to the manufacture of saltpeter and gunpowder. A monopoly was granted to George and John Evlyn. The Evlyn family enjoyed the rent splitting for almost fifty years (until 1635).[32] But steady opposition from both merchants and the common law courts (dating from the initial award) finally brought the monopoly restrictions down. Subsequently, the manufacture of both saltpeter and gunpowder became the object of open competition. Principal opposition came from the merchants and "from the increasing number of town traders and landed gentlemen with money to invest in the new industries, the same persons who were becoming lax about complying with royal industrial legislation. They objected to all industrial monopolies as trenching upon the liberty and the property of the subject, whose rights, they claimed, were guaranteed by the fundamental law of the country."[33]

Other examples may be cited. The rights to the royalties from ores other than gold and silver were removed from the crown in a court decision of 1566, which limited regalian rights to gold and silver only (none in England). Officials charged with dealing with mining leases *on royal lands* were not above the lure of self-interest, moreover. Thus Professor Nef notes, "Even in royal manors and forests, where the king or queen like any other landlord owned the minerals and appointed special officials to deal with their mining lessees, these officials, like the justices of the peace and the sheriffs, were always local men who were frequently more mindful of the wishes of their rich neighbors with investments in the mines than of the interests of their royal masters."[34]

Elizabeth tried to imitate the French king's successful and lucrative salt tax (the *gabelle*), but these efforts were also doomed. In 1564 Elizabeth attempted to establish a patent monopoly in salt, but the patentees gave up after five years, leaving huge salt pans rusting on the

---

[32] Though Elizabeth claimed regalian rights on grounds of national defense, she stood to gain monetarily by the conditions of the rent-split. All unused gunpowder could be sold by her at a profit to both domestic and foreign consumers. Since by law she claimed *all* Evlyn's output, a time of peace meant pure profit to Elizabeth.

[33] Nef, *Industry and Government in France and England*, p. 92. An issue of "illegal search and seizure" was also involved here, since the collection of saltpeter required entry to henhouses and barnyards across England.

[34] Ibid., p. 101.

Mercantilism as a Rent-Seeking Society   255

English coast. At this point private capitalists, without franchise, entered the industry and profitably produced and marketed salt over the next three decades in spite of repeated attempts by the crown to re-establish monopoly rights.

Yet another example of the futile attempt of Elizabeth's councillors to grant monopolies to court favorites was the paper monopoly, originally granted to one John Spilman in 1588. Spilman claimed to have a new process for producing white paper. Although patents issued to protect a new process or invention were ordinarily unopposed by Commons and the common law courts, they were often extended, enabling patentees to "engulf" closely related products. Such was the case with Spilman, who in 1597 was granted a monopoly over *all kinds* of paper. The monopoly privileges were not enforceable, however, and within six years Spilman had to rest content with "such a share of the expanding market for paper as the efficiency of his machinery, the skill of his workmen, and the situation of his mills enabled him to command."[35] Elizabeth's luckless adventures into the creation of monopolies ended in 1603 (the year of her death), when she personally declared, with respect to proposed monopoly on playing cards, that such patents were contrary to common law, and that such issues were to be decided by Commons and the courts.

POST-ELIZABETHAN RENT SEEKING

Opposition to crown attempts to monopolize industries during Elizabeth's reign grew, culminating in civil war, during the next forty years. Generally, it may be said that after 1603—despite even more vigorous attempts to establish monopolies on the part of Elizabeth's successors—no acts establishing national monopolies were enforceable that reduced the profits of merchants and the interests of those represented by Commons and the courts. At this point we find the de facto end of monarchial mercantilism when, in the context of expanding industries, the net benefit from open competition outweighed the net benefit from crown protection. The *demand* for regulation was reduced owing to rising franchise costs in the form of taxes, together with the uncertainties of regulation by the crown. Potential competition for investment outlets and political pressures upon Commons by

[35] Ibid., p. 106.

affected merchants must have greatly increased the uncertainty of gains from crown-created monopoly.

James I and Charles I revived Elizabeth's early policy of patent grants as sources of revenue, but both met with very limited success (principally in the cases of alum and soap manufacture). Meanwhile, Commons gathered all its strength to fight the king's prerogative to seek rents via monopolization. After a protracted struggle with James over the issue, Commons revived impeachment as a means of punishing monopolists within their ranks and of reminding the king of their total intolerance for his claimed prerogative to seek rents in this manner. Thus, in 1621, for the first time in almost two hundred years, Commons impeached Sir Giles Mompesson and Sir Francis Mitchell for "fraud and oppression committed as patentees for the exclusive manufacture of gold and silver thread, for the inspection of inns and hostelries, and for the licensing of ale houses."[36] The House of Lords rendered the judgment and imposed fines and imprisonment on both men. Commons's objection to the crown's supposed right to supply regulation reached its zenith in 1624, when the famous act concerning monopolies legally stripped the king of all prerogative in patents and other means to monopolize industry.[37]

In 1625 Charles I came to the throne and promptly set about attempting to restore the "divine right of kings," which, of course, included a reassertion of rights to grant monopoly via letters patent or by order of privy council. In doing so, Charles was led to a direct confrontation with constitutionalists, a battle he ultimately lost, along with his head, in 1649. Together with his persuasive and powerful minister Francis Bacon, who supported the royal prerogative to supply regulation, Charles found a loophole in the 1624 statute: the statute did not apply to corporations for benefit of trade or to companies of merchants. Thus, after the repeated refusal of Parliament to fund the king's military adventures and the king's dissolution of Parliament in 1629, Charles tried to make deals with large producers in many indus-

---

[36] Hannis Taylor, *The Origin and Growth of the English Constitution*, Part II (Boston: Houghton, Mifflin and Company, 1898), p. 246.

[37] Exceptions granted were for "patents of Invention" and the alum and soap monopolies. The latter were excepted because the patents were soon to expire and, further, because the privy council agreed not to renew them.

Mercantilism as a Rent-Seeking Society 257

tries:[38] Alum and soap monopolies had been exempted from the 1624 act, but the king encouraged the formation of huge corporations in coal, salt, brickmaking, and others, to which monopoly protection was given (for fourteen years) in return for rents to the crown. Between 1629 and 1640 the alum patent brought in £126,000, with an additional revenue from soap (between 1630 and 1640) of £122,000, but the *new* rent seeking of Charles was doomed to failure.[39] The circumstances of this failure should be, by now, very familiar. The king's monopoly protection and taxing arrangements were *too costly* for *all* the merchants to continue to acquiesce to them. A competitive system in this period of rapid industrial expansion yielded them higher rents than could be obtained through legalized entry control, price fixing, *and* taxation. Thus, cartel arrangements broke down as participants blithely evaded price-fixing agreements or laws when profitable. Moreover, these attempted new monopolies aroused the hostile and vociferous opposition of those merchants left out. The nonmerchant voices correctly perceived monopoly (recall the wool trade example) as inimical to their interests.

Thus the cartel breakdown and the more fundamental problems of enforcement brought on by strong consumer and excluded merchant objections combined to yield the patents of Charles I ineffective three years after they were issued. Antimonopoly interests opposed to the king—reflected in self-interested inaction or adverse decisions by justices of the peace and by Commons—joined forces with legal and religious objections to the king's blatant and audacious assertion of supreme rights and signaled an end to his authority. In a landmark reassertion of rights, Parliament ended the despotism of monarchy and established fundamental constitutional rights. Included in this legislation was the passage in 1640 of a statute putting an end to all but one of the exceptions in the statute of 1624.[40] Monarchial mercantilism

---

[38] Parliament was demanding a restoration of sovereignty and other constitutional rights in return for the subsidy.

[39] Nef, *Industry and Government in France and England*, p. 115.

[40] Although some of the more scientifically minded merchants and gentlemen supported the exemption of limited "patents for invention" in the Statute of 1650 in order to encourage inventors (i.e., in permitting internalization of benefits), the self-interest of members of Parliament, judges, and magistrates may have been a larger factor in this decision. Nef notes, in this connection, that "the increasing industrial investments of the

was repulsed by sharply limiting the ability of the king to *supply* regulation. More important for understanding the course of constitutional history and regulation, the monarch lost this ability largely because actual and potential demanders found the effects of these regulations very uncertain, and most often of negative benefit, given the salubrious state of the competitive system in the English economy of the time.

As argued in the theoretical section of this paper, future attempts to demand and supply monopoly privileges through regulation were far more costly to participants because of the higher transactions costs associated with collective decision-making in a representative body such as Parliament. Thus, the attempt by merchants in the short run to wrest power to confer monopoly from the monarch (culminating in the mid-seventeenth century) led to a long-run situation, lasting until the latter part of the nineteenth century, which severely inhibited the possible formation of rent-seeking regulation.

Customs, Monopoly, and Dualism

Of special interest in a mercantile context is the issue of tariffs and quotas, that is, the issue of tariffs and quotas in protection or encouragement in international competition. Clearly, the nexus of power to levy customs duties ("tonnage and poundage") shifted often from the medieval period through the seventeenth century. Indeed, one of the major factors leading to the constitutional revolt in the reign of Charles I was exactly the matter of prerogative in customs duties. Charles claimed an "ancient right" to customs, but Parliament finally seized the exclusive power to set these duties in 1641.[41] While Parliament was dissolved, however, an event took place that reveals that vested interests were operative in the matter of trade policy. In the

---

wealthy merchants and the improving landlords, represented in parliament, in the courts, and in the town governments, led them to welcome any invention designed to reduce costs of production and to increase profits. . . . Such industrial adventurers and their political representatives saw in the granting of patents a means of encouraging the search for the new inventions with which their prosperity was increasingly bound up" (ibid., p. 119).

[41] Parliament later gave William and Mary customs and port duty for *limited* terms of four years, partially a ploy to guarantee frequent parliaments (Taylor, *The Origin and Growth of the English Constitution*, pt. II, p. 419).

Mercantilism as a Rent-Seeking Society   259

interim in which Charles claimed absolute authority to levy taxes, merchant importers refused (in their own interests) to pay customs to the king, obeying a remonstrance of Parliament to refuse to pay any duties not authorized by Parliament. The king ordered the seizure of goods, whereupon several merchants resisted and were brought before the privy council. One of them, Richard Chambers, declared that "merchants are in no part of the world so screwed as in England. In Turkey they have more encouragement." [42]

This incident, small in itself, reveals that, although motives of unification and state power building may be pressed to explain protectionist trade policies, self-interest was never far from the surface in shaping those policies which we regard as typically mercantile in nature. That is to say, there is a commonality about rent seeking, whether its subject is international trade controls or domestic industrial regulation. [43] Although a number of writers have noted a "dualism" in *mercantile writers'* approach to domestic controls on the one hand and to protectionist "mercantile" policies in trade on the other, the apparent contradiction may be resolved when mercantilism is viewed in terms of rent-seeking activity. [44]

An example drawn from Heckscher will illustrate this point:

[42] Quoted in ibid., p. 274. Prison was the cost to Chambers for his flippancy.

[43] Adam Smith made this point very emphatically: ". . . in the mercantile system, the interest of the consumer is almost constantly sacrificed to that of the producer; and it seems to consider production, and not consumption, as the ultimate end and object of all industry and commerce. . . . In the restraints upon the importance of all foreign commodities which can come into competition with those of our own growth, or manufacture, the interest of the home-consumer is evidently sacrificed to that of the producer. It is altogether for the benefit of the latter, that the former is obliged to pay that enhancement of price which this monopoly almost always occasions" (*Wealth of Nations*, ed. Edwin Cannan [New York: Random House, 1937], p. 625). All restrictions, domestic and international, were for the benefit of merchants and manufacturers. Smith even extends the self-interest axiom to an explanation for the Navigation Acts and to colonial policy: "To found a great empire for the sole purpose of raising up a people of customers, may at first sight appear a project fit only for a nation of shopkeepers. It is, however, a project altogether unfit for a nation of shopkeepers; but extremely fit for a nation whose government is influenced by shopkeepers" (p. 579).

[44] That there was a contradiction in English mercantile *statements* concerning the desirability and efficacy of applications of natural law and free trade is beyond doubt. See A. F. Chalk, "Natural Law and the Rise of Economic Individualism in England," *Journal of Political Economy* 59 (August, 1951): 330–347; or W. D. Grampp, "The Liberal Element in English Mercantilism," *Quarterly Journal of Economics* 66 (November, 1952): 465–501. Their observation that the emergence of a philosophical defense of the domes-

> . . . from the end of the Middle Ages onwards, the import of wool cards
> into England was prohibited. They constituted an important means of
> production in the textile industry, which normally enjoyed greater favour
> than any other. A decree of 1630 went so far as to proscribe the sale of
> cards produced within the country from worn-out patterns. The mainte-
> nance of employment was given as the official motive for the measures,
> but in fact, as least as regards the latter prohibition, the object was to
> assist one of the oldest industrial joint-stock companies, the Mineral and
> Battery Works.[45]

The point that this quotation illustrates is that the "official" motive for
protectionist measures was, in all likelihood, seldom if ever the real
motive. Most writers on mercantilism identify some sort of "homogeneous" mercantile trade policy, employment policy, population policy,
domestic policy, and so on, as if interests independent of those which
drive economic man in all ages were responsible for the economic policy called "mercantilism." We, however, agree with Smith's assessment that mercantilism was but a tissue of protectionist fallacies
supported by merchants, and we go further and argue that thinly var-
nished rent seeking by merchants, monarch, and ultimately by the
masses represented by Parliament explains the sum total of the economic intervention, as well as a good deal of the political and legal
change, over the period. A "philosophical dualism" may have existed,
as philosophers were converted to individualism (Locke) and natural
law as a guide to economic conduct (Mandeville, Petty, Cantillon,
Hume, and Smith). But, as we have seen, the philosophical revolution
was fostered by the conduct of rent seekers, constrained by a particular form of polity. The form of that polity, moreover, changed fundamentally through the interplay of these self-interested economic
forces. Mercantilist writers, Jacob Viner suggests, created "an elaborate system of confused and self-contradictory argument."[46] Our ap-

---

tic market economy came in the late sixteenth century is indisputable. But to defend
free trade internally and simultaneously support import and export controls is not "du-
alistic," if both are of net benefit to the individual involved. When mercantilism is
viewed as a rent-seeking process, moreover, the explanation for why mercantilism as a
system has eluded all attempts at characterization by historians of economic thought becomes readily understandable. Thus, our conclusion extends Viner's belief that "pleas for
special interests, whether open or disguised, constituted the bulk of the mercantilist literature. The disinterested patriot or philosopher played a minor part in the development of mercantilist doctrine" (*Studies in the Theory of International Trade*, p. 115).

[45] Heckscher, *Mercantilism*, I, 148.

[46] Viner, *Studies in the Theory of International Trade*, p. 109.

Mercantilism as a Rent-Seeking Society 261

plication to mercantilism of the theory of the rent-seeking society suggests that the practitioners of mercantilism were anything but confused and self-contradictory. Through their actions, self-interested individuals ultimately altered the constraints within which rent-seeking activity took place.

France: The Venal Society

The French experience at rent seeking and the environment under which it took place contrast at almost every point with the case in England. If mercantilism means "a system of extensive economic controls," one could hardly find a better example than France from the thirteenth to eighteenth centuries. The source of this difference lies in large measure with the absolutist property rights in taxation vested in the crown from 1439 through the French Revolution of the late eighteenth century. With minor alterations the tax system of the Old Regime followed that of the Renaissance. Characterized by institutionalized venality, French monarchs shared the power to tax with the French aristocracy over the entire mercantile period. Rent seeking by the monarch in the form of contracting to enterprises or to "tax farmers" was common as early as the thirteenth and fourteenth centuries. A scholar of fiscal systems of the period aptly describes the situation: " . . . the most important local revenues were 'farmed out' to enterprisers, who received the right to collect the domaines in return for lump sum payments. Amounts in excess of this sum became the revenue farmers' profits; and, if they collected less than the amounts paid, it was their loss—not the king's."[47] Corruption permeated a gigantic fiscal bureaucracy, and, as in certain modern political systems, it became a way of life. Property rights shifted as the centuries passed, with tax farming and other "leases" becoming hereditary. Legal and judicial offices were sold by the crown, for example, and provide an interesting example of venality. Revealing the utter hypocrisy of the system, the oath of office in the case of justices and crown lawyers required a state-

[47] Wolfe, *The Fiscal System of Renaissance France*, p. 12. Also see B. F. Hoselitz, "The Early History of Entrepreneurial Theory," in *Essays in Economic Thought: Aristotle to Marshall*, ed. J. J. Spengler and W. R. Allen (Chicago: Rand McNally & Co., 1960), pp. 234–257; and R. B. Ekelund and R. F. Hebert, "A Tale of Two Theories: Concepts of Competition in Economic Literature," unpublished manuscript, Auburn University, 1978.

ment that they had not paid any money for their position. It has been observed that "for the whole sixteenth century the justices and royal lawyers began their careers with an act of perjury."[48]

Royal venality was of such magnitude at the end of Louis XIII's reign (between 1636 and 1642) that the French monarch was collecting between three and four times the per capita taxes from his subjects as Charles I, who was locked in a death battle with Parliament at the time. The mercantile writer Gregory King estimated the "general income" of France in 1688 at £80,500,000 sterling and that of England at £41,700,000, estimates rough in themselves but sufficient to indicate a much larger success of royal rent seeking in France over the "mercantile" period.[49]

THE INSTITUTIONAL FRAMEWORK OF RENT SEEKING IN FRANCE

The rent-seeking coalition of crown and aristocracy was facilitated in France by a number of institutional features stemming from and related to the absolute power to tax by the crown. There are the interrelated matters of (1) the enforcement of industrial regulation, (2) the degree of *effective* crown rent-seeking interference with old and new industries, and (3) the incidence of the tax structure and the incentives established thereby.

The guild system in France grew stronger from the time of the Middle Ages onward, in contrast with the English experience. At the opening of the sixteenth century, most local industry was done by free craftsmen, but by the reign of Henry IV (1589–1610), the guild regime was dramatically strengthened. Two crown edicts (1581 and 1597) laid down uniform rules for the organization of handicrafts all over France and permitted master craftsmen who were not members of guilds to organize and obtain from rent-seeking royal officials all the advantages of formal guild membership—regulated apprenticeships and entry, hours of work permitted, and so forth. Guild regulations, moreover, were confirmed by royal letters patent. The result of these activities was a massive extension of royal prerogative, superseding guild and local prerogative in the matter of decentralized royal control over

[48] Wolfe, *The Fiscal System of Renaissance France*, p. 297.

[49] Gregory King, quoted in Nef, *Industry and Government in France and England*, p. 128.

Mercantilism as a Rent-Seeking Society   263

industrial activity. Entry control, the imposition of maximum wage rates upon journeymen, price controls, and the establishment of rent-seeking offices, which all this engendered, became centralized crown prerogatives.

Although these developments set the stage for a venal society with centralized property rights, further developments significantly strengthened the control of the king's officers over municipal authority. *Intendants des provinces*, tried servants of the crown, were sent as commissioners to the provinces to establish administrative reforms. Gradually, under the aegis of Richelieu and Louis XIII, these well-paid *intendants* took over and consolidated most of the functions of earlier royal provincial administrators, thereby permitting crown ministers far greater assurance that the crown's policies would be undertaken. Adjudication of regulatory disputes at the local level was also more and more becoming the business of the crown courts by invocation of the principle of *cas royaux*, whereby disputes over guild regulations and other industrial encumbrances could be tried in royal courts due to "crown interests." Certainly Colbert, minister of France between 1661 and 1683, must have found these inherited institutions a great advantage in implementing the intensified rent seeking of Louis XIV.

Over this important period, then, the institutions of legislative and judicial enforcement over industry and trade were developing along sharply opposed lines in England and France. During the crucial century from 1540 to 1640, institutions that facilitated rent seeking by crown and aristocracy were greatly strengthened in France, while such "enforcement" institutions, legal and administrative, were becoming atrophied in England. The French crown did not have to brook the *combined* opposition of enforcers, those disgruntled by regulation, and the public in its quest for economic rents.

The administrative machinery that served rent seekers vis-à-vis local handicraft regulation was duplicated over specific industries in a manner that could only be pitifully imitated by the English. Tight royal control over mines, saltpeter and gunpowder, and salt was greatly facilitated by decentralized local production, with centralized control over rent-producing "franchises."

In the matter of saltpeter and gunpowder manufacture, the "grand master of the artillery" (the Minister Sully served for a long while) was given exclusive management. In imitation of the tax-collection system, these rights were "farmed out" to commissioners, who represented the grand master in granting or revoking rights to produce. Commissioners, in turn, exacted a split in the rents created for themselves. Concession rights to the produce of mines were likewise farmed out to court favorites through an elaborate administrative machinery. Revenues in the form of lump-sum payments went to the crown, as did a regalian tax on ores (*droit du dixième*). Entry, exit, and abandonment were all regulated to the mutual advantage of aristocratic franchise holders (*concessionaires*) and the king.

The French crown, in common with its English counterpart, granted patents for new inventions and, along with them, money subsidies and official salaried help for inventors. But the French went much further, determining the entire direction of technology. By granting a large number of limited tax-exempt concessions, kings from Henry IV and Louis XIII directed technological change by shifting emphasis toward new branches of *artistic* craftsmanship (cloth, glass, tapestries) and away from cost-reducing devices necessary for the introduction of quantity-oriented, large-scale production. Though patents for the latter were not refused, crown advisors were establishing conditions that greatly favored the establishment of high-quality artistic productions. Such emphasis expanded into the well-known government studios and art factories of Louis XIV and his royal successors.

Perhaps the single most successful application of venality by the French crown related to the salt monopoly. Claiming regalian rights (which roughly corresponded to the salt tribute of the imperial Roman state) in most of the provinces of France, the crown imposed intricate regulations on salt producers, requiring them to sell all salt produced to royal storehouses at prices fixed by the king's officers. Consumers were then forced to purchase salt, with required quantities per parish, at rates four times as high as free market rates.[50] Although there were infractions, monopoly conditions were rigorously enforced, in large measure because of the fidelity of royal representatives at the local levels.

The *gabelle* and other taxes on salt became the single most important revenue source next to the infamous *taille*. The *taille* was a tax

---

[50] These are Nef's estimates.

Mercantilism as a Rent-Seeking Society   265

levied on the income and real property of peasants, shopkeepers, and craftsmen, who were not exempted by virtue of participation in royal manufactures. In real terms receipts from the *gabelle* rose eight or ten times between 1523 and 1641.[51] The imposition of both the *gabelle* and the *taille* had stark implications for the distribution of income and economic growth. Both these taxes and the indirect taxes on commodities fell heavily upon the poor, discouraging capital formation. Unbridled taxing powers facilitated redistributions to the nobility and to the clergy, who utilized wealth redistributions for "artistic consumptions."

A POSTSCRIPT ON THE VENAL SOCIETY

Institutionalized rent seeking had a number of implications for the ultimate form of the French mercantile state. Growth in real output lagged far behind that of England due to a dearth of investment opportunities and, more importantly, to a lack of incentive for capital formation. Absolutism created so much uncertainty in property rights that, as has been remarked of the Spanish mercantile system of the time, one became a student, monk, beggar, or bureaucrat, since there was nothing else to be.[52] The best minds, as in all controlled societies, were attracted to the areas of highest return. In France this meant that they sought a bureaucratic sinecure that could be passed on through hereditary rights.

The certainty of absolute power and of an imposed system of rent seeking contrasted sharply with the uncertainty of private entrepreneurial returns in France. The high *private* returns of a relatively unfettered competitive system, which proved sufficient to bring down mercantile monarchy in the English case, were not possible in France. The tradition of the venal system created there was so strong that the emergence of a liberal order was postponed until the late eighteenth century.

Conclusions

Historical episodes from France and England appear to fit the theory of mercantilism as rent-seeking activity, as well as to provide a solid

---

[51] Nef, *Industry and Government in France and England*, p. 83.
[52] North and Thomas, *The Rise of the Western World*, p. 131.

base for explaining its decline in England. In the latter case, higher cost due to uncertainty and growing private returns reduced industry demands for regulation and controls. All this strengthened the emergent constitutional democracy, which created conditions making rent-seeking activity on the part of both monarch and merchants more costly. When the locus of power to seek rents shifted from the monarch to Parliament via more stringent controls on the king, the costs of supplying regulation through legislative enactment rose because transaction costs to rent seekers went up. Moreover, a competitive judiciary created massive uncertainty about the durability of *any* monopoly right. In addition, the inability of the monarch to enforce even simple local regulations was premised upon the political structure of England and, as we have seen, upon the changing cost-benefit structure to royal representatives charged with such enforcement.

The pattern of mercantile rent-seeking in France until the late eighteenth century was manifestly different. Absolute tax powers and ever more efficient royal enforcement at local levels permitted and supported a system of outright venality administered by an institutionalized aristocratic bureaucracy. Monarchial controls over technology further altered the cost-benefit structure of the demand for monopoly franchises by reducing the returns to production and participation in the private economy. Along with monopoly in the supply of franchises, it is easy to understand the persistence and growth of venality in France. The absence of meaningful representative institutions or conditions that would facilitate their emergence is sufficient to explain the historical pattern.

We have argued that the application of the theory of the rent-seeking society to the mercantile period yields new insights into the rise and decline of mercantile restrictions in England and France. Surely our argument would not have surprised Adam Smith, and we view it as an extension of Smith's (admittedly) fragmentary analysis of the rent-seeking modes of the period.[53] As noted throughout the pres-

---

[53] One of Smith's principal themes in the *Wealth of Nations* was that mercantilism was equivalent to the demand for regulation and rents by merchants and manufactures (see pp. 250, 403, 420, 425, 460–461, 695). Smith attributes mercantile restrictions of all kinds—colonization, restrictions designed for specie accumulation, and so forth—to the self-seeking interests of merchants. Typical of Smith's "capture" theory is the following "It cannot be very difficult to determine who have been the contrivers of this whole mercantile system; not the consumers, we may believe, whose interest has been entirely

Mercantilism as a Rent-Seeking Society   267

ent paper, however, there is no dearth of arguments concerning the decline of overt mercantile policies in England, although the reasons for this significant episode of deregulation are largely unexplored in the literature. Credit is given implicitly to Adam Smith and his "liberal" predecessors, who advocated the advantages of the free and spontaneous coordination of economic activity, for making such a forceful intellectual case for their point of view that it was translated into public policy. Our interpretation of mercantilism as a rent-seeking society does not suggest that intellectual developments will have much impact on public policy. We thus tend to disagree with Keynes, who was certain "that the power of vested interests is vastly exaggerated compared with the gradual encroachment of ideas."[54] As fine an academic scribbler as Adam Smith was, we suspect that the roles of special interests and ideas were either reversed or subsidiary to other forces in the ascension of free enterprise over mercantilism. Certainly Smith himself characterized mercantilism correctly as a system built entirely upon self-interest.[55]

We believe, in short, that commentators on mercantilism, such as Heckscher, have "overscholarized" the period. It is not that these renowned writers have not greatly added to our knowledge of the pe-

---

neglected; but the producers, whose interest has been so carefully attended to; and among this latter class our merchants and manufactures have been by far the principal architects" (p. 626). Although Smith featured the monarch as a rent seeker, he did not elaborate much on the self-interested aspects of politicians, but probably more so than Professor Stigler believes (see G. J. Stigler, "Smith's Travels on the Ship of State," *History of Political Economy* 3 [Fall, 1971]: 265–277).

[54] Keynes, *The General Theory*, p. 383.

[55] Other types of explanations are equally unlikely. For example, within the context of our rent-seeking model, the movement to free enterprise might be explained as a general process of Pareto-optimization. The inefficiencies concommitant to monopoly organization offer a range of mutually beneficial gains from exchange. Presumably, consumers could offer to buy monopolists out to the net benefit of both parties. The difficulty with such a solution is the existence of prohibitively high transaction costs to consumers, which implies that monopoly and regulation will persist despite the potential social gains (Buchanan and Tullock, "The 'Dead Hand' of Monopoly"). Moreover, perhaps there were fewer consumers in mercantilist times and more such Pareto-superior bargains could be struck. If this were operationally so, the movement to free enterprise from the monopolistic policies of mercantilism would be susceptible to rational explanation. This is, however, an extremely unlikely explanation of the decline of mercantilism, since the mathematics of transaction costs imply that the number of transactors must be very small before meaningful reductions in transaction costs obtain. It is therefore quite likely that in mercantilist times the organizing costs to consumers would have dominated the returns from abolishing monopoly via Pareto-superior moves.

riod, but rather that they have implicitly emphasized ideas as primary causal forces of change rather than as (sometimes interesting) rationalizations based upon one's position in the rent-seeking game of income redistribution. The motives of mercantile writers, as Smith cunningly indicated, should always be suspect. Heckscher, for example, has pointed out, with reference to "intellectual arguments," that "there was little mysticism in the arguments of the mercantilists. . . . they did not appeal to sentiment, but were obviously anxious to find reasonable grounds for every position they adopted."[56] We certainly do not disagree that writers of *all* persuasions sought reasonable grounds for their arguments, but we argue that these grounds in the main were laid over the underlying self-interested forces of the times. It is our thesis, in short, that rent seeking engendered forces that drastically altered institutions in England, while producing, in a milieu of French constraints, a mercantile rigidity lasting until the nineteenth century. As such, our view is a reassertion of Smith's primitive analysis of mercantilism. It is, moreover, an elaboration of that view, in that it finds a crucial link between rent-seeking activities and fundamental institutional change.

[56] Heckscher, *Mercantilism*, I, 308.

Efficient Transactors or Rent-Seeking Monopolists? The Rationale for Early Chartered Trading Companies

S. R. H. JONES AND SIMON P. VILLE

Although the modern multinational corporation is usually regarded as a product of changes in the scale and nature of business that have occurred since the middle of the nineteenth century, there are examples of large, integrated firms dating back to the sixteenth century. Perhaps the most celebrated of these are the English and Dutch East India companies, established in 1600 and 1602, respectively, with a national monopoly of trade with Asia. Other English companies to be granted trading monopoly charters included the Muscovy Company (1553), the Hudson's Bay Company (1670), and the Royal African Company (1672), and similar rights were granted to foreign companies by the governments of France, Spain, Sweden, and Denmark.

The grant of exclusive trading rights to particular areas had long been enjoyed by chartered companies, a notable example being the Company of Merchant Adventurers. The earliest companies, which handled well-established trades, were organized as regulated companies in which the governing body, having negotiated trading treaties and established warehouse facilities, merely set broad operational parameters within which members traded on their own account. Entry to the regulated companies was relatively unimpeded, often through payment of a small fine.

The companies that appeared from the middle of the sixteenth century were rather different, their monopoly status being seen as encouragement and recompense for forging new trading links. Entry was by the purchase of shares in a joint-stock company, which exploited monopoly powers by trading as a corporate enterprise. Some shareholders were merchants actively engaged in trade, but others were passive investors who delegated management to paid officials directed by a governor and assistants elected from amongst their ranks. Adam Smith, no friend of the chartered companies, argued that this separation of ownership from control contributed to gross administrative inefficiency, inattention to detail, and the pursuit of managerial goals, which raised prices to consumers and reduced returns to shareholders. He believed that only the extraction of monopoly rents ensured the success and continuance of such companies.[1]

In a recent series of articles, Ann Carlos and Stephen Nicholas have cast doubt upon this traditional interpretation. They argue that the joint-stock chartered companies, far from being comparatively inefficient institutions, represented the optimal organizational form for conducting long-distance trade. The chartered companies' business, like that of the late-nineteenth-century multinationals, was "characterized by a large volume of transactions in many different locations," which prompted a similar organizational response, namely, the adoption of a vertically integrated structure and an administrative hierarchy that enabled them to economize on transaction costs and overcome the limits to management encountered by owner-managed firms. Like modern multinationals, the chartered companies adopted control systems that were intended to limit opportunistic

The Journal of Economic History, Vol. 56, No. 4 (Dec. 1996). © The Economic History Association. All rights reserved. ISSN 0022-0507.

S. R. H. Jones is Senior Lecturer in Economics, Department of Economic Studies, University of Dundee, Dundee DD1 4HN, Scotland. Simon P. Ville is Reader in Economic History, Australian National University, Canberra, ACT 0200, Australia.

We are grateful to Helen Bridge for research assistance and to Santhi Hejeebu and Dr. A. M. Endres and seminar participants at the London School of Economics, King's College, London, the Institute of Historical Research, London, and the universities of Hull and Bangor for their criticisms and suggestions.

[1] Smith, *Wealth of Nations*, pp. 754–57.

898

behavior by their servants. In terms of transaction cost economizing and administrative control, "the charter companies were analogues to the modern business corporation."[2]

Although joint-stock chartered companies shared some features with modern corporations, we do not believe that they constituted the least-cost transactional mode for conducting foreign trade. There is ample evidence to indicate that in spite of the systems and structures employed, they experienced significant transaction cost disabilities. However, the fact that a comparatively inefficient transactional mode was widely preferred for the conduct of long-distance trade suggests that chartered companies offered benefits that more than offset relatively high transaction costs.

The principal benefit of operating as large-scale, vertically integrated enterprises was that the companies were better able to appropriate and maximize monopoly rents than franchisees trading individually. Like manorial lords who farmed their own demesnes, chartered companies were able to control operations and implement systems in such a way that yielded maximum returns, and the enhanced returns from direct exploitation more than offset transaction-cost disabilities. Coalitions of franchisees with agreed operating procedures and effective sanctions, by economizing on the costs of hierarchy, may have been able to outperform the larger companies. However, the uncertainty and information asymmetries involved in long-distance trade and the inherent difficulties in writing efficient contracts, suggest that the hierarchically organized joint-stock company was the most effective way of appropriating and sharing in rents.[3]

Chartered companies were thus adopted not because they represented a transactionally efficient form for conducting long-distance trade but because they were a contractually efficient form for extracting monopoly rents. Before we turn to the question of rent extraction, however, we will first consider the transaction-cost arguments advanced by Carlos and Nicholas and assess how successful the companies were in reducing the costs of hierarchy.

HIERARCHIES VERSUS MARKETS

Chartered companies were generally organized in a similar fashion. Formed as joint-stock companies on the basis of monopoly privileges conferred by executive or legislature, they were run by a court of directors and headquarters staff with substantial powers delegated to governors and factors overseas who negotiated trading rights and treaties and conducted trade from forts, factories, and trading posts. The foreign establishments sold trade goods procured and shipped by headquarters staff and used company vessels (chartered or owned) to ship home locally acquired goods. The return cargoes were usually compiled according to fairly specific instructions from the head office although, in the case of the Royal African Company, slaves were also shipped to the West Indies where they were exchanged for cargoes of cotton, sugar, and other commodities. Bullion might be exported to cover trade deficits whereas overseas, the companies were occasionally involved in local production.

Carlos and Nicholas believe the companies developed as large vertically integrated enterprises "not because a private market did not exist, but because operating by managerial fiat inside the hierarchical firm was less costly than using the market." Their superior efficiency is viewed as the product of organizational innovations that enabled them to handle a large volume of recurrent transactions at less cost than small individual

---

[2] Carlos and Nicholas, "Giants," p. 400. In subsequent articles they focus mainly on the Hudson's Bay and Royal African companies. We provide coverage of a broad range of companies.

[3] Fenoaltea, "Authority," p. 698. An interesting example of merchant coalitions providing some of the advantages of vertical integration without the costs is provided by Greif, "Reputation." However, special cultural factors played an important part in reducing opportunism and enhancing the effects of sanctions.

enterprises of more limited scope. Of particular importance was the development of administrative structures that enabled them to acquire and process complex market information; "it was the efficient processing of information . . . that gave the early trading companies their advantage over the market." Only for the Royal African Company was the choice of vertical integration inappropriate, and that was principally because the volume of trade was apparently insufficient to bear the charges of supporting overseas establishments.[4]

The explanation offered by Carlos and Nicholas is an application of the internalization thesis advanced by Peter Buckley and Mark Casson, the central feature of which is the relationship between set-up and direct costs.[5] Set-up costs were substantial for chartered companies which, in addition to headquarters staff, often incurred heavy expenditure on forts and factories overseas. The set-up costs for individual traders, who might procure domestic cargoes themselves and use supercargoes to trade from vessels overseas, were correspondingly light. In addition to set-up there were also direct costs involved in transacting business, and with freight and insurance constituting a major cost, these probably rose roughly in proportion to goods traded. However, direct trading costs were generally less for chartered companies than individual traders as they might rely on permanent shore establishments to economize on search, negotiation, and enforcement expenditures.[6] Taking the set-up and direct costs of transacting together, trading via the internal markets of a chartered company may be illustrated by the cost function FF' while the costs of individual traders transacting via a series of market exchanges may be described by cost function MM' (see Figure 1). From this it may be deduced that, on the basis of transaction costs alone, individual trading would be preferred when volumes of trade were below $0q^*$ and chartered companies preferred when volumes were above $0q^*$.

That the chartered trading companies chose to exploit their monopolies via hierarchically organized firms does not necessarily confirm that such hierarchies possessed superior transaction-cost properties relative to other organizational modes. Stefano Fenoaltea and Michael Dietrich have each pointed out that governance structures gain their rationale both from transaction-cost minimization and other benefits that might accrue, something that Carlos and Nicholas do not consider. Thus, it would be rational to adopt a structure with higher transaction costs provided that the additional costs were more than compensated by gains elsewhere, such as the more effective appropriation of monopoly rents.[7]

Conclusive historical evidence would thus be necessary to support Carlos and Nicholas's contention that hierarchy was adopted because of its superior transaction-cost properties. Detailed comparisons of the relative costs of operating through markets or a hierarchy are difficult to make. Nevertheless, there are authoritative statements concerning the economics of trading from ships as opposed to shore establishments, and it is possible to draw inferences concerning relative costs from an analysis of market structures and the operations of private traders.[8] Rather than explore this evidence, however, Carlos and Nicholas outline the administrative structures and systems that, on an a priori basis, might be expected to have reduced transaction costs. They discuss the way in which responsibility for the procurement of European trade goods, shipping, gathering information, and conducting correspondence was handled at home by a system of committees and how the establishment of forts and factories abroad was designed to eliminate middlemen and improve scheduling.

It is far from clear that the combination of scale and internalization yielded "an enormous advantage over the market." Indeed, there was a large discrepancy between what

---

[4] Carlos and Nicholas, "Giants," pp. 404, 407, 411.

[5] Buckley, "New Theories," pp. 42–43.

[6] Carlos and Nicholas, "Giants," p. 407.

[7] Fenoaltea, "Authority," p. 698; and Dietrich, *Transaction Cost Economics*, p. 37.

[8] Davies, *Royal African Company*, pp. 259–60.

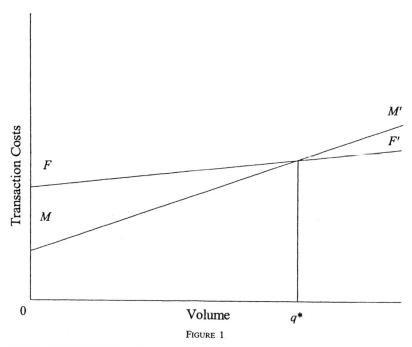

FIGURE 1

TRANSACTION COSTS FOR CHARTERED COMPANY VERSUS INDIVIDUAL TRADERS

Notes: *FF'* is the transaction cost function of the chartered trading company. *MM'* is the transaction cost function of individual traders. q^* is the point beyond which the chartered trading company becomes the lower transaction cost mode of production.
Source: See the text.

the systems were designed to achieve and what happened in practice, the technological constraints from poor communications posing a severe handicap for companies with widely dispersed operations. Although systems were designed to overcome asymmetries, information was often slow to be processed, books were sometimes years out of date, and not all company servants understood the significance of what lay before them or had the capacity or freedom to respond appropriately. The efficient utilization of information was further impeded by the mingling of company operations with the private ventures of shareholders and company servants, a situation that increased the level of confusion and the scope for opportunistic behavior. In spite of a plethora of committees, extensive reporting systems, and a mass of paperwork, specific orders were not always met, freight rates were not invariably the most advantageous, goods might be both overpriced and deficient in quantity and quality, and warehouses were sometimes swollen with unsaleable stock.[9]

Whether internalizing shipping operations yielded efficiency gains must also be doubted. Both the English and Dutch East India companies initially owned their fleets, although from 1639 the former moved towards chartering. The specialized nature of the vessels,

[9] Carlos and Nicholas, "Giants," p. 407; Galenson, *Traders*, p. 148; Chaudhuri, *Trading World*, pp. 58, 65, 208–10, 458–59; *Letters*, pp. 278–85; Rich, *Publications*, vol. 1, pp. 75–77, 102–03, 113, 153–57, 230–32, 263, 538–39; Tattersfield, *Forgotten Trade*, pp. 39–40, 85–86; Davies, *Royal African Company*, pp. 147–49, 155–56; Furber, *Rival Empires*, pp. 128–29; Willan, *Early History*, p. 26; and Wood, *History*, p. 216.

however, encouraged English shipowners to combine, highly profitable rates being set by a clique of owners amongst whom English East India Company directors were prominent. Even so, direct costs per ton of the two companies were still broadly comparable up to 1740. In the second half of the eighteenth century the Dutch East India Company periodically chartered vessels at an average freight rate of £14 per ton plus demurrage charges, whereas their own shipping costs were £28. Better and lighter vessel design, fewer guns, and competition in freight markets helped keep down charter rates. Although comparing this with the company's own cost structures cannot be entirely accurate, the margin is still substantial. A Dutch East India Company report in 1795 recognized that hiring would have yielded major cost savings. A comparison of the shipping costs of the Ostend Company with a private trader in the early eighteenth century, using identical cost components, found the latter to be 15 percent lower.[10]

The ownership of forts and factories along with the employment of a corps of highly skilled factors is also seen by Carlos and Nicholas as yielding decisive trading advantages. They explain such investment by the "frequent and recurring nature of transacting and the type of trade goods sold," with forts and factories providing secure trading and warehousing facilities in an uncertain environment. This, they suggest, represented a credible commitment by chartered companies to an ongoing and substantial trade, especially helpful when negotiating with foreign potentates, contracting with suppliers, or establishing new market networks. Company staff abroad also developed trading expertise, buying keenly and helping to ensure that vessels were fully laden and promptly dispatched.[11]

Although trading via permanent establishments abroad afforded some advantages, it is not generally apparent that "forward integration reduced the costs of transacting below those of market trading." Commodity markets in Asia were highly developed with major entrepots well served by a wide range of specialists, including brokers, wholesale merchants, and shipowners. Seventeenth-century Surat was said to be the equivalent of Amsterdam, Masulipatnam able to supply the needs of 20 large ships, and Canton merchants capable of supplying complete cargoes. Market imperfections did exist, but buyers were generally able to overcome problems of hold-up and opportunism by having recourse to highly competitive spot and forward markets. Financial markets were also well developed in Asia, with the English East India Company borrowing heavily in local markets to overcome liquidity problems.[12] Moreover, the conduct of the entire China tea trade by supercargoes, the extensive and private involvement of overseas servants in trade throughout Asia, and a sharp increase in the number of interloping voyages that occurred each time the English East India Company's monopoly charter came under challenge all indicate that it was possible to trade profitably in the Far East without relying upon forts and factories for low-cost commercial services.[13]

In other regions the commercial infrastructure was far less developed, and systems of exchange were often rudimentary. However, in Rupert's Land, where the Hudson's Bay Company engaged in the fur trade with Indians, interlopers soon appeared in an effort to emulate the company's success by conducting a profitable shipboard trade. The Indians proved adaptable traders, with a number of the Cree and Assinboine middlemen linking hunters inland with trading settlements on the shore. That no interloper succeeded was probably due to the strategic location of the Hudson's Bay Company's forts and the rigorous enforcement of its monopoly through the seizure of interlopers and the confiscation by customs of goods believed to have been shipped illicitly from Hudson's Bay. The

---

[10] Dillo, "Made to Measure," pp. 59–61, 63–64; Degryse and Parmentier, "Maritime Aspects," pp. 148–50; and Postma, *Dutch*, pp. 141, 144.

[11] Carlos and Nicholas, "Giants," pp. 411–13.

[12] Ibid, p. 411; and Chaudhuri, *Trading World*, pp. 63, 141–44, 175.

[13] Chaudhuri, *Trading World*, pp. 42, 65–66; Furber, *Rival Empires*, pp. 75–76, 98–99; Keay, *Honourable Company*, pp. 170–75; and Prakash, *Precious Metals*, p. 90.

West African trade proved more difficult to defend from interlopers. Regular interloping voyages led native traders to keep back slaves for them. Competition from domestic and overseas traders progressively undermined the viability of the Royal African Company, for it barely broke even in the relatively good years of the 1670s and 1680s. In 1698 Parliament threw open the trade on condition that merchants pay the company 10 percent of export values to offset the costs of providing defense and other public goods along the African coast. Despite these payments, private trade flourished whereas that of the company languished, and by 1708 it was effectively bankrupt. Interloping voyages also undermined the viability of the Russia Company, and competition between rival merchants trading to the eastern Mediterranean resulted in a change of status for the Levant Company, which by 1600 had changed from a joint-stock into a regulated company. Henceforth, trade was conducted on a quasi-franchise basis, with members using the brokerage and warehouse facilities provided by the company in Turkey and paying fixed rate "impositions" on all goods exported and imported.[14]

Despite the success of individual traders, Carlos and Nicholas believe that the superior efficiency properties of chartered companies enabled them to sustain a competitive advantage in trades in which large volumes were involved. Yet the fact that the comparatively small Hudson's Bay Company survived whereas the larger Royal African Company failed calls into question their general thesis. Carlos seeks to allay doubts by arguing that the Royal African Company was singularly unsuccessful in solving the principal-agent problems that beset chartered companies.[15] It is to these problems that we now turn.

THE PERSISTENCE OF PRINCIPAL-AGENT PROBLEMS

The geographically dispersed nature of chartered companies' operations meant that significant responsibility was delegated to company servants. Poor communications systems gave rise to considerable information asymmetries, with head offices struggling to determine whether trading outcomes were the result of exogenous factors or the degree of employee honesty and efficiency. Carlos and Nicholas believe that managerial performance had a critical bearing upon profitability and "the major problem facing the trading companies, therefore, was that of managing the managers at a distance." They argue that the introduction of sophisticated control mechanisms that included individual incentives, monitoring systems, and a corporate ethos, enabled most companies to reduce inefficiency and opportunism to acceptable levels. Only in environments such as the West African coast, where high mortality rates made it difficult to introduce efficient employment contracts and where there was ample scope for managers to trade on their own account, were control mechanisms—and companies—likely to fail. In areas such as Hudson's Bay where the environment was different, "agency was not a serious problem."[16]

Hierarchical organizations generally face high incentive and enforcement costs for long-term implicit contracting. This was true for the chartered companies where the wide range of control mechanisms described by Carlos and Nicholas would have needed to be highly effective to cover their costs.[17] We do not believe their systems to have been

---

[14] Rich, *Publications*, vol. 1, pp. 37–38, 103–04, 144–50; Ray and Freeman, *"Give Us Good Measure,"* pp. 20, 29–36, 42–43, 60, 256; Davies, *Royal African Company*, pp. 78–79, 90, 107, 114–15, 134; Willan, *Early History*, pp. 67–77, 278–79; and Wood, *History*, pp. 18–22, 209.

[15] Carlos, "Principal-Agent Problems," p. 144. The Danish Asiatic Company was vertically integrated in spite of the very small size of its operations. Gobel, "Danish Country Trade Routes," pp. 99–100, 115–16:

[16] Carlos and Nicholas, "Agency Problems," p. 855; Carlos, "Agent Opportunism," p. 150; and Carlos and Nicholas, "Managing the Manager," p. 255.

[17] Market-based and intermediate production modes can often mitigate contractual costs. Fenoaltea, "Authority," p. 697; and Greif, "Reputation," p. 874.

cost-effective. Major difficulties were encountered in attenuating agency costs, which is confirmed by wide-ranging evidence of persistent managerial malfeasance in many companies over long periods.[18]

Contracts and Incentives

Incentive structures face the difficulty of relating rewards to output, particularly when teamwork and imperfect information are encountered. Where individual work can be measured, the level and nature of incentives necessary to mitigate opportunism depends upon the opportunity costs of such behavior, which varies over time and between individuals. This creates a series of unique situations that makes efficient contracting based on precedent very difficult. If incentives are too high the company will incur unnecessary costs, and if too low opportunism will continue. The difficulties in designing appropriate incentives are reflected in a lack of consensus over the relative merits of promotion and bonus-based incentives and, more broadly, between monetary and nonmonetary rewards.[19]

Notwithstanding these difficulties, Carlos and Nicholas believe that the employment contracts offered by chartered companies were well structured, with a system of rewards and sanctions in place that was largely able to overcome opportunism. A key element was the level of remuneration, with principals willing to write "a generous employment contract for their managers." Salaries for managers at the Hudson's Bay and Royal African companies ranged between £100 and £200, while senior servants with the English East India Company were also rewarded with "high and generous salaries." Gratuities and bonuses were paid, and some private trade periodically permitted. A system of bonds was also instituted, apparently to raise the opportunity cost of cheating, and such securities were to be forfeited should malfeasance occur. Bonds typically ranged from £300 to £2,000 for governors and managers in the Hudson's Bay Company, and those for senior staff of the Royal African Company might be ten times their annual salary. Management and staff were also required to swear oaths to the company.[20]

Although companies addressed agency problems, the material provided by Carlos and Nicholas only demonstrates that such problems existed, not that they were resolved. Company salaries were no larger on average than those earned elsewhere and did not contain a premium to compensate for private trade forgone. Their sources indicate that engineers and lawyers were generally paid more than senior trading-company officials, and that the clergy received a similar level of remuneration. In Asia salaries were of limited relevance due to the lucrative private trade of staff who dominated commerce in the Indian Ocean and South China Seas.[21]

Remuneration for lesser staff was also modest. Hudson's Bay Company and Royal African Company masters and crew earned no more than prevailing occupational rates, and in 1768 seamen went on strike for improved wages. Nor were the wages paid to personnel on station in Hudson's Bay particularly generous, the terms offered in 1711 proving insufficient to offset the effects of wartime press gangs and attracting none of the "lusty young labouring men" that were so urgently needed. Unable to recruit suitable servants in London, the company turned first to Scotland and then to the Orkney Isles. Rumors of arbitrary treatment of Royal African Company servants on the African coast, the failure to repatriate men on time, danger, discomfort, disease, and unsatisfactory arrangements for remitting the effects of the deceased adversely affected recruitment and discipline. Conditions of employment in the East Indies were, if anything, worse, with modest wages

---

[18] See Ville and Jones, "Principal-Agent Question."

[19] Baker, Jensen, and Murphy, "Compensation," pp. 594–95, 600–01.

[20] Carlos and Nicholas, "Giants," pp. 414–16 and "Agency Problems," pp. 862–65; and Carlos, "Agent Opportunism," p. 146.

[21] Williamson, "Structure of Pay," p. 48; and Prakash, *Precious Metals*, pp. 11–12.

and the brutal enforcement of discipline leading to desertion and a permanent shortage of European labor until at least the middle of the eighteenth century.[22]

Wage and salary levels do not, therefore, appear to have been particularly generous, being largely determined by seniority, length of service, and skills. Such premiums that were paid probably reflected productivity gains resulting from "learning by doing" and the risks involved in living in an alien and inhospitable environment. Carlos notes that wages may have been inflated by a small risk and productivity premium. Her argument that the Royal African Company paid an efficiency wage because "on occasions more people are listed as having applied for the position than hired" is unpersuasive, for it is quite possible that many applicants were unsuitable for vacant positions whereas the remainder were hired at a market clearing wage. Further doubt must be cast on this application of the efficiency-wage hypothesis by the conspicuous absence of sanctions, such as dismissal and bond forfeiture, resorted to by the Royal African Company.[23]

Whether bonds and oaths were effective instruments of control is doubtful given the many employees found guilty of private trade, some of whom continued to rise through company ranks. In 1732 the entire Calcutta Council of the English East India Company was dismissed for corruption and disobedience. Occasionally companies called home those suspected of wrongdoing; although this might result in suits in chancery and ultimately dismissal, attempts were rarely made to realize bonds. Carlos and Nicholas, "found little evidence . . . that bonds were forfeited, implying that they were successful in reducing opportunism."[24] We, too, have found little evidence of bonds being forfeited but, given repeated instances of private trading and gross inefficiency, would question whether bonding was seriously regarded as a means of tackling opportunism. The fact that the "warehouse keeper or husband" within the head-office structure of the Royal African Company in London posted a very large bond suggests that the system was primarily a means of ensuring that the company was able to obtain financial restitution in the event of misappropriation. This appears to be borne out by an instruction that "bonds would not be delivered up until the company was satisfied that all accounts were in order."[25] With bonding employed to secure financial restitution, their nonforfeiture merely indicates that company servants may have been "effective" accountants, not that they were honest and efficient, or eschewed private trade.

Monitoring and Internal Control

Successful monitoring requires effective reporting systems that convey comprehensive, accurate, and up-to-date information. Appropriate measures must be devised as imperfect observation, such as a focus upon quantity rather than quality, may elicit an inappropriate response. Agents will generally be reluctant to share superior information with their principals because it will inhibit rent gathering; indeed, they may even sabotage monitoring systems. Mutual monitoring by agents may check such behavior but it might also produce

[22] Davis, *Rise*, pp. 134–45; Innis, *Fur Trade*, pp. 130, 158; Ville, *English Shipowning*, pp. 80–83; Rich, *Publications*, vol. 1, pp. 315, 389, 498–99, notes that the companies were able to gain some protection from impressment; Davies, *Royal African Company*, pp. 253–57; Tattersfield, *Forgotten Trade*, p. 83; Postma, *Dutch*, pp. 65–66; and Furber, *Rival Empires*, pp. 303–06.

[23] Carlos, "Principal-Agent Problems," p. 142 and "Agent Opportunism," pp. 149–50 and "Bonding," pp. 321–22, 331. Besides being used as a control mechanism, other reasons for paying an efficiency wage include the reduction of turnover and adverse selection, together with a range of social conventions. The hypothesis is generally applied to the primary sector. Akerlof and Yellen, *Efficiency Wage Models*, pp. 1–8.

[24] Mackay, *Honourable Company*, pp. 72–74; Chaudhuri, *Trading World*, p. 448; Tattersfield, *Forgotten Trade*, p. 86; and Carlos and Nicholas, "Agency Problems," p. 864.

[25] Carlos, "Bonding," pp. 325–26, 330.

Jones and Ville

additional costs associated with overmonitoring.[26] Monitoring also becomes difficult in larger companies where managerial specialization and teamwork are common and cooperation occurs amongst opportunistic agents. Irrespective of the quality of information received, companies must have in place systems capable of rapid and efficient information appraisal and an executive structure that responds promptly and effectively. In an environment of gross uncertainty, organizational design is of paramount importance.

Chartered companies may have been innovative in terms of organizational design, but unlike Carlos and Nicholas, we do not believe that their control systems were particularly effective. As we have seen, information was sometimes inaccurate and often out of date, a situation that got worse as companies expanded, while data transmitted was often narrow in scope and limited in usefulness. Thus servants tended to focus primarily on the type of trade goods required beyond Europe and the state of the market in imported produce. Even in this respect information was often incomplete, the Royal African Company recording auction but not contract sales. Accounting practices were also deficient. The Dutch East India Company lacked cost-price calculations and simply set costs against total sales without showing the prices of imports and exports, although it was not alone in its failure to adopt a systematic method for identifying costs. The complexities of international trade provided further opportunities for misinformation and fraud. A plethora of weights and measures, a range of fluctuating currencies, variations in freight rates, and volatile prices, especially in commodities such as sugar and coffee, made effective monitoring very difficult. Uncertainty in the terms of trade provided scope for collusive fraudulence between employees and local traders. Gift-giving policies and sanctioned bribery provided further scope for opportunistic "trimming."[27]

Carlos and Nicholas emphasize the large volume of information generated by companies but give little indication as to how it was used. Many historians believe that although companies attempted to act on information received they were frequently overburdened with detail. K. G. Davies observes that the Royal African Company made little attempt to "digest or summarize the information," and Holden Furber's comments on the Dutch East India Company are particularly illuminating:

> There is no doubt that hundreds of pages sent home were never even read. Anyone working among the company's records at the Dutch National Archives is likely to open a volume to find thousands of grains of sand used to blot the ink lying undisturbed between its pages.[28]

The periodic arrival of large volumes of information accentuated processing problems. Douglas Mackay shows that the Hudson's Bay Company's London office sometimes took two years to respond to outposts with operational decisions.[29] Although suspicions might be aroused when information was processed, proving a case might be difficult, scarcely worth the time and effort and, in some instances, rather too late.

Direct monitoring through the search of company vessels made it more difficult for servants to repatriate the proceeds of illicit trade. The process, however, was fraught with deception and bribery, with searches conducted by the Royal African Company often ineffective and slaves concealed or written off as dead but landed in the West Indies before the company's agents came aboard. There were many points on the French Coast where illegal cargoes might be landed while the growth in size of the Dutch East India Company fleets, arriving together, made the task of searching more difficult. By delegating monitoring to minor officials the companies risked collusive opportunism and bribery. Overseas

---

[26] Baker, Jensen, and Murphy, "Compensation," p. 606.

[27] Furber, *Rival Empires*, pp. 128–29, 191, 196–97, 263; Davies, *Royal African Company*, pp. 156, 361, 366; Rich, *Publications*, vol. 1, pp. 186–87; Gaastra, "Shifting Balance," p. 54; Ville, *English Shipowning*, p. 174; Chaudhuri, *Trading World*, pp. 125, 357, 378–81; and Innis, *Fur Trade*, p. 146.

[28] Furber, *Rival Empires*, p. 191; and Davies, *Royal African Company*, p. 111.

[29] Mackay, *Honourable Company*, p. 134.

monitoring was even more difficult, with senior officials reluctant to expose others for fear of their own misdeeds being revealed, collusion and fraud being rife at all levels.[30] The problems involved in both mutual and indirect monitoring raise serious questions about the effectiveness of the whole exercise. Indeed, those to whom monitoring responsibilities had been delegated were best placed to make judgments about the risks and rewards of opportunism. Given that many monitors turned to private trading, the rewards would appear to have been worth the risks.[31]

Agent Opportunism and Company Culture

The problems associated with incentives and monitoring led Herbert Simon to argue that there are "other powerful motivations that induce employees to accept organizational goals and authority as bases for their actions." A company culture concerns the development of behavioral norms such as pride, loyalty, docility, and identification that all discourage opportunism. It may be doubted, however, whether "most human beings are gifted with a considerable measure of docility."[32] The appropriate level of docility would require some element of fostering by the firm, a not entirely costless exercise that would probably only work under particular conditions, such as close and regular interaction within the enterprise. Although docility and conformism may be appropriate values amongst the unskilled, a firm would expect individualism and initiative from its managers.

Carlos and Nicholas make much of the development of company culture, attributing the success of the Hudson's Bay Company to the creation "of a social system in which managers and workers were made to feel part of a family." Yet evidence of company culture is tenuous and at odds with a working environment in which censorship, searches, and harsh discipline were the norm, and where servants were offered incentives to spy on each other. Of course, the Hudson's Bay Company correspondence was "replete with positive encouragement" for managers and men, as was the correspondence of other companies, but its little homilies were insufficient to prevent desertion by senior staff, drunkenness on a stupefying and stupendous scale, gross immorality, and a desire by Orkney men to escape the company's service once they had scraped together a few pounds.[33]

Whether the Hudson's Bay Company was successful in creating a homogeneous workforce with shared values must be doubted. By no means all senior officers began as company apprentices at Christ's Hospital whereas the recruitment of Orkney men was, at least initially, a matter of expediency, their suitability being dictated as much by the fact that the Orkney Isles was the last port of hire as the characteristics of sobriety and steadiness for which the islanders were renowned. Nor was a homogeneous workforce necessarily loyal or industrious, especially when group values were at odds with those of their managers and directors in London. Thus one Hudson's Bay Company manager ruefully commented of Orkney men:

---

[30] Galenson, *Traders*, p. 27, believes it is difficult to determine the extent of slave concealment; Davies, *Royal African Company*, pp. 110, 255–56, 366; Furber, *Rival Empires*, p. 142; Glamann, *Dutch-Asiatic Trade*, p. 238; Chaudhuri, *Trading World*, pp. 208–13; Keay, *Honourable Company*, p. 235; Rich, *Publications*, vol. 1, p. 602; and Tattersfield, *Forgotten Trade*, pp. 83–85.

[31] Carlos and Nicholas argue that the monitoring system employed by the Hudson's Bay Company was highly effective. See "Managing the Manager," pp. 243–56. We believe that the model they employ is misspecified, their data unrepresentative, and their conclusions at variance with the results of an internal review carried out by the Hudson's Bay Company. See Casson, Jones, and Ville, "Modelling Agency."

[32] Simon, "Organizations," pp. 24, 36.

[33] Carlos and Nicholas, "Agency Problems," pp. 872–73; Rich, *Publications*, vol. 1, pp. 587–88, 597; Innis, *Fur Trade*, p. 165; and Rich, *Publications*, vol. 1, pp. 496–99, 547–48 and vol. 2, pp. 9, 28.

they are the slyest set of men under the Sun; and their universal propensity to smuggling, and Clandestin dealings of every kind, added to their Clannish attachment to each other, puts it out of the power of any one English man to detect them.

The Orkney men, although capable of enduring great privations, were viewed as dull and unenterprising by many observers, and in 1812 it was suggested that the Hudson's Bay Company would have been better served by recruiting native Canadians.[34]

Given the apparent lack of an esprit de corps amongst Hudson's Bay Company servants, it is difficult to accept Carlos's argument that the differing fortunes of the Hudson's Bay Company and Royal African Company were due to the former's ability to inculcate an appropriate company culture. Moreover, the environment that supposedly undermined the attempts of the Royal African Company to back up its incentive and monitoring systems with an appropriate company culture, namely, an openness to outside influences and a shortness of employment contracts, was not dissimilar to the environment in which the managerial hierarchies of the English and Dutch East India companies operated successfully. There is little evidence of a strong corporate culture in either of these companies, both of which employed a self-serving and highly cosmopolitan staff. Fringe benefits that companies offered, such as wartime payments for injury and pensions in the event of death, should therefore be seen as attempts to keep men at their posts in a hostile environment, not as a means to foster a family environment amongst exceedingly disparate individuals. Similar employment practices were adopted by private shipowners, equally concerned to retain the services of valued staff.[35]

The historians of trading companies have emphasized the seriousness of the agency problem, which may have actually increased over the course of the seventeenth and eighteenth centuries. For the English East India Company, K. N. Chaudhuri concluded "the company was never able to solve satisfactorily the difficult task of controlling officials in Asia and extracting compliance to its orders." Davies noted the "lethargy and dishonesty" of officials of the Royal African Company, and Om Prakash doubted whether the Dutch East India Company ever solved the agency problem.[36] Attempts were made to align the interests of companies and individuals by granting servants trading and other privileges, but our review of the evidence strongly suggests that, in spite of a variety of monitoring and incentive systems, technological constraints and opportunistic behavior by company servants resulted in the excessive dissipation of monopoly rents.

CHARTERED COMPANIES AS RENT-SEEKING MONOPOLISTS: A RESTATEMENT

The notion that chartered companies were rent-seeking monopolists was discussed by pamphleteers and regularly debated in Parliament long before the publication of the *Wealth of Nations* in 1776. Grievances against the indiscriminate granting of monopolies by the crown had led to a number of grants being overturned by the Statute of Monopolies of 1624. The chartered trading companies, although far from popular, were allowed to retain their privileges in recognition of the fact that they financed the cost of public goods necessary to prosecute trade in new and hitherto undeveloped markets. Adam Smith accepted that "a temporary monopoly of this kind may be vindicated upon the same principles upon which a like monopoly is granted to its inventor." Nevertheless, he was opposed to permanent monopolies, believing that trade should be thrown open to all after

[34] Rich, *Publications*, vol. 1, pp. 498–99 and vol. 2, p. 128; and Innis, *Fur Trade*, p. 165.

[35] Innis, *Fur Trade*, p. 158; Carlos, "Agent Opportunism," p. 150; Carlos and Nicholas, "Giants," p. 419; Furber, *Rival Empires*, p. 211; and Ville, *English Shipowning*, p. 74.

[36] Carlos and Nicholas, "Agency Problems," pp. 855–56; Chaudhuri, *Trading World*, p. 40; Davies, *Royal African Company*, p. 165; Prakash, *Dutch East India Company*, p. 83; and Wood, *History*, p. 56.

Rationale for Early Chartered Trading Companies 909

a period of time and "forts and garrisons, if it was found necessary to establish any, to be taken into the hand of government, their value paid to the company."[37]

A monopoly granting exclusive trading privileges constituted a potentially valuable property right and there developed a continual struggle between their corporate owners and those who wished to share in or acquire the right to trade. The value of the property right varied both between companies and over time, but generally it was not insignificant. In 1687 private traders to West Africa paid a premium of 40 percent of the value of their cargoes for the right to trade while the value of the English East India trade in 1698 was used by the crown as security to raise a loan of £2 million.[38] The Hudson's Bay Company was an altogether more modest affair, but its exclusive rights were regarded as a valuable privilege by shareholders who spent considerable sums defending their trading monopoly in Parliament, court, and the Bay.

In view of the value attached to monopoly rights by contemporaries, it seems strange that Carlos and Nicholas should have made little attempt to analyze the ways in which a desire to appropriate monopoly rents may have affected company structure and organization. We believe that this is a serious oversight as there is a substantial literature examining the nature of organizational choices open to those wishing to exploit monopolies.[39] The question of organizational form was widely discussed amongst those involved with the chartered companies, although when faced with a choice of selling licences to private traders, operating as a regulated company, or trading as a vertically integrated enterprise, the owners of monopoly rights opted for the latter. Such a choice, we believe, was motivated by the desire to maximize monopoly rents and not to capture internalization advantages that, as we have demonstrated, were difficult to realize.

Monopoly Powers, Public Goods and the Vertically Integrated Trading Enterprise

The charter provisions of the companies did not prescribe organizational form; although it was assumed that trading would probably take place on a joint-stock basis, franchising, either through a regulated company or a system of licences, was also regarded as appropriate. Thus when questioned by Lord Burghley in 1591, members of the Levant Company replied that they wished to continue to operate as a joint-stock company although within a few years it had become a regulated company. Members of the English East India Company were equally indecisive, framing a charter that although intended for a joint-stock company "contained many expressions that would be more appropriate to a regulated one." The Hudson's Bay Company charter included an even wider range of organizational options, with shareholders permitted to exploit the company's monopoly by issuing licences to trade, operating as a regulated company, employing a system of terminable or permanent joint stocks, or undertaking trade via the "Cape Merchant" system in which settlers conducted local trade while the company engrossed the import and export trade via a "Magazeen Ship." According to the company's historian, it "only stumbled into its firm adherence to close control and joint-stock trading as circumstances made opposition to private trade possible and necessary."[40] Several reasons have been advanced to explain the general preference for the joint-stock form, including the high levels of risk and the considerable fixed and sunk costs involved in the politics and defense of long-distance trade. The companies themselves stressed that "Trafique with infidels and barbarous nations" could only be developed and sustained by companies willing to finance the construction of forts and factories and bear the costs of commercial negotiations with

[37] Smith, *Wealth of Nations*, pp. 754–55.

[38] Davies, *Royal African Company*, pp. 125–26; and Scott, *Constitution*, vol. 1, p. 362.

[39] For example, see Rich, *Publications*, vol. 1, p. 55; Scott, *Constitution*, vol. 2, pp. 84–88; and Anderson, McCormick, and Tollison, "Economic Organization," pp. 233–36.

[40] Scott, *Constitution*, vol. 2, pp. 84–88, 97; and Rich, *Publications*, vol. 1, p. 55.

910   *Jones and Ville*

princes and potentates. It was hardly fair, they argued, that having established a trade at such vast expense and trouble, others should benefit "that have had nothing of the burden and the charge."[41]

Not everyone viewed chartered companies as necessary for the conduct of long-distance trade. It was pointed out that in four years of open trade between 1667 and 1671, 135 vessels had sailed for West Africa without the benefits of Royal African Company services. In particular, the value of shore establishments was questioned for they were thinly spread and often underutilized in a trade where much business was conducted by vessels standing off. Their value lay in watching over local rulers many of whom had been coerced into monopsonistic agreements. However, this stationary system, restricted by heavy sunk investments in fortified stations, was inflexible in response to changing economic and political conditions. Hudson's Bay Company forts were described as "no better than pig styes" and built to "resist the cold and not the arms of those who might attack from the land." The forts on the edge of Hudson's Bay were not ideally located, with many prime furs being lost to Canadian backwoodsmen who intercepted Indian traders far inland. The experience of the English East India Company also suggests that permanent establishments were not always cost effective, with many closed after 1660 as the company turned to local brokers.[42]

It seems unlikely, therefore, that most interlopers were free-riders, taking advantage of essential public goods. Frequent episodes of interloping suggest that in most markets for most of the time, trade might just as easily have been conducted via market exchanges as through vertically integrated corporations. Companies chose to adopt the vertically integrated joint-stock form because it was the most effective mode for capturing and manipulating the size of monopoly rents.

Vertical Integration and the Appropriation of Rents

As we have previously seen, one advantage of vertical integration was that chartered companies could point to the expenditure on forts and factories and use it as a basis to plead for the continuation of their trading privileges. It was an argument regularly employed by all English companies, to the extent that sceptics might argue that their forts afforded greater protection at home than they did abroad. There were more immediate reasons for adopting the joint-stock form, not the least being that it provided royalty, courtiers, and other passive investors with a convenient means of participating in the profits of a monopolized trade. A regulated company or other type of franchise would have mostly excluded such investors who had neither the skill nor inclination to engage directly in mercantile ventures but whose political influence was instrumental in securing and preserving monopoly charters. The crown also preferred joint-stock companies both as a medium for investment and because of the scope for raising loans from such bodies.[43]

The direct appropriation of monopoly rents removed the costs of franchise management, especially those of monitoring and enforcement, which, in the case of the Merchant

[41] Davies, *Royal African Company*, pp. 33–37, 107–08; Rich, *Publications*, vol. 1, p. 12; and Scott, *Constitution*, vol. 2, p. 149.

[42] Davies, *Royal African Company*, pp. 98–99, 106, 121, 126–29, shows that the Royal African Company charter contained explicit provisions to ensure the enforcement of its monopoly including courts on the West African coast to deal with interlopers; Tattersfield, *Forgotten Trade*, pp. 81, 109–15; and Postma, *Atlantic Slave Trade*, p. 206. Rich, *Publications*, vol. 1, pp. 120, 268, 524–25, 589; and Winius and Vink, *Merchant-Warrior*, pp. 63–64, 70. Boogaart, "Trade"; and Eltis, "Relative Importance," debate the timing of the Royal African Company's shift of emphasis towards the slave trade, although its forts were intended for the gold trade. The Danish Asiatic Company closed its Tranquebar factory in 1796 when the focus of its trade changed from Coromandel to Bengal. Gobel, "Danish Country Trade Routes," pp. 112–13; and Chaudhuri, *English East India Company*, p. 68 and *Trading World*, p. 45.

[43] Scott, *Constitution*, vol. 1, pp. 70–71 and vol. 2, p. 166; and Davies, *Royal African Company*, p. 37.

Adventurers with its large membership and many statutes and ordinances, might be considerable. The wide range of commodities traded in diverse markets suggests that the cost of writing complex franchise contracts that sustained monopoly prices in final markets may well have been prohibitive.[44] With a joint-stock company engrossing the trade it was, so to speak, patently obvious who possessed the right to trade and what their obligations might be. Optimum pricing, which involved companies manipulating the terms of trade in their favor, was carried out more easily by the vertically integrated enterprise. So were other aspects of rent extraction.

There is ample evidence that chartered companies attempted to extract rents wherever they achieved market dominance. Generally speaking, they were better able to influence the prices at which they sold goods at home than the prices at which they purchased goods at home and abroad. Nevertheless, companies sometimes achieved monopsonistic power in their territory over the sale of certain domestically produced items whereas bribery and coercion might enable them to secure favorable buying terms and deny trading rivals access to cargoes. At sea this was reinforced by restrictions in the movement of competitors' cargoes.[45]

The Dutch East India Company was probably the most successful at monopolizing trades, restricting English access to the spice trade by force of arms and using a combination of military might and commercial chicanery to exercise control over the production of cloves, nutmeg, and cinnamon in Ceylon, Java, and the Moluccas. Clove production was controlled by the destruction of trees enabling the company to hold Dutch prices stable from 1677 to 1744. In Surinam planters complained of the low supply and high prices of imported slaves and in 1703 petitioned for the abolition of the Dutch West India Company's monopoly. Neither English companies particularly scrupulous as to the methods they employed, often using their military and naval capability to improve purchasing leverage. A letter to the Royal African Company in 1705 noted "the perpetual force and constraints put on blacks to trade nowhere but the forts, and this prosecuted to such a height as panjarding [confiscating] their goods, killing people from the forts, and brandering their persons." In Hudson's Bay bribery was more commonly resorted to although both the French and the rival North West Company were known to use homicide as a competitive device.[46]

Although chartered companies rarely achieved a complete monopoly of goods shipped home, their position of dominance enabled them to raise prices. Some companies exercised market power quite crudely, the Russia Company, for example, raising the price of cordage by 50 percent by not importing for three years.[47] The Hudson's Bay Company also sought to control competition on the London market, encouraging customs officers to enforce their monopoly by arranging to buy from them, at market price, all beaver furs confiscated for not having been shipped from their country of origin. The Hudson's Bay Company was not entirely free to manipulate the market in furs, Parliament bowing to public pressure in 1690 by stipulating that there should be two public auctions each year. Furthermore, its

---

[44] Scott, *Constitution*, vol. 1, pp. 10–11; and Anderson, McCormick, and Tollison, "Economic Organization," pp. 233–36.

[45] Winius and Wink, *Merchant-Warrior*, p. 78.

[46] Furber, *Rival Empires*, p. 88; Davies, *Royal African Company*, p. 367; Rich, *Publications*, vol. 2, chap. 3; and Postma, *Dutch*, pp. 183–84. The Dutch East India Company also used "dumping" to eliminate competitors. Prakash, *Dutch East India Company*, paper 2, p. 122.

[47] "to sell their ware dear they have contracted with the buyer not to bring any more of that commodity within three years after." U.K., *Journal*, p. 220. Scott, *Constitution*, vol. 1, p. 126, accepts uncritically lobbyist claims that a lack of imports was due to the company's indebtedness. However, the enduring debts of this and other companies did not prevent them trading in many other years. The Royal African Company found barter solutions to working capital shortages. Galenson, *Traders*, p. 148; and Willan, *Early History*, pp. 185, 254–55.

power to act as a discriminating monopolist was limited by the proviso that private sales to large furriers should be at the same price as the last public sale.[48]

The English East India Company adopted a more sophisticated pricing strategy since commodities were to be re-exported to Europe where it faced competition from other companies. "Supplies were controlled over time according to calculations that took into account the strategy of rival Dutch or French Companies, the cost of holding inventories, the elasticity of demand, and the level of current prices." Overseas factors bought goods in quantities and prices stipulated by head office, shipping them home to the company's warehouse from which they were subsequently released onto the domestic market via a system of quarterly public auctions. Attempts were made to maintain the prices at home by printing sales catalogues that included indicative prices, quantities sold being adjusted so as to ensure that indicative prices were reached. Price discrimination was enforced where appropriate, with care taken that commodities sold for "transportation" overseas were not resold in the home market.[49]

The desire to manipulate prices helps to explain why companies expended so much time and money in attempting to limit the trading activities of interlopers and company servants. Recognition that some private trade would always occur led companies to experiment with trading privileges in their employment contracts. Although the companies were prepared to sacrifice some of their rents in this way, the schemes were rarely successful and substantial rent dissipation continued. There was also the problem of the division of rents among shareholders, with auction sales viewed as a way of preventing certain groups purchasing company wares on favorable terms. Whether it was so easy to prevent shareholders selling trade goods to the company at high prices is more difficult to determine although the English East India Company was known to have chartered vessels from such a group at highly remunerative rates. Notwithstanding such rent dissipation, the returns from trade were generally sufficient to cover the costs of the hierarchy that was vital to sustain the process of rent extraction.

CONCLUSION

The contention that chartered trading companies represented the optimal organizational form for conducting long distance-trade in the seventeenth and eighteenth centuries does not stand up to scrutiny. There is no specific historical evidence to support the Carlos and Nicholas hypothesis that vertically integrated organizations enjoyed lower costs than individual traders. Set-up investments may have reduced direct costs, but there is no reason to suppose that overall costs were lower. Relatively sophisticated markets were well established in many trading areas, the continual breaching of official monopolies by interlopers suggesting that free trade alternatives were, in fact, competitive. As Chaudhuri concluded, "the relative benefits of open trading as against closed was never properly put to the test and the decision to adopt a monopolistic form of organization was derived on the basis of conditions in Europe rather than those in Asia."[50]

Principal-agent problems were not easily resolved, company histories providing abundant evidence of persistent opportunism. Attempts to improve the conduct and efficiency of employees appear to have met with limited success. In addition to the general problem of devising effective incentive and monitoring structures in large organizations in which teamwork is common, the companies faced difficulties in acquiring and processing up-to-date information. Thus although bonds were required from employees, they were rarely forfeited, while a system of efficiency wages, if in fact instituted, was unlikely to succeed in an environment of gross uncertainty in which opportunity costs and rates of

[48] Rich, *Publications*, vol. 1, pp. 269, 319.
[49] Chaudhuri, *Trading World*, pp. 134–35, 318–19.
[50] Ibid., p. 47.

Rationale for Early Chartered Trading Companies 913

discount might vary enormously over a short space of time. Whether much progress was made in engendering cooperative cultural values amongst a workforce subject to brutal treatment must also be doubted.

Although chartered companies reaped few efficiency gains from a vertically integrated structure, there were other notable benefits. The erection of forts and factories and the provision of public goods overseas, while conferring limited operational advantages, provided a justification for the grant and retention of monopoly powers. At the same time, integration removed the costs of franchise management and facilitated more effective rent appropriation through the closer manipulation of markets. The adoption of the joint-stock form enabled royalty, courtiers, and other influential investors to share in monopoly profits. The companies also served as a useful means of projecting state power in an age of mercantilism, initiatives in the form of gifts, letters of goodwill, and the deployment of diplomatic, naval, and military personnel being an integral part of foreign policy.[51] This link between privilege, patronage and policy provided a useful bulwark against attacks by interlopers and others jealous of companies' monopoly powers.

During the course of the eighteenth century, chartered companies came under growing pressure to relinquish their monopolies. The extension of formal empire by the leading European powers, particularly Britain, the decline of mercantilism, and the growth of free-trade philosophies, added weight to these demands. In order to fend off criticism companies adjusted their structure and membership, with the Dutch and English East India companies and the Hudson's Bay Company merging with actual or potential competitors. However, the easing of barriers to entry gradually eroded monopoly rents so that in later years many companies struggled to survive and sometimes relied on government support. The loss of monopoly status usually spelled rapid decline and ultimate collapse, with only the Hudson's Bay Company managing to survive. Thus, far from being an efficient trading institution, the vertically integrated chartered company was generally uncompetitive. Furber was, perhaps, not so wide of the mark in viewing it as "a most cumbersome organization."[52]

[51] Ibid., p. 455; and Wood, *History*, pp. 181–84.
[52] Furber, *Rival Empires*, p. 187.

REFERENCES

Akerlof, George A. and Janet L. Yellen. *Efficiency Wage Models of the Labor Market*. Cambridge: Cambridge University Press, 1986.

Anderson, Gary M., Robert E. McCormick, and Robert D. Tollison. "The Economic Organization of the English East India Company." *Journal of Economic Behaviour and Organization* 4, no. 10 (1983): 221–38.

Baker, George P., Michael C. Jensen, and Kevin Murphy. "Compensation and Incentives: Practice vs Theory." *Journal of Finance* 43, no. 3 (1988): 593–616.

Boogaart, Ernst van den. "The Trade Between Western Africa and the Atlantic World, 1600–90: Estimates of Trends in Composition and Value." *Journal of African History* 33 (1992): 369–85.

Buckley, Peter J. "New Theories of International Business: Some Unresolved Issues." In *The Growth of International Business*, edited by Mark Casson, 34–50. London: Allen & Unwin, 1983.

Carlos, Ann M. "Agent Opportunism and the Role of Company Culture: The Hudson's Bay and Royal African Companies Compared." *Business and Economic History*, 2d ser., 20 (1991): 142–51.

914 *Jones and Ville*

_____. "Principal-Agent Problems in Early Trading Companies: A Tale of Two Firms." *American Economic Review, Papers and Proceedings* 82, no. 2 (May 1992): 140–45.

_____. "Bonding and the Agency Problem: Evidence from the Royal African Company." *Explorations in Economic History* 31, no. 3 (1994): 313–35.

Carlos, Ann M., and Stephen Nicholas. "Giants of an Earlier Capitalism: The Early Chartered Trading Companies as Modern Multinationals." *Business History Review* 62 (autumn 1988): 398–419.

_____. "Agency Problems in Early Chartered Companies: The Case of the Hudson's Bay Company," this JOURNAL 50, no., 4 (1990): 853–75.

_____. "Managing the Manager: An Application of the Principal Agent Model to the Hudson's Bay Company." *Oxford Economic Papers* 45 (1993): 243–56.

Casson, M., S. R. H. Jones, and S. Ville. "Modelling Agency in the Hudson's Bay Company: A Critique." *Discussion Papers in Economics*. University of Reading. 322 (1995): 1–22.

Chaudhuri, K. N. *The English East India Company: The Study of an Early Joint Stock Company, 1600–1640*. London: Frank Cass, 1965.

_____. *The Trading World of Asia and the English East India Company, 1660–1760*. Cambridge: The University Press, 1978.

Davies, K. G. *The Royal African Company*. London: Longmans Green, 1957.

Davis, Ralph. *The Rise of the English Shipping Industry in the Seventeenth and Eighteenth Centuries*. Newton Abbot: David and Charles, 1962.

Degryse, K. and Parmentier, J. "Maritime Aspects of the Ostend Trade to Mocha, India and China (1715–32)." In *Ships, Sailors and Spices. East India Companies and their Shipping in the 16th, 17th, and 18th Centuries*, edited by Jaap R. Bruijn and Femme S. Gaastra, 139–75. Amsterdam: NEHA, 1993.

Dietrich, Michael. *Transaction Cost Economics and Beyond: Towards a New Economics of the Firm*. London: Routledge, 1994.

Dillo, Ingrid G. "Made to Measure? A Comparative Approach to the System and Costs of English and Dutch Shipping to Asia in the 18th Century." In *Anglo-Dutch Mercantile Marine Relations, 1700–1850*, edited by J. R. Bruijn and W. F. F. Morzer Bruyns, 57–65. Leiden: Leiden University Press, 1991.

Eltis, David. "The Relative Importance of Slaves and Commodities in the Atlantic Trade of Seventeenth-Century Africa." *Journal of African History* 35 (1994): 237–49.

Fenoaltea, Stefano. "Authority, Efficiency, and Agricultural Organization in Medieval England and Beyond: a Hypothesis." this JOURNAL 35, no. 3 (1975): 693–718.

Furber, Holden. *Rival Empires of Trade in the Orient 1600–1800*. Minneapolis: University of Minnesota Press, 1976.

Gaastra, Femme. "The Shifting Balance of Trade of the Dutch East India Company." In *Companies and Trade*, edited by Leonard Blusse and Femme Gaastra, 47–69. Leiden: Leiden University Press, 1981.

Galenson, David W. *Traders, Planters and Slaves: Market Behavior in Early English America*. Cambridge: Cambridge University Press, 1986.

Glamann, Kristof. *Dutch Asiatic Trade, 1620–1740*. The Hague: Nijhoff/Kluwer, 1981.

Gobel, E. "Danish Country Trade Routes in Asian Waters in the Seventeenth and Eighteenth Centuries." In *Asian Trade Routes*, edited by Karl Reinhold Haellquist, 104–16. Stockholm: Curzon Press, 1991.

Greif, Avner. "Reputation and Coalitions in Medieval Trade: Evidence on the Maghribi Traders." this JOURNAL 49, no. 4 (1989): 857–82.

Innis, Harold A. *The Fur Trade in Canada: An Introduction to Canadian Economic History*. New Haven: Yale University Press, 1930.

Keay, John. *The Honourable Company: A History of the English East India Company*. London: Harper Collins, 1991.

Letters From Hudson's Bay. Vol. 25. London: Hudson's Bay Record Society, 1965.

Rationale for Early Chartered Trading Companies   915

Mackay, Douglas. *The Honourable Company; A History of the Hudson's Bay Company*. London: Cassell & Co. 1937.

Postma, Johannes Menne. *The Dutch in the Atlantic Slave Trade, 1600–1815*. Cambridge: Cambridge University Press, 1990.

Prakash, Om. *The Dutch East India Company and the Economy of Bengal 1630–1720*. Princeton, NJ: Princeton University Press, 1985.

_____. *Precious Metals and Commerce. The Dutch East India Company in the Indian Ocean Trade*. Aldershot: Variorum, 1994.

Ray, Arthur J. and Freeman, Donald B. *"Give us Good Measure": An Economic Analysis of Relations Between the Indians and the Hudson's Bay Company before 1763*. Toronto: University of Toronto Press, 1978.

Rich, E. E. *The Publications of the Hudson's Bay Record Society: Hudson's Bay Company 1670–1870*. 2 vols. London: Hudson's Bay Record Society, 1958.

Scott, William Robert. *The Constitution and Finance of English, Scottish and Irish joint Stock Companies to 1720*. 3 vols. Cambridge: The University Press, 1912.

Simon, Herbert. "Organizations and Markets." *Journal of Economic Perspectives* 5, no. 2 (1991): 25–44.

Smith, Adam. *An Inquiry into the Nature and Causes of the Wealth of Nations*, edited by R. H. Campbell, A. S. Skinner and W. B. Todd. Oxford: Clarendon Press, 1976.

Tattersfield, Nigel. *The Forgotten Trade*. London: Cape, 1991.

United Kingdom. *Journal of the House of Commons*. Vol. 1. 1604.

Ville, Simon P. *English Shipowning During the Industrial Revolution*. Manchester: Manchester University Press 1987.

Ville, S. and S. R. H. Jones. "The Principal Agent Question: the Chartered Trading Companies." *Working Papers in Economic History* (London School of Economics and Political Science) 27 (1995): 1–26.

Willan, T. S. *The Early History of the Russia Company*. Manchester: Manchester University Press, 1956.

Williamson, Jeffrey G. "Structure of Pay In Britain, 1710–1911." *Research in Economic History* 7 (1982): 1–54.

Winius, George D. and Vink, Marcus P. M. *The Merchant-Warrior Pacified. The VOC (The Dutch East India Company) and its Changing Political Economy in India*. Delhi: Oxford University Press, 1991.

Wood, Alfred C. *A History of the Levant Company*. London: Frank Cass, 1964.

ELSEVIER

Journal of Economic Behavior & Organization
Vol. 42 (2000) 1–17

JOURNAL OF
Economic Behavior
& Organization

www.elsevier.com/locate/econbase

The open constitution and its enemies: competition, rent seeking, and the rise of the modern state

Oliver Volckart

Max-Planck-Institut zur Erforschung, von Wirtschaftssystemen, Unit 1: International Economics, Kahlaische Strasse 10, 07745 Jena, Germany

Received 20 August 1998; received in revised form 23 March 1999; accepted 31 December 1999

Abstract

The article presents a simple non-mathematical model that helps to explain how states emerged in medieval and early modern Central Europe. Classical feudalism is modelled as an essentially state-less political system, that is, as a market for military security characterized by intensive competition. The emergence of states is interpreted as the consequence of rent seeking taking place in this market after the medieval growth of population and the simultaneous reduction in transaction costs changed the market power of the parties contracting for the supply of security. ©2000 Elsevier Science B.V. All rights reserved.

JEL classification: H1; H4; N4

Keywords: Constitutional economics; Constitutional history; State formation

1. Introduction

The fact that German medieval and early modern politics were characterized by intensive competition has often been noticed but never analyzed from an economic point of view. Occasionally it has even been perceived that this competition played an important part in the rise of the modern state. As early as in 1943, Theodor Mayer, one of the most distinguished scholars of medieval German history, noted that "the numerous struggles between king and nobility can be correctly understood only when they are interpreted as competition for the creation of the fundaments and forms of the emerging state, but not as a struggle for power within an already existing state" (Mayer, 1943, p. 1). Mayer's statement shows that the existence of states in the modern sense of the word — that is, of political organizations with a territorially defined monopoly of force and the competence of creating ultimately binding legal rules — cannot be taken for granted. In other words, the assumption shared by most economists and economic historians that the use and control of violence was a natural

2   O. Volckart / J. of Economic Behavior & Org. 42 (2000) 1–17

monopoly (cf. Lane, 1958, p. 402; North and Thomas, 1973, p. 30) does not agree with the facts of constitutional history. In Central Europe states in the above sense of the word are a rather young phenomenon: they go back only to the 17th or 18th centuries (Vierhaus, 1985, p. 450f; Boldt, 1990, p. 30; Moraw, 1995, p. 54f).

With this article I want to contribute to clarifying the question of how modern states emerged in Germany. [1] The paper starts out from the proposition that this is impossible without taking premodern political competition into account. By that I do not mean competition between or within territorially defined political units that initially did not even exist. Rather, several individuals or organizations within one geographical region were supplying the same goods which today have been monopolized by the state, among these goods being military security. The political system which served as a frame for their activities — feudalism — was based on the fact that protection was provided within bilateral contracts as a non-public good, that is, as a good which cannot be defined by non-rivalry in consumption and impossibility of exclusion. In feudalism, there were no institutions limiting the freedom to enter into agreements about the provision of military security. The only relevant restriction was a simple kind of budget constraint: Potential lords needed at least so much land that they could grant part of it as a fief or a peasant's holding. As there were no institutions restricting the entry into the feudal market for security, the constitution of the high Middle Ages was an 'Open Constitution' in the true sense of the word. [2]

In contrast to Mayer's statement cited above, the article shows that the emergence of the modern state was not so much the result of competition among premodern political authorities itself than of the successful endeavors of some authorities to restrict competition by creating discriminating institutions. [3] In analogy to activities on product markets, such endeavors can be interpreted as a kind of rent seeking. The rules that allowed the appropriation of rents prevented potential suppliers of military security from providing this good. In consequence of the removal of their competitors, the suppliers who were not excluded had the chance to realize profits in excess of those they could have made under competitive conditions. Seen from this perspective, the emergence of the modern state appears as the result of a special kind of rent seeking.

---

[1] Constitutional historiography claims that in Western Europe modern states emerged in principle in the same way as in Germany (Moraw, 1995, p. 55). Therefore, the model presented here might be helpful to explain state formation in, e.g., England or France, too. To test the model against the history of these countries is, however, beyond the scope of this article. For some tentative remarks see Footnote 13 below.

[2] In the context of German constitutional history, this term was coined by Peter Moraw. He, however, is using it with a slightly different meaning. Moraw (Moraw, 1989, p. 21) does not argue economically but sees the 'Open Constitution' as 'characterized by the reduction of the institutionalized components to a minimum, by the participation of very few persons in all-German politics, and by the very few duties of the members of the Empire'.

[3] A comprehensive overview over state formation models hitherto developed is presented by Tilly who is distinguishing between several main approaches: The 'statist model' presents state formation chiefly as a consequence of events within particular states, whereas 'geopolitical arguments' claim that interstate relations influence state formation. 'Mode of production analyses' represent the form of government as a function of the way production is organized within its territory, and 'world system analyses' stress the division of labor in world economy (Tilly, 1990, p. 6–11). Evidently, the focus of these models of state formation is rather on the growth and evolution of government; the a priori existence of some kind of minimal state is always taken for granted. Tilly's own model which is stressing military competition and the acquisition of coercive means by rulers is based on a similar assumption: the rulers and conquerors he is analyzing have, if no monopoly of force, then at least a clear comparative advantage of its employment (Tilly, 1990, p. 14ff).

O. Volckart / J. of Economic Behavior & Org. 42 (2000) 1–17
3

Analyzing this kind of rent seeking requires first studying political and social conditions as they were when competition was not yet restricted. I am here assuming that this was the case in the high Middle Ages, that is, roughly in the time between the 11th and the 14th centuries. Therefore, in the first main part of this paper (chapter 2) I will present a model of the classical feudal system existing at that time. Starting out from the hypothesis that actors on the supply side as well as on the demand side of the market are always interested in restricting competition among themselves — that is, in reducing the openness of the system, I will then analyze what were the results of the competitive processes when a number of the assumptions contained in the model are dropped (chapter 3). These assumptions are a low density of population and high transaction costs. The study will close with the time when in most parts of Germany monopolies of force were established, that is, with the 17th or 18th centuries. In a final part (chapter 4) I will briefly sum up the model and hint at some of its implications for German history.

2. The political economy of the feudal system

2.1. Assumptions and actors of the model

In 1980, Richard Posner published an article on the 'Theory of Primitive Society' where he presented a model of society that in many respects bears close similarity to conditions as they were in high medieval central Europe. This model is based on the assumption of high transaction costs, that is, of costs connected with the creation, use, or change of institutions or organizations (cf. Furubotn and Richter, 1991, p. 8). Here, they consisted mainly of high information costs that were due to the lack of familiarity with natural laws and to the lack of writing (Posner, 1980, p. 5ff). Writing was used in high medieval Europe, of course, but as its knowledge was mainly restricted to the clergy, the conclusions Posner reached on the basis of his assumption are valid for the society analyzed here, too: due to the lack of written records governments were weak, most consumption goods could not be stored because technology did not allow this, and trade was weak because of the high risk connected with non-simultaneous transactions (Posner, 1980, p. 9).

Still, archaic society in Germany — as in all Europe — shows a number of peculiar traits that are not explicitly contained within Posner's model. Because commerce was weak, money played only a small role in economic relations. Moreover, the population was extremely small, its growth being limited by the low productivity. Most important, however, were the peculiarities in the field of politics. In comparison to Posner's model, European society at the close of the Dark Ages was characterized by extreme military insecurity that was caused on the one hand by the wars among the successors of Charlemagne, and on the other hand by the incursions of Vikings, Magyars, and Moslems. Of course the degree of insecurity differed in different places and times, but it nevertheless contributed not only to the high transaction costs — again, especially information costs — but also gave rise to an extremely high demand for military protection that formed the basis for the political

Oliver Volckart

relationships emerging in medieval Europe. [4] These relationships, today called feudalism, were defined by the Belgian historian François Louis Ganshof (Ganshof, 1964, p. XVI) as "a body of institutions creating and regulating the obligations of obedience and service — mainly military service — on the part of a free man (the vassal) towards another free man (the lord), and the obligations of protection and maintenance on the part of the lord with regard to his vassal. The obligation of maintenance had usually as one of its effects the grant by the lord to his vassal of a unit of property known as a fief".

Ganshof's brief description points out the central trait of feudalism which consisted in the contractual exchange of military services against military protection and a fief. Nevertheless, a number of comments are in order. First it should be noted that the lord, when granting a fief, transferred only certain property rights to his vassal, usually those called usus and usus fructus in property rights theory (cf. Furubotn and Richter, 1991, p. 6). Other rights, for example the right to reclaim the fief at the death of the vassal or to impose an inheritance duty, were retained by the lord (Ganshof, 1964, p. 129ff).

Another point that needs to be taken into account is that though the term 'vassal' was only used for noblemen who performed military services for their lord, similar relationships existed with members of other social groups. Both lords and vassals concluded contracts with peasants who were obliged to render services-in their case agricultural labors-in exchange for the security provided for them (Ganshof, 1964, p. 25). [5] In principle it did not matter whether the peasant was free and able to dispose of a piece of property of his own which he transferred to his lord, retaining certain rights for himself, or whether he was unfree and therefore obliged to work for his lord who now settled him on a piece of land.

Furthermore, relations based on implicit contracts concerning the supply of security did not only exist among lords, vassals and peasants, but in principle within every household managed by an individual who was economically independent. The members of the household — relatives and servants — depended on its head for a certain measure of protection. In this respect, conditions in the households of peasants, vassals, and lords were alike (Brunner, 1992, p. 211ff).

One last remark is necessary. Ganshof's definition of feudalism might give rise to the impression that the lord's part of the contract consisted in supplying protection to his partners. This is not altogether correct: hardly anybody would have been able to that on his own (Fenoaltea, 1975, p. 388). Lords who had concluded contracts exclusively with peasants depended on the support of other noblemen. What they really did was therefore organizing the military activities of other individuals. Like modern entrepreneurs they provided the organization that their partners required to overcome the dilemma arising from the freerider

---

[4] A number of scholars, notably Mann (Mann, 1989, p. 13) and Hall (Hall, 1995, p. 235f), stress the importance of Christianity for the emergence of competitive markets in medieval Europe: religion is supposed to have provided a common social identity that supported the general recognition of a number of institutions regarding property rights and their exchange. In contrast to this, my hypothesis is that, as the parties partaking in the market for security expected to co-operate repeatedly, their interest in establishing a reputation as trustworthy and reliable was often sufficient to prevent defection even in the absence of a common social identity. Cf. p. 5 below.

[5] The contractual interpretation of this relationship is disputed; it is claimed that there was no element of voluntariness on the side of the peasants (North and Thomas, 1971; cf. Kahan, 1973, p. 95f; Fenoaltea, 1975, p. 389f). It is useful to analyze relations as they were at the moment of the conclusion of the contract as distinct from later developments. An initial voluntariness does not preclude later opportunistic behavior.

O. Volckart / J. of Economic Behavior & Org. 42 (2000) 1–17   5

problem connected with collective action (Olson, 1965, p. 11). Lords were prepared to do this as long as their gain in security — and in agricultural products that otherwise could not be grown — was greater then the costs arising from their organizational efforts (cf. Hardin, 1982, p. 39). Feudal contracts created authority relations as vassals and peasants transferred the right to control certain of their activities to their lord (cf. Coleman, 1990, p. 72f). The lord entered into obligations, too, but the fact that he provided the organization necessary for the provision of security precluded any authority his partners might have over him.

The costs incurred when acquiring information about where and when military security was needed and whether vassals fulfilled their contractual obligations frequently led to the creation of supplementary feudal relations or even to the total dissolution of the original contracts. The higher these costs were (possibly because of a temporary or local rise in military insecurity), the more advantageous did it become to provide protection within smaller organizations that could be set up and were able to be on the spot more quickly. High enforcement costs prevented lords from hindering their vassals to organize military security on their own. In effect, anybody who was physically and economically able to do that — who, in other words, could fight and who had land that could be granted to vassals or peasants — had the chance to become a lord himself (Brunner, 1992, p. 209f). This leads to a central hypothesis of this study: The kind of political system preceding the modern state, that is, feudalism in its classic form as described by Ganshof, was based on the fact that there was freedom of contract in respect of the provision of military security.

High information costs were furthermore responsible for military security being not a public good. At first sight it might here be supposed that military technology was the important or even decisive factor. However, this was not the case, as shown by a comparison between conditions in Antiquity and in the high Middle Ages. Rome (which had an excellent road network and a functioning postal service so that information costs were comparatively low) provided security as a public good, whereas feudal knights were unable to do that in spite of the fact that their military technology was more advanced then Rome's (e.g. because of the use of the stirrup). What was really relevant in this context were the information costs. Because of them, lords were unable to react quickly enough to military threats to be able to provide security for whole territorial units. Instead, their offer of security applied to specific individuals with whom they concluded pertinent contracts which they either fulfilled by trying to protect their partners on the spot or by allowing them to seek refuge within their fortification.

From this security individuals, whether peasants or vassals, could be excluded. To do that a lord just needed to refuse to protect this person or to exclude him from the fortification he defended together with his vassals (Fenoaltea, 1975, p. 388). Within castles, space was limited so that the criterion of rivalry in consumption applies, too, at least when a certain number of persons was reached. It can be imagined, of course, that especially in the direct vicinity of the castle there were positive external effects from which individuals profited even when they had entered into no agreement with the lord. Still, excluding these persons was possible at comparatively low costs. Altogether in a study of high medieval political economy military protection can therefore be treated as a private good.

The assumptions of high military insecurity and high transaction costs lead to the conclusion that political rule in its modern form as the authoritative and monopolistic supply of certain public goods did not exist in the high Middle Ages. Archaic rule can rather be defined

6   *O. Volckart / J. of Economic Behavior & Org. 42 (2000) 1–17*

as providing a nexus for contractual relations between political entrepreneurs who offered to organize military security and individuals who made use of this offer.[6] Graphically, feudal relations may be depicted thus:

A simplified model of a feudal organization

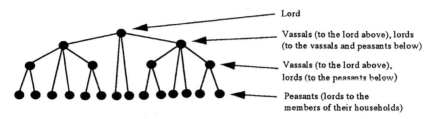

Lord

Vassals (to the lord above), lords
(to the vassals and peasants below)

Vassals (to the lord above),
lords (to the peasants below)

Peasants (lords to the
members of their households)

Every lord has direct relations with peasants; the lords on the top two levels have relations with vassals, too. None of the individuals shown here has a monopoly of force in any given geographical area. What is distinguishing this kind of organization from a modern federal state is that there is no clear division of competencies between individuals on different levels and that no one has the competence to create ultimately binding legal rules (there is no 'federal government').

2.2. Political competition in feudalism: the process of exchange

That in feudalism the provision of military security was characterized by freedom of contract points to the fact that there was a market for this good where actors on the supply side and on the demand side competed with each other. Competition was a complex phenomenon as most vassals were lords themselves and most lords had other lords above them. Still, for simplicity's sake its analysis can be restricted to a study of how lords competed for vassals and for peasants, and of how vassals competed for peasants. Just as competition on product markets, feudal political competition can be subdivided into two distinct but interlocked processes: on the one hand, there was a process of exchange that linked the supply and the demand sides of the market, and on the other hand, there was a parallel process which consisted of the activities of actors on one and the same side of the market. In the process of exchange, buyers chose goods or services provided by the sellers; in the parallel process, sellers tried to improve their situation vis à vis their competitors (Hoppmann, 1967, p. 88f).

Regarding exchange between lords and vassals, it can be assumed that both parties found the contracts advantageous, at least at the moment of their conclusion. However, because of the scarcity of labor lords were more interested in establishing feudal relationships than vassals. In principle, everybody able to fight and owning land that could be granted as a fief or a peasant's holding could become a lord as well as a vassal. Still, individuals who were prepared to organize military security needed more than one warrior to provide protection, whereas every warrior needed only one lord. For this reason the market power of potential vassals was relatively great — a fact that may explain why lords had to grant them not only

---

[6] As Jensen and Meckling (Jensen and Meckling, 1976, p. 310) note, just as most organisations firms are "legal fictions which serve as a nexus for a set of contracting relationships among individuals". In this respect, too, feudal organizations resembled modern firms.

O. Volckart / J. of Economic Behavior & Org. 42 (2000) 1–17   7

protection within their castles but fiefs, too. In the absence of any superior authority with the competence to enforce feudal contracts vis à vis defective partners — that is, against vassals who refused to fight when called upon and against lords who failed to protect vassals — the agreements were probably stabilized by reputation and by the threat of exclusion from the security organization. [7]

In spite of this stabilizing factor, the process of exchange — that is, the choice between several suppliers — was connected with few costs for actors on the demand side of the market. Because of the private character of security, a vassal did not need to be mobile: He did not have to cross a territorial border whether he was to be excluded from his lord's supply of protection, or whether he wanted to choose another lord. Usually, he had property of his own that was only supplemented by his fief (Ganshof, 1964, p. 67). Therefore, anybody who did not live too far away to contribute to its protection was eligible as a lord.

In comparison to a world of closed territorial units, the fact that mobility was no necessary condition for choice among lords lowered costs. These were primarily not transaction costs, as acquiring information about alternatives, formulating the contract, and enforcing it would have required resources even when the vassal would have had to be mobile. What was influencing his calculus were rather the migration costs — a fact that should not be underrated in view of the poor infrastructure, and that contributed to the intensity of competition.

Intensity of competition was high, too, because the vassal did not make specific investments that made it difficult to terminate a once established relationship (about the importance of specific investments for the intensity of competition see Williamson, 1985, p. 30). As a knightly vassal might forcibly appropriate the property rights over his fief which the lord had reserved for himself, he was able to use a castle he had built even after he had dissolved his original feudal contract and had chosen a different lord (cf. Ganshof and Verhulst, 1966, p. 309). In spite of the loss of reputation a vassal incurred through this behavior, competition among lords is frequently testified in medieval sources because resources vassals spent on fortifications or for other purposes were no specific investments that prevented them from exiting to a different lord. Any analysis of this competition must, though, take the fact into account that the protection provided within feudal organizations was rather a means than an end in itself. Of course, security was a physical necessity, but moreover it was a precondition for agricultural production, the increase of which was the real aim of political actors. Consequently, relations to peasants were essential for both lords and vassals.

Exchange between them and peasants was mutually advantageous, too. Peasants who entered into a feudal relationship with a lord improved their situation. If they were free and had property of their own, the protection supplied to them was a distinct improvement over the near anarchic conditions under which they would otherwise have had to live. If they were unfree, being settled on a peasant's holding which they could work for themselves enlarged their freedom of action. The lord, on the other hand gained the labor of hitherto independent peasants, and furthermore certain property rights applying to their land (as for instance the right to impose an inheritance due), but no rights over the output produced there. How this

---

[7] The medieval merchant guilds that were organizations for the provision of military security, too, were based on the same mechanisms (cf. Volckart and Mangels, 1999).

8
O. Volckart / J. of Economic Behavior & Org. 42 (2000) 1–17

were to be used, could be determined by the peasants themselves, so that their incentives to productive activities were not negatively affected. When the lord granted a holding to unfree peasants who before had had a slave-like status, he increased their productivity, as the property rights granted to them lessened their incentives to shirk (cf. Homann, 1989, p. 45).

For peasants choice among lords was more costly then for vassals. Unlike vassals, they needed to be mobile to make use of the option to exit to a different lord. In contrast to vassals who specialized in fighting, peasants concentrated on agricultural labor. They were increasingly unable to use force and had consequently fewer chances to usurp the property rights over their holdings that the lord had reserved for himself. Because of their military inferiority, resources they spent on improving the quality of the land had the character of specific investments which reduced the intensity of competition. Still, as because of the scarcity of labor many lords were prepared to bear the costs of informing peasants about opportunities they provided for them (for example by assigning agents to recruit settlers: Ganshof and Verhulst, 1966, p. 295; Aubin, 1966, p. 462), exit costs altogether seem to have been low in spite of the fact that transaction costs in general were high.

2.3. The parallel process and the consequences of competition

As mentioned above, the primary aim of lords and vassals in the parallel process, that is, in competing among each other for peasants, was to create conditions that allowed them to increase their agricultural output. Every lord and vassal stood at the head of his own agricultural enterprise, his manor, that he worked partly with unfree laborers and partly with peasants with whom he had concluded feudal contracts and who rendered him agricultural services (Brunner, 1992, p. 207f, 218). The manor's output depended on how much land the lord could productively use. In principle, he had to find the optimal combination of land worked under his own supervision, land given out as peasants' holdings, and land granted to vassals. If he kept too much under his own supervision, the labor services he received from his peasants were insufficient to work it; if he transferred too much to his peasants — which was attractive for reasons of productivity — there was not enough left to grant to his vassals in order to provide the necessary security, and if he gave too much to his vassals, they were able to outdo him economically. However, as long as the population was so small that land was abundant, feudal lords had a strong incentive not only to concentrate on working their own demesnes but also to try and gain as many peasants and vassals as possible.

In the parallel process, a lord had few options. When competing for vassals, he could improve his own position for example by demanding fewer military services then other lords. However, in this way he impaired the quality of his security organization. His other option was to grant larger fiefs or more comprehensive property rights. In competition for peasants, basically the same parameters were important. However, because of their specialization in agricultural work, it seems plausible that the quality of the protection organized by the lord was more important for peasants then for vassals. A lord could directly influence this quality only by concluding contracts not only with peasants, but with vassals, too; otherwise he depended on cooperating in the security organization of his own lord. Therefore, the most important parameters were the price he demanded for his services and the property rights he

O. Volckart / J. of Economic Behavior & Org. 42 (2000) 1–17

9

transferred to the peasants. Here, an institutional competition (fundamental: Tiebout, 1956; Hirschman, 1970; Wohlgemuth, 1995; Streit, 1996) did not develop. In classical feudalism, lords had no competence to create legal rules (Ebel, 1958/1988, p. 16–20; Wolf, 1973, p. 517); they were no greater providers of new institutions than of other public goods. [8] In the high Middle Ages, restrictions of conduct were consciously created only within the frame of contracts that were mutually advantageous. Therefore, competition for labor induced many lords to reduce their peasants' obligations or to grant them nearly comprehensive property rights — including, for example, the right to inherit their holdings (cf. Ganshof and Verhulst, 1966, p. 327).

Altogether in the high Middle Ages a lord who did not want to loose his labor force had to improve his peasants' situation. His freedom of conduct was therefore restricted less by abstract legal, moral, or ethic institutions then by the existence of other lords and therefore by his own interest. Here, too, competitive conditions contributed to the reduction of social and political discrimination (cf. Friedman, 1962/1982, p. 109): they were the factor behind the decreasing importance of the distinction between free and unfree peasants. Without a central political authority influencing this process, a 'mobile agrarian society' developed where 'almost always horizontal mobility was the condition of vertical mobility' (Irsigler, 1976/1977, p. 10; cf. Ganshof and Verhulst, 1966, p. 294).

As a preliminary result of this study it can be noted that social and political conditions during the high Middle Ages were characterized by intensive competition. Military security, today monopolized by states, was no public good; there was a market for protection the entry of which was not institutionally restricted. In fact, every economically independent individual acted as a supplier on this market as he provided protection at least to the members of his own household. If he was economically able to enlarge his household and to extend his supply for instance by employing more servants or concluding contracts with more peasants or vassals, he competed with other suppliers. This was a sign of the openness of the high medieval political system. Still, unavoidably in a stateless social order, there was no authority to safeguard this openness. In other words, there was no authority that enforced institutions ensuring open access to the supply side of the market for protection or that prevented the emergence of rules that restricted entry. This was of prime importance for future development.

3. Rent seeking and the rise of the state

3.1. Population size and the intensity of competition

At the beginning of chapter 2, I specified a number of assumptions — among them a small population and high transaction costs — that I will now drop. First, the competitive processes described in the previous section will be analyzed under the assumption that there was a high density of population, as was really the case at the close of the 13th and

---

[8] High medieval law was a mainly unintentionally developed and non-codified customary law. Judicial courts, composed of peasants or vassals, played an important part in its development (Willoweit, 1980, p. 108).

the beginning of the 14th century. [9] As will be shown, this was a necessary condition for successful attempts to appropriate rents arising on the market for military security.

One of the main consequences of the change of the relative prices of labor and land resulting from the growth of population was that it gave lords the chance to reformulate the contracts they had concluded with peasants and vassals. Under the conditions of a small population, their compliance with these contracts was mainly due to the fact that their partners could threaten convincingly to exit to a different supplier of security. However, by the end of the high Middle Ages the scarcity of land and the correspondingly large supply of labor had blunted this threat. Unused land was hard to find; moreover, lords lost their interest in contracting with more peasants when they received enough labor dues to work their demesnes. Under these conditions, it was possible for lords to renege on agreements, that is, to impose new contracts with unfavorable terms for their peasants. Two consequences of this development should be distinguished: as land was a good in limited supply, lords could appropriate a rent for granting it to peasants. And as exit was now difficult for peasants, lords had enough bargaining power to demand higher prices for their organization of security, too. This development affected knightly vassals in a lesser degree than peasants. As mentioned above, the vassals' ability to fight allowed them to forcibly appropriate the property rights over their fief which their lord had reserved for himself. They still did not need to be mobile to exit to a different lord. Still, altogether a high density of population caused a reduced openness of the feudal constitution because it made it difficult for actors on the demand side of the market for protection to choose between suppliers.

3.2. Population size and the emergence of a law giving competence

In the course of the high Middle Ages, the effects of higher exit costs were aggravated by attempts to restrict competition for vassals and peasants and thereby further to reduce the constitutional openness. These attempts were aimed at monopolizing the market for military security and at appropriating monopoly rents arising there. As long as the entry to this market was unrestricted, it can be assumed that the prices paid by peasants and vassals for the services provided by their lords came much closer to competitive prices then the taxes modern states raise for their supply of public and non-public goods. Therefore, any restriction of competition on the supply side of the market allowed suppliers to raise their prices. Alternatively, they might form cartels the importance of which regarding modern political competition is analyzed by Streit (1996, p. 234).

It is striking that up to now attempts to appropriate monopoly rents through the creation of entry barriers to a market seem to have been studied only under conditions characterized by the fundamental division between state and society. Here, economic actors who are interested in forming policy-backed monopolies must spend resources on influencing political

---

[9] Eleventh century Germany is supposed to have had a population of about 3 million; 300 years later it was about 12 million (Cipolla, 1980, p. 3). In the model presented here, the growth of population is treated as an exogenous variable. Still, it should be noted that historically this was only partially the case. True enough, there were a number of technical and organizational improvements (e.g. the heavy plough, the yoke, and the open field system) that contributed to growth and are really exogenous to the model. However, the increase in population was also a consequence of the incentive structure provided by the peasants' changed (mostly improved) property rights and by the better military security provided for them.

O. Volckart / J. of Economic Behavior & Org. 42 (2000) 1–17   11

actors who are in position to create institutional barriers to the entry into the market. It is this activity that is usually called rent seeking (cf Tollison, 1982). [10] In feudalism conditions for rent seeking were quite different. Here, every economically independent individual who had land to grant to peasants or to vassals was a political actor. He did not necessarily need to spend resources to influence others. Rather, under certain conditions some participants in the market became powerful enough themselves to create institutions which excluded their competitors.

As noted above, in classical feudalism there were no authorities who had the competence to create legal rules. However, the 13th or 14th century scarcity of land gave the lords the chance not only to enforce specific orders against their peasants and in a lesser degree against their vassals, but also to create institutions. When such rules restricted the ability of vassals or peasants to act as suppliers of protection, their introduction can be interpreted as an attempt at gaining a monopolistic position on the market for security and at appropriating a monopoly rent. Nevertheless, the lords' market power was seldom sufficient for the formation of monopolies of force and of the creation of legal rules. Frequently, his contractual partners on the demand side of the market developed a counter strategy that allowed them to avoid competing with each other. This strategy involved the collective action respectively of peasants and vassals; it was made possible by the lords' attempts to reformulate feudal contracts which increased the opportunity costs of acting alone.

Here, it is important to note that peasants and vassals were acting on both sides of the market for protection: They did not only use the security organizations provided by their respective lords, but supplied protection to their own dependents, too. Therefore they had a two-fold motive for acting collectively: On the one hand, they were interested in obtaining a collective good, namely contractual regulations that allowed them to acquire the services their lords provided at a lower price then they would have had to pay when each acted on his own. In so far the formation of peasant or vassal organizations can be interpreted as the restriction of competition among the demanders of military protection. On the other hand, however, village communities and their counterparts formed by vassals functioned as cartels of suppliers. [11] The regulations they negotiated with their lords did not only affect themselves but also their direct dependents. They were consciously created institutions, that is, public goods that harmonized the conditions under which the members of the peasants' households and the contractual partners of the vassals themselves worked. In this way, they restricted competition for labor and for individuals who made use of the lords' supply of protection. [12] The costs of overcoming the problem of collective action were frequently borne by members of the upper stratum of the peasantry or of the territorial nobility who had a lot to gain by avoiding competition.

---

[10] Modern rent seeking is blurring the distinction between state and society (or between political and economic actors) because it allows special-interest groups to influence the state's supply of public goods (e.g. the institutional system) or to gain the competence authoritatively to supply public goods of their own. Still, the fundamental existence of the above mentioned distinction is a precondition for rent seeking in its modern form.

[11] Remember that every vassal had entered into contractual relations with vassals of his own and/or with peasants, and that every peasant had done the same in respect of the members of his household.

[12] This is the consequence of the formation of suppliers' cartels in institutional competition that is stressed by Streit (Streit, 1996, p. 234).

Altogether, the most important consequence of the high density of population was a decline in the bargaining position of the demanders on the market for protection. This made their threat to exit less credible and allowed the emergence of authorities who were able to use force against their dependents. In some exceptional cases, such authorities were lords who managed to gain the competence to create institutions, but mostly they were organizations of peasants or vassals who introduced new rules for themselves and their dependents.

It should be remembered, though, that medieval and early modern authorities were at best able to enforce institutions vis à vis their direct subjects. Enforcement became more difficult when the geographical distance between rulers and the ruled or the number of intermediate authorities grew (cf. Wolf, 1973, p. 542). The vassals of a lord who were themselves such an intermediate authority were seldom prepared to enforce directives that reduced their authority or that negatively affected their interests (Vann, 1984, p. 19; cf. Schremmer, 1972, p. 45, 58). Therefore, while a change in the relative prices of land and labor caused by the growth of population lead to the emergence of political authorities — thus transforming the open constitution of the high Middle Ages into the constitution of a hierarchically structured corporate society — it usually did not lead to the formation of monopolies of force and of the creation of legal rules.

3.3. The growth of product markets and the intensity of competition

In addition to the assumption of a small population, I now drop that of high transaction costs. This, too, is suggested by historical developments as literacy became more common and the familiarity with natural laws increased in the late Middle Ages. In terms of my analysis the increasing use of written records in administration and the development of a road system that allowed a quicker spread of news are of special importance. Along with the spread of a money economy they caused a sharp reduction in transaction costs, especially of information costs. It is useful to distinguish between three areas affected by these developments: the intensity of competition, the character of the goods that were exchanged, and the ability to restrict competition.

One consequence of the growth of population was the urbanization of many parts of Germany where until then towns had not existed. As a result, a market for agricultural goods developed where peasants could sell their products. This was the precondition for the replacement of labor services by payments of money which many lords introduced in the course of the high Middle Ages. Occasionally, the lords gave up working their demesnes and granted all their land to peasants, but usually they kept a smaller part for themselves (Ganshof and Verhulst, 1966, p. 313).

As shown by North and Thomas, the development was closely linked to a reduction in transaction costs (North and Thomas, 1971, p. 795). Whether this, as claimed by them, caused the reduction of labor services, we need not discuss (for criticism of this view see Fenoaltea, 1976). What is important in the present context is rather a consequence of the switch to monetary payments. Previously, lords had lost their interest in extending their supply of protection to more persons when their demand for labor services was accommodated. However, when they turned to demanding monetary payments, the old labor constraint was

O. Volckart / J. of Economic Behavior & Org. 42 (2000) 1–17   13

no longer relevant, so that they could continue competing for individuals who made use of their supply of protection and institutions even when they received enough labor dues to work their shrunken demesnes. Therefore, in spite of land being scarce, the suppliers of military security regarded the subjects of their own vassals as potential contractual partners of their own, and their vassals as competitors who were to be excluded from the market.

3.4. Military security as a public good

This development was intensified because the character of military security changed. In classical feudalism it had been a private good. Due to the late medieval reduction in information costs, its provision increasingly gave rise to positive external effects. Not all lords were equally affected by this development. Noblemen with few vassals or peasants whose range of activity was small continued to provide security as a private good, in effect supplying it only within their castles. In contrast, lords who could dispose of large tracts of land that they had granted to many peasants from whom they received monetary rents profited from the sinking information costs, as these gave them the chance to react quickly enough to military threats to defend whole territories. They were interested in doing this because their income depended on the preservation of the labor force within their area of activity, and this labor force might be too large to take refuge within their castle.

As security was provided for whole territories, exclusion became more difficult. Consequently the incentives to freeride and the interest of the suppliers to make potential freeriders pay increased. Negotiations to internalize externalities — as analyzed by Coase — were impossible, though, because the conclusion of a contract with every single inhabitant of the territory that was to be protected would have caused prohibitive transaction costs in spite of the fact that these costs were generally being reduced (cf. Coase, 1960; Olson, 1969, p. 481). Furthermore, those intermediate authorities who supplied protection to their own subjects would have regarded this as an assault on their autonomy. When a higher authority wanted to make the subjects of its subordinate authorities pay for the protection it supplied, it needed the consent of these subordinate authorities which could be withheld especially when they were able to act collectively. Therefore, the share of taxes in the overall income of a political authority tended to be the greater, the more subordinate authorities it had and the more heterogeneous their interests were.

3.5. The restriction of competition

While the late medieval reduction in information costs allowed the transformation of military security from a private into a public good supplied on a territorial base, and the replacement of labor services by monetary payments intensified competition within these territories, how did the reduction of transaction costs affect the chances of political actors to restrict competition? Answering this question makes it necessary to study the interests of the several authorities participating in the political process. There was not only competition on the market for protection, but on the growing product markets, too. In both cases authorities had the chance to appropriate monopoly rents if they succeeded in introducing institutions that restricted entry. Still, the interests of authorities on different levels of hierarchy were diverging — a fact that provided an opportunity for cooperation.

An authority's interest in restricting competition on product markets was directly related to the share that the yields of its own economic activities had in its overall income. Lords who derived their income mainly from their subjects' monetary dues were primarily interested in increasing the number of persons from whom they received payments. In contrast, authorities who had few subjects from whom they received monetary payments and who mostly depended on producing and selling on the market themselves were in the first place interested in seeking rents arising on product markets. However, to create institutions that prevented their own peasants from competing with them, they usually had to cooperate on a regional scale or over several levels of hierarchy. This opened the prospect for fruitful negotiations which became possible when transaction costs sank. Thus, in 1577 the vassals of the duke of Prussia managed to push through a law forbidding their peasants to sell grain on any but the nearest markets (Schmelzeisen, 1968, p. 391–402). Under these conditions, trading centers like Danzig and Königsberg, where grain-exporting merchants from western Europe gathered, were inaccessible to most peasants, while noblemen gained a chance to appropriate monopoly rents. Such measures were not uncommon. From the 15th century onward, sources show that there were frequent discussions between lords and vassals over the introduction of rules that were to the damage of the vassals' subjects (Malowist, 1957, p. 31ff).

The monopolization of the supply of certain public goods by the state which emerged in this process was therefore the result of an exchange: Subordinate authorities received economic privileges or were supported in enforcing them, while they conceded a monopoly of the supply of public goods like security and institutions to their superior authorities who gained a state-like character (Oestreich, 1967, p. 70). Hence the emergence of the state did not entail the emergence of anything approaching Franz Böhm's (Böhm, 1966) normative ideal of a private law society where relations between individuals are regulated by a private law equal for all. On the contrary, the rise of the state depended on subordinate authorities acquiring privileges relevant for activities on product markets. In exchange for these privileges, superior authorities acquired the right to exclude other suppliers from the market for security and institutions, the rules allowing them to do that being at the core of the emerging public law. Altogether, state formation was a process in which special-interest groups negotiated to the disadvantage of third parties over the distribution of monopoly rents arising either on product markets or on political markets.

4. Conclusion

The model of the rise of the modern state which I present here is based on the assumptions that in high medieval feudalism military security was a non-public good, that in its supply there was freedom of contract, that there was a market for protection, and that there was intensive competition among actors on the supply and the demand side of this market. I am interpreting the emergence of states as a process of monopolization through the creation of discriminating institutions that made it possible to exclude potential suppliers from the market for security.

O. Volckart / J. of Economic Behavior & Org. 42 (2000) 1–17   15

The necessary conditions for creating such entry barriers were on the one hand the growth of population, and on the other hand a reduction in transaction costs. A growing population increased exit costs. It allowed feudal lords ex post to change contracts they had concluded with actors on the demand side of the market. These actors reacted by forming organizations. Thus, in the course of the high Middle Ages political authorities developed who could create legal rules. Still, they were able to enforce these institutions — introduced with the aim to appropriate monopoly rents — at best partially. Alone, the growth of population did not lead to the emergence of territorial monopolies of force and of the creation of legal rules.

A further enforcement of discriminating institutions created by political authorities became possible through the reduction in transaction costs. Lower information costs transformed military security from a private into a public good; lower negotiation costs allowed transactions between authorities on several levels of the feudal hierarchy. Thereby authorities on the lower rungs of hierarchy could exchange their right to provide security and institutions against privileges that improved their chances on product markets. In this way, authorities developed that held both a monopoly of force and a monopoly for the creation of legal rules, that became, in other words, states in the modern sense of the word.

A convincing explanation of why in medieval and early modern Germany a large number of relatively small states developed instead of one large centralized state needs a more detailed investigation, but the model presented here might be of some help because it draws attention to a number of factors hitherto neglected in constitutional history, notably to the importance of transaction costs. It suggests that the all-German feudal organization that developed in the 10th century was based — apart from dynastic chance — on linguistic and other cultural similarities shared by the several German tribes. Such similarities tended to reduce negotiation costs. Still, the growth of population caused the emergence of local or regional authorities at a relatively early date, that is, towards the end of the high Middle Ages. At this time, in Germany the enforcement of rules on a supra-regional scale was prevented by high transaction costs. [13] When the increasing literacy and the improving infrastructure allowed a reduction in these costs, regional authorities were already firmly established, had developed the competence to create legal rules, and supplied security as a public good. Altogether, the political fragmentation of Germany seems to have been the consequence of a reduction in transaction costs that occurred only after the growth of population had made the emergence of regional authorities possible.

References

Aubin, Hermann, 1966. Medieval Agrarian Society in its prime: the lands east of the Elbe and German colonization eastwards. In: Postan, Michael Moissey (Ed.), The Cambridge Economic History of Europe, Vol. 1, The Agrarian Life of the Middle Ages, Cambridge, New York, New Rochelle, Melbourne, Sidney, Cambridge University Press, Cambridge, pp. 449–486.

---

[13] In England and France transaction costs may have been considerably lower as both countries had been former Roman provinces where literacy had either never disappeared or had been redeveloped at a relatively early date, and where a rudimentary network of roads continued to exist into the Middle Ages. Because of her insular character, in England exit costs were from the outset comparatively high; in France they seem to have risen at about the same time as in Germany. This suggests that the respective timing of the rise in exit costs and the fall in transaction costs may have been an essential determinant for the political structures emerging in the area under study.

Böhm, Franz, 1966. Privatrechtsgesellschaft und Marktwirtschaft ORDO — Jahrbuch für die Ordnung von Wirtschaft und Gesellschaft 17, 75–151.

Boldt, Hans, 1990. Deutsche Verfassungsgeschichte, Vol. 1. Von den Anfängen bis zum Ende des älteren deutschen Reiches 1806 (München, dtv).

Brunner, Otto, 1992. Land and Lordship: Structures of Governance in Medieval Austria. University of Pennsylvania Press, Philadelphia.

Cipolla, C.M., 1980. Before the Industrial Revolution: European Society and Economy. Cambridge, Cambridge University Press, pp. 1000–1700.

Coase, R.H., 1960. The problem of social cost Journal of Law and Economics 3, 1–44.

Coleman, James S., 1990. Foundations of Social Theory. Cambridge/Mass., London, Belknap.

Ebel, Wilhelm, 1958/1988. Geschichte der Gesetzgebung in Deutschland. Otto Schwarz & Co., Göttingen.

Fenoaltea, S., 1975. The rise and fall of a theoretical model: the manorial system Journal of Economic History 35, 386–409.

Fenoaltea, Stefano, 1976. Risk, transaction costs, and the organization of medieval agriculture Explorations in Economic History 13, 129–151.

Friedman, Milton, 1962/1982. Capitalism and Freedom. Chicago University Press, Chicago, London.

Furubotn, E., Richter, R., 1991. The new institutional economics: an assessment. In: Furubotn, Eirik, Richter, Rudolf (Eds.), The New Institutional Economics, Tübingen, Mohr, pp. 1–32.

Ganshof, François Louis, 1964. Feudalism. Longmans, London.

Ganshof, F.L., Verhulst, A., 1966. Medieval Agrarian Society in its Prime: France, The Low Countries, and Western Germany. In: Michael Moissey Postan (Ed.), The Cambridge Economic History of Europe, Vol. 1: The Agrarian Life of the Middle Ages. Cambridge, New York, New Rochelle, Melbourne, Sidney, Cambridge University Press, pp. 291–339.

Hall, J.H., 1995. A theory of the rise of the west METU Studies in Development 22 (3), 231–241.

Hardin, Russel, 1982. Collective Action. John Hopkins University Press, Baltimore.

Hirschman, A.O., 1970. Exit, Voice, and Loyalty: Respones to Decline in Firms. Organizations, and States, Harvard University Press, Cambridge/Mass.

Homann, Karl, 1989. Vertragstheorie und Property-Rights-Ansatz — Stand der Diskussion und Möglichkeiten der Weiterentwicklung. In: Biervert, Bernd, Held, Martin (Eds.), Ethische Grundlagen der ökonomischen Theorie: Eigentum, Verträge, Institutionen. Frankfurt, New York, Campus, pp. 37–69.

Hoppmann, E., 1967. Wettbewerb als Norm der Wettbewerbspolitik ORDO-Jahrbuch für die Ordnung von Wirtschaft und Gesellschaft 18, 77–94.

Irsigler, F., 1976/1977. Freiheit und Unfreiheit im Mittelalter: Formen und Wege sozialer Mobilität Westfälische Forschungen 28, 1–15.

Jensen, M.C., Meckling, W.H., 1976. Theory of the firm: managerial behavior, agency costs and ownership structure Journal of Financial Economics 2, 305–360.

Kahan, A., 1973. Notes on Serfdom in Western and Eastern Europe Journal of Economic History 33, 86–99.

Lane, F.C., 1958. Economic consequences of organized violence Journal of Economic History 18 (4), 401–417.

Malowist, M., 1957. Über die Frage der Handelspolitik des Adels in den Ostseeländern im 15 und 16 Jahrhundert. Hansische Geschichtsblätter 75, 29–47.

Mann, M., 1989. European Development: Approaching a Historical Explanation. In: Baechler, John, Hall, John A., Mann, Michael (Eds.), Europe and the Rise of Capitalism, Oxford, Basil Blackwell, pp. 6–19.

Mayer, T., 1943. Adel und Bauern im Staat des deutschen Mittelalters. In: Baechler, John, Hall, John A., Mann, Michael (Eds.), Adel und Bauern im deutschen Staat des Mittelalters, Leipzig, Koehler & Amelang.

Moraw, P., 1989. Von offener Verfassung zu gestalteter Verdichtung: Das Reich im Späten Mittelalter 1250 bis 1490. Frankfurt, Berlin, Propyläen.

Moraw, P., 1995. Neue Ergebnisse der deutschen Verfassungsgeschichte des späten Mittelalters. In: Schwinges, Rainer Christoph (Ed.), Über König und Reich: Aufsätze zur deutschen Verfassungsgeschichte des späten Mittelalters, Sigmaringen, Thorbecke, pp. 47–71.

North, D.C., Thomas, R.T., 1971. The rise and fall of the manorial system: a theoretical model Journal of Economic History 31, 777–803.

North, D.C., Thomas, R.P., 1973. The Rise of the Western World: A New Economic History. Cambridge University Press, Cambridge.

Oestreich, G., 1967. Ständetum und Staatsbildung in Deutschland Der Staat 6, 61–73.

O. Volckart / J. of Economic Behavior & Org. 42 (2000) 1–17   17

Olson, Mancur, 1965. The Logic of Collective Action: Public Goods and the Theory of Groups. Harvard University Press, Cambridge/Mass., London.

Olson, Mancur, 1969. The Principle of 'Fiscal Equivalence': the Division of Responsibilities Among Different Levels of Government. American Economic Review: Papers and Proceedings, Vol. 59, pp. 479–487.

Posner, R., 1980. A theory of primitive society with special reference to law Journal of Law and Economics 23, 1–53.

Schmelzeisen, Gustaf Klemens (Ed.), 1968. Polizei- und Landesordnungen, Vol. 1. Reich und Territorien, Weimar, Böhlau.

Schremmer, E., 1972. Agrarverfassung und Wirtschaftsstruktur: Die südostdeutsche Hofmark — eine Wirtschaftsherrschaft? Zeitschrift für Agrargeschichte und Agrarsoziologie 20, 42–65.

Streit, M.E., 1996. Systemwettbewerb und Harmonisierung im europäischen Integrationsprozeß. In: Cassel, Dieter (Ed.), Entstehung und Wettbewerb von Systemen, Berlin, Duncker & Humblot, pp. 223–244.

Tiebout, C.M., 1956. A pure theory of local expenditures Journal of Political Economy 64, 416–424.

Tilly, Charles, 1990. Coercion, Capital, and European States, AD 990–1990. Cambridge/Mass., Basil Blackwell.

Tollison, R.D., 1982. Rent seeking: a survey Kyklos 35, 575–602.

Vann, James Allen, 1984. The Making of a State: Württemberg, 1593–1793. Ithaca, London, Cornell University Press.

Vierhaus, Rudolf, 1985. Deutschland im Zeitalter des Absolutismus (1648–1763). In: Moeller, Bernd, Heckel, Martin, Vierhaus, Rudolf (Eds.), Deutsche Geschichte, Vol. 2, Frühe Neuzeit, Göttingen, Vandenhoeck & Ruprecht, pp. 355–512.

Volckart, O., Mangels, A., 1999. Are the roots of the Modern Lex Mercatoria really medieval? Southern Economic Journal 65 (3), 427–450.

Williamson, Oliver E., 1985. The Economic Institutions of Capitalism: Firms, Markets, Relational Contracting. The Free Press, New York, London.

Willoweit, D., 1980. Gebot und Verbot im Spätmittelalter — vornehmlich nach südhessischen und mainfränkischen Weistümern Hessisches Jahrbuch für Landesgeschichte 30, 94–130.

Wohlgemuth, M., 1995. Institutional competition-notes on an unfinished agenda Journal des Economistes et des Etudes Humaines 6, 277–299.

Wolf, A., 1973. Die Gesetzgebung der entstehenden Territorialstaaten. In: Coing, Helmut (Ed.), Handbuch der Quellen und Literatur der neueren europäischen Privatrechtsgeschichte, Vol. 1, Mittelalter (1100–1500): Die gelehrten Rechte und die Gesetzgebung, München, Beck, pp. 517–799.

International Review of Law and Economics (1986), *6* (87–99)

ILLEGAL ECONOMIC ACTIVITIES AND PURGES IN A SOVIET-TYPE ECONOMY: A RENT-SEEKING PERSPECTIVE

ARYE L. HILLMAN

Department of Economics, Bar-Ilan University, Ramat Gan 52100, Israel
Department of Economics, University of California, Los Angeles, CA 90024, USA

AND

ADI SCHNYTZER

Department of Economics, Bar-Ilan University, Ramat Gan 52100, Israel
School of Social and Industrial Administration, Griffith University, Qld. 4111, Australia

May you be made to live off your official salary (contemporary Russian curse).

1. INTRODUCTION

Whether in the setting of Western developed or Third World developing societies, the substantial literature on rent seeking or directly unproductive profit-seeking activities has focussed on the activities of agents in decentralized market economies.[1] The literature describes how resources are expended as private agents lobby governments for the creation of rents via interventionist activity and how individuals seek rents which have arisen as the consequence of prior government regulatory activities. Redistributive transfers in market economies, whether governmental or private charity, also evoke rent-seeking behavior. At the same time, incumbents who are the beneficiaries of rents confront the incentive to expend resources in preempting those aspiring to their positions. On the supply side of the political market, government officials have an incentive to engage in rent creation via regulatory activity and protection. These various unproductive activities would of course be absent from an idealized decentralized competitive economy. Nor is such behavior consistent with the idealized planned economy, where, just as in its idealized decentralized competitive dual, no rents arise to be sought or protected. In the perfectly planned economy centralized resource allocation simply forestals the discretionary use of resources in unproductive rent-seeking quests.

However, in practice, just as Western decentralized market economies are not perfectly laissez-faire but 'mixed', so planned economies exhibit various degrees of

0144-8188/86/01 0087-13 $03.00 © 1986 Butterworth & Co (Publishers) Ltd market-determined resource allocation. Agricultural surpluses in planned economies are often sold directly by peasants or collectives to consumers. Such parallel economies are generally tolerated by the authorities and are a source of legal income.

There is however a further economy which is a source of illegal income. This economy, which is characterized by economic crimes and corruption, has been the subject of considerable recent attention, in particular in relation to the Soviet Union.[2] The evidence reveals that the illegal economy is not marginal to the official and officially-sanctioned systems. Participants are representative of all tiers of the social, political and economic hierarchy. The most detailed accounts to date have been provided by Konstantin Simis in his book *U.S.S.R.: Secrets of a Corrupt Society.*[3] Simis' study, facilitated by access to privileged information obtained via his activities as a defence attorney, provides accounts of large-scale economic corruption. In this paper we show how Simis' observations and those of others, in particular Gregory Grossman, tie together within an analytical framework consistent with the perception of the 'corrupt' planned economy as a rent-seeking society. Rather than view individuals' activities in terms of economic crime and corruption, we interpret behavior in the manner proposed by the theory of the rent-seeking society. In particular, we are led to a characterization of that recurrent aspect of Soviet-type systems, the purge, in terms of rent-seeking and rent-protecting behavior.

Gregory Grossman has observed many of the essential features of the illegal economy and has suggested the analytical framework of kleptocracy to describe individuals' illegal behavior within Soviet-type systems:

> The next logical step in the development of corruption would seem to be capitalization of expected future streams of graft, and hence the purchase and sale of lucrative official positions. This step, too, seems to have been taken in the USSR. . . . At the very least one can deduce that the purchase and sale of positions for large sums of money signifies the profound institutionalization in the Soviet Union of a whole structure of bribery and graft, from the bottom to the top of the pyramid of power; that considerable stability of the structure of power is expected by all concerned; and that very probably there is a close organic connection between political–administrative authority, on the one hand, and a highly developed world of illegal economic activity, on the other. In sum, the concept of *kleptocracy*, developed by sociologists with reference to corrupt regimes and bureaucracies in underdeveloped countries, does not seem inapplicable to at least certain portions and regional segments of the Soviet party-government hierarchy.[4]

An alternative to Grossman's notion of a kleptocratic society is the behavioral optimizing framework for economic activity provided by the theory of the rent-seeking society. Adaptation of the predictions of this theory highlights the social costs of a Soviet-type system of social and economic organization, while explaining the occasional periods of political instability to which such systems are prone.

II. DISCRETIONARY RESOURCES, RENTS, AND HIERARCHICAL STRUCTURE

In principle, central planning implies prior designation of use of all inputs. This ought then suffice to forestal the use of productive resources in potentially unproductive rent-seeking and rent-protecting activities. Indeed, according to the official ideology, with resources preallocated and consumption allocations made according to 'needs', *Homo Sovietus* would have no incentive to seek resources for use in rent-seeking or rent-protecting quests. Even if there should be miscalculations in the plan, *Homo Sovietus* would respond in a manner consistent with the collective benefit, and, cognizant of the 'needs' of his comrades, would not take personal advantage of the opportunity to become the beneficiary of a surplus payment such as a rent. In practice, however, motives of personal advantage result in departures from this idealized norm. Individuals do not behave in the manner of the altruistic *Homo Sovietus* but follow the norms of self-interested *Homo Economicus*. The quests for personal gain (utility and profit maximization) give rise to rent-seeking and rent-protecting activities as individuals allocate resources to increasing and protecting their incomes. Notwithstanding attempts at centralized designation of resource use, resources facilitating these personal quests are readily available.

Of course, monitoring of individuals' time allocation is difficult in both decentralized and centralized economic systems. Particular difficulties however confront central planners in a Soviet-type economy. At the plant and product-distribution levels the managerial incentive to monitor is reduced because those charged with monitoring the operations of the state's enterprises are not residual claimants. Individuals are, however, residual claimants to the rewards derived from their rent-seeking activities[5] and hence there is a strong incentive to allocate discretionary time to supplanting and replacing a superior. Likewise, discretionary time is at the disposal of the superior for rent-protecting activity aimed at preempting those individuals aspiring to his position and his rents. Labor or time is moreover not the only available discretionary input. There is abundant evidence of non-labor resources 'hidden' from the central planners.[6] These hidden resources have an insurance function, in that they permit random shortfalls in output to be met, thus avoiding penalties for not attaining official targets. There is of course no incentive to use discretionary and hidden resources to exceed output targets, as this would only increase the future output target for officially-specified inputs. There *is* an incentive to use these resources where possible for personal gain in activities wherein agents are residual claimants.

The evidence that hidden or discretionary resources exist for use outside the plan does not in itself imply socially wasteful resource usage. On the contary, insofar as illegal activities in conjunction with hidden and discretionary resources are directed towards satisfying consumers' demands for various goods and services which the state refuses to provide, there is social gain. As has been stressed by Ericson, illegal markets based on 'hidden' intermediate goods may yield constrained first best outcomes by efficiently rationing discretionary resources in a centrally-planned economy.[7] Still, hidden resources also give rise to rents which appear in the form of transfers or bribes made to facilitate the ongoing functioning of the illegal economy. As we shall see, these transfers involve individuals at levels from ministers and regional party chiefs down to workers on the factory floor and the salespeople charged with distributing output to consumers. Bribes are transferred upwards within the hierarchy to facilitate the supply of material inputs and distribution of output and downwards to ensure labor inputs and, most importantly, to buy silence. Since the activities constitute economic crimes, transfers are made to the security authorities, so giving rise to rent seeking (and rent-protecting activities) within that hierarchy as well. The rents extend into the political hierarchy. Indeed, bribes are so central a feature of the Soviet economic system that for a private entrepreneur engaging in illicit production activities such payments appear to be an unavoidable cost of production. Simis observes:

The only major ongoing expense which can be connected to underground costs is the money spent on bribes without which no single private factory would last for more than a month.[8]

An indication of how transfers are distributed is provided by the case of a private entrepreneur named Laziashvili who operated in Georgia. A list of bribe recipients was presented at his trial:

> The list began with district police officials, and went on to name heads of the DCMSP [the state body charged with the regulation of economic crimes] (including the chief of the Republic's DCMSP) and the Ministry for Internal Affairs (including the Minister) and public prosecutors from the district level on up to the Public Prosecutor of the Republic. A prominent place on the list was occupied by employees—from the lowest levels right up to the ministers themselves—of ministries on which Laziashvili's enterprises depended. The list of the state officials regularly bribed by Laziashvili was crowned by the name of the Chairman of the Council of Ministers and his deputies. But the heftiest bribes found their way to Party, rather than state, leaders: these included officials ranging from the first secretaries of the 'raikoms' to the first and second secretaries of the Central Committee.[9]

III. THE VALUE OF THE RENT-SEEKING PRIZES

How significant are the above-reported transfers relative to official incomes? The value of the outlays which an individual will be prepared to make in rent-seeking and rent-protecting activities depends on the value of the rents contested. In general, the larger the prize, the larger the outlay.[10]

In Western market economies, the prizes sought or defended are generally specified in terms of expected present values of income flows. In the Soviet-type system, in contrast, rent seeking and rent protection transcend income flows. In the top echelons of the hierarchy, individuals receive their monetary remuneration from legal and illegal sources, but incumbency also provides benefits tied to claims over apartments, chauffered cars, servants, country dachas, travel, entertainment of various sorts, privileged shopping, and ostensibly more.[11] If supplanted, an incumbent not only loses his claims to current and future income flows, but also forfeits rights to these latter benefits. In a capitalist economy, the forfeiture by an incumbent of his position is a far less drastic event. Capitalist property rights will have allowed the incumbent to accumulate private assets. Ownership of these assets is independent of future tenure in the position which allowed the assets to be accumulated. Due to differences in the nature of property rights assignment, the prizes sought and defended are therefore of greater relative significance in the Soviet rent-seeking quest. Correspondingly, more resources can be expected to be allocated to rent seeking by aspirants to various positions and to preemptive defensive activity by incumbents.

Absent or restricted property rights also influence the supply of rent *creating* intervention. The Soviet official is aware that in the event of his being supplanted by a successful lower-echelon rival, the assets of apartment, car, etc., most of which would be retained under a private property rights system, are lost, but that illicit private assets can be accumulated from illegal transfers or bribes. Hence, the otherwise puzzling phenomenon arises of high-echelon officials engaging in bribe-seeking (or rent-creating) activities when such activities yield meagre returns relative to the officials' perceived *official* wealth and status.

Given the nature of the activities involved, there are understandable difficulties in obtaining data on the value of rent-seeking prizes contested. There is, however, some interesting information available on the values attached to republican ministerial posts in the Soviet Union. Grossman cites official claims of

> widespread purchases and sale around 1970 of high Party and high govern-ment positions in Azerbaijzhan for sums ranging from 10,000 rubles for lesser posts to 250,000 rubles for that of minister of trade.[12]

Similarly, Hosking quotes an Azerbaidjani official as claiming that, in the 1970s, the post of regional procurator cost 30000 roubles, that of police chief 50000 roubles and that of regional party secretary 200000 roubles.[13]

These sums must be judged remarkable given the official average monthly earnings of a minister of around 2000 roubles.

Evidence is also available on the nature of the bidding mechanism underlying the seeking of the above positions:

> . . . when a post did come up, a competition began. The first round was nominated by a top official such as a secretary in the Republic's Party Central Committee, personnel chief to the Central Committee or the Chairman of the Council of Ministers or one of his deputies. A decisive factor in these nominations was often a family connection between the candidate and his proposer, especially in Central Asian and Trans-Caucasian Republics.
>
> Even at this early stage, the size of the bribe to be paid for the nomination would have been discussed, but the real battle only began when it became clear just who the possible candidates were. Then . . . an auction would take place behind the scenes, although the victor was not always the highest bidder. That is because the competition was not merely among the aspirants to the vacant post but also a competition among the recipients of their bribes, so the most influential patron had the best chance of winning.[14]

With respect to values bid, again the evidence is that the prizes were large relative to official incomes:

> . . . there was a going rate in those years for ministerial posts, ranging from 100,000 rubles for the not very important (or lucrative) post of minister of Social Security, up to 250,000 to 3,000,000 rubles for such bottomless feeding troughs as the Ministries of Trade or of Light Industry. The acquisition of these posts was not cheap, of course, but, once installed, the minister would be able to derive considerable income from it by peddling, in his turn, jobs as sector and territory chiefs, which, in a ministry like that of Light Industry, could fetch 100,000 to 125,000 rubles.[15]

These transfers sought by high government and party officials have their origins in the rents associated with production and distribution activities. Just as monopoly power and regulation give rise to artificial scarcity in market economies, so the scarcities consequent upon imperfect planning provide the opportunities for appro-priately placed individuals to benefit from differences between the willingness to pay for goods and the costs of production and distribution. A fascinating example of these activities is provided by the operation of Food Store Five in Moscow. Simis' description warrants quotation at length. To begin with, there is evidence on the value of transfers within the production and distribution hierarchy. Again the values are high relative to official incomes:

> The illegal profits extracted from customers' pockets by the sales clerks are very large indeed compared with their official wages. The average salary for a sales clerk in a Moscow food store is 120 to 130 rubles a month, but the illegal earnings could range from 500–700 rubles for someone working the delicatessen or another department to 1,500 or 2,000 rubles for a butcher. The store managers' illegal earnings could average 40,000 to 50,000 rubles a month . . .[16]

However, this was not the store managers' gross return. There were various overhead expenses incurred outside of the plan:

> Since, in the case in question, the assistant manager had kept her 'black' ledger with great accuracy, the investigation and trial turned up detailed facts about both illegal income and illegal expenses . . . The managers had to pay the loaders, as well as skilled workmen hired off the books to repair all the minor breakages which are inevitable in any large store. In addition, there were 36 sales clerks in the store, each of whom took food home each day without paying for it. The resulting shortages had to be made up by the manager and his assistant. This amounted to the quite sizable sum of 4,000 to 5,000 rubles a month.[17]

Such expenses may be anticipated in the course of conducting business operations outside the official plan. But there were also expenses incurred in consequence of the need to keep government and party officials compliant, and these costs were more substantial:

> Food Store Number Five supplies the district elite with food at less than full price, also the store's management made regular tribute payments, in cash and merchandise, to all the various inspectors, auditors and police employees. Nearly 9,000 rubles were spent each month on these gifts.[18]

Bribes were also necessary within the state vertically-integrated production system to ensure the ongoing supply of goods:

> So that the store could fulfil its sales plan and make sufficient illegal income besides, it needed good and scarce products. In order to get such items . . . the managers of Food Store Number Five had to pay further, regular bribes. The assistant manager's ledger recorded 9,000 to 11,000 rubles a month for such bribes.[19]

Furthermore, there was an evident link to the senior political hierarchy. This link underlay the competition which we have observed for positions in that hierarchy:

> . . . the assistant manager paid a monthly visit to the municipal administration of the chain of food stores to deliver a package of money—10,000 to 12,000 rubles—to the administration's head or one of his deputies. The documents in this case gave indications that a portion of that money had a higher destination than the municipal administration; namely the Depart-

ment of Trade of the Moscow Committee of the Communist Party and the Trade Department of the Moscow Municipal Executive Committee.[20]

These various transfer payments still left some considerable rents for the managers of the store:

> . . the great bulk of the illegal income received by the managers of Food Store Number Five—35,000 to 40,000 rubles per month—went on business expenses and various kinds of bribes. Even after that, however, there was still a profit of 5,000 to 10,000 rubles a month left over for them.[21]

The overall prizes for rent seekers include all the transfers accruing within the economic and political hierarchies. Hence, it is the gross sum of 40000 to 50000 roubles per month which provides an indication of the value of the resources which the operations of Food Store Number Five might attract into rent seeking and protecting activities. The profits of 5000 to 10000 roubles reflect only the value of the resources which might be allocated to supplanting the enterprise managers.

IV. THE PURGE: LARGE-SCALE RENT SEEKING AND RENT PROTECTION

We turn now from the value of the rent-seeking prizes to a characteristic of Soviet-type economies—the purge.

The perception of the centrally-planned economy of the Soviet type as a rent-seeking society leads to a theory of the purge which differs in substance from previous theories. Purges are commonplace in Marxist–Leninist systems. They vary in scope and severity, ranging from the enormity of Stalin's great terror to the demotion of an anonymous bureaucrat. Different cultural attributes appear to affect the nature of purges: for example, at high levels of the Party, the Albanian purge is 'short, nasty, and brutish';[22] in China, until the crushing of the Gang of Four, high level purgees suffered perhaps no more than house arrest.

Such differences of implementation aside, previous explanations of the phenomenon of the purge have fallen into two categories. The general historical-empirical view is that each purge can be accounted for by the specific influences—historical, political, economic and social—prevailing at the time. This approach has appeal if one is interested in the specifics of a particular political system[23] but does not lend itself to theoretical generalization. An alternative view emphasizes the psychological factors underlying the behavior of the communist leader. Most studies in this vein have centered upon the personality of Joseph Stalin. However, the most sophisticated analysis along these lines is that of the behavior of Mao-Tse-Tung.[24] These studies may provide insights about behavioral characteristics of particular dictators but, again, fail to provide general hypotheses—unless one proposes that *every* communist leader has been a paranoid schizophrenic. Moreover, such a personalized theory based on idiosyncratic behavior of the leadership could not account for the great many purges at lower levels of the hierarchy in which leaders play no part.

The theory of rent-seeking and rent-protecting behavior does, however, provide a general explanation for purges at *all* levels of the hierarchical structure. The purge may have its origins from above and so may be rent-protecting in nature; in such instances, lower-level rent seekers who have engaged in activities directed at supplanting an incumbent are eliminated, thereby protecting the incumbent's rents.

Alternatively, the origins of the purge may be from below, in which case the purge reflects rent-seeking rather than rent-protecting activity. Moreover, once a purge has been set into motion one may as well look to the future and eliminate rivals at the same hierarchical level in addition to the upper-level incumbents whose positions are the focus of rent-seeking activity.

Thus, consider an official in the hierarchy whose position brings with it a given rent directly associated with incumbency. In general, the official will have under his control a number of subordinates and, ultimately, a set of enterprises. The official must be bribed if illegal activities in these enterprises are to be permitted to proceed unchecked, in particular if resource requirements for successful plan fulfillment are to be obtained in desired above-plan quantities. The official is in effect a monopolist with respect to the enterprises under his control. He confronts potential competitors. There is, however, no prospect of market sharing or other strategic accommodating responses to entry. Successful entry by a rival completely eliminates the official's rents. Thus the official can be expected to seek to protect his rents by undertaking activities to protect his continuing claim to his position.[25] To the extent that prior positioning and political skills are required to attain the position in question, rent seeking to supplant the incumbent official will be a small-numbers activity. This allows those aspiring to the official's position to be identified and a well-directed purge is an effective means of preemptive behavior.

A proper analysis of purge behavior requires careful consideration of the nature of the barriers to entry protecting an official in the hierarchy. The official has in effect property rights conferred upon him by the party leadership.[26] To the extent that contestability is not sanctioned from above, any rent-seeking quests set in motion will be unsuccessful and significant expenditures on rent protection by incumbents will be unnecessary. This would have been the case in times of political stability such as experienced in the Soviet Union during most of the Khruschchev and Brezhnev eras.

During Stalin's reign there were, on the other hand, frequent changes in property rights specification; property rights could not be taken for granted and contestability was often sanctioned. This manifested itself in many forms: the launching of an anti-bureaucracy campaign in the press, a keynote speech which counselled vigilence against agents of imperialism or enemies of the revolution. The sudden dismissal of one or more senior officials could provide the indication that property rights to rents had become contestable.

Triggers sanctioning the contestability of rents are not unique to the Stalin period. It was during the Great Terror, however, that the Soviet Union took on the character of a rent-seeking society par excellence. It may be that a time of such instability will not again plague Soviet society. On the other hand, recent high-level purges in the Kremlin underlying Gorbachev's attempts to strengthen his power base may indicate a further period of instability.

One of the beneficiaries of the recent purges has been the newly-appointed Soviet Foreign Minister, Eduard Sheverdnadze. His earlier ascent to the Georgian leadership provides an interesting example of a successful rent-seeking purge initiated from below in the hierarchy. Georgia is a republic noted for its venality and illegality. Grossman has observed that private activity in the urban sector prior to 1972 was 'carried out on an unparalleled scale and with unrivalled scope and daring'.[27] In particular, rents abounded in Georgia because:

> . . . for climatic reasons Georgia has a monopoly on citrus fruit production
> in the USSR and shares with only a few other regions considerable

advantage in growing out-of-season fruits and flowers. The state attempts to obtain these goods for distribution throughout the country at prices that are a fraction of what the products bring growers in the open markets of the Soviet Union's northern population centres. Naturally, Georgian peasants prefer the open markets. In effect, there has been for some time now an undeclared war going on between state authorities and the peasants, a contest in which the peasants have shown an enormous determination and remarkable ingenuity in overcoming the formidable obstacles which the state has placed in the way of their pocketing the large economic rent offered by the open market.[28]

Given these rents, the theory predicts that rent seeking and preemptive defensive behavior will come into play, with the official hierarchy seeking to acquire or protect its share.

The conventional wisdom is that in the thoroughly corrupt party and state hierarchies there stood out a man of impeccable moral fibre, the Minister for Internal Affairs, Eduard Sheverdnadze. Of course, how an honest communist could rise to become chief of secret police in a place like Georgia is explained by none of the commentators. Even Simis argues that Sheverdnadze was

> ... in part motivated by ambition, but he apparently also felt genuine hatred for corruption and was pained by the decadence he witnessed. 'Once, the Georgians were known throughout the world as a nation of warriors and poets; now they are known as swindlers', he commented bitterly at a closed meeting.[29]

Simis goes on to describe the groundwork for the purge:

> For several years, agents of Shevarnadze's ministry for International Affairs shadowed all the leading functionaries in the Party and state apparat of Georgia, as well as their families, and much compromising evidence was gathered. . . . Shevarnadze made careful, unhurried preparations for his exposure of the corrupt ruling elite . . . even within the Ministry no one was informed about the Minister's intentions.[30]

By the middle of 1972, it had become clear to Sheverdnadze that the First Party Secretary, Mzhavarnadze, had been alerted to the situation. Not wishing to fall victim to a rent-protecting purge, Sheverdnadze rushed to Moscow where he presented his evidence to Brezhnev. The consequence of Sheverdnadze's visit was that

> ... a sudden, extraordinary plenary session of the Georgian Central Committee was convened, which 'complied with the Mzhavarnadze's requests that he be permitted to retire on pension, for reasons of age' and 'elected Shevarnadze as First Secretary of the Central Committee on instructions from Moscow'.
>
> Virtually the entire ruling apparat of Georgia (both Party and State) was removed for reasons of health, pensioned off, or, indeed, dismissed without any reason being given.[31]

A successful purge had been implemented, from below. Nonetheless, corruption in Georgia persisted.[32] We presently suggest general reasons for the failure of reform, but a careful reading of Simis reveals a possible reason specific to this case. Underground millionaire Laziashvili whom we met in Section II was exposed in 1973 in the wake of the purges. On his above-cited list of bribe takers is included none other than the Minister for Internal Affairs, 'honest' Eduard Sheverdnadze! It should, therefore, surprise no one that corruption did not end in Georgia. Sheverdnadze's purge was a successful rent-seeking endeavour. The illegal activities underlying the rents continued with a newly specified property rights designation.

V. RENT SEEKING AND THE FAILURE OF REFORM

Failure of reform in Georgia is but one example of the lack of success of attempts to eliminate 'corruption' and 'economic crimes' in economic systems of the Soviet type. The perception of the Soviet-type system as intrinsically a rent-seeking society provides a natural explanation for the failure of reform attempts. Successful reforms eliminate rents via elimination of the transfers (or bribes) which give rise to the rents, whereas incumbents will have invested in securing access to their rents, and aspiring rent seekers will have made outlays to secure vantages for upward movement in the hierarchy. Within the political, managerial, and security hierarchies, neither incumbents nor well-placed aspirants have an interest in reform.

Indeed, the theory of the rent-seeking society predicts quite generally, without regard for the peculiarities of Soviet-type systems that piecemeal attempts at reform will be unsuccessful.[33] The evidence goes beyond confirming that in the Soviet system attempts at elimination of corruption fail to gain support. More significantly, when viewing the system from the vantage of the theory of a rent-seeking society, there is evidence that when piecemeal reforms are instituted, the economic subsystem surrounding the source of the reform breaks down. Thus, return to Food Store Five, where a purge took place—not a rent-seeking purge, but rather an impeccably honest administrator was placed in charge in an attempt to eliminate corruption. Simis' account is as follows:

> In the 1960s, 'in order to improve the situation in Moscow's commercial network' (as the Moscow Committee's decree put it), several dozen retired officers, all members of the Communist Party with irreproachable reputations, were sent out to work as managers of shops, restaurants and cafes. One of the officers was Lieutenant-Colonel Boris Adamov, who was assigned the post of manager of Food Store Number Five. Adamov was an honest officer, educated in military concepts of discipline and obedience, and when he arrived at his new post he could not accept the fact that the normal functions of a state enterprise could only be carried out with the help of bribes and by cheating the customers. He started out by operating in strict compliance with the law of the land: he took no money from his sales personnel, sold nothing at speculative prices to professional retailers, and categorically refused to pay bribes to top people in the municipal administration of the chain responsible for the shop or to the managers of the wholesale depots, cold storage facilities and meat-packing plants which supplied the store with merchandise.[34]

The consequence of the reform was that Food Store Five simply ceased functioning:

> Since the municipal administration officials were not receiving their monthly payments from the new manager, they began to carp at any petty

blunder made by an inexperienced employee. At the same time, the managers of the various supply facilities, since they too were going without their regular bribes, stopped providing the store with goods which were in short supply and even made great difficulties about supplying things which were available in abundance. Consequently, Food Store Number Five did not fulfil its sales plan and its income fell sharply. The official wages fell too, as they are not paid in full unless the plan is met.[35]

This led the honest administrator to modify his approach to reform:

Adamov could not stand the pressure and accepted a compromise. He took no money for himself, but permitted his highly experienced assistant to run the business according to the unwritten rules of Soviet trade—to take money from the sales clerks, to sell goods at inflated prices, to cheat the customers, and, of course, to bribe the top people in the municipal administration, and all the store's suppliers.[36]

Evidently, in the case of Food Store Five, rent-seeking activities sustained general productive activity. Consumers benefitted from the provision of goods which in the absence of illegal activities would not have been available. If consumers were 'cheated', some positive consumer surplus presumably remained. However, concomitant with this satisfaction of consumer demand which would otherwise not have taken place, transfers were made which become the focus of individuals' activities. These transfers underlay the incentives for the quests to become the beneficiaries of or to protect rents accruing to particular positions.

VI. CONCLUDING REMARKS

An analysis of Soviet-type economic planning in light of the theory of the rent-seeking society reveals a contradiction between the goals implied by Marxist–Leninist ideology and the rational behavior of economic agents. To the extent that a centrally-planned economy generates rents—at least while 'perfect' computation of the plan is not a realistic option—it is rational for individuals to engage in rent-seeking and, consequently, rent-protecting activity. As long as this remains the case, the replacement of the 'capitalist law of anarchy in production' by the 'law of planned and proportional development' under socialism cannot proceed in accord with official Soviet rhetoric. The uncertainties of the market remain, while the bureaucratization of society and the illegality of most market operations give rise to a plethora of rents.

A rent-seeking perspective on Soviet-type economies provides a general framework for understanding phenomena such as the purges which have been previously viewed as having their rationale entirely outside the scope of economic incentives. Further, the recognition of the role of the theory of rent-seeking behavior has important implications for comparative studies of centrally-directed and market economies.[37] Just as rent seeking and rent protection add a dimension of cost to the social loss due to monopoly power and government regulation in market economies, so may additional cost be imputed to the imperfectly functioning planned economy. In a market economy monopoly and regulation result in inefficiencies in resource allocation, and under central planning inefficiencies due to resource misallocation arise because allocational decisions are made under conditions of imperfect information. It is the relative magnitudes of these inefficiencies which have been the focus of theoretical and empirical study in investigations of the comparative social costs of imperfectly centralized and decentralized economies. Incorporation of the cost of rent-seeking and rent-protecting activities has substantially increased the range of estimates of social loss associated with monopoly and regulation in market economies;[37] acknowledgement of the prevalent role of rent-seeking and rent-protecting behavior under planned socialism similarly increases the magnitudes of social cost associated with such economic systems.

Finally, we observe that analyses of income distribution in the Soviet system are incomplete without reference to the resources expended in seeking to change or maintain income distribution via respective rent-seeking and rent-protecting activity. While it appears that the practice of Soviet socialism provides the conditions and incentives for a functioning rent-seeking society, enquiries into income distribution in the Soviet system[38] have not availed themselves of the theoretical framework offered by the theory of rent-seeking and rent-protecting behavior. Likewise, projections of future performance of Soviet-type systems[39] which do not encompass recognition of the resources expended in the seeking and protection of rents omit from their accounts a central feature of economic activity in such economies.

REFERENCES AND NOTES

1. *See* R. D. Tollison, 'Rent Seeking: A Survey', (1982) Kyklos, 35. *See*, however, R. B. Ekelund Jr, and R. D. Tollison, *Mercantilism as a Rent-Seeking Society: Economic Regulation in Historical Perspective*, (1982), Texas A. and M. Press, for an application of the theory to explain activity in a pre-capitalist economy.
2. Recent contributions include G. Grossman, 'The Second Economy of the USSR', (1977) Problems of Communism 26, reprinted in M. Bornstein (ed.), *The Soviet Economy: Continuity and Change*, Westview Press, Boulder, Colorado (1981); G. Grossman, 'Notes on the Illegal Private Economy and Corruption', in *The Soviet Economy in a Time of Change*, Compendium of papers, Joint Economic Committee, US Congress, Washington, DC, (1979), US Government Printing Office, Vol. 1; A. Katsenelinboigen, 'Coloured Markets in the Soviet Union', (1977) Soviet Studies 29; A. Katsenelinboigen and M. S. Levine, 'Market and Plan, Plan and Market: The Soviet Case', (1977) Am. Econ. Rev. 67; D. K. Simes, 'The Soviet Parallel Market', (1975) Survey 21; K. Simis, 'The Machinery of Corruption in the Soviet Union', (1977) Survey 23; D. Law, 'Corruption in Georgia', (1974) Critiques 3.
3. (1982), Dent, London.
4. Grossman, (1977), *supra*, note 2.
5. *See* W. M. Crain and A. Zardkoohi, 'X-Inefficiency and Non-Pecuniary Rewards in a Rent-Seeking Society: A Neglected Issue in the Property Rights Theory of the Firm', (1980) Am. Econ. Rev. 70.
6. *See* the pioneering paper by J. S. Berliner, 'The Informal Organisation of the Soviet Firm', (1952) Quart. J. Econ. 56.
7. R. E. Ericson, 'The "Second Economy" and Resource Allocation Under Central Planning', in P. Desai (ed.), *Marxism, Central Planning and the Soviet Economy*, MIT Press, Cambridge, Mass. (1983), and 'The Second Economy and Resource Allocation Under Central Planning', (1984) J. Comparative Econ. 8. For a similar viewpoint in a Third World context, *see* N. H. Leff, 'Economic Development through Bureaucratic Corruption', (1964) The Am. Behavioral Scientist 7.
8. Simis, *supra*, note 2, p. 118.
9. *Ibid.*, pp. 118–119.
10. On the relation between the value of a rent-seeking prize and the value of the resources expanded in quest of the prize, *see* G. Tullock, 'Efficient Rent Seeking', in J. M. Buchanan, R. Tollison and G. Tullock (eds), *Toward a Theory of the Rent Seeking*

Society, Texas A. and M. Press (1980); P. Rogerson, 'The Social Cost of Monopoly and Regulation', (1982) Bell J. Econ. 13; A. L. Hillman and E. Katz, 'Risk-averse Rent Seekers and the Social Cost of Monopoly Power', (1984) Econ. J. 94; R. Higgins, W. Shuggart II and R. D. Tollison, 'Free Entry and Efficient Rent Seeking', (1985) Public Choice 46; E. Appelbaum and E. Katz, 'Transfer Seeking and Avoidance: On the Full Social Costs of Rent Seeking', (1986) Public Choice 48; A. L. Hillman and D. Samet, 'Dissipation of Contestable Rents by Small Numbers of Contenders', Public Choice, forthcoming.

11. *See* the accounts given in M. Mathews, *Privilege in the Soviet Union*, Allen and Unwin, London (1978).
12. Grossman, *supra*, note 2, p. 79.
13. G. Hosking, *A History of the Soviet Union*, Fontana, London (1985).
14. Simis (1982), *supra*, note 2, pp. 35–36.
15. *Ibid.*
16. *Ibid.*, pp. 150–151.
17. *Ibid.*, p. 151.
18. *Ibid.*
19. *Ibid.*, p. 152.
20. *Ibid.*, p. 153.
21. *Ibid.*
22. *See* A. Schnytzer, *Stalinist Economic Strategy in Practice*, Oxford University Press (1982).
23. For a fine recent example, *see* A. Pipa, 'Party Ideology and Purges in Albania', (1984) Telos 59.
24. R. J. Lifton, *Revolutionary Immortality*, Penguin, London (1970).
25. There is an evident analogy to an incumbent monopolistic firm in a market economy seeking to protect its rents by preempting entry of competitors: *see* A. L. Hillman, 'Preemptive Rent-Seeking and the Social Cost of Monopoly Power', (1984) Int. J. Ind. Org. 2.
26. On property rights and entry barriers in the context of a capitalist firm, *see* H. Demsetz, 'Barriers to Entry', (1982) Am. Econ. Rev. 72.
27. Grossman, *supra*, note 2, p. 81.
28. *Ibid.*
29. Simis, *supra*, note 2, p. 35.
30. *Ibid.*, pp. 37, 38.
31. *Ibid.*, p. 39.
32. *See* Grossman, *supra*, note 2.
33. J. M. Buchanan, 'Reform in the Rent-Seeking Society', in J. M. Buchanan, R. Tollison and G. Tullock (eds), *Toward a Theory of the Rent-Seeking Society*, Texas A. and M. Press (1980).
34. Simis, *supra*, note 2, pp. 155–156.
35. *Ibid.*
36. *Ibid.*
37. *See* K. Cowling and P. C. Mueller, 'The Social Costs of Monopoly Power', (1978) Econ. J. 88; reprinted in J. M. Buchanan, R. Tollison and G. Tullock, *supra*, note 33.
38. *See* the review by A. Bergson, 'Income Inequality under Soviet Socialism', (1984) J. Econ. Literature 22.
39. For example, A. Bergson and H. Levine, *The Soviet Economy: Toward the Year 2000*, Allan and Unwin, Winchester, Mass. (1983).

Applied Economics, 2005, **37**, 705–711

Rent seeking and taxation in the Ancient Roman Empire

Charles D. DeLorme Jr, Stacey Isom and David R. Kamerschen*

Economics Department, University of Georgia, Terry College of Business, Athens, GA 30602-6254, USA

Historians maintain that an increase in taxation of the peasant farmers, government corruption and misuse of its revenue by the ruling class led to a weakening of the Roman Empire that culminated in its western demise in the fifth century. But it was not just the taxation issue doomed the Roman Empire, but political change from a Republic to an emperor that exacerbated the climate of rent-seeking behaviour by the ruling classes that culminated in the misallocation of tax resources. One category of rent seeking involves the spending of money that the average taxpayer sees as foolish but that benefits a particular group. The groups who bear the costs can stop the rent seeking if they are informed. These average citizens were peasant farmers who no doubt recognized the costs but were unable to form political coalitions to protect themselves because military control of Roman legions was under the tight control of the emperor. This was not the case under the Republic. With the emperors, public funds were being diverted from the public infrastructure such as road building and repair to more frivolous activities.

I. Introduction

The tax system of the ancient Roman Empire, from the time the Republic began in 509 BC throughout the empire that Octavian (Caesar Augustus) established in 27 BC, operated with efficiencies and inefficiencies. Historians argue that an increase in taxation and government corruption led to a weakening of the Empire that culminated in the western downfall in 476 AD. Taxation extends benefits to citizens in the form of public works as well as costs if the governing bodies impose excessive, unequal or unfair taxes. Taxpayers see the tax collector as a necessary evil, but when the taxing power falls under the control of one emperor or a few powerful people, these people use their position and the revenue generated as they see fit – most likely for personal gain. In this case the average taxpayer was the peasant farmer who bore the costs. This study shows the political change of Rome from a Republic or more democratic form of government to an emperor who increased the wasteful taxation that doomed the Empire. Even though the peasants may have recognized their plight, they could not do anything about it.

Rent is the return to owners of resources in excess of opportunity cost. Rent seeking is the outlay of resources to capture these returns in excess of opportunity costs. Formally, rent seeking involves wasting scarce resources to secure or maintain rents, or profitable position (see e.g., Tollison, 1982; Colander, 1984; Rowley *et al.* 1988; Tollison and Congleton, 1995).[1] For actual empirical calculations of rent-seeking activities, see e.g., DeLorme *et al.* (1986, 1992, 1994), Ampofo-Tuffuor *et al.* (1991) and Basurto *et al.* (2001).

* Corresponding author. E-mail: davidk@terry.uga.edu
[1] Ekelund *et al.* (1996, pp. 60–1) have even demonstrated, using neoclassical theory, that the medieval Catholic Church acted as a firm that tried to block entry by potential rivals.

705

The limits to the magnitude of rent seeking were generalized by DeLorme and Snow (1990), who show within a general equilibrium framework that the precise limits to rent-seeking waste depend on the extent to which government subsidizes rent seekers through tax-financed grants, contracts, and favours. Tullock (1985, p. 233) has divided rent seeking into three categories, one of which is pertinent to this study. It concerns 'spending money in a way that in the standpoint of the average tax payer is foolish but that benefits a particular group'. He points out that rent seeking can most often be stopped if the groups that are bearing the cost can be informed. However, this was not the case for the peasant farmers in Ancient Rome because they could not form a political coalition; the military power or Roman legions were directly under the control of the emperor and owed their own personal allegiance and income to the emperor. Analysis of a system such as that of Ancient Rome provides insight into the long and early history of rent seeking and the necessity and abuse of taxation by those directly in power. It is our belief that increased rent seeking by the emperor in power and the increase in taxes of Roman peasant farmers led to the weakening and fall of the Roman Empire.

II. Description of the Roman Tax System

Taxation has been prevalent throughout time and among societies as the means by which governments must raise money. Citizens talk about the topic and make efforts to avoid, or at times, evade the taxes. The burden of taxation falls differently among socioeconomic classes. With a progressive tax, the burden, expressed as a percentage of income, increases as income increases. With a regressive tax, the burden falls as income increases. With a proportional tax, the burden is the same as income increases. For instance, the USA now uses a mildly progressive federal tax system in which the rate of taxation increases with income.[2] Rome did not have a progressive tax system. Hopkins (1980, p. 121), Jones (1986, p. 10), and others who study the Roman economy make the point that taxation was regressive. The Late Roman Empire taxed its populace heavily,[3] but upper classes, members of the elite, did not pay a higher percentage than the peasant class. Engels (1990, p. 19) describes how the right to elect officials disappeared along with

the Republic and led to an abuse of power by the Roman elite, who could now oppress the poor in each province without punishment. The powerful provincial governors collected taxes and the populace of the Empire remained helpless under the control of the emperor, unless they revolted. The emperor had no checks on his power.

Jones, a renowned scholar on the Roman economy, points out that the Roman Empire possessed an agricultural economy. Imperial revenue was derived from the land tax and rents, since the income of the rich was invested in land. The greatest percentage of the Roman population was peasants, and unprogressive taxation fell most heavily on them, sometimes to the extent that it forced them to abandon their land, their livelihood. Jones writes (1974, p. 135), 'If I may venture a generalization on the economic effects of the Roman Empire I would say that its chief effect was to promote an ever increasing concentration of land in the hands of its governing aristocracy at the expense of the population at large'. Jones explains (1974, p. 136) that the small group of the wealthy made their fortunes in politics and in administration or the law. 'The rich men of the Empire mostly made their money by booty, governmental extortion and corruption, the profits of government contracting, and to a lesser extent official salaries'. His arguments provide evidence for the rent-seeking tendencies leading to the corruption of the ruling class. Becker and Stigler (1975), Rose-Ackerman (1975, 1998) and Klitgaard (1988, 1991) have analysed bureaucratic corruption as a principal–agent problem. This result is especially true when the emperors ruled the Roman Empire since the peasant farmers had no one to plead their case. Recently, Van Rijckeghem and Wender (1997) have shown that there is a negative relationship between corruption and civil service wages. This result, however, does not appear to be as strong as the principal–agent problem during the Roman Empire.

Diocletian, emperor from 284–305 AD, can be called the founder of the late empire. Taxes in the later Roman Empire, in the fourth century and the fifth century, including the *iugatio* and the *capitatio* instituted by Diocletian, assessed on the land and the rural population, produced tax revenue used to support the army. Roman soldiers needed

---

[2] It is mildly regressive since the federal taxes are dominated by the progressive individual tax that overcomes the regressive payroll tax. Under reasonable assumptions about the shifting and incidence, local and state taxes are mildly regressive. The corporate tax is progressive as it falls largely on owners and since the profits and capital income that accrued to owners are a larger part of the incomes of high-income households. See e.g. Case and Fair (1999, Ch. 18).

[3] Wickham (1994, p. 13) says, 'The weight of taxation in the late empire is well-known, and often used as a standard formula in discussions of why the empire fell'.

food and uniforms, state employees who produced the arms needed pay, and everyone needed the roads and the postal service (*cursus publicus*). The land tax, paid in kind by all landowners, would be calculated by the assessment of fiscal units based on the extent and quality of land, type of crops grown, number of settlers and cattle and amount of equipment.

Other taxes, the *gleba*, the *aurum oblaticium* and the *aurum coronarium*, were levied on senators who were landowners. Traders (*negotiatores*, literally 'businessmen', including all who made their living by buying and selling – merchants, moneylenders, prostitutes) had to pay the *collatio lustralis* (Jones, 1974, p. 35). The *publicani*, the contracted tax collectors, did not carry out the system uniformly in every region, but Diocletian's new system did result in an improved accounting of the empire's revenues. Jones points out (1974, p. 83) that the main tax was imposed on agriculture and this tax accounted for over 90% of national revenue: 'It was a combined land and poll tax, being assessed partly on agricultural land (*iugatio*) and partly on the rural population (*capitatio*).' The high rate of taxation in the economy that fell on the peasant farmers resulted in smaller yields of agricultural products (i.e. food), depopulation of the rural areas, and depopulation of the whole empire (1974, p. 84). Explanations for *agri deserti*, 'abandoned land', include exhaustion of the soil, shortage of agricultural labour, and growing insecurity caused by barbarian raids. But most plausibly, as Lactantius puts it (1984, p. 86), 'the resources of the farmers were exhausted by the outrageous burden of all the taxes, the fields were abandoned, and the cultivated land reverted to waste'. Jones concludes (1974, p. 88):

> The evidence does suggest that over-taxation played a significant role in the decline of the empire. It can be established that the taxes rose from Diocletian's time until they absorbed a very

high proportion of the yield of the land. It can plausibly be argued that the high rate of tax was the main reason for the abandonment of marginal land and the consequent impoverishment of the empire. It is at any rate probable that it was a major factor in reducing the manpower of the empire, and thereby contributed directly to its military collapse.

III. Change in Government Structure

The reign of Julius Caesar marks the transition from the Republic to the Empire.[4] The Republic was theoretically democratic, but the senators, their friends and families held power and made the rent seeking laws, including the tax laws, to benefit themselves. The senatorial order exhibited the notion of supremacy. Ancient Rome, from the Republic through the Empire, operated a tax system that hurt the peasants. Two people attempted to institute fairness and justice in the Roman Republic. Gaius Sempronius Gracchus, a tribune, attempted to relieve the problem of overcrowding and a troubled economy by intensive building programmes that would lessen the power of senatorial nobility. Marcus Tullius Cicero fought to uphold the ideals of the republic. He prosecuted Lucius Sergius Catilina, the main actor in the Catiline conspiracy to seize consular power and control of the government.

The transition from the Republic to the Empire brought gains to the provincial aristocracy who benefited from the increased wealth of the Empire. The privileged, who received their titles usually by inheritance, lived and met in grand buildings and attended games, festivals, gladiatorial combats, all evidence of the prosperity of the wealthy few.[5] Meanwhile, the peasants saw little improvement in their standard of living. The plebeians, the commoners, served the patricians in their homes as household slaves,

---

[4] According to legend, Romulus and Remus originally founded Rome in 753 BC and a succession of seven kings ruled until 309 BC. When the virtuous wife of Lucius Tarquinius Collatinus was raped by the son of the king, Lucius Tarquinius Superbus, the populace overthrew the monarchy. The Rape of Lucretia marks the beginning of the Republic, and the assassination of Julius Caesar marks the end of the Republic and the beginning of the Empire.

[5] The excess spending programmes of the Roman emperors are evident in the writing of Imperator Caesar Augustus, who wrote in *Res Gestae Divi Augusti* ('The Achievements of the Divine Augustus', see any search engine on the Internet such as Google, Yahoo, etc. for *Ancient History Sourcebook*) about the 23 temples he built and the 82 temples he repaired, as well as the bridges and roads he either constructed or repaired. He says, 'I gave gladiatorial shows 3 times in my own name, and 5 times in the names of my sons or grandsons; at these shows about 10 000 fought. Twice I presented to the people in my own name an exhibition of athletes, invited from all parts of the world, and a third time in the name of my grandson. I presented games in my own name 4 times, and in addition 23 times in the place of other magistrates. On behalf of The Quindecimviri Sacris Faciundis ("The Fifteen"), as Master of the College with Marcus Agrippa as my colleague, I celebrated the SECULAR GAMES (May 31 –June 3 [17 BC]). In [2 BC] I was the first to celebrate the Mars Games, which subsequently, by Senatorial Decree and statute, the consuls have regularly celebrated in succeeding years. I provided hunting spectacles of African wild beasts 26 times, in the Circus or in the Forum or in the amphitheaters, in my own name or in the names of my sons or grandsons; in these exhibitions about 3500 animals were killed'.

on stage as actors, and in the arena as sacrificial gladiators. Jones (1974, p. 127) remarks about the tax system: 'While not in general oppressive it could at times hit the humble class of taxpayer hard, and it no doubt forced many to mortgage or sell their land, and thus promoted the concentration of landed property in the hands of the rich.' Personal scandals tainted the reputation of public figures, and poets were sent into exile for lascivious writings.[6] The Empire seemed to be in a state of decay, both moral and economic. Romans subject to the early and late Empire rule of, for example, Nero, Caligula, Lactantius, and Valentinian III were no better off than Romans under the Republican system of senators and elected officials.

Duncan-Jones (1994, pp. 47–63) uses Egypt[7] as a case study of taxation in the Roman Empire. Rome taxed its province, Egypt, as it did all its provinces. One must distinguish between the Early Roman Empire, the Principate (27–305 AD, from Augustus to Diocletian, so named because of the title of *princeps*, meaning leader, that Augustus gave himself) and the Late Roman Empire, the Dominate (305–410 AD, from *dominus* meaning lord or master and used by Diocletian and his successors). There were Roman governors who 'notoriously enriched themselves' in the Principate just as many had done in the Republic.[8] Tax collection in the province of Egypt, which was under imperial Roman control, was inefficient, and tax-debt accumulated with which the emperors and the emperors had to contend. Duncan-Jones (1994, p. 59) demonstrates that 'Hadrian prided himself on writing off more tax-debt than any of his predecessors. Julian at one point suspended the practice, after discovering that it helped the rich, who could postpone payment, but not the poor, who had to pay up promptly.' Duncan-Jones (1994, p. 63) calls the system of collection 'open to abuse', with intermediaries[9] taking too much personal profit and states, 'The long-term drop in revenue in Egypt over a period of centuries may reflect the drain on the taxpayer of the way tax was collected, as well as the tendency for heavy taxes

to drive marginal land out of cultivation'. Jones expresses the same sentiment with his explanation for the *agri deserti*.

IV. The Taxed, the Beneficiaries, the Fallen

Heavy taxation does harm the productiveness of an economy (Wickham, 1994, p. 14), but taxes are necessary to build roads, pay teachers, maintain public buildings and parks, keep a large prepared military, and support the displaced and disabled in society. 'The power to tax is the one great power upon which the whole national fabric is based. It is as necessary to the existence and prosperity of a nation as is the air he breathes to the natural man.' It is not only the power to destroy but also the power to keep alive (Rosen, 1999, p. 253 citing *Nicol v. Ames*, 173 US 509, 515 (1899)). But when emperors and members of the government used rent-seeking tactics to administer the system corruptly, the nation fell.

Lactantius,[10] Aurelius Victor, Themistius, Emperor Valentian III and Procopius all wrote that taxes increased in the late Empire, negatively affecting agricultural productivity (Engels, 1990, p. 192). The emperors and provincial governors did not necessarily use the taxes to build roads, aqueducts, public buildings or any sort of public infrastructure that could increase productivity. Instead, as when the city of Corinth was given the city-state of Argos along with the right to tax the Argives, 'the Corinthians abused their power by levying unlawful taxes on the Argives, in part to fund wild beast hunts in their theaters – a situation that required the intervention of the Emperor Julian in 362' (Engels, 1990, p. 21).

However, Wickham (1994, p. 17) claims that Rome needed the great amount of taxes that it collected to pay the army, much needed against the Germanic invasions in the late fourth century, and for public works. Hopkins (1980, pp. 104–5) shows that rents, as well as taxes, were charged according to the surplus, the amount above subsistence level,

---

[6] The emperor Augustus banished Ovid to Tomis, in modern-day Romania. Ovid gave two reasons for the exile – his book, *Ars Amatoria* (1930) ('The Art of Love'), and a scandal involving the adultery of Augustus' granddaughter, Julia, who was also banished.
[7] Augustus conquered Egypt, the kingdom of Cleopatra, in 30 BC, and subjected it to Roman rule.
[8] 'Extortion by provincial governors and their staffs began early; the first complaint recorded is that of the Spanish provinces in 182 BC'. (Jones, 1974, p. 117).
[9] The tax farmer was an intermediary who collected taxes for a share of the proceeds.
[10] Lactantius (1984: 13), early fourth century Christian teacher of Latin rhetoric, lashed out against Diocletian and other non-Christian emperors. 'He appointed three men to share his rule, dividing the world into four parts and multiplying the armies, since each of the four strove to have a far larger number of troops than previous emperors had had when they were governing the state alone. The number of recipients began to exceed the number of contributors by so much that, with farmers' resources exhausted by the enormous size of requisitions, fields became deserted and cultivated land was turned into forest'.

produced by peasants. The Roman elite (senators and knights) grew wealthier. While the rents and taxes were drawn from the local peasants, this revenue was not spent in their local regions. Taxes and rents were used by the local landowners and provincial elite to establish trade networks.

The decrease in agricultural production brought about by these taxes resulted in a decrease in the quantity of wheat on the market, and higher wheat prices. Rome was experiencing a great inflation when Diocletian became emperor in 284 AD. With his *Edictum de Maximis Pretiis,* Diocletian attempted to stabilize the economy by several reforms. He minted sterling silver coins and fixed their value in relation to the gold standard. He set up the *jugatio-capitatio*[11] tax system. In an attempt to prevent further inflation, he fixed wages and placed price controls on wheat, the price of which had risen two hundred times in a century and a half (Jones, 1974, p. 200). 'In the fourth, fifth and sixth centuries then, it would seem, the increased cost of defense and administration, enhanced by inefficiency and corruption, overstrained the economic resources of the empire' (Jones, 1974, p. 135). The military took an incredible amount of man-hours and money to sustain. Higher military expenditures required higher taxes. The higher taxes levied on land discouraged agricultural production. Malnutrition reduced the number and strength of Roman soldiers. Alaric[12] therefore sacked a vulnerable empire in 410 AD.

V. Similarities to the Modern Tax System

Today, economists and politicians search for a fair or equitable way to tax.

Verri[13] once stated the following: 'A nation may fall into decay through taxation in two ways. In the first case, when the amount of taxes exceeds the powers of the nation and is not proportional to the general wealth. In the second case, when an amount of taxation, proportioned on the whole to the powers of the nation, is viciously distributed'

(cited in Rosen, 1999, p. 308). Historians may use these two adjectives, 'vicious' and 'nonproportional', to describe the Roman system of taxation.

The Roman government of neither the Republic nor the Empire serves as a good basis for a modern government because of the rent-seeking behaviour of the ruling class. Today in US government, lobbyists and legislators act in their own self-interest, not necessarily for the good of all, the public good, much espoused in the Roman writings of Cicero.[14] Cicero attached himself to the ideas behind the Republic. In reality, self-interest overrides the public interest and politicians hold their own agenda. Typically previously wealthy before taking office, they fix the tax system as they see fit. In their introduction to Cicero's speeches against Catiline, Gould and Whiteley (1996, p. ix) make an argument as to why Cicero dedicated his career to trying to save the Republic. Unlike many other Roman senators and officials, Cicero worked his way through the political ranks first as a lawyer, then senator, then provincial governor in Cilicia. Idealistic, he was unable to see the rent-seeking of the ruling class (the senatorial order) and 'its failure to provide a strong and efficient government either in Rome or in the provinces'. The senators were also unable to recognize the danger of the generals and armies, who stretched the boundaries of the Empire by conquering faraway lands. The same generals and armies were plotting to overthrow the government.

The USA uses a mix of income and sales taxes, as well as property taxes that tax wealth. The marginal income tax rate in the USA in 1986 for the top bracket has decreased from 70% to 28% (Rosen, 1999, p. 375). In contrast, the Roman system primarily taxed wealth and had no concept of income tax. Kay writes (1987, p. 849), 'Dependence on personal income tax has been seen to imply excessive rates. The result has been some moves back towards broadly based indirect taxes, particularly the value added tax, which has been introduced throughout the European community and in about thirty other states'. Kay explains the difference between a direct

---

[11] *Jugatio* means 'agricultural land', and *capitatio* means 'rural population'.
[12] Alaric was leader of the Visigoths, a Germanic tribe north of the Danube River, the boundary of the Roman Empire. Alaric had connections with the Roman Empire – he served for a short time as commander of the Gothic troops in the Roman army. Alaric was upset when the Roman senate did not pay him the subsidies promised. He and his army crossed the Danube. Other tribal soldiers in the Roman army joined with Alaric. The western Roman emperors, Honorius and Attalus, could not negotiate with him, so the Visigothic army besieged and occupied Rome, ending the Western Roman Empire.
[13] Pietro Verri (1728–1797) was an eighteenth century Italian political economist and philosopher who developed a theory of taxation, including the notion that taxation affects consumption decisions, that proceeded the modern economic concepts of shifting of taxes and excess burden.
[14] In 80 BC, the dictator Sulla instituted proscriptions, a system by which those with political opinions considered dangerous were put to death with impunity. The triumvirate of Octavian (Augustus), Antony, and Lepidus executed Cicero in 43 BC.

tax and an indirect tax: 'Direct taxes are those for which the legal liability and the incidence are identical: indirect taxes are those where the tax is shifted, most usually to final consumers' (1987, p. 847). Broad-based taxes affect a larger group of people. Other ideas proposed for tax reform include a national sales tax, the value-added tax, and a flat tax. Representative Andrew Jacobs of the US Congress has said, 'If you evade your taxes, you go to the penitentiary. If you want to avoid taxes, you go to the US Congress – and see what they can do for you' (Rosen, 1999, p. 371). Lobbyists with special interests will always take part in the US political process seeking rents.

VI. Summary and Conclusions

Taxes have affected citizens from ancient to modern times. Historians maintain that an increase in taxation of the peasant farmers and government corruption and misuse of its revenue by the ruling class led to a weakening of the Roman Empire that culminated in its western demise in the fifth century. This study shows that it was not just the taxation issue that helped to doom the Roman Empire, but the political change from a Republic to an emperor that exacerbated the climate of rent-seeking behaviour by the ruling classes that culminated in the misallocation of tax resources. One category of rent seeking involves the spending of money that the average taxpayer sees as foolish but which benefits a particular group. The groups who bear the costs can stop the rent seeking if they are informed. The average Roman citizens were peasant farmers, no doubt recognized the costs but were unable to form political coalitions to protect themselves because military control of Roman legions was under the tight control of the emperor. This was not the case under the Republic, which had some degree of democracy. During the period of the emperors, public funds were being diverted from the public infrastructure such as road building and repair, which had employed the citizens and soldiers during periods of unemployment, to more frivolous activities of the emperors and their minions.

The USA, for example, will not collapse under over-taxation because of the many checks and balances in its political structure. Although legislators have followed and always will follow their own agendas, tax laws and the government's budget stay under scrutiny and criticism by the electorate. The US federal tax system is mildly progressive as it levies a higher percentage tax on the citizens with the most income according to the ability to pay theory.

In contrast, the Roman tax system was regressive and operated inefficiently. The government officials practised rent-seeking behaviour and with their tax collectors taxed the peasants and farmers at the same rate as the wealthy and misused the money for their own entertainment. The farmers were taxed off their land, the population decreased, the military weakened, and barbarians from the north sacked Rome.

Acknowledgements

We are indebted to Dr David B. Robinson for his comments and suggestions.

References

Ampofo-Tuffuor, E., DeLorme Jr, C. D. and Kamerschen, D. R. (1991) The nature, and significance, and cost of rent seeking in Ghana, *Kyklos*, 44(4), 537–59.

Ancient History Sourcebook, available at various Internet search engines.

Becker, G. S. and Stigler, G. J. (1974) Law enforcement, malfeasance, and compensation of enforcers, *Journal of Legal Studies*, 3(3), 1–18.

Basurto, L., DeLorme Jr, C. D. and Kamerschen, D. R. (2001) Rent seeking, the Bracero program and current Mexican farm labor policy, *International Economic Journal*, 15(1), 21–40.

Case, K. E. and Fair, R. C. (1999) *Principles of Microeconomics*, 5th edn, Prentice Hall, Upper Saddle River, NJ.

Cicero (1996), in *Catilinam I and II* (Eds) H. E. Gould and J. L. Whiteley, Bristol Classical Press, London.

Colander, D. C. (Ed.) (1984) *Neoclassical Political Economy: The Analysis of Rent Seeking and DVP Activities*, Balinger Publishing, MA.

DeLorme Jr, C. D., Kamerschen, D. R. and Mangel, J. H. (1994) Rent seeking and the byproduct theory of labor movements, *Rivista Internazionale Di Scienze Economiche E Commerciali* (*International Review of Economics and Business*), 41(4), 399–422.

DeLorme Jr, C. D., Redman, D. C. and Kamerschen, D. R. (1992) The first US food stamp program: an example of rent seeking and avoiding, *American Journal of Economics and Sociology*, 51(4), 421–33.

DeLorme Jr, C. D. and Snow, A. (1990) On the limits to rent-seeking waste, *Public Choice*, 67, 129–54.

DeLorme Jr, C. D., Mbaku, J. M. and Kamerschen, D. R. (1986) Rent seeking in the Cameroon economy, *American Journal of Economics and Sociology*, 45(5), 413–24.

Duncan-Jones, R. (1994) *Money and Government in the Roman Empire*, Cambridge University Press, Cambridge.

Ekelund, R., Hébert, R. F., Tollison, R. D. Anderson, G. M. and Davidson, A. B. (1996) *Sacred Trust: The Medieval Church as an Economic Firm*, Oxford University Press, Oxford.

Engels, D. (1990) *Roman Corinth*, University of Chicago Press, Chicago, IL.

Gould, H. E. and Whiteley, J. L. (Eds) (1996) *Catilinam I and II*, Bristol Classical Press, London.

Hopkins, K. (1980) Taxes and trade in the Roman Empire (200 B.C.–A.D. 400), *The Journal of Roman Studies*, **70**, 101–25.

Jones, A. H. M. (1974) *The Roman Economy*, Basil Blackwell, Oxford.

Jones, A. H. M. (1986) *The Later Roman Empire*, Johns Hopkins University Press, Baltimore, MD.

Kay, J. (1987) Direct taxes, in *The New Palgrave, A Dictionary of Economics* (Eds) J. Eatwell, M. Milgate and P. Newman, The Macmillan Press Ltd, London, pp. 847–49.

Klitgaard, R. (1988) *Controlling Corruption*, University of California Press, Berkeley, CA.

Klitgaard, R. (1991) Gifts and bribes, in *Strategy and Choice* (Ed.) R. Zeckhauser, MIT Press, Cambridge, MA.

Lactantius (1984) *De Mortibus Persecutorum* (Ed. and Trans.) J. L. Creed, Clarendon Press, Oxford.

Nicol v. Ames (1989) 173 US 509, 515.

Ovid (1930) *Ars Amatoria*, Parity Press, New York.

Rose-Ackerman, S. (1975) The economics of corruption, *Journal of Public Economics*, **4**, 187–203.

Rose-Ackerman, S. (1998) Corruption, in *New Palgrave Dictionary of Law and Economics* (Ed.) P. Newman, Macmillan Press, London.

Rosen, H. S. (1999) *Public Finance*, 5th edn, Irwin/McGraw-Hill, Boston, MA.

Rowley, C. K., Tollison, R. D. and Tullock, G. (Eds) (1988) *The Political Economy of Rent Seeking*, Kluwer Academic Publishers, Boston, MA.

Tollison, R. D. (1982) Rent seeking: a survey, *Kyklos*, **35**, 575–601.

Tollison, R. D. and Congleton, R. D. (Eds) (1995) *The Economic Analysis of Rent Seeking*, Edward Elgar Publishing Company, Brookfield, Vermont.

Tullock, G. (1984) How to do well while doing good, in *Neoclassical Political Economy: The Analysis of Rent-Seeking and DUP Activities* (Ed.) D. C. Colander, Ballinger Publishing Company, MA, pp. 229–39.

Van Rijckeghem, C. and Wender, B. (1997) Corruption and the rate of temptation: do low wages in the civil service cause corruption?, IMF Working Paper, 73.

Wickham, C. (1994) *Land and Power: Studies in Italian and European Social History 400–1200*, British School at Rome, London.

Part 5

The Firm

Acta Oeconomica, Vol. 25(3–4), pp. 231–246 (1980)

J. KORNAI

"HARD" AND "SOFT" BUDGET CONSTRAINT

Hungarian economic literature in recent years has much discussed the behaviour of enterprises and, in this context, the impacts of economic coercion on the enterprise. This study wishes to contribute to the subject. Its main task is to clarify some notions: what should be meant by "budget constraint", by the "hardness" and "softness" of this constraint.*

Introductory example

The concept of "budget constraint" had been introduced by the theory of household consumption** and then it was taken over by the general equilibrium theory. In this context, "budget" is of general nature and serves to denote the plan for revenues and expenditure of any economic unit: household, enterprise, non-profit institution. It is thus not restricted exclusively to the (fiscal) plan of the central government. For those less familiar with the literature on microeconomics it will be useful to explain this notion with the aid of a highly simplified example and a related figure.

A factory plans a technological reconstruction, for which a definite sum, say 50 million Forints, are available. It may choose at discretion from various degrees of mechanization and automation. In the figure two *isoquant curves* can be seen. Let us consider the lower curve T_1. Each point of the curve represents identical amounts of output: 1000 tonnes annually. This amount can be produced with many combinations of "machine" and "labour": with more labour and fewer machines, and conversely: with less labour and more machines. The parallel T_2 curve above it represents higher annual amounts, 1250 tonnes, T_3 1500 tonnes, etc.

The two straight lines in the figure express two possibilities for spending the budget with two constellations of the price of "labour" and the price of "machines". The straight line with the smaller slope expresses that the firm may buy 7 units of labour for 50 million forints, if it spends nothing on machines, and 3 and a half machines, if it

*A new book by the author [6] has been recently published under the title of "Economics of shortage". The present article takes over *Chapter 13* of the book – with some modifications, sometimes shortening, sometimes complementing the original text. The book itself consists of 22 chapters; the present article thus excerpts a part of the book, the "centre" of a longer line of reasoning. It is unavoidable that the article should leave many questions unanswered, to which the book tries to give an answer.

**As far as I know, it was introduced by the Russian theoretical economist *Slutsky* in his classical study [8] on the household.

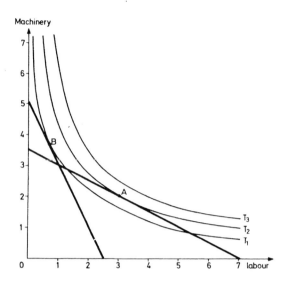

Fig. 1. Choice of the input combination and the budget constraint

spends nothing on labour. And, of course, every linear combination of the two kinds of input can be realized from the same amount. The steeper line presents the state when labour has become expensive relative to machinery. Now, for the same 50 million forints only 2 and a half units of labour can be had, but 5 units of machinery.

However strong the simplifications may be, the figure expresses important relationships. In this model the decision-maker can take into account exclusively those alternatives which do not fall above the actually valid budget line. *Precisely on this account,* he is forced to react on prices directly. If the budget line shifts, he too *must* shift the point representing the decision.

Anyone acquainted in another context with mathematical programming (e.g. applied a programming model to drawing up an investment or production plan of a firm), obviously recognizes that our figure presents a simple two-variable decision problem. The budget constraint delimits the set of feasible decisions. The question we want to examine is: under what circumstances is the constraint *effective,* that is, when does it really influence the enterprise's behaviour, and under what conditions does it become ineffective.

Relationship between the financial balance and the budget constraint

Let us come nearer from the schematic example to economic reality. It will help clarification of the notions if, for the moment, we leave it open whether we have to deal with a capitalist or a socialist enterprise. In a later part of the article *the historical realization* of the categories to be clarified now will be reviewed in socio-economic systems of different periods.

Everyone knows *the financial balance of the firm.* In its most comprehensive and general form it gives the following relationship as a summary reflection of financial processes in a period:

Terminal stock of money − terminal stock of debts ≡

$\equiv$ initial stock of money − initial stock of debts +

$+$ credits raised during the period +

$+$ other receipts during the period −

$-$ credits repaid during the period −

$-$ other outlays emerging during the period.

The left-hand and the right-hand sides of the balance are linked by the sign of identity. This identity of the two sides always holds tautologically. *This* balance cannot be "infringed upon". Even if the enterprise simply does not pay for the commodity delivered, the balance-identity remains: an item of the credits raised during the year will be the credit forced upon the supplier, forcibly extorted by our firm. This is why we say that the financial balance sheet, the *ex post* accounting of monetary sources and their uses is an *"accounting" identity.*

The financial balance may be also written in the form of inequality. All uses may be taken to the left-hand side and all sources to the right-hand side and it may be stated that uses must not exceed sources. This is again an upper constraint of tautological nature, which is necessarily observed.

In the budget constraint the same items appear as in the financial balance, and in the constraint derived from it: uses must not exceed sources. But the budget constraint is not an *ex post,* but an *ex ante* category. It is not an "accounting" identity, but a *behavioural regularity.* More exactly: it is a summary expression of a whole series of partial rules which jointly restrict the behaviour of the firm. For understanding it, we must break it down into its components.

Hard budget constraint: the pure case

First we examine the *pure* case of a hard budget constraint. We shall indicate five conditions the fulfilment of which guarantees hardness of the constraint. A theoretical construction is presented; one or another of the five conditions is never perfectly satisfied in reality. This will be explained later.

The five conditions together are *sufficient* to guarantee *perfect* hardness of the constraint. We do not claim that only this set of conditions guarantees it. However, these five conditions provide a good starting-point for further steps in our reasoning. To facilitate subsequent comparisons we shall add the letter H (hard) to the serial numbers of the conditions.

Condition 1-H. Exogenous prices. Purchase prices for inputs and selling prices for outputs are given for the firm. The firm is a *price-taker* and not a price-maker. From this point of view it does not matter who determines the price: an atomized market process that cannot be influenced by a single buyer or seller; a seller more powerful than our firm in fixing the purchase price, or a buyer more powerful in fixing the selling price; or a state authority. It may be anybody; the main point remains that our firm is unable to influence the price.

Condition 2-H. The tax system is hard. This does not mean that taxes are high, but that the following principles are strictly observed:

a) The formulation of tax rules (laws, regulations) cannot be influenced by our firm; they are given exogenously for it.

b) The tax system links taxes to various objectively observable and measurable criteria.

c) The firm cannot receive any individual exceptional exemption.

d) The tax imposed is collected unconditionally on the prescribed terms.

Condition 3-H. No free state grants. The state does not give any grants to cover current expenses, nor make any free contributions to investment.

Condition 4-H. No credit. All inputs purchased must be paid for exclusively in cash. Interfirm credit cannot be taken up either by agreement with the seller, or by breaking the contract, failing to make payments and thus forcing the creditor's role upon him. Nor can credit be obtained from any other source.

Condition 5-H. No external financial investment. Our argument does not cover the foundation of the firm, that is, the question of how the initial financial investment in the firm was made. We consider only existing firms. Condition 5 says: the owners can draw profit from the firm. Yet if they do so, they cannot re-invest it in the firm.*

Conditions 1-H, . . . ,5-H set *ex ante* behavioural constraints on the items in the financial balance of the firm. If these constraints are strictly observed, then the budget constraint summing up their effects indeed restricts the freedom of choice of the firm, that is, it becomes a true constraint on *behaviour.*

Let us now examine the implications of these five conditions in detail.

How does hardness of the budget constraint manifest itself? (We shall again add the letter H to the serial numbers.)

Consequence (i-H): Survival. The firm's survival depends exclusively on the proceeds from sales and on the costs of inputs. If, for a short time the latter is greater than the former, the owners can avail themselves of the money stock to cover the loss, and can renounce the withdrawal of profit. But, if they have fully renounced the withdrawal of profit and used up the money stock and the loss is still not eliminated, they are compelled to reduce expenditures. Fewer inputs lead to less output, proceeds will decrease, and

---

*Conditions 4-H and 5-H give *abstract conditions* which can be interpreted only for a stationary economy, that is for simple reproduction. It is necessary to state them in order to define the *pure* case of hard budget constraint. We shall return later to the problem.

finally the firm becomes insolvent and goes bankrupt. *The hard budget constraint is a form of economic coercion: proceeds from sales and cost of input are a question of life and death for the firm.*

Consequence (ii-H): Growth. Technical progress and growth of the firm, which require investment, depend on the same factors. *Financial resources to purchase additional inputs necessary for expansion of the firm are created exclusively by internal accumulation within the firm.*

Consequence (iii-H): Adjustment to prices. Prices being given exogenously, *the firm must adjust to prices.* Adjustment must be performed basically by *real* actions, first of all by increasing or reducing the level of production, or by modification of the input-output combination. These changes are internal to the producing plant and are, therefore, not directly linked to prices. Indirectly, however, they are all the more closely connected to them, by purchases of input which permit modifications in production, as well as by sales of output which are made possible by modifications in production.

The firm may be helped in its adjustment by two *internal* financial variables: it may use its money stock and it may reduce or suspend the withdrawal of profit. The money stock, however, may be exhausted, and withdrawals of profit can only be reduced to zero. The firm cannot maneuver by using *external* financial resources. Finally, therefore, no other means is left than to adjust through *real* actions.

Under such circumstances price is not merely a "signal" which the firm observes in controlling real actions if it feels like it, but need not observe if it does not feel like it. It *has to* observe it because otherwise it will be incapable of development or expansion, and might even go bankrupt.

At this point we can entirely ignore the properties of prices. "Optimal" prices or "nonoptimal" ones, "equilibrium" prices or "nonequilibrium" ones—it is all the same from the point of view of *hardness* of the budget constraint. It matters only that prices do not depend on the firm and that in the case of a hard constraint the firm has to adjust to them. This was expressed in the figure by the shift of the decision from point A to point B under the impact of changes in price.

Consequence (iv-H): Uncertainty. The firm does not share its risks. It bears the consequences of external circumstances as well as of its own actions.

Since prices are exogenous, they may bring disaster or good luck for the firm. In either case it will be the firm's own bad or good luck. If it is bad luck, nobody will help it to get out of it; if it is good luck, nobody will skim off the result.

Consequence (v-H): Demand of the firm. The consequences enumerated above together imply that the firm's *demand for inputs is finite.* It depends closely on the purchase price of inputs and on the current and expected income of the firm, on its sales receipts. (In the figure the finite nature of demand was expressed by the fact that only points on or below the budget line were attainable. The firm can buy only as much "machinery" and "labour" as is allowed by its budget constraint.)

Almost-hard budget constraints

In every actual economic system there are several phenomena at work which shift the budget constraint away from the pure case of perfect hardness as described above. We shall examine below under what conditions the budget constraint should be at least *almost-hard*. The expression "almost-hard" indicates that although the constraint is not so hard as in the theoretically pure case, it is approximately hard. This will be indicated by the *consequences*. A budget constraint is almost hard if it causes the consequences (i-H/–/v-H) of the preceding section. Again we shall be content to give a set of *sufficient* conditions; there may be other sets of conditions able to cause consequences (i-H/–/v-H). (The letters AH following the serial numbers of the conditions indicate the qualification "almost hard".)

Condition I-AH: Price-making within narrow limits. Some of the firms are price-makers for some inputs and outputs. However, in deciding on prices they are constrained by the resistance of their trading partners and, finally, by the level of total demand.

Conditions 2-AH and 3-AH: No state redistribution among firms. Here conditions (2-H) and (3-H) of the pure case must fully stand. The state cannot redistribute the financial receipts of fims either by differentiating taxes and other methods of skimming off profits, or by subsidies and other grants.*

Condition 4-AH: Credit on hard conditions. This does not mean that the creditor demands high interest, but that certain *principles*–which are "orthodox" and "conservative" – are employed in granting credit:

The creditor (bank, etc.) grants credit to a firm only if it is creditworthy, i.e. it is fully guaranteed that the firm is able to repay it from the proceeds of its sales of output. That is, credit is an "advance payment".

If the firm has taken a loan, it must always fulfill every obligation in the credit agreement: instalments must be paid on time, and interest must be added according to the agreement. The adherence to credit agreements is enforced with the full rigour of the law.

The buyer cannot force the seller to grant credit by failing to pay immediately – without preliminary agreement – for the goods delivered.

Condition 5-AH: External financial investment on hard conditions. The internal financial resources of the firm can be supplemented by monetary investment by the owners. This may finance only technical progress and expansion of the firm and must be reimbursed from increased proceeds. No external financial resource can be used to surmount short-run financial difficulties.

We wish to avoid repetition. Reconsideration of what we said in the preceding section can convince the reader that consequences (i-H/–/v-H) listed there will occur in

---

*This condition only excludes redistribution of money incomes *among firms.* This is compatible with state redistribution of incomes among various groups of the population: with high taxes levied on some groups and with monetary supports given to other groups.

this case too. It must be added, however, that they cannot be guaranteed as strictly as in the theoretically pure case. It is true that conditions 2–3 have not changed: the possibility of state redistribution is still excluded. Yet even so difficulties may arise with conditions 1, 4, and 5. They deal with phenomena about which a simple "yes or no" statement cannot be made. We cannot say, for example that credit is given either on hard or on soft conditions. There are many intermediate degrees possible. The situation is the same with price-making or price-taking, as well as with the hardness or softness of external financing conditions.

Soft budget constraint: the pure case

Intermediate cases will be discussed later. At this point, however, we shall omit them and discuss the other extreme.

When can we say that the budget constraint has become totally soft, that is it does not bind *ex ante* the freedom of choice of the firm? We shall go over the five conditions discussed above. (This time we shall put a letter S after the serial number.) In fact, a single condition – or perhaps even a single part of a condition – is sufficient to render the constraint soft, though usually several conditions apply simultaneously.

Condition 1-S: Price-making. The majority of firms are not price-takers but price-makers. Price is not exogenous for most firms.

Theoretically this could be the case on both sides of the market: in input prices as well as in output prices. In practice, however, it is usually the latter which soften the budget constraint. The firm is able to impose its own cost increases on the buyer. This may be because, in the case of free contract price, it is the seller who is stronger than the buyer. (For example, it is a large monopolistic seller faced with many scattered buyers. Or, there may be chronic shortage, and he can dictate the price for this reason.) Or it can influence the price because, although it is formally determined by an administrative price authority, the firm has a large influence on the authority's decision.

Continuous imposition of all costs on the buyer is made possible ultimately by the fact that total demand in money terms is not strictly limited but adjusts more or less passively to the rising level of costs.

Condition 2-S: The tax system is soft. A few of its characteristic manifestations are these:

a) the formulation of tax rules is influenced by the firm;

b) the firm may be granted exemption or postponement as an individual favour; and

c) taxes are not collected strictly.

Condition 3-S: Free state grants. The firm can get these in various forms:

a) contributions to investment expenditures, without repayment obligations;

b) permanent subsidies paid continuously in compensation for a lasting loss or to encourage some activity over a long period; and

c) *ad hoc* nonrecurrent subsidies to counterbalance an occasional loss or to encourage a special activity.

Acta Oeconomica 25, 1980

Condition 4-S: The credit system is soft. It does not follow "orthodox" and "conservative" principles.

The firm is granted credit even if there is no full guarantee of its ability to repay it on schedule from its proceeds from sales. Credit is not strictly an "advance payment"; its granting is not closely related to expected production and sales.

The firm is permitted to fail to fulfill its repayment obligations undertaken in the credit agreement. Moreover, the firm, in the role of buyer of inputs, is allowed arbitrarily to postpone payment without previous agreement with the seller.

Condition 5-S: External financial investment on soft conditions. In the case of a firm in state ownership this cannot be distinguished from condition 3-S, free state grants. Phenomena of this kind may also be observed with private enterprise: owners invest money from their own resources in the firm — not in order to develop and enlarge it but to help it out of its financial difficulties.*

We can now contrast the signs accompanying phenomena and direct consequences of a soft budget constraint with those of a hard one.

Consequence (i-S): Survival. Survival of the firm does not depend only on whether it is able permanently to cover the costs of its purchases of inputs from the proceeds of its sales. Even if the former permanently exceed the latter, that may be counterbalanced by tax exemptions, state subsidies, soft credit, etc. The difference between the proceeds from production and the costs of production is *not a question of life and death.*

Consequence (ii-S): Growth. Technical progress and growth of the firm do not depend solely on whether it is able to raise the financial resources for investment from *internal* financial accumulation (whether from its money stock, i.e. from savings from previous profit, or from hard investment loans which have to be repaid later from its own receipts.) The financial resources needed to buy additional inputs for development and expansion may be provided by the state in the form of free subsidies or soft investment credits.

Consequence (iii-S): Adjustment to prices. The firm is not compelled to adjust to prices under all circumstances, for two reasons.

Either the budget constraint has softened as a consequence of above-mentioned condition 1-S. The firm is not a price-taker but a price-maker. For example, let us take the case when it is able to influence the selling price of its own product. It need not take much notice of the relative prices of inputs. However much they change, it will be able to adjust the selling price of its own products to cover cost increases.

Even if this method does not operate and the firm is a price-taker, it still does not have to adjust to prices by altering its input-output combination. Even if it disregards prices and suffers losses as a consequence, these may be compensated for by remission of tax, state subsidy, postponement of credit repayment, extra credit granted under soft conditions, and so on.

---

*For example, a family enterprise in difficulties which the owners try to refloat at the cost of their personal wealth. This is, of course, limited by the size of that wealth.

Survival and growth of the firm do not depend on prices. The firm takes note of prices if it feels like it and does not take note of them if it does not feel like it. In the latter case it can still survive and even expand.

The firm may react to changes in prices in its *real actions,* namely, by a suitable change of its input-output combination. This changes the real quantity of inputs purchased as well as the real quantity of sales, and thereby affects the firm's financial situation. Yet the firm may also react in another way. It may try to influence purchase and sales prices, as well as the *financial variables* (tax, state subsidies, credit terms, etc.).

In the first case the firm reacts in the real sphere, in the second case in the control sphere. In the first case it acts in the *factory,* in the second case in the *offices* of the ministry, the tax authority, or the bank. In the first case the main element in the reaction is *production*; the adjustment of the input and output combination to the new situation. In the second case the main elements are: requests, complaints, and bargaining—in other words, attempts to *manipulate* all those on whom tax remissions, subsidies, soft credit, and so on, depend.

Softening of the budget constraint does not exclude the first reaction, but it does not enforce it either. At the same time it offers large scope for — and even temptations to — the second kind of reaction.

Consequence (iv-S): Uncertainty. The firm does not bear risk alone, but shares it with the state. If circumstances develop favourably, it cannot be sure that it can keep the additional profit: probably it will be skimmed off. However, if it has bad luck, or cannot adjust itself adequately to conditions, it will probably be able to shift the consequences onto somebody else: onto the buyer by a price increase; onto the creditors; and primarily onto the state.

The financial situation of the firm and its budget-constraint suffer from a double uncertainty. One is the kind of uncertainty that is present for every firm (also that with a hard budget constraint): prices and markets are uncertain. In addition, uncertainty is also caused by the continuous redistribution of the financial receipts of firms. The firm cannot foresee exactly how much the state will take away from it, or how much it will give.

Consequence (v-S): Demand of the firm. As a result of the consequences enumerated above the *demand of the firm for inputs is almost-insatiable.* It does not depend either on the purchasing price of inputs, or on current and expected income of the firm. Sooner or later it can expect to be able to cover its costs on inputs; and, if its proceeds from sales of outputs are not enough, it will be able to cover costs from an external financial source.

After all, a soft budget constraint does not bind the firm in its action in the real sphere, namely production and trade. *The soft budget constraint — as opposed to the hard one — is unable to act as an effective behavioural constraint, but exists only as an accounting relationship.*

Let us have a glance again at the figure. In the case of a hard constraint, the budget line is impenetrable, as if it were of stone, while in the case of soft constraint, it can be easily expanded, as if it were of rubber. Therefore, it does not determine the place of points A or B. The decision-maker forms the input-output combination *not* by adjusting to prices.

Elementary events and general behaviour

In previous sections we have considered the factors that harden or soften the firm's budget constraint. These factors influence the life of the firm at the submicro-level, through millions of elementary events. Objective events take place which are subjectively *perceived* by decision-makers in the firm. The latter are affected not only by their own experience, but also by their observation of other firms. Finally, all these experiences form *expectations*. The hardness or softness of the budget constraint reflects what the manager of the firm expects for the future. The more he expects that the existence and growth of the firm will depend *solely* on production costs and on proceeds from sales, the more he will respect the budget constraint, and therefore the harder that constraint will be. And the less he expects this to be so, the less seriously he takes the constraint, the softer it will become.

It follows – as we noted earlier – that the constraint need not assume one of only two different values: *either* hard *or* soft. There are also intermediate stages, for two reasons. First, one or other decision-maker may himself expect an intermediate value. Secondly, within the same system the expectations of different decision-makers may vary; some expect a harder budget constraint, others a softer one.

There are, however, tendencies that lead toward uniform and extreme expectations. If an event occurs frequently enough which gives the impression of a soft budget constraint, and if its frequency goes beyond some critical value, a "public opinion" will develop that regards the constraint as soft.

The degree of hardness of the budget constraint is *observable and measurable*. Since it is a very complex group of phenomena, it cannot be described by a single cardinal indicator. It can only be measured ordinally, by several indicators together.

By making observations over a longer perod the *normal degree* of hardness of the firm's budget constraint within the system can be established for given social conditions.

Observations about capitalist and socialist economies

Up to this point in the present study we have discussed the budget constraint on an abstract level. We wished to elaborate the *analytical tools* (concepts, relations of cause and effect, principles of observation and measurement, etc.), for the examination of historically materialized specific systems. Now, in possession of the analytical tools, we shall begin to tackle this task.

First of all we shall make a few remarks about the hardness of the firm's budget constraint in a *capitalist economy*. Differences between countries are considerable. Nevertheless, looking back over a long period a common trend is evident.

The normal degree of hardness of the constraint seems to have shifted: *the trend is in the direction of softening*. Perfect hardness in its absolute purity may never have existed, even though the capitalist system came close to this abstract extreme point in the then leading countries in the nineteenth century. Bankruptcy was real bankruptcy; the firm that failed was not helped out by anyone but crushed ruthlessly by more successful competitors. The receiver selling up the bankrupt businessman's personal belongings and the debtor's prison were symbols of the hard system of taxation and credit. With a few exceptions (the railways, shipping, insurance, a few big companies engaged in colonial trade) firms were not big; prices were in fact formed mainly by anonymous market processes and were thus given exogenously for the firm.

Significant changes have taken place since the initial period of classical capitalism, and these move the budget constraint away from the point of "perfect hardness". Although they are well-known, we shall briefly review them.

The economy is becoming highly concentrated; huge corporations are being founded. They are no longer price-takers, but price-makers. This is one of the basic factors from the point of view of softening the budget constraint. A large capitalist corporation is able to react to input price changes not by adopting its input-output combination, but by adjusting output price to actual costs plus the expected mark-up. By its price-making power it can almost "automatically" guarantee its survival, its self-perpetuation.

Historical experience draws the attention of society towards employment, and not only the attention of workers directly suffering from unemployment but also the attention of capitalists and other strata of society. Bankruptcy is not solely a problem for the capitalist owner, since it always affects employment. Workers in the shut-down factory are dismissed. What is more, modern economics has shown that there are multiplier and accelerator effects; every bankruptcy reduces aggregate demand, thereby endangering employment at other places as well. It is not only the owners who are involved, but trade unions as well, and almost the whole society presses the state to save the threatened firm: it should be given a tax allowance, subsidy, and credit with governmental guarantees. Rescue action sometimes takes the form of nationalization.

Protectionist state intervention is growing in numerous fields. The state protects domestic companies left behind in international competition, if their performance either in exporting or in import substitution is weak. For various socio-political reasons it subsidizes unprofitable products and services.

The growth of a firm depends not only on its success in atomistic markets but also on its power: the pressure it can put on its business partners, the connections it has with banks and, last but not least, the extent to which it can influence state decisions, taxes, subsidies, and government orders.

Principles of credit are softened: in the Keynesian spirit they deviate from "conservative" and "orthodox" principles. A budgetary deficit is deemed to be permissible and even desirable in certain conditions.

We repeat that all the above-mentioned phenomena are well known from Marxist literature* as well as from works of non-Marxist economists.** Here we have collected them according to a single criterion: we wished to point out that these processes all contribute to the softening of the capitalist firm's budget constraint. Today's capitalist firm does not react to circumstances merely through *real* actions. The bigger and more powerful the firm, the better our observation applies. The firm can influence its life in numerous other ways: from price-making to "lobbying" the authorities.

As regards the degree of hardness of the budget constraint of the capitalist firm, no general proposition can be made. The normal degree of hardness is different in each country, depending on the level of concentration, on the economic activity of the state, and on other social factors. It also varies within one country; it is different for the powerful and the weak firm. There is a sphere in which it could be said that the budget constraint is still "almost-hard", and other spheres where it is „not very hard" or "rather soft" — although nowhere under capitalist conditions has the budget constraint reached full softness, with an automatic guarantee of the firm's survival.

It is not the task of the present article to analyse in more detail the position of the capitalist economy. We have gone into the question this far mainly to avoid distorted comparison. We may compare theoretical cases: the "pure hard" and the "pure soft" budget, as defined at an abstract level. Or we may compare one *real* system with another *real* system. And in this case we must compare the empirically observable behaviour of the modern capitalist firm with what we can also observe empirically about the socialist firm. In respect of the latter our main hypotheses are as follows:

1. *In the traditional socialist economy* (prior to the reform of economic control and management) *the budget constraint of the firm is soft.*

2. *A partially decentralizing reform like the 1968 Hungarian reform shifted the normal degree of hardness of the firm's budget constraint — but only a little. The constraint remained basically rather soft.****

---

*The historical importance of the concentration of capital was first stressed by *Marx,* and later it played an important role in the thought of *Hilferding, Lenin,* and *Luxemburg.*

**The price-making role played by the big firm was first stressed in the literature of imperfect competition; starting-points were works by *Robinson* and *Chamberlin.* The work of *Galbraith* on the relation between the contemporary capitalist corporation and the state raised great interest.

The theoretical starting point for active government economic policy pursued in the interest of full employment is Keynes' activity; related pro- and anti-Keynesian literature is plentiful. The neo-liberal school must be mentioned especially: *Hayek, Friedmann* and their followers who, while feeling nostalgic about the classical free market period, point out sharply several aspects of the softening budget constraint.

***This hypothesis is indirectly supported by the following comparison. First I quote from an article on Japan in an American weekly ". . . the combination of slow economic growth, competition from abroad and the rapid appreciation of the yen has proved fatal to many companies . . . Last year, a record 18,000 companies went bankrupt . . . the transformation may be painful . . ." (*Nagorski* [7]). On the contrary, in Hungary, following the price explosion perhaps one or two firms were subjected to a procedure of financial rehabilitation.

J. KORNAI: "HARD" AND "SOFT" BUDGET CONSTRAINT   243

3. *The budget constraint is not uniformly soft for every firm. It is relatively softer in the preferred industries and for the biggest companies.*

It is not mere chance that I have called the above ideas "hypotheses" and not "statements". True, they are verified by hundred kinds of experience; also many articles were published in the Hungarian economic literature which support them by facts.* Nevertheless, further comprehensive empirical investigations are needed in order that the hypotheses might be considered fully proven.**

The validity of hypothesis (2) was confined to the end of 1979, leaving open the question of the hardness of the budget constraint beginning with 1980. It is known that one of the basic ideas justifying the introduction of the control system of 1980 was to "harden" the financial and credit system, to strengthen the economic pressure on the firm. It would be too early to make any statement on the extent to which this has been realized. The normal degree of hardness or softness of the budget constraint cannot change from one month to the next. As we have emphasized, this is a rule of behaviour and human behaviour is shaped by much experience, long observation and "ingrained habit". Economic executives will have to experience repeatedly themselves or observe what is happening to their colleagues in order to understand that loss is a serious matter, that transgression of the budget constraint is impossible and that the life and death of the firm, its growth, depend on the financial position — until the recognition becomes deeply ingrained in their consciousness and governs their decisions almost unconsciously, as a "conditional reflex". Therefore, an opinion about the impact of the 1980 control system can be formulated in this respect after 2—3 or 5 years.

Budget constraint and profit-motive

Having reached the end of my article, it may be stated that much more questions have remained open than I have succeeded to answer. We have torn out merely a single link from the chain of causes and consequences. At this place we could not discuss at length what factors do really explain the normal degree of hardness or softness of the budget constraint, and the direction of a possible change: whether it tends towards hardening or softening. And, on the other side, we have not shown all possible consequences of the soft (or rather soft) budget constraint: how it affects the adaptability of the firm, its demand and supply, the equilibrium of the national economy, the emergence of shortage, etc.

*We should like to stress from among them the following ones: Csanádi Demeter, M. [1], Deák, A. ed. [2] Deák, A. [3], Faluvégi, L. [4] Fenyővári, I. [5], Szabó, B. [9] Tallós, Gy. [10] and Vincze, I. [15].

**The author — together with some colleagues from the State Development Bank: A. Deák, A. Ferge, K. Sztahó and M. Simek — is now processing the financial balances of state enterprises in recent years in order to draw some conclusions regarding the phenomena discussed in the present article. An attempt will be made to measure the hardness and softness of the budget constraint.

244   J. KORNAI: "HARD" AND "SOFT" BUDGET CONSTRAINT

Instead of digressing to all these problems at this place, I shall confine myself to a single remark. Those well versed in the literature on reforms of economic control systems will have noticed that we touched on several problems amply discussed in that literature. Yet the focus of the reform dispute in this connection was "profit-incentive", whereas in this article the focus is on "softness of the budget constraint". This would not be worth mentioning if it were just a terminological difference. In that case this article might be blamed for changing terminology unnecessarily.

Yet the issue here is not merely a change of words, but differences in the logic of the argument and in the order of importance of the explanatory factors. The fact that the owners, managers, and workers of a firm are interested in increasing profits does not in itself determine their behavior. When profit incentives are combined with a hard budget constraint, efforts are directed towards the line of real actions. Combining profit incentives with a soft budget constraint gives at least an equal role to the manipulation of financial variables, price increases, running after state donations, etc.

The crucial question affecting the situation of the socialist firm is not whether the managing director's personal share in the profit amounts to zero, 10, or 50 per cent of his basic salary. Nor is it crucial by what formula profit shares are distributed among workers, or how welfare funds or tax paid on profit are linked to profit. All this is important, but *not primarily* important. In the case of a hard budget constraint the managing director would not be indifferent to profit even if his personal share were zero in the short run — since he has identified himself with the survival and expansion of the firm. We do not seek to change the terminology, but to draw attention to the fact that the main question — both theoretically, and in practical economic policy — is not the actual form of incentive, but the rules for the survival and growth of the firm and, linked to these phenomena, the relation between firm and state.

References

1. CSANÁDINÉ DEMETER, M.: *A vállalatnagyság, a jövedelmezőség és a preferenciák néhány összefüggése* (Some interrelations between the size of the firm, profitability and preferences.) Pénzügyi Szemle, 1979. No. 2, pp. 105–120
2. DEÁK, A. (ed.): *Pénzügyi megkülönböztetések rendszere* (The system of financial distinctions.) Budapest, 1972. Ministry of Finance. Mimeo.
3. DEÁK, A.: *Állami pénzügyi befolyásolás, preferenciák és diszpreferenciák* (Government influencing, preferences and dispreferences through fiscal measures.) Budapest, 1972. Ministry of Finance. Mimeo.
4. FALUVÉGI, L.: *Állami pénzügyek és gazdaságirányítás* (State finances and economic control.) Budapest, 1977. Közgazdasági és Jogi Könyvkiadó.
5. FENYŐVÁRI, I.: *The role of profit in the Hungarian economy.* Acta Oeconomica, (1979) Vol. 22, Nos 1–2
6. KORNAI, J.: *Economics of shortage.* Amsterdam, 1980. North-Holland Publishing Co. Vol. 1–2
7. NAGORSKI, A.: *Japan vs. the world.* Newsweek, 17 July, 1978. pp. 8–12
8. SLUTSKY, E. E.: *On the theory of the budget of the consumer.* Giornale degli Economisti, 1915. pp. 1–26

J. KORNAI: "HARD" AND "SOFT" BUDGET CONSTRAINT   245

9. SZABÓ, B.: *Vállalati adóztatás, nyereségelvonás* (Enterprise taxation, the withdrawal of profit.) Valóság, 1977, No. 8, pp. 91–95

10. TALLÓS, GY.: *A bankhitel szerepe gazdaságirányítási rendszerünkben* (The role of bank credit in the Hungarian system of economic control.) Budapest, 1976. Kossuth Könyvkiadó.

11. VINCZE, I.: *Árak, adók, támogatások a gazdaságirányítás reformja után* (Prices, taxes and subsidies after the reform of economic control and management.) Budapest, 1971. Közgazdasági és Jogi Könyvkiadó.

«ЖЕСТКИЕ» И «МЯГКИЕ» БЮДЖЕТНЫЕ ОГРАНИЧЕНИЯ

Я. КОРНАИ

Выражение «бюджетное ограничение» вошло в обиход в микроэкономике. Под этим понимается обусловленность поведения, отражающая то, что хозяйственная единица (домашнее хозяйство, предприятие, учреждение) при планировании своих расходов не может превысить имеющихся в ее распоряжении финансовых ресурсов. Статья посвящена поведению предприятий. Сначала в теоретическом плане уясняется, когда ограничение является «жестким» и когда «мягким», то есть когда оно эффективно ограничивает свободу действий предприятия и когда практически не оказывает воздействия. Для последнего достаточно, чтобы имело место хотя бы одно из следующих условий: предприятие решающим образом определяет цены сбыта своей продукции; получает даровые государственные субсидии; система налогообложения и кредитования «мягка» и т. д. Наиболее характерные последствия «мягких» бюджетных ограничений: выживание предприятия гарантируется автоматически, его рост весьма мало зависит от его финансового положения, оно не реагирует чутко на цену затрат, его текущие расходы и спрос на капитальные ресурсы могут оторваться от его собственной выручки от реализации.

Затем в статье дается анализ степени жесткости — мягкости бюджетных ограничений в условиях различных исторически сложившихся экономических систем. В заключение рассматривается связь заинтересованности в прибылях и бюджетных ограничений.

Oxford Economic Papers 39 (1987), 813–820

WORKERS AS INSURANCE: ANTICIPATED GOVERNMENT ASSISTANCE AND FACTOR DEMAND

By ARYE L. HILLMAN, ELIAKIM KATZ *and* JACOB ROSENBERG

I. Introduction

GOVERNMENTS are often subject to political pressure to protect "jobs" which are threatened by import penetration of domestic markets. The pressure for intervention is increased when the industry is geographically concentrated; then the pro-protection coalition comprises not only firms and workers in the industry directly impacted, but also the interests standing to lose from regional decline. Typical of the political response to such pressure is the pronouncement of a senior cabinet minister in Israel that "the government would not stand idly by and preside over pockets of unemployment in development towns". These towns are often specialized in production, and hence local employment is sensitive to price movements in one good. In the above instance, the reference was to the impending closure of the Ata textile plant in the northern Israeli town of Kiryat Ata. The plant had benefitted from government assistance in the past. Threat of closure led to considerable pressure for further assistance, or a direct government buyout. There were also proposals that the government pay for private interests to take over the running of the plant. After considerable public debate and prolonged demonstrations by workers whose jobs were threatened, the government decided against intervention, and the plant closed down. However, at various times during the Ata "crisis", it appeared that the government might succumb to the political pressure to intervene to forestall unemployment in the development town.

The phenomenon of such political pressure to preempt localized unemployment appears quite common. In the U.S., a recent protectionist bill, which was passed by Congress in 1985 and then subsequently narrowly failed to find sufficient support to override a presidential veto, was argued by its proponents to be justified because of the loss of domestic jobs in the geographically concentrated shoe and textile industries. Speaking before the vote on the presidential-veto override, a representative from Maine pointed out that 32 shoe factories had closed and 6,200 jobs had been lost in her state during the previous year. In the case of textiles, workers whose jobs the bill sought to protect tended to be women, who it was argued were concentrated in rural areas, and who, because of family obligations, lacked geographical mobility.

A further example, from the U.K., of public opinion in an impacted region favoring assistance to local industry is provided by Robert Dore

We are grateful to an anonymous referee of this journal for helpful comments.

(1982) who reports that "we have not met a single person in Lancashire who does not think that it is wicked of the government of Britain and the European Community to deny textile firms protection and so force them into closure. Everyone concerned will always lobby for protection rather than face closure."

However, despite political pressures, as the above instances indicate, protection is not a certain outcome. Governments are responsive to countervailing domestic interests which would lose from protection (see Baldwin, 1982; Hillman, 1982; Findlay and Wellisz, 1982; Becker, 1983; Godek, 1985) and are also sensitive to the possibility of foreign retaliation. The expected profits of a firm producing an import-competing good therefore encompass contingencies that, in the event of threatened trade-related unemployment of its workers, the government will intervene and that it will not.[1] Past policy responses may suggest to the firm that the government's susceptibility to intervene increases with the scope of threatened unemployment. In that case workers take on an insurance function for the firm[2] and uncertainty concerning a government bail-out (or a protectionist response) becomes endogenous to the firm via its factor-input decisions. In this paper we investigate the effects of such endogenous uncertainty on a firm's factor-input choices.

Section 2 introduces a risk-neutral firm which confronts a contractually specified nominal wage and is the prominent employer of labor in its region. The firm produces a traded good, the price of which is variable. The possibility of a protectionist response[3] is internalized in the firm's perceiving unemployment to be politically disadvantageous to the government. The likelihood of intervention to "protect jobs" is subjectively perceived as increasing with the number of workers whose jobs are threatened. Factor-input decisions under these circumstances are described in Section 3, and

[1] For example, uncertainty regarding intervention may derive from lack of foreknowledge as to whether industry decline will be accepted as due primarily to import competition, or will be attributed to other causes; see Grossman's study (1986) of the cause of injury to the U.S. steel industry. Also, intervention if forthcoming need not take the form of protection but may entail programs of adjustment assistance for displaced workers. See Cassing (1980), Richardson (1982). Firms and their employees whose jobs are threatened would appear to have reason to prefer a protectionist response to adjustment assistance. Wallerstein (1987) stresses the special interests of trade unions in lobbying for protection in times of unemployment. Protection preempts losses for the firm's residual claimants, and employees may confront uncompensated costs of adjustment. Regional unemployment may lead to a decline in the value of all regional-specific assets, and adjustment assistance may hasten regional decline by encouraging exit from the region. For a regionally-based view of protectionist interests, see Cassing, McKeown and Ochs, (1986).

[2] The firm is assumed to have no opportunity to transact in insurance markets which provide coverage against adverse realizations of the price of the output. For other perspectives on insurance, incomplete markets and trade policy, see Eaton and Grossman (1985), Cassing, Hillman and Long (1986), Falvey and Lloyd (1986).

[3] The protectionist response may take any one of a number of forms, such as subsidization of the firm's output, tariffs, quotas, voluntary export restraints, or a guaranteed market share for the domestic producer. We do not address here the question of the determination of the mode of intervention. This choice may also be politically-motivated; see Cassing and Hillman (1985).

the choice of relative factor intensities in Section 4. In the final section we note an adverse selection problem which arises via the incentives affecting firms' regional location decisions.

II. The firm

We begin with a risk-neutral firm producing a traded good in the absence of government intervention. The firm makes initial factor-employment decisions before the realization of the random price of its output. The output price takes on values of P_A or $P_B(<P_A)$ with probabilties q_A and q_B. On the basis of this information, a nominal wage w is contractually specified. The wage is binding upon the firm and its employees, but the firm can change labor employment ex-post, after the realization of price.[4] Output is produced via the strictly-concave decreasing-returns production function $F(L, K)$. Capital is competitively available to the firm at a nominal rental price r.

The firm determines its inputs as follows: Initially, before the price of output is revealed, K and L are chosen. Once chosen, the value of K cannot be altered and the firm incurs costs of rK regardless of the state of the world. The labor decision allows for more, though still limited, flexibility. Once chosen, L can be altered to zero if circumstances warrant. That is, the firm can close its plant. Other than a shutdown, the value of L is unchangeable.

In particular, we assume that if P_B is the world price, variable costs cannot be covered at any output level, so the firm closes down its operations, losing rK. Note, however, that the assumption of the shutdown response is adopted only for expositional simplicity. Allowing a more variable labor force will not affect the essence of the results.

Expected profits in the absence of government intervention are accordingly:

$$E\pi = q_A[P_A F(K, L_A) - wL_A] - rK. \tag{1}$$

If the realized price is P_B and the government does not intervene to "bail out" the firm, the firm shuts down and lays off all its employees. Alternative employment is not available to the workers who are laid-off. Labor either emigrates or remains in the region unemployed, and regional-specific asset values decline in value. This is however politically costly to the government, and there is a positive probability p that intervention will take place to forestall the closure of the plant and thereby protect the jobs of the firm's employees.[5] The probability of a "bail out" increases with the number of workers whose jobs are threatened: hence $p = p(L)$ and $p'(L) > 0$. Incorporating the probability of intervention into the firm's expected profits

---

[4] Hence we have an implicit-contract format; see for example Katz and Rosenberg (1983).
[5] There are potentially more complex political-support related interactions between protection and the level of employment. See Cassing and Hillman (1986).

yields

$$E\tilde{\pi} = q_A\pi_A + q_B[(1 - \rho(L))\pi_B + \rho(L)\tilde{\pi}_B] \tag{2}$$

where $\tilde{\pi}_B$ denotes profits when the price realized is P_B and the government intervenes to preempt unemployment and thereby at the same time bail out the firm. We shall assume that $\tilde{\pi}_B = \pi_A$. That is, intervention is a perfect substitute from the firm's perspective for the favorable realization of price P_A. Hence (2) becomes

$$E\tilde{\pi} = [q_A + \rho(L)q_B](R_A - wL) - rK \tag{2'}$$

where R_A is revenue in state A. $[q_A + \rho(L)q_B]$ in (2') is the endogenous probability that the firm will cover its variable costs and labor will remain employed. This occurs if either the price P_A is realized, or if subsequent to the realization of P_B (which occurs with probability q_B) the government acts to "bail out" the firm (which occurs with probability $\rho(L)$).

III. Factor employment

Employment of capital must be chosen before the price of output is realized. Hence, given the probability of intervention, $\rho(L)$, the expected-profit maximizing condition for capital inputs is

$$(q_A + \rho(L)q_B)P_A F_K = r, \tag{3}$$

where $(q_A + \rho(L)q_B) < 1$ if $\rho > 0$. Clearly, in the absence of intervention $\rho(L) = 0$ and $q_A P_A F_K = r$. Thus the anticipation of intervention increases the firm's capital input choice. More capital is employed because the (imperfect) insurance provided via the increased employment of labor increases the expected value of the marginal product of capital.

Labor employment which maximizes expected profits (for $L > 0$) is given by

$$(q_A + \rho(L)q_B)(P_A F_L - w) = -(R_A - wL)q_B\rho'(L) < 0. \tag{4}$$

Clearly, if changes in L do not alter the probability of intervention, i.e., if $\rho'(L) = 0$, (4) reduces to the state-A contingent labor-employment condition that the value of the marginal product of labor (for the precommitted choice of K) equals the wage:

$$P_A F_L = w. \tag{5}$$

Likewise, (5) is the condition for choice of labor employment (for given K) when there is no price variability and P_A is realized with probability one.

From (3) and (5) it is therefore clear that the conditions determining employment of capital and employment of labor depend on different considerations. For capital, the expected value of marginal product is set at less than the cost of capital if and only if the probability of intervention ρ if positive. The sign of ρ' is immaterial here. On the other hand, for the marginal revenue product of labor to be set at less than the cost of labor ρ' must be positive.

A comparison of the labor choices implied by (3) and (4) therefore reveals that in the presence of price variability more labor is employed, *ceteris paribus*, when the firm anticipates an interventionist response. In the absence of direct insurance markets for adverse realizations of price, the firm uses labor employment as a means of insurance. Manipulation of the labor employment decision cannot however provide a perfect substitute for an absent insurance market. The firm can do no more than increase the probability of intervention by playing on the government's political sensitivity to unemployment, and there is no assurance of an interventionist response. *Expected* profits are nevertheless increased by increasing labor employment beyond the level at which the value of the state-A marginal product equals the wage.

The linear homogeneous technology implies that $F_{LK} > 0$. Relative to the case where no intervention is anticipated, the employment of *both* labor and capital is therefore increased; and since we have no inferior input, output (in state A where the firm does not close down) is necessarily increased by the firm's internalizing the likelihood of intervention.

IV. Relative factor intensities

Does the anticipation of intervention introduce a bias one way or the other in relative factor intensities? One might surmise that since increased labor employment increases the likelihood of a bail-out in the event of an unfavorable realization of price, a bias is imparted towards labor employment. We shall see however that this is not necessarily the case.

Combining (3) and (5) we have when intervention is anticipated,

$$\frac{F_L}{F_K} = \frac{\alpha w - \beta}{r} \tag{6}$$

where

$$0 < \alpha = q_A + \rho(L)q_B < 1$$

and

$$\beta = (R_A - wL)q_B\rho'(L) > 0.$$

On the other hand, when intervention is not anticipated,

$$\frac{F_L}{F_K} = \frac{q_A w}{r}. \tag{7}$$

Hence, for both the intervention and non-intervention cases, a decrease in the firm's perceived probability of the realization of the more favorable output price results in choice of more labor-intensive production methods.

This is because the risks associated with the realization of the low price P_B relate to capital employment, which is wholly irreversible.

However, to determine the effect of the anticipation of intervention on the relative factor intensity in production, we compare $q_A w$ with the term $\{q_A w + \rho(L)q_B w - (R_A - wL)q\rho'(L)\}$. Anticipation of intervention therefore increases or decreases relative labor intensity as respectively

$$[\rho(L)w - (R_A - wL)\rho'(L)] \lessgtr 0. \tag{8}$$

Clearly, if ρ is large in relation to ρ' the anticipation of intervention increases relative capital intensity, whereas if the opposite is the case the firm chooses more labor-intensive production methods.

Thus the anticipation of government intervention to preempt unemployment of labor may lead the firm to substitute capital for labor. This possibility arises, of course, because as noted the underlying cause of loss due to an unfavorable world price is the irreversible capital commitment.

V. Concluding remarks

We conclude that if firms adapt factor input decisions to internalize the political sensitivity of governments to labor unemployment, more labor is employed, but also more capital, and more output is produced, though not necessarily by more labor-intensive methods than would be chosen in the absence of the anticipation of intervention. An ex-ante protective effect is therefore revealed, together with an implicit factor-usage subsidy which could favor capital rather than labor.

In responding to the anticipation of government intervention, the firm is engaging in a form of unproductive profit or rent-seeking activity; the firm is allocating and using resources inefficiently but to its own advantage.[6] Still, an outcome of increased output and increased labor employment need not be contrary to government objectives. For example, in Israel, it is an objective of policy to encourage decentralized output and population dispersion to development towns and settlements. Our analysis reveals, however, that the government's political sensitivity to unemployment of labor in these towns and settlements may lead firms to choose more *capital*-intensive factor-input proportions.

A locational bias can also be identified. Because of the implicit insurance provided by location, a firm which confronts relatively greater probabilities of adverse price outcomes has the greater incentive to choose a location where unemployment is politically more sensitive. But insofar as the firm is the principal local employer of labor, a bias is imparted towards periodic trade-related employment "crises" associated with adverse realizations of the price of the firm's output. Hence, an adverse selection problem arises.

---

[6] See Tullock (1967), Bhagwati (1982). The social cost of such activity can be related to the firm's perceived benefit: see for example Tullock (1980), Hillman and Katz (1984), Appelbaum and Katz (1986), Hillman and Samet (forthcoming).

Paradoxically, in circumstances where employment stability may be desired because of the immediate lack of alternative employment opportunities, potential instability is increased.

Finally, while we have considered unemployment in the context of an industry producing an internationally traded good, the conclusions derived are applicable to regional unemployment due to domestic rather than international changes affecting an industry's competitiveness. Our reference to traded goods can be interpreted as referring to interregionally as well as to internationally traded goods.

Bar-Ilan University, Israel and University of California, Los Angeles, U.S.A.
Bar-Ilan University, Israel and York University, Canada
Bar-Ilan University, Israel and Vanderbilt University, USA.

REFERENCES

APPELBAUM, E. and KATZ, E. "Transfer Seeking and Avoidance: On the Full Social Costs of Rent Seeking," *Public Choice*, 1986, 48, 175–181.

BALDWIN, R. E. "The Political Economy of Protectionism," in J. N. Bhagwati editor, *Import Competition and Response*, University of Chicago Press, for the National Bureau of Economic Research, 1982, 263–286.

BECKER, G. "A Theory of Competition Among Pressure Groups for Political Influence," *Quarterly Journal of Economics*, August 1983, 98, 371–400.

BHAGWATI, J. N. "Directly Unproductive Profit-Seeking (DUP) Activities," *Journal of Political Economy*, August 1982, 90, 988–1002.

CASSING, J. H. "Alternatives to Protectionism," in I. Levenson and J. Wheeler, editors, *Western Economies in Transition: Structural Change and Adjustment Policies in Industrial Countries*, Westview, Croon Helm, 1980, 391–424.

CASSING, J. H. and HILLMAN, A. L. "Political-influence Motives and the Choice Between Tariffs and Quotas," *Journal of International Economics*, November 1985, 19, 279–290.

CASSING, J. H., HILLMAN, A. L. and LONG, N. V. "Risk Aversion, Terms of Trade Uncertainty and Social-consensus Trade Policy," *Oxford Economic Papers*, June 1986, 38, 234–242.

CASSING, J. H. and HILLMAN, A. L. "Shifting Comparative Advantage and Senescent Industry Collapse," *American Economic Review*, June 1986, 76, 516–523.

CASSING, J. H., McKEOWN, T. and OCHS, J. "The Political Economy of the Tariff Cycle," *American Political Science Review*, September 1986, 80, 843–862.

DORE, R. P. "Adjustment in Process: A Lancashire Town," in J. N. Bhagwati, editor, *Import Competition and Response*, University of Chicago Press, for the National Bureau of Economic Research, 1982, 295–317.

EATON, J. and GROSSMAN, G. M. "Tariffs as Insurance: Optimal Commercial Policy when Domestic Markets are Incomplete," *Canadian Journal of Economics*, May 1985, 18, 258–272.

FALVEY, R. and LLOYD, P. J. "The Choice of Instrument of Industry Protection," in R. Snape, Editor, *Issues in World Trade Policy: GATT at the Crossroads*, Macmillan, 1986.

FINDLAY, R. and WELLISZ, S. "Endogenous Tariffs, the Political Economy of Trade Restrictions, and Welfare," in J. N. Bhagwati, editor, *Import Competition and Response*, University of Chicago Press, for the National Bureau of Economic Research, 1982, 238–243.

GODEK, P. E. "Industry Structure and Redistribution Through Trade Restrictions," *Journal of Law and Economics*, October, 1985, 28, 687–703.

GROSSMAN, G. M. "Imports as a Cause of Injury: The Case of the U.S. Steel Industry," *Journal of International Economics*, May 1986, 20, 201–223.

HILLMAN, A. L. "Declining Industries and Political-support Protectionist Motives," *American Economic Review*, December 1982, 72, 1180–87.

HILLMAN, A. L. and KATZ, E. "Risk-averse Rent seekers and the Social Cost of Monopoly Power," *Economic Journal, March* 1984, 94, 104–110.

HILLMAN, A. L. and SAMET, D. "Dissipation of Contestable Rents by Small Numbers of Contenders," *Public Choice*, forthcoming.

KATZ, E. and ROSENBERG, J. "Inflation Variability, Real Wage Variability and Production Inefficiency," *Economica*, November 1983, 50, 469–475.

RICHARDSON, J. D. "Trade Adjustment Assistance under the U.S. Trade Act of 1974," in J. N. Bhagwati, editor, *Import Competition and Response*, University of Chicago Press, for the National Bureau of Economic Research, 1982, 321–357.

TULLOCK, G. "The Welfare Costs of Tariffs, Monopolies and Theft," *Western Economic Journal*, June 1967, 5, 224–232; reprinted in J. M. Buchanan, R. D. Tollison and G. Tullock, editors, *Toward a Theory of the Rent Seeking Society*, Texas A & M Press, 1980, 269–282.

TULLOCK, G. "Efficient Rent Seeking," in J. M. Buchanan, R. D. Tollison and G. Tullock, editors, *Towards a Theory of the Rent Seeking Society*, Texas A & M Press, 1980, 97–112.

WALLERSTEIN, M. "Unemployment, Trade Unions and the Demand for Protection," *American Journal of Political Science*, forthcoming November, 1987.

Review of Agricultural Economics—Volume 21, Number 2—Pages 358–373

Rent Seeking and Rent Dissipation in State Enterprises

Steven T. Buccola and James E. McCandlish

We reflect on the use of state power in state-owned enterprises. An African case study is first recounted in which a private coffee exporting firm seeks to compete against a government-owned monopoly marketing board. A principal theme of the study is that state enterprises retain de facto control of their markets long after surrendering any *de jure* monopoly privileges. Managers of the state firm and their supervisors within the civil service form a coherent lobbying group whose interest is to defend the enterprise from competition. With this study as a backdrop, we offer a theory of rent seeking in state-owned enterprises. We argue that state firms in less-developed countries seek to maximize costs within the limits of the subsidies offered them by international donors. *Government rent* is the difference between such maximized cost and minimum cost. The portion of government rent determined by valuing inputs at competitive factor prices is dissipative in the sense that it vanishes from productive output. Dissipated government rent likely is larger than in the classical (Tullock) rent-seeking paradigm because a state firm's managers have little incentive to limit their rent-seeking activities. Hence, renewed calls for state regulation can be expected once the present deregulation trend has run its course.

"The market system provides no mechanism for its own survival."
—P.T. Bauer, *Reality and Rhetoric* (p. 36)

The most significant event of the past quarter century has been the global retreat of the public sector. Licensing regulations have been eased, prices and exchange rates floated, trade barriers slashed, and state-owned enterprises sold off. It is tempting to think these have been spontaneous reactions to the massive failure of statist economies. Fail massively statism did, but none would have realized it in the absence of a mental yardstick, a theory of human choice. Chief among such yardsticks has been the notion that humans seek rents, that government preferences are an especially lucrative and durable source of rents for the few who obtain them,

■ *Steven Buccola is professor, Department of Agricultural and Resource Economics, Oregon State University.*
■ *James McCandlish is an attorney in private practice in Portland, Oregon.*

Figure 1. Classical rent from government preferences: the buyer case

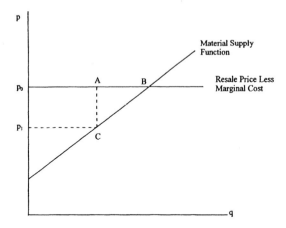

and that such preferences reduce aggregate wealth and economic opportunity. If this notion is true, then deregulation is a two-edged sword, at once enhancing growth and providing an incentive for new state-sponsored rents and thus for reregulation.

The best known rent-seeking theory (in Buchanan, Tollison, and Tullock and their followers) is scripted for a world of circumscribed government power. A private firm buying raw materials, say, on a competitive market asks government to use its tax or regulatory authority to restrict competition from the firm's potential rivals. The situation is depicted in figure 1, where the buyer is assumed to have a constant returns technology so that p_0 represents resale price less buyer's marginal cost. If the lobbying effort is successful, material prices are depressed from p_0 to p_1, generating rent equal to area p_0ACp_1. To obtain this rent, however, the firm must expend resources, either to buy lobbying services on the private market or to offer rewards to bureaucrats or legislators. In a competitive rent market where no firms have rent-seeking advantages like specialized human capital, search expenditures exhaust the present value of expected future rents, leaving only a normal return to the rent search efforts. Of course, competition likely isn't perfect and human capital certainly is unevenly distributed, so some net rents probably remain in bidders' hands.

Regulations restricting competition reduce aggregate wealth for the simple reason that they reduce output, inflating consumer prices or (as in the present buyer-side case) reducing factor prices. The least wealth dissipated is Harberger or deadweight loss triangle ABC in figure 1, familiar to every student of economic theory. A potentially greater loss, however, is the very expenditure our rentier firm would make to secure and protect its privileges. The most it would spend is the sum of transfers it would expect in turn to receive from factor owners, namely the "Tullock rectangle" p_0ACp_1. Yet as Higgins and Tollison point out, rent-seeking payments to private or public entities really are "eaten up" only if they divert activity from the production of valued products. With some effort, one could imagine a world in which state employees' efforts to confer preferences on their chosen clients divert little time from their other tasks, the production of truly public goods. In that event, the portion of rent-seeking payments going to the state would consist of transfers from consumers or producers to state employees. The corresponding portion of the Tullock rectangle would be saved from dissipation, regardless of our opinions about the morality of the transfers.

This insight about private firms' bids for state favors is useful only to the extent that private goods production is in private—albeit government-influenced—hands. It does not well explain the search for rents in situations where government itself wants to produce private goods, to engage in its own corporate activity. Governments of such sort are now in intellectual disfavor, but we must not suppose that state-owned firms are unworthy of our consideration. They remain numerous in Asia, and privatization attempts in Russia are seriously threatened. Many state enterprises in Africa, introduced by colonial rulers during the 1940s and enthusiastically embraced by their nationalist successors, dissolved in the 1980s under donor pressure. Others stubbornly have persisted in some form (Adam, Cavendish, and Mistry) and a political counterattack against privatization is underway (Jayne and Jones, p. 1,523). Understanding these conflicts is difficult without a theory of rent seeking in *dirigiste* economies, where state power is poorly circumscribed and government has customary access to private goods production.

Our purpose is to provide some thoughts about the direction such a theory should take. We make few claims to deductive rigor, preferring instead to think discursively and thematically. To this end, it seems best to use our own experience as a point of departure for expanding on the insights of other scholars.

Malawi Smallholder Coffee

We begin with a first-hand story. It takes place in the remote, semitropical mountains of northern Malawi, where coffee has been the principal cash crop since the 1950s. Villagers' dwellings are widely dispersed in these mountains, carved onto narrow terraces above breathtaking views of canyon and river and flanked above and below with maize, beans, sweet potatoes, and coffee. The Tumbuka and Sukwa speakers living here and in the intermittent valleys are renowned for their energy, enterprise, and educational performance; yet incomes average about $200 per year, near the lowest in the world. In many huts, the only purchased goods are a few articles of clothing, iron cooking pots, wooden chair, salt, and soap. Land is so plentiful in some areas that outsiders often are invited in to establish farms, yet the average household keeps only 0.15 hectare of coffee, indifferently.

Ripe coffee on the tree is called "cherry," looking and nearly tasting like that. After harvest, it is carried by head to a village pulpery, an acre or so of donor-constructed cement channels, holding tanks, pulping machine, and drying tables. Here the red pulp is removed and the twin beans within are washed, left to ferment for several days, and sun-dried. They are now called "parchment," after the yellowish husk enclosing the green bean. Coffee at parchment stage is ready to be shipped out of the village and into town because the husks can be removed efficiently only by large hulling machinery. Upon hulling, polishing, and grading, it is ready to be shipped overseas as green coffee.

The Heady Era of Centralization

During the early days, Malawi's small farmers exported their own coffee through village-level cooperatives and a regional cooperative union. But the government newly liberated in 1964 from British rule distrusted cooperatives, pointing with some legitimacy to corruption and mismanagement in them. It abolished the cooperative union and reduced the local cooperatives to captive agents of the Farmers' Marketing Board, a government corporation that recently had been granted control of the nation's agricultural markets. Under the new dispensation, village coffee co-ops received cherry from their farmer members, processed it into parchment, and delivered it to the Board for hulling and export. No other export channels were allowed. Farm prices, and allowances for the local cooperatives' pulping expenses, were determined each year by the Agriculture and Finance Ministries and enforced by statute.

Further centralization came in the 1970s. A 1971 act of Parliament replaced the Farmers Marketing Board with the Agricultural Development and Marketing Corporation, which supplemented its nationwide marketing monopsonies by moving aggressively into farming, food processing, and transportation. In the companion Special Crops Act, a Smallholder Coffee Authority was instituted to take specialized control of small-farm coffee marketing. The Coffee Authority abolished the village cooperatives and assumed direct control of cherry processing at the numerous village pulpery sites. A holistic approach to government involvement was in the air. Backed by substantial new support from the European Community, the Authority took charge not only of coffee processing and marketing but of extension services and local road maintenance as well. Large state-owned coffee farms were planted on the steep hillsides and in the sheltered ravines, tended by a small army of employees. Impressive new red-brick training schools and dormitories were built to host coffee management courses for farmer groups. Rows of substantial houses were constructed to accommodate an expanded corps of extension workers. The Authority's headquarters themselves were ensconced in a new five-acre facility, replete with conference hall, three separate accounting departments, workshops, and a large fleet of trucks and all-terrain vehicles. The Big Push to develop smallholder coffee was on.

Or was it? To give an idea of the size of the effort involved, it is well to note that smallholder coffee production in Malawi averages about 225 metric tons annually. At current prices, this represents about $330,000 in annual FOB value. Divided among some 4,300 growers, the 225 metric tons amounts to 52 kg of green coffee per farmer, for an annual sale value of $76. In 1996, well past its heyday and already moving into receivership, the Coffee Authority still had 657 employees on hand to support and market this $330,000 crop. Fifty-seven of these staff were "established," considered professional and entitled to extensive benefit packages. Many more than the 57 were accommodated in the sorts of houses to which only the four or five richest coffee farmers could aspire. The Authority's General Manager and Assistant General Manager alone each had a 3,000 square-foot house on an acre of gardened property, attended by numerous vehicles, drivers, and messengers.

A still clearer picture of the Great Leap Forward can be had by examining the Authority's capitalization and operating costs. In a 1996 consultant's report (Lincoln Bailey), Coffee Authority buildings were valued at $989,780 and vehicles at $98,067.

Total capital valuation, that is, was $1,087,847, more than four times higher than annual farm receipts.[1] The Authority's operating cost picture was similar. Between 1991 and 1994, its coffee marketing expenses averaged 80%, and never fell below 50%, of revenues. "Expenses" for this purpose exclude depreciation, the cost of farmer loan defaults, and debt interest, which in 1994/1995 were collectively one-third as large as marketing expenses. Thus, total processing and handling cost could not have averaged much less than 90% of revenue.[2] It is no surprise that little was left to pay farmers for their coffee.

Time to Decentralize: Competition and Cooperatives

Like most poor nations, Malawi began participating in World Bank structural adjustment loans (SALs) in the early 1980s. By the end of its second SAL (1983–1987), it was to be well on its way toward eliminating exchange controls, reducing consumer subsidies, and decontrolling agricultural markets. The Bank however observed in March 1985 that Malawi was complying "with some but not all conditions requested," and grouped it with three other nations (Thailand, Cote d'Ivoire, Philippines) meriting Index of Compliance scores between 60% and 90% (Mosley, p. 54). In fact, Malawi's legislative compliance with the SALs' agricultural liberalization objectives did not come until March 1996, when Parliament officially eliminated marketing board monopsonies. A companion bill abrogated the Special Crops Act of 1971. Finally, private traders could buy, sell, and export coffee at freely negotiated prices.

The 1996 Liberalization Acts were fully anticipated. After thirty years of Kamuzu Banda's dictatorship, the Muluzi Government had been elected in 1994 on a promarket platform. Encouraged by the new spirit, we asked the principal secretary of the Ministry of Agriculture in 1994 for permission to buy and export Malawi smallholder coffee. He warmly accepted the idea, assuring us the Smallholder Coffee Authority would soon be disbanded and that in the meantime we would compete with it "on a level playing field."

Our decision to enter the market with our new firm, African Gourmet Coffee (AGC), began with some simple arithmetic. On 23 August 1994, we observed that Colombian green coffee on the New York spot market had reached $4.49/kg. Shipping cost from southern African ports to New York City that year was $0.25/kg, so the coffee border price in southern Africa, in Colombian coffee equivalent, was $4.24/kg green. At the same time, the Smallholder Coffee Authority was paying Malawi smallholders $0.078/kg cherry, or equivalently $0.43/kg green. That is, farmers were receiving only 10% of the Colombian benchmark border price. Of the Malawi-coffee-equivalent border price they were receiving even a smaller share, since Malawian arabica typically brings a $0.77/kg premium over Colombian arabica.[3]

To confirm this arithmetic, we toured extensively through Malawi's mountain villages. The luscious and productive coffee farms we had known in the late 1960s had devolved into thickets of unpruned bare wood. Farmers were resigned more than angry; most made weekly treks to the lowlands to grow tobacco. The coffee industry had simply collapsed under the weight of government monopsony.

Unfortunately, the industry was not all that had collapsed. Twenty-five years of Coffee Authority benevolence—in the form of direct control of village coffee pulping, pricing, accounting, and feeder road maintenance—had eliminated all but the vestiges of local farmer organization and energy. Indeed, the evisceration of local institutions was a key source of the Authority's collapse, and more generally of the failure of the government's 1970s centralization drive. By the same token, it seemed that a revitalized cooperative sector would be essential to any successful market liberalization effort.

The reasons for thinking so were twofold. First, Malawi's economy has, like most poor nations, two personalities: an unregulated "rural" sector and a regulated "urban" sector. Investor-owned and state-owned firms are regulated and hence subject to minimum wage and employee benefit laws, regardless of how rural their actual activity. In contrast, local farmer cooperatives are largely exempt from wage regulation, in practice if not in law. They hire and fire at will, paying workers on the basis of local opportunity costs. They also rely heavily on traditional village networks, where individual privacy and, therefore, employee monitoring costs are low. Thus also, cooperatives are positioned to operate rural pulperies, administer farmer accounts, and arrange local transportation more efficiently than are investor-owned firms.[4]

The second reason cooperatives appear, at least in the present instance, essential to rural market liberalization is technological rather than regulatory. At current output volumes, size economies in Malawi cherry pulping are so strong that it is inefficient to situate pulping facilities less than three or four miles apart. Because cherry must be carried by head from farm to pulpery over difficult terrain, few farmers have a credible choice about which pulpery to use. Coffee pulping, in short, is a natural local monopsony and investor ownership of the pulping stage would create its own market power problems.[5] The most competitive option is for democratically run cooperatives to purchase cherry from their members, operate the pulping facilities, and sell parchment to exporters of their choice, returning any profits to the membership (Sexton).[6] Motivated by this reasoning, and after consulting with the Ministry of Agriculture, we began organizing village marketing cooperatives late in the 1994 season.

Battle is Joined

By the middle of the 1995 season, African Gourmet Coffee had developed the logistics to buy coffee in villages, operating through a patchwork of partly assembled farmer cooperatives, buying clubs, and individual growers. New York prices, meanwhile, had dropped from their 1994 highs around $4.50/kg to near $3.30/kg. AGC announced a grade I cash farm price of $1.88/kg green equivalent, more than four times as large as the Coffee Authority's 1994 price of $0.43/kg.[7] The Authority responded immediately by raising its grade I farm price to $1.10/kg. The latter would be paid at end of season when inflation would reduce its present value to around $0.94/kg, so it represented barely one-half the AGC offer. Nevertheless, the Authority captured 90% of the 1995 smallholder crop. The key to its success was control of the twenty-seven village-level pulperies. Soon after AGC's appearance, the Authority declared that farmers intending to sell to non-Authority entities would be barred from pulpery use. They would have to process their cherry at home, a labor-intensive task hardly compensating for the price premium it afforded. The level playing field had developed a pronounced tilt.

Conflict intensified in 1996. Following a slight decline in world prices, and conscious of a $21,000 loss on its 1995 operations, AGC announced a 1996 grade I cash farm price of $1.67/kg green equivalent, down from $1.88 the previous year. In response, the Coffee Authority *increased* its farm price from $1.10 to $1.30/kg green ($1.10 on a present-value basis), modestly closing the gap with AGC's offer. This move could be explained only as a bid to maintain market share, since even with its higher margins in 1995, the Authority had reported a loss of $35,800, more than one-fifth of revenues.

The Authority's urge to raise farm prices at all was conditioned by diplomatic events earlier in the year. After extensive negotiations, AGC had obtained an agreement with the minister of agriculture that the new farmer cooperatives would be permitted "equal access" to village pulping facilities. Local co-op representatives were to discuss with the Coffee Authority manager at their own pulpery site how to apportion pulpery time between cooperative-purchased and Authority-purchased cherry. Processing time would be allocated proportionately to the volume of cherry each had purchased. The pulpery access problem seemed to have been solved, opening the door to "level-playing-field" competition.

Retreating to a Second Defense Line: User Fees

But the Smallholder Coffee Authority was far from surrendering its privileged trading position. In July 1996, just as harvest was beginning, it announced the following Catch-22: farmers wishing to sell cherry to a cooperative would first have to pay a pulpery user fee of $0.044/kg cherry ($0.26/kg green), while those selling to the Authority would be exempt. Few growers could pay such a fee even if they wished to, since little money is available in mountain villages until the cherry has been processed and payment for it received. As angry farmers held their crop back to dry on the tree, or sold reluctantly to the Authority at two-thirds of the AGC price offer, a flurry of political activity ensued to seek cancellation of the user fee. AGC petitioned the Ministry—which, it transpired, had never authorized the fee—to intervene. In one locale, co-op members took forcible control of four pulperies, chasing Coffee Authority personnel into the woods. The Ministry commissioned its chief trouble-shooter to come to the North to make peace.

Conflict resolution in African agricultural communities is lengthy and ambiguous, a fact conducive to the power of incumbency. The Ministry's trouble-shooter toured coffee villages and held tense, noisy meetings, which the Coffee Authority packed with its employees to create a sense of political support. Cooperatives, and AGC on their behalf, besieged senior officials with letters protesting the fees and demanding they be canceled. The Ministry's Pricing Branch inaugurated a study of pulpery costs, saying results could be used to establish a sensible use charge. But sensibleness depended more on ethical and legal questions than on economic ones.

For example, a principal issue was whether fees should be based on the variable or total cost of pulpery use. The answer depended upon on whose behalf the pulperies were assumed to have been built. Did the donors financing construction intend government to sell pulpery services to local farmers, recoup full cost, and spend it elsewhere in the economy, or did they vest a pulpery's ownership in government only as custodian for the farmers who would use it? In the latter event, a pulpery's opportunity cost is essentially zero since the facilities are largely immobile and have just one possible use.[8] An equally important issue was whether such fees should be assessed on every farmer or only on those selling to a co-op (and thus to a private exporter). The Coffee Authority argued that farmers selling to the Authority should not be assessed, inasmuch as a pulpery user fee "was already deducted from these farmers' receipts." However, the presence of such a fee in the Authority's price structure was impossible to ascertain since farm prices were affected by the Authority's operating expenditures, which bear no relationship to minimum cost. In a word, the Authority's farm prices were politically considered, and one consideration was to ward off competition from the private sector.

The user fee controversy dragged on for two months, into the middle of the 1996 harvest season. Then, with no apparent attention to the conceptual questions AGC had posed, the Ministry announced merely that it would cut the $0.26 user fee in half and require payment only at the end of the year, when farmers would have the necessary cash. The decision was Solomonic because collection arrangements were nonexistent and everyone knew postseason payments could not be enforced. Meanwhile, however, the Authority had captured most of the early harvest through its user fee pronouncement.

And, as the teeth in its user fee threat dissolved, the Authority showed it had other weapons in its market share arsenal: it began simply to renege on its earlier agreement to share pulpery time on a volume-proportionate basis with farmer cooperatives. This move was illegal, so the Authority's general manager never formally announced it. Instead, it worked its will adventitiously, through the individual Coffee Authority supervisors who kept the keys to the twenty-seven village pulperies. In several villages, co-ops had organized strongly enough to resist the coercion and to continue to negotiate adequate processing time. In most areas, however, Authority supervisors successfully intimidated cooperative officers into accepting the *fait accompli*, forcing members to sell to the Authority or process their cherry at home. Formal complaints to the general manager brought denials of wrongdoing. The Ministry of Agriculture said it would investigate . . . .

But the harvest season was slipping away. By year-end the Coffee Authority had, despite farm prices effectively 34% lower than its competitor's, purchased 75% of the smallholder crop. In the face of substantial size economies and lobbying costs, AGC lost $83,000, bringing its total two-year loss to $104,000. Authority losses, yet unreported, certainly were substantial. Indeed, the government's continual promises to disband its coffee venture had borne much of their fruit. The spacious offices and meeting rooms, the workshops, the cavernous warehouse at Authority headquarters were largely empty. Most of the once-proud vehicle fleet sat helpless in neat rows of rust. Bank credit had evaporated and some tangible assets had been seized. The general manager had received early retirement notice, replaced by a custodian who would oversee transition to "a new modality for marketing smallholder coffee." The new modality would not be attracting much entrepreneurial capital. In mid 1997, African Gourmet Coffee informed the Agriculture Ministry that it was withdrawing its investments. The competition that had tripled farm incomes had evaporated.

Rent-Seeking in Government Enterprises

In opting to foil rather than foster private capital formation, the Malawi Government had shown how not to privatize a state company. Were this an isolated story, it would be an interesting curiosity only. But false starts in marketing board privatization have been more the rule than the exception (Adam, Cavendish, and Mistry; Krueger, Schiff, and Valdes). State firms seem to die hard, even when donors have decreed they should go and recipients have agreed to abolish them. Why is this so? And if state enterprises show vigor even at the stake, will they not soon rise from their own ashes? The answers to these questions, it seems to us, require an improved theory of rent seeking in government-rich economies.

Just as the classical rent-seeking drama is scripted for two players, the firm and the state, so we must locate the principal actors in the rent-seeking drama where governments produce private goods. The latter are, unsurprisingly, the same governments that typically seek foreign aid. It is a mistake to focus in these societies on the interaction between a state firm's managers and the ministries which oversee them. A company is "para"statal only in its license to seek bank loans and to avoid civil service labor regulations. A state firm is no more independent, in a policy sense, of its ministry supervisors than is one layer of a ministry hierarchy independent of that above it. Indeed, state enterprises and their governing ministries form a cohesive interest group, a main goal of which is to seek rents from donors.[9] For the fact in our own story is that the Malawi Government forced its Coffee Authority into receivership not because it had passed too little of its revenues onto farmers or because its losses were too high, but because donors refused any longer to cover those losses. If, in liberal societies, for-profit firms seek rents from their government regulators, in illiberal ones, governments and their captive enterprises seek rents from international donors.

The Malawi Government's energetic defense of its coffee monopsony's market share in the face of immitigable international pressure to relinquish it is itself notable. State enterprise profits and losses accrue to the public treasury, not to the enterprise managers or to their supervisors in the civil service. Government's urge to compete with the private sector could not, therefore, be explained as a quest for monopsony profits. One must look elsewhere for the rewards that government managers envision.

State Firms Want to Maximize Their Budgets

Unquestionably, state employees seek paid activity. On this, all theoreticians of bureaucracy seem to agree (Bates, Jackson, James, Niskanen).[10] To the manager of an export marketing board, which purchases farm produce and sells it on a foreign market, paid activity is the board's budget. Thus, a natural marketing board objective is to maximize budget in a manner that is financially feasible. Board budgets are financed in two ways: (*a*) through the excess of sale revenues over payments to farmers and (*b*) through subsidies from donors via the domestic treasury. A reasonable board maximand, then, is to choose a farm price and inefficiency level that maximizes total budget, provided the budget does not exceed the maximum donor subsidy plus the excess of revenue over payments to farmers.

To fix this idea more clearly, define C as the board's budget or total marketing cost, q the quantity of product purchased from farmers, D a vector of cost function parameters, β a parameter indicating the extent of technical and allocative inefficiency in marketing ($\beta = 1$ for minimum-cost operation), w a vector of marketing input prices, P the expected international market price, p the price paid to farmers,

Figure 2. Classical rent from government preferences: a marketing board

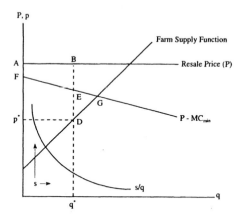

F a vector of other factors affecting farm supply, and s the maximum donor subsidy. The government's optimization problem is

(1) $\max_{\beta, p} C(q, \beta; \mathbf{w}, \mathbf{D})$

subject to

$$C(q, \beta; \mathbf{w}, \mathbf{D}) \le q(P - p) + s \qquad q = q(p, \mathbf{F})$$

where $\partial C / \partial q, \partial C / \partial \beta > 0$, and in which roman letters are used to signify parameters $(\mathbf{w}, P, \mathbf{D}, \mathbf{F}, s)$ assumed to be beyond government's direct control. Optimal inefficiency level β may or may not exceed unity depending upon vector $(\mathbf{w}, P, \mathbf{D}, \mathbf{F}, s)$.[11]

Farm price p has a dual effect on a marketing board's budget. Lowering p enhances per-unit margin $(P - p)$ and thus the budget size per unit of volume; but it also reduces volume q itself, which dampens the budget inasmuch as marginal costs $\partial C / \partial q$ are positive. Hence, the government's problem is to find the budget-maximizing balance between a farm price reduction's margin-enhancing and output-suppressing effects. This balance, like the choice of inefficiency level β, depends on elasticities of the cost and farm supply functions as well as on the subsidy that donors are willing to pay.

Optimal bureaucratic pricing of farm products is characterized in figure 2. An efficient marketing firm's marginal cost function (assumed here to be up-sloping) is designated MC_{min}. Line $(P - MC_{min})$ represents competitive demand for the farm product, the vertical distance of this line from world price P being MC_{min} itself. Competitive farm price and output are, therefore, at point G, where $(P - MC_{min})$ intersects the farm supply curve. Rectangular hyperbola s/q is the donor's maximum subsidy expressed on a per-unit basis. Taking the above information into account along with budget function $C(q, \beta; \mathbf{w}, \mathbf{D})$, government solves problem (1) to find optimal farm price p^*. The latter is, following the preponderance of the literature (Bates; Bauer 1963, 1984; Krueger, Schiff, and Valdes; Pollard and Graham), indicated in figure 2 as below the competitive price. At price p^*, farmers produce q^*, so government's gross margin over farmer payments, $q(P - p)$, is area ABDp^*. Donor subsidy is s, the area below unit subsidy line s/q and to the left of q^*. Hence (ABDp^* + s) is total financing which, insofar as the first constraint in problem (1) is binding, equals total budget.

Government Rent is Part Dissipation, Part Transfer

In the classical rent-seeking literature, a private firm seeks gain from some state-awarded privilege. In the present analysis, it is state employees who seek gain from a state-awarded privilege. This latter gain is usefully called "government rent" to distinguish it from its classical cousin, the rent captured by a private firm.

Understanding rent seeking within government requires that we first identify government rent in figure 2. As Tollison (p. 144) makes clear, rent in general is the return an asset brings in excess of what it could bring in the next-best employment. The principal fixed asset of governments that produce private goods is the legislative sanction to engage in such business, normally on terms that exclude or severely hamper private-sector competition. Sanctions usually are restricted to the goods legally specified; they rarely have "alternative employment" in producing other goods. Because, therefore, governments want to maximize their budgets, one is tempted to call government rent any expenditures the state makes in producing the private goods authorized. Yet this would overstate actual rents, since private firms would have made some of the same factor payments had production taken place in a competitive private sector. Government rent, instead, is the income the government's factor suppliers receive, in the production of private goods, in excess of what they would receive in a competitive private market. Because competitive or minimum marketing cost is area ABEF in figure 2, such rent is the sum of areas FEDp^* and s. This is the gain that bureaucracies naturally seek to protect from privatization.[12]

How much does society lose when a government successfully protects its rents from competitive encroachment? The loss that might conventionally be identified is area EGD in figure 2, analogous to standard Harberger or deadweight loss triangle ABC in figure 1. EGD is the sum of producer and buyer surplus foregone because the state's crop purchases were lower than in a competitive equilibrium. EGD may be quite large. An equally important issue, however, is the disposition of government rent (FEDp^* + s) itself. For both normative and positive purposes, it is important to know which part of such rents is dissipative—lost from national product in the sense of failing to produce valued outputs—and which part represents a mere transfer from farmers and international donors to the government's employees and nonfarm suppliers.

The literature has raised a corresponding question about Tullock rectangle p_0ACp_1 in figure 1: namely, the gross rents a for-profit firm extracts from trade protection, special tax breaks, and the like. The entire such rent is available as profit if resources need not be expended in obtaining the rent. Of course, resources normally do need to be expended for this purpose, but any excess above the expenditure is a net transfer from taxpayers and other private agents to the rent-seeking firm and thus is saved from dissipation. Furthermore, only expenditures on such

Figure 3. The cost of state production of private goods[a]

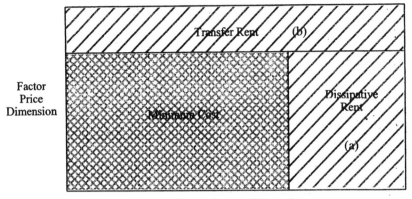

Factor
Price
Dimension

Transfer Rent   (b)

Minimum Cost

Dissipative
Rent

(a)

Factor Quantity Dimension

[a] Transfer rent is assumed, for diagrammatic simplicity, to be positive.

inputs as legal, public relations, and lobbying services, which otherwise would go to output-producing activity, are dissipative. Those which would not (campaign contributions that do not affect a legislator's public good activities, for example) are transfers from suppliers or consumers to government employees. Thus, when profit-seeking firms bid for government preferences, significant opportunities are available for saving some of the rental transfers, despite our views about the fairness of the transfers.

... But the Dissipation Looms Large

Unfortunately the outlook is not so bright when governments bid with international donors for monopsony privileges in private goods production. Indeed, the portion of government rents in figure 2 determined by valuing all government inputs at competitive, private-sector factor prices is pure dissipation. Rents in figure 2 are simply the difference between the government cost and minimum cost of private goods production. This difference consists of two measurably distinct portions: (a) payments to factors at competitive factor prices that a cost-minimizing firm would not have employed to produce q^* and (b) any difference between the government's actual factor payments and the valuation of such payments at competitive factor prices. Assuming private-sector firms would pay only competitive prices, portion (a) corresponds to the resources that would have been available for producing goods additional to q^* had the government not engaged in private goods production. Thus (a) represents technical or allocative inefficiency and is pure waste. By contrast, portion (b) is a pecuniary transfer from farmers and donors to government since it has no opportunity cost in the sense of potentially affecting private-sector output.[13]

Figure 3 summarizes these results: total government cost is divided into minimum cost and government rent, and the latter into dissipative rent (a) and transfer rent (b).

The transfer portion of government rent need not be positive: a state might use its market power to pay subcompetitive rates to its employees and nonfarm suppliers just as it does to farmers. Its chances for doing so depend upon opportunities these agents have of selling their services in other sectors of the economy.[14] Likely, unskilled and semiskilled workers receive little transfer rent, positive or negative, from state marketing firms because markets for their labor are fairly competitive. But there is strong reason to believe that senior employees in state enterprises and in their supervising ministries earn positive pecuniary transfers through supercompetitive benefit packages. The extraordinary housing arrangements for Coffee Authority managers in our own chronicle are a case in point. Extra income for senior personnel provides compensation for their part in the rent-seeking effort and for their support of the coalition needed to sustain government's private good production authority. Thus, part of the conspicuous consumption we see among senior officials in government-dominated economies probably is a simple transfer from consumers and taxpayers rather than wasteful as such. Nevertheless, senior officials in ministries charged with private as well as public good production are necessarily responsible for both sides of the portfolio. Inducements to spend time on the private goods portion reduce the time available for the public goods portion. These inducements are dissipative because they have an opportunity cost in reducing the production of public goods, as Friedman has argued strongly for a number of decades.

The Future of Government Rent Seeking

Our analysis of government rent has strong and worrisome implications for rent seeking in state-owned enterprises. The search for rent in liberal economies always will be constrained for the simple reason that firms engage in it for profit, which declines as search costs grow. Rent-seekers in government, however, face no such obstacle, since search costs do not diminish the compensation received. To the contrary, these costs are impounded into the bureau's budget, which the rentiers wish in any event to maximize.

The same insight may be reworded in the following way. In bureaus with private-good mandates, rent search has both an indirect and direct effect on the budget, and both effects are positive. The indirect effect is the influence brought to bear on domestic politicians and international donors to maintain the state's production authority, monopsony status, and operating subsidies. The direct effect is the cost of this very rent-seeking activity, which bears some similitude to the bureau's legitimate charge. Thus, little incentive exists for economizing on rent-seeking efforts as long as these efforts do not grossly infringe on the production of public and private goods under the bureau's charge. Rent seeking in state-owned firms and in their supervising ministries is, for this reason, especially potent.

If the search for government rents in state-owned firms is so lucrative, why did the Smallholder Coffee Authority go into receivership? What explains the seismic retreat of government marketing boards around the world, and more generally of the public production of private goods? Institutional retrenchments of such dramatic nature, it seems to us, signify overshooting, and one cannot understand overshooting without a dynamic story of rentier behavior. We have portrayed our own model in static form. But the outlines of a dynamic model incorporating excessive and thus self-destructive rent seeking are fairly clear. Output prices, marketing costs, and farm production cannot be fully anticipated. Because marketing boards make annual contractual commitments to employees, suppliers, and farmers, budget restrictions of the form $C(q, \beta; \mathbf{w}, \mathbf{D}) \leq q(P - p) + s$ cannot be strictly enforced in the short run. Subsidies will rise to pay for the excess of actual expenditures over initially announced limits. Subventions of this sort are legion in state-owned firms. Hardly a state enterprise exists which isn't intended, on paper, to operate without treasury support. Subsidies come in through the back door as "short-term" relief for cost overages.

For a number of reasons, the overages may grow continuously for a long time. Consider, for example, an agriculture ministry that underestimates farm supply response. Chronically underestimating supply is, technically speaking, irrational. But it has some claim to empirical validity (Pollard and Graham). It is also ideologically consistent. The argument that poor farmers do not respond well to price incentives is, after all, one of the principal justifications for state intervention in developing nations' economies. A ministry that underestimates farm supply slope $\partial q / \partial p$ in equation (1) will overestimate the rate at which a unit reduction in farm price will increase net margins $q(P - p)$.[15] Thus, government generally will offer farm prices that are too low for a given assumed subsidy, receive lower grower financing $q(P - p)$ than expected, and rely more than expected on donor financing.

What will it learn from these errors? With its ideological predispositions, and in the face of weather-induced ambiguity in farm supply relationships, it will arguably learn more about the elasticity of the donor's willingness to contribute than about the elasticity of farm supply. It will learn, in particular, that a donor can be quite happy for awhile financing successively increasing overages. International financial sources are wealthy and remote, and their agents in the aid bureaucracy have their own interests in maintaining the assistance pipeline. Marketing boards become ensnared in a cycle of declining production, unused facilities, rising unit costs, reduced operating margins, and further farm price cuts to pay for them. The agricultural wealth from which the state had extracted much of its rent deteriorates, leaving the donor itself as the only exploitable asset. Only when taxpayers in donor nations become aware of this does the aid relationship become untenable.

A market liberalization that truly liberalizes, that replaces state monopoly with competitive institutions, eventually will help restore the prosperity which central control had compromised. But renewed prosperity provides new rent-seeking targets. As capital and output grow, so does the rental value of state power. We can expect, therefore, to hear renewed calls for state monopoly and state regulation in the years ahead. In anticipating these cycles, and more generally in calculating the social costs of government power in economic life, one must distinguish clearly between the dissipative and transfer portions of government rent. The precise size of each is a context-specific and thus empirical question. For reasons we have discussed, however, we think the dissipative portion will be found to be much larger than in the classical (Tullock) rent-seeking paradigm.

Endnotes

[1] Indeed, a market-based valuation such as this understates true capital cost. Valued at cost, most of the Authority's rural facilities are beyond the means of private buyers and would sell at substantial losses.

[2] By way of comparison, the average expense-to-revenue ratio in the Kenyan coffee industry was 20% during the 1991–94 period.

[3] Such figures were consistent with the subsequent Lincoln Bailey report indicating that close to 90% of Coffee Authority revenues were being soaked up in marketing costs.

[4] In their excellent historical survey of grain marketing policy in east and southern Africa, Jayne and Jones (p. 1,521) conclude as well that the development of local farmer organizations is essential to successful market reform.

[5] More technically, the total cost of cherry assembly and pulping is, at current output volume, minimized where the long-run average pulping cost curves are negatively sloped.

[6] Sexton shows, in an explicitly spatial setting, that adding a cooperative to a group of incumbent oligopolistic firms is likely to have a more competitive pricing effect than would adding another investor-owned firm to the same group. Evidence of the efficiency of cooperation in small-scale agriculture, where nonconvexities and, hence, natural monopsonies frequently occur, is widespread. Medieval Scottish farmers, for example, typically formed production cooperatives in which each family contributed one ox to a two- or four-ox plow team (Yeoman, p. 108).

[7] Actual prices were quoted for parchment and depended upon parchment grade and upon whether the cherry was pulped at the farmer's home or at the village's centralized facility. Figures discussed here assume a 5:1 weight ratio between cherry and parchment and a 1.25:1 weight ratio between parchment and green bean.

[8] Depreciation costs remain, of course, even if opportunity costs are zero.

[9] James (pp. 72–75) observes that parastatals in Tanzania and Kenya have operated largely independently of their ministerial supervisors. We agree that managers often act with wide latitude at an operational level. They do not, however, set price policy or lobby independently for their budget resources. In particular, parastatal manager and ministerial supervisor have a strong mutual interest in increasing the size of the parastatal's budget.

[10] Although state firms also seek authority, reputation, and patronage, James (p. 149) and Niskanen (p. 38) show that each of these goals is facilitated by budget maximization.

[11] In Niskanen's (pp. 45–46) model of government budget maximization, a state bureau operates where its budget function (reflecting the sponsor's or donor's willingness to pay for given levels of the bureau's service) is a maximum, subject to the restriction that the budget not fall below minimized cost. A marketing board is an instance of what Niskanen calls a "mixed" bureau, one financed both by a sponsor (our international donor) and by a "customer" (our farmer). Niskanen sums the sponsor's and customer's "demands" into an aggregate budget function. Subsidy (s) in our model might be considered an observation on Niskanen's budget function, and farmer financing $q(P - p)$ a version of Niskanen's customer contribution. However, our model remains different from Niskanen's in emphasis, specificity, and amenability to hypothesis testing. Separately, Jackson (pp. 185–88) provides an extensive discussion of the reasons bureaucracies tend to be allocatively inefficient, implying in the present model that β normally exceeds unity. Consistent with this, Jayne and Jones (p. 1,517) note that the legalization of private grain trading in Africa has dramatically reduced marketing costs.

[12] We assume for simplicity that fixed costs are zero. In a shorter run, where fixed costs are positive, rent would consist of $(FEDp^* + s)$ minus minimum fixed costs.

[13] An exception to this rule would arise if wage rate changes affected a worker's output. However, incentive effects normally would be modeled by separating workers into productivity classes, each with its own wage rate.

[14] Marketing boards succeed in paying subcompetitive farm prices principally because farmland resources are relatively immobile.

[15] The derivative of net margins with respect to a decrease in farm price is $-\partial[q(P - p)]/\partial p = q - (\partial q/\partial p)(P - p)$. Thus, net margins actually will fall as p rises if $(\partial q/\partial p)(P - p) > q$. Underestimating $\partial q/\partial p$ reduces the likelihood of anticipating this fall. Pollard and Graham, for example, argue that Jamaican marketing boards have assumed that farm supply response $\partial q/\partial p$ is essentially zero. In such an extreme case, a board would conclude that a unit reduction in p would bring about a net margin increase of q.

References

Adam, C., W. Cavendish, and P.S. Mistry. *Adjusting Privatization: Case Studies from Developing Countries.* Portsmouth NH: Heinemann, 1992.

Bates, R.H. *Markets and States in Tropical Africa.* Berkeley CA: University of California Press, 1981.

Bauer, P.T. *Reality and Rhetoric: Studies in the Economics of Development.* Cambridge MA: Harvard University Press, 1984.

———. *West African Trade.* London: Routledge and Kegan Paul, 1963.

Buchanan, J.M., R.D. Tollison, and G. Tullock. *Toward a Theory of the Rent-Seeking Society.* College Station TX: Texas A&M University Press, 1980.

Friedman, M. *Free to Choose.* New York: Harcourt Brace Jovanovich, 1980.

Higgins, R.S., and R.D. Tollison. "Life Among the Triangles and Trapezoids: Notes on the Theory of Rent-Seeking." *The Political Economy of Rent Seeking.* C.K. Rowley, R.D. Tollison, and G. Tullock, eds. Boston: Kluwer Academic Publishers, 1988.

Jackson, P.M. *The Political Economy of Bureaucracy.* Totowa NJ: Barnes and Noble, 1983.

James, J. *The State, Technology, and Industrialization in Africa.* London: Macmillan Press, 1995.

Jayne, T.S., and S. Jones. "Food Marketing and Pricing Policy in Eastern and Southern Africa: A Survey." *World Develop.* 25(September 1997):1505–27.

Krueger, A.O., M. Schiff, and A. Valdes. *The Political Economy of Agricultural Pricing Policy,* vol. 3, *Africa and the Mediterranean.* Baltimore MD: Johns Hopkins University Press (for World Bank), 1991.

Lincoln Bailey Consultants. *Study on the Smallholder Coffee Authority.* Consultancy Report to the Government of Malawi, Photocopy, 1996.

Mosley, P. "On Persuading a Leopard to Change His Spots: Optimal Strategies for Donors and Recipients of Conditional Development Aid." *Toward a Political Economy of Development.* R.H. Bates, ed. Berkeley CA: University of California Press, 1988.

Niskanen, W.A. *Bureaucracy and Representative Government.* Chicago: Aldine-Atherton, 1971.

Pollard, S.K., and D.H. Graham. "Price Policy and Agricultural Export Performance in Jamaica." *World Develop.* 13(September 1985):1067–75.

Sexton, R.J. "Imperfect Competition in Agricultural Markets and the Role of Cooperatives: A Spatial Analysis." *Amer. J. Agr. Econ.* 72(August 1990):709–20.

Tollison, R.D. "Is the Theory of Rent-Seeking Here to Stay?" *Democracy and Public Choice: Essays in Honor of Gordon Tullock.* C.K. Rowley, ed. New York: Basil Blackwell, 1987.

Yeoman, P. *Medieval Scotland: An Archeological Perspective.* London: B.T. Batsford, 1995.

Discouraging Rivals: Managerial Rent-Seeking and Economic Inefficiencies

By Aaron S. Edlin and Joseph E. Stiglitz *

Managerial theories of the firm have a long and controversial history, beginning perhaps with Adolf A. Berle, Jr. and Gardiner C. Means's classic (1932) study. Such theories postulated that managers had considerable discretion running corporations and exercised it to pursue objectives other than maximizing shareholder market value.

Critics later denied that managers really have discretion, arguing that such behavior could not survive in equilibrium. Either management would be voted from office, the firm would be taken over, or the firm would go bankrupt in a competitive product market.

The more recent literature on information economics emasculated these criticisms. Managers are important to corporate decision-making because of their expertise and the information they acquire about the firm and its prospects. Yet the very information asymmetries that create a *need* for management also limit the discipline that the board of directors can impose on managers. At the same time, neither the shareholder-voting mechanism nor the takeover mechanism provides effective discipline.[1] Small shareholders free ride on the efforts of others, since it does not pay for them to obtain the costly information needed to exercise their proxy vote intelligently. Moreover, if a takeover will enhance the productivity of the firm, it will likewise enhance its market value, so small shareholders are better off holding onto their shares than tendering them. Takeovers can therefore be difficult when ownership is dispersed. Indeed, the theoretical arguments suggest that the takeover mechanism should be even less effective than it seems to be in practice. It has become more of a theoretical puzzle to explain the existence of managerial discipline than of managerial discretion.[2]

These observations argue for a return to the viewpoint of the earlier managerial literature, which presumed that managers have discretion and asked how they will use it (see James G. March and Simon, 1958; Robin L. Marris, 1964; Oliver E. Williamson, 1964; Harvey Leibenstein, 1966). This paper continues that tradition, examining one route—namely, investment choice—by which managerial discretion affords managers the opportunity to obtain "rents" (payments in excess of their opportunity costs). We thereby expand on the theme of Shleifer and Vishny's (1989) insightful paper on "managerial entrenchment."

A somewhat earlier literature on incomplete contracts emphasized the investment consequences of rent-seeking. That literature explained how concern about opportunism can

* Edlin: Department of Economics, 549 Evans Hall, University of California, Berkeley, CA 94720; Stiglitz: Department of Economics, Stanford University, Stanford, CA 94305-6072, and Council of Economic Advisers, Washington, DC. This paper was originally prepared for a conference sponsored by the Center for Economic Policy Research, Stanford, May 1991. We thank the National Science Foundation and the Hoover Institution for financial support and Jeremy Bulow, Eric Emch, Kirsten Landeryou, Peter Klein, Jonathan Paul, Jeffrey Zwiebel, and the anonymous referees, for their comments. The views expressed are solely those of the authors and not necessarily of any organization with which they are or have been affiliated.

[1] The theoretical literature on takeovers includes Stiglitz (1972, 1975) and Sanford S. Grossman and Oliver D. Hart (1980). The empirical literature includes Michael Jensen (1988), David Scharfstein (1988), and Andrei Shleifer and Robert W. Vishny (1988). For discussions of the voting (or proxy) control mechanisms, see Stiglitz (1981), Jensen and Richard S. Ruback (1983), and Randall Morck et al. (1989).

[2] Early literature, such as Berle (1926), stressed the disciplinary role of banks (see also Stiglitz, 1985). More recently, organization theorists and some economists have emphasized social control mechanisms (attempts to make managers *identify* with the company, and adopt the "well-being" of the corporation as their own private goals). On this, see George A. Akerlof (1991) and Herbert A. Simon (1991).

American Economic Review **85**, 1301–1312

lead to underinvestment in such relationship-specific investments such as a manager's investment in firm-specific human capital (see Aaron S. Edlin and Stefan Reichelstein [1993] for citations). We argue here for a broader view of the biases in managers' decisions: In general, managerial rent-seeking affects not only the *level* of investment, but also the *form*.[3]

Our basic hypothesis is simple: given the now well-established *scope* for managerial discretion, managers have an incentive to exercise that discretion to enhance their income. Any managerial contract is subject to renegotiation, and a manager's pay is the outcome of an often bewildering bargaining process between management, the board of directors, and rival management teams or takeover artists. Two critical factors in that bargaining process are the incumbent management's productivity relative to rivals and the wages that rivals demand. A manager may increase her compensation either by increasing her own productivity (the aspect generally stressed) or by decreasing the threat from rival managers.[4] Shleifer and Vishny (1989) consider the latter possibility and show that a manager can increase her rents by choosing to invest in projects she can manage better than her rivals.

Here we explore a new avenue for entrenchment. The prototypical example of the Shleifer and Vishny (1989) effect is a secretary who becomes invaluable by rearranging a filing system to suit his own idiosyncratic search patterns. Yet we observe that managers often retain their jobs without making such investments; they are rehired even when they select assets for which their own idiosyncratic talents are not the best match. We suggest that these managers may preserve their jobs by investing in activities for which information asymmetries are particularly large (our arguments are

in the same spirit as Laurie S. Bagwell and Josef Zechner [1993]). In our theory, managers invest to create these asymmetries, not to exploit their talents. They thus engage in a form of rent-seeking even less productive than that considered by Shleifer and Vishny (1989).

Our theory predicts, for example, that managers will overvalue acquisitions that promise *potential*, but not certain, synergies, since such acquisitions can bring rents to incumbent managers as long as they get earlier or more accurate signals than rivals of whether these synergies materialize. This argument suggests that the recent wave of acquisitions in the media and communications industries is a sensible entrenchment strategy, because the potential synergies are large, even if the expected synergies might not be.

Such possibilities become clearer as the paper unfolds. Section I sets up the framework for discouraging rivals. Section II analyzes how to discourage rivals who can observe investment levels. Section III considers discouraging rivals who cannot observe the mix of investment, and the final section outlines some implications of the analysis both for policy and empirical work.

I. Discouraging Rivals: The Framework

We present a three-stage model. In the first stage the manager chooses investments. In the second, the board of directors decides who will manage the firm's assets, and in the third, the manager manages the assets.

Managers choose investments to maximize the product of the probability that they are rehired in stage 2 and the rents they expect to accrue conditional upon being rehired:

$$\max_{\{I_1, I_2\}} [E[\text{rents} \,|\, \text{incumbent rehired}]$$

$$\times \Pr\{\text{incumbent rehired}\}].$$

This formulation does not imply risk neutrality: instead, these rents are in units of utility and represent the difference between the utility the manager could get from outside opportunities (which we assume to be constant) and the utility from the stage-2 contract, which is a function of the contract she negotiates and

---

[3] See Edlin (1992) for the argument that the important distortions in the incomplete-contracts context are also in the form, not the level, of investment.

[4] Although the contexts differ, there is a strong similarity between our argument and Steven C. Salop and David T. Scheffman's (1983, 1987) analysis of the behavior of firms in imperfectly competitive markets. They argue that firms can enhance their profits not only by increasing their own productivity, but also by reducing the threat of rivals, (i.e., by raising rivals' costs).

VOL. 85 NO. 5   EDLIN AND STIGLITZ: DISCOURAGING RIVALS   1303

the effort she subsequently expends. We will soon be explicit about the sources of these rents, but at a general level, our argument is simply this: as the inherent ability of a manager's rivals falls, as the effort rival managers will exert falls, or as rivals demand higher wages to accept the position, then the incumbent manager will gather increased rents from contract negotiations, other things being equal.

Of course, some students of corporate culture may rebel at the image of a board of directors negotiating with the manager: The manager is often thought simply to name the terms of her contract, with the board providing the rubber stamp. Indeed, boards sometimes do approve contracts with incumbent managers that predictably leave the firm worse off than under rival management. Nonetheless, even those who take an extreme view of the agency problems involved in the board's representation of shareholder interests will concede that *something* limits what managers can successfully demand. We suggest that these limits ultimately stem from the threat of replacement by rivals. We therefore examine how managers can reduce this threat by *discouraging* rivals.

In our formulation, a firm's terminal, or stage-3 return, R, is a product of the effective quality of the manager and the prospects of the firm's ongoing projects:

(1) $$R = (C_1 + C_2)q(e)$$

where q is the effective quality of the manager, which may depend upon effort e, and C_i represents the "prospects" in project i, $i \in \{1, 2\}$. The two projects can be thought of as a "short-run" and "long-run" project, or as two different activities run over the same time horizon. C_i may represent the potential cash flows or underlying "capital" of project i. It is stochastically related to the firm's stage-1 investment according to some risk θ_i, which increases proportionately with investment:

(2) $$C_i = F_i(I_i) + \theta_i$$

where

$$\theta_i \sim \mathcal{N}(0, I_i^2 \sigma_i^2), \qquad i \in \{1, 2\}.$$

We consider two main cases: in the first, outsiders can observe the mix of investment in the two activities; in the second, they only observe total investment $I_1 + I_2$. In both cases, the incumbent observes C_i accurately, while rivals must try to infer C_i from the signals Y_i, defined as

(3) $$Y_i = C_i + \varepsilon_i$$

where

$$\varepsilon_i \sim \mathcal{N}(0, I_i^2 w_i^2), \, i \in \{1, 2\}$$

and where the ε's and θ's are all independent.

The first-best mix of investment maximizes $E[C_1 + C_2]$. Assuming an interior solution, optimal investments are some I_1^* and I_2^* such that $F_1'(I_1^*) = F_2'(I_2^*)$. The next two sections show, however, that these first-best investments do not solve the investment problem for a manager trying to entrench herself. The investment choices will be distorted regardless of whether the mix of investment she chooses is observable to outsiders or remains unobservable. In either case, the manager favors investments in which information is more quickly or fully revealed to her than to outsiders, although the reasons for the distortions differ somewhat between the two cases.

II. Case 1: Observable Investment

Rivals base their expectation of the firm's potential cash flows on their observations Y_1 and Y_2. This expectation is given by

(4) $$E[C_1 + C_2 | Y_1, Y_2]$$

$$= \beta_0 + \beta_1 Y_1 + \beta_2 Y_2$$

where

$$\beta_i = \frac{\sigma_i^2}{w_i^2 + \sigma_i^2} \qquad i \in \{1, 2\}$$

$$\beta_0 = \frac{w_1^2}{w_1^2 + \sigma_1^2} F_1(I_1) + \frac{w_2^2}{w_2^2 + \sigma_2^2} F_2(I_2).$$

We derive this expectation formula in the Appendix. Since in this section's analysis, outsiders can observe the investment mix, the intercept term β_0 is a function of the actual investments I_1 and I_2. This feature differs from Section III, which analyzes unobservable investment.

A. *Investing to Discourage Rivals' Efforts*

After the investments are chosen, the assets must be managed, either by the incumbent manager or by some rival. In either case, the manager chooses her effort level to maximize her expected utility given her information. The firm must provide the manager with some incentive to expend effort, and for simplicity we assume that the manager who is given responsibility for managing the assets has an incentive contract giving her a share in profits.[5] Thus, if W represents manager j's fixed wage income, s her share of profits, U her utility function, $p_j e$ her personal cost of expending effort e (p_j is an index of her ability), and Φ her information set, the manager chooses effort to maximize

(5) $E[U[W + s(C_1 + C_2)q(e) - p_j e] | \Phi]$.

Assuming constant absolute risk aversion, so that the certainty equivalent is linear in the mean and variance of wealth,[6] the manager's problem is to maximize

(6) $W + sq(e)E[(C_1 + C_2)|\Phi]$

$$- ks^2 q^2(e) \mathrm{Var}[(C_1 + C_2)|\Phi] - p_j e$$

where $\mathrm{Var}[(C_1 + C_2)|\Phi]$ is the variance of $C_1 + C_2$ conditional upon the manager's information Φ and where k equals half of the degree of absolute risk aversion. We assume that effective worker quality $q(e)$ increases with effort. Effort is costly and so, all else

---

[5] For one justification of linear incentive schemes, see Bengt Holmstrom and Paul R. Milgrom (1987).
[6] We do not require all the structure of constant absolute risk aversion in order for Lemma 1 to hold and the subsequent analysis to be valid. In particular, the strong linearity is not important: it would be sufficient for our purposes that effort enter separately and that managers' utility be some increasing function of expected wealth and decreasing function of the variance of wealth.

equal, managers with a higher cost of effort p_j exert less effort, and have lower effective quality. However, a manager's effort, and hence effective quality q, also depends upon her appraisal of a firm's prospects.

In our model, a rival who takes over a management role must decide her effort before learning the prospects $C_1 + C_2$. This timing captures important features that we would neglect by assuming that rivals observe C_1 and C_2 before choosing effort. When the rival takes over, he will not be handed the keys to some safe containing the secret information "C_1" and "C_2." That would be a poor caricature of private information. Witness the fact that it took John Sculley four months to discover the desperate condition of Spectrum, and consider that such information is often less concrete than in that case.[7] Relevant information can be quite diffuse, spread among many present and former officials of the firm, and revelation to the new management team is far from immediate. Thus, while our assumption that nothing new is learned after taking the helm is extreme, it neatly captures the fact that much of what was known to the predecessor remains unknown to new management.

We are now prepared to state a useful lemma.

LEMMA 1: *Holding the cost of effort and other factors constant, an interior solution to manager j's effort choice problem e^{*j} increases with $E[(C_1 + C_2)|\Phi]$ and decreases with $\mathrm{Var}[(C_1 + C_2)|\Phi]$.*

PROOF:
The lemma follows from the form of the manager's objective function together with the fact that effective quality q increases with effort. The cross derivative with respect to q and $E[(C_1 + C_2)|\Phi]$ is positive and with respect to q and $\mathrm{Var}[(C_1 + C_2)|\Phi]$ is negative, so Milgrom and Christina Shannon's (1994) Monotone Selection Theorem implies that the solution to manager j's effort-choice problem is weakly increasing in $E[(C_1 + C_2)|\Phi]$ and weakly decreasing in $\mathrm{Var}[(C_1 + C_2)|\Phi]$.

---

[7] See Jonathan Weber (1994) for a description of the Sculley–Spectrum saga.

These results are strict whenever $e*^j$ is interior as assumed, because then if first-order conditions hold for one expectation or variance, they fail for higher ones.

We now proceed to examine how current management's actions can poison the applicant pool for the manager's job by lowering the effectiveness of rival management. The current manager can reduce rivals' efforts by increasing their perceived uncertainty about the firm's prospects. The incumbent's effort and hence effective quality rises relative to rivals with an increase in

$$(7) \qquad \text{Var}[\,(C_1 + C_2)\,|\,\Phi_{\text{riv}}]$$

$$- \text{Var}[\,(C_1 + C_2)\,|\,\Phi_{\text{inc}}]$$

where Φ_{riv} denotes the information of the rivals and Φ_{inc} denotes that of the incumbent.

Recall that the incumbent observes $C_1 + C_2$, so $\text{Var}[(C_1 + C_2)|\Phi_{\text{inc}}] = 0$. In contrast, rival management teams can only infer $C_1 + C_2$ from the noisy signals Y_1 and Y_2. The Appendix shows that

$$(8) \qquad \text{Var}(C_1 + C_2|Y_1, Y_2)$$

$$= \frac{\sigma_1^2 w_1^2 I_1^2}{\sigma_1^2 + w_1^2} + \frac{\sigma_2^2 w_2^2 I_2^2}{\sigma_2^2 + w_2^2}.$$

Equation (8) reveals that the manager will favor highly noisy investments (high w^2 for any given σ^2): such investments decrease the effectiveness of outside managers by increasing expression (7).[8] These gains from increasing noise are larger for higher underlying risks, and in the extreme case where $\sigma^2 = 0$, w^2 becomes irrelevant because the potential cash flows are fully determined by the observable investment levels. Finally, in choosing among projects with similar risk (σ^2) and noise

for outside investors (w^2), incumbents can decrease the effectiveness of rivals by concentrating their investments, because of the convexity of I^2. Accordingly, rent-seeking may cause overspecialization.

B. Discouraging Applicants

In addition to reducing the effective quality of the rivals, the incumbent manager's investment choices can raise rivals' wage demands. For manager j, with reservation utility level $r(j)$, to be willing to work for the firm, she must be offered a high enough wage that

$$(9) \quad W + sq(e*^j)E[\,(C_1 + C_2)\,|\,\Phi] - p_j e*^j$$

$$> r(j) + ks^2 q^2 \text{Var}(C_1 + C_2|\Phi).$$

The right-hand side represents the familiar fact that the manager must be compensated both for her reservation price $r(j)$, and for the risk from the incentive plan given by s. When $\text{Var}(C_1 + C_2|\Phi_{\text{riv}})$ increases, any given compensation package will fall below the reservation wage of some rivals. These managers choose not to apply, weakening the pool of rivals and increasing the chance that the incumbent is rehired.

C. Increasing Rivals' Winner's Curse

A third reason for a manager to invest in noisy projects is that such projects create a winner's curse effect. This effect further discourages applicants from "applying" and makes those who do apply demand higher offsetting compensation. Recall that the incumbent knows $C_1 + C_2$, so that

$$(10) \qquad E(C_1 + C_2|\Phi_{\text{inc}}) = C_1 + C_2.$$

The rival manager does not know $C_1 + C_2$, but knows that, if he were to observe a value of Y_1 and Y_2 such that his expectation of $C_1 + C_2$ is the same as that of the incumbent, the board of directors would likely stick with the incumbent for the two reasons already discussed: (a) all else equal, incumbents work harder because the returns to their effort is more certain; and (b) incumbents are willing to accept the

---

[8] Notice that such a result is quite different from the more standard asset-substitution result of Jensen and William H. Meckling (1976 section 4.1). They argue that equity-holders will be biased to invest in high-risk assets since limited liability cuts off their downside risk. The noise w^2 should be distinguished from the fundamental risk σ^2.

Aaron S. Edlin and Joseph E. Stiglitz

job at lower compensation since their perceived risk is smaller.

Thus, the incumbent will be able to cut a deal with the board of directors, beating out rival management offers unless (a) the incumbent has a very high reservation wage relative to rivals; (b) the board of directors' estimate of the rival's ability is high relative to the incumbent; or (c) the rival has seriously overestimated the value of the project (ε is high). Holding the first two factors constant, the rival manager knows he gets the job only when his signal is overly optimistic. He takes this into account in forming his expectations. (Consider the *Wall Street Journal* headline after John Akers left quietly: ''Akers Quits at IBM'' together with the sub-headline, ''But Who'd Want This Job?'' [Michael W. Miller and Laurence Hooper, 1993]).[9]

In determining whether to apply, the rival manager in fact considers

(11) $E[C_1 + C_2 | Y_1, Y_2, \text{incumbent not rehired}]$

instead of

(12) $E[C_1 + C_2 | Y_1, Y_2].$

This winner's curse further reduces rivals' efforts and their willingness to accept a job,[10] since as explained above,

(13) $E[C_1 + C_2 | Y_1, Y_2, \text{incumbent not rehired}]$

$< E[C_1 + C_2 | Y_1, Y_2].$

Assume that the incumbent manager's rents conditional upon being rehired increase linearly with the wedge,

(14) $C_1 + C_2 - E[C_1 + C_2 | Y_1, Y_2,$

incumbent not rehired]

---

[9] Miller and Hooper (1993) report that ''In the end, International Business Machines Corp. had unraveled so badly that there wasn't any need for a fractious boardroom coup.''

[10] Rivals' management teams' estimates of the relevant variances may also have to be altered to take into account the winner's curse phenomenon, but we assume that the truncation leaves the risk-ordering of investments the same.

and the conditional variance,

(15) $\text{Var}[C_1 + C_2 | Y_1, Y_2,$

incumbent not rehired].

Recall that the incumbent manager's investment problem is

(16) $\max_{\{I_1, I_2\}} [E[\text{rents} | \text{incumbent rehired}]$

$\times \Pr\{\text{incumbent rehired}\}].$

Our analysis indicates that the return to a noisy investment (one with a high value of w^2 for any given σ^2) is larger than the return to one for which Y is a good signal of the project's potential cash flows, for three distinct reasons: (a) the noise directly discourages rivals' efforts and thus makes rivals less attractive as managers; (b) the noise directly discourages rivals from applying (and makes them insist on higher compensation), thus making them a less viable threat; and (c) the noise increases the asymmetry of information and accordingly the winner's curse effect.

Consider the extreme case in which rivals can perfectly observe project 1 but only observe project 2 via a noisy signal. If the fundamentals of the two projects are sufficiently close, we would expect project 2 to be chosen even though shareholders would favor investment in project 1. By investing in the noisy project, managers raise both the probability of being rehired and the average rents they obtain when they are rehired. Section IV argues that some of the recent acquisitions in preparation for the nascent information age probably represent such entrenchment activities.

D. *Extensions: Multidimensional Effort*

A similar analysis could be done to explore a model in which, instead of choosing investment at stage 1, a manager chooses how to allocate his own effort between the projects. Jonathan M. Paul (1992) studied that problem in considering the efficiency of stock-based compensation. In terms of our notation, he found that the manager's effort would be increasing in σ_i^2 and decreasing in w_i^2. Our conclusions for such an analysis would differ from his because, unlike Paul (1992), we imagine that the managerial contract is negotiated or renegotiated after these decisions. Noise (high w_i^2) may discourage rivals and put the incumbent in a better position to extract rent in these renegotiations. In contrast, Paul's (1992) effects would dominate if the contract were preset to include stock-based compensation, and *could not be renegotiated*, since noisy projects have the drawback of having little influence on the stock price, as Paul observes.

III. Case 2: Unobservable Investment

We assume that the manager has a budget $\bar{I}$ to allocate between projects 1 and 2, and that although the financial statements reveal the total investment, they do not disclose the mix of investment dollars between the two projects. Rivals must therefore base their projections of the firm's prospects upon the equilibrium investment mix, together with the observable signals Y_1 and Y_2. The expected value of these prospects conditional upon the observations Y_1 and Y_2 are derived in the Appendix and given by

$$(17) \quad E[C_1 + C_2 | Y_1, Y_2] = \beta_0 + \beta_1 Y_1 + \beta_2 Y_2$$

where

$$\beta_i = \sigma_i^2 / (\sigma_i^2 + w_i^2) \qquad i \in \{1, 2\}$$

$$\beta_0 = \frac{w_1^2}{w_1^2 + \sigma_1^2} F_1(\hat{I}_1) + \frac{w_2^2}{w_2^2 + \sigma_2^2} F_2(\hat{I}_2).$$

Altering the mix of investment alters Y_1 and Y_2, but since rivals do not observe deviations, they will not change the rule, given in equation (17), by which they form expectations. The intercept term here is a function of the *equilibrium* investments $\hat{I}_1$ and $\hat{I}_2$, unlike in equation (4), where *actual* investments are observed.

The incumbent can reduce the effectiveness of rivals by raising $E[C_1 + C_2 | \Phi_{\text{inc}}] - E[C_1 + C_2 | \Phi_{\text{riv}}]$. We can see that she will not generally choose the first-best investments I_1^* and I_2^*, because she would benefit from shifting some investment into the noisier project with the higher w^2 / σ^2 and lower coefficient β. Such

a shift increases the wedge $C_1 + C_2 - E[C_1 + C_2 | Y_1, Y_2]$:[11] To see this, observe that as a first-order approximation for small shifts in investment from I_1^* and I_2^* into the noisier project, for any given realization of ε_i and θ_i, $E[C_1 + C_2 | Y_1, Y_2]$ falls, while $C_1 + C_2$ remains constant, since $F_1'(I_1^*) = F_2'(I_2^*)$.

Shifting investment to noisier projects reduces rivals' effective quality by reducing their optimal effort. A winner's curse problem, analogous to the one in the previous section, exacerbates this effect. In fact, all investment might potentially be in the noisier project in equilibrium. With sufficiently diminishing real returns, however, it will eventually no longer pay the incumbent to create noise, for, when returns are lower in the noisy asset, shifting investment lowers $C_1 + C_2$ to a first-order approximation, just as it lowers $E[C_1 + C_2 | Y_1, Y_2]$. Lowering $C_1 + C_2$ lowers the incumbent's effort under any given incentive contract, making her a less desirable manager. Moreover, to the extent that the manager also places weight on $C_1 + C_2$ in her decision problem (perhaps because she initially holds stock options), lowering $C_1 + C_2$ is directly undesirable.

We should finally observe that since rivals cannot observe the investment mix here, the incumbent cannot affect $\text{Var}[C_1 + C_2 | Y_1, Y_2]$ as she could in the previous section; in this section $\text{Var}[C_1 + C_2 | Y_1, Y_2]$ is determined by the equilibrium investment levels.

IV. Implications

We conclude with some implications and interpretations of our analysis, asking four questions:

---

[11] With full knowledge of her investment level, the incumbent manager forms expectations about what outsiders' uninformed expectations will be. The incumbent's expectations might be written $E_{\text{in}}[E_{\text{out}}(C_1 + C_2 | Y_1, Y_2) | I_1, I_2]$, and it is important to realize that it is an equilibrium condition that at the equilibrium investment levels, $\hat{I}_1, \hat{I}_2$, $E_{\text{in}}[E_{\text{out}}(C_1 + C_2 | Y_1, Y_2) | \hat{I}_1, \hat{I}_2] = E_{\text{in}}[(C_1 + C_2) | \hat{I}_1, \hat{I}_2]$. Because of the information difference of the two expectation operators, this equality would not hold "out of equilibrium" if the incumbent reallocated investment to try to create a wedge to get rents. This equality is a condition reflecting consistent or rational expectations.

(i) Does this model explain management biases toward excessive growth such as those observed by Gordon Donaldson (1984 pp. 36–42)?

In our view, managers' rents are associated with investing in noisy projects. If a firm never invested in new projects but simply maintained old assets, its manager would derive little rent, since past project returns would provide good information about asset values.

Indiscriminate growth will not, however, help management. For instance, replicating established ventures of known value does not benefit management. Growth increases a manager's rents in our model when returns are uncertain and when this uncertainty is resolved sooner for insiders than for outsiders. We think it a fair generalization that in new and emerging enterprises both σ^2 and w^2 are quite high, so we should look at these investments for evidence of entrenchment activities. The model can thus help explain biases toward growth, supplementing more traditional explanations of "empire building."

This bias toward innovative activities is not all bad. A bias toward innovation and expenditures on R&D may countervail tendencies toward excessive conservatism, tendencies such as managerial myopia,[12] or the fact that managers tend to be more risk-averse than their typically better-diversified shareholders.

(ii) What implications does the theory have concerning the efficiency of corporate acquisitions and divestitures?

Traditional takeover theory argued that 1980's-style restructurings are necessarily efficiency-enhancing, since in each case, assets are sold to the manager or management team that can most effectively employ them, as evidenced by the price the winning bidder is willing to pay. Our analysis of information asymmetries enriches our understanding of the patterns of divestiture and acquisition and explains how inefficiencies can arise. If scant rents are associated with "mature" or well-established enterprises, it pays to spin-off such assets to owner-managers (who maximize value). The nonowner managers can use the proceeds to purchase assets whose value is hard for rivals to ascertain. Thus, in an auction for an asset (such as the recent bidding by QVC and Viacom for Paramount), what any manager is willing to pay depends not only on what the firm can extract from the asset, but on the rents she can derive from controlling it. These rents are likely to be larger if she can quickly alter the asset to make its market value more uncertain to outsiders. Thus, the "managerial" value of an asset may differ across firms; and the asset will be sold to the firm with the highest managerial value, not necessarily the one with the highest expected value of returns.

Managerial rents may be quite high for acquisitions that have great potential synergies with a firm's existing assets. Because the returns are supposed to materialize from synergies, they cannot be well established by studying the past results of the target firm. Only time can reveal the returns. Moreover, returns will likely be revealed much sooner to incumbents than to rivals.

The recent wave of acquisitions in the communications, computer, and entertainment industries may promote entrenchment.[13] Managers are seeking long-horizon synergies in what they hope are the key information technologies of the next century. Such acquisitions have significant upside potential, but the downside may be as important to management as the upside. It is the uncertainty inherent to "potential" that creates rents, and as long as potential remains and inside managers see realizations before outsiders, incumbents may expect personal prosperity. Such assets are wise acquisitions for management, even if expected returns are not impressive. In contrast, nonsynergistic acquisitions, such as

---

[12] See Paul (1991) for a short survey of the literature on myopia and for an instructive theory of why managers concentrate on immediate returns to maximize stock-market value in a noisy world.

[13] Examples include the Time-Warner merger, the acquisition of Paramount by Viacom, and the acquisitions of McCaw Cellular Communications by AT&T. See Wall Street Journal (1994) for a discussion of the new merger wave.

typified the formation of diversified conglomerates in the 1960's and 1970's, are not particularly valuable for entrenchment; they invite the sorts of takeovers and spin-offs that dominated the 1980's.

(iii) What can be done to combat or limit the rent-seeking we discuss?

First, by being aware of the natural potential biases in managerial behavior, the board of directors or shareholders can hope to uncover and stop the most flagrant instances of biased investment behavior. One recent example might be the efforts of two large QVC shareholders, Liberty Media and Comcast, to derail Barry Diller's attempted acquisition of CBS (see *Chicago Tribune*, 1994). A major quandary firms face, however, is that many investments that increase profits also increase managerial rents. For instance, profits can be high in new enterprises, but the barriers which serve to enhance firm profits may equally enhance managerial rents (see Benjamin E. Hermalin [1992] for a different view).

Second, the board may seek a way to prevent renegotiation of wages; it might "constitutionalize" the CEO's pay in corporate bylaws. Such an approach, however, has drawbacks: the inertial staying power of some bylaws may itself prove costly (the hazards of inflexibility are well illustrated by the American Tobacco Co.),[14] and some states have acted to limit compensation schemes in bylaws.[15] Perhaps a better way to limit (though not eliminate) the rent-seeking we analyze is the common plan to cope with other agency problems: at the expense of inefficient risk-bearing, boards may require high (initial) stock ownership by management.

A third approach is for either boards or the government to require more stringent and detailed accounting and reporting. For instance, if reports identify the mix of investment, the distortions in Section III are eliminated. Furthermore, all the distortions we identify can be reduced to the extent that managers are required to report inside information faster and more accurately.

We recognize that it is in the nature of private information that calls for revelation are easier made than effectuated. Nonetheless, reporting requirements can have an effect. Few can doubt that because of the U.S. Securities Act of 1933 and the Securities Exchange Act of 1934, important information is public that would otherwise remain private. (Compare the information available about publicly traded companies in the United States with that available in nations that do not have, or do not enforce, such legislation.)

(iv) Finally, what empirical questions does our research open?

Our paper raises a number of empirical questions, most of which will require ingenuity to answer. In principle, one might test the predictions of the model if one were first willing to take a stand on what kinds of investments have returns known better to incumbents than rivals. One could then try to determine whether the marginal return tends to be lower for such investments than for those with returns that are more equally observable to insiders and outsiders. Such a result would imply that managers favor noisy investments and invest beyond the point where returns are equated. Since other papers (e.g., Paul, 1991, 1992) predict that managers who maximize shareholder value will shy away from noisy investments, empirical results would be helpful for understanding managerial objectives.

It would also be valuable to investigate how investment patterns have responded to changes in reporting requirements by the Financial Accounting Standards Board (FASB) and by regulatory bodies such as the Securities

---

[14] In 1912, the shareholders of the American Tobacco Co. adopted a bylaw granting the president a bonus equal to 2.5 percent of net profits, with 1.5 percent going to each vice president. Twenty-eight years later, in 1930, this bylaw yielded the president an $840,000 bonus! The minority shareholders can perhaps be excused their incivility for suggesting in *Rogers* v. *Hill* (289 U.S. 582, 1933), that such a payment constituted waste.

[15] Consider North Carolina Business Corporation Act §16(3) (1973): "No bylaw authorizing compensation of officers measured by the amount of a corporation's income

or volume of business shall be valid after five years from its adoption unless renewed by the vote of the holders of a majority of the outstanding shares regardless of limitation on voting rights."

and Exchange Commission (SEC). Significant responses might indicate that managers do, in fact, exploit information asymmetries when they are allowed.

APPENDIX

We first prove a simple statistical lemma necessary to derive the conditional expectations $E[C_1 + C_2 | Y_1, Y_2]$ and variances $\text{Var}[C_1 + C_2 | Y_1, Y_2]$ given in the paper.

LEMMA A1: *If x and y are independent normal variables and $x \sim \mathcal{N}(0, \sigma^2)$ and $y \sim \mathcal{N}(0, w^2)$, then the distribution of x given that $x + y = s$ is*

$$\mathcal{N}\left(s\frac{\sigma^2}{\sigma^2 + w^2}, \frac{\sigma^2 w^2}{\sigma^2 + w^2} \right).$$

PROOF:

The conditional density of x can be written

$$f(x | x + y = s) = \frac{f(x, x + y = s)}{f(x + y)}$$

$$= \frac{\frac{1}{2\pi\sigma w} \exp\left(-\frac{x^2}{2\sigma^2} \right) \exp\left(-\frac{(s - x)^2}{2w^2} \right)}{\frac{1}{\sqrt{2\pi}\sqrt{\sigma^2 + w^2}} \exp\left(\frac{-s^2}{2(\sigma^2 + w^2)} \right)}$$

$$= \frac{\sqrt{\sigma^2 + w^2}}{\sqrt{2\pi}\sigma w} \exp\left[\frac{-x^2(\sigma^2 + w^2)}{2\sigma^2 w^2} \right.$$

$$\left. + \frac{xs}{w^2} - \frac{s^2}{2w^2} + \frac{s^2}{2(\sigma^2 + w^2)} \right]$$

$$= \frac{\sqrt{\sigma^2 + w^2}}{\sqrt{2\pi}\sigma w} \exp\left[-\frac{\sigma^2 + w^2}{2\sigma^2 w^2} \right.$$

$$\left. \times \left(x - s\frac{\sigma^2}{\sigma^2 + w^2} \right)^2 \right].$$

Thus, the distribution of x given that $x + y = s$ is

$$\mathcal{N}\left(s\frac{\sigma^2}{\sigma^2 + w^2}, \frac{\sigma^2 w^2}{\sigma^2 + w^2} \right).$$

We can use Lemma A1 to find $E[C_1 + C_2 | Y_1, Y_2]$ and $\text{Var}[C_1 + C_2 | Y_1, Y_2]$. Since the investment levels are known,

$$E[C_1 + C_2 | Y_1, Y_2] = F_1(I_1)$$

$$+ F_2(I_2) + E[\theta_1 | \varepsilon_1 + \theta_1 = Y_1 - F_1(I_1)]$$

$$+ E[\theta_2 | \varepsilon_2 + \theta_2 = Y_2 - F_2(I_2)]$$

which by Lemma A1 equals

$$F_1(I_1) + F_2(I_2) + \beta_1(Y_1 - F_1(I_1))$$

$$+ \beta_2(Y_2 - F_2(I_2))$$

where

$$\beta_i = \frac{\sigma_i^2 I_i^2}{(\sigma_i^2 + w_i^2) I_i^2} = \frac{\sigma_i^2}{\sigma_i^2 + w_i^2}.$$

Choosing $\beta_0 = F_1(I_1)[1 - \beta_1] + F_2(I_2)[1 - \beta_2]$, we get the formula in the text for $E[C_1 + C_2 | Y_1, Y_2]$. It also follows that

$$\text{Var}(C_1 + C_2 | Y_1, Y_2)$$

$$= \text{Var}[\theta_1 | \varepsilon_1 + \theta_1 = Y_1 - F_1(I_1)]$$

$$+ \text{Var}[\theta_2 | \varepsilon_2 + \theta_2 = Y_2 - F_2(I_2)].$$

By Lemma A1, this equals half the sum of the harmonic means of $I_1^2\sigma_1^2$ and $I_1^2 w_1^2$ and of $I_2^2\sigma_2^2$ and $I_2^2 w_2^2$, as claimed in the text:

$$\frac{I_1^2\sigma_1^2 w_1^2}{\sigma_1^2 + w_1^2} + \frac{I_2^2\sigma_2^2 w_2^2}{\sigma_2^2 + w_2^2}.$$

REFERENCES

Akerlof, George A. "Procrastination and Obedience." *American Economic Review*, May 1991 (*Papers and Proceedings*), *81*(2), pp. 1–19.

Bagwell, Laurie S. and Zechner, Josef. "Influence Costs and Capital Structure." *Journal of Finance*, July 1993, *48*(3), pp. 975–1008.

Berle, Adolf A., Jr. "Non-voting Stock and Bankers' Control." *Harvard Law Review*, April 1926, *39*(6), pp. 673–93.

Berle, Adolf A., Jr. and Means, Gardiner C. *The modern corporation and private property.* New York: Macmillan, 1932.

Chicago Tribune. "QVC Accepts Sweetened Takeovers." Business Section, 5 August 1994, p. 3.

Donaldson, Gordon. *Managing corporate wealth: The operation of a comprehensive financial goals system.* New York: Praeger, 1984.

Edlin, Aaron S. "Specific Investments, Holdups and the Efficiency of Contract Remedies." Unpublished manuscript, Stanford University, 1992.

Edlin, Aaron S. and Reichelstein, Stefan. "Holdups, Standard Breach Remedies, and Optimal Investment." IBER Working Paper, University of California, Berkeley, 1993; *American Economic Review* (forthcoming).

Grossman, Sanford J. and Hart, Oliver D. "Takeover Bids, the Free-Rider Problem, and the Theory of the Corporation." *Bell Journal of Economics,* Spring 1980, *11*(1), pp. 42–64.

Hermalin, Benjamin E. "The Effects of Competition on Executive Behavior." *Rand Journal of Economics,* Autumn 1992, *23*(3), pp. 360–65.

Holmstrom, Bengt and Milgrom, Paul R. "Aggregation and Linearity in the Provision of Intertemporal Incentives." *Econometrica,* March 1987, *55*(2), pp. 303–28.

Jensen, Michael C. "Takeovers: Their Causes and Consequences." *Journal of Economic Perspectives,* Winter 1988, *2*(1), pp. 21–48.

Jensen, Michael C. and Meckling, William H. "Theory of the Firm: Managerial Behavior, Agency Costs and Ownership Structure." *Journal of Financial Economics,* October 1976, *3*(4), pp. 305–60.

Jensen, Michael C. and Ruback, Richard S. "The Market for Corporate Control: The Scientific Evidence." *Journal of Financial Economics,* April 1983, *11*(1–4), pp. 5–50.

Leibenstein, Harvey. "Allocative Efficiency vs. 'X-Efficiency'." *American Economic Review,* June 1966, *56*(3), pp. 392–415.

March, James G. and Simon, Herbert A. *Organizations.* New York: Wiley, 1958.

Marris, Robin L. *The economic theory of managerial capitalism.* Glencoe, IL: Free Press, 1964.

Milgrom, Paul R. and Shannon, Chris. "Monotone Comparative Statics." *Econometrica,* January 1994, *62*(1), pp. 157–80.

Miller, Michael W. and Hooper, Laurence. "Akers Quits at IBM Under Heavy Pressure; Dividend Is Slashed. Outsiders Will Lead Search for New Chief Executive To Be a 'Change-Master.' But Who'd Want This Job?" *Wall Street Journal,* 27 January 1993, p. A1.

Morck, Randall; Shleifer, Andrei and Vishny, Robert W. "Alternative Mechanisms for Corporate Control." *American Economic Review,* September 1989, *79*(4), pp. 842–52.

Paul, Jonathan M. "Managerial Myopia and the Observability of Future Cash Flows." Unpublished manuscript, University of Michigan, 1991.

_____. "On the Efficiency of Stock-Based Compensation." *Review of Financial Studies,* 1992, *5*(3), pp. 471–502.

Salop, Steven C. and Scheffman, David T. "Raising Rivals' Costs." *American Economic Review,* May 1983 (Papers and Proceedings), *73*(2), pp. 267–71.

_____. "Cost-Raising Strategies." *Journal of Industrial Economics,* September 1987, *36*(1), pp. 19–34.

Scharfstein, David. "The Disciplinary Role of Takeovers." *Review of Economic Studies,* April 1988, *55*(2), pp. 185–200.

Shleifer, Andrei and Vishny, Robert W. "Value Maximization and the Acquisition Process." *Journal of Economic Perspectives,* Winter 1988, *2*(1), pp. 7–20.

_____. "Management Entrenchment: The Case of Manager-Specific Investments." *Journal of Financial Economics,* November 1989, *25*(1), pp. 123–39.

Simon, Herbert A. "Organizations and Markets." *Journal of Economic Perspectives,* Spring 1991, *5*(2), pp. 25–44.

Stiglitz, Joseph E. "Some Aspects of the Pure Theory of Corporate Finance: Bankruptcies and Takeovers." *Bell Journal of Economics,* Autumn 1972, *3*(2), pp. 458–82.

_____. "Information and Economic Analysis," in Michael Parkin and Avelino R.

Nobay, eds., *Current economic problems*. Cambridge: Cambridge University Press, 1975, pp. 27–52.

_____. "Ownership, Control, and Efficient Markets: Some Paradoxes in the Theory of Capital Markets," in Kenneth D. Boyer and William G. Shepherd, eds., *Economic regulation: Essays in honor of James R. Nelson*. East Lansing, MI: Institute of Public Utilities, Michigan State University, 1981, pp. 311–41.

_____. "Credit Markets and the Control of Capital." *Journal of Money, Banking, and Credit*, May 1985, *17*(1), pp. 133–52.

Wall Street Journal. "Big is Back in Style as Corporate America Deals, Buys, and Merges." Western Edition, 4 August 1994, p. A1.

Weber, Jonathan. "Saga of Apple's Ex-Chief Takes an Unusual Turn." *Los Angeles Times*, Home Edition, 8 February 1994, p. A1.

Williamson, Oliver E. *The economics of discretionary behavior: Managerial objectives in a theory of the firm*. Englewood Cliffs, NJ: Prentice-Hall, 1964.

THE JOURNAL OF FINANCE • VOL. LV, NO. 6 • DEC. 2000

The Dark Side of Internal Capital Markets: Divisional Rent-Seeking and Inefficient Investment

DAVID S. SCHARFSTEIN and JEREMY C. STEIN*

ABSTRACT

We develop a two-tiered agency model that shows how rent-seeking behavior on the part of division managers can subvert the workings of an internal capital market. By rent-seeking, division managers can raise their bargaining power and extract greater overall compensation from the CEO. And because the CEO is herself an agent of outside investors, this extra compensation may take the form not of cash wages, but rather of preferential capital budgeting allocations. One interesting feature of our model is that it implies a kind of "socialism" in internal capital allocation, whereby weaker divisions get subsidized by stronger ones.

IN RECENT YEARS, it has become almost axiomatic among researchers in finance and strategy that a policy of corporate diversification is typically value reducing. A variety of empirical evidence lends support to this view. For example, diversified firms apparently trade at lower stock values than comparable portfolios of specialized firms.[1] Moreover, during the 1980s corporate acquirers systematically dismantled diversified firms with the view that the divisions would be more efficiently run as stand-alones.[2]

While it may be clear to most observers that diversification can destroy value, it is much less clear exactly how it does so. One general theme in the literature is that the conglomerate form of organization somehow exacerbates the investment inefficiencies that arise from managerial agency prob-

*MIT Sloan School of Management and NBER, and Harvard University and NBER, respectively. This paper is a completely overhauled version of our March 1997 NBER working paper (#5969) with the same title. We have received research support from the National Science Foundation and the Finance Research Center at MIT. We are grateful to Charlie Hadlock, Oliver Hart, Laurie Hodrick, Bengt Holmström, Preston McAfee, Vik Nanda, Julio Rotemberg, René Stulz, Dimitri Vayanos, Luigi Zingales, Jeff Zwiebel, the referees and seminar participants at Columbia, Harvard, Indiana, the NBER, Boston University, Utah, Ohio State, Stanford, Stockholm, Yale, the ASSA meetings, and the New York Fed for helpful comments. Thanks also to Melissa Cunniffe and Svetlana Sussman for help in preparing the manuscript.

[1] See, for example, Lang and Stulz (1994), Berger and Ofek (1995), and Comment and Jarrell (1995) for evidence from the U.S., and Lins and Servaes (1999) and Fauver, Houston, and Naranjo (1998) for international evidence. In a recent paper Campa and Kedia (1999) challenge some of this evidence.

[2] See Bhagat, Shleifer, and Vishny (1990) and Berger and Ofek (1996).

lems. There are two basic ways that this could happen. First, if one believes that managers have a tendency to overinvest out of free cash flow (Jensen 1986, 1993), it might simply be that conglomerates give managers more resources to play with, and this leads to more overinvestment.[3] Alternatively, it may be that conglomerates do not, on average, have more free cash flow, but that their internal capital markets do a worse job of allocating a given amount of resources than would external capital markets—that is, they tend to engage in inefficient cross-subsidization, spending relatively too much in some divisions, and too little in others.

This latter hypothesis about inefficient cross-subsidization in internal capital markets has been much discussed. And recent evidence suggests that conglomerates do, in fact, engage in active resource reallocation, moving funds from one division to another.[4] But it is far from obvious that any such resource reallocation should be expected to be systematically inefficient, even in a standard agency context. Indeed, Stein (1997), building on Williamson (1975), makes exactly the reverse argument. He notes that even if CEOs derive private benefits from control, and hence have a tendency to engage in empire-building overinvestment, there is a presumption that, conditional on the level of investment, any reallocation of resources across divisions will be in the direction of increased efficiency. This is because the CEO's ability to appropriate private benefits should ultimately be roughly in line with the value of the enterprise as a whole. To put it simply, although agency-prone CEOs may want big empires, it also seems reasonable that, holding size fixed, they will want valuable empires.[5]

Of course, one can think of exceptions to this general tendency. For example, there may be "pet" projects that effectively generate disproportionately high private benefits for the CEO.[6] Nonetheless, it remains hard to explain pervasive allocative inefficiencies in internal capital markets simply by appealing to agency problems at the level of the CEO. This is especially true to the extent that the associated cross-subsidies follow a consistent and predictable pattern across firms and industries.

In this regard, many observers have claimed that the cross-subsidies in internal capital markets often tend to be "socialist" in nature—that is, strong divisions typically wind up subsidizing weak ones. Or, said somewhat differently, one of the fundamental failings of the conglomerate form of organization seems to be its inability to put the weakest divisions in the firm on

---

[3] This might occur, if, for example, coinsurance effects allow a conglomerate to borrow more against its assets than a comparable portfolio of specialized firms. However, recent empirical work by Berger and Ofek (1995) finds that in practice, this extra-borrowing effect is of trivial importance.

[4] See Lamont (1997), and Shin and Stulz (1998).

[5] See also Matsusaka and Nanda (2000) for a similar argument about the potential benefits of an internal capital market.

[6] On a related note, Shleifer and Vishny (1989) argue that CEOs will prefer to invest in industries where they have more personal experience, as this makes them indispensable.

Divisional Rent-Seeking and Inefficient Investment 2539

much-needed diets. Unless one is willing to assume that CEOs systematically derive more private benefits from weak divisions—which seems implausible—such a socialist pattern cannot be rationalized simply by appealing to agency problems at the CEO level.

This suggests that to develop a satisfactory theory of inefficient cross-subsidies in internal capital markets, one has to go a level deeper in the organization, and explicitly examine the incentives and behavior of not only the CEO, but also the division managers. That is what we do in this paper. Specifically, we consider a setting where division managers have the ability to engage not only in productive work, but also in wasteful rent-seeking activities. The effect of such rent-seeking in our model is that it increases division managers' bargaining power when they negotiate a compensation package with the CEO. It turns out that under plausible conditions, rent-seeking is more of a problem with managers of weaker divisions. This is because the opportunity cost to such managers of taking time away from productive work to engage in rent-seeking is lower.

The rent-seeking behavior we model is in some respects similar to the influence activities studied by Meyer, Milgrom, and Roberts (1992), and it has some of the same implications. Their model also predicts that such distortionary behavior is more of a problem in divisions with poor prospects, and like ours, it suggests that firms may often be better off divesting such divisions. But it is important to note that rent-seeking or influence activities at the level of division managers do not by themselves necessarily generate any inefficiencies in the allocation of *investment spending*.[7] After all, even if the CEO has to in some sense "overcompensate" rent-seeking division managers, would it not be more efficient for everybody involved if the extra compensation was in the form of cash? Why use directed investment spending as a means of compensation?

Thus, although a model with just division-level rent-seeking may in some cases deliver socialist outcomes with respect to cash wages—that is, managers of weak divisions receiving salaries that seem to be too high relative to those paid to managers of strong divisions—something else must be added if we are to make predictions with respect to capital allocation. This is where the agency problem between the CEO and the outside capital market comes in. We show that although outside investors would prefer that any extra compensation paid to division managers be paid in cash rather than with distorted capital spending, they have no means to enforce this. For in our setup, the hiring and retention of division managers must be delegated to the CEO. And as an agent, the CEO may not be inclined to pay the division managers in the currency that outside investors would prefer. More

---

[7] In Meyer et al. (1992), there are no investment inefficiencies. The only distortions are the time and effort expended by managers in a fruitless attempt to convince headquarters not to shrink their divisions.

precisely, we demonstrate that given the nature of the optimal financial contract between outside investors and the CEO, the CEO views it as less personally costly to distort investment in favor of those divisions whose managers require extra compensation, thereby conserving on cash payments to these managers.

Overall then, the primary novelty of this paper is to build a model with two layers of agency that can speak directly to the question of how some division managers in a conglomerate are able to extract excessively large capital allocations from the CEO.[8] In addition to providing a theoretical rationale for the existence of inefficient cross-subsidies in internal capital markets, the model also enables us to make fairly precise predictions about both the direction of such cross-subsidies, as well as the circumstances under which they are most likely to be acute. For example, one of our principal results is that large socialist-type inefficiencies are especially likely to arise when there is a great deal of divergence in the strength of the divisions, and when the CEO has low-powered incentives.

Our two-tiered agency approach distinguishes us from another line of work that has also examined the question of why managers may be compensated with extra capital rather than cash. In these other papers, the party making the compensation decision is the principal (as opposed to the CEO, who is an agent in our set-up), so that it is actually efficient, in some constrained sense, to pay with capital. Rotemberg (1993) is an example. In his model, managers are rewarded with the right to make irreversible investment decisions, because this is a way for the principal to precommit not to renege on a long-term deal.[9] Similarly, in Rajan, Servaes, and Zingales (2000), the principal optimally tilts the capital budget towards the weaker division in a firm, because this makes the weaker division behave more cooperatively in joint production with other divisions.[10] Thus, what is relatively unique about our model is that, by incorporating two levels of agency, we not only capture divisional rent-seeking behavior, but also the idea that the allocation of investment by the CEO reflects her own misaligned incentives, and thus can be grossly inefficient from the perspective of outside investors.

The remainder of the paper is organized as follows. We develop the basic model in Section I, and consider some extensions and variations in Section II. Section III discusses several recent empirical papers that speak directly to the model's central predictions. Section IV concludes.

---

[8] Tirole (1986) is one of the first papers to explicitly analyze a multilayer agency problem. However, he does not consider the possibility that agents could be compensated in a form other than cash. See also Holmström and Milgrom (1990) and McAfee and McMillan (1995) for related work on multilayer agency issues.

[9] See also Prendergast and Stole (1996), who provide a number of other reasons why intra-firm transactions might optimally be done in a nonmonetary fashion.

[10] Wulf (1997) also argues that a principal might optimally choose to tilt the capital budget so as to mitigate an agency problem with divisional managers.

I. The Model

A. Overview

Our model considers a firm operating with two divisions and features three basic agents: division managers, a CEO, and outside investors. Within each division, there are both assets already in place, and new investment opportunities. Both division managers and the CEO derive private benefits from the assets under their purview. Thus the manager of a division gets private benefits from the assets of his division only, whereas the CEO gets private benefits from the assets of all divisions.

The CEO plays two important roles. First, she has the authority to allocate new investment across divisions. Second, she is charged with identifying, hiring, and retaining the division managers. As part of this second job, she has to negotiate with the division managers the terms of their employment—that is, set their compensation. We explain in more detail below why these two jobs have to be delegated to the CEO and cannot be accomplished by outside investors.

Much of the focus of our analysis is on how the CEO chooses to compensate division managers—whether she pays them in cash or with an inefficiently large share of the capital budget. However, to facilitate the exposition of the model, we begin by assuming that investment is allocated efficiently across the two divisions, and that any further rewards to division managers are paid in cash. In this setting, we analyze how the magnitude of the cash wage depends on both a division's productivity and the manager's rent-seeking behavior. Next, we describe the contracting environment between the CEO and investors, and show that given the nature of the optimal financial contract, there may be incentives for the CEO, acting as an agent, to substitute capital expenditures for cash in the division manager's compensation.

B. Production and Rent-seeking When CEO Bargains With Cash Only

There are two periods, 1 and 2. At time 1, the CEO hires a new manager for each division, to work with assets that are already in place. The wages of these new managers at time 1 are normalized to zero. The output of division i at time 1 is $\theta_i f(e_i)$, where θ_i is a measure of the productivity of the assets in place, e_i is the productive effort of the division manager, and $f(\cdot)$ is an increasing concave function. The output is fully and costlessly verifiable, and hence can be assigned to outside investors. In addition to this verifiable output, there are also noncontractible private benefits. In particular, division manager i reaps a private benefit of $\gamma \theta_i f(e_i)$ from his own division, and the CEO gets a private benefit of $\phi \theta_i f(e_i)$ from each of the two divisions. These private benefits can be thought of in any number of ways: the usual perks, psychic benefits from empire building, and so forth. They are assumed to be small relative to the verifiable output—that is, γ and ϕ are both much less than one. This is in contrast to recent models of financial contracting—such as Bolton and Scharfstein (1990) and Hart and Moore (1998)—in which managers can "steal" a large share of the cash flows produced by operating assets. What matters for our purposes is that both division managers and the CEO care to some degree about the total amount of output from the assets under their span of control.

At time 2, the old assets in place are fully depreciated, and there is a second round of production with newly invested capital. If the original division manager from time 1 remains on the job, the output of division i at time 2 is $\theta_i k(I_i)$, where I_i is the new investment in division i, and $k(\cdot)$ is an increasing concave function, with $k'(0) = \infty$. However, if the original division manager quits, and has to be replaced, output is reduced. The interpretation is that by time 2, the original division manager has acquired some specific human capital, which makes him particularly valuable. This, in turn, means that the division manager may be able to bargain with the CEO for increased compensation at time 2. In any case, the CEO continues to get private benefits equal to ϕ times the output of each division, and the division manager continues to get private benefits equal to γ times the output of his own division.

One of our key premises is that the division manager anticipates the time 2 bargaining ex ante, at time 1, and may take steps to enhance his negotiating position. This is what we mean by "rent-seeking": rather than spending all his time on productive effort e_i at time 1, division manager i may spend r_i on activity that is not directly productive, but that may enable him to extract more from the CEO when they negotiate at time 2. The division manager is subject to an overall time constraint that $e_i + r_i = h$. The allocation of effort is noncontractible, so that there is no way to directly force a division manager to spend his time in the right way.

We have examined two different formulations of rent-seeking. In the first, which we call "resumé-polishing," the rent-seeking effort r_i goes to improving the division manager's outside option. The interpretation here is that the division manager spends too much time increasing his external visibility, perhaps attending industry conventions, accepting needless speaking engagements, and the like. Thus at time 2, the division manager has an outside option given by $g(r_i)$, where $g(\cdot)$ is an increasing concave function, with $g(0) = 0$. We further assume that if the division manager quits at time 2 and a new manager is brought on, output falls by a fixed amount X, to $\theta_i k(I_i) - X$.

In the second variant, which we term "scorched earth," the rent-seeking effort r_i goes to making it harder for any successor to the division manager to take over the job. One might interpret r_i in this context as time spent creating excessively opaque internal accounting systems, hiding other information, and so forth.[11] In this case, the old manager's outside option re-

---

[11] See also Shleifer and Vishny (1989), Bagwell and Zechner (1993), Edlin and Stiglitz (1995), and Fulghieri and Hodrick (1997) for similar interpretations of rent-seeking inside firms.

Divisional Rent-Seeking and Inefficient Investment   2543

mains at zero, but if a new manager comes in to run the division at time 2, output falls to $\theta_i k(I_i) - g(r_i)$. Note that in both variations, it is important that the old manager be somewhat entrenched at time 2, in the sense of being more productive than any potential replacement. However, with resumé-polishing, the degree of entrenchment is a constant given by X, whereas with scorched earth, the degree of entrenchment depends on r_i. The two variations give broadly similar results, but the former is easier to work with.[12] So to streamline the exposition, we focus on the resumé-polishing formulation in what follows.

To see how the model works with resumé-polishing, let us begin by assuming that it is time 2, and that some nonzero effort r_i has already been devoted to this form of rent-seeking. Therefore, the division manager now has an outside option of $g(r_i)$.[13] Moreover, if he leaves, output falls by X. Now consider the respective bargaining positions of the division manager and the CEO. If the division manager quits at time 2, he goes to his outside option and gets $g(r_i)$. If he stays, he gets utility of $\gamma \theta_i k(I_i) + w_i$, where w_i is the cash wage (if any) agreed to by the CEO. For simplicity, we further assume that: (1) the CEO has all the bargaining power at time 2—that is, she can make a take-it-or-leave-it offer to the division manager; and (2) $\phi X > g(r_i)$, for any value of r_i. The former assumption is not critical; as long as the CEO has *some* bargaining power at time 2, the division manager cares about his outside option $g(r_i)$, which is the important feature of the model. The latter assumption ensures that the CEO has enough of a stake in output that she always deems it privately efficient to retain the division manager, even if the cash wage w_i has to come out of her own pocket.

For the moment, we explore a benchmark scenario where the CEO is constrained to allocate investment efficiently across the two divisions, so that $I_i = I_i^*$, as given by[14]

$$\theta_1 k'(I_1^*) = \theta_2 k'(I_2^*). \tag{1}$$

---

[12] The reason that resumé-polishing is easier to work with is that one can endow the CEO with all the bargaining power at time 2—so that division managers are held to just their outside options—and still get nonzero rent-seeking. In contrast, with the entrenchment formulation, division managers only rent-seek if they get to share the surplus with the CEO. Given that our game has three players (the two division managers and the CEO) solving the model with surplus sharing becomes somewhat complicated.

[13] A natural extension of the model is to allow a division manager's outside option to depend not only on his level of rent-seeking, but also on the productivity of the industry in which he specializes—for example, one might write the outside option as $(1 + \delta\theta_i)g(r_i)$ for some $\delta > 0$. So long as δ is not too large, our basic results about there being more rent-seeking problems in weak (low-θ) divisions continue to apply. This becomes clear as we develop the model further.

[14] We should be a bit careful with the use of the term "efficient" here. As we see below, under certain conditions, even outside investors might wish to deviate slightly from the benchmark where $I_i = I_i^*$.

Moreover, we assume that the CEO also has enough wealth to pay any cash wages. In this setting, the CEO always rehires the division manager at time 2, and faces the following "retention constraint":

$$w_i + \gamma \theta_i k(I_i^*) \geq g(r_i). \tag{2}$$

In words, the CEO simply has to promise the division manager more total utility than he would get if he left. Note that the labor contract implied in this discussion is an easily implementable one. All that we require is that a court be able to verify (1) whether the division manager was in fact employed by the firm at time 2, and (2) whether the promised cash wage was paid. It is not necessary for us to assume that a court can verify capital expenditures at the divisional level. One can imagine that at time 2, the CEO first irreversibly sinks the capital allocations, and then, conditional on these allocations, promises to pay any still-needed cash wage to each division manager if he stays on.

The first observation about the retention constraint is that it may be slack at the efficient level of investment, I_i^*. If division i is very productive (i.e., has a high value of θ_i) and is therefore doing a lot of investing at the efficient level, the division manager gets more than his outside option in utility even without a cash wage, so the CEO can set $w_i = 0$. On the other hand, if the division has a low value of θ_i, it is more likely that the CEO has to pay a positive cash wage to keep the manager at time 2.

Now let us back up and consider the division manager's decision of how to divide his time between productive effort e_i and rent-seeking r_i. If the manager rent-seeks, his time 1 private benefits fall by $\gamma \theta_i [f(h) - f(h - r_i)]$ because of the reduced time 1 output. However, his time 2 outside option rises by $g(r_i)$. If $g(r_i)$ is greater than $\gamma \theta k(I_i^*)$—so that the retention constraint is violated when the wage is zero—then the CEO must pay a wage of $g(r_i) - \gamma \theta_i k(I_i^*)$ to keep the manager. Thus, for a given r_i the manager rent-seeks, provided the time 2 gain in wage compensation exceeds the loss in time 1 private benefits:

$$g(r_i) > \gamma \theta_i [k(I_i^*) + f(h) - f(h - r_i)]. \tag{3}$$

If there is an r_i that satisfies this "rent-seeking condition," we know that there is at least some rent-seeking in equilibrium. Just how much, r_i^*, is determined by equating the marginal gain in time 2 compensation and the marginal loss in time 1 private benefits:

$$g'(r_i^*) = \gamma \theta_i f'(h - r_i^*). \tag{4}$$

Note, however, that if at r_i^* the rent-seeking condition

$$g(r_i^*) > \gamma \theta_i [k(I_i^*) + f(h) - f(h - r_i^*)] \tag{5}$$

Divisional Rent-Seeking and Inefficient Investment   2545

is not met, then the manager does not actually rent-seek. What this means is that the equilibrium level of rent-seeking, $\hat{r}_i$, is given by the following:

$$\hat{r}_i = \begin{cases} r_i^* & \text{if } g(r_i^*) > \gamma\theta_i[k(I_i^*) + \Delta f_i] \\ 0 & \text{otherwise} \end{cases}, \tag{6}$$

where, for shorthand, we define $\Delta f_i \equiv f(h) - f(h - r_i^*)$.

The main implication of this analysis is that managers of weaker divisions (those with lower values of θ_i) do more rent-seeking. More precisely, we can distinguish two regions. In the first, when θ_i is below some cutoff (call it $\bar{\theta}$) the rent-seeking condition (5) is satisfied, so managers choose to actively rent-seek. In this region the level of rent-seeking increases as θ_i falls, because managers in charge of less productive assets at time 1 have a lower opportunity cost of taking time away from productive effort. This is reflected in the first-order condition (4). In the second region, for values of θ_i above $\bar{\theta}$, managers do not rent-seek at all: the rent-seeking condition (5) is not satisfied. At these higher levels of θ_i there is no incentive to rent-seek, both because of the large loss in time 1 private benefits that this would entail, and because the time 2 private benefits, $\gamma\theta_i k(I_i^*)$ are already high.

Correspondingly, the cash wage is greater for managers in low-θ divisions. In the rent-seeking region ($\theta_i < \bar{\theta}$), $w_i = g(r_i^*) - \gamma\theta_i k(I_i^*)$. Because managers in low-θ divisions rent-seek more and derive less private benefits from time 2 investment, they must receive higher wages to get them to stay. In very high-θ divisions ($\theta_i > \bar{\theta}$), managers do not rent-seek at all, and so do not need to be compensated further to be retained in the firm.[15]

Before proceeding, it is worthwhile to interpret the results to this point. Recall that we have not yet introduced the possibility that the CEO attempts to compensate division managers with investment levels above the efficient values of I_i^*; this comes shortly. For the time being, cash wages are the only currency. In this context, w_i is a complete measure of both (1) the magnitude of the rent-seeking problem, and (2) how much "extra" (above and beyond the efficient level of investment) the CEO has to give division managers to get them to stay on. So what we have learned is that the CEO always has a tougher problem with the managers of weak (low-θ) divisions. This is true because of two distinct effects. First, there is what might be called a time 2 "satisfaction effect": efficiency dictates that high-θ division managers are naturally allocated more capital at time 2; this means that their utility from staying on is higher, so that the benefits from rent-seeking are low. Second, there is a time 1 "opportunity-cost-of-rent-seeking effect": even if they do engage in rent-seeking, high-θ division managers will spend less of their time on it, because they view it as more costly to take time away from productive activity.

---

[15] None of this implies that low-θ managers get higher *total utility* than high-θ managers. Even without a cash wage, high-θ managers can be very well off because they get more investment and higher private benefits.

It can be argued that our model is missing a countervailing ingredient. Specifically, one might posit that for a variety of reasons, a division manager working in a better industry might find it easier to generate outside options. For example, one might write the outside option as $(1 + \delta\theta_i)g(r_i)$ for some $\delta > 0$, which corresponds to the marginal productivity of resumé-polishing being greater in high-θ industries. If δ is sufficiently large, this can lead to a situation where, if he chooses to rent-seek, the manager of a stronger division obtains a higher outside option—that is, for an optimally chosen r_i^*, $(1 + \delta\theta_i)g(r_i^*)$ can be *increasing* rather than decreasing in θ_i.

However, it is important to recognize that this countervailing effect need not overturn our central result. Even if $(1 + \delta\theta_i)g(r_i^*)$ increases with θ_i, it does not follow that the *equilibrium outside option*, $(1 + \delta\theta_i)g(\hat{r}_i)$, increases with θ_i. This is because of the strong "satisfaction effect" that we have identified. In equilibrium, a manager of a high-θ division may still be more likely to have $\hat{r}_i = 0$, as is apparent from equation (6). In words, the high-θ manager is getting so much utility from running a profitable division with a large capital budget that he is no threat to leave the firm, and, therefore, his resumé-polishing abilities are irrelevant. Of course, it is always possible to reverse our conclusions by raising δ far enough, but this line of reasoning suggests that they are somewhat robust.

Moreover, as noted above, the basic notion that managers of weak divisions can cause more problems for the CEO is not unique to this model. We are more interested in using it as a point of departure. In particular, now that we know that the CEO has to give more extra compensation to low-θ division managers, we can turn to our central question: what form does this extra compensation take? Is it paid in cash, or with an inefficiently high share of the capital budget? To answer this question, we have to be clearer about the nature of the agency relationship between the CEO and outside investors.

C. CEO-Level Agency and the Form of Division-Manager Compensation

To create an interesting agency problem at the CEO level, we assume that the CEO has no wealth of her own. The first implication of this assumption is that the financing for any new time 2 investment of $I_1 + I_2$ must come from outside investors. The form of the financial contract is very simple. Outside investors have two forms of contractual protection to ensure that they earn a return on their investment in physical assets. First, they can specify $\bar{I}$, the amount of their investment in the firm as a whole that must be converted into physical capital. That is, the act of converting cash into physical capital is verifiable; this is a standard assumption. Second, as we have already noted, once the capital is put into place, it generates future cash flows that are also verifiable, and that outside investors can directly appropriate. Thus on the whole, funding that is put up for capital investment is relatively well protected in this model—besides the potentially small

Divisional Rent-Seeking and Inefficient Investment 2547

amount of perks taken by the CEO and division managers, outside investors recoup everything else coming from physical capital. This contrasts with models such as Bolton and Scharfstein (1990) and Hart and Moore (1998), where managers can steal all the cash flows from physical assets.

One thing that outside investors cannot do is specify how the total firm-wide capital budget of $\bar{I}$ gets split up across divisions. This control right is assumed to reside with the CEO. We take this delegation of capital-allocation authority to the CEO to be a defining characteristic of integration. Thus, we are implicitly assuming that a court cannot enforce a contract that specifies investment at the divisional level (perhaps because it cannot verify unambiguously which division "owns" a given piece of capital). Of course, to the extent that our model generates large inefficiencies, this begs the question of why there should be integration in the first place; that is, why shouldn't the firm be broken up? It is important to be clear that our aim here is not to provide a complete equilibrium model of the costs and benefits of integration. Rather, we simply assume that integration has taken place for some exogenous reason—perhaps, as in Stein (1997), because the CEO has better information than outside investors—and then explore some of its potentially dysfunctional consequences. Thus we are perfectly comfortable with the view that some of the largest inefficiencies implied by the model may not survive in the long run because there will be pressure to break up the firm. Indeed, we like to think that the model has predictive content for the circumstances in which breakups are most likely to occur, a point which we take up explicitly in Section II.B below.

The second key aspect of the agency problem between the CEO and outside investors is that the hiring and compensation of division managers must be delegated to the CEO, that is, the outside investors cannot contract directly with division managers.[16] There are a number of ways to motivate this feature. For example, one might assume that all contracting between the CEO and outside investors takes place at some initial chartering date (denoted "time 0") before any specific candidates for the division manager jobs have been identified by the CEO. After this initial round of contracting, there is no further scope for outside investors to get re-involved; this could be justified by appealing to the notion that the outside investors are a diffuse group, and cannot easily coordinate in such a way as to rewrite contracts on an ongoing basis. This line of argument follows Aghion and Tirole (1997) and Burkart, Gromb, and Panunzi (1997) in emphasizing that the CEO may have de facto authority with respect to certain decisions, even if outside investors are endowed with formal control rights in the sense of Grossman and Hart (1986) and Hart and Moore (1990).

---

[16] An essentially identical assumption is made by McAfee and McMillan (1995) in their analysis of a multitier hierarchy: the "top principal" is assumed to be unable to contract directly with the agent. They argue that this constraint reflects limits on the top principal's time and attention (p. 407).

Given that they cannot write contracts with the division managers themselves, it may be optimal for outside investors to give the CEO additional funds that are not contractually earmarked for physical investment. The potential benefit of doing so is that the CEO may use these other funds to compensate division managers with cash wages rather than with distorted capital budgets. Thus, in addition to the capital budget of $\bar{I}$, we allow for the possibility that there is a total "operating budget" of $\bar{W}$.

As will become clear, our main results are driven by assuming that it is contractually difficult for outside investors to fully protect the operating budget from abuse by the CEO. Or, said differently, we need to assume that if the CEO does not turn the operating budget over to division managers, she can to some degree spend it on herself. To illustrate the ideas most starkly, we begin with an extreme case where the operating budget is totally discretionary for the CEO, that is, outside investors give $\bar{W}$ to the CEO, and anything that she does not spend on wages for the division managers, she can directly divert to herself.

Obviously, this stark assumption about the CEO's ability to take home the operating budget is not intended to be realistic. What we have in mind is that, in a richer model, the operating budget would have to be used to cover a wide range of expenditures other than those verifiable outlays on physical capital that are specified in the capital budget. In addition to division-manager wages, these would include money spent on advertising, administration, travel, and so forth. To the extent that the CEO holds down division-manager wages, she can spend more of the operating budget on things that raise her utility (e.g., excess travel).[17] Our simple formulation corresponds to an extreme case where these discretionary expenditures raise the CEO's utility dollar for dollar; however, this is not at all necessary for our results.

Although the notion that the CEO can divert a portion of the operating budget to herself does not strike us as unreasonable—indeed, it is a standard assumption in the agency literature—it is nevertheless not the only way to tell the story. Ultimately, all we really need is some motivation for the CEO to care about conserving on cash wage payments to division managers. Another way to derive this feature is to assume that the CEO has profit-linked incentive compensation. Then, by holding down wages, she boosts profits and—even if these excess profits are returned to shareholders rather than diverted—also raises her compensation. Somewhat more subtly, the same effect can arise if the CEO has stock in the firm, and she wants to raise reported profits to pump up the near-term stock price, as in the signal-jamming model of Stein (1989). We sketch out this alternative formulation of the model in more detail in Section II.A below.

---

[17] Note the key contracting assumption that we have slipped in with this metaphor. We are implicitly assuming that although outside investors can control the firm's aggregate operating budget, they cannot control it line-by-line. In particular, the auditing/verification technology does not allow outside investors to stipulate: "These funds can be used to pay division-manager wages, but they *cannot* be used for travel expenses."

Divisional Rent-Seeking and Inefficient Investment   2549

To analyze the properties of the model, we now proceed as follows. First, we begin by treating the size of the capital budget $\bar{I}$ as a fixed parameter, and assuming that the operating budget $\overline{W}$ is sufficiently large that the CEO is unconstrained in setting cash wages. Once we have solved the model this way, we can back up and endogenize $\bar{I}$, as well as check whether this approach to setting $\overline{W}$ is optimal from the perspective of outside investors.

The retention constraints faced by the CEO are almost identical to our earlier scenario. In particular, they are now given by

$$w_i + \gamma \theta_i k(I_i) \geq g(r_i). \tag{7}$$

The only difference is that now we allow for the possibility that I_i differs from I_i^*. In other words, the CEO may meet a binding constraint either by using a cash wage or by raising investment above the efficient level.

The CEO seeks to maximize her utility, subject to these constraints.[18] CEO utility at time 2 is given by

$$\phi \theta_1 k(I_1) - w_1 + \phi \theta_2 k(I_2) - w_2 \tag{8}$$

In words, expression (8) says that the CEO cares about two things. On the one hand, she cares about allocating investment efficiently—because she gets more private benefits with higher output—but she only puts a fractional weight of ϕ on this objective. On the other hand, she also wishes to minimize cash wages, because, according to our strong assumption, any cash wages ultimately come dollar-for-dollar out of her pocket. Note that if the CEO instead acts benevolently on behalf of outside investors, the objective function would be of the same form as above, except that we would set $\phi = 1$.

In this version of the model, in which the investment allocation can vary, each division manager's rent-seeking decision is more complex, because it may now depend on the *other* division manager's rent-seeking strategy. In fact, rent-seeking choices may be strategic complements; either manager may have more incentive to rent-seek if the other manager also rent-seeks.

To understand why, recall that if a given manager i rent-seeks, he gets $g(r_i^*)$ at time 2 and loses Δf_i in time 1 private benefits. This is the case no matter what the other manager j does. However, if manager i does not rent-seek, his time 2 private benefits depend critically on manager j's rent-seeking activity. His utility at time 2 in this case comes only from what the CEO decides to allocate in capital to his division i; because he has no outside option there is no reason for the CEO to pay him a wage. And his capital allocation is determined in part by the desire of the CEO to meet manager j's retention constraint. Thus, manager i's time 2 private benefits can be

---

[18] Note that we have guaranteed that the CEO always wishes to satisfy the retention constraints by virtue of our earlier assumption that $\phi X > g(r_i)$.

written as $\gamma\theta_i I_i(r_j)$, where $I_i(r_j)$ denotes the investment allocation to i if i does not rent-seek and the other manager, j, rent-seeks at level r_j. This implies that manager i rent-seeks if

$$g(r_i^*) > \gamma\theta_i[k(I_i(r_j)) + \Delta f_i]. \tag{9}$$

As will become clear, the capital allocation to i tends to be reduced below the efficient level if only j actively rent-seeks: $I_i(r_j^*) < I_i^*$. It follows that i's incentive to rent-seek can be greater if j rent-seeks—this is the sense in which rent-seeking activities can be strategic complements. Note that this is the case even though manager j's rent-seeking does not directly reduce the rents available to manager i.

Now let us make the following further definitions. We say that

$$\theta_i \text{ is ``low'' if } g(r_i^*) > \gamma\theta_i[k(I_i^*) + \Delta f_i] \tag{10}$$

$$\theta_i \text{ is ``medium'' if } \gamma\theta_i[k(I_i^*) + \Delta f_i] \geq g(r_i^*) > \gamma\theta_i[k(I_i(r_j^*)) + \Delta f_i] \tag{11}$$

$$\theta_i \text{ is ``high'' if } g(r_i^*) \leq \gamma\theta_i[k(I_i(r_j^*)) + \Delta f_i]. \tag{12}$$

The interpretation of these definitions is as follows. When θ_i is low, manager i wishes to rent-seek no matter what—even if he conjectures that, absent rent-seeking, he will be allocated the efficient level of investment I_i^*. In contrast, when θ_i is high, manager i never rent-seeks, even if he conjectures that, absent rent-seeking, the capital budget will be tilted to manager j, so that he (manager i) gets a reduced allocation of only $I_i(r_j^*)$. Finally, when θ_i is medium, we have a case where there is the potential for strategic interaction: manager i's rent-seeking decision *depends* on his conjecture about how much capital he gets if he does not rent-seek.

With the definitions in hand, we can now provide a characterization of the solution to the CEO's problem. The full details are in Appendix A. Here we just state the main qualitative results.

PROPOSITION 1: *Assume without loss of generality that $\theta_1 < \theta_2$. There are five regions to be considered:*

(1) *Region 1: θ_1 high or medium; θ_2 high. In this region, neither division manager rent-seeks, and investment is efficient: $I_i = I_i^*$.*

(2) *Region 2: θ_1 low; θ_2 high. In this region, only the manager of division 1 rent-seeks, and investment is distorted towards division 1: $I_1 > I_1^*$.*

(3) *Region 3: θ_1 low; θ_2 low. In this region, both division managers rent-seek. However, investment is efficient: $I_i = I_i^*$. The retention constraints of both managers are met with cash wages: $w_i > 0$.*

(4) *Region 4: θ_1 low; θ_2 medium. In this region, both division managers rent-seek. Depending on parameter values, investment may or may not be distorted towards division 1: $I_1 \geq I_1^*$.*

Divisional Rent-Seeking and Inefficient Investment 2551

(5) Region 5: θ_1 medium; θ_2 medium. In this region, there are two possible equilibria, which we denote by Equilibrium 5a and Equilibrium 5b.

Equilibrium 5a: Neither division manager rent-seeks, and investment is efficient: $I_i = I_i^*$.

Equilibrium 5b: Both division managers rent-seek. Depending on parameter values, investment may or may not be distorted towards division 1: $I_1 \geq I_1^*$.

Region 1, where both divisions are relatively high productivity, represents the simplest and least interesting case. In this portion of the parameter space, both managers are so satisfied with the prescribed levels of capital allocation and would lose so much in time 1 private benefits that they are no threat to rent-seek, and hence the outcome is fully efficient, in terms of the allocation of both managerial effort and physical capital. Note that the CEO's ability to extract private benefits from the operating budget causes no distortions in this case, because outside investors can simply set $\overline{W} = 0$, without worrying that this leads to any problems.

Region 2 gets to the heart of our idea. Here division 1 is low productivity, so that its manager rent-seeks no matter what the manager of division 2 does. In contrast, division 2 is high productivity, so that its manager never rent-seeks, and therefore has a slack retention constraint. To retain the manager of division 1, the CEO has two choices: she can pay him a cash wage or she can tilt the capital budget in his direction. The former costs her dollar for dollar, whereas the latter initially does not. This is because the retention constraint for division 2 is slack, so the CEO can shift resources away from it without having to compensate its manager for the lost investment with a cash wage. Thus at least initially, the CEO only bears a second-order cost (proportional to ϕ) of distorting the capital budget, and this is the preferred means of compensating division manager 1. This logic is sufficient to establish that investment is distorted towards division 1.

Notice that whenever a division manager's retention constraint is slack, his cash wages are zero. This is because the CEO sets wages as low as possible in this region to minimize the division manager's rents. At first glance, this might lead one to doubt the model's relevance, because wages of literally zero are never observed. However, it is trivial to modify the model so that cash wages are strictly positive even when the retention constraint is slack. Suppose that division managers face an additional liquidity constraint, which requires them to earn cash wages of L in order to eat—that is, they cannot live on private benefits alone. Thus if cash wages are below L, no amount of capital expenditures in their division can compensate for this. Then, of course, the CEO has to pay the division manager cash wages of L to meet this liquidity constraint. And it is possible that when this liquidity constraint is met, the retention constraint is slack. Thus everything is the same as before, except the minimal point at which wages can be set is L, not zero. This simple renormalization makes the model more realistic in terms of its literal implications for cash wages, without changing any of the fundamental logic.

Region 3 is interesting because it makes the point that our results on investment inefficiencies require more than just the existence of low θ's and rent-seeking per se—they require a pronounced imbalance between the productivity of the two divisions. When both divisions are low productivity, and therefore both face binding retention constraints, it does the CEO no good to shift capital from division 2 to division 1, because in so doing, she lowers the utility of manager 2 by at least as much as she raises the utility of manager 1, and hence does not make it any cheaper for herself to retain both managers. Instead, the CEO optimally chooses to pay off both rent-seeking managers with cash. As an aside, this case also illustrates that investment inefficiencies do not necessarily follow simply from the assumption that the CEO can abuse the operating budget. In this case, with two weak divisions, the CEO does what investors would consider to be the right thing with the operating budget, and spends it not on herself, but rather to retain the division managers.

Region 4 represents an intermediate case between Region 2 and Region 3, and is consistent with the broad intuition that investment distortions are most likely to occur when there is an imbalance between the two divisions. Here division 1 is still low productivity, but division 2 is medium productivity. In this situation, both division managers rent-seek. The consequences for investment are less clear-cut. Depending on parameter values, we can either have an outcome where investment is tilted towards division 1 (as in Region 2) or one where investment is allocated efficiently (as in Region 3).[19]

Finally, Region 5 is where the potential for strategic complementarities comes into play. In this region, both divisions are of medium productivity, so that each division manager's rent-seeking decision depends on the other's. This implies that there can be two equilibria.[20] The first, 5a, has the same properties as the equilibrium in Region 1: no rent-seeking, and efficient investment. The second, 5b, is like that in Region 4: both managers rent-seek, and investment may (though need not) be distorted towards division 1.

In comparing these two equilibria, one point to note is that equilibrium 5a is Pareto-superior. Clearly, the CEO (as well as outside investors) prefers the outcome with no rent-seeking. Moreover, it is easy to see from definition (11) that the two division managers prefer this equilibrium also. That is, equilibrium 5b represents a "coordination failure" outcome where each division manager defensively rent-seeks only because he expects his counterpart to do the same, and where both wind up worse off as a result. The potential for a firm to get stuck in this sort of dysfunctional equilibrium, where division managers waste their time in a futile tug-of-war over the capital budget, strikes us as a particularly interesting feature of the model.

---

[19] In the latter case of efficient investment, both retention constraints are met with cash wages, also as in Region 3.

[20] Although the models are quite different, our multiple-equilibrium result is similar in spirit to Proposition 3 of Fulghieri and Hodrick (1997).

Divisional Rent-Seeking and Inefficient Investment   2553

From an empirical perspective, however, the single clearest prediction that emerges from Proposition 1 is that investment is most likely to be tilted towards the weaker division in a firm when it is paired with a much stronger division, as in Region 2. When there are more modest differences in productivity (as in Regions 4 or 5) there may possibly be investment distortions, but the prediction is more ambiguous.

Although Proposition 1 tells us about the direction in which the capital budget is tilted, it need not imply economically large distortions relative to the benchmark of $I_i = I_i^*$. Indeed, Proposition 1 as stated even applies when there is no agency problem between the CEO and outside investors; as noted earlier, this just corresponds to a special case where we set $\phi = 1$ in expression (8). Even a principal may be willing to tilt the capital budget *slightly* away from the $I_i = I_i^*$ benchmark when confronted with rent-seeking. After all, the principal's objective is not just to maximize investment output, but rather to maximize output *less* the cost of retaining rent-seeking managers.[21]

Of course, intuition suggests that while a principal might tilt the capital budget slightly, the quantitative effect should be much amplified when the decision is made by the CEO acting as an agent—that is, when we have $\phi \ll 1$. Thus the natural next question to ask is: In those cases where investment is distorted, how big is the distortion? In Appendix A, we prove the following:

PROPOSITION 2: *Any time there is an investment distortion, the CEO shifts capital to division 1 until one of the following limits is hit:*

(1) Division manager 1's retention constraint is satisfied with a zero cash wage, i.e.: I_1 solves $g(r_1^*) = \gamma\theta_1 k(I_1)$; or

(2) The marginal cost to the CEO of distorting investment becomes so high that she is unwilling to distort it further, and prefers to pay the rest of the needed compensation to the manager of division 1 in cash: $\phi(\theta_2 k'(I_2) - \theta_1 k'(I_1)) = \gamma\theta_1 k'(I_1)$; or

(3) The retention constraint of division manager 2 binds when $w_2 = 0$: $g(r_2^*) = \gamma\theta_2 k(I_2)$.

The implication of Proposition 2 is that we are likely to get a large distortion in investment allocation when the following conditions jointly obtain: (1) division 1 is very weak, so that θ_1 is very small and a large value of I_1 is needed to satisfy manager 1's retention constraint; (2) division 2 is very strong, so that manager 2 never rent-seeks and always has a slack retention constraint; and (3) the CEO has low-powered incentives (i.e., ϕ is small) so that she is willing to tolerate a large difference in the marginal product of capital across the two divisions.

To isolate the pure effects of agency at the CEO level, note that from part 2 of Proposition 2, an upper bound on the investment distortion is given by $\theta_2 k'(I_2)/\theta_1 k'(I_1) = 1 + \gamma/\phi$. If ϕ and γ are of the same order of magnitude,

---

[21] When one division manager's retention constraint is slack, and the principal initially shifts a little bit of capital to another manager with a binding constraint, he suffers only a second-order investment inefficiency but realizes a first-order savings in cash wages.

this implies a potentially large distortion. Now consider what happens if instead the CEO acts benevolently on behalf of outside investors, so that effectively, $\phi = 1$. If we continue to maintain that $\gamma \ll 1$, it is easy to see that there can only ever be a very small deviation from the $I_i = I_i^*$ benchmark in this no-agency case. Thus to the extent that there are economically large deviations when $\phi \ll 1$, they are wholly attributable the CEO's weak incentives to maximize value.

Note that our results on distortions in capital expenditures are not critically dependent on the assumption that the CEO has all the bargaining power when making offers to the division managers at time 2. Rather, these distortions arise because of an externality. When the CEO and the division managers sit down to negotiate at time 2, outside investors are not at the table. Thus the CEO and division managers do not internalize the costs to these outside investors of misallocating the capital budget, and instead maximize only their own joint surplus. As a result, there is an incentive to distort the capital budget, regardless of how the resulting surplus is ultimately divided.

D. Investors' Choice of $\bar{I}$ and $\bar{W}$

To this point, we have been treating the amount of total firm-wide investment $\bar{I}$ as a fixed parameter. We have also been assuming that outside investors give the CEO an operating budget $\bar{W}$ that allows her to pay all cash wages she would like. The next step is to ask what values of $\bar{I}$ and $\bar{W}$ emerge from ex ante optimization on the part of outside investors.

Consider the optimal choice of $\bar{W}$ first. The method of analysis is as follows. First, solve the model—as we have above—under the assumption that the CEO is unconstrained with respect to setting cash wages. This implies an amount of cash that is needed to pay any w_1 or w_2. Now ask whether outside investors can gain by reducing $\bar{W}$ below $w_1 + w_2$. (Clearly, they never wish to give the CEO more than this amount.)

Given the specific way we have modeled things, it is easy to show that investors never reduce $\bar{W}$ below $w_1 + w_2$. For if they did, one of two things would have to happen: (1) the CEO might distort the capital budget even further than before, so as to retain manager 1 without using any cash; or (2) the CEO would be simply unable to satisfy both managers' retention constraints—at least one manager would depart to his outside option. Under our assumptions, both of these outcomes are more costly to investors than the incremental savings in wages. Intuitively, the problem here is not with the cash wages that the CEO pays to division managers; rather it is the fact that the CEO would like to economize on cash wages, and hence prefers to use distortions in capital expenditures as a means of compensating division managers. Thus, preventing the CEO from making those cash payments that she is actually willing to make can only worsen matters.

More generally, even if the model is changed so that it is in some circumstances optimal for investors to constrain the CEO's ability to pay cash wages, our results on investment distortions still go through—even more strongly

Divisional Rent-Seeking and Inefficient Investment 2555

and transparently so. To see this, suppose that we are in Region 2 of Proposition 1, where only the manager of the low-θ division rent-seeks. If the CEO does not have the cash to pay any wages, the only possible way for her to retain this manager is to tilt the capital budget in his favor.

The optimal choice of $\bar{I}$ is much less interesting for our purposes, in the sense that it does not interact in any meaningful way with any of our previous results. Everything that we have said thus far holds for any value of $\bar{I}$. Nonetheless, for completeness, it is worth discussing the determination of $\bar{I}$. If outside investors can count on there being no misallocations of the capital budget, they set $\bar{I} = I_1^{**} + I_2^{**}$, where I_i^{**} satisfies $\theta_i k'(I_i^{**}) = 1$. However, in those regions of the parameter space where they can anticipate misallocations, $\bar{I}$ is set at a lower value.

II. Extensions and Variations

A. A Signal-jamming Rationale for Conserving the Operating Budget

Up to now, we have assumed that the auditing/verification technology is such that the CEO has some discretion over the operating budget—if the CEO does not spend the operating budget on division-manager wages, she can instead spend it on something else that raises her utility, such as excess travel. In contrast, the CEO has less discretion with respect to the capital budget—although she can choose in which division to spend it, the funds must be spent on physical capital somewhere in the firm, and cannot be used for other purposes. These assumptions taken together lead to our principal conclusion, namely that the CEO may prefer to tilt the capital budget rather than spend the operating budget to satisfy a division manager's demands.

Thus a natural criticism of our model is that our results are a by-product of an implausible assumption. Why, it might be asked, can't outside investors somehow circumscribe the CEO's ability to divert the operating budget? For example, with a stronger auditing technology, investors might be able to specify that the funds they put up for division-manager wages cannot be used for anything else. This would prevent the CEO from enjoying private benefits when she holds down division-manager wages.

In response to this critique, we should stress that it is not really necessary for our results that the CEO be able to divert the operating budget to herself. All that is really required is the much weaker condition that the CEO have some reason to care about economizing on wage payments to division managers. We now sketch one alternative model—without any diversion of the operating budget—which has this property.

The alternative model is a variation on Stein (1989). Assume that the CEO owns stock in the firm, and that she contemplates selling some of this stock in the not-too-distant future. Thus the CEO wishes to take actions that increase the short-run stock price, even if these actions ultimately reduce the firm's long-run value. At time 2, the CEO has ample cash on hand so that she can, if she chooses, pay any needed wages to the division managers. Any cash that is not spent on such wages is added to operating earnings, which are paid out in the form of a dividend to investors. So the CEO does not get to divert to herself any savings that are realized from holding down division-manager wages.

However, suppose that the division managers' equilibrium outside options—as given by $g(\hat{r}_i)$—are observed only by the CEO, and not by investors. In this case, the CEO still has an incentive to skimp on cash wage payments to the division managers. For by doing so, she can boost reported earnings, and—to the extent that these earnings are informative about future prospects—raise the stock price.

Essentially, by making the outside options unobservable to investors, we have created a situation where reductions in cash wages are exactly analogous to Stein's (1989) notion of "borrowing" in an unobservable way against the future. In particular, investors now cannot tell whether a marginal increase in earnings comes from honestly good performance, or whether it reflects the fact that the CEO has held back on cash wages to the division managers (which is ultimately costly due to the resulting misallocation of capital). As a result, equilibrium necessarily involves some degree of this costly borrowing, and our previous conclusions should continue to apply.

B. Breakups

To this point, we have simply assumed the existence of an integrated firm where the CEO has the authority to allocate the overall capital budget across the two divisions. But given the potential for inefficiencies that we have identified, it is natural to ask whether one can do better than in the integrated setting, by separating the two divisions. We cannot provide a complete answer to this question, because we have not modeled any of the potential benefits of integration, only the costs. But if one is willing to assume that the benefits are relatively constant across the parameter values of our model, we may have something to say about the circumstances under which a breakup is most likely to be a good idea.[22]

In the context of our model, a "breakup" can be conceptualized very simply, as follows. Divisions 1 and 2 are split into two distinct firms, each with their own CEOs, division managers, operating budgets, and capital budgets of I_i^{**}.[23] It is easy to see that a breakup can be beneficial when we are in Region 2 of Proposition 1—that is, when the divisions are relatively unequal in strength and there is a distortion in investment in the integrated equilibrium. Upon breakup, this investment distortion is eliminated. Note however, that in this region a breakup *does not* eliminate the inefficient

---

[22] When we say "good idea," this is from the perspective of outside investors. In reality, of course, good ideas of this kind may not be implemented right away if the CEO enjoys having a large empire and is insulated from shareholder pressure, so large investment inefficiencies may persist for long periods of time.

[23] Note that in our setting, a CEO is still required for each division operating as a stand-alone, because it is the CEO who identifies and hires the division manager.

Divisional Rent-Seeking and Inefficient Investment   2557

rent-seeking behavior on the part of the manager of the weak division. All it does is force the CEO to compensate the rent-seeking manager in cash, rather than with capital from the other division.

Somewhat more subtly, a breakup might also add value in Region 5, if the firm has somehow gotten stuck in the "bad" equilibrium 5b with rent-seeking. This holds true even if there is no investment distortion in equilibrium 5b. For when the divisions are separated, the multiplicity disappears and the unique outcome for these parameters is now one with no rent-seeking in either division. For similar reasons, a breakup can be helpful in Region 4 as well, regardless of whether or not there is an investment distortion. In this region, when a medium-productivity division is separated from a low-productivity division, its optimal strategy shifts from rent-seeking to not rent-seeking. This is an efficiency gain above and beyond any investment effect.

In contrast, a breakup does no good if we are in Region 3, where both managers rent-seek but there is no investment distortion. Postbreakup, there is still the same level of rent-seeking in each division, because, with low productivity, the incentive to rent-seek is so strong that any manager does so irrespective of his counterpart's behavior.

Thus the model is loosely suggestive about the circumstances under which one might expect to see breakups—they should be not so much driven by the absolute weakness of a given division, but rather by differences in productivity across multiple divisions in the same firm. Moreover, this thought experiment reinforces once again a point made earlier: the ability of the CEO to abuse the operating budget, taken by itself, need not lead to any inefficiencies. When there is a breakup, both CEOs spend any operating budgets efficiently, to retain their respective managers.

Of course, this whole line of reasoning is subject to the caveat that we have not endogenized the benefits of integration, and are implicitly treating them as a constant. To see why this simplification could be problematic, note that the beneficial, "winner-picking" aspects of an internal capital market might conceivably also be more pronounced when the divisions in question are more divergent in terms of productivity.[24] If this is so, our predictions for breakups become less clear-cut.

III. Empirical Implications

A few recent empirical papers speak directly to our model's central predictions. Using segment-level data from COMPUSTAT, Shin and Stulz (1998) document that the investment of any given segment in a diversified firm depends on the cash flows of other, unrelated segments. Moreover, this apparent cross-subsidization "does not depend on whether that segment (receiving the transfer) has the best investment opportunities within the firm" (p. 533). As Shin and Stulz argue, this latter finding fits with our notion of socialism in internal capital markets.

---

[24] However, Stein (1997) argues that winner picking may actually work better when the divisions are in related lines of business.

Rajan et al. (2000) use a similar data set, and uncover three noteworthy patterns. First, consistent with the notion of socialism, multisegment firms allocate relatively more than their stand-alone counterparts to segments in "weak" lines of business (as measured either by industry Q ratios or investment rates) and relatively less to segments in "strong" lines of business. Second, this misallocation of resources is most pronounced when there is a wide disparity in the productivity of investment across the lines of business, as proxied for by the dispersion of the corresponding industry Q ratios. This is directly in line with the predictions of our Propositions 1 and 2, which state that large investment inefficiencies are most likely to occur when there is a pronounced differential in divisions' investment opportunities. Finally, the investment distortions have significant value consequences—those diversified firms that have the most heterogeneous segments and that misallocate funds the most also tend to trade at the largest discounts.[25]

Scharfstein (1998) also finds evidence of socialism in a sample of diversified conglomerates, in that the investment of conglomerate divisions is virtually insensitive to their investment opportunities, as measured by the corresponding industry Qs. (In contrast, the investment of stand-alone firms is significantly more sensitive to industry Qs.) But perhaps most interesting from the perspective of our model is Scharfstein's finding that socialism seems to be driven by a misalignment of incentives between outside investors and top management. In particular, he shows that the sensitivity of divisional investment to Q increases as top management's equity stake in the firm goes up. Or, said differently, socialism is more pronounced when the CEO has low-powered incentives. This gets precisely at the heart of the most distinctive aspect of our model—the idea that the agency problem between the CEO and outside investors is a crucial part of the story. As noted earlier, the model of Rajan et al. (2000), where investment levels are set by a principal rather than by an agent, does not make the same prediction.

Some of the evidence put forth by Shin and Stulz (1998), Rajan et al. (2000), and Scharfstein (1998) has been challenged in a recent paper by Chevalier (1999), who argues that there may be biases arising from unobserved differences between conglomerate divisions and stand-alone firms. However, Gertner, Powers, and Scharfstein (1999) demonstrate that even when one controls for these unobserved differences—by examining the same division before and after it is spun out of a conglomerate—investment is markedly less sensitive to Q when a division is inside a conglomerate.

Thus overall, evidence is beginning to emerge that suggests that not only is there a general tendency towards socialism in internal capital markets, but that this problem is more acute when (1) there are wide disparities across divisions in investment prospects, and (2) top management has weak incentives to maximize value. This broad picture squares very well with our theory.

---

[25] Berger and Ofek (1995) also find that the conglomerate discount is greatest in firms that invest the most in low-Q lines of business.

Divisional Rent-Seeking and Inefficient Investment 2559

IV. Conclusions

Although we have couched our model in terms of a CEO allocating capital to divisions, we believe it captures a more general and broadly applicable point about how organizations work. In its most basic form, our key insight is that when any agent *i* inside an organization wishes to get any other agent *j* to do something, she will likely try to pay for this not with cash, but rather by directing to agent *j* an extra share of the resources over which she (*i*) has allocative authority. Our model has considered an especially simple case where it is exogenously assumed that the CEO is the only one with any meaningful authority to allocate resources. But in reality, a wide range of agents throughout any organization have some authority to allocate resources, and nonmonetary exchanges are pervasive.

Because these nonmonetary exchanges are typically inefficient in our framework, a potentially important element of organizational design centers on how spreading or concentrating the power to make resource-allocation decisions affects efficiency. To see the sorts of issues that might arise, consider an example of a business school faculty that must make decisions in two different areas: (1) it must choose which new faculty to recruit; and (2) it must assign existing faculty to teaching particular courses. Now compare two organizational design options. In the first case, a single individual is made department head and given the authority to make both decisions. In the latter, two separate people are put in charge of recruiting and course staffing.

On the one hand, the latter, two-headed option might well offer the advantage of specialized expertise in decision making—in other words, if somebody is responsible for just recruiting and nothing else, he is more likely to become more informed about the candidates. On the other hand, dividing up the authority in this way could conceivably increase the scope for inefficient "favor trading." For example, the course-staffing chair might give a particularly light teaching load to the recruiting chair in exchange for being allowed to hire his favorite candidate. It might be interesting to model these sorts of trade-offs more explicitly, and to draw out their implications for organizational design.

Appendix A.

Proof of Proposition 1: The optimal wage and capital budget at time 1 maximizes the CEO's utility:

$$U \equiv \phi \theta_1 k(I_1) - w_1 + \phi \theta_2 k(\bar{I} - I_1) - w_2 \tag{A1}$$

subject to the retention constraints

$$w_1 + \gamma \theta_1 k(I_1) \geq g(r_1) \tag{A2}$$

$$w_2 + \gamma \theta_2 k(\bar{I} - I_1) \geq g(r_2). \tag{A3}$$

Note that we have made use of the fact that the capital budget is fixed so that $I_1 + I_2 = \bar{I}$.

The first-order conditions of the associated Lagrangian, L, of this constrained maximization are:

$$\frac{\partial L}{\partial w_1} = -1 + \lambda_1 \leq 0 \tag{A4}$$

$$\frac{\partial L}{\partial w_2} = 1 + \lambda_2 \leq 0 \tag{A5}$$

$$\frac{\partial L}{\partial I_1} = \phi[\theta_1 k'(I_1) - \theta_2 k'(\bar{I} - I_1)] + \lambda_1 \gamma \theta_1 k'(I_1) - \lambda_2 \gamma \theta_2 k'(\bar{I} - I_1) = 0, \tag{A6}$$

where λ_1 and λ_2 are the Lagrange multipliers on the retention constraints.[26]

To establish the outcomes in the various regions, it is helpful to characterize $I_2(r_1^*)$, the investment allocation to Manager 2 (M2) when he does not rent-seek but Manager 1 (M1) does. In this case, M2 has no outside option, so his retention constraint is never binding; $\lambda_2 = 0$. Therefore, the relevant first-order conditions are equation (A4) and a simplified version of equation (A6):

$$\frac{\partial L}{\partial I_1} = \phi[\theta_1 k'(I_1) - \theta_2 k'(\bar{I} - I_1)] + \lambda_1 \gamma \theta_1 k'(I_1) = 0. \tag{A7}$$

There are two mutually exclusive solutions in this case, which can only occur when $g(r_1^*) > \gamma \theta_1 k(I_1^*)$. (Otherwise M1 would not rent-seek.)

(i) Define I_1^a as the solution to the retention constraint when $w_1 = 0$:

$$\gamma \theta_1 k(I_1^a) = g(r_1^*). \tag{A8}$$

At an optimum $w_1 = 0$ and $I_1 = I_1^a$ provided,

$$\frac{\partial L}{\partial I_1} = \phi[\theta_1 k'(I_1^a) - \theta_2 k'(\bar{I} - I_1^a)] + \gamma \theta_1 k'(I_1^a) > 0. \tag{A9}$$

Given equation (A9), there exists a $\lambda_1 < 1$ such that the first-order condition (A7) is satisfied for $I_1^a > I_1^*$. Intuitively, at $I_1 = I_1^a$, the marginal reduction in M1's wage made possible by an increase in $I_1, \gamma \theta_1 k'(I_1^a)$, exceeds the marginal cost to the principal of distorting investment, $\phi[\theta_2 k'(I - I_1^a) - \theta_1 k'(I_1^a)]$.

[26] The assumption that $k'(0) = \infty$ guarantees that $I_1 > 0$ and $\partial L/\partial I_1 = 0$ at an optimum.

Divisional Rent-Seeking and Inefficient Investment   2561

(ii) If equation (A9) is not satisfied, then I_1 must be less than I_1^a for the first-order condition (A7) to be satisfied. Thus, $w_1 > 0$ if the retention constraint is to be satisfied, from which it follows that $\lambda_1 = 1$. At an optimum $I_1 = I_1^b$ where I_1^b solves

$$\phi\left[\theta_1 k'(I_1^b) - \theta_2 k'(\bar{I} - I_1^b)\right] + \gamma\theta_1 k'(I_1^b) = 0. \tag{A10}$$

Note that $I_1^a > I_1^b > I_1^*$. The important point is that $I_2(r_1^*) < I_2^*$ when $\gamma\theta_1 k(I_1^*) < g(r_1^*)$; M2 gets less than the efficient allocation of capital if he does not rent-seek but M1 does.

We now show that the equilibrium outcomes correspond to the five regions described in the Proposition.

Region 1: θ_1 high or medium; θ_2 high

In this region, M2 does not rent-seek regardless of what M1 does; it is a dominant strategy for M2 not to rent-seek. To see this, suppose M1 rent-seeks. If M2 also rent-seeks, he receives $g(r_2^*)$ at date 2 but loses $\gamma\theta_2\Delta f_2$ at date 1. If M2 does not rent-seek, he gets $\gamma\theta_2 k(I_2(r_1^*))$ as shown above. This establishes that M2 does not rent-seek when $g(r_2^*) \leq \gamma\theta_2[k(I_2(r_1^*)) + \Delta f_2]$, which is satisfied by the definition of θ_2 being high. If M1 does not rent-seek, then M2 has even less incentive to rent-seek, because when neither manager rent-seeks, the allocation of capital is efficient. So M2 does not rent-seek provided $g(r_2^*) \leq \gamma\theta_2[k(I_2^*) + \Delta f_2]$. Given that $I_2(r_1^*) < I_2^*$, the condition defining this region again implies that M2 does not rent-seek.

Because M2 does not rent-seek, it is straightforward to show that M1 does not rent-seek provided $g(r_1^*) \leq \gamma\theta_1[k(I_1^*) + \Delta f_1]$, which is satisfied for θ_1 high or medium. Thus, neither manager rent-seeks, neither retention constraint is binding, and the allocation of capital is efficient.

Region 2: θ_1 low; θ_2 high

As shown above, if θ_2 is high, it is a dominant strategy for M2 not to rent-seek. However, M1 rent-seeks because when θ_1 is low $g(r_1^*) > \gamma\theta_1[k(I_1^*) + \Delta f_1]$. We have already shown that if M1 rent-seeks and M2 does not, $I_1 = \bar{I} - I_2(r_1^*) > I_1^*$.

Region 3: θ_1 low; θ_2 low

First we show that it is a Nash equilibrium for both managers to rent-seek in this region. If M2 does not rent-seek but M1 does, he receives $I_2(r_1^*)$ in capital, where we know that $I_2(r_1^*) < I_2^*$. Thus, $g(r_2^*) > \gamma\theta_2[k(I_2(r_1^*)) + \Delta f_2]$ because we have assumed that in this region $g(r_2^*) > \gamma\theta_2[k(I_2^*) + \Delta f_2]$. An analogous argument establishes that M1 rent-seeks given that M2 rent-seeks.

We now show that the investment allocation is efficient in this region. First, note that both wages must be strictly positive. If neither wage were positive both retention constraints could not be met. If $w_1 > 0$ but $w_2 = 0$, then $I_2 > I_2^*$. In this case, the first-order condition (A6) implies $\lambda_2 > \lambda_1$. But because $w_1 > 0$, λ_1 must equal 1 and λ_2 cannot be greater than 1 from the first-order condition (A4). Thus, $w_1 > 0$, $w_2 = 0$ is not an optimal solution. An analogous argument establishes that $w_1 = 0$, $w_2 > 0$, is also not optimal. It follows that $w_1 > 0$ and $w_2 > 0$ and that equations (A4) and (A5) therefore imply $\lambda_1 = \lambda_2 = 1$. Substituting into condition (A6) implies that $I_i = I_i^*$ at an optimum.

Region 4: θ_1 low; θ_2 medium

The discussion of Region 3 establishes that if $g(r_2^*) > \gamma \theta_2[k(I_2(r_1^*)) + \Delta f_2]$, M2 rent-seeks if M1 does. And, given that M2 rent-seeks, M1 rent-seeks if $g(r_1^*) > \gamma \theta_1[k(I_1(r_2^*)) + \Delta f_1]$, where $I_1(r_2^*)$ is the investment allocation to M1 when M1 does not rent-seek but M2 does. Because θ_1 being low means $g(r_1^*) > \gamma \theta_1[k(I_1^*) + \Delta f_1]$ and $k(I_1^*) > k(I_1(r_2^*))$, the rent-seeking condition is met and M1 also rent-seeks.

While both managers rent-seek, the investment allocation may or may not be efficient. It is efficient if $\gamma \theta_2 k(I_2^*) < g(r_2^*)$. In this case the argument for the efficiency of the investment allocation in Region 3 goes through unaltered. However, if $g(r_2^*) < \gamma \theta_2 k(I_2^*)$, then it is possible for the investment allocation to be inefficient. Let I_2^c be the investment level such that

$$g(r_2^*) = \gamma \theta_2 k(I_2^c). \tag{A11}$$

Recall that I_1^a and I_1^b are the possible optimal investment allocations when M2's retention constraint is not binding. If $\bar{I} - I_1^a > I_2^c$ or $\bar{I} - I_1^b > I_2^c$, then one of these (either I_1^a or I_1^b) is the solution, because M2's constraint is not binding at these levels. If this is not the case, then another possible solution is to set $w_2 = 0$ and $I_2 = I_2^c$. This is the solution if

$$\phi[\theta_1 k'(\bar{I} - I_2^c) - \theta_2 k'(\bar{I}_2^c)] + \gamma \theta_1 k'(\bar{I} - I_2^c) > 0. \tag{A12}$$

One can verify that in this case $w_1 > 0$, $\lambda_1 = 1$, $0 < \lambda_2 < 1$ satisfies all the first-order conditions for an optimum. This suffices to show that the investment allocation can also be inefficient in Region 4.

Region 5: θ_1 medium; θ_2 medium

Equilibrium 5a: In this equilibrium neither manager rent-seeks. Given that M_j does not rent-seek, M_i does not rent-seek because in this region $g(r_i^*) \le \gamma \theta_i[k(I_i^*) + \Delta f_i]$. If neither manager rent-seeks then neither retention constraint is binding, and the investment allocation is efficient.

Divisional Rent-Seeking and Inefficient Investment   2563

Equilibrium 5b: In this equilibrium both managers rent-seek. The condition for i to rent-seek given that j rent-seeks is $g(r_i^*) > \gamma \theta_i [k(I_i(r_j^*)) + \Delta f_i]$, which is satisfied when θ_i is medium. A similar argument to the one for Region 4 establishes that the investment allocation may or may not be efficient.   Q.E.D.

Proof of Proposition 2: We have already established Proposition 2 in the course of proving Proposition 1. In particular, the three different possible outcomes where $I_1 > I_1^*$ referred to in Proposition 2 correspond to I_1^a, I_1^b, and I_1^c, as defined in equations (A8), (A10), and (A11), respectively.   Q.E.D.

REFERENCES

Aghion, Philippe, and Jean Tirole, 1997, Formal and real authority in organizations, *Journal of Political Economy* 105, 1–29.

Bagwell, Laurie Simon, and Josef Zechner, 1993, Influence costs and capital structure, *Journal of Finance* 48, 975–1008.

Berger, Philip, and Eli Ofek, 1995, Diversification's effect on firm value, *Journal of Financial Economics* 37, 39–65.

Berger, Philip, and Eli Ofek, 1996, Bustup takeovers of value-destroying diversified firms, *Journal of Finance* 51, 1175–1200.

Bhagat, Sanjai, Andrei Shleifer, and Robert W. Vishny, 1990, Hostile takeovers in the 1980s: The return to corporate specialization, *Brookings Papers on Economic Activity: Microeconomics* Special Issue, 1–72.

Bolton, Patrick, and David Scharfstein, 1990, A theory of predation based on agency problems in financial contracting, *American Economic Review* 80, 94–106.

Burkart, Mike, Denis Gromb, and Fausto Panunzi, 1997, Large shareholders, monitoring, and the value of the firm, *Quarterly Journal of Economics* 112, 693–728.

Campa, Jose M., and Simi Kedia, 1999, Explaining the diversification discount, Working paper, Harvard Business School.

Chevalier, Judith A., 1999, Why do firms undertake diversifying mergers? An examination of the investment policies of merging firms, Working paper, University of Chicago.

Comment, Robert, and Gregg A. Jarrell, 1995, Corporate focus and stock returns, *Journal of Financial Economics* 37, 67–87.

Edlin, Aaron S., and Joseph E. Stiglitz, 1995, Discouraging rivals: Managerial rent-seeking and economic inefficiencies, *American Economic Review* 85, 1301–1312.

Fauver, Larry, Joel Houston, and Andy Naranjo, 1998, Capital market development, legal systems and the value of corporate diversification: A cross-country analysis, Working paper, University of Florida.

Fulghieri, Paolo, and Laurie Simon Hodrick, 1997, Synergies and internal agency conflicts: The double-edged sword of mergers, Working paper, Columbia University.

Gertner, Robert G., Eric Powers, and David S. Scharfstein, 1999, Learning about internal capital markets from corporate spinoffs, Working paper, Massachusetts Institute of Technology.

Grossman, Sanford, and Oliver Hart, 1986, The costs and benefits of ownership: A theory of vertical and lateral integration., *Journal of Political Economy* 94, 691–719.

Hart, Oliver, and John Moore, 1990, Property rights and the nature of the firm, *Journal of Political Economy* 98, 1119–1158.

Hart, Oliver, and John Moore, 1998, Default and renegotiation: A dynamic model of debt, *Quarterly Journal of Economics* 113, 1–41.

Holmström, Bengt, and Paul Milgrom, 1990, Regulating trade among agents, *Journal of Institutional and Theoretical Economics* 146, 85–105.

Jensen, Michael C., 1986, Agency costs of free cash flow, corporate finance and takeovers, *American Economic Review* 76, 323–329.

Jensen, Michael C., 1993, The modern industrial revolution, exit, and the failure of internal control systems, *Journal of Finance* 48, 831–880.

Lamont, Owen, 1997, Cash flow and investment: Evidence from internal capital markets, *Journal of Finance* 52, 83–109.

Lang, Larry H.P., and René Stulz, 1994, Tobin's *q*, corporate diversification, and firm performance, *Journal of Political Economy* 102, 1248–1280.

Lins, Karl, and Henri Servaes, 1999, International evidence on the value of corporate diversification, *Journal of Finance* 54, 2215–2239.

Matsusaka, John, and Vikram Nanda, 1997, Internal capital markets and corporate refocusing, *Journal of Financial Intermediation*, forthcoming.

McAfee, R. Preston, and John McMillan, 1995, Organizational diseconomies of scale, *Journal of Economics and Management Strategy* 4, 399–426.

Meyer, Margaret, Paul Milgrom, and John Roberts, 1992, Organizational prospects, influence costs, and ownership changes, *Journal of Economics and Management Strategy* 1, 9–35.

Prendergast, Canice, and Lars Stole, 1996, Non-monetary exchange within firms and industries, NBER Working paper No. 5765.

Rajan, Raghuram G., Henri Servaes, and Luigi Zingales, 2000, The cost of diversity: The diversification discount and inefficient investment, *Journal of Finance* 55, 35–80.

Rotemberg, Julio, 1993, Power in profit-maximizing organizations, *Journal of Economics and Management Strategy* 2, 165–198.

Scharfstein, David, 1998, The dark side of internal capital markets II: Evidence from diversified conglomerates, NBER Working paper No. 6352.

Shin, Hyun-Han, and René Stulz, 1998, Are internal capital markets efficient? *Quarterly Journal of Economics* 113, 531–552.

Shleifer, Andrei, and Robert W. Vishny, 1989, Management entrenchment: The case of manager-specific investments, *Journal of Financial Economics* 25, 123–140.

Stein, Jeremy C., 1989, Efficient capital markets, inefficient firms: A model of myopic corporate behavior, *Quarterly Journal of Economics* 104, 655–669.

Stein, Jeremy C., 1997, Internal capital markets and the competition for corporate resources, *Journal of Finance* 52, 111–133.

Tirole, Jean, 1986, Hierarchies and bureaucracies, *Journal of Law, Economics and Organization* 2, 181–214.

Williamson, Oliver E., 1975, *Markets and Hierarchies: Analysis and Antitrust Implications* (Collier Macmillan Publishers, Inc., New York).

Wulf, Julie, 1997, Influence and inefficiency in the internal capital market: Theory and evidence, Working paper, Columbia University.

ELSEVIER

Journal of Economic Behavior & Organization
Vol. 48 (2002) 155–162

JOURNAL OF
Economic Behavior
& Organization

www.elsevier.com/locate/econbase

Allies as rivals: internal and external rent seeking

Amihai Glazer*

Department of Economics, University of California, Irvine Irvine, CA 92697, USA

Received 12 August 1999; accepted 1 July 2000

Abstract

An owner or other leader can more effectively obtain rents or other benefits for his organization the higher the quality of his staff. These staff may, however, also seek rents inside the firm, with the most able staff best able to do so. The paper finds that an employer will hire better staff the stiffer the competition for external rents, and the smaller the assets of the firm. The relation between the quality of an owner and the quality of his staff is not monotonic: both high- and low-ability owners may prefer staff of low ability. © 2002 Elsevier Science B.V. All rights reserved.

Keywords: Owner; Rent seeking; Principal

1. Introduction

Rent seeking occurs not only between firms or other organizations, but also within them. If the contest is only between organizations, the situation studied in most of the literature, then the organization would benefit from appointing staff who are highly effective in rent seeking. A person, however, who is effective in rent seeking on behalf of the organization (I call this *external* rent seeking) may also effectively rent seek within the organization, appropriating assets to himself (I call this *internal* rent seeking). The tension between these two effects may induce the leader of an organization to appoint staff who are ineffective rent seekers.

External rent seeking takes many forms: pharmaceutical firms may race for a patent, defense contractors may invest in design and development in an effort to win a lucrative contract, firms may lobby to induce Congress to levy tariffs. Rent seeking also appears outside firms: a symphony orchestra may desire to be viewed as the world's best, a president may seek to win a war, or a political party may aim to win a parliamentary majority. Despite all these possibilities, it is convenient to speak of a specific situation. I shall therefore consider a firm which can increase its profits by external rent seeking.

* Tel.: +1-949-824-5974; fax: +1-949-824-2182.
E-mail address: aglazer@uci.edu (A. Glazer).

Internal rent seeking involves a transfer from the owner to the worker. For example, a knowledgeable worker may embezzle from his employer or engage in insider trading. An employee may learn of the firm's trade secrets, which he uses to establish a competing firm. [1] Staff may take credit for the successes of the organization, reducing the glory of the employer. [2] Or, in government, an able worker may gain access to levers of power and to other staff which allows him to stage a coup.

2. Literature

The literature on external rent seeking is extensive, including studies of how the abilities of rent seekers affect the equilibrium outcomes. Nitzan (1994), e.g. considers the effects of an increase in a firm's unit cost of rent-seeking. In choosing a particular function to represent the results of rent seeking, I make use of the classic function introduced by Tullock (1967) and Skaperdas (1996) shows this is a special case in the class of functions which meets plausible conditions such as homotheticity.

The seminal study of internal rent seeking is Milgrom (1988), who terms the behavior influence activities. Rajan and Zingales (2000) examine optimal hierarchical organization when a manager has to be given access to information, but also has to be limited in his appropriative activity. The spirit of my analysis resembles Carmichael (1988) explanation for tenure: members of an academic department may fear that hiring high-quality faculty will reduce the future income of current members. Relatedly, Garfinkel and Skaperdas (2000) and Skaperdas and Syropoulos (1997) show that when economic agents can choose to allocate resources between production and conflict, the agent who is more productive can earn a smaller income. They do not ask, however, as I do, the quality of a team member one member would prefer.

3. Assumptions

The firm consists of two people, the owner and the staff person (or worker) he appoints. I assume, as is common in principal-agent models, that the owner is risk neutral. The effort of the worker and of the owner are fixed; their effectiveness in rent seeking varies with their ability. The reservation utility of the staff is invariant with his ability (perhaps because his skills are useful only to the owner in question).

Since internal rent seeking involves a pure transfer, the owner might be thought to be indifferent about the level of internal rent seeking—whatever the staff gains the owner could recoup by reducing the wage. But that may sometimes be infeasible. If the worker is sufficiently risk averse, then his expected utility from the internal rent seeking may be low, and the owner may be forced to pay a wage equal to the staff's reservation utility. Moreover, credit constraints and imperfect credit markets may make a person unwilling to work for

---

[1] Indeed Bhide (2000, p. 94) reports that 71 percent of the firms included in the *Inc. 500* (a list of young, fast growing firms) were founded by people who replicated or modified an idea encountered in their previous employment.

[2] See Mayhew (1974) for a discussion of credit claiming by congressmen.

A. Glazer / J. of Economic Behavior & Org. 48 (2002) 155–162

a low wage. If the staff person's expected monetary gain is larger than his reservation utility, calling in a first-best solution for the staff to pay the owner, then enforceability can become a problem: the owner may take the payment and then refuse to hire staff, or refuse to give him a position where rent seeking is possible. So such side payments may be impractical.

Another complication is that the owner may attempt to reduce internal rent seeking by firing his staff after the firm won external rents. But such firing may often be infeasible. First, the two rent-seeking games may be simultaneous. Second, once hired, the staff person may have information that allows him to rent seek whether he is employed by the owner or not. Third, the game may be a repeated one, where the owner needs the staff in the future. Thus, the problem addressed here appears plausible.

Let the quality of the owner or manager be exogenously set at θ_m. The quality of the staff person is θ_s; the parameter λ translates his quality into effectiveness in rent seeking for the firm. This parameter allows the staff's effectiveness to differ in internal and external rent seeking. The prize is worth Z. For simplicity, the behavior of only one firm is studied. The behavior of all other external rent seekers is captured by the parameter K. In contrast to most models of rent seeking, which focus on the efforts in rent seeking chosen by each firm, I highlight the tension between internal and external rent seeking by taking effort as fixed, and instead considering only the abilities of the owner and of the staff.

The fraction of the external rents the firm wins [3] is

$$\frac{\theta_m + \lambda\theta_s}{K + \theta_m + \lambda\theta_s}. \tag{1}$$

In addition to any external rent-seeking prize, the firm has assets subject to internal rent seeking, in the amount F.

Internal rent seeking determines the fraction of the firm's appropriable wealth (the sum of F and of the firm's share of Z) retained by the owner. For simplicity, I suppose all workers engage in internal rent seeking. But a similar model would hold if only some do. What is critical is that internal and external rent seeking be positively correlated. The fraction of assets retained by the owner is

$$\frac{\theta_m}{\theta_m + \theta_s}. \tag{2}$$

4. Optimal solution for owner

The owner must choose a quality of his staff, θ_s, which maximizes the owner's expected wealth. Since, for simplicity, the wage does not vary with the worker's ability in rent seeking, it is a constant that can be ignored. Thus, the owner maximizes

$$\Pi = \left(Z\frac{\theta_m + \lambda\theta_s}{K + \theta_m + \lambda\theta_s} + F \right) \frac{\theta_m}{\theta_m + \theta_s}. \tag{3}$$

---

[3] I modify the (Tullock, 1967) function only by introducing the factor λ.

158   A. Glazer / J. of Economic Behavior & Org. 48 (2002) 155–162

Table 1
Optimal quality of staff for various parameter values

θ_m	F	K	Z	λ	θ_s
1	0	10	100	6	1.01
5	0	10	100	6	1.80
10	0	10	100	6	2.06
20	0	10	100	6	1.94
30	0	10	100	6	1.94
1	10	10	100	6	0.70
5	10	10	100	6	1.48
10	10	10	100	6	1.70
20	10	10	100	6	1.52
30	10	10	100	6	0.98

The first-order condition for a maximum with respect to θ_s is that

$$\theta_s = \frac{-Z\theta_m - FK - F\theta_m + \sqrt{ZK}\sqrt{-FK - \theta_m F + Z\lambda\theta_m - Z\theta_m + FK\theta_m}}{\lambda(Z + F)}. \tag{4}$$

4.1. Do able owners hire able staff?

Table 1 gives some numerical solutions that show how θ_s varies with the values of the parameters.

Note that in some intervals θ_s increases with θ_m but that in other intervals it declines. Thus, an increase in the owner's quality may induce him to choose a lower-quality staff: the high ability of the owner makes him worry less about internal rent seeking, but also makes it less important to have effective staff for external rent seeking. The combined effect can be that the owner prefers a lower quality staff. Note also that in an increase in F, the wealth of the firm exclusive of gains from external rent seeking, induces the owner to hire lower-quality staff: the greater wealth of the firm makes internal rent seeking more costly to the owner.

The results show more than that an owner avoids hiring workers with low marginal product. For marginal product in this model depends in part on the quality of the owner. Some owners will hire high-ability staff and others will not. Of course, saying that marginal product depends on other factors of production is unsurprising; one need only think of capital and labor as factors of production whose quantities affect each other's productivity. Determining this relationship, however, can be non-trivial and enlightening. And in the context of rent seeking it can explain how rent seeking can be constrained, how rents are distributed, and whether the best and the brightest will be employed to engage in rent seeking rather than in other activities.

Analytically, consider how the optimal θ_s varies with the owner's own ability in rent seeking:

$$\frac{\partial \theta_s}{\partial \theta_m} = \frac{\sqrt{ZK}(\lambda - 1)}{2\lambda\sqrt{-FK - F\theta_m + Z\lambda\theta_m - Z\theta_m + F\lambda\theta_m}} - 1. \tag{5}$$

A. Glazer / J. of Economic Behavior & Org. 48 (2002) 155–162   159

For $\lambda > 1$ and for sufficiently high Z this expression is positive: better owners will hire better staff.

Consider next the simpler case in which $F = 0$. Then

$$\theta_s = \frac{1}{\lambda}\left(-\theta_m + \sqrt{K\theta_m(\lambda - 1)}\right),\tag{6}$$

and

$$\frac{\partial\theta_s}{\partial\theta_m} = \frac{K(\lambda - 1)}{2\lambda\sqrt{K\theta_m(\lambda - 1)}} - \frac{1}{\lambda}.\tag{7}$$

For $\lambda > 1$ this derivative is positive if

$$\frac{K(\lambda - 1)}{\sqrt{K\theta_m\lambda(\lambda - 1)}} > 2.\tag{8}$$

The inequality is satisfied for sufficiently low values of θ_m, so that θ_s increases with θ_m.

I also want to compare θ_s to θ_m. Of course, for $Z = 0$ and $F > 0$, the value of θ_s is zero, and so $\theta_s < \theta_m$. Can the opposite occur? We have

$$\lim_{Z\to\infty}\frac{\theta_s}{\theta_m} = \frac{\sqrt{K}\sqrt{\lambda\theta_m - \theta_m} - \theta_m}{\lambda\theta_m}.\tag{9}$$

For large K this is greater than 1. Thus, when the stakes are large (Z is large), and the external rent seeker is powerful (K is large), $\theta_s > \theta_m$, or the owner may appoint staff better than himself.

4.2. Effects of an increase in the external prize

Consider next an increase in the importance of external rent seeking, as given by an increase in Z. For general values of F,

$$\frac{\partial\theta_s}{\partial Z} = \frac{KF}{\lambda(Z + F)^2}$$
$$+KF\frac{(-FK - F\theta_m + Z\lambda\theta_m - Z\theta_m + FK\theta_m) - ZK\theta_m + Z\lambda\theta_m + ZK}{2(Z + F)^2\lambda\sqrt{ZK}\sqrt{-FK - F\theta_m + Z\lambda\theta_m - Z\theta_m + FK\theta_m}}.\tag{10}$$

Numerical solutions with various values of the parameters show that $\partial\theta_s/\partial Z$ can be positive, but for no values is it negative.

Some simpler cases of Eq. (10) that are analytically solvable can be instructive. If $F = 0$ and $Z > 0$ then $\partial\theta_s/\partial Z = 0$ and for general values of F, $\lim_{Z\to\infty}\partial\theta_s/\partial Z = 0$. It, thus, appears that an increase in the prize cannot induce a reduction in the quality of the staff, but can induce an increase.

4.3. Dynamics

Clearly, an increase in F, the appropriable assets of the firm additional to those arising from current external rent seeking, reduces the quality of staff the owner desires. Consider

160   *A. Glazer / J. of Economic Behavior & Org. 48 (2002) 155–162*

then an organization which won a large prize from external rent seeking, and is, therefore, wealthier in the following period. That will reduce θ_s in the following period, and thereby reduce the organization's success in external rent seeking in the following period.

If we think of a country as the organization, with the political elite or the decisive voter as the owner, then we may have some explanation for the relative decline of nations. As a nation becomes wealthier, internal rent seeking or redistribution becomes increasingly important, leading to less effort on such activities of external rent seeking as military conquest or industrial innovation. The observed behavior reflects that discussed by Olson (1982), but the explanation differs—instead of claiming that special interest groups become more powerful, it claims that the incentive to appoint aggressive, highly able, leaders declines.

5. Extensions

As just suggested, the interpretation of an owner and his staff can be broad. Consider the public in a country as an owner who may wish to appoint a strong leader. A strong leader may be attractive when the stakes are large, but the danger is that the leader will exploit the public who chose him. The Old Testament (I Samuel 8: 4–19) well explains the problem:

> "Then all the elders of Israel gathered themselves together, and came to Samuel unto Ramah, And said unto him, Behold, thou art old, and thy sons walk not in thy ways: now make us a king to judge us like all the nations. But the thing displeased Samuel when they said, Give us a king to judge us. And Samuel prayed unto the Lord . . . And Samuel told all the words of the Lord unto the people that asked of him a king. And he said, This will be the manner of the king that shall reign over you: He will take your sons, and appoint them for himself, for his chariots, and to be his horsemen; and some shall run before his chariots. And he will appoint him captains over thousands, and captains over fifties; and will set them to ear his ground, and to reap his harvest, and to make his instruments of war, and instruments of his chariots. And he will take your daughters to be confectionaries, and to be cooks, and to be bakers. And he will take your fields, and your vineyards, and your oliveyards, even the best of them, and give them to his servants. And he will take the tenth of your seed, and of your vineyards, and give to his officers, and to his servants. And he will take your menservants, and your maidservants, and your goodliest young men, and your asses, and put them to his work. He will take the tenth of your sheep: and ye shall be his servants. And ye shall cry out in that day because of your king which ye shall have chosen you; and the Lord will not hear you in that day. Nevertheless the people refused to obey the voice of Samuel; and they said, Nay; but we will have a king over us; That we also may be like all the nations; and that our king may judge us, and go out before us, and fight our battles".

The model also suggests that leaders would prefer to appoint staff, or other officials with power, who may be good at external rent seeking but poor at internal rent seeking. In politics that would suggest appointing officials who are unlikely to be political threats. Thus, an elected official may appoint cabinet officers and other officials who could not win an election on their own. Members of disliked minority groups may be attractive for that

A. Glazer / J. of Economic Behavior & Org. 48 (2002) 155–162   161

reason: the Muslim Ottoman Empire relied on the Janissaries, who were originally staffed by Christian youths from the Balkan provinces.

Similar reasoning shows the constraints faced by dictators. The same appointed officials who keep the regime in power may have the ability and skills needed to lead a coup against the current dictator.[4] Stalin understood the problem, and was infamous for his purges. Secret trials in the late 1930s found many prominent Old Bolsheviks guilty of treason and executed or imprisoned them, thereby eliminating the major real and potential political rivals. In addition to these show trials, a series of closed trials of top Soviet military leaders was held in 1937–1938, in which prominent military leaders were eliminated. At the time external threats were relatively small (or in our terms K and Z were small), so that the benefits of high-ability officials to Stalin were low. Of course, during World War II, when the external threat was high, purges of top officers were uncommon. The history of the Janissaries is corroborative. The Janissaries frequently engineered palace coups in the 17th and 18th centuries, and in the early 19th century they resisted the adoption of European reforms by the army. In 1826, they revolted, leading Sultan Mahmud II to declare war on the rebels and direct cannon fire on their barracks. Most of the Janissaries were killed, and those taken prisoner were executed.

The model assumes that a worker's effective marginal product should be measured not simply by the increased output of the firm, but also by the losses to the firm's owners from the worker's internal rent seeking. This view may explain some of the data reported by Frank (1985) showing that highly productive automobile salesmen and professors are paid far less than the revenue they generate. Frank interprets such underpayment as indicating a taste for high relative status by workers. Though status is important, my model offers a different explanation: those workers who generate much income for the employer are also adept at redistributing resources to themselves at the expense of others in the organization. A professor may demand more office space, more secretarial support, a more convenient teaching schedule, and so on. Even if the countervailing efforts of his colleagues results, in equilibrium, in little such redistribution, the increased rent-seeking within the organization can be costly, and therefore the net productivity of the worker may be less than at first appears.

Nevertheless, the threat of internal rent seeking does not always mean that low-ability staff will be appointed. As already indicated, large external threats may justify hiring high-ability staff. But under these conditions, managers may have to institute inefficient procedures that constrain internal rent seeking. Thus, Franklin Roosevelt maintained his power over the federal government in part by inducing competition among his staff and cabinet members; the influence activities by staff were directed against one another rather than against him. Rajan and Zingales (2000) show how the hierarchical organization of the firm can limit internal rent seeking, although at some cost. A manager may appoint family members to his staff. Such family members may appropriate little both because they are altruistic towards the family member who owns the firm, and because they recognize that a mechanism similar to Ricardian Equivalence may cause the owner to reduce his bequest in response to internal rent seeking, thereby reducing its attractiveness. Family-run firms may therefore have higher-ability managers than other firms.

---

[4] For wonderful discussions of dictatorship, see (Wintrobe, 1998, 2001).

References

Bhide, A.V., 2000. The Origin and the Evolution of New Businesses. Oxford University Press, New York.

Carmichael, H.L., 1988. Incentives in academics: why is there tenure? Journal of Political Economy 96 (3), 453–472.

Frank, R. 1985. Choosing the Right Pond. Oxford University Press, New York.

Garfinkel, M.R., Skaperdas S., 2000. Contract or war? On the consequences of a broader view of self-interest in economics. Department of Economics, University of California-Irvine, Working Paper 99-00-12.

Mayhew, D., 1974. Congress: The Electoral Connection. Yale University Press, New Haven.

Milgrom, P., 1988. Employment contracts, influence activities, and efficient organization design. Journal of Political Economy 96 (2), 42–60.

Nitzan, S., 1994 Modelling rent-seeking contests. European Journal of Political Economy 10, 41–60.

Olson, M., 1982. The Rise and Decline of Nations: Economic Growth, Stagflation, and Social Rigidities. Yale University Press, New Haven.

Rajan, R.G., Zingales, L., 2000. The firm as a dedicated hierarchy: a theory of the origin and growth of firms. National Bureau of Economic Research, Working Paper 7546.

Skaperdas, S., 1996. Contest success functions. Economic Theory 7, 283–290.

Skaperdas, S., Syropoulos, C., 1996. The distribution of income in the presence of appropriative activities. Economica 64, 101–117.

Tullock, , Gordon, , 1967. The welfare cost of tariffs, monopolies, and theft. Western Economic Journal 5, 224–232.

Wintrobe, R., 1998. The Political Economy of Dictatorship. Cambridge University Press, New York.

Wintrobe, R., 2001. How to understand and deal with dictatorship. Economics of Governance 2, 35–58.

European Economic Review 31 (1987) 407–416. North-Holland

Theories of Involuntary Unemployment

EFFICIENCY WAGES VERSUS INSIDERS AND OUTSIDERS

Assar LINDBECK*

University of Stockholm, S-106 91 Stockholm, Sweden

Dennis J. SNOWER*

Birkbeck College, University of London, London W1P 1PA, UK

1. Introduction

This paper aims to evaluate two competing microeconomic foundations of involuntary unemployment: the efficiency-wage theory and the insider–outsider theory. These theories compete not by being mutually exclusive, but by identifying different microeconomic sources of involuntary unemployment.

In the efficiency-wage theory, the source is firms' imperfect information about the profitability of their employees. Under this condition, firms may have an incentive to use the wage as a screening device for employees' profitability, implying that an increase in the wage raises not only the marginal labor cost (per unit of time), but the marginal revenue product (net of training costs) of labor as well. Then when wages are set at their profit-maximizing levels, aggregate labor demand may fall short of aggregate labor supply.

In the insider–outsider theory, the source of the unemployment lies in (a) an explicit labor turnover cost and (b) the ability of the full-fledged employees ('insiders') to exercise influence over their wages, without taking full account of the interests of the fledgling employees ('entrants') or the unemployed workers ('outsiders'). The insiders' market power arises from the turnover cost, and this power may also be devoted to augmenting that cost. Due to this cost, the insiders are able to raise their wage above the minimal level required to induce workers to become entrants, but firms nevertheless have no incentive to hire outsiders. For this reason, aggregate labor supply may exceed aggregate labor demand.

Both theories deal with employees who capture economic rent from being employed but whose wages are not underbid by the involuntarily unemployed workers. However, in the efficiency wage theory, underbidding does not occur because lower wages don't appeal to the firms; whereas in the

*We are indebted to Carl Shapiro and Alan Drazen for their insightful comments on a draft of this paper.

insider–outsider theory the insiders use their market power to prevent wages from falling. The existence of involuntary unemployment is related to labor turnover costs in some versions of the efficiency wage theory and in all versions of the insider–outsider theory. However, in the former, the unemployment arises because firms set wages with a view to manipulating the turnover costs under imperfect information, whereas in the latter theory the turnover costs give insiders market power which permits them to drive wages above their market-clearing levels.

The two theories may be interpreted as alternative microfoundations for macroeconomic models of unemployment, where there is deficient demand for labor although the product market clears [viz. the boundary between the 'Keynesian' and 'Classical' regimes in the models of Barro and Grossman (1976), and Malinvaud (1977)]. In particular, the theories provide explanations for why the labor market does not clear and these explanations do not rest on a failure of the product market to clear.

Broadly speaking, we define involuntary unemployment as a state in which there are workers without jobs, even though it is possible to find a wage, less than prevailing wages, which would induce them to work, provided that these workers could be employed under identical conditions of work as the incumbent workers. It is important to emphasize that this type of unemployment is quite distinct from the notion of *suboptimal* (inefficiently low) production and employment, relative to a hypothetical Walrasian equilibruim, in models with imperfect competition, as developed by Benassy (1977) and Negishi (1977), or models with search activity of employees depending on that of employers and vice versa, as developed by Drazen (1985), related to the analysis of Diamond (1982).

To explain the existence of involuntary unemployment as defined in this paper, it is necessary to show why there is no underbidding. By 'underbidding' we mean, quite generally, any wage agreement among the actual and potential parties to a labor contract, whereby unemployed workers are enabled to find jobs at wages which make them less costly (to the firms) than the incumbent employees.

2. The efficiency-wage theory

As mentioned, the centerpiece of the efficiency-wage theory is that wage increases may raise a firm's profit by having

– a positive effect on the average productivity of its workforce and/or
– a negative effect on the average labor cost per time unit.

Let $Q = f(e \cdot L)$ be the firm's production function, where Q is output, L is the number of employees, e is the average labor productivity per employee and $f' > 0$, $f'' < 0$. Furthermore, let W be the firm's wage offer and T its costs of training its employees. Then the effects above may be expressed as[1]

$$e = e(W), \qquad e' > 0,$$

$$T = T(W), \qquad T' < (0). \tag{1}$$

Various rationales for these effects have been proposed: (a) In the 'productivity differential models' [of Weiss (1980), Malcomson (1981)] the firm has imperfect information on the abilities of its employees and when its wage offer falls, the ablest workers quit. (b) In the 'shirking models' [of Calvo and Wellisz (1978), Shapiro and Stiglitz (1984), etc.], the firm cannot perfectly monitor whether its employees are shirking on the job, and the higher the firm's wage offer, the lower the average level of shirking. (c) In the 'search models' [of Snower (1985)], the firm has imperfect information on whether its employees are engaged in on-the-job search, and by raising the offer, the firm reduces the expected returns from search and thereby increases the average productivity of its workforce. (d) In the 'turnover models' [of Stiglitz (1985) and Calvo (1979)], the firm cannot directly observe its employees' propensity to quit, and by raising the wage offer, the firm reduces the quit propensity and thereby lowers its costs of having to train new employees.

A particularly simple way[2] of formalizing the firm's wage and employment decisions in this analytical context is:

$$\text{Maximize } \pi = P \cdot f(\lambda) - (\lambda/e) \cdot [W + T], \tag{2}$$
$$\underset{W, \lambda}{}$$

where $\lambda = e \cdot L$ is the firm's workforce in efficiency units and P is the exogenously given price of its product. The first-order conditions for an interior optimum may be expressed as

$$\partial \pi / \partial W = -\lambda \cdot [\partial \phi / \partial W] = 0, \tag{3a}$$

$$\partial \pi / \partial \lambda = P \cdot f'(\lambda) - \phi = 0, \tag{3b}$$

where $\phi = (W + T)/e$ may be called the 'efficiency labor cost'. By condition (3a) (illustrated in fig. 1a), which implies $\partial \phi / \partial W = 0$ and assuming $\partial^2 \phi / \partial W^2 > 0$, the wage (W^*) is set so that the efficiency labor cost is minimized. By condition (3b) (illustrated in fig. 1b), the level of employment in efficiency units (λ^*) is such that the marginal value product of labor (in efficiency units) is equal to the efficiency labor cost.

[1] In addition, e and T may also depend on other variables (such as the wage offered by other firms and the level of unemployment) but, for simplicity, we ignore these here.

[2] We are deeply indebted to Ben Lockwood to whom the basic idea underlying this simple formulation is due.

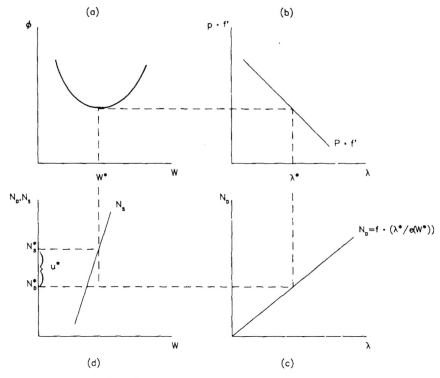

Fig. 1. Unemployment in the efficiency-wage theory.

Suppose that the economy contains a fixed number (F) of identical firms. Then the aggregate level of labor demand is $N_D = F \cdot (\lambda^*/e(W^*))$ as illustrated in fig. 1c. Furthermore, suppose that the aggregate labor supply is positively related to (or independent of) the real wage: $N_S = N_S(W/P)$, $N_S' \geq 0$, as illustrated in fig. 1d (for a given price). At the prevailing wage W^*. the aggregate labor supply may exceed the aggregate labor demand and the difference is the level of unemployment: $u^* = N_S^* - N_D^*$.

The unemployment above may be *involuntary* by our definition, namely unemployed workers receive no jobs even though there exists a wage, an effort level, and a training cost at which they would prefer employment to unemployment and at which their efficiency labor cost is less than that of the current employees. However, the unemployed workers cannot precommit themselves to such an effort level (e) and such a training cost (T) borne by the firm, because the firms cannot monitor e and T directly and the workers would be unwilling or unable to keep such a commitment of their own accord.

3. The insider–outsider theory

The crux of the insider–outsider theory, as suggested in the introduction, is that an 'insider' in a firm faces more favorable conditions of work than an 'entrant' (ceteris paribus). The reason is that insiders can exploit and manipulate labor turnover costs for the purpose of raising their wage rates.

Various sources of these costs have been suggested. For example: (a) Hiring, training and firing activities [see Lindbeck and Snower (1984a) and Solow (1985)]. It is frequently the case that workers become entrants only after advertising, screening and negotiation costs have been incurred; entrants may turn into insiders only after the absorption of training expenses; and the dismissal of insiders may require severance payments and the implementation of costly firing procedures. (b) Cooperation and harassment activities [see Lindbeck and Snower (1985)]. To boost their wage claims and prevent underbidding, insiders may choose to 'cooperate' with each other (individually or by collective action) in the process of production but not to cooperate with undesired entrants, thereby creating an insider–entrant productivity differential. For the same reasons, insiders may 'harass' entrants but not each other (i.e., have worse personal relations with entrants than with each other), thereby raising the entrants' disutility of work above their own. (c) Effort response to labor turnover [see Lindbeck and Snower (1984b)]. As in the efficiency wage theory, firms are assumed to monitor work effort imperfectly; yet unlike this theory, they affect effort via direct control of their labor turnover rate, rather than via the wage. In practice it is quite common that the higher a worker's current effort input, the lower his chances of dismissal (or the higher his chances of promotion) and thus the more likely he is to receive an insider wage in the future. Furthermore, when a firm raises its long-run rate of labor turnover, it reduces the worker's future reward for current effort. It is for this reason that effort may be inversely related to the labor turnover rate.

The distinction between 'insiders' and 'entrants' rests on such labor turnover costs (and not merely on seniority). The insider–outsider theory presumes not only that these costs exist, but also that the insiders may influence them and that firms cannot entirely pass them on to their employees in the form of wage reductions. The main reason is that the insiders have market power (as individuals or collectively, although we will not consider the latter possibility here). Thus, an insider receives a higher wage than an entrant (ceteris paribus), but since the firm bears some of the labor turnover costs, it may nevertheless have no incentive to replace the insider by the entrant. (Insofar as the entrant has market power as well, the wage which he receives will exceed his reservation wage.) In this context, the insider–outsider theory provides a rationale for unionization, since unions may help insiders to raise the firm's labor turnover costs [see Lindbeck and Snower (1984a, 1985b)].

For simplicity, it may be convenient to conceive of outsiders, entrants and insiders as homogeneous groups. When an outsider is hired, he becomes an entrant. The replacement of an entrant is associated with no (or 'low') turnover costs. After passing through an 'initiation period' at the firm, the entrant turns into an insider, whose replacement would require 'high' turnover costs.

Let L_I and L_E be the number of insiders and entrants, respectively, employed by a particular firm. W_I and W_E are their respective wages. The firm's production function is $Q = f(L_I + L_E)$, where $f' > 0$, $f'' < 0$. The 'incumbent workforce' is m (i.e., the number of insiders carried forward from the previous time period). Then, $L_I \leq m$. The firm's cost of dismissing insiders (say, from the sources (a)–(c) above) is $C_I(m - L_I)$, with the following properties: $C_I(0) = 0$ and, for $L_I < m$, $C_I' > 0$ and $\lim_{L_I \to m} C_I' = \tilde{c}_I$, where $\tilde{c}_I$ is a positive constant. (In other words the dismissal costs are finitely large for all L_I less than m.) Finally, the firm's cost of acquiring entrants (say, from sources (a) (c) above) is $C_E(L_E)$, with the following properties: $C_E(0) = 0$ and, for $L_E > 0$, $C_E' > 0$ and $\lim_{L_E \to 0} C_E' = \tilde{c}_E$, where $\tilde{c}_E$ is a positive constant. (In other words, the labor acquisition costs are finitely large for all positive L_E.)

To fix ideas, we suppose that entrants receive the reservation wage ($W_E = R$) and that the insider wage (W_I) is determined by a bargaining process between the firm and its insiders. For simplicity let insiders bargain 'individualistically' (i.e., each insider assumes the wage and employment of all other insiders to be exogenously given) and let them have 'complete market power' (i.e., each insider sets his wage as high as possible consistent with his continued employment).[3] By implication, the insider wage is $W_I = \min[(f'(m) + \tilde{c}_I), (W_E + \tilde{c}_I + \tilde{c}_E)]$, i.e., the insider wage is the smaller of the insider marginal product (net of firing costs) and the sum of the entrant wage and the marginal turnover costs.

With W_E, W_I, and m exogenously given to the firm, the employment decision may be expressed as the solution to the following profit-maximization problem:

$$\text{Maximize } \pi = P \cdot f(L_I + L_E) - W_I \cdot L_I - W_E \cdot L_E - C_I(m - L_I) - C_E(L_E). \quad (4)$$
$$\scriptstyle L_I, L_E$$

Let the optimal solution be (L_I^*, L_E^*). Then supposing that $L_I^* > 0$, the first-order conditions are

$$\partial \pi / \partial L_I = P \cdot f' - W_I + C_I' \geqq 0, \qquad (\partial \pi / \partial L_I^*) \cdot (m - L_I^*) = 0, \qquad (5a)$$

$$\partial \pi / \partial L_E = P \cdot f' - W_E - C_E' \leqq 0, \qquad (\partial \pi / \partial L_E^*) \cdot L_E^* = 0. \qquad (5b)$$

[3] This strong assumption is a convenient simplification but is not necessary for the subsequent analysis. It would be sufficient to assume that the insiders receive some part of the rent generated by the turnover costs and that the greater these costs, the greater are their wages.

Combining (5a) and (5b) we obtain

$$W_I - W_E \lessgtr C_I' + C_E'.$$

These conditions are illustrated in fig. 2a, where the equilibrium locus of (W_I, L) points is given by the boldface curve. While eqs. (5a) and (5b) define the demand functions for insiders and entrants, respectively, eq. (6) tells us that the insider wage cannot exceed the entrant wage by more than the sum of the marginal hiring and firing costs of labor.

As shown in fig. 2a, if the firm has an incumbent workforce of $\hat{m}$, the insider wage is $\hat{W}_I$, all incumbents are employed ($L_I^* = \hat{m}$), and the firm does not find it profitable to hire any entrants ($L_E^* = 0$, by condition (5b)). Moreover, for an economy with F identical firms, aggregate labor demand

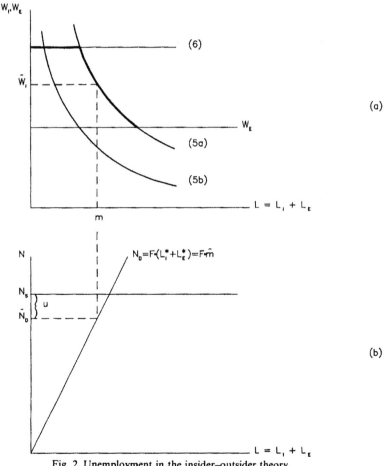

Fig. 2. Unemployment in the insider–outsider theory.

then is $\hat{N}_D = F \cdot (L_L + L_E)$ (illustrated in fig. 1b). Let the number of workers in the economy be $N_S(> \hat{N}_D)$. Then the level of unemployment is $u = N_S - \hat{N}_D$. In short, *the insiders' rent-seeking activity, which generates the turnover costs, depresses entrants' marginal product (net of hiring and firing costs) relative to their reservation wage.* Given this activity, there may, in equilibrium, be no wage for entrants greater than their reservation wage at which they would be more profitable than the insiders. This is illustrated in fig. 2a, where the reservation wage ($W_E = R$) is greater than entrants' net marginal product at employment $\hat{m}$ (given by curve (5b)).

This unemployment is involuntary in the sense that the outsiders are willing to work for a wage which would make them more profitable than the insiders, if only they had the opportunity to work at identical conditions. (We say that two workers face 'identical conditions of work' when they confront the same production technologies and have the same legal and social status, so that the only difference between them – as providers of labor – can lie in their respective levels of skill and effort.) However, this opportunity may be denied to them on account of the incumbents' reactions whenever the outsiders attempt to enter the workforce: they may face a wide variety of adverse conditions, e.g., less cooperation and more harassment from insiders, effort-related turnover costs (as mentioned above) and 'dispensable' hiring, training, and firing costs, viz. those costs which are not intrinsically important to the process of production such as severance pay.

As shown, the outsider and the firm may be unable to find a wage which induces both the outsider to work and the firm to employ him, given the insiders' activities which, in effect, discriminate against outsiders. But, even though time-contracts thus may give rise to involuntary unemployment is it not possible for the firm or the outsiders to make side-payments *to the insiders*, in order to give them an incentive to abstain from these activities? For example, such side-payments may take the form of profit-sharing or wage bonuses per entrant hired. But even though such arrangements may benefit the insiders, they may be unwilling to accept them because the insiders may fear that the admittance of low wage workers into the firm will give the employer an incentive to fire the insiders in the future. Besides, profit-sharing may be difficult for the insiders to monitor and may impose more risk on the insiders than they may be willing to accept at the new insider wage [see Lindbeck and Snower (1985a)]. In this manner, risk-bearing, non-enforceability of contracts which are not subgame perfect, and difficulties in observing or verifying variables such as profits may be effective obstacles to eliminate involuntary unemployment through underbidding by way of side-payments to the insiders.

4. Concluding remarks

The efficiency-wage and insider–outsider theories of involuntary unemployment are built on quite different foundations. The former explain unemployment through firms' imperfect information about the productivities and about costs of their employees; the latter do so through insiders' market power which is used to exploit labor turnover costs in the process of wage formation – and to some extent the turnover costs themselves can be manipulated by the insiders. In the efficiency wage theories, union activity is generally implied to be unimportant in determining the level of unemployment; in the insider–outsider theory, it may augment unemployment by amplifying labor turnover costs. In the efficiency wage theory, the 'involuntariness' of unemployment is traceable to a genuine information cost for firms. In the insider–outsider theory, the 'involuntariness' is mirrored in the more limited employment opportunity set of outsiders relative to insiders – a limitation that may be accentuated by social norms and legislation. In particular, the harassment version of the insider–outsider theory may be useful in explaining why outsiders may feel inhibited from underbidding, and the hiring/firing cost version may provide an underpinning for the notion that 'job security legislation' may be at least partially responsible for unemployment. When comparing the realism of the two theories, the vital issue that remains is whether firms' imperfect information or workers' market power is more important in providing microeconomic foundations for the existence and persistence of involuntary unemployment in market economies.

References

Barro, R.J. and H.I. Grossman, 1976, Money, employment and inflation (Cambridge University Press, Cambridge).

Benassy, J.-P., 1977, A neo-Keynesian model of price and quantity determination in disequilibrium, in: G. Schwödiauer, ed., Equilibrium and disequilibrium in economic theory (Reidel, Dordrecht).

Calvo, G.A., 1979, Quasi-Walrasian theory of unemployment, American Economic Review 69, no. 2, 102–107.

Calvo, G.A. and S. Wellisz, 1978, Supervision, loss of control, and the optimum size of the firm, Journal of Political Economy 86, 943–952.

Diamond, P., 1982, Aggregate demand management in search equilibrium, Journal of Political Economy 90, 881–894.

Drazen, A., 1985, Involuntary unemployment and aggregate demand spillovers in an optimum search model, Mimeo.

Lindbeck, A. and D.J. Snower, 1984a, Involuntary unemployment as an insider–outsider dilemma, Seminar paper no. 282 (Institute for International Economic Studies, University of Stockholm, Stockholm) in: W. Beckerman, ed., Wage rigidity and unemployment (Duckworth, London) 97–125.

Lindbeck, A. and D.J. Snower, 1984b, Labor turnover, insider morale and involuntary unemployment, Seminar paper no. 310 (Institute for International Economic Studies, University of Stockholm, Stockholm).

Lindbeck, A. and D.J. Snower, 1985a, Cooperation, harassment, and involuntary unemployment, Seminar paper no. 321 (Institute for International Economic Studies, University of Stockholm, Stockholm).

Lindbeck, A. and D.J. Snower, 1985b, Strikes, lockouts and fiscal policy, Discussion paper no. 178 (Birkbeck College, London).

Malcomson, J.M., 1981, Unemployment and the efficiency wage hypothesis, Economic Journal 91, 848–866.

Malinvaud, E., 1977, The theory of unemployment reconsidered (Blackwell, Oxford).

Negishi, T., 1977, Existence of an underemployment equilibrium, in: G. Schödiauer, ed., Equilibrium and disequilibrium in economic theory (Reidel, Boston, MA).

Shapiro, C. and J.E. Stiglitz, 1984, Equilibrium unemployment as a worker discipline device, American Economic Review 74, no. 3, 433–444.

Snower, D.J., 1983, Search, flexible wages and involuntary unemployment, Discussion paper no. 132 (Birkbeck College, University of London, London).

Solow, R., 1985, Insiders and outsiders in wage determination, Scandinavian Journal of Economics 87, no. 2.

Stiglitz, J.E., 1985, Equilibrium wage distributions, Economic Journal 95, no. 379, 595–618.

Weiss, A., 1980, Job queues and layoffs in labour markets with flexible wages, Journal of Political Economy 88, 526–538.

Monitoring rent-seeking managers: advantages of diffuse ownership

ROGER D. CONGLETON George Mason University

Abstract. This paper demonstrates that a one-owner firm tends to overmonitor its employees. Because monitoring is imperfect, and penalities imposable on detected rent-seekers are limited by the opportunity cost wage, employees have incentives to engage in rent-seeking activities which both reduce and redistribute the firm's residual. Since owner monitoring will be partly motivated by concerns over the distribution of the firm's residual, a sole owner tends to monitor beyond the level that maximizes a firm's residual. Appropriately diffuse ownership can reduce monitoring effort to efficient levels by diluting incentives for monitoring activities.

A propos du contrôle des gestionnaires chasseurs-de-rentes: avantages d'une propriété répandue. Ce mémoire démontre qu'une firme à propriétaire unique tend à surcontrôler ses employés. Parce que le contrôle est imparfait, et les punitions imposables aux chasseurs-de-rentes qu'on découvre limitées par la taille des coûts salariaux alternatifs, les employés sont incités à s'engager dans des activités de chasse-aux-rentes qui, à la fois, réduisent les gains résiduels de la firme et les redistribuent. Puisque le contrôle du propriétaire est en partie motivé par ses intérêts dans la répartition des gains résiduels de la firme, un propriétaire unique tend à pousser le contrôle au delà du niveau qui maximise la taille des gains résiduels. Une propriété répandue proprement sur un plus grand nombre de personnes peut réduire les efforts de contrôle à des niveaux plus efficients en réduisant les incitations à contrôler.

INTRODUCTION

An important test of a theory is the extent to which it encompasses novel facts or yields predictions outside the domain of alternative theories. Faith, Higgins, and Tollison (1984) demonstrate that the rent-seeking approach to the firm can explain such micro-phenomena as managerial compensation and the use of external labour markets by firms that have well-developed internal labour markets. This paper argues that the rent-seeking approach also offers a possible explanation of the existence of

The author would like to thank Robert Tollison, Robert Blewett, Mark Toma, and the anonymous referees for their helpful comments on previous drafts of this paper. They are, of course, entirely blameless for any errors which remain.

Canadian Journal of Economics   Revue canadienne d'Economique, XXII, No. 3
August Août 1989. Printed in Canada Imprimé au Canada

0008-4085 / 89 / 662–672 $1.50 © Canadian Economics Association

diffuse ownership. In many industries, diffuse ownership may promote firm efficiency by reducing losses from intra-firm rent-seeking.

The basic logic of the rent-seeking approach to intra-firm activities is that a firm's management and owners have incentives to invest resources in socially fruitless disputes over the firm's residual. Losses accrue from these rent-seeking activities in so far as scarce economic resources are consumed by a process of distributional competition. No new wealth is created by rent-seeking activities, but a firm's residual declines as managers and owners invest resources in rent-seeking or rent-avoiding activities. Moreover, any rents actually realized may involve compensation schemes which cost the firm more than gained by employees or owners.

This paper argues that a single-firm owner or residual claimant is likely to commit *too many* resources to monitoring a firm's management. This conclusion contrasts with the usual emphasis on undermonitoring by firm owners.[1] However, there is more than a little anecdotal evidence that supports the contention that post-entrepreneurial firms perform best when dominant shareholders remain at arms length from a firm's operations; that is, when less direct monitoring is done by firm owners.[2]

The over-monitoring result represents a substantial departure from the line of reasoning established by Alchian and Demsetz (1972) in which they suggest that the residual claimant status of firm owners creates incentives for them to adopt monitoring levels that minimize production costs and maximize the size of the firm's residual. Yet if we accept their reasoning, we would expect single-owner firms to out-perform partnerships and corporations with diffuse incentives for monitoring. This paper suggests that in may cases the residual claimant status of firm owners gives rise to a rent-seeking game that tends to be incompatible with minimizing production costs or maximizing the size of the firm's residual. To the extent that firms emerge as a means of economizing on transactions costs, as argued by Ronald Coase (1937) and Oliver Williamson (1964, 1981), the rent-seeking approach predicts the emergence of market arrangements that dilute owner incentives for monitoring management.

1 See Radner (1986) for a concise survey of intra-firm incentive problems. Note that rent-seeking losses differ from those of Liebenstein (1966) and Simon (1959) in so far as they are entirely the result of optimizing behaviour. And while the portion of rent-seeking losses attributable to the activities of management are analogous to agency costs noted by Jensen and Meckling (1976) and Fama (1980), rent-seeking losses include possible failures by owners as well. The rent-seeking problem results from conflict over the production team's residual rather than agency problems, per se.

2 A scenario of the following sort can be found in nearly every successful family enterprise. The founder through innovation, luck, and thrift accumulates a large block of capital wealth. As the firm's rate of innovation declines, either under the founder or his heirs, the family enterprise begins to flounder. The direct management of the firm is turned over to 'professionals,' and the company again expands its market share and prospers. At this point the scenario often repeats itself as family members take back direct control, the firm flounders, and professional managers again assume control. In terms of this paper, less direct monitoring by a firm's owners, here family members, often improves the firm's performance. See for example: Manchester's (1964) book about the Krupp family of Germany, Koskoff's (1978) book on the Mellon family, Woods's (1983) book of the Molson family of Canada, or Lacey's (1986) book on the Ford family. In most of these family biographies the authors emphasize the autocratic (high-monitoring) management style of the firm's owner and the team or committee approach of the professional managers who rejuvenate the firm.

664   Roger D. Congleton

A MODEL OF MANAGERIAL RENT-SEEKING

Consider the following model of managerial rent-seeking in the spirit of models developed by Jensen and Meckling and by Faith, Higgins, and Tollison (hereafter **FHT**). Suppose that managers have sufficient managerial discretion (see Williamson, 1964; Migue and Belanger, 1974; or Congleton, 1982) that they may engage in rent-seeking activity A which allows them to increase their total compensation by generating remuneration in the form of managerial rents, R. Examples of rent-seeking activities include shirking, developing bonds with senior management who directly influence managerial remuneration, and the creation of other informal intra-firm contracts noted in Faith, Higgins, and Tollison (1984).

Naturally, owners will be disinclined to promote rent-seeking and will attempt to penalize it when discovered. Were monitoring a costless activity, owners would be able to discourage rent-seeking activities by simply reducing the normal salaries of any 'successful' rent-seekers to offset exactly the rents being realized. By eliminating the possibility of true managerial rents, such a strategy eliminates incentives for rent-seeking activities and hence any rent-seeking losses associated with them. Unfortunately, monitoring management is neither a costless nor an easy task.[3] Firm owners will generally not be inclined or able to discover every instance of rent-seeking. Nor will owners generally be able to increase penalties imposed on rent-seekers sufficiently to compensate for the resulting positive probability of successful rent acquisition.[4] As a consequence, rent-seeking managers face a choice between relatively certain rents and probabilistic costs associated with their discovery.

Managers are assumed to engage in the level of rent-seeking that maximizes their total expected remuneration. Their expected compensation consists of salary, plus managerial rents, less expected penalties, or:

3 The monitoring task faced by current and potential firm owners tends to be problematic for several reasons. First, appraising managerial performance in an uncertain world is itself extremely difficult. Distinguishing between good (bad) management and good (bad) luck is at best an imprecise craft. Identification of managerial rents will be equally difficult, since such rents are simply compensation not directly linked to managerial marginal product. Second, top management exercises substantial control over the flow of information and the agendas of both board and stockholder meetings. In part, this is simply a desirable aspect of specialization which allows the CEO to exercise considerable control over the direction of corporate policy. However, it also allows management considerable control over both the level of their own remuneration and the cost of monitoring managerial rents.

4 To the extent that penalized rent-seekers may simply leave the firm and realize their opportunity cost wage, an upper bound on effective penalties is created which limits the range of penalties available to firm owners. If salaries are merely adjusted for the capitalized value of realized rents, as argued by **FHT**, rent-seeking will continue to be a rational course of action unless the probability of detection is very large or managers are very risk-averse. Nor are variations in contingent remuneration (stock options and the like) likely to be sufficiently sensitive to the level of managerial rents that rent-seeking becomes unprofitable. As Jensen and Meckling point out, managers receive all of the rents but only bear a fraction of reductions in the value of the firm. It is conceptually possible that salary reductions are so large that all rent-seeking activity is discouraged, but this requires a penalty which more than compensates for the likelihood of detection and punishment. For example, managers who are well known to be rent-seekers might suffer such damaged reputations that they would have difficulty finding comparable employment elsewhere.

$$Y = S(A) + R(A) - P(A, M)K(A). \tag{1}$$

Managerial salary, S, is assumed to be composed of a fixed annual wage and a bonus contingent on the receipts of firm owners. Since rent-seeking reduces shareholder returns, the bonus portion of remuneration tends to decrease somewhat as rent-seeking activity A increases, $S_A < 0$. (Subscripts denote partial derivatives with respect to the subscripted variable.) Rent-seeking activities are presumed to be at least partially successful, so rents increase with increases in rent-seeking, $R_A > 0$. Monitoring techniques are assumed to be such that the probability of detection, P, increases with the scale of rent seeking undertaken, $P_A > 0$, and with the extent of resources committed to monitoring, $P_M > 0$. Increases in monitoring effort also increase the rate at which rent-seeking activities increase the probability of detection, $P_{AM} > 10$. The penalty imposed on any detected rent-seekers ultimately takes the form of salary reductions. Salaries may be reduced directly by demotion or indirectly by diminished reputation and hence reduced prospects for future salary increments. Penalties increase as the level of rent-seeking discovered increases, $K_A > 0$.

The decision to engage in the rent-seeking activity implies that the resulting marginal increase in rent exceeds expected marginal cost of rent seeking over part of the range of interest. That is to say, the appropriate level of rent seeking must be expected to yield a net increase in managerial compensation. The compensation maximizing level of rent-seeking activity may be found by differentiating equation (1) with respect to A and setting the result equal to zero.

$$R_A = P_A K + PK_A - S_A. \tag{2}$$

Managers seek rents until the marginal reductions in contingent salaries plus expected marginal penalties equal the marginal value of managerial rents.

The relationship between total managerial compensation, montoriing, and rent-seeking will be strictly concave if managerial rents increase at a decreasing rate, $R_{AA} < 0$, the contingent portion of managerial salaries falls at an increasing rate, $S_{AA} < 0$, and both the probability of detection and the penalty imposed increase at increasing rates, $P_{AA} > 0$ and $K_{AA} > 0$. Strict concavity implies the existence of a unique expected income maximizing level of rent-seeking for each monitoring level undertaken by firm owners. Given these assumptions, the implicit function rule allows the optimal level of rent-seeking to be specified as a function of the monitoring level chosen by firm owners.

$$A^* = a(M). \tag{3.0}$$

Differentiating with respect to M yields the intuitive result that rent-seeking activities are a decreasing function of owner monitoring effort:

$$A_M^* = \frac{(P_{AM}K + P_M K_A)}{(R_{AA} - P_{AA}K - 2P_A K_A - PK_{AA} + S_{AA})} < 0. \tag{3.1}$$

Thus, increased monitoring effort by owners reduces managerial rent seeking.

The conventions of the rent-seeking literature imply that managerial rent-seeking

666   Roger D. Congleton

is wasteful if the overall cost of obtaining rents exceeds the value of the rents actually captured (see, e.g., Tullick, 1967; Krueger, 1972; Buchanan, Tollison, and Tullock, 1980; Congleton, 1984). This occurs when resources are used to re-distribute existing wealth rather than to produce new wealth. A costless transfer of receipts from owners to managers does not generate a deadweight loss, but the use of costly rent-seeking methods or imperfect transfer mechanisms does – in the absence of compensating external economies. In this last case, the mere existence of managerial rent-seeking generates rent-seeking losses in the form of increased production costs and deterioration of the firm's residual.

MONITORING RENT-SEEKING MANAGEMENT

Naturally, owners have an interest in monitoring rent-seeking activities because rent-seeking affects owner receipts. Successful managerial rent-seeking directly increases the firms production costs in so far as managers are able to realize above market salaries, perquisites, or working conditions. In a perfectly competitive labour market, where rent seeking can be costlessly detected, managerial rents would be eliminated through the processes of monitoring and competition. The discovery of any unusually large benefits accruing to management would generate immediate offsetting reductions in direct salaries or other benefits which return managerial salaries to market levels. However, in circumstances where monitoring rent-seeking activity is itself a costly activity, at least some managers will be able to realize substantial managerial rents.

As **FHT** point out, rent-acquiring managers may be penalized by salary reductions or dismissal. In either case, monitoring costs are borne in order to ascertain the level and distribution of managerial rent-seeking and rent acquisition. In the case of dismissal and replacement, there is the additional cost of finding, hiring, and training new managers. If the labour market for executives is truly competitive, then the transaction cost of replacing rent-acquiring managers with suitable substitutes will be relatively small. On the other hand, if monitoring is a defining characteristic of the 'firm' as suggested by Alchian and Demsetz (1972), monitoring costs are likely to be non-trivial. In this case, the scope for managerial rent-seeking may be significant even if executive labour markets are otherwise efficient.[5]

Reductions in owner receipts may be divided into a combination of efficiency losses and distributional losses. Efficiency losses occur when the rent-seeking activities reduce the technological efficiency of the firm and hence its net income. Distributional losses occur when a portion of the firm's residual is captured by successful rent-seeking managers. For example, suppose that one hour of managerial

5 Casual evidence supports this contention. **FHT** have argued that extensive use of external executive labour markets by firms with well-developed internal labour markets is a symptom of the exis-tence of managerial rents. 'Golden Parachutes' and the extremes to which managers occasionally defend themselves from 'unfriendly' take-overs provide additional evidence of the scale of mana-gerial rents.

shirking reduces owner receipts by \$40, while generating leisure worth \$10 to the manager. In this case, the efficiency loss is \$30, the net reduction in the firm's residual. The distributional loss is \$10. Note that distributional losses are the same thing as managerial rents. Distributional losses do not affect the size of the firm's residual but rather, in effect, make managers de facto residual claimants. Of course, firm owners are indifferent between efficiency losses and distributional losses. A dollar's worth of either reduces owner income by the same amount. Owners will be inclined to monitor managerial rents in either case.

Monitoring affects both the size of the residual and its distribution by reducing rent-seeking activities. Wealth-maximizing owners will monitor at the level that maximizes the present value of their income stream. In a stationary state, this is equivalent to maximizing their net income. For the purposes of this paper, owner net income is simply the total net income of the firm, N, less distributional losses, D, less monitoring costs, C, plus anticipated penalty receipts, PK.

$$W = N(A) - D(A) - C(M) + P(A, M)K(A). \tag{4}$$

$N(A)$ is the firm's total residual associated with rent-seeking level A. $D(A)$ is the distributive loss caused by the managerial claims on the firm's residual at rent-seeking level A. The firm's residual decreases with increases in rent-seeking, $N_A < 0$. Distributive losses increase with increases in rent-seeking, $D_A > 0$. The cost of monitoring, $C(M)$, increases as the level of monitoring, M, increases, $C_M > 0$. $P(A, M)$ is the probability of detecting a rent-seeker given rent-seeking level A and monitoring effort M. $K(A)$ is the penalty in the form of a salary reduction or loss of perks imposed on the person caught. Ignoring monitoring costs, owner income tends to increase with increases in monitoring, since monitoring reduces rent-seeking activities.

Differentiating equation (4) with respect to monitoring effort, M, allows the owner net-income maximizing monitoring level to be characterized.

$$N_A A_M - D_A A_M + P_M K + A_M(P_A K + PK_A) = C_M. \tag{5}$$

The firm owner monitors at the level that sets the marginal increase in efficiency, plus the marginal reduction in distributional losses, plus the marginal increase in penalty receipts equal to the marginal cost of monitoring. Note that as long as increased monitoring reduces distributional losses, and/or increase penalty receipts at the margin, owner choices will be motivated at least partly by distributional goals. This interest in the *distribution* of the firm's residual represents a second possible source of rent-seeking losses.

MINIMIZING RENT-SEEKING LOSSES

In a world where rent-seeking is an inherent facet of utility-maximizing behaviour, the complete absence of rent-seeking losses is probably not possible. Thus, measuring rent-seeking losses relative to some ideal zero level is inappropriate.

668   Roger D. Congleton

Losses in this setting are properly appraised relative to the minimum possible in a manner analogous to that used by Becker (1968) to characterize the optimal level of crime.

Within the microcosm of the firm, rent-seeking losses associated with a particular level of monitoring effort may be represented as

$$L = C(M) - [N(A) - D(A)] - R(A). \tag{6.1}$$

Since distributional losses are the same as the rents actually received by management, equation (6.1) reduces to

$$L = C(M) - N(A). \tag{6.2}$$

Mimizing rent-seeking losses requires the size of the firm's residual to be maximized net of monitoring costs. The monitoring level that minimizes the dead-weight loss of rent-seeking is characterized by the following first-order condition.

$$N_A A_M = C_M. \tag{7}$$

Monitoring should be undertaken at the level where the marginal increase in the *firm's residual* equals the marginal cost of monitoring.

If we compare equation (7) with equation (5), we find that the loss-minimizing level of monitoring is *smaller* than that chosen by a wealth maximizing owner if increased monitoring reduces managerial rents more rapidly than expected penalty receipts decline.[6] Since managers may avoid penalties in excess of their rents by seeking employment elsewhere, penalty receipts are generally small and not much affected by monitoring efforts. As a consequence, a single residual claimant tends to *overmonitor* management in settings where monitoring is effective but not sufficient to reduce managerial rents to zero.

Figure 1 illustrates the relationship between the monitoring level that can be justified in efficiency grounds, labelled M^{**}, and the level a single owner will choose in order to maximize his wealth, labelled M^*. The illustration represents the case where monitoring reduces the distributional losses at a faster rate than expected penalty receipts decline, $A_M(-D_A + P_A K + PK_A) + P_M K > 0$. Triangle ABC is the deadweight loss of monitoring expenditures made for purely redistributive concerns.

---

6 Since penalty receipts are generally limited to the capitalized value of rents realized by rent-acquiring managers, expected penalty receipts will generally be smaller than distributional losses. Thus, in order for the undermonitoring case to hold, increased monitoring must induce a *very* rapid decline in the probability of detection causes by reduced rent-seeking activity. $A_M P_A K$ must dominate $P_M K - (D_A - PK_A)A_M$. Only in the case where penalty receipts fall at exactly the same rate as distributive losses would firm owners monitor at the level that maximizes the firm's gross residual.

It should be noted that expected penalty receipts may be zero. In this case, the undermonitoring case is ruled out, and the overmonitoring result obtains whenever monitoring successfully reduces distributive losses at the margin. If, for example, detected rent-acquiring managers are simply replaced with new managers hired from outside the firm, managers suffer reduced rents and reputations, but owners gain little if anything in the way of penalty receipts. The indirect penalty receipts generated by dismissal are positive only if the replacement manager engages in less rent-seeking than the manager dismissed. In the case where an average rent-seeker is replaced by another manager with similar rent-seeking propensities, the expected direct effect of replacement on distributional losses is zero.

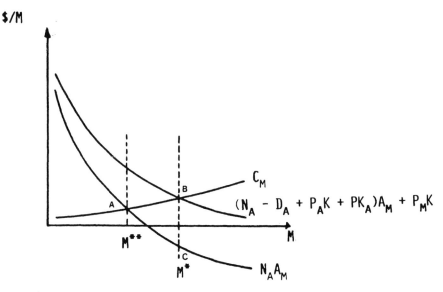

$/M

FIGURE 1

In an extreme case like that illustrated, owners are willing to accept higher production costs and a smaller total residual if their share of the firm's residual increases sufficiently. Attentive monitoring does not always improve a firm's efficiency.[7]

OPTIMALLY DIFFUSE OWNERSHIP

As has often been noted, the existence of more than one owner dillutes incentives for monitoring managers. Generally, this has been considered an undesirable problem that markets have to cope with. Our analysis suggests that an appropriate diffusion of ownership can actually improve monitoring levels over what would occur in the single-owner case.

Suppose that there are S owners, each of whom receives an equal share of owner income and each of whom monitors at the level that maximizes their return from ownership. To simplify, without substantial loss of generality, assume that each owner has the same constant cost of monitoring. An owner's net income in this case is simply

7 The existence of relatively efficient capital markets tends to exacerbate rather than reduce the extent of overmonitoring by firm owners. Since capital markers are essentially markets for ownership, share prices reflect the anticipated receipts accruing to firm owners. Thus, monitoring efforts that increase those receipts yield capital gains for current firm owners. In the long run, investment flows to areas in which monitoring efforts are most productive to firm owners and away from areas where monitoring activities are less rewarding for firm owners. This tends to reinforce the above overmonitoring tendencies. Complete capitalization of managerial rents into firm prices increases incentives for current and future owners to monitor at levels that maximize owner net income rather than at levels that maximize the size of the firm's residual.

670   Roger D. Congleton

$$W' = [N(A) - D(A) - CM' + P(A, M)K(A)]/S, \tag{8}$$

where $M = SM'$. M' is the monitoring level done by a singly owner. M is the total monitoring effort. The income-maximizing monitoring effort for a typical shareholder requires M' such that

$$[N_A A_M - D_A A_M + P_M K + A_M(P_A KPK_A)]/S = C. \tag{9}$$

A quick comparison of equations (9) and (5) reveals that a typical shareholder monitors less than a single proprietor would, because the shareholder bears the whole cost of monitoring but receives only a fraction of the benefits.

Ignoring penalty receipts and combining equations (9) and (7), we find that the optimal diffusion of ownership sets

$$S = 1 - D_A/N_A. \tag{10}$$

Optimally diffuse ownership requires the number of owners to be equal to one plus the ratio of marginal distributive losses to efficiency losses from rent-seeking. (Recall that $N_A < 0$.) Ownership should be more diffuse in markets where efficiency losses are small relative to distributive losses at the margin. In the case where marginal distributive losses are the same as marginal efficiency losses, a two-owner firm is ideal. Only in the case where efficiency losses swamp distributive losses would a unified firm operating under a single residual claimant dominate more diffuse ownership arrangements.

CONCLUSION

Our analysis suggests that the existence of positive monitoring costs tend to generate a variety of rent-seeking losses. To recapitulate briefly: the existence of significant monitoring costs implies that some rent acquisition will go undetected and unpunished. This encourages at least some managers to invest resources in activities that might allow them to obtain above-market compensation in one form or another. Both the rent-seeking activities and any rents realized reduce owner receipts. As a consequence, owners have an incentive to invest resources in monitoring management as a means of enlarging owner receipts. Because owner efforts are partially directed at *redistributing* the firm's residual from managers to owners, monitoring is a rent-seeking or, more accurately, a rent-avoiding activity. In the absence of free-rider problems, wealth-maximizing firm owners tend to *over*monitor rent-seeking managers as a means of increasing their share of the firm's residual. Appropriately diffuse ownership can eliminate any resultant rent-seeking losses by reducing incentives for owners to monitor firm employees.

The losses associated with intra-firm rent-seeking can be considered an example of the inefficiencies or frictional losses often associated with informational imperfections. In this respect, rent-seeking represents another source of internal transactions costs to be minimized by successful firms. It is the cost of determining which managers engage in rent-seeking activities and/or the extent of any rents realized that creates the environment where rent-seeking losses are generated. However, the losses attributed to excess monitoring by owners noted here are not simply frictional losses, since these losses are calculated relative to the best that can be done *given* monitoring costs. Intra-firm rent-seeking losses occur because of the nature of the distributive conflict engendered by costly and imperfect information rather than because of the costly information itself.

To the extent that successful enterprises are those able to avoid the worst effects of rent-seeking losses, one would expect to see successful firms adopt a number of strategies to reduce rent-seeking losses. Faith, Higgins, and Tollison suggest that the use of external labour markets is one policy for dealing with the corrosive effects of intra-firm rent-seeking. An implication of Congleton (1984) is that the delegation of monitoring authority to committees like a firm's board of trustees also tends to reduce the extent of intra-firm rent-seeking. The results of this paper suggest that institutional arrangements which dilute incentives for owners to monitor management may, also on balance, increase a firm's efficiency in some markets. Modest free-rider problems associated with multiple-owner firms tend to increase a firm's efficiency in settings where managerial efficiency or distributive losses are relatively large at the margin.

The optimal level of residual claimant dilution naturally varies with the extent to which monitoring activities affect a firm's output. In settings where managerial talents are highly complementary, monitoring rapidly reaches levels where output declines with increases in monitoring effort. Here, even relatively minor micro-monitoring of management by firm owners may lead to substantial declines in firm productivity. Our analysis suggests that, in efficient markets, ownership will be most diluted in areas where management is most productive rather than where it is least productive, as implied by the principal agent theory. The greater success of multiple-owner firms in large-scale enterprises may partly reflect the fact that the productivity of management is greater in those industries than in others. On the other hand, our analysis parallels the standard analysis in so far as it suggests that the returns to ownership, vis à vis managerial compensation, tends to be reduced somewhat by ownership dilution.

REFERENCES

Alchian, A.A. and H. Demsetz (1972) 'Production, information costs, and economic organization.' *American Economic Review* 62, 777–95
Becker, G. (1968) 'Crime and punishment: an economic approach.' *Journal of Political Economy* 78, 169–215
Buchanan, J.M., R.D. Tollison, and G. Tullock (1980) *Toward a Theory of the Rent-Seeking Society* (Texas A&M University Press)
Coase, R.H. (1937) 'The nature of the firm.' *Economica* 4, 386–405
Congleton, R.D. (1982) 'A model of asymmetric bureaucratic inertia and bias.' *Public Choice* 39, 421–5
—— (1984) 'Committees and rent-seeking effort.' *Journal of Public Economics* 25, 197–209
Easterbrook, F.H. (1984) 'Two agency-cost explanations of dividends.' *American Economic Review* 74, 650–9
Faith, R.L., R.S. Higgins, and R.D. Tollison (1984) 'Managerial rents and outside recruitment in the Coasian firm.' *American Economic Review* 74, 600–72

672   Roger D. Congleton

Fama, E.F. (1980) 'Agency problems and the theory of the firm.' *Journal of Political Economy* 86, 288–307

Jensen, M.C. and W.H. Meckling (1976) 'Theory of the firm: managerial behavior, agency costs and ownership structure.' *Journal of Financial Economics* 3, 305–60

Koskoff, D.E. (1978) *The Mellons: The Chronicle of America's Richest Family* (New York: Thomas Crowell Company)

Krueger, A.O. (1974) 'The political economy of the rent-seeking society.' *American Economic Review* 64, 291–303

Lacey, R. (1986) *Ford: The Men and the Machine* (Toronto: Little, Brown and Company)

Lakatos, I. (1970) 'Falsification and the methodology of scientific research programs.' In I. Lakatos and A. Musgrave, eds, *Criticism and the Growth of Knowledge* (Cambridge: Cambridge University Press)

Liebenstein, H. (1966) 'Allocative efficiency vs. X-inefficiency.' *American Economic Review* 56, 392–413

Manchester, W. (1964) *The Arms of Krupp 1587–1968* (Toronto: Little, Brown and Company)

Migue, J. and G. Belanger (1974) 'Towards a general theory of managerial discretion.' *Public Choice* (Spring), 27–43

Woods, S.E. (1983) *The Molson Saga 1763–1983* (Toronto: Doubleday)

Radner, R. (1986) 'The internal economy of large firms.' *Economic Journal* 66 (supplement: conference papers), 1–22

Simon, H. (1959) 'Theories of decisionmaking in economics and behavioral science.' *American Economic Review* 49, 253–83

Tullock, G. (1967) 'The welfare costs of tariffs, monopolies, and theft.' *Western Economic Journal* 5, 224–32

Williamson, O.E. (1964) *The Economics of Discretionary Behavior: Managerial Objectives in the Theory of the Firm* (New York, Prentice Hall)

—— (1981) 'The modern corporations: origins, evolution, attributes.' *Journal of Economic Literature* 19, 1537–68

RAND Journal of Economics
Vol. 32, No. 3, Autumn 2001
pp. 527–541

Inside versus outside ownership: a political theory of the firm

Holger M. Müller*

and

Karl Wärneryd**

If contracting within the firm is incomplete, managers will expend resources on trying to appropriate a share of the surplus that is generated. We show that outside ownership may alleviate the deadweight losses associated with such costly distributional conflict, even if all it does is add another level of conflict. In case managers have to be provided with incentives to make firm-specific investments, there is a tradeoff between minimizing conflict costs and maximizing output. This suggests, among other things, an explanation of why some firms are organized as partnerships and others as stock corporations.

> [C]ovenants, without the sword, are but words,
> and of no strength to secure a man at all.
> —Thomas Hobbes, *Leviathan*

1. Introduction

■ Suppose a group of agents by making a joint effort could produce something of value. Much of economic theory is based on the idea that such potential gains from trade would be fully exploited. Implicitly, we assume the existence of institutions that ensure the cooperation of all parties involved, such as complete contracts and their enforcement by a legal system. But in reality, contracts are incomplete and courts less than omniscient, and any *ex ante* agreement, such as on how to split the surplus resulting from a joint activity, is subject to opportunistic behavior *ex post*. In this article, we argue that outside ownership of firms may be an institution that fills in the gaps left by imperfect formal enforcement.

Consider the costs that arise from imperfect enforcement. In a joint undertaking, such as a partnership or cooperative, individuals may be able to divert part of the jointly produced surplus

* New York University and CEPR; hmueller@stern.nyu.edu.

** Stockholm School of Economics and CESifo; Karl.Warneryd@hhs.se.

This article has benefited from comments and suggestions by Guido Friebel, Roger Gordon, Bengt Holmström, Roman Inderst, Christian Laux, Paul Milgrom, Kay Mitusch, Stergios Skaperdas, Luigi Zingales, seminar participants at UC Irvine and at the Universities of Berlin (FU), Lund, and Mannheim, two anonymous referees, and, in particular, Joe Harrington. Financial support from Deutsche Forschungsgemeinschaft, Sonderforschungsbereich 504 (Müller), and the Bank of Sweden Tercentenary Foundation (Wärneryd) is gratefully acknowledged.

527

Holger M. Müller and Karl Wärneryd

for their own uses. A partner may use company money to finance private activities but then claim that the money was used for business purposes. Preparing to support such a claim before a court or an arbitrator, the partner may manipulate documents and accounting information, and hire lawyers or expert witnesses. Since the court has no information about the case apart from what is presented by the parties, the outcome depends partly on strategic, costly decisions by the parties themselves. Hence, relying on courts to enforce contracts may in fact exacerbate rather than reduce the total costs of conflict in a business transaction.

The legal literature contains many cases concerning individuals in partnerships engaging in self-dealing or fraud at the expense of their co-partners. Banks (1995) cites, for example, *Bentley v. Craven*, in which a partner had been employed to purchase sugar on the firm's behalf. Without the knowledge of his co-partners he supplied the firm with sugar previously purchased on his own account at a favorable price, for which he charged the firm the full market value. Similarly, in *Dunne v. English*, the plaintiff and the defendant, both partners in the same firm, agreed to buy a mine for £50,000 with a view toward reselling it later at a profit. It was ultimately arranged that the defendant would sell the mine to a third party for £60,000, and that the plaintiff and the defendant would divide the resulting profit of £10,000. As it happened, the defendant sold the mine for a sum far in excess of £60,000, claiming that the price was only £60,000.

A second, perhaps not as obvious, cost of imperfect enforcement arises because an agent may also have to invest effort in guarding his share of surplus against the first, appropriative type of activity on the part of others. As noted by Tullock (1967), the social costs of theft are not just the resources diverted from productive activity into burglary, but also those used to put locks on doors.

To the extent that they involve costly time and effort, both types of activity are wasteful, since they only serve to reallocate income. Using an established term, we shall refer to such behavior as *rent-seeking*.[1]

Thomas Hobbes famously suggested that, but for the institution of government, all of society would be engaged in a wasteful war of every man against every man. Only by giving up their natural liberties to the Sovereign, who would then become a more fearsome threat, would citizens avoid internal conflict. Similarly, by selling the firm to outsiders, the members of a partnership involved in distributional conflict may improve on their situation—even if the only de facto right that comes with ownership is the right to participate in the fight over the surplus.

There is nothing about outside ownership per se that guarantees that the outsiders get anything out of the firm.[2] The insiders in a firm control the accounting machinery. To force the insiders to distribute the produced surplus, the outsiders must first provide evidence that the surplus indeed exists. For instance, they must disentangle book earnings from true earnings. Outside ownership may therefore realistically be viewed as a distributional conflict in which the insiders and outsiders fight over the surplus generated in the firm by investing costly resources in the covering and uncovering, respectively, of information about the true size of the surplus.

In this article we show that outside ownership may reduce total rent-seeking costs even though it adds another level of conflict. In equilibrium, the outsiders extract at least part of the firm's surplus. With less surplus left in the firm to fight about, less resources are wasted by the insiders in the subsequent internal distributional conflict. The outsiders take on the role of a "common enemy," forcing insiders to lower the amount spent on internal conflict. Of course, against this beneficial effect must be counted the extra resources now spent in the conflict between insiders and outsiders. We show that the net effect may well be positive.[3] The distributional-conflict perspective therefore provides a rationale for outside owners who provide no productive input—indeed, in our model they only waste resources—or risk-sharing function, who perform no monitoring (in

---

[1] Alternative expressions are *safeguarding activities* (Williamson, 1985), *influence activities* (Milgrom, 1988), and *power-seeking activities* (Rajan and Zingales, 2000).

[2] Indeed, the notion that managers are reluctant to pay out funds to investors is a fundamental motivation for the recent literature on corporate governance. See Shleifer and Vishny (1997) for a survey.

[3] Wärneryd (1998) uses a related effect to explain federalist structures of jurisdictional interaction.

contrast with Alchian and Demsetz (1972)), do not break the balanced-budget constraint (in contrast with Holmström (1982)), and do not control important physical assets (in contrast with Grossman and Hart (1986) and Hart and Moore (1990)).

Since, in general, there will be less of the surplus left in the firm with outsiders taking part of it, insiders will face dulled incentives to make incontractible firm-specific (e.g., human capital) investments relative to the partnership model. Hence there may be a tradeoff between minimizing the cost of distributional conflict and maximizing surplus. This suggests an explanation of why many partnerships, such as law firms, medical practices, and accounting agencies, are found in areas where human capital investments are important. It also provides a possible explanation of why some firms that start out as partnerships or closed corporations eventually go public. Initially, marginal returns to firm-specific investments are typically high, implying that for incentive reasons inside ownership is the optimal ownership arrangement. With decreasing marginal returns to investment, however, there may come a time when the most profitable investment opportunities have been exhausted. At this point, reducing rent-seeking costs may be more important than promoting firm-specific investments, and going public may become optimal.

Our article is related to, but differs in its focus from, some recent contributions on cooperatives. Both Hart and Moore (1998) and Kremer (1998) study the choice between inside and outside ownership. Hart and Moore focus on price and quality decisions in consumer cooperatives. Kremer discusses why egalitarian sharing rules are often found in practice in partnerships. In both articles, cooperatives are characterized by the use of voting procedures to make collective decisions. In contrast, we focus on costly decentralized conflict, but we find, along with Kremer, that the importance of providing incentives for human capital investments is crucial in determining whether a partnership or outside ownership is optimal.

The rest of the article is organized as follows. Section 2 examines distributional conflicts in partnerships. We show that introducing outside ownership may lower the total cost of distributional conflict in Section 3. The effect of outside ownership on the incentives for insiders to make firm-specific investments, and the resultant tradeoff, is discussed in Section 4. Section 5 discusses the relation between our approach and other theories of the firm, and concludes.

2. Partnerships

■   We consider a group of m agents (to be called *managers*) who by joining forces can potentially carry out a profitable project, if they can agree beforehand on the forms for doing this. We assume no binding contracts can be costlessly written, and that any value produced in the firm is subject to costly distributional conflict. Ultimately, we shall be interested in the constitutional question of which organizational structure maximizes the expected value of the original m managers, without the unanimous agreement of whom the firm cannot be formed.

In this section we consider the option of organizing the firm as a partnership. Under this arrangement, we shall therefore sometimes refer to the managers as *partners*.

The production activity of the firm gives rise to a surplus Y given by

$$Y := (1 - \theta)\, \bar{y} + \theta \sum_{i=1}^{m} e_i,$$

where $\bar{y}$ is a constant, e_i is the firm-specific (human capital) investment of manager i, and $\theta \in [0, 1]$ is a parameter that measures the importance of managerial investments for the value of output. For now, we shall assume that we have $\theta = 0$, i.e., that output is independent of firm-specific investments. We discuss the case where firm-specific investments matter in Section 4.

We assume that contractual incompleteness within the firm gives rise to a costly distributional conflict between the partners over the produced surplus. As we argue in the Introduction, this may be because

(i) a partner may divert part of the surplus to finance private activities, claiming that the money is used for business purposes, and

(ii) a partner may have to take action to safeguard his share against the appropriative activities of others.

To potentially support his claim before a court or arbitrator, partner i may invest costly resources (e.g., time and effort) of value r_i in the production of favorable evidence. We shall assume that the greater a partner's rent-seeking effort relative to the sum total of such efforts, the greater the share of the surplus he can appropriate.

In particular, we assume partner i's share of the surplus is

$$\alpha_i := \begin{cases} r_i/R & \text{if } R > 0 \\ 1/m & \text{otherwise,} \end{cases}$$

where $R := \sum_j r_j$.[4]

For simplicity, we assume the managers are risk neutral and that the disutility of expending r_i is simply r_i. Then partner i's utility is

$$u_i := \alpha_i Y - r_i.$$

We can now look for an equilibrium in rent-seeking expenditures. Clearly, there is no equilibrium such that nobody makes a positive expenditure, since an individual partner could then get the entire surplus by expending an arbitrarily small amount. The optimal rent-seeking expenditure of partner i, given the expenditure of everyone else, is therefore determined by his first-order condition

$$\frac{\partial u_i}{\partial r_i} = \frac{R - r_i}{R^2} Y - 1 = 0.$$

This condition implies that in the unique equilibrium, rent-seeking expenditures are the same for all partners. Let $r(m, W)$ be the common equilibrium expenditure in a contest with m participants and a prize of value W. Then in the partnership model, individual equilibrium expenditures are

$$r(m, Y) = \frac{m - 1}{m^2} Y.$$

Hence total equilibrium rent-seeking expenditures are

$$R_I := mr(m, Y) = \frac{m - 1}{m} Y$$

and each partner receives the share

$$\alpha_i = \alpha := \frac{1}{m}$$

of surplus.

Equilibrium utilities may be expressed as fractions of the surplus Y. Defining

$$\delta_I := \frac{1}{m^2},$$

partner i's surplus share *net* of rent-seeking expenditures, his equilibrium utility under inside ownership is

$$\alpha Y - r = \delta_I Y.$$

Since everybody spends the same amount in equilibrium, the end result of the distributional conflict is the same division of surplus as if contracting were complete and the partners agreed to

---

[4] This particular contest success function was introduced by Tullock (1975, 1980) for the analysis of court proceedings and rent-seeking contests. See also Fullerton and McAfee (1999), who use the same success function, derived from more primitive assumptions, to discuss research contests. Skaperdas (1996) axiomatizes it. Baye, Kovenock, and de Vries (1993) use the related success function where the highest bidder wins with certainty to study lobbying. For more general discussions of models of conflict of this nature, see, e.g., Skaperdas (1992), Dixit (1987), and Nitzan (1994).

an egalitarian sharing rule. The resources spent on rent seeking are wasted. The partners are trapped in a prisoner's dilemma–like situation of escalated rent seeking. A repeated, long-term interaction might offer the possibility of sustaining a more cooperative outcome, but in the following we shall instead explore the effect of changes in the firm's ownership structure.

3. Outside ownership

■ Suppose the partners sell the firm to one or more outsiders. We henceforth refer to the partners as *insiders*. Being the owners, the outsiders have a legal claim to the surplus that is generated. Since the insiders have control over the accounting machinery, this claim is generally worthless unless the owners can prove before a court that a surplus indeed exists. Even though accounting rules and laws potentially constrain what the insiders can do, such rules do not enforce themselves. An outsider may have to take costly action to initiate the enforcement of his claim.[5] Hence we may think of outside ownership as a distributional conflict between the insiders and outsiders, where the parties take costly actions in covering and uncovering, respectively, information about the true size of the surplus. As with the partnership, it is still the case that the insiders must fight against each other over what is left in the firm, but under outside ownership they must also fight as a collective against the outside owners.

That is, we assume that what distinguishes insiders from outsiders is that the former are in control of the surplus when it arrives. Any value generated in the firm first appears within the firm's walls, so to speak, and all of it remains there unless the outsiders take measures to acquire some of it.[6] This naturally gives rise to a two-level procedure for distributional conflict. At the top level, the insiders fight against the outsiders (if any) to retain as much as possible of the surplus within the firm. At the lower level, the insiders fight among themselves over whatever has been retained in the firm.

Whether we think of the rent-seeking investments at the different levels as taking place simultaneously or sequentially shall make no difference, since we abstract from any resource constraints. The equilibrium conditions will look the same under either interpretation. For concreteness, and for a setting in which a time order seems natural, consider the example of a consulting or law firm. Since its mandates and its fee structure may be well known, it may not be difficult for outsiders to reconstruct the firm's revenue. Any direct appropriation of this revenue by the insiders can therefore easily be punished. It may be more difficult, however, to document the firm's cost, including overhead cost and actual working hours by the insiders, and its investment needs. The insiders can therefore inflate the true cost and overstate investment needs. Hence the conflict between the insiders and outsiders takes place not in the form of a fight over the firm's revenue, which may be verifiable, but in the parties collecting or defending claims against this revenue. Once this issue is settled, in or out of court, the insiders are left to fight among themselves over whatever they managed to retain from the conflict with the outsiders.

We shall show that with the optimal number of outside owners, the total deadweight loss from conflict is in fact reduced relative to the partnership model, even though resources are now expended at two levels. In the end, we shall argue that these savings may be internalized by the original insiders if shares are sold to outsiders at competitive rates.

It seems natural to model the higher-level contest between outsiders and insiders analogously with the inside contest, with the single difference that the share retained by the firm is a public good to the managers. Let s_i be the expenditure of manager i in the contest with outsiders and t_j the expenditure of outside owner j, and let S and T be the corresponding aggregate expenditures.

---

[5] A referee points out that a problem for outside investors (most notably in, e.g., the former Soviet Union) may be that the insiders can strip the firm of everything before there is time to do anything about it. Our basic assumption is that enough of a legal order (or equivalent private means of enforcement) is in place that outsiders, by taking costly measures, can guarantee themselves a share of the surplus.

[6] Assuming that there is also a costlessly verifiable, noncontestable part of the surplus that accrues automatically to the outsiders does not change anything in our analysis, which then pertains only to the contestable part of the surplus.

We shall assume that the share of surplus remaining in the firm is

$$\beta := \begin{cases} S/(S+T) & \text{if } S+T > 0 \\ 1 & \text{otherwise.} \end{cases}$$

When deciding on their individual expenditures in the conflict with the outsiders, the insiders take into account the anticipated equilibrium outcome of the internal conflict. Since βY is what will remain to be fought over inside the firm, each manager expects to ultimately receive $\alpha \beta Y$. Hence insider i's objective function in the conflict with the outsiders is

$$v_i := \alpha \beta Y - r(m, \beta Y) - s_i = \delta_I \beta Y - s_i.$$

We assume the insiders make their expenditure decisions independently in the fight against the outsiders. As before, there is no equilibrium in which no party expends a positive amount on conflict. (This of course also means that the boundary condition of the success function is irrelevant in equilibrium.) We return to this issue when discussing the incentives of outsiders below. Hence insider i's optimal rent-seeking expenditure, given the rent-seeking expenditures of the outside owners and the other insiders, is given by the first-order condition

$$\frac{\partial v_i}{\partial s_i} = \frac{T}{(S+T)^2} \frac{Y}{m^2} - 1 = 0.$$

Since the surplus share is a public good to the insiders, the first-order conditions only determine aggregate insider expenditure. Furthermore, this aggregate effort is suboptimal, since first-order conditions for collectively optimal choices would have Y instead of Y/m^2.

Next consider the outsiders. For generality, assume that for any amount Z acquired by the outsiders as a group in the top-level fight against the insiders, each individual outsider gets $v(n)Z$, with $v(n) \in (0, 1/n]$, $v'(n) < 0$, $\lim_{n \to \infty} v(n) = 0$, and $v(1) = 1$. That is, we assume an aggregate deadweight loss of $(1 - v(n)n)Z$ among the outsiders. It appears natural to assume that this loss is zero when there is only a single outsider. We can now consider the cases where the outsiders fight among themselves in exactly the same manner as the insiders (in which case we have $v(n) = 1/n^2$) and where proceeds from the top-level conflict are paid out as well-defined dividends (in which case we have $v(n) = 1/n$), among others.

The utility of outsider i from the viewpoint of the top-level fight is then

$$w_i := v(n)(1 - \beta)Y - t_i.$$

We assume the outsiders make their expenditure decisions noncooperatively. Suppose the insiders expend nothing in the top-level conflict. Then any outsider can increase his expected payoff by expending an arbitrarily small amount. Hence there is no equilibrium in which some party expends zero. The relevant condition for outsider i's optimal choice is therefore the first-order condition

$$\frac{\partial w_i}{\partial t_i} = \frac{S}{(S+T)^2} v(n) Y - 1 = 0.$$

Again, we note that these first-order conditions only determine aggregate rent-seeking expenditures. Hence there is a continuum of equilibria, all involving the same aggregate expenditures from the respective groups. We focus on within-group symmetric equilibria. That is, we shall assume all insiders make the same equilibrium expenditure s, and all outsiders make the same equilibrium expenditure t. The first-order conditions then reduce to

$$\frac{ms}{(ms + nt)^2} v(n) Y - 1 = 0$$

and

$$\frac{nt}{(ms + nt)^2} \frac{Y}{m^2} - 1 = 0.$$

Solving this system of equations for s and t, we have that

$$s = \frac{1}{m\nu(n)\eta^2}Y,$$

where $\eta := (1/\nu(n)) + m^2$, and

$$t = \frac{m^2}{n\eta^2}Y.$$

The equilibrium share of surplus retained in the firm is therefore

$$\beta = \frac{1}{1 + \nu(n)m^2}.$$

We note that the share retained in the firm is a strictly increasing function of the number of outside owners, and that β approaches one as the number of outsiders approaches infinity. Intuitively, since monitoring the insiders is a public good, total resources expended by the outsiders in the distributional conflict with the insiders become less as the number of outsiders increases.

Insider i's equilibrium *ex post* utility under outside ownership is then

$$\frac{1}{m}\frac{1}{\nu(n)\eta}Y - s - r(m, \beta Y) = \delta_O Y,$$

where $\delta_O := (\eta - m)/\nu(n)m^2\eta^2$ is his surplus share *net* of rent-seeking expenditures when both the internal conflict and the conflict with the outsiders are taken into account.

Recall that total rent-seeking expenditures under inside ownership are

$$R_I = \frac{m-1}{m}Y.$$

The total deadweight loss under outside ownership, taking into account the resources expended by the insiders in fighting for individual shares over whatever is left in the firm, is

$$R_O := ms + nt + \frac{m-1}{m}\beta Y + (1 - \nu(n)n)(1 - \beta)Y$$

$$= \frac{m(1 + \nu(n) + m^2\nu(n)(1 - n\nu(n))) - 1}{m\nu(n)\eta}Y.$$

For $m > 1$ and $n \geq 1$ we then have that

$$R_O < R_I \text{ as } \nu(n) > \frac{m+1}{m^2 n}.$$

Since this condition always holds for $n = 1$, total rent-seeking costs can always be made lower under outside ownership than under inside ownership. Hence we have the following result.[7]

Proposition 1. If output is independent of firm-specific investments, total rent-seeking expenditures under outside ownership with an expenditure-minimizing number of outsiders are strictly lower than under inside ownership.

While outside ownership entails additional rent-seeking expenditures of $ms + nt$ incurred in the conflict between the insiders and outside owners, and a deadweight loss of $(1 - n\nu(n))Y$ at the outsider stage, it reduces the rent-seeking expenditures incurred in the internal conflict between the insiders by $mr(m, Y)(1 - \beta)$.

---

[7] We are assuming, of course, that the outsiders own all of the firm. Suppose instead they collectively own some total share $\gamma \in [0, 1]$, equally distributed. Then the share remaining in the firm is $(1 - \gamma) + \gamma\beta$, and that going to outsiders is $\gamma(1 - \beta)$. It is easily seen that manipulating γ is equivalent to manipulating n in its effect on equilibrium conflict expenditure, since increasing γ or reducing n both improve an outsider's incentives in the top-level contest. Without loss of generality, we therefore focus on the case of $\gamma = 1$.

Two main effects are at work in generating this phenomenon:

(i) Under outside ownership with the optimal number of outsiders, part of the surplus is shifted to agents who dissipate less of it.

(ii) There is a free-rider problem among the insiders in the collective conflict with the outsiders.

It is worth considering some robustness issues at this point. Recall that we are ultimately interested in the optimal ownership structure from the point of view of the original insiders. Any reductions in overall deadweight losses can be internalized by the insiders by the selling of shares *ex ante*, as we shall discuss below. Hence we need only consider arrangements that are optimal. For this reason, potential internal conflict and free-riding among outsider groups with more than one member do not affect our conclusions, since we know that total rent-seeking costs are always lower with a single outsider than under inside ownership.

The beneficial effect of outside ownership is reinforced by the fact that the insiders face a free-rider problem in contributing to the contest with the outsiders, implying that only a relatively small share of the surplus is retained within the firm. It can be shown, however, that Proposition 1 continues to hold if the fighting against the outsiders is delegated to a single insider and the cost of fighting is split equally between the insiders.

The central force behind our result is therefore the shifting of part of the surplus to a party that has a higher valuation of it. Although it is inconvenient for our purposes to adopt a more general model of conflict, since we need to be able to compare indirect utilities in order to rank ownership structures, this effect of asymmetric valuations is likely to hold under fairly general conditions.

Now note that

$$\lim_{n \to \infty} R_O = \frac{m-1}{m}.$$

As the number of outside owners approaches infinity, total rent-seeking costs under outside ownership approach total rent-seeking costs under inside ownership, and the share of surplus captured by the outsiders approaches zero. Hence from a distributional conflict perspective, a firm with a large number of outside owners (e.g., a widely held stock corporation) is like a closely held firm.

In the following we shall assume that what the outsiders get out of the firm is paid out in the form of well-defined individual dividends, i.e., that we have $v(n) = 1/n$. This seems natural if for no other reason than that it is a standard way of remunerating owners in real-world corporations.

Then, differentiating R_O with respect to n shows that total rent-seeking costs under outside ownership are strictly increasing in the number of outside owners. It follows that total rent-seeking costs are minimized by having a single outside owner. As we discuss in the next section, this does not automatically imply that the optimal ownership structure is always to have a single outsider. If managerial human capital investments are important, a relatively larger share of surplus may have to be retained in the firm in order to give managers incentives. One way of accomplishing this is by increasing the number of outsiders, since this exacerbates the free-rider problem among the outsiders. In particular, since when the number of outsiders increases, the individual return to an increase in the outside share falls, we have that

$$\frac{\partial \delta_O}{\partial n} = \frac{1}{m} \frac{n(m+1) + m^2(m-1)}{\eta^3} > 0.$$

That is, the share of output ultimately consumed by an individual manager is a strictly increasing function of the number of outside owners. Hence inside ownership or outside ownership with more than one owner may be optimal in such a setting. If we have $\theta = 0$, however, i.e., human capital investments play no role, then clearly outside ownership (with a single outsider) is efficient.

Intuitively, the benefit from having outside owners is that they withdraw part of the surplus from the firm. Since this means there is less left to fight over, this reduces the amount of resources wasted in the internal distributional conflict between the insiders. Having a single outside owner maximizes the amount withdrawn as it overcomes the free-rider problem in monitoring.

If capital markets are perfectly competitive, the insiders can extract the full efficiency gain from selling the firm to outsiders, as then the outsiders can be made to pay exactly their (aggregate) net gain

$$(1 - \beta) Y - nt = \frac{m^2 (\eta - 1)}{\eta^2} Y.$$

Because it seems reasonable to assume that membership in the firm is well defined, each partner can sell his share individually on the capital market. This rules out any conflict over the proceeds from transfers of ownership. Accordingly, if all insiders have an equal share in the firm *ex ante,* insider i's *ex ante* utility (which includes the proceeds from the sale of his share in the firm) is

$$\left(\delta_O + \frac{1}{m} \frac{m^2 (\eta - 1)}{\eta^2} \right) Y = \frac{m^3 - m + n}{m^2 \eta} Y,$$

which, as expected, is strictly greater than his utility $\delta_I Y = Y/m^2$ under inside ownership.

4. Incentives for firm-specific investments

■   We have seen how introducing outside owners lowers rent-seeking costs in the firm. The benefit from having outsiders is that the outsiders extract part of the firm's surplus. Since there is now less left to fight over within the firm, fewer resources are wasted in the distributional conflict between the insiders. Even though additional resources are wasted at the new conflict level, in our model the overall effect is positive.

The net effect is not so clear if the insiders have to be given incentives to make firm-specific investments at an interim stage (i.e., before the distributional conflicts take place but after shares have been sold). Since managers receive a smaller share of the total surplus when there are outside owners, their incentives to make firm-specific investments are dulled. So in choosing an optimal ownership structure, there is a tradeoff between minimizing rent-seeking costs and providing investment incentives. In what follows, we take a step back and consider the determination of these incentives.

Suppose the insiders noncooperatively choose their firm-specific investment levels e_i. The objective function of insider i is

$$\delta \left((1 - \theta) \bar{y} + \theta \sum_{i=1}^{m} e_i \right) - c (e_i),$$

where $\delta \in \{\delta_I, \delta_O\}$ is his net surplus share as determined in the subsequent distributional conflict(s), and c is an increasing, strictly convex function.

There is then a unique equilibrium in which all insiders make the same investment e given by

$$\delta \theta = c' (e).$$

Since c' is increasing, the noncooperatively selected investment levels are strictly lower than the collectively optimal level e^* given by

$$\theta = c'(e^*).$$

This is, of course, an instance of the standard holdup problem discussed by, e.g., Williamson (1975, 1985), Klein, Crawford, and Alchian (1978), and Grossman and Hart (1986). Anticipating that they must share part of the surplus with the other insiders (and possibly also with outsiders), the insiders underinvest. In the present case, this problem is exarcerbated because the sharing takes place through costly conflict, which means that individual shares do not sum to one.

Since we have that

$$\frac{\partial e}{\partial \delta} = \frac{\theta}{c''} > 0 \text{ for } \theta > 0,$$

equilibrium investments are strictly increasing in the share retained by each manager. (Equilibrium investment for $\theta = 0$ is naturally zero.)

So because we have $\delta_O < \delta_I$ for any finite number n of outsiders, the total surplus under outside ownership is strictly lower than under inside ownership. We have already noted that δ_O is increasing in n. In the limit, we have that

$$\lim_{n \to \infty} \delta_O = \delta_I.$$

Thus with respect both to mitigating the costs of distributional conflict and to providing insiders with incentives to make firm-specific investments, a firm with a very large number of outside owners is like a firm with no outside owner at all.

Again, the cost of outside ownership is that it dulls the incentives for insiders to make firm-specific investments, thus leading to a lower surplus. The benefit is that, given whatever surplus has been produced, the total amount of resources wasted in the conflict(s) over the surplus is strictly less than under inside ownership. Trading off the costs and benefits, we can determine an optimal ownership structure.

When deciding whether to sell shares to outsiders or not, the managers consider the value of the firm, i.e., the value of output minus managerial investment and rent-seeking costs, under the different possible arrangements. Under inside ownership, the value of the firm is

$$V_I := \left(1 - \frac{m-1}{m}\right) Y(e(\delta_I)) - mc(e(\delta_I)).$$

Under outside ownership with n outsiders, it is

$$V_O := \left(1 - \frac{m - n + mn}{m\eta}\right) Y(e(\delta_O)) - mc(e(\delta_O)).$$

Assume we have $\theta > 0$ and, as a first step, consider the problem of selecting the optimal number of outsiders given outside ownership. Since V_O is not necessarily a concave function of n, the optimum is not readily characterized.

It is easily seen, however, that the optimal number of outsiders may be greater than one. Suppose there was a single outsider. As we have already seen, this corresponds to minimal total rent-seeking costs. But since the share of each individual manager under outside ownership is strictly lower than under inside ownership, managers have less incentive to invest in human capital than under inside ownership, and hence the value of output is lower. Adding more outsiders will (i) increase each manager's net surplus share δ_O, leading to more output as managers' incentives improve, but (ii) increase total rent-seeking costs. The net effect may be positive. Hence the optimal number of outsiders may be greater than one.

The complete problem consists of comparing the net value of the firm under inside ownership with that under outside ownership with the *optimal* number of outsiders. In the following, we present a specific numerical example with quadratic cost function. This example has the property that there is a threshold value of θ such that for all values of θ below the threshold, outside ownership is optimal, and for all values above the threshold, inside ownership is optimal. This reflects the basic intuition that outside ownership may not be desirable if firm-specific investments are important.

Suppose we have $c(e_i) = e_i^2/2$, $m = 2$, and $\bar{y} = .025$. To evaluate whether inside ownership or outside ownership is optimal, we consider the difference in net firm values $V_O - V_I$. The net firm value under inside ownership is

$$V_I = \frac{1 - \theta}{80} + \theta e(\delta_I) - (e(\delta_I))^2,$$

and the net firm value under outside ownership is

$$V_O = \left(\frac{1-\theta}{80} + \theta e(\delta_O)\right)\frac{n+6}{n+4} - (e(\delta_O))^2 .$$

Given the cost function $c(e) = e^2/2$, equilibrium effort is determined by the first-order condition

$$\theta\delta = e.$$

Hence we obtain

$$V_O - V_I = \frac{1-\theta}{40(4+n)} - \theta^2 \frac{n^3 + 29n^2 + 144n + 192}{4(4+n)^4} .$$

Figures 1–4 show the graph of $V_O - V_I$ for different values of θ. As expected, in all the examples the difference $V_O - V_I$ converges to zero as n approaches infinity.

In Figure 1, where we have $\theta = .1$, the difference $V_O - V_I$ is positive and strictly decreasing for all $n \geq 1$, implying that outside ownership with a single owner is the optimal ownership structure.

Increasing θ to .16, as in Figure 2, we find that outside ownership is still the dominant ownership structure, but the optimal number of outside owners is strictly greater than one. At $\theta = .16$ the optimal number of outside owners is $n \approx 6$. Intuitively, as firm-specific investments become more important, enlarging the number of outside owners—and thereby reducing the share of the surplus that is withdrawn from the firm—is desirable.

In Figure 3, where we have further increased θ to .2, there is a threshold $\bar{n} > 1$ such that the difference $V_O - V_I$ is positive for all $n \geq \bar{n}$ and negative for all $n < \bar{n}$. Hence the optimal number of outside owners is again strictly greater than one.

At $\theta = .3$, as in Figure 4, inside ownership dominates outside ownership for all $n \geq 1$. Here, firm-specific investments are so important that merely enlarging the number of outside owners is not enough to provide the insiders with sufficient incentives to invest. The optimal ownership arrangement is therefore to have no outside owner at all.

Table 1 shows the optimal numbers of outside owners of the firm, rounded to integers, for a variety of values of m and θ. That inside ownership is never optimal for $m > 2$ under these

FIGURE 1

$\theta = .1$

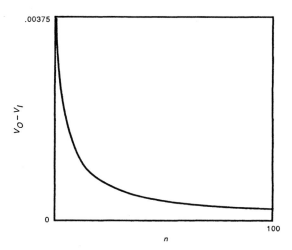

FIGURE 2

$\theta = .16$

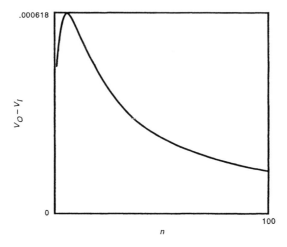

conditions is an artifact of our chosen cost function. In general, there will be some threshold number of insiders such that if there are more, outside ownership is always optimal.

From a dynamic perspective, our examples suggest why firms may over time go from being partnerships to being corporations, a not-uncommon phenomenon. Firm-specific investments by founders may have an especially important role to play at the outset of a project. Hence it may be efficient to provide the members of the firm with relatively powerful incentives. Later on, such investment opportunities may become exhausted. At this point, the objective of minimizing rent-seeking costs through outside ownership may become dominant.

FIGURE 3

$\theta = .2$

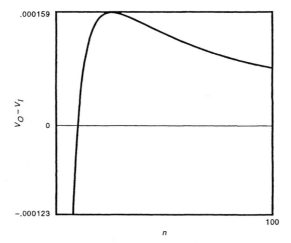

FIGURE 4

$\theta = .3$

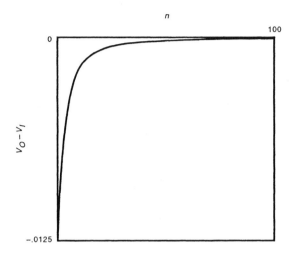

5. The theory of the firm

■ Why are some firms owned by insiders (e.g., partners) and others by outsiders not involved in the firm's business? The received literature on this fundamental question focuses mainly on the problem of providing the participants in a firm with the right incentives for productive activities.

Alchian and Demsetz (1972) argue that in partnerships, free-rider problems lead to an undersupply of productive inputs. In view of this problem, it may be optimal to bring in a third party to monitor the activities of the insiders. For this outsider to have the correct incentives, he should be entitled to the firm's residual income, which makes him effectively the firm's owner.

TABLE 1   **Approximate Optimal Numbers of Outside Owners**

θ	2	5	20	100	500
			m		
0	1	1	1	1	1
.1	1	1	1	1	1
.2	26	1	1	1	1
.3	0	1	1	1	1
.4	0	16	1	1	1
.5	0	27	1	1	1
.6	0	35	128	1	1
.7	0	40	239	1	1
.8	0	44	331	1,254	1
.9	0	46	402	5,405	1
1.0	0	48	456	10,256	251,255

540 / THE RAND JOURNAL OF ECONOMICS

Alternatively, the insiders could write an incentive contract, which, if designed appropriately, induces each agent to supply the efficient amount of effort. Such an incentive contract, however, requires bonuses and penalties that occasionally deviate from the produced surplus. As a solution, Holmström (1982) suggests that the firm hire an outsider whose only role is to break the budget-balancing constraint. As with Alchian and Demsetz, outside ownership in this theory entails only benefits, no costs.

More recently, Grossman and Hart (1986) and Hart and Moore (1990) emphasize the costs and benefits of ownership of indispensable physical assets in providing incentives for one party while diminishing the incentives for another party. There is no meaningful distinction between inside and outside ownership in terms of this theory, however.

In contrast, the present article addresses the question of inside versus outside ownership in a setting where contractual incompleteness in firms leads to costly distributional conflicts over the produced surplus. We show that outside ownership may ameliorate the cost of such conflict, even though it adds a second conflict in which the outsiders fight against the insiders. In this conflict, the insiders invest costly resources in, for example, the manipulation of accounting data, claiming that the surplus is low, whereas the outsiders as the legal claimants to the firm's surplus invest resources in proving the contrary. In equilibrium, the outsiders always manage to extract at least part of the surplus, implying that fewer resources are wasted in the subsequent distributional conflict between the insiders. Hence the owners of a firm may play a role similar to Hobbes's Leviathan in presenting the insiders with an outside threat or common enemy sufficient to lessen their internal squabblings.

In our analysis, outside ownership plays a role much like that of debt in the literature on free cash flow (e.g., Jensen, 1986). There, debt is used to force managers to pay out funds, thereby reducing the amount of funds invested in negative net present value projects. In our model, it makes no difference whether the insiders take on debt or sell the firm to outsiders. As the insiders are generally reluctant to pay out funds, they will default on repaying the debt, implying that the debtholders effectively become the firm's new outside owners. In the same fashion as the outside owners in our model, the former debtholders must then engage in a contest with the insiders over the distribution of the surplus.

References

ALCHIAN, A.A. AND DEMSETZ, H. "Production, Information Costs, and Economic Organization." *American Economic Review,* Vol. 62 (1972), pp. 777–795.

BANKS, R.C.I. *Lindley & Banks on Partnership.* London: Sweet & Maxwell, 1995.

BAYE, M.R., KOVENOCK, D., AND DE VRIES, C.G. "Rigging the Lobbying Process: An Application of the All-Pay Auction." *American Economic Review,* Vol. 83 (1993), pp. 289–294.

DIXIT, A. "Strategic Behavior in Contests." *American Economic Review,* Vol. 77 (1987), pp. 891–898.

FULLERTON, R.L. AND MCAFEE, R.P. "Auctioning Entry into Tournaments." *Journal of Political Economy,* Vol. 107 (1999), pp. 573–605.

GROSSMAN, S. AND HART, O. "The Costs and Benefits of Ownership: A Theory of Vertical and Lateral Integration." *Journal of Political Economy,* Vol. 94 (1986), pp. 691–719.

HART, O. AND MOORE, J. "Property Rights and the Nature of the Firm." *Journal of Political Economy,* Vol. 98 (1990), pp. 1119–1158.

―――― AND ――――. "Cooperatives vs. Outside Ownership." Working Paper no. W6421, National Bureau of Economic Research, 1998.

HOLMSTRÖM, B. "Moral Hazard in Teams." *Bell Journal of Economics,* Vol. 13 (1982), pp. 324–340.

JENSEN, M.C. "Agency Costs of Free Cash Flow, Corporate Finance, and Takeovers." *American Economic Review,* Vol. 76 (1986), pp. 323–329.

KLEIN, B., CRAWFORD, R.G., AND ALCHIAN, A.A. "Vertical Integration, Appropriable Rents, and the Competitive Contracting Process." *Journal of Law and Economics,* Vol. 21 (1978), pp. 297–326.

KREMER, M. "Worker Cooperatives as Economic Democracies." Working paper, MIT, 1998.

MILGROM, P.R. "Employment Contracts, Influence Activities, and Efficient Organization Design." *Journal of Political Economy,* Vol. 96 (1988), pp. 42–60.

NITZAN, S. "Modelling Rent-Seeking Contests." *European Journal of Political Economy,* Vol. 10 (1994), pp. 41–60.

RAJAN, R.G. AND ZINGALES, L. "The Tyranny of Inequality." *Journal of Public Economics,* Vol. 76 (2000), pp. 521–558.

SHLEIFER, A. AND VISHNY, R.W. "A Survey of Corporate Governance." *Journal of Finance,* Vol. 52 (1997), pp. 737–783.

SKAPERDAS, S. "Cooperation, Conflict, and Power in the Absence of Property Rights." *American Economic Review,* Vol. 82 (1992), pp. 720–739.

———. "Contest Success Functions." *Economic Theory,* Vol. 7 (1996), pp. 283–290.

TULLOCK, G. "The Welfare Costs of Tariffs, Monopolies, and Theft." *Western Economic Journal,* Vol. 5 (1967), pp. 224–232.

———. "On the Efficient Organization of Trials." *Kyklos,* Vol. 28 (1975), pp. 745–762.

———. "Efficient Rent Seeking." In J.M. Buchanan, R.D. Tollison, and G. Tullock, eds., *Toward a Theory of the Rent-Seeking Society.* College Station, Tex.: Texas A&M University Press, 1980.

WÄRNERYD, K. "Distributional Conflict and Jurisdictional Organization." *Journal of Public Economics,* Vol. 69 (1998), pp. 435–450.

WILLIAMSON, O.E. *Markets and Hierarchies: Analysis and Antitrust Implications.* New York: Free Press, 1975.

———. *The Economic Institutions of Capitalism.* New York: Free Press, 1985.

Part 6

Societal Relations

Journal of Economic Behavior and Organization 11 (1989) 175–190. North-Holland

EFFICIENT STATUS SEEKING: EXTERNALITIES, AND THE EVOLUTION OF STATUS GAMES

Roger D. CONGLETON*

George Mason University, Fairfax, VA 22030, USA

Received June 1987, final version received July 1988

Status-seeking games are games in which an individual's utility is determined by his relative expenditure on status-seeking activities rather than his absolute consumption. There are a number of parallels between status-seeking and rent-seeking activities, for example, a tendency for Pareto excessive private investment. However, many status-seeking activities differ from rent-seeking activities insofar as they generate significant benefits to individuals not actively involved in the game. Given an array of more or less productive status-seeking games, it is likely that relatively efficient status conferring mechanisms will tend to displace less efficient ones.

'The activity which we call economic, whether of production or of consumption or of the two together, is also, if we look below the surface, to be interpreted largely by the motives of a competitive contest or game, rather than those of mechanical utility functions to be maximized'.

Frank Knight, *The Ethics of Competition and Other Essays*, p. 301.

1. Introduction

In the orthodox economic model of consumer behavior, consumers maximize utility given opportunity sets determined by the market value of inherited and/or accumulated personal assets. The orthodox model assumes that each consumer's decisions are independent of those of other consumers. Thus, the utility level assigned to a particular bundle of goods is not affected by the consumption levels of others. While this model continues to dominate economic research, a new literature examining the implications of interdependent utility functions emerged during the 1970s which stresses links between individual choices. See Hochman and Rogers (1969) for an altruism-based

*The author wishes to thank the Clarkson University School of Management for summer research support and the Lynde and Harry Bradley Foundation for support at the Center for Study of Public Choice. The author would also like to thank Randall Bennett, James Buchanan, Robert Tollison, Viktor Vanberg, Ulrich Witt, and especially Timur Kuran for helpful comments on previous drafts of the paper. They bear no responsibility for any errors or misconceptions that remain.

theory of taxation and transfers, Barro (1974) for an intergenerational theory of the public debt, or Becker (1981) for a theory of the family. One strand of this literature has explored the implications of competition between consumers for relative position in a consumption hierarchy.

Hirsch (1976) and Frank (1985a, 1985b) argue that the quest for social position is an important argument in individual utility functions.[1] In Hirsch's view, a substantial portion of individual satisfaction results from the consumption of what he calls positional goods. Satisfaction from positional goods arises not from absolute levels of consumption, but rather, from the social rank generated by them. Since rank is inherently scarce, the prospect of increasing social welfare by expanding ordinary production is severely limited. Frank points out that individuals tend to overinvest in positional goods. Like rent-seeking activities, expenditures on positional goods redistribute, rather than create, social wealth.[2] Consequently, a substantial portion of the investment in positional goods may be regarded as a dead-weight loss.

These conclusions are based largely on the observation that each person's quest for status imposes external costs on other status-seekers. Within a particular status game, one person's gain in status is another's loss. However, the external effects of status-seeking activities are not always limited to those borne by fellow status seekers. Many status games involve activities which provide benefits for individuals not actively involved in the game of interest. In such games, the activities by which status seekers acquire status may benefit rather than harm society.

Moreover, if some status games are more productive than others, one might expect institutional arrangements to emerge which promote games generating positive externalities and discourage those which do not. Thus, existing status-assigning systems may be less wasteful than implied by the positional goods literature. This paper explores the extent to which wasteful status-seeking games tend to be displaced by games which reduce social losses or which increase social welfare by providing non-monetary incentives for individuals to engage in activities which generate positive externalities.

The paper is organized as follows. Section 2 characterizes status-seeking games and suggests that such games are commonplace. Section 3 demonstrates that the private quest for status does not necessarily become a 'rat

---

[1]Economic antecedents to the work of Hirsch and Frank include Veblen (1899/1953), Leibenstein (1948), Duesenberry (1949), and Easterlin (1973). Easterlin reviews survey evidence which suggests that happiness is based more on relative wealth than absolute wealth. Veblen writes: 'If as is sometimes assumed, the incentive to accumulation were the want of subsistence or of physical comfort, then the aggregate economic wants of a community might conceivably be satisfied at some point in the advance of industrial efficiency; but since the struggle is substantially a race for reputability on the basis of an invidious comparison, no approach to a definitive attainment is possible' (p. 39).

[2]For examples of the methodology of the rent-seeking literature, see Tullock (1967), Posner (1975), and Congleton (1980).

race'. It shows that the extent of investment in status-generating activities varies with the status-assigning mechanism. Section 4 contrasts the privately optimal level of status-seeking effort in micro-status games with the Pareto optimal level. Here we note that the normative appeal of alternative status-seeking activities varies widely, and that in certain status-seeking games, *too few* resources may be devoted to status-seeking activities. Section 5 discusses the benign evolution of micro-status games. Section 6 explores the extent to which a similar case might be made for macro-status games. Section 7 summarizes the paper and suggests extensions.

2. Status games

There are a wide range of activities by which an individual may seek and gain status. A contemporary scholar gains status as the number and quality of his scholarly publications increase relative to others in his field of inquiry. An athlete gains status by increasing his speed, physical strength and stamina relative to his competitors. An alpinist's relative status varies with the number and difficulty of the peaks he has climbed. Within each of these relatively small groups, there are even smaller groups concerned with even more specialized status-assigning measures. A brief reflection on the numerous methods by which the modern Olympic Games measure the relative performance of athletes, or of the numerous fields of specialization in academia or gourmet cooking, provides a glimpse of the scope of status-seeking activities. Status-seeking behavior occurs in virtually every activity where a *cognoscente* may be said to exist, from groups as varied as religious orders to serious imbibers of alcoholic beverages.

Each of these methods of obtaining status has its own metric for measuring the relative merit of its participants. In some cases, an individual's status is measured by events beyond his control. For example, an individual's relative status might reflect the achievements of his ancestors, or be the result of a random process, as might be said of the survivors of a major battle in modern warfare. In other cases, the ones of interest here, status is measured by personal achievements linked to individual decisions. This may be said of the homage paid to outstanding athletes, scholars, entrepreneurs, politicians, warriors, or culinary experts. In these cases, personal status is the result of individual decisions to employ scarce economic resources in status-generating activities.

Conceptually, measures of status may be ordinal or cardinal. If status is a pure positional good, absolute magnitude comparisons are without interest, and status is purely ordinal. The winner of a race has only to be faster than the person coming in second. On the other hand, status might be determined relative to some norm. An individual whose collection includes twice as many rare coins as some other numismatist might be deemed twice as good a collector irrespective of the number of collectors with greater or lesser holdings. What matters for the purposes of this paper is that individuals are sufficiently interested in acquiring status that they invest economic resources in order to obtain it.

Given a measure of status and individual proclivities to invest in status-generating activities, the result is a game whose payoffs are various assignments of status. There are essentially two levels of games in which the quest for relative status takes place. Macro-status games are those in which essentially all members of society gain or lose status from the activities involved. Socio-economic status in modern western societies is largely a matter of one's relative wealth, education, and influence, the pursuit of which occupy non-trivial portions of most people's time. In other societies, one's geneology, bravery and/or access to those in political power determine macro-status. Micro-status games are those in which the number of status seekers is much smaller than the population as a whole. In these games, status-seeking efforts affect principally the status of a small segment of society. Such games include competitive foot races, cooking and beauty contests, admission to exclusive colleges or careers, and most determinations of relative merit within firms. The common element of all status games is that relative performance rather than absolute performance ultimately determines individual utility levels, where 'performance' is measured by the status-assigning rules of the game of interest.

The rich variety of micro-status games suggests that attempts to represent status with a single broad social index will miss much that is significant about the quest for personal status. For example, if all status games have the properties of the positional games explored by Frank (1985b), the total deadweight loss of status-seeking activities will be substantially larger than indicated by an examination of personal investments in macro-status games. More important for the purposes of this paper is the fact that analysis of macro-status games tends to shift attention away from the existence of alternative status-assigning mechanisms, and thereby neglects the possibility of the benign evolution of status-assigning mechanisms.

For example, some of Fank's illustrations of institutional arrangements which reduce expenditures on positional goods appear to be instances of the substitution of productive for non-productive status games rather than consciously chosen limitations on status seeking. Frank (1985a) argues that unions promote savings and health plans as mechanisms to shield workers from useless expenditures on positional goods. However, it seems more likely to be the case that unions compete with each other for worker enlistments, and that workers naturally prefer unions which offer the best results. Union performance has been measured by such indices as strike time, wage rates and fringe benefit levels. To the extent that health and retirement benefits have replaced strike time as an index of union quality, competition to be the best union becomes a status game which indirectly improves the health of labor and extent of capital in the economy, a productive status-seeking game.

3. A model of status-seeking behavior

To demonstrate that different status-assigning mechanisms generate different investments in status-seeking activities, the paper analyzes a relatively stark model of the quest for status. In order to focus sharply on status seeking, status is assumed to be the result of relative investments in status-generating activities which are not themselves elements of an individual's utility function. While many status-seeking activities do generate non-status benefits as well as personal status, this assumption simplifies the analysis and strengthens our argument by putting the worst possible face on status-seeking activities. If we can demonstrate that some status-seeking games are more appealing than others in this environment, extensions can be readily made to less extreme settings.

Assume that individual utility is a function of two goods, a non-status good purchased in a competitive market and personal status. Let, status be generated by purchasing pure status goods in a competitive market. This allows the individual's pursuit of status to be represented as a utility maximizing allocation of personal wealth among the status and non-status goods, S and X respectively. The individual chooses S to maximize

$$U = u(\tilde{S}, X) \qquad \text{subject to} \tag{1}$$

$$W = X + PS \quad \text{and} \quad \tilde{S} = s(S, S^a) \quad \text{with} \tag{2}$$

$$U_{\tilde{S}} > 0, \ U_X > 0, \ \tilde{S}_S > 0 \quad \text{and} \quad \tilde{S}_{S^a} < 0.$$

Subscripts denote partial derivatives. W is the individual's wealth; $\tilde{S}$ is the status generated by his purchase of the status good; S^a is the average level of status seeking by others in the relevant group; and P is the price of the status good, with the non-status good used as the numeraire good. The representation of status used here is similar to one previously used by Boskin and Sheshinski (1978). Status increases as one's holding of the pure-status good increase relative to the average holdings of the rest of the game players. Naturally, any explicit representation of a status production function reduces the generality of the analysis based on it, but the purpose of the model is fairly modest.

Substituting for S and X in (1) yields an expression for utility in terms of status-seeking effort

$$U = u(s(S, S^a), W - PS). \tag{3}$$

Differentiating with respect to S and setting the result equal to zero yields the first order condition for the utility maximizing level of status seeking

$$U_{\tilde{S}}/U_X = P/\tilde{S}_S. \tag{4}$$

Thus, utility is maximized by seeking status up to the point where the marginal rate of substitution between status and non status consumption equals the relative price of status and non-status goods. At the margin, individuals are indifferent between status and non-status goods.

Note that as long as $\tilde{S}_S$ does not change, there is little difference between status and non-status consumption. However, $\tilde{S}_S$, the rate at which the status-generating activity generates status, is affected by the efforts of others in the status game, $\tilde{S}_{SS}a < 0$. It is this link between the consumption choices of individuals which distinguishes status seeking activities from ordinary consumption.

The usual assumptions about utility functions imply that the individual's preferred investment in the status good can be characterized with an implicit function based on eq. (4).

$$S = s(P, W, S^a). \tag{5}$$

Eq. (5) represents the individual's demand for status goods in this game. We see that the optimal level of status seeking effort depends on (i) the price of the status good, (ii) an individual's wealth, and (iii) the average level of status seeking by others in the game. Partial derivatives of eq. (5) with respect to these variables reveal the effect that they have on the individual's preferred purchase of the status good. To simplify notation a bit, U is assumed to be a separable function of $\tilde{S}$ and X.

$$S_P = (U_X - PSU_{XX})/K < 0, \tag{6}$$

$$S_W = (PU_{XX})/K > 0, \tag{7}$$

$$S_S a = (U_{\tilde{S}\tilde{S}}\tilde{S}_S a\tilde{S}_S + U_{\tilde{S}}\tilde{S}_{SS}a)/K, \qquad \text{where} \tag{8}$$

$$K = U_{\tilde{S}\tilde{S}}\tilde{S}_{\tilde{S}}^2 + U_{\tilde{S}}\tilde{S}_{SS} + P^2 U_{XX} < 0. \tag{9}$$

The first two partial derivatives demonstrate the fact that in this game investment in status goods is analogous to the purchase of ordinary consumer goods. Eq. (6) shows that, other things being equal, an increase in the relative price of the status-generating activity reduces an individual's incination to invest in it. Eq. (7) demonstrates that individuals invest more resources in the quest for status as their wealth increases.

The last partial derivative, whose sign is ambiguous, is of greater interest for the purposes of this paper. The ambiguity is caused by the fact that an increase in aggregate status seeking or decrease in the number of status seekers has two effects on a typical status seeker. An increase in average status-seeking effort reduces the status generated by a given amount of the status good and thereby increases the marginal utility of additional status. At the same time, it decreases the rate at which additional purchases of the status good generate additional status. The net effect thus depends on which of the two effects dominates. Note that both $\tilde{S}_s a \tilde{S}_s$ and $\tilde{S}_{ss} a$ are properties of the status assigning mechanism rather than of the desire for status. What is significant here is that not all measures of status lead to an escalating 'rat race' among status seekers.

The possibility that status-seeking efforts might de-escalate contrasts with Frank's (1985b) characterization of the quest for positional goods. Escalation was the result of his particular mathematical representation of the status-generating process. Other representations generate different results. This suggests that a broad range of equilibrium status-seeking levels is possible according to the opportunity cost of status seeking, tastes for status, and the particular measure of status in the game of interest. Possible equilibria range from all-consuming contests to those which attract no investments whatever. Thus, it will be possible to control or at least influence the overall investment in status-seeking by changing either the cost of status-seeking activities or the method by which status is measured.

4. Pareto-efficient status seeking

If status-seeking activities affect only the welfare of others in the status game, it is relatively straightforward to demonstrate that too many resources will be invested in the quest for status [see Frank (1985a)]. In this case, a status-seeking game is analogous to a rent-seeking game. The pool of status distributed among game players is essentially fixed, and individual status-seeking investments affect the distribution of status without generating social gain. Since any equilibrium assignment of status can be reproduced using a trivial amount of scarce resources, say 1/1,000 of the actual investment, the bulk of status-seeking efforts can be considered a dead-weight loss similar to those of rent-seeking activities.

However, while some status-seeking games, like alpine competition, do have minimal impacts beyond those on fellow status seekers, many others impose externalities on non-game players. Fortunately, most of these games appear to create spillover benefits rather than costs for non-participants. In some, the benefits involve direct consumption benefits. Such is the case with a competitive footrace which generates entertainment for spectators. Other games generate technological externalities. For example, the pursuit of academic status often generates knowledge which reduces the cost of producing both status and non-status goods. Still other status games provide indirect status for non-participants; in what might be called complementary status games, attainment of high status in one game indirectly increases the status of individuals in other games. For example, less than generous comments made regarding the complex reasoning of intellectuals indicates that increased intellectualism by one person may indirectly increase the status of others in games where status is inversely related to revealed intellectualism.

Pareto optimal status-seeking requires the sum of individuals' marginal rates of substitution between status and non-status consumption to equal the marginal technical rate of substitution between status and non-status generating goods. In other words, the social marginal benefit from status seeking by any given individual must equal the marginal opportunity cost of that status seeking in terms of non-status consumption. It also requires the total production of the status and non-status goods, S and X, to be on the production possibility frontier.

Suppose there are N status seekers in the game characterized above, and M members of the society at large, with $N < M$. Let $T(S, X) = R$ be society's production possibility frontier and $\tilde{S}_i = s(S_i; S_1, S_2, \ldots, S_N)$ represent the method by which status is measured. Pareto efficiency requires the ith status seeker to pursue status at the point on the production possibility frontier where S_i sets

$$\sum_{j=1}^{N} (U_{\tilde{S}j}\tilde{S}_{Si}/U_{Xj}) + \sum_{j=N+1}^{M} (Uj_{Si}/U_{Xj}) = T_S/T_X. \tag{10}$$

In a game with a fixed pool of status, i's status seeking imposes status losses on other status seekers equal to his gain, so the first sum is approximately zero. The second sum is the effect of i's status seeking effort on non-participants, Uj_{Si}/U_{Xj}. Since extra-game externalities can be either positive or negative, this sum may be greater or less than zero.

Given the results of eq. (4), and the fact that in competitive markets $P = T_S/T_X$, the Pigovian tax or subsidy required to internalize the externalities generated by i's choice is

$$T_i = \sum_{j \neq i}^{N} (U_{\tilde{S}j}\tilde{S}_{Si}/U_{Xj}) + \sum_{j=N+1}^{M} (Uj_{Si}/U_{Xj}). \tag{11}$$

Only in the case where the lost status of other game players exactly offsets the gains of non-players at the margin would the appropriate externality internalizing tax be zero. As the literature on positional goods maintains, private status-seeking levels are unlikely to be Pareto optimal. In cases where external benefits are small or non-existent, a Pigovian tax will be appropriate.[3] However, in cases where external benefits are substantial, Pareto-efficient status seeking requires Pigovian subsidies. Subsidies reduce the cost of the status-generating activity and thereby increase the extent of beneficial game externalities.

Alternatively, efficiency can be increased by changing the method by which status is measured. Increased investment in status can be induced by encouraging the use of status measures which tend toward escalation. Note that firms often attempt to create escalating games in which relative productivity determines the status and/or salaries of their employees. In cases where too much status-seeking effort is forthcoming, status measures which induce de-escalation can replace ones leading to excessive investment.

5. Evolution of micro status games

Hayek's (1973) notion of *kosmos*, a societal process of coordination and improvement, suggests that the personally gratifying quest for status will tend to be channelled into games that minimize the social cost of status seeking. In other words, status-seeking games that generate dead-weight losses will be gradually supplanted by games that generate significant positive externalities. As it turns out, the choices of both status seekers and the non-playing majority tend to moderate social losses from micro-status games.

The case for the benign evolution of micro-status games is relatively straightforward. Since the number of active status seekers in a micro-status game is substantially smaller than the number of non-players, the non-participating majority can easily promote status games that provide positive externalities and discourage those that generate negative externalities by changing the returns of alternative status games. Sanctions may take the form of monetary fines or subsidies, or the assignment of more or less macro-status to participation in burdensome micro-status games. Examples of status games curtailed by majority rule legislation include dueling, street racing, and the destructive potlatches of the North Pacific Coast Cultue [see Drucker (1965, p. 492)]. The pursuit of artistic and academic status have long been subsidized by both governments and private individuals.

Moreover, the fact that the participants of micro-status games *choose which game to play* implies that relative unproductive status assigning

---

[3]Note that in the case where taxes are called for, the status assigning mechanism used above implies that taxes on status seeking activities will be progressive. Eq. (7) implies that an increase in wealth shifts the individual's MRS curve to the Northeast. This, Pigovian taxes will be an increasing function of wealth, a progressive consumption tax. This result differs from Frank's results, but is analogous to a point made by Thompson (1972, 1974) with respect to wealth taxes as means of financing national defense. In that case individuals with relatively greater coveted wealth would face relatively greater taxes to internalize the effects of that wealth on others.

mechanisms have short lives. For example, during the late nineteenth century, Galbraith (1977, p. 65), citing Veblen, notes that 'the ceremonies at which wealth was displayed – costly entertainments such as the potlatch or the ball – were of particular importance in the competition for esteem'. Beebe (1966, p. 129) relates the details of several of the most spectacular instances in the U.S. in which more than a million dollars was spent on party festivities. However, investment in this form of status seeking peaked in the late nineteenth century as parties were scaled down and redirected toward less wasteful activities. Beebe (p. 131) reports that 'a later generation would have taken to itself the social prestige that derived from these flamboyant [parties] while excusing their cost in the name of some public benevolence'. In the end, status-generating parties moved away from simple ostentation toward charitable activities.

Individuals tend to prefer status-seeking activities which serve non-status purposes at the same time that they generate status, other things being equal. Sponsorship of charity balls demonstrates socio-economic status while simultaneously advancing the altruistic interests of the sponsor. In such cases, status-seeking may still cause excessive expenditures on the activities by which status is measured, the parties may still be more elaborate than they should be, but the dead-weight loss of status seeking is smaller than it would have been had the entire expenditure been motivated by status. Moreover, if status seekers have different skills at different games, they will opt for games in which they have a comparative advantage. If only least cost producers participate in a given status game, losses will be smaller than would have been the case had individuals chosen games at random. Thus, there are a variety of reasons why particularly wasteful micro-status games tend to be supplanted by less wasteful games.

In cases where changes in the status assigning mechanism do not occur, as Frank (1985a) has noted, status seekers may adopt rules or institutional arrangements which limit or reduce expenditures on status seeking. For example, status seekers often erect barriers to entry in games where an increase in the number of competitors erodes the status of those already in the game. Most exclusive clubs restrict eligibility for membership in arbitrary ways. Many clubs require new members to be acceptable to current members and/or limit membership to persons of a particular genology, creed, or sex.

It bears noting that barriers to entry can be productive in status games. In contrast to competition in markets where dissipated economic rents are simply transferred to third parties not directly involved in the competitive contest, namely consumers, third parties do not necessarily benefit from the

---

[4]This is not to say that excluded individuals do not gain or lose status from the status game of interest. However, rigid entry barriers discourage active pursuit of club membership. These inactive participants in status games may gain or lose status as a consequence, but they do not engage in potentially wasteful status-seeking activities.

dissipation of status-seeking rents.[4] On the other hand, in cases where status-seeking activities confer benefits on non-game players, the non-playing majority has an interest in eliminating entry barriers erected by game players. Recent efforts to open up membership in public service clubs like the Rotary and Lions clubs seem to be consistent with promoting productive status-seeking activities.

If it is true that more efficient status-seeking mechanisms tend to displace less efficient ones, we should observe at least a few status-seeking games in which non-participants subsidize those actively involved in the quest for status. This is in fact the case. For example, public and private subsidies to both amateur and professional athletic and scholarly activities are commonplace. Moreover, status games are often created as a means of generating positive externalities. Thus, we observe numerous contrived contests which reward individuals for superior public service, architecture, journalism, athleticism, and scientific contributions.

Demsetz (1967) argues that societies which adopt efficient rules will be better able to accumulate wealth and prosper in the long run. From the perspective of this paper, prosperous societies will be those which most effectively channel the quest for status into productive activites.

6. Efficient macro-status games

Unfortunately, the case for the benign evolution of macro-status games is more difficult to make because macro-status games do not exhibit extra-game externalities similar to those of micro-status games. This follows from the fact that essentially all members of society are involved in that society's macro-status game. On the other hand, the normative appeal of alternative methods of assigning macro-status varies substantially. For example, there are important differences between wealth-consuming and wealth-creating macro-status games.

Consider the previous two-good world with one pure-status good and one non-status good. Let the number of status seekers equal the number of members of society, $M = N$. Suppose that some status generating activities have direct effects on the available productive resources. In other words, suppose that

$$R = r(S) = T(S, X). \tag{12}$$

In this setting, status seeking effort causes both movement along, and shifts of, the production possibility frontier.

Pareto optimal seeking for the ith member of society now requires

$$\sum_{j}^{N} (U_{Sj}\tilde{S}j_{Si}/U_{Xj}) = (T_S - R_S)/T_X. \tag{13}$$

The new term in the numerator of the right hand side of eq. (13), R_S, is the effect that status seeking has on the production possibility frontier. In the case of a productive status game, R_S is positive and the social opportunity cost of status seeking is smaller than it would be in non-productive or destructive games. Consequently, the Pareto efficient level of the status–seeking activity is larger in productive games than in non-productive games.[5]

Moreover, status goods tend to be relatively labor intensive, since the scale economies of mass production tend to reduce the exclusivity of the goods produced. In physical form, status goods generally consist of limited production runs by skilled artisans. Given this, games which promote the accumulation of productive wealth also tend to reduce the relative price of non-status goods. On the other hand, games which promote wealth desctruction tend to reduce the pool of productive capital and thereby cause the price of non-status goods to increase relative to status goods. Wealth-destroying games reinforce status-seeking waste whereas wealth-creating games create relative price changes encouraging consumption of non-status goods.

While it is easy to demonstrate that not all macro-status assigning mechanisms have the same normative appeal, it is difficult to motivate an evolutionary process by which wealth enhancing macro-status games supplant less efficient mechanisms. The fact that essentially all members of society actively participate in macro-status games reduces individual incentives to adopt or promote alternative status assigning measures. An individual or small group that opts out of an existing game generally does so at substantial personal cost. In most cases, the combination of status and economic losses borne by individual 'drop-outs' induces continued participation by many who find existing status-generating activities personally disaggreeable.

In a somewhat different context, Kuran (1987) argues that collective conservatism is a consequence of incentives for individuals to hide their

---

[5]In the case of competition between equals, the left hand term of eq. (13) is zero since j's gain in macro-status is offset by losses by other players. This implies that status-seeking activities are desirable only if they create more wealth than they consume, namely if $R_{S^*} > T_{S^*}$. In this case, the marginal opportunity cost of status seeking is negative over some range and worthwhile up to the point where $T_{S^*} = R_{S^*}$. Thus, individuals in macro-status games may engage in too little status-seeking effort if external economies in production more than offset the status losses of other game players. Here a subsidy on the status generating activity or a tax on the non-status goods will be appropriate. On the other hand, wealth-reducing mechanisms *necessarily* generate Pareto excessive status-seeking efforts with losses in excess of the resources directly employed by status seekers.

personal beliefs in order to avoid punishments or obtain rewards. In his model, individuals may benefit from revealing false but conventional beliefs rather than their own true beliefs. A similar process can keep relatively efficient macro-status assigning systems from displacing less efficient ones. To take a somewhat mundane example, 'dressing for success' is an important part of the modern wealth-seeking status games of Western societies. An individual who drops out of this game as a means of reducing personal expenditures on clothing, is likely to find that his job prospects are substantially diminished. Thus, substantial investments in uncomfortable shoes and suits continue to be made for public purposes, although most individuals slip into more comfortable clothing as soon as they reach home.

It is also difficult to tax or otherwise regulate unproductive macro-status generating activities. Taxation is difficult to motivate for two reasons. Since each person or subgroup benefits if their status-seeking costs are reduced relative to others, coalitions favoring taxation of macro-status generating activities tend to be unstable. Moreover, the required consensus that a particular status generating activity is undesirable, and should be taxed, is difficult to obtain. Such a consensus might be generated if there were some common method of assessing the relative merits of various status-seeking activities. However, since this is largely what macro-status assigning mechanisms entail, lobbying for taxes requires one to argue that some widely accepted method of gaining respect should be differentially taxed – a difficult task.[6]

On the other hand, subsidizing macro-status-seeking activities is fairly common. While coalitions favoring subsidies also tend to be unstable, since everyone prefers larger subsidies for themselves than for others, subsidies are consistent with the values embedded in every macro-status assigning mechanism. Examination of the U.S. tax code reveals a number of macro-status generating activities that receive tax preferences. Religious activities and organizations have long been granted special treatment. Charitable contributions are deductible from taxable income. Income from capital goods and entrepreneurship are treated differently than ordinary labor income. Unfortunately, the politics of subsidies appear to be nearly the same whether the macro-status game is productive or not.

Transformation of macro-status games is at best a slow process. Yet, there is some evidence of the benign evolution of macro-status games. One macro-status game that exhibits productive economies is the one used to character-

---

[6]The implicit values of macro-status assigning mechanisms are often used to rank alternative social states. For example, if religious fervor is the dominant method of acquiring personal status, it is natural to rank societies according to the extent to which they encourage religious fervor. Militarists tend to rank societies by their ability to project military force. Wealth-seekers naturally tend to use GNP (or per capita GNP) as a method of ranking alternative social arrangements.

ize capitalist society. In this game, status is measured by relative holdings of productive capital. To the extent that capital is accumulated through the market-based activities of saving and entrepreneurship, the game itself requires production rather than consumption of economic resources. This contrasts with pre-capitalist macro-status games in which abstinence from worldly activities or actively destructive activities are sources of relative status. Thus, the gradual replacement of pre-capitalist (or non-capitalist) status games with capitalist games is consistent with Hayek's view of the process of social evolution.

Consider Takizawa's (1927) account of the end of the feudal system in Japan. Under the feudal system, macro-status was the result of family position, filial and political loyalty, and holdings of land. Land was passed on to family members and could only be subdivided down to about twenty five acre parcels (ten *koku*). Land reverted to the Shogun in the absence of an heir. Awards were granted to commoners for great filial piety. However, Takizawa reports that 'this time-honored family system began to show signs of disintegration in the late Tokugawa period.... Great forces were transforming the whole economic and social system' (p. 356). The latter was largely the emergence of a thriving merchant class. 'As more and more avenues of work opened up for those who left their village homes, the family became less and less significant.... Peasants were parting with their ancestral land more and more willingly' (p. 357). 'Even the courts inclined to treat as individuals those who brought up money actions' (p. 361). In sum, 'the invasion of money into the family called forth new attitudes and brought new opportunities which undermined the old system at its very roots – the family' (p. 362).

It bears noting that, to a large extent, the relative wealth of contemporary capitalist and non-capitalist societies parallels the extent to which capitalist status games have become macro-games. Both sorts of societies have access to modern technology, global capital markets and the ubiquitous forces of markets; but capitalists gain status by accumulating productive wealth whereas the elite of other cultures gain status through maintained relationships *within* the elite itself. Accumulation of wealth in most non-capitalist settings is not based on productive entrepreneurship but rather on what might be called social entrepreneurship, the effects of which are largely confined to the status game. Perhaps relatively prosperous and stable societies like those of the Ottoman Turks and Chinese lost ground to Western Europe during the eighteenth and nineteenth centuries not because of a lack of stable property rights or significant technological and capital bases, but because the accumulative status games of capitalists never succeeded in becoming macro-status games.

This provides evidence of the limits of Hayek's notion of *kosmos*. If the process of social evolution were sufficiently strong, only efficient status games would remain. Unfortunately, wealth-consuming status games seem to remain dominant for substantial periods of time.[7]

7. Conclusion

As in the case of other rivalrous games, the particular institutional framework and mechanisms for distributing the fuits of conflict have important effects on the extent of status seeking effort and any dead weight loss associated with it. Frank has argued that institutional arrangements tend to emerge which curtail unproductive status-seeking activities. Another possibility emphasized here is that inefficient status games may be replaced by more efficient ones. Games which create negative externalities may be replaced by games generating no externalities or, better still, by games generating positive externalities.

A good many status-seeking activities do generate positive externalities. The feats of athletes provide mass entertainment, those of scholars provide the foundation of improved productive technology and/or institutional arrangements.[8] Capitalists in their quest for status, produce and accumulate the capital necessary for mass production and widespread material wealth. These status games are efficiency enhancing. This is not to say that all status-seeking activities are consistent with economic efficiency. The analysis and illustrations of this paper suggest a tendency rather than an inexorable law. Yet it is clearly the case that many, if not most, status-seeking games are less wasteful than one would imagine based on an analysis of the quest for personal status alone.

[7]For more on the limitations of Hayek's theory of social evolution, see Vanberg (1986).

[8]Contributions to the positional goods literature are motivated partly by the pursuit of academic status. Note that this status game might be a socially-productive game if theoretical advances facilitate the benign evolution of status-seeking games.

References

Barro, Robert J., 1974, Are government bonds net wealth?, Journal of Political Economy 82, 1095–1117.

Becker, Gary, 1980, A treatise on the family (Harvard University Press, Cambridge, MA).

Beebe, Lucius M., 1966, The big spenders (Doubleday, New York).

Bell, Daniel, 1945/1978, The cultural contradictions of capitalism (Basic Books, New York).

Boskin, Michael J. and Eyton Sheshinski, 1978, Optimal redistributive taxation when individual welfare depends upon relative income, Quarterly Journal of Economics 92, 589–601.

Buchanan, James M., Gordon Tullock and Robert D. Tollison, eds., 1980, Towards a theory of the rent-seeking society (A&M Press, College Station, TX).

Burke, Peter, 1980, Sociology and history (Allen and Unwin, London).

Congleton, Roger, 1980, Competitive process, competitive waste, and institutions, in: Buchanan et al., eds., Towards a theory of the rent-seeking society, 183–194.

Demsetz, Harold, 1967, Towards a theory of property rights, American Economic Review 57, 347–360.

Drucker, Philip, 1965, Cultures of the North Pacific coast. Reprinted in Dalton, G., 1967, Tribal and peasant economies (University of Texas Press, Austin, TX).

Duesenberry, James S., 1949, Income, saving and the theory of consumer behavior (Harvard Univerity Press, Cambridge, MA).

Easterlin, Richard A., 1973, Does money buy happiness?, Public Interest 30, 3–10.

Frank, Robert H., 1985a, The demand for unobservable and other nonpositional goods, American Economic Review 75, 101–116.

Frank, Robert H., 1985b, Choosing the right pond: Human behavior and the quest for status (Oxford University Press, New York).

Galbraith, John K., 1977, The age of uncertainty (Houghton Mifflin, Boston, MA).

Hayek, Friedrich A., 1973, Law legislation and liberty (University of Chicago, Chicago, IL).

Hirsch, Fred, 1976, Social limits to economic growth (Harvard University Press, Cambridge, MA).

Hochman, Harold M. and James D. Rodgers, 1969, Pareto optimal redistribution, American Economic Review 59, 542–547.

Kuran, Timur, 1987, Preference falsification, policy continuity and collective conservatism, Economic Journal 97, 642–665.

Leibenstein, Harvey, 1948, Bandwagon, snob, and Veblen effects in theory of consumers' demand, Quarterly Journal of Economics, 165–201.

Long Ngo V. and Neil Vousden, 1987, Risk-averse rent seeking with shared rents, Economic Journal, 971–985.

Posner, Richard A., 1975, The social costs of monopoly and regulation, Journal of Political Economy 83, 807–827.

Sen, Amartya, 1983, Poor relatively speaking, Oxford Economic Papers 35, 153–169, July.

Takizawa, Matsuyo, 1927, The disintegration of the old family system, Chapter VII, from the penetration of money economy in Japan and its effects on social and political institutions (Columbia University Press, NY); Reprinted in Tribal and peasant economies, 1967 (University of Texas Press, Austin, TX).

Thompson, Earl, 1972, The taxation of wealth, American Economic Review 62, 329–330.

Thompson, Earl, 1974, Taxation and national defense, Journal of Political Economy 82, 755–782.

Tullock, Gordon, 1967, The welfare costs of tariffs, monopolies, and theft, Western Economic Journal 5, 224–232.

Tullock, Gordon, 1980, Efficient rent seeking, in: Buchanan et al., Towards a theory of the rent-seeking society, 97–112.

Vanberg, Victor, 1986, Spontaneous market order and social rules, Economics and Philosophy 2, 75–100.

Veblen, Thorstein, 1899/1953, The theory of the leisure class (Mentor Books, New York).

A Signaling Explanation for Charity

By Amihai Glazer and Kai A. Konrad *

The standard model of voluntary provision of public goods considers utility to be a function $u = u(x, G)$ of consumption of a private good x and of the sum of contributions to a public good G. Recent theoretical analyses derive the following properties of the Nash equilibrium. 1) In large economies only the very rich contribute to the public good (James Andreoni, 1988; Timothy L. Fries et al., 1991); the share of contributions in total income is negligible. 2) Governmental supply of the public good crowds out private supply. If all individuals donate in the original equilibrium this crowding out is complete (Peter G. Warr, 1982; B. Douglas Bernheim, 1986; Theodore C. Bergstrom et al., 1986).

These theoretical results conflict with empirical evidence on private charity. According to Arthur H. White (1989), nine out of ten Americans report giving, and many studies show that crowding out is only partial (Richard Steinberg, 1989). Such evidence led some theorists to suppose that donations enter directly into a person's utility function, that is, $u = u(x, g, G)$, where g is his donation (see, for example, Andreoni, 1989, 1990; Richard Cornes and Todd Sandler, 1984, 1994; Bruce R. Kingma, 1989; Robert McClelland, 1989; Russel D. Roberts, 1987; Sandler and John Posnett, 1991; Steinberg, 1986, 1987). In this warm-glow approach the act of giving directly enters the utility function (Kenneth J. Arrow, 1972).

We consider here an additional motive— the desire to demonstrate wealth, perhaps because individuals prefer to socialize with individuals of the same or higher social status. Though we suppose individuals seek to signal high absolute wealth, much of our analysis also applies when individuals signal relative wealth. Over a century ago John Rae (1834) and John S. Mill (1847) considered such a motive. The behavior of consumers who signal income is studied by other economists, and most elegantly in the work of Robert H. Frank (1984a, 1984b, 1985a, 1985b).

Though people may signal status by conspicuously consuming private goods, we do not think they will be used exclusively. First, conspicuous consumption may be banned by social norms[1] when charitable donations are not.[2] Second, ownership of luxury goods may be difficult to observe reliably. A consumer who wants to impress others may therefore buy a zirconium ring instead of a diamond one, an imitation Rolex watch instead of a genuine one, or may rent an expensive automobile for special occasions rather than incur the greater expense of purchasing one.[3] Such behavior can ruin the use of expensive goods as signals.

Third, charitable donations may be especially good signals to people who belong to a peer group but cannot see the big house or luxury car of another member. Impressing former college roommates who may live in other

* Glazer: Department of Economics, University of California, Irvine, CA 92717; Konrad: Department of Economics, Free University of Berlin, D-14195 Berlin, Germany. We are grateful for suggestions by Richard Cyert, Roger Gordon, Daniel Klein, Charles Lave, Kjell Erik Lommerud, Richard Romano, Larry Rothenberg, Herbert Simon, Stergios Skaperdas, and three anonymous referees. Glazer is grateful for the support of the Graduate School of Industrial Administration at Carnegie Mellon University.

[1] Anton Velleman (1900) gives a historical overview of laws forbidding consumption of luxury goods. Roger D. Congleton (1989) suggests that status seeking through charitable activities may be the result of an evolution towards status-seeking games with positive external effects.

[2] Donations and inter-vivos transfers to children may also signal income, and some of the conclusions on charitable donations may apply.

[3] This argument is loosely related to that of Bernheim (1991) and Laurie Simon Bagwell and Bernheim (1992) who show that agents may have to choose the more wasteful signal to generate separating.

1019

American Economic Review **86**, 1019–1028

parts of the world may require a notice in the alma mater's alumni magazine. Such contributions are large. In 1991 U.S. universities received $10.2 billion in voluntary support. Of this, $5 billion was from individuals, and of the $5 billion, $2.3 billion was from alumni. Thus, about one fourth of private support for higher education came from alumni (*Statistical Abstract of the United States,* 1993). Similarly, Britain's upper ten thousand find that London's charities provide perfect services in publicizing donations in a discreet but still observable way.[4,5] Thus, a person may want to signal income to several different peer groups. He may use conspicuous luxury consumption in some status games and may use donations to signal income to those who cannot see his consumption of luxury goods.

Fourth, when people receive a warm glow from charitable donations, the donations generate intrinsic utility like luxury goods do. If the rich have particularly strong warm-glow feelings then giving reveals high wealth. Some less rich but particularly status motivated people could then try to pool with this group of rich people by making donations. Thus, if warm glow is important to some persons, it can stimulate donations by persons who care little about warm glow but much about status.

Fifth, when at least some people make donations to increase the supply of a public good

---

[4] An example of publicity which is considered tasteful and that reveals the size of donations is the program of London's Royal Academy of Arts. They have 5 donation categories. Invitations to exclusive events are contingent on the donation category and membership cards (plain, bronze, silver, gold, gold and silver) reveal the participant's donation to the members of the peer group that self-select into the same social event.

[5] Jon Elster (1989, p. 52) expresses this view well: "Sometimes the motivating force [for contributions] seems to be the desire to give, and be known as giving, more than other donors. I was first struck by this motivation at the Art Institute in Chicago, where the size of the plaques honoring the donors is carefully adjusted to the size of the donation." Similarly, Derek Fraser (1984 p. 118) reports about charitable donations in the Victorian period in England: "Charitable activity was imbued with social snobbery and a royal patron could considerably enhance any society's prospects. The published subscription list was a very fruitful stimulus to increased contributions, as people could reflect smugly on their own offerings and scorn the parsimony of their neighbors."

(that is, when we observe private provision of a public good), then crowding out effects may make signaling of income by donations more effective than signaling by conspicuous consumption of private goods. To see how, recall that a central result in the standard game of private provision of a public good is that, with a large but finite group of possible contributors, and with homogeneous preferences, only those with incomes above a critical level contribute to the public good (Andreoni, 1988). Therefore, if initially only people who do not care about status make contributions, the contribution equilibrium would reveal income. Signaling can also appear for other observable goods, but the effect is more pronounced for private provision of a public good: rich peoples' donations crowd out the donations of the less wealthy. That is, any donations by people seeking status would cause a decline in donations by those who care only about provision of the public good. But the reduced donations occur not uniformly among initial donors, but instead among the least wealthy of them, thereby shifting upward the income distribution of donors. For some utility functions and distributions of wealth it is possible that a signaling equilibrium appears with donations to public goods, but not with purchases of private goods.

We will not model these interactions because we simplify matters by assuming infinitely many individuals: in our framework people have no motivation to contribute for the purpose of increasing provision of the public good. This allows us to show most clearly that status reasons for contributions can lead to excessive voluntary contributions.

The paper proceeds as follows. Section I gives evidence for status-motivated giving. Section II presents a fully revealing signaling game. Extensions of this model in Section III show that status-motivated giving can lead to excessive private provision of a public good and that the model applies to a very general concept of status preferences. Section IV concludes.

I. Empirical Evidence for Conspicuous Giving

The data on charitable giving support the hypothesis that donors donate at least partly for signaling purposes rather than only to aid

VOL. 86 NO. 4   GLAZER AND KONRAD: CHARITY AS SIGNAL   1021

the recipient or to obtain satisfactions unrelated to status.

Individuals who donate to signal their income will not make anonymous donations. In contrast, both the standard and the warm-glow models are consistent with anonymous donations. The data we collected show that anonymous donations are rare. Here are some examples. The Pittsburgh Philharmonic received 2,240 donations from individuals in 1991. Only 29 (1.29 percent) were anonymous. The fall 1991 *Yale Law Report* (sent to all alumni of Yale Law School) names donors to the Yale Law School Fund. Of the 1,950 entries, only four are anonymous. Incidentally, to ease the task of discovering which classmates donated how much, the names of donors are listed by graduation year in each category. Donations to Harvard Law School show the same pattern: donations are listed by size, and fewer than 1 percent of donations were anonymous. Similarly, in 1989–1990 Carnegie Mellon University received donations from 5,462 individuals. Only 14 (0.3 percent) were anonymous. Perusal of all reports by nonprofit organizations on file at the Pittsburgh Business Library found no institution with rates of anonymous donations higher than in these examples.

Donors may have several motivations for giving. The paucity of anonymous donations indicates that concern about status is one of them. We can further distinguish the motivations of individuals by examining semipublic donations—those where the names of donors are public, but where the amount each donated is only approximately inferable. Consider donations to the Cameron Clan at Carnegie Mellon University. The university's annual report names all people who gave between $500–$999, but does not separately report each donation amount. A person motivated solely by status who gives in this category should give exactly $500; a prediction the standard and warm-glow models do not make. The average gift in 1988–1989 was $525, which suggests that most gifts were very close to $500. Similar distributions appear in other categories. The 1993–1994 report of the Harvard Law School Fund shows the same pattern. For example, 980 people contributed in the category of $500–$999. Contributions of exactly $500

would constitute 93 percent of the total raised in this category.

Further analysis is possible with a smaller data set from a unit at Carnegie Mellon University which listed the dollar amount of each contribution. We find, for example, that of 82 contributions made in the range $1,000–$4,999, 56 (or 68 percent) were exactly $1,000. Also, people that give primarily for signaling purposes should be more likely to give a bit more than the minimum in a category rather than a bit less; no such motivation appears under the warm-glow and private-provision models. As one measure of such a bias, we tabulate the number of donations that lie within 10-percent above the minimum in a category, and the number that lie within 10-percent below the minimum of a category. We find, for example, that for the $1,000 minimum 17 people gave just above the minimum, while only 4 gave just below. Together with the 56 who exactly gave $1,000, this is 73 of 82 individuals in this category. Tabulations with different cutoffs yield similar results.

II. A Signaling Equilibrium

Though charitable organizations usually report donations within categories, thus not allowing perfect revelation, for analytical tractability we shall consider an equilibrium with perfect revelation and a continuum of types, as characterized in George J. Mailath (1987) and Norman J. Ireland (1994).[6]

Consider a set I of individuals $i \in I$. The income distribution is described by a density function $f(y)$ on the interval $[y_{min}, y_{max}]$; a consumer gets utility from a private good x_i consumption of which is unobservable, and from his income status. Status of individual i is determined by his signaled net income $\hat{y}_i - g_i$, defined as the belief by other individuals about i's income net of donations. This belief

---

[6] As in other models with signaling, multiple equilibria may exist. In particular, some belief functions lead to a pooling equilibrium with $g^*(y) \equiv 0$, some belief functions lead to partially revealing equilibria, and some different fully revealing equilibria arise if the distribution of income has discrete jumps.

Amihai Glazer and Kai A. Konrad

is derived from observable donations, g_i, to a charity. The utility function

$$(1) \qquad u^i = u(x_i, \hat{y}_i - g_i)$$

$$= v(x_i) + w(\hat{y}_i - g_i)$$

is the same for all individuals. It is twice differentiable. Marginal utility of each argument is strictly positive and decreasing. An individual gets no direct utility from aggregate donations to charity.[7] Each cares only about the signaling effect of his own donation. Also, we assume $u(y_i, y_{min}) > u(0, y_{max})$; nobody would ever want to donate all his income. The individual's budget constraint is

$$(2) \qquad y_i = x_i + g_i.$$

Income y_i is exogenous, and differs across individuals. Let g_i be observable or be made observable by the charitable institution, whereas x_i and y_i are not observable by others. Then beliefs about individual i's income is a function only of the observable donation, $\hat{y}_i = \hat{y}_i(g_i)$.

In our model the equilibrium is defined by individuals' choices of donations $g^*(y)$ as a function of their incomes, and by a strictly monotonic function of beliefs $\hat{y}_i(g_i)$ such that, for each i with income y_i, the vector $(y_i - g^*(y_i), \hat{y}_i(g^*(y_i)) - g^*(y_i))$ maximizes (1) subject to the budget constraint (2), to $g_i \geq 0$, $x_i \geq 0$, and subject to

$$(3) \qquad \hat{y}_i(g^*(y_i)) = y_i,$$

that is, beliefs are correct in the equilibrium. Strict monotonicity of the belief function and of $g^*(y)$ in combination with (3) makes the equilibrium a fully revealing equilibrium.

PROPOSITION 1: *A perfectly revealing equilibrium exists.*

---

[7] If individuals also get intrinsic utility from making donations, we could add a "warm-glow" element to our model. The extension would not invalidate our analysis; the warm-glow model would become a special case—one in which status signaling is absent. But to work out the new aspects of the signaling approach it is more useful to concentrate on the element that is distinct from the warm-glow model.

The proof is in the Appendix. Some properties of the equilibrium are as follows.

PROPERTY 1: *A replication of the economy has no effect on any individual's donation* $g^*(y_i)$.

PROPERTY 2: *Let government fund a charity providing a public good, and let revenue for this funding be raised by a lump-sum tax that does not change the support of the income distribution. Then crowding out is partial.*

PROPERTY 3: *Income redistribution among donors is generically not neutral. If $g^*(y)$ is convex (concave), then an income redistribution that reduces income inequality but does not change y_{min} reduces (increases) donations. The function*

$$(4) \qquad g^*(y) \text{ is concave if and only if}$$

$$[(-v''/v') - (-w''/w')] < 0.$$

PROPERTY 4: *Assume that poor people are added to a population such that the support of incomes increases from $[y_{min}, y_{max}]$ to $[y_{min} - \theta, y_{max}]$, with $\theta > 0$. Then in the new equilibrium the original donors make higher donations.*

Proofs of these properties are in the Appendix.

The crowding-out properties of our model, as given by Property 2, are the same as in the warm-glow model (see Andreoni, 1989 p. 1453): both models predict less than perfect crowding out. Empirical results show that crowding out depends—among other things—on the type of charity that receives governmental contributions (Steinberg [1989] surveys studies of crowding out). The differing relevance of the signaling approach for different types of charities may partially account for this fact.

Properties 3 and 4 most notably distinguish our approach from other models. The relations between the convexity of $g^*(y)$, income redistribution, and aggregate contributions, and between the support of the income distribution and aggregate donations are specific to our signaling model.[8] Property 3 can be rephrased:

---

[8] For a related result in a different model see Frank (1985a p. 105).

suppose that $(-v''/v') < (-w''/w')$. Individuals are less "risk averse" with respect to utility from intrinsic consumption, $v(y_i - g_i)$, than with respect to utility from signaling income, $w(\hat{y}_i - g_i)$. Then a mean-preserving spread reduces per capita contributions.[9] Property 4 considers a situation in which the smallest possible income becomes smaller: donations for any given income increase. If lower-income individuals enter the group, all other individuals contribute more.

Though we do not have the data to test the effects of additional consumers on donations, the prediction does have empirical applications. For signaling wealth, people will make donations only when income in the community is heterogeneous. If, for example, everyone at a university has the same income after graduation, then none will make any donations as alumni. A university may be able to elicit greater aggregate contributions by increasing the heterogeneity of its student body. This can motivate a university to give scholarships to the middle class: they may increase future donations by rich alumni.[10] Similarly, management of some clubs may want to provide lower fees to poorer members (without making public the incomes of such members). The increased heterogeneity of members may make each more willing to signal his income by donating to that club.

We now turn to considering a subsidy for donations.

PROPERTY 5: *Suppose government subsidizes individuals' donations g_i with a proportional subsidy rate, that is, if an individual spends a dollar on the public good, government reimburses the fraction $\alpha/(1 + \alpha)$. Let* the subsidy be financed by exogenous sources or by a reduction of the government's direct contributions to the public good. Then each individual contributes $g^{**}(y) = (1 + \alpha)g^*(y)$ in the new signaling equilibrium.

For the proof see the Appendix.

In the warm-glow model, a dollar spent on subsidies stimulates charity more than does a dollar of direct grants (Andreoni, 1990 p. 470).[11] Intuitively, with matching grants, an additional dollar on public goods buys more of the public good, and, hence yields higher marginal utility. In the signaling model matching grants reduce the signaling value of an increased donation: the cost of each dollar donation is reduced to $1/(1 + \alpha)$, so that a donor who wants to generate an equivalently strong signal as without reimbursement, must make a gross contribution of $(1 + \alpha)$.

Property 5 has some implications. First, if government finances the matching grants by reducing its funding for the public good, then the per capita provision of the public good in the economy is unchanged. Second, private contributions net of reimbursement are independent of α, provided that the government finances the matching grants in a way that does not affect the individuals' own budgets.

III. Extensions

The results in this paper can be extended in different ways.

A) Suppose the donations are used to provide a public good, Γ, which is a function $\Gamma = \Gamma(\bar{g}, I)$, where I is the set of individuals normalized to the unit interval, and $\bar{g}$ is the per capita donation,[12]

$$(5) \qquad \Gamma(\bar{g}, I) = \Gamma\left(\int_{i \in I} g_i \, di, I\right).$$

---

[9] Condition (4) is identical with a condition in Konrad and Kjell Erik Lommerud (1993) that determines whether status seeking leads to excessive insurance demand and is discussed there.

[10] Students, however, prefer a college with uniformity among themselves because they save on donations later. Heterogeneity increases future contributions of a given set of students, but reduces rich families' willingness to pay for an education at this college. Whether a college will actively increase heterogeneity depends on which of these effects is stronger, which, in turn, depends on the market power of colleges.

[11] Andreoni and Bergstrom (1992) show in the standard model that whether matching grants induce higher contributions depends on whether the government chooses a clever tax scheme for financing these grants. If not, neutrality of matching grants may indeed apply.

[12] This way of modeling a public good in an economy with an uncountable set of individuals is borrowed from Jean-Jacques Laffont (1975) who uses this setup to model a macroeconomic externality.

Let the public good enter the utility function in an additively separable way: $u^i = v(x_i) + w(\hat{y}_i - g_i) + z(\Gamma)$. In (5) $d\bar{g}/dg_i = 0$ and, therefore, $d\Gamma/dg_i = 0$, since a single individual has zero measure. This fact together with additive separability implies that the term $z(\Gamma)$ does not affect donation behavior. Accordingly, in the signaling equilibrium Γ is strictly positive, but may be larger or smaller than the socially optimal level.

How does this extended model relate to the standard model in which concern for income status is absent? To consider a continuum of contributors we had to use Laffont's description of a public good as in (5), and we need to compare our results to a modified standard model that applies a similar description of the public good. With a finite number, n, of contributors, the analogue to (5) has utility depend on private consumption and on $\Gamma \equiv (1/n)G = \sum_{i=1}^{n} g_i/n$. For this modified standard model, if n is constant, the results concerning existence and uniqueness of equilibrium, redistribution neutrality and perfect crowding out are identical to those in the standard model. For the modified standard model, where we can speak of $n \to \infty$, the sum of contributions converges to zero. Hence in both the standard model and in the modified standard model, contributions are an infinitesimally small share in aggregate expenditure if the number of possible contributors is large. In our model, in contrast, charitable contributions can constitute a significant share of expenditures.

In the warm-glow model, the "warm glow" of giving yields an additional private incentive to donate. However, in the warm-glow equilibrium a joint increase in donations by all individuals that makes everyone better-off is always feasible. The effect of additional donations on welfare is ambiguous in our signaling model: the negative externalities of status signaling via donations have to be weighed against the positive externalities of donations. The outcome can be under-provision or over-provision of the public good.

B) Suppose that individuals are interested in signaling not a high absolute income, but instead a high relative income. The utility function is then the functional

(6) $\quad u^i = v(x_i) + w(\hat{y}_i - g_i, F(y - g))$,

where $F(y - g)$ describes the aggregate distribution of net income. How does this change our results?

Proposition 1 holds without change. Taxes and redistribution of income, however, usually change $F(y - g)$. As a result, $g^*(y)$ may (but need not) change as $\partial w/\partial(\hat{y}_i - g_i)$ changes. If, for example, utility is affected only by properties of $F(y - g)$ that do not vary with income redistribution,[13] then most of the properties of Section II hold. That is, the results can apply when individuals care about relative rather than about absolute status.

IV. Discussion

This paper examines a novel but plausible motive for charitable giving. Charitable donations which are observable can signal wealth or income. The signaling equilibrium of charitable donations has attractive properties. Donations increase proportionally with population size. Governmental funding for public goods affects private charity only through an income effect. Crowding out need not be complete. Income redistribution is generically nonneutral. Increasing the spread between the poorest and richest person in a community tends to increase private donations.

Our theory is based on the assumption that people are willing to make charitable donations even if they will not increase provision of the public good. Why then do the organizations receiving these donations provide any service at all? An answer is given in our model. We assume that donors want others to know about their donation. In other words, a consumer is more willing to donate to an organization the more likely is the intended audience to hear about that donation. Successful organizations must therefore attract many patrons. A good orchestra will have its published program read by more people, and will therefore give a wider audience to the names of its donors published in that program. Thus, though we do not require organizations to provide services with the money they raise, mar-

---

[13] This is frequently assumed in the literature on status seeking, and is particularly true when relative income is defined as a function of one's income and of others' average income (see, for example, Richard Layard, 1980).

VOL. 86 NO. 4   *GLAZER AND KONRAD: CHARITY AS SIGNAL*   1025

ket forces lead them to provide services. Under the standard view of private provision of a public good, consumers should prefer to donate to organizations with low costs of raising money. Yet we observe that many successful nonprofit organizations have high fund-raising costs. In our model this is understandable to the extent that such fund-raising activities publicize the amounts donated by others. Dinners, benefit concerts, and promotional literature can fall into this category.

APPENDIX

PROOF OF PROPOSITION 1:

It is sufficient to show that a belief function $\hat{y}_i(g_i)$ exists that is one-to-one, and a donation function $g^*(y)$ exists, such that: i) for any individual with income $y_i \in [y_{min}, y_{max}]$ the value $g^*(y_i)$ solves the problem of maximizing (1) globally subject to the belief function; ii) $g^*(y)$ is one-to-one; iii) $g^*(y_i)$ is feasible [that is, $g^*(y_i) \in [0, y_i] \,\forall y_i$]; and iv) $g^*(y_i)$ fulfills $\hat{y}_i(g^*(y_i)) = y_i$.

We try the following belief solution. Let $\hat{y}_i(g_i)$ be the definite solution of the first-order differential equation[14]

$$\text{(A1)} \quad \hat{y}_i'(g_i) = \frac{v'(\hat{y}_i(g_i) - g_i)}{w'(\hat{y}_i(g_i) - g_i)} + 1$$

$$\equiv \phi(\hat{y}_i(g_i), g_i)$$

with the initial condition $\hat{y}_i(0) = y_{min}$. This belief function is strictly increasing. Hence, $\hat{y}_i(g_i)$ is one-to-one. The function has finite slope $\phi > 1$ as $\infty > v' > 0$ and $\infty > w' > 0$ is assumed. Further,

$$\text{(A2)} \quad \hat{y}_i''(g_i)$$

$$= \frac{v''(\hat{y}_i - g_i) \times w'(\hat{y}_i - g_i)}{(w'(\hat{y}_i - g_i))^2} \times (\hat{y}_i' - 1)$$

$$- \frac{v'(\hat{y}_i - g_i) \times w''(\hat{y}_i - g_i)}{(w'(\hat{y}_i - g_i))^2} \times (\hat{y}_i' - 1).$$

Consider the inverse of the belief function $\hat{y}_i(g_i)$; call it $g^*(y)$. By the slope ϕ in (A1), this inverse exists with $g^*(y_{min}) = 0$ and slope $0 < g^{*\prime} < 1$. We show that $g^*(y)$ fulfills i), ii), iii) and iv).

If individuals with income y_i choose $g^*(y_i)$ then iv) is fulfilled by definition of $g^*(y_i)$. The slope $0 < g^{*\prime} < 1$ implies ii). For iii), by construction, $g^*(y_{min}) = 0$. Further, $0 < g^{*\prime} < 1$ for all $y_i \in (y_{min}, y_{max}]$, and, hence, $0 \leq g^*(y_i) < y_i$.

It remains to show that the individuals' choice of $g^*(y_i)$ yields a unique global maximum of utility. Individual i's choice of $g^*(y_i)$ fulfills i's first-order condition

$$\text{(A3)} \quad -v'(y_i - g_i) + (\hat{y}_i'(g_i) - 1)$$

$$\times w'(\hat{y}_i(g_i) - g_i) = 0,$$

since for the choice $g^*(y_i)$, we get $y_i = \hat{y}_i$ and, hence (A3) becomes identical with (A1). The second-order condition for a local maximum is also fulfilled:[15] using (A1) and (A2) we obtain

$$\text{(A4)} \quad \frac{d^2u^i}{(dg_i)^2_{|y_i = \hat{y}_i}} = v''(\hat{y}_i - g_i)$$

$$\times \hat{y}_i'(g_i) < 0.$$

Further, $g^*(y_i)$ is the only local maximum for the given belief function $\hat{y}_i(g_i)$ that is implicitly defined in (A1): suppose for some y_i that some other $\tilde{g}(y_i) \neq g^*(y_i)$ fulfills (A3). Then, by (A1),

$$-v'(y_i - \tilde{g}(y_i)) + w'(\hat{y}_i(\tilde{g}(y_i)) - \tilde{g}(y_i))$$

$$\times [\hat{y}_i'(\tilde{g}(y_i)) - 1] = -v'(y_i - \tilde{g}(y_i))$$

$$+ w'(\hat{y}_i(\tilde{g}(y_i)) - \tilde{g}(y_i))$$

$$\times \frac{v'(\hat{y}_i(\tilde{g}(y_i)) - \tilde{g}(y_i))}{w'(\hat{y}_i(\tilde{g}(y_i)) - \tilde{g}(y_i))} = 0$$

---

[14] The global solution of the first-order differential equation in (A1) exists and is unique for a given initial value since, in particular, $(\hat{y}_i(g_i), g_i)$ is differentiable with respect to $\hat{y}_i$ (Heinrich Behnke et al., 1962 pp. 302, 316).

[15] The discussion of sufficiency of the first-order condition below relates to the single-crossing property in Mailath (1987).

or,

$$v'(y_i - \tilde{g}(y_i)) = v'(\hat{y}_i(\tilde{g}(y_i)) - \tilde{g}(y_i)),$$

or,

$$y_i = \hat{y}_i(\tilde{g}(y_i)),$$

or

$$\tilde{g}(y_i) = g^*(y_i).$$

Finally, this unique local maximum is also the global maximum. To confirm this we have to check the corner solutions. It follows from $u(y_i, y_{min}) > u(0, y_{max})$ that $g_i = y_i$ is not a maximum. Except for $y_i = y_{min}$ for which $g^*(y_{min}) = 0$ is also the interior maximum, $g_i = 0$ is also not a maximum. To confirm this we note that $du^i/dg_i = 0$ at $g_i = 0$ and $y_i = y_{min}$, and $d^2u^i/(dg_i dy_i) = -v''(y_i) > 0$.

PROOF OF PROPERTIES 1–5:

Property 1 follows from the fact that donations $g^*(y_i)$ depend on y_{min} but not on the size of I.

For Property 2 note first that governmental contributions have no effect on $g^*(y)$. Hence, if government contributes some amount (c) and finances this by a lump-sum tax that is imposed on some individual i such that i's income becomes $y_i - c > y_{min}$, this individual reduces his contributions by $\Delta g_i = g^*(y_i) - g^*(y_i - c)$. Crowding out is partial because $g^{*\prime} < 1$.

Moreover, Δg_i differs for different initial incomes y_i, and is a decreasing (increasing) function of income y_i if $g^*(y)$ is concave (convex). This yields the intuition for Property 3: consider redistributing some amount c from i to j, with $y_{min} < y_j < y_j + c < y_i - c < y_i \le y_{max}$. This redistribution reduces donations if and only if $(d/dy)(g^*(y_i)) > (d/dy)(g^*(y_j))$. Hence, a sufficient condition for a redistribution of income, that reduces income inequality (in the sense of a mean-preserving contraction) to reduce donations, is that $g^*(y)$ be convex. Further, $g' = w'/(v' + w')$ by (A1), and hence $g'' = (w''v' - v''w')/(v' + w')^2$ which is negative if and only if $(w''/w') < (v''/v')$.

To prove Property 4 consider an initial distribution of incomes on the support $[y_{min}, y_{max}]$. Add a set of consumers with incomes $[y_{min} - \theta, y_{max}]$ where $\theta > 0$. This changes $g^*(y)$ to $g^{**}(y)$, the inverse of the solution of (A1) for the initial condition $\hat{y}_i(0) = (y_{min} - \theta)$. Hence, the new solution has $g^{**}(y_i) > g^*(y_i)$ for all $y_i \in [y_{min}, y_{max}]$.

Finally we prove Property 5. Consider the new belief function $\hat{y}_i$ with $\hat{y}_i((1 + \alpha)g_i) = \hat{y}_i(g_i)$. Without subsidy, $g^*(y_i)$ fulfilled the first-order condition (A3). Given the subsidy, the new maximization problem is to maximize $v(y_i - g_i/(1 + \alpha)) + w(\hat{y}_i(g_i) - g_i/(1 + \alpha))$ and yields a first-order condition $-v' - w' + (1 + \alpha)w'\hat{y}_i' = -v' - w' + w'\hat{y}_i' = 0$ that is fulfilled for $g^{**}(y_i) = (1 + \alpha)g^*(y_i)$, since this choice yields

$$(A5) \quad x_i = y_i - g^{**}(y_i) + \frac{\alpha}{1 + \alpha} g^{**}(y_i)$$

$$= y_i - g^*(y_i)$$

and signaled net income

$$(A6) \quad \hat{y}_i(g_i^{**}) - g_i^{**}(y_i) + \frac{\alpha}{1 + \alpha} g_i^{**}(y_i)$$

$$= \hat{y}_i(g^*(y_i)) - g^*(y_i).$$

REFERENCES

Andreoni, James. "Privately Provided Public Goods in a Large Economy: The Limits of Altruism." *Journal of Public Economics*, February 1988, *35*(1), pp. 57–73.

———. "Giving with Impure Altruism: Applications to Charity and Ricardian Equivalence." *Journal of Political Economy*, December 1989, *97*(6), pp. 1447–58.

———. "Impure Altruism and Donations to Public Goods: A Theory of Warm-Glow Giving." *Economic Journal*, June 1990, *100*(401), pp. 464–77.

Andreoni, James and Bergstrom, Theodore C. "Do Government Subsidies Increase the Private Supply of Public Goods?" Working

Paper No. 9207, University of Wisconsin–Madison, February 1992.

Arrow, Kenneth J. "Gifts and Exchanges." *Philosophy and Public Affairs*, Summer 1972, *1*(4), pp. 343–62.

Bagwell, Laurie Simon and Bernheim, B. Douglas. "Conspicuous Consumption, Pure Profits, and the Luxury Tax." National Bureau of Economic Research (Cambridge, MA) Working Paper No. 4163, September 1992.

Behnke, Heinrich; Bachmann, Friedrich; Fladt, Kuno and Süss, Wilhelm. *Grundzüge der mathematik, Vol. 3: Analysis*. Göttingen: Vandenhoeck and Ruprecht, 1962.

Bergstrom, Theodore C.; Blume, Lawrence and Varian, Hal. "On the Private Provision of Public Goods." *Journal of Public Economics*, February 1986, *29*(1), pp. 25–49.

Bernheim, B. Douglas. "On the Voluntary and Involuntary Provision of Public Goods." *American Economic Review*, September 1986, *76*(4), pp. 789–93.

_____. "Tax Policy and the Dividend Puzzle." *RAND Journal of Economics*, Winter 1991, *22*(4), pp. 455–76.

Congleton, Roger D. "Efficient Status Seeking: Externalities, and the Evolution of Status Games." *Journal of Economic Behavior and Organization*, March 1989, *11*(2), pp. 175–90.

Cornes, Richard and Sandler, Todd. "Easy Riders, Joint Production, and Public Goods." *Economic Journal*, September 1984, *94*(375), pp. 580–98.

_____. "The Comparative Static Properties of the Impure Public Good Model." *Journal of Public Economics*, July 1994, *54*(3), pp. 403–21.

Elster, Jon. *Nuts and bolts for the social sciences*. Cambridge: Cambridge University Press, 1989.

Frank, Robert H. "Interdependent Preferences and the Competitive Wage Structure." *RAND Journal of Economics*, Winter 1984a, *15*(4), pp. 510–20.

_____. "Are Workers Paid Their Marginal Products?" *American Economic Review*, September 1984b, *74*(4), pp. 549–71.

_____. "The Demand for Unobservable and Other Nonpositional Goods." *American Economic Review*, March 1985a, *75*(1), pp. 101–16.

_____. *Choosing the right pond, human behavior and the quest for status*. Oxford: Oxford University Press, 1985b.

Fraser, Derek. *Evolution of the British welfare state*. London: MacMillan, 1984.

Fries, Timothy L.; Golding, Edward and Romano, Richard E. "Private Provision of Public Goods and the Failure of the Neutrality Property in Large Finite Economies." *International Economic Review*, February 1991, *32*(1), pp. 147–57.

Ireland, Norman J. "On Limiting the Market for Status Signals." *Journal of Public Economics*, January 1994, *53*(1), pp. 91–110.

Kingma, Bruce Robert. "An Accurate Measurement of the Crowd-Out Effect, Income Effect, and Price Effect for Charitable Contributions." *Journal of Political Economy*, October 1989, *97*(5), pp. 1197–207.

Konrad, Kai A. and Lommerud, Kjell Erik. "Relative Standing Comparisons, Risk Taking, and Safety Regulations." *Journal of Public Economics*, July 1993, *51*(3), pp. 345–58.

Laffont, Jean-Jacques. "Macroeconomic Constraints, Economic Efficiency and Ethics: An Introduction to Kantian Economics." *Economica*, November 1975, *42*(4), pp. 430–37.

Layard, Richard. "Human Satisfactions and Public Policy." *Economic Journal*, December 1980, *90*(360), pp. 737–50.

Mailath, George J. "Incentive Compatibility in Signalling Games with a Continuum of Types." *Econometrica*, November 1987, *55*(6), pp. 1349–65.

McClelland, Robert. "Voluntary Donations and Public Expenditures in a Federalist System, Comment and Extension." *American Economic Review*, December 1989, *79*(5), pp. 1291–96.

Mill, John S. *Principles of political economy*. London: Longmans, Green and Co., 1847/1911.

Rae, John. *The sociological theory of capital*. London: MacMillan, 1834.

Roberts, Russel D. "Financing Public Goods." *Journal of Political Economy*, April 1987, *95*(2), pp. 420–37.

Sandler, Todd and Posnett, John. "The Private Provision of Public Goods: A Perspective on Neutrality." *Public Finance Quarterly*, January 1991, *19*(1), pp. 22–42.

The statistical abstract of the United States. Washington, DC: Government Printing Office, 1993.

Steinberg, Richard. "Charitable Giving as a Mixed Public/Private Good: Implications for Tax Policy." *Public Finance Quarterly,* October 1986, *14*(4), pp. 415–31.

———. "Voluntary Donations and Public Expenditures in a Federalist System." *American Economic Review,* March 1987, *77*(1), pp. 24–36.

———. "The Theory of Crowding Out: Donations, Local Government Spending, and the 'New Federalism'," in Richard Magat, ed., *Philanthropic giving.* Oxford: Oxford University Press, 1989, pp. 143–56.

Velleman, Anton. "Der Luxus in seinen Beziehungen zur Sozialökonomie, II. Teil: Die volkswirtschaftspolitische und finanzielle Behandlung der Luxuskonsumption." *Zeitschrift für die Gesamte Staatswissenschaft,* September 1900, *56*(3), pp. 498–549.

Warr, Peter G. "Pareto Optimal Redistribution and Private Charity." *Journal of Public Economics,* October 1982, *19*(1), pp. 131–38.

White, Arthur H. "Patterns of Giving," in Richard Magat, ed., *Philanthropic giving.* Oxford: Oxford University Press, 1989, pp. 65–71.

Yale Law Report, Fall 1991, *38*(1), pp. 37–69.

KYKLOS, Vol. 55 – 2002 – Fasc. 3, 335–360

Competition for Sainthood and the Millennial Church

Mario Ferrero*

I. INTRODUCTION

The Roman Catholic Church is certainly foremost among the few human institutions that have proven able to survive and thrive for over a millennium. This plain fact in itself invites analysis, given the paucity of like examples. One might note that most of the other millennial institutions in existence are themselves churches or organized religions, testifying to the endurance of religious sentiment across human history. Yet the Catholic Church is unique among religions in the degree of centralization of belief and behavior, a centralization which seems to have steadily increased to this day; and given the extent and intensity of the challenges it has had to withstand by contestants and competitors from within and without over the centuries, the church's apparent prosperity as it enters its third millennium is all the more puzzling. To the believer, such a remarkable accomplishment will simply be testimony to the fact that the church embodies the Truth, which is bound to prevail over error. But to the scholar committed to the paradigm of rational choice it raises the question of how the church has been able to overcome the tendencies to ossification and decay that seem to be inherent in all centralized institutions in the course of time. Judging by Iannaccone's (1998) thorough survey, such a basic question seems not to have been asked in the young but burgeoning field of economics of religion. This paper is a first attempt to address the question. In a nutshell, our approach is to view the church as a bureaucracy of salvation, and to look for the inner

* Department of Public Policy and Public Choice (POLIS), University of Eastern Piedmont, Corso Borsalino 50, 15 100 Alessandria, Italy, e-mail: ferrerom@sp.unipmn.it. An earlier draft of this paper was presented at a panel on Public Choice and the Millennium in the annual meeting of the European Public Choice Society, Siena, 26–29 April, 2000, whose participants provided interesting discussion. The author is particularly indebted to George Akerlof, Vani Borooah, Alberto Cassone, Joan Delaney Grossman, Gregory Grossman, Ronald Wintrobe, Robert Young, and a referee of this Journal for useful comments and suggestions. The revised version was completed while the author was visiting professor at the Department of Economics of the University of California at Berkeley, whose support is gratefully acknowledged.

335

competitive elements that alone can keep a bureaucracy going. Among these competitive elements, we will focus exclusively on one central mechanism: the competition for sainthood, which sets the church apart from all other churches, including those which also have a cult of saints of sorts. The cult of saints, and the mechanism through which it is sanctioned and promoted by the church, is here arranged competitively in a way analogous to a rent-seeking contest, and this, we submit, is one of the mainsprings of the continuing supply of participation and militancy 'from the bottom up' that counters bureaucratic inertia and pushes the organization forward. While we make no claim that this is the only rational explanation to the puzzle of the church's continuing prosperity, Catholic saint-making clearly is sufficiently important to warrant close analysis.

The paper is organized as follows. Section II sketches out the background view of the church as a centralizing bureaucracy. Section III surveys the essentials of the saints' cult and the canonization procedure as it has been evolving with time. Section IV offers an interpretation of saintly competition as an incentive mechanism that makes the bureaucracy efficient in the pursuit of its own goals, and provides supporting statistical evidence from the sociology of canonizations. Section V offers an instructive comparison with another centralizing bureaucracy which embodies a competition for sainthood, a communist regime. The final Section concludes.

II. BACKGROUND: THE CATHOLIC CHURCH AS A BUREAUCRACY

It took a very long time and a protracted struggle for the Catholic Church to become the centralized institution that we know today[1]. It began as a diffuse network of local communities, and even after becoming the official religion of both the Western and Eastern Roman Empires in the fourth century A. D., it remained a loose constellation of local dioceses, making collective decisions on matters of doctrine and behavior through periodic general councils of bishops. The pope, who was then just the bishop of Rome, was slow to gain predominance and finally to secure the unquestioned authority that we know today. Basic features of the church which we now take for granted – such as the papal

---

1. For modern historical accounts of the Catholic Church the reader is referred to the classic work of Hughes (1952), which carries the reader up to the outbreak of the Reformation, and to his compendium volume (Hughes 1967) which brings the story up to our day. Another useful summary is Holmes and Bickers (1983). Latourette (1953) is especially detailed on the political and territorial implications.

336

COMPETITION FOR SAINTHOOD AND THE MILLENNIAL CHURCH

appointment of bishops, the papal control over monastic and other orders, the celibacy of the clergy, the infallibility of the pope on theological matters, the designation of saints (on which more below), a geography of the afterlife crucially including the Purgatory (Le Goff 1981), and the promulgation and enforcement of rules of good Christian conduct for the laity (Bossy 1970, 1975, 1983, 1988) – took centuries to be firmly established. Thus the history of the church can be read as an unbroken, though wavering, trend toward increasing centralization of both decision-making and implementation control.

From a different angle, the growth and consolidation of the church can be seen as a continuing struggle for effective territorial monopoly over religious affairs. From the beginning, decisions were based on the rule of unanimity: one is not supposed to vote over truth, so agreement over the content and implications of divine revelation must be reached by unanimous consent, after which obedience to official rulings is mandatory – even if the pope's vote came to be the decisive one in councils. Thus the church never allowed the kind of pluralism, or coexistence of alternative interpretations of the Book, that occurs in the Jewish or the Islamic religions among others. Nor was coexistence with nonchristian religions ever allowed: the Gospel is for all of mankind, superseding all previous or subsequent doctrines. Therefore the church was from the beginning engaged in active missionary activity on the outward boundaries of Christendom. In both endeavors, it found it essential to rely on the coercive power of the state. Thus the church was bent on stamping out dissident or unruly behavior, branded as heresy and handled by the Inquisition, from inside its domain through the end of the Middle Ages and beyond, and on mass conversion of nonchristian peoples wherever its arm could reach. The church's monopolistic drive was stalled for a time when in the XVI century a number of heretics, unlike their forerunners, were able to secure sanctuary or active endorsement from princes and kings: there followed the Protestant Reformation, a time of lively competition entailing, however, a century of civil strife and regular warfare across Europe. The turning point was the treaty of Westphalia (1648), which ended the Thirty Years War and established between Catholics and Protestants the principle *cuius regio eius religio*, i.e., one's religion is to be that of the sovereign ruling the territory of one's abode. Thus the church forsook all claims to the lands lost to the Reformation in exchange for exclusive monopoly rights over the Catholic countries; and this territorial principle naturally extended to the overseas possessions of European powers. From then on, the church's control, though curtailed in space, became pervasive and unchallenged as never before in its homelands, at least until the rise of secular social movements, such as the liberal bourgeoisie and later the socialist working class, began to unravel the tangle of church and state.

337

MARIO FERRERO

In the modern era, then, the church emerges from centuries of struggle as almost a textbook example of a Weberian-type bureaucracy[2]. It has effectively suppressed competition of all kinds in its domain, both for the field and within the field (Demsetz 1968). On a formal level, it is organized as a rigidly hierarchical, territorially-based bureaucracy: the parishes at the bottom, next the dioceses, then the national diocesan synods (councils), and finally the papacy at the peak. It is not a democracy: unanimity rule prevails at all levels and peaks at the Vatican's doorstep where only the pope has the power to override any decision or rule except his predecessors' formal rulings (because they were infallible). Subject to the pope's formally unconstrained authority, subordinates at all levels, called the 'secular' clergy, are expected not to argue over, or to interpret, but stricly to carry out orders. Positive rewards for loyal and effective behavior are extremely slim: the enormous venality and corruption of the later Middle Ages that almost turned the church into a profit-seeking business and sparked the Reformation was effectively curbed after the Council of Trent, so about the only reward is promotion to higher ranks, which is awarded from above. But given the ratio of positions at adjoining levels, the chances for the average priest ever to become a bishop are next to insignificant. Obedience therefore is enforced almost entirely through penalties, which may range from admonition up to full loss of clerical status. No wonder then that the performance of the average clergyman has hardly lived up to the paragon of Christian virtues[3]. Outside the secular hierarchy, on the other hand, there mushrooms a sundry world of religious orders and lay organizations, such as Marian congregations, confraternities, devotional groups, and others, which channel and organize the efforts of zealots and militants. These bodies are usually not entrusted with the burden of ministering to the general needs of a territorial section of the populace and are therefore freer to specialize in their own chosen inclinations, subject, however, to strict supervision over doctrinal orthodoxy and propriety of behavior and to the ultimate discipline of the official hierarchy.

This summary description of the clerical bureaucracy, however, naturally invites the question: where is the motive power that keeps the organization run-

---

2. A comprehensive description and insightful discussion of church structure and operation is McKenzie (1969). See also his short, excellent chapter on saints, called the church's 'finest product' (p. 227), which broadly supports our general approach.
3. As Italian parents have been instructing their children from time immemorial, 'always do as the priest says, never do as the priest does'. Such a glaring gap between principle and practice in the secular clergy has of course been a major item of criticism from Protestant quarters ever since the Reformation; but even such a residual competitive pressure is being now muted by the ecumenical drive towards collusion of all churches that Pope John Paul II is so actively promoting and that many, though not all, Protestant denominations seem to welcome.

338

COMPETITION FOR SAINTHOOD AND THE MILLENNIAL CHURCH

ning? Modern bureaucratic theory teaches us that no bureaucracy can carry on for long by simply giving and taking orders: private incentives to subordinates, formal or informal, are needed as much as punishments or repression to elicit loyal behavior in the organization's best interests. In other words, there has to be some competitive pressure to breathe life and motion into a hierarchical organization, which would otherwise be bound to ossify and collapse. The Catholic Church has arranged the main avenues of competition not within and through the secular clergy but alongside it, in the parallel world of the so-called 'regular' clergy and the lesser or non-clerical organizations alluded to above[4]. These organizations, specializing in specific virtues or worthy pursuits, have always been a field of free competitive enterprise, escaping the narrow bounds of clerical routine (Chatellier 1989). Nowhere is this competitive entrepreneurship more evident than in the cult of saints and the competition for saintliness, to which we now turn.

III. FROM THE CULT OF SAINTS TO THE CONTEST FOR SAINTHOOD

Today, and in the modern Catholic church generally, saintliness is not a title of virtue that comes by degrees, nor is it a matter for argument or subjective evaluation: sainthood is an official status granted to a dead person by the pope alone upon completion of a formal procedure of evaluation by a central body of the church. This yields an official list of persons who alone are entitled to a public cult, i.e., a cult performed by an ordained cleric of the church on its behalf (private cults of other saintly individuals are always allowed). But it has not always been so[5].

---

4. This is official church terminology, somewhat at variance with everyday language. Secular refers to a priest who lives in the world (*saeculum*) as opposed to a person who lives secluded in a monastery – the only two options available until the XII century. A regular is a person belonging to an order and bound by the order's rule (*regula*), who may now also live in the world as countless noncloistered orders have sprung up since the XIII century. So the seculars make up the official church hierarchy. The regulars, on the other hand, may or may not be ordained priests: all members of female orders obviously are not, and many males also are not, or not yet, ordained depending on the particular order's rule and the nature of the vows taken. A priest is a man whom the church empowers to hold the mass, give out the Eucharist, and minister the penance.
5. The information given in this section, and many hints that support the interpretation offered in the next section, are based on Delooz (1969, 1983), Brown (1981), Weinstein and Bell (1982), Wilson (1983), and Woodward (1996). The last mentioned work is a highly readable, yet thoroughly researched, first-hand account by a journalist who managed to worm his way into the saint-makers' offices in the Vatican.

339

The cult of saints was from the beginning a feature that sharply distinguished the Christian faith from the polytheism of the ancient world. In the Early Church the saints were the martyrs, those who had given their lives for the faith during the Roman persecutions. To these soon began to be added holy persons of various sorts who had escaped the wordly goods to pursue spiritual perfection. These saints' shrines and relics attracted the spontaneous devotion of the people who thought that various benefits flowed from their physical proximity, ranging from miracles to the cure of illnesses to protection from evil forces and misfortune. With these visits and pilgrimages came donations, alms, and legacies. The clergy, both secular and regular, were quick to learn the lesson and try to secure a share of the available shrines to their location; thus the late Antiquity and early Middle Ages were marked by frequent 'translations' of shrines and relics across the Mediterranean and the Frankish and Hiberian territories, as each diocese and abbey tried to secure possession of them and thereby enhance its prestige among the faithful, its influence and material wealth (Brown 1981). However, there was nothing even remotely resembling a formalized canonization procedure. Basically, saints were either inherited from the past and sanctioned by a tradition of popular worship, or designated by a local community who had known them to be blessed and virtuous in life and believed them to be able to work miracles and other benefits after death. In the course of time the bishops were ever more frequently called in to ratify and lend authority to a saint's cult, but throughout the first millennium Christianity knew only local saints: the idea of a saint whose cult was mandatory for the whole of the church was unknown. This local nature of the saint-making process and of the territorial domain of the cult has remained basically unchanged in the acephalous Eastern Orthodox churches to this day.

In the West, this localism apparently led to unchecked multiplication of saints, cults, and shrines, competing for the devotion and donations of the faithful. It was probably a move to displace the competitors that prompted one bishop to raise the contest one step above the battleground and solicit an intervention of the pope to lend the weight of his authority to the proclamation of a new saint, yielding the first papal canonization in 993 (Delooz 1969, p. 28). From then on, popes were increasingly solicited to step into the saint-making process and gladly seized the opportunity, until they realized that they could make it into a monopoly: in 1234 pope Gregory IX decreed that the right of canonization was henceforth reserved to the papacy. In the following four centuries, an increasingly complex judicial procedure to examine candidates to sainthood was developed and finally entrusted to a specialized body of Vatican professionals, the Congregation of Rites, established in 1587. As saints offi-

340

COMPETITION FOR SAINTHOOD AND THE MILLENNIAL CHURCH

cially entered the liturgy of the church, they also entered its liturgical calendar (Wilson 1983, p. 11). For all these centuries, however, the papacy did not have sufficient power to effectively enforce its canonization monopoly: local churches and bishops had continued all along to sanction new saints who remained the object of local cults as before, in spite of the pontifical reserve and without papal approval.

This double track to sainthood, local versus universal, was finally terminated in 1634, when a brief by pope Urban VIII ruled that no further episcopal canonizations were henceforth to be permitted and drew up the rules of procedure which remained operative until 1982. The Roman canonization process was to be a posthumous trial (*processus*) in which the candidate was assumed guilty until proven innocent: his/her case was argued by a canon lawyer appointed by the candidate's Roman 'postulator' on behalf of his/her local promoters, and was countered by the Promoter of the Faith (popularly known as the Devil's Advocate) who did everything in his powers to find fault with the cause. The pope had the last word only on those candidates who had weathered this judicial process. Urban VIII's brief further legislated a distinction between two degrees of sanctity, the blessed (*beatus*) and the saint proper (*sanctus*), both to be proclaimed by the pope alone upon official examination of the case by the Congregation of Rites. The first step, called beatification, is indispensable to allow a public cult, but this step only permits the cult to be performed by and for particular communities; the second step, canonization proper, requires evidence of new miracles produced by the blessed after beatification, and it not just permits but enjoins the cult as universal and mandatory for the whole church.

The criteria for sainthood slowly evolved over the centuries and appear never to have been formally laid down in the period covered by papal canonizations according to the old canon law, i.e., before 1634. Since then, however, the new canon law establishes four criteria for the judicial determination of sanctity, which have been routinely applied to every candidate by the Congregation of Rites. They are (1) doctrinal orthodoxy, (2) miracles, (3) heroic virtue, (4) martyrdom.

The first criterion is obviously to guard against heresy; to this end, anything a candidate to sainthood may have written is closely scrutinized. This is then mainly a negative criterion designed to screen out improper candidates. Miracles have nearly always been considered by the church as an obligatory requirement for both beatification and canonization of nonmartyrs, a proof that the dead person is in a special relation with God and can intercede with Him on behalf of his/her living devotees (only miracles occurring after death count, miracles occurring in life are not required nor normally evaluated). Today this

341

means miracles which have been juridically established as such. However, 'miracles', or supernatural feats infringing the laws of nature, can also be the work of white or black magics, performed by devil's agents masquerading as holy Christians. Guarding against this danger seems to have been the original rationale for the requirement that the candidate must have practised Christian virtues 'to a heroic degree', that is, better than ordinary mortals, whatever that may mean. Thus canonization proceedings routinely provide a summary of the candidate's behavior, virtue by virtue. The official catalog of virtues, by a long tradition dating back at least to Thomas Aquinas, includes seven items: the three theological virtues of faith, hope, and charity, and the four moral or 'cardinal' virtues of fortitude, justice, prudence, and temperance; for members of religious orders, to these is added observance of the three vows of poverty, chastity, and obedience. The same tradition further allows any number of additional virtues to be included under one or another of the seven headings, whose formulation is broad enough to allow for a convenient latitude in interpretation. Finally, martyrdom is a unique criterion in that it overrides all the others and excuses everything: if someone dies for the faith, behavior and belief in life do not matter anymore, so (s)he can dispense with both orthodoxy and heroic virtues. Miracles too have not been required for beatification under recent popes: only the further step of full canonization requires, for martyrs as for all others, the occurrence of new miracles after beatification. Martyrdom is also special because it allows for collective canonizations, bundling into one case a whole group of people who were executed on the same occasion as witnesses of the faith: thus the modern era supplied a plentiful crop of martyrs who fell in scores during the Protestant Reformation or in the overseas missions. As Delooz (1969, ch. 13) points out, given the long, expensive, and demanding nature of an individual canonization cause, group martyrdom offers an easier path to sainthood.

We have just seen how demanding the modern requirements for canonizations are. A single case may stretch over very long periods: canonizations are usually proclaimed several decades, and often several centuries after death, with the case typically lying dormant for a long time and then resuming its course when some group resumes sufficient pressure to press it on. The financial costs of a canonization cause seem to have been truly enormous in the early modern period and then to have fallen substantially over the centuries. To get some sense of the endpoint of this evolution, a conservative estimate for the early 1960s, assuming that expenditures were made all in one year (which they were not, as we have just seen) and that relative prices have not changed in almost four decades, yields figures in 1999 Euros of ca. 160.000 for a simple beatification and a further 240.000 for canonization proper, totalling 400.000 Eu-

342

COMPETITION FOR SAINTHOOD AND THE MILLENNIAL CHURCH

ros for the complete procedure[6]. However, it should be noted that these cash disbursements are only a fraction of the real social opportunity cost of a cause, which should include the value of labor time of the many unpaid volunteers and consultants paid only nominal fees, as well as the value of the services of the many church officials who work on the cause but are financially supported by their orders or by the diocese which formally initiates the cause.

While taking note of the steady centralizing trend in the canonization process over the centuries, it is important not to lose sight of the bottom-up nature of the initiative that sets each cause into motion. Overt political use of canonizations by popes, irrespective of popular initiative, for example, by making a convenient monarch or a pope's relative into a saint for reasons of state, has been very rare and confined to the Middle Ages. Canonization causes have always been, and still are, initiated from below, by a group of followers or believers of the would-be saint who are willing and able to press the case through. Popes have been responding to pressures from below first by filtering candidates through the ordeal of the judicial procedure described above and then passing their verdict on those who had survived it. It is this dual feature of the process – free, unsolicited initiative from below, exclusive, autocratic adjudication from above – that solves the church's twin problems of providing incentives to members and keeping their efforts in line with the overall interests of the organization. To this interpretation we now turn.

IV. COMPETITION FOR SAINTHOOD AS AN INCENTIVE MECHANISM

The foregoing description provides the basis for an interpretation of the canonization process as a rent-seeking contest. Of course those who do the competing are not the would-be saints, who by definition are dead[7], but their followers,

---

6. Author's own calculations based on the scanty data reported in Delooz (1969, Appendix 2). This calculation roughly compares with unadjusted, current-price figures for an American canonization cause lasting from 1929 to 1975 and totalling USD 250.000 and for an American beatification cause lasting from 1965 to 1988 and totalling some USD 333.000 (Woodward 1996, pp. 111–114). Unlike the Delooz calculations just cited, these figures include postulation costs, which are substantial. All these data are too crude to tell with any certainty whether 'marginal cost' (i.e., the cost of the second step, canonization proper) is increasing, as the figures reported in the text would seem to suggest.

7. I believe a good case could be made for the proposition that achieving sainthood after death was indeed a conscious, purposeful endeavor of many saints during their lifetime, as suggested by several writers such as Woodward (1996, p. 224). Proving such a proposition, however, would go beyond the limits of this paper. All we need to claim here is that the candidates' followers have incentives to participate in the competition.

343

who are alive and stand to profit from their candidate achieving canonization. The gains are in the form of donations in kind and cash, legacies, political clout in a given society, and power and influence within the church apparatus. By all accounts, the likelihood of successful completion of a canonization cause is an increasing function of the total effort that followers manage to put into it in the course of time. This effort takes the form of providing witness to the candidate's holy behavior in life, words and deeds, witness to martyrdom if such is the case, evidence of miracles and, crucially, of their connection with the saint, financial backing to the furtherance of their case before the Vatican bureaucracy, continuing devotion by the ordinary people, and dedication to the saint's chosen mission by the rank-and-file. But first and foremost, an adequate candidate worth all such effort is required. The spontaneous efforts of local zealots, which had been sufficient to establish a cult of a saint in the early church, clearly are no longer equal to such a formidable task. As Delooz (1983, p. 199) puts it,

'as soon as a judicial procedure before a bishop or the Holy See became obligatory or at least general practice, pressure from an unorganized community became insufficient. And so we see groups being formed to take up causes and press them towards a successful conclusion. Moral reputation and financial credit, competence in canon law and perseverance well beyond a single human life-span became essential elements here. Religious, whose orders could play the necessary role of pressure groups, thus came to have a considerable advantage over lay candidates for canonization',

and also over candidates from the secular clergy. The postulators, who are responsible for each cause once it reaches Rome, are nearly all members of religious orders: they are 'the system's entrepreneurs' (Woodward 1996, p. 107).

Seen from another angle, sainthood is not a scarce good per se in Catholic doctrine, as Heaven has room for infinite numbers of saints. It is papal control of canonizations that made it into a scarce good, to be rationed out and allocated to the most deserving applicants through a contest. Specifically, it is a volunteer contest (Cugno and Ferrero 1999), in which participants invest their time and effort for zero current reward in the expectation of a probabilistic future return in the form of the perpetual rent stream from a successful canonization. Since, however, maximum participation in the contest is to be encouraged subject to a minimum level of individual effort, i.e., church-oriented militancy is to be stimulated all around, the contest is designed not as a single-prize tournament but provides for multiple, rank-ordered prizes for some, though not all, of the performers below the top, in the form of more delayed canonizations. The elaborate, exacting bureaucratic procedure that screens candidates is designed to ensure that applicants do not cheat but exert themselves in the best interests of the church. Applicants, in turn, participate in the contest only if they can trust the procedure to be fair. Now, leaving aside exceptional cases of pat-

344

COMPETITION FOR SAINTHOOD AND THE MILLENNIAL CHURCH

rimonial use of their position by a few popes, and assuming that the pope embodies the overall interests of his organization (on which see below), then he has no reason to be unfair and cheat on contest outcomes by favoring the second-best contestant over the first best, because by so doing he would increase the expected costs of participation and reduce militancy at no gain to the church[8].

The reasons for such an epoch-making change in church policy from decentralized to centralized canonizations at the inception of the second millennium are easy to grasp. If saints are made and worshipped at a local level, as in the first millennium, there is no use for a central institution in the church, the number of saints and cults grows without limit, the flows of donations and patronage leak away in a thousand tiny streams, the relative influence of competing shrines and cult places tends to cancel out, and the church's overall interests are not well served. If, in contrast, saints are made at the center, the competitive dissipation of rents is prevented, and efforts and resources are channelled into a vertical exchange between the papacy and the local bodies and orders, making the role of the papacy indispensable and enforcing a loyalty to it that holds the organization together and furthers its overall interests and aims[9]. The 'bureaucratization of sanctity' (Woodward 1996, p. 73) thus fits well in the overall pattern of church centralization over the centuries sketched out in the second section above. However, while centralization in other respects was detrimental to bureaucratic incentives, centralization of canonizations into a rent-seeking contest provided the needed incentives to participants in a way that paralleled and supplemented the shortcomings of the official hierarchy. The contrast between decentralized and centralized cult of saints is thus an instance of the general contrast between horizontal exchanges, which accumulate loyalty and trust between subordinates that are detrimental to the hierarchy's goals, and vertical

8. On the inefficiency of unfair contests see O'Keeffe, Viscusi, and Zeckhauser (1984).
9. This contrast between inefficient decentralization and efficient centralization of saint-making has close parallels in less esoteric problems analyzed in the economics literature. Rose-Ackerman (1982) shows that unlimited free entry into a charity market drives each charity to engage in wasteful, excessive fundraising expenditures, which tends to dissipate net donation revenues away and makes restriction of entry and centralization or cartelization of fundraising drives Pareto-improving. From another angle, our contrast is similar to the contrast between certification and licensing of professionals' human capital (Shapiro 1986). Voluntary certification may drive good professionals to overinvest in human capital to separate themselves from lower-quality colleagues in a signalling equilibrium. On the other hand licensing, by raising the mandatory minimum quality standards, hurts or even drives out low-quality providers, raises average quality in the market, and reduces the need for costly investments in reputation by high-quality providers, being therefore Pareto-superior to certification if demanders (in our case, the church) value quality highly.

345

exchanges, which accumulate loyalty and trust between subordinates and supe-riors that enhance the organization's cohesion and efficiency (Breton and Win-trobe 1982).

The rent-seeking model does not tell the whole story, however. Granted that the contest provides incentives for groups to further a canonization cause, why and how should their actions work to the benefit of the church? Put differently, the criteria for sainthood reviewed above seem to force all candidates into one mold: all saints either underwent martyrdom, or must all have been strictly or-thodox, all work miracles, and all show an outstanding record in all virtues. But if the canonized saints were all the same, all replicas of the same prototype, in what ways could their actions and their legacies serve the manifold interests of the church? The key to this question lies in the notion of 'heroic virtues' and the way in which this notion has been implemented in the canonization process.

As we have seen above, the definition of the seven virtues is broad and ge-neric enough that virtually anything and everything can be included in each – provided it is beneficial to the church. For example, telling the truth in social relations is notoriously not held in great esteem in Catholic doctrine and prac-tice, because only intentions deep in the soul, not words, count for salvation; and so Delooz (1983, p. 204) pointedly notes that sincerity does not seem to have been examined as a virtue by the Congregation of Rites. But otherwise, the thing that is counted as a given virtue, practiced to a heroic degree, in each case is the candidate's novel contribution to the organization's overall well-be-ing. What being heroically virtuous in a given situation involves is not, and could not be, written in theology books nor spelled out from the top of the hierarchy: it is the candidate's challenge to find it out, and since there can be no heroism in doing what is routine in the surrounding environment, the candidate has to look for spots or aspects of social behavior which ought to be, but cur-rently are not, adequately emphasized by a Christian. Viewed this way, the con-test for sainthood is really a permanent, unbounded invitation to innovate and break new grounds, subject to the ex-post check that overall church interests be thereby adequately furthered[10]. As a first approximation, church interests can be taken to be the protection of its monopoly power, i.e., the expansion of its reach on the outward frontiers of Christendom and the strengthening of its grip on the people inside its domain against such threats as heresy, secularization, and corruption of behavior, so as to ward off such cataclysms as new schisms

10. 'What, then, does the Roman Church mean by heroic virtue? The Roman Church believes that when it appears it will be recognized. There is no pattern which the saint must meet; he can do what he must do wherever he is and whatever he does ... The Roman Church does not tell the saints how to practice heroic virtue; it learns from them how to practice such virtue' (McKenzie 1969, p. 232).

346

COMPETITION FOR SAINTHOOD AND THE MILLENNIAL CHURCH

and reformations. As any centralized bureaucracy, the church is beset by chronic information and incentive problems: it cannot know at the top where and when problems arise and then take timely and adequate action to solve them by central planning and command. Let therefore volunteers on the spot search out comparatively neglected areas, sections of society, or aspects of behavior, take on the risk, and do whatever they think the situation requires, knowing that the church will keep its implicit commitment to reward its most loyal and successful servants. The volunteer contest for sainthood then amounts to providing incentives for a completely decentralized implementation of church goals.

This yields a secular pattern of sainthood which is hugely diverse: each saint is different from the others, each specializes in some activity or behavioral trait which becomes his or her preserve and that of his or her followers. Specialization of individual innovators brings specialization of organizations that survive them and continue their mission. Typically, a would-be saint is the founder of a new order, congregation, or confraternity, or of a special branch or section thereof, which is often looked on with suspicion and resisted by the entrenched church officialdom. His followers continue his work and finally succeed in having the founder canonized, which is like the licensing of the new enterprise. Order members across generations are brought up in the cult of the founder and naturally continue and develop his special brand of saintly action in new directions, which eventually brings in new saints, who in turn further enhance the power of the order and therefore its capacity to promote new canonization causes, and so on in a virtuous circle – that is, as long as this specialized brand of sanctity is in demand, i.e., it furthers the church's overall cause as judged by the church itself. When demand shifts away from a given brand of saintly action and toward new ones, a symmetric cycle of decline sets in: fewer saints are made, which entails a reduction in popularity, resources, and power, which in turn entails a reduced activity, which brings in still fewer saints, and so on. In this way, adaptation and flexibility are built into the mechanism, and the supply of religious actions responds to changing social demand over time without any need for traumatic devices like dismissals or terminations of a branch of activity which has outlived its usefulness. Thus the historical profile of saints reveals an extraordinary variety that closely mirrors the evolution of church structure and power through the second millennium.

The available quantitative evidence lends strong support to our interpretation of the working of Catholic saint-making. We will rely on the seminal work by Pierre Delooz (1969), a Belgian sociologist who did a thorough statistical study of the saints of the second millennium based on official canonization proceedings and a huge mass of additional historical documentation. He came up

347

MARIO FERRERO

with a net total of 2.610 saints and blessed made from 993 to 1967, including all pontifical canonizations carried out under both the old and the new canon law, all beatifications carried out from the XVII century onward, and a 'best' list, necessarily incomplete, of local saints proclaimed by a local church authority without papal sanction, or (after 1234) despite papal reservation[11]. The detailed statistical breakdown of these lists is a mine of information, from which we summarize the findings most relevant to our argument.

First of all, the data overturn a conclusion reached earlier by Sorokin (1950) on the basis of an inadequate list of saints (Delooz 1969, ch. 9). Sorokin thought he had detected a dramatic fall in numbers of saints after the XVII century, which he attributed to the increasing secularization of modern society which entails a drying up of the supply of saints. Delooz shows that no such fall is shown by his data, that the number of saints and blessed (ordered by date of death) remains very high in the XIX century (322 in total) and promises to be at least as high in the XX century once the many, lengthy canonization causes under way will have been completed, and that the only significant low in the time series occurs in the XIV and XV centuries, mirroring the deep crisis of the church that eventually sparked the Reformation. Now as the secularization of Western society pointed out by Sorokin is real enough, the Delooz findings would remain unexplained if the number of saints were driven by the social supply of saintliness, as Sorokin saw it. Instead, such findings are easily explained on our interpretation, which sees the number of saints as driven by demand: secularization implies that the power and influence of the church are jeopardized, which calls for action, and the call is answered by volunteers who search out corners where the church was losing influence, such as the new classes created by the industrial revolution (the middle class and the working class, see Delooz 1969, ch. 17), the women, and the racial or ethnic minorities (see below).

Secondly, the overwhelming importance of religious orders throughout the history of canonizations comes out unambiguously from Delooz's analysis (chs. 15 and 16). Both the diocesan clergy and the laity represent modest percentages of the totals, whether by century or by category. Both groups are overwhelmingly made up of martyrs, who were canonized or beatified as a group. In these cases, with the political exceptions of as many as 137 priests beatified in one shot as martyrs of the French Revolution and 63 priests beatified in one shot as martyrs of the English Reformation (p. 407), each martyr group invari-

---

11. Delooz's list is considered the most authoritative and reliable, superseding all previous attempts and marking the starting point for any further study of saints. See Wilson (1983, p. 314) and Weinstein and Bell (1982, pp. 277–278).

348

COMPETITION FOR SAINTHOOD AND THE MILLENNIAL CHURCH

ably included some regular cleric whose order took charge of the case and carried along both priests and lay people, the latter including large numbers of non-Europeans in the overseas missions (pp. 408–409). The tiny proportion of secular clergy who were not martyrs are either powerful bishops or popes, who are fairly well represented in the High Middle Ages alongside lay members from the royalty or the nobility, or in recent centuries are founders of, or otherwise connected with, some religious congregation or order which took them in charge (p. 401). The simple parish priest, it seems, has absolutely no chance in this peculiar contest. Similarly, the tiny proportion of laity who were not martyrs nor aristocrats were almost invariably associated with some religious family which considered them as its 'stepchildren' (pp. 353–356, 361–362).

Thirdly, all the founders of a religious order or congregation of any kind, or of an important branch or extension thereof, have been pontifically canonized or beatified. Reciprocally, the founders make up as much as one quarter of all saints fully canonized by a pope and more than half of the women made saints under the new canon law (pp. 390, 402). As to the blessed, the founders account for almost a third of the number of beatification *causes* (which is much less than the number of blessed due to massive group beatifications of martyrs, which account for the vast majority of this class) (p. 408).

Lastly, the breakdown of canonizations by religious orders clearly shows the changing directions of demand for volunteer effort across the centuries and translates into a changing structure of church power. The beginning of the second millennium saw the preeminence of cloistered monastic orders, islands of spiritual escape from the world and of higher learning: the Benedictine order first, and then the reformed orders reacting to its incipient corruption. The development of urban society and the concurrent spread of heresy gave birth to the Mendicant orders in the XIII century, mainly the Franciscans devoted to proselytizing the cities and the Dominicans devoted to fighting heresy and preaching doctrinal observance. The record of both papal and episcopal canonizations through the Middle Ages clearly shows this evolution (pp. 388, 391, 393; see also Goodich 1983).

The corruption and decay of both some of the religious orders and the secular clergy at the end of the Middle Ages and the ensuing Reformation, occurring at about the same time as the founding of European empires overseas, brought home to the church the dire need for renewed militancy both inward and outward. Thus the XVI and XVII centuries were the heyday of the Jesuit saints, which together with the Franciscans account for about a third of total canonizations in those centuries (p. 410), roughly half of which due to martyrdom (pp. 403, 407). The Jesuits were like clerical soldiers of the Christian cause, undertaking vast missionary activity overseas and promoting sister con-

349

gregations in Europe. On the other hand, monastic orders disappear altogether from the list of saints to this day (p. 399), except for a number of blessed nuns (p. 407). The Counter-Reformation period also saw the birth of many lesser, more differentiated orders and congregations, including many noncloistered female congregations, aimed at specific target groups in the population: they devoted themselves to Christian schooling, preaching, charity, hospitals, missionary work, and more. This is mirrored in the time distribution of founder saints, which shows a significant cluster of people born in the late XV and XVI centuries (p. 403). Another time of crisis for the church was brought on by the Enlightenment, the French Revolution, and the rise of liberalism and socialism in the wake of the industrial revolution: thus another strong cluster of founder saints were born between 1750 and 1850 (p. 403). It is the time of the socially-minded saint, devoted to worker education, the disabled, the destitute girl or single mother, the stranded boy, the orphan, the elderly, the criminal serving a life sentence or awaiting execution, and so forth. This time pattern is replicated in the profile of the blessed category, showing a very large, unprecedented dispersion of the blessed (mostly martyrs) across orders and congregations of every description (pp. 406–407).

Finally, in an organization like the Catholic church so gender-biased as to deny women the access to priesthood, to impose celibacy on the secular clergy, and to admit almost no married women to the ranks of its saints and blessed, the rise of women to sainthood is a late, delayed, but still noticeable development (ch. 11). Women represent about one in six of all saints canonized by a pope in the millennium, but half of these have been canonized in the XX century, accounting for 30 percent of the century's total; they represent slightly over one in five of the blessed, but more than four fifths of them have been beatified in the XX century, accounting for a quarter of the century's total (pp. 268, 271). The women's way to sainthood is not mainly martyrdom, at least relative to men (p. 269), but again life in a religious order. Of the 31 women fully canonized in the XX century, 27 were religious, and 8 of these 27 had died before the XIX century and therefore reveal a recent increase in women's capacity for pressure; out of these same 27 saints, 19 were founders of female congregations, of which 15 were founded in the XIX century (pp. 272–273). Thus, in this as in other respects, innovation and response to social demand develops at a grassroot level via religious organizations, this effort is channelled into the sainthood contest, and its outcome is reflected in the canonization record.

Extending Delooz's lists and statistical analysis, which stop at 1967, to the date of this writing would go far beyond the limits of this paper. However, Pope John Paul II's activism in saint-making has raised the whole process to unprecedented magnitude and scope. From the inception of his pontificate in 1978 to

350

COMPETITION FOR SAINTHOOD AND THE MILLENNIAL CHURCH

October 2, 2000, he canonized a total of 447 saints, more than the cumulative total of pontifical canonizations before him (Stanley 2000); and to April 22, 2000, he beatified 984 people (The Economist 2000), which is even more remarkable in absolute numbers and comes close to 80 percent of the cumulative total of beatifications made by previous popes since the XVII century. Though large numbers in both categories are accounted for by group canonizations of martyrs, such as the 120 Chinese and European missionaries killed in China between 1648 and 1930 (Stanley 2000), these figures imply a dramatic acceleration of upward secular trends in saint-making. Also, continuing the recent trends outlined above, the range of these canonizations has kept broadening to accommodate saints or blessed from 'underrepresented' countries and especially from occupations, peoples, and minorities with no previous saints[12]. Nearly all of the new saints and blessed were founders or members of, or taken in charge by, religious orders, as before. Women are slowly on the rise, and nearly always founders of orders if not martyrs, as before. Nonmartyr lay saints continue to be rare, and normal married laity completely absent.

We can only speculate that John Paul II's spectacular drive to increase and differentiate the flow of canonizations is his answer to the hard challenge that the high-information society and globalization, with their enhanced opportunities for denominational competition and secularization, pose to the church's monopoly over souls. But whatever his reasons, in view of the tight rules of procedure that govern the saint-making process, a more pertinent question here is, by what means could John Paul II manage such an astonishing number and variety of canonizations? Now as before, the supply of candidates comes from the church's grassroots, the processing of causes is carried out by the bureaucracy of the Congregation for the Causes of Saints (as the former Congregation of Rites is now called), and no pope may declare a saint until and unless his/her cause has been successfully processed by the congregation. Only then can the pope exercise his discretion in picking which candidates will be ratified first, if at all (candidates may be put on hold for political or pastoral reasons). To that extent the pope enjoys a kind of agenda-setting power. But such power is augmented if the pope manages to increase the flow of completed causes at a given time. As the backlog of pending causes was well above 1.000 in the 1980s and the congregation can process only so many causes per year, John Paul II had the congregation's staff strengthened and thus the annual output of completed

12. For example, a former Sudanese slave, an American heiress, a Mohawk Indian woman, a Spanish friar who founded the California missions system, as well as politically sensitive cases such as martyrs of the Mexican revolution, the Spanish civil war, and the Nazi occupation of Europe (Weigel 2000, Woodward 1996).

351

causes doubled, thereby expanding the range of candidates ready for him to choose from (Woodward 1996, pp. 119–120). Furthermore, the order of consideration of pending causes by the congregation is subject to papal pressures, e.g., in view of having a given cause ready in good time for John Paul II to present overseas peoples with 'their' new saint or blessed on the occasion of his frequent travels (Woodward 1996, pp. 116–117).

More fundamentally, John Paul II enacted in 1983 a reform of the saint-making procedure, the first since Urban VIII, which makes the path to sainthood faster and easier, thereby substantially increasing the output of successful causes out of a given pool of candidates, and thus widening the pope's scope for discretion and priority (Woodward 1996, pp. 91–99). First, the number of miracles required was reduced by half, from two to one for the beatification of nonmartyrs and again from two to one for the final canonization of both martyrs and nonmartyrs, while the already customary waiving of any miracle requirements for the beatification of martyrs was confirmed. Second, instead of two canonical processes (one local and one in Rome) as before, there was henceforth to be only one, directed by the local bishop, who was entrusted with the entire responsibility for marshalling all the evidence in support of a cause. Third, and most important, the reform fundamentally overhauled the Roman process. The courtroom model of an adversarial legal process between the candidate's lawyer and the Devil's Advocate, which had been in place for 350 years, was replaced by an academic model of researching and writing a doctoral dissertation: both sides of the previous trial process are now replaced by a relator, appointed by the congregation, who is in charge of supervising the writing of a historical-critical biography of the candidate. As a result,

'the spirit was to be cooperative rather than adversarial. Everyone involved in the preparation of a cause would have an incentive to see it succeed, and none more than the relator who was to assume responsibilty for the cause's success once it reached Rome' (Woodward 1996, p. 95).

The church's changing demands for sainthood, as understood and articulated by the incumbent pope, can now be met more fully, promptly, and flexibly than ever before, as John Paul II's canonization record remarkably testifies.

V. A COMPARISON

While many organized religions (from Islam to Orthodox Christianity, from Hinduism to Buddhism) have a cult of saints or holy persons of some kind, none has a centralized saint-making process like the Catholic church. For a useful comparison we must leave the religious realm and enter the political realm,

352

COMPETITION FOR SAINTHOOD AND THE MILLENNIAL CHURCH

where we find a politico-economic system which features a centralized cult of saints: a classic communist regime. The analogies are striking, and only a summary overview can be offered here[13].

Catholicism and communism are totalitarian orders at their heights, each in its respective domain[14]. Though the label may seem too strong as applied to Catholicism, consider the following parallels. No pluralism or coexistence of alternative doctrinal interpretations or policies is allowed inside a communist party and regime: argument is fine but final decisions are binding on everyone (which is called 'democratic centralism'), which is equivalent to a unanimity principle that can be overruled only by the top leader (like the pope). No coexistence with capitalism is conceivable, only temporary truces in difficult times, otherwise mass conversion is the general policy. Thus the party, like the church, is bent on fighting heresy (Trotsky) even before paganism (Hitler) because the former is closer and therefore more threatening. The joint outcome of both drives, once the revolution has succeeded, is the establishment of a territorial monopoly of politics and economics, that is, an exclusive economic order backed by government coercion, like the religious monopoly of the church backed by the state.

Once communists are firmly in power, the party doubles into a formally separate hierarchy taking charge of the administration of the economy to replace the suppressed market mechanism; so we have a territorially and sectorally structured bureaucracy ministering to the day-to-day business of production, distribution, and general government, much like the secular clergy. This is, however, ultimately supervised by the parallel hierarchy of the party – as one well-known expert, Mao Zedong, used to say, politics is always in command and takes priority over economics. The party can and does step in at all times and places to fill the gaps and solve the coordination, information, and incentive problems created by the missing market mechanism and only defectively remedied by the administrative bureaucracy. This latter, being a secular organization, has somewhat more scope for material incentives than the secular

13. The interpretation of communist campaigns and purges, and more generally of communist mobilization regimes, offered in this section relies on the extensive discussion in Ferrero (1994). Among the literature cited therein, see especially Shirk (1984), who has an explicit, illuminating analysis of what she calls 'virtuocracy' in China, and Grossman (1983), who highlights the dual role of the Soviet communist party as manager, which fills in the coordination gaps, and entrepreneur, which fills in the incentive gaps, both gaps arising from the chronic inability of central planning to fully substitute for the market mechanism. The political analogy between the Christian revolution in the Roman Empire and the socialist revolution in XIX century Europe is strongly emphasized by Friedrich Engels (1982), who was a serious student of church history and had a unique first-hand knowledge of the socialist movement of his day.
14. Wintrobe (1998) is a basic reference for a political economy approach to totalitarianism.

353

clergy, and some intra-bureaucratic competition does indeed take place to build loyalty to superiors. But here too the range of incentives is severely constrained by the egalitarianism and avoidance of conspicuous consumption which are supposedly the regime's hallmarks. Party members, on the other hand, unlike members of the secular bureaucracy, are not burdened by the daily routine of administration and can play the role of all-purpose caretakers who direct themselves wherever and whenever problems arise. By so doing they signal themselves to their superiors as best performers of political service and thereby earn not just public praise and medals but promotion and other material benefits. Thus members of the party, and of its countless sister, dependent, or collateral organizations, are analogous to the religious regulars of the Catholic church: here as there, the competition that keeps bureaucratic inertia in check and rejuvenates the secular bureaucracy is arranged mainly in a parallel organizational network, which is a field for volunteer enterprise and results in a contest for sainthood.

Communists had from the beginning a cult of martyrs, those who had fallen for the cause both before and after the revolutionary takeover or in defense of it; they were officially proclaimed martyrs of the revolution and their associates and relatives were awarded benefits. As with Catholics, martyrdom excused everything because only death counts, not belief or behavior in life. Otherwise, communist saints, unlike Catholic saints, were living persons: they were the most loyal and effective performers in a drive to fulfill a task, meet a need, fight an enemy, counter an emergency, or ward off a threat in the best interest of the party and the regime. They were personally rewarded in life by promotion to higher positions, possibly displacing a disloyal or ineffective official in the secular bureaucracy, up to the uppermost ranks of party and state power. This was in fact the standard career pattern up through the party hierarchy under classic communist regimes. Although the rewards accrued mainly to the saints themselves, however, once they achieved success and recognition they could and did distribute part of their rewards to their followers and supporters, whose support they crucially needed as helpers in the action and witnesses in the 'trial' before the higher party bosses. For communist saints, like modern Catholic saints, were not designated by the rank-and-file or the local activists: they were proclaimed by the apex of the regime as winners of a contest. No grassroot or episcopal canonizations, only papal canonizations, were allowed under communism. It is this centralized nature of the saint-making process that gave the local section or constituency within or around the party the crucial role of a pressure group in the canonization procedure, much like the orders or congregations in the church that press a case through and stand to gain from it. The criteria for sainthood were again as close to the Catholic criteria as they could be: miracles

354

COMPETITION FOR SAINTHOOD AND THE MILLENNIAL CHURCH

were not required of course, but the negative criterion of doctrinal orthodoxy was a *sine qua non*, while the chief positive criterion, besides martyrdom, was the practice of (communist) virtues to a heroic degree. And here again, as there could be no heroism in practicing what was commonplace behavior, each communist saint specialized and earned his/her degrees in the performance of some task or duty which was valuable to the regime but heretofore neglected or shirked by others.

Here, however, comes a major difference with the Catholic model. As we have seen, in the latter, since overall church goals are relatively straightforward or one-dimensional and can be summarized in the protection of its monopoly over souls, their implementation can be left to decentralized initiative that searches out neglected areas and situations and acts accordingly, with the church evaluating outcomes and awarding prizes only ex post. By contrast, communist goals involved the management of a whole economy and were therefore so complex, multi-dimensional, and interdependent that their implementation could not possibly be left to amateurish improvisation and decentralized initiative: the center had to set the tasks or priorities of a volunteer drive at any one time. Except in the early, hectic days of the revolution or under extraordinary calamities, the communist volunteers and would-be saints never were individualistic pioneers who started out on their own and at their own risk: they answered a call from the center that took the typical form of a mobilization campaign[15]. The campaigns on successive, different priorities or goals worked like a self-selection mechanism by which those who invested most in party loyalty signalled themselves as reliable candidates for promotion and reward, as they had voluntarily incurred a sunk cost whose capitalized value could be recouped only through continuing loyal service to the regime. Usually a campaign ended with the proclamation of the saints selected through it, until a next round was started on yet another task. This often turned out canonizations of whole groups of signal activists, and since here collective canonization did not require martyrdom as with the Catholics, there were incentives for individuals to join the bandwagon and try the easier path to sainthood. Thus the communist saint-making process was centralized not only in the adjudication of the contest

---

15. The anarchists, who also had a cult of the saints and martyrs of their cause, resorted neither to directed campaigns nor to centralized canonization but, as dictated by their totally individualistic, non-authoritarian ideology, had their heroes 'canonized' through a spontaneous, decentralized process carried out by local collectives and groups and spread across groups by example, as in the early church. This inefficient contest design may have substantially contributed to the general ineffectiveness of the anarchist movement and so to its eventual disappearance from the stage of working-class politics (see Hobsbawm 1971 and Joll 1979).

355

and the awarding of prizes, as in the Catholic church, but also in the setting of the timing, sequencing, and object of the effort of successive contests.

The campaign technique of policy implementation is necessarily clumsy, as it implies that a typical campaign will overshoot its target and require correction by a counter-campaign, which gave classic communist regimes their typically cyclical pattern of 'advances' and 'retreats'. More important perhaps, the campaign mode of sainthood contest lacks the in-built incentive to decentralized innovation and initiative in policy implementation that makes the Catholic contest design so efficient. Furthermore, the fact that communist saints were living persons and must be rewarded in life by hierarchical promotion made it impossible for communism to replicate the flexibility of adaptation to changing political demand that is built into the Catholic process, in which for example cloistered monastic orders, when their saintly services are no longer useful, are left to slowly die out and their old saints are slowly forgotten by the new generations, as they are overtaken by newcomers in the sainthood contest. Under communism the living saints issued by previous campaigns had to be brushed aside to make room for newcomers. This was accomplished by the purge, a traumatic device that kicked saints out of Heaven, i.e., turned the erstwhile saints into enemies of the people. The purge was itself a campaign in reverse, launched from above and calling on activists to search out and denounce the 'enemies' to the higher authorities, thereby incurring the cost of alienating themselves from their peers and expecting a proper return on this investment. Thus the purge was yet another, centrally promoted contest for sainthood, in which, however, candidate saints were required to do harm, not good, something unknown to the Catholic church.

The campaign-purge complex could not be continued for ever: by its very nature it made insecurity of one's position (and often life) pervasive, bred resentment, suspicion, and enmity among the people, broke the morale of even honest, rule-abiding bureaucrats, and turned social life into a daily gamble. Sooner or later, a powerful constituency would form and demand security of managerial and administrative tenure, rule of law, and termination of the campaign-purge complex, that is, an end to the saints and the contests for sainthood – something that has never occurred in the Catholic church so far. But on our interpretation, this would take away the main device that kept an all-encompassing, centralized bureaucracy going. The end of the mobilization (or Stalinist) era in the long run spelled the doom of the Soviet Union and its satellites. The Chinese communist regime survived the end of Maoism only because it gave its people a new contest to engage in and gamble on, a direct contest for personal wealth as a substitute for the sainthood contest. Cuba is still carrying on as a mobilization regime, but arguably thanks to its unique device of letting

356

COMPETITION FOR SAINTHOOD AND THE MILLENNIAL CHURCH

the losers exit the country instead of keeping them in as a hostile, revengeful group of saints-turned-devils. While all this is happening, the Catholic church is turning out saints at a faster pace than ever before.

VI. CONCLUSION

This paper has offered a rational interpretation of the central role that saint-making has always played, and continues to play, in the Roman Catholic church. As a background, we sketched out a description of the church in modern times as a centralized bureaucracy striving to achieve and maintain a religious monopoly over a given territory. To maintain and expand its control over society, the church must solve two problems, which are typical of all centralized bureaucracies but are here magnified to a forbidding degree: incentives and information. The incentive problem is inordinately acute due to the priests' self-denial which has been the church's hallmark at least in modern times, and the information problem is staggering due to the hugely diverse and constantly evolving facets of society that are being targeted at any one time and to the lack or distortion of incentives for the ordinary clerics to pass the relevant information upwards. So the papacy cannot simply watch out for problem spots and then order its clergy appropriate action. Detection of problem spots and consequent action have to be left to decentralized initiative at a grassroot level, with the top hierarchy evaluating outcomes ex post and awarding prizes to the best performers in the church's interests. Paramount among such prizes is sainthood, which is awarded through a judicial evaluation procedure as the outcome of a competitive, open-access rent-seeking contest. Participants in the contest are the followers of the would-be saint, who almost invariably turn out to be members of religious orders. For orders are long-lived institutions, capable of sustained pressure for decades or even centuries; on the other hand, the canonization of a new saint brings benefits to his/her followers in the form of enhanced power of their order, a form which is compatible with austerity in personal consumption, and therefore the followers have incentives to press their champion's canonization cause through and to field and promote new potential candidates. Thus the modern Catholic saint-making process, by combining competitive initiative and pressure from below with exclusive adjudication from above, is able to provide effective incentives to participants while avoiding the need to centrally process all the information that would be required for central direction of local efforts.

This interpretation, if correct, implies that the varieties and 'specializations' of saints in the course of time should mirror the changing needs for action in

357

society from the church's point of view; that is, the structure of supply, as embodied in the canonization record, should be driven by demand rather than by an exogenous supply of saintly souls. Our review of the statistical evidence from the sociology of canonizations, spanning the whole second millennium of the Christian era, strongly confirms this hypothesis. It suggests that canonizations have been highly responsive to problem areas and emerging social and territorial groups, via the changing fortunes of orders – a responsiveness that John Paul II's unprecedented saint-making drive has further enhanced.

Today, as the third millennium begins, the fact that the Catholic church keeps looking for evidence of miracles and proclaiming new saints is often looked down on as an oddity, an archaic survival that lingers on despite globalization and the information society. Yet this feature is as central as ever to the church's life, and the church itself seems to be in a pretty good shape overall. By contrast, as we have seen in the last section, communist regimes, which tried out a secularized, seemingly much more rational version of the contest for sainthood, have all but passed away in less than a century. All the difference between the two versions stems from two basic facts: Catholic saints are dead whereas communist saints were alive, and Catholic saints are simply to uphold church popularity and influence whereas communist saints were supposed to manage an economy – something that could not be sustained for long. This paper has then argued the counterintuitive notion that the church's 'oddity' is just doing the right thing in the right way for the purpose at hand.

REFERENCES

Bossy, J. (1970). The Counter-Reformation and the People of Catholic Europe, *Past and Present*. 47: 51–70.
Bossy, J. (1975). The Social History of Confession in the Age of the Reformation, *Transactions of the Royal Historical Society*. 25: 21–38.
Bossy, J. (1983). The Mass as a Social Institution, 1200–1700, *Past and Present*. 100: 29–61.
Bossy, J. (1988). Moral Arithmetic: Seven Sins into Ten Commandments, in: E. Leites (ed.), *Conscience and Casuistry in Early Modern Europe*. Cambridge: Cambridge University Press: 214–234.
Breton, A. and R. Wintrobe (1982). *The Logic of Bureaucratic Conduct*. Cambridge: Cambridge University Press.
Brown, P. (1981). *The Cult of the Saints*. Chicago and London: University of Chicago Press.
Chatellier, L. (1989). *The Europe of the Devout: The Catholic Reformation and the Formation of a New Society*. Cambridge: Cambridge University Press.
Cugno, F. and M. Ferrero (1999). Competition among Volunteers, mimeo, Department of Economics, University of Turin.
Delooz, P. (1969). *Sociologie et Canonisations*. The Hague: Martinus Nijhoff.
Delooz, P. (1983). Towards a Sociological Study of Canonized Sainthood in the Catholic Church, in: S. Wilson (ed.), *Saints and their Cults*. Cambridge: Cambridge University Press: 189–216.

358

COMPETITION FOR SAINTHOOD AND THE MILLENNIAL CHURCH

Demsetz, H. (1968). Why Regulate Utilities?, *Journal of Law and Economics*. 11: 55–65.

Engels, F. (1895/1982). *Zur Geschichte des Urchristenthums*, translated as *On the History of Early Christianity*, in: K. Marx and F. Engels, *On Religion*. Chico: Scholars Press, American Academy of Religion: 120–142.

Ferrero, M. (1994). Bureaucrats Versus Red Guards: A Politico-Economic Model of the Stability of Communist Regimes, in: R. W. Campbell (ed.), *The Postcommunist Economic Transformation*. Essays in Honor of Gregory Grossman. Boulder: Westview Press: 281–316.

Goodich, M. (1983). The Politics of Canonization in the Thirteenth Century: Lay and Mendicant Saints, in: S. Wilson (ed.), *Saints and their Cults*. Cambridge: Cambridge University Press: 169–187.

Grossman, G. (1983). The Party As Manager and Entrepreneur, in: G. Guroff and F. Carstensen (eds.), *Entrepreneurship in Imperial Russia and the Soviet Union*. Princeton: Princeton University Press: 284–305.

Hobsbawm, E. J. (1971). The Andalusian Anarchists, *Primitive Rebels*. Manchester: Manchester University Press: 74–92.

Holmes, J. D. and B. W. Bickers (1983). *A Short History of the Catholic Church*. London: Burns & Oates.

Hughes, P. (1952). *A History of the Church*. New York: Sheed & Ward.

Hughes, P. (1967). *A Short History of the Catholic Church*. London: Burns & Oates.

Iannaccone, L. (1998). Introduction to the Economics of Religion, *Journal of Economic Literature*. 36: 1465–1496.

Joll, J. (1979). *The Anarchists*. London: Methuen.

Latourette, K. S. (1953). *A History of Christianity*. New York: Harper & Bro.

Le Goff, J. (1981). *La Naissance du Purgatoire*. Paris: Gallimard.

McKenzie, J. L. (1969). *The Roman Catholic Church*. London: Weidenfeld & Nicolson.

O'Keeffe, M., K. Viscusi and R. Zeckhauser (1984). Economic Contests: Comparative Reward Schemes, *Journal of Labor Economics*. 2: 27–56.

Rose-Ackerman, S. (1982). Charitable Giving and Excessive Fundraising, *Quarterly Journal of Economics*. 97: 193–212.

Shapiro, C. (1986). Investment, Moral Hazard, and Occupational Licensing, *Review of Economic Studies*. 53: 843–862.

Shirk, S. L. (1984). The Decline of Virtuocracy in China, in: J. L. Watson (ed.), *Class and Social Stratification in Post-Revolutionary China*. Cambridge: Cambridge University Press: 56–83.

Sorokin, P. A., (1950). *Altruistic Love*. A Study of American 'Good Neighbors' and Christian Saints. Boston: Beacon Press.

Stanley, A. (2000). Pope Canonizes 120 Killed in China and One American, The New York Times, October 2.

The Economist (2000). Miracles Under the Microscope, April 22.

Weigel, G. (2000). A Century of Saints, The Wall Street Journal, October 4.

Weinstein, D. and R. M. Bell (1982). *Saints and Society*. Chicago: University of Chicago Press.

Wilson, S. (1983). Introduction, in: S. Wilson (ed.), *Saints and their Cults*. Cambridge: Cambridge University Press: 1–53.

Wilson, S. (ed.) (1983). *Saints and their Cults*. Cambridge: Cambridge University Press.

Wintrobe, R. (1998). *The Political Economy of Dictatorship*. Cambridge: Cambridge University Press.

Woodward, K. L. (1996). *Making Saints*. How the Catholic Church Determines Who Becomes a Saint, Who Doesn't, and Why. New York: Simon & Schuster.

359

MARIO FERRERO

SUMMARY

The Roman Catholic Church has been turning out new saints for two millennia. The argument advanced here is that the saint-making process is arranged as an open contest for sainthood: by combining competitive initiative and pressure from below with exclusive adjudication from above, it provides effective incentives for participants to direct their efforts toward the best interests of the church. This is a key factor that counters bureaucratic ossification and keeps the church thriving. The argument implies that the secular pattern of canonizations should mirror the changing pattern of church demand rather than any exogenous supply of saintly persons, and should translate into a pattern of rise and decline of religious orders which specialize in particular virtues meeting particular demands. Statistical data on canonizations in the second millennium strongly support this empirical implication.

ZUSAMMENFASSUNG

Die römisch-katholische Kirche hat über zwei Jahrtausende immer neue Heilige hervorgebracht. Hierzu wird die These vertreten, dass das Verfahren der Kanonisation Heiligkeit in einem offenen Wettbewerb organisiert. Indem konkurrierende Initiativen und Druck von unten mit exklusiver Jurisdiktion von oben verbunden werden, lassen sich dabei effektive Anreize für die Beteiligten schaffen, ihre Anstrengungen auf die bestmögliche Verwirklichung der Interessen der Kirche zu richten. Diese Schlüsselinstitution beugt bürokratischen Verknöcherungen vor und lässt die Kirche gedeihen. Die These impliziert, dass das Modell der Kanonisation langfristig wohl eher die wechselnden Strukturen der kirchlichen Bedürfnisse als das Angebot von heiligen Persönlichkeiten abbildet und in ein Modell zum Aufstieg und Zerfall von religiösen Ordnungen einzubetten ist, die sich auf die Entwicklung besonderer Tugenden für besondere Bedürfnisse spezialisieren. Die statistischen Daten der Kanonisationen des zweiten Jahrtausends stützen diese empirische Implikation.

RÉSUMÉ

Depuis presque deux mille ans, l'Eglise catholique n'a cessé de proclamer de nouveaux saints. Cet essai va soutenir la thèse selon laquelle le processus de canonisation a été organisé comme une compétition pour la sainteté ouverte à tout le monde. Libre initiative et pression exercée par la base combinées avec un pouvoir de décision exclusif reservé au sommet de la hiérarchie ont pour but d'encourager les participants à la compétition à s'employer à un meilleur service de l'Eglise. Cela fonctionne comme un antidote contre la sclérose bureaucratique et donne à l'Eglise le dynamisme nécessaire. Il s'ensuit que le déroulement des canonisations à travers les siècles reflète l'évolution des attentes de l'Eglise plutôt qu'une offre spontanée d'âmes saintes. Il s'insère donc dans l'ascension et le déclin d'ordres religieux spécialisés dans le développement de vertus spécifiques correspondant à des besoins particuliers. Les données statistiques sur les canonisations pendant le deuxième millénaire vérifient cette implication empirique.

360

Public Choice **116**: 205–223, 2003.
© 2003 *Kluwer Academic Publishers. Printed in the Netherlands.*

205

Publishing as prostitution? – Choosing between one's own ideas and academic success

BRUNO S. FREY*
Institute for Empirical Economic Research, University of Zürich, CH-8006 Zürich, Switzerland; e-mail: bsfrey@iew.unizh.ch

Accepted 3 September 2002

Abstract. Survival in academia depends on publications in refereed journals. Authors only get their papers accepted if they intellectually prostitute themselves by slavishly following the demands made by anonymous referees who have no property rights to the journals they advise. Intellectual prostitution is neither beneficial to suppliers nor consumers. But it is avoidable. The editor (with property rights to the journal) should make the basic decision of whether a paper is worth publishing or not. The referees should only offer suggestions for improvement. The author may disregard this advice. This reduces intellectual prostitution and produces more original publications.

1. Prostitution of ideas and academic career

When writing this paper, I never expected that it would be published in a (refereed) economics journal because it would not be able to pass the refereeing

* I wish to thank Rosemary Brown for helping to formulate the paper in English and I am grateful for helpful comments from William Baumol, Gary Becker, Matthias Benz, Mark Blaug, Brian Coplin, Andreas Diekmann, Egon Franck, Robert Frank, Joshua Gans, Steven Hanke, Gebhard Kirchgässner, Reto Jegen, Axel Lejonhufvud, Alfred Kieser, Rafael Lalive, Simon Luechinger, Casey Mulligan, Margit Osterloh, Stephan Meier, Karl-Dieter Opp, Colin Robinson, Dan Rubinfeld, Bob Tollison, Gordon Tullock, Richard E. Wagner and Hannelore Weck-Hannemann. I sent an earlier version of this paper to a considerable number of editors of professional economics journals, many of whom were kind enough to provide me with useful remarks. They agreed and disagreed with much of what I write, but there is nearly no consensus among them. I plan to publish (some) of the responses in a forthcoming book entitled "Economics of Economics". I thank the following editors for their responses: Morris Altman (J. Socio-Economics), Iain Begg (J. Common Market Studies), Ben Bernanke (Am. Ec. Rev.), Dominique Demougin (Eur. Ec. Rev.), James Dow (Rev. Ec. Stud.), David de Meza (Ec. J.), Edward Diener (J. Happiness Studies), Peter Earl (J. Ec. Psychology), René L. Frey (Kyklos), Donald George (J. Ec. Surveys), Reiner Eichenberger (Kyklos), Daniel Hamermesh (J. Population Ecs.), Ken Koford (Eastern Ec. J.), Kai A. Konrad (Ecs. Governance), Robert Kunst (Empirical Ec.), Sam Peltzman (J. Law & Ecs.), James Poterba (J. Public Ecs.), Rudolf Richter (J. Inst. & Theor. Ecs.), Barkley Rosser Jr. (J. Ec. Beh. & Organ), Charles K. Rowley (Public Choice), Friedrich Schneider (Public Choice), Günther Schulze (J. Cult. Ecs.), Mark Schuster (J. Cult. Ecs.) and Diana Strassmann (Feminist Ecs.).

process within a reasonable period of time, if at all. But in the case of *Public Choice*, I was lucky thanks to the quick and resolute action of the (European) editor.

The author knows that, normally, he would be lucky if, after something like a year or so, he gets an invitation to resubmit the paper *according to the demands* exactly spelled out by the two to three referees and the editor(s). For most scholars, this is a proposal that cannot be refused, because their survival in academia crucially depends on publications in refereed professional journals. They are well aware of the fact that they only have a chance to get the paper accepted if they slavishly follow the demands formulated. The system of journal editing existing in our field at the present time virtually forces academics to become prostitutes: they sell themselves for money (and a good living). Unlike prostitutes who sell their bodies for money (Edlund and Korn, 2002), academics sell their soul to conform to the will of others, the referees and editors, in order to gain one advantage, namely publication. Most persons refusing to prostitute themselves and to follow the demands of the system are not academics: they cannot enter, or have to leave, academia because they fail to publish. Their integrity survives, but the persons disappear as academics.

This paper discusses the process forcing persons wanting to pursue a university career to act as intellectual prostitutes (Section 2). Intellectual or academic prostitution is defined here as acting against one's convictions in order to get a reward. The reason for such academic prostitution is seen to lie in the institutions of journal editing currently existing in economics. This system essentially accords veto power to every referee.[1] A prospective author therefore has to meet the demands formulated by the referees in order to have a chance of having the paper accepted for publication.

Some readers may feel that intellectual prostitution is not morally objectionable *per se*, but simply a particular choice made by would-be authors. This is correct; prostitution can be looked at as a normal market activity without any moral connotation.[2] The problem is that both the production and consumption activities going with academic prostitution produce undesirable outcomes. It is neither beneficial to the suppliers of academic prostitution nor to its consumers. A major reason for this failure to produce good results lies in the fact that the (anonymous) referees have no property rights on the journals they advise (Section 3).

Other readers may think that the kind of prostitution discussed here is unavoidable. The fundamental fact of scarcity forces all of us to adjust our behavior in order to survive. Suppliers wanting to sell their goods and services must carry out the wishes of the potential customers. Section 4 proposes a different point of view. Scholars are seen as performing a similar activity to artists, in particular painters who, since the Renaissance, are expected to express their own beliefs and convictions – which led to an explosion of creativity in the arts. The almost dictatorial demands advanced by the referees are difficult, or even impossible, to reconcile with authors wanting to publish their own ideas in economics journals.

Section 5 advances a modest proposal designed to substantially reduce the "need" to prostitute oneself in order to publish and be academically successful. It seeks to overcome the veto power of (anonymous) referees. My proposal is that the editor makes an initial decision whether a paper is worth publishing or not. The referees are only asked to give suggestions on how to improve the paper. The author is free to follow or to disregard this advice. Section 6 concludes.

2. How academic prostitution evolves

The author's first decision is whether he wants to submit an article to a scholarly paper or not. Only if he is willing to submit does he have a chance of eventually publishing the paper and entering and staying in academia. After considerable time has passed (today one year is not unusual[3]), the editor of the journal either rejects the paper in the first round or *demands the revisions found necessary by the referees*. The author's second decision is whether to make revisions according to these demands and therewith prostitute himself academically, or withdraw. In the latter case, the author has the gratification of keeping his intellectual purity, but time has been lost and the chance of a university career vanishes. If the author revises according to the demands of the referees, the editor takes the final decision[4] of whether to reject or accept the paper for publication with a given probability. In the case of rejection, the author has expended considerable work effort to please the referees, has lost even more time (something like two years is not unrealistic), and has to carry the moral cost of having had to prostitute himself. The effort, time and moral costs also apply in the case of acceptance, but they are counterbalanced by the benefits of having an article published, and therewith being able to enter or stay in academia. An author is more likely to intellectually prostitute himself (i.e., to revise) rather than withdraw, the higher the (subjectively expected) chance of final acceptance and the lower the (expected) revision work effort, the higher the cost of time for the revision and the lower his moral cost of prostitution.

This game captures the essence of the academic publication process as I see it.[5] It allows us to focus on the crucial determinants of the process.

208

2.1. *Revisions demanded*

All authors would like to receive referee reports helping them to improve their paper. Alas, this is rarely the case. Normally, the referees want to see substantial changes basically altering the paper. Often, an almost completely new paper is demanded. At the very least, the author is asked to write things he or she would not otherwise have written. The more fundamental and numerous the changes demanded by the referees are, the less it pays to submit a paper and to engage in an academic career.

Many economic scholars are likely to be in complete disagreement with this interpretation of the behavior of the referees. They like to think that the referees only ask for changes improving the paper in the interests of the author, but refrain from interfering any further.

Surprisingly enough, the (economic) literature on journal publication[6] does not offer any theory about the behavior of referees. The implicit assumption is that referees act in the interests of science as a whole. Engers and Gans (1998, reprinted in Gans 2000: 140) explicitly assume that "referees are motivated by a concern for the quality of research". The notion that individuals act according to general social interest is totally inconsistent with the traditional rational choice model of man (e.g., Becker, 1976; Frey, 1999). Nor is there any well-worked out theory on the behavior of editors. Laband and Piette (1994, reprinted in Gans 2000: 119) state: "to our knowledge, no widely accepted theory of editorial behavior has ever been articulated". In the literature, similar implicit assumptions as those made for referees are current (see Vandermeulen, 1972; Laband and Piette, 1994).

A useful starting point for a rational choice theory of referees' and editors' behavior is to acknowledge the difference between the two groups of actors[7] on property rights to journals. Anonymous referees have no property rights to the journal they advise. They are not concerned with the effect their advice has on the journal. The absence of property rights must be expected to lead to shirking. The interests of the journal and the referees are not aligned. The referees find themselves in a classical low cost situation (Kirchgässner, 1992). Their decisions with respect to the evaluation of the papers in their hands has little or no consequences for them, provided they keep to the *formal* rules of the profession. But with respect to the *content* of the evaluation, they are free to do whatever they please. In a low cost situation, the referees attribute some weight to what *they* consider to be the "common good". But it would be naive to assume that they only do that. Personal interests must also be expected to play a role. Many referees will be tempted to judge papers according to whether their own contributions are sufficiently appreciated and their own publications quoted. They carry, for instance, no costs when they advise rejection of a paper they dislike (e.g., because it criticizes their own work), even

Complete property rights			No property rights	
private owner and editor	sole editor	group of editors	identified referees	anonymous referees

Figure 1. Extent of property rights to journals.

if they expect that it would be beneficial for economics as a discipline. It is important to recognize that no "bad" behavior is subsumed here, but simply a behavior in line with what economic theory assumes as a matter of course in all other areas.

In contrast to referees, *editors* enjoy property rights to "their" journal. The editors' reputation is enhanced by the quality of their journal even if they do not own it. In contrast to the referees, editors are not anonymous; rather, their names are well known in the profession and are closely connected with "their" journal. Well-known examples are Keynes and the *Economic Journal* and Stigler and the *Journal of Political Economy*. The property rights of editors work indirectly through their reputation. As a consequence, editors are interested in the influence and quality of their respective journals. Such effects of reputation, and therefore the extent of property rights, are the weaker, the larger the group of editors is. Scholars outside the United Kingdom would, for example, find it difficult to name the five managing editors of today's *Economic Journal*. The extent of property rights to a journal thus varies according to organizational forms and actors, as illustrated in Figure 1.

Complete property rights are owned by a journal edited by its owner, but this organizational form does not seem to exist in economics (at least not with any well-ranked journal).[8] A sole, and therefore well-identified, editor owns stronger implicit property rights than a group of editors. When referees are identified (for instance by putting their names at the beginning of a published article[9]), their reputation is to some extent connected with the journal. Anonymous referees have no property rights in the journals they advise. Therefore they must be expected to act least in line with the interests of the respective journals. Following economic theory, the more one moves to the right in Figure 1, the stronger the private interests of editors and referees to reveal themselves is to be expected.

Some authors may subjectively perceive that all that the referees ask is also in their own best interests and in no case leads to a distortion of their own thinking. But such perception can also be viewed as the result of having so much internalized the existing publication process that even the idea of intellectual prostitution is alien. This is a striking case of a reduction in cognitive dissonance (see Festinger, 1957, in economics Akerlof and Dickens, 1982): those individuals prepared to follow the demands of the referees to the

210

letter experience less personal cost if they can convince themselves that this in no way distorts their own thinking.[10] Viewed *ex ante*, however, intellectual prostitution remains an issue.

2.2. *Cost of time*

Authors experience the opportunity cost of time throughout the whole publication decision process. It becomes particularly visible when the paper is rejected in the first or in a later round because then it is not counterbalanced by any potential or actual benefit of publication. The size of the time cost varies according to institutional conditions and one's career achievements.

In a competitive academic system, such as in the United States, and increasingly also in Europe and elsewhere, graduate students and assistant professors are under extreme time pressure. In some cases, it is an "all or nothing" issue: either they are able to publish in a "core" refereed journal, or they have to bury their dream of an academic career. The number of such publications determines the ranking of the university offering a position. Getting off to a good start is important,[11] as it is quite difficult to move upwards once one has left top universities. But the time available as a graduate student or assistant professor is generally severely limited, so that a time loss is a serious matter. It follows that for scholars starting a university career, the time costs are high, which *ceteris paribus* raises the option of not submitting the paper and looking for an alternative occupation.

For more advanced scholars, both the time cost and benefits of journal publication is lower. Empirical evidence (Oster and Hamermesh, 1998) suggests that, on balance, the lower benefits of journal publishing at a higher age outweigh the lower cost and that therefore older researchers submit less papers to journals.

2.3. *Moral costs of intellectual prostitution*

The utility loss experienced by scholars[12] who are confronted with undesired demands for revisions by referees depends on various factors. It is useful to distinguish between two extreme types:

(a) An "autonomous person" with a strong identity has well-developed ideas of his own and therefore suffers high costs from intellectual prostitution. Older and more successful persons are more likely to belong to this category than young and less successful ones. As a consequence, the former are less likely to engage in the publication process and pursue an academic career. Young scholars, in contrast, may find it less taxing to yield to the demands of referees and therefore are more likely to submit papers to refereed journals.

(b) "Other-directed persons" have low costs to adjust to the demands of other persons. This may be due to their genetic inheritance (these might be called *"born intellectual prostitutes"*) while others have learned the need to adjust in order to be able to publish (they might be called *"learned intellectual prostitutes"*).

Some of the born or learned academic prostitutes are masters at predicting what the referees and editors want to see, and from the very beginning introduce it into their papers.[13] The extent of prostitution can then no longer be identified by looking at the changes undertaken in the course of the publication process. The more perfectly the authors are able to anticipate the demands, the less they need to change. Due to the lower cost of meeting the demands for revision, born and learned intellectual prostitutes are more likely to engage in the publication game and to stay in academia.

A comparison between autonomous and other-directed persons suggests that the members of a competitively oriented academia tend to be more malleable and more directed towards fulfilling what they see to be the prevailing standards.

2.4. *Benefits of publication*

Rankings of individuals, departments and universities in modern economics are based to a large extent on publications in refereed journals (see e.g. Graves, Marchand and Thompson, 1982; Laband, 1985; Dusansky and Vernon, 1998). Publications in such journals provide substantial benefits in terms of career, income and internal recognition (see Tuckman and Leahey, 1975; Hansen, Weisbrod and Strauss, 1978, Hamermesh, Johnson and Weisbrod, 1982; Diamond, 1986; Saurer, 1988). As already pointed out, scholars at the beginning of their careers derive larger benefits than already established scholars, and therefore are more inclined to undertake journal submissions.

In competitive academic systems, citations have become increasingly used as a ranking device (see Blaug, 1999; Frey and Eichenberger, 2000). This reduces the importance of journal publications because citations refer to any kind of "publication", including papers put on the web. Some working paper series have started to introduce a refereeing system also for web publications, so that the costs caused by intellectual prostitution are transferred to this publication outlet. In principle, however, anyone can put their papers on the web without having to go through a refereeing process. While attention will be smaller than in well-established official working paper series, it nevertheless opens an effective way of evading intellectual prostitution. The higher level of original and unconventional ideas published on the web may enliven and benefit economics.[14]

212

The discussion of the publication decision process has shown that there are various determinants affecting the likelihood of submitting and revising a paper, and therewith accepting academic prostitution. The weight of these determinants depends not only on personal characteristics ("type of person") but most importantly also on the existing academic system (especially the extent of its competitiveness) and one's position on the career ladder.

3. Intellectual prostitution and no fun

So far the cost of conforming to the demands of the referees for the would-be authors has been analyzed. But what about the consequences of imposing the refereeing system for prospective readers of the articles? Perhaps the cost of intellectual prostitution to the authors is fully compensated by the benefits to the readers.[15]

The initial purpose of the refereeing system was to select or screen the "best" papers. Only gradually has it evolved into a "censuring" system, making it most difficult to have unconventional ideas accepted. Consider the case of several referees, each having veto power. The probability of an unconventional idea not being vetoed by any of them, nor by the editor(s), is very small because it is highly likely that one of them dislikes a new thought for one of three reasons: the idea is new and therefore more difficult to grasp and appreciate for the referees than are more conventional contributions; the referees are normally leading researchers in the topic treated (see the evidence in Hamermesh, 1994). They fear the loss of some of their reputation if a new idea is introduced; the new idea is less well formulated than are the well-established ideas and therefore is rejected for lack of rigor.

For these reasons, the present refereeing system tends to work against originality, but it may still make a good job of choosing the "good" papers. It is, of course, not possible to state in an absolute way what a "good" paper is. It is only possible to evaluate whether a paper corresponds to the generally accepted criteria which have emerged in a discipline. Circumstantial evidence lends some support to the notion that the present system of academic journal publication does not lead to beneficial outcomes from a broader point of view (except in part for those who have made it in the profession[16]):

(1) Many authors state that the refereeing process has indeed helped them to improve their papers. According to an empirical analysis undertaken by Laband (1990), referees "add value" to papers.[17] But more importantly in our context, they also often confirm that in order to have their papers accepted, they were "forced" to delete those parts of the paper particularly dear to them. Many authors feel that the refereeing process robbed them of the chance of really contributing what they find important and innovative. An

example is given by Brian Arthur, who states that "I put the paper ("Competing Technologies, Increasing Returns, and Lock-In by Historical Events", finally published in the *Economic Journal* 1989) through eight rewrites in this (revision) process; each time it became stiffer, more formal, less informative, and as a result more publishable" (Gans and Shepherd, 1994, reprinted in Gans, 2000: 35). Sometimes the papers published reflect more the referees' than the author's ideas. Such stories can often be heard in informal discussion within our profession.

(2) Many preliminary articles circulating in paper form, or available on the web, are known, appreciated and fruitfully used by other scholars. In those cases, the established refereeing process does not seem to be necessary to spark interest in the academic community. One may even advance the hypothesis that the "censored" versions emerging after passing the refereeing process have less impact.[18]

(3) Non-economists are using the results produced in modern economics and its publication system less and less, because they judge them to be far from relevant.[19] There is substantial evidence that economists have gradually been losing their position as important advisors to governments. *The Economist* (1997: 13; 2000: 90), for example, wonders about the "Puzzling Failure of Economics", and asks "in the long run, is the subject dead?", or the *New Yorker* (Cassidy, 1996: 50-1) remarks: "... a good deal of modern economic theory, even the kind that wins Nobel Prizes, simply does not matter much". This apparent failure has been reflected on the market for students. In most countries, economists have lost much ground to other disciplines, in particular to management.[20]

At least according to such evidence, it is not easy to defend the position that the existing journal publication process contributes greatly to making economics a generally relevant, innovative[21] and exciting discipline.

4. Scholars should be treated like artists

Is it possible to avoid intellectual prostitution at all? Is it not simply the reflection of scarcity forcing scholars to adjust? Room for publication, especially in renowned journals, is much smaller than the number of articles that scholars want to place. Rejection rates of 95 percent are quite common with many journals. As elsewhere in the economy, the suppliers of services – here ideas contained in articles – must adjust to the demanders' wishes. In this sense we are all prostitutes (in which case the term is without any meaning).

But a different view may be entertained. Scholars may be compared to artists, who we expect to express their own original ideas and convictions. We do not simply expect them to produce what the market wants. Production

214

for the market was the rule in the Middle Ages, and painters and musicians were simple artisans who had to do what their customers wanted. But the Renaissance brought a complete reorientation: artists were given the right to express themselves with as few restrictions as possible. The result was an explosion in *creativity*, Leonardo da Vinci and Michelangelo Buonarotti being the best-known examples.[22]

If scholars are to be original in a similar way to artists today, they have to be given as much independence as possible. This principle has been accorded to universities a long time ago, and is rightly guarded by them. It has also brought about an explosion of innovation never seen before.[23] Nevertheless, economics scholars have managed to establish a journal publication system, tending to turn them into intellectual prostitutes.

But how is the scarcity problem inherent in scholarly journal publication to be solved? It is important to acknowledge that many different procedures are feasible and are used in other disciplines. While the present system in economics is similar, for instance, to the one in psychology, it differs strongly from that existing in legal research. The institutional setting of journal publications presently existing in economics is special, because it tends to attribute veto power to the anonymous referees, whose interests are not aligned with those of the journal they advise, and via competition with the overall interests of economics as a discipline. The next section presents an alternative proposal, which seeks to redress this imbalance and provides more scope for individual scholars to be able to express their own ideas rather than to intellectually prostitute themselves.

5. A proposal to reduce intellectual prostitution

Prostitution, be it sexual or academic, involves choice. It is useful to distinguish between the possibilities individuals have to evade prostitution, given the existing journal editing system, and changing the journal publication system.

5.1. *Individual options*

There are three major ways of reducing the burden of being forced to intellectually prostitute oneself:

(a) Revising papers according to the demands of referees and editor(s) can be taken as purely instrumental to gain entry and tenure into the academic system. But once in, one stops conforming to the undesirable demands. Given reasonable magnitudes of the relevant costs, benefits and parameters (like the probability of final rejection), this normally means that it is more attractive to turn to publication activities with no, or at least less stringent[24] refereeing demands. Conventional possibilities are to write and edit books,[25] contribute to collections of articles or *Festschriften*, or write newspaper columns – or not to publish at all. Increasingly it is possible to put one's articles on the web or in some working paper series (provided there is no refereeing process similar to printed journals).

However, as is the case with many other resolutions, it is not easy to act in a time-consistent way. Once one has entered academia, incentives change. There are moral costs to change course once one has been successful and to refrain from intellectual prostitution. As Oster and Hamermesh (1998) empirically show, success breeds later success, i.e., once one has been able to publish in refereed journals, it is easier to continue. Finally, once one belongs to a group or – as Leijonhufvud (1973) states – to a "caste" (here the tenured professional economists in the universities), one tends to identify with it,[26] and finds it costly to deviate from convention. For these cost reasons, it has to be expected that few academics are willing to change once they are in academia.[27]

(b) One can totally refuse to intellectually prostitute oneself by submitting papers to journals accepting papers without the formal refereeing process. This is almost impossible nowadays because non-refereed journals count little, if anything, with respect to crucial academic career decisions. In tandem, the respective articles must be expected to receive less attention, and to be quoted less.

To many readers, this option probably seems naive, or even ridiculous. But at least one noted economist successfully pursued this strategy.[28] He knew that the referees would demand changes he was not prepared to make. He therefore submitted his papers, some of which became "classics", to non-refereed journals. This risky strategy paid off in the case of Reinhard Selten: he was awarded the Nobel Prize.

(c) One can fight the demands made by the referees and editors. This is again a risky strategy. Academics tend to be prima donnas and do not easily change their conclusions, especially when writing the referee report has cost them much time and effort. To fight back is much easier with formal aspects than with matters of content, which are sometimes tied to ideological preconceptions. Fighting back has, moreover, costs in terms of self-respect. Some authors are too proud to start haggling about a decision taken by other persons.

5.2. *Changing the journal publication system*

A modest change in the publication procedure would greatly reduce the incidence of intellectual prostitution. The journal's editor(s) should take the *basic*

216

decision of whether to accept or reject a paper at the outset, based on how interesting they judge the content to be. In some cases, it may be useful to consult other scholars about this basic decision. The appropriate body is the board of editors, which has no function with most journals today.

The board exists to provide academic weight to the journal, but also to serve as a clue for what type of papers the journal is interested in. Under this provision, the managing editor(s) should be able to judge whether a paper's content is valuable enough to merit publication in the journal. Because the editor(s) (and possibly the members of the board consulted) would only have to decide whether to accept or reject a paper, the decision can be quickly made. This procedure would greatly reduce two types of cost to the prospective authors: the time cost would be much lower than today, and there would be no prostitution cost, because the acceptance decision would not be conditional on meeting the referees' demands.

Only in the second phase would referees be invited to collaborate. They should solely make suggestions on how the paper can be improved. Then the authors can use what *they* find useful, and can disregard what *they* do not like. The role of the referees would change. Instead of having to mainly demonstrate how clever they are in destroying the author's ideas,[29] they would now be invited to be supportive. The referees would lose some of their power, in particular they could no longer veto a paper they did not like (for instance, because their own ideas are not sufficiently appreciated). As a consequence, there would be an incentive problem. It would become more difficult to get referees. This could be counteracted by giving them the right to publish their dissenting views, together with the original paper.[30] The space allotted for this purpose could be short (say one printed page or less).

It might be argued that the difference in procedure would have no effect on the papers published. Editors would choose the papers they like. The born or learned intellectual prostitutes would again win because they are best able to predict what the editors like. But there is a major difference in the result, due to the different property rights to the journal. The anonymous referees, who have no property rights to the journal, might become active only *after* the basic acceptance decision has been made. The editor(s) who have (some) property rights on the journal due to their reputation, would have no incentive to simply accept those papers they personally like. At least to some extent they would be induced to accept papers expected to raise the journal's reputation.[31] They would actively compete for papers they expect to make a future impact on the field; i.e., to be cited much in the future.

It may also be claimed that the proposal made is futile because a "good" journal already follows the procedure that the editor(s) decide(s) and the referees only advise. But in most cases, this remains at best an ideal and is not put into practice. Generally, the editors can only accept papers if *all* the referees agree *after* one or more rounds of revisions.[32] Under the present system, an editor cannot accept a paper he or she likes when the referees advise rejection. Only when the referees' opinions differ and are in clear contradiction, has the editor some discretionary power. Seasoned (sole) editors develop skills to extend their discretionary power, mainly by choosing the "right" referees. But there are clear limits to such attempts. With some journals, the decisions are taken by the group of managing editors. While, with the help of their reputation, they have stronger property rights than outside referees, authors only have a chance if they muster the support of the majority, and do not provoke a veto. This system again creates incentives for intellectual prostitution.

It may further be questioned whether the authors whose papers have been accepted have sufficient incentive to improve their paper. But rational authors wish to integrate good suggestions offered by the referees. It is in the authors' own best interests to carefully listen to the suggestions for improvement – but this is quite distinct from being "forced" to follow the changes demanded by the referees.

Yet another concern may be that the editors are unable to fulfil the more extensive role attributed to them. The major role of the referees cannot be discarded without loss of quality in publications. This is debatable because, due to the missing property rights, the referees' interests are not in line with the journal seeking their advice. Scholars are asked to referee a paper without knowing anything about the quality of the *other* papers under consideration for publication. Referees thus have to try to decide according to some mystical absolute standards rather than be able to select the *relatively best* paper from those submitted. The editors, in contrast, do have this knowledge and are therefore well equipped to make the basic initial decision.

When judging the proposal advanced here, it should not be overlooked that, according to many observers, the present journal publication system attributing veto power to referees does not function that well.[33] This has become clear from the responses by 140 leading economists about their journal submission experiences and the list of "classic" papers once, and often more than once, rejected (Gans and Shepherd, 1994). A well-known example is Akerlof's "Market for Lemons", which was rejected by the *American Economic Review* and the *Review of Economic Studies* as being "trivial", and by the *Journal of Political Economy* for being "too general" before it was accepted by the *Quarterly Journal of Economics*, which was instrumental in him winning the Nobel Prize. But whatever one's opinion about the state of economics, a *comparative* perspective is required. No publication procedure, *including* the one existing at present, produces perfect results. It is therefore

218

necessary to compare the imperfect results produced by the modest change in the publication process suggested here to the equally imperfect results of the present system.

6. Conclusions

The existing refereeing process commonly used in economics journals essentially grants veto power to any referee. But the interests of the referees are not aligned with those of the journal. Due to reputation effects, the editors' incentives are more in line but they are certainly not identical with those of the journal. Editors accept referees' vetoes not least because it relieves them of some of the burden of the many rejections that scarcity of journal space imposes. Yet the results of this publication process are most unsatisfactory:

(a) The authors are forced to follow closely, if not slavishly, referees' demands, as they know that they otherwise cannot publish and pursue an academic career. An even more advanced form of intellectual prostitution is to try to predict and steer who the referees will be, and to write and cite accordingly.

(b) Economics is inundated with boring and irrelevant papers. They lack originality and produce only small variations on themes commonly accepted within the discipline. Economics loses its importance for advising governments and becomes increasingly less attractive as a field for students.

The proposal developed here considers scholars to be like artists, who must be given much room for expressing themselves. This can be achieved by three changes, which make the proposal superior to the existing publication procedure:

(1) The *editors* decide autonomously whether a submitted paper is interesting and original and accept or reject it for publication. This makes their work more attractive.

(2) *Referees* are invited to suggest non-binding improvements. Those with fundamental objections to the paper are invited to summarize their views on one ore two pages after the published article. This provides an incentive to referee more carefully.

(3) The *authors* of accepted papers introduce those recommendations they find useful. They keep full control over their paper and can be more innovative.

These changes should be able to:
– reduce authors' incentives to intellectually prostitute themselves;
– speed up the publication decision process; and
– bolster authors' creativity, leading to more innovative and relevant articles in economics.

Notes

1. That editors reject papers if only one referee advises rejection irrespective of the other referees' judgement is based on the author's own experience, and is supported by confirming impressions by many other economics scholars the author consulted on this point. See also Seidl, Schmidt and Grösche (2002) who take it as a matter of course that a referee has veto power despite the fact that referees' recommendations may be highly contradictory (Cicchetti, 1991). They also refer to much literature establishing the fact for other disciplines.

2. Much prostitution is indeed voluntary and undertaken because of the good pay; see Edlund and Korn (2002: 209–210 and 188–192).

3. Ellison (2000) finds on average somewhat shorter periods between initial submission and final acceptance, varying from 3–6 months to 2–3 years. My impression is that the time until authors get the first reaction has increased considerably. The notion that the reviewing process has lengthened is supported by the empirical evidence collected by Coe and Weinstock, 1967; Yohe, 1980; Laband, McCormick and Maloney, 1990. A recent (non-representative) survey of the refereeing process of 166 journals in economics (Seidl, Schmidt and Grösche, 2002) asked the question: "After submission, how long did it take on average to get a reply other than just a confirmation that your paper had been received?" It turns out that hardly any journal decides in less than 10 weeks, and more than half need 20 weeks and more to take a decision. The average length is 21 weeks, i.e., more than five months.

4. It is easy to envisage further rounds of revisions.

5. I believe I have some experience and competence in this area. I have published more than 350 papers in over 140 refereed journals during the period 1965–2002. Among them are leading economics journals such as *AER*, *JPE*, *RES*, *REcsStats*, *EJ*, *JEcLit* and *JEcPersp.*, but also in political science (e.g., *APSR*), psychology, law and sociology journals. I have also tried the alternatives to journal publications by writing 16 books and by being a columnist for a leading weekly newspaper. I have served as one of the two (and later three) managing editors of *Kyklos* since 1970, am a member of the board of editors of 23 journals and over the years have served as referee for numerous journals.

6. See, for instance, Laband, 1990; Blank, 1991; Hamermesh, 1994; Laband and Piette, 1994; Engers and Gans, 1998; Coupé, 2000.

7. This distinction has been disregarded in the literature. Laband (1990) is a notable exception, but he does not analyze the behavioral consequences.

8. But it would be interesting to analyze why this is not the case, especially in view of the fact that it is possible to derive sizeable profits from running an academic journal, see Bergstrom (2001).

9. Some journals seek to raise the reputation of individual editors on their board of managing editors by explicitly stating which editor is responsible for having accepted a particular article.

10. A similar process of cognitive adaptation seems to happen to sexual prostitutes, most of whom report no feeling of regret about their choice of occupation (Bullough and Bullough, 1987).

11. That especially the first article published is of great importance for economics' scholars is shown by Siow (1991).

12. Many economics authors are dissatisfied with the refereeing process. In the empirical study by Seidl, Schmidt and Grösche (2002) it turns out that out of 106 professional journals only 36 are considered to perform in a satisfactory or better way with respect to

the way they handle submissions. 23 were judged to do so in an unsatisfactory or even bad or very bad way, among them many of the most prestigious journals included in the well-known list compiled by Diamond (1989).

13. It has become quite common for authors to attempt to predict who will be the referees. By citing some authors they expect to be favorable to their paper, they raise the chance of them being chosen by the editor as referee.

14. Gordon Tullock long ago suggested that scholars should be able to recommend papers they find particularly good. If, for instance, a paper is recommended by Kenneth Arrow or William Baumol, a valuable signal is provided to other scholars inducing them to consult the paper.

15. This seems to be the case for sexual prostitution because otherwise it is difficult to explain the large demand in all periods and countries (for evidence see Edlund and Korn 2002).

16. But even among extremely successful economists, awarded the Nobel Prize, there are some who harshly criticize the existing journal publication system. Examples are Leontief (1971), Coase (1994) or Buchanan (2000); see more generally Leijorihufvud (1973) and Cassidy (1996).

17. But Laband (1990) explicitly warns the readers in his second footnote: "The search for value-added necessarily is grounded on the *assumption* that the review process in economics is intended to add value to manuscripts." (my emphasis).

18. This hypothesis is in principle empirically testable. One could, for example, study the development over time of the proportion of censored papers to uncensored papers quoted by other scholars in their work. But this indicator is difficult to construct because many papers appearing in working paper series on paper and the web had to pass some sort of refereeing process. Moreover, scholars possibly quote unpublished papers less than published ones, and this tendency may have increased over time. This is not necessarily due to an effort to appear more original than one really is, but perhaps even more to the fact that one remembers an unpublished paper less vividly than a published one when sitting down to write an article.

19. Most academic economists do not share this evaluation at all, but rather side with Summers (2000: 1), proclaiming that "What economists think, say, and do has profound implications for the lives of literally billions of their fellow citizens". It is, of course, not surprising that economists, like any other self-interested group, fight for their profession and tend to reject criticism.

20. These aspects are more fully discussed in e.g., Blaug (2002), van Bergeijk et al. (1997), Middleton (1998), Reder (1999), and Frey (2002) where a large amount of literature is quoted.

21. It has often been stated that it is very difficult to publish unorthodox papers under the present journal publication system; see, for instance, the evidence collected in Gans and Shepherd (1994).

22. I here draw on the literature on the economics of art; see Towse (1997), Throsby (2000), Frey (2000).

23. Commercially driven research within firms may also be innovative, but it is characteristic that such institutions often act as if they were universities, leaving their researchers considerable freedom.

24. Established economists often have good personal contacts to editors. This is normally the case for inhouse journals. It has been argued that this helps them to get their articles through with less changes demanded, and allows them to publish in invited special issues. Gans and Shepherd (1994), reprinted in Gans (2000: 34) report: "Editors at several journ-

als apparently sometimes permit certain authors to bypass the journals' normal refereeing process" (see also Gerrity and McKenzie, 1978; Laband, 1985).

25. But more and more editing houses ask outside referees to evaluate book proposals and manuscripts. Normally, referees interfere here much less than in journal publishing, especially when it comes to evaluating a completed manuscript. Therefore, with books, the need to intellectually prostitute oneself is considerably lower.

26. Leijorihufvud (1973) suggests that economists are solely motivated by peer acceptance.

27. There is an analogy here to sexual prostitution: many women forced into prostitution in order to be able to pay off their debts choose to stay in the profession even when they are debt-free (Muroi and Sasaki, 1997 for Thai prostitutes in Japan).

28. Personal communication to the author.

29. Anonymity certainly contributes to referees being very critical. See the controlled experiments made in the late 1980s at the *American Economic Review* by Blank (1991), finding lower acceptance rates and more critical reviews when both the referees' and the author's identities are unknown (double-blind refereeing).

30. I owe this idea to Reto Jegen.

31. The question of how editors are to be selected is beyond the scope of this paper. It must suffice to state that it would be mistaken to rely on performance compensation, for the reasons given in Frey (1997) and Frey and Osterloh (2002).

32. The editors of some journals may reject papers clearly below the journal's standards without consulting the referees. But most journals do not reject without adding lengthy referee comments. This looks "fair" and takes pressure off the editors, but disregards the (often high) cost of having to wait for this decision (nowadays often one year or even longer).

33. In response to the shortcomings of the present journal publishing system some preliminary efforts have been undertaken to improve it. An example is the *Berkeley Electronic Journals in Economic Analysis and Policy* which guarantees a 10-week turnaround, simultaneous consideration in four journals of different quality levels, and immediate publication after acceptance.

References

Akerlof, G.A. and Dickens, W.T. (1982). The economic consequences of cognitive dissonance. *American Economic Review* 72: 307–319.

Becker, G.S. (1976). *The economic approach to human behavior*. Chicago: Chicago University Press.

Bergstrom, T.C. (2001). Free labour for costly journals? *Journal of Economic Perspectives* 15: 183–198.

Blank, R.M. (1991). The effects of double-blind versus single-blind reviewing: Experimental evidence from the American Economic Review. *American Economic Review* 5: 1041–1068.

Blaug, M. (1999). Who's who in economics (3rd Edn), Cheltenham, UK: Edward Elgar.

Blaug, M. (2002). Ugly currents in modern economics. In: Maki U. (Ed.), *Fact and fiction in economics*. Cambridge: Cambridge University Press.

Buchanan, J.M. (2000). Saving the soul of classical economics. *Wall Street Journal*, January 1st.

Bullough, V.L. and Bullough, B. (1987). *Women and prostitution: A social history.* Buffalo: Prometheus Books.

Cassidy, J. (1996). The decline of economics. *New Yorker* 2: 50–60.

Cicchetti, D.V. (1991). The reliability of peer review for manuscripts and grant submissions: A cross disciplinary investigation. *Behavioral and Brain Sciences* 14: 119–186.

Coase, R.H. (1994). *Essays on economics and economists.* Chicago and London: Chicago University Press.

Coe, R.K. and Weinstock, I. (1967). Editorial policies of the major economics journals. *Quarterly Review of Economics and Business* 7: 37–43.

Coupé, T. (2000). Revealed performances. Worldwide rankings of economists and economic departments. Working Paper, ECA RES, Université Libre de Bruxelles.

Diamond, A. (1986). The life-cycle research productivity of mathematicians and scientists. *Journal of Gerontology* 41: 520–525.

Diamond, A. (1989). The core journals in economics. *Current Contents* 1: 4–11.

Dusansky, R. and Vernon, C.J. (1998). Rankings of U.S. economics departments. *Journal of Economic Perspectives* 12: 157–170.

Economist, The (1997). The puzzling failure of economics. *The Economist,* August 23rd: 13.

Economist, The (2000). Economics forum: The future of economics. *The Economist,* March 4th: 90.

Edlund, L. and Korn, E. (2002). A theory of prostitution. *Journal of Political Economy* 110: 181–214.

Ellison, G. (2000). The slowdown of the economics publishing process. NBER Working Paper No. W 7804, July.

Engers, M. and Gans, J.S. (1998). Why referees are not paid (enough). *American Economic Review* 88: 1341–1350.

Festinger, L. (1957). *A theory of cognitive dissonance.* Stanford: Stanford University Press.

Frank, R. (1987). If homo economicus could choose his own utility function, would he want one with a conscience? *American Economic Review* 77: 593–604.

Frey, B.S. (1997). *Not just for the money.* Cheltenham, UK and Northampton, USA: Elgar.

Frey, B.S. (1999). *Economics as a science of human behaviour.* 2nd rev. and extended ed., Boston and Dordrecht: Kluwer.

Frey, B.S. (2000). *Arts and economics: Analysis and cultural policy.* Berlin, Heidelberg, New York: Springer-Verlag.

Frey, B.S. (2002). Do economists affect policy outcomes? Working Paper Series, Institute for Empirical Research, University of Zürich.

Frey, B.S. and Eichenberger, R. (2000). The ranking of economists and management scientists in Europe. A quantitative analysis. *Journal des Economistes et des Etudes Humaines* 10: 575–581.

Frey, B.S. and Osterloh, M. (Eds.) (2002). *Successful management by motivation.* Berlin, Heidelberg and New York: Springer.

Gans, J. (2000). *Publishing economics: Analyses of the academic journal market in economics.* Cheltenham, UK, and Northampton, MA, USA: Elgar.

Gans, J.S. and Shepherd, G.B. (1994). How are the mighty fallen: Rejected classic articles by leading economists. *Journal of Economic Perspectives* 8: 165–180.

Gerrity, D.M. and McKenzie, R.B. (1978). The ranking of southern economics departments: New criterion and further evidence. *Southern Economic Journal* 11: 161–166.

Graves, P.E., Marchand, J.R. and Thompson, R. (1982). Economics departmental rankings: Research incentives, constraints, and efficiency. *American Economic Review* 72: 1131–1141.

Hamermesh, D.S. (1994). Facts and myths about refereeing. *Journal of Economic Perspectives* 8: 153–164.

Hamermesh, D.S., Johnson, G.E. and Weisbrod, B.A. (1982). Scholarship, citations and salaries: Economic rewards in economics. *Southern Economic Journal* 49: 472–481.

Hansen, W.L., Weisbrod, B.A. and Strauss, R.P. (1978). Modeling the earnings and research productivity of academic economists. *Journal of Political Economy* 86: 729–741.

Kirchgässner, G. (1992). Towards a theory of low-cost decisions. *European Journal of Political Economy* 8: 305–320.

Laband, D.N. (1985). Publishing favoritism: A critique of department rankings based on quantitative publishing performance. *Southern Economic Journal* 52: 510–515.

Laband, D.N., McCormick, R.E. and Maloney, M.T. (1990). The review process in economics: Some empirical findings. Mimeo.

Laband, D.N. (1990). Is there value-added from the review process in economics?: Preliminary evidence from authors. *Quarterly Journal of Economics* 2: 341–352.

Leijorihufvud, A.(1973). Life among the econ. *Western Economic Journal* 11: 327–337.

Leontief, W. (1971). Theoretical assumptions and nonobserved facts. *American Economic Journal* 61: 1–7.

Middleton, R. (1998). *Charlatans or saviours? Economists and the British economy from Marshall to Meade*. Northampton MA: Edward Elgar Publisher.

Muroi, H. and Sasaki, N. (1997). Tourism and prostitution in Japan. In: Sinclair, M.T. (Ed.), *Gender, work and tourism*. London: Routledge.

Oster, S.M. and Hamermesh, D.S. (1998). Aging and productivity among economists. *Review of Economics and Statistics* 80: 154–157.

Reder, M.W. (1999). *Economics. The culture of a controversial science*. Chicago and London: University of Chicago Press.

Sauer, R. (1988). Estimates of the returns to quality and co-authorship in economic academia. *Journal of Political Economy* 96: 855–866.

Seidl, C., Schmidt, U. and Grösche, P. (2002). A beauty contest of referee processes of economics journals: Preliminary results. Mimeo, Department of Economics, University of Kiel.

Siow, A. (1991). Are first impressions important in academia? *Journal of Human Resources* 26: 236–255.

Summers, L.H. (2000). International financial crises: Causes, preventions and cures. *American Economic Review* 90: 1–16.

Throsby, D.C. (2000). *Economics and culture*. Cambridge: Cambridge University Press.

Towse, R. (1997). *Cultural economics: The arts, the heritage and the media industries*. 2 Vols. Cheltenham, U.K. and Lyme, U.S.: Edward Elgar.

Tuckman, H.P. and Leahey, J. (1975). What is an article worth? *Journal of Political Economy* 83: 951–967.

van Bergeijk, P.A.G., et al. (Eds.) (1997). *Economic science and practice: The roles of academic economists and policy-makers*. Cheltenham, UK, and Lyme, NH: Elgar.

Vandermeulen, A. (1972). Manuscripts in the Maelstrom: A theory of the editorial process. *Public Choice* 13: 107–111.

Yohe, G.W. (1980). Current publication lags in economics journals. *Journal of Economic Literature* 18: 1050–1055.

Journal of Public Economics 44 (1991) 65–86. North-Holland

Ideological conviction and persuasion in the rent-seeking society

Roger D. Congleton*

Center for Study of Public Choice, George Mason University, Fairfax, VA 22030, USA

Received June 1989, revised version received April 1990

The paper develops a model of rent-seeking in a democratic political context where voting, as well as rent-seeking, matters. In this context, the paper demonstrates that voter ideology is a constraint on the rent-seeking game as well as a possible avenue of rent-seeking. In a setting where there are both rent-seeking and ideological interest groups, rent-seekers can free ride on the efforts of ideologues, which tends to reduce rent-seeking effort. In a setting where complementary economic and ideological interest groups coordinate their efforts, both rent-seeking and ideological conflict tend to increase.

'Error and ignorance often are not due to low mental capacity but to "prejudice", which can blind men even to the obvious' – Frank Knight (1950).

1. Introduction

For the most part, the literature on rent-seeking has operated under the assumption that special interest groups seek and gain *economic* rents from favorable legislation by investing economic resources in the lobbying process.[1] Large rents are considered to be consequences of large investments in rent-seeking activities, other things being equal. Little attention has been focused on the role of ideology or ideological interest groups in this process. Yet, as Tullock (1981, 1987) has observed, the rent-seeking industry is smaller than one would expect based on the standard models. Moreover, rent-conferring programs are rarely as efficient as they might have been.

---

*William Hunter, Chris Paul, Gordon Tullock, Al Wilhite, and an anonymous referee made helpful comments on previous drafts of the paper. They, of course, bear no responsibility for any errors or misconceptions that remain, or for the use to which I put their good advice. A previous version of the paper was presented at the 1989 meetings of the Public Choice Society.
[1]Buchanan, Tollison and Tullock (1980) contains a good sampling of the methodology of the rent-seeking approach. Bhagwati et al. (1984) prefer the term DUP, directly unproductive activities.

Quotas and price supports are more common than lump-sum payments in cash.

This paper argues that a proper accounting of the effects of ideology can shed considerable light on both the rhetoric and reality of the politics of redistribution. In polities where voting matters, ideology is both a constraint on the rent-seeking domain and an element of that domain. In order to demonstrate this, a model of the interplay between economic interest groups, ideological interest groups and voters is developed which includes roles for preference and message filtering aspects of ideology. While little generally can be said about the relationship between ideology and rent-seeking without specifying the specific content of an ideology, the analysis demonstrates that the strength of the electorate's ideological convictions does have systematic effects on the extent and scope of rent-seeking activities. The analysis also demonstrates that interaction between economic and ideological groups affects the level of rent-seeking activities.

Ideology constrains the process of rent seeking in a democratic polity in several ways. For example, transfer activities are constrained by institutional rules based, at least partly, on the ideological beliefs of past participants in the political process. Under the U.S. Constitution, one is not allowed to expropriate private property without compensating its owner. To the extent that institutions change more slowly than the ideological beliefs of those affected by them, the ideological beliefs of past participants in the political process constrain the feasible realm of current transfer schemes. [See North (1988) for a discussion of ideology and institutions.] Yet, while institutional arrangements often increase the cost of such transfers, they do not rule them out. As a consequence, it is often profitable for individuals to promote public policies which directly or indirectly transfer wealth to their own accounts.

The range of transfers one might obtain is also constrained by current ideology insofar as the ideological preferences of those with ultimate political control affect the transfer policies finally adopted. Political ideologies normally include a notion of the good society towards which the actual, naturally imperfect, society should move. New transfer schemes which are said to move society closer to an accepted ideal naturally have greater appeal than those which go against the ideological grain. If the prevailing ideology leads voters to prefer transfers from the rich to the poor to other transfer schemes, such transfers will be more likely, other things being equal. In this manner, the current ideology of political decision-makers partly determines the range of *politically* feasible transfer schemes.

Ideology also constrains the range of transfers insofar as it affects the domain of political debate. Success in policy debate is obviously an important matter. Special interest groups rarely have sufficient votes to directly determine the policy sought. Consequently, successful enactment usually requires the support of individuals who are not direct beneficiaries of the proposed program. This can be a matter of log rolling, where several special interest groups join forces to assure simultaneous passage of a melange of transfer programs. See Tullock (1970). Or, of greater interest here, a majority coalition can be assembled by *persuading* enough voters who are not direct beneficiaries of a particular redistribution scheme that their indirect interest in a more perfect society is served. Such arguments are generally ideological in nature and serve to legitimize the transfer programs sought. Because not all arguments are equally persuasive, the ideological filters of the relevant population of voters shape the domain of the policy debate. Ideological filters thereby affect both the rhetoric and reality of transfers.

It is the *information processing* aspect of ideology that is the focus of analysis in this paper. Ideological aspects of political institutions and voter tastes are taken as given. It is clear that the informational aspects of ideology are important in a rent-seeking society. Political persuasion becomes the principle legitimate door left open for rent-seekers in a setting where tastes and institutional arrangements are relatively unsusceptible to change. Since the information filters of voters determine just how persuasive a given line of argument is, these filters also determine ultimately who gets what.

As evidence of ideologically oriented debate, observe that arguments for farm programs, which tend to benefit individuals with large farms more than those with small farms, are publicly cast in terms of the Jeffersonian ideal of a rural agrarian society rather than power politics. Sympathy for the poor hard-working independent farm family is evoked, almost as an endangered species, rather than respect for a politically powerful coalition. Appparently, it is not sufficient to be the most exuberant lobbyist favoring transfers to wealthy land owners. Neither voters not their representatives are persuaded by arguments based solely on 'I want'. Since the median voter is not a farmer, he must be convinced to favor such transfers on other grounds.

Both informational and preference aspects of ideology have previously attracted the attention of researchers interested in political outcomes. For example, evidence that ideological concerns affect presidential elections is discussed in Enelow and Hinich (1984, ch. 9). Kau and Rubin (1982) provide statistical evidence from role-call votes in the U.S. Congress that ideological preferences influence legislation.[2] Kalt and Zupan (1984) find evidence of

---

[2]There is by no means a complete consensus on the importance of ideology in political decision-making. Several prominent economists argue that what appears to be ideology is actually personal economic interest rather than an interest in the 'good society', however conceived. See, for example, Stigler (1976) or Peltzman (1984). However, if politics is only about economic interests it is difficult to explain the ideological *language* of political debates. Unless ideological arguments are more persuasive than economic arguments, there is no obvious reason to expect individuals seeking to advance their economic interests to cloak their efforts in ideological terms. Moreover, it is difficult to explain why ideological arguments are persuasive unless voters and/or representatives are at least partly motivated by ideological concerns.

what they refer to as ideological shirking in their examination of Senate votes on strip mining. Poole and Daniels (1985) suggest that more than 80 percent of roll-call voting can be explained by a one-dimensional ideological spectrum. Enelow and Hinich (1982) argue that ideological labels allow voters accurately to estimate candidate positions on a variety of issues with a minimal investment in information. However, little attention has been focused on ideology's role in political debate or on the level of resources invested in political contests.

In order to analyze the effect that ideology has on political debate, a model of political persuasion is developed in the next section of the paper. Voters are assumed to have Bayesian priors over the consequences of policy alternatives which can be affected by messages sent by rent-seeking and/or ideological groups. Messages affect political outcomes by changing voter estimates of the probable *consequences* of the policy alternatives to be voted on. Economic interest groups are modelled as groups that sponsor messages in order to increase (or protect) their economic rents. Ideological interest groups are assumed to sponsor messages to advance their vision of the ideal world.

The model developed is sufficiently general that it can be interpreted in non-ideological terms as a model of investment in the manipulation of voter information in a world of uncertainty. It sheds light on the role of ideology in political debate only insofar as the link between political messages and expected policy consequences can be given an ideological interpretation. However, this link is fairly direct. In Bayesian terms, an individual's ideological theories and conviction can be characterized as a distribution of prior probabilities used to interpret political messages and forecast the consequences of political or other policies. Seen in this light, ideology and ideological conviction affect the conclusions (posterior probabilities) that voters draw from political messages. Insofar as interest groups sponsor political messages because of their effects on policy outcomes, ideology and ideological conviction affect both the content and intensity of policy debates. The analysis that follows suggests that, other things being equal, fewer resources will be invested in political debate as the level of ideological conviction increases.

The remainder of the paper is organized as follows. Section 2 models the effects of rent-seeking in a democratic polity populated by voters who are more or less persuadable. Section 3 characterizes equilibrium levels of rent-seeking in such an environment. Section 4 explores the extent to which the efforts of ideological groups affect rent-seeking activities. Section 5 summarizes the results and suggests possible extensions.

2. A model of the effects of ideology and rent-seeking on elections

The essential features of ideology's effect on politics can be demonstrated by focusing on an ordinary day-to-day choice of some public service level. Consider the politics of a world in which there are two goods, a public service produced by government, G, and a private consumption good, C, where the method of finance is pre-determined. Suppose that the output of the public service level is to be determined by a direct vote (or by a subset of representatives chosen randomly from the population of voters), and that the extent of the public service is far easier to determine than its production and finance costs are. (A brief reflection on the wide range of professional estimates of the burden of the national debt or of the cost of public funds will make this assumption seem plausible.)

Voters opt for the public service level which maximizes their expected utility subject to personal and public budget constraints. However, this cannot be done without forecasting the tax price of the public service. Given models of government production and taxation, the result is a probabilistic representation of the link between service levels and personal tax burden. Final estimates of the consequences of policy are based on posterior probabilities generated from pre-campaign priors and new information processed in the period immediately preceding the policy choice.

The individual's subjective posterior probability distribution of possible tax burdens associated with a particular service level is conditioned on the service level, past experience, and the range and number of new policy messages confronted. Similar structures have been previously used by Congleton (1986) and Austin-Smith (1987). Ideology plays a role in the estimation of tax burden insofar as it affects both the choice of models used to forecast tax burdens and production costs, and one's confidence in them. That is to say, ideological theories partly determine the shape of an individual's posterior probability function for given values of the service level, experience, and political messages. An individual's ideological conviction is simply the extent to which his priors for specific theories approach unity.[3]

Special interest groups are assumed to sponsor messages as a means of altering the electorate's anticipated tax price for the public services. Groups with an interest in greater service levels attempt to convince voters that their tax costs will be smaller than initially believed. Those opposed to an increase in service levels attempt to persuade voters that their tax costs will be higher than initially thought. The extent to which a voter is open to influence by political messages is determined by his past experience with political

---

[3]The extent to which an individual has strong beliefs is, in principle, independent of the particular preference content of his ideology. One can be more or less committed to principles of democratic tolerance or to more extreme ideologies like Maoism or Fundamentalist Islam. One can be more or less confident that particular policies doom society or lead to nirvana. Although the term ideologue is rarely used as a complement, the essential feature of an ideologue is his confident view of the world rather than his particular beliefs.

messages and policy which, for the purposes of this paper, is represented by parameter I, denoting the extent of an individual's ideological conviction.[4]

To the extent that interest groups can be classified into those favoring more of the government service and those favoring less of the service than a typical voter, one can represent interest group activities as a contest between two groups. Suppose that each group sponsors a single message honed for maximum impact. Let M_1 be the number of messages confronted by the voter which imply that the tax burden of the program will be small, and M_2 be the number of messages suggesting that the tax burden will be large.

The typical voter's preferred service level is the one that maximizes:

$$U^e = P^0 U(G, Y) + \int_0^{+} P U(G, C)\, dT,$$

$$(1)$$

$$U_G > 0, \quad U_C > 0, \quad U_{CG} > 0, \quad U_{GG} < 0, \quad U_{CC} < 0,$$

where

$$P = p(T \mid G, I, M_1, M_2),$$

$$(2)$$

$$P^0 = 1 - \int_0^{+} P\, dT,$$

and

$$C = Y - T,$$ $$(3)$$

with

$$P_G > 0, \quad P_I < 0, \quad P_{M1} < 0, \quad P_{M2} > 0,$$

$$P_{GM1} > 0, \quad P_{GM2} < 0, \quad P_{IG} = 0,$$

$$P_{GG} = 0, \quad P_{M1M1} < 0, \quad P_{M2M2} > 0 \quad \text{and} \quad P_{M1M2} < 0.$$

(Letter subscripts designate partial derivatives with respect to the variable subscripted.) P is the voter's conditional subjective probability distribution

---

[4]See Congleton (1986) for an analysis of the messages that policy proponents tend to transmit to the voters. It bears noting that message filtering is both more necessary and more difficult in the area of politics than in most other areas. A good deal of the information available to voters is directly or indirectly provided by rent-seeking groups with a direct interest in the policy under review. For example, defense contractors often sponsor messages that attempt to persuade voters to favor a strong national defense; while educators sponsor messages rationalizing new schools or higher salaries for educators. Because the sponsors of political messages are known to be building a case for particular policies, their messages cannot be taken at face value. At the very least, the information provided tends to have a selectivity bias.

over possible *positive* tax burdens. The probability of a zero tax, P^0, is one minus the probability of a tax greater than zero. Y is the voter's pre-tax income.[5]

The general shape of the conditional probability distribution reflects the voter's initial beliefs about tax burdens and the plausibility of alternative political messages. His Bayesian priors are this distribution conditioned on no political messages. His Bayesian posteriors are this distribution conditioned on the actual series of political messages confronted.

Conviction parameter I represents the extent to which messages affect prior beliefs about tax burdens. A pure ideologue ignores all new political messages, P_{M1} and P_{M2} approach zero as I approaches infinity. Naturally, the effect that ideological conviction has on the probability of a particular tax burden depends on the content of the ideology deemed most plausible by the voter. For convenience, it is arbitrarily assumed that an increase in ideological conviction causes a decrease in the expected tax price of the public service, $P_I < 0$. That is to say, voters are assumed to be ideologically predisposed to be a bit left of center.

Differentiating eq. (1) with respect to G and setting the result equal to zero characterizes the voter's preferred service level:

$$\int_0^+ P_G(U - U^0)\,dT + \int_0^+ P(U_G - U_G^0)\,dT = 0, \tag{4}$$

where

$$U^0 = U(G, Y).$$

Each voter prefers the public service level that sets the marginal utility from the public service equal to his expected marginal tax cost for the service in terms of utility sacrificed from reduced private consumption.

The implicit function theorem implies that eq, (4) can be used as a basis to characterize a voter's preferred public service level, G^*, as a function of the variables beyond his control:

$$G^* = g(Y, I, M_1, M_2). \tag{5}$$

Each voter's preferred service level is a function of his income, ideological conviction and the combination of policy messages confronted. Partial

---

[5]Life-cycle problems are ignored to simplify analysis and allow a sharper focus on rent-seeking effort levels. The analysis is not very much changed if one takes account of intergenerational and lifetime problems. In this case, one would expect that the current median voter's expected *lifetime* utility would be maximized rather than his instantaneous utility. See Congleton and Shughart (1990) for an application of this sort of framework.

derivatives with respect to ideological conviction and the number of pro and
con messages are of particular interest here:

$$G^*_{M1} = \left[\int_0^+ P_{GM1}(U-U^0)\,dt + \int_0^+ P_{M1}(U_G - U_G^0)\,dT \right] \Big/ -K > 0, \qquad (6.1)$$

$$G^*_{M2} = \left[\int_0^+ P_{GM2}(U-U^0)\,dt + \int_0^+ P_{M2}(U_G - U_G^0)\,dT \right] \Big/ -K < 0, \qquad (6.2)$$

$$G^*_I = \left[\int_0^+ P_{GI}(U-U^0)\,dt + \int_0^+ P_I(U_G - U_G^0)\,dT \right] \Big/ -K > 0, \qquad (6.3)$$

$$K = \int_0^+ +2P_G(U_G - U_G^0)\,dT + \int_0^+ P(U_{GG} - U_{GG}^0)\,dT < 0 \qquad (6.4)$$

K is the second derivative of eq. (3) and is negative as required for eq. (4)
to characterize utility-maximizing levels of government services. The derivatives of utility under a zero tax exceed those under a positive tax, since
$U_{GC} > 0$. Thus, the qualitative effects of income and political messages on a
voter's preferred public service level are determined by the signs of the
numerators, all of which are determined unambiguously.

Note that $K < 0$ implies that voter preferences are single peaked in policy
domain G. This, in turn, implies that electoral competition tends to generate
policy outcomes that maximize the median voter's utility subject to his
constraints.[6] In this context, eqs. (6.1), (6.2), and (6.3) imply that the public
service level increases as the median voter's income increases, and 'pro-
service' messages persuade him that his personal tax cost will be smaller than
initially believed. Service levels tend to decline as the median voter is
persuaded by 'anti-service' messages that his tax cost for the public service
will be larger than initially thought.

Note that the effects of ideological conviction on government output are
determined by the *particular content* of the median voter's ideology. As the
assumed ideological inclinations of the median voter lead him to expect a

[6]The median voter result follows from the two-good, one policy, structure of the model. In
more complex settings, a number of severe symmetry restrictions would have to be added to
ensure median voter results. See, for example, those developed by Plott (1967). However, Hinich
and Enelow's (1982) theoretical work suggests that if there is a monotone mapping of policies
into a one-dimensional ideological space, median voter results tend to obtain. In conjunction
with the empirical work of Poole and Daniels (1985) showing that a one-dimensional ideological
spectrum does an excellent job of predicting the voting pattern of U.S. Congressmen, this
suggests that median voter models may be more broadly applicable than analysis of voting
models generally implies.

relatively small tax price for this particular public service, the public service level increases as ideological conviction increases, thus $G_I > 0$. The reverse would have held were the median voter assumed to be a 'conservative' with P_I and P_{GI} greater than zero.

3. Rent-seeking in an ideological environment

The effect that ideological conviction has on rent-seeking activities is less arbitrary. The model of public policy formation developed above characterizes a mechanism by which special interest groups can influence political outcomes by sponsoring appropriate policy messages. Since ideological conviction directly affects the productivity of such messages, it also directly affects incentives to sponsor them. Consequently, as demonstrated below, rent-seeking activities tend to decline as ideological conviction increases.

This section examines the effect of ideological conviction on the rent-seeking activities of economic interest groups. Ideological interest groups are taken up in the next section of the paper. Economic groups differ from ideological groups chiefly in their motivation. Rent-seeking groups have a specific pecuniary interest in public policy outcomes. Ideological groups have no particular economic interest at stake, but rather an ideological interest in the general thrust of public policies. The National Education Association and National Farmers Organization are economic interest groups. The American Civil Liberties Union and the American Conservative Union are ideological interest groups. Rent-seekers maximize their own private pecuniary income, while ideological groups try to advance their vision of the 'good' society through 'proper' legislation. Both sorts of groups send political messages, although the content of their messages may differ substantially. To facilitate analysis, the activities of ideological groups are neglected initially in order to focus attention on the strategies of ordinary rent-seekers.

Returning to the model, suppose that there are two groups (or coalitions of groups) whose economic interests are affected by the public service level to be decided. Group 1's profits, R_1, increase as the public services increase, and Group 2's profits, R_2, fall as service levels increase. Group 1 might own inputs used to produce the public service, or be a group that faces unusually low tax costs for the public service. Group 2 might be an alternative employer of those inputs, or a group that faces an unusually high tax price for expanded government services. Both groups sponsor the number of messages that maximize their net income from the government service.

Group 1's net income, N_1, is simply the rent generated by the public service level, $r(G)$, less the cost of sponsoring political messages. Suppose that message transmission services are purchased in a competitive market at a cost of m dollars per message sent. Group 1's net income is:

$$N_1 = r(G) - mM_1, \tag{7}$$

with $R1_G > 0$ and $R1_{GG} \leq 0$. Service level, G, is as previously characterized by eq. (5) for given levels of median voter income, ideological conviction, and policy messages.

Differentiating eq. (7) with respect to M_1 and setting the result equal to zero yields:

$$0 = R_G G_{M1} - m. \tag{8}$$

The pro-service group sends messages up to the point where the marginal increase in personal income derived from the public service equals the marginal cost of sending messages, other things being equal. Group 2 would send its messages up to the point where the marginal reduction in losses from the public service equals its message cost.

Applying the implicit function theorem to eq. (8) allows the net rent-maximizing number of messages for Group 1 to be written as:

$$M1^* = m1(Y, I, m, M_2). \tag{9}$$

The optimal number of messages for Group 1 to sponsor is a function of the median voter's income and ideological conviction, the cost of sponsoring messages, and the number of opposing messages sent by Group 2.

The effect of ideological conviction on Group 1's rent-seeking effort can be appraised by differentiating eq. (9) with respect to I:

$$M1^*_I = (R_{GG} G_I G_{M1} + R_G G_{IM1})/- K', \tag{10}$$

with

$$K' = R_{GG} G^2_{M1} + R_G G_{M1M1}.$$

Unfortunately, signing eq. (10) requires additional assumptions about the geometry of eqs. (1) and (2). Third derivatives of P and U come into play. Suppose that these are such that G is concave. That is to say, suppose that:

$$G_{M1M1} > 0, \quad G_{M2M2} < 0, \quad \text{and} \quad G_{II} < 0,$$

with

$$G_{M1M2} < 0, \quad G_{IM1} < 0 \quad \text{and} \quad G_{IM2} > 0.$$

Given these, the numerator of eq. (10) is unambiguously negative, and the denominator is unambiguously positive, so $M1^*_I < 0$.

Group 1 sends fewer messages as ideological conviction increases because the marginal productivity of message transmissions falls as ideological conviction increases. Thus, less persuadable voters attract relatively smaller rent-seeking investments by pro-service group(s). A similar result can easily be obtained for Group 2's efforts to oppose production of the public service.

It bears noting that this result is *independent* of the particulars of the ideologies held by the median voter. The point here is that the more firmly rooted the beliefs of decisive voters are, the more costly it is for rent-seekers to influence political outcomes through persuasion, other things being equal. Consequently, *fewer* resources, $m(M_1 + M_2)$, tend to be devoted to public rent-seeking activities in ideologically committed societies.

However, other things are not equal. Each group's efforts are partly determined by the efforts of its opposition, which are likewise affected by the persuadability of voters. This interaction between economic interest groups can also be characterized with reference to eq. (9). Given values for the median voter's income, ideological conviction and message costs, eq. (9) is the Cournot–Nash reaction function of the pro-service group. A similar function can be found for Group 2.

The overall effect of an increase in ideological conviction can be modelled as a change in the Nash equilibrium of this rent-seeking game. The geometry of a typical equilibrium can be characterized by differentiating eq. (9) with respect to M_2:

$$M1_{M2} = (R_{GG}G_{M2}G_{M1} + R_G G_{M1M2})/ - K'. \tag{11}$$

K' is as previously defined, so terms in the numerator determine the slope of Group 1's reaction curve. However, the numerator cannot be signed. The first term is positive, and the second is negative. Because the income received from government programs is subject to diminishing returns, $R_{GG} < 0$, an increase in messages by the opposition reduces the service level, $G_{M2} < 0$, and thereby increases the marginal benefit generated by an additional message. On the other hand, increased message levels by the opposition reduce the productivity of messages sent by the pro-service group, $G_{M1M2} < 0$. The slope of the reaction function is determined by the relative sizes of these two effects. Escalation occurs if the first effect dominates, as would be the case when economic rents are subject to substantial diminishing returns. De-escalation occurs if the second effect dominates, as would be the case where rents are proportional to the size of the government service. For example, Group 1 might be composed of 'cost plus' contractors.

In either case, eq. (10) implies that rent-seeking activities fall as ideological conviction increases if the rent-seeking game is reasonably symmetric. Fig. 1 depicts a Nash equilibrium for the case where both groups have upward-sloping reaction functions. Eq. (10) implies that an increase in ideological conviction shifts Group 1's curve toward the M2 axis and Group 2's curve

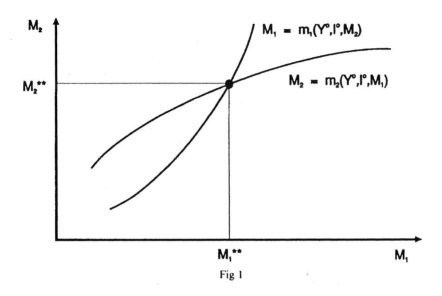

Fig 1

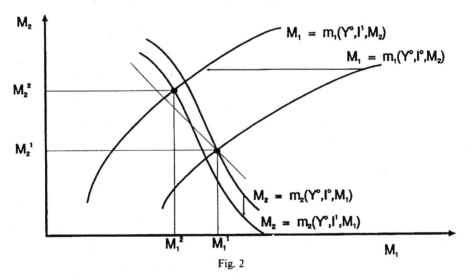

Fig. 2

toward the M1 axis. This implies an unambiguous decrease in rent-seeking activities by both groups. While one group may be less affected by ideological conviction than the other, the total resources devoted to political persuasion clearly decline.

Only in the case where the *economic* situation facing rent-gainers and rent-losers is extremely asymmetric could an increase in ideological conviction increase rent-seeking activities. [The *ideological* terms in eq. (10) are the same for each group.] For example, it is possible that Group 2's gains are subject to constant returns while Group 1's losses are subject to diminishing marginal returns. Fig. 2 illustrates the effect of ideological conviction in an economically asymmetric game. In the case depicted, the reaction functions of the two groups can have opposite slopes. Eq. (10) implies that an increase in ideological conviction shifts the $M1^*$ reaction curve towards the $M2$ axis and the $M2^*$ reaction curve towards the $M1$ axis. In this case, reductions in the rent-seeking effort of Group 1 causes Group 2 to increase its investment. If Group 2's increase is large enough to generate a new equilibrium beyond a 45° line passing through the original equilibrium, aggregate rent-seeking efforts increase.

In both the symmetric and asymmetric cases, the scale and composition of rent-seeking are directly affected by the ideological environment in which it takes place. Ideological conviction affects the number of messages sponsored by each group.

In cases where the disputed policies have symmetric effects on pro and anti service groups, as in the usual rent-seeking (zero-sum) transfer game, ideological conviction reduces expenditures on politicized information by rent-seekers. Insofar as this form of competition generates a deadweight loss, an increase in ideological conviction increases economic efficiency.[7] Consequently, societies populated by individuals with firmly held priors are less prone to rent-seeking losses than those with a less rigid world view or in the process of changing from one ideology to another.[8]

4. Ideological conflict in a rent-seeking society

Ideology and ideological conviction have to this point been taken as given. To a large extent, this is a reasonably good approximation of the situation facing rent-seekers during the course of a single election or referendum. Ideological perspectives appear to be relatively stable on a day-to-day or

---

[7]Expenditures on political persuasion are not necessarily a deadweight loss in total. The messages sponsored may benefit voters. The normative question of whether social welfare is increased by increased ideological conviction depends on whether or not the reduced cost of rent-seeking activities exceeds any benefits lost from political messages no longer sent. The polity clearly benefits if fewer fraudulent or irrelevant claims have to sorted through by voters. On the other hand, greater ideological certainty may cause voters to neglect political messages which they could have in fact (were it to be known) benefited from while reducing incentives to transmit such beneficial messages.

[8]This is one possible explanation of the empirical estimates of rent-seeking losses in the Third World. See, for example, Krueger (1974). Third World countries generally are in a greater state of ideological turmoil than countries at more advanced or more primitive stages of economic and political development. The above analysis implies that there will be greater rent-seeking in Turkey or India than in New Guinea or Canada.

year-to-year basis. Poole and Daniels (1985) report only modest ideological drift in their twenty-year study of role-call voting in the U.S. Congress. Moreover, to the extent that ideology or ideological conviction do change, it is probably more often the result of undirected personal experience than the persuasive efforts of ideologically oriented interest groups. On the other hand, it is clear that changes in ideology can also be the result of directed experience, as in public education, or be stimulated by public debate. The possibility that ideology and/or ideological conviction can be systematically altered creates another avenue by which interest groups can affect policy outcomes.

To simplify a bit, it is assumed that the ideological groups sponsor only ideological messages and that the rent-seeking groups sponsor only policy messages. Ideological messages are assumed to be aimed at general normative and conceptual issues relevant for a variety of public policy issues. Policy messages are assumed to focus on somewhat narrower issues especially relevant for the policy at issue. For example, an ideological group might attempt to promote equity by sponsoring message that emphasize the *desirable* progressive nature of the tax used to finance the public service. To the extent that this reinforces the ideological propensities of voters, it makes them more confident of their world view. That is to say, it increases their ideological conviction. The analysis of the previous section indicates that even if this is the *only* effect that such messages have, these messages will affect the extent of political debate. The analysis below indicates that such modest effects are also sufficient to motivate ideological messages.

Given this somewhat exaggerated distinction between policy and ideological messages, a minor revision to the previous model allows it to be used to analyze ideological conflict in the course of a single election or referendum. Political outcomes continue to reflect the preferences and expectations of the median voter, subject to anticipated financial constraints. Ordinary policy messages continue to affect particular beliefs about the tax consequences of the policy at issue. However, now ideological conviction becomes an endogenous variable, influenced by the messages sent by ideological groups. (Ideological messages are assumed to raise doubts or reinforce the world view of targeted individuals rather than induce sudden wholesale revisions in ideological preferences or theories.)

To the extent that ideological interest groups either prefer greater or lesser service levels than the median voter, little is lost by assuming that there are two ideological interest groups, Group 3 and Group 4, with opposite interests in the size of government. Let Group 3 prefer a large public sector, and sponsor messages that strengthen the median voter's assumed predilection to support relatively large public service levels as his ideological conviction increases. (Recall that the assumed ideological predisposition of the median voter implies than an increase in ideological convicion reduces the median voter's estimated tax cost, $P_I < 0$, and so increases his demand for the public service.) Group 4 prefers a small government sector and therefore sponsors messages that attempt to reduce the median voter's confidence in his ideology. Note that even ideological messages are affected by the ideological predilections of voters.

The political process in this setting can be modeled using eqs. (1), (2), and (3), plus eq. (12) below which characterizes the relationship between ideological messages and ideological conviction:

$$I = i(D_3, D_4),\qquad(12)$$

with

$$I_{D3} > 0, \quad I_{D4} < 0, \quad I_{D3D4} < 0, \quad I_{D3D3} < 0, \quad I_{D4D4} > 0.$$

D_3 is the number of messages sent by the pro-service group and D_4 is the number of messages sent by the more conservative ideological group. I is the resulting ideological conviction of the median voter.

The first-order condition characterizing political outcomes is as before in eq. (4). However, the function describing the median voter's preferred service level now includes ideological messages rather than ideological conviction:

$$G^* = g(Y, D_3, D_4, M_1, M_2).\qquad(13)$$

The median voter's tastes and message-filtering process continue to affect the shape of this function, while pretax income, together with the number of political and ideological messages, determine its value.

Ideological groups sponsor messages as a means of moving the political outcome, G^*, closer to their ideal points. That is to say, ideological groups are motivated by ideological aspects of their utility functions. Their interest is in living in a more free, just or perfect world rather than greater personal income, per se. Members of ideological groups can be thought of as altruists or individuals with meddlesome preferences, since for them the 'good society' is an end in itself rather than a means to an end.

Ideological organizations invest their resources in political messages to minimize the extent to which actual policy, G, deviates from their ideal subject to various economic and political constraints. Cast in net-benefit terms, smaller deviations from the ideal are preferred to larger ones, so the benefit associated with a particular policy outcome by the ith group, V_i, is a monotone decreasing function of the difference between the actual policy, G, and the group's ideal policy, G_i''. If it costs d dollars to transmit an ideological message, the net advantage that Group i derives from D_i ideological messages can be represented as:

$$N_i = V_i(G_i') - dD_i,$$ (14)

with

$$G_i' = |G - G_i''|$$

and

$$V_{G'} < 0, \quad V_{G'G'}^+ < 0$$

To reduce notational complexity, Group 3's ideal point is assumed to be larger than the service level favored by the median voter, and Group 4's ideal point is assumed to be smaller than the median voter's preferred service level. This allows the absolute value signs to be dispensed with.

The essential features of an ideological interest group's decision to participate in policy debate can be characterized by focusing on either interest group. The net advantage of Group 3 is maximized if it chooses D_1 such that

$$-V_{G'}^i G_{D3} = d.$$ (15)

Recall that $G_{G'} = -1$, $I_{D3} > 0$ and $G_I > 0$, which implies that $G_{D3} > 0$. Group 3's ideological messages attempt to strengthen the median voter's ideological conviction as a means of increasing his inclination to opt for relatively large service levels. $V_{G'}^i$ is less than 0, and represents the extent to which moving the actual policy closer to Group 3's ideal point diminishes their dissatisfaction with 'inadequate' government services. The left-hand side of eq. (15) thus represents the extent to which an additional ideological message increases Group 3's satisfaction with the policies chosen by the electorate. Group 3 will sponsor ideological messages up to the point where the marginal value of induced increases in public service levels equals the marginal cost of its messages. Group 4 would similarly sponsor messages up to the point where the value of induced reductions in public service equals the marginal cost of its messages.

Eq. (15) can be used as the basis for characterizing Group 3's message levels as a function of variables beyond their control:

$$D_3^* = i(Y, d, D_4, M_1, M_2).$$ (16)

Group 3's messages are affected by median voter income, the cost of ideological messages, and the number of messages sent by other ideological and non-ideological interest groups. Given values for median voter income and the cost of ideological messages, eq. (16) can be used as the basis for Group 3's Nash reaction function. A similar equation can easily be developed for Group 4.

The effects of the messages of the other special interest groups can be determined by differentiating eq. (16) with respect to D_4, M_1, and M_2:

$$D3_{D4} = [V_{G'} G_{D4} G_{D3} + V_{G'} G_{D3D4}]/ - K'' > 0, \qquad (17.1)$$

$$D3_{M1} = [V_{G'} G_{M1} G_{D3} + V_{G'} G_{D3M1}]/ - K'' < 0, \qquad (17.2)$$

$$D3_{M2} = [V_{G'} G_{M2} G_{D3} + V_{G'} G_{D3M2}]/ - K'' > 0, \qquad (17.3)$$

with

$$K'' = -[V_{G'G'} G_{D3}^2 + V_{G'} G_{D3D3}] < 0. \qquad (17.4)$$

Note that ideological conflict differs from ordinary rent-seeking in that ideological conflict between extreme groups *always tends towards escalation.* $D3_{D4}$ is unambiguously greater than zero. On the other hand, the existence of independent rent-seeking groups with similar *policy* interests moderate efforts by ideological groups, here $D3_{M1} < 0$. Rent-seekers whose messages run at cross purposes intensify the efforts of ideological groups, $D3_{M2} > 0$.

The overall effect of ideological messages on the level of rent-seeking depends on (a) whether the net effect is to increase or decrease the median voter's ideological conviction, and (b) the extent to which symmetry characterizes the rent-seeking game. In the case where ideological conviction is increased and the game is more or less symmetric, the rent-seeking efforts of economic interest groups tend to decline. On the other hand, if ideological messages reduce the confidence that the median voter has in his model of the world, by for example reopening issues previously thought settled, ideological conflict can encourage additional efforts by rent-seekers.

The pattern of relationships between interest groups can also affect the level of rent-seeking activities. An overall Nash equilibrium of interest groups requires a combination of messages such that eqs. (16) and (9), along with their counterparts for the opposing ideological and economic interest groups, are simultaneously satisfied. Fig. 3 illustrates the geometry of a partial equilibrium between rent-seeking Group 1 and ideological Group 3 whose messages are substitutes for one another. The reaction functions characterized by eqs. (16) and (9) are both downward-sloping in the $M \times D$ plane, both $D3_{M1}$ and $M1_{I_{D3}}$ are less than zero. (Similar geometry holds for Groups 2 and 4.)

In the absence of ideological messages, the rent-seeking group would have sent messages at the point where their reaction curve intersects the M-axis. The downward-sloping reaction function implies that the existence of an active complementary ideological group, $D_3 > 0$, necessarily *reduces* the number of rent-seeking messages transmitted, ceteris paribus. Here, Group 3's efforts reduce rent-seeking expenditures by Group 1 because they reduce

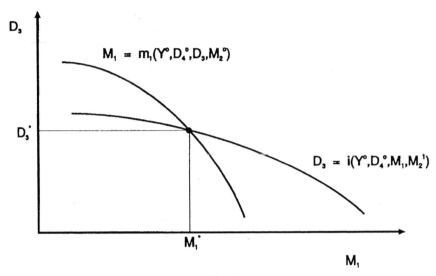

Fig. 3

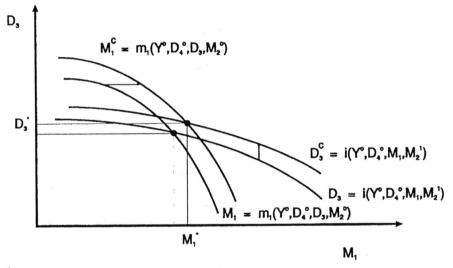

Fig. 4

Group 1's returns from sponsoring additional policy messages. Group 1's messages have a similar effect on Group 3's ideological messages. At the Nash equilibrium, complementary interest groups can free ride on each other's efforts.

On the other hand, suppose, instead of independently participating in the policy debate, that complementary interest groups *coordinate* their efforts. In this case, the existence of a complementary interest group tends to *increase* the resources devoted to political conflict. To see this, recall that the optimal combination of messages for a particular confederation of interest groups to sponsor is the one that maximizes the sum of their net advantages:[9]

$$N = R(G) + V(|G'' - G|) - dD - mM. \tag{18}$$

Functions R and V are as previously defined for Groups 1 and 3. The optimal combination of messages satisfies:

$$(R_G - V_{G'})G_I I_{D3} = d \tag{19.1}$$

and

$$(R_G - V_{G'})G_{M1} = m. \tag{19.2}$$

Comparing the equations for joint optimization with their counterparts for independent optimization, eqs. (8) and (15), it is clear that there will be both more rent-seeking and more ideological messages sent in a confederation of interest groups, other things being equal. Accounting for the benefits that fellow travellers receive causes more messages of each sort to pass muster. R_G and $-V_{G'}$ are both positive over the range of interest. Similar results obtain for Groups 2 and 4. Coordination allows the external benefits of complementary group activities to be internalized.

[9]There are four general types of relationships that complementary economic and ideological interest groups can have. (1) Their behavior can be independent of one another. This sort of behavior yields the Nash game examined above. (2) Ideologues might know the reaction functions of rent-seekers and take their anticipated responses into account when sending messages. In this case, the result is a Stackleburg equilibrium between ideological groups and economic interest groups, and a Cournot–Nash equilibrium between the ideological groups. (3) The third possibility is the mirror image of the second. It is possible that ideological groups might be sponsored by rent-seekers in a manner calculated to make their preferred policy outcome more likely. In this case, rent-seekers would, in effect, send two sorts of messages: direct policy messages, and indirect ideological messages by manipulating the ideological groups. (4) Ideological and rent-seeking groups with complementary goals might cooperate with each other. This is the second case examined. Here, the equilibrium to the message game is a Nash–Cournot equilibrium between opposing confederations of interest groups. The second and third structures can be thought of as special cases of the fourth which highlight relationships within a federation of interest groups.

Relationships within and between ideological and economic interest groups are often complex. For example, economic interest groups can hire employees with the appropriate ideological zeal for lower money wages than would be the case for employees entirely motivated by money wages. As a consequence, trade organizations may find themselves with an unintentional ideological agenda. For example, one occasionally observes a trade organization providing economic resources to ideological groups whose stated agenda runs counter to the trade organization's economic interest. The National Education Association is said to provide funds for Planned Parenthood groups. Naturally, this indirectly tends to reduce the number of children born, and thereby reduces the demand for teachers. On the other hand, it may be the result of coalitional logrolling. In many cases, it is difficult to determine whether such trade groups are engaged in ordinary rent-seeking activities or have an ideological agenda of their own.

Fig. 4 superimposes solutions for eqs. (19.1) and (19.2), denoted with a superscript c, over those for eqs. (8) and (15), previously used in fig. 3, to illustrate this result. The semi-cooperative equilibrium lies generally to the northeast of the Nash Equilibrium. Cooperation implies that more messages will be sponsored regardless of whether or not both groups participate in the policy debate of interest. Note that eq. (19.1) intersects the M-axis somewhat above the point where eq. (9) strikes it. Properly accounting for the interests of ideologues requires rent-seekers to sponsor additional policy messages even if the ideological groups transmit no additional messages themselves. Similar results hold for ideological groups at the other extreme. In general, coordination by complementary economic and ideological groups causes an increase in the extent to which resources are devoted to political conflict.

5. Overview and conclusions

The purpose of this paper has been to explore some of the effects that the ideological filtering of messages has on rent-seeking activities. The analysis has demonstrated that individuals who are relatively certain of their beliefs generally attract smaller efforts by special interest groups. The analysis also demonstrates that relationships among special interest groups affect the extent of rent-seeking activities. Interest groups with similar policy interests invest less than they otherwise would be inclined to if they can free ride on each others' efforts. Thus, overall investments in political messages are affected by the persuadability of the targeted group of individuals and the extent to which relevant interest groups coordinate their efforts.

Interpreted in ideological terms, the paper has shown that the ideological environment in which rent-seeking takes place has a variety of effects on both the level and content of rent-seeking activities. The more certain voters are of their pre-campaign ideologies, the less inclined economic interest groups are to invest in rent-seeking activities: political messages and the like. Ideological conviction reduces the productivity of public rent-seeking activities. And since ideological filters make some political messages more plausible than others, ideology affects both the content and mix of messages that rent-seeking and ideological groups sponsor. Conclusions drawn from the messages, in turn, affect policy outcomes. Ideology and ideological conviction thereby affect the rhetoric and reality of political redistribution.

Prospects for ideological conflict widen the domain of political competition, while ideological conviction constrains it. If the second effect dominates the first, the analysis suggests that ideological transitions will be difficult times as the polity confronts extensive rent-seeking coupled with intense ideological competition. On the other hand, the analysis suggests that societies strongly committed to particular ideologies will exhibit relatively little public debate because the returns from both rent-seeking and ideological messages are relatively low. Ideological conviction may blind (or bind) one to the truth, but it also blinds one to many of the blandishments of interest groups.

The analysis has neglected some interesting problems associated with ideological conflict. Associated ideological preferences or visions of the good society were subsumed into voter tastes assumed to be exogenously predetermined. Persuasion rather than violence was assumed to be the vehicle of policy change. Political arrangements were taken as given. The paper sheds little light on the extent to which ideological messages might convert a person from one sort of ideologue to another. Nor does it illuminate ideology's substantial role in shaping institutional arrangements except insofar as these arrangements are determined by ordinary legislation. However, even without these additional complexities, the analysis has demonstrated that ideology and ideological conviction matter. And while the analysis has focused on a democratic political setting, many of its conclusions would apply to authoritarian regimes or to the bureaucracy to the extent that such policy-makers can be modelled as forward-looking utility maximizers who rely at least partly on ideological filters.

References

Austin-Smith, D., 1987, Interest groups, campaign contributions, and probabilistic voting, Public Choice 54, 123–140.

Becker, G.S. 1983, A theory of competition among pressure groups for political influence, Quarterly Journal of Economics 98, 371–399.

Bhagwati, J.N., T.A. Brecher and T.N. Srinivasan, 1984, DUP activities and economic theory, in: D.C. Colander ed., Neoclassical political economy: The analysis of rent-seeking and DUP activities (Cambridge MA).

Buchanan, J.M., R.D. Tollison and G. Tullock, 1980, Toward a theory of the rent-seeking society (Texas A&M Press, College Station, Texas).

Congleton, R.D., 1986, Rent-seeking aspects of political advertising, Public Choice 49, 249–263.

Congleton, R.D. and W.F. Shughart, 1990, The growth of social security: Electoral demand or political pull, Economic Inquiry 28, 109–132.

Crain, W. and R. Tollison, 1976, Campaign expenditures and political competition, Journal of Law and Economics (April), 177–188.

Downs, A., 1957, An economic theory of democracy (Harper and Row, New York).

Enelow, J. and M.J. Hinich, 1984, The spatial theory of voting (Cambridge University Press, Cambridge Mass).

Good, I.J., 1976, The Bayesian influence, in: Harper and Hooker, eds., Foundations of probability theory, and statistical theories of science, vol. 2 (D. Reidel Publishing Company, Boston).

Hinich, M.J. and J. Enelow, 1982, Ideology, issues, and the spatial theory of elections, American Political Science Review 76, 493–501.

Jacobson, G., 1980, Money in congressional elections (Yale University Press, New Haven).

Kalt, J.P. and M.A. Zupan, 1984, Capture and ideology in the economic theory of politics, American Economic Review 74, 279–300.

Kau, J.B. and P.H. Rubin, 1982, Congressmen, constituents and contributors (Martinus Nijhoff Publishing, Boston).

Knight, F.H., 1950, Economic and social policy in democratic society, Journal of Political Economy 58, 513–522.

Kramer, G., 1971, Short-term fluctuations in U.S. voting behavior, American Political Science Review 65, 131–143.

Krueger, A., 1974, The political economy of the rent-seeking society, American Economic Review 64, 291–303.

Kuran, T., 1987, Chameleon voters and public choice, Public Choice 53, 53–78.

North, D.C., 1988, Ideology and political/economic institutions, Cato Journal 8, 15–27.

Olson, M., 1965, The logic of collective action (Harvard University Press, Cambridge).

Peltzman, S., 1984, Constituent interest and congressional voting, Journal of Law and Economics 27, 181–210.

Plott, C.R., 1967, Equilibrium and majority rule, American Economic Review 62, 787–806.

Poole, K.T. and R.S. Daniels, 1985, Ideology, party and voting in the U.S. Congress, 1959–1980, American Political Science Review 57, 373–399.

Rowley, C.R., 1984, The relevance of the median voter theorem, Journal of Institutional and Theoretical Economics 40, 104–135.

Simon, H., 1986, Rationality in psychology and economics, Journal of Business 39, 209–224.

Stigler, G.J., 1976, Do economists matter?, Southern Economic Journal 42, 347–354.

Tullock, G., 1970, A simple algebraic logrolling model, American Economic Review 60, 419–426.

Tullock, G., 1981, The rhetoric and reality of redistribution, Southern Economic Journal 47, 895–907.

Tullock, G., 1987, Why is the rent-seeking industry so small? A nugatory solution (University of Arizona Discussion Paper).

Public Choice **96:** 219–239, 1998.
© 1998 *Kluwer Academic Publishers. Printed in the Netherlands.*

Political economy and political correctness *

ARYE L. HILLMAN
Department of Economics, Bar-Ilan University, Ramat Gan 52900, Israel

Accepted 28 October 1997

1. Introduction

Political correctness is a complex topic, if only because those who hold that something is politically correct are not inclined to be open to critical evaluation of the merits of their political correctness. Such unwillingness to entertain open discourse is a characteristic of all social systems with supreme values (see Bernholz, 1991, 1993); thus under communism questioning the politically correct position that the society was on the path to Marxist Utopia could result in confinement in an asylum for the insane.

Socialism espouses that the proper functioning of an economic system requires political allocation, and the subjugation of individual preferences and freedoms to a higher social order of priorities. The economic and social philosophy of political economy of the economic right takes the precisely opposite view, that market allocation is preferable to political allocation, and that individuals are better judges of the requisites of their own welfare than social planners.

Yet, in the western economics literature, neither political economy, that of the left nor that of the right, has been politically correct. The political incorrectness of the political economy of the left can be understood in the denial of personal freedoms, if not in the inadequacies of the results achieved in practice by economic systems that sought to apply socialist principles.[1] My purpose here is to evaluate the basis for the political incorrectness of the political economy of the *right*, and to consider how this political incorrectness has influenced the literature of economics, with particular reference to the manner in which government is portrayed in economic models. In order to proceed, we shall require consensus on a definition of political correctness.

* Presidential address, European Public Choice Society, Prague, April 1997. In preparing the paper for publication, I have benefitted from the helpful comments of Vani K. Borooah, Jack Hirshleifer, Dennis Mueller, Pierre Salmon, and Christian Seidl.

220

That is, we require an acceptable specification of political correctness which neutralizes the controversies associated with the designation of a proposition as politically correct or incorrect.

The criterion which I propose for political correctness is educational. We should accept as politically correct a position or proposition which conforms to the norms of behavior and conceptual thinking which a society wishes to designate as exemplary for its young.

This leaves open the possibility that, beyond the education of the young, those who so wish can view political correctness as an intellectually unworthy restriction on open intellectual academic debate. A broader disdain for political correctness in intellectual discourse need not contradict the position that societies should be permitted to choose fundamental moral and ethical norms as the basis of a desirable education of their young.

I would admit that the educational criterion for political correctness is not devoid of potential controversy. Indeed the controversy regarding the principles that should be chosen to form the basis of the education of the young is central to my subsequent discussion. The margins can be also fine in defining who are the *young*, and the simple non-discretionary norms appropriate for small children can differ from less qualified educational principles that societies may choose to set before more mature students. A criterion of educational paternalism nonetheless appears reasonable for political correctness – and we are confronted with the observation that all societies do in practice choose principles of education for their young. By this criterion, the question of political correctness becomes one of designating the educational principles that should be chosen by an enlightened society.[2]

As indicated, in considering the political incorrectness of the economic right, I narrow the focus to the conception of government, and thereby to the question: *when is an economic model of government politically correct, by the criterion of setting desirable educational norms before the young?* An appropriate point of departure for seeking an answer to this question is the concept of rent seeking.

2. Rent-seeking models as politically incorrect political economy

Models of rent-seeking behavior describe the use of resources and time in contests for influence over political allocation.[3] Although the objective of rent seeking is distributional (to evoke favorable change in income distribution or asset ownership), the activity of rent seeking gives rise to losses of an efficiency nature, and the unproductive resource allocation which is due to rent seeking thereby supplements the deadweight efficiency losses that an economy incurs because of market imperfections.[4] The idea of social loss due to rent-seeking incentives was first expounded by Tullock (1967).[5] Nitzan (1994) provides an excellent survey of the subsequent extensive literature.[6] The models of this literature provide the analytical underpinnings for the proposition that societies are impoverished by discretionary political allocation of income and wealth.[7] The rent-seeking models also explain why governments intervene to *create* rather than to correct market inefficiencies or distortions, and why government policies might benefit the more fortunate in society at the expense of the less fortunate.

The nature of rent seeking limits the empirical evidence. Government statistical offices cannot be sources of data, nor can evidence in general be based on direct observation, since in most societies it is dishonorable and politically costly to be openly seen to be seeking or dispensing rents, and attempts are accordingly made to hide rent seeking.[8] The evidence is, as a consequence, often indirect or informal, and is reflected more in the outcome of rent-seeking activities than in the observation of the activities themselves.[9]

Since the prizes secured by successful rent seekers are often quite visible while the underlying rent-seeking behavior is not, the literature has focused on inferring the value of the resources used in the contests from the observed value of the prize, by considering the outlays that would be made by rational individuals who are confronted with rent-seeking opportunities.

Although it is the case that the *incentives* for rent seeking by individual optimizing agents are in place *wherever* there is discretionary political allocation of income or wealth, there is an identifiable schism between economic models which recognize rent seeking as a component of rational economic behavior, and models where rent seeking is absent. To explain the schism, I propose that we look to the educational criterion for political correctness. For *educationally unsatisfactory* behavioral attributes are present in all rent-seeking models. The unsatisfactory behavioral attributes concern the manner of behavior of both political agents and private-sector individuals.

Regarding first political behavior, when economies are modeled as guided by benevolent welfare-maximizing governments, no rents exist to be sought and there can be no role for rent seeking. A belief in *modeling* virtuous benevolent government thus eliminates rent seeking from economic analysis. Models that do incorporate rent-seeking behavior on the other hand raise questions concerning the origins of the rents that are contested, and draw into question the motives of policy makers in creating and assigning rents. A line of inquiry is initiated that leads in directions away from allocation by the invisible hand of the market, to allocation by political discretion. This line of inquiry can become compelling if there is evidence that rents are assigned by deliberate political calculation, and if the political assignment is seen to benefit the political agents assigning the rents. In these circumstances, it is difficult to

222

avoid the supposition that rents are politically created in order to be politically assigned for political or personal benefit – in which case political-support and private-benefit motives of political agents become intertwined with economic incentives in ways that are inconsistent with benevolent government.

Regarding further private-sector behavior, rent-seeking models portray personal income and wealth as attained by individuals' seeking politically assigned privilege and favor. Unproductive activity is rewarded and personal gains are ill-gotten. A more educationally exemplary description of sources of incomes and wealth would point to the roles of education, human capital, competence, and experience in determining market-assigned rewards, and would portray individuals whom government assists not as successful rent seekers but as the deserving unfortunate and disadvantaged in society.

That is, to summarize, the rent-seeking models depart from an educationally satisfactory model of government by portraying people who have made their careers *within* government as creating and dispensing rents for personal gain. And people *outside* government are shown in an educationally unsatisfactory manner, as seeking wealth and income not from productive personal endeavor, but by devoting time and effort to influencing political allocation. To see how this perceived political incorrectness has influenced economic analysis, I turn now to the literature on international trade policy and then literature on broader endogeneous economic policy.

3. Political economy and political correctness in international trade policy

3.1. *Contradictions and reconciliations*

The idea that free trade is desirable has a long history that has survived many assaults (see Irwin, 1996). Because of the broad consensus that free trade is the socially optimal policy for governments to follow, political correctness has required conciliation of the politically correct model of benevolent government with the manifestly present protectionist policies. The conciliation has taken different forms. Bhagwati (1971) has shown how, in a second-best world, protectionism can be efficiency-enhancing. Another approach looks not to efficiency justifications for government intervention, but to social justice as the basis for conciliation: Corden (1974) has proposed that protectionist policies permit benevolent governments to ensure that their citizens are not unreasonably disadvantaged by changes in international comparative advantage.[10] Bhagwati and Corden have both explained protectionist policies in politically correct ways. For Bhagwati, benevolent government does its best to achieve efficiency, subject to the presence of pre-existing market distortions, and the efficient policy could be protection, so if a benevolent government is choosing protection rather than free trade, there could be a second-best reason. For Corden, a benevolent government helps the disadvantaged. In neither case can the political discretion that is required for rent seeking be present.

Political-economy models of international trade policy do not seek conciliation between socially desirable and the observed distortionary policies. The political-economy models begin from the premise that policy makers have personal and political objectives which are not necessarily consistent with efficiency or social justice.[11] Rent seeking is present, if not necessarily by that name, and implicitly if not explicitly.[12]

The co-existence of politically correct and incorrect views of government behavior with regard to the same phenomenon is demonstrated by answers given to a fundamental question of the international trade policy literature: why do governments grant protection to retard the decline of domestic industries that are losing their comparative advantage in international markets? The second-best answer is that protection is the efficient policy given other market distortions in place, and the social-justice answer is that governments are benevolently assisting people who have been disadvantaged by a change in a country's comparative advantage. The same policy of protection for declining industries is however *also* predicted by a politically incorrect model which shows self-interested policy makers as choosing trade policies to maximize political support (see Hillman, 1982). The politically correct and incorrect explanations of protection are complemented by similarly politically correct and incorrect ways to answer the question why governments choose to *liberalize* international trade. A politically-correct benevolent government liberalizes trade to correct for past protectionist misadventures. In a political-economy model consistent with the "exchange of market access" terminology that *trade negotiators themselves use to describe reciprocal trade liberalization*, trade liberalization reflects political self-interest in allocating rents between export and import-competing industries.[13] For policies that restrict or liberalize international trade, the literature thus confronts us with a choice between politically correct and incorrect explanations.

Besides the *answers* that are given, political correctness affects the permissible *questions* that can be asked about international trade policies. A politically incorrect political-economy model permits questions to be asked such as, what leads governments to choose different policy instruments to create rents by restriction of trade (see Cassing and Hillman, 1985; and Hillman and Ursprung, 1988), why do governments at times permit precipitous collapse of import-competing industries (see Cassing and Hillman, 1986), and with whom are third parties such as environmentalists or multinational firms to

224

be expected to be bedfellows in seeking to influence international trade policies (Hillman and Ursprung, 1992, 1993)? Such questions are incompatible
with a politically correct model wherein governments are necessarily benevolent and are not susceptible to rent-seeking approaches of private agents.
Questions relating to contingent protection (anti-dumping actions, etc.) also
require a rent-seeking context (see Leidy, 1994). Implicit political incorrectness is also present in Cassing's (1996) very elucidating portrayal of the
principal-agent problem between diversified shareholders and management
of import-competing firms. Cassing observes that diversified shareholders
benefit from free-trade policies that maximize both a country's aggregate
national income and the value of a diversified personal investment portfolio.
Incentive-performance schemes for management also benefit shareholders,
but provide an incentive for management to lobby for protectionist policies
– against the interest of the diversified shareholders. The questions raised by
Cassing could not be asked if the implicit model were one of politically correct government. The shareholder-management principal-agent problem can
only exist because of a more fundamental principal-agent problem between
shareholders (as voters) and policy makers. That is, if policy makers were
not susceptible to the rent seeking of managers, the principal-agent problem
described by Cassing would not arise to confront shareholders.

3.2. *Strategic trade policy*

The politically-incorrect political-economy models also have in particular
shared the stage with another politically-correct model of government intervention in international trade, that of "strategic trade policy". A "new"
international trade theory[14] beginning in the 1980s has developed on the
assumption of imperfect competition in international markets. The imperfect
competition gives rise to the presence of rents. "Strategic trade policy", which
can be placed in the taxonomy of Bhagwati's second-best cases for intervention, asks how a government can best go about ensuring that the rents accrue
to "home" rather than "foreign" firms. Once the government has intervened
to ensure that the "home" firm has secured the rents, the captured rents can be
used to improve national welfare. James Brander, one of the pioneers of the
literature, has written an excellent survey of the literature (Brander, 1995).[15]
It is notable that although rents are present, and are sought and redistributed,
rent seeking plays no part in the theory of strategic trade policy. Yet one can
well expect that there will be many potential private domestic beneficiaries of
the government-induced foreign rent transfers;[16] there will indeed be as many
potential industry-specific beneficiaries as there are imperfectly competitive
international markets with domestic and foreign participants (see Moore and
Suranovic, 1993). A political-economy perspective on the behavior of self-

interested private and political agents finds it difficult to avoid pointing to the incentives that are *inherently present* for governments to shift rents to domestic firms *without* the strategic trade policy advice. Governments in the strategic trade policy models are of course politically correct. The models portray a government which shifts rents to chosen meritorious domestic firms, from whence the rents are benevolently dispensed for the social (national) good.

I wish to point now to the anomalous relation between the attention which the literature has devoted to theory of strategic trade policy, relative to the empirical content of the theory. Political-economy theories of international trade policy are complemented by a vast number of empirical studies confirming the principles that policy decision makers are not always concerned with the efficiency consequences of their decisions (distortions are introduced rather than corrected), and are not always concerned with social justice (the shareholders and other owners of capital who gain when industries are protected from foreign competition are not necessarily the unfortunate and disadvantaged in society). The empirical discussion of strategic trade policy has however consisted of the *possibilities* offered by the mainframe airline industry (Boeing and Airbus), supplemented by some other few *possibilities* where the policy has been conjectured to be prospectively applicable. Although there is this remarkable imbalance between the dearth of empirical cases and the intensity of the intellectual effort which has gone into theorizing about the nuances of variants of strategic trade policy, politically correct strategic trade policy, as the policy accompaniment of the "new" international economics, has constituted mainstream policy analysis of international trade theory. Strategic trade policy is a triumph of political correctness over observation.

4. Interest group competition

The propensities of governments to intervene to establish differentially unfavorable conditions for market transactions with foreigners makes international trade policy a prominent focus of study of politically endogenous policies. The conditions under which international trade takes place are however but one of many instances where interest groups compete for influence over policy determination (see the review of the empirical evidence by Potters and Sloof, 1996). An influential *general model* of interest group competition is that of Becker (1983). Becker's model portrays two interest groups, one of which is potentially to provide a transfer *via* government redistribution to the other. Because of deadweight losses, the potential losers from redistribution have a political advantage over the gainers; the advantage is reflected in the

226

willingness of the potential losers to spend more in political outlays to protect their incomes, than potential gainers are prepared to spend in political outlays to secure income transfers.[17] Becker proposes that since everybody (whether a potential loser or gainer from the income transfer) wishes deadweight losses to be minimal, there is a presumption that the least-distorting means of redistribution will be chosen. Any political redistribution that takes place will therefore be efficient. *Becker can thus complement the efficiency of the market with efficiency of political allocation.*

Becker's measure of inefficiency is standard Harberger deadweight losses. Yet, in his model, interest groups expend resources to influence political allocation. One might well ask, then, what has become of the social losses incurred in the resources that are used in the competition for political influence between the interest groups? A complete computation of social loss due to interest group competition includes the resources used by rent seekers and rent defenders in the competition to influence policy. Politically incorrect rent seeking is missing from Becker's analysis of contestable endogenous distribution.

The consequences of the missing rent-seeking allocations are far-reaching. For if resources used in rent seeking are added to deadweight losses, and if redistributional transfers are perceived as rents in the rent-seeking and rent-defending contests that "interest-group" competition entails, then the social costs of redistribution are correspondingly greater. In general it is voters at large who constitute the countervailing interest to special-interest redistribution. Since voters in Becker's model are rationally ignorant (see Baba, 1997), rent-seeking interests have reason to seek policies that depart from the most efficient means of redistribution. Magee's (Magee, Brock, and Young, 1989) observations on discretionary policy design therefore come into play. That is, rational ignorance permits the means of intervention to be optimized. The trade-off confronting the policy maker is between political benefits from more obscure means of income transfers (voters have greater difficulty perceiving what is going on), against the greater deadweight efficiency losses that are in general associated with more circuitous means of transfers. The policy obfuscation trade-off is not present in the endogenous policy mechanism of Becker's interest-group competition. Yet if there is a political cost to greater public visibility of government rent allocations, the benefits from more surreptitious, hidden rent seeking provide the incentive for choosing inefficient yet politically beneficial circuitous means of political allocation. With rent seeking and these related considerations absent, and political allocation as efficient, Becker's model appears as politically correct as is possible for a theory of endogenous income redistribution determined by interest-group competition for political influence.

To compare with a corresponding politically-incorrect political-economy model of interest group competition, we can consider Ursprung's (1990) portrayal of the same endogenous redistribution process. In Ursprung's model, candidates for political office announce policies which provide collective benefit to their respective constituencies, and the constituencies provide financial contributions to influence candidates' policy choices. The political agents who make the policy decisions are explicitly present, and rent-seeking activity is explicitly taking place. The objective of the political agents is to win political office, for which purpose they court their constituencies with favorable policies. The political agents' announced policies do not necessarily mirror the preferred policies sought by the constituencies, since political contributions are responsive to the difference between the political candidates' policy pronouncements. If the candidates announce the same policy, as they would in a back-to-back Hotelling policy equilibrium, they would receive no financial contributions, for nothing would distinguish them in the eyes of the competing interest groups. A Hotelling back-to-back outcome with identical policy pronouncements is the Nash equilibrium for candidates who maximize their probabilities of political success. Ursprung proposes however that political candidates also value financial contributions independently of the implications for the probability of winning the political contest (they keep some of the money for themselves). They therefore have reason to depart from the common Hotelling back-to-back equilibrium to announce different policies. Ursprung's model of interest-group and political competition reflects many elements of observed political behavior (see, for example, Stern, 1988) but must be given a low score on the scale of political correctness.

Indeed, rent seeking appears intrinsic to theories of collective action aimed at policy influence. Olson (1965), writing before Tullock's (1967) paper on the social cost of rent seeking, pointed how, in the quest for political influence it is disadvantageous to be a member of too large a group. An investigation of why this is so leads on to rent-seeking models, and on to political incorrectness. Olson's theory of group behavior coalesces with rent seeking, since individuals usually do not rent seek alone, but do so as members of coalitions (see Ursprung, 1990) compromised of individuals with a common cause (generally maximization of their personal wealth or incomes *via* an appropriate government policy). Rent-seeking contributions consequently take the form of private contributions to finance a public good (a policy) or to secure a private good (money) that is ultimately to be shared. And, so returning to Olson, because of the collective character of contributions to rent seeking and also the rents acquired, the effectiveness of the rent-seeking coalition can be compromised if the coalition is too large.[18]

228

5. The "new" political economy and political correctness

My intent in the above consideration of endogenous international trade policy in particular and interest-group competition in general has been to illustrate how political correctness has influenced economic modelling. There is of course a substantial literature that has not been constrained by political correctness. This includes, beyond the rent-seeking models, the broader public-choice view of the world (see Mueller, 1989), the political-competition models of endogenous policy equilibria referred to above (see the overview by Ursprung, 1991), and the Stigler-Peltzman capture theory of regulation of industry (Stigler, 1971; Peltzman, 1976) which views governments as choosing regulatory policies to maximize political support from both producer interests and consumers. The models of the above literature, which allow for the presence of rent-seeking behavior (by this name or another), are part of the "old" political economy, which can be contrasted with a "new" political economy that has arisen toward the end of the 1980s and in the 1990s. Thus, for example, a recent NBER review of current research publications describes political economy as a "hot" area (Rose, 1996); or interpreting the remark, political economy has become a popular field of research, ostensibly for a new population of researchers who have recently "discovered" political economy.

A characteristic of the "new" political economy is a focus (although by no means exclusively) on the collective decision making mechanisms of *direct democracy*.[19] Under direct democracy, there is *no political discretion*. Voters decide on the desired policy (the median voter decides with majority voting, or there is another voting rule), and an executive implicitly implements the chosen policy. And since there is no political discretion, there is no role for rent seeking. The "new political economy" therefore conforms to the requisites of political correctness. Rent seeking remains excluded from the analytical framework and from the lexicon of exposition.[20]

There are of course unpleasant difficulties with median-voter models (see Tullock, 1959). A majority can unjustly exploit a minority, and nor does the equilibrium that emerges necessarily have desirable efficiency properties.[21]

Yet overall majority-voter models are politically correct. I return to international trade policy to illustrate the limitations of politically correct direct democracy. Mayer (1984), writing before median-voter political economy was "hot", has shown how direct-democracy median-voter models can explain inefficient trade policies. Mayer's elegant analysis is based on the dispersion of ownership of capital in a Hecksher-Ohlin model where capital is a generic factor of production, and where the self-interest of a voter thus depends on how much capital he or she owns. Mayer would readily concur that where the beneficiaries of protection are a small group (import-competing industry interests), protection is an unlikely equilibrium outcome of a direct vote, since the median voter would certainly always be in the larger group of losers from protectionist policies. Models of endogenous international trade policy have been more generally set against the background of representative democracy (see Rodrik, 1995). And then, given that there exists a principal-agent problem between voter and representative (see Magee, Brock, and Young, 1989), political incorrectness becomes avoidable. The question is only one of degree of the political incorrectness that is portrayed.

To illustrate the matter of degree, consider the model by Grossman and Helpman (1994) which the authors describe as "protection for sale". The model portrays a policy maker who takes bids on trade policies from interested parties. In offering "protection for sale", the policy maker is, as described by Applebaum and Katz (1987), "seeking rents by creating rents" (see also Spiller, 1990). The policy maker is here politically quite incorrect (by our educational criterion), and in the degree of political incorrectness, at least in the rhetoric, Grossman and Helpman's political incorrectness advances a step beyond political agents portrayed in previous political economy models of international trade policy. In the previous models, compulsions of political life and the requisites of electoral success lead policy makers to offer to implement inefficient protectionist policies. Grossman and Helpman's elected representative betrays public trust to "sell" protection for personal gain to the detriment of society at large, and is, by the educational criterion for political correctness, a very much less worthy public official than the political agent pulled by the tides of political competition and needs of political support.[22]

Yet Grossman and Helpman are but observing – in the spirit of the public choice literature that preceded them[23] – that opportunistic politicians have nothing to sell but their policies, and that the professional and personal success of a politician under the institutions of representative democracy is often tied to financial contributions (see Potters, Sloof, and van Winden, 1997). These observations, which accord with the basic premise of rent-seeking models, are politically incorrect but are not necessarily untrue. Public trust is however betrayed when representatives of the people cater to special interests (including their own) rather than seeking the common good. Desirable social norms require that, when confronted with opportunities for personal gain, a representative of the people should refrain from entering into exchange which compromises the social good. That is, economic policies are "invaluable goods" for which market offers should not be entertained (see the discussion by Arrow, 1997). From "invaluable goods", it is a small step to the educational criterion for political correctness, and to the political incorrectness of rent seeking.

230

6. Educating the young (again): Why modeling rent seeking is politically correct

Corruption of the young is a most serious charge. The official reason for Socrates' indictment and trial (and subsequent death by enforced taking of hemlock) was corrupting the young (see Plato, The Socratic Dialogues). The true reason for Socrates' demise was that his quest for truth was at the expense of the credibility of his intellectual mainstream antagonists, who found themselves hard pressed to provide answers to Socrates' inquiries regarding the foundations of their (politically correct) propositions.

I have thus far adhered to the idea that the educational criterion of political correctness can be applied to declare rent-seeking models as politically incorrect, on the grounds of corruption of the young. I have adhered to this position to allow a reasoned explanation for the schism in the economics literature regarding rent seeking and political correctness. Yet I now wish to propose that the same educational criterion that renders rent seeking politically incorrect on the contrary makes *rent seeking a politically correct concept which the young should (therefore) be taught*. To make the case, I return to the two reasons posed for educational political incorrectness of rent seeking.

The first reason is that rent-seeking models expose the young to undesirable political behavior, when they should be exposed to benevolent government as part of a desirable vision of a world to which they should taught to aspire. The implicit assumption is then that the pursuit of the virtuous society is furthered by withholding from the young the (potential) inadequacies of a society's political institutions. Rent-seeking models however offer the desirable educational message of the need for vigilance and caution when individuals who have chosen to make their careers in politics or government bureaucracy[24] are left to make discretionary economic decisions. An education fostering *belief* in only benevolent government is inconsistent with citizens' awareness of their self-interest in opposing opportunistic rent-creating policies.[25] Education which provides awareness of the consequences of political discretion is at the same time not inconsistent with educating the young about the good that enlightened government can in principle do, and should do.

The second basis which was proposed by the educational criterion for the political incorrectness of rent seeking is that socially inappropriate signals are provided to the young regarding private behavior in the acquisition of income and wealth. The question then is, is it indeed socially virtuous that the young be made to believe that all incomes and wealth reflect market-determined rewards, when because of political allocation the truth may be otherwise. There is personal loss incurred when an individual believes that all rewards are awarded fairly by the merits of personal effort; for since rent seeking is privately rational behavior, honest but naive individuals are disadvantaged in the asymmetric Nash equilibrium of a Prisoner's Dilemma. This is a self-inflicted personally undesirable outcome that the young may well wish to be taught to avoid. Avoidance need not take the form of participating in rent seeking, but participating in collective activities to eliminate the institutional basis for discretionary political allocation. The education that espouses resistance is impaired if rent seekers are able to misconstrue their politically assigned gains as due to personal productive endeavor. For failure to educate the young about rent seeking spares the winners of the rent-seeking contests the stigma of being known as successful rent seekers, and spares politicians the political cost of being seen to be dispensing rents. If the young are protected from exposure to rent-seeking models, an educational failure occurs which aids and abets rent seeking.

It should be clear that, in making the case here for educational political correctness of rent-seeking models, I am not advocating that rent seeking is a desirable activity. Nor am I proposing that "there should be no government redistribution" or that "no-one is deserving of government transfers". In models of benevolent government where rent seeking cannot be present, only *deserving* individuals (however defined) receive government transfers. Rent-seeking models expose the prospect to the young that the people benefiting from government largesse may not be deserving under any acceptable criteria of worthiness or misfortune – which opens the question (for the young, and for the voter) why did the (people in) government decide to make the transfers? This is a question, I propose, that the young should be taught to ask when they observe political allocation.

To summarize, rent seeking may be educationally politically incorrect, but not the rent-seeking models, which have a meritorious educational role.

7. The intellectual and social consequences of political incorrectness

My acceptance thus far of the educational criterion of political correctness has permitted an investigation of the attributes of a so-defined politically correct model. However, the characteristic of politically correct propositions, of not being open to intellectual challenge or debate, must surely make the concept of political correctness *unsatisfactory at higher levels of intellectual analysis*. As Arrow (1997: 763) observed, "the usual doctrine is that conduct may be regulated, if that is socially desirable, but that speech must be unrestricted".

In any intellectual discipline, political correctness is divisive, in that one who challenges a politically correct position has no place in the reference group for which the politically correct position is the designated norm. It is in consequence often the case that, in discussions of political correctness,

232

one has to conduct the debate with oneself, or with one's fellow agnostics. True believers in the political correct positions (or those who profess to believe, see Kuran, 1993) may not be prepared to participate in discussion on the grounds that it is *politically incorrect to question or debate a politically correct proposition.* Acknowledgment that there is room to question compromises the essence of political correctness.

There is a social as well as intellectually inhibiting character to political correctness. By not conforming to political correct positions, a researcher risks losing acceptance within the reference group that adheres to those positions. For the professional economist living in a world of political correctness, political *in*correctness can mean conference invitations foregone, denial of access to research funding, and retribution in the evaluation of professional research. And at higher levels, the ultimate awards of professional recognition may not be offered.

My use of rent seeking as the standard bearer for perceived political incorrectness leads us in intellectual history to Tullock who made the seminal contributions (his 1967 and his 1980 papers, and see also his books 1988 and 1993). And, as observed, his 1959 paper on direct democracy is also not politically correct. Tullock's propositions are often "outrageous" in being disparaging of democratic institutions. Yet as Salmon (1994) has eloquently proposed, outrageous arguments have a central role in a critical open society, in focusing attention and in encouraging critical thinking. Outrageous statements are likely to be politically incorrect, but they may have merit. Political correctness stands in the way of any merit that may be present being established.[26]

8. Why is political economy becoming politically correct?

My final question relates to the origins of the changes in perceptions that are making the political economy models of the right politically correct. The answer which I wish to propose for the new political correctness of the political economy of the right returns us to the political economy of the left. To illustrate the relation, before the first post-communist democratic elections took place in Hungary (in March 1990), I was asked in a seminar at the Karl Marx (now Budapest) University of Economic Sciences to summarize the elements of rent-seeking models, but succumbed to the self-censorship of political correctness. It appeared inappropriate to introduce conceptions that might compromise the dreams of a better world by people who had only recently been freed from the political correctness of socialist principles. By the mid-1990s, few dreams remained to be spoiled in the post-socialist transition economies. The previous inhibitions were no longer present to deter publication of a paper in Russian (Hillman, 1996) which explained the behavioral assumptions and predictions of rent-seeking models, and was intended to familiarize Russian economists with a body of western economic theory that could take in its stride an economy contaminated by Mafia and pervaded by the private self interest of political and bureaucratic agents engaged in private distribution of the prior "social property". A politically correct exposition of behavioral incentives of political and economic agents that omitted rent seeking would under the circumstances have little to say, except about what ought to be and was not.

Conditions in other post-socialist countries were similar (see Gelb, Hillman, and Ursprung, 1996). Although an admittedly extreme case, the Bulgarian economy collapsed in the latter part of 1996 and a street-revolution brought down the government in early 1997.[27] Although privatization had been pressed upon policy makers as an essential prerequisite for economic transformation (see the World Bank, 1996), Bulgarian governments had been remarkably lax in privatizing the large state enterprises. One could propose that failure of progress with privatization was due to the intrinsic lack of worth of the assets involved (who would wish to buy the unprofitable state factories?), that bureaucratic obstacles impeded privatization (absence of the requisite legal framework), or that the unprofitable state factories were kept alive out of a perception of social responsibility to workers. To whatever extent these considerations were present, a closer study reveals the conditions and predicted behavior of a rent-seeking model (see Bogetić and Hillman, 1995). Rents were created by permitting privileged transactions between private agents and state firms – by private supply of inputs to state firms and private purchases of state firms' outputs. The losses that were in consequence incurred by state enterprises had the complementary role of making the enterprise unattractive for privatization. This can be described by the analogy of feeding and milking a cow that belongs (ambiguously but formally) to the state. Deferred to the future was the issue of the longer-term health of the cow. That health could be adversely affected by greed (a short time horizon), and by the rational belief that a well-fed good-looking cow might indeed be privatized, so putting an end to the sources of the rents. In the environment of ambiguous property right, the rents from feeding and milking the state cow were contestable – and were contested – drawing individuals' attention and resources way from productive activity. A rent-seeking model explains the behavior of agents, and could predict the profound economic collapse that was to come.

The copious prizes for rent-seeking contests that have characterized the transition from socialism reflect the designation of private ownership to much of the prior social property; the contestability necessary for rent seeking re-

234

flects the initial ambiguous property rights from which the transition was initiated.

It is perhaps significant that the increasing political correctness of the political economy of the economic right (and of rent seeking in particular) coincides with the end of socialism and the beginning of the transition. Perhaps for so long as the communist world persisted to offer a competing model, it was politically incorrect to emphasize (by modeling) the inadequacies of economic decision making of western market political and collective-decision making institutions. With the contest declared over, the inhibitions have diminished, and the formerly politically incorrect political economy has become correct.

Notes

1. As observed by Hayek (1988) and others, there has often been broad sympathy for the idealized general principles of the political economy of the left.
2. We do not need to go back far in history to find instances where the educational criterion as practiced fails to satisfy enlightened ethical norms. The children of the Hitlerjugend of Germany and Austria were presented with anti-semitism and mass murder of (other) young children as politically correct. The children of Chinese Red Guards were educated to fall cruelly on those among their own people who strayed from the true (politically correct) path.
3. Rent-seeking activities reach maximal heights when an economic system allows *only* political allocation, as in planned communist economies (see Hillman, 1994).
4. Hence, in the case of monopoly power, the efficiency losses are two-fold, the traditional deadweight losses due to inefficient resource allocation and the resources which are used in sustaining (and resisting) the underlying institutional structure that preempts warranted competitive entry (see Posner, 1974). Similarly, in the case of protectionist trade policies, the social losses consist of the traditional losses due to inefficient resource allocation and the resources used in influencing trade policy determination (see Hillman, 1989: Ch. 6).
5. The terminology "rent seeking" is from Krueger (1974).
6. See also the collections of papers in the edited volumes by Buchanan, Tollison, and Tullock (1980), Rowley, Tollison, and Tullock (1988), and Congleton and Tollison (1995).
7. The extent of social loss via rent dissipation (that is, the value of the resources attracted into the unproductive quest to determine political allocation) depends on a number of characteristics of the rent-seeking "contest", including risk aversion (Hillman and Katz, 1984), the nature of the function which translates resources used into prospective success (Hillman and Samet, 1987; Hillman and Riley, 1989), the collective nature of the endeavor and/or the rent sought (Ursprung, 1990; Nitzan, 1991), the presence of countervailing opposition (Hillman and Riley, 1989; Fabella, 1995), and the institutional structure or stages of the contest (Katz and Tokatlidu, 1996).
8. Culture plays a role, and reticence is not always the case. In some societies wealth provides honor independently of how the wealth is acquired, and it is not contrary to accepted norms for those who have attained political power to use that power openly (rather than surreptitiously) for personal economic gain. For a study of rent seeking in such contexts, see Kimenyi and Mbaku (1995).

9. Much of the evidence comes from journalistic reporting of "scandals" where politicians, and also bureaucrats, have been discovered to have betrayed the public interest for their own personal advantage. For a summary of some of this, see Tullock (1988, 1993). Stern (1988) provides a picture of the U.S. Congress. Potters and Sloof (1996) provide a broad review of the empirical evidence on the rent-seeking activities of interest groups.

10. This is similar to the social insurance explanation for protectionist policies (see my survey, 1989: Ch. 9).

11. For reviews of the literature on the political economy of trade policy, see Hillman (1989), Magee (1994), and Rodrik (1995).

12. See in particular the perspectives offered by Baldwin (1982, 1984, 1985).

13. See Hillman, Long, and Moser (1995) for elaboration on the different approaches to explaining trade liberalization.

14. See, however, Baldwin (1992) for observations on the "newness".

15. See also the books of readings edited by Krugman (1986) and Grossman (1992).

16. Strategic trade policy does not necessarily require that governments subsidize their firms: taxes are indicated when firms compete in price (Bertrand) and subsidies when firms are Cournot-quantity competitors, and there are other interventionist solutions that depend on the circumstances modeled (see Brander, 1995). In practical discussions of strategic trade policy, only the subsidy (or protection) and never the tax has ever appeared to have arisen.

17. Losers from redistribution are defending their incomes and wish to avoid the deadweight loss that they would incur because of the transfer, so they are willing to spend more in defending their incomes than the monetary sum they stand to lose. The beneficiaries value the transfer less than the monetary value, again because of deadweight losses, and so are willing to expend less than the value of the transfer in "rent seeking".

18. In a non-cooperative equilibrium for private contributions to the collective objective of the interest group, the change in effectiveness of the coalition as reflected in the resources marshaled depends on countervailing income and substitution effects as the size of the coalition is enlarged (see Cornes and Sandler, 1996). On other collective aspects of rent seeking, see Ursprung (1990), Nitzan (1991), and Gradstein (1993).

19. The "new" political economy literature using median-voter equilibria is vast and any citations can be but arbitrary.

20. This is true of the models of the "new" political economy. However, where practiced, direct democracy is also susceptible to attempts by interest groups and political agents to influence policy outcomes, for example by the manner in which the question put to popular vote is framed, and by the use of resources to convince voters of the merits or demerits of a particular position.

21. Adolf Hitler was placed in power through democratic institutions, and a majority proceeded to determine and implement policies that had tragic consequences for a minority.

22. The *rhetoric* of "protection for sale" overstates Grossman and Helpman's (1994) political incorrectness. They model a common-agency policy menu problem and provide underpinnings for a conventional political-support function which has been extensively used in the endogenous protection and regulation literature by endogenizing the determination of sectoral political weights. However, also the order of moves in the game between the politician offering to sell protection and the private agents bidding for protectionist rents can be interpreted on a scale of political correctness. The Grossman-Helpman politician is in this regard less politically correct than, for example, the Ursprung (1990) candidates for political office.

23. See Mueller (1989), and in particular on the premises of the public-choice approach to international trade policy, Frey (1984).

236

24. The career as politician or regulator may also be a preliminary activity before entering private-sector employment. See Brezis and Weiss (1997).
25. Bloom (1987) in his study *The closing of the American mind* observes that the conceptions which have guided the politically correct norms of behavior of the American young have been self-ironical niceness, egalitarianism stemming from non-discrimination, and offering a pleasant face to the world. Rent-seeking models contradict each of these facets.
26. Of course many outrageous statements have no merit. For example, staying within the previous theme of the politically correct propositions set before Hitlerjugend, there are those who would deny that the murder of six million Jews, or some one and a half million children, ever took place. If we allow outrageous statements, we must allow such propositions, which question history. Such questioning of history is quite different from a recommendation placed before the young that the killing of innocent people has merit. The denial that the murders took place is an outrageous statement that can be confronted with evidence, and confirmed to be outrageous with intended malice.
27. The change of government was subsequently confirmed in democratic elections.

References

Applebaum, E. and Katz, E. (1987). Seeking rents by setting rents: The political economy of rent seeking. *Economic Journal* 97: 685–699.

Arrow, K.J. (1997). Invaluable goods. *Journal of Economic Literature* 35: 757–801.

Baba, S.A. (1997). Democracies and inefficiency. *Economics and Politics* 9: 99–114.

Baldwin, R.E. (1982). The political economy of protectionism. In J. Bhagwati (Ed.), *Import competition and response*. Chicago: Chicago University Press, 263–286.

Baldwin, R.E. (1984). Rent seeking and trade policy: An industry approach. *Weltwirtschaftliches Archiv* 120: 662–677.

Baldwin, R.E. (1985). *The political economy of US import policy*. Cambridge, MA: MIT Press.

Baldwin, R.E. (1992). Are economists' traditional trade policy views still valid? *Journal of Economic Literature* 30: 804–829.

Becker, G. (1983). A theory of competition among pressure groups for political influence. *Quarterly Journal of Economics* 98: 371–400.

Bernholz, P. (1991). The constitution of totalitarianism. *Journal of Institutional and Theoretical Economics* 147: 424–440.

Bernholz, P. (1993). Necessary conditions for totalitarianism, supreme values, power, and personal interest. In G. Radnitzsky and H. Boullion (Eds.), *Government: Servant or master*. Amsterdam and Atlanta: Rodopi, 267–312.

Bhagwati, J. (1971). The generalized theory of distortions and welfare. In J. Bhagwati, R.W. Jones, R.A. Mundell, and J. Vanek (Eds.), *Trade, the balance of payments and growth: Essays in honor of Charles P. Kindleberger*, 69–90. Amsterdam: North-Holland.

Bloom, A. (1987). *The closing of the American mind: How higher education has failed democracy and impoverished the souls of today's students*. New York: Simon and Schuster.

Brezis, E. and Weiss, A. (1997). Conscientious regulation and post-regulatory employment restrictions. *European Journal of Political Economy* 13: 517–536.

Bogetić, Z. and Hillman, A.L. (Eds.). (1995). *Financing government in transition, Bulgaria: The political economy of tax policies, tax bases, and tax evasion*. Washington, DC: The World Bank.

Brander, J. (1995). Strategic trade policy. In G.M. Grossman and K. Rogoff (Eds.), *Handbook of international economics*, Vol. 3, 1395–1455. Amsterdam: North-Holland.

Buchanan, J., Tollison, R.D. and Tullock, G. (Eds.). (1980). *Toward a theory of the rent-seeking society*. College Station: Texas A&M Press.

Cassing, J. (1996). Protectionist mutual funds. *European Journal of Political Economy* 12: 1–18.

Cassing, J. and Hillman, A.L. (1985). Political influence motives and the choice between tariffs and quotas. *Journal of International Economics* 19: 279–290. Reprinted in J. Bhagwati and P. Rosendorff (Eds.), *Readings in the political economy of trade policy*, Cambridge, MA: MIT Press, forthcoming.

Cassing, J. and Hillman, A.L. (1986). Shifting comparative advantage and senescent industry collapse. *American Economic Review* 76: 516–523. Reprinted in J. Bhagwati and P. Rosendorff (Eds.), *Readings in the political economy of trade policy*, Cambridge, MA: MIT Press, forthcoming.

Congleton, R. and Tollison, R. (Eds.). (1995). *The economic analysis of rent seeking*. Oxford: Edward Elgar.

Corden, M. (1974). *Trade policy and economic welfare*. Oxford: Clarendon Press.

Cornes, R. and Sandler, T. (1996). *The theory of externalities, public goods, and club goods*. Cambridge, UK: Cambridge University Press.

Fabella, R.V. (1995). The social cost of rent seeking under countervailing opposition to distortionary transfers. *Journal of Public Economics* 57: 235–248.

Frey, B. (1984). *International political economics*. Cambridge, UK: Basil Blackwell.

Gelb, A., Hillman, A.L. and Ursprung, H.W. (1995). Rents and the transition. *World Development Report Background Paper*. Washington, DC: The World Bank.

Gradstein, M. (1993). Rent seeking and the provision of public goods. *Economic Journal* 103: 1236–1243.

Grossman, G. (Ed.) (1992). *Imperfect competition and international trade*. Cambridge, MA: MIT Press.

Grossman, G. and Helpman, E. (1994). Protection for sale. *American Economic Review* 84: 833–850.

Hayek, F.A. (1988). *The fatal conceit: The errors of socialism*. London: Routledge.

Hillman, A.L. (1982). Declining industries and political-support protectionist motives. *American Economic Review* 72: 1180–1187. Reprinted in J. Bhagwati and P. Rosendorff (Eds.), *Readings in the political economy of trade policy*, Cambridge, MA: MIT Press, forthcoming.

Hillman, A.L. (1989/1994). *The political economy of protection*. New York: Harwood Academic Publishers.

Hillman, A.L. (1994). The transition from socialism: An overview from a political-economy perspective. *European Journal of Political Economy* 10: 191–225.

Hillman, A.L. (1996). Western economic theory and the transition: *Economics and mathematical methods. Journal of the Central Economic and Mathematical Institute of the Russian Academy of Sciences* 32: 77–90. (in Russian. Transl. M. Levin).

Hillman, A.L., Long, N.V. and Moser, P. (1995). Modeling reciprocal trade liberalization: The political-economy and national-welfare perspectives. *Swiss Journal of Economics and Statistics* 131: 503–515.

Hillman, A.L. and Katz, E. (1984). Risk-averse rent seekers and the social cost of monopoly power. *Economic Journal* 94: 104–110. Reprinted in C. Rowley, R. Tollison, and G. Tullock (Eds.), *The political economy of rent seeking*, 81–90. Boston: Kluwer Academic

238

Publishers, 1988, and in R. Congleton and R. Tollison (Eds.), *The economic analysis of rent seeking*. Oxford: Edward Elgar, 1995.

Hillman, A.L. and Riley, J. (1989). Politically contestable rents and transfers. *Economics and Politics* 1: 17–39. Reprinted in J. Bhagwati and P. Rosendorff (Eds.), *Readings in the political economy of trade policy*, Cambridge, MA: MIT Press, forthcoming.

Hillman, A.L. and Samet, D. (1987). Dissipation of rents and revenues in small-numbers contests. *Public Choice* 54: 63–82.

Hillman, A.L. and Ursprung, H.W. (1988). Domestic politics, foreign interests and international trade policy. *American Economic Review* 78: 729–745. Reprinted in *International library of critical writings in economics: International trade*, edited by J.P. Neary. Cheltenham: Edward Elgar, 1996, and in J. Bhagwati and P. Rosendorff (Eds.), *Readings in the political economy of trade policy*, Cambridge, MA: MIT Press, forthcoming.

Hillman, A.L. and Ursprung, H.W. (1992). The influence of environmental concerns on the political determination of international trade policy. In R. Blackhurst and K. Anderson (Eds.), *The greening of world trade issues*, 195–220. New York: Harvester, Wheatsheaf.

Hillman, A.L. and Ursprung, H.W. (1993). The multinational firm, political competition, and international trade policy. *International Economic Review* 34: 347–363.

Irwin, D. (1996). *Against the tide: An intellectual history of free trade*. Princeton: Princeton University Press.

Katz, E. and Tokalidu, J. (1996). Group competition for rents. *European Journal of Political Economy* 12: 599–607.

Kimenyi, M.S. and Mbaku, J.M. (1995). Rents, military elites, and political democracy. *European Journal of Political Economy* 11: 699–708.

Krugman, P. (Ed.). (1986). *Strategic trade policy and the new international economics*. Cambridge, MA: MIT Press.

Krueger, A. (1974). The political economy of the rent-seeking society. *American Economic Review* 64: 291–303.

Kuran, T. (1993). Mitigating the tyranny of public opinion: Anonymous discourse and the ethic of sincerity. *Constitutional Political Economy* 4: 41–78.

Leidy, M. (1994). Trade policy and indirect rent seeking: A synthesis of recent work. *Economics and Politics* 6: 97–118.

Magee, S.P. (1994). The political economy of trade policy. In D. Greenaway and L.A. Winters (Eds.), *Surveys in international trade*, 139–176. Oxford: Basil Blackwell.

Magee, S.P., Brock, W.A. and Young, L. (1989). *Black hole tariffs and endogenous policy theory: Political economy in general equilibrium*. Cambridge, UK: Cambridge University Press.

Mayer, W. (1984). Endogenous tariff formation. *American Economic Review* 74: 970–985.

Moore, M.O. and Suranovic, S.M. (1993). Lobbying and Cournot-Nash competition: Implications for strategic trade policy. *Journal of International Economics* 35: 367–376.

Mueller, D. (1989). *Public choice II*. Cambridge, UK: Cambridge University Press.

Nitzan, S.I. (1991). Collective rent dissipation. *Economic Journal* 101: 1522–1534.

Nitzan, S.I. (1994). Modeling rent seeking contests. *European Journal of Political Economy* 10: 41–60.

Olson, M., Jr. (1965). *The logic of collective action: Public goods and the theory of groups*. Cambridge, MA: Harvard University Press.

Peltzman, S. (1976). Toward a more general theory of regulation. *Journal of Law and Economics* 19: 211–240.

Posner, R.A. (1974). The social costs of monopoly and regulation. *Journal of Political Economy* 83: 807–827.

Potters, J. and Sloof, R. (1996). Interest groups: A survey of empirical models that try to assess their influence. *European Journal of Political Economy* 12: 403–442.

Potters, J. and Sloof, R. (1997). Campaign expenditures, contributions, and direct endorsements: The use of information and money to influence voter behavior. *European Journal of Political Economy* 13: 1–31.

Rodrik, D. (1995). Political economy of trade policy. In G.M. Grossman and K. Rogoff (Eds.), *Handbook of international economics*, Vol. 3, 1457–1494. Amsterdam: North-Holland.

Rose, A. (1996). Program report: International finance and macroeconomics. *NBER Reporter, National Bureau of Economic Research.* Cambridge, MA.

Rowley, C., Tollison, R. and Tullock, G. (Eds.). (1988). *The political economy of rent seeking.* Boston and Dordrecht: Kluwer Academic Publishers.

Salmon, P. (1994). Outrageous arguments in economics and public choice. *European Journal of Political Economy* 10: 409–426.

Stern, P. (1988). *The best Congress money can buy.* New York: Pantheon Books.

Stigler, G.J. (1971). The theory of economic regulation. *Bell Journal of Economics and Management Science* 2: 3–21.

Spiller, P.T. (1990). Politicians, interest groups, and regulators: A multiple principals agent theory of regulation (or let them be bribed). *Journal of Law and Economics* 33: 65–101.

Tullock, G. (1959). Problems of majority voting. *Journal of Political Economy* 67: 571–579.

Tullock, G. (1967). The welfare costs of tariffs, monopoly, and theft, *Western Economic Journal* 5: 224–232. Reprinted in J. Buchanan, R.D. Tollison, and G. Tullock (Eds.), *Toward a theory of the rent-seeking society*, 39–50. College Station: Texas A&M Press.

Tullock, G. (1980). Efficient rent seeking. In J. Buchanan, R.D. Tollison, and G. Tullock (Eds.), *Toward a theory of the rent-seeking society*, 97–112. College Station: Texas A&M Press.

Tullock, G. (1989). *The economics of special privilege and rent seeking.* Boston and Dordrecht: Kluwer Academic Publishers.

Tullock, G. (1993). *Rent seeking.* Aldershot, UK: Edward Elgar.

Ursprung, H.W. (1990). Public goods, rent dissipation, and candidate competition. *Economics and Politics* 2: 115–132.

Ursprung, H.W. (1991). Economic policies and political competition. In A.L. Hillman (Ed.), *Markets and Politicians: Politicized Economic Choice*, 1–25. Dordrecht and Boston: Kluwer Academic Publishers.

World Bank. (1996). *From plan to market* (World development report). Washington, DC: The World Bank.

Acknowledgements

The contributions to this volume are reprinted from the following publications, with permission from the respective publishers:

Richard A. Posner, 1975. The social costs of monopoly and regulation. Journal of Political Economy 83, 807–27.

Keith Cowling and Dennis C. Mueller, 1978. The social costs of monopoly power. Economic Journal 88, 727–48.

Stephen C. Littlechild, 1981. Misleading calculations of the social costs of monopoly power. Economic Journal 91, 348–63.

Arye L. Hillman, 1982. Declining industries and political-support protectionist motives. American Economic Review 72, 1180–87.

Arye L. Hillman and Heinrich W. Ursprung, 1988. Domestic politics, foreign interests, and international trade policy. American Economic Review 78, 729–45.

Gene M. Grossman and Elhanan Helpman, 1994. Protection for sale. American Economic Review 84, 833–50.

Anne O. Krueger, 1974. The political economy of the rent-seeking society. American Economic Review 64, 291–303.

Jakob Svensson, 2000. Foreign aid and rent seeking. Journal of International Economics 51, 437–61.

Philip Verwimp, 2003. The political economy of coffee, dictatorship, and genocide. European Journal of Political Economy 19, 161–81.

Kevin M. Murphy, Andrei Shleifer, and Robert W. Vishny, 1993. Why is rent seeking so costly to growth? American Economic Review 83, 409–14.

Arye L. Hillman and Heinrich W. Ursprung, 2000. Political culture and economic decline. European Journal of Political Economy 16, 189–213.

Halvor Mehlum, Karl Moene, and Ragnar Torvik, 2006. Institutions and the resource curse. Economic Journal 116, 1–20.

Gil S. Epstein, Arye L. Hillman, and Heinrich W. Ursprung, 1999. The king never emigrates. Review of Development Economics 3, 107–21.

Peter Nannestad, 2004. Immigration as a challenge to the Danish welfare state? European Journal of Political Economy 20, 755–67.

Roger D. Congleton, 1986. Rent-seeking aspects of political advertising. Public Choice 49, 249–63.

Fred S. McChesney, 1987. Rent extraction and rent creation in the economic theory of regulation. Journal of Legal Studies 16, 101–18.

Michael R. Baye, Dan Kovenock, and Casper G. de Vries, 1993. Rigging the lobbying process: An application of the all-pay auction. American Economic Review 83, 289–94.

Yeon-Koo Che and Ian L. Gale, 1998. Caps on political lobbying. American Economic Review 88, 643–51.

Kai A. Konrad, 2004. Inverse campaigning. Economic Journal 114, 69–82.

Gordon Tullock, 1975. On the efficient organization of trials. Kyklos 28, 745–62.

Amy Farmer and Paul Pecorino, 1999. Legal expenditure as a rent-seeking game. Public Choice 100, 271–88.

Francesco Parisi, 2002. Rent-seeking through litigation: Adversarial and inquisitorial systems compared. International Review of Law and Economics 22, 193–216.

Michael R. Baye, Dan Kovenock, and Casper G. de Vries, 2005. Comparative analysis of litigation systems: An auction-theoretic approach. Economic Journal 115, 583–601.

James M. Buchanan, 1983. Rent seeking, noncompensated transfers, and laws of succession. Journal of Law and Economics 26, 71–85.

Kevin Sylwester, 2001. A model of institutional formation within a rent-seeking environment. Journal of Economic Behavior and Organization 44, 169–76.

J. Atsu Amegashie, 2006. The 2002 Winter Olympics scandal: Rent seeking and committees. Social Choice and Welfare 26, 183–89.

Barry Baysinger, Robert B. Ekelund Jr., and Robert D. Tollison, 1980. Mercantilism as a rent-seeking society. In: James M. Buchanan, Robert D. Tollison, and Gordon Tullock (Eds.), Toward a Theory of the Rent-Seeking Society. Texas A&M University Press, College Station, 235–68.

S. R. H. Jones and Simon P. Ville, 1996. Efficient transactors or rent-seeking monopolists? The rationale for early chartered trading companies. Journal of Economic History 56, 898–915.

Oliver Volckart, 2000. The open constitution and its enemies: Competition, rent seeking, and the rise of the modern state. Journal of Economic Behavior and Organization 42, 1–17.

Arye L. Hillman and Adi Schnytzer, 1986. Illegal economic activities and purges in a Soviet-type economy: A rent-seeking perspective. International Review of Law and Economics 6, 87–99.

Charles D. DeLorme Jr., Stacey Isom, and David R. Kamerschen, 2005. Rent seeking and taxation in the Ancient Roman Empire. Applied Economics 37, 705–11.

J. Kornai, 1980. "Hard" and "soft" budget constraint. Acta Oeconomica 25, 231–46.

Arye L. Hillman, Eliakim Katz, and Jacob Rosenberg, 1987. Workers as insurance: Anticipated government assistance and factor demand. Oxford Economic Papers 39, 813–20.

Steven T. Buccola and James E. McCandlish, 1999. Rent seeking and rent dissipation in state enterprises. Review of Agricultural Economics 21, 358–73.

Aaron S. Edlin and Joseph E. Stiglitz, 1995. Discouraging rivals: Managerial rent-seeking and economic inefficiencies. American Economic Review 85, 1301–12.

David S. Scharfstein and Jeremy C. Stein, 2000. The dark side of internal capital markets: Divisional rent-seeking and inefficient investment. The Journal of Finance 55, 2537–64.

Amihai Glazer, 2002. Allies as rivals: Internal and external rent seeking. Journal of Economic Behavior and Organization 48, 155–62.

Assar Lindbeck and Dennis J. Snower, 1987. Efficiency wages versus insiders and outsiders. European Economic Review 31, 407–16.

Roger D. Congleton, 1989. Monitoring rent-seeking managers: Advantages of diffuse ownership. Canadian Journal of Economics 22, 662–72.

Holger M. Müller and Karl Wärneryd, 2001. Inside versus outside ownership: A political theory of the firm. Rand Journal of Economics 32, 527–41.

Roger D. Congleton, 1989. Efficient status seeking: Externalities, and the evolution of status games. Journal of Economic Behavior and Organization 11, 175–90.

Amihai Glazer and Kai A. Konrad, 1996. A signaling explanation for charity. American Economic Review 86, 1019–28.

Mario Ferrero, 2002. Competition for sainthood and the millennial church. Kyklos 55, 335–60.

Bruno S. Frey, 2003. Publishing as prostitution: Choosing between one's own ideas and academic success. Public Choice 116, 205–23.

Roger D. Congleton, 1991. Ideological conviction and persuasion in the rent-seeking society. Journal of Public Economics 44, 65–86.

Arye L. Hillman, 1998. Political economy and political correctness. Public Choice 96, 219–39.